*Ninth Edition*

# MANAGERIAL ACCOUNTING

JOSEPH G. LOUDERBACK III
CLEMSON UNIVERSITY

JAY S. HOLMEN
UNIVERSITY OF WISCONSIN - EAU CLAIRE

GERALDINE F. DOMINIAK
TEXAS CHRISTIAN UNIVERSITY

**South-Western College Publishing**
Thomson Learning™

Australia • Canada • Denmark • Japan • Mexico • New Zealand • Philippines
Puerto Rico • Singapore • South Africa • Spain • United Kingdom • United States

*Managerial Accounting*, 9e, by Joseph G. Louderback, Jay S. Holmen, and Geraldine F. Dominiak

Accounting Team Director: Richard Lindgren
Acquisitions Editor: Rochelle J. Kronzek
Developmental Editor: Rebecca Glaab
Marketing Manager: Dan Silverburg
Media & Technology Editor: Diane Van Bakel

Media Production Editor: Lora Craver
Production Editor: Mike Busam
Manufacturing Coordinator: Doug Wilke
Cover Design: Jennifer Martin-Lambert
Cover Illustration: Sally Wern Comport/Stock Illustration Source
Production House: Cover to Cover Publishing, Inc.
Compositor: Sandy Thomson, Cover to Cover Publishing, Inc.
Printer: Westgroup

Printed in the United States of America
1 2 3 4 5 02 01 00 99

For more information contact South-Western College Publishing, 5101 Madison Road, Cincinnati, Ohio, 45227 or find us on the Internet at http://www.swcollege.com

**For permission to use material from this text or product, contact us by**
• **telephone: 1-800-730-2214**
• **fax: 1-800-730-2215**
• **web: http://www.thomsonrights.com**

**Library of Congress Cataloging-in-Publication Data**
Louderback, Joseph G.
    Managerial accounting / Joseph G. Louderback III, Jay Holmen,
Geraldine F. Dominiak. -- 9th ed.
      p.   cm.
    Dominiak's name appears first in previous edition.
    Includes index.
    ISBN 0-324-01208-X
    1. Managerial accounting. I. Dominiak, Geraldine F. II. Holmen,
Jay. III. Title.
HF5657.4.D66 1999
658.15--dc21                               99-27838

This book is printed on acid-free paper.

# PREFACE

The business environment has changed dramatically over the twenty-five years since our book was first published. Technology has automated industry, and the Internet is transforming and streamlining commerce. Some things never change, though; managers need to make decisions, and they want to make informed decisions. In the tradition of the first eight editions, *Managerial Accounting*, ninth edition, continues its leading-edge coverage of management accounting topics within a decision-making framework. *Managerial Accounting*, 9e parallels the shift in today's business world, focusing not just on the numbers but on the functions of management: planning, decision making, controlling, and performance evaluation. This emphasis is apparent even in the chapters on product costing (Chapters 13–15), a topic that accounting textbooks seldom discuss with the nonaccountant in mind. These chapters approach product costing from the standpoint of analyzing results under different costing systems, rather than concentrating on cost-accumulation procedures or the accounting problems related to those procedures.

Because the book emphasizes the uses of managerial accounting information, it is appropriate not only for accounting majors but also for other business majors (marketing, management, finance, etc.). It can also be used by majors in nonbusiness areas such as engineering, mathematics, and the physical sciences. The real-world examples and decision situations illustrated throughout the text and the assignment material help students put information into a business perspective, rather than strictly an accounting focus.

The ninth edition of this book is intended for an introductory course in managerial accounting. Though we wrote the book with the undergraduate student in mind, it has seen successful use in graduate courses and in management development programs. The wide variety of assignment material allows instructors to use the book at various levels by selecting assignments consistent with students' backgrounds.

We assume that a student has had one or two terms of financial accounting or a working exposure to basic financial statements. We expect some understanding of the most basic principles on which financial statements are based. The journal-entry/T-account framework appears only in Chapter 15 and is not otherwise necessary to understanding the concepts. For those instructors wanting to cover the statement of cash flows and financial statement analysis, we have included two chapters (Chapters 17 and 18) on these topics.

## OBJECTIVES

The overall goal of our text is to present clearly and understandably the most important conceptual and practical aspects of managerial accounting. In order to achieve this we have arranged our book with the following objectives:

1. To order the material in a way that allows the reader to build from elementary concepts to more complex topics and thus to integrate and expand early understanding.

2. To illustrate some of the interrelationships between managerial accounting and other courses in a normal business curriculum.

3. To show students, through discussion, illustration, and assignment material, the manifold applications of managerial accounting principles to decision making in economic entities of all types (including personal decisions).

4. To help students recognize that *people*, not entities, make decisions and are responsible for the results of those decisions.

5. To acquaint students with new approaches such as the balanced scorecard, Theory of Constraints, and total quality management to enhance their appreciation of managerial accounting in strategy development and value-chain analysis.

We use various means to achieve these objectives. First, we use examples and illustrations liberally. Second, we proceed through the text (and its increasingly complex concepts) in a building-block fashion. We begin with the principles of cost behavior and cost-volume-profit analysis, which underlie virtually all of managerial accounting, and use this basis to approach the more complex problems encountered in decision making, comprehensive budgeting, responsibility accounting, and product costing. A reader will see the reliance on previously developed concepts by the use of references to earlier chapters.

Throughout the book we emphasize that decisions are based on estimates and that some factors important to a decision are difficult to quantify. Our intentions are to underscore (1) the presence of uncertainty and (2) the importance of recognizing all the available alternatives and all the factors relevant to each alternative. Both the text and many of the problems emphasize that a major problem in managing any enterprise is determining the right questions to ask and what kinds of information to seek.

## NEW TO THIS EDITION

Based on user and reviewer feedback, we have added new features to the ninth edition.

**A Full Chapter on Activity-Based Costing.** In response to the widespread usage of activity-based costing (ABC) in today's business world, we devote all of

Chapter 4 to ABC. We continue to integrate ABC into virtually every succeeding chapter. Chapter 3 is now devoted to cost management and cost estimation.

**More on Strategy.** We discuss several managerial accounting principles and techniques in the context of corporate strategy. Most apparent is the discussion of the value chain in Chapter 1 and elsewhere, the introduction of the balanced scorecard in Chapter 10, and more attention to strategic issues in Chapters 4, 5, 8, 9, 10, and 11 and in some of the product costing material.

**Integration of Additional Aspects of Cost-Volume-Profit Material.** In editions past this material was all in one chapter. In the ninth edition the discussion of contribution margin variances is now found in Chapter 10; cost-volume-profit analysis of a multiple product setting is now an appendix to Chapter 2. Segment margin reporting is now tied more closely to ABC and remains in Chapter 4.

**Theory of Constraints.** We have greatly expanded the coverage of Theory of Constraints, devoting half a chapter (16) to this topic that is receiving increasing attention in managerial accounting.

**Increased Coverage of Quality Costs.** Chapter 16 now includes an expanded discussion of quality costs.

**Internet Activities.** Every chapter has an internet activity for students. We believe it important that students understand how to access information and how to use it. These activities do not have specific solutions because we cannot predict how students will seek information and what they will find. An alternative, to send students to specific Web sites, does appear a few times, but only to Web sites whose names we were sure would remain the same.

## ADDITIONAL FEATURES

**Learning Objectives.** Each chapter begins with a set of learning objectives designed to provide an overview of chapter concepts and serve as a framework for study and comprehension.

**Real-World Examples.** Each chapter opens with a vignette that uses real-world material to set the stage for the chapter material. Throughout the text there are more examples from the real world with more references to actual companies. Much of the real-world material appears in boxed Insights. Assignment material also includes items related to activities and policies of real companies. Real-company names are highlighted throughout the text for easy identification. A company index appears at the back of the text.

**Chapter Links.** A strength of our text has always been its building-block approach using the basic concepts and principles of managerial accounting as a basis for learning about more complex topics. Link margin icons help students quickly identify references to related concepts. A left arrow represents a concept that was covered in an earlier chapter, while a right arrow indicates a concept that will be covered in more detail in a later chapter.

**Ethics.** Material on ethics has been incorporated and includes a reprint of the IMA Standards for Professional Conduct. Most chapters have assignments dealing with ethical issues.

**International Coverage.**  We have maintained attention to international matters, such as cultural differences and currency translation.

**Guidelines for Preparing Memoranda.**  Virtually all chapters have assignments that require preparing memoranda with regard to the Accounting Education Change Commission. Appendix A gives guidelines for preparing memoranda.

## ASSIGNMENT MATERIAL

One of the strongest features of this book is the assignment material, because of its integration with the text, its volume, and its variety with respect to degree of difficulty and economic entities. Users of previous editions have told us that these factors make it possible to teach this course, and the individual topics therein, at various levels of difficulty. Users cite the same factors in successful offerings of the course to students with widely diverse backgrounds.  Notes to the Instructor in the Solutions Manual aid in the judicious choice of assignment items to accommodate different objectives.

End-of-chapter material for every chapter includes Internet activities, questions for discussion, exercises, problems, and cases. Discussion questions are designed to increase students' understanding of concepts and use of critical-thinking skills; thus, many have no clearly correct answers. Both exercises and problems are generally arranged in order of increasing difficulty.

For most cases, students must propose an analytical approach appropriate to the available, relevant information.  These assignments are designed to encourage students to think, since this is what a manager must do.

## ALTERNATIVE SEQUENCES

The text contains more material than is needed for a one-term course, and we expect most users to omit one or more chapters. Several users have found alternative sequencing to be practical. The text does offer considerable flexibility in the order of coverage.

Chapter 16, which discusses quality costs, theory of constraints, and learning curves, can be covered early, perhaps after Chapter 4. Instructors wishing to review the basic financial statements may wish to discuss Chapter 18 (and possibly Chapter 17) immediately after Chapter 1.

Instructors desiring earlier and greater emphasis on product costing can move to Chapters 12 through 15 after Chapter 4. (Beginning product costing early requires incorporating Chapter 12 in the coverage of that topic rather than as part of the study of responsibility accounting, because some understanding of standard costs is assumed in Chapters 14 and 15.) Some users increase the time available to cover product costing by omitting Chapters 10 and 11. Alternatively, some users omit all product costing material, or omit all or parts of Chapters 14 and 15. One or both chapters on capital budgeting (Chapters 8 and 9) can be omitted without serious loss of continuity.

Appendix B, which deals with the time value of money, is available for use with Chapters 8 and 9 on capital budgeting. It assumes no previous exposure to the principles of present and future value, but those who have had such exposure are likely to find this material useful for review.

## SUPPLEMENTARY MATERIAL

**Check Figures.** Key figures for solutions to selected assignment material are provided at the back of the text.

**Study Guide.** The study guide is designed to help students obtain full value from the study of this text. This supplement, which offers key statements to use as guides in reading the chapters, includes not only objective questions but also a variety of short- and medium-length problems (solutions included) to test understanding. The final section of the study guide for each chapter identifies those concepts, practices, or approaches that cause the most difficulty or greatest misunderstanding for students.

**Solutions Manual.** The solutions manual contains solutions for all assignment material and suggested times for completing assignments. It also provides notes to the instructor regarding class use of the material. These notes offer (1) alternative approaches for arriving at solutions, (2) suggestions for eliciting class discussion, and (3) suggestions for expanding individual assignments to cover new issues, pursuing existing issues in more depth, or highlighting relationships between managerial accounting concepts and concepts studied in other business disciplines. The solutions manual also contains suggested time allocations for alternative course lengths and chapter sequencing.

**Solutions Transparencies.** Acetate transparencies for many solutions are available to adopters.

**Test Bank.** The test bank, which contains true-false and multiple-choice questions and short problems, allows for the preparation of several exams without the repetition of material due to the large number of questions available.

**Spreadsheet Templates.** (Prepared by Marvin Bouillon, Iowa State University) Excel templates for various end-of-chapter assignments are complimentary to adopters.

**PowerPoint Slides.** (Prepared by Marvin Bouillon, Iowa State University) PowerPoint slides provide an electronic slide-show outline of each chapter, including key concepts, examples, and exhibits from the text.

**Cases in Cost Management: A Strategic Emphasis.** (Written by John K. Shank, Dartmouth College) The thirty-four case studies examined in this supplement helps professionals develop the ability to apply managerial cost analysis in decision-making.

**Readings and Issues in Cost Management, 2e.** (Edited by James Reeve, University of Tennessee) This supplement is designed to expose students to the concepts and information they need to become responsive and flexible managers. Articles cover topics such as TQM, employee empowerment, reengineering, continuous improvement, and short-cycle management.

**Managerial Accounting Activities Book.**  (Written by Neal Hannon, Bryant College) For those students and professors that want to explore additional classroom, business-related, and Internet activities for managerial accounting information and topics, this is the perfect companion text.

## ACKNOWLEDGMENTS

We wish to thank the many instructors and students whose comments and suggestions have helped us significantly in the preparation of all nine editions of this book. In particular, we want to thank the reviewers of the ninth edition:

Maurice L. Hirsch, Jr.
*Southern Illinois University, Edwardsville*

Noel McKeon
*Florida Community College at Jacksonville*

Leonard Stokes
*Siena College*

Olin Scott Stovall
*Abilene Christian College*

Sherri Hill Watters
*Limestone College/Coker College*

Special thanks goes to James Emig, Villanova University, for verifying the accuracy of the solutions manual, test bank, and study guide.

We also express our appreciation to the American Institute of Certified Public Accountants and Institute of Management Accountants for their generous permission to use problems adapted from past CPA and CMA examinations, respectively.

Many people at South-Western have been extremely helpful. We particularly appreciate the work of our Developmental Editor, Rebecca Glaab and our Acquisitions Editor, Rochelle Kronzek.  Others who made the work go more smoothly were Mike Busam (Production Editor) and Rick Lindgren (Accounting Team Director).

Finally, we thank our respective institutions, and our colleagues at those institutions, without whom the development of this volume, in its current and prior editions, would have been a much less pleasant task.

*Joseph G. Louderback*
*Jay S. Holmen*
*Geraldine F. Dominiak*

# BRIEF CONTENTS

# CONTENTS

*Chapter One*

# INTRODUCTION

## LEARNING OBJECTIVES

*After reading this chapter, you should be able to*
- *Describe four managerial functions and their relationships to accounting.*
- *Describe the value chain and explain how it relates to competitive strategies.*
- *Distinguish between financial accounting and managerial accounting.*
- *Describe some of the problems that arise in conventional manufacturing and how advanced manufacturing techniques overcome them.*
- *Describe the activities of managerial accountants.*
- *Describe the code of ethics that managerial accountants follow.*
- *Discuss some factors influencing the development of managerial accounting.*

*Electric utilities are facing increasing competition. Deregulation is causing both utilities and private companies to view their value chain in a different light. It is expected that many utilities will become far smaller by selling off their massive generating plants and becoming distribution companies. **Southern California Edison** builds and operates power plants for the exclusive use of private customers. **Enron** and **Louisville Gas & Electric** have traders that buy and sell electricity on the open market like a commodity. **AlliedSignal** has developed a line of small generators that is suitable for individual office and apartment buildings.\**

*Factory work has changed radically over the past few decades. At the **Toyota** plant in Georgetown, Kentucky, workers have multiple duties, rather than one duty as characterized by traditional production systems. Toyota workers can stop the production line when they find a defective unit, while at traditional plants, workers do not inspect work in progress. Instead, someone inspects at the end of the process. Two days every month, more than 50 automotive executives and engineers from competing firms tour the plant to learn how Toyota makes cars.\*\**

*The Institute of Management Accountants (IMA), the leading professional organization of management accountants, has established a Continuous Improvement Center (CIC) that offers services to financial managers in four areas: Assessment Assistance, Benchmark Database, Performance Improvement and Best Practices, and Recognition Programs. The first three assist managers in developing opportunities for improvement and enable managers to determine how well they are performing in relation to similar organizations and to the best organizations.*

> *The common thread in these descriptions is that change has made it necessary for organizations to operate differently—deregulation for the utility companies, foreign and domestic competition for many others. The need to streamline and improve financial processes to be competitive in the global marketplace lies behind the IMA's CIC. The study and practice of managerial accounting itself faces many changes brought on by globalization, the adoption of advanced manufacturing techniques, and new discoveries in various areas affecting what managerial accountants do and how they do it.*

*\*"Transforming the Power Business,"* Fortune, *September 29, 1997, 143–156.*
*\*\*"How Toyota Defies Gravity,"* Fortune, *December 8, 1997, 100.*

Accountants develop and communicate much of the economic information used by managers of businesses and other economic organizations and by external parties, such as creditors, stockholders, and governmental agencies. Providing information to outsiders is **financial accounting**. **Managerial accounting** (or *management accounting* or sometimes *internal accounting*) has to do with providing information to help meet the needs of managers inside an organization. Managerial accounting defies attempts at comprehensive, concise definition; it changes constantly to adapt to technological changes, changes in managers' needs, and new approaches to other functional areas of business—marketing, production, finance, organizational behavior, and corporate strategy. Managerial accounting is an indispensable part of the system that provides information to managers—the people whose decisions and actions determine the success or failure of an organization.

Managerial accounting is relevant to many activities of managers. Managers develop strategies for achieving goals, evaluate the performance of workers and of other managers, and make decisions. Managers decide what prices to charge for their products, whether to continue selling particular products, and whether to build a new factory. Many activities performed by managers have to do with acquiring and using economic resources (money, people, machinery, buildings), and managers need information to help them make those decisions. Managerial accountants generate much of the information managers use to plan operations and make decisions.

Managerial accounting applies to businesses because it deals with economic information, and businesses seek profits and other economic goals. Managerial accounting also applies to organizations that do not seek profits—government units, universities, hospitals, and churches—because those organizations, like businesses, use economic resources to meet their objectives. Hence, an understanding of the concepts of managerial accounting is important to managers in any organization. Therefore, in this book we do not assume that you plan to major in accounting or to become an accountant; we assume only that you are interested in managing.

## MANAGEMENT FUNCTIONS AND ACCOUNTING

Planning and control are two important management functions for which managers require information. The managerial accountant is the primary, though not the only, provider of information required for these functions. Useful information includes historical data such as prices of materials, wages paid to employees, rent on leased facilities or equipment, costs of fringe benefits, and various taxes. Managerial accountants prepare performance reports that assist managers in controlling their operations. They also provide information about the probable effects of proposed actions; for example, managerial accountants will estimate the profit that is likely to result from a successful advertising program. Managers also use information originating outside the firm. For example, statistics on the state of the economy are helpful in forecasting sales; patterns of population growth are relevant to decisions about locations for stores, warehouses, and manufacturing plants; statistics on the state of each industry in which a company operates are useful in forecasting both sales and related expenses.

## PLANNING

**Planning** is setting goals and developing strategies and tactics to achieve them. Some planning is routine, recurring, and relates principally to periods of a year or less. Such planning includes the important process of **budgeting**, which is relating goals to the means for achieving them. For example, if a $1 million profit is a goal, budgets will determine what machinery, cash, labor force, and other resources will be needed to achieve that goal and how to acquire the necessary amount of each resource. Without careful planning, a company achieves its goals only by accident.

A company that budgets a profit for a year must also determine how to reach that target. For example, what products should it emphasize, and at what prices? Managerial accountants develop data that help managers identify the more profitable products. Often, managerial accountants determine the effects of alternatives, such as different prices and selling efforts. (What will profit be if we cut prices 5 percent and increase volume 15 percent? Would spending $250,000 on advertising, or offering a 10 percent sales commission, be wise if it led to a 20 percent increase in sales?)

Managerial accountants prepare budgeted financial statements, often called **pro forma statements**. Among the most important statements is the budget of cash receipts and disbursements. The finance department uses forecasts of cash requirements to determine whether borrowing will be necessary. The management of cash is extremely critical; more companies fail because they run out of cash as a result of inadequate planning than because they are unable to make a profit. Making profits and maintaining adequate cash are two very different things; managers must understand that profitability does not guarantee generating enough cash to pay the bills.

Long-term planning, often called *strategic planning*, is also critical to organizations. Managerial accountants play an important role in formulating and implementing long-term strategies that relate to cost. There increasingly is an emphasis on strategic concerns such as value chains and supply chains. Today companies often join forces with their suppliers and customers to benefit all parties. A **value chain** is the entire set of processes that transforms raw materials into finished products. A single company operates in only a portion of the value chain; the chain also includes suppliers and customers.

Consider the value chain for the petroleum industry. The value chain would include exploring for oil, developing an oil field, pumping the crude oil, piping and shipping the oil, and refining the crude into gasoline. The value chain would continue with pipelines for gasoline, terminal operations where the gas is transferred from pipelines to trucks, transportation of the gasoline, and the retail operation of a service station or convenience store. **Chevron** spans a wide portion of the petroleum value chain as do other major integrated oil companies. Chevron has divisions that explore for oil as well as refine and market the oil. Chevron also owns pipelines, oil tankers, and trucks. Other companies, such as **Apache**, operate only in the oil exploration or the production portion of the value chain. Still other companies such as **QuikTrip** operate only in the retail operations portion of the chain.

The value chain in sports shoes and apparel includes designing, procuring materials, manufacturing the goods, marketing, distribution, and retailing. **Nike** participates in only a portion of the value chain, designing and marketing its shoes and apparel but subcontracting out the actual manufacturing of the goods. The accompanying Insight provides a summary of the petroleum value chain (see below).

An understanding of the value chain enables a company to evaluate how it competes. To sustain a competitive advantage, a company will follow either a **lowest cost strategy** or a **differentiation strategy**. The focus of a lowest cost strategy is to have the lowest cost relative to competitors. A firm with the lowest cost can control prices paid by customers by threatening other competitors with a price war. The focus of a differentiation strategy is to create a perception of uniqueness that will allow the company to charge a higher price. Some approaches to differentiation include brand loyalty, superior customer service, and product design. The value chain allows a company to understand the behavior of its costs and to determine sources of differentiation. The accompanying Insight describes the strategies of several companies (see next page).

## **IN** SIGHT

### Value Chain

In late March 1998 the average retail price for a gallon of gasoline fell to around a dollar—a record low, adjusted for inflation. Here's a rough breakdown of where that dollar goes when you pull away from the pump.

- $0.34: Your contribution to the folks drilling crude oil.
- $0.06: For the refining process, which turns raw crude into gas via heat and chemical treatment.
- $0.05: Grist for the middleman. After gas is refined, wholesalers sell it to your local station, receiving a nickel per gallon for their trouble.
- $0.43: Average federal, state, and local taxes. The federal cut is 18.3 cents, but state excise taxes run from 7.5 cents (Georgia) to a crippling 36 cents (Connecticut).
- $0.12: The service stations' just reward.

*Source: Ed Brown, "Where Your Gas Money Goes," Fortune, April 27, 1998, 72.*

**SIGHT**

### Competitive Strategies

**Lowe's** 1996 Annual Report stated their strategy as follows: "As a dedicated low cost operator, our strategy is to lower operating costs as a percentage of sales, which will enable us to lower our retail prices. Lower prices will bring us more customers, which will increase sales and allow us to lower prices even more."

**Home Depot's** 1996 Annual Report stated that it is looking "for additional ways to become more efficient and reduce costs. A major area of focus was our supply chain, getting merchandise from our suppliers into the hands of our customers. We are developing ways to flow goods through the distribution channels that offer the lowest handling and transportation costs while meeting target in-stock levels . . . to have the potential to lower our cost of goods sold and shorten the time it takes to get merchandise on the shelves."

**Gucci**, the maker of handbags, shoes, and accessories, has a differentiation focus. Gucci's concern is to have a careful balance between the maintenance of its brand image and over-exploitation through mass consumption.

*Source: Annual Reports.*

**Decision Making.**  Much of the information provided by managerial accountants is used in **decision making**, which is an important part of planning. Some decision making is carried on continually. Managers decide daily or weekly how many units of a product to buy or make, or how much advertising to place in specific newspapers or on specific radio stations. They also set prices for products or services.

Some decisions are made infrequently, such as whether to build a new factory, buy a new warehouse, introduce a new product line, or enter a foreign market. Accounting systems do not routinely generate data for such analyses, so managerial accountants do special analyses. They determine what data are needed, present the data in an understandable way, and explain the analyses to the managers making the decisions.

Managerial accountants assist managers in making decisions not only by providing information, but by using analytical techniques that help managers understand the implications of a decision. For example, managerial accountants can tell managers how many units of a new product they must sell to earn a desired profit or what cost savings are necessary to justify buying new machinery. We discuss many of these techniques in this book.

**Decision Making and Behavior.**  Although managers use accounting data extensively in making decisions, such data do not *answer* the questions that managers face. *People* make decisions, and people bring to decision making their experience, values, and knowledge that usually cannot be incorporated into quantitative analyses. Managers might take actions because of some qualitative factor not captured in the accounting data. For example, managers of a company whose strategies include technological leadership might launch a new product that they expect to be unprofitable. Quantifying the benefits of such leadership is very difficult. A report of the quantitative analysis likely would include a comment about those benefits. That is, reports from managerial accountants recognize factors whose financial implications are not incorporated in the quantitative analyses.

## CONTROL

**Control** is determining whether goals are being met, and if not, what can be done. What changes might we make to achieve our goals? Should we change our goals? Managerial accounting is used extensively in control because many goals are expressed in dollar terms—so much sales, so much cost—and because managerial accountants use analytical tools to help managers understand the reasons for not achieving goals. Implicit in control is **performance evaluation**—managers reviewing the accomplishments of their employees and weighing them against standards. Many such evaluations use managerial accounting information. For many managers, **control reports**, which often show actual and budgeted results, are the most common contact with managerial accounting information.

Low-level managers and managers of small enterprises control through close physical supervision, but the size of modern organizations precludes such close contact across several organizational levels. Even managers in relatively small companies usually cannot exercise constant oversight of the activities of their staffs. The principle of management by exception helps managers to control operations. Applying this principle, managers rely on reports to keep informed. Reports reduce the need for minute-by-minute, physical supervision and allow managers time to perform their other functions. Many of these reports detail costs for which managers are responsible and usually relate those costs to budgeted costs. As a rule, when budgeted and actual results are close, managers conclude that operations are going according to plan and need no special investigation. When budgeted and actual results differ significantly, managers usually investigate to determine what is going wrong and who might need help. Thus, accounting reports partially substitute for managers' personal supervision of activities.

Control reports do not tell managers what to do. That actual results differ significantly from planned results does not tell managers why the results differed. Control reports provide feedback to help managers determine where attention might be required. They do not tell managers how to correct any problems that might exist nor do they establish who performed satisfactorily or unsatisfactorily. Substandard performance could result from conditions outside a manager's control.

**Performance Evaluation.**    Performance evaluation and control are closely related. Managers are evaluated partly on the basis of how well they control their operations: whether they achieve budgeted sales, meet budgeted cost levels, or produce budgeted quantities of product. Higher-level managers who are not involved directly in day-to-day activities rely on the information reported by management accountants about the performance of lower-level managers.

Developing suitable measures of performance for a given manager is a behavioral problem. Many people think of accounting data as factual, neutral, or objective. On the contrary, accounting data and reports can motivate people to act in various ways—some desirable, some not. For example, evaluating the performance of sales managers on the basis of total sales dollars, a seemingly objective accounting figure, will motivate them to concentrate on obtaining the highest dollar sales without regard to the *profitability* of the products sold. The result might be very high sales but very low profits. Gross profit or other measures that reflect costs as well as revenues are better measures. Similarly, evaluating production managers by whether they meet budgeted costs might tempt them to ignore product quality, postpone preventive maintenance, or take other actions that harm the company in the long run. Selecting appropriate measures of performance is a constant concern of both managers and managerial accountants.

Effective performance evaluation requires that performance measures capture the essential aspects of the job. Failure to do so can be counterproductive to the company's best interests as the previous examples show. Managerial accountants continue to research the ways in which the form and content of reports influence the actions of those who receive them. The reports developed by managerial accountants should continue to improve as a result of such research. In any case, the likelihood of misdirected managerial efforts is reduced when a manager is fully informed about the bases on which his or her performance will be evaluated.

## MANAGERIAL ACCOUNTING AND FINANCIAL ACCOUNTING

Both managerial and financial accounting deal with economic events. Both require quantifying the results of economic activity, and both are concerned with revenues and expenses, assets, liabilities, and cash flows. Both, therefore, involve financial statements, and both suffer from the difficulties of capturing, in quantitative terms, the many aspects of an economic event. The major differences between financial and managerial accounting arise because they serve different audiences.

Financial accounting serves persons outside the firm, such as creditors, customers, government units, and investors. Hence, financial accounting reports are concerned mostly with the company as a whole. In contrast, managerial accounting reports usually deal with segments of a firm; managers receive information related to their own responsibilities rather than to the entire firm. The different audiences for accounting information use information for different purposes. Creditors and investors use information to decide whether or not to extend credit to the firm, and whether to buy, sell, or hold its stock. People inside the company use accounting information to make decisions such as which of several products to sell, whether to issue bonds or stock, which employees to reward for good performance, and what prices to charge.

The classification schemes used in managerial accounting reports usually differ from those in financial accounting reports. In financial accounting, costs are usually classified by the object of the expense (salaries, taxes, rent, repairs) or by the function of the expense (cost of goods sold, selling expenses, administrative expenses, financing expenses). In contrast, reports for managerial accounting purposes often follow other cost classification schemes. Some reports are based on the behavior of costs, separating costs that change when activity levels change from costs that do not change regardless of the level of activity. Other managerial accounting reports concentrate on the concepts of responsibility and controllability; costs are classified according to whether or not a particular manager is responsible for the cost and can control it. These classification schemes—behavior, responsibility, and controllability—underlie much of the material in this book and are critical to almost all aspects of planning and control.

Information in financial accounting reports might also differ in source and nature from that in managerial accounting reports. Financial accounting reports are developed from the basic accounting system, which captures data about completed transactions. Some managerial accounting reports incorporate information that is not found in the financial accounting system. Such information might relate to expected future transactions (such as budgeted sales and costs) or alternatives to past transactions (such as showing what income would have been if we had sold more units at a lower price). Some very important analyses in managerial accounting use hypothetical transactions. As later chapters describe, one of the costs associated with product quality is the cost of external failure, which is all of the costs of selling a unit that fails when used by the customer. Perhaps the most important cost is the lost sales from the ill will such failures cause, a cost that will never be recorded in the company's accounting system. These external failure costs occur in a very late portion of the value chain—the customer. The cause of the failure is likely due to activities that occur much earlier in the chain, perhaps even in portions of the chain prior to the start of manufacturing.

Managerial accounting reports are specifically designed for a particular user or a particular decision; financial accounting reports are general purpose. For this reason, a particular cost might appear on one internal report and not on another; the cost might be relevant for some internal decisions and not for others. We can illustrate this point with an example from everyday life. Suppose you own a car and pay $450 for insurance per year. That cost is part of the total cost of owning the car, but it is irrelevant if you are trying to determine how much it will cost to take a 200-mile trip. Because you pay the same $450 for insurance whether you take the trip or not, you can ignore it in determining the cost of the trip. The phrase "different costs for different purposes" describes the idea that relevance depends on the specific purpose.

Financial and managerial accounting information differ in that the former is primarily historical while the latter is concerned more with the future. Although many items in financial statements incorporate expectations (e.g., estimated useful life and residual value in the computation of depreciation, estimated warranty work to be done on items sold, and so on), financial accounting reports concentrate on the results of past decisions. Internal reports to managers often concentrate on what is likely to happen in the future.

Managerial accounting has no external restrictions such as the generally accepted accounting principles (GAAP) that govern financial accounting. For managerial purposes, relevance is the important concern, and managerial accountants respond to specific information requirements. For example, market price (replacement cost, fair market value, or some other measure) will be used in a managerial accounting report if it will help the manager make a better decision. Such alternatives are usually not allowed in financial accounting.

Advances in computer technology, especially in the ability to store and retrieve large amounts of information, have been accompanied by an unfortunate side effect called information overload. Some managers receive far more information than they can possibly use. One challenge in managerial accounting is to develop ways to determine what information is relevant for particular managers, summarize the information, and present it in a usable form. The general manager of a factory employing 500 people cannot effectively use weekly reports showing the actual costs in 823 categories. That manager could, however, use a report showing which costs differed significantly from their budgeted amounts. Communication between managers and managerial accountants is important so that managers receive the information they need and need the information they receive.

## ADVANCED MANUFACTURING

One of the driving forces behind many recent developments in managerial accounting is profound changes in manufacturing. These changes have carried over to service and merchandising organizations as well. At various points throughout this text we use terms such as advanced manufacturing environment, **advanced manufacturing**, world-class manufacturing, or just-in-time manufacturing to describe such developments. To help you better understand these references, we discuss those changes and some of their implications here.

### CONVENTIONAL MANUFACTURING: ITS BACKGROUND AND ITS PROBLEMS

Following World War II, American companies were the unchallenged world leaders in manufacturing. They had strong advantages in product quality, capacity, and distribution facilities and, exaggerating only a little, they could sell nearly anything they made. Production was the critical activity and the philosophy was to "get it out the door."

In this environment, many U.S. manufacturers adopted practices that reflected a "just-in-case" philosophy. As insurance against production delays caused by defects in components or the unavailability of materials, companies routinely purchased more than required to meet production needs. (They inspected all incoming shipments, though they often adopted sophisticated statistical techniques to cope with this growing task.) To avoid production shortfalls caused by manufacturing errors (or by delays because of defects in materials), companies produced more than required and also scheduled production much earlier than required to meet shipping dates. As a result, **lead time** or **cycle time**—the period that begins with the arrival of materials and ends with shipment of a finished unit—extended well beyond the time needed for the manufacturing process alone. A product that could be manufactured in a day or two might have a lead time of one, two, or even three months. This type of manufacturing is called "push," because parts and components push their way through the system whether they are needed or not.

Not surprisingly, these manufacturing practices generated significant costs. The high inventories of materials and finished units increased the risk of spoilage and obsolescence, as well as the costs of storage, insurance, financing, and handling. Inspecting raw materials, component parts, and finished units also was costly. Inevitably, prices rose to cover the increased costs. An unfortunate outcome of striving to meet output requirements on a timely basis was that waste, scrap, and the reworking of defective units came to be thought of as normal. This attitude did not encourage high quality and might even have discouraged quality control efforts. Thus, practices that were wise if quality was suspect actually contributed to lowering quality.

Philosophies and practices that characterize the new manufacturing environment surfaced as overseas companies began to compete with U.S. manufacturers. In searching for a competitive edge, overseas manufacturers concentrated on the weaknesses of conventional manufacturing practices, particularly mediocre quality and high inventories. Terms used to describe a manufacturing environment that eliminates those weaknesses include just-in-time manufacturing, world-class manufacturing, and advanced manufacturing.

## JUST-IN-TIME (JIT) MANUFACTURING

**Just-in-time (JIT) manufacturing** is a philosophy that focuses on timing, efficiency, and quality in meeting commitments. Companies that employ JIT strive for continual improvement and relentlessly search out and eliminate waste of materials, time, and space. One aspect of this philosophy is to increase customer satisfaction by reducing lead time. Advocates of the JIT philosophy continually strive to promote a smooth and rapid flow of materials and components into finished products.

**Inventory and Lead Time.**    The term "just in time" refers to one way of characterizing the goals of advanced manufacturing techniques. Under ideal conditions, purchased materials and components arrive just in time to be used, partly assembled units arrive at work stations just in time for the next step in production, and finished units emerge from production just in time to meet the shipping date requested by the customer. This is a "pull" environment, where the need for a finished unit pulls the parts and components along. Of course, ideal conditions are virtually impossible to achieve, but they serve as goals against which to measure progress, and progress has been dramatic in many cases. As examples, some factories receive deliveries of some items several times a day, and some have eliminated loading docks in favor of entrances allowing trucks to deliver materials directly to work stations. The delivery system reduces space requirements and eliminates the steps of placing materials in storage and then later taking them to work stations when needed.  The trucks also carry away finished products so that they do not have to be stored and then taken out again for delivery to customers. (**Allen-Bradley** reports that its "factory within a factory" can take an order one day, produce the required units, and ship the order the following day, with only a small amount of material and no finished or unfinished units on hand at the end of the day.)  Progress toward achieving just-in-time goals means shortened lead times, as well as reduced inventories and inventory costs. The accompanying Insight describes a computer company's inventory strategy.

The JIT philosophy is concerned with all aspects of cycle time, not just inventory reduction. Managers continually scrutinize each step in the production process itself, trying to determine which cost-producing and time-consuming activities add value to the final product and which do not. For example, moving partially finished units from one work station to another is a non-value-adding activity. Hence, work stations in a JIT environment are often adjacent, rather than being spread throughout a factory, so that as much work as possible is done in a small cluster of machinery and workers, called a **manufacturing cell**. Coupling the use of cells with reduced needs for space to store inventories of various types, JIT operations use less space than conventional operations. Exhibit 1-1 (page 12) illustrates production flows in a conventional operation and a JIT operation.

### Dell Computer Strategy

**Dell Computer Corporation**, the third largest personal computer manufacturer, has focused its strategy solely on a direct market approach. Customers (large corporations such as **Ford**, **Boeing**, and **Texaco**; federal, state, and local governments; and individuals) deal directly with Dell rather than with a retailer. Eliminating the middleman in the distribution channel, coupled with a just-in-time production system that can assemble, test, and pack—complete with installed software—a customized personal computer in just eight hours from the time an order is received, enables Dell to minimize the risks of carrying a rapidly changing inventory of parts. One risk is to hold inventory that does not meet customer demands while chips are becoming faster and hard drives larger. Another risk is to not be able to protect inventory in the distribution channel from drops in prices. This is extremely important in an industry where component prices are falling 1% per week. In 1998, Dell held an average of seven days of supply in inventory compared with an average of 80 days or more for competitors that sell through retail stores or resellers.

*Source: Annual Report.*

**Multiskilled Workers.**   People are critical to any organization and especially so in JIT companies that give workers much more responsibility than do conventional manufacturers. Workers in a JIT company must master all of the skills required in cells. They must do much of their own maintenance and repair work. Some JIT companies, such as **Harley-Davidson**, give raises only to employees who learn new skills. People work in teams and often earn bonuses based on the performance of their teams. **New Balance**, the maker of athletic shoes, recently changed from assembly line to team manufacturing.

**Flexible Manufacturing.**   In their efforts to reduce production time, JIT managers also have emphasized reducing setup time, the time required to change machine settings from making one product to making another. Conventional manufacturers often make long production runs of each product, which result in setup times measured in hours. The term **flexible manufacturing system** describes a JIT operation with a setup time of a few minutes that can respond very quickly to customer orders. For example, some plants that manufacture wearing apparel, which often has a high risk of obsolescence, can make and ship an order of ten pairs of walking shorts, in various sizes, colors, and patterns, within 24 hours of receiving the order. A manufacturer's ability to achieve flexible manufacturing depends partly on the available technology. But the goal of a flexible manufacturing system is to produce by units, rather than by batches.

   **Computer-integrated manufacturing (CIM)** goes beyond flexible manufacturing so that a factory is virtually all automated and controlled by computer. Some versions of CIM include integration of all aspects of products, from design through development into production.

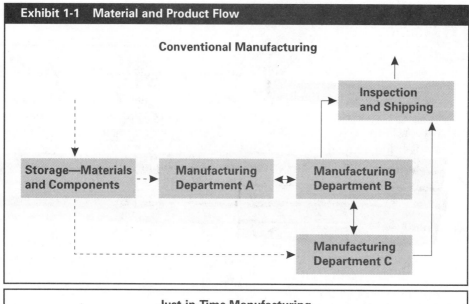

**Exhibit 1-1    Material and Product Flow**

**Conventional Manufacturing**

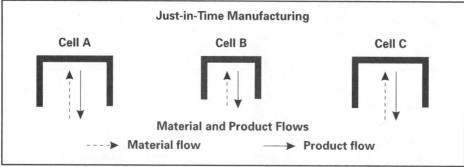

**Just-in-Time Manufacturing**

**Material and Product Flows**

- - - ▸ **Material flow**        ⟶ **Product flow**

**Total Quality Control.**    Of course, total quality control or total quality management is critical to the success of JIT operations. If little or no inventory of materials and components exist, everything received must be without defects or production could be delayed. Manufacturing errors leading to defective units cannot be tolerated. Several practices have evolved to achieve this condition, which is often referred to as *zero defects*. JIT companies stop inspecting incoming shipments when they are convinced that a supplier is providing components of the desired quality, and they stop buying from suppliers who do not meet that standard.

Similarly, JIT operations pinpoint problems early because workers inspect units throughout production instead of only at a few formal inspection points. Moreover, to reduce costs and increase quality, JIT manufacturers design quality and ease of manufacturability into products. Because of this lack of coordination in conventional manufacturing, product designers rarely talk with production people. Production engineers develop a manufacturing process to accommodate the design specifications, even though a minor design change might greatly simplify production. Design flaws often surface as manufacturing difficulties or in customer dissatisfaction. The conventional company is often described as a field of silos, with no connections among marketing, production, design, and customer service.

JIT companies stress cooperation and the blurring of lines of authority. **Nokia**, the Finnish manufacturer of cellular telephones, built research and development laboratories next to each of its five major factories so that it could move quickly from the lab to the factory. It engineers "concurrently" with research and development, saving valuable time and ensuring coordination of the two functions. Cellular phones have short life cycles, so quick response is critical. **Culp, Inc.** is a $260 million manufacturer of decorative fabrics for the home furnishings industry, where design is important. The company has determined that over 80 percent of total costs are built into products at the design stage. The company's cost management and design people now work together. The company uses redesign as a strategic tool with new products that do not meet profit targets, rather than simply trying to reduce their manufacturing costs.

The following table summarizes and contrasts JIT and conventional manufacturing.

| JIT Manufacturing | Conventional Manufacturing |
| --- | --- |
| Manufacturing cells concentrating on one product | Departments working on all products |
| Multiskilled workers | Single-skilled workers |
| Small batches, smooth flows | Large batches, erratic flows |
| Total quality control | Some defects seen as inevitable |
| Short production cycle | Long production cycle |
| Zero or trivial inventories | Large inventories held as buffers |
| Daily delivery of materials/components | Large deliveries at irregular intervals |
| Relentless search to improve, eliminate all waste | Achieve acceptable performance |
| Integrate design and manufacturing | Design and manufacturing separate |

## ACTIVITIES OF MANAGERIAL ACCOUNTANTS

Managers of line functions are concerned with the primary operating activities of the organization—manufacturing (or buying) and selling a physical product or performing a service. A staff manager manages a department that serves other departments. For example, financial managers obtain the cash to keep operations running smoothly. The manager of the legal department advises other managers regarding the legal ramifications of actions.

Accounting is a staff function, with managerial accountants providing information to other managers. Information can relate to financial statements, tax problems, dealings with governmental authorities, and other matters. The managerial accountant, like other staff managers, often recommends courses of action to those using the information. But neither the managerial accountant, nor any other staff manager, can impose recommendations on line managers. Nevertheless, because of their expertise, staff managers can influence decisions. Staff managers, like all managers, also manage their own departments.

Managerial accountants in businesses include people in the controller's office, as well as budget analysts, cost analysts, and financial analysts. A large company, or a division of a large company, might have several hundred people performing managerial accounting functions. In small businesses the controller and an assistant might carry out all of the other managerial accounting functions. Many managers look at managerial accountants as people who can identify and solve problems; help in implementing programs of continuous improvement and total quality management; and evaluate actions, products, and decisions.

The specific duties of managerial accountants include (1) assisting in the design of the organization's information system, (2) ensuring that the system performs adequately, (3) periodically reporting information to interested managers, and (4) undertaking special analyses.

The information system must meet the needs of all people who require information to perform their jobs. Managers responsible for sales of a particular product might need weekly sales reports for each territory. Their supervisor, who also supervises other sales managers, might need only a weekly report for a group (or line) of products. The chief sales executive might want only monthly, not weekly, reports of sales by product groups and sales territories. Managerial accountants must ensure that the system meets these varying needs.

Computers usually record transactions in journals and ledgers. Accountants are responsible for supervising the gathering of data and for monitoring the system, making sure it functions as intended and is used appropriately. Regular, periodic reporting is the heart of managerial accountants' work in many organizations. One of the challenges here is ensuring that other managers receive relevant information and are not overwhelmed by irrelevant information. For some years, many people believed that managers should receive all of the information that could possibly be relevant. This view no longer prevails; managers' time is too valuable to spend sifting through material until they find what they need.

Special analyses are required when managers consider nonroutine actions. In some cases, such as the location of a new plant, relevant data might not be available in a form that enables managers to decide on the best course of action. Accountants must develop relevant information to serve such special purposes.

Managerial accountants have gained status in recent years as they now spend more time analyzing a company's operations and less with the problems of recording and computing costs of products. The Institute of Management Accountants (IMA), the principal organization of managerial accountants in the United States, has instituted a program to provide certifications for managerial accountants and financial managers. The Certified Management Accountant (CMA) examination was first given in 1972. A listing of the required subject areas in the CMA examination indicates the breadth of knowledge expected of the professional managerial accountant. The examination consists of the following four parts: Economics, Finance, and Management; Financial Accounting and Reporting; Management Reporting, Analysis, and Behavioral Issues; and Decision Analysis and Information Systems. The Certified in Financial Management (CFM) examination was first given in 1996. The CFM examination is similar to the CMA examination with one major difference: the Financial Accounting and Reporting section is replaced with Corporate Financial Management. The IMA also promulgated a code of ethics for management accountants, which is discussed in the next section.

The role of the management accountant is expanding in many ways, in many companies. A manager at **ITT Automotive** stated "now the accountants are not only the interpreters, but they help drive management toward the proper response to what the numbers are telling us and toward helping them tie together the financial results with the business strategies. In a nutshell, going from a number-crunching-type mode to a business partnership, more strategic approach." A **Hewlett-Packard** finance manager summed up the change: "We are not accountants; we are analysts and business partners."[1]

## ETHICS

In 1983, the Institute of Management Accountants published the Standards of Ethical Conduct for Management Accountants. The Institute also established an Ethics Committee and an Ethics Counseling Service. Management accountants are expected to abide by the Standards, which are reproduced in Exhibit 1-2.

---

**Exhibit 1-2   Standards of Ethical Conduct**

### STANDARDS OF ETHICAL CONDUCT FOR MANAGEMENT ACCOUNTANTS

Management accountants have an obligation to the organizations they serve, their profession, the public, and themselves to maintain the highest standards of ethical conduct. In recognition of this obligation, the Institute of Management Accountants, formerly the National Association of Accountants, has promulgated the following standards of ethical conduct for management accountants. Adherence to these standards is integral to achieving the *Objectives of Management Accounting.** Management accountants shall not commit acts contrary to these standards nor shall they condone the commission of such acts by others within their organizations.

#### COMPETENCE

Management accountants have a responsibility to:

- Maintain an appropriate level of professional competence by ongoing development of their knowledge and skills.
- Perform their professional duties in accordance with relevant laws, regulations, and technical standards.
- Prepare complete and clear reports and recommendations after appropriate analyses of relevant and reliable information.

#### CONFIDENTIALITY

Management accountants have a responsibility to:

- Refrain from disclosing confidential information acquired in the course of their work except when authorized, unless legally obligated to do so.
- Inform subordinates as appropriate regarding the confidentiality of information acquired in the course of their work and monitor their activities to assure the maintenance of that confidentiality.
- Refrain from using or appearing to use confidential information acquired in the course of their work for unethical or illegal advantage either personally or through third parties.

#### INTEGRITY

Management accountants have a responsibility to:

- Avoid actual or apparent conflicts of interest and advise all appropriate parties of any potential conflict.
- Refrain from engaging in any activity that would prejudice their ability to carry out their duties ethically.
- Refuse any gift, favor, or hospitality that would influence or would appear to influence their actions.

---

1  Gary Siegel and C.S. "Bud" Kulesza, "The Practice Analysis of Management Accounting," Management Accounting, *April 1996, 20–28.*

- Refrain from either actively or passively subverting the attainment of the organization's legitimate and ethical objectives.
- Recognize and communicate professional limitations or other constraints that would preclude responsible judgment or successful performance of an activity.
- Communicate unfavorable as well as favorable information and professional judgments or opinions.
- Refrain from engaging in or supporting any activity that would discredit the profession.

## OBJECTIVITY

Management accountants have a responsibility to:

- Communicate information fairly and objectively.
- Disclose fully all relevant information that could reasonably be expected to influence an intended user's understanding of the reports, comments, and recommendations presented.

## RESOLUTION OF ETHICAL CONFLICT

In applying the standards of ethical conduct, management accountants may encounter problems in identifying unethical behavior or in resolving an ethical conflict. When faced with significant ethical issues, management accountants should follow the established policies of the organization bearing on the resolution of such conflict. If these policies do not resolve the ethical conflict, management accountants should consider the following course of action:

- Discuss such problems with the immediate superior except when it appears that the superior is involved, in which case the problem should be presented initially to the next higher managerial level. If satisfactory resolution cannot be achieved when the problem is initially presented, submit the issues to the next higher managerial level.

  If the immediate superior is the chief executive officer, or equivalent, the acceptable reviewing authority may be a group such as the audit committee, executive committee, board of directors, board of trustees, or owners. Contact with levels above the immediate superior should be initiated only with the superior's knowledge, assuming the superior is not involved.
- Clarify relevant concepts by confidential discussion with an objective advisor to obtain an understanding of possible courses of action.
- If the ethical conflict still exists after exhausting all levels of internal review, the management accountant may have no other recourse on significant matters than to resign from the organization and to submit an informative memorandum to an appropriate representative of the organization.

Except where legally prescribed, communication of such problems to authorities or individuals not employed or engaged by the organization is not considered appropriate.

* Institute of Management Accountants, formerly National Association of Accountants, Statements on Management Accounting: Objectives of Management Accounting, Statement No. 1B, New York, N.Y., June 17, 1982.

Should you work as a controller or in some other managerial accounting position, you will be expected to comply with the Standards. Even if you are not subject to the code, there are two reasons why it is important that you know something about it. First, as a manager you have the right to expect ethical behavior from the managerial accountants with whom you work. Second, you should be aware that managerial accountants are prohibited from committing unethical acts on behalf of managers in the company by which they are employed.

The Standards have four sections: competence, confidentiality, integrity, and objectivity. The competence provisions require management accountants to develop their knowledge and skills and to do their tasks in accordance with relevant laws, regulations, and standards. The confidentiality provisions forbid them to act on, or even appear to act on, confidential information they acquire in doing their work. This provision thus forbids "insider" actions such as selling the company's stock upon learning that it is likely to lose a major lawsuit. The integrity provisions cover avoidance of conflicts of interest, improprieties of accepting gifts or favors, and other matters generally associated with professional behavior. The objectivity provisions require management accountants to "communicate information fairly and objectively" and to "disclose fully all relevant information. . . ."

Management accountants ethically cannot ignore relevant data or use wildly optimistic projections to justify a course of action. Managers in charge of a product line that is not doing well, who fear for their jobs, might pressure management accountants to use exceedingly optimistic sales projections in an analysis. For management accountants to do so would compromise their professionalism. Moreover, management accountants could not ethically recommend buying office equipment from a company owned by a family member unless they disclosed the family member's interest to the persons making the decision.

The Standards require professional behavior, especially in avoiding conflicts of interest. They require management accountants to bring bad news to the attention of their supervisors, and to work competently. They also recognize that management accountants faced with a serious ethical conflict might have to resign and explain why to "an appropriate representative of the organization." Periodically, the Standards are reprinted in *Management Accounting*, the monthly magazine of the Institute, and the magazine's monthly column on ethics contains case studies and other materials that serve to remind management accountants of their ethical responsibilities.

## INTERNATIONAL ASPECTS OF MANAGERIAL ACCOUNTING

In today's global economy, managers face new and more complex decisions. Should capital be raised in the United States or elsewhere? Where should the company manufacture the products it sells to customers in and outside of the United States? What products should the company make and in which countries? Should the company make some parts for its products in one country and complete the manufacturing process in others? Would it be profitable to change some products to accommodate differences among countries in tastes and culture? These decisions expand the information needs that managerial accountants must meet and influence the development of managerial accounting.

Perhaps the most pervasive problem facing multinational companies is the management of foreign currency. **The Toronto Blue Jays** illustrate the problem of changing currency values. The Blue Jays pay their players in U.S. dollars, but collect gate receipts in Canadian dollars. (They pay some expenses in Canadian dollars, but player salaries are the major expense.) Suppose the Canadian dollar is worth 0.90 U.S. dollars ($0.90). Then the U.S. dollar is worth $1.111 Canadian dollars ($1.00/$0.90). Paying each dollar of salary requires 1.111 Canadian dollars. If the value of the Canadian dollar drops to $0.80, is the team better off or worse off? It is worse off because each U.S. dollar in salary now requires 1.25 Canadian dollars ($1.00/$0.80). The team must take more of its Canadian dollars to the bank to exchange for U.S. dollars than it previously did. Of course, if the Canadian dollar rises to $0.95, the team is better off. The Blue Jays and other organizations with similar dealings can hedge against unfavorable foreign currency movements by purchasing futures contracts that allow them to buy U.S. dollars at future dates at specific prices. Such actions make certain what the companies will have to pay, but eliminate the possibility of their making money from a favorable move in the dollar.

The following excerpt from a **Dell Computer Corporation** annual report indicates the importance of foreign currency management.

"The Company's objective in managing its exposure to foreign currency exchange rate fluctuations is to reduce the impact of adverse fluctuations in earnings and cash flows associated with foreign currency exchange rate changes. Accordingly, the Company utilizes foreign currency option contracts and forward contracts to hedge its exposure on anticipated transactions and firm commitments. The principle currencies hedged are the British pound, Japanese yen, German mark, French franc and Canadian dollar. The Company monitors its foreign exchange exposures daily to ensure the overall effectiveness of its foreign currency hedge positions. However, there can be no assurance the Company's foreign currency hedging activities will substantially offset the impact of fluctuations in currency exchange rates on its results of operations and financial position."

At various points in this text we consider some of the special issues raised when analyzing the decisions confronting managers of international companies.

## DEREGULATION

Deregulation is increasingly important to many companies and is among the factors that are influencing management accounting. In some regulated environments companies are guaranteed a stipulated rate of profit. Such companies do not need to control costs because they can pass them along to consumers. Many such companies now face competition and the market sets prices, not a regulatory agency. Electric utilities will soon be able to compete with other utilities for commercial electric customers. The regional **Bell** telephone companies have also begun to face competition from cellular companies and personal service communications enterprises. Such competition requires different information, especially measures of performance. Airlines were deregulated in the early 1980s, which required them to pay much more attention to costs and allowed carriers such as **Southwest Airlines** to grow profitably while offering very low fares.

## SUMMARY

Managerial accounting and financial accounting both deal with economic events and reports about them. But the two areas of accounting differ in many ways, primarily because they serve different audiences. Managerial accounting serves internal managers in organizations. In businesses, top executives and managers in sales, production, finance, and accounting use accounting data for planning and control, including decision making and performance evaluation. Managers of not-for-profit organizations perform many of these same functions and use much of the same accounting data as managers in businesses.

As you study managerial accounting, you will be introduced to some of the activities managers carry out in several areas of a business or other economic organizations. Changes in the manufacturing environment continue to prompt changes in managerial accounting as well as in related disciplines. Some managerial accounting concept or type of report relates to almost every area of managerial activity, and managerial accounting draws heavily on the concepts from related business disciplines. Management accountants are expected to carry out their activities in a manner consistent with their ethical responsibilities.

## KEY TERMS

advanced manufacturing   *(9)*
budgeting   *(3)*
computer-integrated manufacturing
   (CIM)   *(11)*
control   *(6)*
control reports   *(6)*
cycle time   *(9)*
decision making   *(5)*
differentiation strategy   *(4)*
financial accounting   *(2)*

flexible manufacturing system   *(11)*
just-in-time (JIT) manufacturing   *(10)*
lead time   *(9)*
lowest cost strategy   *(4)*
managerial accounting   *(2)*
manufacturing cell   *(10)*
performance evaluation   *(6)*
planning   *(3)*
pro forma statements   *(3)*
value chain   *(3)*

## ASSIGNMENT MATERIAL

### INTERNET ACTIVITY

Two different professional organizations to which accountants may belong are the American Institute of Certified Public Accountants (AICPA) and the Institute of Management Accountants (IMA). Use a Web search engine such as Yahoo to find the AICPA and IMA websites. Search these sites to find out about the CPA, CMA, and CFM examinations. Be prepared to describe and discuss what you discovered.

## QUESTIONS FOR DISCUSSION

**1-1  *Everyday planning and control***   For each of the following activities, find an analogy to the planning and control process described in the chapter. Describe the process to be undertaken in these activities and compare with the process described in the chapter.

(a) Taking a course in college, including preparation and study, taking examinations, and evaluating test results.
(b) Taking a long automobile trip.
(c) Decorating your room or apartment.
(d) Coaching an athletic team.

**1-2   *Ethics*** For each of the following situations, indicate which, if any, of the Standards of Ethical Conduct are violated.

(a) Frank Wright, an assistant controller, informs his sister, a financial analyst, that the company he works for will report record earnings in the coming quarter. Frank's sister has given him some profitable tips in the past and he wants to repay her.
(b) In order to please his superior, Bart Roberts, an ambitious management accountant, slants an analysis on building a new factory that makes the project appear profitable when it probably will not be. His superior will be promoted to controller if the plant is built and told Roberts she "sure hoped the analysis would be favorable."

**1-3   *Who needs financial accounting?*** The chapter points out that differences between financial and managerial accounting relate to differences in the decisions made by managers and those made by parties external to the firm. If managerial accounting is supposed to serve the information needs of managers, why should managers know and understand financial accounting?

**1-4   *Conventional versus world-class manufacturing*** Indicate whether each of the following costs should be higher or lower for a world-class (or JIT) manufacturer than for a conventional manufacturer. Briefly state why.

(a) Product warranty costs.
(b) Salaries of quality control inspectors.
(c) Amounts paid to vendors for parts and components.
(d) Wage *rates* for direct laborers.
(e) Total supervisory salaries.
(f) Warehousing costs, including rent or depreciation on space, salaries and wages of employees, utilities, etc.

**1-5   *Value chain*** Acme Motors, a major automobile manufacturer, is considering requiring its suppliers to be certified to a quality standard known as ISO 9000.

(a) What impact will this have on Acme Motors' quality costs?
(b) What will be the impact on the relative costs of all of the companies along the value chain?

## PROBLEMS

**1-6   *Review of financial statement preparation*** Following is the balance sheet for Illustrative Company as of December 31, 20X1, and selected information relating to activities in 20X2.

**Illustrative Company**
**Balance Sheet**
**as of December 31, 20X1**

Assets

Current assets:

| | | |
|---|---:|---:|
| Cash | | $ 20,000 |
| Accounts receivable | | 50,000 |
| Inventory | | 70,000 |
| Total current assets | | $140,000 |
| Property, plant, and equipment: | | |
| Cost | $520,000 | |
| Less: Accumulated depreciation | 208,000 | |
| Net | | 312,000 |
| Total assets | | $452,000 |

Equities

Current liabilities:

| | | |
|---|---:|---:|
| Accounts payable | | $ 20,000 |
| Taxes payable | | 22,000 |
| Total current liabilities | | $ 42,000 |
| Long-term debt: | | |
| Bonds payable, 7%, due 20X5 | | 100,000 |
| Total liabilities | | $142,000 |
| Stockholders' equity: | | |
| Common stock, no par value, | | |
| 10,000 shares issued and outstanding | $200,000 | |
| Retained earnings | 110,000 | |
| Total stockholders' equity | | 310,000 |
| Total equities | | $452,000 |

During 20X2 the following events occurred.

(a) Sales on account were $450,000.
(b) Collections on receivables were $440,000.
(c) Credit purchases of inventory were $280,000.
(d) Cost of goods sold was $290,000.
(e) Payments to suppliers for inventory were $265,000.
(f) Cash paid for operating expenses was $70,000; interest on bonds was also paid.
(g) Plant and equipment were bought for $70,000 cash.
(h) Taxes payable at December 31, 20X1, were paid.
(i) Depreciation expense was $40,000.
(j) Income taxes are 40% of income before taxes. No payments were made on 20X2 taxes in 20X2.
(k) A dividend of $10,000 was declared and paid.

*Required*
1. Prepare an income statement for Illustrative Company for 20X2.
2. Prepare a balance sheet for Illustrative Company as of December 31, 20X2.

*1-7  Review of the cash flow statement*  Using the information from the previous assignment, prepare a cash flow statement for 20X2 for Illustrative Company.

**1-8  Review of financial statement preparation**   Following is the balance sheet for Example Company as of December 31, 20X1, and selected information relating to activities in 20X2.

**Example Company**
**Balance Sheet**
**as of December 31, 20X1**

| | | |
|---|---:|---:|
| Assets | | |
| Current assets: | | |
| Cash | | $ 20,000 |
| Accounts receivable | | 80,000 |
| Inventory | | 120,000 |
| Prepaid expenses | | 8,000 |
| Total current assets | | $228,000 |
| Property, plant, and equipment: | | |
| Cost | $350,000 | |
| Less:  Accumulated depreciation | 130,000 | |
| Net | | 220,000 |
| Total assets | | $448,000 |
| Equities | | |
| Current liabilities: | | |
| Accounts payable | | $ 40,000 |
| Taxes payable | | 25,000 |
| Accrued expenses | | 12,000 |
| Total current liabilities | | $ 77,000 |
| Long-term liabilities: | | |
| Bond payable, 6%, due 20X4 | | 200,000 |
| Total liabilities | | $277,000 |
| Stockholders' equity: | | |
| Common stock, $10 par value, | | |
| 8,000 shares issued and outstanding | $ 80,000 | |
| Retained earnings | 91,000 | |
| Total stockholders' equity | | 171,000 |
| Total equities | | $448,000 |

Other data relating to activities in 20X2 were as follows.
(a)  Sales on account were $480,000.
(b)  Collections on accounts receivable were $430,000.
(c)  Credit purchases of goods for resale were $220,000.
(d)  Cost of goods sold was $240,000.
(e)  Payments of accounts payable were $210,000.
(f)  Interest expense on bonds payable was paid in cash.
(g)  Prepaid expenses at the beginning of the year expired and new prepayments in the amount of $6,000 were made in 20X2.
(h)  Accrued taxes payable at the beginning of the year were paid.
(i)  Accrued expenses payable are for wages and salaries. Total cash payments for wages and salaries during 20X2 were $95,000. At the end of 20X2, $7,000 was owed to employees.
(j)  Other cash payments for expenses during 20X2 were $65,000, not including the $6,000 prepayments in (g).

(k)  The company issued common stock to the public for $40,000 (4,000 shares).
(l)  Plant and equipment were purchased for $30,000 cash.
(m) Depreciation expense was $40,000.
(n)  The income tax rate is 40%. Income taxes for 20X2 were unpaid at year end.
(o)  A dividend of $5,000 was declared and paid.

**Required**
1. Prepare an income statement for Example Company for 20X2.
2. Prepare a balance sheet for Example Company as of December 31, 20X2.

*1-9  Review of the cash flow statement*   Using the information from the previous assignment, prepare a cash flow statement for 20X2 for Example Company.

*1-10  Different costs for different purposes*   Suppose you are going to drive home this weekend, a round trip of 150 miles. Your car gets 30 miles per gallon of gas and you expect gas to cost $0.95 per gallon. Insurance and depreciation are $1,000 per year. You usually drive 12,000 miles per year. A friend asks you to take her along. She lives a mile from your home.

**Required**
1. What are the costs of taking your friend along, as opposed to going by yourself?
2. Suppose now that you are not planning on going home. Your friend asks for a ride and you are willing to go. What are the costs of going, as opposed to not going?

*1-11  JIT*   You have been telling your fellow managers about the potential benefits of adopting the JIT philosophy, but some remain unconvinced. A couple of them seem not to hear what you have been saying. Manager A says, "Look, we just can't hit production right on the nose so that stuff arrives just when a guy finishes the last batch. We need some extra units so that our people aren't waiting around for the guys before them to finish." Manager B chimes in, "It all sounds great, but we're doing fine the way we work now. Some of our problems are caused by bad design of products, but we have to please our customers."
    The quality control manager says, "We use the latest techniques to inspect both incoming shipments of parts and components and outgoing shipments of finished product. We are sure our quality is good on what goes out the door.  And we catch plenty of stuff before we ship it, maybe 10 to 15 percent defectives that have to be reworked or scrapped. So we earn our keep around here."  The production manager argues that the functional factory arrangement, with all machines of a given type in the same area, makes the company more efficient because the workers ". . . can really learn how to operate that one machine they're responsible for."

**Required**
Comment on each of the statements and indicate how JIT could help the company.

*1-12  Ethics*   You are the newly hired controller of QT Products, a large manufacturer of industrial products. Yesterday morning the president of the company called you and other senior executives to her office where she stated that a competitor was about to file suit against QT for patent infringement. Regardless of the merits of the case, it will tie up company talent for a long while and will be quite costly to fight. The effects on the company's prospects cannot be measured, but it is possible that they will be severe.
    This evening your father called from Arizona, where he and your mother have lived in retirement for a few years. You chatted about the weather, the children, dad's golf game, and other such things. Then he told you that he had just bought shares

of stock in QT Products because he knew that any company you worked at would do well.

**Required**
What do you say to your father?

**1-13  *Ethics***  You work as the data processing manager of Quick Clean, a franchiser of cleaning services. You recently asked for bids on a new client/server network and asked the controller's office to assist you in evaluating the costs and benefits of the suppliers' proposals. Eventually, you settled on systems offered by Integrated Technologies, a relatively new company with a good reputation. The decision was based partly on a favorable analysis by Ann Taylor, an assistant controller.

A week or so after deciding on the Integrated systems, you happen to see Taylor eating lunch with Susan Ventura, one of Integrated's sales engineers. You later ask Taylor about it, and she says that she and Susan were college classmates. She says that she didn't mention their friendship because it wasn't relevant; she did her analysis strictly on the facts.

**Required**
1. Has Taylor violated the IMA Standards of Ethical Conduct? If so, which standard?
2. Suppose instead of seeing Taylor and Ventura at lunch, you saw them at the airport. Taylor waved to you and said Ventura was paying for a weekend of sun and surf in the Bahamas. Has Taylor violated the Standards now? If so, which?

**1-14  *Conventional and JIT manufacturing***  Jason Company manufactures five basic products that are similar and relatively standard. That is, they are not made-to-order. Product design and features are updated periodically in response to customer suggestions. Product designers come up with improvements, and production is responsible for re-tooling and other activities required to implement the redesign.

Jason receives orders from customers, then fills the orders from stock or manufactures the required units. The company has a warehouse where it keeps finished units, raw materials, and components. The Quality Control Department inspects all incoming shipments of raw materials and components and rejects those with defects above a certain percentage. The percentage differs for different items. For instance, a relatively high percentage, say 10 percent, of defectives is considered acceptable for sophisticated, hard-to-manufacture components, while a low percentage, say 1 percent, is acceptable for mass-produced items like simple valves.

The company usually buys a two- or three-month supply of high-volume raw materials. Jason receives a 1 percent average discount on prices by buying in large quantities. Jason's purchasing manager is responsible, and rewarded, for obtaining raw materials and components at the lowest possible cost and so scours the country looking for the best deals. Jason therefore deals with a great many suppliers.

Production begins by withdrawing the necessary raw materials and components from the warehouse, inspecting them for possible deterioration during storage, and transporting them to the first station that will work on the batch of product. No job begins until all raw materials and components are available. Each station does one function, such as drilling, planing, welding, or various assembly operations.

Each station has an area to store raw materials and components for work that has not yet started. The raw materials wait there until the station is ready to begin the job. Significant setup time is required in changing over from one product to another at some stations. After the workers at the station have finished their part of the job, they send the semi-completed units along with the raw materials and components not yet installed to the next station. At that station the same process is repeated and so on until all work is completed. In some cases a job will go to the same station more than once during production because it requires the same operation at different stages of production.

At the conclusion of the process, the finished units go to the Quality Control Department where they are tested and inspected. They then are sent to the warehouse to await shipment. The company usually makes 10 percent more units than needed for an order to allow for defects. Any spare good units are held in the warehouse until another order arrives. Defective units sometimes are reworked or sold as scrap. Reworked units are stored in the warehouse. If the work station that produced the defective part has been determined, the work station's manager is held responsible. (Bonuses for station managers are based largely on total goods output.) In many cases, determining the source of the defect is not possible, so no one is held responsible.

The factory manager has said that "it gets pretty hectic at the end of each month when we're trying to finish up jobs and get the stuff out to the warehouse."

Cycle time varies among types of products, but spans from 10 to 45 days depending on various factors.

### Required

Prepare a memorandum describing how Jason differs from a JIT company and what changes in its operations you would recommend. Use the guidelines in Appendix A.

# Part One

# cost-volume-profit analysis and decision making

The first part of this book discusses the basic principles of decision making, the principles of cost-volume-profit analysis. These principles underlie the chapters in Part One and most of the material in the rest of the book. Much planning and decision making depends on classifying costs according to their behavior and on understanding what activities drive costs. An understanding of cost drivers and behavior is essential if a manager is to have the best information for making rational decisions.

The principles and techniques developed in this section are discussed and illustrated primarily in a business context. But nearly all are applicable to not-for-profit economic entities, such as hospitals, universities, charitable institutions, and government units.

## Chapter Two

# PROFIT PLANNING

**LEARNING OBJECTIVES**

*After reading this chapter, you should be able to*
- *Describe and apply the concepts of fixed and variable costs.*
- *Describe and apply the concept of contribution margin.*
- *Prepare contribution margin format income statements.*
- *Describe and discuss the significance of the relevant range.*
- *Construct and interpret a cost-volume-profit graph.*
- *Determine the sales volume or selling price needed to achieve a target profit.*
- *Describe and illustrate target costing.*
- *Describe and discuss the importance of cost structure.*
- *Discuss the assumptions that underlie cost-volume-profit analysis.*

The schedule below shows percentage increases in sales and income before taxes for two recent years for four large, successful companies.

| | Percentage Increase in | |
| | Sales | Income before Taxes |
| --- | --- | --- |
| **Gillette** | 3.8% | 50.4% |
| **Wal-Mart** | 12.4% | 15.4% |
| **Seagate Technology** | 4.1% | 208.6% |
| **Compaq** | 35.8% | 41.3% |

Why did **Seagate** and **Gillette** show increases in income many times their increases in sales? Why were **Compaq's** and **Wal-Mart's** income increases only slightly more than their sales increase? What factors besides sales determine a company's profit performance? One important reason for the differences in sales and profit increases of the listed companies is their cost structures. Some companies' costs remain relatively constant, so that even small increases in sales filter down to income. Other companies' costs rise and fall as sales rise and fall, so they experience much lower increases in profit from increases in sales. Other factors act on sales/profit relationships as well. The sales/profit street runs both ways, though. If Seagate's sales fall, its profit will fall more rapidly than that of Compaq or Wal-Mart. The ability to raise prices to meet cost increases is also an important factor. Gillette has more ability to raise prices than does Wal-Mart, which competes fiercely on its low prices. As you study this chapter, you will learn more about the relationships among sales volume, costs, and profits.

Companies must earn profits to stay in business. Managers want to increase profitability and therefore need to predict how their actions will affect profits. For example, what will happen to profits if increasing promotional efforts by $250,000 increases sales by 50,000 units? Managers also are concerned with questions such as the following: How many units must we sell to earn $50,000? What selling price should we set? Should we hire another salesperson? Would staying open another two hours each day be profitable?

Cost-volume-profit analysis helps managers plan for change and answer questions such as those posed above. **Cost-volume-profit (CVP) analysis** is a method for analyzing the relationships among costs, volume, and profits. Managers use these relationships to plan, budget, and make decisions. The first step in CVP analysis is classifying costs according to behavior.

Classifying costs according to behavior is distinctive to managerial use of accounting information. In financial accounting reports prepared for external use, costs normally are grouped according to the functional areas of business: production (cost of goods sold), marketing (selling expenses), administration (general and administrative expenses), and financing (interest expense). A functional classification does not provide the necessary information to predict what is likely to happen to costs and profits if circumstances change, and a manager must plan for change and take actions to make changes.

## COST BEHAVIOR

A cost is classified as either fixed or variable, according to whether the *total* amount of the cost changes as activity changes. *Activity* is a general term denoting anything that the company does; examples of activity include units of product sold or produced, hours worked, invoices prepared, and parts inspected. *Volume* is a common measure of activity. In this chapter, we use sales as the measure of volume and classify costs as either fixed or variable with respect to sales. Not all costs fall into these categories, and other measures of activity are often needed to explain how costs behave. We consider other measures of activity in

Chapter 3. For CVP analysis we care how a cost behaves, not whether it is cost of goods sold, salaries, or depreciation.

## VARIABLE COSTS

**Variable costs** change, in total, in direct proportion to changes in volume. To illustrate this concept, consider Exeter Company, a wholesaler of backpacks. The following schedule shows data for Exeter.

| Exeter Company Data | | |
|---|---|---|
| Selling price of backpacks | $20.00 | |
| Cost of backpacks from manufacturer | $10.00 | |
| Variable cost to pack and ship | 1.00 | |
| Sales commission at 5% of $20 | 1.00 | per backpack at $20 price |
| Total unit variable cost | $12.00 | |
| Total monthly fixed costs (rent, salaries, depreciation, etc.) | $40,000 | |

Notice that the $1.00 commission depends on the selling price, but that the per-unit amounts of the other variable costs do not. All three costs vary *in total* with the volume of sales. That is, the costs are incurred each time a backpack is sold, and the total of each increases or decreases in proportion to changes in sales.

## CONTRIBUTION MARGIN

**Contribution margin** is the difference between selling price per unit and variable cost per unit. The term often is used to denote *total contribution margin*, the difference between total sales and total variable costs. In some cases, expressing contribution margin as a percentage is useful and convenient. The **contribution margin percentage** is per-unit contribution margin divided by selling price, or total contribution margin divided by total sales dollars. (Both calculations give the same result.) The percentage of variable costs to selling price, per unit or in total, is called the **variable cost percentage**.

We use the term *contribution* because what is left from a sale after variable costs are covered *contributes* to covering other costs and producing profit. In Exeter's case, contribution margin per unit is $8 ($20 – $12) and contribution margin percentage is 40 percent ($8/$20).

## FIXED COSTS

**Fixed costs** remain the same in total over a wide range of volume. The schedule shows that Exeter has monthly fixed costs of $40,000. As well as the items listed, these costs include utilities, insurance, property taxes, advertising, and others that do not change in response to changes in sales volume. Note that we do not say that fixed costs never change. A company can hire more salaried personnel, increase or decrease advertising, turn up the air conditioning, and take other actions that change costs. But the costs do not change *automatically* as volume changes. For planning purposes, we think of them as fixed. Knowing total monthly fixed costs and unit variable costs, we can determine total costs as

*Total costs = fixed costs + (variable cost per unit × unit volume)*
*= $40,000 + ($12 × units sold)*

Knowing how to determine total costs, we can also determine profit as

*Profit = (selling price × unit sales) – total variable costs – total fixed costs*

## CONTRIBUTION MARGIN INCOME STATEMENT

The following income statements for Exeter show the effects of fixed costs and of changes in sales. Unlike financial accounting income statements, these statements group costs only as variable or fixed and show contribution margin as a subtotal.

Exeter Company
Income Statements at Various Sales Levels

|  | 5,000 Units | 6,000 Units | 7,000 Units |
|---|---|---|---|
| Sales ($20 per unit) | $100,000 | $120,000 | $140,000 |
| Variable costs ($12 per unit) | 60,000 | 72,000 | 84,000 |
| Contribution margin ($8 per unit) | $ 40,000 | $ 48,000 | $ 56,000 |
| Fixed costs | 40,000 | 40,000 | 40,000 |
| Income | $        0 | $  8,000 | $ 16,000 |

Notice that the $8,000 change in contribution margin as sales increase by 1,000 units is also the change in income. *As sales change, income changes by unit contribution margin multiplied by the change in sales.* We can also calculate income by multiplying per-unit contribution margin by unit sales and then subtracting total fixed costs.

Thus, to calculate Exeter's income for sales of 6,000 backpacks, we can multiply the $8 contribution margin by 6,000. This gives total contribution margin of $48,000, and when we subtract fixed costs of $40,000 we find income of $8,000. We also could determine total contribution at that level of sales by multiplying sales of $120,000 (6,000 × $20) by the 40 percent contribution margin percentage, giving $48,000. Again, income is total contribution margin minus fixed costs.

An important use of CVP analysis is to help managers predict how income will change if volume changes. If Exeter managers wonder what will happen to income if sales increase by 100 backpacks per month, CVP analysis can tell them that income will increase by $800, the 100-backpack increase multiplied by the $8 per-backpack contribution margin. The $800 change in income also can be determined by computing the increase in sales revenue (100 units × $20 = $2,000) and multiplying by the contribution margin percentage of 40 percent. Note that the increase in income is $800 no matter what the current level of sales.

## EMPHASIS ON EXPECTATIONS

At this early stage we are dealing with a simplified case, looking at the costs in a single period (a month, a quarter, or perhaps a year) and predicting costs and income for the following period. The important point is that predictions are about the future. To expect either per-unit variable costs or total fixed costs to remain the same month after month, or year after year, is unreasonable. Total fixed costs, per-unit variable costs, and selling prices can change for many reasons.

Inflation is a major cause of changes in both fixed and variable costs—suppliers might raise their prices, lessors might raise rents, salaries might rise, and so on. Profit planning must take into account expected changes in costs. Based on expectations, CVP analysis does not assume that costs remain constant over time. Thus, if Exeter managers expect the price they pay for backpacks to go up by $2.50 next month, they will use $12.50 (instead of $10.00) in planning for next month. Rapid inflation is a serious problem for managers in many countries and forces them to be creative. In the early 1990s in Russia, for example, a manufacturer of shirts raised prices 15–20 times per month to cover rising costs. Having a good idea of how cost increases affect fixed and variable costs is necessary to make such adjustments.

Because of inflation, competition, or for other reasons, managers might change selling prices. For example, Exeter might raise its price to $24 to counter an increase in the price it pays for backpacks. (Of course, an increase in the selling price will also increase Exeter's per-unit commission, so it would use both the new price *and* the new variable cost in its plans.)

As mentioned earlier, managers can change some costs. Exeter could hire another employee at a monthly salary, increasing fixed costs, or it could increase advertising (also increasing fixed costs). In a more complex company, many cost changes are the result of managerial actions. A large company could increase (or decrease) its office staff or change its level of spending on such items as travel and employee training. Thus, fixed costs might change during a period. But they are still fixed because they do not change with the level of activity. For planning purposes, then, managers predict fixed costs based on what they expect for the coming period, knowing they might change costs to meet changing conditions.

As a general rule, managers can change some fixed costs more easily than they can change per-unit variable costs, especially over short periods of time (more about this in Chapter 3). Some accountants, therefore, use the term **nonvariable costs** instead of *fixed costs*. The point, as we briefly introduced earlier, is that fixed costs are not fixed in the sense that they cannot be changed, but rather that, unlike variable costs, fixed costs do not change automatically when volume changes. In this book, we call such costs *fixed* because that term is more common. Regardless of terminology, the emphasis in planning is on expectations. If actual conditions (selling prices, prices from suppliers, etc.) do not coincide with expectations, or if managers later change decisions, differences will occur between actual and predicted costs and profit. Such differences between actuality and expectations are inherent in business but do not reduce the need to plan. The accompanying Insight illustrates various cost and profit plans by automakers in recent years.

**CHAPTER 3**

## IN *SIGHT*

### Cost and Profit Expectations at Automakers

**Ford Motor** set ambitious productivity goals: North America would make a return on sales of 4 percent, and total automotive costs would be reduced by $1 billion. At the time, Ford had the lowest profit per car of the Big Three and an after-tax profit margin on car sales of just 1.5 percent. Management quickly drew up a plan to cut costs by, among other things, eliminating seven slow-moving models and shifting production capacity to higher-profit lines. Ford handily beat all of the targets. North American auto operations returned 5.1 percent last year, and cost savings exceeded $3 billion.

**Chrysler's** CEO claims the company should be able to earn profits of 8 percent on sales; it is currently earning 6 percent. Margins in the auto industry resemble those of supermarkets: razor thin. The CEO says Chrysler can do better because it spends less and employs fewer people per car than its competitors. Its product development process, measured by speed, efficiency, and innovative design, is the best in the world. It continues to get significant savings and improvements from its manufacturing operations and its suppliers.

**Volvo** must shorten product cycles and reduce costs to compete effectively. "We have to learn to get more out of existing facilities," Volvo's CEO says. At Volvo's biggest assembly plant inventory is stacked high and workers move in slow motion. Volvo spends 35 hours assembling each car; a manufacturing consultant claims Volvo should be able to do the job in 30 hours.

*Sources:* Fortune *articles by Alex Taylor III. "The Gentlemen at Ford Are Kicking Butt," June 22, 1998; "Chrysler's Great Expectations," December 9, 1996; "Volvo and Saab," June 21, 1997.*

## INCOME STATEMENT FORMATS—FINANCIAL ACCOUNTING AND CONTRIBUTION MARGIN FORMATS

The format used for income statements in this chapter and throughout most of this book differs from that used in financial accounting. As stated earlier, in financial accounting costs are usually classified by function or by object. The income statements in Exhibit 2-1 highlight the differences between the two approaches. Notice that the sales and income figures are the same under both approaches, but the costs are classified in different ways. The statements are for a month when Exeter sells 6,000 backpacks.

The obvious differences between the statements are in terminology and the placement of costs. The principal difference is that a manager who receives a statement in the financial accounting format cannot perform CVP analysis, because that format tells little about cost behavior. The manager must determine how much of each cost is fixed and variable, which is not possible without additional analysis. One unfortunate result is the tendency of some managers to treat fixed costs as if they were variable and to use average total cost per unit for planning.

## UNIT COSTS

You should see that, because total fixed costs remain the same at different levels of activity, the average fixed cost per unit changes whenever volume changes. Thus, the average fixed cost per unit when Exeter sells 5,000 units is $8.00 ($40,000/5,000), while the average at 7,000 units is about $5.71 ($40,000/7,000). The average *total* cost per unit, then, depends on the level of activity, with the average total per-unit cost for Exeter being $20.00 ($8.00 fixed plus $12 variable) at 5,000 units, and $17.71 ($5.71 fixed plus $12 variable) at 7,000 units. Notice that Exeter earns zero profit at 5,000 units and that its average *total* cost of $20 at that

---

**Exhibit 2-1   Comparison of Contribution Margin and Financial Accounting Income Statements**

| Financial Accounting Format (Functional) | | Contribution Margin Format (Behavioral) | |
|---|---|---|---|
| Sales, 6,000 × $20 | $120,000 | Sales, 6,000 × $20 | $120,000 |
| Cost of sales, 6,000 × $10 | 60,000 | Variable costs: | |
| Gross profit | $ 60,000 | Cost of sales | $ 60,000 |
| Operating expenses: | | Packing and shipping | 6,000 |
| Packing and shipping | $  6,000 | Commissions | 6,000 |
| Commissions | 6,000 | Total variable costs | $ 72,000 |
| Rent, salaries, | | Contribution margin | $ 48,000 |
| depreciation, etc. | 40,000 | Fixed costs | 40,000 |
| Total operating expenses | $ 52,000 | | |
| Income | $  8,000 | Income | $  8,000 |

volume equals its $20 selling price. Exeter earns a $16,000 profit at 7,000 units because only its variable costs increase and its fixed costs remain constant.

Failing to recognize that average total per-unit cost changes as activity changes creates problems for managers who—unwisely—use averages to predict future costs. Managers should not use the average total per-unit cost for one level of activity to predict total costs at another level.

To illustrate this point, suppose Exeter uses the $17.71 average total cost per unit (at 7,000 units) to predict total costs at a volume of 8,000 backpacks. The predicted cost is $141,680 ($17.71 × 8,000 backpacks). But Exeter's income statements at volumes of 7,000 and 8,000 backpacks are as follows:

|  | 7,000 Backpacks | 8,000 Backpacks |
| --- | --- | --- |
| Sales ($20 per unit) | $140,000 | $160,000 |
| Variable costs ($12 per unit) | 84,000 | 96,000 |
| Contribution margin ($8 per unit) | $ 56,000 | $ 64,000 |
| Fixed costs | 40,000 | 40,000 |
| Income | $ 16,000 | $ 24,000 |
| Average cost per unit | $17.71 | $17.00 |
| Profit per unit | $2.29 | $3.00 |

Total costs at sales of 8,000 backpacks are $136,000 ($96,000 + $40,000), not $141,680. What appears to be additional profit per unit at the higher level of activity is simply the result of spreading the fixed costs over a larger number of units. The *behavior* of Exeter's costs has not changed at all; variable costs remain at 60 percent of sales ($12 per unit) and fixed costs remain at $40,000. Using average total cost per unit to predict total costs works only if all costs are variable.

In the preceding example, notice that income as a percentage of sales (called **return on sales**, or **ROS**) differs at the two levels of volume. At sales of 7,000 units, income is about 11.4 percent of sales ($16,000/$140,000), while at sales of 8,000 units, income is 15 percent of sales ($24,000/$160,000). Perhaps the most common mistake managers make is to use the ROS percentage at one level of volume to predict income at another volume level. If a company has *any* fixed costs, its income as a percentage of sales increases as volume increases. Moreover, the percentage increase in income is greater than the percentage increase in sales. In the income statements just shown, a 14.3 percent increase in sales ($20,000/$140,000) produced a 50 percent increase in income (from $16,000 to $24,000).

Notice that a relatively small percentage increase in sales generated a larger percentage increase in profits. This is due to fixed costs and is called **operating leverage**. In a physical sense, leverage is the use of a smaller object to move a larger object. In an operating sense, the unchanging fixed costs are used as a lever to increase the profits. Operating leverage is calculated as

$$Operating\ leverage\ =\ contribution\ margin/profit$$

For Exeter, operating leverage at 7,000 units sold is 3.5 ($56,000/$16,000). Operating leverage is used to calculate the percentage increase in profits, since a 1 percent increase in sales will generate a 1 percent × operating leverage increase in profits. For Exeter, a 14.3 percent increase in sales will generate a 50 percent (3.5 × 14.3%) increase in profits.

## RELEVANT RANGE

As stated earlier, per-unit variable costs and total fixed costs change over time. They might also change when activity changes by a large amount. That is, the per-unit variable cost and total fixed cost will behave as expected only over some limited range of activity.

For example, Exeter might be able to handle up to 10,000 backpacks with its current level of staff. But above that level of sales it will need additional help, increasing fixed costs. If Exeter orders more than 10,000 backpacks per month it might get a discount on the purchase price, thus reducing per-unit variable costs.

The examples illustrate an important assumption underlying CVP analysis: that the company will operate within a **relevant range**, a range of volume over which it can reasonably expect selling price, per-unit variable cost, and total fixed costs to be constant. Managers cannot expect these factors to remain constant when they operate outside the relevant range.

A company might have more than one relevant range, within each of which a particular price/cost combination prevails. For instance, a company could go from one shift to two shifts per day. Two-shift operation necessitates leaving the heat and lights on, hiring additional supervisors, and taking on other fixed costs. For planning purposes, managers forecast the approximate range of activity and use the selling price and costs they believe will hold within that range.

A special case of operating outside the relevant range occurs when a business shuts down for a short period. A company that closes for a week or a month should find its total costs for that period to be less than its normal total fixed costs. A company closing for a month would turn out the lights, turn down the heat, and probably not advertise. The company might also lay off some employees. Thus, to think of fixed costs as the costs that the company would incur at zero activity is not appropriate. Fixed costs are better thought of as the planned costs that will not change in total as volume changes within the relevant range.

Exeter's volume, and relevant range, are expressed in units of product or dollars of sales. Businesses that sell services, rather than goods, often charge their clients for the hours that they work. CPA firms, law firms, and consulting firms are examples. For these firms, chargeable hours (the number of hours worked that are chargeable to client business) is an appropriate and useful measure of activity. Still other companies use percentage of capacity as the measure of volume. Airlines use seat-miles or passenger-miles to measure volume. (A seat-mile is one seat flown one mile. A passenger-mile is a seat-mile occupied by a paying passenger.) Annual reports of airlines cite various statistics regarding seat-miles and passenger-miles. For example, **Delta Airlines** stated that its break-even point in 1997 was about 63 percent of available seat-miles.

Alternative measures are usually available and managers might use several of them, perhaps relying more on one than on others. According to a recent annual report, **The Coca-Cola Company** ". . . measures soft drink volume in two ways: gallon shipments of concentrates and syrups, and equivalent unit cases of finished product. . . . Management believes unit case volume more accurately measures the underlying strength of the global business system because it measures trends at the retail level and is less impacted by inventory management practices at the wholesale level."

## COST-VOLUME-PROFIT GRAPH

Exhibit 2-2 gives a graphical representation of the CVP picture for Exeter. The revenue line shows total sales dollars at any volume, which is simply the selling price per unit multiplied by the level of unit volume. At any volume, the vertical distance between total costs and fixed costs is total variable costs at that volume.

Although the lines on the graph extend far to the right and back to the vertical axis on the left, doing so is not legitimate because of the relevant range. As suggested earlier, Exeter's fixed costs should be less than $40,000 if the store is closed for the month (zero activity), and either per-unit variable or total fixed costs, or both, are likely to change if volume exceeds 10,000 backpacks per month. We extend the lines to zero volume and to 10,000 units to make it easier to read the graph.

At any volume, the vertical distance between the revenue line and the total cost line is the amount of profit or loss (shaded areas) at that volume. The graphical presentation directs attention to the **break-even point**—the point at which profits are zero because total revenues equal total costs. A company operating above the break-even point makes profits; below that point it incurs losses. Managers of

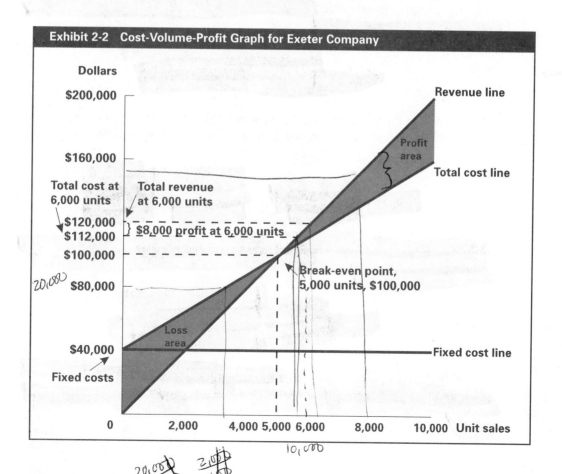

**Exhibit 2-2    Cost-Volume-Profit Graph for Exeter Company**

business firms do not want to break even—they want to earn profits. But they still want to know how low volume can be before losses appear. Knowing the break-even point is useful for many purposes. Managers of not-for-profit organizations frequently seek to break even, or show only a small profit or loss, on some of their activities. The graph highlights an important lesson. As long as selling price exceeds variable cost (contribution margin is positive), selling more units will benefit the company, either by increasing profits or by decreasing losses. Thus, companies can often do better by staying open because their losses would be greater if they closed. Such is often the case with seasonal businesses. Businesses in summer resort areas expect losses during the winter, but might remain open. Many seasonal businesses continue to operate in the off-season because they recognize that the contribution margin from the additional, though lower, sales reduces their losses. Chapter 3 considers this point in more detail.

## ACHIEVING TARGET PROFITS

### BREAK-EVEN POINT AND TARGET DOLLAR PROFITS

The break-even point is of interest, but managers of profit-seeking organizations are concerned more with meeting a desired or **target profit**. Managers can express targets as absolute dollar amounts, ROS percentages, or in other ways. We can use the same general relationships to find both the break-even point and the volume required to earn a target profit. Profit equals total sales minus total variable costs minus total fixed costs. That is,

$$Profit = \begin{matrix} total \\ sales \\ dollars \end{matrix} - \begin{matrix} total \\ variable \\ costs \end{matrix} - \begin{matrix} total \\ fixed \\ costs \end{matrix}$$

Understanding the relationships in either format allows you to solve virtually any CVP problem. Using Q to denote the quantity of units sold, we can restate the formula as

$$Profit = \left( \begin{matrix} per\text{-}unit \\ selling \\ price \end{matrix} \times Q \right) - \left( \begin{matrix} per\text{-}unit \\ variable \\ cost \end{matrix} \times Q \right) - \begin{matrix} total \\ fixed \\ costs \end{matrix}$$

Knowing that selling price minus variable cost per unit equals contribution margin per unit, we can combine those two components. We then add fixed costs to both sides, and get

$$Profit + \begin{matrix} total \\ fixed \\ costs \end{matrix} = \left( \begin{matrix} contribution \\ margin \\ per\ unit \end{matrix} \times Q \right)$$

Let us first use the above equation to find the break-even point (where profit is zero). At break even, the profit term drops out. Now we can solve for Q (the break-even sales in units) by dividing both sides by contribution margin per unit, producing

$$Q \text{ (break-even sales in units)} = \frac{\text{total fixed costs}}{\text{contribution margin per unit}}$$

Exeter managers can interpret this formula as saying: "How many units must we sell to cover fixed costs of $40,000, if each unit contributes $8 to cover those fixed costs?" Applying the formula, Exeter can determine that the break-even point is 5,000 backpacks.

$$\text{Break-even sales in units} = \frac{\$40,000}{\$20 - \$12} = \frac{\$40,000}{\$8} = 5,000 \text{ backpacks}$$

At the break-even point, total contribution margin equals total fixed costs. We can therefore find the volume required to achieve a target profit (zero is a target) by finding the sales required to earn total contribution margin equal to the sum of total fixed costs and the target profit.

Suppose Exeter wishes to earn a profit of $5,000 per month. How many backpacks must it sell? We know that total contribution margin must equal fixed costs of $40,000 for Exeter to break even. Hence, to achieve a profit of $5,000, total contribution margin must be $5,000 greater than fixed costs, or $45,000. To achieve total contribution margin of $45,000 when contribution margin per unit is $8 ($20 − $12), Exeter must sell 5,625 units. Expressed in general terms, our basic equation is

$$\left( \begin{array}{c} \text{Sales, in units,} \\ \text{to achieve} \\ \text{target profit} \end{array} \times \begin{array}{c} \text{contribution} \\ \text{margin} \\ \text{per unit} \end{array} \right) - \begin{array}{c} \text{total} \\ \text{fixed} \\ \text{costs} \end{array} = \begin{array}{c} \text{target} \\ \text{profit} \end{array}$$

Restating this equation to solve for the needed level of sales yields

$$\frac{\text{Sales, in units, to}}{\text{achieve target profit}} = \frac{\text{fixed costs} + \text{target profit}}{\text{contribution margin per unit}}$$

Applying this formula in Exeter's case, we have

$$\frac{\text{Unit sales to}}{\text{achieve target profit}} = \frac{\$40,000 + \$5,000}{\$20 - \$12} = \frac{\$45,000}{\$8} = 5,625 \text{ units}$$

Notice that the numerator of the formula is the total contribution margin required to earn the target profit, consisting of the $40,000 contribution margin required for break even plus the $5,000 required for the target profit. Target dollar sales is $112,500 (5,625 × $20).

An alternative approach also can be useful. We can construct an income statement filling in what we know and solving for what we do not know. First, we know profit and fixed costs, which enable us to determine total contribution margin.

| | |
|---|---|
| Sales ($20 per unit) | ? |
| Variable costs ($12 per unit) | ? |
| Contribution margin ($8 per unit) | $45,000 |
| Fixed costs | 40,000 |
| Profit | $ 5,000 |

We know that total contribution margin of $45,000 is unit contribution margin of $8 multiplied by volume, so we can divide total contribution margin by unit contribution margin to get the same 5,625 ($45,000/$8) unit result we obtained with the equation.

## CONTRIBUTION MARGIN PERCENTAGE

Both the graph in Exhibit 2-2 and the target profit formula just derived show sales in units. At times it is more convenient to measure volume in sales dollars. The following equation shows the contribution margin percentage alternative applied to Exeter. We can rearrange the terms in the basic equation to yield

$$Profit \ = \ (sales \ dollars \ \times \ contribution \ margin \ percentage) \ - \ fixed \ costs$$

So the volume required for a target profit is

$$\frac{Sales, \ in \ dollars, \ required}{to \ earn \ target \ profit} \ = \ \frac{total \ fixed \ costs \ + \ target \ profit}{contribution \ margin \ percentage}$$

Exeter can interpret this version of the formula as saying: "How many dollars of sales must I have to cover fixed costs of $40,000 and earn a target profit, given that each sales dollar yields $0.40 of contribution margin (the 40 percent contribution margin percentage, $8/$20)?"

For break even,

$$Break\text{-}even \ sales, \ in \ dollars \ = \ \frac{\$40,000 \ + \ \$0}{40\%} \ = \ \$100,000$$

The units required to break even are still 5,000 ($100,000/$20 selling price per unit), and both this formula and the one using sales units give the same answer for the break-even point, 5,000 units or $100,000.

For a $5,000 profit, Exeter needs sales of $112,500.

$$Sales \ dollars \ = \ \frac{\$40,000 \ + \ \$5,000}{40\%} \ = \ \$112,500$$

Once again, the answer is the same regardless of approach. Target sales in units are 5,625 units, whether computed directly or as a result of the computation of target sales dollars ($112,500/$20), and target sales in dollars are $112,500 (5,625 × $20).

A single-product company can use either way of stating contribution margin (and of determining required sales); the choice depends on computational convenience. The contribution margin percentage approach is especially useful to companies that sell numerous products. For instance, managers of a convenience store that sells hundreds of items cannot easily work with unit sales. (It makes little sense to speak of sales of 12,500,000 units when the units are as diverse as gallons of gasoline, liters of soda, bags of chips, and bottles of aspirin.) They prefer to work with sales dollars because their experience allows them to interpret numbers such as $400,000 of sales.

## TARGET RETURN ON SALES

Managers might also state a profit target as an ROS (profit divided by sales). Managers with such a profit target are saying that their desired dollar profit varies with sales.

Suppose that Exeter wishes to earn a 15 percent ROS. We already know that variable costs are 60 percent of sales (12/$20). Therefore, it wants 75 percent of its sales to cover variable costs and profit, leaving 25 percent to cover fixed costs. We use a variation of the break-even formula based on contribution margin percentage to find target sales. Starting with the basic equation, then substituting the values we know,

$$Profit = sales - variable\ costs - fixed\ costs$$
$$15\% \times sales = sales - (60\% \times sales) - \$40,000$$

Gathering terms,

$$15\% \times sales = 40\% \times sales - \$40,000$$
$$25\% \times sales = \$40,000$$
$$Sales = \$40,000/25\% = \$160,000$$

Or,

$$\frac{Sales,\ in\ dollars,\ to}{achieve\ target\ ROS} = \frac{fixed\ costs}{contribution\ margin\ percentage - target\ ROS}$$

$$\frac{Sales,\ in\ dollars,\ to}{achieve\ target\ ROS} = \frac{\$40,000}{40\% - 15\%} = \frac{\$40,000}{25\%} = \$160,000$$

The logic of this later formula is that Exeter needs 75 percent of sales for variable costs and profit (60 percent for variable costs, 15 percent for profit), so 25 percent is left to cover fixed costs. Exeter's income statement shows that logic. We could have approached this problem by filling in the percentages in the income statement, with contribution margin at 40 percent and profit at 15 percent. We then see that fixed costs must be 25 percent of sales.

|  | Dollars | Percentages |
|---|---|---|
| Sales | $160,000 | 100% |
| Variable costs (60% of sales) | 96,000 | 60% |
| Contribution margin | $ 64,000 | 40% |
| Fixed costs | 40,000 | 25% |
| Income | $ 24,000 | 15% |

To achieve sales of $160,000, Exeter has to sell 8,000 backpacks ($160,000/$20). Warning: Don't forget that the percentages of fixed costs and of profit to sales are valid only at this volume.

We could also translate Exeter's goal of a 15 percent ROS into a $3 profit per backpack ($20 × 15%). Subtracting the variable costs of $12 and the $3 profit from the $20 selling price leaves $5 to cover fixed costs. In a variation of the basic break-even formula (fixed costs/contribution margin), we could determine the sales volume needed for a target 15 percent ROS as 8,000 units ($40,000/$5). Note that this answer agrees with the one computed earlier.

## CHANGING PLANS

The concepts of contribution margin and target profit are useful when managers are contemplating changes in plans in the hope of increasing profits. A typical example is an increase in advertising, with the expectation of increasing sales.

Suppose that Exeter's marketing manager has proposed an advertising campaign that will cost $10,000 and is expected to increase sales by 2,000 units. Total contribution margin will increase by $16,000 (2,000 × $8), but fixed costs will be $10,000 higher, so that profit will be $6,000 higher than it would have been without the extra advertising. But suppose that some managers are concerned that sales might not increase by 2,000 units. They wonder how many additional units they must sell to make the additional advertising pay off. We can apply the target profit formula to determine the sales increase that is needed to cover the additional advertising.

$$Additional\ sales\ required\ =\ \$10,000/\$8\ =\ 1,250\ units$$

Exeter needs 1,250 units just to cover the increase in fixed costs. Total profit will increase only if the advertising can increase sales by more than 1,250 units.

The preceding analysis does not require knowing what sales the company expected without the advertising campaign. That is, knowing if sales expected without the additional advertising were 0, 5,000, or 10,000 units does not matter. As long as the increase in volume is greater than 1,250 units, taking the proposed action increases profits over what they would have been.

## TARGET SELLING PRICES

Exeter's target is $10,000 per month and it expects to sell 6,000 backpacks per month. Remember that Exeter's variable costs are $10.00 to purchase a backpack, $1.00 for packing and shipping, and a 5 percent sales commission. Thus, per-unit variable cost is $11.00 plus 5 percent of selling price. We still use the basic income statement equation,

| Profit | = | sales | – | variable costs | – | fixed costs |
|---|---|---|---|---|---|---|
| $10,000 | = | S | – | [(6,000 × $11.00) + 5%S] | – | $40,000 |
| $10,000 | = | S | – | $66,000 – 5%S | – | $40,000 |
| $116,000 | = | 95%S | | | | |
| $122,105 | = | S | | | | |

Dividing the required sales of $122,105 by the expected volume of 6,000 backpacks yields a target price of $20.35 (rounded). Notice that we cannot use the contribution margin percentage approach because that percentage changes when we change the selling price. If Exeter's variable costs did not depend on selling price (as the $11.00 does not), the calculation is simpler. In fact, a rearrangement of the basic equation gives

$$Price = \frac{total\ fixed\ costs\ +\ target\ profit}{unit\ volume} + unit\ variable\ cost$$

Notice that the first term on the right side is the required contribution margin per unit, the total required contribution margin divided by unit volume. Adding contribution margin to unit variable cost gives the selling price. For Exeter,

$$Price = \frac{\$40,000\ +\ \$10,000}{6,000} + \$11.00 + (5\% \times price)$$

$$Price = \$8.33 + \$11.00 + 5\%\,Price$$

$$95\%\,Price = \$8.33 + \$11.00$$

$$Price = \$20.35\ rounded$$

Whatever the basis used for setting a target profit, the manager must then ask: Are we likely to sell 6,000 units at $20.35? CVP analysis cannot answer this question. The more competitive the market, the less control a company has over selling prices. Most companies have some discretion in pricing, but the amount of discretion changes as market conditions change. Personal computers used to be high priced because people needed support and wanted to be able to call someone when they could not get the computer to work correctly. Now users are more sophisticated, so many buy from mail-order companies or from large retailers who offer little or no support but charge very low prices.

## TARGET COSTING

Some companies use a planning technique called **target costing** to help decide whether to enter a new market or bring out a new product. The essence of target costing is to determine how much the company can spend to manufacture and market a product, given a target profit. That is, the price and volume are estimated first, then the costs. Target costing is useful especially in deciding whether to enter an established market where selling prices are relatively stable. Proponents of target costing argue that its use increases the involvement of manufacturing, designing, and engineering people in planning because they have a cost to aim at, and will be encouraged to be creative in reaching the target cost. Recall from Chapter 1 that much of a product's cost is determined during the design stage, so close cooperation among the functional areas is important.

CHAPTER 1

Analytically, the technique simply requires solving the basic CVP equation for total cost, variable cost, or fixed cost. For instance, if the managers agree on a target profit of $300,000 and that unit volume of 100,000 is achievable at a $20 price, the total allowable cost is

| | |
|---|---|
| Revenue (100,000 × $20) | $2,000,000 |
| Target profit | 300,000 |
| Total allowable cost | $1,700,000 |

If managers expect total fixed costs to be $1,200,000, total variable costs can be $500,000, or $5 per unit. The $5 then, along with the $1,200,000 fixed cost, becomes an objective for the managers responsible for designing and manufacturing the product. Note, however, that as with target pricing, the answer given by the analysis might not be achievable with existing manufacturing techniques. The managers responsible for manufacturing might be unsuccessful in reaching the target cost objective. In such cases, the top managers might decide against introducing the new product or entering the new market. Or they might decide to re-examine their profit target and estimates of price and volume. For example, reconsidering the profit target is more likely when the new product (or market) is one the managers believe is especially important for, say, the company's reputation as an innovator, or for pursuing a long-range strategy. The accompanying Insight describes several uses of the technique.

CHAPTER
12

Chapter 12 will describe a related technique called Kaizen popularized by some Japanese manufacturers. Kaizen is a form of continuous improvement that seeks to reduce costs by target amounts each period.

## COST STRUCTURE AND MANAGERIAL ATTITUDES

Businesses can operate in different ways. A company can use a great deal of labor and little machinery or vice versa. Salespeople might be on salary, commission, or a combination of the two. When making choices, managers must consider the effects of their decisions on the *cost structure*—the relative proportions of fixed and variable costs. For example, a company might take on higher fixed costs to reduce variable costs and thereby increase contribution margin. (Automation does exactly that.) Such an action increases potential profitability, but also increases risk. The break-even point will probably rise and, if volume drops, profits will fall more rapidly with the higher contribution margin.

To illustrate, consider Caldwell Company. Its managers decide to introduce a new product. They expect to sell 20,000 units at $10. They can make the product in either of two manufacturing processes. Process A uses a great deal of labor and has variable costs of $7 per unit and annual fixed costs of $40,000. Process B uses more machinery, with unit variable costs of $4 and annual fixed costs of $95,000. Given these estimates, Process B yields more profit, as shown in the following income statement.

|  | Process A | Process B |
|---|---|---|
| Sales (20,000 × $10) | $200,000 | $200,000 |
| Variable costs at $7 and $4 | 140,000 | 80,000 |
| Contribution margin at $3 and $6 | $ 60,000 | $120,000 |
| Fixed costs | 40,000 | 95,000 |
| Profit | $ 20,000 | $ 25,000 |

If the managers are certain that the numbers are correct, they will choose Process B. But the numbers are estimates, so the managers should do some additional analysis before deciding which process to use. One item the managers should look at is the break-even point for each process.

SIGHT

> ### Uses of Target Costing
>
> **ITT Automotive,** a major worldwide maker of automotive parts with $4.8 billion sales, uses target costing to maintain its profitability and increase its market share in a competitive environment. Achieving the target cost is accomplished through several techniques, including the use of cross-functional teams, setting early cost targets, value engineering, and forming partners with suppliers.
>
> **H. J. Heinz Pet Products** took a similar approach with its 9-Lives cat food. Prices in the industry had fallen for several years. Heinz raised prices and lost so much volume that its profits dropped significantly. The 9-Lives unit then approached the problem from the consumers' point of view. The managers estimated the price that consumers were willing to pay for cat food, then worked on cost targets. It has reduced costs by closing old plants and automating new ones and forming partnerships with vendors to ensure stable supplies at favorable prices.
>
> In developing the target cost of an excavator's cooling system, **Komatsu** determined that the most important performance factor was the surface area of the system's radiator. They calculated the target cost of the radiator to reflect both the least square area needed and the minimum cost per unit of area.

*Sources: George Schmelze, Rolf Geier, and Thomas Buttross, "Target Costing at ITT Automotive,"* Management Accounting, *December 1996, 26–30.*
*"How to Escape a Price War,"* Fortune, *June 13, 1994, 84.*
*Robin Cooper and W. Bruce Chew, "Control Tomorrow's Costs Through Today's Designs,"* Harvard Business Review, *January–February 1996, 88–97.*

*Process A: $40,000/$3 = 13,333 units*

*Process B: $95,000/$6 = 15,833 units*

Process B's higher break-even point is one indication that it is riskier, but that analysis ignores sales expectations. To incorporate those expectations in their assessment of the alternatives, managers often express risk by referring to the margin of safety.

## MARGIN OF SAFETY

The decline in volume from the expected level of sales to the break-even point is called the **margin of safety (MOS)**. As the name suggests, the MOS is the difference between expected sales and the break-even point. The MOS can be expressed as a unit amount, dollar amount, or percentage. In our example, the MOS for Process A is 6,667 units (20,000 expected – 13,333 break even), or $66,670 (6,667 units at $10 each), or 33.3 percent (6,667/20,000). For Process B it is 4,167 units (20,000 – 15,833), $41,670 (4,167 units at $10), or 20.8 percent (4,167/20,000). Generally, the higher the MOS, the lower the risk. Our illustration shows the MOS for a single product, but the concept can be applied to a group of products or to an entire company.

## INDIFFERENCE POINT

Another tool that managers use to help them choose between alternative cost structures is the indifference point. The **indifference point** is the level of volume at which total costs, and hence profits, are the same under both cost structures. If the company operated at that level of volume, the alternative used would not matter because income would be the same either way.

We calculate the indifference point by setting up an equation where each side represents total cost under one of the alternatives. (Because selling price is the same under both of these alternatives, profits will be the same when total costs are the same.) At unit volumes below the indifference point, the alternative with the lower fixed cost gives higher profits; at volumes above the indifference point, the alternative with the higher fixed cost is more profitable. The indifference point for Caldwell's new product is 18,333 units, calculated as follows, with Q equal to unit volume.

$$
\begin{array}{rcl}
\textit{Total Cost for Process A} & = & \textit{Total Cost for Process B} \\
\textit{Fixed cost} + \textit{variable cost} & = & \textit{Fixed cost} + \textit{variable cost} \\
\$40,000 + \$7Q & = & \$95,000 + \$4Q \\
\$3Q & = & \$55,000 \\
Q & = & 18,333 \ (\textit{rounded})
\end{array}
$$

At volumes below 18,333 units, Process A gives lower total costs (and higher profits); above 18,333 units, Process B gives higher profits.

The line $\$3Q = \$55,000$ gives a clue to the trade-off between the alternatives: Caldwell gains $3 per unit in reduced variable costs by increasing fixed costs $55,000. The indifference point shows that the company needs 18,333 units to make the trade-off desirable; that volume is only 1,667 units (or 8 percent) below the estimated volume of 20,000. If Caldwell's managers believe that a high likelihood exists that volume will be lower than their estimate of 20,000 units, they might decide to use Process A.

Exhibit 2-3 shows Caldwell's choices in a variation of the CVP graph shown earlier. As in the earlier graph, the axes represent volume and dollars. Each line represents profit at each level of volume for the associated alternative. Notice that the line for each process begins at a negative point equal to fixed costs for that process and crosses zero at the break-even point for that process. Where profit is the same under both alternatives, the two lines cross. This form of the graph is useful especially in examining alternatives because it reduces the number of lines needed to represent an alternative.

Caldwell's managers have no correct answer in their choice of cost structure. Analytical tools such as the indifference point, margin of safety, and CVP graph help them evaluate alternatives, but the decision depends on their attitudes about risk and return. If they want to avoid risk, they will choose Process A, forgoing the potential for higher profits from Process B. If they are venturesome, they probably will be willing to take some risk for the potentially higher returns and choose Process B. The accompanying Insight on page 48 describes the risk-reward characteristics of two prominent U.S. companies.

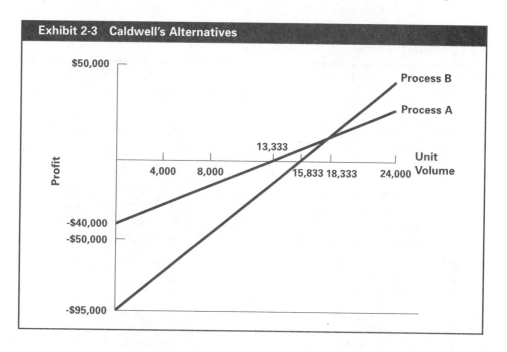

**Exhibit 2-3    Caldwell's Alternatives**

## ASSUMPTIONS AND LIMITATIONS OF CVP ANALYSIS

We have already mentioned some of the conditions necessary for CVP analysis to give useful predictions. It must be possible to graph both revenues and total costs as straight, rather than curved, lines within the relevant range. This requirement means that selling price, per-unit variable cost, and total fixed costs must be constant throughout the relevant range. We introduce two additional assumptions here, but we discuss them in detail in later chapters.

First, CVP analysis assumes that (1) the company sells only one product or (2) the sales of each product in a multiproduct company are a constant percentage of total sales. The term **sales mix** describes the percentage of each product's sales to total sales. If a change in sales mix occurs, the contribution margin percentage probably will change. Appendix 2 discusses multiproduct CVP analysis.

The second assumption is relevant only to manufacturing companies, not to merchandising and service companies. To apply CVP analysis to a manufacturing firm, production must equal sales. (That assumption was implicit in the analysis of Caldwell Company's alternative cost structure.) Because of certain requirements of financial accounting (and tax laws) for manufacturing companies, income reported for financial accounting (or tax) purposes usually does not agree with income predicted by CVP analysis. Chapter 14 explains how those requirements cause differences between reported income and income predictions using CVP analysis.

The companies in our illustrations, Exeter and Caldwell Company, are relatively simple operations compared with most companies today. Analyzing a bigger, more diverse company in its entirety is more difficult. Yet CVP analysis is a tool that is used, in various forms, by managers of the largest and most complex organizations. Managers apply CVP analysis to segments of their companies, such as products or product lines and geographical areas.

CHAPTER
14

 SIGHT

### Cost Structures and Strategies

Managers can use CVP relationships to evaluate strategies and tactics. The following data are from the 1997 annual report of **Delta Airlines**, in millions, except for percentages.

|                                | 1997     | 1996     |
|--------------------------------|----------|----------|
| Operating revenues             | $13,590  | $12,455  |
| Operating expenses             | $12,060  | $11,992  |
| Operating loss                 | $1,530   | $463     |
| Available seat-miles (ASM)     | 136,821  | 130,751  |
| Revenue passenger miles (RPM)  | 97,758   | 88,673   |
| Load factor, RPM/ASM           | 71.4%    | 67.8%    |
| Break-even load factor         | 62.7%    | 65.1%    |

An available seat-mile is a seat flown one mile. An airplane with 100 seats flying a 200-mile trip has 20,000 available seat-miles (100 × 200). A revenue passenger mile is one passenger flown one mile. If the 100-seat airplane carries 60 passengers it generates 12,000 RPMs (60 × 200). The load factor and break-even point are expressed as percentages of available seat-miles, so the airplane has a 60% load factor (12,000/20,000).

What are the keys to success for an airline? Its fixed costs are relatively high and variable costs relatively low. Moreover, its product, seat-miles, is perishable because once a plane is in the air Delta cannot sell another seat.

Companies with high fixed costs and perishable products (hotels, radio and TV stations) often lower prices to increase volume, but many times wind up pricing so low that they cannot be profitable without extraordinarily high volumes. Contrast these problems with those of a company such as **Wal-Mart**, some of whose results appear below, in millions of dollars.

| Sales              |          | $117,958 |
|--------------------|----------|----------|
| Cost of sales      | $93,438  |          |
| Operating expenses | 19,358   | 112,796  |
| Operating income   |          | $ 5,162  |

Wal-Mart has much higher variable costs than Delta (cost of sales is variable as are some operating expenses, though we cannot tell how much), so it will not have the feast or famine characteristic of high fixed cost companies. Wal-Mart must pay careful attention to prices, because slight changes can have major effects.

## SUMMARY

Cost-volume-profit analysis is critical to planning and requires classifying costs by behavior. A cost is either fixed or variable depending on whether the total amount of the cost changes as activity changes. Contribution margin, the difference between price and variable cost, is important in CVP analysis. Contribution margin can be expressed as a per-unit amount, a total, or a percentage of selling price. The critical points in the chapter are the recognition of the fixed/variable cost classification scheme, the analytical value of this classification, and the usefulness of contribution margin.

Managers use cost-volume-profit analysis to answer questions such as the following: What profits are earned at different levels of sales? What sales are needed to earn a particular profit? What are the effects of changes in selling prices? What price must we charge to earn a particular profit?

With varying degrees of ease, managers can change both costs and prices. Within limits, managers also can control the relative proportions of fixed and variable costs in their cost structure. The usefulness of CVP analysis as a planning tool depends, therefore, on managers' estimates about future conditions, not those prevailing in the past. A basic CVP graph presents a single set of conditions that managers expect. The indifference point, margin of safety, and a variation of the basic CVP graph help managers assess the risks and returns of alternative cost structures. Managers' attitudes toward risk-return relationships influence decisions about cost structure.

Managers in multiproduct and/or manufacturing companies can apply CVP analysis if they recognize that certain assumptions underlie that analysis.

## KEY TERMS

break-even point  *(37)*
complementary products  *(54)*
  *appendix 2*
contribution margin  *(31)*
contribution margin percentage  *(31)*
cost-volume-profit (CVP) analysis
  *(30)*
fixed costs  *(31)*
indifference point  *(46)*
margin of safety (MOS)  *(45)*
nonvariable costs  *(33)*
operating leverage  *(35)*

relevant range  *(36)*
return on sales (ROS)  *(35)*
sales mix  *(47)*
substitute products  *(59) appendix 2*
target costing  *(43)*
target profit  *(38)*
variable costs  *(30)*
variable cost percentage  *(31)*
weighted-average contribution margin
  percentage  *(54) appendix 2*
weighted-average contribution margin
  per unit  *(58) appendix 2*

## KEY FORMULAS

$$\text{Break-even sales, in units} = \frac{\text{total fixed costs}}{\text{contribution margin per unit}}$$

$$\text{Break-even sales, in dollars} = \frac{\text{total fixed costs}}{\text{contribution margin percentage}}$$

$$\text{Operating leverage} = \frac{\text{total contribution margin}}{\text{profit}}$$

$$\text{Profit} = \text{sales} - \text{variable costs} - \text{fixed costs}$$

$$\text{Sales, in dollars, to achieve target profit} = \frac{\text{total fixed costs} + \text{target profit}}{\text{contribution margin percentage}}$$

$$\text{Sales, in units, to achieve target profit} = \frac{\text{fixed costs} + \text{target profit}}{\text{contribution margin per unit}}$$

$$\text{Sales, in dollars, to achieve target return on sales} = \frac{\text{fixed costs}}{\text{contribution margin percentage} - \text{target return on sales}}$$

$$\text{Total costs} = \text{fixed costs} + (\text{variable cost per unit} \times \text{unit volume})$$

## REVIEW PROBLEM

Cost-volume-profit analysis assumes that important variables (selling price, variable cost per unit, total fixed costs) do not change within the relevant range. Nevertheless, as we saw in the section on price determination, a manager may want to know what value for one of these variables is consistent with a particular target profit. Moreover, because prices and costs can change quickly, a manager must be alert to the effects of such changes. The following problem tests your basic understanding of CVP analysis. Solve the problem, one part at a time, and check your answers with those provided. Consider each question independently of the others.

   Clayton Company sells its one product at $30 per unit. Variable costs are $22 per unit and fixed costs are $100,000 per month.

### Required

1. If Clayton can sell 15,000 units in a particular month, what will be its income?
2. What is the break-even point in units?
3. What is the break-even point in sales dollars?
4. What unit sales are required to earn $50,000 for the month?
5. What sales, in dollars, are required to earn $50,000 for the month?
6. Suppose Clayton reduces its selling price to $28 because competitors are charging that amount. What is its new break-even point (a) in units? (b) in dollars?
7. Suppose that fixed costs are expected to increase by $10,000 (to $110,000 per month). What is the new break-even point (a) in units? (b) in dollars? Price remains $30.
8. Suppose that Clayton is currently selling 10,000 units per month. The marketing manager believes that sales would increase if advertising were increased by $5,000. How much would sales have to increase, in units, to give Clayton the same income or loss that it is currently earning? (Although you know how many units are now being sold, you do not need this fact to solve the problem.)
9. Suppose Clayton is selling 20,000 units per month at $30. What is its margin of safety?
10. Clayton currently pays its salespeople salaries that total $40,000 per month, but no commissions. The vice president of sales is considering a plan whereby the salespeople would receive a 5 percent commission, but their salaries would fall to a total of $25,000 per month (a drop of $15,000). At what sales level is the company indifferent between the two compensation plans?

### ANSWER TO REVIEW PROBLEM

1. Clayton will earn $20,000. An income statement is shown on the next page.

| | |
|---|---|
| Sales (15,000 × $30) | $450,000 |
| Variable costs (15,000 × $22) | 330,000 |
| Contribution margin (15,000 × $8) | $120,000 |
| Fixed costs | 100,000 |
| Income | $ 20,000 |

A shortcut is to multiply contribution margin per unit of $8 by 15,000 units (which gives $120,000 in contribution margin), then subtract fixed costs of $100,000 to get $20,000 income.

2. 12,500 units. The break-even point in units is the result of dividing fixed costs ($100,000) by the $8 contribution margin per unit.

3. $375,000. This amount can be determined either by multiplying the break-even point in units (from requirement 2) by the selling price per unit (12,500 × $30) or by applying the break-even formula using the contribution margin percentage ($100,000/26.67%). The contribution margin percentage is determined by dividing the selling price of $30 into the contribution margin of $8 (from requirement 2).

4. 18,750 units. The profit of $50,000 is added to the fixed costs of $100,000, and the target profit formula is then applied. Thus, the total to be obtained from sales is $50,000 plus $100,000 in fixed costs. If Clayton gets $8 per unit and desires total contribution margin of $150,000, it must sell 18,750 units ($150,000/$8).

5. $562,500. This amount can be determined either by multiplying the 18,750 units (from requirement 4) by the $30 selling price per unit or by applying the formula using the contribution margin percentage. To return the fixed costs of $100,000 plus a profit of $50,000 when the contribution margin percentage is 26.67 percent requires sales of $562,500 ($150,000/26.67%).

6. (a) 16,667 units. If fixed costs of $100,000 must be covered when each unit carries a contribution margin of $6 ($28 selling price – variable cost of $22), a total of 16,667 units must be sold ($100,000/$6).

(b) $466,676. This amount can be determined either by multiplying the number of units (16,667) computed in part (a) by the selling price of $28 or by using the formula with the contribution margin percentage. Thus, 16,667 × $28 is $466,676 or $100,000/[($28 – $22)/$28] = $466,676 (rounded).

7. (a) 13,750 units. With fixed costs of $110,000 and a contribution margin per unit of $8, the number of units to produce a contribution margin equal to the fixed costs is 13,750 ($110,000/$8). Another approach is to determine what additional sales volume (beyond that required to break even with the current cost structure) provides sufficient contribution margin to cover the additional fixed costs. It will take the contribution margin from an additional 1,250 units ($10,000/$8 per unit) to cover the added fixed costs, and the break-even point is already 12,500 units, so the total number of units required to break even with the new cost structure is 13,750 (12,500 + 1,250).

(b) $412,500. The most direct approach to this answer is to multiply the number of units (13,750) computed in part (a) by the selling price per unit ($30). Or the answer could be determined by dividing the fixed costs ($110,000) by the contribution margin percentage (26.67%).

8. 625 units. Income will not be affected as long as the contribution margin from the additional units sold is sufficient to offset the expenditure for advertising. Hence, we need to determine only what additional sales will produce contribution margin sufficient to cover the cost of the advertising. Because contribution margin per unit is $8, the number of units needed to cover the $5,000 advertising campaign is $5,000/$8 or 625 units. (Note that the current level of sales is irrelevant

to the decision of whether or not to undertake the advertising campaign. As long as the campaign will increase sales by 625 units, Clayton will be neither better nor worse off than it would have been without it.)

9. 7,500 units, or 37.5%. At sales of 20,000 units Clayton earns $60,000 (20,000 × $8 − $100,000) and the break-even point is 12,500 units (from requirement 2).

10. 10,000 units. Fixed costs fall to $85,000 under the proposal and variable costs increase to $23.50 ($22 + 0.05 × $30).

| Total Costs Now | | Total Costs Under Proposal |
|---|---|---|
| $100,000 + $22Q | = | $85,000 + $23.50Q |
| $1.50Q | = | $15,000 |
| Q | = | 10,000 |

Below 10,000 units the proposed method is more profitable for Clayton, while above 10,000 units the existing method gives higher profit. Note that this situation differs from one in which the company was changing the way it manufactures a product. The method of manufacture probably does not affect the sales of the product (quality remaining constant). But for Clayton motivational questions might arise. The salespeople might sell more units under one method than they would under the other. We cannot be certain which method would better motivate the salespeople.

This review problem has emphasized the possibility of changes in the structure of costs and selling prices. Managers must be alert for changes from outside (for example, a supplier raising prices) and should understand their effects on profits. Additionally, managers can analyze proposed changes to see if they will increase profits. Requirement 8 of this problem gave an important practical example: an increase in a fixed cost was expected to lead to some increase in volume. If the marketing manager believes that the added cost will generate additional sales in excess of 625 units, the proposal for additional advertising would be wise.

## APPENDIX 1: INCOME TAXES AND PROFIT PLANNING

Income taxes are a cost of doing business and should be considered, as should all costs, in the planning process. Income taxes are based on the amount of income before taxes. For our purposes, it is reasonable to assume that income taxes are a constant percentage of income before taxes. In most large corporations, this assumption is reasonable, but we hasten to point out that tax law is exceedingly complex, not all businesses are incorporated, and generalizations are risky.

Income taxes must be considered if managers seek an after-tax target profit. An after-tax target requires a revision of the basic target profit formula. The revision requires converting the after-tax target profit to a before-tax profit, which is accomplished by dividing the after-tax target profit by 1 minus the income tax rate. For example, suppose Exeter wants to earn an after-tax profit of $6,300 and its tax rate is 30 percent. To earn $6,300 after taxes, Exeter must earn $9,000 before taxes ($6,300/70%). Of the before-tax income of $9,000, $2,700 goes to the government ($9,000 × 30%), leaving $6,300 ($9,000 − $2,700). Accordingly, when the target is an after-tax profit, the basic formula for calculating the volume needed to achieve the target is as follows:

$$\begin{array}{c} \text{Sales to achieve} \\ \text{target after-tax profit} \end{array} = \frac{\text{fixed costs} + \dfrac{\text{after-tax profit}}{1 - \text{tax rate}}}{\text{contribution margin percentage}}$$

$$\text{or}$$

$$\text{contribution margin per unit}$$

We already know that Exeter's fixed costs are $40,000 and that its contribution margin percentage is 40 percent. Solving the above formula for sales dollars to achieve a $6,300 profit after taxes gives

$$Sales = \frac{\$40,000 + \dfrac{\$6,300}{70\%}}{40\%}$$

$$= \frac{\$40,000 + \$9,000}{40\%} = \frac{\$49,000}{40\%}$$

$$= \$122,500$$

We could calculate the unit sales required either by dividing the $122,500 sales by the $20 selling price, or by dividing the $8 contribution margin per unit into the $49,000 (fixed costs plus required before-tax profit). Either way, the answer is 6,125 backpacks.

You needn't concern yourself with any formulas beyond those in the chapter if you recognize that the key step in both of the above calculations was converting an after-tax target ($6,300) to a before-tax target ($9,000). That conversion is the key whether the target is an absolute dollar amount of profit or a specific ROS.

To demonstrate, suppose Exeter's target is an after-tax ROS of 14 percent. Once again, its after-tax target is 70 percent (1 minus the 30 percent income tax rate) of a before-tax target; so its before-tax ROS target is 20 percent (14%/70%). Using the formula on page 41, the sales target is $200,000, as shown below.

$$\begin{array}{c} \text{Sales, in dollars, to} \\ \text{achieve target ROS} \end{array} = \frac{\$40,000}{40\% - 20\%} = \$200,000$$

The income statement below, with both dollar amounts and percentages of sales, shows that sales of $200,000 will produce the after-tax ROS target of 14 percent.

| | | |
|---|---|---|
| Sales | $200,000 | 100% |
| Variable costs | 120,000 | |
| Contribution margin | $ 80,000 | 40% |
| Fixed costs | 40,000 | |
| Income before taxes | $ 40,000 | 20% |
| Income taxes, at 30% | 12,000 | |
| Net income | $ 28,000 | 14% |

One final reminder. Planning for income taxes is important if the entity is subject to income taxes and if there is income to tax. Therefore, income taxes do not affect the determination of the break-even point, at which there is no income to tax.

## APPENDIX 2: MULTIPLE PRODUCTS

CVP analysis assumes either a single product or a constant sales mix. (Recall that sales mix is the proportion of each product in total sales, expressed in units or in dollars.) If products have widely differing contribution margins, and if the mix changes, the company's contribution margin could change and results could be much different from those predicted. Multiple-product companies can nonetheless use CVP analysis for individual products or for groups of products with approximately equal contribution margins (per unit or percentage). They also can use CVP analysis when contributions differ greatly, provided that the sales mix remains relatively constant.

Companies have relatively constant sales mixes for several reasons. Some companies sell products that are used together, so that the sales of one affect the sales of the other. Common examples are cameras and film, ice cream and toppings, and tables and chairs. Such products are **complementary products**. Even with no apparent complementary relationship among products, the sales mix still might remain fairly constant. A department store might consistently derive 40 percent of its sales from clothing, 25 percent from furniture and housewares, and 35 percent from its other departments. These percentages might be relatively constant over time despite the absence of obvious causes. Whatever the reasons for the predictability of sales mix, managers of a multiple-product company can apply CVP analysis by using a weighted-average contribution margin.

In applying CVP analysis in a multiproduct company, managers often group similar products together. A natural grouping of products is called a *product line*. An example is a hair-care line, consisting of shampoos, conditioners, colorings, creams, tonics, and restorers. Before proposing a program that could influence sales mix, a manager needs to know price and cost data for each product as well as the current sales mix. These data give the manager some idea of profitability by product and how the sales mix might be enriched. In many cases, managers will treat the entire line as a single "product." Several reasons influence managers to take this simplified approach for analytical purposes.

First, the products might have such similar contribution margins (either per unit or percentages) that little is gained by examining them individually. After all, planning does involve estimates; moreover, minor differences that result from grouping products with slightly different contribution margins are not likely to affect decisions. A second reason is that the sheer number of products might make analyzing them individually difficult and time-consuming.

A third reason for grouping products relates to the level of the manager receiving the analysis. The president of a department store does not look at sales and cost details for every product stocked by the store. However, a lower-level manager—say one in charge of sporting goods—does look at individual products in that line. That manager is concerned about each product and makes decisions about adding and dropping individual products. The president is more concerned with the product line as a whole and makes decisions about adding or dropping entire departments.

### WEIGHTED-AVERAGE CONTRIBUTION MARGIN PERCENTAGE

As the term suggests, the **weighted-average contribution margin percentage** is the overall contribution margin percentage. It consists of the individual products' percentages weighted by their relative sales. Managers also can use the weighted-average contribution margin percentage just as they use the contribution margin percentage for a single product.

Suppose that Exeter has expanded its business. It now sells tote bags and bookbags, as well as backpacks. Increasing the diversity of the business has increased fixed costs to $60,000 per month for additional employees and larger rented quarters. Data for the individual products follow.

|  | Backpacks | | Tote Bags | | Bookbags |  |
|---|---|---|---|---|---|---|
| Selling price | $20 | | $16 | | $20 | |
| Variable cost | 12 | | 4 | | 10 | |
| Contribution margin | $ 8 | | $12 | | $10 | |
| Contribution margin percentage | 40% | | 75% | | 50% | |
| Percentage in sales mix | 60% | + | 10% | + | 30% | = 100% |

The percentages shown for sales mix are the proportions of *total sales dollars* coming from each product. (These percentages must total 100 percent.)

Exeter has the same questions it had earlier: What is the break-even point? What sales are required to achieve a particular profit target? When Exeter had only one product, it could work equally well with either sales units or sales dollars. With multiple products, it might be more convenient, and simpler, to work with sales dollars, using the weighted-average contribution margin percentage. (As we shall see, some companies could just as easily use sales units.)

We can calculate the weighted-average contribution margin percentage in at least two ways. One way is to prepare a hypothetical partial income statement, such as the one below, down to contribution margin, which assumes total sales of $100,000 and the sales mix that Exeter expects.

|  | Backpacks | Tote Bags | Bookbags | Totals |
|---|---|---|---|---|
| Sales mix | 60% | 10% | 30% | 100% |
| Sales | $60,000 | $10,000 | $30,000 | $100,000 |
| Variable costs | 36,000 | 2,500 | 15,000 | 53,500 |
| Contribution margin | $24,000 | $ 7,500 | $15,000 | $ 46,500 |

The weighted-average contribution margin percentage is 46.5 percent ($46,500/$100,000).

A more direct way to find the weighted-average contribution margin percentage is to multiply the contribution margin percentage for each product by its percentage in the sales mix and add the results. This calculation appears below.

|  | Backpacks | | Tote Bags | | Bookbags | | Total |
|---|---|---|---|---|---|---|---|
| Contribution margin percentage | 40% | | 75% | | 50% | | |
| Multiplied by percentage sales mix | 60% | | 10% | | 30% | | |
| Weighted average | 24% | + | 7.5% | + | 15% | = | 46.5% |

Let's look at the logic of this calculation. With the 60/10/30 percent sales mix, the average sales dollar is composed of $0.60 from backpacks, $0.10 from tote bags, and $0.30 from bookbags. The $0.60 sales from backpacks provides $0.24 in contribution margin because the contribution margin percentage on backpacks is 40 percent. The contribution margin of $0.24 is the 24 percent in the backpacks column. Similarly, the $0.30 sales of bookbags in the average sales dollar provides $0.15 contribution margin because the rate on bookbags is 50 percent. The following schedule shows the calculations in dollars.

|  | Backpacks | Tote Bags | Bookbags | Total |
|---|---|---|---|---|
| Average sales dollar | $0.60 | $ 0.10 | $0.30 | $ 1.00 |
| Contribution margin percentage | 40% | 75% | 50% |  |
| Contribution margin | $0.24 + | $0.075 + | $0.15 = | $0.465 |

Because the average sales dollar yields $0.465 in contribution margin, the weighted-average contribution margin percentage is 46.5 percent.

Using the 46.5 percent weighted-average contribution margin percentage, Exeter now can do the same analyses it did earlier. The break-even point is $129,032 ($60,000/46.5%). To earn a $20,000 target profit requires sales of $172,043 [($60,000 + $20,000)/46.5%].

The following income statement shows that the weighted-average contribution margin of 46.5 percent works.

|  | Backpacks | Tote Bags | Bookbags | Total |
|---|---|---|---|---|
| Sales mix | 60% | 10% | 30% | 100% |
| Sales | $103,226 | $17,204 | $51,613 | $172,043 |
| Variable costs | 61,936 | 4,301 | 25,806 | 92,043 |
| Contribution margin | $ 41,290 | $12,903 | $25,807 | $ 80,000 |
| Fixed costs |  |  |  | 60,000 |
| Profit |  |  |  | $ 20,000 |

## CHANGES IN SALES MIX

Sales mix is very important when the contribution margin percentages differ greatly among products. (If all products have the same contribution margin percentages, that percentage *is* the weighted-average contribution margin percentage.) Suppose that Exeter sees a trend that is likely to change the sales mix to 30 percent backpacks, 40 percent tote bags, and 30 percent bookbags (a shift from backpacks to tote bags). The new weighted-average contribution margin is 57 percent, an increase of 11.5 percentage points. The increase results from tote bags having a much higher contribution margin percentage than backpacks.

|  | Backpacks | Tote Bags | Bookbags | Total |
|---|---|---|---|---|
| Contribution margin percentage | 40% | 75% | 50% |  |
| Percentage in sales mix | 30% | 40% | 30% |  |
| Weighted average | 12% + | 30% + | 15% = | 57% |

Exhibit 2-4 shows Exeter's CVP chart. Note that the horizontal axis shows sales in dollars rather than in units because we are working with contribution margin per-

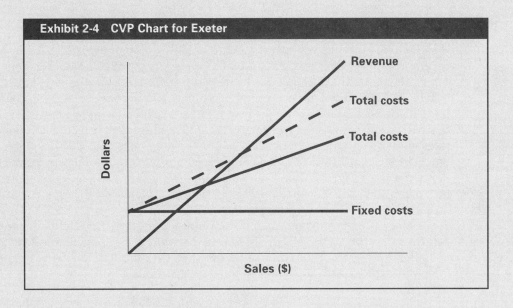

**Exhibit 2-4   CVP Chart for Exeter**

centage. The chart shows two total cost lines to represent two sales mixes. The dotted line shows the 53.5 percent variable cost percentage, which holds when the weighted-average contribution margin percentage is 46.5 percent (as computed when the sales mix was 60 percent backpacks, 10 percent tote bags, and 30 percent bookbags). The solid total cost line uses a 43 percent variable cost percentage, which holds when the weighted-average contribution margin is 57 percent (the second computation, when the sales mix was 30 percent backpacks, 40 percent tote bags, and 30 percent bookbags).

At any level of sales, the break-even point is lower and profits are higher when contribution margin is 57 percent than when it is 46.5 percent. Other things being equal, a richer sales mix—one with a higher overall contribution margin percentage—is better, which explains why managers routinely try to enrich sales mix. Under some circumstances, if a company can increase its total sales by some dollar amount, or shift a dollar in sales from one product to another, the product that should be emphasized is the one with the higher contribution margin percentage. Accordingly, managers might shift the emphasis in their advertising towards products with higher contribution margin percentages, while reducing advertising space for products carrying lower percentages. At a simpler level, a salesperson learning that a customer intends to spend $20 for a gift should consider emphasizing suitable $20 items that also have relatively high contribution margin percentages. For a real-life example, **British Airways** richened its sales mix by various tactics aimed at filling more premium-priced seats. The airline recently had 15 percent of its passengers fly first-class and business class, but earned 33 percent of its revenues from these premium seats. The growth that the company experienced in these premium-priced seats increased overall passenger revenue per mile by 2.7 percent, a very hefty increase in the airline industry.

Note, however, that some efforts to enrich sales mix might make "other things" unequal. For example, increasing advertising to enrich sales mix also increases fixed costs. If products are substitutes, shifting sales from one to the other might not be profitable. That case is best considered in the next section, which deals with contribution margin per unit.

## WEIGHTED-AVERAGE CONTRIBUTION MARGIN PER UNIT

Some multiple-product companies use units, rather than dollars, to measure volume and express sales mix. For instance, managers of an automobile manufacturer are primarily concerned with the number of cars sold, rather than total dollars of sales. (They are concerned, of course, about dollar sales, but most of their analyses use units—cars—instead of dollars.) Similarly, managers of service businesses, such as firms of CPAs, lawyers, and management consultants, express sales volumes in terms of chargeable hours, the hours that their personnel spend on client business. These managers also consider sales mix in unit percentages, not dollar percentages. While Exeter says that 40 percent of dollar sales are from backpacks, a manager of an automaker says that 40 percent of the cars it sells are sedans.

Companies that think and plan in unit terms can calculate weighted-average contribution margin percentages, but they often find it more useful to calculate a weighted-average contribution margin per unit. Consider the following data for Corbin Company, a manufacturer of three models of desks.

|  | President | Senior VP | Junior VP |
|---|---|---|---|
| Selling price | $1,000 | $800 | $500 |
| Unit variable cost | 600 | 500 | 250 |
| Unit contribution margin | $ 400 | $300 | $250 |
| Percentage in sales mix, in units | 20% | 30% | 50% |

The **weighted-average contribution margin per unit** is calculated in basically the same way as the weighted-average contribution margin percentage. The per-unit contribution margin of each product (in dollars, not as a percentage) is multiplied by its percentage in the sales mix.

|  | President | Senior VP | Junior VP | Total |
|---|---|---|---|---|
| Unit contribution margin | $400 | $300 | $250 | |
| Times mix percentage, in units | 20% | 30% | 50% | |
| Weighted-average unit contribution margin | $ 80 + | $ 90 + | $125 = | $295 |

So long as the sales mix holds, managers can use the weighted-average unit contribution margin of $295 just as they would if the company made a single product. Thus, if Corbin's fixed costs are $500,000, its break-even point is about 1,695 desks (fixed costs of $500,000 divided by the weighted-average per-unit contribution margin of $295). To prove that the per-unit calculation works, suppose that Corbin sells 1,000 desks in the expected mix. Its income statement, through contribution margin, is as follows.

|  | President | Senior VP | Junior VP | Total |
|---|---|---|---|---|
| Sales in units* | 200 | 300 | 500 | 1,000 |
| Sales | $200,000 | $240,000 | $250,000 | $690,000 |
| Variable costs | 120,000 | 150,000 | 125,000 | 395,000 |
| Contribution margin | $ 80,000 | $ 90,000 | $125,000 | $295,000* |

*1,000 × 20%, 30%, 50%

Total contribution margin is $295,000, which is $295 times 1,000 *total* units. Note also that the weighted-average contribution margin percentage is about 42.8 percent ($295,000/$690,000). Corbin's managers could use either form of weighted-average contribution margin in their analyses.

Would Corbin's profits increase if its managers tried to shift the sales mix toward the President, the model with the highest per-unit contribution margin? The answer is it depends. Corbin manufactures **substitute products**. That is, customers who buy a desk of one model are unlikely to buy a desk of another model, though they might buy chairs and other accessories. Because Corbin earns the contribution margin on only one desk, its managers would certainly prefer to receive the highest contribution margin possible. But managers must recognize that attempting to persuade customers to upgrade to a more profitable model might backfire if customers don't buy *any* desk and go elsewhere. (An unethical, and illegal, effort to persuade customers to buy models carrying higher contribution margins is known as "bait and switch." This scheme involves advertising a very low price on a popular style or model when the company has only a very small quantity of that item available to sell.)

Past sales provide clues to sales mix and managers can influence sales mix. But if some products are substitutes or complementary, managers should not adopt strategies to influence the volume of one product unless they have considered the effects on sales of the related products.

## ASSIGNMENT MATERIAL

### INTERNET ACTIVITY

Companies that operate in different industries often will have different targets for return on sales (ROS). Various lists such as the Fortune 500 or the Standard & Poor's (S&P) 500 present each company's ROS. Use a Web search engine such as Yahoo to find listings of the Fortune 500 and the S&P 500 companies. Search these sites to determine the ROS for companies that interest you. Be sure to analyze companies in several industries. Be prepared to describe and discuss what you discovered.

### QUESTIONS FOR DISCUSSION

**2-1  *Assumptions and misconceptions about CVP analysis***  A classmate is having trouble with CVP analysis and asks for your help. He has the following questions.

1. "How can CVP analysis work when you really don't know what's going to happen? You might change your selling price. Your suppliers might change their prices. Inflation can cause other costs to go up. You might not sell the number of units you need to sell in order to earn a target profit. All sorts of things can happen that will invalidate your calculations."

2. "When I took economics, I learned that the higher the price, the less you sell. So how can you draw a straight revenue line?"

3. "I don't see how you can say that some costs are fixed. I'll accept depreciation and a few others, but salaries can be raised or lowered easily, your insurance premiums can go up or down, you can spend more or less on advertising, travel, and all sorts of other elements that you would call fixed."

4. "Most companies cannot sell everything at their normal prices. A clothing store has to discount goods at the end of a season."

**Required**
Answer your classmate's questions.

**2-2   Effects of events**   The newsletter of a national brokerage firm stated the following points about the profitability of **Cooper Tire & Rubber**.
1. Industry-wide selling prices are rising, including Cooper's.
2. Raw material costs are rising.
3. The rise of the yen against the dollar should increase Cooper's export business.

**Required**
State the effect of each item, if any, on Cooper's CVP graph.

**2-3   Effects of keeping up with technology**   The following statement appeared in a recent **Amazon.com** annual report.

"To remain competitive, the Company must continue to enhance and improve the responsiveness, functionality and features of the Amazon.com online store. The Internet and the online commerce industry are characterized by rapid technological change, changes in user and customer requirements and preferences, frequent new product and service introductions embodying new technologies and the emergence of new industry standards and practices that could render the Company's existing Web site and proprietary technology and systems obsolete."

**Required**
Discuss this statement in relation to the concepts introduced in Chapter 2.

## EXERCISES

**2-4   Income statement and CVP analysis**   The following data are available for Melrose Company's one product.

| | |
|---|---|
| Unit selling price | $15 |
| Unit variable cost | $10 |
| Total fixed costs | $90,000 |
| Unit volume | 60,000 |

**Required**
1. Prepare an income statement using the contribution margin format.
2. Determine the break-even point in (a) units and (b) sales dollars.
3. Determine the (a) unit volume and (b) dollar volume required to earn a 10% return on sales.
4. Determine the price that the company must charge to double the profit you determined in requirement 1, still selling 60,000 units.

**2-5   Income statement and CVP analysis**   The following data relate to McFarland, Inc.

| | |
|---|---|
| Sales | $800,000 |
| Variable cost percentage | 40% |
| Total fixed costs | $450,000 |

**Required**

1. Prepare an income statement using the contribution margin format.
2. Determine the break-even point in sales dollars.
3. Determine the dollar volume required to double the profit you determined in requirement 1.

**2-6  Income statement and CVP analysis with taxes (Appendix 1)**   Use the data from Exercise 2-4 for this assignment. Assume a 30% income tax rate.

**Required**

1. Prepare an income statement that incorporates income taxes.
2. Determine the (a) unit volume and (b) dollar volume required to double the after-tax profit you determined in requirement 1.
3. Determine the selling price that will double the before-tax profit at the original volume.

**2-7  Income statement and CVP analysis with taxes (Appendix 1)**   Use the data from Exercise 2-5 for this assignment. Assume a 40% income tax rate.

**Required**

1. Prepare an income statement that incorporates income taxes.
2. Determine the dollar volume required to double the after-tax profit you determined in requirement 1.

**2-8  Basic CVP analysis**   Trailfood, Inc. sells high-energy bars to supermarkets for $40 per case. Variable cost is $15 per case and annual fixed costs are $1,000,000.

**Required**

1. Determine the break-even point in (a) units and (b) dollars.
2. Determine the volume required to earn a $120,000 profit in (a) units and (b) dollars.
3. Determine the volume required to earn a 10% return on sales in (a) units and (b) dollars.
4. If Trailfood can sell 55,000 cases, what price would it have to charge to earn a $100,000 profit?
5. Redo requirement 4 assuming that the variable cost of $15 consists of $9 related to the case and a 15% commission on sales ($6 per case at the $40 price).

**2-9  Basic CVP relationships, with income taxes (Appendix 1)**   In one of its factories, Clarion Corporation manufactures a water pump that it sells to auto parts dealers throughout the country. Clarion sells the pump for $40. Variable costs are $25 and annual fixed costs are $3,000,000. The tax rate is 40%.

**Required**

1. Determine the volume required to earn a $600,000 after-tax profit in (a) units and (b) dollars.
2. If Clarion can sell 300,000 pumps, what price must it charge to earn a $600,000 after-tax profit?
3. Redo requirement 2 assuming that the $25 variable cost consists of $21 for manufacturing and a 10% commission on sales ($4 per unit at the $40 price).

**2-10  Relationships among variables**  Fill in the blanks for each of the following independent situations.

| Case | (a) Selling Price per Unit | (b) Variable Cost Percentage | (c) Number of Units Sold | (d) Contribution Margin | (e) Fixed Costs | (f) Income (Loss) |
|---|---|---|---|---|---|---|
| 1. | $50 | 40% | — | — | $50,000 | $28,000 |
| 2. | $80 | — | 3,000 | $60,000 | — | $(20,000) |
| 3. | $25 | — | 15,000 | — | 25,000 | $50,000 |

**2-11  Relationships among variables**  Fill in the blanks for each of the following independent situations.

| | 1 | 2 | 3 |
|---|---|---|---|
| Selling price per unit | — | $5 | — |
| Variable cost per unit | $6 | $3 | $6 |
| Number of units sold | 1,000 | — | 4,000 |
| Total contribution margin | $2,000 | $4,000 | $16,000 |
| Total fixed costs | — | $1,500 | $8,000 |
| Income | $1,200 | — | — |

**2-12  CVP graph**  The following graph portrays the operations of Richmond Company.

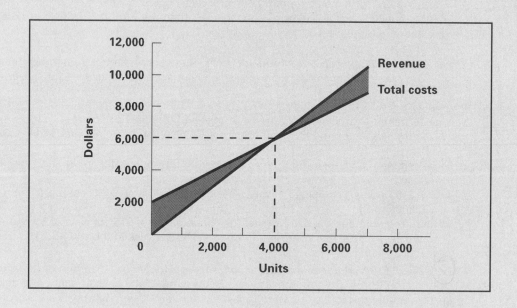

**Required**

Determine the following.

1. Sales dollars at the break-even point.
2. Fixed costs at 4,500 units sold.
3. Total variable costs at 4,000 units sold.
4. Variable cost per unit at 2,000 units sold.
5. Variable cost per unit at 5,000 units sold.

6. Selling price per unit.
7. Total contribution margin at 3,000 units sold.
8. Profit (loss) at sales of 3,000 units.
9. Profit (loss) at sales of 5,000 units.
10. Break-even sales, in units, if fixed costs were to increase by $500.

**2-13  Basic sales mix (Appendix 2)**  The general manager of Lo-Price Grocery Stores reviewed the following data.

|  | Produce | Meat/Dairy | Canned Goods |
|---|---|---|---|
| Contribution margin percentage | 40% | 50% | 40% |
| Sales mix percentage, in dollars | 20% | 30% | 50% |

Fixed costs are $1,290,000 per month.

**Required**
1. Determine the weighted-average contribution margin percentage.
2. Determine the break-even sales volume per month.
3. Determine the sales necessary to earn $300,000 per month.

**2-14  Improving sales mix (Appendix 2)**  Davis Exterminating Company performs a wide variety of pest control services. George Davis, the owner, has been examining the following forecasts for 20X2.

| Type of Service | Expected Dollar Volume for 20X2 | Contribution Margin Percentage |
|---|---|---|
| Termites | $160,000 | 50% |
| Lawn pests | 120,000 | 60% |
| Interior pests | 120,000 | 80% |

Davis expects total fixed costs of $150,000 in 20X2.

**Required**
1. What is the weighted-average contribution margin percentage?
2. What profit should Davis earn?
3. The actual sales mix turned out to be 20% termites, 30% lawn pests, and 50% interior pests. Total actual sales were $400,000 and total fixed costs were $150,000. Determine (a) the actual weighted-average contribution margin percentage and (b) profit.

**2-15  Margin of safety**  Strategy Inc. plans to market a new electronic game. The game would sell for $90, and Strategy expects sales to be 16,000 units. Per-unit variable manufacturing cost is $52. The only other variable cost is a 20% sales commission. The fixed costs associated with this game are $275,000.

**Required**
Compute the margin of safety at the expected sales volume.

**2-16  Alternative CVP graph (continuation of 2-15)**  The managers of Strategy Inc. have determined that the new game also could be brought out using a different combination of production and marketing strategies. The alternative strategies would reduce per-unit variable manufacturing cost to $41, but annual fixed costs would increase to $325,000 and the sales commission would be raised to 25%.

**Required**

In a CVP graph like Exhibit 2-3, plot the results of the two alternatives that Strategy is considering.

**2-17  CVP graph, analysis of changes**  You have prepared a CVP graph for NMA Shoes. It reflects the following expectations.

| | |
|---|---:|
| Selling price | $40 |
| Unit variable cost | $22 |
| Total fixed costs | $4,000,000 |

NMA's managers are wondering what the effects will be on operations if some changes take place, either by management decision or by some outside force such as the prices charged by a supplier. The following specific changes are the most likely possibilities.

1. A decrease in the selling price resulting from greater-than-expected competition.
2. A decrease in unit variable cost arising from a decision to use less expensive leather in the shoes.
3. An increase in total fixed costs accompanied by a decrease in unit variable cost from introducing labor-saving machinery.
4. A decrease in the number of units expected to be sold.
5. An increase in the selling price combined with an increase in unit variable cost resulting from a decision to increase the quality of the product.

**Required**

Treat each change independently of the others. For each, state the effects on (a) the revenue line, (b) the total cost line, and (c) the break-even point. Some changes will have no effect on one or more of the items. In at least one case, the effect on the break-even point cannot be determined without additional information. Note that both the intercept and slope of the total cost line could be affected by a set of changes.

**2-18  Converting an income statement**  Leslie Clayton, president of Clayton Enterprises, has given you the following income statement for a recent month.

| | | |
|---|---:|---:|
| Sales | | $400,000 |
| Cost of goods sold | | 240,000 |
| Gross profit | | $160,000 |
| Operating expenses: | | |
|   Salaries and commissions | $71,000 | |
|   Utilities | 10,000 | |
|   Rent | 15,000 | |
|   Other | 25,000 | 121,000 |
| Profit | | $ 39,000 |

Clayton sells one product, a stadium chair, at $25 per unit. Cost of goods sold is variable. A 10% sales commission, included in salaries and commissions, is the only other variable cost. Clayton tells you that the income statement is not helpful, for she cannot determine such things as the break-even point or the price that will achieve a target profit.

**Required**

1. Redo the income statement using the contribution margin format.
2. Determine the break-even point in (a) units and (b) dollars.
3. Determine the price that will give a $45,000 profit at 15,000 units.

**2-19   *Target costing*** Managers of TNC Enterprises are thinking about a new product in the industrial electronics area. TNC has considerable technical expertise in the field but has never entered the segment of the market in which the new product would compete. Before writing specifications for performance, the managers want to determine what costs are allowable. They estimate sales of 200,000 units per year at a $100 selling price. They also want a profit of $6,000,000.

**Required**

1. Determine the total costs that TNC can incur and meet its profit objective.
2. Suppose that the designers, engineers, and manufacturing managers estimate that annual fixed costs will be about $9,000,000 per year. Find the maximum per-unit variable cost that TNC can incur and meet its profit objective.

**2-20   *Profit planning*** Zaldec Company, a wholesaler of jeans, had the following income statement.

| | | |
|---|---:|---:|
| Sales (40,000 pairs at $35) | | $1,400,000 |
| Cost of sales | | 800,000 |
| Gross margin | | $ 600,000 |
| Selling expenses | $350,000 | |
| Administrative expenses | 190,000 | 540,000 |
| Income | | $ 60,000 |

Mr. Zaldec informs you that the only variable costs are cost of sales and $2 per-unit selling costs. All administrative expenses are fixed. In planning for the coming year, Mr. Zaldec expects his selling price to remain constant, with unit volume increasing by 20%. He also forecasts the following changes in costs and is concerned about how they will affect profitability.

| | |
|---|---|
| Variable costs: | |
| Cost of goods sold | up $1.50 per unit |
| Selling costs | up $0.10 per unit |
| Fixed costs: | |
| Selling costs | up $40,000 |
| Administrative costs | up $30,000 |

**Required**

1. Prepare an income statement for the coming year using the contribution margin format and assuming that all forecasts are met.
2. Determine the number of units that Zaldec will have to sell in the coming year to earn the same profit as the current year.
3. Mr. Zaldec is disturbed at the results of requirements 1 and 2. He asks you how much he must raise his selling price to earn $60,000 selling 48,000 units.

**2-21   *Basic income taxes (Appendix 1)*** Hughes Company is introducing an electronic printer that will sell for $140. Unit variable manufacturing cost is $92, and

Hughes pays a 10% sales commission. Fixed costs for the printer are $250,000 per year. The tax rate is 40%.

**Required**
1. Determine the profit after taxes that Hughes would earn selling 12,000 printers.
2. Determine the number of units that Hughes has to sell to earn an after-tax profit of $120,000.
3. Determine the price that Hughes has to charge to earn a $180,000 pretax profit selling 11,000 units.

**2-22   Basic sales mix (Appendix 2)**  Allen Cosmetics makes two facial creams, Allergy-free and Cleansaway. Data are as follows.

|  | Allergy-free | Cleansaway |
|---|---|---|
| Price per jar | $18 | $24 |
| Variable cost per jar | 9 | 6 |

Monthly fixed costs are $180,000.

**Required**
1. If the sales mix in dollars is 60% for Allergy-free and 40% for Cleansaway, what is the weighted-average contribution margin percentage? What dollar sales are needed to earn a profit of $60,000 per month?  At that level, how many  units of each product, and total units, will the company sell?
2. If the sales mix is 50% for each product in units, what is the weighted-average unit contribution margin? What unit sales are needed to earn $60,000 per month? Why is this number of units different from the answer you found in requirement 1?  What are total dollar sales and why is this figure different from your answer to requirement 1?
3. Suppose that the company is operating at the level of sales that you calculated in requirement 1, earning a $60,000 monthly profit. The sales manager believes that it is possible to persuade customers to switch to Cleansaway from Allergy-free by increasing advertising expenses. He thinks that $8,000 additional monthly advertising would change the mix to 40% for Allergy-free and 60% for Cleansaway. Total dollar sales will not change, only the mix. What effect would the campaign have on profit?

**2-23   Weighted-average contribution margin (Appendix 2)**  Blue-Room Products sells three types of simulated brass soap dishes, Necessary, Frill, and Luxury. Detailed selling price and cost data for the products are as follows.

|  | Necessary | Frill | Luxury |
|---|---|---|---|
| Selling price | $10 | $20 | $25 |
| Variable cost | 4 | 12 | 50% of selling price |

Fixed costs for these products are $286,000.

**Required**
1. If the company has a choice of selling one more unit of any one of its products, which product should it choose?
2. If the company could sell $1,000 more of any one of its products, which product should it choose?

3. Assume that the sales dollar volume of the company is distributed 40% from Necessary, 20% from Frill, and 40% from Luxury.
   (a)  What is the weighted-average contribution margin percentage?
   (b)  What is the break-even point for the company in sales dollars?
   (c)  At the break-even point, how many units of Luxury are sold?
4. Assume, instead, that the company's sales in units are 40% for Necessary, 20% for Frill, and 40% for Luxury.
   (a)  What is the weighted-average unit contribution margin?
   (b)  What is the break-even point in units?
   (c)  At the break-even point, how many units of Luxury are sold?

## PROBLEMS

**2-24  Indifference point**   Travelco sells one of its products, a piece of soft-sided luggage, for $60. Variable cost per unit is $34, and monthly fixed costs are $60,000. A combination of changes in the way Travelco produces and sells this product could reduce per-unit variable cost to $28 but increase monthly fixed costs to $104,000.

*Required*
1. Determine the monthly break-even points under the two available alternatives.
2. Determine the indifference point of the two alternatives.

**2-25  Cost structure**   Ben Skove, the owner of SKE Company, is trying to decide which of two machines to rent. He needs a machine to sand the surfaces of a picnic table that SKE manufactures. The following data are related to the two alternatives.

|  | Hand-Fed Machine | Automatic Machine |
|---|---|---|
| Annual rental payments | $ 14,000 | $ 36,000 |
| Other annual fixed costs | 100,000 | 110,000 |

Skove expects the variable cost per table to be $34 using the hand-fed machine and $27 using the automatic machine. He also expects annual volume of about 3,000 tables.

*Required*
1. Determine the total annual cost to manufacture 3,000 tables under each alternative.
2. Determine the annual volume of tables at which total manufacturing cost would be the same for each machine.

**2-26  Changes in contribution margin**   Mr. Hughes, owner of Trimtown, a specialty clothing store, asks you for some advice. Last year, his business had the following income statement.

| | |
|---|---|
| Sales (20,000 units at $10) | $200,000 |
| Variable costs | 100,000 |
| Contribution margin | $100,000 |
| Fixed costs | 50,000 |
| Income | $ 50,000 |

Mr. Hughes expects variable costs to increase to $6 per unit next year.

**Required**
1. Determine the volume Mr. Hughes needs to earn $50,000 in the coming year.
2. Mr. Hughes decides to increase his selling price so that he can earn $50,000 next year with the same unit volume he had last year. (a) What price will achieve that objective? (b) What dollar sales will he have?
3. Suppose that Mr. Hughes raises his price so that the contribution margin percentage is the same as it was last year. (a) What price will he set? (b) What dollar volume will give a $50,000 profit? (c) What is the unit volume?

**2-27  Pricing and return on sales**   Rogers Construction builds steel structures for commercial and industrial customers. The buildings are various shapes and sizes, with the average price being $30 per square foot and the average variable cost $18 per square foot. Annual fixed costs are $5,000,000.

**Required**
Answer each of the following items independently.

1. Determine the volume that will give Rogers a 20% return on sales in (a) sales dollars and (b) square feet of construction.
2. If Rogers can sell 600,000 square feet of construction in the coming year, what selling price will give a $400,000 profit?
3. If Rogers can sell 600,000 square feet of construction in the coming year at $30, how high could variable cost per square foot rise and still allow Rogers to earn a $280,000 profit?
4. If variable cost increases to $22 per square foot and Rogers can sell 500,000 square feet, what price will give a $280,000 profit?

**2-28  CVP  analysis for a service firm**   Rhonda McConnell, a graphic designer, has estimated the following fixed costs of operation for the coming year.

| | |
|---|---:|
| Office salaries | $52,000 |
| Rent, utilities | 31,000 |
| Other | 14,000 |
| Total | $97,000 |

McConnell's operation has no variable costs. She charges clients $80 per hour for her time.

**Required**
1. How many hours must McConnell work to earn a profit of $50,000?
2. McConnell is thinking about hiring one or two senior design majors from a local university for $8 per hour to do some routine work for her clients. She expects each to work about 300 hours, but about 30 of those hours (training and temporary idle time) will not be chargeable to clients. McConnell wants each student to provide at least $3,000 profit. What hourly rate must she charge for their time to achieve her objective?

**2-29  Pricing decision—nursery school**   The Board of Directors of First Community Church is considering opening a nursery school. Members of the board agree that the school, which would be open to all children, should operate within $100 of the break-even point.

The school will be open for nine months each year with two classes, one in the morning and one in the afternoon. The treasurer prepares an analysis of the expected costs of operating the school, based on conversations with members of other churches that run similar programs.

| | |
|---|---|
| Salaries—teacher and assistant | $28,000  for nine months |
| Utilities | $1,200  for nine months |
| Miscellaneous operating costs | $800  for nine months |
| Supplies, paper, paint | $2  per child per month |
| Snacks, cookies, juice | $4  per child per month |

The best estimate of enrollment is 20 children in each of the two classes, which is all that the teacher and assistant can handle and still achieve the quality that the board thinks is essential.

### Required

1. Determine the monthly fee per child that would have to be charged for the school to break even (round to nearest dollar) with its maximum enrollment.
2. If the monthly fee is $80, what is the break-even point in enrollment?

**2-30  Sensitivity of variables**  Cranston Jellies expects the following results for the coming year.

| | |
|---|---|
| Planned sales in cases | 50,000 |
| Selling price | $25 |
| Variable costs | $18 |
| Total fixed costs | $300,000 |

### Required

Answer the following questions, considering each independently.

1. Which of the following would reduce planned profit the most?
   (a) A 10% decrease in selling price.
   (b) A 10% increase per case in variable costs.
   (c) A 10% increase in fixed costs.
   (d) A 10% decrease in sales volume.
2. Which of the following would increase planned profit the most?
   (a) A 10% increase in selling price.
   (b) A 10% decrease per case in variable costs.
   (c) A 10% increase in sales volume.
   (d) A 10% decrease in fixed costs.
3. If the selling price declined by 10%, how many cases would have to be sold to achieve the planned profit?
4. If the selling price increased by 20%, by how much could variable cost per case increase and the planned profit be achieved?

**2-31  CVP analysis—changes in variables**  During two recent months, Thompson Company had the following income statements.

| | March | April |
|---|---|---|
| Sales | $200,000 | $222,000 |
| Variable costs | 130,000 | 154,200 |
| Contribution margin | $ 70,000 | $ 67,800 |
| Fixed costs | 40,000 | 40,000 |
| Income | $ 30,000 | $ 27,800 |

You learn that the price of the product Thompson sells generally changes each month, though its purchase cost is stable at $11 per unit. The only other variable cost is a 10% commission paid on all sales.

**Required**
Determine the selling price, unit volume, and variable cost per unit in each of the two months.

**2-32   Changes in cost structure**   Newberry Company makes a product with variable production costs of $14 per unit. The production manager has been approached by a salesperson from a machinery maker. The salesperson offers a machine for rent for five years on a noncancelable lease at $48,000 per year. The production manager expects to save $1.20 per unit in variable manufacturing costs using the machine.

**Required**
1. Determine the annual unit production that would make renting the machine and continuing with current operations yield the same profit to the firm.
2. Suppose that the expected volume is 60,000 units per year. Determine the change in annual profit that would occur if the company were to rent the machine.
3. Would you be more likely or less likely to rent the machine if the lease were cancelable at your option rather than noncancelable for a five-year period? Explain your answer.

**2-33   CVP analysis on new business**   Managers of Harter Enterprises, a medium-sized manufacturer of dress gloves, want to branch out from the company's traditional business into exercise gloves. Doing so requires leasing additional equipment for $550,000 per year. Other fixed costs associated with the new venture—including new personnel, advertising, and promotion—are estimated at $380,000 annually.
   The variable cost of the new gloves is expected to be about $7 per pair and the selling price about $15 per pair. The managers are reluctant to try the new gloves unless they can be fairly confident of earning $150,000.

**Required**
1. Determine how many pairs of gloves Harter must sell to earn the target profit.
2. The marketing people believe that unit sales will be 120,000 units. What selling price will yield the target profit at that volume?
3. Suppose again that 120,000 units is the best estimate of volume and that Harter will stick with the $15 price. How much must Harter reduce the expected variable cost to meet the profit target?

**2-34   CVP analysis for a hospital**   The administrator of the Caldwell Memorial Hospital is considering methods of providing X-ray treatments to patients. The hospital now refers about 200 patients per month to a nearby private clinic, and each treatment costs the patient $65. If the hospital provides the treatment, a machine will be rented for $2,200 per month and technicians will be hired for $3,600 per month. Variable costs are $10 per treatment.

**Required**
1. The administrator considers charging the same fee as the clinic. By how much will the hospital increase its income if it provides the service?
2. How much must the hospital charge to break even on the treatments?

**2-35   CVP in a service business**   Web Designs develops Web pages to customer order, primarily for business applications. The company charges its customers $40 per hour for programming time. The managers are planning operations for the coming year and have developed the following estimates.

| | |
|---|---|
| Total estimated chargeable hours | 80,000 |
| Total fixed costs, salaries, rent, etc. | $1,750,000 |

Web Designs employs 15 full-time programmers at an average salary of $30,000. These salaries are included in the cost figure given above. Each programmer works about 2,000 chargeable hours per year. The company does not wish to hire additional programmers, but rather wants to use freelancers to meet demand. Freelancers charge an average of $25 per hour.

**Required**
1. If the company meets its goal of 80,000 chargeable hours, what profit will it earn?
2. How many chargeable hours must it obtain from freelancers, in addition to the hours its full-time programmers work, to earn a $300,000 profit?

**2-36  Developing CVP information**   The manager of Sans Flavour Food Store, a franchise operation, is confused by the income statements she has received from her accountant. She asks you to help her with them. She is especially concerned that her return on sales dropped much more than sales from April to May.

| | April | May |
|---|---|---|
| Sales | $100,000 | $80,000 |
| Cost of sales | 40,000 | 32,000 |
| Gross profit | $ 60,000 | $48,000 |
| Operating expenses: | | |
| Rent | $  1,200 | $  1,200 |
| Salaries, wages, commissions | 34,500 | 30,500 |
| Insurance | 1,100 | 1,100 |
| Supplies | 2,000 | 1,600 |
| Utilities | 1,500 | 1,500 |
| Miscellaneous expenses | 6,000 | 6,000 |
| Total operating expenses | $ 46,300 | $41,900 |
| Income | $ 13,700 | $  6,100 |
| Return on sales | 13.7% | 7.6% |

The manager informs you that the salaries, wages, and commissions account includes the salaries of several clerks and herself, as well as commissions. All salespeople earn commissions of 20% of sales. Supplies are primarily wrapping paper and tape and vary directly with sales. The manager had expected the $20,000 decline in sales, but expected income of $10,960, 13.7% of expected sales. She is now concerned that income will continue to be 7.6% of sales.

**Required**
Prepare income statements using the contribution margin format for April and May, and explain to the manager the advantages of this format.

**2-37  Margin of safety**   Nelson Wallets is considering two new wallets for introduction during the coming year. Because of a lack of production capacity, only one will be brought out. Data on the two wallets follow.

|                                        | Model 440         | Model 1200         |
| -------------------------------------- | ----------------- | ------------------ |
| Expected sales                         | $200,000          | $250,000           |
| Expected contribution margin           | $ 60,000 (30%)    | $150,000 (60%)     |
| Expected fixed costs for production, advertising, promotion, etc. | 39,000 | 120,000 |
| Expected annual profit                 | $ 21,000          | $ 30,000           |

### Required

1. Determine the margins of safety for each wallet, in dollars and as percentages of expected sales.
2. Suppose that the company is relatively conservative; its top managers do not like to take significant risks unless the potential profits are extremely high. Which wallet would you recommend be introduced? Why?

**2-38   *Changes in operations***   Bart Packard operates the 15th Street Parking Lot, leasing the lot from the owner at $12,000 per month plus 10% of sales. Packard is thinking about staying open until midnight. He now closes at 7 p.m. Keeping the lot open requires paying an additional $800 per week to attendants, with increases in utilities and insurance being another $100 per week. The lot pays a 5% city tax on its total revenue. The parking charge is $0.80 per hour.

### Required

1. Suppose that Packard expects additional business amounting to 2,000 hours per week. Should he stay open until midnight?
2. How much additional business, stated in hours, does Packard need to break even on the additional hours of operation?

**2-39   *CVP analysis—product mix (Appendix 2)***   Horngrosen Brewery produces and sells two grades of beer: premium and regular. Premium sells for $10.50 per case, regular for $7.40. Variable brewing costs per case are $5.10 (premium) and $4.25 (regular). Sales of regular beer, in cases, are double those of premium. Fixed brewing costs are $600,000 monthly and fixed selling and administrative costs are $375,000 monthly. The only variable cost besides variable brewing costs is a 10% sales commission.

### Required

1. Compute the break-even point in total cases per month.
2. How many cases of each kind of beer are sold at break even?
3. The brewery is now selling about 350,000 cases per month. The advertising manager believes that sales of premium beer could be increased by 20% if an extensive advertising campaign were undertaken. The campaign would cost $80,000 per month. However, sales of regular beer are expected to fall by about 5% because some customers now buying the regular grade would merely switch to premium. Should the campaign be undertaken?
4. If the campaign were undertaken, what is the weighted-average unit contribution margin?
5. What is the new break-even point in unit sales?

**2-40   *Unit costs***   John Anderson owns a chain of shoe stores. He recently opened a store in a shopping mall and was not pleased with the results for the first month.

| | | |
|---|---:|---:|
| Sales | | $100,000 |
| Cost of sales | | 50,000 |
| Gross margin | | $ 50,000 |
| Salaries and wages | $30,000 | |
| Utilities, insurance, rent | 3,500 | |
| Commissions at 15% of sales | 15,000 | 48,500 |
| Profit | | $  1,500 |

Noting that sales were 4,000 pairs at an average price of $25, Anderson calculates the per-pair cost at $24.625 ($98,500/4,000), leaving only a $0.375 profit per pair. He did expect sales to rise to 5,000 pairs at an average price of $25 over the next month or two, but he figured that profit would increase only to about $1,875 (5,000 × $0.375), which still was not adequate.

Anderson asks for your advice and, in response to your questions, says that even with the increase in sales additional salaried personnel will not be needed and that utilities, insurance, and rent will remain about the same. The cost of sales percentage will also remain at 50%.

**Required**

Prepare an income statement based on sales of 5,000 pairs of shoes. If profit is different from Mr. Anderson's estimate, explain the fallacy in his reasoning.

**2-41  CVP analysis and break-even pricing—municipal operation**   Gardendale operates a municipal trash collection service. Analyses of costs indicate that monthly fixed cost is $15,000 and variable cost is about $0.80 per pickup per customer. The city collects trash in the business district 12 times a month and in the residential districts 4 times a month. The difference in frequency results from the much larger volume of trash in the business district. There are 250 businesses and 1,500 residences served by trash collection.

**Required**

1. The city manager is aware that other cities charge business customers $20 per month and residential customers $6 per month. What profit or loss would the operation generate at these prices?
2. The city manager would like to break even or show a small profit on trash collection. She believes it is fair to charge businesses three times as much as residences because the businesses get three times as much service. What monthly prices would make the operation break even?

**2-42  Product profitability (Appendix 2)**   Messorman Company produces three models of pen and pencil sets, regular, silver, and gold. Price and cost data are as follows.

| | Regular | Silver | Gold |
|---|---|---|---|
| Selling price | $10 | $20 | $30 |
| Variable costs | 6 | 8 | 15 |

Monthly fixed costs are $200,000.

**Required**

1. Which model is most profitable per unit sold?
2. Which model is most profitable per dollar of sales?
3. Suppose the sales mix in dollars is 40% Regular, 20% Silver, and 40% Gold.
   (a) What is the weighted-average contribution margin?
   (b) What is the monthly break-even point?
   (c) What sales volume will yield a profit of $30,000 per month?
4. Suppose the sales mix in dollars is 30% Regular, 30% Silver, and 40% Gold.
   (a) What is the break-even point?
   (b) What sales volume is necessary to earn $30,000 per month?
5. Suppose that the sales mix in units is 40% Regular, 20% Silver, and 40% Gold.
   (a) What is the weighted-average unit contribution margin?
   (b) What is the break-even point in total units?
   (c) How many total units must Messorman sell to earn $30,000 per month?

**2-43  Alternative cost behavior—a movie company (continued in 2-44 and 3-26)**
Blockbusters Incorporated, a leading producer of movies, is currently negotiating with Harrelson Frodd, the biggest box-office attraction in the movie industry, to star in *Hurricane*, an adventure film. For a starring role, Harrelson normally receives a salary of $10,000,000 plus 5% of the receipts to the producer. (The producer normally receives 40% of the total paid admissions wherever the movie is shown.) However, Harrelson is quite optimistic about the prospects for *Hurricane* and has expressed some interest in a special contract that would give him only 25% of his normal salary but increase his portion of the receipts to the producer to 20%. Other than Harrelson's pay, costs of producing the picture are expected to be $25,000,000.

**Required**

Answer the following questions, calling the alternative compensation schemes N (for the normal contract) and S (for the special contract).

1. What are the break-even receipts to the producer under each of the compensation schemes?
2. If total paid admissions in theaters are expected to be $100,000,000, what will be the income to the producer under compensation schemes N and S?
3. At what level of receipts to the producer would Harrelson earn the same total income under compensation schemes N and S?

**2-44  Multiple products—movie company (Appendix 2) (continuation of 2-43)**
Both the producing company and prospective star have given further thought to the contract terms and concluded that some provision probably should be made for revenues to be earned from contracts authorizing showings of the movie on television. After lengthy negotiations, Frodd's agent proposed the following terms: (a) a payment of $5,000,000, plus (b) 15% of the receipts to the producer from theater admissions, plus (c) 10% of the revenues from sales of television rights. Blockbusters' negotiating team leaves the negotiations to study the potential effect of the new offer.

A study of past productions indicates that the producer can expect revenues from sales of television rights to be approximately one-eighth (12.5%) of producer's revenues from theater admissions. Blockbusters' president is pleased with the opportunity to lower the fixed-payment part of the contract but is concerned about the magnitude of the two off-the-top percentages.

**Required**

1. At what level of receipts to the producer will Blockbusters break even under the new contract proposal?

2. Considering the additional information about the sale of television rights, at what level of receipts to the producer will Blockbusters break even under Frodd's normal contract terms ($10,000,000 plus 5% of the producer's receipts)?
3. Assume that, because of Blockbusters' delay in accepting the contract offer, Frodd's agent decides that his client should also receive a percentage of the revenues Blockbusters will derive from the sale of screening rights in foreign countries, revenues which typically amount to 10% of domestic receipts. If the agent proposes a 5% cut of those revenues for Frodd, what is the break-even point for Blockbusters Incorporated?

**2-45   *Conversion of income statement to contribution margin basis*** The controller of Rudolf Company prepared the following budgeted income statement. Materials and labor are both variable costs.

Rudolf Company
Budgeted Income Statement

| | | |
|---|---:|---:|
| Sales (20,000 units) | | $150,000 |
| Cost of goods sold: | | |
|   Materials | $20,000 | |
|   Labor | 10,000 | |
|   Other manufacturing costs: | | |
|     Variable | 25,000 | |
|     Fixed | 50,000 | 105,000 |
| Gross profit | | $ 45,000 |
| Selling and administrative expenses: | | |
|   Variable | $19,000 | |
|   Fixed | 35,000 | 54,000 |
| Loss | | $ (9,000) |

**Required**
1. Prepare a new income statement using the contribution margin format.
2. What is the break-even point in units?
3. The president believes that spending an additional $15,000 on advertising will increase sales by 8,000 units. His son, the general manager, says that would be silly because the company is losing enough already. Is the son right?

**2-46   *Occupancy rate as measure of volume*** Norman Motels is a chain operating in small cities throughout the Midwest. Its most relevant measure of volume is the occupancy rate, the percentage of available rooms rented to guests. Monthly revenue is $100,000 per percentage point of occupancy. (For example, at 40% occupancy, revenue is $4,000,000.) Contribution margin is 70%, and monthly fixed costs are $4,200,000.

**Required**
1. Find the monthly break-even point in (a) dollars and (b) occupancy rate.
2. Determine Norman's profit at a 75% occupancy rate.
3. Determine the occupancy rate Norman needs to earn $700,000 per month.
4. Determine whether Norman should increase advertising $100,000 per month if doing so increases the occupancy rate by two percentage points.

**2-47   *Changes in variables*** Last year you were engaged as a consultant to Thompson Products Company and prepared some analyses of its CVP relationships.

Among your findings was that the contribution margin percentage was 40% at the planned selling price of $40. The company expected to sell 10,000 units, which you estimated would yield a $46,000 income. You told Ms. Thompson, the owner, that profit would change at the rate of $0.40 per $1 change in sales.

Ms. Thompson has just called to tell you that the results did not come out as you had said they would. The company earned $69,600 on sales of $442,800. Variable costs per unit were incurred as expected, as were total fixed costs. Ms. Thompson was very pleased at the results. However, she asks you why profit did not increase by 40% of the added sales volume of $42,800, but rather by somewhat more.

**Required**

1. Prepare an income statement for the year, based on the actual results.
2. Determine (a) the number of units sold and (b) the selling price per unit.
3. Write a memorandum to Ms. Thompson explaining why the results were not as you had forecast. Use the guidelines in Appendix A.

**2-48   *Cost structure***   Wink Company manufactures replacement parts for automobiles and sells them to distributors in the northeastern United States. Barton Wink, the president of the company, wishes to begin selling in the Southeast but is uncertain how to expand most profitably. Two alternatives have been selected for final consideration. Under the first, Wink would use the services of independent sales representatives who would sell to distributors for a 15% commission. This plan would increase costs at the company's central office by $80,000 per year. Under the second alternative, Wink would hire additional salespeople to work on salary. Salaries for salespeople are estimated to be $180,000 per year; additionally, an office would be opened in the region and would cost $20,000 per year to operate.

Variable manufacturing and distribution costs on parts total 35% (without considering commissions). The president is uncertain about demand in the Southeast and asks that you analyze profitability under both plans at various volumes. He selects $600,000, $1,000,000, and $1,200,000 as the sales volumes to be used for comparison.

**Required**

Prepare a memorandum. Choose an alternative and defend your choice. Describe any qualitative factors you believe Mr. Wink should consider. Use the guidelines in Appendix A.

## CASES

**2-49   *Opening a law office (CMA adapted)***   Don Masters and two of his colleagues are considering opening a law office in a large metropolitan area that would make inexpensive legal services available to those who could not otherwise afford these services. The intent is to provide easy access for their clients by having the office open 360 days per year, 16 hours each day from 7 a.m. to 11 p.m. The office would be staffed by a lawyer, paralegal, legal secretary, and clerk-receptionist for each of the two 8-hour shifts.

In order to determine the feasibility of the project, Masters hired a marketing consultant to assist with market projections. The results of this study show that if the firm spent $500,000 on advertising the first year, it could expect about 50 new clients each day. Masters and his associates believe the estimate to be reasonable and are prepared to spend the $500,000 on advertising. Other pertinent information about the operation of the office is given on the next page.

The only charge to each new client would be $30 for the initial consultation. All cases that warranted further legal work would be accepted on a contingency basis with the firm earning 30% of any favorable settlements or judgments. Masters estimates that 20% of new client consultations will result in favorable settlements or judgments averaging $2,000. Masters expects no repeat clients during the first year of operations.

The hourly wages of the staff are projected to be $25 for the lawyer, $20 for the paralegal, $15 for the legal secretary, and $10 for the clerk-receptionist. Fringe benefit expense will be 40% of the wages paid.

Masters has located 6,000 square feet of suitable office space that rents for $28 per square foot annually. Associated expenses will be $22,000 for property insurance and $32,000 for utilities. The group will purchase malpractice insurance for $180,000 annually. The initial investment in office equipment will be $60,000, which will be depreciated over four years. The cost of office supplies has been estimated at $4 per expected new client consultation.

### Required

1. Determine the income the law office can expect if all goes according to plan.
2. Determine how many new clients must visit the law office for the venture to break even during its first year of operations.
3. Write a memorandum using the guidelines in Appendix A stating whether Masters and his associates should proceed.

**2-50   A concessionaire**   Ralph Newkirk is considering a bid for the hot dog and soft drink concession at the 14 football games for the season. There will be 7 college games and 7 professional games. Average attendance at college games is 30,000; at professional games attendance is 60,000. Ralph estimates that he sells one hot dog and one soft drink for each two persons attending a game.

Revenue and cost data are as follows.

|  | Hot Dogs | Soft Drinks |
|---|---|---|
| Selling price | $1.50 | $1.00 |
| Variable costs: |  |  |
| Hot dog | 0.32 |  |
| Roll | 0.14 |  |
| Mustard, onion, etc. | 0.02 |  |
| Soft drink and ice |  | 0.22 |

In addition, salespeople earn a 20% commission on all sales. Fixed costs per game are $8,000 for rentals of heating, cooking, mixing, and cooling equipment.

The stadium management requested that bids be made in the form of royalties on sales. The highest percentage of sales bid will win the contract.

### Required

1. What percentage of sales can Newkirk pay as royalty to the stadium and earn $180,000 for the season? (Round to nearest one-tenth of a percentage point.)
2. If Newkirk bids 12% of sales, what income can he expect? (Is your answer consistent with your answer in requirement 1?)
3. Assume that Newkirk gets the concession at a royalty of 12% of sales. He wants to know how much margin of safety he has in two ways. He is uncertain about total attendance and about the percentage of total attendees who buy a hot dog and drink. What is his break-even point for the season, expressed as (a) total attendance assuming one hot dog and drink per two attendees, and (b) the percentage of attendees who must buy a hot dog and drink if total attendance is as expected but the number of hot dogs and drinks each buys is uncertain?

4. What kinds of information does Newkirk need if he is also deciding to bid for the concession at baseball games at the same stadium?
5. After forecasting attendance for football games, Newkirk learns that the star quarterback of the local professional team will retire before the coming season. What effect does this information have on his planning?

**2-51  Hockey camp**   Since Jean Oldcraft has been head women's hockey coach at Casco College, she has enjoyed considerable success. Oldcraft has coached at summer camps previously and now is considering a summer camp for Casco. The college would provide room, board, and ice time for the campers at a price and would also take 10% of revenue. Oldcraft asks you for advice. You say that some of the important factors are setting a price, estimating enrollment, and estimating costs. After a few weeks, Oldcraft returns with the following information, gathered from various sources.

| | |
|---|---|
| Average enrollment | 90  campers |
| Average price for one-week camp | $225 |
| Costs: | |
| Food, charged by college | $50  per camper |
| Insurance and T-shirts | $15  per camper |
| Room rent charged by college | $18  per camper |
| Coaches' salaries | $550  per coach |
| Ice arena charge | $1,000  total |
| Brochures, mailing, miscellaneous | $3,700  total |

Oldcraft also says that other camps have typically employed one coach for each 15 campers, excluding the director (Oldcraft in this case). One problem is that you generally need to hire the coaches before you know the enrollment, although it is usually possible to find one or two at the last minute. It is, however, necessary to hire some of the coaches early so that you can use their names in brochures. Furthermore, while the enrollment and price given are averages, wide variations exist, with enrollments ranging from 40 to 120 and prices ranging from $160 to $330. As might be expected, the better-known camps have higher enrollments at higher prices, but they also pay better, as high as $1,000 per week for a well-known coach. Oldcraft will keep the profits and suffer the losses, so she wants to be fairly confident before proceeding.

**Required**
1. If Oldcraft hires enough coaches to meet the average enrollment and achieves all of the averages given above, what will be her profit?
2. What price will enable her to earn $4,000 enrolling 100 campers?
3. The college offers to take over the cost of brochures, mailing, and miscellaneous ($3,700 estimated) in exchange for a higher share of the revenue. If Oldcraft achieves the results from requirement 1 (meets the averages), what percentage of revenue will she be able to pay the college and earn the same profit expected in requirement 1?
4. Write a memorandum to Oldcraft explaining the advantages and disadvantages to her and to the college of the proposed arrangements. Use the guidelines in Appendix A.

## Chapter Three

# COST ANALYSIS

## LEARNING OBJECTIVES

*After reading this chapter, you should be able to*

- *Understand the importance of cost management.*
- *Describe the two aspects of managing costs.*
- *Distinguish between value-adding and non-value-adding activities and costs.*
- *Describe and use methods of analyzing cost behavior.*
- *Understand the limitations of methods of cost behavior analysis.*
- *Classify costs along several dimensions including whether managers can change them at short notice.*

*Pick up a recent annual report of any company and you are almost certain to find references to increasing quality and reducing costs. **General Motors** and other automakers are reducing the number of basic platforms they use to build cars. (For instance, many Chevrolets, Buicks, and Oldsmobiles share the same platform.) GM is also striving to increase the number of parts that are common to more than one vehicle.*

*Service stations now accept credit cards at the pump. **United Airlines** allows employees to make such important decisions as waiving charges on customers who buy cheap tickets well in advance, then change their plans. Such changes usually entail penalties of 40 percent or more of the ticket price.*

***Cisco Systems**, the giant networking company, has leveraged its Internet Website to allow customers to order products, saving considerable dollars. The company also allows customers to download software upgrades and receive technical support from the Web. These two features save Cisco $325 million annually. Cisco also uses the Web to reduce paperwork. The company now has paperless internal purchasing, saving over $2 million per year. Cisco receives 70 percent of its resumes over the Web, reducing recruiting costs by $8 million annually.*

*What do these actions have in common? They are all intended to manage costs better, often increasing some costs in order to reduce others and to provide better value to customers. Some cost-reduction efforts, such as GM's, aim at performing essential functions in less expensive ways, without reducing the quality of the products and services the organizations provide to their customers. Customers using credit cards at the pump save time, have a record of the transaction, and delay payment, each feature*

> being attractive to some customers. The service station benefits from lesser loads on clerks and the need to carry less cash.
>
> The other actions described aim to reduce, or eliminate, a special category of costs called non-value-adding costs—*costs that do not benefit customers. Processing paper purchase orders and shipping software upgrades through the mail do not add value to a company's offerings.*

*Sources: Annual Reports.*
*Carleen Hawn, "The (Truly) Friendly Skies," Forbes, January 13, 1997, 39.*

Chapter 2 introduced cost behavior, stating that at first it was reasonable to categorize costs as either fixed or as variable with sales. Some costs do not vary with sales, but with some other activity. For example, some costs of a purchasing department vary with the number of vendors the company uses and the number of parts and components the company buys. Some costs have both fixed and variable components. An example is maintenance, which typically includes a fixed component for regularly scheduled work and a component that varies with the use of the machinery. In this chapter we introduce other cost categories and refine the concepts of Chapter 2.

## OBJECTIVES OF ANALYZING COSTS

Chapter 2 stressed that managers must understand cost behavior to plan and make decisions. To plan income for a period, managers must be able to predict costs for that period, which requires estimates of fixed and variable costs. Managers also need good estimates of variable cost so they can compute contribution margin. Much important planning and decision-making activity requires knowledge of contribution margin. Many important decisions, such as setting prices, determining whether to continue carrying a particular product or service, and determining whether to continue selling to a particular type of customer, require careful and relevant cost analyses.

## COST MANAGEMENT

Managers must also understand cost behavior to manage and control operations. Chapter 1 described changes in the competitive environment, especially the emergence of worldwide competition. Reducing costs and increasing quality are critical success factors. Cost reduction is one key to increasing competitiveness and profitability. Of course, not all cost reduction is desirable; reductions might sacrifice product quality, prompt delivery, technological superiority, or quick response to changing conditions, style, and fashion. The accompanying Insight describes some companies' attitudes about cost management.

Managing costs has two basic aspects: One is managing the cost itself—for instance, buying materials, parts, and components at better prices. This aspect has traditionally been the principal focus of managerial accounting. The second, and usually more important, aspect is managing the *activity* that causes the costs—for instance, reducing the material content of a product without sacrificing quality.

Managers now pay much more attention to this latter aspect. Chapter 4 takes up this subject in greater detail.

## **IN** *SIGHT*

### Cost Management Programs

**Quaker Oats** has been reducing costs through careful analysis of its value chain. The company has developed a Supply Chain Management program that seeks to reduce the costs of purchasing, manufacturing, and delivery. The program also aims to increase product availability, order-filling rates, and on-time delivery percentages, all important concerns of its customers. The company now has over one-third of its customers in its continuous replenishment delivery program. Those customers have higher rates of growth in market share and are significantly more profitable than their competitors' averages, indicating that the program is successful.

**Cypress Semiconductor** operates in highly competitive markets, where selling prices decline rapidly. The typical Static Random Access Memory (SRAM) chip that the company makes sells for $20 immediately after its introduction, for $10 when the critical level of volume is reached, and for $5 within two years of introduction. The price eventually falls to $2. In such an environment, cost management is absolutely critical. The company continually redesigns manufacturing processes and wafers to pack more, and faster, chips into less space. In 1989 the company put 400 chips on a wafer, in 1996 it squeezed in 2,800. Cypress designed a new plant that would reduce assembly cost by $0.06 per unit. While $0.06 is not much, over 50 million chips, the savings are $3 million. The company also squeezes costs out of its testing process. Its second-generation equipment tested 8 chips at a time; the third-generation equipment handles 64, saving another $0.02 per unit, or $1 million annually.

**General Mills** expects to grow by generating strong unit growth through innovation, increasing contributions from international operations, and improving productivity. The company seeks to improve productivity through investments in manufacturing operations and adopting high-performance work methods. The company has been successful; its most efficient lines have achieved manufacturing cost reductions of 33 percent compared to the least efficient lines.

One technique that General Mills found useful is benchmarking, which is finding the best practices and evaluating your operations against those practices. The company benchmarked the equipment changes of professional race-car pit crews and applied the lessons to cereal production. In one case the company applied those lessons and reduced changeover time from eight hours to ten minutes. Such an improvement means that the company not only saves costs, it also increases output because equipment is idle for less time.

*Sources: Annual Reports.*

Cost management is especially important for companies that cannot compete by differentiating their products or service. As Chapter 1 noted, most companies select one of three basic strategies: (1) cost leadership (exemplified by such companies as **Wal-Mart**), (2) differentiation of products or services (**Mercedes Benz**,

Calvin Klein), or (3) focusing on a market niche (publishers of narrow-interest magazines such as *Golf Digest*). Companies that produce commodities, products that are virtually the same regardless of who makes them, must be cost leaders to survive. These companies need good estimates of the costs of all of their products and must be able to manage those costs and their underlying activities to thrive. But even companies that follow differentiation or niche strategies must also pay attention to costs, as the accompanying Insight below shows.

## MANAGING ACTIVITIES—COST DRIVERS AND COST POOLS

To manage costs effectively, managers associate costs with activities. Activities that cause costs are **cost drivers** and include sales, production, and various others such as the number of products the company makes and the number of customers it serves. A group of costs driven by the same activity is a **cost pool**. A cost pool might consist of all of the costs incurred by a department, such as the assembly department in a factory. A pool also could consist of only some of the costs of a department. For instance, the number of purchase orders drives some costs of the purchasing department and the number of vendors drives others, while four or five other drivers might drive other costs. A pool could also consist of costs from more than one department. The number of employees drives some costs of both the payroll and personnel departments.

As later sections of this chapter show, identifying cost drivers and their associated cost pools is an important step in estimating the behavior of the cost. Identifying cost drivers also enables managers to focus their attention where it is

 **SIGHT**

### Cost Management at Tiffany

Very few companies have differentiated themselves as successfully as **Tiffany & Co.**, the jewelry chain. The company enjoys great brand loyalty and excellent profit margins. For example, one analyst commented that, in Japan, it is decidedly "uncool" to give an engagement ring that did not come from Tiffany. Yet the company still works hard at managing costs. Much of its success in a recent quarter came through its emphasis on inventory management and associated cost advantages. The company has a new distribution facility that replaced three others. The facility can handle 50,000 units per day and at much lower delivery costs than did the old facilities. People in the facility use advanced picking and packing systems that include radio-frequency devices linked to inventory management. The facility also provides better process flow than its predecessors. The improved inventory management helps Tiffany stores keep stock up-to-date, which allows stores to devote more space to selling and less to storage, which in turn increases profits.

*Source: Alex Schay, "Tiffany Sparkles," The Motley Fool Evening News, August 17, 1998.*

likely to do the most good. Suppose setting up machines to run particular products drives a pool of $250,000 annual costs, and storing materials and components drives a pool of only $30,000 annual costs. Managers are likely to reduce costs more by concentrating on doing fewer machine setups, or doing them faster, than by trying to streamline storage procedures. Of course, *all* cost savings are helpful, but managers should concentrate their attention where the payoff will probably be the highest.  Even if most of the costs of setups are fixed, large reductions in setups almost certainly will reduce the costs in the related pool.

After identifying a cost driver, managers estimate the fixed and variable components of each cost that is driven by that activity. They use methods that we explain in this chapter. But even if managers fail to estimate successfully how much of a cost is fixed and how much is variable, they can still manage costs better when they know what drives them. A manager who knows that increasing the number of parts in a product will increase particular costs can make some decisions even without knowing how much of each cost is fixed or variable.

For many years, labor time drove most other manufacturing costs. As manufacturing became more sophisticated, machines and computers took over many of the tasks that people had performed, and labor requirements declined. Now, more costs are driven by such activities as procurement, machine setup, and recordkeeping than was once the case. This newer environment therefore has more cost drivers.

## VALUE-ADDING AND NON-VALUE-ADDING ACTIVITIES

As managers came to understand the changing environment, they looked harder at why cost-driving activities occur and whether they were necessary. Activities that do not add value to products and services are wasted. Some activities, such as sewing together shoe soles and uppers, are clearly necessary to making products. These activities are **value-adding activities** and their costs are value-adding costs. Activities such as moving materials into and out of warehouses are **non-value-adding activities** because they do not make the product more valuable to the customer. The costs that non-value-adding activities drive are non-value-adding costs. Classifying activities as value-adding or non-value-adding is not always easy and disagreements will arise about many activities.

Managers strive to perform value-adding activities more efficiently and at lower costs consistent with quality and other objectives. The goal with non-value-adding activities is simple: eliminate them. No company has eliminated all non-value-adding activities, but the goal is nonetheless valid.  Trying to perform non-value-adding activities more efficiently is a poor tactic because it treats symptoms, not causes. For instance, workers in many companies now inspect for defects as they make products instead of making a separate, final inspection that is a non-value-adding activity. From efforts to eliminate the non-value-adding activities of final inspection and reworking defective units came the emphasis on quality work—doing things right the first time.

Non-value-adding activities and costs are themselves usually driven by other factors.[1] Think a moment about some non-value-adding activities and costs.

---

1 Michael R. Ostrenga and Frank R. Probst, "*Process Value Analysis: The Missing Link in Cost Management,*" Journal of Cost Management, *Fall 1992, 4–14.*

From Chapter 1 we know that a functional factory arrangement, where machines of a given type are grouped together in departments, causes excessive movement of materials and semi-finished products. The *factory arrangement* is therefore driving the activity and cost of moving materials and product. Or consider supervision, an activity that many managers would not classify as non-value-adding. Organizations employ supervisors because management does not believe workers can, or will, perform their jobs without supervision. For those organizations, management attitude, or policy, is driving a non-value-adding activity and cost. Many companies have greatly reduced or eliminated supervision and experienced increased productivity as workers become better motivated through their greater autonomy and responsibility. Teams of workers take full responsibility for their jobs in many companies today. Many companies' annual reports comment on reducing layers of management, or bureaucracy, and empowering workers to do their jobs without close supervision.

Service organizations also benefit from identifying non-value-adding activities. For example, many service companies discovered that the activity of following up on customers' complaints seldom added to customers' perception of value received. Such companies determined that improving the quality of service was less costly than following up complaints.

The accompanying Insight on the next page describes how **Southwest Airlines** eliminated non-value-adding activities and became one of the most productive companies in America.

## ESTIMATING COST BEHAVIOR

Managers use several methods to estimate the fixed and variable components of costs. The methods range from simple to sophisticated. Each method has advantages and disadvantages, and managers in most companies will use more than one method.

A **mixed** (or **semivariable**) **cost** has both a fixed component and a variable component. For example, maintenance costs are likely to have a fixed component related to normal preventive maintenance performed routinely every month. There is also likely to be a variable component related to the amount of machine use. Exhibit 3-1 on page 86 shows the behavior of a mixed cost. The pattern is like that of total costs when both fixed and variable costs are present.

## ACCOUNT ANALYSIS

A simple, yet often effective, method of classifying the behavior of a cost is **account analysis**. Applying this method, the manager decides how to classify a cost by looking at its name and then checking this judgment by scanning the account for that cost for several periods. For instance, costs such as rent, depreciation, salaries, and advertising are generally fixed. If the amounts in the account for a cost vary only a little from month to month, it is likely that the cost is fixed. If the cost varies considerably from month to month, it is probably variable or mixed.

One weakness of account analysis is that it shows only what costs have been, not what they should be. Another is that considerable misclassification is possible. For example, stores in some malls pay rent as a percentage of sales, making rent a variable cost. But rent is fixed for most companies, and someone looking at

## SIGHT

### Cost Reduction Practices

**Southwest Airlines** was the only major U.S. airline to be profitable in the early 1990s, which was a very difficult time for airlines. Much of the credit belongs to Herb Kelleher, its founder and president. The company is admired as a place to work, and its people are very loyal and very productive. Average salaries rival those of competitors and Southwest has excellent profit-sharing and pension plans.

Southwest calls itself the "nation's low fare, high Customer Satisfaction airline" and wants to continue to be the airline with the lowest cost structure. Southwest concentrates on short flights at low fares, eliminating meals and frills. Passengers cannot check baggage through if they are connecting with another airline. Southwest has pared non-value-adding activities to a bare minimum. It does not use the computerized reservation system that virtually all travel agents use. Travelers and travel agents alike must call the company to make a reservation. This policy alone saves $30 million annually. (It is interesting to note that other major airlines recently announced that they would stop compensating travel agents at the standard 10 percent of the fare and impose a $50 limit on the commission. This action not only reduced costs, but also changed the way consumers purchase airline services. It should be obvious that the cost to a travel agent of booking a flight does not depend on the fare for the flight, although one cost driver is probably the number of legs on the flight.) But Southwest does not scrimp on service: it is the only airline to lead the industry in the categories of Ontime Performance, Baggage Handling, and Customer Satisfaction, and it led all three categories two years in a row.

Time that aircraft spend on the ground is non-value-adding. Southwest turns its planes around in 15–20 minutes, while other airlines take close to an hour. Such speed enables Southwest to operate its schedule with fewer aircraft and fewer flight crews. Southwest planes make about twice as many flights per day as those of other major carriers, spending about eleven hours per day in the air. By flying only one type of aircraft, the Boeing 737, Southwest saves millions of dollars because mechanics, pilots, and flight attendants need learn how to maintain and operate only one airplane.

Southwest has the lowest operating costs in the industry. For airlines, the most-watched measure of productivity/cost control is cost-per-seat-mile, the average cost of flying a seat, occupied or not, one mile. Southwest, at about seven cents per seat-mile, was two to four cents below its major competitors. Southwest flies over 2,400 passengers per employee, compared with as few as 800 for other major carriers. Southwest employs only 81 people per airplane, while other airlines employ over 100 people per airplane, some over 150.

*Source: Southwest Airlines Annual Reports.*

accounts would probably so classify it. Perhaps the most important weakness of this method is that it ignores the importance of identifying the cost-driving activity. Hence, account analysis is of limited usefulness.

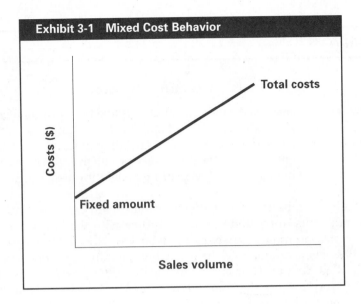

Exhibit 3-1   Mixed Cost Behavior

## ENGINEERING APPROACH

Another widely used method of ascertaining cost behavior is the **engineering approach,** which has been used most successfully to determine per-unit variable costs in manufacturing firms or for repetitive, standard activities such as processing insurance claims. Under this method, engineers study the material and labor requirements of products and related operations, then make per-unit estimates of the costs that should vary with production.

An important advantage of the engineering approach is that it indicates what costs *should be* rather than what they have been. This is important because simply knowing that, for instance, labor cost per unit of product has been $3.50 does not tell you that the labor is being used efficiently. It could well be that the company should be using a good deal less labor and that a cost of $2.80 is readily achievable if workers make changes in the way they do their jobs.

## INTERVIEWS

A simple but useful tool for determining what drives many costs is interviewing managers to determine what will happen to particular costs, given specific actions. For instance, the purchasing manager probably could estimate the increase in workload that might follow the introduction of a new product that requires parts not used in any other products. Using such parts would require evaluating new vendors, establishing testing procedures, doing paperwork, and so on. The new parts also could require additional personnel in purchasing and perhaps in receiving and inspection.

Interviewing does not help determine how much of a particular cost is fixed or variable. However, it does help identify cost drivers, which is an important part of applying the methods discussed in the remainder of this section. Interviewing might be useful in developing ballpark estimates of the effects of various decisions. For instance, a manufacturing manager might be able to tell a cost analyst how many additional people might be needed to speed up the introduction of a new product. The analyst could then assign dollar amounts to the additional needs.

To aid the presentation of the remaining methods, we will use the following data related to maintenance costs of RFC Manufacturing Co. In this situation, we assume RFC already has identified hours of machine use as the cost-driving activity, and that all of the observations are within the relevant range. The remaining methods provide numerical estimates of the fixed and variable components of costs.

| Machine Hours | Maintenance Cost |
|---|---|
| 5,000 | $14,800 |
| 10,800 | 28,200 |
| 12,200 | 27,300 |
| 7,300 | 19,100 |
| 10,000 | 25,400 |
| 8,100 | 24,900 |
| 18,000 | 40,800 |
| 13,400 | 31,800 |
| 5,400 | 18,100 |
| 14,100 | 31,900 |
| 15,100 | 36,100 |
| 17,300 | 35,900 |

## HIGH-LOW (TWO-POINT) METHOD

A relatively unsophisticated, yet widely used, method of estimating the components of a mixed cost is the **high-low** (or **two-point**) **method**. This method uses two past levels of activity and the amounts of the cost incurred at those levels. The high and low points selected should be the highest and lowest levels of activity (as opposed to the highest and lowest costs) *within the relevant range.* To find the variable component of the cost, divide the difference in cost at the two levels by the difference in volumes of the cost-driving activity. The formula for finding the variable cost factor in a mixed cost is

$$\frac{\text{Variable cost component}}{\text{of mixed cost}} = \frac{\text{change in cost}}{\text{change in activity}} \qquad \frac{\Delta y}{\Delta x}$$

Using our example,

$$\frac{\text{Variable cost component}}{\text{of mixed cost}} = \frac{\$40,800 - \$14,800}{18,000 - 5,000}$$

$$= \$26,000/13,000$$

$$= \$2 \text{ per machine hour}$$

Because the total cost at any volume equals total variable cost at that volume plus total fixed cost, the fixed component of the total cost equals the difference between the total cost and the total variable cost at that volume. In formula notation this becomes, using the high volume,

$$\frac{\text{Fixed cost component}}{\text{of mixed cost}} = \frac{\text{total cost at}}{\text{high volume}} - \frac{\text{high}}{\text{volume}} \times \frac{\text{variable cost}}{\text{component}}$$

At 18,000 machine hours,

| | |
|---|---|
| Total cost at high volume | $40,800 |
| Less variable portion (18,000 × $2) | 36,000 |
| Fixed component | $ 4,800 |

We get the same answer using the low volume at 5,000 machine hours.

| | |
|---|---|
| Total cost at low volume | $14,800 |
| Less variable portion (5,000 × $2) | 10,000 |
| Fixed component | $ 4,800 |

The formula that RFC can then use to predict maintenance cost is

*Total maintenance cost   =   $4,800   +   ($2 × machine hours)*

This method simply uses the formula for a straight line, $y = a + bx$, with $b$ being the slope of the line and $a$ the point where the line intercepts the $y$ axis. The formula given above for determining the variable component of a mixed cost computes $b$, the slope of the line. The formula for the fixed component is solving the general formula for $a$ when you know $b$ (the slope), $x$ (a level of the cost-driving activity, or independent variable, represented on the $x$ axis), and $y$ (the value of the dependent variable, total cost, at that activity level).

Please remember that the volume levels used when applying the high-low method must be within the relevant range if the resulting cost prediction formula is to be useful. (Remember from Chapter 2 that the relevant range is that over which per-unit variable cost and total fixed cost should remain constant.) The two-point method has some serious disadvantages, which will become clearer as we discuss the next method.

CHAPTER 2

## SCATTER-DIAGRAM METHOD

Like the high-low method, the **scatter-diagram (or graphical) method** requires cost and volume data from prior periods, and derives an equation (cost prediction formula) based on those data. Again, the goal is a cost prediction formula of the form $y = a + bx$.

The first step is to plot points that represent total cost at various levels of activity within the relevant range. The dots in Exhibit 3-2 show the maintenance cost that RFC incurred at various levels of machine hours. The second step is to draw a line as close to all the points as possible. (Exhibit 3-2 shows such a line.) The placement and slope of the line are matters of judgment; the manager "eyeballs" the data and fits the line visually. Because the fitting is done by hand and eye, as is the determination of the intercept (fixed component) and slope (variable component), different users will get different results. We obtained the following formula to predict maintenance cost for RFC.

*Total maintenance cost   =   $7,200   +   ($1.82 × machine hours)*

Like the high-low method, the scatter-diagram method suffers from its reliance on what costs have been, rather than what they are likely to be in the future. But

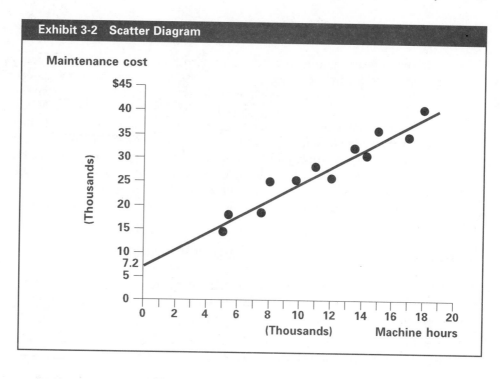

**Exhibit 3-2   Scatter Diagram**

Maintenance cost

the scatter-diagram method is preferable for two reasons. First, because the high-low method relies on only two observations, it carries the risk that one point or the other (or both) was affected by a random oddity or unusual event. If RFC did a great deal of preventive maintenance in the low-activity month, the resulting prediction formula could be useless. Because the scatter-diagram method uses more observations and permits the manager to see the pattern of costs, the formula is less likely to be influenced by such events and oddities. The second advantage of the scatter-diagram method is that by looking at the plotting of costs at various levels of the activity, a manager will get some idea of how closely the cost follows changes in the cost-driving activity. (This issue is discussed in more detail later.)

Whichever formula it uses, RFC cannot expect to predict maintenance costs exactly. The spread of points on the scatter diagram shows that differences can be expected. Several reasons might explain these differences. One reason is that factors other than machine hours (e.g., the types of materials put through the machinery) might affect maintenance costs. Another is that random elements influence cost, just as they do an automobile's gas mileage.

## REGRESSION METHOD

Regression analysis (or just regression) is a more sophisticated method for estimating the fixed and variable components of a mixed cost. Like the high-low and scatter-diagram methods, regression uses cost and volume data from prior periods to yield an equation of the form $y = a + bx$, or Total cost = fixed cost + (variable cost per unit of activity × level of activity). In contrast to the high-low method, regression uses more than two observations. And in contrast to the scatter-diagram method, regression relies on statistical concepts, rather than on the judgment of the manager drawing the line. Regression fits the mathematically best line to the data.

In recent years, accountants have increased their efforts to find techniques for planning administrative costs, partly because such costs have increased more rapidly than many others. A tool that managers are employing with some success in analyzing administrative and other costs is *multiple regression analysis,* which uses two or more independent variables, or cost drivers, to predict the behavior of a cost. Knowledge of some important statistical principles is required before you can understand and apply either simple or multiple regression analysis. But you should be aware that advanced techniques such as these are available for solving cost estimation problems. A discussion of the basic terms and procedures of simple and multiple regression analysis appears in the Appendix to this chapter.

## PROBLEMS AND PITFALLS IN COST BEHAVIOR ANALYSIS

The methods we have discussed for estimating the behavior of mixed costs are all subject to problems that could decrease the usefulness of cost prediction formulas.

### HISTORICAL DATA

The common thread in the high-low, scatter-diagram, and regression methods is that they all use historical information. As we stated earlier, formulas based on historical data can give useful predictions only if past conditions will prevail in the future. The usefulness of a cost-prediction formula also can be impaired by nonrepresentative historical data. Remember that the analyst should consider only observations within the relevant range. But even those observations might not be representative of normal circumstances. A company might use temporary, less efficient workers for a few months, making those months nonrepresentative. Formulas developed using nonrepresentative data can lead to major misestimates of costs. Managers should use cost estimation methods only after they review and understand the operating conditions under which cost and activity data were gathered. The scatter-diagram method offers an advantage here because it highlights out-of-line points. Managers often plot data even when they use regression analysis. An out-of-line observation (called an *outlier*) should be ignored.

Finally, cost prediction formulas given by all of the methods are based on observations within a specific range of activity, usually the relevant range. The formulas describe behavior within the range over which the observations fell, so predicting costs at activity levels outside that range (called *extrapolation*) is unwise.

Apart from the problems created by using historical data, analysts must consider the possibility that their predictions will be ineffective because they collected the wrong data. We discuss some of the flaws of data collection in the next section.

### CORRELATION AND ASSOCIATION

For an equation to be useful for planning, the relationship between the cost and the activity must be fairly close. The closeness of the relationship is called

**correlation** or association. Consider the costs of preparing customer invoices. The scatter diagram in Exhibit 3-3 relates the total costs of preparing invoices to activity measured by number of invoices. It shows a wide spread of costs around the cost-prediction line, so that using the number of invoices to predict the cost won't work. The spread indicates that the number of invoices does not drive invoice preparation costs.

Exhibit 3-4 shows invoice preparation costs, which are primarily clerical costs, plotted against another driver, the number of items ordered, or lines per invoice. Because individual sales orders vary in dollar value, it is not surprising that the total cost for invoice preparation varies more closely with the number of lines than with the number of invoices represented by the orders. Finding this better correlated activity measure is important for cost management as well as for cost prediction. Knowing the cost driver, managers can try to reduce the cost by various means. One way is to allow customers to order electronically, perhaps through the Internet. Or the company might encourage customers to place larger, but fewer, orders.

As stated earlier, the visual aspect of the scatter-diagram method is an important advantage; it allows the manager to see whether the activity chosen as the independent variable is likely to be a good predictor of the dependent variable (cost). Virtually all computer programs for regression analysis, including spreadsheets such as Lotus 1-2-3®, also provide information about correlation. The high-low method, because it includes only two points, does not provide this important information.

## SPURIOUS CORRELATION

Determining what activity drives costs is an important objective of cost analysis, enabling managers to monitor and control both the cost and the activity. Computers make it possible to do regression and correlation for hundreds of

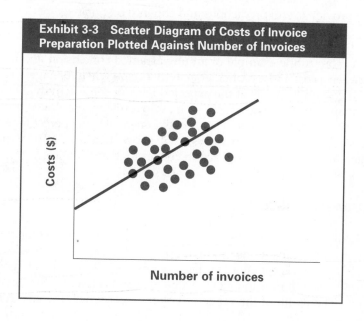

**Exhibit 3-3   Scatter Diagram of Costs of Invoice Preparation Plotted Against Number of Invoices**

Costs ($)

Number of invoices

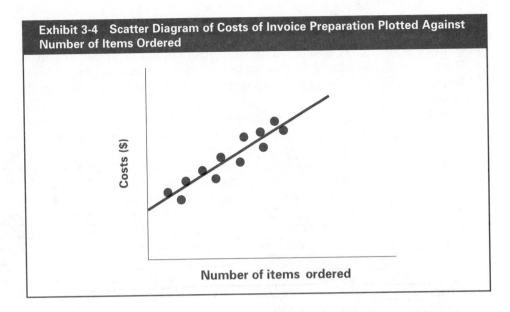

**Exhibit 3-4   Scatter Diagram of Costs of Invoice Preparation Plotted Against Number of Items Ordered**

combinations of activity and cost very quickly. It is quite possible that some analyses will show a high correlation between a cost and an activity even though no causal relationship exists. Such a correlation is called *spurious* and presents problems for the unwary.

For example, some electric utilities have a high correlation between the number of kilowatt hours they generate and the cost of outside maintenance of their property (cutting the grass, etc.). Obviously, producing electric power cannot drive maintenance costs (or vice versa), so why the high correlation? The logical reason for the high correlation is that both depend on another factor: the weather. Both electric power output and outside maintenance are highest in the summer; both are also low in the winter. Because both are related to the same factor, they *appear* to be related to one another. The key, then, in seeking a relationship that will provide useful predictions and enhance cost management is to question high correlations that seem to have no causal basis. The measure of activity used to predict a cost must make sense.

A more subtle example of an unwarranted conclusion about the relationship between a cost and a particular activity occurs when managers *plan* the level of a fixed cost on the basis of the expected level of some activity. For example, many companies budget fixed costs such as advertising, employee training, charitable contributions, and research and development at some percentage of sales. A scatter diagram or regression analysis will show such costs to be variable with sales, when in reality managerial action creates that appearance.

## STEP-VARIABLE COSTS

Exhibit 3-5 shows a pattern of cost behavior that fits neither the fixed-variable classification scheme nor the pattern of a typical mixed cost. A cost exhibiting such behavior is commonly called a **step-variable cost**. It is fixed over a range of volume, then jumps to a new level and remains fixed at that level until the next jump. The width of the range of volume over which the cost remains fixed de-

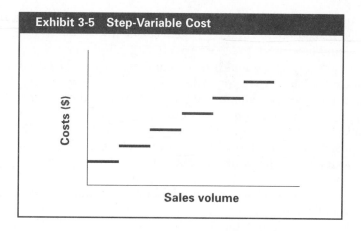

pends on the particular cost. Step-variable behavior often occurs because of company policy, such as having one supervisor for every 20 workers, or one clerk for every 1,000 customer accounts.

Step-variable costs exist because of indivisibility of resources; many resources cannot be acquired in infinitely divisible increments. An airline can't fly fractions of planes to provide exactly as many seats as passengers demand; it can fly only an entire airplane. Similarly, companies usually cannot rent space one cubic foot at a time. Nor can they hire part-time people for some jobs; it is difficult to hire a sales manager or controller for six or eight months of the year. However, the growing use of temporary employees ("temps") is a way of confronting the indivisibility problem.

Should we plan step-variable costs as if they were mixed, though the fixed component changes within the relevant range? Should we consider them variable, even though they do not vary between steps? Both approaches are used in practice, which means that actual costs will differ from cost predictions under either alternative. Managers are more likely to treat a cost as variable if the steps are relatively short and as fixed if the steps are relatively long (measured horizontally).

Isolating the activity that drives a step-variable cost is often difficult because such costs do not change in direct proportion to short-term changes in activity, but rather respond to changes in activity only over longer periods. Analysts therefore can fail to identify the activity driving the cost, and the real cost-driving activity is less likely to be carefully monitored and controlled. Interviewing can be helpful in analyzing step-variable costs. Many companies have reported success in controlling some types of step-variable costs after interviewing provided clues to the cost-driving activity, enabling managers to concentrate on reducing the level of that activity. For example, companies that have worked closely with suppliers to achieve a high level of quality in purchased materials have reduced inspection and rework costs after recognizing that those costs were driven by the quality, rather than the number, of incoming shipments.

## COMMITTED AND DISCRETIONARY FIXED COSTS

Recall from Chapter 2 that classifying a cost as "fixed" does not imply that the cost cannot be changed, only that it does not vary automatically as volume changes. Some fixed costs can be quickly altered by managerial action and are called **discretionary costs.** Managers frequently decide whether to incur the cost at all and how much to incur. Advertising, employee training, and research and development are examples of discretionary costs. Fixed costs that cannot be changed so quickly are **committed costs,** so called to express the idea that managers have made a commitment that cannot be readily changed. Depreciation is a committed cost. Like other committed fixed costs, depreciation arises from past managerial decisions—some made years ago—and cannot be changed without disposing of the asset to which the depreciation applies.

Deciding whether a cost is committed or discretionary is not always possible just by knowing what the cost is for (rent, salaries, research and development, etc.). For example, rent might or might not be a committed cost depending on the terms of the rental agreement.

Do not misinterpret the discretionary-committed classification as distinguishing between unnecessary and necessary costs, respectively. Advertising is a discretionary fixed cost, but some type of advertising—a sign, a Yellow Pages listing, something—is necessary for many enterprises. Similarly, depreciation is a committed fixed cost; yet most companies could probably operate successfully without one or more of several cash registers, telephone lines, or display racks.

Discretionary costs present unique problems in cost management because managers must determine whether the level of the discretionary activity—the cost driver—is appropriate. For example, should the company hire another research scientist? Should it reduce the number of pages in the annual report? Should it discontinue a particular training program? The larger question is often whether the company should even be performing the activity at all. Should the company pay tuition for employees taking courses? Should the company make charitable contributions?

Unfortunately, discretionary costs are often the first to be attacked in cost-reduction programs, perhaps partly because their effects are not immediately apparent. Consider the long-run effects of cutting such discretionary costs as research and product development, management training programs, and programs to upgrade worker skills.

Research and product development are crucial to the success of companies in such high-technology fields as pharmaceuticals, computers, aircraft, and some consumer products. Reducing expenditures for personnel development can lead to reduced morale, high turnover, and lessened productivity. Another problem is that cutting discretionary costs does not always reduce the workload, and the morale of the remaining employees might suffer. Corporate downsizing, so much in the news today, seems to have had significant effects on morale and loyalty of employees. The accompanying Insight describes the importance of discretionary costs.

## AVOIDABLE AND UNAVOIDABLE COSTS

Another useful subdivision of costs hinges on whether the company could avoid the cost by adding, dropping, or curtailing some activity. (Variable costs are nearly always avoidable if we decide to increase or decrease an activity, so for the most part we are concerned with fixed costs.) A particular cost, such as sales salaries, might be partly avoidable, partly not, depending on the decision. A

**SIGHT**

### Discretionary Costs?

**Amazon.com** reported in March 1998, that it spent $6,279,000 on product development, which was 7.2 percent of sales of $87,375,000. The company said the following.

> Product development expenses consist principally of payroll and related expenses for development, editorial, systems and telecommunications operations personnel and consultants, systems and telecommunications infrastructure, and costs of acquired content. The increases in product development expenses were primarily attributable to increased staffing and associated costs related to enhancing the features, content and functionality of the Company's Web site and transaction-processing systems, as well as increased investment in systems and telecommunications infrastructure. . . . The Company believes that continued investment in product development is critical to attaining its strategic objectives and, as a result, expects product development expenses to increase significantly in absolute dollars.

An annual report of **First Union** stated that "A handful of banking organizations have the capital strength and size necessary to make discretionary investments in technology and in national brand awareness campaigns that are necessary to enhance revenues."

**Yahoo** recently filed a quarterly report that stated

> "Sales and marketing expenses consist primarily of advertising and other marketing-related expenses. . . . The increase in absolute dollars from the year ago periods is primarily attributable to an increase in advertising and distribution costs associated with the Company's aggressive brand-building strategy, increases in compensation expense associated with growth in sales and marketing personnel . . . sales and marketing expenses in absolute dollars will increase in future periods as it continues to pursue an aggressive brand-building strategy and continues to build its direct sales organization. . . .
>
> Product development expenses consist primarily of employee compensation relating to developing and enhancing the features and functionality of Yahoo! online media properties. . . . The Company believes that significant investments in product development are required to remain competitive.

What is important about these statements is that the companies view discretionary costs as extremely important from a strategic point of view. The companies need not make the expenditures, but recognize that they must in order to compete successfully.

For the effects of cutting discretionary costs, consider **Vlasic**, the maker of pickles and Swanson frozen dinners. Vlasic suffered severe losses in sales and profits during 1998 at least partly because of "significantly lower advertising."

**IN**SIGHT                                                                                          **(continued)**

Advertising fell from $15 million to $7.6 million. Sales of pickles fell 20 percent and sales of frozen dinners fell 4 percent. While sales of these brands were falling, leading competitors' sales were rising.

*Sources: Annual Reports.*
*Vanessa O'Connell, "Vlasic Hopes New Marketing Plan Will Perk Up Sales,"* The Wall Street Journal, *May 26, 1998, B11.*

company that stops selling in a geographical region could reduce its salesforce. One that drops a product line might not be able to reduce its salesforce because it still needs all of the salespeople to cover its customers, even though each salesperson would carry fewer lines. Thus, the ideas of avoidability and unavoidability apply only when a decision is at hand. Avoidable if we do, or do not do, what?

At first glance, the avoidable-unavoidable categories might seem to parallel the discretionary-committed categories. This is sometimes so, but significant exceptions may exist, and determining whether or not a cost is avoidable typically requires a case-by-case analysis. Chapters 4 and 5 delve into this topic more deeply.

## DIRECT AND INDIRECT (COMMON) COSTS

Another refinement of our basic cost classification scheme is often useful. Costs may be classified as direct or indirect. A **direct cost**, also called a **separable cost** or **traceable cost**, is incurred specifically because of a particular activity of the firm, like a product, product line, or geographical area. (All costs are direct to some activity, if only to the company as a whole.) An **indirect cost**, also called a **common cost** or **joint cost**, does not relate to one specific activity, but rather to several.

Variable costs are direct to a particular product or activity. Some fixed costs are direct to particular products or activities, and some are not. For example, salaries of salespeople who cover particular geographical regions are direct to those regions. But if the salespeople sell several products, their salaries are indirect to each of the products. Thus, to classify a cost as direct or indirect, it is necessary first to specify the activity in which the manager is interested.

Direct costs usually are avoidable, although there certainly are exceptions. If a company rents a sales office and the lease has ten years to run, the rent is direct to the office, but is unavoidable. Indirect costs generally are unavoidable; by definition they are incurred to support two or more activities, so they will continue to be incurred if only one of the activities is discontinued. Even here, though, the individual circumstances determine the classification. Consider a large company with six major production departments in a single factory building. Dropping one department could enable the company to reduce such indirect costs as those of operating the payroll and personnel functions, even though no one person in either of those departments works exclusively on the production department being dropped. Thus, some portion of the indirect cost is avoidable.

## MANUFACTURING COSTS

A manufacturer incurs costs to make products, so the behavioral classification and management of manufacturing costs concentrates on activities having to do with production.

A typical manufacturer has three types of manufacturing costs: materials and purchased components, direct labor, and manufacturing overhead. The cost of **materials** (sometimes called **raw materials** or **direct materials**) and components that the company buys and transforms into its products (steel, wood, valves, fenders, etc.), normally varies with the volume of production. The cost of **direct labor**, wages paid to employees who work directly on the product, also usually varies with the volume of production. However, in some European countries where it is difficult, or even impossible, to lay off workers in slow times, labor becomes a fixed cost. Some U.S. companies also follow no-layoff policies as well. **Manufacturing overhead**, consisting of all production costs other than materials, purchased components, and direct labor, includes costs that are fixed, variable, and mixed. Many such costs vary with production, but many others are driven by other activities. Activity-based costing (discussed in the next chapter) is concerned with analyzing these costs, determining their drivers, and relating the costs to products. Some examples of manufacturing overhead costs appear in Exhibit 3-6.

From the brief listing in Exhibit 3-6, you should see that companies have several pools of manufacturing overhead costs, each driven by a different activity. Some pools of manufacturing overhead will be mixed costs, with variable components based on activities such as labor hours or machine hours. Some pools will

### Exhibit 3-6   Examples of Manufacturing Overhead Costs

- Costs of acquiring materials and components, which include finding acceptable vendors and carrying out routine purchasing functions
- Wages of indirect laborers (those who do not work directly on the products), such as maintenance workers, materials handlers, and cleaners
- Costs of data processing related to manufacturing activities
- Salaries of production supervisors
- Costs of changing machinery over from making one product to another (setup costs)
- Accounting and recordkeeping related to manufacturing operations
- Quality control costs, such as salaries of workers responsible for inspecting incoming shipments of materials and components in conventional manufacturers
- Wages of workers responsible for the storage and control of materials
- Heat, light, and power costs for factory
- Depreciation and property taxes on factory buildings and factory machinery
- Salary and office expenses of plant managers and their staffs
- Salaries and expenses of industrial engineers, computer programmers, and other manufacturing support personnel

be fixed in the short term because they are driven by factors that do not change significantly over short periods. (One example is the costs of some administrative functions that change only as the factory increases the number of products it makes.)

One objective of cost management is to determine the costs of each product so that managers can make decisions about those products. For instance, should we continue to make a particular product or phase it out over the coming year? Should we raise prices on some products? Lower prices on others? A multiproduct company can seldom relate the behavior of most manufacturing overhead costs, as well as selling and administrative expenses, to a single, broad measure of output such as the number of units produced or sold, or to the labor content of each product. For example, a company that makes refrigerators, ovens, and toasters could not expect each type of manufacturing overhead cost to vary with the total number of units produced because the units are so different. (Making a toaster does not cause as much overhead as making a refrigerator because a refrigerator requires more labor and machine time, has many more parts, and is a much more complicated product.) Activity-based costing, discussed in the following chapter, addresses these issues.

## SUMMARY

Cost analysis and management are important because managers can control costs directly or control the activities (drivers) that generate them. Many costs vary with activities other than sales, necessitating the identification of their drivers. Identifying value-adding and non-value-adding activities and costs is crucial for cost management. A company's objectives are to perform value-adding activities more efficiently and eliminate non-value-adding activities and their associated costs.

Some costs are mixed, containing both fixed and variable elements. Step-variable costs are fixed over small ranges of activity but at different levels for different ranges. Scatter diagrams, high-low estimates, and regression analysis are useful tools for analyzing cost behavior, but must be used with care. Whatever the method used to analyze cost behavior, actual costs will probably differ from planned costs.

Other classifications of costs include discretionary or committed, avoidable or unavoidable, and direct or indirect. Discretionary fixed costs can be changed on relatively short notice. Committed fixed costs normally cannot be changed quickly. Costs are avoidable or unavoidable only in relation to specific decisions, such as dropping a product. Direct costs relate to a specific activity, while indirect (or common) costs benefit more than one activity.

## KEY TERMS

account analysis    *(84)*          correlation    *(91)*
committed costs    *(94)*          cost drivers    *(82)*

cost pool   *(82)*

direct (separable or traceable) cost
   *(96)*

direct labor   *(97)*

discretionary costs   *(94)*

engineering approach   *(86)*

high-low (or two-point) method   *(87)*

indirect (common or joint) cost   *(96)*

manufacturing overhead   *(97)*

materials (raw or direct)   *(97)*

mixed (semivariable) cost   *(84)*

non-value-adding activities   *(83)*

regression analysis   *(89)*

scatter-diagram (graphical) method
   *(88)*

step-variable cost   *(92)*

value-adding activities   *(83)*

## KEY FORMULAS

$$\text{Variable cost component of mixed cost} = \frac{\text{change in cost}}{\text{change in activity}}$$

$$\text{Fixed cost component of mixed cost} = \text{total cost at high volume} - \text{high volume} \times \text{variable cost component}$$

## REVIEW PROBLEM

Bobbie Marvin, owner of Interior Solutions, has been trying to get a handle on her supplies costs. She has amassed the following monthly data for you to consider. A plot of the data also appears on page 100.

| Sales | Supplies Cost |
|-------|---------------|
| $23,500 | $3,420 |
| 25,450 | 3,645 |
| 27,250 | 3,622 |
| 31,500 | 3,880 |
| 22,000 | 3,456 |
| 24,600 | 3,445 |
| 22,570 | 3,280 |

### Required

1. Determine the fixed and variable components of the cost using the high-low method.
2. Determine the cost that Bobbie would predict at sales of $30,000.
3. Use the scatter diagram to derive a cost-prediction equation.

### ANSWER TO REVIEW PROBLEM

1.

$$\text{Variable component} = \frac{\text{Cost at high volume} - \text{cost at low volume}}{\text{High volume} - \text{low volume}}$$

$$= \frac{\$3,880 - \$3,456}{\$31,500 - \$22,000}$$

$$= \$424/\$9,500$$

$$= \$0.0446$$

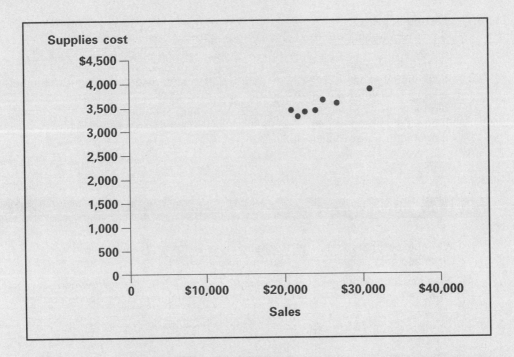

Fixed component:

| | |
|---|---:|
| Cost at high volume | $3,880 |
| Variable cost at high volume, $0.0446 × $31,500 | 1,405 |
| Fixed cost | $2,475 |

The cost is $2,475 per month fixed and $0.0446 variable with sales dollars.  This equation might not be the best predictor. She might want to try other drivers such as the number of clients, or the hours her people work.

2. $3,813; $2,475 + ($0.0446 × $30,000)
3. Your line will vary according to your dexterity and how you believe the line should look. The "correct" line as found by regression analysis is $2,140 + $0.055 × sales. The high-low method understates variable costs and overstates fixed costs.

## APPENDIX: REGRESSION ANALYSIS

Regression analysis fits a straight line to a set of data. In contrast to the high-low method, regression analysis uses more than two observations. In contrast to the scatter-diagram method, regression analysis fits a mathematically precise line, rather than one that depends on the judgment of the manager drawing the line. You can easily set up and solve a regression using a computer spreadsheet. Some hand-held calculators can solve regressions.

Although regression analysis is used for many purposes, our main interest here is predicting cost behavior—determining the fixed and variable components of a cost or pool of costs associated with a cost driver. Regression provides an equation of the same form as do the high-low and scatter-diagram methods.

$$Total\ cost\ =\ fixed\ component\ +\ (variable\ rate\ \times\ activity)$$

Regression analysis also provides measures that indicate how well the costs are associated with the measure of activity (cost driver) used. Thus, you can test several drivers to determine which seems to predict costs best. The first step, then, in using regression analysis is deciding which cost driver to use—sales dollars, production in units, number of sales invoices prepared, hours worked by direct laborers, or number of parts and components in a product.

We present two techniques, simple and multiple regression, in this Appendix. In simple regression, the equation uses one cost driver (independent variable) to explain costs (dependent variable). In multiple regression, the equation uses more than one independent variable to explain the dependent variable. Assignments in the text do not require the use of multiple regression so we discuss it only briefly.

## SIMPLE REGRESSION

We show below the regression results that Lotus 1-2-3 gives using the data in the example in the chapter (page 87).

|  Regression Output |  |
| --- | ---: |
| Constant | $7,731.78 |
| Std Err of Y Est | $1,763.16 |
| R Squared | 0.954921527 |
| No. of Observations | 12 |
| Degrees of Freedom | 10 |
| X Coefficient(s) | $1.766778 |
| Std Err of Coef. | $0.121390 |

The constant, $7,731.78, is the value for $a$, the estimate of the fixed component of cost. The variable component, $b$, is the $1.766778 shown as the X Coefficient(s). (Lotus 1-2-3 allows you to do multiple regression, where you have more than one $b$ value, hence the (s).) We used 12 observations, shown as No. of Observations. The value for Degrees of Freedom, 10, is not important to us. The other three items relate to the goodness of fit of the regression line. We shall not discuss the standard error of the coefficient, $0.121390, but we take up the other measures below.

## CORRELATION AND THE STANDARD ERROR

Managers using any equation to predict costs want to have some idea about their likely accuracy. Measures of *goodness of fit* tell us how well the regression line fits the data, and therefore suggest to managers how good their predictions are likely to be. The two measures we discuss are the coefficient of determination, often called $r^2$ (R Squared in the 1-2-3 output) and the standard error of the estimate (Std Err of Y Est in the output). The coefficient of determination measures how well the regression line accounts for the changes in Y, the dependent variable. The value (0.9549 above) is the percentage of the variation in Y that is associated with changes in X, so its value can range from zero through 1. A value of 1 means that the regression line is perfect: all points fall on it. A value near zero means that the values of Y are randomly scattered with no relationship to the values of X. The coefficient of determination ($r^2$) for our example, 0.9549, indicates an excellent fit, so predictions using the regression equation should be good. Again, however, we have only 12 observations to keep down the calculations. Using more observations, say 20 to 30, would make us more confident of the equation.

Exhibit 3-7 shows scatter diagrams for two cases, one with high correlation and one with low correlation. Using machine hours as the independent variable, your predictions of Cost W would be closer to their actual results than those of Cost T. Perhaps you could better predict Cost T using some other measure of activity, or perhaps Cost T is not driven by any activity but is just random. The coefficient of determination for Cost W will be high, for Cost T it will be low.

You might find it helpful to know how the coefficient is calculated.

$$r^2 \;=\; 1 \;-\; \frac{\Sigma(Y - Y_c)^2}{\Sigma(Y - \overline{Y})^2}$$

The differences, $Y - Y_c$, are the differences between the actual values of Y and those predicted by the regression equation. The differences, $Y - \overline{Y}$, are the differences between the actual values of Y and the mean, or average of the values of Y. (The differences are squared for reasons we shall not discuss here.)

A rough interpretation of $r^2$ follows. If you had no values for X and had to predict Y using only the past values of Y, your best prediction is the average of previous costs. The variation around that average is the denominator of the last term of the equation and, because that variation is large, your predictions will be well off most of the time. For instance, the average value of Y is $27,858. But the actual values that you would have tried to predict range from $14,800 to $40,800. Your predictions for those months would have been off by about $13,000. In some months you would have been closer, but not as close as you would have been using the regression equation.

The numerator of the last term of the equation is the unexplained variation; the variation that remains after incorporating the independent variable. If $r^2$ is 1, the unexplained variation is zero, and all of the observations fall on the regression line.

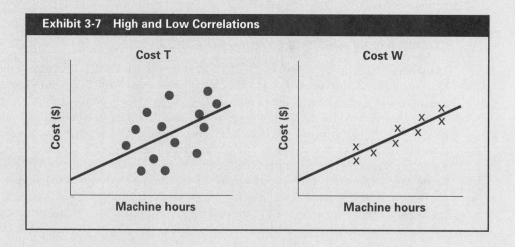

**Exhibit 3-7    High and Low Correlations**

The standard error of the estimate of Y ($S_e$) is a measure of the variation around the regression line as is shown by its calculation.[2]

$$S_e = \sqrt{\frac{\Sigma(Y - Y_c)^2}{n - 2}}$$

The lower the standard error of the estimate, the better. The standard error is zero if the regression line is perfect and all observations fall on it. (Note that the numerator in the standard error calculation uses the same values as the numerator in the $r^2$ calculation.) In our example, the standard error is 1,763.16, shown as Std Err of Y Est.

Roughly 68 percent of the actual values of cost lie within one standard error of their predicted values, about 95 percent within two standard errors.[3]  With the standard error of $1,763, actual cost will be within $1,763 of its predicted value about 68 percent of the time, and within $3,526 (2 × $1,763) about 95 percent of the time. Assuming a cost prediction at the average of about $28,000, 95 percent of the time actual cost should differ by no more than 12.6 percent ($3,526/28,000). Thus, the standard error of the estimate, like $r^2$, suggests a good fit of the regression line to the data.

## SELECTING A COST-PREDICTION EQUATION

We now have three cost-prediction formulas for maintenance cost. The high-low method result is on page 88, the scatter-diagram result on page 88.

| | | | | | |
|---|---|---|---|---|---|
| *high-low* | *maintenance cost* | = | *$4,800* | + | *$2* | *× machine hours* |
| *scatter-diagram* | *maintenance cost* | = | *$7,200* | + | *$1.82* | *× machine hours* |
| *regression analysis* | *maintenance cost* | = | *$7,732* | + | *$1.77* | *× machine hours* |

Which one should the company use? The regression method gives the best results. It is objectively determined, uses all observations, and has good measures of goodness of fit. Note that both other equations overstate the variable component of the cost. The variable component is especially important because it enters into the calculation of contribution margin, which is important for a variety of decisions. The regression equation gives the best estimate of variable maintenance cost.

## PROBLEMS AND PITFALLS

A basic assumption in using regression analysis is that the data are representative. That is, the conditions under which each of the observations was collected were about the same and can be expected to continue. As we suggested in the chapter, if one or more of the observations used in the analysis are not representative of normal conditions, the regression line will not be as useful.

---

2 *The divisor is actually the number of observations minus the number of coefficients estimated in the equation. We estimate a and b here. In multiple regression, we could have three or more coefficients and the divisor will increase accordingly.*
3 *The following is very rough. We are simply illustrating the principle of the standard error of the estimate. The actual intervals within which predicted costs are likely to fall are wider than the standard error of the estimate.*

Consider the scatter diagram in Exhibit 3-7 for Cost W. Suppose Cost W is maintenance and repairs plotted against machine hours. Picture an observation of a very high cost at a very low volume, well up the left-hand part of the scatter diagram. Such an observation, called an outlier, has a disproportionate effect on a regression equation. Such an observation is clearly unusual and might best be ignored in developing the equation. That observation might have been from a month in which the plant was shut down for a considerable period for extensive repair work. The high cost of repairs combined with the low volume of machine hours makes the observation nonrepresentative. Great care must be taken in "throwing out" observations, but if a particular observation occurred for an unusual reason, it is best to ignore it.

One final caution. Like the predictions from using the high-low and scatter-diagram methods, those resulting from regression analysis depend for their validity on observations over a particular range of activity, that is, the range over which the observations were gathered. Care must be taken in using any of these methods to predict costs for levels of activity not included within the range over which the observations were gathered. For example, if costs of power to operate machines have been analyzed in a range from 500 to 800 hours of machine time per week, there is no reason to assume that the relationships that held over that range will hold also at 350 hours or 1,100 hours.

## MULTIPLE REGRESSION

Multiple regression analysis uses more than one independent variable to generate a cost-prediction equation. In a modern business, many costs depend on more than one activity. The cost of heating a factory depends both on the number of hours it is open and on the outside temperature. Shipping costs depend on both the weight of the goods and the distance over which they must travel.

A multiple regression equation has the following general form.

$$Y = a + b_1X_1 + b_2X_3 \dots b_nX_n$$

where

$$
\begin{aligned}
Y &= \text{the dependent variable to be predicted} \\
X_1 \dots X_n &= \text{the values of the various independent variables influencing the value of Y} \\
b_1 \dots b_n &= \text{the coefficients of the various independent variables} \\
a &= \text{the fixed component (as in simple regression)}
\end{aligned}
$$

Suppose the manager of a factory that makes a number of products has requested an analysis of manufacturing overhead costs. The managerial accountant, working in conjunction with a statistician, came up with the following analysis.

| | |
|---|---|
| Fixed component of manufacturing overhead cost | $32,500 per month (a) |
| Variable components (independent variables): | |
| Direct labor hours ($X_1$) | $2.40 per hour ($b_1$) |
| Machine hours ($X_2$) | $1.80 per hour ($b_2$) |
| Number of setups ($X_3$) | $80.00 per setup ($b_3$) |

The accountant has found that variations in three variables (direct labor hours, machine hours, and number of setups) better describe variations in total overhead costs than do variations in any one or combination of two such variables. Such a conclusion is reasonable when one considers that many overhead costs (fringe benefits, for example) are related to labor time and some (like power, supplies, and lubricants) are readily associated with machine time. Still others, such as the wages paid to workers who set up machines and the materials they use, depend on the number of setups or hours spent doing setups.

Suppose, now, that the factory manager expects the following activity in the coming month.

| | |
|---|---:|
| Direct labor hours | 20,000 |
| Machine hours | 15,000 |
| Setups | 200 |

The manager would predict total manufacturing overhead of $123,500.

$$
\begin{array}{l}
\begin{matrix}
Total \\
manufacturing \\
overhead
\end{matrix}
=
\begin{matrix}
fixed \\
cost
\end{matrix}
+
\begin{matrix}
costs \\
variable\ with \\
direct\ labor \\
hours
\end{matrix}
+
\begin{matrix}
costs \\
variable\ with \\
machine\ hours
\end{matrix}
+
\begin{matrix}
costs \\
variable\ with \\
setups
\end{matrix}
\end{array}
$$

$$= \$32,500 + (\$2.40 \times 20,000) + (\$1.80 \times 15,000) + (\$80.00 \times 200)$$

$$= \$32,500 + \quad \$48,000 \quad + \quad \$27,000 \quad + \quad \$16,000$$

The cautions associated with simple regression also apply here, plus one more. Multiple regression analysis requires the assumption that the independent variables are not correlated with each other. In our example, for instance, knowing whether direct labor hours and machine hours (or some other combination of the three independent variables) are closely associated is important. If two (or more) of the independent variables are highly correlated, the results of multiple regression analysis must be used with care and the underlying statistical problems must be understood. Your statistics courses will address these problems.

A multiple regression equation also has a coefficient of determination and a standard error of the estimate, but the calculations are somewhat different than they are for simple regression and we shall omit them.

In summary, when using either simple or multiple regression analysis, you must understand the statistical principles that underlie these approaches. Critical to the production of useful results under either approach is the need for the observations to be representative of conditions expected to prevail during the period for which predictions are being made.

## REVIEW PROBLEM—APPENDIX

The controller of Tuscany Products has just received the following results from the company's statistician.

$$Y = \$326,389 + \$8.625X, \ r^2 = 0.712, \ S_e = \$16,352$$
$$Y = monthly\ factory\ power\ cost, \ X = machine\ hours$$

The statistician collected the data in a range of 20,000 to 30,000 machine hours.

**Required**

1. Calculate the expected power cost at 22,000 machine hours.
2. Explain the meaning of the equation and of each component of the equation and the measures of goodness of fit. Also indicate the usefulness of each item in cost analysis.

**ANSWER TO REVIEW PROBLEM**

1. $516,139; $326,389 + $8.625 × 22,000
2. The equation itself tells us that factory power cost has a fixed component of $326,389 per month and a variable component of $8.625 per machine hour. We can therefore predict power cost by using the equation, as we did in requirement 1.

   We can find the total variable cost of power for a product or component that we manufacture by multiplying $8.625 by the number of machine hours the manufactured item requires.

   The coefficient of determination, $r^2$ of 0.712, or 71.2%, tells us the percentage of the variation in power cost that is associated with changes in machine hours. The relatively high value for $r^2$ indicates a good fit.

   The standard error of the estimate, $S_e$, tells us how close our predictions are likely to be to the actual results. In this case, we expect predictions to be within $16,352 about 68% of the time and within $32,704 (2 × $16,352) about 95% of the time.

   It is also helpful to understand what the results do not tell you. The equation is not necessarily the best available. Some other factor might predict better. Multiple regression with some other factors might give better results, higher $r^2$, and a lower standard error.

   One last point. The intercept, $326,389, is *not* the estimate of total cost at zero machine hours. The data were collected in the range of 20–30 thousand hours and it is unsafe to extrapolate outside that range.

## ASSIGNMENT MATERIAL

### INTERNET ACTIVITY

Go to the Internet and find annual reports from three or four companies that discuss their cost management programs. Write a short description of how each company is managing costs, what kinds of costs (manufacturing, distribution, service) they are concentrating on, and how much progress they have made. A good place to start is Yahoo.com, which will direct you to company Web sites. Not all companies post their annual reports on the Web, so you will have some false starts. Some good industries to look for companies are computers, consumer products, and automobiles.

### QUESTIONS FOR DISCUSSION

**3-1  Cost classification**  Indicate whether each of the following costs is likely to be discretionary or committed. If in doubt, describe the circumstances under which the cost would fall into one or the other category. If the cost is mixed, consider only the fixed portion.

(a) Straight-line depreciation on office equipment.

(b) The cost of preparing the company's income tax return.

(c) Research and development.

(d) Salaries of president and vice-presidents for marketing and finance.

(e) Fees for consultants on plant relocation.

(f) Utilities for factory—heating and lighting.

(g) Management development costs—tuition reimbursements, costs of attending seminars, training programs, etc.

**3-2  Limitations of high-low method**   The assistant controller of HashCo, Inc. recommended the following approach to estimating the fixed and variable components of manufacturing overhead costs such as utilities, maintenance, supervision, indirect labor, and supplies.

  Estimate the total cost the company would incur if it shut down, and treat that amount as fixed cost. Then estimate the total cost working at 100% of capacity, stated in machine hours. Divide the difference in the two cost figures by machine hours at capacity and treat that as the variable component.

*Required*

Comment on the suggested procedure. Would the formula derived from it work well for the company if it normally operated between 75% and 90% of capacity?

**3-3  Methods of cost behavior analysis (Appendix)**   Discuss the advantages and disadvantages of the high-low, scatter-diagram, and regression methods of cost estimation.

**3-4  Cost classification**   Cramer Company is a large distributor of household products. It operates in eight regions, maintaining a sales office in each. State whether each of the following costs is likely to be (a) avoidable or unavoidable in deciding whether to stop selling in the South-Central region, and (b) direct or indirect to the South-Central office.

(a) Salaries of salespeople in the South-Central region.

(b) Rent on the South-Central office. The lease has five years left.

(c) Rent on equipment used in the South-Central regional office. The equipment can be returned with one week's notice.

(d) Salaries of the national vice-president for sales and her staff.

(e) National advertising.

(f) Travel expenses of salespeople working in the South-Central region.

**3-5  Cost classification—directness and avoidability**   Talley Industries makes small fiberglass boats. It has two production departments, the Forming Department and the Finishing Department. The company is considering closing the Forming Department and contracting out the work the department does. State whether each of the following costs is likely to be (a) avoidable or unavoidable with regard to contracting out the work now done by the Forming Department, and (b) direct or indirect to the Forming Department.

(a) Wages of workers in the Forming Department.

(b) Property taxes on the factory building.

(c) Depreciation on machinery used only in the Forming Department.

(d) Salaries of the plant controller and her staff.

(e) Salary of the Forming Department manager.

(f) Wages of maintenance workers who tend all machinery in the factory.

## EXERCISES

**3-6  Accuracy of predictions**  The scatter diagrams below show two costs plotted against production.

**Required**
Which cost can you predict and plan for more easily? Explain.

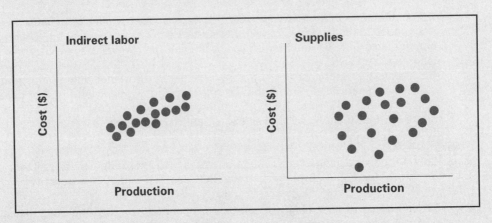

**3-7  Mixed costs**  Gorman Research Labs performs various scientific tests for its customers. The controller is trying to analyze cost behavior and has asked you to develop a behavioral classification for indirect labor cost. You have the following data from two recent months.

| Testing Hours | Indirect Labor Cost |
|---|---|
| 38,000 | $90,240 |
| 52,000 | $96,820 |

**Required**
1. Compute the fixed and variable portions of indirect labor cost based on testing hours.
2. Determine estimated indirect labor cost at 45,000 testing hours.
3. Why should the controller be interested in the variable component of cost?

**3-8  Cost behavior (Appendix)**  Benton Market Research operates several regional offices. Its managers have been concerned about the cost of supplies and need an analysis of its behavior. A record of service revenues and corresponding supply costs in one of the offices follows.

| Monthly Service Revenues | Cost of Supplies |
|---|---|
| $430,000 | $21,640 |
| 480,000 | 24,860 |
| 340,000 | 21,150 |
| 520,000 | 25,210 |
| 370,000 | 23,150 |
| 380,000 | 24,640 |
| 450,000 | 27,280 |
| 560,000 | 29,840 |
| 500,000 | 26,520 |

### Required

1. Determine the variable cost percentage of service revenues and the fixed costs using the high-low method.
2. Do a regression analysis using a spreadsheet. Comment on the differences between the cost prediction equations given by the two methods.
3. Comment on the measures of goodness of fit the regression analysis generates. Will the equation predict supplies costs well?

**3-9 Cost analysis—high-low method** The controller of Clarkson Furniture, a retail store, wants to develop CVP relationships for planning and control. She is not sure how this might be done and asks your assistance. She has prepared income statements for recent months.

|  | October | November |
|---|---|---|
| Sales | $80,000 | $90,000 |
| Cost of goods sold | 48,000 | 54,000 |
| Gross profit | $32,000 | $36,000 |
| Operating expenses: | | |
| Selling expenses | $ 8,500 | $8,800 |
| Administrative expenses | 9,200 | 9,400 |
| Total expenses | $17,700 | $18,200 |
| Income | $14,300 | $17,800 |

### Required

1. Determine the fixed and variable components of cost of goods sold, selling expenses, and administrative expenses.
2. Prepare a contribution margin income statement based on sales of $100,000.

**3-10 Understanding regression results (Appendix)** Boynton Solutions is a management consulting firm that employs both full-time and part-time consultants. The president has been concerned about the level of use of part-time consultants and has asked for your assistance. You have developed the following regression results.

$Y$ = monthly part-time consultant cost, $X$ = monthly consulting revenues
$Y = \$28,331 + \$0.1647X$, $r^2 = 0.6181$, $S_e = \$10,113$

The data were collected in a range of $800,000 to $1,200,000 monthly consulting fees. The controller wants your assistance in explaining these results to a group of managers.

### Required

Write a memorandum that explains the meaning and significance of each of the items in the regression results. Use the guidelines in Appendix B.

**3-11 Interpreting behavior patterns** The graph on page 110 depicts the costs experienced by Magma Enterprises.

### Required

1. Give some reasons why costs might behave as depicted.
2. How would you plan for costs that exhibited this type of behavior?

**3-12 High-low method for manufacturing company** The chief accountant of Dearborn, Inc. prepared the following income statements, in thousands.

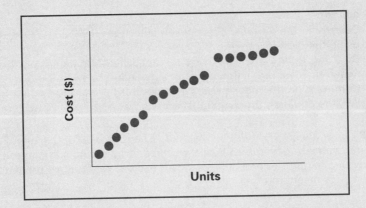

|  | June | July |
|---|---|---|
| Sales | $550.0 | $580.0 |
| Cost of sales | 335.0 | 344.0 |
| Gross margin | $215.0 | $236.0 |
| Selling and administrative expenses | 185.0 | 191.0 |
| Income before taxes | $ 30.0 | $ 45.0 |

**Required**

1. Determine the fixed and variable components of cost of sales and of selling and administrative expenses.
2. Prepare income statements for June and July using the contribution-margin format. Comment on the differences between the statements above and the ones that you prepared.

**3-13  Relationships**   Answer the following questions, considering each situation independently. You might not be able to answer the questions in the order they are asked.

1. A company earned $200,000 selling 100,000 units at $8 per unit. Its fixed costs are $400,000.
   (a)  What are variable costs per unit?
   (b)  What is total contribution margin?
   (c)  What would income be if sales increased by 5,000 units?
2. A company has return on sales of 20%, income of $50,000, selling price of $10, and a contribution margin of 40%.
   (a)  What are fixed costs?
   (b)  What are variable costs per unit?
   (c)  What are sales in units?
   (d)  What are sales in dollars?
3. A company has return on sales of 15% at sales of $400,000. Its fixed costs are $90,000; variable costs are $25 per unit.
   (a)  What are sales in units?
   (b)  What is contribution margin per unit?
   (c)  What is income?

**3-14  Per-unit analysis**   The controller of E&G Company has prepared the following per-unit analysis of profitability, based on sales of 80,000 units.

| Sales | | $6.00 |
|---|---|---|
| Variable costs | $2.40 | |
| Fixed costs | 2.70 | 5.10 |
| Profit | | $0.90 |

**Required**
Answer the following questions independently of one another.

1. What are total fixed costs?
2. How many units must the company sell to earn a profit of $90,000?
3. If E&G could sell 70,000 units, what selling price will yield a $90,000 profit?
4. E&G can undertake an advertising campaign for $6,000. Marketing expects volume to increase by 3,000 units at the $6 selling price. By how much and in which direction (increase or decrease) will the company's profit change if it takes the action?

**3-15   Percentage income statement**   The president of Millard Industries has developed the following income statement showing expected percentage results at sales of $800,000.

| Sales | 100% |
|---|---|
| Cost of sales | 60% |
| Gross margin | 40% |
| Other expenses | 30% |
| Income | 10% |

The president tells you that cost of sales is all variable and that the only other variable cost is commissions, which are 10% of sales, and are included in the "other expenses" category.

**Required**
1. Determine the profit that the company expects to earn.
2. Determine fixed costs, the break-even point, and the margin of safety.
3. If sales are $700,000, what will profit be?
4. The president wants a $120,000 profit. Expected unit volume is the same as for the statement above. By what percentage must the company increase its selling price to achieve the goal? Assume the per-unit cost of sales remains constant.

**3-16   Cost behavior graphs (AICPA adapted)**   Graphs and descriptions of cost elements follow on page 112.

**Required**
For each description, select the letter of the graph that best shows the behavior of the cost. Graphs may be used more than once. The zero point for each graph is the intersection of the horizontal and vertical axes. The vertical axis represents total cost for the described cost and the horizontal axis represents production in units. Be prepared to discuss any assumptions you might have to make in selecting your answers.

1. Depreciation of equipment, using the units-of-production method.

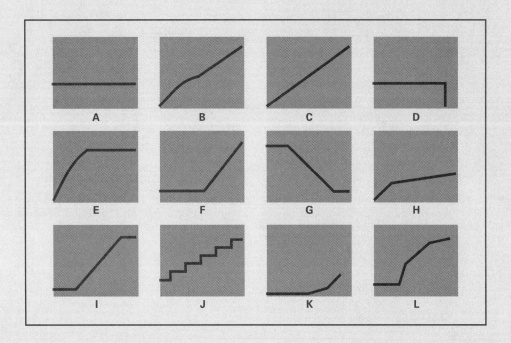

2. Electricity bill, a flat charge plus a variable cost after a certain number of kilowatt-hours are used.
3. City water bill, computed as follows:

| | | |
|---|---|---|
| First 1,000,000 gallons or less | $1,000 | flat fee |
| Next 10,000 gallons | 0.003 | per gallon used |
| Next 10,000 gallons | 0.006 | per gallon used |
| Next 10,000 gallons | 0.009 | per gallon used |
| etc., etc., etc. | | |

4. Cost of lubricant for machines, where cost per unit decreases with each pound of lubricant used (for example, if one pound is used, the cost is $10.00; if two pounds are used, the cost is $19.98; if three pounds are used, the cost is $29.94; with a minimum cost per pound of $9.25).
5. Depreciation of equipment, using the straight-line method.
6. Rent for a factory building donated by the city, where the agreement calls for a fixed-fee payment unless 200,000 person-hours are worked, in which case no rent need be paid.
7. Salaries of repairpeople, where one repairperson is needed for every 1,000 hours of machine time or less (i.e., 0 to 1,000 hours requires one repairperson, 1,001 to 2,000 hours requires two repairpeople, etc.).
8. Federal unemployment compensation taxes, where the labor force is constant in number throughout the year and the average annual wage is $16,000. The tax is levied only on the first $8,500 earned by each employee.
9. Rent for production machinery, computed as follows:

| | |
|---|---|
| First 10,000 hours of use | $20,000 flat fee |
| Next 2,000 hours of use | $1.90 per hour |
| Next 2,000 hours of use | $1.80 per hour |
| Next 2,000 hours of use | $1.70 per hour |
| etc., etc., etc. | |

10. Rent for a factory building donated by the county, where the agreement calls for rent of $100,000 less $1 for each hour laborers worked in excess of 200,000 hours, but a minimum rental payment of $20,000 is required.

**3-17  CVP review**   Tina's Handicrafts sells handmade sweaters at $100 apiece. Tina buys sweaters from Ms. Posey at $30 apiece, but the agreement also requires an extra fee of 10% (of selling price) for each sweater sold. Tina's monthly fixed costs are $5,000.

**Required**

Answer each of the following questions independently.

1. If Tina wants to earn a profit of $6,000 a month, how many sweaters must she sell?
2. What price must Tina charge to earn a $6,000 profit selling 150 sweaters per month?
3. Suppose that Tina is selling 150 sweaters per month at $100 and making a profit of $4,000.  Ms. Posey offers to renegotiate the agreement so that she would receive $25 per sweater plus 15% (based on selling price) for each sweater sold. How many sweaters must Tina sell under the new agreement to earn the same $4,000 profit?  Why might Ms. Posey propose this arrangement?

## PROBLEMS

**3-18  Profit improvement alternatives**   Leslie Meriwether, president of Meriwether Associates, was not happy with the 20X8 income statement.

| | |
|---|---:|
| Sales (100,000 × $10) | $1,000,000 |
| Variable costs (100,000 × $6) | 600,000 |
| Contribution margin | $ 400,000 |
| Fixed costs | 360,000 |
| Profit | $ 40,000 |

Ms. Meriwether wanted a profit of at least $100,000 in 20X9, and believed that it was a reasonable target. She instructed the controller to analyze each component of the statement and determine the change in each component that would allow the company to earn the target profit of $100,000. (For example, what change in per-unit selling price would produce the target profit if sales volume, fixed costs, and per-unit variable costs remained constant; or what change in sales volume would be needed, assuming that prices and costs did not change?)

**Required**

Write a memorandum to Ms. Meriwether that summarizes your findings and indicates what changes might be easier to achieve. Use the guidelines in Appendix A.

**3-19  Interpreting data**   Your assistant at Valchon Limousine used the scatter diagram on page 114 to separate maintenance expenses on its limousines into fixed and variable components. She derived the following equation: Monthly total cost = $350 + ($0.80 × hours driven), which is represented by the line drawn on the diagram.

**Required**

Comment on the way in which your assistant fitted the line to the data and make an alternative recommendation.

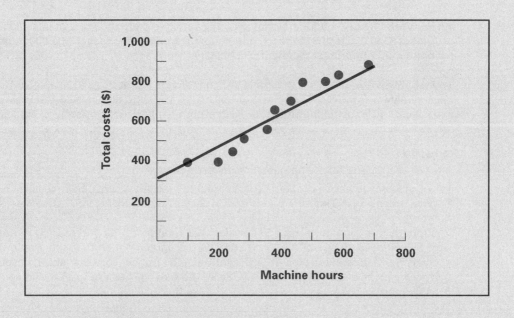

**3-20    Delta Airlines CVP relationships**    A recent annual report of **Delta Airlines** contained the following data, in millions of dollars.

| | |
|---|---:|
| Operating revenues | $8,582.20 |
| Operating expenses | $8,162.70 |
| Operating income | $419.50 |
| Load factor (percentage of available seat-miles occupied) | 61.15% |
| Break-even load factor | 57.96% |

**Required**
1. Determine the variable cost as a percentage of revenue for Delta Airlines.  (Hint: Find total revenue and total cost at break even, then use the high-low method.)
2. Determine fixed operating costs for Delta Airlines.
3. Determine what operating income Delta Airlines would have earned had it flown its aircraft 62.15% full (one percentage point higher than it actually did).
4. What does your answer to requirement 3 tell you about how to be successful in the airline industry?

**3-21    Using multiple regression (Appendix)**    The chief statistician of AJK, Inc. has developed the following regression analysis.

$$Y = \$49,272 + \$1.78L + \$2.68M$$

where

Y  = total monthly manufacturing overhead cost
L  = labor hours
M  = machine hours

The measures of goodness of fit are good and no evidence of multicollinearity exists. AJK will use 12,000 labor hours and 2,000 machine hours next month. Your boss has asked you the following questions.

**Required**

1. Determine the total manufacturing overhead cost that AJK should incur next month.
2. AJK makes a product that has $6 in materials cost. It requires two hours of labor time and 30 minutes of machine time. Laborers earn $10 per hour. What is the product's per-unit variable manufacturing cost?
3. Suppose that AJK could reduce the labor time for the product described in requirement 2 by 30 minutes, to 1.5 hours. Machine time will remain the same. By how much would the per-unit variable manufacturing cost fall?

**3-22   Understanding regression results (Appendix)**   The controller of the Cromwell Plant of TAYCO Enterprises has the following regression results prepared by the plant's statistician.

$$Y = \$61,424 + \$2.067X, \; r^2 = 0.7731, \; S_e = \$12,206$$
$$Y = monthly\ power\ cost, \; X = machine\ hours$$

The results are based on the past 30 months of operations during which monthly machine hours ranged from 80,000 to 140,000. The controller wants you to explain the results to some of her staff.

**Required**

1. If the plant will work 100,000 machine hours next month, what is the predicted power cost?
2. If the plant shuts down next month, should power cost be $61,424?
3. The company is considering a new product that requires 45 machine hours per batch of 100 units. What is the variable cost of power for the product?
4. How close are your predictions of power costs likely to be to the actual results? For example, can you state the range within which actual cost should be some specified percentage of the time?
5. Can you tell whether this equation is the best available to predict power costs?

CHAPTER 2

**3-23   Review problem, including income taxes, Chapters 2 and 3**   After reviewing its cost structure (variable costs of $7.50 per unit and monthly fixed costs of $60,000) and potential market, Forecast Company established what it considered to be a reasonable selling price. The company expected to sell 50,000 units per month and planned its monthly results as follows.

| | |
|---|---:|
| Sales | $500,000 |
| Variable costs | 375,000 |
| Contribution margin | $125,000 |
| Fixed costs | 60,000 |
| Income before taxes | $ 65,000 |
| Income taxes (at 40%) | 26,000 |
| Net income | $ 39,000 |

**Required**

Using the preceding information, answer the following questions independently.

1. What selling price did the company establish?
2. What is the contribution margin per unit?
3. What is the break-even point in units?
4. If the company determined that a particular advertising campaign had a high probability of increasing sales by 3,000 units, how much could it pay for such a campaign without reducing its planned profits?

5. If the company wants a $60,000 before-tax profit, how many units must it sell?
6. If the company wants a 10% before-tax return on sales, what level of sales, in dollars, does it need?
7. If the company wants a $45,000 after-tax profit, how many units must it sell?
8. If the company wants an after-tax return on sales of 9%, how many units must it sell?
9. If the company wants an after-tax profit of $45,000 on its expected sales volume of 50,000 units, what price must it charge?
10. If the company wants a before-tax return on sales of 16% on its expected sales volume of 50,000 units, what price must it charge?
11. The company is considering offering its salespeople a 5% commission on sales. What would the total sales, in dollars, have to be in order to implement the commission plan and still earn the planned pretax income of $65,000?

**3-24  Cost formula, high-low method**  The owner of Bed and Bath Boutique regularly uses part-time help in addition to full-time employees. Some part-time help is needed every day for miscellaneous chores, and the owner arranges for additional hours based on her estimates of sales for the following week. The following is a record of the wages paid to part-time employees at recent monthly sales volumes.

| Sales | Wages Paid to Part-Time Help |
|---|---|
| $ 8,210 | $   629 |
| 1,950 | 558 |
| 6,340 | 710 |
| 17,650 | 1,360 |
| 18,100 | 1,350 |
| 13,800 | 1,130 |
| 15,040 | 1,466 |
| 5,050 | 675 |
| 11,000 | 1,014 |

The owner considers these months to be relatively normal; however, in the month with sales of $1,950, the Boutique was closed for over two weeks for repainting and installing new carpeting.

**Required**
Determine the variable cost rate and fixed costs using the high-low method.

**3-25  Fixed costs and decisions**  Warren Keith owns a bistro in a suburb of a large city. The bistro does little business during August, and Keith is considering closing down and taking a vacation for the month. He develops the following budgeted income statement for August.

| | | |
|---|---:|---:|
| Sales | | $21,800 |
| Cost of sales | | 8,900 |
| Gross margin | | $12,900 |
| Wages to part-time help | $ 3,900 | |
| Utilities | 1,800 | |
| Rent on building | 1,550 | |
| Depreciation on fixtures | 600 | |
| Supplies and miscellaneous | 4,700 | 12,550 |
| Income | | $    350 |

Keith believes it is not worthwhile to stay open unless he can net at least $2,500 for the month. He works hard when the bistro is open and believes that he deserves at least that much to compensate him for the work he does.

He also tells you that if he closes, he will have to pay a minimum utility bill of $450. Supplies and miscellaneous expenses are fixed, but avoidable if he closed.

**Required**
Write a memorandum that advises Mr. Keith about the desirability of staying open for August. Use the guidelines in Appendix A.

**3-26 Alternative cost structures—a movie company (continuation of 2-43 and 2-44)** The president of Blockbusters Incorporated has reviewed the preliminary analysis of the two contract alternatives and wishes to give further consideration to the arrangements with Frodd. Frodd's agent is also having second thoughts about the alternatives and is wondering what is best for his client.

**Required**
Answer the following questions.

1. If total paid admissions are expected to be between $90 and $100 million, which compensation scheme is best for (a) Blockbusters and (b) Frodd? (Hint: Refer to your answers in Problem 2-43 regarding break-even points.)
2. If total paid admissions are expected to be about $250 million, which scheme is better for (a) Blockbusters and (b) Frodd?

**3-27 Regression analysis (Appendix)** Your new assistant has just handed you the following results of a regression analysis.

*Factory overhead = $262,203 + ($13.19 × units produced)*

You are surprised because your company makes several models of lawn mowers, and you had not thought it possible to express factory overhead so simply. Your assistant assures you that the results are correct, giving you the following data.

| Month | Units Produced | Factory Overhead |
|---|---|---|
| January | 1,700 | $260,000 |
| February | 1,100 | 280,000 |
| March | 2,800 | 300,000 |
| April | 2,300 | 260,000 |
| May | 2,000 | 360,000 |
| June | 1,800 | 320,000 |
| July | 2,400 | 320,000 |
| August | 2,000 | 200,000 |
| September | 2,100 | 300,000 |

**Required**
Comment on your assistant's results. You should do a regression analysis using a spreadsheet or other program.

**3-28 Alternative CVP graph** Managers of Sanders Company are considering alternative strategies for one of their products. The differences result from alternatives such as salaries versus commissions and different levels of product quality, advertising, and promotion.

| Alternative | Price | Variable Cost | Fixed Costs |
|---|---|---|---|
| 1 | $20 | $12 | $180,000 |
| 2 | $20 | $8 | $240,000 |
| 3 | $18 | $10 | $120,000 |

When evaluating alternative strategies, the firm's managers prefer the following alternative graphical approach. It represents a graph with Alternative 1 already plotted.

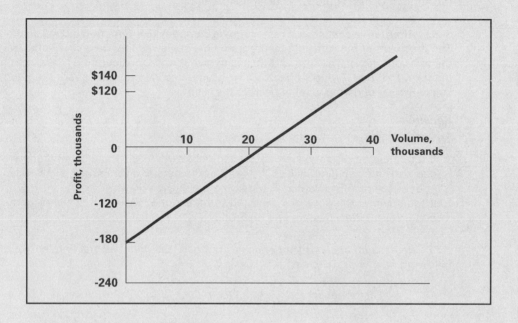

**Required**

1. Plot the profit lines for alternatives 2 and 3.
2. What general conclusions can you draw from the completed graph? Could you select the best alternative based on the graphical results?

**3-29  CVP analysis with changes in costs**  Stoneham Company manufactures a complete line of toiletries. The average selling price per case is $20 and cost data appear below.

| | |
|---|---|
| Variable costs per case: | |
| Materials | $4.00 |
| Labor | 2.00 |
| Other variable costs | 2.00 |
| Total variable costs | $8.00 |
| Annual fixed costs: | |
| Manufacturing | $1,500,000 |
| Selling and administrative | $2,500,000 |

Art Stoneham, the president, expects to sell 350,000 cases in the coming year. After gathering the above data, Stoneham learned that materials costs will increase by 25% because of shortages.

*Required*

1. Determine the profit that Stoneham expected before the increase in materials prices.
2. Given the increase in materials costs, determine the price that Stoneham has to charge to earn the profit you calculated in requirement 1.
3. Suppose that Stoneham decided to raise the price enough to maintain the same contribution margin percentage it had before the cost increase.
   (a) Determine the required price.
   (b) Would Stoneham earn more or less than your answer to requirement 2 if it charged that price and sold 350,000 cases?

**3-30   Cost structures and average costs**   At a dinner meeting of a local association of company accountants, the following conversation took place.

*Ruth Hifixed:* "My company has enormous fixed costs, and volume is our critical problem. My cost per unit is now $6, at 100,000 units, but if I could get 200,000 units, cost per unit would drop to $4. My selling price is also too low, only $6."

*Jim Lofixed:* "You are lucky. My cost per unit is $5 at 200,000 units, but we can't produce any more than 200,000. At least we're now better off than we were when sales were 80,000 units. At that volume we lost $0.50 per unit at our $6 price. We kept the same selling price at all volumes."

*Required*

1. Compute the profit earned by each company at its current level of sales.
2. Determine fixed costs, variable cost per unit, and contribution margin per unit for each firm.
3. Compute the break-even point for each firm.
4. Which company earns more at 150,000 units?
5. Which company earns more at 100,000 units?

**3-31   Avoidable costs**   Halton's Flower Shop buys and sells floral arrangements. The average selling price is $30, and average purchase cost is $10. Weekly fixed costs are $3,000. Because the arrangements are perishable, the shop cannot sell any units after they have been in inventory for one week. The shop must order a full week's supply at one time.

Mr. Halton, the owner, would like to earn $1,000 per week from the business. A friend has explained CVP analysis to him and made the following calculation.

$$\text{Unit volume required for \$1,000 profit} = \frac{\$3,000 + \$1,000}{\$30 - \$10}$$
$$= 200 \text{ arrangements}$$

*Required*

1. Is the above equation correct in the sense that if Mr. Halton orders 200 arrangements per week, he will earn $1,000? Why or why not?
2. Is the purchase cost fixed or variable? Explain.
3. Can you tell Mr. Halton how many arrangements he must sell to earn $1,000 if he purchases 300? If he purchases 400?

**3-32   Cost estimation—service business**   William Jarvis operates his own firm of Certified Public Accountants. For planning purposes, he is interested in developing information about the cost structure of the firm. At times, he hires part-time employees, usually accounting majors from the nearby university.

The best measure of activity for the company is chargeable hours, the number of hours that employees work on client business. The company charges the clients for these hours at hourly rates. Jarvis has the following data regarding wages of part-time employees from recent months.

| Total Chargeable Hours | Part-Time Wages |
|---|---|
| 3,000 | $3,000 |
| 3,500 | 3,100 |
| 2,800 | 2,990 |
| 3,200 | 3,090 |
| 4,800 | 5,400 |
| 5,200 | 6,180 |
| 5,600 | 6,900 |

**Required**

Plot the data on a scatter diagram and comment on the results. Can Mr. Jarvis use your results for planning? What reasons might there be for the pattern that you observe?

**3-33  CVP analysis for an airline**  Icarus Airlines flies a number of routes in the southwestern United States. The company owns six airplanes, each of which can hold 150 passengers. All routes are about the same distance, and all fares are $66 one way. The line is obligated to provide 250 flights per month. Each flight costs $4,000 for gasoline, crew salaries, and so on. Variable costs per passenger are $6, for a meal and a head tax imposed for each passenger at every airport to which Icarus flies. Other costs, all fixed, are $130,000 per month.

**Required**

1. How many passengers must Icarus carry on its 250 flights in order to earn $70,000 profit per month? What percentage of capacity is this number?
2. If the company could cut its flights to 200 per month, how many passengers are required to earn $70,000 per month? What percentage of capacity does this number represent (using 200 flights as capacity)?
3. Is the $4,000 cost per flight fixed or variable?
4. What is the chief problem faced by a company with this type of cost structure?

**3-34  Promotional campaign**  Ajax Publishers sells magazine subscriptions. Its managers are considering a large promotional campaign in which it will award prizes of $10,000,000. Other costs associated with the campaign appear below.

| | |
|---|---:|
| Television time | $ 4,400,000 |
| Fee to Fred Mahon, TV spokesperson | 700,000 |
| Mailing | 5,300,000 |
| Total | $10,400,000 |

Ajax plans to mail 20,000,000 packages containing entry blanks and forms for subscribing to magazines. Ajax receives 25% of total subscription revenue. Experience indicates that about 15% of those receiving a package take out one or more subscriptions. The average subscription revenue from a respondent is $35.

**Required**

1. What profit will Ajax earn if the campaign meets all expectations?

2. What is the break-even point for the campaign expressed as a response rate, assuming that each respondent orders $35 in magazine subscriptions?

**3-35   Brain teaser—calculating contribution margin percentage**   Bell Company has a 25% margin of safety. Its after-tax return on sales is 6%, and its tax rate is 40%.

**Required**
1. Determine Bell's contribution margin percentage.
2. Assuming that current sales are $120,000, determine total fixed costs.

**3-36   Cost structure and risk**   Gladack Company makes a number of products and uses a great deal of machinery. A new product this coming year will require the acquisition of a new machine. The machine can only be leased, not purchased. There are two alternative leasing arrangements: (1) a month-to-month lease that can be canceled on 30-days' notice by either Gladack or the lessor, at a monthly rental of $6,000, and (2) a five-year noncancelable lease at $5,200 per month. The new product is expected to have a life of five years, during which annual revenues will be $250,000 and annual variable costs $100,000. There are no new fixed costs other than the lease payments. The president is concerned that the five-year lease removes a great deal of flexibility; if the product does not pan out as expected, the company is stuck with the machine and there are no other uses for it. He does, however, like the idea of saving $800 per month.

**Required**
Why would the president hesitate between the choices? What could happen to make him regret choosing (a) the month-to-month lease? (b) the five-year lease?

**3-37   Loss per unit**   A company had a loss of $3 per unit when sales were 40,000 units. When sales were 50,000 units, the company had a loss of $1.60 per unit.

**Required**
1. Determine contribution margin per unit.
2. Determine fixed costs.
3. Determine the break-even point in units.

**3-38   CVP analysis—measures of volume**   Acme Foam Rubber Company buys large pieces of foam rubber (called "loaves") and cuts them into small pieces that are used in seat cushions and other products. A loaf contains 5,000 board feet of foam rubber (a "board foot" is one foot square and one inch thick), of which 10% becomes scrap during the process of cutting up the loaf. A loaf costs $700, including freight, and the company is currently processing 100 loaves per month.

The company charges $0.22 per board foot for its good output and $0.07 per board foot for the scrap. Variable costs of cutting the loaf are $100 for labor and power to run the cutting machines. Fixed costs are $18,000 per month. The president of the company has asked for your assistance in developing CVP relationships.

**Required**
1. Determine the firm's income when it processes 100 loaves per month.
2. Determine the firm's break-even point expressed as number of loaves processed.
3. The president tells you that your analyses in requirements 1 and 2 are not what he had in mind. He says that he is accustomed to thinking in terms of board feet of good output sold. He would like to know how many board feet he would have to sell to earn $6,000 per month. Determine the firm's contribution margin per board foot of good output sold and sales required to earn $6,000 per month.

## CASES

**3-39  Measures of volume**  The controller of Throckton Company has been to a seminar on CVP analysis and wants to use some of the techniques she learned. She gives you the following data and asks that you analyze each cost into its fixed and variable components. She plans to use the information for profit planning. You prepare the following schedules of costs and measures of activity for the previous six months.

| Sales | Labor Hours | Production Costs | Selling Expenses | Administrative Expenses |
|---|---|---|---|---|
| $12,000 | 500 | $ 9,100 | $3,250 | $3,200 |
| 10,000 | 700 | 11,000 | 2,980 | 3,300 |
| 21,000 | 1,200 | 14,300 | 4,130 | 4,100 |
| 30,000 | 1,300 | 15,300 | 4,950 | 4,500 |
| 33,000 | 900 | 11,980 | 5,370 | 4,300 |
| 35,000 | 800 | 11,200 | 5,560 | 4,800 |

**Required**

Analyze the cost behavior patterns in accordance with the request of the controller. Determine the most likely driver for each cost.

**3-40  Selecting a regression equation (Appendix)**  The controller's office is trying to develop cost estimating equations for planning and control. One of your assistants has performed regression analyses on two possible drivers of power cost. The first equation used direct labor hours as the independent variable.

$$Y = \$182,938 + \$0.5612X, \ r^2 = 0.2691, \ S_e = \$79,982$$
$$Y = \text{monthly power costs}, \ X = \text{labor hours}$$

The second equation used machine hours as the independent variable.

$$Y = \$61,122 + \$1.4651X, \ r^2 = 0.7314, \ S_e = \$8,982$$
$$Y = \text{monthly power costs}, \ X = \text{machine hours}$$

The number of labor hours per month runs between 15,000 and 25,000. The number of machine hours is between 70,000 and 125,000, depending on the mix of products being made.

The controller hopes that this preliminary study will show that regression is a feasible tool for developing cost-estimating equations. She has asked you for a memo indicating which equation to use, and whether it will do the job. After she has read your memo you will meet with her to discuss the results.

**Required**

Write a memorandum to the controller. Justify your recommendation. Use the guidelines in Appendix B.

**3-41  Value-adding and non-value-adding activities and costs**  MUL Company manufactures six types of products. The products are relatively standard, not made-to-order. MUL takes orders from customers, then fills the orders from stock or manufactures the required units. The company keeps finished units in a warehouse that it also uses for materials and components.  The Quality Control Division inspects all shipments of materials and components, as well as all finished products before they are shipped.

The company holds a two- to three-month supply of parts and components that it uses to make high-volume products. MUL's purchasing manager is responsible for obtaining materials and components at the lowest possible cost and so scours the country looking for the best deals. MUL therefore uses a good many vendors.

Production begins by withdrawing the necessary materials and components from the warehouse, inspecting them for possible deterioration during storage, and transporting them to the first station that works on the product. Each station does one function, such as drilling, planing, welding, and various assembly operations.

Each station has an area to store materials and components for jobs that it has not yet started. The materials wait in the area until the station is ready to begin the job. Setup time in going from one product to another is often substantial at some stations. After the workers at the station have finished with their part of the job, they send the semi-completed units along with the materials and components not yet installed to the next station. There the same process is repeated and so on until all work is completed. In some cases, a job will go to the same station more than once because it requires the same operation at different stages of production.

At the conclusion of production, units go to the Quality Control Division to await testing and inspection. They then go to the warehouse for shipment. The company usually makes 10% more units than needed for an order to allow for defects. Any spare good units are held in the warehouse until another order arrives. Defective units are sometimes reworked and sometimes sold as scrap. Reworked units are stored in the warehouse. If it is possible to determine which work station caused the defect, its manager is held responsible. (Bonuses for station managers are based largely on total good output.) In cases where it is not possible to determine the source of the defect, no one is held responsible.

The factory manager has said that "it gets pretty hectic at the end of each month when we're trying to finish up jobs and get the stuff out to the warehouse."

The cycle time varies among types of products, but runs from 10 days to 45 days depending on various factors.

### Required

What activities described above do not add value to products? What changes in operations can you recommend?

## Chapter Four

# ACTIVITY-BASED COSTING AND MANAGEMENT

## LEARNING OBJECTIVES

*After reading this chapter, you should be able to*

- *Explain and illustrate the traditional method of calculating average costs of products.*
- *Explain why the traditional method does not adequately serve modern organizations.*
- *Explain how complexity and diversity are important cost drivers.*
- *Explain and illustrate the activity-based costing method of calculating average costs of products.*
- *Explain and illustrate activity-based management.*
- *Prepare ABC-formatted income statements.*

*Amazon.com*, the world's largest bookstore, operates solely on the Internet. Amazon.com charges $3.95 shipping and handling for the first item a customer orders and $0.95 for each additional item. Most companies charge shipping and handling based on the dollar value of the order, not the number of items. For instance, **L. L. Bean**, in its Spring 1998 catalog, charged $3.50 on orders up to $25, $5.50 on orders up to $75, and $7.50 on orders over $75. Suppose that both Amazon.com and L. L. Bean want the shipping and handling charge to cover costs of filling and shipping the order. What are those costs? Someone must process the order, someone must pick out the items for the order, someone must pack the order, and finally, someone must ship it. The companies must also pay the shipper, often **UPS**. In this light, which method of charging, by item or by dollar value, makes more sense to you? What are some alternative ways to charge? We shall return to this question later in the chapter.

Managers are always concerned about the profitability of segments of their organizations. Such segments include product lines, geographical areas, types of customers, and services. To analyze profitability, managers need estimates of the total costs of the segments. A manufacturer of several products wants to know which products are the most profitable and which are the least profitable. On the basis of profitability analyses, managers might decide to drop some products, raise the prices of others, and increase promotional efforts on still others.

Managers of banks need to know whether providing free checking accounts increases profits. Wholesalers and distributors are interested in whether they should continue to serve all of their customers or whether they should drop some, and what kinds of customers they should try to acquire in the future.

Estimating the variable costs of such segments requires using techniques discussed in Chapter 3. But estimates of total costs of segments must also include estimates of fixed costs. Again, as Chapter 3 showed, managers can often estimate the amounts of direct fixed costs associated with particular segments. But Chapter 3 did not explore the question of how to associate indirect fixed costs with such segments as products. Estimating fixed costs associated with segments is the principal focus of this chapter. In the past, companies found the cost driver with which variable costs varied most closely and used that driver to estimate the fixed costs of individual segments.

## THE TRADITIONAL APPROACH

Historically, managers have been most concerned with estimating the total costs of manufactured products and, for convenience, we shall discuss the traditional techniques in that context. Please bear in mind that our discussion applies also to service and merchandising organizations. For many years, companies developed and refined cost-estimation methods, and they typically associated indirect fixed costs with products through an allocation process that employed the medium of an input factor. Recall from Chapter 3 that manufacturers of diverse products do not reasonably expect a significant amount of overhead costs to vary with the number of units produced. An appliance maker will build refrigerators and toasters, which require vastly different quantities of input factors. We also discussed in Chapter 3 the concept of a cost driver, an activity that generates costs. For many years, manufacturers used a single driver, typically direct labor hours or machine hours, to allocate overhead costs to products. Examples of cost drivers include direct labor hours, machine hours, and the quantity of raw materials processed. Costs that are indirect to products are by definition not traceable directly and unequivocally to those products. Costs that are indirect to products are nonetheless direct to *some* activity (after all, there is some underlying reason for the cost), so the task was to select the activity with which costs most closely related and assign costs to products based on their relative use of the activity. Chapter 3 was largely about how companies determine just what activities drive what costs. For example, we found that some manufacturing overhead costs are associated with machine hours. The more machines run, the higher are costs such as maintenance and power. Consequently, assigning such costs to products based on the machine time they use makes sense. The problem for many years was that companies assigned virtually all of their indirect manufacturing costs on labor hours or machine hours.

The process is very simple. Compute an average overhead rate per direct labor (or machine) hour by dividing total overhead cost by total hours. Then multiply this rate by the number of hours spent on each product and assign that amount to the product. Each product then received its proportionate share of overhead cost based on its relative use of the cost driver.

For example, suppose a company makes two products, A and B, and believes that machine hours drive overhead costs. Data are:

|  | A | B | Total |
|---|---|---|---|
| Machine hours per unit | 2 | 4 |  |
| Total units | 100,000 | 25,000 |  |
| Total hours | 200,000 | 100,000 | 300,000 |
| Total overhead cost |  |  | $900,000 |

The overhead rate is $3, $900,000/300,000, and the allocations of overhead to products are:

|  | A | B | Total |
|---|---|---|---|
| Total hours | 200,000 | 100,000 | 300,000 |
| Rate | × $3 | × $3 | × $3 |
| Total overhead | $600,000 | $300,000 | $900,000 |

You can also see that each unit of Product A is allocated $6 (2 hours × $3) and each unit of B $12 (4 × $3). Managers would then use these numbers to set prices and make various other decisions. Of course, they would use variable costs to make short-term decisions about increasing or decreasing volume, but for longer-term decisions they would use average total costs. Such allocations worked well for many years, but problems arose.

## ACTIVITY-BASED COSTING APPROACH

From Chapter 3 we know that many activities drive costs. Volume is one major driver, measured either in output (units produced) or input (labor hours, machine hours, etc). Accountants today recognize two other major influences on cost: complexity and diversity of operations. As a company's products become more complicated, having more parts and requiring more operations, costs will increase even though total output does not increase. Similarly, if a company increases the variety of its product offerings, costs will increase even if total output remains constant. That is, complexity and diversity of operations drive costs just as does volume. Activity-based costing seeks to estimate the costs of products (and other segments) by estimating the costs of many activities and in turn using those estimates to estimate the costs of products by reference to how much of the activity each product uses. ABC is concerned with resource consumption. It provides a way to trace resource consumption to products and other segments.

## COMPLEXITY AND DIVERSITY AS COST DRIVERS

Let's consider a few examples. First, assuming that you will take a 15-hour class load, would you prefer to take five 3-hour classes or 15 one-hour classes? Clearly, taking 15 subjects would be much harder and more time-consuming than taking five subjects, even though the total amount of material covered would be about the same. The complexity and diversity of the 15 classes would impose much greater time requirements than the 5 classes, not to mention the financial and physical demands of buying and carrying more books.

In a business context, imagine two manufacturers of bricks. UniBrick makes 10,000,000 red bricks of a single size, shape, and texture and sells them all to a few customers. *All* of UniBrick's costs relate to its one product and volume is the principal, and perhaps the only, cost driver. MultiBrick also makes 10,000,000 total bricks, but in a dozen colors, four textures, and eight sizes/shapes, a total of 384 (12 × 4 × 8) possibilities. MultiBrick mixes and bakes 10 to 18 batches of bricks per day. Some batches are relatively small, some large, but each batch requires changing and cleaning molds, getting the required materials from storage, and adjusting oven temperatures. MultiBrick sells to over 1,000 customers, whose orders typically include 15 to 20 different kinds of bricks.

 MultiBrick's much more complex and diverse operation generates higher costs than UniBrick. MultiBrick's office deals with many more customers, increasing its costs of order-taking, billing, credit-checking, collection, and customer service. MultiBrick's shipping department incurs higher costs because making up an order requires picking up and taking to the shipping dock various quantities of several kinds of bricks. A forklift truck must find 15 to 20 types of bricks and pick up the correct quantities of each. It must make several stops to pick up each order, and probably must make more trips to fill orders than would a truck at UniBrick that goes to a single location and loads up.

 Manufacturing operations also will differ. Because it makes varying quantities of many types of bricks, MultiBrick must carefully schedule production to be sure of getting the right quantities of each type of brick its customers require. MultiBrick needs skilled people to determine the best production schedule, communicate that schedule to the factory floor, monitor actual progress, and record results.

 MultiBrick must change over from making one type of brick to another 10 to 18 times a day. These changeovers, or setups, can be very costly. Workers in MultiBrick must clean the old color out of the vats, then mix and pour the new color. They must change molds if they change the sizes of the bricks. They must change the recipe to accommodate different textures and must get the appropriate ingredients from storage. All of these activities require people and add to costs. UniBrick has no such costs because it cranks out its one model all day long.

 MultiBrick must stock several pigments, rather than one, and several grades of clay. Because it must take care not to run out of any given ingredient, it must keep much more inventory than UniBrick. MultiBrick therefore needs more storage space, which increases occupancy costs, more people to monitor and move inventory, more purchase orders, and so on. Failure to perform these activities could result in the inability to meet customers' orders promptly, which could lose sales. MultiBrick will have more idle time and be less efficient than UniBrick. MultiBrick will probably have more scrap and more defective bricks because it must change operations so often.

 Even though both companies have the same sales and production volumes, MultiBrick's total costs will exceed UniBrick's because so many of MultiBrick's costs will be driven by activities other than volume. The numbers of setups, production orders, sales orders, and other non-volume activities will drive significant amounts of cost. UniBrick's costs will probably vary only with volume. Of course, despite its higher costs, MultiBrick can still be profitable, perhaps more profitable than UniBrick; MultiBrick is likely to command higher prices for its speciality bricks than UniBrick can for its one model. The accompanying Insight tells of one company's recognition of the costs of complexity and its response.

## ADVANTAGES OF ABC

From a managerial accounting perspective, the significance of diversity and complexity as cost drivers is that managers cannot use a single, volume-based

**SIGHT**

### Reducing Complexity at Carrier Corporation

**Carrier Corporation** is the world's largest maker of heating and air conditioning equipment. Its objectives include providing its customers high quality, innovative products that will differentiate it from competitors and at a low cost with zero defects. Carrier's management recognized that reaching these objectives required that it reduce the complexity of its operations because complexity increased costs. Complexity was one of Carrier's principal drivers of costs and reducing it was the common thread across its strategic initiatives. These initiatives included JIT, product and process standardization, and careful management of the value chain.

The company adopted ABC and used it to manage its program to reduce complexity. Carrier classifies all batch-related and product-sustaining costs as costs of complexity. The company has developed measures that reflect how much complexity it has removed, such as the number of common product components it uses (as opposed to special components that appear in only one or a few products). The company has Cost of Complexity teams, uses Complexity Reduction Forms, and keeps a Complexity Reduction Log.

Carrier uses ABC analyses to determine how much it has saved from completed efforts and could save from additional initiatives. Managers believe that quantifying the potential benefits of reducing complexity makes operating managers more likely to undertake such projects.

*Source: Dan W. Swenson, "Managing Costs Through Complexity Reduction at Carrier Corporation,"* Management Accounting, *April 1998, 20–28.*

measure to determine overhead costs of individual products. *Of special importance is that using volume-based measures alone overcosts high-volume products and undercosts low-volume products.* Setup costs mount as changeovers increase, and setups increase as the company makes more low-volume products. One key to success for MultiBrick is reasonable estimates of the total costs that each of its products generates. Managers will use these estimates to make many decisions, including whether to drop some models from the line or emphasize some models over others. **National Semiconductor** eliminated nearly 45 percent of its product line after an ABC analysis showed these products contributing very little to overall profits.

Activity-based costing (ABC) developed as managers understood that low-volume products could be less profitable than they appeared, and high-volume products could be more profitable than they appeared. Under ABC, each product or other segment is apportioned costs based on its consumption of resources as indicated by the cost drivers. MultiBrick needs to develop costs for each of the principal activities that its individual bricks require.

Exhibit 4-1 shows how MultiBrick might determine manufacturing costs using the volume measure, number of bricks, as the sole driver. This analysis is repre-

---

### Exhibit 4-1   MultiBrick Cost Determination Data

Total manufacturing overhead:   $800,000
Total output:                    10,000,000 bricks

|                          | Model A-42 | Model A-88 | Model C-11 |
|--------------------------|-----------|-----------|-----------|
| Total production         | 6,000     | 4,000     | 100,000   |
| Material cost per brick  | $0.05     | $0.04     | $0.03     |
| Direct labor cost per brick | $0.06  | $0.07     | $0.04     |

Overhead rate  =  total manufacturing overhead costs/total units produced
               =  $800,000/10,000,000
               =  $0.08 per brick

Cost calculations:

|                          | Model A-42 | Model A-88 | Model C-11 |
|--------------------------|-----------|-----------|-----------|
| Material cost per brick  | $0.05     | $0.04     | $0.03     |
| Direct labor cost per brick | 0.06   | 0.07      | 0.04      |
| Overhead cost at $0.08   | 0.08      | 0.08      | 0.08      |
| Total unit cost          | $0.19     | $0.19     | $0.15     |

---

sentative of what companies did for many years prior to ABC. Models A-42 and A-88 are low-volume, specialty bricks, while Model C-11 is a high-volume brick. MultiBrick makes Model C-11 in long production runs. Model C-11 requires no special ingredients or special handling. The company molds the bricks in machines. MultiBrick makes Models A-42 and A-88 in short production runs, and each requires special ingredients, different oven temperatures and settings, and special hand molding. These three bricks are obviously not the only ones the company makes. We limit the example to three types for simplicity.

One major point to note about this traditional analysis is every brick carries the same overhead cost no matter what that brick contributes to costs. The low-volume, specialty bricks have the same $0.08 overhead cost as the high-volume bricks. This result is certainly counter-intuitive. The specialty bricks do show higher costs ($0.19 to $0.15), but only because their material and direct labor costs are higher.

## HOW COMPANIES MAKE ABC ESTIMATES

ABC introduces some new terms. One is **cost object**, which simply refers to whatever segment for which you are estimating the cost. Products are often cost objects, as are customers, geographical areas, and channels of distribution. We used the term *cost driver* in Chapter 3 and will use it again here. We also use the term **resource driver** to refer to activities that drive resource requirements, such as people, machinery, space, and utilities, and therefore drive costs. Finding such drivers usually involves finding out how people spend their time.

The resource driver, *process customer returns*, drives costs of receiving and handling the returned goods, inspecting the returned goods, reworking them if possible and putting them back into stock, issuing credit memos, making entries in the customers' accounts, and so on. People perform the functions listed above, but space is also required, as is equipment, such as handling equipment and computers. The accountant who identified processing returns as a driver probably interviewed people in several areas, including receiving, manufacturing, inventory control, and accounts receivable. She found that people in each area spent some time dealing with returns and therefore made it a separate driver.

An **activity driver** relates resource-driving activities to products, customers, geographical areas, or other segments of interest. Customer returns might be related to the number of returns a customer makes, the dollar amount of the returns, or a combination of the two factors.

ABC also requires that accountants identify *cost pools* related to each driver. In some cases, such pools might be made up of costs of a particular department, such as purchasing or personnel. But more often pools will be smaller than departments, particularly if departments perform several distinct activities. For instance, the number of purchase orders will probably drive some routine costs of a purchasing department. The number of vendors might drive other of the department's costs, as might the number of parts and components that the department orders. Finally, special orders will drive some costs, as for instance if someone orders a machine that the company has never before bought.

Accountants might determine what costs belong in what pools by interviewing managers. For example, a storeroom supervisor might tell you that two of his people spend 20 percent of their time checking incoming shipments of parts and components and the other 80 percent moving incoming parts and components into their proper storage places. Another worker might process requisitions of materials from the shop floor. Two other workers might spend all of their time moving components to the shop floor. From such conversations we could estimate the cost of each activity. We can treat checking incoming shipments and moving them into storage as either one activity or as two. How far we break down activities depends on whether further breaking down would likely provide information with more benefit than the additional cost. At some point we should stop decomposing activities.

Estimating ABC costs is a two-step process. First, you must identify resources, their drivers, and costs. Second, you must determine the amounts of activity that each cost object uses and assign costs accordingly. An example should make the principle clear.

MultiBrick's managers have identified three major resource drivers, baking bricks, setting up to change from one model to another, and production orders. (In real life the company would have many more drivers, but the principle would remain the same. We also limit this example to manufacturing costs, but the same analyses apply to selling and administrative expenses as well.) The managers have also determined the activity drivers and the quantities of each driver used by three models of bricks. (Again, the real company would have many more models, but the principles would still hold.) The managers have also determined the amounts of cost associated with each activity. The activity-based information appears in Exhibit 4-2, along with the quantities of each driver used by the three models.

Exhibit 4-3 shows the ABC cost calculations. Notice that we are still using the $800,000 total overhead. Using ABC does not change total costs, it only arranges them differently, by assigning them to bricks through activities other than vol-

## Exhibit 4-2   MultiBrick Data for Illustration

| Resource Driver | Costs in Pool | divided by | Total Amount of Driver | equals | Rate |
|---|---|---|---|---|---|
| Setups | $120,000 | / | 10,000 setups | = | $12 |
| Baking time | 600,000 | / | 300,000 hours | = | $2 |
| Customer orders | 80,000 | / | 5,000 orders | = | $16 |
| Total cost | $800,000 | | | | |

Activity data, per year:

| | Model A-42 | Model A-88 | Model C-11 |
|---|---|---|---|
| Number of setups | 150 | 180 | 30 |
| Baking time, hours | 60 | 50 | 300 |
| Number of customer orders | 30 | 40 | 20 |

Costs, excluding overhead:

| | Model A-42 | Model A-88 | Model C-11 |
|---|---|---|---|
| Material cost per brick | $0.05 | $0.04 | $0.03 |
| Direct labor cost per brick | 0.06 | 0.07 | 0.04 |

ume.  Note, however, that baking time is a volume-based driver.  ABC does not deny the importance of volume, ABC denies only that volume is the sole driver.

Exhibit 4-4 compares the total cost of each brick model using traditional analysis with the cost per brick using the ABC approach. An important question to consider is "why are the costs different under the two approaches?"

## Exhibit 4-3   ABC Analysis of Bricks

| | Model A-42 | Model A-88 | Model C-11 |
|---|---|---|---|
| Material cost* | $   300 | $   160 | $   3,000 |
| Direct labor cost** | 360 | 280 | 4,000 |
| Overhead: | | | |
| Setups based at | | | |
| $12 x 150, 180, 30 | 1,800 | 2,160 | 360 |
| Baking time at $2 x 60, 50, 300 | 120 | 100 | 600 |
| Customer order based | | | |
| at $16 x 30, 40, 20 | 480 | 640 | 320 |
| Total cost | $3,060 | $3,340 | $   8,280 |
| Divided by annual volume | 6,000 | 4,000 | 100,000 |
| Average cost per brick | $   0.51 | $0.835 | $   0.083 |

* $0.05 × 6,000, $0.04 × 4,000, $0.03 × 100,000
** $0.06 × 6,000, $0.07 × 4,000, $0.04 × 100,000

### Exhibit 4-4    Comparison of Traditional Costs and Activity-Based Costs

**Traditional Cost Approach**

|                  | Model A-42 | Model A-88 | Model C-11 |
|------------------|-----------:|-----------:|-----------:|
| Material cost    | $ 300      | $160       | $ 3,000    |
| Direct labor cost| 360        | 280        | 4,000      |
| Overhead cost    | 480        | 320        | 8,000      |
| Total cost       | $1,140     | $760       | $15,000    |

**Activity-Based Cost Approach**

|                  | Model A-42 | Model A-88 | Model C-11 |
|------------------|-----------:|-----------:|-----------:|
| Material cost    | $ 300      | $ 160      | $3,000     |
| Direct labor cost| 360        | 280        | 4,000      |
| Overhead cost    | 2,400      | 2,900      | 1,280      |
| Total cost       | $3,060     | $3,340     | $8,280     |

The answer to this question can be found in comparing consumption ratios. A **consumption ratio** is the resource utilized by a given product divided by the total amount of the resource available. For example, in the traditional cost approach overhead is assigned to each model based on the number of bricks produced. Since MultiBrick is producing a total of 10,000,000 bricks, the ratio of each model is:

*Model A-42:*     *6,000 bricks   /   10,000,000 total   =   0.06%*
*Model A-88:*     *4,000 bricks   /   10,000,000 total   =   0.04%*
*Model C-11:*   *100,000 bricks   /   10,000,000 total   =   1.00%*

Notice that Model A-42 is assigned 0.06% × $800,000 = $480 overhead. If, however, we look at the consumption ratios for the resources used to assign overhead costs under activity-based costing we see a very different pattern. Consumption ratios for the resource "number of setups" are:

*Model A-42:*     *150 setups   /   10,000 total     =   1.50%*
*Model A-88:*     *180 setups   /   10,000 total     =   1.80%*
*Model C-11:*      *30 setups   /   10,000 total     =   0.30%*

The amount of setup cost assigned to Model A-42 is 1.50% × $120,000 = $1,800. Consumption ratios for the resource "baking time" are:

*Model A-42:*     *60 hours   /   300,000 total   =   0.0200%*
*Model A-88:*     *50 hours   /   300,000 total   =   0.0167%*
*Model C-11:*   *300 hours   /   300,000 total   =   0.1000%*

The amount of baking cost assigned to Model A-42 is 0.02% × $600,000 = $120. Consumption ratios for the resource "customer orders" are:

| *Model A-42:* | *30 orders* | / | *5,000 total* | = | *0.60%* |
|---|---|---|---|---|---|
| *Model A-88:* | *40 orders* | / | *5,000 total* | = | *0.80%* |
| *Model C-11:* | *20 orders* | / | *5,000 total* | = | *0.40%* |

The amount of customer order cost assigned to Model A-42 is 0.60% × $80,000 = $480. The important thing to notice is the variation of the consumption ratios for a given line of bricks. The traditional costing approach does not recognize this variation. The traditional approach assumes that each product consumes all resources in one single proportion.

What is the significance of these differences? Many companies set prices based on costs, or at least consider costs in their pricing decisions. Virtually all companies analyze the profitability of products (and other segments). A company that uses the traditional approach will tend to set prices too high on its high-volume products and too low on its low-volume products. If the company does not have pricing discretion, that is, the market sets prices, profitability analyses will be misleading. Overcosted high-volume products will appear less profitable, while undercosted low-volume products will appear more profitable.

How might a company recognize that its existing cost system is providing misleading costs? Some signs of poor cost data are:[1]

- Competitors' prices for high-volume products appear much too low. "How can they be making money at that price when we are barely profitable at a higher price?"
- The company seems to have a highly profitable niche all to itself. No other company tries to compete with us on a low-volume product.
- Customers don't balk at price increases for low-volume products.
- Difficult to produce, pain-in-the-neck products that managers would like to drop show high profits.

Other counter-intuitive indications might crop up in a given situation. For instance, a distributor might have cost data indicating that small customers are more profitable than large ones. Such a conclusion is not surprising if costs of serving customers are allocated based on dollar sales, a common practice. But analyzing the activities necessary to serve customers should show that small customers generate much higher service costs than do large customers.

Although ABC developed in manufacturing environments, its principles also apply to merchandising and service. The accompanying Insight describes two such applications.

## ABC AND COST BEHAVIOR ANALYSIS

ABC is not a method of identifying fixed and variable components of costs. Rather, it is concerned with resource consumption, and therefore with long-term average costs. Unit costs developed using ABC should not be used to predict total costs at various levels of output in the short run. ABC is excellent for identifying long-term costs. For example, if the average annual cost of dealing with a vendor

---

1 Robin Cooper, *"You Need a New Cost System When . . . ,"* Harvard Business Review, *January–February 1989,* 77–82.

 **SIGHT**

### ABC in Service Organizations

Growth in the use of ABC in health maintenance organizations such as hospitals is partly the result of changes in programs such as Medicare and Medicaid. The rise of managed care, exemplified by HMOs, also contributed to increasing use. Such organizations now face payment systems based on Diagnosis Related Groups (DRGs). Under this system, hospitals are not reimbursed for the services they provide, but by a fee based on the patient's DRG. An appendectomy has a specific fee, as does a day in the Intensive Care Unit. Health care providers must now be on top of their costs to ensure that their revenues are sufficient for them to survive. Obviously, cost containment is critical, and ABC helps health care managers deploy resources successfully. For instance, some health care organizations have dropped procedures and activities that proved unprofitable.

One major reason for using ABC is the growing use of *capitation*, where an HMO or other provider bids a fixed per-person fee for the employees of an organization or other group. If the bid is accepted, the total fee then is the same regardless of what services each employee actually needs. In such an environment, cost management is critical and understanding cost drivers helps managers submit capitation bids that will ensure financial viability.

The Internal Revenue Service began a re-engineering/cost management program in the early 1990s. The IRS now uses ABC and related techniques we discuss later to improve its operations and reduce costs through a variety of initiatives. For instance, the IRS now offers electronic filing, where error rates are running about 0.5 percent, compared to 17 percent with paper returns.

*Sources: Timothy D. West and David A. West, "Applying ABC to Healthcare,"* Management Accounting, *February 1997, 22–33.*
*John B. MacArthur, "Cost Management at the IRS,"* Management Accounting, *November 1996, 42–48.*

is $12,324, we cannot say that adding one vendor will increase costs $12,324 per year, but we can say that as we add batches of vendors over time, the average cost increase might be about that. If we then plan new products or manufacturing processes and plan to add 20 vendors, our costs could increase by about $12,300 per vendor. Step-variable costs are common in ABC analysis. So cost reduction is not accomplished linearly, but in chunks, as a company either redeploys people or does not have to hire additional people as soon as it had thought it would. In the long run, companies can change the amount of capacity and personnel they need for such functions as purchasing, machine setups, and customer billing. Thus, costs that are fixed, in the sense of not changing automatically as volume changes in the short term, *will* change as managers adjust to resource requirements. Focusing attention on individual activities helps managers in many areas.

For instance, a design engineer revising the specifications of a product might incorporate a component the company does not now use. Unless the company uses ABC, it will not have a good estimate of the costs associated with introducing a new component and will be much less likely to question the designer's decision. Introducing that component will require that the purchasing department first find vendors who supply it, and then evaluate each potential vendor's prices, quality control, and ability to meet delivery schedules. The storeroom will allot space for the component, add the component to its list of stocked items, and probably generate other paperwork. Until the vendor has satisfied the company that the quality of the component is acceptable, the company will inspect incoming shipments. The data processing department must incorporate the component into whatever computer files are used by various departments. The accounts payable section will process more invoices and pay more bills. The company's internal auditors will have to count the component. In short, a seemingly simple change might send ripples of cost through many areas of the company, which, though relatively small, can accumulate as more and more such changes occur.

All of the costs described above must be considered in making such decisions. Evaluating the profitability of products or of geographical areas are examples of where ABC is helpful in identifying cost-driving activities. ABC thereby plays a role in cost reduction and continuous improvement which JIT operations pursue. Many companies use ABC as a competitive tool.  For instance, an ABC analysis could show customers that your product, though priced higher than the competition's, is less costly overall because of lower returns, quicker delivery, or smaller lots.

ABC also encompasses selling and administrative activities and costs.  Later in this book we shall illustrate how companies account for the costs of manufactured products for financial reporting and income tax purposes.   Selling and administrative costs do not enter into these calculations.  However, for the managerial purpose of analyzing the profitability of individual products or lines, all costs are relevant, not just manufacturing costs. The accompanying Insight describes different types of use of ABC at three large companies.

## KINDS OF VARIABILITY

Chapter 3 stated that some costs are variable with some activities, but not with others.  ABC distinguishes four major categories of activities and costs.

1.  **Unit-level activities** are those performed each time a unit is produced or sold.  The amount of the activity increases and decreases proportionately with unit volume.  The costs associated with these activities are the classic variable costs that we introduced in Chapter 2. Materials and components are one example.  Operations such as drilling or welding are another.

2.  **Batch-level activities** are those that a company performs when it makes a group of units, regardless of how many units are in the batch.  Machine setups are a good example. Many of these costs will vary with the number of batches, but some will be fixed over a wide relevant range.

3.  **Sustaining activities** arise because a company does particular types of business, or maintains a particular product or service.  Virtually all companies perform product-sustaining activities and incur related costs.  Product-sustaining activities and costs do not depend on the volume of production or sales of the particular product.  That is, they are fixed with respect to the volume of production. Such activities and costs include fixed manufacturing costs related to the product, advertising devoted to the product, and engineering and development related to the product.  Other types of sustaining

SIGHT

### Other Uses of ABC

**Stratus Computer** does not have a full-blown ABC system because a pilot study showed that such a system was not cost-effective. Nonetheless, the company has found that estimates of savings from buying parts, rather than manufacturing them, were often erroneous unless it applied ABC concepts. The problems arose principally because the variable overhead associated with parts was based on direct labor time, and all variable overhead elements were averaged across all parts and products using the direct labor base. One type of problem arose with parts that had especially long or especially short production runs. The former were overcosted and the latter undercosted by the use of averages. Parts with long production runs required less setup time, less inspection of first pieces to be sure settings were correct, and less production scheduling and control.

Additionally, ABC analyses showed that the company had previously misestimated costs associated with having longer lead times and lesser quality of parts made by outsiders. For instance, for some assemblies, Stratus shipped kits of parts to an outside contractor that did the assembly work, then sent the finished assembly back to Stratus. An ABC analysis showed that Stratus would benefit by paying the contractor to buy the parts itself, instead of Stratus buying the parts and shipping them to the assembler. The traditional system indicated that Stratus's overhead rate for materials was about 10 percent, but an activity-based analysis showed that avoidable costs were far more than 10 percent of material costs.

**Weyerhauser** uses ABC throughout the organization for various purposes. The company used ABC to make its payroll operation more efficient, reducing expected annual costs by over half a million dollars. The payroll operation provides services for 16,000 employees, about 14,000 salaried and the rest hourly. The department provides several major services ranging from producing payroll checks to processing employee stock options. Among the activities of the department are such diverse items as updating employee records, coordinating direct bank deposits, and preparing state and federal tax reports.

Among the actions taken to reduce costs were to reduce the number of reports, process special paychecks less frequently, and use the same time period for all hourly employees. Weyerhauser took these and other steps after a careful activity analysis that included asking employees of the payroll department to indicate how much time they spent with each of some 70 activities.

**Carolina Power and Light** (CP&L) studied activities related to planned outages, times when the company deliberately shuts down power-generating plants. The company once hired outside contractors to do a great deal of the work involved with these outages. A few years ago, the company began rotating employees from one plant to another during planned outages. Doing so resulted in hiring fewer outside contractors, doing higher-quality work, and broadening the skills of employees. CP&L also uses self-directed work teams, which reduces the need for supervision.

Sources: Mark Boisoneault, "Activity-Based Costing for Make/Buy Decisions at Stratus Computer," Target, March/April 1992, 20–24.
R. Brian Pederson, "Weyerhauser: Streamlining Payroll," Management Accounting, October 1991, 38–41.

activities include capacity-sustaining, customer-sustaining, distribution-channel sustaining, and geographical area-sustaining. The number of sustaining activities an organization performs depends on how much attention it must devote to the entities with which it does business and the ways in which it does business. **Barnes and Noble** sells books in retail stores and also over the Internet, while **Amazon.com** sells only over the Internet. Some mail-order companies take orders only by telephone, while some also use the Internet. Some operate retail outlets, some do not. Each company will have costs associated with each channel and each can analyze its channel-sustaining activities and costs to determine whether to continue using those channels, whether to emphasize one or another channel, or whether to offer customers incentives to use one channel vis-à-vis others. Stockbrokers charge much lower commissions to customers who place orders over the Internet than to those who telephone orders to offices.

4. **Facility-sustaining** or **company-sustaining activities** and costs relate to an entire plant, office, or company as a whole. Rent of the corporate headquarters building is a good example.

ABC authorities differ on estimating the facility-sustaining costs that a product should bear. Some believe that including such costs is unwise because they are so indirect. Few authorities advocate using company-sustaining costs in the estimations for the same reason. Nonetheless, companies do include all such costs in their ABC estimates.[2] The amounts of such costs are often relatively low, so significant differences are unlikely.

The above distinctions among costs help managers make decisions that involve more than just volume changes. In Chapter 2 we were content to pose questions such as, "Should we increase advertising in order to increase unit sales?" The Chapter 2 solution was, in the absence of complicating factors, simple: multiply contribution margin per unit by the expected increase in volume. If the additional contribution margin exceeds the increased advertising cost, go ahead. This simple analysis is fine so long as all cost variability is unit-based. Traditional methods assumed that virtually all variable overhead cost was unit-based. The simple analysis will not work if batch-level costs are significant. We would also have to know how many batches of the additional units we would have to make before we could reach a decision. If production scheduling was such that we would need to make a great many batches, the batch-level costs could overwhelm the expected contribution margin.

ABC also explains much of the uneasiness that managers have experienced over the years when they looked only at unit-based variable costs. For many years, accountants and other managers have introduced fudge factors to recognize that decisions were likely to increase costs by more than the associated unit-based variable costs. Managers knew that product-sustaining costs grew over time, as companies brought out new products. They knew that having more products and adding more suppliers led to increased costs for changeovers, record-keeping, receiving, and purchasing. But because such costs were not directly related to changes in unit volume, managers had no systematic way to incorporate them into their analyses.

---

2 Robin Cooper, "Cost Classification in Unit-Based and Activity-Based Manufacturing Systems," Journal of Cost Management for the Manufacturing Industry, *Fall 1990, 4–14.*

Let us now return to the vignette at the beginning of the chapter. We posed the question whether charging for shipping and handling on a per-item basis made more or less sense than charging by the dollar value of the order. We believe that **Amazon.com's** method of charging $3.95 for the first item and $0.95 thereafter makes more sense. The question is, what drives order-filling and handling costs? In all likelihood, companies incur some costs simply processing an order. Orders generate records, perhaps credit checks, invoices, and shipping labels, no matter how many items or how much dollar value. An employee must set up the box to pack the order, attach the shipping label, and send the filled box to be shipped. Other costs, perhaps the larger part of total costs, relate to people who go from shelf to shelf to pick articles for the order. These costs almost certainly depend more on the number of picks than on the dollar value of the items picked. A $150 art book is no more difficult to pick and pack than a $30 dictionary. One alternative is to charge by weight. Because books weigh quite different amounts, Amazon.com might lose out on actual shipping costs (such as UPS charges) on heavy books, while clothing sellers probably do not because clothes do not vary much in weight. This aside, the per-item charge still seems superior, based on our hypothetical ABC analysis.

So why do companies still charge based on dollar value of orders? Such charges are convenient, easy to compute, and customers are familiar with them. Recall that **L. L. Bean's** charges increase less than proportionally with the increase in the value of the order. This characteristic is common to most mail-order operations. This aspect of the charge encourages customers to order fewer times, but more items at a time. So does Amazon.com's $3.95 charge for the first item.

## ABC AND ETHICS

Because some costs are on the borderline between being direct or indirect to a product or line, managerial accountants must use some judgment in assigning costs to products. Whenever decisions involve judgment, the potential for an ethical conflict exists. For example, managers responsible for products want to keep their costs low and might pressure accountants to treat particular costs as common costs on the income statements for their products. Suppose a product manager, who is also a friend, argues that you should not include a particular cost in the *line's* income statement because the cost cannot be controlled. You then have an ethical conflict: should you treat the cost as common even though you believe it belongs with direct costs? The IMA's Standards of Ethical Conduct, page 15, show that the need for management accountants to maintain professional objectivity outweighs feelings of loyalty to a friend.

## ACTIVITY-BASED MANAGEMENT

As we have seen already, insights gained by ABC have led managers down several fruitful paths. One logical outgrowth of ABC is activity-based management (ABM). ABM, as the term suggests, is using information about activities to manage many aspects of an organization, rather than simply managing costs. ABM requires information about activities that goes beyond what is required for ABC. ABM typically focuses on processes, and on tasks and activities within processes. ABM consists of analyzing activities, ferreting out opportunities for improvement, and exploiting those opportunities. ABM includes identifying value-adding and non-value-adding activities within processes. It also includes increasing the efficiency of value-adding activities and determining how to eliminate non-value-adding activities. ABM also includes cross-functional analyses aimed at finding needless duplications of effort and gaps in effort. For instance, a company might have several organizational units dealing with the same suppliers or customers. Several units might duplicate each others' training programs.

ABM information does not necessarily lead to changes in estimates of product costs or costs of other segments. ABM might stop short of such estimates because it is concerned with the management of processes, not products. An ABM analysis applies wholly to the examined set of activities, without necessarily linking those activities with products or other segments. In other words, although an ABM analysis of the accounts payable process might have implications for certain products (perhaps ones using special components from special vendors) the analysis need not go beyond the simple question of how the accounts payable function might be improved. The term **re-engineering** describes developing new ways to perform existing activities and ways to stop performing non-value-adding activities. Descriptions of re-engineering efforts often occupy considerable space in annual reports.

**Benchmarking** is often an important part of an ABM project. To determine whether you are performing a task efficiently you must have some idea of what "efficient" is. Companies that use benchmarking often look to the best practices of industry leaders. For example, **L. L. Bean**, the mail-order retailer, was for many years epitomized as the best company in the land at filling customer orders. Bean filled orders quickly, and with very, very few errors. Other companies studied Bean not only to gain insights into the best ways to fill orders, but also to develop benchmarks regarding the time to fill an order, error rates, time to ship an order, and so on. **Carolina Power and Light** began a benchmarking program that included goals related to operating costs, safety, sales growth, customer satisfaction, and return to shareholders.

The results of ABM should include better understanding of processes, which should in turn lead to improvements in operating the processes, both through reduced costs and better service. For instance, reducing the time required to process accounts payable will improve relations with vendors. Because an ABM project necessarily includes people from several areas of an organization, it fosters cross-functional cooperation and communication. When people see how activities in one area affect other areas, they gain useful perspective. Often people in one area have little or no idea how their actions might affect people in other areas.

In fact, one reason for the rapidly growing interest in ABC and ABM is that traditional accounting systems focused on factory departments, such as machining, milling, and assembly, and on non-manufacturing departments, such as marketing and finance. Consequently, managers did not have information about how their decisions affected others in the organization. We discussed this point as early as Chapter 1. Thus, engineers submitted change orders without knowing how much they were increasing manufacturing costs. Salespeople garnered new customers without reference to their likely profitability. **General Electric** (GE) was an early user of ABC/ABM techniques, which it called "activity cost analysis." GE was motivated by the inability to trace the impact of decisions through the affected departments.

One common cross-departmental problem arises when purchasing managers seek out opportunities to buy large quantities of a material or component at less-than-normal prices. But the savings in purchase price might be more than offset by increased costs in other areas. Large orders flowing into the receiving department could clog up its work flow, delay processing and storage of other materials and components, and require pulling workers from other areas to cope with the arrival of a large order. The manager of the storage area might have to move other materials to accommodate the large orders, and might even have to acquire outside storage space. Material kept in storage might deteriorate.

## PROCESS VALUE ANALYSIS (PVA)

PVA is another tool that uses activity analysis to manage costs. PVA focuses on manufacturing processes and seeks to reduce or optimize the activities performed within a process. PVA examines the conditions that drive the need for specific activities. PVA seeks out underlying drivers of cost and stresses the value-adding, non-value-adding categories. One objective of PVA is to reduce activities and costs through understanding, managing, and eliminating such underlying drivers, or root causes, of activities and costs. These root causes can be external to the company or can be managerial policies. They need not be quantifiable, such as material moves.

For an example of an underlying driver, ask: What drives supervisory costs? One answer is the number of supervisors; a better answer is the number of workers under supervision, because companies often maintain a specific ratio of workers to supervisors (such as one supervisor for every 20 workers). But those answers are superficial. Instead of asking, in effect, how many supervisors do we need, we could ask: Why do we have supervisors at all? Answers to this question could include because workers do not always know what to do; or because workers need training, motivation, guidance, and direction; because workers are lazy and will not work unsupervised. All of these answers are degrading to workers who, research has shown, will perform quite well when conditions are favorable. One favorable condition is control over the job, the ability to decide what to do and when to do it. Job control, often called *empowerment*, is at the heart of JIT manufacturing cells. **Mercedes Benz** empowered its workers a few years ago in response to problems with quality. The company eliminated supervisors and now workers make all decisions and are also accountable for performance.

Other examples of underlying drivers include poor plant layout, which generates handling costs and other inefficiencies; poor quality of materials and parts; and poorly designed products. PVA thus focuses on activities in a different way from that which ABC uses, and also focuses on different activities.[3]

PVA requires careful documentation of the activities and flows within each process, generally using flowcharts that detail carefully how products (or other work such as insurance claims or college applications) move through. The team of analysts also relates the activities of the process to the customers' requirements. That step helps the team identify activities as value-adding or non-value-adding.

---

3 *Excellent sources for PVA are: Michael R. Ostrenga, "Activities: The Focal Point of Total Cost Management,"* Management Accounting, *February 1990, 42–49 and Michael R. Ostrenga and Frank R. Probst, "Process Value Analysis: The Missing Link in Cost Management,"* Journal of Cost Management, *Fall 1992, 4–13.*

The team must also determine the root causes of activities, the underlying drivers. Often this step takes a question-and-answer format repeatedly asking "why?" until the root cause has been determined. "Why do we have one supervisor for every ten workers?" "Because one person can only supervise ten others." "What is there about the work that requires supervision?" "The workers cannot solve all of the problems themselves." "Is that because they are lazy, insufficiently trained, or what?" "Well, some of each, I guess." From such examinations can come insights into deeper problems with managerial policies and attitudes. PVA also develops performance measures that alert managers to how well activities are carried out within processes. These measures can be financial but are often nonfinancial, such as percentages of defects, percentage of on-time delivery, or number of non-standard parts in a new product design.

## CAVEATS

ABM does not automatically produce results. Organizations cannot reduce costs until they reduce, or eliminate, the underlying activities. Managers must be careful to avoid a variety of pitfalls. Companies that use teams consisting only of finance and accounting people rarely get the results they expect. Cross-functional teams are necessary to develop accurate pictures of operations and to convince other managers that an ABM analysis is not just an accounting project. Teams must also talk with the people directly responsible for activities, workers and supervisors, not just higher-level managers. Teams must avoid the temptation to overcomplicate the analysis by selecting too many cost drivers. They should look at all activities and costs, not just manufacturing.[4]

Introducing an ABC/ABM system is a major organizational change, and success or failure depends on several factors. One study concluded that the support of top management is important, along with employee involvement in the implementation of this system. People were more satisfied with their systems when the objectives of the system were clearly stated, when they received appropriate training with the system, and when the system was linked to performance evaluation.[5]

Some advocates of ABM are uneasy with the "value-adding" and "non-value-adding" classification of activities and their related costs. Their point is that identifying what people performing a specific task do as non-value-adding is unlikely to raise their morale and increase their commitment and productivity. Picture your response to someone telling you that your efforts do not add value. Moreover, these advocates argue that separating activities into the two categories is at best arbitrary at the edges. Virtually everyone agrees that time products spend waiting to be worked on is not value-adding; products sitting around are not becoming more valuable. But once we go past such obvious activities, the going gets much tougher. How does processing accounts payable add value to a product? What customer cares how well you process payables? But processing payables is necessary to stay in business. So processing payables is value-adding in the sense that staying in business makes it possible for the company to create

4  R. Steve Player, "The Top Ten Things That Can Go Wrong with an ABM Project (And How to Avoid Them)," *As Easy As ABC, Summer 1993, 1–2.*
5  *Annie S. McGowan and Thomas P. Klammer, "Satisfaction with Activity-Based Cost Management Implementation,"* Journal of Management Accounting Research, *vol 9, 1997, 217–37.*

value for its customers. Of course, reducing the time and resources required to process payables is a worthwhile objective, as we noted previously.

## ABC/ABM AND WORLD-CLASS MANUFACTURING

ABC is most beneficial for companies with a great deal of complexity and diversity in their products and operations. JIT functions best when a company can use manufacturing cells to make standard products. Because JIT cells make many costs direct to products, a JIT operation need not use ABC for analyzing products because the amount of cost to be treated using ABC is relatively small. Nonetheless, JIT operations can use ABC to analyze customers, distribution channels, or other segments.

ABC supports many other new management philosophies, including Total Quality Management (TQM) and continuous improvement. ABC is invaluable in identifying costs that are related to quality, which we consider in more detail in Chapter 16. By developing cost pools driven by efforts to increase quality, or by failure to achieve acceptable quality (including warranty costs, and perhaps even estimates of customer ill will), ABC provides a starting point for managers to select areas where improvements are most likely to have significant economic effects. ABC also helps managers set goals for improvement, such as reducing the costs of inspection by a given percentage or so that companies can see tangible progress toward TQM.

Continuous improvement is often a matter of reducing or eliminating batch-level activities and associated costs. Toyota generally receives credit as the originator of JIT, and as the company that pioneered efforts at reducing setup time. The less the batch-level activities and costs, the more flexible the company becomes, with all of the attendant benefits. More flexible companies have greatly reduced cycle times. They are able to respond quickly to customer orders, produce small lots at the same unit cost as larger lots, and offer a wider product line without increasing the costs of diversity and complexity. If MultiBrick, our earlier example, could change over from one type to another with little time and cost, it would be in a much better competitive position. It could charge lower prices (or earn higher profits at the same prices), meet customer orders more quickly (making customers happier), and produce and sell more bricks with the same size plant.[6]

The accompanying Insight describes some examples of organizations paring down activities, gaining focus, and improving operations. Some examples relate to reducing complexity, including complexity of support activities. ABC is not just for manufacturing.

## ABC/ABM ANALYSIS AND INCOME REPORTING

Chapter 3 introduced the concepts of committed/discretionary, direct/indirect, and avoidable/unavoidable fixed costs. These concepts are important in evaluating products, product lines, geographical areas, and other activities, or segments,

---

6 *Peter B. B. Turney and James M. Reeve, "The Impact of Continuous Improvement on the Design of Activity-Based Cost Systems,"* Journal of Cost Management, *Summer 1990, 43–50.*

 **SIGHT**

### Simplifying Operations

In the mid-1990s, **Procter & Gamble**, the consumer-products behemoth, began a program to pare down its product offerings, standardize its products, and reduce trade promotions and coupons. The company once offered 31 versions of Head & Shoulders shampoo and 52 varieties of Crest. P&G is "hacking away at layers of complexity in a drive to cut costs, serve customers better, and expand globally." For example, the company has found that reducing special price promotions has reduced the percentage of customer invoices requiring manual correction from 31 to 6 percent.

After **Whirlpool** acquired European appliance maker **Philips**, it began reducing the number of parts in its appliances. Philips had allowed its subsidiaries to make their own models in every European country, so shared parts were minimal. By standardizing products, thereby reducing product diversity, the company was able to save $400 million annually, reduce the number of suppliers from 1,600 to 800, reduce the number of warehouses from 36 to 16, and cut inventories by one-third.

**Chrysler** learned that new model introductions are major cost drivers, partly because the company is slower than other automakers to retool its factories. On learning about its relative slowness, the company developed a program to shorten the required time. Designing these expensive tools once took 30 months, but Chrysler has cut the time to 24 months and expects to reduce it further.

*Sources: Zachary Schiller, et. al., "Make It Simple,"* Business Week, *September 9, 1996, 96–104.*
*Patrick Oster and John Rossant, "Call It Worldpool,"* Business Week, *November 28, 1994.*
*Neal Templin, "Chrysler Designs A Computer-Aided Manufacturing Plan,"* The Wall Street Journal, *August 2, 1995, B3.*

of a company. The classification of a particular cost depends on the segment being examined. For example, nationwide advertising for a product line is discretionary, avoidable, and direct to the line. But the cost is indirect and unavoidable to any particular geographical region. Similarly, regional advertising promoting several product lines is discretionary, direct, and avoidable to the region, but is indirect and unavoidable to any single line. Nonetheless, because managers can include or exclude any line of products from a particular advertisement, an ABC estimate of the advertising cost of each line is perfectly reasonable (as a product-sustaining cost).

The importance of a particular classification, such as direct or avoidable, depends on the purpose of the analysis. If a manager is trying to decide whether to drop a segment (a product, a line, or a region), the important issue is whether a cost is avoidable. If the manager is assessing a segment's profitability, then avoidability is important, but it is also important to know whether a cost is direct or indirect to that segment. Decisions to drop segments are multifaceted and are

CHAPTER
5

discussed in detail in Chapter 5. Our focus here is on developing information that will help managers evaluate segments.

Exhibit 4-5 shows one type of segmented income statement for Patterson Homewares, which makes three general types of products. The statement has three important subtotals: unit-level contribution margin, batch-level contribution margin, and product margin. Generally speaking, a segment with a negative contribution margin, either unit-level or batch-level, is unprofitable and a candidate for immediate divestiture. A segment with a negative product margin is not profitable in the long-term, and is a candidate for gradual liquidation.

Because Flooring has a relatively low product margin, Patterson might begin to explore alternatives. Dropping Flooring would not result in an immediate loss of $11.5 thousand. The loss would be higher because some of the product-sustaining costs are avoidable. The company would lose the $100.7 thousand batch-level contribution margin.

Other formats are possible, depending on the intended use. For example, a manager might wish to separate avoidable and unavoidable product-sustaining costs. We would calculate revenue less all avoidable costs if we were deciding whether to drop a product immediately.

---

**Exhibit 4-5    Patterson Homewares Income Statement**

**Patterson Homewares, Inc.**
**Income Statement for 20X2, in thousands**

|  | Flooring | Tile | Carpet | Total |
|---|---|---|---|---|
| Sales | $300.4 | $503.5 | $623.3 | $1,427.2 |
| Unit-level variable costs | 190.1 | 161.1 | 249.3 | 600.5 |
| Unit-level contribution margin | $110.3 | $342.4 | $374.0 | $ 826.7 |
| Batch-level variable costs | 9.6 | 26.4 | 52.8 | 88.8 |
| Batch-level contribution margin | $100.7 | $316.0 | $321.2 | $ 737.9 |
| Product-sustaining costs | 89.2 | 56.7 | 73.7 | 219.6 |
| Product margin | $ 11.5 | $259.3 | $247.5 | $ 518.3 |
| Facility-sustaining costs |  |  |  | 220.5 |
| Income |  |  |  | $ 297.8 |

---

## SUMMARY

ABC is a response to problems created by using a single cost driver to assign costs to manufactured products, and to other cost objects such as channels of distribution. The traditional approach overcosted high-volume products and undercosted low-volume products because drivers were volume-related. Direct labor hours and machine hours were two commonly selected drivers.

Managers now realize that complexity and diversity of operations drive many costs, sometimes more than volume drives. Capturing the effects of complexity and diversity requires identifying resource drivers, which are responsible for consuming resources. Managers then determine what activity drivers to use to relate the costs to products or other segments.

ABC has generated a flurry of outgrowths that aim to use activity analysis to improve organizational performance. Activity-based management and process value analysis are two notable examples. ABM and PVA strive to eliminate, or at least reduce, non-value-adding activities, and to perform value-adding activities more efficiently.

## KEY TERMS

activity driver   *(131)*
batch-level activity   *(136)*
benchmarking   *(140)*
consumption ratio   *(133)*
cost object   *(130)*

facility-sustaining or company-
   sustaining activities   *(138)*
re-engineering   *(140)*
resource driver   *(130)*
sustaining activity   *(136)*
unit-level activity   *(136)*

## REVIEW PROBLEM

TriTech Company incurs about $860,000 in manufacturing overhead costs each month. The company's former controller had been allocating overhead to individual product lines based on the lines' relative shares of direct labor hours (DLH). The company works about 100,000 DLH per month, so the average overhead cost per DLH is $8.60. The new controller is concerned that using DLH is inappropriate because some costs are driven by other activities. She has developed the following information regarding cost pools and drivers.

| Cost Driver | Amount in Pool | Amount of Activity |
|---|---|---|
| Direct labor hours | $520,000 | 100,000 |
| Number of batches | 280,000 | 500 |
| Engineering/design changes | 60,000 | 120 |
| Total overhead costs | $860,000 | |

The controller asks you to analyze two product lines using the existing method of allocating overhead costs based on DLH and using activity-based rates. She gives you the following data regarding two product lines. Bells are a bread-and-butter line that the company makes in large batches, while whistles are a specialty line that only a few customers buy.

| | Bells | Whistles |
|---|---|---|
| Direct labor hours | 1,600 | 200 |
| Number of batches | 4 | 12 |
| Engineering/design changes | 2 | 14 |

### Required

1. Determine the overhead to be allocated to each line using DLH as the only cost driver.
2. Determine the overhead to be allocated to each line using the three drivers identified on the previous page.
3. Comment on the differences between your results in requirements 1 and 2. Why should the differences be so large? What are some implications of the differences for pricing and analyzing the profitability of product lines?

### ANSWER TO REVIEW PROBLEM

1.

| | Bells | Whistles |
|---|---|---|
| Overhead cost, $8.60 × 1,600, $8.60 × 200 | $13,760 | $1,720 |

2. Computation of rates

| Cost Driver | Amount in Pool | Amount of Activity | Rate |
|---|---|---|---|
| Direct labor hours | $520,000 | 100,000 | $   5.20 |
| Number of batches | 280,000 | 500 | 560.00 |
| Engineering/design changes | 60,000 | 120 | 500.00 |

| | Bells | Whistles |
|---|---|---|
| Direct labor hours, $5.20 × 1,600, $5.20 × 200 | $ 8,320 | $ 1,040 |
| Number of batches, $560 × 4, $560 × 12 | 2,240 | 6,720 |
| Engineering/design changes, $500 × 2, $500 × 14 | 1,000 | 7,000 |
| Totals | $11,560 | $14,760 |

3. The differences are so large because Whistles consume much more of the non-volume-driven resources, which account for significant amounts of cost. Bells are relatively more labor-intensive and so draw much more overhead cost under the single-driver method. Some implications are:

- The apparent profitability of the two lines, and others, will change considerably under the two methods. Using ABC should give the company a better idea of what product lines are contributing, because it better shows how the lines demand use of resources.
- Prices set under the two methods will differ. The ABC-based prices will better reflect the consumption of resources, especially as between high-volume, bread-and-butter lines and specialty, niche lines.

## ASSIGNMENT MATERIAL

### INTERNET ACTIVITY

Many companies offer consulting services in activity-based costing and management. Find some of their Web sites. See how they view ABC, what services they offer, and what benefits they say they can provide. See if they offer examples of successful implementations of ABC and ABM. Be prepared to describe and discuss what you discovered. Take the viewpoint that your boss has asked you to make a preliminary survey to see whether it is feasible for your company to look into an ABC/ABM system.

## QUESTIONS FOR DISCUSSION

**4-1   *Benefits of ABC***   Betty Jane Confections operates several plants. The Brazos Mill buys wheat and grinds it into flour, then transfers the flour to other Betty Jane plants. The River City Bakery buys flour from the Brazos Mill. It also buys sugar, spices, butter, and other materials from outside vendors. It bakes 23 types of cakes and pastries that vary widely in unit volume, selling price, ingredients, baking time, and other factors, such as icing and other finishes.

***Required***

Should the Brazos Mill use ABC? Why or why not? How about the River City Bakery? Why or why not?

**4-2   *Cost analysis***   A few years ago, **Levi Strauss** announced that it would stop selling to stores that did not order at least $10,000 worth of product annually.

***Required***

How do you think Levi Strauss come to this decision? What analyses might have prompted the decision?

**4-3   *Cost drivers***   **Intuit**, the software company that sells the popular Quicken® finance programs, recently stated that

"The majority of these costs [customer service and technical support costs, mainly for telephone assistance] consist of fixed costs such as salary expense for permanent, full-time employees, and as such do not fluctuate as a direct function of seasonal variations in the Company's product sales."

***Required***

What activities do you think drive these costs?

**4-4   *Cost and activities***   *Fortune* (September 19, 1994, p. 226, "Companies to Watch") reported that **DIY Home Warehouse** carries fewer models than its competitors, such as 20 types of hammer to 70 for other companies, and that DIY's break-even point is lower because of its lack of variety.

***Required***

Why do you think its break-even point is lower?

**4-5   *Costs of complexity***   A friend of yours wonders why complexity is a cost driver. He asks "Don't costs depend solely on the total number of units you make? What does it matter whether you make 1,000 of one kind of widget, or 100 of each of ten kinds?"

***Required***

Answer your friend.

## EXERCISES

**4-6   *Basic allocation***   Jim Roberts runs a landscaping business that has two major segments, residential and commercial. Data on the operations follow.

| | Residential | Commercial | Totals |
|---|---|---|---|
| Annual revenues | $100,000 | $300,000 | $400,000 |
| Annual labor costs | 60,000 | 100,000 | 160,000 |

The business also has overhead costs for maintenance, supplies, transportation, and others of $180,000. Roberts wants to determine the profitability of each segment.

**Required**
1. Allocate the overhead costs to the segments based on labor cost.
2. Determine the income of each segment.

**4-7    ABC estimates (continuation of 4-6)**   Mr. Roberts was surprised to see that residential business appeared to be so unprofitable. That business did not use as much expensive equipment as did the commercial business, the customers were closer together, and it was much easier to schedule residential work because some commercial customers wanted work done only at certain hours.   At your urging, he developed the following estimates.

| Cost Pool | Cost in Pool | Cost Driver |
|---|---|---|
| Maintenance | $75,000 | hours of equipment operation |
| Scheduling and transport | 45,000 | travel time |
| General | 60,000 | labor cost |
| Total | $180,000 | |

| | Residential | Commercial | Totals |
|---|---|---|---|
| Hours of operation | 5,000 | 20,000 | 25,000 |
| Travel time, hours | 1,000 | 4,000 | 5,000 |

**Required**
1. Determine the overhead rates for each activity and allocate the costs to each segment.
2. Determine the incomes for each segment.
3. What recommendations might you make?

**4-8    Basic allocations**   MicroGraph makes several types of graphics workstations. One factory specializes in two types, the A-3 and the W-6. The A-3 has been a bread-and-butter product for a number of years, while the W-6 is relatively new and struggling to gain acceptance. Data on the two machines follow.

| | A-3 | W-6 |
|---|---|---|
| Material cost | $20 | $45 |
| Assembly time | 10 hours | 20 hours |
| Expected volume for coming year | 10,000 | 500 |

Assembly labor cost is $20 per hour and overhead costs are budgeted at $660,000 for the coming year.

**Required**
1. Determine the total number of labor hours the company will work in the coming year.
2. Determine the overhead rate per labor hour.
3. Determine the total cost of each workstation.

**4-9 ABC estimates (continuation of 4-8)** The managers of Micrograph are concerned about the costs you calculated in Exercise 4-8. The A-3 is now selling for $320, providing very little margin, while the W-6 now fetches $950, yielding a hefty margin. The controller develops the following information.

|  | A-3 | W-6 |
|---|---|---|
| Number of setups, annually | 100 | 250 |
| Testing time, annually | 2,000 hours | 2,750 hours |

Thus, the company performs one setup for every 100 units of A-3 (100/10,000) and one setup for every two units of W-6 (250/500). Similarly, the company spends 0.20 hours (2,000/10,000) testing an A-3 and 5.5 hours (2,750/500) testing a W-6.

The controller also determined that, of the total overhead of $660,000, about $140,000 related to setups and $190,000 to testing. The remaining $330,000 related to assembly labor.

**Required**
1. Determine the overhead rates for each activity: setups, testing, and assembly.
2. Determine the cost of each workstation using the new information.
3. Comment on the differences between your results here and those in Exercise 4-8.

**4-10 Basic allocations** Myers and Wilson is an accounting firm that performs three basic services: assurance, tax, and consulting. Melli Varner, the firm's accountant, plans to revise and update the fee structure. Somewhat simplified, her plan is to charge each client a percentage of the cost of the service, with the cost including both salary of the accountants performing the services and a provision for overhead. She has collected the following data.

| | |
|---|---|
| Total annual chargeable hours | 100,000 |
| Total annual salaries | $4,000,000 |
| Total annual overhead costs | $1,800,000 |

Ms. Varner is unsure whether to use chargeable hours or salary cost to apportion overhead costs.

**Required**
1. Calculate an overhead rate per chargeable hour.
2. Calculate an overhead rate per dollar of salary.
3. Suppose that client Wyse Industries had the following activity during the year.

| | |
|---|---|
| Chargeable hours | 1,400 |
| Salary cost | $71,000 |

Determine the amounts of overhead that would be charged to Wyse Industries under each of the alternatives in requirements 1 and 2. Can you tell why the amounts differ? How might Wyse argue that the lower charge better reflects costs?

**4-11 ABC estimates (continuation of 4-10)** Ms. Varner is not happy with either of the charging methods from the previous assignment. She knows that overhead costs actually differ according to the service provided because of different levels of support each type requires. After much effort, she determines the following.

|  | Assurance | Tax | Consulting | Total |
|---|---|---|---|---|
| Annual chargeable hours | 50,000 | 30,000 | 20,000 | 100,000 |
| Annual salaries | $2,000,000 | $1,600,000 | $1,400,000 | $4,000,000 |
| Annual overhead | $400,000 | $900,000 | $500,000 | $1,800,000 |

She also believes that chargeable hours, not salary dollars, drive overhead cost. She analyzed the Wyse account and found the following.

|  | Assurance | Tax | Consulting | Total |
|---|---|---|---|---|
| Chargeable hours | 900 | 400 | 100 | 1,400 |
| Salary cost | $42,000 | $22,000 | $7,000 | $71,000 |

**Required**
1. Compute overhead rates for each type of service, based on chargeable hours.
2. Determine the amount of overhead to be charged to the Wyse account.
3. Which basis for charging clients, the one here or either one from Exercise 4-10, makes the most sense to you? Why?

## PROBLEMS

**4-12   ABC for shipping department**   Boswell Company, a large wholesaler of grocery and household products, has been implementing ABC in several functions. The shipping department, which averages about $626,000 in monthly costs, is now ready for analysis. The controller is interested in attributing shipping costs to two principal types of customers, supermarkets and convenience stores, but wonders whether it is worthwhile to use ABC. Boswell has been using dollar volume of orders to evaluate customers and the controller believes this practice is probably working well.

The controller's assistant worked up the data below using very rough, preliminary estimates to see whether a more careful study might be likely to produce results significantly different from the current method.

| Cost Pool/Driver | Amount in Pool | Amount of Activity | Rate |
|---|---|---|---|
| Dollar volume of orders | $246,000 | $6,000,000 | $0.04100 |
| Number of customers | 180,000 | 280 | 642.86 |
| Number of orders | 80,000 | 680 | 117.65 |
| Number of stocks | 120,000 | 3,200 | 37.50 |
| Total shipping costs | $626,000 |  |  |

The number of stocks is a weighted average of the number of items in each order and the number of units of each item. Orders containing many items in small quantities require more time for the fork-lift operators. The assistant left costs that she could not easily identify with other drivers in the pool driven by dollar volume. Dollar volume also drives some costs, such as credit checking.

The following data relate to the two main classes of customers.

|  | Supermarkets | Convenience Stores |
|---|---|---|
| Dollar volume of orders | $4,500,000 | $1,500,000 |
| Number of customers | 80 | 200 |
| Number of orders | 220 | 460 |
| Number of stocks | 2,000 | 1,200 |

**Required**

1. Allocate the costs of the shipping department based on the dollar volume of orders.
2. Allocate the costs of the shipping department using ABC rates.
3. Does it appear that the company might benefit from pursuing the use of ABC for the shipping department?

**4-13   Cost drivers**   For each of the following costs, indicate which listed activity might drive it. Some activities might drive more than one cost; some might drive none of the listed costs. You may also suggest activities not listed below.

| Costs | Activities |
|---|---|
| Machine maintenance | Direct labor hours |
| Wages of workers who reset machinery when products change | Number of parts in a product |
| | Number of employees |
| Costs of inspecting incoming materials and components | Number of products |
| | Number of sales orders |
| Costs of keeping records on workers—how much they produce, what they earn | Number of customers |
| | Number of components/parts stocked |
| Costs of inspecting finished products | Number of suppliers |
| Costs to rework defective units | Number of incoming shipments |
| Building maintenance | Number of outgoing shipments |
| Personnel department costs, including payroll processing costs | Number of production runs of individual products |
| Purchasing department costs, including soliciting bids from vendors and preparing, reviewing, and auditing purchase orders | Production in units |
| | Sales in dollars |
| | Machine hours |
| Customer billing | Space in factory |

**4-14   Activity-based cost analysis**   The controller of the Wellcome Plant of RKD Industries has been analyzing costs of support departments to identify the major cost drivers and is seeking ways to reduce costs. He has just finished analyzing the costs and activity of the production scheduling department. The schedulers determine when particular products will be made, what machinery will be used, and how large the batch will be. Scheduling has come under increasing pressure as the number of products the plant manufactures has increased. The controller has assembled the following information regarding scheduling costs and the number of different products being made. All amounts are in thousands.

| Quarter | Number of Products | Costs of Production Scheduling Department |
|---|---|---|
| 20X2 Q4 | 5.2 | $93.0 |
| 20X2 Q3 | 5.2 | 84.0 |
| 20X2 Q2 | 4.2 | 83.8 |
| 20X2 Q1 | 4.1 | 82.3 |
| 20X1 Q4 | 4.0 | 75.1 |
| 20X1 Q3 | 3.2 | 74.0 |
| 20X1 Q2 | 3.2 | 67.0 |
| 20X1 Q1 | 2.7 | 66.0 |

**Required**
Analyze the scheduling department costs using a scatter diagram or regression analysis. Comment on the usefulness of the results for pursuing cost reduction.

**4-15  Product-line report**   Karen Bell is president of Bell & Company, which distributes consumer products to supermarkets. Ms. Bell has been trying to analyze the profitability of her lines. She has available the following information.

| Line | Annual Sales | Gross Profit Percentage | Line-Sustaining Fixed Costs |
|------|------|------|------|
| Paper products | $2,000,000 | 30% | $110,000 |
| Detergents | 1,200,000 | 40% | 150,000 |

The only variable cost, besides cost of goods sold, is a 10% commission paid on all sales. Bell incurs $350,000 in fixed costs that are common to both lines.

**Required**
Answer each item independently.

1. Prepare an income statement using the format shown in Exhibit 4-5.
2. Ms. Bell believes that she could increase the volume of either line by 10% by increasing promotion of the line by $30,000. Which, if either, line should she select? She cannot select both.
3. Ms. Bell believes that she could increase the volume of either line by 10% if she raised the commission rate on that line to 12%. Which, if either, line should she select? She cannot select both.
4. How does the report format you used for requirement 1 provide better information than would an income statement showing only combined results for the two lines?

**4-16  ABC, value-chain**   Trent Machining charges $3.50 for a machined part that is one of its biggest sellers.  RKL Industries is one of its largest customers and has recently begun complaining about the price.  Jill Green, Trent's new controller, has been sympathetic to RKL because she believes Trent is overcharging its large customers and undercharging smaller ones.  In response to similar complaints over the past year, the previous controller, recently retired, had done the following analysis of customer profitability.

| | Typical Large Customer | Typical Small Customer |
|------|------|------|
| Number of units per order | 8,000 | 1,000 |
| Number of orders annually | 60 | 40 |
| Total annual volume | 480,000 | 40,000 |
| Revenue | $1,680,000 | $140,000 |
| Variable manufacturing costs | 672,000 | 56,000 |
| Variable manufacturing margin | $1,008,000 | $ 84,000 |
| Fixed manufacturing costs | 288,000 | 24,000 |
| Manufacturing margin | $ 720,000 | $ 60,000 |
| Selling and administrative | 168,000 | 14,000 |
| Profit | $ 552,000 | $ 46,000 |

The fixed manufacturing costs allocation was based on total production. Selling and administrative expenses amount to about 10% of revenue, so the controller allocated that percentage to each type of customer.

Green did not dispute the fixed manufacturing cost allocation because those costs are the same no matter who the customer, but she pointed out that a significant portion of selling and administrative expenses, about $800,000, related to order-filling. The company fills about 5,000 orders annually.  The rest of the selling and administrative expenses are company-sustaining, and Green sees no useful purpose in assigning them to customers.

**Required**
Determine whether Trent is charging its two classes of customer reasonably.  If not, recommend an alternative.

**4-17   ABC for a distributor**   RST Company is a distributor serving two general types of customers, supermarkets and convenience stores.  The controller has prepared the following income statement for a typical month.

|  | Supermarkets | Convenience Stores |
|---|---|---|
| Sales | $500,000 | $100,000 |
| Cost of sales | 300,000 | 50,000 |
| Gross profit | $200,000 | $ 50,000 |
| Operating expenses* | 150,000 | 30,000 |
| Income | $ 50,000 | $ 20,000 |

*\* Allocated on sales dollars*

The president is uneasy with the statement because she knows that convenience stores require more effort than supermarkets. In response to her request, you amass the following information about operating expenses.

| Expense | Amount | Driver |
|---|---|---|
| Delivery | $60,000 | Number of deliveries |
| Stocking | 30,000 | Number of items stocked |
| Recordkeeping | 40,000 | Number of transactions, purchases, payments, etc. |
| Other | 50,000 | Sales dollars |

You also determine the following amounts of use of drivers.

|  | Supermarkets | Convenience Stores |
|---|---|---|
| Deliveries | 400 | 100 |
| Stocking | 4,000 | 11,000 |
| Recordkeeping | 800 | 1,200 |

**Required**
1. Prepare an income statement that uses ABC analyses to determine the costs of servicing each type of customer.
2. What recommendations might you make?

**4-18   Cost drivers, activity-based analysis**   The controller of the Summerton Division of KPL Industries was concerned that costs of some departments normally thought to be fixed had been rising over the past few years. The purchasing department had come in for special review because its costs had been rising rapidly. The purchasing manager argued that the division's increasing number of products and of component parts had strained his resources. The division's products are similar, but product designers use parts that differ in size or other characteristics. Purchasing is responsible for finding and evaluating vendors, inspecting incoming shipments, re-ordering parts when needed, and other tasks associated with managing component parts.

The controller developed the following data related to quarterly costs of the purchasing department and the number of different component parts used in the division's products (not the total number of parts put into products). All amounts are in thousands.

| Quarter | Number of Parts | Purchasing Department Costs |
|---------|-----------------|-----------------------------|
| 20X2 Q4 | 14.2 | $123.1 |
| 20X2 Q3 | 14.1 | 115.1 |
| 20X2 Q2 | 12.8 | 111.7 |
| 20X2 Q1 | 11.0 | 109.0 |
| 20X1 Q4 | 10.9 | 106.7 |
| 20X1 Q3 | 10.8 | 106.6 |
| 20X1 Q2 | 10.1 | 104.6 |
| 20X1 Q1 | 10.1 | 100.1 |

**Required**

Analyze the purchasing department's costs using a scatter diagram or regression analysis. What do your results tell about cost reduction?

**4-19   ABC for receiving department**   Wilson Company is a medium-sized manufacturer of industrial products. The company has implemented ABC for its manufacturing operations and is extending it to other functions. One of the managers involved in the study believes that receiving department costs should be allocated based on total manufacturing costs because it is simple. "I can understand using ABC for manufacturing, but not for some of these minor functions." The controller disagrees, and the two decide to do a brief, preliminary analysis to see if ABC makes sense for the receiving department.

They accumulate the following data.

| Cost Driver | Amount of Overhead Cost in Pool | Amount of Activity |
|-------------|--------------------------------|--------------------|
| Total manufacturing costs | $440,000 | $8,600,000 |
| Number of shipments received | 180,000 | 1,400 |
| Number of orders requiring inspection | 80,000 | 240 |
| Total overhead cost | $700,000 | |

Orders requiring inspection are from vendors who have not yet passed Wilson's tests. All vendors go through this probationary period and the predominance of such orders is for specialty products that are continually undergoing design and manufacturing changes. The following data relate to Wilson's three major product lines.

| | Line A | Line B | Line C |
|---|--------|--------|--------|
| Total manufacturing costs | $4,500,000 | $2,200,000 | $1,900,000 |
| Number of shipments received | 440 | 320 | 640 |
| Number of orders requiring inspection | 10 | 25 | 205 |

**Required**

1. Determine the receiving department costs to be apportioned to each line using total manufacturing costs as the only cost driver.
2. Determine the receiving department costs to be apportioned to each line using ABC.
3. Comment on the differences. Should Wilson extend ABC to the receiving department?

**4-20   Product line income statements**   The president of Mifflan Tool Company has just received the firm's income statement for January 20X8. He is puzzled because you had told him last year, when working as a consultant to the firm, that sales of $500,000 should produce a profit of about $46,500 before income taxes.

Mifflan Tool Company
Income Statement for January 20X8

| | | |
|---|---|---|
| Sales | | $500,000 |
| Cost of sales | | 307,500 |
| Gross profit | | $192,500 |
| Operating expenses: | | |
| Rent | $40,000 | |
| Salaries | 70,000 | |
| Shipping and delivery | 23,000 | |
| Other expenses | 30,000 | 163,000 |
| Income before taxes | | $ 29,500 |

The company sells three lines of power tools, and your analysis assumed the following sales mix in dollars: saws, 30%; drills, 20%; and sanders, 50%. The actual mix in dollars in January was 40%, 30%, 30%, respectively. The company does not manufacture its products. Cost of sales and shipping and delivery are variable costs. All others are fixed. Data per unit for each product follow.

| | Saws | Drills | Sanders |
|---|---|---|---|
| Selling price | $50 | $20 | $40 |
| Cost of sales | $30 | $15 | $20 |
| Shipping and delivery | 2 | 1 | 2 |
| Total variable costs | $32 | $16 | $22 |
| Contribution margin | $18 | $ 4 | $18 |

No fixed costs are associated with any particular product line. All costs were incurred as expected, per unit for variable costs, in total for fixed costs. Selling prices were as expected.

**Required**

1. Prepare a new income statement by product, based on actual results in January. Show both gross profit and contribution margin for each product.
2. Prepare an income statement by product for January, assuming that the expected sales mix had been achieved.
3. Explain the reasons for the differences between the two statements.

**4-21   Product line reporting, activity analysis**   Kelly Company is a retail store specializing in men's clothing. The company has three major product lines: suits, sport clothes, and accessories. The most recent monthly income statement follows.

## Kelly Company
### Income Statement for April 20X7
### (thousands of dollars)

| | | |
|---|---:|---:|
| Sales | | $800.0 |
| Cost of sales | | 572.0 |
| Gross profit | | $228.0 |
| Operating expenses: | | |
| Commissions | $48.0 | |
| Salaries | 71.4 | |
| Rent | 21.4 | |
| Shipping and delivery | 15.2 | |
| Insurance | 14.0 | |
| Miscellaneous | 20.8 | 190.8 |
| Income before taxes | | $ 37.2 |

The president wants a product-line income statement. She gives you the following additional data:

1. The sales mix in April was 30% suits, 50% sport clothes, and 20% accessories, expressed in dollars of total sales.
2. The cost of sales percentages are 80% for suits, 75% for sport clothes, and 50% for accessories.
3. Sales commissions are 6% for all product lines.
4. Each product line is the responsibility of a separate manager, and each manager has a small staff. The salaries that are directly related to each product line are $12,000 for suits, $8,000 for sport clothes, and $5,200 for accessories. All other salaries are common to the three lines and considered to be facility-sustaining.
5. Rent is for both office and warehouse space, all of which is in a single building.
6. Shipping and delivery costs are for operating expenses and depreciation on the firm's three trucks. Each truck serves a particular geographical area and delivers all three product lines.
7. Insurance is for basic liability coverage.
8. Miscellaneous expenses are directly traceable to lines. The amounts are $6,000 to suits, $8,800 to sport clothes, and $6,000 to accessories.

### Required
Prepare an income statement by product, using the format shown in Exhibit 4-5. You will not have batch-level variable costs.

**4-22  ABC for a Distributor**   TriCo Distribution handles various household products, selling to supermarkets, retail drug stores, and discounters. The controller has become concerned about the profitability of some of the company's customers and has prepared the following analysis of some representative accounts.

| | Customer | | | | |
|---|---:|---:|---:|---:|---:|
| | A | B | C | D | E |
| Sales | $200,000 | $220,000 | $330,000 | $400,000 | $700,000 |
| Gross profit | $ 96,000 | $101,200 | $138,600 | $148,000 | $238,000 |
| Operating costs | 32,432 | 35,676 | 53,514 | 64,865 | 113,514 |
| Margin | $ 63,568 | $ 65,524 | $ 85,086 | $ 83,135 | $124,486 |

The controller allocated operating costs on the basis of relative sales. He commented that customers such as "E" should be considerably more profitable given the high sales they generate, while smaller accounts should be less profitable. Gross margins differ among customers because of different product mixes and some quantity discounts.

The assistant controller thought that the analysis did not capture all of the costs of servicing a customer. She had developed the following data as part of an ABC study that was not yet complete.

| Customer | Average Number of Deliveries | Items Per Delivery | Units Per Delivery |
|---|---|---|---|
| A | 140 | 70 | 600 |
| B | 125 | 30 | 1,000 |
| C | 90 | 40 | 1,200 |
| D | 60 | 50 | 3,500 |
| E | 75 | 20 | 3,800 |

She had also worked out the following preliminary cost analysis.

| | |
|---|---|
| Order costs | $120 per order plus $2.50 per item ordered |
| Delivery costs | $250 per delivery |
| Shelf-stocking costs | $0.08 per unit stocked |

The company makes a separate delivery for each order.

### Required

1. Prepare an ABC analysis of the five customers.
2. Compare your results with the controller's analysis. Which makes better sense? What might you recommend?

**4-23  Line of business reporting (CMA adapted)**   Riparian Company produces and sells three products. Each is sold domestically and in foreign countries. The foreign market has been disappointing to management because of poor operating results, as evidenced by the income statement for the first quarter.

| | Total | Domestic | Foreign |
|---|---|---|---|
| Sales | $1,300,000 | $1,000,000 | $300,000 |
| Cost of goods sold | 1,010,000 | 775,000 | 235,000 |
| Gross profit | 290,000 | 225,000 | 65,000 |
| Selling expenses | 105,000 | 60,000 | 45,000 |
| Administrative expenses | 52,000 | 40,000 | 12,000 |
| | 157,000 | 100,000 | 57,000 |
| Income | $ 133,000 | $ 125,000 | $ 8,000 |

Management decided a year ago to enter the foreign market because of excess capacity, but is now unsure whether to continue devoting time and effort to developing it. The following information has been gathered for consideration of the alternatives that management has identified.

| | Products | | |
|---|---|---|---|
| | A | B | C |
| Sales: | | | |
| Domestic | $400,000 | $300,000 | $300,000 |
| Foreign | 100,000 | 100,000 | 100,000 |
| Variable manufacturing costs (percentage of sales) | 60% | 70% | 60% |
| Variable selling expenses (percentage of sales) | 3% | 2% | 2% |

Of the $190,000 total fixed manufacturing costs, $30,000, $40,000, and $70,000 are line-sustaining costs of products A, B, and C, respectively. Additionally, $90,000 in fixed manufacturing costs are market-sustaining to the domestic market, $20,000 to the foreign market.

All administrative expenses are fixed and unrelated to the three products and to the two markets. Fixed selling expenses are market-sustaining. Some $40,000 of fixed selling expenses are product-sustaining. The percentages of the $40,000 applicable to each product are 30% to A, 30% to B, and 40% to C.

Management believes that if the foreign market was dropped, sales in the domestic market could be increased by $200,000. The increase would be divided 40%, 40%, 20% among products A, B, and C, respectively.

Management also believes that a new product, D, could be introduced by the end of the current year. The product would replace product C and would increase fixed costs by $30,000 per quarter.

**Required**
1. Prepare an income statement for the quarter by product, using the format shown in Exhibit 4-5.
2. Prepare an income statement for the quarter by market, using the format shown in Exhibit 4-5.
3. Determine whether the foreign market should be dropped.
4. Assume that the foreign market will not be dropped. Determine the minimum quarterly contribution margin that product D would have to produce in order to make its introduction desirable.

## CASES

*4-24  Determining variable costs of products—activity-based analysis* Shelly LaMoy, controller of VoTech Industries, has not been satisfied with the cost analysis her staff has been doing. The staff had developed several regression equations to predict future costs, but none has worked very well. All of the equations used direct labor hours to predict manufacturing overhead costs. Predictions have been consistently well off the mark and managers have complained about poor information on which to base their decisions.

LaMoy believed that the staff had failed to recognize that drivers other than direct labor hours are at work. She therefore conducted a study of cost pools and drivers and developed the following analysis, showing the fixed and variable components of various cost pools and drivers.

| Cost Driver | Variable Amount |
| --- | --- |
| Direct labor hours (DLH) | $3.00 per DLH |
| Machine hours (MH) | $18.00 per MH |
| Number of parts/components | $0.05 per part |
| Total processing time | $3.00 per hour |

LaMoy has instructed you to determine the variable cost of two products using the data she has developed. Variable costs for materials and labor and other data for the products follow.

|  | Product 816 | Product 389 |
| --- | --- | --- |
| Materials cost | $13.00 | $11.00 |
| Direct labor cost at $14 per DLH | 7.00 | 14.00 |
| Other data: |  |  |
| Machine hours | 0.50 | 0.20 |
| Number of parts | 120 | 185 |
| Total processing time | 10.00 hours | 15.00 hours |

### Required

1. Determine the total variable cost of each product.
2. Suppose that the staff had estimated variable overhead cost at $40 per direct labor hour. Determine the cost of each product using that estimate.
3. Comment on the differences between your answers to requirements 1 and 2.

**4-25   *Segmented income statements for a distributor, activity analysis, ethics***   Vic Kemp, executive vice president of Taylor, Inc., is examining the most recent monthly income statements, segmented by geographical area (see page 160). Each area is the responsibility of a regional manager. Taylor distributes products used by paper manufacturers and began operations in the western part of the United States 20 years ago. The company expanded into the southern and eastern markets only a year ago. Taylor does not manufacture its products, but rather buys them for resale to its customers.

Because Taylor has a good reputation and strong product lines, it has done well in the new markets, or at least Kemp thinks it has. Other than salespeople, Taylor has relatively few people and other assets in the market areas. The bulk of expenses are incurred at the home offices in Corvallis, Oregon.

Kemp is happy with the results in the new territories, but at the same time mistrusts them, not knowing exactly how the statements are prepared. Kemp is also concerned that the push into the new territories has caused managers to neglect the western territory, which seems to be slipping from past levels of profitability. He is quite concerned that the income statements do not give him the kind of information he needs to make decisions. He has asked the chief accountant for an explanation of the income statements, but to little avail. The chief accountant usually puts him off by saying that it is very complicated and that he does not have the time to explain every number.

Taylor's chief accountant has been allocating costs to the markets using a set of formulas based on relative sales volume in both unit and dollar terms. No one else quite knows how the chief accountant prepares the statements. Kemp finally goes to the controller and asks for a special study to help him get the information he feels is needed. The controller has been concerned with the allocation methods for some time and has collected the following information based on analyses of the activities in each territory.

## Taylor, Inc.
## Income Statement, October 20X9
## (in thousands of dollars)

|  | Total | Eastern | Southern | Western |
|---|---|---|---|---|
| Sales | $2,896.0 | $589.0 | $752.0 | $1,555.0 |
| Cost of sales | 1,231.9 | 200.3 | 300.8 | 730.8 |
| Gross margin | 1,664.1 | 388.7 | 451.2 | 824.2 |
| Selling expenses: |  |  |  |  |
| Salaries and commissions | 754.2 | 156.2 | 192.6 | 405.4 |
| Shipping and warehousing | 187.3 | 43.2 | 67.1 | 77.0 |
| Other selling expenses | 84.5 | 12.1 | 27.6 | 44.8 |
| Total selling expenses | 1,026.0 | 211.5 | 287.3 | 527.2 |
| Administrative expenses: |  |  |  |  |
| Salaries | 147.2 | 42.6 | 36.8 | 67.8 |
| Building occupancy | 61.7 | 22.7 | 26.5 | 12.5 |
| Other | 56.1 | 12.3 | 22.1 | 21.7 |
| Total administrative expenses | 265.0 | 77.6 | 85.4 | 102.0 |
| Total operating expenses | 1,291.0 | 289.1 | 372.7 | 629.2 |
| Income before taxes | $ 373.1 | $ 99.6 | $ 78.5 | $ 195.0 |

The controller explains that she has developed the information by analyzing the cost-driving activities associated with each category. For instance, the eastern territory has relatively heavy selling expenses for several reasons. First, there are more established competitors in that region, and new customers are harder to cultivate. Second, shipping costs tend to be higher because orders from the east are smaller than those from the other regions, thus losing economies of large shipments. Other reasons contribute to the differences between the activity-based direct costs and the costs as allocated in the income statement.

|  | Eastern | Southern | Western |
|---|---|---|---|
| Variable costs, percentage of sales: |  |  |  |
| Cost of sales | 34.00% | 40.00% | 47.00% |
| Selling expenses | 14.00% | 13.00% | 16.00% |
| Administrative expenses | 0.00% | 0.00% | 0.00% |
| District-sustaining costs: |  |  |  |
| Cost of sales | $0 | $0 | $0 |
| Selling expenses | 152 | 155 | 207 |
| Administrative expenses | 9 | 12 | 19 |

### Required
1. Prepare a segmented income statement using the contribution margin format. Work with totals only for selling expenses and administrative expenses. Ignore the individual components of those cost categories.

2. Write a memorandum to Mr. Kemp telling him how each territory is doing.  Use the guidelines in Appendix A.

3. Write a memorandum indicating the ethical issues that might arise from your analysis, such as what the regional managers have a right to expect from you or another managerial accountant. Refer to Exhibit 1-2 on page 15.

**4-26  *Segmented income statements—costs of activities, ethics***   Hunter Inc. manufactures and distributes three principal product lines: sporting goods, housewares, and hardware. The company has suffered reduced profitability in the past few quarters, and the top managers have taken a number of actions to try to improve the situation. The most recent quarterly income statement, segmented by product line, follows. Indirect, common fixed costs are allocated to the lines based on relative sales or labor content.

Claxton Industries
Income Statement, Second Quarter, 20X9
(in thousands of dollars)

| | Total | Sporting Goods | Housewares | Hardware |
|---|---|---|---|---|
| Sales | $3,337.0 | $650.0 | $921.0 | $1,766.0 |
| Cost of sales | 1,928.8 | 357.3 | 545.7 | 1,025.8 |
| Gross margin | $1,408.2 | $292.7 | $375.3 | $740.2 |
| Operating expenses: | | | | |
| Selling expenses | $787.6 | $157.1 | $225.9 | $404.6 |
| Administrative expenses | 514.6 | 94.2 | 135.6 | 284.8 |
| Total operating expenses | $1,302.2 | $251.3 | $361.5 | $689.4 |
| Income before taxes | $106.0 | $41.4 | $13.8 | $50.8 |

The managers are still not happy with the 3.2% return on sales (ROS), but the $106 thousand pretax profit was a bit higher than the previous quarter's profit. The consensus of the managers is that they should concentrate on sporting goods and hardware because their ROS's are higher than that of housewares. One manager even wants to ignore housewares because its ROS was only 1.5%. "If we only keep a cent and a half from a dollar's sales, why even bother with it?"

When asked to confirm the judgments about relative profitabilities, the controller said that some indirect costs are allocated to the product lines and that some distortions might result from those allocations. Therefore, her assistant has been asked to prepare an alternative income statement. The assistant's analysis of Hunter's cost structure reveals the following (in thousands of dollars).

| | Sporting Goods | Housewares | Hardware |
|---|---|---|---|
| Variable costs, unit and batch percentage of sales: | | | |
| Cost of sales | 28.00% | 32.00% | 35.00% |
| Selling expenses | 2.00% | 1.50% | 1.80% |
| Administrative expenses | 0.90% | 0.70% | 2.00% |
| Product-line-sustaining costs | | | |
| Cost of sales | $158 | $141 | $197 |
| Selling expenses | 56 | 87 | 133 |
| Administrative expenses | 13 | 22 | 43 |

The assistant evaluated the costs by examining the activities that generate them. For example, sporting goods require relatively more attention from manufacturing support personnel, such as engineers, than hardware and so is assigned relatively higher direct fixed manufacturing costs. By the same token, hardware consumes considerably more relative administrative time than sporting goods, giving it relatively more cost. All remaining costs are company-sustaining and the controller believes they should not be assigned to product lines.

### Required

1. Prepare a new segmented income statement using the assistant's findings. Show company-sustaining costs only in the total column, as in Exhibit 4-5.
2. Write a memorandum to the controller that comments on the differences between your statement and the one above. Indicate for example, what decisions are easier, or more difficult, to make with your statement. Use the guidelines in Appendix A.
3. Each line is controlled by a manager. From an ethics standpoint, what can these managers expect from the people who develop the information and prepare the reports? Refer to Exhibit 1-2 on page 15.

## Chapter Five

# SHORT-TERM DECISIONS AND ACCOUNTING INFORMATION

## LEARNING OBJECTIVES

*After reading this chapter, you should be able to*

- *Explain why decision making requires information not included in regular accounting reports.*
- *Determine what costs and revenues are relevant to decisions.*
- *Analyze the quantitative factors relevant to typical decisions.*
- *Explain the importance of complementary effects to decisions of a segment of a larger entity.*
- *Identify nonquantitative or long-term considerations that influence short-term decisions.*
- *Describe some of the legal constraints on managers' decisions.*

As we pointed out very early in this book, decisions relate to future actions. Managers can never be sure whether their decisions were wise or unwise, because

1. unexpected events can influence subsequent results and
2. what would have happened had the decision been different can never be known.

In the mid-1990s **Chrysler** planned a new luxury automobile to compete against Cadillac, Mercedes, Lexus, and Infiniti. By building capacity to produce only a few more cars than they thought they could sell, Chrysler's top managers planned to keep their fixed costs low, about $1,000 to $1,500 per car below their competitors' costs at the expected annual volume of 30,000. Yet, the company eventually dropped the project because the managers believed that the contribution margin would not be sufficient to cover fixed costs and provide a reasonable profit. One problem was the prevalence of leasing, which cuts into margins. As president Robert Lutz was quoted, "You start using $6,000 to $7,000 to $8,000 to $9,000 of your variable margins to subsidize your lease sales: by the time you do the per-unit fixed-cost allocations you're underwater."

**Best Buy**, the electronics chain, decided to offer CDs at very low prices, barely above cost, to stimulate traffic through its stores and increase sales

> of VCRs, stereos, and other high-margin items. A typical Best Buy store stocked 60,000 CDs, more than the average record store. Best Buy sold plenty of CDs, but its profitability declined. Margins fell and the company earned only $1.7 million in 1996, down from $58 million the year before. Moreover, Best Buy's decision might well have accelerated the decline of the traditional record store. Six record chains declared bankruptcy from 1995 through early 1997, affecting over 900 stores.
>
>   Did these companies make mistakes? Were their decisions bad? Again, we cannot say because we don't know what would have happened had they taken other paths. Perhaps Chrysler's car would have been highly profitable, perhaps not. Best Buy might have done better using a different loss leader to generate traffic through its stores, but it might not have. All we can say is that managers making decisions should use the available information wisely.

*Sources: Jerry Flint, "The Car Chrysler Didn't Build," Forbes, August 12, 1996, 89–91.*
*Tim Carvell, "These Prices Really Are Insane," Fortune, August 4, 1997, 109–116.*

Making decisions is choosing among alternatives. Should we raise the price of our product, lower it, or leave it alone? Should we drop a product (or product line) or keep it? Should we add a new product? Should we make a component of our product in our factory or buy it from another company? Managers continually evaluate such sets of alternatives.

This chapter focuses on short-term decisions. Most managers and accountants consider a decision to be short term if it involves a period of one year or less. This cutoff is arbitrary but commonly used, though a better distinction is that long-term decisions normally require substantial investments that will not pay off for several years, and short-term decisions do not. Short-term decisions are more easily reversed than long-term ones. (You can almost always change prices or your method of compensating salespeople, but you can't so quickly dispose of a factory or a specialized piece of equipment.) The basic principles of short-term decisions also apply in the long run, but long-term decisions require additional considerations. Chapters 8 and 9 focus on long-term decisions.

One other matter. Virtually all decisions, especially important ones, have both quantitative and qualitative aspects, and managers must understand both. The analytical approaches we present concentrate on quantifiable, economic aspects of decisions, but we usually describe qualitative issues as well. Such qualitative considerations often override quantitative factors; managers might select an alternative that is not as economically sound as others because of company policy or strategy. The accompanying Insight describes several such situations. Managers acting in the ways described in the Insight cannot be called wrong. But it is critical that managers be aware of the costs of policies. The techniques described in this chapter help managers to determine such costs.

## THE CRITERION FOR SHORT-TERM DECISIONS

The economic criterion for making short-term decisions is simple: *Take the action that you expect will give the organization the highest income (or lowest loss).* Applying this rule is not always simple, and two subrules are often helpful:

 *SIGHT*

### Policy and Profit

**Mitsubishi Electronics America** stopped selling its products to **Circuit City**, even though it was then Mitsubishi's largest customer. A Mitsubishi official said "we will not be in a national chain" and argued that smaller retailers offer better service. **Taco Inc.**, a company that makes pumps and valves, operates an on-site learning center where employees attend courses—not all of them work-related—both during and after work hours. Asked about the company's commitment to the learning center, Taco's chief executive said "I don't have any idea why the hell it happened except I wanted to do it." **Ben & Jerry's Homemade Inc.** is widely known for policies that reflect its management's interest in social issues. Its most recent annual report stated:

> "The Company's Social Mission. The Company's basic business philosophy is embodied in a three-part mission statement, which includes a social mission to "operate the Company in a way that actively recognizes the central role that business plays in the structure of society by initiating innovative ways to improve the quality of life of a broad community: local, national and international. . . . The Company believes that implementation of its social mission, which is integrated into the Company's business, has been beneficial to the Company's overall financial performance. However, it is possible that at some future date the amount of the Company's energies and resources devoted to its social mission could have some material adverse financial effect.

*Sources: Marcia Berss, "'We will not be in a national chain'," Forbes, March 27, 1995, 50.*
*Thomas A. Stewart, "How a Little Company Won Big By Betting on Brainpower," Fortune, September 4, 1995, 121-122.*
*Annual Reports.*

1. The only revenues and costs that are *relevant* in making decisions are the expected *future* revenues and costs that will *differ* among the available choices. These are called **differential revenues and costs**. (Because many decisions result in increases in revenues and costs, some managers use the terms **incremental revenues and costs**.)

2. Revenues and costs that have already been earned or incurred are *irrelevant* in making decisions. Their only use is that they might aid in predicting future revenues and costs.

### DIFFERENTIAL (INCREMENTAL) REVENUES AND COSTS

The term *differential* is more inclusive than *incremental*. The latter term suggests increases, and some decisions produce decreases in both revenues and costs. But the terms are not as important as what they denote. Differential costs are *avoidable* costs, as we discussed in Chapter 3. If a company can change a cost by taking one

CHAPTER 3

action as opposed to another, the cost is avoidable and therefore differential. Suppose a company could save $50,000 in salaries and other fixed costs if it stopped selling a product in a particular geographical region. The $50,000 is avoidable (differential) because it will be incurred if the company continues to sell in the region and will not be incurred if the firm stops selling in that region. Of course, the company will lose revenue if it discontinues sales in the region. Hence, the lost revenue is also differential in a decision to stop selling in the region.

## SUNK COSTS AND OPPORTUNITY COSTS

The emphasis on differential revenues and costs gives rise to two other related concepts you might have encountered in your study of economics: *sunk costs* and *opportunity costs*. A **sunk cost** is one that has already been incurred and therefore will be the same no matter which alternative a manager selects. Sunk costs are *never* relevant for decision making because they are not differential.

The opening vignette described a car that Chrysler developed but did not market. Chrysler spent a great deal of money developing the car. That development cost was relevant at the time Chrysler was deciding whether to develop the car or not. But the cost was irrelevant after Chrysler had spent it and was deciding whether to market the car. The development cost already spent was going to be the same whether or not Chrysler marketed the car. Similarly, depreciation on a machine is irrelevant in deciding which products to make with that machine. *All historical costs*, including the costs of assets, whether original cost or book value (cost minus accumulated depreciation), *are sunk costs*.

Even though the historical cost of a resource is sunk, the resource can have a cost for decision-making purposes. If a resource can be used in more than one way, it has an opportunity cost. An **opportunity cost** is the benefit lost by taking one action as opposed to another. The "other" action is the best alternative available other than the one being contemplated.

A company that owns a warehouse can use it either to store its own products or rent it to another company. Using the space for storage requires that the company forego the opportunity to rent it. When the company considers any action that requires using the space for storage, the relevant cost of the space is its opportunity cost, the rent the company will not collect. Of course, the space might have other uses.

Perhaps the main problem in decision making is identifying the alternatives and analyzing all of their likely effects. The importance of examining all of the effects of a decision is highlighted in the accompanying Insight.

The example described in the next section uses the concepts of differential revenues and costs, sunk costs, and opportunity costs. As you read, look for examples of these concepts.

## BASIC EXAMPLE

Kyron Computers recently manufactured 100 specialized computer monitors for a customer that has since gone bankrupt. Because they are made-to-order and bear the customer's logo, the monitors cannot go to Kyron's regular customers. A rival company has offered to buy the monitors for $12,000. The cost to manufacture the monitors was $17,000. The president says he'd rather throw them away than sell them at a loss of $5,000 ($17,000 manufacturing costs − $12,000 revenue).

### What is the Product?

Internet search engines such as Yahoo! and Excite have decided to *give away* their major product, access to information. Why? Because advertisers are willing to pay to display their banners on the search engines' Web pages. Some companies give away software on the Internet to stimulate sales of other products. Companies offer landscape planning, golf lessons, and many other products associated with their software.

A less dramatic example is that of **America Online's** statement that "An important component of the Company's business strategy is an increasing reliance on advertising, commerce and other revenues, which include advertising and related revenues, the sale of merchandise and transaction fees associated with electronic commerce."

AOL seeks to increase its subscriber base not only for the revenue its membership fees provide, but also because "Among the Company's business objectives are . . . continuing to accelerate the change in its business model into one in which more profits are generated from sources other than online service revenues, such as advertising and electronic commerce. The Company expects that the growth . . . will provide the Company with the opportunity and flexibility to fund the costs associated with the increased usage resulting from flat-rate pricing. . . ."

The flat-rate pricing AOL refers to makes little sense without the complementary effects described above. AOL's move to flat-rate pricing is the subject of a Chapter 6 vignette.

*Sources: Annual reports and SEC filings.*

Is his reasoning sound? If there's no likelihood of getting a better offer, the president is wrong, and Kyron should accept the chain's offer.

Kyron has two alternatives: (1) throw the monitors away or (2) sell them to the rival company. Throwing them away yields no revenue and requires no additional costs. But the rival's offer yields $12,000 revenues and no additional costs, so Kyron should accept the rival's offer. The differential revenues and costs for selling to the chain as opposed to throwing out the monitors are as follows.

| Decision: Sell to Rival (*Rather* than Throw Monitors Away) | |
| --- | --- |
| Differential revenues | $12,000 |
| Differential costs | 0 |
| Differential profit | $12,000 |

You understand the concepts of differential and sunk costs if you saw that the $17,000 cost to make the monitors is sunk. It has already been incurred and will not change regardless of the alternative chosen. True, Kyron will have a $5,000 book loss if it sells the monitors to the chain ($17,000 – $12,000). But if Kyron simply throws the monitors out, the book loss will be $17,000. (Note that Kyron is better off selling the monitors for $12,000, whether the cost to manufacture them was $2,000, $17,000, or even $50,000, if the only alternative is to throw them away.)

Let's add another alternative: A computer maker offers to pay $20,000 for the monitors provided that Kyron disguises the original logo and makes a few other modifications. The production manager estimates the incremental cost of the modifications at $6,000. The president isn't happy about this alternative either, because the $23,000 total cost [$17,000 + $6,000] is greater than the $20,000 offer.

Three alternatives are now available, but we already know that the as-is sale is preferable to throwing the monitors away. So, we need only compare the new alternative with the as-is sale. Which of those two alternatives should Kyron choose? It should do the work and sell the monitors for $20,000. To understand why, consider the differential revenues and costs to rework and sell the monitors as opposed to selling them to the chain as is.

| Decision: Rework and Sell (*Rather* than Sell As Is) | |
|---|---|
| Differential revenues ($20,000 – $12,000) | $8,000 |
| Differential costs ($6,000 – $0) | 6,000 |
| Differential profit | $2,000 |

Kyron is $2,000 better off reworking the monitors rather than selling them as is. Some people prefer to analyze the alternatives separately. Following are analyses of the alternatives using that approach.

| | Throw Out Monitors | Sell Monitors As Is | Rework and Sell |
|---|---|---|---|
| Incremental revenue | $— | $12,000 | $20,000 |
| Incremental costs | | | (6,000) |
| Incremental profit (loss) | $— | $12,000 | $14,000 |

Once again, the rework alternative is the best choice, and the as-is sale is preferable to throwing the monitors away. Either method of analysis gives the same result. As before, the $17,000 cost of manufacturing the monitors is irrelevant. To emphasize the irrelevance of this sunk cost, consider Kyron's income statement for each of the alternatives.

| | Throw Out Monitors | Sell Monitors As Is | Rework and Sell |
|---|---|---|---|
| Revenues | $    0 | $ 12,000 | $ 20,000 |
| Costs: | | | |
| Manufacturing | (17,000) | (17,000) | (17,000) |
| Rework | | | (6,000) |
| Profit (loss) | $(17,000) | $ (5,000) | $ (3,000) |

Reworking the monitors yields the smallest loss, confirming the results of the differential analyses, which showed that alternative to be the best of the three. The loss incurred by selling the monitors immediately is $12,000 less than that from throwing them out, which is equal to the $12,000 differential profit shown in the first analysis. The $3,000 loss reported for reworking the monitors is $2,000 less than the loss from the as-is sale, which is exactly the $2,000 differential profit we found when comparing those choices.

Let us revise our original example one last time to show that the relevant cost might be the cost of *replacing* the resource. Kyron still has the 100 monitors manufactured at a cost of $17,000. But now it can sell them at their regular price of $35,000. A computer maker again offers Kyron $20,000 for the monitors. The difference now is that Kyron will have to make similar monitors to meet future sales if it sells the ones on hand. Moreover, the production manager says that the cost of making 100 monitors has risen to $22,000. What should Kyron do now?

The key to the analysis is to understand that, *whatever* Kyron decides to do, it wants to have 100 monitors available to meet the expected demand at the regular price. The revenue from selling them at the regular price will be the same no matter what Kyron does with the monitors now on hand. Hence, the expected $35,000 revenue from selling 100 monitors at regular prices is irrelevant to the decision about accepting the $20,000 offer.

Kyron has two alternatives. First, it can hold the monitors to meet expected sales needs at regular prices. Choosing this alternative, Kyron receives no revenues it wouldn't otherwise receive and incurs no additional costs, for a net of zero. Second, Kyron can sell the on-hand monitors and make others to meet regular sales needs. Here, Kyron receives $20,000 revenue and incurs a cost of $22,000 (to produce the units needed for regular sales), for an incremental loss of $2,000. The better choice is to do nothing (that is, sell through the regular channel); Kyron will be $2,000 better off by choosing that action.

## DEVELOPING RELEVANT INFORMATION

Most decisions involve a proposed change in a segment of a company—for example, a product, product line, factory, or geographical area. Finding or developing the information relevant to a decision about a segment isn't a simple task, because the necessary information is seldom available in a routine accounting report.

Suppose a company makes several models of copiers, fax machines, and other office equipment, sells them in several geographical regions to different types of customers (e.g., businesses, schools, and hospitals), and operates several factories, some of which make only one product or line and others that make several products. Regular accounting reports might show sales by model, product line, factory, sales region, or customer type. But those reports might not show information for a specific model of one product by sales region, factory, or customer type, which might be the information needed for a particular decision.

An existing accounting report for the segment of concern might include some of the information needed for a decision. (The product-line income statement in Exhibit 4-5 on page 144 is an example of such a report.) But decisions are about what to expect in the future, so information about past levels of revenues and costs is relevant only if it helps to predict future levels. Estimates of expected future sales of a product or service come from marketing people, and production and design engineers provide information about expected needs for materials, labor, and other aspects of manufacturing. Modern information technology makes more information available to managers, and makes possible looking at information in various ways. Internal databases contain details of information that appear only in summary form on reports.

Unfortunately, determining avoidable costs requires more than access to sophisticated computer systems and databases because, as we said in Chapter 3, avoidability depends on the decision at hand. Consider further the office equipment maker just described. Suppose salespeople are paid salaries, concentrate on specific types of customers, and sell all of the company's products. Neither sales salaries nor travel costs are avoidable costs when a manager is analyzing a particular model of copier; if the company drops a single model, salespeople will still call on the same customers. However, a manager analyzing the profitability of a particular type of customer will see that some sales salaries and related expenses are avoidable if the company stops selling to those customers. Similarly, if salespeople cover specific geographical regions, their salaries and other expenses are avoidable in an analysis by region. Thus, costs that are avoidable, and therefore differential, when reviewing one segment might be unavoidable when looking at a different segment. Of course, analyzing the activities that will be added or dropped as a result of a decision helps managers to predict cost changes.

*In general, the smaller the segment, the less the avoidable cost.* Avoidable costs of a copier model sold in one particular region might be limited to the variable costs of producing that model. Those associated with the entire line of copiers in the same region include variable production costs and probably some selling expenses. Some fixed manufacturing costs might also be saved, especially if copiers sold in that region are made in a factory that does not make other product lines. As the segment expands to an entire product line, more costs become avoidable. The most important point about decisions relating to segments is that the analyses will differ with the decisions. There is no magic formula for identifying costs and revenues relevant to decisions, even when accounting reports exist for the segment. As the next section shows, existing accounting reports might even be misleading.

## ALLOCATED COSTS

The accounting practice of allocating indirect (common) costs to segments complicates the task of identifying the costs relevant to a particular decision. Recall from Chapter 4 that *cost allocation* is the process of assigning indirect costs to individual segments to which the costs are common. For reasons discussed in Chapter 10, cost allocations are often incorporated into internal reports that serve as a starting point for decision making. Chapter 4 also stated that activity-based cost estimates were not estimates of costs avoidable in the short term. Activity-based cost estimates relate to longer-run resource consumption, not to decisions that will play out over a very short period. Thus, ABC analyses might become less useful as segments narrow and the time period shortens.

Earlier in this chapter we emphasized that the basis for decision making was information about the future. In Chapter 2, we showed that per-unit fixed costs—the result of allocations—are not useful in predicting future total costs *in the short-run.* Hence, per-unit fixed costs are not relevant for short-term decision making. Allocating common costs to individual segments does not make the allocated amount avoidable in the future. Hence, for making decisions about a segment, common costs allocated to that segment are not relevant; the only relevant costs are those that will change (be differential) if a firm chooses one course of action rather than another.

Although the presumption is that an allocated cost is unavoidable, it is sometimes possible to reduce common costs if a large enough segment is eliminated. For example, suppose that each of the 20 employees of a payroll department works on some part of the payrolls of all six factories that the company operates. The salaries of all of the employees in the payroll department are then common to the six factories. But if one large factory closes, the payroll department might be able to reassign work and people, reducing the staff to 17 or 18 and so reducing some of the common cost. As you saw in Chapters 3 and 4, determining these types of changes in costs is part of analyzing costs in an activity framework.

The appearance of allocated costs on segment reports raises an important point about internal use of information from existing accounting reports about segments. An information system must provide data for preparing financial statements, completing tax returns and other government paperwork, and making decisions. The system is usually designed around the information needs for external reports, because the information needed for such reports is well-known and regularly needed. Segment reports produced by the information system often reflect practices required for external reporting. Hence, a manager consulting such reports for information about the costs relevant to a particular decision must understand the basic concepts of both financial and managerial accounting.

## ACTIVITY-BASED ESTIMATES

Organizations that use activity-based costing estimate costs only after making careful studies of cost pools and related cost drivers. Using ABC helps managers focus on what activities change as the result of a decision. Therefore, organizations using ABC should be better able to identify costs that will change with a particular decision, at least over a reasonable period, and should have fewer problems with allocations getting in the way of good decisions.

If, as is the case with companies using ABC, the only costs assigned to segments are those that are clearly driven by activities of the segments, then significant amounts of such costs might be avoidable. Managers who can determine how activities will change as a result of taking particular courses of action should be better able to estimate the effects of the changes on costs. Good estimates are especially likely if the segment will cease certain activities. Even in that case, however, the cost reduction might not be immediate. Moreover, changing the level of an activity might not have a direct, proportional effect on costs; that is, a normal ABC analysis does not automatically determine how much cost is avoidable in any given situation. Activity-based allocations do not substitute for careful analyses of the likely effects of decisions, but they should make those analyses less difficult to develop.

Of great importance in analyzing decisions is whether they truly fit the short-term category, and do not presage longer-term commitments. Companies should use incremental analysis for pure short-term, one-shot decisions such as whether to sell a single batch of goods outside normal channels. But whether to sign a contract to supply a discount chain with private branded goods over the next year is not such a one-shot decision, and requires an ABC analysis. Similarly, dropping a product that accounts for 1 percent of sales might not have significant effects beyond the lost contribution margin. Dropping products that amount to 20 percent of business will have much more widespread effects.

## TYPICAL SHORT-TERM DECISIONS

Most of the remainder of this chapter is devoted to typical examples of short-term decisions. Although the situations appear to be quite different, the basic principle we stated earlier applies to all: *Find the most profitable alternative by analyzing the differential revenues and costs.* In some cases, it will be relatively easy to determine the differentials and choose among the alternatives. In others, you might find it easier to make your choice by preparing complete income statements for the alternatives. But the two approaches should lead to the same decision.

## DROPPING A SEGMENT

You already know there are many ways to segment a company. Determining the best mix of segments is a continual problem for managers, who sometimes have to decide whether to drop a segment, or perhaps to replace one segment with another. For example, managers of supermarkets regularly consider whether to carry nongrocery products or services such as flowers, video rentals, and photo processing. Managers of department stores face similar decisions.

LeBranna Fashions uses its available space for three product lines. Following is the income statement for a recent month, and LeBranna's managers expect these results to continue in the foreseeable future.

|  | Clothing | Shoes | Jewelry | Total |
|---|---|---|---|---|
| Sales | $45,000 | $40,000 | $15,000 | $100,000 |
| Variable costs | 25,000 | 18,000 | 11,000 | 54,000 |
| Contribution margin | $20,000 | $22,000 | $ 4,000 | $ 46,000 |
| Fixed costs: | | | | |
| Direct—all avoidable | (4,000) | (3,400) | (1,500) | (8,900) |
| Indirect (common), | | | | |
| allocated on sales | (9,450) | (8,400) | (3,150) | (21,000) |
| Income (loss) | $ 6,550 | $10,200 | $ (650) | $ 16,100 |

Should the store drop the jewelry line because it shows a loss? To answer that question we must know what would change if LeBranna dropped the line.

Let's begin with a choice between two simple alternatives: keep jewelry or drop it and rent the available space to another company for $400 per month. If it dropped jewelry, LeBranna would lose the $15,000 of sales but could avoid the $11,000 of variable costs of those sales as well as the $1,500 avoidable fixed costs shown on the segment report. A careful analysis of the cost drivers for the various common (indirect) fixed costs would show LeBranna's managers how much of those costs might be avoided by dropping the line. (Remember the example of the payroll department.) The accompanying Insight describes one such analysis.

Suppose LeBranna's analysis shows that dropping jewelry would reduce common costs by $1,000, so that they would drop to $20,000. The changes (differentials) are summarized as follows.

**IN** *SIGHT*

### Using ABC to Determine the Cost of a Segment

**Mahaney Welding Supply** is a distributor of welding supplies and compressed gases in the upstate New York area. Mahaney performed an ABC analysis to determine whether certain parts of the company were profitable or not. The ABC analysis indicated that fifteen different activities drove costs. The analysis identified the costs of servicing different customers. After the ABC analysis, it appeared that a specific route was unprofitable. Rather than drop the route, Mahaney explored various ways that the route could be made more profitable. The company had to be careful about dropping the route because some customers on the route also brought business into the shop and some customers on the route were clearly profitable. Among the possible remedies were reshuffling the route, imposing a delivery charge, and requiring a minimum sales charge. The authors, one of whom works for Mahaney, stressed that the ABC analysis did not make the decisions, managers made them, and that ABC was simply one tool for doing so.

*Source: Michael Krupnicki and Thomas Tyson, "Using ABC to Determine the Cost of Servicing Customers," Management Accounting, December 1997, 40–46.*

| Decision: Rent Out the Space (*Rather* than Sell Jewelry) | | |
|---|---:|---:|
| Differential revenues: | | |
| Lost sales from jewelry | $15,000 | |
| New rent revenue | 400 | |
| Net revenue *lost* | | $14,600 |
| Differential costs: | | |
| Variable costs saved on jewelry | $11,000 | |
| Direct fixed costs saved | 1,500 | |
| Indirect fixed costs saved | 1,000 | |
| Total cost saving | | 13,500 |
| Differential *loss* from dropping jewelry | | $ 1,100 |

Keeping jewelry seems the better choice because dropping it and renting out the space will *reduce* income by $1,100. The analysis shows separately the lost revenues and the savings of variable costs, but we could have shown only a $4,000 differential for contribution margin lost. Another way to determine the change in income is to prepare a new income statement that includes only the remaining product lines, the rent revenue, and the lower common costs. (Total income drops from $16,100 to $15,000, a $1,100 difference.)

Realistic decisions about dropping a segment usually involve alternatives for using freed-up resources. For example, LeBranna might be able to use the space to expand one of its other lines, or for an altogether new line. Let's examine a slightly more complicated alternative. Suppose LeBranna could operate a music department in the space now occupied by jewelry. LeBranna's managers estimate that a music department would generate revenues of $20,000 and variable costs of $8,000, for a $12,000 contribution margin, and would have $2,700 of direct fixed costs. If LeBranna substitutes the music department for jewelry, it will not reduce common costs. Should LeBranna make the substitution? What will change? Contribution margin will increase $8,000 ($12,000 from music vs. $4,000 from jewelry) but direct fixed costs will increase by $1,200 ($2,700 for music vs. $1,500 for jewelry). The substitution would increase income by $6,800 ($8,000 − $1,200). The differential analysis of the substitution option is as follows.

| Decision: Substitute Music for Jewelry | |
| --- | --- |
| Differential contribution margin—increase  ($12,000 − $4,000) | $8,000 |
| Differential costs—increase in <br> direct fixed costs ($2,700 − $1,500) | 1,200 |
| Differential profit *favoring substitution* | $6,800 |

If you prepared a complete income statement for the new sales mix, income would be $22,900, $6,800 higher than the current $16,100.

We emphasize that the decision is whether to substitute music for jewelry. The purpose of that decision is to find the best way to use *existing* resources. The analysis would differ if LeBranna were considering *adding* music to its existing product lines. Adding a line requires investment in new resources (e.g., display equipment, furniture and fixtures, etc.), a characteristic that distinguishes long-term from short-term decisions.

The alternatives considered thus far serve to remind you that whether a cost is avoidable depends on the decision. If the decision is whether to drop jewelry altogether, the $1,000 potential reduction in common costs is relevant because it is avoidable and, therefore, differential. But if the decision is whether to substitute music for jewelry, none of the common costs are relevant because they are all unavoidable.

### Complementary Effects

The facts of the preceding example didn't include any likelihood that dropping or adding a segment (product line, in this case) would affect the sales of other segments. But as noted in the discussion of sales mix in the appendix to Chapter 2, a change in the sales of one product is often accompanied by a change in the sales of another. When such a relationship exists, a decision about one product is said to have **complementary effects**. Marketing studies of shopping habits often help quantify the effects of such complementary relationships.

Suppose LeBranna's managers believe that some people coming to shop for music are also likely to buy clothing. After reviewing the results of market studies, the managers estimate that clothing sales will increase 7 percent if music is substituted for jewelry. Considering this new information, should LeBranna make the substitution?

You should see that a differential analysis of the substitution decision includes everything in the previous analysis *plus* the impact of the complementary effects. Following is such an analysis.

| Decision: Substitute Music for Jewelry | |
|---|---|
| Differential contribution margin: | |
| Increase due to selling music vs. jewelry | $8,000 |
| Increase due to higher clothing sales | |
| (7% × $20,000 contribution margin on current sales) | 1,400 |
| Net increase in contribution margin | $9,400 |
| Differential costs—increase in direct fixed costs | |
| ($2,700 – $1,500) | 1,200 |
| Differential profit favoring substitution | $8,200 |

The advantage of the substitution is greater than computed earlier ($8,200 vs. $6,800), and the substitution is still profitable. Again, we could have determined the outcome of the substitution by preparing an income statement to reflect the new sales mix including the complementary effects. (You might want to prepare such a statement to confirm the answer reached using only differentials.) The statement should show total income of $24,300, which is $8,200 greater than the $16,100 income with the current mix.

**Loss Leader**

A particularly interesting case of complementary effects is the **loss leader**, a product or line that shows a negative profit in the sense that its contribution margin does not cover its avoidable fixed costs. In an extreme case, the product might even have a negative contribution margin. If complementary effects between the loss leader and the firm's other products are large enough, even such an extreme pricing policy could be beneficial.

Consider the manager of a local pizzeria who is concerned by the lack of business at lunchtime. He attributes this problem to specials at competing restaurants and wants to change the situation. (Note that the *segment* in this case is a time period rather than a product or product line.) He has prepared the following income statement, based on a normal week, for the 11 a.m. to 2 p.m. period. The costs shown are all incremental.

| | Pizza | Soft Drinks | Total |
|---|---|---|---|
| Sales (200 pizzas @ $1.80) | $360 | $100 | $460 |
| Variable costs | 120 | 40 | 160 |
| Contribution margin | $240 | $ 60 | $300 |
| Wages of part-time employees | | | 80 |
| Income | | | $220 |

He is thinking about offering free soft drinks with each pizza. He believes the offer could double lunchtime pizza sales. On the basis of his experience and judgment, he anticipates that soft drink consumption will increase to two and one-half times the present level. He also estimates that the cost of additional part-time help needed for the additional business would increase by $40 per week. Soft drinks will generate no revenue, but the costs will continue, so he will obviously lose money on beverages. Can he gain enough on the sales of pizza to offset the loss?

The following expected income statement for the lunchtime period shows the effects of the special, using the manager's estimates (which are the best information available).

|  | Pizza | Soft Drinks | Total |
|---|---|---|---|
| Sales | $720 | $ 0 | $720 |
| Variable costs | 240[a] | 100[b] | 340 |
| Contribution margin | $480 | $(100) | $380 |
| Wages of part-time employees ($80 + $40) |  |  | 120 |
| Income |  |  | $260 |

a  *Variable costs computed at the same rate as before, one-third or 33 1/3% of selling price.*
b  *Variable costs computed as two and one-half times the previous costs.*

Soft drinks show a negative contribution margin. Yet if expectations about increased sales are realized, total income increases by $40 per week ($260 – $220). In this case, developing a new income statement is probably easier than determining differentials for specific items.

The potential for complementary effects is more obvious in some cases than in others. For example, one can readily see the relationship between sales of toothbrushes and toothpaste. The relationship is also clear in **Little Caesar's Pizza** offers of a free liter of Coca-Cola with an order of a large pizza. But the loss-leader rationale is also behind many low prices that are expected to encourage sales of products that are not complementary. Examples include buy-one, get-one-free offers and offers of extremely low prices for some name-brand item—a can of Campbell's tomato soup for 10 cents—to customers spending $10 (or some other specific amount) on other grocery items. In these examples, the complementary products are all other products in the store.

Considering the company as a whole is important in evaluating any decision. A product that is selling at a loss—even at a negative contribution margin—might be so essential to the sales of other products that it should not be dropped (recall the previous Insight). Or perhaps a qualitative issue, such as a reputation for offering a complete product line, will be relevant to a decision that could affect that reputation. Of course, a company's managers should want to know the cost of maintaining such a policy. Marketing managers might argue for retaining low-volume products because the company should offer a full line. An ABC analysis can indicate whether products are unprofitable, but cannot determine whether the marketing managers are correct. As did **Mahaney**, cited in an earlier Insight, a company might look for ways to make the segment less unprofitable.

## MAKE-OR-BUY DECISIONS

Manufactured products consist of several components that are assembled into a finished unit. Many of these components can be bought from an outside supplier or made by the assembling firm. For each component, a company's managers must decide whether to make or buy. Besides cost, flexibility and reduction of risk are reasons that some companies outsource, as described in the accompanying Insight.

As with other decisions, the quantitative factors are the differential costs to make and to buy. Suppose XYZ Company now makes a component for its major

**SIGHT**

## Outsourcing Manufacturing

Buying goods and services outside the company is now so common that an Outsourcing Institute exists. The September 29, 1997 issue of *Fortune* contained a 48-page advertising supplement devoted solely to outsourcing.

Some companies do little besides manufacture goods for sale under other companies' names. They now form an industry called *contract manufacturers*. They are becoming increasingly important in high-tech. Companies such as **Solectron** and **Jabil Circuit** have been successful in contract manufacturing for several reasons. One is that demand for personal computers is so volatile and unpredictable that PC makers often find they lack the capacity to produce popular models. Because of the short life cycles of computers, sales lost because of inability to meet customer demand are probably lost forever. PC makers then must turn to contract manufacturers, which maintain sufficient capacity to absorb peaks in demand. For instance, Solectron has three types of assembly lines, one for high-volume products, one for medium-volume, and one for low-volume, but is able to switch some products from one line to another. This flexibility allows it to absorb unexpectedly high demand for some products. Solectron now manufactures cellular phone products for **Mitsubishi Electric**, the Japanese company.

**Western Digital**, a large disk drive maker, buys 70 percent of its parts, while **Seagate Technologies**, another large drive maker, makes nearly all of its parts. Seagate therefore has higher fixed costs than Western Digital, which hurts its performance in lean years. Seagate also earns higher profits in good years, but Western Digital has more stable earnings.

*Sources: Scott Wooley, "Get Off Your Assets," Forbes, January 13, 1997, 54.*
*G. Pascal Zachary, "Solectron to Take Over Manufacturing of Some Mitsubishi Electric Products," The Wall Street Journal, July 30, 1998, A4.*

product. A manager has prepared the following estimates of costs at the normal volume of 20,000 units.

| | |
|---|---:|
| Materials at $2 per unit | $ 40,000 |
| Direct labor at $5 per unit | 100,000 |
| Variable overhead at $3 per unit | 60,000 |
| Allocated indirect fixed costs (building depreciation, heat and light, etc.) | 120,000 |
| Total costs | $320,000 |

An outside supplier offers to supply the component at $14 per unit or $280,000 for 20,000 units. Should XYZ accept the offer?

Because unit sales of the final product will be the same whether XYZ makes or buys the component, revenues are the same either way. Hence, the decision depends on which alternative results in the lower cost. The cost of making the component depends on whether alternative uses can be found for the space and equipment now used to make the component, and whether the total of any of the other allocated fixed costs will change if the company buys the component from an outsider supplier. If no alternative use is available and total allocated fixed costs won't change, the analysis is quite straightforward. The following schedule focuses on the relevant costs for each available course of action.

|  | Decisions | |
|---|---|---|
|  | Make | Buy |
| Materials | $ 40,000 | $        0 |
| Direct labor | 100,000 | 0 |
| Variable overhead | 60,000 | 0 |
| Purchase price | 0 | 280,000 |
| Total | $200,000 | $280,000 |

XYZ saves $80,000 by making the component. (Note that including the fixed overhead of $120,000 under both alternatives would not change the $80,000 advantage of making the component.) Of course, if XYZ could reduce the indirect fixed costs by outside purchase of the component, the avoidable cost should be part of the total cost of making the component internally.

The following analysis shows only the differentials of a decision to make the component.

| Decision: Make the Component (*Rather* than Buy) | | |
|---|---|---|
| New cost—purchase from outside supplier |  | $280,000 |
| Cost savings—materials | $ 40,000 |  |
| —labor | 100,000 |  |
| —variable overhead | 60,000 |  |
| Total savings |  | 200,000 |
| Difference *favoring* making the component |  | $ 80,000 |

XYZ is better off making the component unless it can obtain more than $80,000 by using the space and equipment in some other way. Considering only the quantitative data, XYZ should use the available space and equipment to make the component until some other opportunity arises such that the opportunity cost—the benefit to be gained by using the space and equipment for that other purpose—exceeds the $80,000 cost savings available by using those resources to make the component. Such a benefit could come from renting the space and equipment or using them to make a product that would bring more than $80,000 in incremental profit. XYZ might even consider using the resources to make a component it is currently buying from an outsider.

### Long-Term Considerations

We remind you that this chapter focuses on short-term decisions, which concern the best way to use existing resources. Thus, our example mentioned possible other *uses* for the equipment devoted to making the component; it did not mention disposing of the equipment. Selling the equipment has long-term consequences, because it eliminates the company's ability to return quickly to in-house production should an outside supplier prove unsuitable. The same is true when managers are considering *making* a component now purchased outside, if in-house production requires new equipment. Chapter 8 presents techniques managers use to analyze long-term decisions.

### Qualitative Issues

Managers consider many qualitative issues when deciding whether to purchase or make a component. Will the quality of purchased components be as good as the company can achieve by producing the part in-house? Will the supplier meet delivery commitments? A few years ago, a major question was "Will the supplier raise the price later?" That question is still important in some situations, but cost-cutting efforts by large manufacturers have increased pressure on suppliers to *reduce* component prices. Hence, the relative sizes, and bargaining power, of the buyer and supplier are also relevant to a make-or-buy decision.

Deciding whether to acquire a service internally or externally requires considering all of the costs of providing the service and all of the costs of purchasing the service. If you are going to produce the item or service internally on a long-term basis, you must consider long-term costs such as continuing R&D, human resource development, etc. You should also consider the headquarters and support costs that are necessary to monitor the production of the good or service. The best approach to use in determining these costs is the activity-based costing approach presented in Chapter 4. The costs of purchasing, receiving, and monitoring the purchase of the goods or services will also create costs.

Outsourcing is a way for a company to achieve increased effectiveness of functions within the company that are not core competencies. From a strategic viewpoint, core competencies are the activities that offer the company a long-term competitive advantage and must be controlled very closely. Peripheral activities are those that are not critical to the company's competitive edge. Activities such as building security, maintenance, distribution, logistics, and even product design are being outsourced. Outsourcing is no longer limited to manufacturing operations, as the accompanying Insight shows.

Make-or-buy decisions are especially important in an advanced manufacturing environment. A just-in-time manufacturer is concerned with quality and delivery schedules and will not buy a component unless both are guaranteed.

An additional consideration is how purchasing a good or service fits with the company's value chain. As discussed in Chapter 1, some companies choose to participate in many sectors of the value chain while others choose to participate in only a few sectors. **Nike** participates in the research and development portion of the athletic footwear value chain and the marketing, distribution, and sales portion. The company made a strategic decision to stay out of the manufacturing portion of the value chain.

## JOINT PRODUCTS

When a single manufacturing process invariably produces two or more separate products, the products are called **joint products**. The process that makes the products is called a **joint process**, and the costs of operating such a process are called **joint costs**. (Joint costs are one type of what we call **common costs**.) Petroleum refiners and meat packers operate joint processes. Refining crude

**SIGHT**

### Outsourcing is Not Just for Manufacturing

A 1995 study by Arthur Andersen and the Economist Intelligence Unit examined the scope of outsourcing in the finance function. The survey revealed 42 percent of the companies surveyed already outsource pension management, 40 percent tax, 28 percent payroll, 19 percent leasing, 12 percent internal auditing, and 12 percent short-term investment management. A second survey reported that companies outsource to reduce their administrative costs and to improve the quality of the service.

The whole process of procurement, through purchase orders to accounts payable to payment, is one non-core area where much outsourcing exists. Various personnel and accounting functions are also candidates. Many universities contract with outsiders to provide food services and to operate the campus bookstore.

As the controller of **Strategic Materials, Inc.** put it, "We are an $80 million company in a very competitive industry [glass products], and we do not choose to allocate our investments into improving our support processes. Our time is better spent focusing on the acquisition and sale of glass, not on nonstrategic purchasing and accounts payable." One study suggested that companies should consider outsourcing any activity that " . . . is not part of your company's core competence," and even to consider outsourcing activities that are ". . . close to the core, but you simply cannot do well."

Perhaps the ultimate in outsourcing was the plan of Connecticut to have all of its information technology contracted out. Some 65 state agencies in Connecticut now spend about $250 million annually on information technology, which the state thinks could drop by $50 million with a private contractor. Many people are delighted at the prospect of getting their driver's licenses from a source other than the Department of Transportation.

*Sources: Robert Kralovetz, "A Guide to Successful Outsourcing,"* Management Accounting, *October 1996, 32-38.*
*Celia Renner & Darin Tebbe, "Who is Outsourcing and Why?"* Management Accounting, *July 1998, 45-47.*
*Wendy Zellner, "The Promised Land for Outsourcing?"* Business Week, *July 6, 1998, 39.*
*Charles E. Davis and Lee Ann Moore, "Outsourcing the Procurement-Through-Payables Process,"* Management Accounting, *July 1998, 38–44.*
*Michael Useem and Joseph Harder, "Lateral Leadership for Organizations That Are Outsourcing,"* Wharton Center for Leadership and Change Management, *quoted in* Wharton Alumni Magazine, *Summer 1998, 26.*

petroleum yields various products, including auto and aircraft fuel, various grades of oil, and kerosene. Processing cattle results in hides, hoofs, various cuts of meat, and other items (fat, bones).

In some joint processes, the company can control how much of each product emerges, within limits. An oil refiner can change the amounts of motor oil and gasoline that emerge from the refining process, but cannot get a barrel of gasoline out of a barrel of crude petroleum. In other joint processes, the company has no control over which products emerge from the process, and in what quantities. Some joint products are valuable; some have little or no value. Some can be sold just as they emerge from the joint process or can be processed further. For example, a meat packer might sell hides to a tanner. Or, if the meat packer has the expertise and the facilities, it could tan the hides, or even use the tanned hides to make shoes, gloves, and other products.

Companies that operate joint processes must decide whether to sell each of the joint products at the **split-off point**—the point at which they emerge from the joint process as separate products—or to process each further into another saleable product. Such a decision can't be based on the total costs of the individual final products or even on the total variable costs. To produce *any* of the joint products, the company must undertake the joint process and so incur all the costs to perform that process. For example, a meat packer might pay $300 per animal. This cost does not relate to particular cuts of meat, to hides, or to by-products, because the packer must buy the entire animal to get *any* of those products. The total cost of purchasing animals varies with the number of animals entering the joint process, but the $300 cost per animal is the same whether any or all of the joint products are sold immediately or processed further. Hence, the costs incurred prior to split-off—the costs of the joint process—are irrelevant to decisions about the joint products. In determining whether to sell a product at the split-off point or process it further, all costs incurred prior to the split-off point are sunk, whether such costs are fixed or variable with respect to the volume of input material that goes through the joint process.

Consider the following example. QBT, a chemical company, operates a joint process that results in two products, Alpha and Omega. Each 1,000 pounds of materials yields 600 pounds of Alpha and 400 pounds of Omega. QBT can sell both Alpha and Omega at the split-off point, or process each product further. Selling price and cost data per batch (1,000 pounds of materials) are as follows.

|  | Alpha | Omega |
|---|---|---|
| Selling price at split-off | $1,200 ($2 per pound) | $1,600 ($4 per pound) |
| Selling price after additional processing | $3,600 ($6 per pound) | $2,000 ($5 per pound) |
| Costs of additional processing, all variable | $900 ($1.50 per pound) | $500 ($1.25 per pound) |

We can analyze the results of both alternatives for each product. We analyze Alpha as follows.

| Decision Alternatives for Alpha | | |
|---|---|---|
|  | Sell at Split-Off | Process Further |
| Sales value | $1,200 | $3,600 |
| Incremental cost | 0 | 900 |
| Incremental profit | $1,200 | $2,700 |

QBT should process Alpha beyond split-off because profit will be $1,500 higher ($2,700 − $1,200). The following differential analysis of the decision to process Alpha further gives the same conclusion.

| Decision: Process Alpha Further (*Rather* than Sell at Split-Off) | |
|---|---|
| Differential revenue ($3,600 – $1,200) | $2,400 |
| Differential costs | 900 |
| Differential profit, favoring additional processing | $1,500 |

A similar analysis of the alternatives for Omega reveals that QBT should sell it at split-off, not process it further.

| Decision: Process Omega Further (*Rather* than Sell at Split-Off) | |
|---|---|
| Differential revenues ($2,000 – $1,600) | $ 400 |
| Differential costs | 500 |
| Differential loss, favoring sale at split-off | $(100) |

QBT would be $100 worse off processing Omega further.

The preceding analytical approaches are appropriate when all incremental costs of additional processing are variable. As a practical matter, additional processing will almost surely require space, equipment, and people. Some of those costs might be avoidable. Let's assume that further processing of Alpha requires avoidable fixed costs of $10,000 per month and that QBT usually processes ten batches per month. Note that the $10,000 is common to *all* Alpha further processed during the month. Hence, to compare costs and revenues, the focus must be on the *monthly* output of 6,000 pounds (10 × 600 pounds per batch). The following analysis indicates a $5,000 advantage ($17,000 – $12,000) to processing Alpha beyond split-off.

| Decision Alternatives for Alpha | | |
|---|---|---|
| | Sell at Split-Off | Process Further |
| Sales: 10 × $1,200 per batch | $12,000 | |
|        10 × $3,600 per batch | | $ 36,000 |
| Incremental costs: | | |
|    Variable (10 × $900 per batch) | — | (9,000) |
|    Fixed and avoidable | — | (10,000) |
| Incremental profit | $12,000 | $ 17,000 |

A differential analysis would show the $24,000 additional revenue from selling after further processing ($36,000 – $12,000) and the additional costs of further processing ($19,000), giving the same $5,000 difference in favor of processing Alpha beyond the split-off point. Still another way to look at the decision is to say that the opportunity cost of processing further is the $12,000 given up by not selling at split-off. Incorporating the opportunity cost into the analysis of the decision to process further gives total costs of $31,000 ($9,000 variable costs + $10,000 avoidable fixed costs + $12,000 opportunity cost to use the output for further processing). Subtracting $31,000 from the $36,000 revenue gives the same $5,000 advantage of processing Alpha further.

The joint products case exemplifies a critical point made earlier: the relevance or irrelevance of a cost depends on the specific decision. The variable costs of the joint process are relevant in deciding whether to operate that process at all, because they are avoidable if the joint process is not operated. But they are irrelevant in deciding whether to sell a given joint product at the split-off point or to process it further. Thus, a managerial accountant cannot respond to the question "What does it cost?" without knowing why the manager wants the answer to that question.

### Long-Term Considerations

In analyzing further processing decisions we are dealing with companies that already have the facilities and expertise to carry out the additional processing. (Otherwise, the decision is not short term.) Such a company has the flexibility to respond quickly to changes in selling prices of a joint product, either at the split-off point or after further processing. If additional capital investment is required, the decision about further processing becomes long term. Similarly, a decision about reducing short-term flexibility by eliminating facilities needed for additional processing of joint products is long term.

One type of joint product that creates interesting strategic problems is the unit that does not meet the specifications of the standard product, but is nevertheless serviceable, and which the company cannot reduce to zero with available manufacturing methods. Most people are familiar with factory outlets and other stores that sell seconds, damaged clothing, and other products. The accompanying Insight describes the problem that besets computer chip makers.

 *SIGHT*

#### Product Seconds

**Intel**, the world's largest chipmaker, processes silicon wafers containing perhaps a thousand chips. But not all of the chips work according to specifications. Some are total losses. A single dust mote will ruin an entire chip, necessitating the clean room manufacture seen in Intel's advertisements. Phenomena as subtle as air currents can harm chips as well. Some chips will not perform as well as their mates on the wafer, but are still adequate for some purposes. Intel's Pentium 60 and Pentium 90 chips were actually Pentium 66 and Pentium 100 chips that would not run at the faster speeds, but which ran fine at slower speeds. Intel and other chipmakers want to reduce sub-standard chips to zero, but that objective is not achievable with current manufacturing methods and equipment. Intel, and every other chipmaker, must then decide what to do with rejects. Selling them at reduced prices seems attractive, but might reduce sales of their own standard chips. Some customers who buy the standard chips would be perfectly happy with slower, cheaper chips. The decision can be complicated. If demand is strong, so that the company can sell all of its high-quality output, no harm is likely from selling seconds. But if demand is weak, sales of seconds might replace regular sales one-to-one, so the company could lose money.

## SPECIAL ORDERS

Companies that make products to be sold under their own brand names often make nearly identical products and sell them at lower prices under the brand names of chain stores (called *house brands*). For example, at one time **Whirlpool Corp**. sold over 40 percent of the appliances it made to **Sears**, which marketed them under the Kenmore name. Some manufacturers might also sell to chains at lower prices than to smaller dealers selling under the manufacturer's brand name. In addition, manufacturers might accept special one-time orders at lower-than-usual prices when the level of actual sales is lower than that expected when planning production volume.

Griffith Company's income statement for 20X8 is based on planned production and sales of 60,000 units, with sales at $15 per unit. Griffith has the capacity to produce 100,000 units, and could hire additional hourly workers to achieve production in excess of 60,000. A chain store has just approached Griffith with an offer to buy 20,000 units at $10. The variable portion of selling and administrative costs is a 2 percent sales commission ($0.30 per unit on regular sales), which Griffith would not have to pay on the special order. The president is hesitant to accept the order because the average manufacturing cost of $13 per unit ($780,000/60,000) is greater than the $10 price offered.

|  | Per Unit | Total | |
|---|---|---|---|
| Sales (60,000 units) | $15 | | $900,000 |
| Manufacturing costs: | | | |
|   Materials | $ 4 | $240,000 | |
|   Direct labor | 3 | 180,000 | |
|   Overhead (one-third variable) | 6 | 360,000 | |
|   Total | $13 | | 780,000 |
| Gross margin | | | $120,000 |
| Selling and administrative expenses | | | 80,000 |
| Operating income | | | $ 40,000 |

As always, only the differential elements should be considered in making a decision. Following is a summary of the differentials.

| Decision: Accept the Special Order (*Rather* than Reject It) | | | |
|---|---|---|---|
|  | Per Unit | Total | |
| Differential revenues (20,000 units) | $10 | | $200,000 |
| Differential costs: | | | |
|   Materials | $ 4 | $80,000 | |
|   Direct labor | 3 | 60,000 | |
|   Variable overhead | 2 | 40,000 | |
|   Total | $ 9 | | 180,000 |
| Incremental profit favoring acceptance | | | $ 20,000 |

Accepting the order increases income by $20,000; therefore, Griffith should accept it unless its managers believe that nonquantifiable factors outweigh that benefit.

In this example, the only differential costs for the order were variable manufacturing costs. In another situation, variable selling and administrative expenses and perhaps some incremental fixed costs might apply. For example, when a special order requires a large increase in production, additional fixed costs might be incurred because the higher production level involves one or more steps in step-variable manufacturing or administrative costs. Those cost increases should also be incorporated in the analysis.

An important concern of accepting many special orders is their potential for affecting sales at regular prices. For instance, an appliance manufacturer deciding whether to supply a discount chain with 100,000 washing machines must consider whether its sales to regular dealers will fall because some customers will buy from the chain instead of from regular dealers. Or perhaps the special order is larger than available capacity, or would cause production delays, so that accepting the order requires foregoing some sales at regular prices. (Even a company having the capacity to accommodate both the planned sales and the special order risks lost sales if actual demand is greater than planned.) **Polk Audio**, a maker of loudspeaker systems, was well aware of potential problems when it began selling its products to **Circuit City** stores. Polk's 1997 annual report noted that while the agreement with Circuit City guaranteed more national exposure for Polk products, it would make some Polk dealers unhappy. Accordingly, one of Polk's stated missions for 1998 was to do even better serving its dealers.

We can illustrate the problem of lost sales, and a basic approach for dealing with it, by continuing the example of Griffith Company. Suppose that due to a labor shortage, Griffith can expect to produce only 75,000 units despite its physical capacity for 100,000 units. Accepting the special order means that Griffith can make only 55,000 units for sale at the regular price (capacity of 75,000 – 20,000 units on the special order). A differential analysis that includes the new information follows. (Remember that there is a commission, a variable selling cost, on regular sales.)

|  | | |
|---|---:|---:|
| **Decision: Accept the Special Order (*Rather* than Reject It)** | | |
| Differential revenues: | | |
| New revenues from the order (above) | $200,000 | |
| Lost revenues on regular sales (5,000 × $15) | 75,000 | |
| Total differential revenues | | $125,000 |
| Differential costs: | | |
| Costs for the special order (earlier) | $180,000 | |
| Costs saved by not making regular sales: | | |
| Variable manufacturing cost | | |
| 5,000 units × $9 ($4 + $3 + $2) | (45,000) | |
| Commissions | | |
| 5,000 × $0.30 | (1,500) | |
| Total differential costs | | 133,500 |
| Differential loss, favoring rejecting the order | | $  (8,500) |

Another approach is to compare the contribution margin on the special order with the contribution margin lost on regular sales.

|  | |
|---|---:|
| **Decision: Accept the Special Order (*Rather* than Reject It)** | |
| New contribution margin—special order | |
| 20,000 × ($10 – $9 variable manufacturing cost) | $20,000 |
| Lost contribution margin—regular sales | |
| 5,000 × ($15 – $9 – $0.30 = $5.70) | 28,500 |
| Loss from accepting order | $ (8,500) |

Both analyses show the special order to be unprofitable under the revised conditions (total output of 75,000 units).

Consider another example. Suppose Griffith has no capacity constraint but its managers believe that *some* sales at the regular price would be lost because of customers buying from the chain. How many units of sales would Griffith have to lose at the regular price to make the special order unprofitable? At a $5.70 per-unit contribution margin for regular sales (shown on previous page), Griffith could lose sales of up to 3,509 units ($20,000 incremental profit on order/$5.70 contribution margin) at regular prices without hurting overall profits. The managers must then assess the likelihood that lost sales would approach that critical number.

### Long-Term Considerations

Because managers view special-order decisions as short term, they might focus on variable costs when quoting a price. Managers do understand, however, that these decisions can have long-term consequences. Companies might accept so much private branding that they need additional manufacturing capacity to meet the continuing growth of their regular sales. Special orders can also stress other resources, so that indirect costs could increase. This possibility is a reason for using ABC, which highlights resource consumption and can sound warnings about approaching problems. Another long-term aspect of accepting special orders at prices based primarily on variable costs is that a company cannot long survive without covering *all* of its costs. Smaller companies, especially, must be careful not to devote too much capacity to special orders that could dominate their businesses. These companies, which are often delighted to acquire large customers such as **Sears**, **Wal-Mart**, or **JC Penney**, can become captives as their large customers demand more and more of their capacity. Victor Coppola, then Director of National Emerging Business Services for an international public accounting firm, was quoted in *The Wall Street Journal* as saying that there are no success stories of captive suppliers.[1]

### RESOURCE CONSTRAINTS

In the special-order example, Griffith's production was constrained, limited to 75,000 units because of a shortage of labor. A shortage of some other productive factor, such as space, machine time, or workers with critical skills, might also restrict operations. Multiproduct companies facing constraints must decide how to use the limited quantity of the constraining factor. Theory of Constraints, which we discuss in detail in Chapter 16, is an important approach to constraint management. For now, we look only at a simple case.

Consider RSLtech, which makes two types of controller chips: one for disk drives, the other for modems. RSLtech can sell all it can make of either product. Both products require processing on machines with total capacity of 1,000 hours per week. Data relating to these two products are as follows.

|  | Drive Chip | Modem Chip |
|---|---|---|
| Selling price | $10 | $6 |
| Variable cost | 6 | 4 |
| Contribution margin | $ 4 | $2 |
| Number of chips that can be made per machine hour | 60 | 150 |

---

1   *June 10, 1988, 36R.*

 **SIGHT**

### House Brands

Perhaps one of the boldest moves in the house-brand arena in many years was the announcement by **AutoNation** that it was considering offering a house-brand automobile to be built by one or more of the major car companies. AutoNation is a chain of auto stores owned by **Republic Industries**. About 25-30 percent of the price of a new car is marketing and distribution. AutoNation expected to be able to slash those costs and offer the cars at very attractive prices. One reason for considering such a move is that the auto industry is plagued by overcapacity. Another is that increasing standardization of parts and modularization (building modules of cars in various factories and assembling them at a central location) makes the idea of producing a unique car possible. The cars would have to be different from the standard models that the companies now make.

**Gerber Childrenswear** manufactures about 12 percent of its output for private brands. The company even develops new brands for customers such as **Wal-Mart**, which does not want to sell the same brand in its Wal-Mart stores as it does in its **Sam's Clubs**. Because of the need for quick responses to customer orders, Gerber produces a large quantity of goods in the United States. Its U.S. operations can deliver within three to five days, while eight weeks is the norm for an overseas plant. Rapid delivery makes the company competitive with foreign-based suppliers in the hotly contested business.

*Sources: Fara Warner, "AutoNation Is Considering Offering a House-Brand Car," The Wall Street Journal, July 21, 1998, b4.*
*Jim DuPlessis, "Selling Small Packages," Greenville News, July 5, 1998, B10-14.*

To decide which product to make, RSLtech's managers cannot look only at contribution margin, because the company can make (and sell) more modem chips than drive chips. If the managers are to make the best possible use of the available machine time, they must consider both the difference in contribution margin and the difference in the production demands on the scarce production factor, machine time.

Two equivalent approaches are available. The first compares total contribution margin from the products over some specific time period, such as a week (100 machine hours available).

Alternative Uses of Machine Time

|  | Drive Chip | Modem Chip |
|---|---|---|
| Maximum weekly production |  |  |
| (60 × 1,000) | 60,000 |  |
| (150 × 1,000) |  | 150,000 |
| Contribution margin per unit | × $4 | × $2 |
| Total weekly contribution margin | $240,000 | $300,000 |

The analysis shows that producing modem chips is the more profitable use of machine time. The answer does not depend on the time period chosen, as we show using the second approach. This approach also shows differences in contribution margin but concentrates on a unit of the scarce input. That is, the second approach determines the *contribution margin per unit of the scarce factor*. In RSLtech's case, the scarce factor is machine time, so the second analysis compares contribution per machine hour.

|  | Drive Chip | Modem Chip |
|---|---|---|
| Number of units that can be made per machine hour | 60 | 150 |
| Contribution margin per unit | × $4 | × $2 |
| Contribution margin per hour | $240 | $300 |

The second analysis, like the first, shows that it is more profitable to produce modem chips; they contribute more than drive chips, *per hour of machine time. The optimal policy is to make the product that has the highest contribution margin per unit of the constraining factor.*

RSLtech's managers can also use the information derived from the preceding analyses for setting prices. For example, suppose the managers are considering raising the price of the drive chip. What price must they charge for the drive chip to make using machine time for it as profitable as using the time to make modem chips? To achieve that objective, the contribution margins *per machine hour* must be equal, which means that the margin for making drive chips has to be $300 per hour. Since RSLtech can make 60 drive chips per hour, contribution per chip has to be $5 ($300/60). Adding the $5 margin to the $6 variable cost per chip gives a selling price of $11. At that price, devoting machine time to making drive chips yields the same contribution margin as spending the time making modem chips. The accompanying Insight illustrates how managers applied their understanding of cost and contribution margin data to analyzing the effects of the constraint in a more complex operating situation.

This section described analytical approaches for decisions under a single production constraint. Chapter 6 extends the analysis to situations with other types of constraints.

## DECISION MAKING UNDER ENVIRONMENTAL CONSTRAINTS

When deciding among available courses of actions, managers must, of course, follow any laws that might apply. Antitrust laws forbid actions that might substantially reduce competition. Anti-dumping laws address aspects of unfair competition in international trade. Environmental protection laws restrict actions that could harm wildlife or increase pollution. At various times controls on wages and prices have restricted price increases. We shall limit our discussion to the major laws dealing with pricing practices.

The Sherman Act, Clayton Act, Robinson-Patman Act, and the statutes of many states prohibit predatory pricing. **Predatory pricing** is pricing below cost in the short term to drive competitors out of business. Often, the question in cases under these laws is about what is meant by "cost." For the most part, courts have held

**SIGHT**

## Analyzing Capacity

Even operating at full capacity, a plant of the very successful Latex Division of **GenCorp Polymer Products** could not meet the demand for all of its products. The plant's managers faced a difficult problem in analyzing product profitability. The constraining factor was the capacity of reactors, vessels in which the ingredients for each product are cooked. Any product can be made in any reactor. But the reactors differ in size, and the time required to process a product depends on the size of the reactor. Hence, a product's contribution margin per unit of processing time, and any ranking of product profitability based on such a contribution, applies only to reactors of a particular size. The managers wanted to choose products independent of the reactor size, because they wanted the flexibility of scheduling production in whatever reactors were available at a given time.

To solve their problem, the managers selected a single reactor size and stated the processing time for each product in relative terms, calling the result "product standard processing time." These standardized times were incorporated into a measure called the Product Profit Velocity (PPV), which was used to analyze product profitability. The measure is calculated as follows (materials and freight-out are the only variable costs).

$$PPV = \frac{\text{revenue per}}{\text{reactor run}} - \frac{\text{materials and}}{\text{freight-out}} = \frac{\text{contribution margin}}{\text{product standard processing time}}$$

The products were then ranked, and the lower-ranked products were cut back when capacity was reached. Because of concerns about customer ill will, the plant manager chose to increase prices rather than drop lower-ranking products. The rankings were also used to highlight products to study for ways to reduce costs (for example, by changing the materials mix).

*Source: Gary B. Frank, Steve A. Fisher, and Allen R. Wilkie, "Linking Cost to Price and Profit," Management Accounting, June 1989, 22-26.*

that prices below average variable costs are predatory. Occasionally, incremental costs have been used as the standard, particularly in cases involving manufacturers who could show they had excess capacity. In some cases, the determining factor has been an offending company's intention. For example, several pharmacies in Arkansas claimed that **Wal-Mart** engaged in predatory pricing. In refusing to find Wal-Mart guilty, the state supreme court noted that the plaintiffs were still profitable and distinguished between "a sustained effort to destroy competition" and attracting customers by selling items below cost.[2]

---

2   Louise Lee, "Wal-Mart Wins Ruling on Pricing Policy," The Wall Street Journal, January 10, 1995, B8.

The Robinson-Patman Act forbids charging different prices to different customers unless there are intrinsic cost differences in serving the different customers; in other words, this act forbids discriminatory pricing. The Federal Trade Commission (FTC) is the regulatory agency responsible for enforcing the act. Defendants charged with discriminatory pricing under Robinson-Patman can avoid liability by showing that the differences in prices from one customer to another emanate from different methods of manufacturing, different quantities purchased, or attempts to meet competition in good faith. (The last is not a cost issue.)

Justifications based on different methods of manufacture must show that the company sold different products to different customers. Companies that sell private brands usually modify the products to meet this criterion. Companies that custom-make products for different customers also can use this defense. For example, **Pittsburgh Plate Glass** successfully defended itself against a price discrimination suit by showing that it sold to the plaintiff, in smaller quantities than to other customers, a nonstandard size of glass that cost more to make.

One key to a successful defense against price discrimination or predatory pricing is for the company's management accountants to have a thorough understanding of costs. They must be able to amass cost data that support the company's position. Of course, potential ethical problems arise in developing cost studies. Management accountants' objectivity and competence are put at risk if they falsify, or even shade, data to meet the company's needs. The IMA Standards expressly forbid such acts.

In the mid-1990s, after several years with few lawsuits, the FTC renewed efforts to combat a vertical price-fixing arrangement known as resale price maintenance. That practice occurs when, by threatening to cut off deliveries, a manufacturer coerces retailers to agree to maintain the retail prices of its products within a specified range. The most notable of the recent price-fixing cases involved **Stride Rite** (Ked shoes) and **Reebok International Ltd**, but the FTC also pursued cases involving manufacturers of hockey skates, suntan products, and toys.[3] In 1995, two Japanese companies pleaded guilty to conspiring to fix prices of paper for fax machines. Costs play no part in price-fixing arrangements, only the ethics of a company's managers and legal advisors.

Many countries, including the United States, have anti-dumping laws to prevent unfair competitive practices in international trade. These laws, as well as some trade agreements, prohibit a company in one country from selling its products in another country at less than fair value. A company might take such action to establish its position in a new country quickly or to avoid lowering prices during a period of oversupply in its home country. The International Trade Administration, part of the Commerce Department, deals with charges of dumping in the United States. During the 1990s, U.S. producers have alleged dumping of many products, ranging from steel, color televisions, and components for computers to disposable lighters and fresh roses. Cost data are relevant to a defense against dumping charges, but such cases also involve political considerations.

---

3   *Viveca Novak and Joseph Pereira, "Reebok and FTC Settle Price-Fixing Charges,"* The Wall Street Journal, *May 5, 1995, B1, B8.*

## SUMMARY

Managerial accountants supply information for short-term decision making. The quantitative factors influencing such decisions are differential revenues and costs, including opportunity costs. Costs and revenues that will be the same whatever action is taken should be ignored. Historical costs are sunk and are irrelevant for decisions because they cannot be changed by any current action. Avoidable fixed costs are relevant. Whether a cost is relevant to a particular decision does not always depend on whether the cost is variable or fixed.

Typical examples of short-term decisions are whether to drop a product or product line, whether to produce a component internally or purchase it from an outside supplier, whether to further process joint products, whether to accept a special order, and how best to use the limited supply of an input factor. As a general rule, the action that is expected to result in the highest income for the firm should be pursued, subject always to constraints imposed by law. This decision rule considers only the quantifiable factors in a given situation. Most decisions involve some factors that can have monetary effects but for which no reliable estimates can be made. Still other factors, such as a company policy prohibiting certain types of products, may not lend themselves to quantification at all. These qualitative factors should not be ignored.

## KEY TERMS

complementary effects  *(174)*

differential revenues and costs  *(165)*

incremental revenues and costs  *(165)*

joint (common) costs  *(179)*

joint process  *(179)*

joint products  *(179)*

loss leader  *(175)*

opportunity cost  *(166)*

predatory pricing  *(188)*

split-off point  *(181)*

sunk cost  *(166)*

## REVIEW PROBLEM

Kottal Systems makes three products. Following are the revenue and cost data for a typical month.

|  | Product X | Y | Z | Total |
|---|---|---|---|---|
| Sales | $300 | $500 | $800 | $1,600 |
| Variable costs | 100 | 200 | 400 | 700 |
| Contribution margin | 200 | 300 | 400 | 900 |
| Fixed costs: |  |  |  |  |
| Avoidable | 80 | 100 | 120 | 300 |
| Common, allocated on the basis of sales dollars | 60 | 100 | 160 | 320 |
| Total fixed costs | 140 | 200 | 280 | 620 |
| Profit | $ 60 | $100 | $120 | $ 280 |

## Required

Answer each of the following questions independently.

1. What will total profit be if Kottal drops product X?
2. Kottal is considering selling a new product, P, in place of X. P will sell for $7 per unit, have variable costs of $5 per unit, and have avoidable fixed costs of $130. How many units of P would Kottal have to sell to maintain its total income of $280?
3. Kottal charges $10 per unit for product Z. A chain store offers to buy 40 units of Z per month at $8 per unit. The additional sales would not affect total fixed costs or variable costs per unit. Kottal has the capacity to produce 110 units of Z per month. If Kottal accepts the offer, what will its total monthly income be?
4. Closer analysis reveals that X, Y, and Z are joint products of a joint process and all are now being processed beyond the split-off point. The cost of the joint process, including raw material, is the $320 joint allocated fixed cost. All of the other reported costs are incurred to process the individual products beyond the split-off point. If the sales values of X, Y, and Z at split-off are $110, $220, and $230, respectively, could Kottal increase its profits by selling one or more products at split-off? If so, which product(s) should be sold at split-off and what will the increase in total profit be?
5. Unit sales of X and Z are 100 and 200, respectively. Both products are made on a single machine that has a limited capacity. The machine can make five units of X per hour, or eight units of Z.
   (a) If Kottal can sell all that it can make of either product, should it continue to make both products? If not, which product should Kottal make?
   (b) Assume the machine is being operated at its capacity of 45 hours per month. What will happen to monthly profits if Kottal makes only the more profitable product as determined in part (a)? Give the dollar increase in profits. (Hint: Remember that if only one product is made, the company will save the avoidable fixed costs on the product that it drops.)

## ANSWER TO REVIEW PROBLEM

1. $160. Kottal would lose the $200 contribution margin from selling X but would save the $80 avoidable fixed costs. Subtracting the net reduction in profit of $120 ($200 – $80) from the current profit of $280 gives $160. (The $120 drop is the incremental profit on X.)
2. 125 units. To achieve the same total profit, selling P must produce the $120 incremental profit lost by dropping X (per requirement 1). Hence, selling P must provide contribution margin sufficient to cover both the new avoidable fixed costs and the $120 profit. The new fixed costs are $130, so the contribution margin needed is $250 ($130 fixed costs plus the $120 desired profit). P's contribution margin is $2 per unit ($7 – $5), so Kottal must sell 125 units of P ($250/$2).
3. $350. The important factor is that Kottal will lose some sales at the regular price if it accepts the special order. Capacity is 110 units and planned sales are 80 units ($800/$10 selling price). If Kottal sells 40 units to the *new* customer, it can sell only 70 units at the regular price, 10 units fewer than planned.

| | |
|---|---:|
| Gain from contribution margin on special order ($8 – $5) × 40 units | $120 |
| Lost contribution margin because of loss of sales of 10 units at regular price, ($10 – $5) × 10 units | 50 |
| Gain on special order | $ 70 |
| Planned profit | 280 |
| New monthly income | $350 |

4. Kottal could increase profits by $20 per month by selling product Y at the split-off point, as shown by the following analysis.

|  | X | Y | Z |
|---|---|---|---|
| Sales with further processing | $300 | $500 | $800 |
| Additional processing costs: | | | |
| Variable costs | 100 | 200 | 400 |
| Avoidable fixed costs | 80 | 100 | 120 |
| Total additional processing costs | 180 | 300 | 520 |
| Profit if further processed | 120 | 200 | 280 |
| Split-off values | 110 | 220 | 230 |
| Advantage (disadvantage) of further processing | $ 10 | $(20) | $ 50 |

5. (a) Kottal should concentrate on product Z rather than product X. The decision is independent of the number of hours available, because the contribution margin *per hour of machine time* is higher for Z.

|  | X | Z |
|---|---|---|
| Contribution margin per unit | $ 2 ($200/100) | $ 2 ($400/200) |
| Units that can be made in one hour | × 5 | × 8 |
| Contribution margin per hour | $10 | $16 |

   As long as the company can sell all the units it makes of either product, total contribution margin will be greater by making only Z.

   (b) Profit will increase by $200. If Kottal uses its capacity of 45 hours to produce only Z, it can make 360 units (45 × 8) for total contribution margin of $720 (360 × $2 per unit). This is an increase of $320 ($720 − $400 contribution margin already anticipated). However, Kottal loses the current $120 *incremental profit* from product X (see requirement 1). Thus, if Kottal concentrates on product Z it would gain $200 ($320 additional contribution margin from Z − $120 incremental profit lost from not producing X).

## ASSIGNMENT MATERIAL

### INTERNET ACTIVITY

One of the decisions that companies continually make is whether to make or buy parts, components, and even entire products. Go to the Internet and look for contract manufacturers, companies that manufacture for others. Find out what specific services they offer and why they believe they can be of service to their customers, i.e., what can they do that the customers cannot do as well.

### QUESTIONS FOR DISCUSSION

**5-1   *"Where do you start?"***   One of your classmates believes he thoroughly understands the principle of incremental cost and so places the following ad in the school paper.

Wanted—Ride to Bordenton

I will pay all of the extra costs involved in taking me to Bordenton.
Call Bob at 555-6202.

Bob believes that someone who is planning on going to Bordenton will answer the ad and that he will therefore pay virtually nothing because the incremental cost will be trivial. Bordenton is 200 miles from the university. How might someone answer the ad and give Bob a shock?

**5-2   Unit costs**  While standing in line to use a telephone, you hear the following part of a conversation. "I'm going to play golf today, dear." (Pause) "Yes, honey, I know it costs $10 for a cart and $6 for drinks after the round, but it really does get cheaper the more I play. Look, the club dues are $1,800 per year, so if I play 50 times it costs, ah, let's see, $52 per round. But if I play 100 times it only costs, um, just a second, yeah, about $34 per round." (Pause) "I knew you'd understand. See you at dinner. Bye." How did the golfer figure the cost per round? Comment on her analysis.

**5-3   The generous management**  Several years ago, a leading newspaper ran an advertisement for itself. The advertisement stated that the paper, which cost the customer $1.50, was a bargain because it cost the publisher nearly $2.00 ($0.93 for paper, $0.17 for printers' labor, $0.10 for ink, $0.35 for salaries of editorial employees and $0.42 for other operating expenses such as executives' salaries, rent, depreciation, and taxes). Is the buyer actually paying less than cost? What assumptions did you make to arrive at your answer? How can the publisher be so generous to readers?

**5-4   Short-term pricing policy**  You enter the departure area of an airline just before a flight to Los Angeles is to take off. The plane is about 80% full, and the regular fare for the flight is $300. You have neither a ticket nor a reservation for the flight, but you offer to pay $50 to take the flight. Assume there are no variable costs associated with the number of passengers. Should the airline accept your offer if it employs the incremental principle? Will the airline accept your offer? Why or why not?

**5-5   Economic and qualitative factors**  The lay trustees at the Central Westcliff Church are discussing ideas for making more use of church facilities. One trustee suggests that the church sponsor monthly dances for the church's young people in its activity hall. Discuss the costs, revenues, and perhaps unquantifiable factors relevant to a decision about using the activity hall for this purpose.

## EXERCISES

**5-6   Special order**  Glo-bright Lamps expects to make and sell 500,000 units in 20X1 at $25 per unit. Per-unit manufacturing costs at that level of production are as follows.

| | |
|---|---|
| Variable manufacturing costs | $11 |
| Fixed manufacturing costs | $7 |

Early in the year, a new customer approaches Glo-bright offering to buy 25,000 lamps at $14 each. Glo-bright can produce additional units with no change in fixed manufacturing costs, though filling the order will require incremental packing and shipping costs of $4,200. Filling the special order will not affect regular sales.

**Required**

Determine the effect of accepting the special order on profit for the year.

**5-7   Joint products**   Rox Company produces two families of chemicals, orides and octines. The production phase of each chemical group begins with a joint process. Following are production, sales, and cost data for the products that result from each 100-gallon batch of materials going through the joint process that produces orides.

|  | Boride | Doride | Foride |
|---|---|---|---|
| Gallons produced | 40 | 10 | 50 |
| Selling price per gallon at the split-off point | $5 | $5 | $0 |
| Selling price per gallon after further processing | $12 | $9 | $4 |
| Per-gallon variable cost of further processing | $5 | $6 | $1 |

**Required**

Determine which of the joint products should be sold at the split-off point and which should be processed further.

**5-8   Joint products (continuation of 5-7)**   Rox normally processes 120,000 gallons of oride mixture per month. You have determined that, in addition to the variable costs of the additional processing of boride, doride, and foride, there are the following monthly fixed costs associated with such added processing.

|  | Boride | Doride | Foride |
|---|---|---|---|
| Avoidable fixed costs of additional processing | $98,000 | $18,000 | $17,000 |
| Unavoidable fixed costs of additional processing, allocated | 25,000 | 30,000 | 4,000 |

**Required**

1. Does the information about the fixed costs of additional processing of the joint products change your answer from Exercise 5-7 as to whether any of those products should be processed after the split-off point?
2. Assume that Rox takes the most profitable course of action with respect to each of the joint oride products. Ignoring the costs of the joint process, what will be the total monthly profit from orides?

**5-9   Dropping a segment**   LeClothes, Inc. expects the following monthly results for the coming year.

|  | Hats | Shirts | Jeans | Total |
|---|---|---|---|---|
| Sales | $ 90,000 | $110,000 | $350,000 | $550,000 |
| Variable costs | $ 50,000 | $ 30,000 | $160,000 | $240,000 |
| Fixed costs | 60,000 | 40,000 | 100,000 | 200,000 |
| Total costs | $110,000 | $ 70,000 | $260,000 | $440,000 |
| Profit (loss) | $ (20,000) | $ 40,000 | $ 90,000 | $110,000 |

**Required**

Answer each of the following questions independently.

1. Suppose that fixed costs, all unavoidable, are allocated based on the floor space each segment occupies. What will total profit be if LeClothes drops the hats segment?
2. Suppose that $25,000 of the fixed costs shown for the hats segment is avoidable. What will total profit be if LeClothes drops the hats segment?
3. Suppose that LeClothes could avoid $25,000 in fixed costs by dropping the hats segment (as in requirement 2). However, the managers believe that if they do drop hats, sales of each of the other lines will fall by 10%. What will profit be if LeClothes drops hats and loses 10% of the sales of each of the other segments?

**5-10  Capacity constraint**   Winston Company makes three models of shoes, all of which require the use of a special machine. Only 200 hours of machine time are available per week. Data for the three products are as follow. Winston can sell as much of any product as it can make.

|                          | Walker | Runner | Aerobic |
|--------------------------|--------|--------|---------|
| Selling price            | $15    | $20    | $28     |
| Variable cost            | 8      | 11     | 14      |
| Contribution margin      | $ 7    | $ 9    | $14     |
| Machine time in minutes  | 6      | 10     | 15      |

**Required**

1. If all products required the same amount of machine time, which product should Winston make?
2. Given the capacity constraint, determine which product Winston should make and what total monthly contribution margin Winston would earn by making only that product.
3. How much would the selling price of the next most profitable (per machine hour) product have to rise to be as profitable as the product you selected in requirement 2?

**5-11  Make or buy**   CalRex Company is introducing a new product. The managers are trying to decide whether to make one of its components or to buy it from an outside supplier. The space that could be used to make the part has no alternative use. The outside supplier will sell the part to CalRex for $16 per unit. Following is an estimate of per-unit costs if CalRex makes the part.

| Materials                       | $ 4.50 |
|---------------------------------|--------|
| Direct labor                    | 5.00   |
| Variable manufacturing overhead | 4.50   |
| Fixed manufacturing overhead    | 6.50   |
| Total cost                      | $20.50 |

The estimate reflects expected volume of 20,000 units of the part. Fixed manufacturing overhead consists of depreciation on machinery and a share of the costs of the factory (heat, light, building depreciation, etc.) based on the floor space that manufacturing the part would occupy.

**Required**

Determine whether CalRex should make or buy the part.

**5-12  *Special order***  Hi-Flight produces high-quality golf balls. A sporting-goods chain offers to buy 80,000 dozen balls at $9 per dozen. The chain would sell the ball to customers for $16 per dozen, which is $5 less than usually charged by Hi-Flight's normal outlets. Hi-Flight would put X's on the balls to indicate that they are rejects. Hi-Flight can produce 1,200,000 dozen balls per year. Following are budgeted results for the coming year without considering the special order from the chain.

| | |
|---|---:|
| Sales (1,000,000 dozen at $14 per dozen) | $14,000,000 |
| Cost of goods sold | 9,000,000 |
| Gross profit | $ 5,000,000 |
| Selling and administrative expenses, all fixed | 3,800,000 |
| Income | $ 1,200,000 |

Cost of goods sold includes variable costs of $6 per dozen balls. The rest of the cost is fixed.

**Required**

1. Determine whether Hi-Flight should accept the order.
2. Might your answer to requirement 1 change if the balls would not carry the X's that indicate they are rejects?

**5-13  *Short-term decisions***  Nickolai Company expects the following results in 20X5. Fixed costs, all unavoidable, are allocated based on relative sales dollars.

| | Product A | Product B | Total |
|---|---:|---:|---:|
| Sales | $450 | $400 | $850 |
| Variable costs | 200 | 100 | 300 |
| Contribution margin | $250 | $300 | $550 |
| Fixed costs | 110 | 180 | 290 |
| Profit | $140 | $120 | $260 |

**Required**

Answer each of the following questions independently, unless otherwise instructed.

1. The managers are considering increasing advertising for product A by $40. They expect to achieve a 30% increase in volume for product A with no change in selling price, but some of that increase will be at the expense of product B. Sales of B are expected to decline by 5%. What will total profit be if the managers approve the proposed action?
2. What is the maximum percentage decline in volume of product B that would leave the action in requirement 1 just barely desirable?
3. The managers are considering dropping product A and replacing it with product C. Introducing product C would increase total fixed costs by $60. C's contribution margin percentage is 50%. What dollar sales of product C are needed to maintain the original profit of $260?

**5-14  Product-line emphasis**  Expected results for the coming year for Porter Communications, which manufactures two lines of computer connectors, are as follows, in thousands of dollars.

|  | Internet Connectors (ICs) | Local Area Connectors (LACs) | Total |
|---|---|---|---|
| Sales | $6,600 | $5,400 | $12,000 |
| Variable costs | 3,300 | 1,620 | 4,920 |
| Contribution margin | $3,300 | $3,780 | $ 7,080 |
| Direct, avoidable fixed costs | 1,250 | 3,430 | 4,680 |
| Product margin | $2,050 | $ 350 | $ 2,400 |
| Common, unavoidable fixed costs |  |  | 1,570 |
| Profit |  |  | $   830 |

**Required**

1. Porter uses the same production facilities for both products. Demand is such that Porter could sell $1 million more of either product line but it would have to reduce output and sales of the other line by the same amount. Which line should the company make more of and what is the effect on total profit?
2. Suppose Porter could introduce a new line that is much more profitable than either of the existing ones. To introduce the new line, however, Porter must drop one of the existing lines entirely. The line that Porter retains will continue as originally planned. Which line should Porter drop?

**5-15  Special order for service firm**  Burns and Cross, CPAs, face a seasonal business. Their summers are relatively light and the staff cannot stay busy on fee-producing work. The managers of Oak Park have decided that the town needs an annual audit. They approach Burns and Cross, stating that they will pay $10,000 for an audit to be performed in June, a very light month for Burns and Cross. The partners develop the following information.

| | |
|---|---|
| Time required for audit | 500 hours |
| Normal average billing rate | $100 per hour |
| Average monthly salary of staff | $4,000 |

The 500 hours the audit should take is about the total time for three staff members for one month. Available staff time is ample to perform the audit and would not displace any other business. Burns and Cross do not lay off staff during the summer because they would have to rehire them later and they might go to other firms. Moreover, they feel an obligation to their employees.

**Required**

Determine whether Burns and Cross should accept the assignment.

**5-16  Joint products**  BAT Company produces four joint products at a joint cost of $110,000. The company currently processes all products beyond the split-off point, and the final products are sold as follows.

| Products | Sales | Additional Processing Costs |
|---|---|---|
| M | $450,000 | $360,000 |
| N | 140,000 | 70,000 |
| O | 45,000 | 10,000 |
| P | 20,000 | 15,000 |

BAT could sell the products at the split-off point for the following amounts: M, $120,000; N, $40,000; O, $35,000; and P, zero.

**Required**

1. Which products should BAT sell at the split-off point?
2. What would BAT's profit be if it took the most profitable action with respect to each of its products?

**5-17  Dropping a product—complementary effects**  The Face Care Division of DeVoe & Co. makes three products in the same factory. Following are the revenue and cost data for a typical month, in thousands of dollars.

|  | | Product | | |
|---|---|---|---|---|
|  | Razors | After-Shave | Shaving Cream | Total |
| Sales | $ 400 | $600 | $400 | $1,400 |
| Variable costs | 300 | 240 | 120 | 660 |
| Contribution margin | $ 100 | $360 | $280 | $ 740 |
| Fixed costs | | | | |
|   Avoidable | $ 120 | $150 | $ 70 | $ 340 |
|   Unavoidable, allocated on basis | | | | |
|     of relative sales dollars | 80 | 120 | 80 | 280 |
| Total fixed costs | $ 200 | $270 | $150 | $ 620 |
| Income (loss) | $(100) | $ 90 | $130 | $ 120 |

**Required**

1. Determine total income if the division dropped razors from the product line.
2. Suppose that if razors were dropped, the sales of after-shave would decline by 20% and those of shaving cream by 10%. Determine income for the company if razors were dropped.

**5-18  Inventory values**  James Company has 300 pounds of a chemical compound called bysol, bought at $6.50 per pound several months ago. Bysol now costs $5.10 per pound. The company could sell it for $4.10 per pound (shipping costs account for the $1.00 difference between the cost to buy and the selling price).

**Required**

Answer each of the following questions independently.

1. Suppose James has stopped making the product for which it used bysol and will sell it or use it to make a special order. The special order has a price of $2,300, and incremental costs, excluding the bysol, are $900. What is the relevant cost of using the bysol in the special order? Should the company accept the order?
2. Suppose the company has alternative uses for bysol so that if it accepts the special order it will have to buy more for its regular production. What is the relevant cost of using the bysol in the special order? Should James accept the order?

**5-19  Make or buy**  Walls, Inc. manufactures 100,000 units of part A-996 annually, which it uses in one of its products. The controller has collected the following cost data related to the part.

| | |
|---|---:|
| Materials | $ 40,000 |
| Direct labor | 90,000 |
| Variable overhead | 80,000 |
| Fixed overhead | 180,000 |
| Total costs | $390,000 |

Laidlaw Company offers to supply a functionally equivalent part for $3.10 per unit. If Walls accepts the offer, it will be able to rent some of the facilities it devotes to making the part to another company for $20,000 annually and will also be able to reduce its fixed overhead costs by about $50,000.

**Required**
1. Should Walls accept the offer?
2. What is the maximum price that Walls should be willing to pay for the part—the price that would give it the same income it would have if it continued making it?
3. Expected use of the part might vary from the 100,000 normal level. At what annual unit volume will Walls earn the same income making the part as it would buying it?

**5-20   Capacity constraint**   Gray Mfg. Inc. can produce either of two products, Product Q and Product Z, with its existing machinery. Making either product requires the use of grinding machines. Gray has 10 grinding machines, each of which can be operated 200 hours per month. Following are the comparative per-unit data for the two products.

| | Product | |
|---|:---:|:---:|
| | Q | Z |
| Selling price | $11 | $18 |
| Variable cost | $7 | $10 |
| Required grinding time, minutes | 2 | 2.5 |

**Required**
1. If Gray can sell as many units of either product as it can make with its limited supply of grinding machines, which product should Gray make and what will Gray's total contribution margin be per month if it makes that product?
2. The selling price of Product Z has only recently risen to $18. Gray's managers now estimate that the maximum sales volume of Z at that price is 40,000 units per year. They also believe that at the $11 price they can sell all of Product Q they can make. How should Gray use its grinding machine capacity over the coming year? (That is, how many of each product should Gray produce?)

## PROBLEMS

**5-21   Joint products**   High Plains Packers slaughters cattle and processes the meat, hides, and bones. It tans the hides and sells them to leather manufacturers. The bones are made into buttons and other sundries. In a typical month, it processes about 3,000 cattle. An income statement for such a month follows, in thousands of dollars. The cost of cattle and the unavoidable processing costs are allocated based on relative sales of each product group.

| | Totals | Meat | Hides | Bones |
|---|---|---|---|---|
| Sales | $ 800 | $600 | $150 | $50 |
| Cost of cattle | 400 | 300 | 75 | 25 |
| Gross profit | $ 400 | $300 | $75 | $25 |
| Additional processing costs, avoidable | (130) | (60) | (40) | (30) |
| Allocated costs | (80) | (60) | (15) | (5) |
| Income (loss) | $ 190 | $ 180 | $20 | $(10) |

### Required

1. Is High Plains losing money by processing the bones into buttons and sundry items? How much better or worse off is the company processing bones?
2. A tanner offers to buy the hides as they are sheared off the cattle for $10 each. He contends that High Plain's income from hides would be $30,000 (3,000 hides × $10), $10,000 more than the company currently earns tanning the hides. Should High Plains accept the offer?
3. If High Plains could sell the bones without further processing, how much would have to be received per month to keep total profits the same as they are now?

**5-22   Opportunity cost pricing**   Grogan Company makes three products. Data are as follows.

| | Product | | |
|---|---|---|---|
| | Audio Tapes | CDs | Video Tapes |
| Current selling price, case | $14 | $21 | $35 |
| Variable cost | 4 | 6 | 10 |
| Contribution margin | $10 | $15 | $25 |
| Machine time required, in minutes | 5 | 10 | 15 |

Grogan has 40,000 minutes of machine time available per week. It can sell all of any of the three products that it can make.

### Required

1. Determine which product Grogan should make.
2. Determine the selling prices that Grogan would have to charge for each of the other two products to make them equally profitable per minute of machine time as the one you selected in requirement 1.

**5-23   Comprehensive review of short-term decisions**   The following data relate to the planned operations of Kimble Company before considering the changes described later. All fixed costs are direct, but unavoidable.

| | Product | | |
|---|---|---|---|
| | Chair | Table | Sofa |
| Unit selling price | $120 | $400 | $600 |
| Unit variable cost | 40 | 160 | 360 |
| Unit fixed costs | 30 | 120 | 180 |
| Total unit cost | $ 70 | $280 | $540 |
| Profit per unit | $ 50 | $120 | $ 60 |
| Annual volume | 8,000 | 3,000 | 4,000 |

## Required

Answer each of the following questions independently, unless otherwise instructed.
1. What is Kimble's expected total profit?
2. What will happen to profit if Kimble drops sofas?
3. What will happen to profit if Kimble drops chairs, but is able to shift the facilities to making more sofas so that volume of sofas increases to 7,000 units? (Total fixed costs remain constant.)
4. Variable cost per sofa includes $60 for parts that the company now buys outside. The company could make the parts at a variable cost of $45. It would also have to increase fixed costs by $35,000 annually. What would happen to profit if the company took the proposed action?
5. Kimble has received a special order for 1,000 tables at $245. Capacity is sufficient to make the units, and sales at the regular price would not be affected. What will happen to profit if Kimble accepts the order?
6. Repeat requirement 5 assuming now that the order is for 1,500 tables and that capacity is limited to 4,000 tables.

**5-24  Using per-unit data**   The managers of Ferrara Company expect the following per-unit results at a volume of 200,000 units.

| | | |
|---|---:|---:|
| Sales | | $10 |
| Variable costs | $6 | |
| Fixed costs | 3 | |
| Total costs | | 9 |
| Profit | | $ 1 |

## Required

Answer each of the following questions independently.
1. Ferrara has the opportunity to sell 20,000 units to a chain store for $8 each. The managers expect that sales at the regular price will drop by about 8,000 units as some customers will buy from the chain store instead of from the regular outlets. What will happen to the company's profit if it accepts the order?
2. Of the total unit variable cost of $6, $2.80 is for a part that Ferrara now buys from an outside supplier. Ferrara could make the part for $2.25 variable cost plus $100,000 per year fixed costs for renting additional machinery. What will happen to annual profit if Ferrara makes the part?
3. The company is considering a new model to replace the existing product. The new model has a $6 unit variable cost and the same total fixed costs as the existing product. The new model has expected sales of 100,000 units per year. At what selling price per unit will the new model give the same total profit as the existing one?

**5-25  Just-in-time, costs of activities**   Racine Machinery recently began to change one of its plants to a just-in-time operation. So far, Racine has set up one manufacturing cell to make a product that had formerly been made in large batches. The following analysis of April operations for the cell was disappointing to the controller who had expected dramatic improvements with JIT.

| | |
|---|---:|
| Units produced | 20,000 |
| Costs: | |
|    Materials | $ 55,000 |
|    Labor | 67,000 |
|    Overhead | 35,000 |
|    Total | $157,000 |
| Per-unit cost | $7.85 |

The overhead cost shown is mostly allocated costs. Roughly $9,000 is incremental, avoidable cost. The per-unit cost to manufacture the product under the old system follows.

| | |
|---|---:|
| Materials | $2.90 |
| Labor | 2.80 |
| Overhead | 1.80 |
| Total | $7.50 |

Overhead is based on 22,000 units and is 40% variable, 60% fixed at that level. Under the old system quality control was weak, so the company had to produce about 22,000 units to obtain 20,000 good units. With the JIT cell, workers do their own inspection during production, and only 20,000 total units are produced to obtain 20,000 good units.

Under the old system, manufacturing the product required personnel in addition to direct laborers. The costs given include fringe benefits.

| | |
|---|---|
| Inspection | $4,000 per month |
| Production scheduling | $5,000 per month |
| Maintenance | $3,600 per month |

When setting up the cell Racine reassigned the people described above to other departments.

**Required**

Determine the incremental cost to produce 20,000 good units in a month under the old method and using the JIT cell. Using the guidelines in Appendix A, prepare a memorandum explaining your results.

**5-26   Choosing a product**   Hare Company operates a cannery that buys raw carrots from local farmers. Hare can produce three types of canned carrots: sliced, mashed, and pickled. Fixed production costs for a season are $80,000. This season, Hare contracted to buy 500,000 pounds of raw carrots at $0.25 per pound. Following are the price and other data for Hare's three products.

| | Sliced | Mashed | Pickled |
|---|---|---|---|
| Selling price per case | $7.50 | $6.00 | $8.25 |
| Variable processing cost per case | $2.50 | $2.75 | $4.00 |
| Pounds of raw carrots required per case | 5 | 2.5 | 5 |

**Required**

1. Hare can sell as many cases as it makes of any product. Which type should Hare produce?
2. Assuming Hare has no costs other than those already mentioned and that it follows the advice you offered in requirement 1, what is the maximum profit Hare can make this season?
3. Assume that, despite your advice in requirement 1, Hare's managers want to produce and sell sliced carrots and are convinced that they can slightly reduce the volume of carrots in each can of sliced carrots without affecting the selling price. How many pounds of carrots would Hare have to use in each case of sliced carrots to make that product as profitable as the type you selected in requirement 1?

4. What other factors should Hare's managers consider before deciding to implement the plan proposed in requirement 3?

**5-27   Product pricing—off-peak hours**   Marie Angelo, owner of Gino's Pizzeria, is considering a luncheon special to increase business during the slow time from 11 a.m. to 1 p.m. on weekdays. For $5.00 on any weekday, she will give customers all the pizza they can eat. Marie has prepared the following data for weekly business during those hours when she typically serves 150 pizzas.

|  | Pizza | Beverages | Total |
|---|---|---|---|
| Sales | $1,020 | $150 | $1,170 |
| Variable costs | 450 | 60 | 510 |
| Contribution margin | $ 570 | $ 90 | $ 660 |
| Avoidable fixed costs—wages of students hired |  |  | 380 |
| Current profit, lunch period |  |  | $ 280 |

She estimates that at the special price she will serve about 300 pizzas per week to about 250 customers. (Some customers will eat more than one pizza, given the lower price.) She also anticipates that variable costs per unit will be about 10% higher because people will want more toppings than they now order. Beverage sales will bear the same relationship to the number of customers that they do now when each customer eats one pizza. The increase in the number of customers will entail an increase in personnel during the hours of the special, increasing wage costs by 20%.

**Required**
Evaluate the monetary effects of the proposed luncheon special.

**5-28   Car pool—relevant costs**   You and your neighbor carpool to work, driving on alternate days. A colleague at work has injured his hand and will not be able to drive for the next three months. He inquires about riding with you and your neighbor and offers to pay "a fair price." You know that he could ride a bus for $2 per day.

From your house it is a 10-mile round trip to work. If you pick up your injured colleague, the round trip is 14 miles. Last year, your car cost you the following for 15,000 miles. (Your neighbor's car cost the same for the same number of miles.)

| | |
|---|---|
| Gasoline and oil | $1,350 |
| Maintenance | 450 |
| New tires (life of 30,000 miles) | 300 |
| Insurance and registration | 600 |
| Decline in market value | 3,000 |
| Total | $5,700 |

**Required**
1. Quote a daily price to your colleague that seems fair to you.
2. What do you think your colleague would say is a fair price?

**5-29   Product line analysis for service firm**   Foelber & Foelber, Architects, is a large diversified practice in a growing area. The firm has been plagued by shortages of qualified staff for some time and the situation does not appear to be improving. The firm's practice includes three major types of work: office buildings, public buildings, and homes. The staff members can perform all types of work. The firm charges fees based on a percentage of the cost of each project, ranging from 10% down to 3% depending on circumstances.  A typical month's income statement by line shows the following, in thousands of dollars.

|  | Office Buildings | Public Buildings | Residences | Total |
|---|---|---|---|---|
| Fee income | $34.5 | $28.1 | $14.4 | $77.0 |
| Cost of fees* | 13.2 | 15.3 | 9.4 | 37.9 |
| Gross margin | $21.3 | $12.8 | $ 5.0 | $39.1 |
| Other expenses | 7.9 | 9.2 | 5.6 | 22.7 |
| Profit | $13.4 | $ 3.6 | $ (0.6) | $16.4 |

\* *Salaries of architects working on specific projects and other direct expenses such as travel*

You learn that *other expenses* are company-sustaining costs allocated based on relative cost of fees.

**Required**
1. Should the firm stop doing residential work?  Show why or why not.
2. If the firm could not do all of the work it was offered, in which lines should it concentrate?

**5-30  *Hours of operation***   Hughes Stationers opens from 8 a.m. to 8 p.m. six days per week. The store sells cards, paper supplies, magazines, and a few books. Following are annual results.

| | | |
|---|---|---|
| Sales | | $464,900 |
| Cost of sales | | 162,700 |
| Gross margin | | $302,200 |
| Operating expenses: | | |
| Salaries | $97,300 | |
| Rent | 39,000 | |
| Utilities | 12,500 | |
| Insurance | 8,500 | |
| Other | 27,200 | 184,500 |
| Profit | | $117,700 |

As an experiment, the owner kept the store open for six hours one Sunday. Sales were $860 and additional payroll costs were $135. Doing a few calculations, the owner came up with $591 as the estimated daily cost of operations, exclusive of cost of sales, without Sunday hours. He therefore concluded that about $910 in sales is necessary to make staying open on Sundays worthwhile.

**Required**
1. Try to determine just what calculations the owner made to get his figures of $591 and $910.
2. With the information available, does it appear profitable to stay open on Sundays?
3. Using the guidelines in Appendix A, prepare a memorandum that describes other information you wish to have before making a final decision.

**5-31  Special order—alternative volumes**  Wilderness Products makes outdoor shirts. Data relating to the coming year's planned operations are as follows.

| | |
|---|---:|
| Sales (230,000 shirts) | $4,140,000 |
| Cost of goods sold | 2,760,000 |
| Gross profit | $1,380,000 |
| Selling and administrative expenses | 805,000 |
| Income | $ 575,000 |

The factory has capacity to make 250,000 shirts per year. Fixed costs included in cost of goods sold are $690,000. The only variable selling, general, and administrative expenses are a 10% sales commission and a $0.50 per shirt licensing fee paid to the designer.

A chain store manager has approached the sales manager of Wilderness Products offering to buy 15,000 shirts at $14 per shirt. These shirts would be sold in areas where Wilderness's shirts are not now sold. The sales manager believes that accepting the offer would result in a loss because the average total cost of a shirt is $15.50 ([$2,760,000 + $805,000]/230,000). He feels that even though sales commissions would not be paid on the order, a loss would still result.

**Required**
1. Determine whether the company should accept the offer.
2. Suppose that the order was for 40,000 shirts instead of 15,000. What would the company's income be if it accepted the order?
3. Assuming the same facts as in requirement 1, what is the lowest price that the company could accept and still earn $575,000?
4. How many units of sales at the regular price could the company lose before it became profitable to accept the order in requirement 2?

**5-32  Make or buy**  Hollis Electric is bringing out a new VCR. The VCR requires a type of electric motor not used for the current line of products. The purchasing manager has received a bid of $29 per motor from Wright Motor Company for any number that Hollis needs. Delivery is guaranteed within two weeks after order.

Hollis's production manager believes the company could make the motor internally by extensively converting an existing model. Additional space and machinery would be required if Hollis were to make the motors. The company currently leases, for $27,800 per year, space that could be used to make the motors. However, the space is now used to store vital materials, so Hollis would have to lease additional space in an adjacent building to store the materials. That space could be rented for $38,000 per year. It is suitable for storage, but not for converting the motors. The equipment needed to convert the motors could be rented for $55,000 per year.

The treasurer has developed the following unit costs based on the expected demand of 18,000 units per year.

| | |
|---|---:|
| Materials | $11.80 |
| Direct labor | 10.60 |
| Rent for space | 2.20 |
| Machinery rental | 2.50 |
| Other overhead | 8.20 |
| Total cost | $35.30 |

The "other overhead" figure includes $5.40 in fixed overhead that would be allocated to conversion of the motors. The remainder of "other overhead" is variable.

**Required**

1. Determine whether Hollis should make or buy the motors.
2. Determine the volume of motors at which Hollis would show the same total income whether it bought or made the motors.
3. Suppose that Hollis has decided to make the motors. Hollis has signed one-year contracts for the additional space and equipment. These contracts cannot be canceled. Determine the price that Wright Motor would have to offer Hollis to induce it to buy the motors.

**5-33  Dropping a product—opportunity costs**  Dayhuff Enterprises has a variety of product lines, all related to sports. The managers are not happy with the expected results of the apparel line (below) and are considering dropping it. If they did so, the company could recover the investment in receivables and inventory related to the line and pay off debt of $320,000 that bears 14% interest.

|  | Apparel Line |
|---|---|
| Sales | $200,000 |
| Variable costs | 125,000 |
| Contribution margin | $ 75,000 |
| Avoidable fixed costs | 40,000 |
| Product margin | $ 35,000 |
| Investment in receivables and inventories | $320,000 |

**Required**

Determine whether Dayhuff should drop the apparel line.

**5-34  Joint process (continuation of 5-7 and 5-8)**  Rox's production manager for orides is following the advice you gave in your answer to Exercise 5-8. The vice president of manufacturing is satisfied with the results but is now wondering whether Rox should continue competing in the oride market. The controller has provided the following information about the joint process that is the first phase in producing the chemicals in the oride family.

| | |
|---|---|
| Variable costs per 100-gallon batch | $160 |
| Monthly fixed costs: | |
| Avoidable | $110,000 |
| Unavoidable | $90,000 |

**Required**

Assume that Rox has no alternative uses for the facilities now devoted to operating the joint process that starts the production of orides. Determine whether the company should continue to operate the joint process.

**5-35  Salesperson's time as scarce resource**  Lombard Distribution sells to both wholesalers and retailers. Lombard has 30 salespeople and cannot easily increase the size of the sales force. An analysis has shown that a salesperson's call on a wholesale customer yields an average order of $500 and on a retail customer, $300.

However, prices to wholesalers are 20% less than those to retailers. Cost of goods sold (all variable) is 60% of prices charged to retailers, 75% of prices charged to wholesalers. A salesperson can call on 8 wholesalers or 14 retailers per day. (The greater number of retailers reduces travel time between calls.)

**Required**
1. Should salespeople concentrate on wholesalers or retailers? Provide an analysis based on one salesperson for one week showing the difference.
2. Using the guidelines in Appendix A, write a memorandum describing other factors that require consideration.

**5-36   Special order—capacity limitation**   Weston Tires has been approached by a large chain store that offers to buy 80,000 tires at $17. Delivery must be made within 30 days. Weston can produce 320,000 tires per month and has an inventory of 10,000 tires on hand. Expected sales at regular prices for the coming month are 300,000 tires. Weston's sales manager believes that about 60% of sales lost during the month would be made up in later months. Price and cost data are as follows.

| | | |
|---|---:|---:|
| Selling price | | $25 |
| Variable costs: | | |
|    Production | $12 | |
|    Selling | 3 | 15 |
| Contribution margin | | $10 |

Variable selling costs on the special order are only $2 per unit.

**Required**
1. Determine whether the company should accept the special order.
2. Determine the lowest price Weston could charge on the special order and not reduce its income.
3. Suppose now that the chain offers to buy 60,000 tires per month at $17. The offer is for an entire year. Expected sales are 300,000 tires per month without considering the special order. Also assume that there is *no* beginning inventory and that any sales lost during the year would not be made up in the following year. Determine whether the offer should be accepted and determine the lowest price that Weston could accept.
4. Return to your answer to requirement 1. Suppose that total monthly fixed costs are $2,400,000. Would you accept the special order?

**5-37   Special orders and qualitative factors**   SuperFi, Inc. has had a reputation for high-quality audio products for many years. The company is owned by descendants of its founder, Walter Gordon, and continues the policy of producing and selling only high-quality, high-priced stereo components.

Recently Paul O'Donnell, president of a chain of discount stores, proposed that SuperFi make and sell him a less expensive line of components than SuperFi currently produces. O'Donnell knows that SuperFi has excess capacity and that many other companies produce lower-quality lines for sale in discount stores. O'Donnell believes that buyers will become aware that SuperFi makes the components even though the SuperFi name will not appear on them. O'Donnell tries to convince the management that its major potential for growth lies in the private-brand field.

O'Donnell proposes that SuperFi sell to the chain at 70% of its current selling price to other outlets. Variable costs are now about 60% of normal selling price but would be reduced by 20% per unit for the less expensive components. The first-year order is to be for $4,000,000, for which SuperFi has enough excess capacity.

**Required**

1. Evaluate the monetary effects of the proposed deal.
2. Using the guidelines in Appendix A, write a memorandum that evaluates qualitative factors such as the attitudes of the management and the family owners and the reputation of the firm.

**5-38  Cost of being your own boss**   Ellen and Doug Taylor own a bistro in a large city. Their most recent year's income statement showed the following results.

| | | |
|---|---:|---:|
| Sales | | $276,000 |
| Cost of sales | | 98,000 |
| Gross profit | | $178,000 |
| Other expenses: | | |
|   Salaries | $55,000 | |
|   Rent (monthly lease) | 4,800 | |
|   Utilities | 3,450 | |
|   Advertising | 7,000 | |
|   Supplies | 5,700 | |
|   Insurance | 6,150 | |
|   Licenses and fees | 380 | |
|   Miscellaneous | 720 | 83,200 |
| Income | | $ 94,800 |

In discussing the results, Ellen and Doug were reminded of their struggle to develop the business. Before they started the bistro, he'd been earning $40,000 per year and she'd been earning $45,000. The first few years were difficult, but the place has caught on and become very popular. Ellen said how nice it was to own one's own business and not have to work for someone else and Doug agreed. "True," she said, we *do* put in more hours at the bistro than we worked in our other jobs." She went on, "Of course, we have $150,000 invested in the business, which is a lot, but we also don't have to fight the traffic to get there."

**Required**

Assume that the Taylors could sell the bistro for $150,000, invest the proceeds at 10% interest, and go back to their former jobs. Should they do so?

**5-39  Pricing policy and excess capacity**   Electric utilities face several problems in achieving optimal use of their facilities. First, because electricity cannot be stored economically, utilities must be able to generate enough electricity to meet demand at all times. Second, the use of electricity is seasonal, especially in warmer climates where air-conditioning produces high-peak requirements in the summer months.

Executives of Southern Electric Company are evaluating a proposal by the sales manager to offer discounts on electrical service to customers who will use electrical heating equipment. The controller has amassed the following data at the request of the sales manager.

| | |
|---|---|
| Current generating capacity—monthly | 20  million kilowatt-hours (kwh) |
| Annual sales | 120  million kwh |
| kwh sold—typical winter month | 7  million |
| kwh sold—typical summer month | 18  million |
| Price per 1,000 kwh | $35 |
| Variable cost per 1,000 kwh | $19 |

The sales manager's proposal is to reduce the price of electricity to $29 per 1,000 kwh if the customer uses electrical heating equipment. He anticipates that about 5 million additional kwh per month could be sold in the winter, a total of about 22 million additional hours per year. Users expected to convert to electrical heating now consume a total of about 30 million kwh per year. Sales to customers currently using electrical heating equipment, who would also qualify for the discount, are about 10 million kwh per year.

**Required**

Evaluate the monetary effects of the proposed decision.

**5-40  Processing decisions**  Ayers Sawmill buys pine logs and saws them into boards of two grades, A and B. The grade is determined by factors such as the number of knotholes and quality of the grain. Bark and sawdust also emerge from the sawing operation. Each log usually produces, by volume, about 35% A-grade boards, 55% B-grade boards, and 10% bark and shavings. Charles Ayers, the owner, has just received the income statement for a typical month's operations. Ayers expects much the same results in the foreseeable future.

|  | Total | Grade A | Grade B | Bark/ Shavings |
|---|---|---|---|---|
| Sales | $80,000 | $ 36,000 | $41,000 | $ 3,000 |
| Costs: |  |  |  |  |
| Logs | $42,000 | $ 14,700 | $23,100 | $ 4,200 |
| Sawing | 17,000 | 5,950 | 9,350 | 1,700 |
| Trimming | 3,200 | 2,340 | 860 |  |
| Sanding | 7,700 | 4,320 | 3,380 |  |
| Shipping | 4,500 | 1,550 | 2,430 | 520 |
| Total costs | $74,400 | $ 28,860 | $39,120 | $ 6,420 |
| Income (loss) | $ 5,600 | $ 7,140 | $ 1,880 | $(3,420) |

Sawing costs include wages, depreciation, and other nonitemized costs of running the sawmill. The cost of logs and of sawing are allocated based on volume (35%, 55%, 10%). Trimming, sanding, and shipping costs are direct and avoidable. Ayers was disturbed at the results. He told an employee, "The bark and shavings are really hurting me. I might as well throw the stuff out rather than sell it."

**Required**

1. Tell Ayers whether he should continue selling bark and shavings or throw it out. Explain the reasons for your decision.
2. A chain of lawn and garden stores has offered to buy Ayers's output of bark and shavings if Ayers will grind it into mulch. The grinding would cost about $1,500 per month for wages and equipment rental. The chain will pick up the mulch at the mill, so Ayers will not incur shipping costs. What monthly revenue does Ayers need to make it profitable to do the grinding?
3. A furniture manufacturer has approached Ayers with an offer to buy all of the sawmill's output of grade B lumber for $30,000 per month as it comes out of the sawing operation. Ayers would not have to trim or sand the lumber. Shipping costs would be $1,200. Determine whether Ayers should accept the offer.

**5-41  Evaluating a decision—costs of activities**  Six months ago the marketing manager of Arcon Company approved the sale of sizable quantities of the company's principal product to a chain store in a geographical region where the company's products are not currently sold. The sales were made monthly. The sales manager recently asked the controller for an analysis of the business to see whether it should be renewed for another six months as the chain wants to do. The controller prepares the following income statement related to the special order.

| | |
|---|---:|
| Sales | $320,000 |
| Cost of sales | 247,000 |
| Gross margin | $ 73,000 |
| Operating expenses | 61,000 |
| Profit | $ 12,000 |

The controller concludes that a $12,000 profit over six months is not enough to justify the added time and effort, as well as the risk of being unable to supply regular customers. Although the company has not operated at capacity during the period, it has come close on occasion.

The sales manager is surprised at the results and asks for more information. The controller provides the following additional data regarding the income statement.

(a)  Cost of sales includes the following.

| | |
|---|---:|
| Materials | $ 86,000 |
| Labor | 41,000 |
| Overhead, 60% variable | 120,000 |
| Total | $247,000 |

(b)  Operating expenses:

| | |
|---|---:|
| Sales salaries | $27,000 |
| Clerical | 12,000 |
| Other | 22,000 |
| Total | $61,000 |

The sales manager is confused about some items and receives the following additional explanation. The sales salaries are for the time of a sales representative who services the account. The representative spends about 80% of her time on the account, and the $27,000 is 80% of her six-month salary. The clerical costs are for a part-time clerk who works exclusively on this account. The bulk of the "other" category is a $16,000 administrative charge. This charge, equal to 5% of sales, is levied on all products to cover administrative expenses of the company. The remaining $6,000 are all incremental costs of various activities as estimated by the controller.

The sales manager seeks your help in understanding the statement and evaluating the order. He is confused and wonders whether to bother discussing renewal of the arrangement.

### Required

Prepare a new income statement that will assist the sales manager in evaluating the business.

**5-42  *Relevant range***   The president of Ipswick Company has received an offer to purchase 20,000 of the tables made by his firm. The offer is to be filled any time during the coming year, and the offer price per table is $60. The planned income statement for the year without this order is as follows.

| | | |
|---|---:|---:|
| Sales (45,000 tables at $100) | | $4,500,000 |
| Cost of goods sold: | | |
| Materials | $ 900,000 | |
| Direct labor | 810,000 | |
| Overhead | 1,340,000 | |
| Total cost of goods sold | | 3,050,000 |
| Gross profit | | $1,450,000 |
| Selling, general, and administrative expenses | | 1,220,000 |
| Income | | $ 230,000 |

The president believes that the order should be rejected because the price is below average production cost of $67.78 per table. He asks you to check the matter further because he knows that some costs are fixed and would not be affected by the special order. In your analysis you find that $800,000 in overhead is fixed and that a 10% commission is the only variable selling, general, and administrative expense.

### Required
Answer the following questions, considering each situation independently.
1. Assume the relevant range for the firm is between 30,000 and 70,000 tables, that existing sales would not be affected, and that the 10% sales commission would not have to be paid on the special order. What effect would there be on income if the order were accepted? Should it be accepted?
2. The relevant range is the same as in requirement 1, and existing sales would be unaffected, but the 10% sales commission would have to be paid. Should the order be accepted?
3. The relevant range is now 30,000 to 55,000 tables. If the special order is accepted, sales at regular prices would fall to 35,000 units. The 10% sales commission would not be paid on the special order. Should the order be accepted?

4. The relevant range is the same as in requirement 3, but production could be increased to meet the special order as well as regular planned sales. For all units produced above 55,000, labor cost per unit and per-unit variable overhead would be 20% higher than planned. Fixed production overhead would increase by $47,000. No sales commission would be paid on the order, and other selling, general, and administrative expenses would remain the same as planned. Should the order be accepted?

**5-43   Value of new products—complementary effects**   Jackman's Grocery is a medium-sized operation in a suburb of a large city. Joe Jackman, the owner, is contemplating the addition of a department to sell either hardware or beer and wine. He has talked to owners of several similar stores and has reached the following conclusions.

1. A hardware department would generate sales of $40,000 per year with a gross profit of 60%. No other variable costs would be added. Fixed costs added would be $12,000. Sales of groceries would increase 5% because of increased traffic through the store.
2. A beer and wine department would generate sales of $60,000 per year with a gross profit of 40%. No other variable costs would be added, and additional fixed

costs would be $18,000. Sales of groceries would increase by 8%. The income statement for a typical year for grocery sales alone is as follows.

| | |
|---|---:|
| Sales | $600,000 |
| Cost of goods sold (variable) | 240,000 |
| Gross profit | $360,000 |
| Other variable costs | 120,000 |
| Contribution margin | $240,000 |
| Fixed costs | 140,000 |
| Income | $100,000 |

### Required

1. Ignore the effects on sales of groceries for the moment. Compute the change in income that would result from adding (a) the hardware department and (b) the beer and wine department.
2. Recompute the effects on income of adding each department, considering the effects on sales of groceries. Which department should be added and why?
3. What can be learned from this problem?

**5-44   Special orders—effects on existing sales**   Hunt Company makes high-quality calculators that are sold only by department stores and office equipment dealers. A large discount chain has offered to buy 30,000 calculators this year at an average price of $30. The income statement expected for the coming year shows the following without considering the special order.

| | |
|---|---:|
| Sales (90,000 units at average price of $50) | $4,500,000 |
| Variable production costs (average of $20) | 1,800,000 |
| Contribution margin | $2,700,000 |
| Fixed costs (production and selling, general, and administrative) | 2,200,000 |
| Income | $ 500,000 |

The 30,000 units to be bought by the chain are in the same mix as Hunt currently sells. Hunt has the capacity to produce 140,000 units per year.

### Required

1. Should the order be accepted if there would be no effect on regular sales?
2. Suppose that accepting the order will result in a 10% decline in sales at regular prices because some current customers would recognize the chain store's product and make their purchases at the lower price. The sales mix would remain unchanged. Should Hunt accept the special order?
3. By how much could sales at regular prices decline before it became unprofitable to accept the order?
4. Assuming the same facts as in requirement 2, what other factors should Hunt's managers consider before deciding whether to accept the order?

**5-45   Alternative uses of product (CMA adapted)**   So-Clean Corporation manufactures a variety of cleaning compounds and solutions for both industrial and household use. Some of its products share ingredients and some can be refined into others. Grit 337 is a coarse, industrial cleaning powder that sells for $2.00 per pound and has variable costs of $1.60 per pound, all for manufacturing costs. The company currently uses a portion of Grit 337 in making a silver polish that sells for $4.00 per jar. Each jar requires a quarter pound of Grit 337. Other variable production costs for the silver polish are $2.50 per jar and variable selling expenses are $0.30 per jar. Monthly avoidable fixed costs of making the silver polish are $5,600.

**Required**

1. Assuming that the company cannot sell all of the Grit 337 it can produce, how many jars of silver polish must So-Clean sell monthly to justify continuing to sell it?
2. Suppose now that So-Clean can sell all of the Grit 337 that it can make. How many jars of silver polish must the company sell per month to justify further processing Grit 337 into silver polish?

**5-46   *Processing decision***   Most beef bought in stores comes from cattle that have been fattened on feedlots. A feedlot is an area consisting mainly of pens and barns in which cattle are closely packed and fed diets designed to increase their weight rapidly. The cattle are bought from ranchers when they weigh about 500 pounds, at a cost of $260 including freight. After the cattle are fattened, their selling price is $0.50 per pound and the buyer pays the freight to deliver the cattle.

The average animal gains weight in the following pattern.

| | |
|---|---|
| First month | 140  pounds |
| Second month | 130 |
| Third month | 120 |
| Fourth month | 100 |
| Total potential gain | 490  pounds |

For each month that an animal is on the feedlot, it eats $52 worth of feed. The lot can hold 5,000 head of cattle at a time.

**Required**

1. Assume that there is a shortage of animals available for fattening. The lot is only able to buy 600 head per month. Determine the number of months that each animal should be kept on the lot before being sold.
2. Suppose, instead, that the supply of animals is very high so that the lot is operating at full capacity. Determine the number of months each animal should be kept.

**5-47   *Special order (CMA adapted)***   Anchor Company manufactures jewelry cases. The firm is currently operating at 80% of its capacity of 7,500 direct labor hours per month. Its sales manager has been looking for special orders to increase the use of capacity. JCL Company has offered to buy 10,000 cases at $7.50 per case provided that delivery is within two months. Per-case cost data for the order are as follows.

| | |
|---|---|
| Materials | $2.50 |
| Direct labor (1/2 hour at $6) | 3.00 |
| Manufacturing overhead | 2.00 |
| Total unit cost | $7.50 |

Variable overhead is $1.50 per direct labor hour and the company allocates fixed manufacturing overhead to units of product based on their direct labor time. Without the order, Anchor has enough business to operate at 6,000 direct labor hours (80% of 7,500) in each of the next two months. The normal selling price of the jewelry case is $10.50. JCL would put its own label on the case. The production manager is concerned about the labor time that making 10,000 cases would require. She cannot schedule more than 7,500 labor hours per month because Anchor has a policy against overtime. Thus, the company will have to reduce some regular-price sales of the jewelry case if it accepts the order. JCL will not take fewer than 10,000 cases.

**Required**

1. Determine whether Anchor should accept the order.
2. Determine the price per case for the order that would make Anchor indifferent between accepting and rejecting the order (the price that would give Anchor the same profit under both alternatives).

## CASES

**5-48   *Services of an athlete—jumping leagues*   The Fort Bluff Titans of the Cross Continental Football League (CCFL) have been approached by an agent for Flinger Johnson, the star quarterback of the Snidely Whips, a team in the other major football league—the Nationwide Football League (NFL). Johnson's current contract, at a salary of $300,000 per year, runs out this year and he is free to consider other offers. His goal is a salary of at least $500,000, and he's willing to jump leagues if that's what it takes to meet his goal.

The six teams in the CCFL play each of the other teams twice, for a total of ten games. (Each team plays every opponent once at home and once away.) Tickets sell for $10 per game and variable costs are about $2 per ticket. The home team keeps $7 of the admission price and gives $3 to the visiting team. The home team pays the variable costs, which are about $2 per ticket.

J.J. Box, owner of the Titans, believes that acquiring Johnson would be a boon to attendance. No team in the CCFL, including the Titans, comes close to filling its stadium. Box estimates that having Johnson in the league would be worth 10,000 additional admissions at every game he played, whether at home or on the road, and sellouts are unlikely even with Johnson in the league. Box recognizes that bringing Johnson to his team would affect all owners in the league.

After considering his own financial situation as well as those of his fellow owners, Box decides to meet with the owners of the other CCFL teams before pursuing further negotiations for Johnson's services. At that meeting, Box proposes that, because all owners would benefit from having Johnson in the league, the other owners should be willing to help cover the cost of bringing Johnson to the CCFL. Box says he's willing to do his share, but that he doesn't think he can or should bear the entire cost of bringing in Johnson. Box's legal counsel appeared at the meeting to provide assurance that reasonable financial cooperation among the owners on this matter would not produce legal action by any unit of government.

As might be expected, the press reported whatever it could find out about Johnson's interest in bettering his financial package. After reading about a potential meeting of CCFL owners, Whips' owner, Sal Mindinow, arranged for the owners of NFL teams to meet and discuss the impact of Johnson's possible departure.

The financial facts in the NFL differ somewhat from those in the CCFL. Variable costs are about the same, around $2 per ticket. But tickets to NFL games are $12, NFL teams play 12 games per season, and about 50% of the games of each team are sellouts. (For sold-out games, teams usually have requests for about 3,000 more tickets than seats available.) After much arguing, the owners at the meeting called by Mindinow agreed that if Johnson left the NFL the total number of tickets requested for games in which Johnson's old team plays would drop by about 8,000. Like his counterpart at the meeting of CCFL owners, Mr. Mindinow's legal counsel assured those at the meeting that reasonable financial cooperation among the owners was not likely to prompt government intervention.

### Required

Assume that "signing" bonuses are prohibited in both leagues.

1.  Develop a proposal that the various owners of teams in the CCFL would consider an economically sound as well as fair way to meet Johnson's salary demands.
2.  Develop a proposal that the various owners of teams in the NFL would consider an economically sound as well as fair way to meet Johnson's salary demands.

### 5-49    Peanuts for peanuts*

*The Time:*    Hopefully never, but then everybody knows the outcome of wishful thinking.

*The Scene:*    A small neighborhood diner in a small New Jersey town about 25 miles from New York City. The operator-owner, Mr. Joseph Madison, is preparing to open for the day. He has just placed a shiny new rack holding brightly colored bags of peanuts on the far end of the counter. As he stands back to admire his new peanut rack, his brother-in-law, Harry, a self-styled efficiency expert, enters from the back door.

*Harry.* Morning Joe. What're you looking so pleased about?

*Joe.* I jus' put up my new peanut rack—the one I tole you about the other night.

*Harry.* Joe, you told me that you were going to put in these peanuts because some people asked for them. But I've been thinking about it and I wonder if you realize what this rack of peanuts is costing you.

*Joe.* It ain't gonna cost. Gonna be a profit. Sure, I hadda pay $25 for a fancy rack to hol' the bags, but the peanuts cost 6 cents a bag and I sell 'em for 10 cents. I figger I can sell 50 bags a week to start. It'll take twelve and a ha'f weeks to cover the cost of the rack and after that I make a clear profit of 4 cents a bag. The more I sell, the more I make.

*Harry* (shaking his finger at Joe). That is an antiquated and completely unrealistic approach. Fortunately, modern accounting procedures permit a more accurate picture which reveals the complexities involved.

*Joe.* Huh?

*Harry.* To be precise, those peanuts must be integrated into your entire operation and be allocated their appropriate share of business overhead. They must share a proportionate part of your expenditures for rent, heat, light, equipment depreciation, decorating, salaries for counter help, cook . . .

*Joe.* The cook? What's he gotta do wit' the peanuts? He don't even know I got 'em yet.

*Harry.* Look, Joe. The cook is in the kitchen; the kitchen prepares the food; the food is what brings people in; and while they're in, they ask to buy peanuts. That's why you must charge a portion of the cook's wages, as well as a part of your own salary to peanut sales. Since you've talked to me I've worked it all out. This sheet contains a carefully calculated cost analysis which clearly indicates that the peanut operation should pay exactly $1,278 per year toward these general overhead costs.

*Joe* (unbelieving). The peanuts? $1,278 a year for overhead? That's nuts!

*Harry.* It's really a little more than that. You also spend money each week to have the windows washed, to have the place swept out in the mornings, to keep soap in

---

* *Used with the permission of Rex H. Anderson, Senior Vice President of INA Reinsurance Company.*

the washroom and provide free colas to the police. That raises the actual total to $1,313 per year.

*Joe* (thoughtfully). But the peanut salesman said I'd make money—put 'em on the end of the counter, he said—and get 4 cents a bag profit.

*Harry* (with a sniff). He's not an accountant. And remember, he wanted to sell you something. Do you actually know what the portion of the counter occupied by the peanut rack is worth to you?

*Joe.* Sure. It ain't worth nuttin'. No stool there—just a dead spot at the end.

*Harry.* The modern cost picture permits no dead spots. Your counter contains 60 square feet and your counter business grosses $15,000 a year. Consequently, the square foot of space occupied by the peanut rack is worth $250 per year. Since you have taken that area away from general counter use, you must charge the value of the space to the occupant. That's called opportunity cost.

*Joe.* You mean I gotta add $250 a year more to the peanuts?

*Harry.* Right. That raises their share of the general operating costs to $1,563 per year. Now then, if you sell 50 bags of peanuts per week, these allocated costs will amount to 60 cents per bag.

*Joe* (incredulously). What?

*Harry.* Obviously, to that must be added your purchase price of 6 cents a bag, which brings the total to 66 cents. So you see, by selling peanuts at 10 cents per bag, you are losing 56 cents on every sale.

*Joe.* Something's crazy!!

*Harry.* Not at all. Here are the figures. They prove your peanut operation just can't stand on its own feet.

*Joe* (brightening). Suppose I sell lotsa peanuts—1,000 bags a week mebbe, 'stead of 50?

*Harry* (tolerantly). No. Joe, you just don't understand the problem. If the volume of peanut sales increased, your operating costs will go up—you'll have to handle more bags, with more time, more general overhead, more everything. The basic principle of accounting is firm on that subject: "The bigger the operation the more general overhead costs must be allocated." No, increasing the volume of sales won't help.

*Joe.* Okay, you so smart, you tell me what I gotta do.

*Harry* (condescendingly now). Well—you could first reduce operating expenses.

*Joe.* Yeah? How?

*Harry.* You might take smaller space in an older building with cheaper rent. Maybe cut salaries. Wash the windows biweekly. Have the floor swept only on Thursdays. Remove the soap from the washrooms. Cut out the colas for the cops. This will help you decrease the square-foot value of the counter. For example, if you can cut your expenses 50%, that will reduce the amount allocated to peanuts from $1,563 down to $781.50 per year, reducing the cost to 36 cents per bag.  Joe. That's better?

*Harry.* Much, much better. Of course, even then you'd lose 26 cents per bag if you charged only 10 cents. Therefore, you must also raise your selling price. If you want a net profit of 4 cents per bag, you would have to charge 40 cents.

*(Harry is looking very confident now, but Joe appears flabbergasted.)*

*Joe.* You mean even after I cut operating costs 50%, I still gotta charge 40 cents for a 10-cent bag of peanuts? Nobody's that nuts about nuts! Who'd buy 'em?

*Harry.* That's a secondary consideration. The point is, at 40 cents, you'd be selling at a price based upon a true and proper evaluation of your then-reduced costs.

*(Joe does not look convinced; then, he brightens.)*

*Joe.* Look! I gotta better idea. Why don't I jus' throw the nuts out—so I lost $25 on the rack. I'm outa this nutsy business and no more grief.

*(Harry is shaking his head vigorously.)*

*Harry.* Joe, it just isn't that simple. You are in the peanut business! The minute you throw those peanuts out, you are adding $1,563 of annual overhead to the rest of your operation. Joe—be realistic—can you afford to do that?

*Joe* (by now completely crushed). It's unbelievable! Last week I wuz makin' money. Now I'm in trouble—jus' becuz I think peanuts on the counter is gonna bring me some extra profit. Jus' becuz I believe 50 bags of peanuts a week is easy.

*Harry* (by now smiling and satisfied that his brother-in-law will not be so quick to argue with him in the future). That is the reason for modern cost studies, Joe—to dispel those false illusions.

*Curtain falls.*

**Required**

1. Who's nuts?
2. Write a memorandum that evaluates the position(s) that Harry takes.

**5-50   *Dropping a segment***   Tom Johnson, owner-manager of Johnson's Drugstore, is opposed to smoking and wants to drop the tobacco counter from the store. He has determined from industry statistics and opinions of other drugstore managers that the tobacco counter creates a good deal of other business because many people who come in just for cigarettes, cigars, and pipe tobacco buy other articles. Moreover, some people will go elsewhere for drugs and sundries if they know that tobacco is not being sold.

Johnson estimates that sales of drugs would drop by 5% and sundries by 10% if the tobacco counter were removed. The space now occupied by the tobacco counter would be devoted to greeting cards, which Johnson does not now sell. Estimated annual sales for greeting cards are $8,000, with cost of sales of $3,000.

If the tobacco counter is dropped, one clerk earning $4,000 could be dropped. But a pharmacist would have to handle the greeting card sales, which would result in a further drop in drug sales of 2% (from the current level). Carrying costs of the inventory of greeting cards are expected to be about $300 less per year than those associated with tobacco products.

Johnson has asked you to advise him in this decision. He's provided you with an income statement for the coming year showing his expectations if tobacco products are retained.

| Johnson's Drugstore Budgeted Income Statement for the Coming Year | | | | |
|---|---|---|---|---|
| | Tobacco | Drugs | Sundries | Total |
| Sales | $31,000 | $128,000 | $36,000 | $195,000 |
| Cost of goods sold | 10,500 | 54,000 | 10,500 | 75,000 |
| Gross profit | $20,500 | $ 74,000 | $25,500 | $120,000 |
| Operating expenses: | | | | |
| Salaries | 9,200 | 40,000 | 10,800 | 60,000 |
| Occupancy costs (rent, utilities, maintenance, etc.) | 3,000 | 7,000 | 4,000 | 14,000 |
| Miscellaneous | 1,500 | 6,700 | 1,800 | 10,000 |
| Total operating expenses | $13,700 | $ 53,700 | $16,600 | $ 84,000 |
| Income before taxes | $ 6,800 | $ 20,300 | $ 8,900 | $ 36,000 |

You learn that occupancy costs are allocated to each product group based on percentages of space occupied for display of those products. These costs will not change in total if greeting cards are substituted for tobacco. The manager's salary, $28,000, is arbitrarily allocated to departments and included in the salaries amount in the income statement. Miscellaneous expenses are allocated based on relative sales volume and would be unaffected by the change except for the cost of carrying inventory.

**Required**

Comment on the cost to Mr. Johnson of implementing his convictions about smoking.

**5-51 *Alternative uses of space*** Several years ago the Star Department Store began leasing space to Clothes Horse, Inc., a chain of boutiques specializing in high-priced women's clothing and accessories. The boutiques are usually separate stores in shopping centers, but the management of Clothes Horse wished to experiment with an operation in a department store and Star was willing, as the space was not then needed for its own operations.

Clothes Horse pays Star a monthly rental of $3,000 plus 5% of its gross sales, and the arrangement has been profitable for both parties. Star pays all electricity, gas, and other costs of occupancy, which are negligible when considered incrementally because the space would have to be lighted and heated anyway. The lease is about to expire, and Clothes Horse is eager to renew it for another year on the same terms. However, some of Star's department heads have indicated a desire to take over the operation of the boutique, and others have requested the use of the space to expand their selling areas.

After reviewing all the requests, Ron Stein and Margot Miller, Star's executive vice president and general manager, respectively, have narrowed the range of choices to the following: (1) renew the lease with Clothes Horse; (2) keep the boutique, but place it under the women's wear department head, Bill Rausch; (3) use the space to expand the shoe department, which is located next to the boutique.

The boutique had total sales of $400,000 in the first ten months of the current year, and the monthly rate is expected to double for the last two months, which come at the height of the Christmas season. Stein and Miller expect a 10% increase in sales in the coming year if Clothes Horse continues to operate the boutique. Mr. Rausch has presented the following expected income statement for the coming year, which he believes he could achieve if he took over the operation of the boutique.

| | | |
|---|---:|---:|
| Sales | | $380,000 |
| Cost of sales | | 171,000 |
| Gross profit | | $209,000 |
| Operating expenses: | | |
| Salaries | $75,000 | |
| Advertising and promotion | 14,000 | |
| Supplies | 7,000 | |
| Miscellaneous | 8,000 | 104,000 |
| Profit | | $105,000 |

Mr. Stein commented that Mr. Rausch is generally too optimistic and that his estimate of sales volume was probably about 10% too high. He also noted that Rausch had provided for fewer salespeople than were employed by Clothes Horse and that the somewhat reduced level of service would not help business. Stein felt that expenses other than cost of sales would probably be about as Rausch had estimated, even at the lower volume that Stein thought would be achieved.

The manager of the shoe department believed that if the space were used to expand his department his sales would increase by about $200,000 with a gross profit rate of 45%. He would need to add one salesperson, who would work on a 10% commission like the other employees in that department. Virtually all other store employees work on salary, not commission.

Miller and Stein both brought up the subject of traffic through the store and both agreed that traffic had increased since Clothes Horse opened the boutique. They were uncertain about the effects of the increased traffic on sales in the store's own departments, so Miller said that she would investigate the matter.

Miller instructed several of her assistants to interview people in the store, particularly in the boutique, regarding their shopping habits. Several days later, the results were in, and she went to Stein's office to discuss them. The following major conclusions were contained in the reports Miller had received.

1. About 40% of sales made in the boutique are to people who come especially to shop there. These people have to walk through parts of the store to get to the boutique and spend about 20% as much in the store as they do in the boutique.
2. The remainder of the boutique's sales are to people who come for other reasons. Many drop in on their way in or out of the store; some plan to shop in the store's other departments as well as in the boutique. These people spend about twice as much in the store's own departments as they do in the boutique.

After a discussion lasting nearly an hour, Stein and Miller decided that the people who came in especially to shop in the boutique would not patronize the store at all if Clothes Horse did not operate it. The executives believed that only the popularity of the Clothes Horse name induced these people to come in.

Of the other group, they believed that about 10% of the patronage would be lost if Clothes Horse did not operate the boutique. This loss of sales would be spread fairly evenly throughout the store. The average gross profit rate in the store is 45%, and other variable costs are an additional 8% of sales.

### Required
Determine the best course of action for the store.  Using the guidelines in Appendix A, write a memorandum supporting your position.

**5-52   Product processing**   Taylor Company makes wall paneling used in homes and offices. The company buys walnut logs and processes them into thin sheets of veneer that are then glued to sheets of plywood to make paneling. Taylor also makes the plywood. The company has enough capacity to make 1,000,000 square feet of veneer per month and 1,200,000 square feet of plywood. Capacity in the gluing operation is 1,300,000 square feet per month. Substantial markets exist for plywood and veneer as well as for paneling, though Taylor's managers think of the company as a paneling manufacturer.

Taylor's senior operating managers meet monthly to discuss recent operating results and their expectations about the coming months. Jim Chen, Taylor's controller, regularly attends these meetings to assist the managers in their deliberations.  To facilitate the monthly discussions, Chen developed the following cost data, per 1,000 square feet of product.

|              | Plywood | Veneer | Paneling |
|--------------|--------:|-------:|---------:|
| Materials    | $18     | $16    | $ 34     |
| Direct labor | 25      | 20     | 55       |
| Overhead     | 32      | 29     | 93       |
| Total        | $75     | $65    | $182     |

When presenting the cost data, Chen pointed out that the figures shown for paneling were cumulative. That is, the amount for each component of paneling cost was the sum of the costs of veneer and plywood plus the additional costs associated with the gluing operation. (Thus, no new materials are added in the gluing operation.) When he first provided the data to operating managers, Chen also pointed out that the variable portion of overhead was approximately 80% of labor cost. After some discussion at that meeting about individual components of fixed overhead, the group agreed that all such costs were probably unavoidable.

At their meeting in March of 20X4, Taylor's managers reviewed operating results for January and February, when the prevailing prices (per 1,000 square feet) of Taylor's products were $178, $74, and $81 for paneling, veneer and plywood, respectively. Mario Franks, Taylor's sales manager, began the meeting with a smile and kind words for everyone present. "I think even Jim Chen will agree we've learned how to use cost data in making our decisions. Our prediction of the selling price for paneling was right on target, and we sold all the paneling we could make in both months."

Sam West, the factory manager, agreed, though with reservations. "Yes, I can see that we did the right thing. But you guys don't have to deal with the flack I'm getting about the layoffs of workers in the plywood shop. And almost every week the manager of the gluing shop—you all know Phyllis—hits me with some new scheme for using the people and equipment in her area to work on jobs that have nothing to do with making paneling."

Anxious that the discussion move on to decisions about what to do in the future, Franks said "All water over the dam. What we need to do now is decide whether we should make any changes in production plans for the near future. Some of my people tell me plywood prices could go up soon, probably to around $86. I hate to say this, because I know that paneling got us where we are; but maybe we should consider other alternatives." To Franks' surprise, Jim Chen chimed in at this point to support consideration of alternatives, though not for the same reason. Said Chen, "I haven't yet seen anything to indicate an increase in plywood prices, Mario, though your field people may be right. But everything I read about new construction projects and the market for remodeling suggests that the price for paneling is in for a drop, perhaps to as low as $164. Even if the field people are wrong and the price of plywood holds at about what it is now, the potential drop in the price for paneling should make us reconsider our position about concentrating on producing paneling."

Gene Draper, the recently hired chief operating officer, entered the discussion with the following comments. "I know I'm the new kid on the block here, but I've tried to do my homework, and it seems to me that whatever the prices for what we produce, a major stumbling block for our company is the unequal capacities of our veneer, plywood, and gluing operations. I know that long-term increases in capacity would involve substantial investments in new assets, and we should discuss such investments at a future meeting. But it seems to me that we should at least be considering ways to equalize capacities in the short run. For example, I'd be willing to authorize spending up to $2,000 a month this year for renting whatever equipment would increase our production capacity of either veneer or plywood by 100,000 square feet, but you'll have to tell me which one to spend the money on."

### Required

Evaluate the operating managers' understanding of Taylor's cost structure and the new CEO's offer of short-term support to move toward equalizing capacities.

# Part Two

# budgeting

Economic enterprises engage in many activities that require not only planning but also coordination of plans. We explore the relationships among those activities in this part.

The comprehensive budget is a tool to make planning effective and provides a means for monitoring whether activities are going according to plan. In a formal and integrated way, the budget captures and reflects the results of planning decisions, from decisions about prices, product mix, and cost structure, to those about dividends and major new investments.

CVP analysis and knowledge of cost behavior are important in budgeting for the relatively near future—the coming year. Those concepts are also important in analyzing the potential of longer-term projects, the expenditures for which might have to be made in the near future. In addition, some of the principles from financial accounting are important in budgeting because a comprehensive budget includes financial statements normally prepared for external reporting.

Budgeting is more than a technical or mechanical exercise. Because it is people who plan and people who act (according to or contrary to plans), the ways that budgets are developed and used can affect people's behavior and vice versa. In this part we introduce some behavioral problems entailed in the budgeting process. A more comprehensive treatment of these problems is given in Part Three.

## Chapter Six

# OPERATIONAL BUDGETING

## LEARNING OBJECTIVES

*After reading this chapter, you should be able to*

- *Explain how budgeting relates to the major functions of management.*
- *Describe the components and organization of a comprehensive budget.*
- *Describe several methods managers use to forecast sales and some of the problems of using each method.*
- *Explain the concept of expected value and its application to forecasting.*
- *Describe two approaches to setting budget allowances for costs and the types of costs for which each is likely to be used.*
- *Describe several behavioral problems associated with the preparation and use of budgets.*
- *Prepare a budgeted income statement, a purchases budget, and a simple production budget.*
- *Explain why a company's inventory policy is important to budgeting.*

***America Online**, the giant Internet and Web provider, changed its pricing structure late in 1996. Prior to December 1, 1996, the Company's standard monthly membership fee for its AOL service, which included five hours of service, was $9.95 per month, with a $2.95 hourly fee for use in excess of five hours per month. The company offered some new alternatives, the most important of which was a standard monthly membership fee of $19.95, with no additional hourly charges. Subscribers could also choose to prepay for one year in advance at the monthly rate of $17.95.*

*The response was immediate and much greater than expected. Membership soared and use soared even more, from a per-customer monthly average of 7 hours to 23 hours. AOL did not have enough connections to satisfy the increased demand and customers could not get through. People referred to "America Off Line," dissatisfied customers complained, members of Congress threatened inquiries, Attorneys General of several states sued AOL, and the stock price plummeted. The next annual report stated that the "Company recorded a charge of $24.3 million related to a legal settlement reached with various State Attorneys General to resolve potential claims arising out of the Company's introduction of flat-rate pricing and its representation that it would provide unlimited access to subscribers."*

> *AOL also agreed to make payments to subscribers "who may have been injured by their reliance on the Company's claim of unlimited access. These payments do not represent refunds of online service revenues, but are rather the compromise and settlement of allegations that the Company's advertising of unlimited access under its flat-rate pricing plan violated consumer protection laws." AOL wound up paying nearly $30 million.*
>
> *AOL also stated that a potential risk it faced was "The Company's inability to manage its growth and to adapt its administrative, operational and financial control systems to the needs of an expanded and evolving entity; and the failure of management to anticipate, respond to and manage changing business conditions."*
>
> *How could such a well-run company misestimate so greatly? The question is all the more pertinent because AOL had tested various pricing models. In the fall of 1996, AOL was testing seven pricing plans, including the ones it adopted.*
>
> *One lesson of this tale is that success, in the form of higher sales, can lead to strains on resources, which can turn success into failure if the company does not respond quickly.*

Sources: *AOL annual and quarterly reports.*
Randy Befumo, *"The Economics of a Flat Fee,"* The Motley Fool Evening News, *October 28, 1996.*

The functional areas of a business (marketing, production, personnel, finance, administration) are interdependent and must work in harmony to achieve goals. Production people must make all, or nearly all, of the units that marketing can sell, but must not overproduce, because having too much inventory causes excessive costs for storage, insurance, taxes, and interest. For the same reason, a purchasing manager must not overpurchase, yet must ensure that materials and components are available to meet production schedules. Finance personnel must make cash available to pay for materials, labor, and other operating costs, as well as for dividends, acquisitions of assets, and debt repayments.

The plans of the business must be specified in sufficient detail that the managers of functional areas know what they must do to ensure smooth performance for other areas and for the company as a whole. Companies use comprehensive budgets to coordinate all of these activities.

## COMPREHENSIVE BUDGETS

A **comprehensive budget** is a set of financial statements and other schedules showing budgeted, expected, or pro forma results for a future period. A comprehensive budget normally contains an income statement, a balance sheet, a cash budget (statement of cash receipts and disbursements), and schedules of production, purchases, and fixed-asset acquisitions. The budget package also might have other components, depending on the entity's needs.

Comprehensive budgeting requires careful studies of cost behavior patterns. Budgeted income statements are similar to the income statements you developed for CVP analysis and for making short-term decisions. But budgeting involves more than CVP analysis. For instance, budgeting cash collections requires both predicting sales *and* estimating the pattern of cash collections (how much do we collect within 30 days? within 60 days?). Predicted cash collections from sales combine with cash receipts from planned borrowing and other sources to become a cash receipts budget. Exhibit 6-1 offers an overview of the relationships among the components of a typical comprehensive budget. You should refer to this exhibit as we discuss these relationships and the components in detail in this and the next chapter.

> CHAPTER
> **7**

Comprehensive budgeting is more complex than CVP analysis because a change in a single assumption affects the whole set of budgets, not just one or a few items in an income statement. For example, changing budgeted sales for a particular month affects not only budgeted variable costs and profit, but also plans for purchasing, the timing and amounts of expected cash receipts, payments for purchases, and perhaps even loans that must be negotiated. The ripple effects of changes in budgets make budgeting ideal for using computer spreadsheets. Spreadsheet users can develop sophisticated budgeting models.

All levels of management are, or should be, involved in putting together some part of the interrelated statements and schedules that make up the comprehensive budget. That is, dealing with budgets is a part of the overall job of managing and helps develop other management skills. (See the accompanying Insight.) Top managers are interested in overall results. Lower-level managers deal only with segments of the total package, and the degree of detail in the schedules they use varies with the breadth of each manager's responsibilities. Thus, a production manager might deal only with schedules of production data. In general, most managers have budgets showing what is expected of *them*—what objectives *they* are to achieve and at what costs. We should point out that some organizations

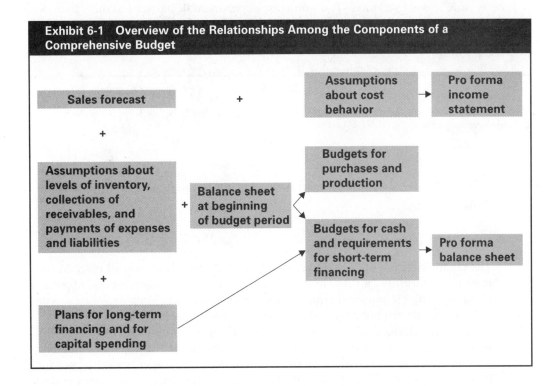

**Exhibit 6-1   Overview of the Relationships Among the Components of a Comprehensive Budget**

### Two Views on Budgeting

Viewing budgets as an integral part of managing is important for managers. For many years, the accounting department at **Elgin Sweeper Company** prepared the company's budgets without participation by the affected managers. Consequently, those managers were not committed to meeting their budgets and didn't view budgets as plans that incorporated or affected their decisions. Top managers made a series of changes in the budgeting process, but it took a long time to get front-line people to prepare budgets. Now Elgin's managers believe that the ". . . key to a successful cost management program was to educate and entrust responsibility to those front-line managers who made the decisions that drive costs."

**IKEA**, headquartered in Scandinavia, is the world's largest furniture manufacturer and retailer. IKEA abandoned budgeting in 1992. Now IKEA's managers merely have to keep costs within certain revenue ratios. Several other Scandinavian companies are also at various stages of abandoning traditional budgets. **Borealis**, a large Danish petrochemicals company, completely abandoned traditional budgeting in 1995. Managers use new mechanisms to steer the company, including scorecards, rolling financial forecasts, trend reporting, and activity-based management.

These companies see traditional budgeting as an "evil" for several reasons. It strengthens the vertical chain of command and control rather than empowering the front-line. It constrains the organization rather than increasing its flexibility and responsiveness. It reinforces departmental barriers rather than encouraging knowledge sharing across the organization. And it is bureaucratic, internally focused, and time consuming.

*Sources: John P. Callan, Wesley N. Tredup, and Randy S. Wissinger, "Elgin Sweeper Company's Journey Toward Cost Management,"* Management Accounting, *July 1991, 24.*
*Jeremy Hope and Robin Fraser, "Beyond Budgeting . . . Breaking through the Barrier to the 'Third Wave',"* Management Accounting (U.K.), *December 1997.*

prefer not to budget, as illustrated in the Insight, but they seem to be in a distinct minority.

## BUDGETS AND PLANNING

The comprehensive budget is part of a formal strategy and overall plan, in contrast to an intuitive, ad hoc approach to operations. A major benefit of formal planning is that it requires explicit statements not only of objectives (such as sales volume and profit) but also of the means required to achieve them.

Some objectives that managers thought achievable might turn out to be unachievable after the budget is finished. For example, the budget calls for high sales in the early part of the year, but the production manager finds that productive capacity is insufficient. Or perhaps the financial manager sees that the company cannot achieve the production needed to achieve budgeted sales unless it obtains short-term financing. If securing financing is undesirable (or even impossible), the budgets must be modified to be consistent with the amount of cash available. The comprehensive budget also incorporates the current effects of plans for long-term financing and for acquisitions of major long-lived assets. The development of those long-term plans, and the related decision making, are discussed in Chapters 7, 8, and 9. Companies change their objectives through time, as the accompanying Insight describes.

As you know from Chapter 1, decision making is part of the overall planning process. Chapter 5 showed that decision making relies on estimates about future results under alternative courses of action, and one of the alternatives in virtually all decisions is to maintain the status quo (that is, to keep things as they are). Managers use the information in budgets as the status quo, the baseline for determining incremental revenues and costs.

## BUDGETS AND CONTROL

Budgets express targets or goals. Actual results express achievements. Comparing budgeted and actual results helps managers control future operations and provides a useful basis for evaluating performance. Problems showing up in the comparisons prompt managers to take corrective action. The preceding statements are oversimplified but fair statements of the role of budgets in control and performance evaluation. (As reported earlier, analyzing variances from budgets and pursuing corrective action is one of the principal factors important to using budgets effectively.)

 *SIGHT*

### Changing Objectives

**Boeing** shifted its major objective from market share to profitability upon determining that it could not have both. The company raised its prices 5 percent because it found its production lines clogged. Boeing had dropped prices on aircraft to keep **Airbus Industrie** from taking some of its traditional customers. The resulting surge of orders will cost billions to untangle. **Toyota** stressed market share and forsook profits for sales until recent years. **Cypress Semiconductor's** recent annual reports discussed a conflict between two of the company's major objectives: market share and profitability. "The company that focuses on redesigning high-volume products to improve efficiency (profitability) cannot use these same design resources to create new products to generate new revenue." Engineers and designers are scarce resources and the company must decide how to use them.

*Sources: Seanna Browder, "Course Change at Boeing," Business Week, July 27, 1998, 34.*
*Alex Taylor III, "How Toyota Defies Gravity," Fortune, December 8, 1997, 100.*

Comparisons are meaningful only if expectations are reasonable and consider all available information. For two reasons, past performance is usually inappropriate as the standard for comparison. First, circumstances change. A company might change its marketing strategy by lowering selling prices and spending less on sales-promotion efforts (the strategy adopted by **General Mills** in the mid-1990s). Or perhaps managers believe that, in the second year of producing one of its products, some production costs will be lower than in the first year because workers are more familiar with their tasks. (The cost effects of learning are presented in some detail in Chapter 17.) Second, comparisons with past performance tell nothing about whether current performance is as good as it should be. A student who gets 38 percent on one examination and 42 percent on the next has improved but is still not performing adequately. This example confirms the need for a standard of comparison that reflects an acceptable level of performance. Companies adopting the continuous improvement (Kaizen) philosophy, which is discussed more extensively in Chapter 12, set specific cost reduction targets based on past performance.

## CHAPTER 17

## ORGANIZATION OF BUDGETS

Budgets usually cover specific time periods. Most companies prepare a budget for the upcoming fiscal year, and for monthly or quarterly periods within that year. Many companies also prepare budgets for longer periods such as two, three, or five years.

Because of forecasting difficulties, annual budgets and segments of longer-term budgets are less detailed than are budgets for periods closer at hand. Thus, the budget for one year hence is more detailed than one for periods beyond one year, and budgets for segments of the current year are more detailed than the budget for the full year. Chapter 7 presents the most common approaches to long-term budgeting.

Virtually all companies prepare a separate **capital budget**—a schedule of planned expenditures for long-lived assets. A capital budget often covers several years into the future. Forecasted expenditures from the capital budget become part of the cash budgets for the appropriate periods. Chapters 8 and 9 treat capital budgeting in detail.

The budget for the current year is normally supplemented by budgets for shorter periods, because monitoring progress toward meeting the goals in the annual budget is easier for managers if checkpoints are available along the way. More important, what actually happens is often different from even the most sophisticated plans, so managers might need to make changes in operating plans for the remainder of the period.

Factors in the business environment also dictate that budgets be developed for periods shorter than a year. Seasonal businesses must make or buy large quantities of goods in advance of the selling season. Doing so creates a need for cash considerably in advance of cash collections from customers. Cash collections also lag behind cash needs during the busy season of service-providing businesses that are seasonal, such as accounting firms and landscape-maintenance companies. Too, cash requirements vary over the year because some costs are not paid evenly throughout the year. Companies normally pay property taxes in two installments; some insurance premiums are due annually; interest payments might be required annually, semiannually, or quarterly; and dividends are usually paid quarterly or annually. It makes a big difference whether a $100,000 payment for taxes or dividends must be made in January or July, because the funds must be available when the payment falls due. Cash budgets are an important part of the total budget package, and budgets prepared for the year as a whole conceal these irregular funds requirements and therefore hinder planning.

Companies whose managers want to have plans for at least a year in advance often use continuous budgets. **Continuous budgets** are maintained by adding a budget for a month (or quarter) as one of these periods goes by. Thus, a 12-month budget exists at all times, and managers are aware of the needs for the next 12 months, regardless of the time of the year. The accompanying Insight describes one company's experience with continuous budgeting.

Although comprehensive budgets focus attention on time periods, many managers also find project budgets helpful for controlling operations and evaluating performance. **Project budgets** reflect expectations for various stages of completing specific projects. A company building a new plant will have a time schedule (finish the exterior by June, the interior by November, begin production by March). The focus in developing a project budget is on completing each stage of the project. Project budgets affect periodic budgeting because cash expenditures for projects must be incorporated in the cash budget. Therefore, project budgets supplement, rather than replace, regular periodic budgets.

## DEVELOPING THE COMPREHENSIVE BUDGET

Well in advance of the start of a new budget year, managers begin discussing prospects for the coming year. The earliest discussions normally focus on overall goals relating to profit or growth, such as a 10 percent increase in income, a 2

**IN** SIGHT

### Continuous Budgeting at HON Company

**HON Company** is the largest maker of mid-priced office furniture in the United States and Canada. Managers found that incorporating the effects of innovation into an annual budget was difficult because the actions taken and the outcomes that result unfold as the year progresses. It was very difficult to forecast the evolutionary changes. To counter this, HON decided to use a continuous three-month budget cycle.

Using a continuous budget system has enabled senior managers to push decisions down to the production floor and helps to gain employee commitment and fast adoption of productivity improvements. All departments work together to produce a four-quarter budget that is updated at the beginning of each quarter. This ensures that the front-line workers translate the corporate strategies into a well-coordinated action plan.

*Source: Ralph Drtina, Steve Hoeger and John Schaub, "Continuous Budgeting at the HON Company,"* Management Accounting, *January 1996, 20–24.*

percent increase in return on sales or assets, a 15 percent increase in sales, or perhaps a 2-point increase in market share. (The overall goals are likely to be derived from longer-term goals and strategies adopted by the firm's top managers.) At least at the outset, most budgets are driven by desired results. But whatever the initial concerns, in every case the budget for the coming period begins with a **sales forecast**, the sales a company expects to achieve. The forecast is critical because expected sales determine the requirements for product, people, other operating costs, cash flows, and financing. The interrelationships among these various elements depend on managerial policies (how much inventory to keep, what credit terms to offer to customers) and operating characteristics (cost structure, cycle time).

Chapters 2 through 5 introduced you to the task of preparing income statements based on expected sales and information about cost behavior. With minor exceptions, preparing a budgeted income statement is an extension of CVP analysis. Other budgets, especially the cash budget and the budgeted balance sheet, present some technical difficulties because of the *leads* and *lags* involved. For example, cash collections usually lag behind the recording of the revenue from credit sales. Similarly, cost of goods sold is recognized when revenue is recorded, but costs to purchase or produce goods for sale are normally incurred before the sale. That is, the costs lead (precede) the sale. Cash payments of incurred costs might be required immediately or might be delayed for varying periods. These leads and lags produce critical technical problems in comprehensive budgeting.

In the remainder of this chapter we present and illustrate sales forecasts, purchases budgets, and expense budgets. These budgets are usually called **operating budgets**. In Chapter 7 we complete the process by considering **financial budgets** (the budgeted balance sheet and the cash budget).

## SALES FORECASTING

The sales forecast is the foundation for the comprehensive budget. For a large company, developing the sales forecast is complex and time consuming. When **Xerox's** seven-member forecasting team adopted a sophisticated computer program, developing a forecast took 50 percent less time—but it still took three months. Businesses use many methods to forecast sales. Not all companies use all of the methods we mention, but most use one or more. A later Insight discusses some companies' experiences.

## INDICATOR METHODS

Sales of many industries are closely associated with one or more factors in the overall economy. Sales of long-lasting consumer goods (cars, washing machines) generally correlate well with published indicators of general economic activity such as Gross Domestic Product (GDP) and personal income. Sales of baby food are associated with the number of births, and sales of housing units with the formation of new households. Companies in such an industry might first use an indicator (e.g., personal income) to predict total sales for their industry, and then develop a sales budget by estimating the share of the total market they will commit themselves to achieving. Scatter diagrams and regression analysis, which we introduced in Chapter 3, are widely used in forecasting sales, just as they are in predicting costs.

Sales in many industries depend to a great extent on sales of *other* industries. For example, makers of bottles and cans look at forecasts for sales of beer and soft drinks, and steel and tire companies keep abreast of developments affecting the auto industry. In these situations, too, a company might develop a forecast for its industry and then for itself, but the indicator is a forecast for *another* industry.

To be useful for sales forecasting, the value of the indicator must be known, or predictable, in advance of the period for which a budget is being prepared, and the farther in advance the better. For example, an equally strong relationship between their sales and the number of births would be more useful to makers of toddlers' clothes than to makers of baby food, because the value of the indicator is available farther in advance of the expected change in sales. The availability of predictions of an indicator's value enhances the usefulness of an observed relationship for budgeting purposes, especially if the sales for the industry (baby-food makers, for example) correlate well with actual values of an indicator in the same or *later* periods. In any case, managers must continue to monitor relationships with indicators over time for hints that changes in other factors have made previously observed relationships less useful.

Managers obtain information about indicators from a variety of sources. Various segments of the U.S. government (e.g., the Departments of Commerce and Labor) develop and report data on broad indicators such as GDP, personal income, housing starts, and consumer prices. Some broad indicators originate with the Federal Reserve, private-sector entities such as **Dow Jones & Company** and **Dun & Bradstreet**, and widely distributed business publications such as *Business Week* and *Forbes*. For industry-specific indicators, managers often can refer to data developed by trade publications or associations (e.g., *Ward's Automotive Reports* and the American Iron & Steel Institute.)

The scatter-diagram in Exhibit 6-2 shows sales of residential carpeting (an industry) plotted against housing starts. Not surprisingly, the correlation is imperfect, partly because replacement sales do not depend on housing starts. Managers might use either regression analysis or a visual fit of a line to develop a sales forecasting equation. They then would adjust the results for changes they expect to influence the demand in the new and replacement markets.

Sometimes managers can obtain predictions of their industry's sales directly from trade associations, many of which publish forecasts or studies that provide

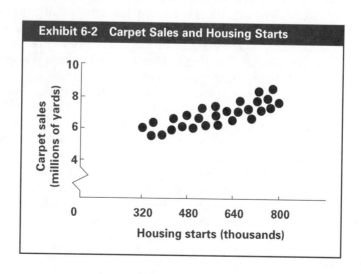

**Exhibit 6-2   Carpet Sales and Housing Starts**

guidance in sales forecasting. For example, an association of appliance dealers might conduct studies to determine the likely sales of various kinds of appliances. Its forecast for the sales of washing machines might consider the overall economic outlook, forecasts for new housing units, previous sales of washing machines, and the results of a survey of consumers about the age of machines currently in use. The forecast wouldn't indicate how these factors affect the sales of any single dealer, but individual dealers obtain a picture of what is likely to happen to industry sales and can apply it to their own companies.

## HISTORICAL ANALYSIS

Companies that operate chains of retail stores (e.g., **Radio Shack**, **Sears**, **The Gap**, **Circuit City**) develop sales data and trends by age of store (i.e., new stores, second-year stores) and begin their forecasts for the coming year by projecting sales from such data and trends. Other companies analyze their total sales of previous years and project the trend to arrive at a forecast. Thus, if sales have been rising at 10 percent per year, the company will start with a forecast based on last year's sales plus 10 percent. However a preliminary forecast is developed, managers then look for factors that suggest the likelihood of higher or lower sales. Were last year's sales abnormally high or low because of a strike or unusual weather conditions? (For example, ice cream, beer, golf balls, and many other products sell better in hot weather.) Are there discernible changes in taste that could affect sales? The past can be used for guidance on what might happen, but differences in conditions can cause the future to differ from the past.

Several sophisticated statistical techniques are available for making predictions from historical data. These techniques are beyond the scope of this book, but you may learn about some of them in other courses.

## JUDGMENTAL METHODS

Some companies budget sales using judgment based on experience with their customers and products. For example, each regional sales manager, in consultation with the sales staff, might estimate sales in that area, by customer or product line. The chief sales executive will review and discuss the forecasts with the regional managers, then develop a sales budget for each area and for the entire company to submit to top management for approval.

The analysis underlying judgment-based forecasts follows the lines of the other methods described here, but is less formal. Instead of using regression analysis or some other mathematical tool, managers will rely on their own experience and perceptions of changing circumstances to develop a forecast of the prospects for the industry and for the company. For example, a manager may notice an increasing number of newspaper and magazine articles about the decreasing length of the work week and reason that people will have increased leisure time. If the company's products are used for leisure-time activities, the manager is likely to forecast increased sales for the industry and for the company. Perceptive monitoring of world events prompted the top managers of **O'Gara-Hess & Eisenhardt** (a company based in Fairfield, Ohio) to forecast an increase in demand for armor-plated cars. News stories attracting the managers' attention included continuing reports of for-ransom kidnappings and of increasing violence to individuals by advocates of various causes.[1]

---

1 Neil Weinberg, editor (Follow-through), "When Bad News is Good News," Forbes, January 30, 1995, 14–15.

## WHICH METHOD TO USE

You should not underestimate the vast differences among companies or the difficulties of applying any one or more of them at any company. The applicability of any of the methods mentioned depends on the characteristics of the company, such as its age, its size, and the industry (or industries) in which it operates. For some companies or industries, no reliable—or predictable—indicators may exist. (Witness the maker of armor-plated cars.) Utilities rely heavily on historical analysis, adjusted for changes in population. In contrast, historical analysis is of little use to relatively new companies, companies in relatively new industries, and companies operating in industries heavily influenced by technological developments, such as companies engaged in electronic commerce.

Relying on any single forecasting method is risky. Forecasts using judgment alone might reflect unwarranted optimism of the sales manager and sales force. Even where indicators or industry forecasts are available and used, current conditions may differ from those in effect when the relationships among the indicators or forecast and the sales of the company or industry were developed. For example, in 1990 the Institute of Clean Air Companies forecast 1993 sales of one type of pollution-control system at $1.2 billion, but actual 1993 sales totaled only $226 million. Apparently, industry experts failed to anticipate how hard utilities would look for less expensive ways to meet limits set in 1990 for releasing pollutants into the air.[2]

Most companies use a combination of forecasting methods, and successful forecasting tends to result from combining sound and experienced business judgment with the judicious use of quantitative tools. Whatever methods are used to forecast, the sales budget for the company as a whole is likely to evolve from several forecasts made on a smaller scale. The original forecasts may be by product, product line, geographical area, department, or some combination of these. The scope of the original forecasts and the methods used depend on the entity's organization.

## EXPECTED VALUES AND FORECASTING

Some companies generate several forecasts by using different indicators or methods or by consulting several managers. When different methods are used, or different persons are preparing forecasts, the resulting forecasts are likely to differ. Even a single manager might come up with several forecasts based on different assumptions and judgments about conditions for the coming period. With several forecasts at hand, the concept of expected value is sometimes used to reach a single forecast figure to use in budgeting.

An **expected value** is the result of applying a probability assessment to each member of a set of possible future events. For example, to determine an expected value of sales from a collection of forecasts, managers assign a probability to each alternative sales forecast that they believe merits serious consideration. The probabilities reflect the managers' judgments of the likelihood of each forecast actually coming about. Suppose the vice president for sales and the regional managers believe there is a 30 percent probability of sales being $6,000,000 next year, a 50 percent probability that they will be $7,000,000, and a 20 percent probability that they will be $8,000,000. The following schedule shows the expected value of sales to be $5,050,000.

---

2 *Seth Lubove, "The Bureaucrat as Businessman,"* Forbes, *August 15, 1994, 64 and 66.*

| (1) Forecast | (2) Assigned Probability | (1) × (2) Expected Value |
|---|---|---|
| $6,000,000 | 0.30 | $1,800,000 |
| 7,000,000 | 0.50 | 3,500,000 |
| 8,000,000 | 0.20 | 1,600,000 |
| Expected value | 1.00 | $6,900,000 |

The probabilities must, of course, add up to 1, or 100 percent. The vice president would use the $5,050,000 expected value in the budget but would recognize that sales could run from $6,000,000 to $8,000,000. The vice president would monitor actual results and be prepared to revise the budget if conditions warranted. (Although we introduce the expected value concept in connection with forecasting sales, it also applies to budgeting costs.)

Probability assignments are usually based on the manager's judgment and experience, sometimes refined by other statistical techniques. The probabilities are, therefore, said to be *subjective* in that different managers might assign different probabilities. As with any managerial tool, the quality of the final information or decision rests heavily on the quality of a manager's judgment.

## INTERIM PERIOD FORECASTS

The forecasting methods discussed apply to sales forecasts of three distinct types: (1) annual forecasts, (2) longer-term forecasts (three to five years), and (3) quarterly or monthly forecasts. Once a forecast for the year has been approved as a basis for planning, it is necessary to break it down into *interim periods*.

Often the data used to forecast annual sales (economic indicators, sales for other industries) are also available for quarters. In such cases, managers can base quarterly forecasts on the same indicator used for the annual forecast. Many companies have developed other reliable ways for breaking down annual forecasts. For example, experience might show that consistent percentages of yearly sales occur in particular quarters or months (15 percent of annual sales are concentrated in March, 40 percent in the first quarter, and so on).

Whatever the methods used to develop the sales forecast, and whatever the length of the forecast period, managers revise budgets when they obtain more information. (Remember the earlier example of revising the budget in the light of heavier-than-expected sales early in the year.) A budget is a plan, not a straitjacket; changing it in the face of changing conditions is sound practice.

The accompanying Insight describes some companies' experiences and their difficulties with sales forecasting, and steps taken to achieve goals in face of adverse circumstances.

 **SIGHT**

### Techniques of Sales Forecasting

**General Mills's** 1997 annual report pointed to its basis for expected growth. According to General Mills, per-capita consumption of cereal was about 11

SIGHT **(continued)**

pounds in the United States. However, those under 18 years of age ate about 13.5 pounds, and those over 45 about 14.3 pounds. The company pointed to demographic data indicating that these two age groups would grow faster than others. The company therefore was planning for increased growth in cereal sales. But pricing had become a problem in the cereal industry and, because of price decreases, the company increased its efforts to improve productivity across the supply chain, from purchasing through manufacturing to distribution.

An annual report of **Sara Lee** described how its unit, Sara Lee Hosiery, maker of various types of hosiery, saw that the market for women's sheer hosiery was declining because many organizations were moving toward casual dress and telecommuting. The company's response was to offer more tights and opaque products, including socks. The company was also able to change over its manufacturing operations from sheer to opaque.

American automobile manufacturers seriously misestimated sales in 1998. They offered special incentives early in the year to increase sales, but wound up running short of cars later in the year. Auto inventories dropped to below a 50-day supply. Automakers try to keep a 60–65 day supply of finished cars.

**Cisco Systems's** 1997 annual report warned investors that results for individual quarters were becoming increasingly unpredictable because sales patterns were becoming more volatile. Cisco has reduced its lead times in response to customer demands, but is still sometimes unable to fill orders. Compounding matters, Cisco cannot always get timely deliveries from its suppliers, though it has worked with them to reduce their lead times. Cisco budgets many of its expenses based on its sales budgets, but cannot always change these expenses if sales differ from budget because most expenses are relatively fixed in the short term. Finally, Cisco sees inventory management, especially reducing lead times, as critical in responding to changing sales patterns.

**Seagate Technology**, the world's largest manufacturer of disk drives, optimistically overforecasted demand for personal computers and therefore for their hard drives. The company produced far too many drives and had to sell them through regular channels at seriously reduced prices. Seagate was especially hurt because the company is highly integrated, making about 70 percent of the parts of its drives. The result was less flexibility (as an insight in Chapter 5 commented on contract manufacturers) in responding to changes in demand.

**Cypress Semiconductor's** managers predicted that both unit sales and selling prices of their principal product would decline during the year because of industry-wide factors. The company responded by aggressively reducing costs through continual product redesign and increased manufacturing efficiency. For example, the company designed a new facility that could reduce assembly costs of a memory chip from $0.20 to $0.14 per unit over a two-year period. A six-cent reduction does not sound like much, but Cypress sells over 50 million units of the chip per year.

*Sources: Annual reports.*
*Gregory L. White and Emily R. Sendler, "Strike or No, Auto Price Wars are Unlikely to End,"* The Wall Street Journal, *June 11, 1998, B1.*
*Randy Befumo,* The Motley Fool Evening News, *May 12, 1998.*

## EXPENSE BUDGETS

Each manager in an organization is responsible for specific tasks and their costs. So managers should have budget allowances, or **expense budgets**, stating the limits for costs they may incur in accomplishing their tasks.

There are two general ways to develop budget allowances for expenses. One way sets the budget at a single amount. An allowance set in this way is called a **static budget**, and this approach is used with most fixed costs. Budget allowances for committed costs can generally be set by referring to existing obligations (because costs to be incurred have largely been set by actions already taken). Managerial policies usually determine the budget allowances for discretionary fixed costs, and static budget allowances are often used for such costs.

The second approach sets a variable budget, or **flexible budget allowance**, based on some measure of activity. Budget allowances are set in this fashion for variable costs and mixed costs, and occasionally for discretionary fixed costs. The character of flexible budget allowances is best exemplified by the budgeting of variable and mixed costs, which we discuss in the next section. Later in the chapter we discuss some special problems relating to the budgeting of discretionary fixed costs.

## BUDGETING VARIABLE AND MIXED COSTS

Chapter 3 introduced the concept that the total amount of a variable or mixed cost varies with the level(s) of the cost-driving activity (activities) identified through cost behavior studies. To develop budget allowances for such costs, managers rely on estimates of the *expected* levels of the relevant activities. For example, the budget allowance for sales commissions is derived from the sales budget. But a budget cannot fulfill its function of revealing deviations from plan unless budget allowances for variable and mixed costs are revised when the *actual* levels of the relevant activities are known. Using the same example, to know whether the cost of sales commissions is under control, managers need a revised budget allowance based on actual sales. Thus, there are two budgeted amounts for costs using a flexible budget allowance: a "before" and an "after."

To illustrate more clearly the need for and use of the flexible budget allowance, consider the budgets of production managers. Some costs are variable, some fixed, and some mixed, and the cost-driving activity will most likely be some measure of production activity. Suppose the manager and supervisor of the Mixing department in a factory agree on the following flexible budget allowances for the listed components of factory overhead in the department. Note that the cost-driving activity for the department's mixed costs is direct labor hours.

| Cost | Fixed Amount per Month | Variable Amount per Direct Labor Hour |
|------|------------------------|----------------------------------------|
| Indirect labor | $2,400 | $0.40 |
| Supplies | 200 | 0.40 |
| Maintenance | 1,600 | 0.20 |
| Depreciation | 1,200 | 0.00 |
| Miscellaneous | 700 | 0.10 |
| Total | $6,100 | $1.10 |

Suppose further that 1,000 direct labor hours are budgeted for the coming month. The budget allowance for each cost element for the month is computed using the following formula.

$$\begin{array}{c}\textit{Flexible} \\ \textit{budget} \\ \textit{allowance} \end{array} = \begin{array}{c}\textit{fixed cost} \\ \textit{per month} \end{array} + \left( \begin{array}{c}\textit{direct} \\ \textit{labor} \\ \textit{hours} \end{array} \times \begin{array}{c}\textit{variable} \\ \textit{cost per} \\ \textit{hour} \end{array} \right)$$

The formula for a flexible budget allowance is essentially the same as the cost prediction formula introduced in Chapter 3. The equivalence is logical, because a flexible budget allowance is simply a prediction of the cost to be incurred at a particular level of activity.

The *original* budget allowance for each cost element in the example is computed and reported in the first column of Exhibit 6-3. For example, the original budget amount for indirect labor is $2,800 [$2,400 + (1,000 × $0.40)]. As you can see, Exhibit 6-3 is actually the beginning of a performance report that will be completed later when actual labor hours are known.

Evaluating the manager's performance in controlling costs requires a *revised* budget allowance, the flexible budget allowance, that is based on the actual level of the cost-driving activity. For example, suppose direct laborers in the department actually work 1,300 hours. The flexible budget allowance for indirect labor would be revised to $2,920 [$2,400 + (1,300 hours × $0.40)], and so on. The revised budget allowances represent goals for the manager's performance.

In Exhibit 6-4, we complete the performance report by inserting the flexible budget allowances for the achieved level of production. We also insert some *assumed* actual costs, and compute a variance between the revised budget and the actual costs. When actual costs are less than the budget allowance, the variance is favorable; when the reverse is true, the variance is unfavorable. Hence, the variances for supplies, maintenance, and total costs are favorable. In Chapter 12 we introduce methods for analyzing variances.

---

**Exhibit 6-3    Production Performance Report**

| Month | *March* | | Department | *Mixing* |
|---|---|---|---|---|
| Manager | *E. Jones* | | | |

| | **Budget Allowances** | | | |
|---|---|---|---|---|
| | **Budgeted Hours** | **Actual Hours** | **Actual Costs Incurred** | **Variance** |
| Direct labor hours | 1,000 | | | |
| Indirect labor | $2,800 | | | |
| Supplies | 600 | | | |
| Maintenance | 1,800 | | | |
| Depreciation | 1,200 | | | |
| Miscellaneous | 800 | | | |
| Total | $7,200 | | | |

## Exhibit 6-4    Production Performance Report

Month _____ *March* _____        Department _____ *Mixing* _____

Manager _____ *E. Jones* _____

|  | Budget Allowances | | Actual Costs Incurred | Variance |
|---|---|---|---|---|
|  | Budgeted Hours | Actual Hours |  |  |
| Direct labor hours | 1,000 | 1,300 |  |  |
| Indirect labor | $2,800 | $2,920 | $2,870 | $ 50 |
| Supplies | 600 | 720 | 705 | 15 |
| Maintenance | 1,800 | 1,860 | 1,900 | (40) |
| Depreciation | 1,200 | 1,200 | 1,200 | — |
| Miscellaneous | 800 | 830 | 840 | (10) |
| Total | $7,200 | $7,530 | $7,515 | $ 15 |

CHAPTER 3

CHAPTER 3

The activities driving many costs are not related directly to sales, labor hours, or production volume. As we showed in Chapter 3, activities such as the number of vendors from whom the company buys materials and components, the number of employees in a department, or the number of different types of products manufactured often generate significant costs. The analytical methods introduced in Chapter 3 help managers identify activities that are useful for budgeting purposes. But the usefulness of the identified relationships for budgeting purposes depends on the availability of estimates or predictions of the level of the cost-driving activities.

## BUDGETING DISCRETIONARY COSTS

As stated earlier, discretionary cost allowances are generally set by managerial policies. Static allowances are appropriate for most such costs, but flexible allowances are appropriate when the company's *policy* is to spend an amount equal to some percentage of another factor. For example, some companies budget costs such as advertising, research and development, and employee training as percentages of sales.

The major problem with budgeting discretionary costs is determining what level of expenditures is desirable. What *is* optimal spending for employee development? for improving current products? for research on potential products? for in-house legal counsel? Managers must establish budget allowances for such costs without knowing what level of spending is best for their company.

Part of the problem of deciding how much to spend on discretionary items is that expenditures seldom produce immediately measurable output or benefits. Research and development activities might not show results for several years. In some cases, budgets for discretionary items are related to some variable input factor, such as the number of employees being given training or the number of research projects. But, note that the variable factor (e.g., number of employees to be trained or projects to be undertaken) is *also* usually a matter of managerial choice for which there is no right answer.

Managers can sometimes specify what benefits could come from a particular level of spending on a discretionary item. For example, the data processing manager might be able to say that a software package would speed customer billing by one or two days. (Getting bills out quicker means that payments come in sooner.) Managers might then compare the benefit of faster collections—a reduction of funds tied up in accounts receivable—with the cost of the software.

Because managers cannot determine optimal spending levels for discretionary items, they often set static budget allowances through negotiations between the affected managers and upper levels of management. Sometimes top managers establish budgets for these areas by specific policy decisions. **Kodak** mandates a minimum of 40 hours of training for every employee, every year. Such training is targeted at continuous improvement and personal renewal. Commitments to specific levels of R&D spending are also common, especially in high-tech companies. **Merck** describes itself as ". . . a global research-driven pharmaceutical company." Whatever the goal accepted by top management, managers of the affected areas have a right to know the reason behind a stated policy so that they authorize actions (and the related expenditures) consistent with the goal.

## BUDGETING AND HUMAN BEHAVIOR

Budgeting necessarily involves people, their behavior, their beliefs, and even their personalities. Behavioral problems arise when managers' interests conflict, when budgets are imposed from above, when stretch goals are used, and when budgets are viewed as checkup devices or ends in themselves. For both managers and management accountants, budgets and the budgeting process can also raise the most common of behavioral problems, ethical conflicts. Moreover, cultural differences can challenge the effectiveness of budgeting, especially at companies operating in more than one country.

## CONFLICTS

We can illustrate the problem of conflicts in budgeting by looking at likely disagreements among managers when a company establishes an inventory policy. An **inventory policy** states the level of inventory the company plans to have on hand at all times. The sales manager of a retailer wants high inventory levels because it's easier to make sales if the goods are available for the customer to see and purchase immediately. The sales manager at a manufacturing company also prefers to have inventory ready for immediate delivery. A financial manager prefers low inventories because of their costs (storage, insurance, taxes, interest, and so on). The production manager at a manufacturer wants low inventory for  all of the reasons described in Chapter 1 and throughout this book, and is also concerned with maintaining steady production—no interruptions for rush orders, no unplanned overtime—and other conditions that minimize production costs. Thus, three managers have different views on the desirable level of inventory. They will be evaluated by reference to how well they do their job, so each has an interest in the company's inventory policy.

In a conventional manufacturing environment, the conflict can be serious and the managerial accountant might be called in to help negotiate the final policy. A manufacturing company committed to the JIT philosophy already has established an inventory policy for the level of its materials and finished products:

little or none. The company-wide commitment to this common goal not only drops the financial manager's concerns from the conflict, but also encourages the other managers to work together to achieve the maximum sales at the minimum cost.

The conflicting interests of the sales and finance managers persist for retail enterprises. Many retailers have begun to emulate the inventory-reduction efforts of manufacturers by negotiating with their suppliers for quicker and more frequent deliveries. To facilitate speedy replenishment of stock, some retailers maintain computer links with suppliers, providing up-to-date sales data and even sales forecasts. **Wal-Mart** is widely recognized as the pioneer of just-in-time retailing, and many of its suppliers have made major operating changes to accommodate this important customer. For example, the maker of Lee and Wrangler jeans now has a computerized reordering system "so precise that if a Wal-Mart sells a pair of jeans on Tuesday, a replacement pair is back on the shelf by Thursday."[3] But however fast replacements arrive, Wal-Mart's managers must still decide how much inventory to have available on the shelf.

Inventory management is especially critical in industries undergoing price declines, as is the case with many high-tech industries. The accompanying Insight describes some problems and highlights how some companies respond.

 **IN SIGHT**

### Importance of Inventory

The personal computer industry is beset by rapid changes in price, performance, and availability of features. Holding significant inventory in such an environment is very risky. Disk drives, CD-ROM drives, and processors are among the highest-risk parts and components. Prices of these components often fall rapidly, leaving companies with high-cost parts and less profit than had they waited to buy. Processor prices can drop 15 percent in one week. Performance upgrades can render large numbers of parts obsolete. A manufacturer that paid $175 for a disk drive will earn less profit on a PC than one that waited to buy until the price fell to $150. These factors weigh against carrying inventory. But failing to be able to meet demand is also risky because purchasers typically will not wait for you to fill their orders, but will find alternative suppliers. In a recent year, **IBM** lost an estimated $100 million sales because it underbudgeted demand for a new line, but earlier in the year it had to reduce prices on a line for which it overbudgeted sales.

Some manufacturers cope with such uncertainty by carrying only partly assembled machines. They avoid installing high-risk parts until a customer actually places an order. Some do not. **Compaq Computer** experienced a below-budget quarter in 1998 that was attributed to "channel stuffing," meaning that the company pushed sales into earlier quarters by shipping product to distrib-

---

3 *"Just Get it to the Stores on Time,"* Business Week, *March 6, 1995, 66–7.*

utors faster than the distributors could sell it. Compaq was pursuing a strategy of "channel assembly," wherein it shipped PC components to its resellers and other distributors who then assembled the components into a branded computer. Compaq also gave its distributors price protection, crediting them for declines in prices of a PC between the time the distributor bought the parts and the time the distributor sold the assembled product. Price protection motivates distributors in exactly the wrong direction; they have no incentive to sell product quickly and no disincentive for holding onto it.

Compaq was crediting distributors $27 for price protection on the CPU and $12 for the memory and disk drive if the distributor held the inventory for four weeks. Because Compaq typically held inventory for another three weeks, it could have lost nearly $70 per PC just in inventory holding losses.

**Dell Computer** is a leading example of a JIT operation. The Austin, Texas, based computer maker puts made-to-order machines on delivery trucks 36 hours after the customer places the order. Dell's three plants in Austin, Texas; Penang, Malaysia; and Limerick, Ireland carry no inventories. Suppliers deliver parts within an hour of receiving Dell's orders. The company maintains no finished goods inventory. Inventory management is an important component of Dell Computer's strategy. CEO Michael Dell said the company's success has followed from its focus on fine-tuning its direct delivery model.

Dell managed to reduce inventories by the end of 1997 to a 7-day supply, versus 11 days in the third quarter and 13 days a year ago. By contrast, Compaq's best effort to follow Dell's lead left it with 24 days of inventory at the end of its fourth quarter. Tight control over inventories allows Dell to take advantage of falling component prices more quickly, thus offering lower sales prices while still claiming higher margins than its competitors.

**General Electric's** 1997 annual report stated that its future leaders in manufacturing would be " . . . people who consider inventory an embarrassment, . . . who understand how to drive asset turns and reduce inventory while at the same time increasing our readiness to serve the customer."

Catalog retailer **Lands' End** increased its sales in the first quarter of 1998, but its stock price fell because the company warned that future quarters could be adversely affected by inventory policy. The company increased its inventory by 68 percent in the quarter to improve customer service, which increased the availability of products and contributed to higher sales. However, Lands' End stated that the higher inventory levels might lead to increased liquidations at higher markdowns in the future.

**General Motors** suffered a strike at a stamping plant in July 1998. Within days most of the company's U.S. operations had been shut down because that plant served nearly all of GM's assembly plants, which held very little inventory. Becoming a JIT operation requires a reliable, safe source of supply, which GM has not enjoyed with its company-owned plants and the United Auto Workers union.

*Sources: Elisa Williams, Orange County Register, "Build-To-Order Demands Reshape Personal Computer Manufacture," Greenville News, June 1, 1995, 10D.*
*Dale Wettlaufer, "Valuing Hypergrowth," The Motley Fool Evening News, May 1, 1998.*
*Andrew Serwer, "Michael Dell Turns the PC World Inside Out," Fortune, September 8, 1997, 76–86.*

Budgeting discretionary costs also presents opportunities for conflicts if for no other reason than that no one knows the "right" answer. For example, the manager of human resources probably favors more employee training programs than do the managers of the employees receiving additional training. The concern of the affected managers is the impact of training time on evaluations of their own performance. If training interferes with timely completion of work assigned to their areas, their ability as managers may be questioned. And if the assigned work is completed despite the training time, higher-level managers might conclude that current staffing levels are higher than necessary.

## IMPOSED BUDGETS

Unfortunately, it's not uncommon for upper-level managers to set performance goals (budgets) without consulting the managers responsible for meeting those goals. In such cases, the budgets are said to be *imposed*, and serious behavioral problems can arise depending on the attitudes of the managers imposing the performance goals.

Some managers who impose budgets believe the performance goals they set should be very high (budgeted costs very low)—so high that almost no one could be expected to meet the budget. Such managers sometimes justify their position on the grounds that it "keeps people on their toes" and express the belief that people will be lax in their performance if they can easily meet a budget. Other managers who impose budgets say that budgets should be achievable given a good, but not exceptional, performance.

Sooner or later, imposing unachievable budgets produces problems. Managers will become discouraged and feel no commitment to meeting budgeted goals. Or perhaps managers will take actions that *seem* to help achieve goals (such as scrimping on preventive maintenance to achieve lower costs in the short run) but are actually harmful in the longer run (when machinery breaks down and production must be halted altogether).

A major problem with imposed budgets is that, if unrealistic, they are not useful for planning, when planning is one of a budget's primary purposes. Consider the implications of setting unrealistically high sales goals. The unrealistic sales budget will be the basis for production plans, including perhaps commitments for materials and components and the hiring and training of factory workers. Based on the sales budget, the company also will have planned cash receipts and estimated its needs for short-term financing. What happens if the sales goals are not realized? Unless the company operates under the JIT philosophy, inventory will be higher than expected, and additional storage space may have to be acquired at unfavorable rates. Whatever the company's operating philosophy, cash receipts will not materialize as planned, and it might have to acquire additional short-term financing on unfavorable terms. If managers adjust subsequent production schedules to bring them into line with lower sales (and to reduce inventory), employee relations may suffer as workers are laid off, and requested delays in delivery of materials may harm relations with suppliers. At their worst, unrealistic budgets can have serious financial effects on the company. At the very least, unrealistic budgets will probably be ignored by those whose actions they were intended to guide.

Even imposed budgets that "imposing" managers believe to reflect achievable, realistic performance goals can produce less-than-optimal performance. There are at least two reasons for adopting a budgeting approach that involves participation by the individuals expected to meet the performance goals in a budget. First, the "imposing" managers can never be as knowledgeable about the costs to perform specific tasks as are the persons actually performing them. Second, a considerable body of empirical evidence suggests that allowing people a say in their expected levels of performance is conducive to better performance than when those individuals are not consulted.

## STRETCH GOALS

A recent development in the area of setting performance goals is the use of stretch goals, or more accurately, stretch targets. **Stretch targets** are exceptionally ambitious goals not likely to be achieved without making fundamental changes in the way a job is done. The following are examples of stretch goals at some well-known companies.[4]

- Produce a new product with half the parts in half the time at half the price (a new VCR introduced by **Toshiba Corporation**).
- Cut the manufacturing cost of a plane 25 percent and its production time more than 50 percent (**Boeing Corporation**).
- Obtain 30 percent of sales revenue from products introduced within the past four years (**3M Company**).
- Raise annual improvement in productivity from 0.3 to 3 percent (**Mead Corporation**).

Not surprisingly, top managers of companies using stretch goals praise them for spurring innovation in ways not prompted by a commitment to the continuous improvement philosophy mentioned earlier in the chapter. (See the accompanying Insight on page 246 for examples.)

## BUDGETS AS "CHECKUP" DEVICES

Behavioral problems do not arise solely because of the procedure followed to set goals or develop budget allowances. Comparisons of budgeted and actual results and subsequent evaluation of performance also introduce difficulties. Ideally, managers use actual results to evaluate their own performance, to evaluate the performance of others, and to correct elements of operations that seem to be out of control. That is, the budget serves as a *feedback device*, letting managers know the results of their actions. Having seen that something is wrong, they can take steps to correct it.

Unfortunately, budgets often are used more for checking up on managers than for providing feedback. Where this is the case, managers are constantly trying to think of ways to explain unfavorable results. The time spent thinking of ways to defend the results could be used more profitably to plan and control operations. Some evaluation of performance is necessary, but the budget ought not to be perceived as a club to be held over the heads of managers. More attention is given to behavioral problems of performance evaluation in Chapters 10, 11, and 12.

---

4 Shawn Tully, "Why to Go for Stretch Targets," Fortune, *November 14, 1994, 145–6, 148, 150, 154, 158.*

**IN** *SIGHT*

### Meeting Stretch Goals

One expression of a stretch goal is Six-Sigma quality. The concept was developed at **Motorola**, and is now in use at, among other companies, **AlliedSignal**, **General Electric**, and **Kodak**. For Kodak, Six-Sigma quality means about 3.4 defects per million units. (Those of you who have already taken statistics recognize that six sigmas from the mean takes in virtually the entire distribution. A man seven feet, two inches tall is probably about six sigmas above the mean height of men.) Kodak seeks 50 percent improvement in quality and in cycle time each year, which it believes will not only improve customer satisfaction, but also reduce costs.

General Electric's 1997 annual report devotes nearly four pages to describing its commitment to Six-Sigma. The company believes that employees have been ahead of management in embracing Six-Sigma principles and implementing them throughout. Among the accomplishments cited were

- a ten-fold increase in the life of CT scanner X-ray tubes,
- a quadrupling of the return on investment of GE's industrial diamond business, and
- a 62 percent reduction in turnaround time at repair shops in the railway car leasing business.

The company now budgets operating margins (income before interest and taxes/sales) of 15 percent, once thought impossible. GE characterizes its future leaders as "A" players, and describes how such people will perform in several areas. In the controllership function, an "A" player will be " . . . a full-fledged participant in driving the business to win in the marketplace—a role far bigger than the dreary and wasteful budget 'drills' and bean-counting that once defined and limited the job."

**Hewlett-Packard** now spends nine months to develop a new product; the company once spent nearly six years to do so. H-P consults with customers to determine what features to include and to exclude. It stresses common parts, and buys software and physical components outside even if it could develop them inside, so long as the outside purchase saves time.

*Sources: Annual reports.*
*Robert D. Hof, "Hewlett-Packard," Business Week, February 13, 1995.*

## UNWISE ADHERENCE TO BUDGETS

Expense budgets set limits on levels of cost to be incurred, allowances managers are not supposed to exceed. If managers view their budget allowances as strict limits on spending, they may spend either too little or too much.

Exceeding a budget might benefit the company. Suppose a sales manager believes that an out-of-town trip to visit several important customers or potential customers will lead to greatly increased sales. The sales manager will be reluctant to authorize the trip if it will result in exceeding the travel budget. At the other extreme, a manager who has kept costs well under budget might be tempted to spend frivolously so that expenditures will reach the budgeted level. The manager may fear a cut in the budget for the following year if costs incurred during the current year are lower than budgeted. The manager might take an undesirable action—for example, authorize an unnecessary trip—so as not to be given a lower budget next year.

Managerial actions influenced by budget concerns in one area are likely to affect the actions taken by managers in other areas. A realistic example involves a manufacturing supervisor who was running a machine at 50 percent of its rated capacity. Asked why, the supervisor said that the machine needed new bearings and would produce only scrap if run faster. A request for maintenance had been ignored for several months because the maintenance supervisor had been controlling costs by not replacing employees who left.

## BUDGETING AND ETHICS

For both operating managers and management accountants, budgeting is a fertile field for behavioral problems involving ethical issues. Each of the items we've already discussed offers opportunity for questionable practices.

Managers in some areas might consider preparing—and ask management accountants to help them in doing so—budgets with a great deal of slack so that the managers will be able to meet them with a minimum of effort. Top-level managers who impose budgets on subordinates could ask management accountants to develop budgets so tight that there is little chance of achieving them. Knowing the problems such budgets are likely to create, the management accountants could view responding to the managers' requests to be an ethical problem.

Ethical issues also arise about the reporting of *actual* results for a budget period. When budgets are viewed as checkup devices and budget allowances as strict limits, a manager might be inclined to misclassify some expenditure or to ask the management accountant to delay recording some costs until the next budget period. Actual results also are influenced by revenue-recognition practices, and evidence exists of some managers accelerating recognition of revenues so as to meet sales budgets. The experiences of one company, **Bausch & Lomb** (presented in the accompanying Insight on pages 248–249), include premature revenue recognition and many of the other problems mentioned in this chapter.

Management accountants are particularly uncomfortable if their role appears to be to act as enforcers for upper-level management, because they recognize that necessary requests for explanations are likely to generate distrust (and perhaps misleading information). Some management accountants might believe that continued pursuit of explanations would reduce managers' inclination to seek assistance needed in the future with resultant harm to the firm as a whole.

## INTERNATIONAL ASPECTS OF BUDGETING

Companies with foreign operations face several problems that their domestic counterparts do not. One technical problem is translating budgets and actual results from the local currency to the currency of the company's home country. (Chapter 11 addresses this issue.) Both legal and cultural differences among countries affect the effectiveness of budgets and the budgeting process. The differences in laws among countries are too numerous and complex to present here. We will point out, however, that the legal environment of a country affects the flexibility of managers to achieve their goals. For example, the fringe benefits mandated by

## Pressure to Make Numbers

**Bausch & Lomb** (B&L) makes several products (including contact lenses and solution, Ray-Ban sunglasses, and binoculars) and had sales of $1.9 billion in 1993. Consistent with goals publicly announced by its top managers, B&L reported double-digit growth in sales and operating income (excluding nonrecurring events) for the 12 years prior to 1994. Maintaining that pace had become increasingly difficult as growth slowed in the markets for the company's products, but the company's budgets continued to reflect the same annual goals.

Several of the company's past and current managers reported tremendous pressure to meet quarterly and annual goals and say they had virtually no part in setting the goals. According to those managers, the chief executive officer's standard advice to managers having trouble meeting budget goals was "Make the numbers, but don't do anything stupid."

Managers adopted a variety of tactics to achieve sales goals. At one or another of B&L's segments, all of the following reportedly occurred.

- End-of-quarter promotions so regular that customers learned to delay their normal purchases to take advantage of the lower prices.
- Sales at exceptionally favorable credit terms. (Customers of one B&L unit pressing for exceptionally large orders were told they wouldn't have to pay until the ordered products were sold.)
- Threats to stop selling to some regular customers unless they placed unusually large orders.
- Sales of significant quantities of product to customers known to be directing the merchandise elsewhere for sale at discount prices.
- Shipping orders early or shipping unordered merchandise to regular customers.
- Repackaging expensive regular contact lenses as frequent-replacement lenses, which were then sold at lower prices by the unit and its customers.

The last tactic generated a class-action suit by users of the regular product who had paid full price for their lenses. Company officials contend that volume discounts were responsible for the lower prices.

Loading sales into the closing days of a budget period had predictable effects on other aspects of the company.

- Receivables remained uncollected for several months. (B&L began selling receivables as collections fell behind budgeted cash receipts.)
- Inventories rose because of higher-than-planned sales returns and production levels budgeted to meet announced sales goals.
- Distribution costs increased because handling the surge of shipments near the end of a budget period required hiring temporary employees and paying overtime to regular employees.

**IN SIGHT**                                                    *(continued)*

- Sales at regular prices suffered as some overstocked distributors sold to discount outlets in the United States and elsewhere.

In mid-1994, the company started an internal investigation of revenue-recognition practices at its Hong Kong unit and announced that profits would probably be below forecasts. After the Securities and Exchange Commission announced in late December 1994 that it would investigate another unit, B&L's top managers are reported to have ordered all units to follow conservative revenue-recognition practices. B&L's sales and operating earnings for 1994 were both lower than in 1993. The company's top managers admitted that some wrongdoing occurred at the two units investigated but denied that either corporate policies or the corporate culture encouraged the actions of managers at those units. Specialists in corporate ethics observe that senior managers don't necessarily perceive the message their comments and actions convey to lower-level managers.

*Source: Developed from "Blind Ambition: How the Pursuit of Results Got Out of Hand at Bausch & Lomb," Mark Maremont,* Business Week, *October 23, 1995, 78-82, 86, 90.*

many countries in western Europe and elsewhere reduce managers' willingness (or ability) to adjust the work force to sales expectations. Of equal or greater importance are the beliefs and behavior of the people of different countries.

Both profit and participation in setting goals are still relatively new ideas in the formerly communist countries of eastern Europe and the now independent countries of the former Soviet Union. Managers in such countries had long been accustomed to doing what a central authority said—produce so much of this, so many of that. To many of those managers, thinking in terms of profit is still a formidable task, and many find it difficult to make the transition to responding to the market. For good or ill, some of the individuals adapting well to the changed circumstances were engaged in enterprises illegal under prior regimes. Such individuals bring to their jobs the creativity and independent thinking needed to respond to the market, but their disdain for established guidelines might also carry over to the new environment.

Some cultures foster fatalistic attitudes, and their members see little reason to plan anything. After all, if certain things are going to happen no matter what you do, why bother? In such cultures it is difficult, even impossible, to motivate managers to budget at all. Increased contact with foreigners usually reduces some of the opposition to budgeting, but the change may come about slowly.

The prevailing economic system aside, people in some cultures are inclined to accept authority uncritically. Here, the problem is that anything upper-level managers say is fine with lower-level managers. Lower-level managers will not question their supervisors, nor will they take active roles in developing budgets. Instead, they will wait for clues as to what their managers are looking for and respond only then (and only in line with what they perceive is expected). Home-office managers might also receive the same deferential treatment. As a result, the company loses the benefit of the insights and understanding of its lower-level managers, and those insights might be critical to the company's success.

Whatever the constraints on an individual company, it will benefit from developing a comprehensive budget that reflects its managers' carefully considered plans. The next sections illustrate the development of the initial segments of such a budget for a retailer and present the special problem confronted by a manufacturer. The illustration will be completed in the next chapter.

## ILLUSTRATION OF A COMPREHENSIVE BUDGET FOR A MERCHANDISER

We illustrate the preparation of a comprehensive budget by working with Home Effects, a retailer whose managers have prepared the needed sales forecasts and developed a sales budget. (That is, we do not illustrate the sales forecasting process that produced the sales budget.) The illustration will be done in two parts. In this chapter we prepare the tentative budgeted income statement and a purchases budget. In Chapter 7 we prepare the cash budget, which requires some of the data in the budgets developed here. We shall then see how the operating and financial budgets are related, especially how the results in a tentative cash budget could prompt managers to look again at the operating budgets and possibly make changes in them.

The managers at Home Effects are developing a comprehensive budget for the first three months of 20X4. As the first step, they've developed the following sales budget, which extends through May. (Shortly, you will see why the managers must budget sales beyond the three-month period in order to complete the budget for that period.)

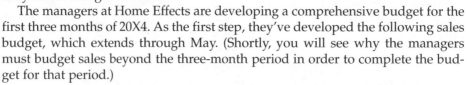

| Month | Sales Budget |
|---|---|
| January | $400 |
| February | $500 |
| March | $800 |
| April | $700 |
| May | $600 |

Sales are seasonal; they increase through March, then drop off. We shall see in Chapter 7 that such seasonality can create liquidity problems.

## BUDGETED INCOME STATEMENT

First, we develop a budgeted, or pro forma, income statement. To do so, we must know something about the behavior of the company's costs. We shall assume that the company's managers have done the necessary cost behavior studies and that they believe the following estimates of cost behavior are a good basis for planning.

- Cost of goods sold is 60 percent of sales.
- Total monthly fixed costs are $150, of which $15 is depreciation expense.

With this information we can develop the budgeted income statement for the three months, as shown in Exhibit 6-5.

The next step is to prepare a purchases budget.

**Exhibit 6-5   Home Effects, Budgeted Income Statement for the Three Months Ending March 31, 20X4**

|  | January | February | March | Three-month Total |
|---|---|---|---|---|
| Sales | $400 | $500 | $800 | $1,700 |
| Cost of goods sold | 240 | 300 | 480 | 1,020 |
| Gross profit and contribution margin | $160 | $200 | $320 | $ 680 |
| Fixed costs | 150 | 150 | 150 | 450 |
| Income | $ 10 | $ 50 | $170 | $ 230 |

## PURCHASES BUDGET

A **purchases budget** shows how much merchandise must be acquired during the budget period. How much merchandise a company needs to acquire during a period depends on how much it expects to sell, how much is on hand, and how much its managers want to have on hand to start the next period.

Retailers must have *some* merchandise on hand, though the amount considered desirable depends on such things as the products carried and normal delivery times. Hence, to develop Home Effects's purchases budget we need to know what level of inventory Home Effects's managers consider desirable. Retailers stock goods in anticipation of sales. (Witness the well-stocked shelves and extra in-aisle displays of department stores early in the Christmas shopping season.) Accordingly, companies usually state their inventory policy as some function of expected sales.

We've already suggested the complexity of a decision about the desired level of inventory, so we'll assume the interested managers at Home Effects have agreed that inventory should be maintained at a level of two months' sales. That is, Home Effects's inventory policy is that, at the end of each month, the company should have merchandise on hand to cover the sales expected in the following two months. (Such a policy does *not* mean that everything Home Effects sells has been on hand for two months. Home Effects might purchase fast-moving items more than once a month and slow-moving items only three or four times a year.) We chose the specific relationship (two months' sales) so that our illustration would emphasize the importance of expectations in determining purchases.

Moving from budgeting sales to budgeting purchases and inventory, you must also move from using selling prices to using costs. (Remember that merchandise is purchased at cost and carried in inventory at cost until it is sold.) To determine purchasing requirements for any period, we can use the general formula for cost of goods sold (from financial accounting):

$$\text{Cost of goods sold} = \text{beginning inventory} + \text{purchases} - \text{ending inventory}$$

Purchases is the unknown, so we restate the formula to obtain

$$\text{Purchases} = \text{cost of goods sold} + \text{ending inventory} - \text{beginning inventory}$$

A purchases budget follows the revised formula, as you can see in Exhibit 6-6, Home Effects's purchases budget for the three months. Amounts for cost of sales come from the pro forma income statements in Exhibit 6-5. The sum of the cost of sales for two consecutive months is the amount shown as "budgeted ending inventory" at the beginning of that two-month period. For example, the inventory required at the end of January ($780) is the sum of the cost of sales for February ($300) and March ($480). The circled items show the derivations of the ending inventory for January. (Now you see why Home Effects must forecast sales beyond the three-month period for which it is preparing its budget. Home Effects could budget purchases only through April if it didn't have sales forecasts beyond June, because the budgeted ending inventories for February and March depend on such forecasts. Whenever a company bases its inventory policy on expected sales, the company must forecast sales beyond the period being budgeted for.)

The *total* requirement for any one month is the amount needed to cover that month's sales plus what the company has determined must be on hand at the end of that month. The total requirement can be met from two sources: goods already on hand—beginning inventory—and purchases during the month. Of course, the beginning inventory for any month is the ending inventory in the previous month. Thus, required purchases are total requirements less beginning inventory. Work through Exhibit 6-6 to be sure you understand the calculations.

The rows in Exhibit 6-6 for cost of goods sold and purchases add across to the totals for the three-month period, but the inventory rows and total requirements row do not. The beginning inventory in the three-month column is the beginning inventory for the three-month period. The ending inventory is the required inventory at the end of the last month being budgeted. You could arrive at the numbers in the final column if you budgeted only for the three-month period as a whole, but the month-by-month budgets are important for other reasons. As you will see in Chapter 7, the monthly purchases budgets provide information for the monthly cash budgets, and the inventory amount at any month-end will appear on the budgeted balance sheet at that date.

### Exhibit 6-6   Home Effects, Purchases Budget for the Three Months Ending March 31, 20X4

|  | January | February | March | Three-month Total |
|---|---|---|---|---|
| Cost of goods sold | $ 240 | $ 300 | $ 480 | $1,020 |
| Budgeted ending inventory | 780 | 900 | 780 | 1,800 |
| Total requirements | $1,020 | $1,200 | $1,260 | $1,800 |
| Beginning inventory | 540 | 780 | 900 | 540 |
| Purchases | $ 480 | $ 420 | $ 360 | $1,260 |

Inventory at January 1 is assumed to be consistent with company policy, $540 = $240 + $300.
Budgeted ending inventories equal cost of sales for the following two months.
February ending inventory of $900 equals $480 plus $420, March and April cost of sales.

## PURCHASES BUDGET—MANUFACTURER

Retailers purchase merchandise to meet sales goals and adhere to inventory policy. Manufacturers *produce* merchandise in keeping with expected sales and inventory policy. Thus, a manufacturer must prepare a **production budget**. But to meet production requirements, a manufacturer must purchase sufficient materials and components to meet production goals. Hence, both types of companies must plan purchases. The basic idea of such planning is the same, but developing the purchases budget is somewhat more complex for the manufacturer because a manufacturer must develop a budget for production *in units* before developing a purchases budget in dollars. Units must be used first because variable production costs (such as materials) will vary with the number of units produced.

Suppose that Brandon Company, a conventional manufacturer, wishes to keep an inventory of its finished product equal to the budgeted sales for the following one and one-half months (a variation of the policy for Home Effects). Brandon's managers have gathered the following budgeted data for 20X8.

| | |
|---|---:|
| Units of product on hand at December 31, 20X7 | 200 units |
| Pounds of material on hand, December 31, 20X7 | 3,000 pounds |
| Budgeted sales for the next six months: | |
| January | 120 units |
| February | 180 units |
| March | 240 units |
| April | 330 units |
| May | 310 units |
| June | 280 units |
| Variable manufacturing costs, per unit produced: | |
| Materials (8 lbs. at $0.50) | $4.00 |
| Direct labor | 3.00 |
| Manufacturing overhead: | |
| Fringe benefits | 0.40 |
| Power | 0.30 |
| Supplies | 0.30 |
| Total | $8.00 |
| Fixed manufacturing costs, per month: | |
| Rent of machinery | $ 400 |
| Supervisory salaries | 600 |
| Insurance | 100 |
| Managerial salaries | 800 |
| Total | $1,900 |

Brandon's sales, like Home Effects's, are seasonal. Also like Home Effects, Brandon has identified its costs as variable or fixed. But for Brandon, the variable manufacturing costs will vary with the number of units produced, not with the number of units sold. Hence, the production budget must show the number of units that must be produced each period to meet sales and inventory requirements.

Exhibit 6-7 shows Brandon's completed production budget for January, February, March, and April. Note that even though a sales forecast is available for

**Exhibit 6-7    Brandon Company, Production Budget for the First Four Months in 20X8 (in units)**

|  | Jan. | Feb. | Mar. | Apr. | May | June |
|---|---|---|---|---|---|---|
| **Budgeted sales** | 120 | 180 | 240 | 330 | 310 | 280 |
| **Ending inventory required**[a] | 300 | 405 | 485 | 450 | ? | ? |
| **Total units required** | 420 | 585 | 725 | 780 | | |
| **Beginning inventory**[b] | 210 | 300 | 405 | 485 | 450 | ? |
| **Required production** | 210 | 285 | 320 | 295 | ? | ? |

a  *Sales for the following month + 50% of sales for the second following month. For example, January ending inventory of 300 units is February sales (180 units) + 50% of March sales (50% × 240 = 120).*
b  *Inventory at January 1 is assumed to be consistent with company policy.*

the first six months of 20X8, we can prepare a production budget for only the first four months. This is true because the company's inventory policy for finished units is based on the expected sales for the following two months, and we do not know the expected sales beyond June.

Ideal JIT operations allow manufacturers to buy materials and components only as needed. Both conventional manufacturers and JIT manufacturers operating under less than ideal conditions maintain some inventory of materials as a buffer. These manufacturers must have a policy regarding how much material should be on hand. Referring to Brandon's cost data we see that the $4 material cost per unit of product consists of eight pounds of material at $0.50 per pound. Let us assume that Brandon's managers desire to keep materials inventory equal to 150 percent of the coming month's budgeted production needs. (An inventory policy for materials is based on production, not on sales, because materials are needed when the product is made, not when it is sold.)

Exhibit 6-8 shows completed budgets for materials purchases in January, February, and March. Brandon's inventory policy for materials makes it impossible to budget purchases for April because such purchases depend on an unknown, the budgeted production for May. This example offers further evidence of the problem that lead times can create, and of the need for planning if the company is to operate efficiently.

A retailer needs a purchases budget to develop a cash budget, because the payments for purchased items are not likely to be made at exactly the time of purchase. A manufacturer needs *both* a production budget and a purchases budget in order to budget cash, because payments for purchases of materials and components are not likely to be required at the same time as the payments for other costs associated with production. The development of a cash budget, one of the most critical of the schedules included in a comprehensive budget, is discussed in detail in Chapter 7.

## SUMMARY

Comprehensive budgeting is vital to effective planning and control. The comprehensive budget is the major near-term planning document that a company develops and consists of a set of financial statements and other schedules showing the

**Exhibit 6-8   Brandon Company, Purchases Budget—Materials, January, February, and March 20X8**

|  | Jan. | Feb. | Mar. | Apr. |
|---|---|---|---|---|
| Budgeted production, in units[a] | 210 | 285 | 320 | 295 |
| Needed for current production, budgeted production × 8 | 1,680 | 2,280 | 2,560 | 2,360 |
| Ending inventory required[b] | 3,420 | 3,840 | 3,540 | ? |
| Total pounds of material needed | 5,100 | 6,120 | 6,100 | ? |
| Beginning inventory[c] | 2,520 | 3,420 | 3,840 | 3,540 |
| Required purchases, in pounds | 2,580 | 2,700 | 2,260 | ? |
| Required purchases at $0.50 per lb. | $1,290 | $1,350 | $1,130 | |

a  From Exhibit 6-7.
b  150% of budgeted production needs for the following month. For example, January ending inventory of 3,420 lbs. is 150% of February's production needs for 2,280 lbs.
c  Inventory at January 1 is assumed to reflect company policy.

expected results for a future period. Developing a comprehensive budget formalizes management objectives and helps coordinate the many activities performed within a single firm.

Sales forecasting is critical to budgeting because the sales budget drives all other budgets. Several approaches are used for forecasting sales. The approach adopted depends on the reliability of available data, the nature of the product, and the experience and sophistication of the managers. A company must have an inventory policy and information about the behavior of its costs in order to prepare the purchases, production, and expense budgets and a pro forma income statement (called operating budgets).

Flexible budget allowances are appropriate for variable and mixed costs, and occasionally for discretionary fixed costs, because such allowances are useful for identifying problems that require managerial action and for evaluating performance. The production budget for a manufacturer is the equivalent of the purchases budget for a retailer. A manufacturer also needs a purchases budget, but the production budget is the basis for developing the purchases budget of a manufacturer.

Budgeting entails numerous behavioral problems, which can be particularly severe if managers do not participate in the development of the budget for their areas or if budget goals are perceived as unachievable. Budgeting is less effective if the concepts of planning, profit, or participation are inconsistent in some way with the prevailing culture.

## KEY TERMS

capital budget  *(230)*
comprehensive budget  *(226)*
continuous budget  *(231)*
expected value  *(235)*
expense budget  *(238)*

financial budget  *(232)*
flexible budget allowance  *(238)*
inventory policy  *(241)*
operating budget  *(232)*
production budget  *(253)*

project budget    *(231)*
purchases budget    *(251)*
sales forecast    *(232)*

static budget    *(238)*
stretch target    *(245)*

## KEY FORMULAS

$$\text{Purchases}^a = \frac{\text{cost of}}{\text{goods sold}} + \frac{\text{ending}}{\text{inventory}} - \frac{\text{beginning}}{\text{inventory}}$$

$$\frac{\text{Budgeted}}{\text{production, in units}} = \frac{\text{units needed}}{\text{for current sales}} + \frac{\text{desired ending}}{\text{inventory}} - \frac{\text{beginning}}{\text{inventory}}$$

*a  For budgeting purchases in a manufacturer, "cost of current sales" becomes "cost of units of materials and components needed for current production."*

## REVIEW PROBLEM

Using the following data for Harlow Stores, prepare a budgeted income statement and a purchases budget in units and dollars for January 20X4.

| | | |
|---|---|---|
| Budgeted sales for January | 6,000 units at $20 | $120,000 |
| Budgeted sales for February | 8,000 units at $20 | $160,000 |
| Cost data: | | |
|    Purchase price of product | $6 per unit | |
|    Commission to salespeople | 10% of sales | |
|    Depreciation | $2,000 per month | |
|    Other operating expenses | $40,000 per month | |

Harlow's policy is to maintain inventory at 150% of the coming month's sales requirements. Inventory at December 31, 20X3, is $48,000 (8,000 units at $6).

### ANSWER TO REVIEW PROBLEM

| Harlow Stores, Budgeted Income Statement for January 20X4 | | |
|---|---|---|
| Sales | | $120,000 |
| Cost of sales (6,000 units at $6) | | 36,000 |
| Gross profit | | $ 84,000 |
| Other variable costs, commissions (10% × $120,000) | | 12,000 |
| Contribution margin | | $ 72,000 |
| Fixed costs: | | |
|    Depreciation | $ 2,000 | |
|    Other operating expenses | 40,000 | 42,000 |
| Income | | $ 30,000 |

Harlow Stores, Purchases Budget for January 20X4

|  | Units | Dollars |
|---|---|---|
| Cost of sales | 6,000 | $36,000 |
| Desired ending inventory (8,000 × 150%) | 12,000 | 72,000 |
| Total requirements | 18,000 | $108,000 |
| Beginning inventory | 8,000 | 48,000 |
| Purchases | 10,000 | $60,000 |

## ASSIGNMENT MATERIAL

### INTERNET ACTIVITY

Most annual reports give some description of how the companies expect to reach their objectives. Read several of these and relate them to the principles discussed in the chapter. For example, suppose a company follows a strategy of developing brand loyalty. How will it do so? High advertising and promotion? Increasing quality? What steps will the company take to reach its objectives?

### QUESTIONS FOR DISCUSSION

**6-1  "I'm too busy to budget"**   The following statement is representative of what many businesspeople say about budgeting. "Budgets are fine for companies that can plan ahead, but I can't. Things are too uncertain for me to make plans. And besides, I have to spend my time looking after day-to-day operations and trying to figure out what is wrong."

**6-2  Expense allowances**   Indicate whether a company is likely to use a static or a flexible budget allowance for each of the following costs. Explain your answers.

(a) Commissions to salespeople
(b) Electricity
(c) Taxes on land and buildings
(d) Taxes on personal property (physical assets other than land and buildings)
(e) Charitable contributions
(f) Office salaries

**6-3  Sales forecasting**   What do you think are the most important factors in forecasting sales for the following companies?

(a) A marketer of high-fashion clothing.
(b) A manufacturer of carpeting.
(c) A grocery chain.
(d) A television station (advertising revenues).

**6-4  Are budgets bad at GE?**   Jack Welch, the CEO of General Electric, has long been known for distrust of budgets. GE does not operate under the typical budgeting system. Welch has argued that participation by managers in the budgeting process is unlikely to produce good results and that stretch goals are the best motivators.

Welch says that budgets can be very deceptive, noting that, while GE's plastics business was up over 10% in 1994, it should have been up over 30%. The business was caught in a price squeeze and failed to respond in time. He reduced bonuses to the plastics managers. On the other hand, GE's aircraft engine business dropped about 10%, but those managers received significant bonuses. The aircraft business was more successful than its competitors and responded better to the severe drop in military purchases that hurt companies all over the world. Had GE operated under a budget system, the plastics business would have appeared very successful and the aircraft business very unsuccessful, when the opposite was the case.

### Required

Should budgeting as described in this chapter produce the results Welch deplores? What is wrong with budgeting that yields the described results?

**6-5   Sales forecasting—effects of external events**   You have just finished your sales forecast. Indicate what effect each of the following events is likely to have on that sales forecast. Explain your reasoning.

(a) Your company makes appliances. The federal government just announced a cutback in its program to assist low-income families in buying their own homes.

(b) Your company distributes jewelry. The government announces that personal income is increasing and unemployment decreasing.

(c) You make parts for the computer industry. Computer makers are announcing price decreases on their products.

(d) You make heating and air conditioning equipment. The prices of electricity, heating oil, and natural gas are expected to rise rapidly.

(e) You make insulation for houses and other buildings. The prices of electricity, heating oil, and natural gas are expected to rise rapidly.

(f) You publish college textbooks. Recent statistics show that the numbers of high school seniors and juniors have fallen off from previous years.

**6-6   Production budgets**   From its sales budget, a manufacturer prepares a production budget in units and then budgets for production costs.

### Required

Why must the company prepare a production budget in units before one for production costs?

**6-7   Effects of JIT on suppliers**   Mattel, the world's largest toy maker, recently announced that it would suffer a decline in sales and profits because many of its customers, retail stores, were cutting inventories deeply, partly as they adopted JIT inventory management techniques.

### Required

Does this news mean that Mattel's future is bleak beyond the current year?

**6-8   What's happening here?**   Jack Rolland, the assistant to the controller of Dayton Company, was looking at the following report for the marketing department. Dayton's fiscal year ends December 31.

| Cost Category | Annual Budget | Expenditures Through November | Expenditures Through December |
|---|---|---|---|
| Salaries | $360,000 | $330,000 | $360,000 |
| Travel | 45,000 | 32,000 | 45,000 |
| Other | 110,000 | 100,000 | 110,000 |

Rolland said to you: "I wonder why Cal, the marketing department manager, waited so long to spend his travel money. Maybe a lot of his business is concentrated in December?"

**Required**
Why else might Cal be spending so much on travel in December?

## EXERCISES

**6-9 Purchases budget (continued in 6-10 and Chapter 7)** Shoetown has budgeted May sales at $300,000 and June sales at $350,000. Cost of sales is 60% of sales. Shoetown's policy is to have inventory equal to budgeted sales needs for the following month. Shoetown began May with inventory of $105,000.

**Required**
Prepare a purchases budget for May.

**6-10 Budgeted income statement (continuation of 6-9, continued in Chapter 7)**
Shoetown's variable costs other than cost of sales are 10% of sales, and its monthly fixed costs are $45,000, including $5,000 depreciation.

**Required**
Prepare budgeted income statements for May and June.

**6-11 Budgeted income statement and purchases budget (continued in Chapter 7)**
Jordan Clothing has the following sales forecast for the first four months of 20X9.

| | |
|---|---|
| January | $ 70,000 |
| February | 90,000 |
| March | 110,000 |
| April | 120,000 |

Jordan's cost of sales is 60% of sales. Fixed costs are $15,000 per month. Jordan maintains inventory at 150% of the coming month's budgeted sales requirements and has $60,000 inventory at January 1.

**Required**
1. Prepare a budgeted income statement for the first three months of 20X9.
2. Prepare a purchases budget for the first three months of 20X9, in total and by month.

**6-12 Budgeted income statement and purchases budget (continued in Chapter 7)**
Thomas Stationery, a large retailer of cards and gifts, has developed the following information.

| Sales Forecast 20X4 | |
|---|---|
| January | $100,000 |
| February | 120,000 |
| March | 150,000 |
| April | 160,000 |

Cost of sales is 40% of sales. Other variable costs, principally commissions, are 30% of sales. Fixed costs are $25,000 per month. Thomas maintains inventory at twice the budgeted sales requirements for the following month. The beginning inventory is $80,000.

**Required**
1. Prepare budgeted income statements for the first three months of 20X4 and for the quarter as a whole.
2. Prepare a purchases budget, by month, for the first quarter.

**6-13  Expected values**  The marketing department has just prepared the following material regarding the expected monthly sales, in cases, of a new detergent your company will introduce shortly.

| Sales | Probability |
|-------|-------------|
| 40,000 | 0.10 |
| 60,000 | 0.50 |
| 70,000 | 0.30 |
| 90,000 | 0.10 |

**Required**
Determine the expected value of sales.

**6-14  Budget for service company**  Deborah Davis owns and operates Davis Design, an interior design company. Ms. Davis has been having problems with the business side of the operation and has asked for your help. One of the first steps you suggest is the preparation of a budget. Davis Designs sells furniture and accessories to its clients as well as charging design fees. Ms. Davis provides the following estimates for the next quarter.

|       | Sales of Merchandise | Design Fees |
|-------|----------------------|-------------|
| April | $12,000 | $8,000 |
| May   | 15,000 | 7,500 |
| June  | 18,000 | 9,500 |

Davis Designs buys furniture and accessories at 90% of the price it charges. All other costs are fixed at $3,500 per month.

**Required**
Prepare budgeted income statements for each of the three months.

**6-15  Purchases budget—units and dollars**  Nash, Inc. expects the following unit sales over the next few months.

| Month | Unit Sales |
|-------|-----------|
| February | 3,500 |
| March | 4,100 |
| April | 4,200 |
| May | 4,500 |
| June | 2,900 |

Nash's policy is to maintain inventory equal to 50% of budgeted sales needs for the following month. The beginning inventory is expected to be 1,500 units. Each unit costs $4.

**Required**

1. Prepare purchases budgets for as many months as you can in (a) units and (b) dollars.
2. Explain why you had to stop where you did.

**6-16   Budgeted income statement for a manufacturer (continued in 6-17, 6-18, and Chapter 7)**   Odell Company manufactures a small cabinet for cassette tapes. Its sales budget for the first three months of 20X0 is as follows.

| | |
|---|---|
| January | $2,000 (50 units) |
| February | $2,200 (55 units) |
| March | $1,800 (45 units) |

Variable manufacturing costs are $26 per unit, of which $12 is for materials. Odell's fixed manufacturing costs are $150 per month, including $40 of depreciation. Its only variable selling cost is a 15% sales commission. Fixed selling and administrative costs are $70 per month. Odell maintains no inventory of finished cabinets.

**Required**

Prepare a budgeted income statement for Odell for January.

**6-17   Production budget for a manufacturer (continuation of 6-16)**   Because Odell carries no inventory of finished cabinets, its production, in units, is the same as its sales. Odell's $12-per-unit materials cost is for four pounds of materials at a price of $3 per pound.

**Required**

Prepare Odell's production budget for January, in dollars, showing as much detail as the facts permit.

**6-18   Purchases budget for a manufacturer (continuation of 6-16 and 6-17)**   Odell's policy is to maintain an inventory of material at 20% of production in the upcoming month. At December 31, 20X9, Odell had 34 pounds of material that cost $102.

**Required**

Prepare a materials purchases budget for Odell for January, in units and dollars.

**6-19   Expense budgets and variances**   Pendleton Company has found the following formula useful in predicting the monthly cost of utilities for its factory:

$$Total\ utilities\ cost = \$19{,}850 + \$0.65X$$

where X is the number of machine hours worked.

Budgeted production for July was 45,000 units. Each unit requires 20 minutes of machine time, so Pendleton budgeted the use of 15,000 machine hours. Actual production in July was 48,000 units, using 16,000 machine hours. Actual utilities were $29,650.

**Required**

1. Determine the amount and direction of the July budget variance for utilities assuming that Pendleton uses a flexible budget for utilities.
2. Determine the amount that Pendleton budgeted for utilities cost before the month began.

3. If Pendleton had used a static budget for utilities, its variance would have been the difference between the $29,650 actual cost and your answer to requirement 2. Compute that variance. Which variance, the one you calculated in part 1, or the one you just calculated, based on the static budget, is more useful to Pendleton's managers? Explain your reasons.

**6-20   Budgeted income statements**   Home Builders operates a chain of building supply stores in a large metropolitan area. The sales manager has retained an economist to develop sales forecasting methods to enable the company to plan better. The economist reports that the following equation fit historical sales quite well and should predict future sales well if past patterns of behavior continue.

$$\textit{Monthly sales in dollars} = \$136,000 + \left(\$0.052 \times \begin{array}{c} \textit{dollar value of building} \\ \textit{permits issued in} \\ \textit{prior month} \end{array}\right)$$

The sales manager shows you the following data regarding building permits. The forecasts were developed by the local Builders' Association, whose previous forecasts have been reasonably accurate.

| | |
|---|---|
| March | $3,000,000   (actual) |
| April | 4,750,000   (forecast) |
| May | 6,900,000   (forecast) |
| June | 7,100,000   (forecast) |

It is now April 3, and the sales manager would like forecasts of sales and income for as many months as you can prepare. She tells you that cost of goods sold, which is all variable, is 45% of sales, other variable costs are 8% of sales, and fixed costs are $140,000 per month.

**Required**

Prepare budgeted income statements for as many months as you can, given the data available. Round to the nearest $100.

## PROBLEMS

**6-21   Flexible budget and variances**   Birdhomes, Inc. makes a popular house for purple martins. Materials for a unit of the birdhouse cost $6, direct labor is $2, and manufacturing overhead is $80,000 per month fixed, plus $8 per unit variable (with production). In one month, production was 25,000 units and actual costs were as follows: materials, $152,800; direct labor, $47,100; variable overhead, $201,000; and fixed overhead, $80,000.

**Required**

1. Prepare a flexible expense budget formula for total production cost.
2. What should costs have been to produce 25,000 units? (Consider each element of cost separately.)
3. What were the variances between actual and budgeted costs for each element of cost?

**6-22   Income statement and purchases budget**   The managers of Learning Centers, a retailer of books and other educational materials, have developed the following data about the company's main product and its operations.

| | |
|---|---|
| Selling price per unit | $40 |
| Purchase cost per unit | $14 |
| Sales commission | 20% of selling price |
| Fixed costs per month | $122,000 |

The managers plan to maintain inventory equal to twice the budgeted sales needs of the following month. Budgeted unit sales for March, April, and May are 8,000, 11,000, and 12,000, respectively.

**Required**
1. Prepare budgeted income statements for March and April.
2. Prepare a purchases budget for April, in units.
3. If sales for June are expected to be $520,000, how many units should the company plan to purchase in May?

**6-23   Flexible and static budgets—service department**   You recently became the supervisor of the Claims Processing department of GHJ Insurance. The financial vice-president, Carl Mintz, has expressed concern to you about the use of supplies in your department and has, after discussions with you, come up with the following monthly budget formula:

$$\text{Budgeted supplies expense} = \$21,400 + (\$0.74 \times \text{claims processed})$$

Budgeted output of processed claims for April was 100,000, giving a budget allowance of $95,400. Your department actually processed 112,500 claims and used supplies costing $101,340. Mintz attached a note to your monthly report saying that you needed to get better control of supplies because you exceeded the budget by $5,940.

**Required**
Using the guidelines in Appendix A, write a memorandum to Mr. Mintz about your use of supplies in April.

**6-24   Inventory policy—carrying costs**   Jack Grant, Frank Milano, and Jill Beary, Steele Company's managers for production, sales, and finance, respectively, are discussing production and inventory policies. Milano believes that if inventory were increased by 10,000 units, sales would be 1,000 units per month higher, and he wants Steele to stock the additional units. Grant is willing to revise production schedules to do so, but Beary is not in favor of the change. She argues that the cost of storing, insuring, and financing the additional inventory would be prohibitive. She says that it costs Steele about $1.50 per month per unit to cover these costs and that they are variable with the number of units on hand. Contribution margin per unit is $8.

**Required**
1. What is the value (per month) of the additional sales that would be generated by the increased inventory?
2. What additional monthly costs are associated with carrying the additional 10,000 units in inventory?

3. Using the guidelines in Appendix A, write a memorandum to the three managers giving and supporting your recommendation regarding production and inventory.

*6-25    Production budget*    Jalisto Pottery manufactures various products. It has the following sales budget, in sets, for its Sonora line of dishes: April, 25,000; May, 30,000; June, 35,000. Jalisto keeps its inventory at twice the coming month's budgeted sales. At April 1, Jalisto expects inventory to be 47,000 sets.

**Required**
Prepare production budgets for April and May.

*6-26    Purchases budget (continuation of 6-25)*    Making one set of Sonora dishes requires 15 pounds of materials that cost $1.50 per pound. Jalisto keeps its inventory of materials at 150% of the coming month's budgeted production. At the beginning of April, Jalisto expects to have 540,000 pounds of materials on hand.

**Required**
Prepare a materials purchases budget for April in (a) pounds and (b) dollars.

*6-27    JIT manufacturing (continuation of 6-25 and 6-26)*    Jalisto's managers are considering adopting just-in-time and flexible manufacturing principles. Some of the managers have studied other companies and believe Medina can implement some aspects of JIT now. They believe the company could cut finished goods inventory to a constant 1,000 sets of Sonora dishes and materials inventory to a two-day supply (1/15 of a month). They believe the company can eventually achieve even greater reductions, with zero inventories as the objective.

**Required**
1. Prepare production budgets for April and May, and a purchases budget for April. Assume that April's beginning inventories conform to the new policies.
2. Using the guidelines in Appendix A, write a memorandum to the factory manager about the advantages you see in reducing inventory as indicated here.

*6-28    Budgeting production and purchases*    The production manager of TriMeld Systems wishes to maintain an inventory of materials equal to budgeted production needs for the next two months. Each unit of product takes five pounds of materials. Budgeted inventory of finished goods is the following two months' budgeted sales. The sales budget for the first five months of the coming year, in units, is as follows.

|  | January | February | March | April | May |
|---|---|---|---|---|---|
| Sales | 22,000 | 24,000 | 12,000 | 26,000 | 28,000 |

Inventories expected at December 31 are 160,000 pounds of materials and 30,000 units of finished product.

**Required**
Prepare budgets of production and purchases of materials in units and pounds, respectively, for as many months as possible.

*6-29    JIT manufacturing (continuation of 6-28)*    TriMeld's managers have begun to use some principles of just-in-time manufacturing. They have been able to reduce finished goods inventory to a ten-day supply (one-third of the coming month's budgeted sales requirements) and materials inventory to a three-day supply (one-tenth of the coming month's budgeted production). Inventories at August 31 reflect these policies. The sales budget for the coming months, in units, is as follows.

|  | September | October | November | December |
|---|---|---|---|---|
| Sales | 22,000 | 18,000 | 12,000 | 15,000 |

### Required

Prepare budgets of production and purchases of materials for as many months as you can. (Round all items to the nearest hundred units or pounds.) Comment on the differences between these budgets and those in the preceding assignment and on the advantages of the JIT operation.

**6-30   Preparing flexible budgets**   As a new assistant to the controller of Gloire Company, you have been assigned the task of preparing a set of flexible budget allowances for overhead costs. You have the following data available.

| Cost | Variable Amount per Direct Labor Hour | Fixed Amount |
|---|---|---|
| Supplies | $0.40 | $24,000 |
| Repairs | 0.08 | 11,500 |
| Power | 1.20 | 15,600 |
| Depreciation | 0 | 14,700 |

Supervision, the only other overhead item, is a step-variable cost. Gloire budgets supervision as $8,000 at 10,000 direct labor hours, rising by $1,500 for each additional 1,000 direct labor hours.

### Required

Prepare a schedule showing the budgeted amount of each cost element, and of total budgeted overhead cost, at 10,000, 12,000, and 14,000 direct labor hours.

**6-31   Relationships**   Following is the pro forma income statement for Habib Company for April. The company has budgeted no change in inventories.

| | | |
|---|---|---|
| Sales (900 units at $60) | | $54,000 |
| Variable costs: | | |
|   Materials ($6 per unit) | $5,400 | |
|   Direct labor ($7 per unit) | 6,300 | |
|   Overhead—manufacturing ($4 per unit) | 3,600 | |
|   Selling expenses ($1 per unit) | 900 | 16,200 |
| Contribution margin | | $37,800 |
| Fixed costs: | | |
|   Manufacturing | $9,000 | |
|   Selling and administrative | 9,100 | 18,100 |
| Income | | $19,700 |

### Required

Fill in the blanks.

1. Budgeted production for April is _____ units.

2. Total variable manufacturing costs for April are $_____.
3. The sale of an additional 10 units would increase income by $_____.
4. Total costs and expenses if 910 units were sold would be $_____.
5. Break-even volume in units is _____.
6. If variable manufacturing costs increased by $2 per unit, income at 900 units sold would be $_____.
7. If fixed costs increased by $4,800, and the firm wanted income of $19,700, sales in units would have to be _____.
8. If ending inventory were to be 30 units higher than beginning inventory, manufacturing costs incurred during the period would be $_____.

**6-32   Multiple components—manufacturing firm**   Soreto Company expects the following sales by month, in units, for the first five months of the coming fiscal year.

|  | January | February | March | April | May |
|---|---|---|---|---|---|
| Budgeted sales | 1,800 | 1,900 | 2,500 | 1,900 | 2,100 |

The company's one product, the Tow, is a combination of two components: Tics and Tacs. Each Tow requires three Tics and two Tacs. Soreto follows the policy of having finished goods equal to 50% of budgeted sales for the following two months. Soreto often experiences problems with the quality of components received from suppliers, so inventories of components are maintained at 150% of budgeted production needs for the coming month. Inventories at January 31, 20X8, reflect these policies.

**Required**
1. Prepare a production budget for Tows for as many months as you can.
2. Prepare purchases budgets for Tics and Tacs for as many months as you can.

**6-33   Budgeted income statements—expected values**   Burke Company's executives are working on the comprehensive budget for 20X7. After lengthy discussions with regional sales managers, Burke's sales vice president does not wish to pin down a single estimate of sales. He would prefer to give three forecasts, along with his estimates of the probabilities he attaches to them.

| Sales Forecast | Probability |
|---|---|
| $  500,000 | 0.5 |
| 800,000 | 0.3 |
| 1,000,000 | 0.2 |

Variable costs are 60% of sales and total fixed costs are budgeted at $250,000.

**Required**
1. Prepare budgeted income statements based on each of the three forecasts.
2. Prepare a budgeted income statement based on the expected value of sales.

**6-34   Smoothing production**   Maynard Inc. makes swimsuits, with its sales falling heavily in the April-June period, as shown by the sales budget (in thousands of units).

|  | January | February | March | April | May | June |
|---|---|---|---|---|---|---|
| Sales | 100 | 100 | 110 | 160 | 200 | 250 |

Maynard's normal inventory policy has been to have a two-month supply of finished product. The production manager has criticized the policy because it requires wide swings in production, which add to costs. He estimates that per-unit variable manufacturing cost is $3 higher than normal for each unit produced in excess of 180,000 units per month. Maynard's treasurer is concerned that increasing production in the early months of the year would lead to high costs of carrying inventory. He estimates that it costs the firm $0.80 per unit per month in ending inventory, consisting of insurance, financing, and handling costs. He emphasizes that these costs are incremental.

All of the managers agree that Maynard should have 450,000 units on hand by the end of April. The production manager wants to spread the required production equally over the four months, while the treasurer believes that the firm should stick to its current policy unless it turns out to be costlier.

**Required**
1. Prepare a budget of production for January through April following Maynard's current policy. Inventory at January 1 is 200,000 units.
2. Prepare a production budget using the production manager's preference.
3. Determine which budget gives lower costs.

**6-35   *Relationships among sales and production budgets*** Following are partially completed sales and production budgets for Firmin Company. Firmin maintains an inventory equal to 150% of the budgeted sales for the coming month.

**Required**
Fill in the blanks.

### Sales Budget (in units)

| Jan. | Feb. | Mar. | Apr. | May | June | July |
|------|------|------|------|-----|------|------|
| 3,000 | 3,400 | _____ | _____ | _____ | _____ | _____ |

### Production Budget (in units)

|  | Jan. | Feb. | Mar. | Apr. | May | June |
|--|------|------|------|------|-----|------|
| Ending inventory | _____ | 6,300 | _____ | _____ | 8,700 | _____ |
| Sales | 3,000 | _____ | _____ | _____ | _____ | 5,800 |
| Total requirements | _____ | _____ | _____ | 13,900 | _____ | _____ |
| Beginning inventory | _____ | 5,100 | _____ | 6,900 | _____ | _____ |
| Production | 3,600 | _____ | _____ | 7,000 | _____ | 5,200 |

**6-36   *Budgeting in a CPA firm*** LaKerra Watson is a certified public accountant practicing in a large city. She employs two staff accountants and two clerical workers, paying them a total of $10,800 per month. Her other expenses, all fixed, for such items as rent, utilities, subscriptions, stationery, and postage, are $5,300 per month.

Public accounting is, for most firms, highly seasonal, with about four months (January through April) that are extremely busy and eight months that have less activity.

The most relevant measure of volume in a CPA firm is charged hours—the hours worked on client business for which the clients are charged. Ms. Watson expects her two staff accountants to work an average of 120 charged hours each month during the eight slower months, and 200 hours each per month during the January–April busy season. Clerical personnel work about 600 charged hours each per year, and

Ms. Watson works about 1,400. For both the clerical personnel and Ms. Watson, approximately 40% of their charged hours fall in the four-month busy season.

Ms. Watson charges her clients $100 per hour for her time, $50 for the time of a staff accountant, and $15 for the time of clerical personnel.

**Required**

Prepare a budget of revenues and expenses for a year for Ms. Watson's firm. Separate the budgets for the periods January–April and May–December.

**6-37 Sales forecasting—scatter diagram and regression** Seneca Concrete Products has engaged you as a consultant to help in its sales forecasting. After a long discussion with Louis Ridley, president of the company, you develop the following data.

| Year | Housing Units Built (in thousands) | Sales of Seneca Company (in thousands) |
|------|------|------|
| 20X1 | 1,300 | $2,440 |
| 20X2 | 1,400 | 2,610 |
| 20X3 | 1,900 | 3,380 |
| 20X4 | 1,500 | 2,760 |
| 20X5 | 2,000 | 3,520 |
| 20X6 | 1,600 | 2,875 |

**Required**

1. Develop an equation to be used to forecast sales for Seneca. Use a scatter diagram and regression analysis.
2. Mr. Ridley has learned that the forecast for housing units to be built in 20X7 is 1.8 million. What is your forecast for Seneca's sales? Are you relatively confident about your forecast? Why or why not?

**6-38 Comprehensive budget (continued in Chapter 7)** The managers and managerial accountants of Arctic Products Company have been developing information for the comprehensive budget for the coming year. The managers have decided to use the following estimates and policies for planning.

| | |
|------|------|
| Sales forecast, in units: | |
| January | 20,000 |
| February | 24,000 |
| March | 30,000 |
| April | 25,000 |
| May | 22,000 |
| Selling price | $30 per unit |
| Materials cost | $8 per unit of product |
| Direct labor and variable overhead | $6 per unit of product |
| Variable selling costs | $2 per unit sold |
| Fixed manufacturing costs | $125,000 per month |
| Fixed selling, general, and administrative costs | $55,000 per month |

The managers plan to keep inventory of finished goods equal to budgeted sales for the following two months, and inventory of materials equal to twice budgeted production for the coming month. The planned December 31 inventories are finished goods, 35,000 units and materials, 66,000 units (one unit of material per unit of product).

**Required**

1. Prepare budgeted income statements for January, February, and the two-month period, using the contribution margin format.
2. Prepare production budgets for January, February, and March.
3. Prepare purchases budgets for materials for January and February.

**6-39  Indicators for sales forecasting**  The following economic indicators and other data might be useful in forecasting sales for certain kinds of firms: income per capita, population, car sales, and rate of unemployment.

**Required**

For each type of business listed below, state which, if any, of the economic indicators you think would be relevant in forecasting sales. Indicate briefly why you think each indicator is relevant or irrelevant.

(a) food company
(b) maker of outboard motors
(c) home construction firm
(d) tire maker
(e) textbook company
(f) jewelry maker
(g) maker of nonprescription drugs

**6-40  Budgeting for a hospital (AICPA adapted)**  Dr. Gale, the administrator of Taylor Memorial Hospital, has asked for your help in preparing the 20X7 budget that she must present at the next meeting of the hospital's board of trustees. The hospital obtains its revenues through two types of charges: charges for use of a hospital room and charges for use of the operating room. Use of the basic rooms depends on whether the patient undergoes surgery during the stay in the hospital. Estimated data as to the types of patients and the related room requirements for 20X7 are as follows:

| Type of Patient | Total Expected | Average Stay in Days | Percentages Selecting Kinds of Rooms | | |
|---|---|---|---|---|---|
| | | | Private | Semiprivate | Ward |
| Surgical | 2,400 | 10 | 15% | 75% | 10% |
| Medical only | 2,100 | 8 | 10% | 60% | 30% |

Basic room charges are $100, $80, and $40 for private, semiprivate, and ward, respectively.

Charges for using the operating room depend on the length of the operation and the number of persons involved in the operation. The charge is $0.40 per person-minute. (A person-minute is one person for one minute; if an operation requires three persons for 40 minutes, there would be a charge for 120 person-minutes at $0.40 per person-minute, or $48.) Based on past experience the following is a breakdown of the types of operations to be performed on surgical patients.

| Type of Operation | Number of Operations | Average Number of Minutes per Operation | Average Number of Persons Required |
|---|---|---|---|
| Minor | 1,200 | 30 | 4 |
| Major—abdominal | 400 | 90 | 6 |
| Major—other | 800 | 120 | 8 |
| | 2,400 | | |

***Required***

1. Prepare a schedule of budgeted revenues from room charges by type of patient and type of room.
2. Prepare a schedule of budgeted revenues from operating room charges by type of operation.

**6-41   *Flexible budget, multiple drivers***   The controller of Ames Industries has ana-lyzed the costs of the Linden Plant. She comes up with the following cost drivers. Data are quarterly.

| | Fixed Component | Variable Component | Cost Driver |
|---|---|---|---|
| Inspection | $72,500 | $120.00 | Shipments |
| Maintenance | 61,200 | 2.40 | Machine hours |
| Data processing | 9,700 | 0.25 | Transactions |
| Purchasing | 63,600 | 180.00 | Number of vendors |
| Other | 278,800 | 2.20 | Labor hours |

Some of these costs are step-variable, so the variable components do not apply to small changes in activity, but only to relatively large movements. You may assume for this assignment that all changes are large.

***Required***

Develop flexible budget allowances for each element of cost, and for total cost, for the following two cases.

| | Case A | Case B |
|---|---|---|
| Shipments | 110 | 75 |
| Machine hours | 15,000 | 22,000 |
| Transactions | 220,000 | 360,000 |
| Number of vendors | 120 | 40 |
| Labor hours | 7,000 | 11,000 |

**6-42   *Manufacturing cost budget***   Horton Company makes a variety of household products, usually in about the same mix. On the average, each unit requires $3 in materials and $2 in variable manufacturing overhead. Direct labor averages $4 per unit at production volumes up to 100,000 units per month. Making more than 100,000 units requires Horton to pay its workers an overtime premium, so that direct labor cost rises to $6 per unit for units over 100,000. The remainder of manufactur-ing overhead is step-variable, with the following pattern.

| Monthly Unit Production | Other Costs |
|---|---|
| Up to 100,000 | $230,000 |
| 100,001–120,000 | 245,000 |
| 120,001–140,000 | 275,000 |

The pattern of these costs reflects increased supervision, utilities, and other costs as-sociated with operating beyond the normal eight-hour day.

Budgeted unit production for the next four months is 440,000 units, scheduled as follows.

|  | March | April | May | June |
|---|---|---|---|---|
| Production | 90,000 | 115,000 | 130,000 | 105,000 |

### Required

1. Prepare budgets for manufacturing costs for each month, and in total.
2. What would total production costs be for the four-month period if the company could equalize production at 110,000 units per month?
3. If Horton needs to produce only 440,000 units for the entire four-month period, how should it produce by month to obtain the lowest possible total production cost?
4. What reasons might there be for Horton to stick to the original monthly production budget despite its higher costs?

**6-43  Budgeting and behavior**  Rydell Company sets sales budgets for its salespeople, who are evaluated by reference to whether they achieve budgeted sales. The budget is expressed in total dollars of sales and is $200,000 per person for the first quarter of 20X3. Rydell makes two products, for which price and cost data are as follows.

|  | A-1303 | D-165 |
|---|---|---|
| Selling price | $10 | $15 |
| Variable costs | 4 | 10 |
| Contribution margin | $ 6 | $ 5 |

A-1303 is a new product that Rydell's president, Sid Koleski, thinks should become a big seller. At a regular meeting with his sales manager, Koleski said that the sales staff probably would have to seek out customers for A-1303 and convince them of the high quality of the product. D-165 has been popular for some years, and Koleski believes it unlikely that customers who have been buying D-165 will buy A-1303.

The $200,000 budgeted sales per person is a fairly high goal, but is attainable. During the first quarter of 20X3, all salespeople met the $200,000 sales budget.

### Required

1. Which product should Rydell's salespeople stress?
2. Under the circumstances described, which product do you think sold most?
3. If your answers to requirements 1 and 2 conflict, what changes would you suggest for the company's budgeting process?

**6-44  Production and purchases budgets—units and dollars**  Drummond Company manufactures several products, including a frying pan with a wooden handle. Each frying pan requires a blank sheet of iron that Drummond buys from a single supplier at $2 per sheet and then molds into the appropriate shape. Handles are purchased in ready-to-use condition from another supplier at $0.40 each.

Sales forecasts for the frying pan for the next five months are as follows, in units.

|  | April | May | June | July | August |
|---|---|---|---|---|---|
| Budgeted sales | 2,500 | 3,100 | 2,800 | 3,500 | 2,400 |

Drummond is able to forecast its total sales for the year fairly well but has experienced less success in breaking down the forecast by month. Finished goods inventory is budgeted at twice the quantity needed for the coming month's sales.

Drummond's policy is to maintain the inventory of handles equal to the coming month's production needs. The current supplier of blank iron sheets provides a product of satisfactory quality but is not willing to deliver more frequently or in relatively small quantities. Drummond's purchasing manager has had difficulty finding an alternative supplier that can provide quick delivery of blank iron sheets of the needed quality, so Drummond budgets its inventory of the sheets equal to budgeted production for the coming two months.

Labor costs for shaping the iron and putting on a handle are $1.50 and variable manufacturing overhead costs are $0.80. Fixed manufacturing costs are $4,500 per month.

At the end of March, the company expects to have the following inventories.

| | |
|---|---|
| Finished pans | 5,300 |
| Blank iron sheets | 5,600 |
| Handles | 4,600 |

### Required

1. Prepare production budgets for April through July, by month, in units and in dollar costs.
2. Prepare purchases budgets in units and dollars for blank iron sheets and handles for April and May.

**6-45  *Conflicts in policy***  Timmons Fashions has the following sales budget, in units, for its best-selling line of women's wear.

| | | | | | |
|---|---|---|---|---|---|
| January | 65,000 | March | 60,000 | May | 100,000 |
| February | 90,000 | April | 60,000 | June | 80,000 |

Timmons manufactures the line in a single factory. Because of union agreements and employment policies, the only feasible amounts of monthly production are 72,000 and 90,000 for a four-day week and five-day week, respectively.

Timmons's policy is to keep inventory of at least 15,000 units at the end of each month to serve as a buffer in case of slow deliveries by suppliers or other problems that could lead to lost sales. Storage space is limited, such that having inventory greater than 40,000 units results in abnormally high costs. The inventory at January 1 is 20,000 units.

### Required

Develop a production budget for the six months. If you cannot keep inventory within the limits stated, be prepared to defend the reasoning you used in making your selection.

**6-46  *Budgeting administrative expenses***  The controller of Kaufman Company has asked you to prepare a flexible budget for costs in the purchasing department. The normal volume of work in the department is 800 purchase orders per week.

Data entry clerks in the department are paid $5 per hour and work a 35-hour week. The clerks can enter about 100 lines per hour and the average purchase order has 10 lines. When they are not entering orders, the clerks file and perform other work. Order clerks prepare the purchase orders for entry. They are paid $6 per hour for a 35-hour week and generally take 20 minutes to prepare an order. When not preparing orders, the order clerks work at other tasks, such as investigating potential vendors. The purchasing agent is paid $500 per week. Supplies, stationery, etc., average $0.40 per purchase order.

### Required

1. Under normal circumstances, how many clerks of each type are required and how much slack time does each type of clerk have available to perform other duties?
2. If salaries for the clerks and costs for supplies and stationery are to be budgeted as variable costs, what is the flexible budget formula for total purchasing costs for each week, and what variance would you expect for a normal week?
3. What is the per-week capacity of the purchasing department given the personnel requirement derived in requirement 1?
4. What is the flexible budget formula for total weekly purchasing costs if the personnel requirements in requirement 1 are treated as fixed costs?

**6-47   Sales forecasting, budgeted income, and budgeted production (continued in Chapter 7)**   Spark Company makes ignition systems for automobile engines. The company has developed the following equation that has been successful in predicting annual sales, in units:

$$Sales = 80,000 + (0.009 \times automobile\ sales)$$

According to two different sources in the automobile industry, this coming year's automobile sales are expected to be 8,000,000 cars.

   Each system sells for $80 and contains materials costing $5. Direct labor is $10 per unit and variable manufacturing overhead is $12. Spark's only other variable cost is a sales commission of 10% of dollar sales. Fixed manufacturing costs are $1,200,000 per year; fixed selling and administrative expenses are $1,800,000 per year. Both are incurred evenly over the year.

   Sales are seasonal; about 60% of sales are in the first six months of the fiscal year, which begins June 1. The sales forecast for the first six months, in percentages of annual sales, is as follows.

| | | | | | |
|---|---|---|---|---|---|
| June | 5% | August | 9% | October | 14% |
| July | 8 | September | 12 | November | 12 |

Spark has a policy of keeping inventory of finished product equal to budgeted sales for the next two months. Materials are bought and delivered daily, so no inventory is kept. The inventory of finished product at May 31 is expected to be 19,000 units.

### Required

1. Prepare a budgeted income statement for the coming year and for the first six months of the year.
2. Prepare a production budget by month for the first three months, in units.
3. Determine Spark's break-even point (in units) for a year. How might the company's managers interpret that information in light of their successful sales predictions using the given formula?

**6-48   Comprehensive budget (adapted from a problem prepared by Professor Maurice L. Hirsch, and continued in Chapter 7)**   Banana City is a wholesaler of bananas and nuts. Mr. Bertram A. Nana, the company's president, has asked for your assistance in preparing budgets for fiscal year 20X7, which begins on September 1, 20X6. He has gathered the following information for your use.

(a) Sales are expected to be $880,000 for the year, of which bananas are expected to be 50%, nuts 50%.
(b) Sales are somewhat seasonal. Banana sales are expected to be $77,000 in November, with the rest spread evenly over the remaining eleven months. Sales

of nuts are expected to be $40,000 per month except in October and November, when they are expected to be $25,000 per month, and in April and May, when they are expected to be $35,000 per month.

(c) Cost of sales, the only variable cost, is 40% for both products.

(d) Inventory of bananas is generally kept equal to a one-month supply. Inventory of nuts is usually held at a two-month supply.

(e) Income taxes are 40% of income before taxes.

(f) Annual fixed costs, all incurred evenly throughout the year, are expected to be as follows.

| Rent | $ 24,000 | Depreciation | $ 36,000 |
|---|---|---|---|
| Insurance | 12,000 | Interest | 6,000 |
| Wages and salaries | 120,000 | Other fixed costs | 156,000 |

(g) Inventories expected at August 31, 20X6, are bananas, $14,300 and nuts, $27,500.

(h) The company expects to sell some land that it purchased several years ago for $8,000. The sale is expected to occur in October at a price of $6,000.

### Required

1. Prepare a budgeted income statement for the fiscal year ending August 31, 20X7.
2. Prepare a budgeted income statement for each month of the first quarter of the fiscal year and for the quarter as a whole.
3. Prepare a purchases budget by product for each month of the first quarter of the fiscal year and for the quarter as a whole.

## CASES

**6-49  *Constraints on scheduling production***  Robertson Company experiences some seasonality in its sales. Following are its sales forecasts (in units) for the first eight months of 20X5.

| January | 3,000 | March | 4,200 | May | 5,400 | July | 4,800 |
|---|---|---|---|---|---|---|---|
| February | 3,800 | April | 5,000 | June | 5,900 | August | 4,200 |

The inventory of finished units at January 1 is expected to be 6,800 units and Robertson's policy is to keep inventory equal to a two-month supply.

Robertson's current work force of 100 people is organized into 20 five-member teams. Each team takes responsibility for the product throughout the production process, so that workers can be hired only in groups of five. The 20 teams can produce 4,000 units per month, but overtime can be used to increase output by 10%.

Unlike some companies that face seasonality in sales, Robertson is not constrained by union contracts requiring some guaranteed level of employment for its employees. Nevertheless, Robertson's top managers prefer not to hire and lay off workers when only moderate changes in production are contemplated. As explained to you by Martha Martinez, Robertson's president, this preference is based partly on a perceived responsibility to provide regular employment and partly on a concern about a potential decline in the available work force if skilled workers leave the community due to unstable employment conditions.

### Required

Using the guidelines in Appendix A, write a memorandum to Martinez about production and labor needs for the first six months of 20X5. Include in the memorandum a production budget (in units), a budget of worker requirements, any assumptions you made, and any reservations you have about the budgets you propose.

*6-50   Budgeting step-variable costs*   Corman Company manufactures several products using a great deal of machinery. Since it is critical to keep the machines running well, Corman pays a good deal of attention to maintenance. Corman's chief engineer has determined that routine maintenance requires a complete shutdown and cleaning every 200 hours a machine has been running. This job costs $250. Excluding the major cleanings, maintenance costs for ten machines have been as follows for the past eight months. Each machine runs about the same amount of time each month as every other machine.

| Month | Hours for Ten Machines | Maintenance Costs |
|---|---|---|
| 1 | 2,200 | $1,400 |
| 2 | 2,100 | 1,380 |
| 3 | 1,950 | 1,260 |
| 4 | 2,000 | 1,290 |
| 5 | 1,700 | 1,190 |
| 6 | 2,400 | 1,505 |
| 7 | 2,300 | 1,455 |
| 8 | 1,800 | 1,200 |

**Required**
1. Using the high-low method, prepare a flexible budget formula for maintenance costs, excluding the major cleaning at 200 hours.
2. Determine the budgeted cost levels for 1,600 hours and at 100-hour intervals up to 2,500 hours. Include maintenance cost using the formula you developed in requirement 1 and the major cleaning costs.
3. Discuss your reservations about the use of flexible budgets when such costs are present.

*6-51   Reporting budget variances*   Wilkinson Company uses monthly budgets. At the end of each month, the accounting department prepares reports of budgeted and actual results. The reports are circulated to the managers whose operations are being reported on and to their supervisors. Following are excerpts from the reports for the latest two months on the costs in one production department.

| | April | | | May | | |
|---|---|---|---|---|---|---|
| | Budget | Actual | Variance | Budget | Actual | Variance |
| Production in units | 8,000 | 7,000 | 1,000 | 10,000 | 10,500 | (500) |
| Costs: | | | | | | |
| Material | $16,000 | $14,600 | $1,400 | $20,000 | $20,800 | $ (800) |
| Direct labor | 24,000 | 21,600 | 2,400 | 30,000 | 31,300 | (1,300) |
| Indirect labor | 4,000 | 3,900 | 100 | 5,000 | 5,300 | (300) |
| Power | 7,000 | 6,700 | 300 | 8,000 | 8,400 | (400) |
| Maintenance | 5,200 | 4,700 | 500 | 6,000 | 6,200 | (200) |
| Supplies | 4,600 | 4,580 | 20 | 5,000 | 5,050 | (50) |
| Total costs | $60,800 | $56,080 | $4,720 | $74,000 | $77,050 | $(3,050) |

Heated discussions between Wilkinson's production manager, Orel Rhodes, and the heads of production departments are common, and Daniel Dabich, Wilkinson's manufacturing vice president, has often asked Rhodes to explain the heated exchanges. Dabich asks you, his new assistant, to study the budget reports and write a memo for his signature to Retha James, the controller, about the usefulness of the reports his managers receive.

### *Required*

Using the guidelines in Appendix A, comply with Dabich's request. (You will find it helpful to analyze the budgeted amounts of each cost and determine its fixed and variable components.)

## Chapter Seven

# FINANCIAL BUDGETING

## LEARNING OBJECTIVES

*After reading this chapter, you should be able to*

- *Describe the leads and lags that complicate the budgeting of cash receipts and disbursements.*
- *Prepare a cash budget.*
- *List several ways that managers might resolve cash deficiencies revealed by a cash budget.*
- *State the sources of the items appearing on a typical budgeted balance sheet and prepare a budgeted balance sheet.*
- *Describe the basic technique managers use to develop annual and long-term budgets.*
- *Explain why long-term planning focuses managers' attention on financing decisions.*
- *Describe similarities and differences between the budgeting processes in for-profit and not-for-profit entities.*

- *State how zero-based budgeting and program budgeting differ from other budgeting processes illustrated in Chapters 6 and 7.*

In its May 15, 1998 filing with the SEC, **Amazon.com** stated the following.

*The Company has rapidly and significantly expanded its operations and anticipates that further expansion will be required to address potential growth in its customer base, to expand its product and service offerings and its international operations, and to pursue other market opportunities. The expansion of the Company's operations and employee base has placed, and is expected to continue to place, a significant strain on the Company's management, operational and financial resources. . . . The Company will be required to improve existing and implement new transaction-processing, operational and financial systems, procedures and controls, as well as to expand, train and manage its growing employee base. . . . If the Company is unable to manage growth effectively, such inability could have a material adverse effect on the Company's business, prospects, financial condition and results of operations.*

**Merck & Co.**, however, in its 1997 annual report, stated about its situation, "Working capital levels are more than adequate to meet the operating *requirements of the Company. " Merck went on to say that it had, over the past three years, repurchased $8.3 billion of its own common stock on the open market.*

*Why the differences? Why is Amazon.com warning stockholders that its financial (and other) resources might be strained, while Merck seems to have so much cash that it considers its best investment to be buying back its own shares? The answer is growth. Merck is growing at roughly 15 percent to 20 percent per year, which still puts it into the growth stock category. But Amazon.com was growing at over 100 percent annually. Growth strains resources and this chapter shows how.*

*Sources:   Annual Reports, SEC Filings*

Chapter 6 introduced comprehensive budgeting and some of the major concepts of budgeting, and illustrated the preparation of operating budgets. Financial budgets are at least as important and this chapter completes the illustration by developing the cash budget and pro forma balance sheet.

We also show how financial statement data are used in the preparation of annual budgets and long-term budgets. Finally, we look at some of the special issues associated with budgeting in not-for-profit entities.

## COMPLETION OF ILLUSTRATION

In Chapter 6 we prepared the budgeted income statement and purchases budget for Home Effects for the first three months of 20X4. We now proceed to the cash budget for the period and the **pro forma balance sheet** (budgeted balance sheet) at March 31, 20X4.

Exhibit 7-1 shows Home Effects's balance sheet at December 31, 20X3, the beginning of the three months the managers are planning for. We need the balance sheet at the beginning of the budget period because it shows (1) the resources (assets) already available for use during the budget period and (2) the existing liabilities that require payment during the budget period. For example, we needed (and used) the inventory figure at December 31 when preparing the purchases  budget in Chapter 6. Exhibit 7-1 also contains information about Home Effects's collections of accounts receivable and payments for expenses.

For ease of reference, we reproduce in Exhibit 7-2 the pro forma income state-  ment and the purchases budget from Chapter 6 (Exhibits 6-5 and 6-6).

## CASH BUDGET

A **cash budget** shows total cash receipts, total cash disbursements, and expected cash balances at various dates, and incorporates loans needed to cover temporary cash deficits. We begin preparing Home Effects's cash budget by looking at cash receipts.

### Cash Receipts
Home Effects receives cash when it collects from customers for sales, so preparing a cash receipts budget requires the sales budget. But we need more informa-

## Exhibit 7-1   Home Effects, Balance Sheet at December 31, 20X3

| Assets | | Equities | |
|---|---|---|---|
| Cash | $ 80 | Accounts payable | $ 195 |
| Accounts receivable | 310 | | |
| Inventory | 540 | | |
| Fixed assets, net | 1,580 | Stockholders' equity | 2,315 |
| Total | $2,510 | Total | $2,510 |

Other data:

Home Effects collects 70% of its sales in the month of sale, 30% in the following month.

Home Effects pays for purchases 60% in the month of purchase, 40% in the following month.

Home Effects pays all other expenses requiring cash disbursements as incurred.

Home Effects tries to keep at least $50 cash as a buffer against unexpected cash needs.

## Exhibit 7-2   Home Effects, Income Statements and Purchases Budget

### Budgeted Income Statements for the Three Months Ending March 31, 20X4

| | January | February | March | Three-month Total |
|---|---|---|---|---|
| Sales | $400 | $500 | $800 | $1,700 |
| Cost of goods sold | 240 | 300 | 480 | 1,020 |
| Gross profit and contribution margin | $160 | $200 | $320 | $ 680 |
| Fixed costs | 150 | 150 | 150 | 450 |
| Income | $ 10 | $ 50 | $170 | $ 230 |

### Purchases Budgets for Three Months Ending March 31, 20X4

| | January | February | March | Three-month Total |
|---|---|---|---|---|
| Cost of goods sold | $ 240 | $ 300 | $ 480 | $1,020 |
| Budgeted ending inventory | 780 | 900 | 780 | 780 |
| Total requirements | 1,020 | 1,200 | 1,260 | 1,800 |
| Beginning inventory | 540 | 780 | 900 | 540 |
| Purchases | $ 480 | $ 420 | $ 360 | $1,260 |

tion, because companies do not usually collect sales immediately. Exhibit 7-1 tells us that Home Effects normally collects 70 percent of its sales in the month of sale, the other 30 percent in the month after sale. It is worthwhile to note that this collection pattern indicates that Home Effects allows its customers nine days, on average, to pay their accounts. (Because Home Effects collects 70 percent of sales in the month of sale, it collects 21 days worth of current month sales. Twenty-one days is 70 percent of a 30-day month. Or, Home Effects has uncollected at month-end 30 percent of a month's sales, or nine days worth.) People developing budgets usually have information about credit terms, or days sales in accounts receivable, which they must translate into percentages of monthly sales collected.

We now can determine cash inflows for the three months. Exhibit 7-3 is a good general format for budgeting cash receipts. The first line, budgeted sales, comes from the pro forma income statements (Exhibit 7-2). The circled items show the pattern of collection of January sales; the total is given below the schedule. The uncollected portion of sales from March will appear as an *asset* (accounts receivable) on Home Effects's balance sheet as of March 31, 20X4. Notice that cash receipts are less than sales in February; in March this is a consequence of rising sales.

If, as is usually the case, a company pays cash to stock goods in advance of sales, but collects cash well after the point of sale, it can run out of cash while sales are rapidly increasing. That situation, which is commonly experienced by growth companies, will be more obvious when we examine cash disbursements.

### Cash Disbursements—Purchases

Home Effects's major cash disbursement is for purchases. To determine cash disbursements for purchases, we need more than the purchases budget reproduced in Exhibit 7-2; we must know the timing of disbursements for purchases. In the unlikely event that a company pays for goods on delivery, cash disbursements for purchases equal purchases in each month. Home Effects takes advantage of credit terms extended by its suppliers. These terms average 12 days, so that Home Effects pays for 60 percent of its purchases in the month of purchase and 40 percent in the month after purchase. (At month-end, Home Effects has not paid for its purchases of the previous 12 days, which is 40 percent of a 30-day month. So at month-end Home Effects has paid for 18 days worth of purchases, which is 60 percent of a 30-day month. If Home Effects had 30 days of credit, it would pay in the month after purchase, and so on.)

To derive cash disbursements for purchases, we need only apply the stated percentages, as in Exhibit 7-4. The January payment is for December purchases,

---

**Exhibit 7-3    Cash Receipts Budgets**

|  | January | February | March | Three-month Total |
|---|---|---|---|---|
| Sales for the month | $400[a] | $500 | $800 | $1,700 |
| From prior month, 30% | $310 | $120 | $150 | $580 |
| From current month, 70% | 280 | 350 | 560 | 1,190 |
| Total receipts | $590 | $470 | $710 | $1,770 |

*a  $400 = total January sales, collected in January and February ($120 + $280 = $400).*

**Exhibit 7-4  Cash Disbursements for Purchases**

|  | January | February | March | Three-month Total |
|---|---|---|---|---|
| From prior month, 40% | $195* | $192 | $168 | $ 555 |
| From current month, 60% | 288 | 252 | 216 | 756 |
| Total | $483 | $444 | $384 | $1,311 |

*\* from beginning balance sheet*

which are accounts payable at December 31, 20X3 (from Exhibit 7-1). The other amounts come from the purchases budget reproduced in Exhibit 7-2.

### Other Cash Disbursements

Exhibit 7-1 tells us that Home Effects pays all of its other expenses requiring cash as incurred. Those expenses are fixed costs requiring cash. Recall from Chapter 6 and Exhibit 7-2 that Home Effects' fixed costs of $150 per month include $15 depreciation. Depreciation does not require cash payments, so Home Effects's fixed costs requiring cash disbursement are $135 per month. Exhibit 7-5 shows all cash disbursements.

The data developed thus far are combined in the cash budget, shown in Exhibit 7-6. This budget shows a decline in cash in January, and a cash shortage in February. It also shows the borrowings that Home Effects must make to overcome the shortfall and keep a minimum balance of $50. (Exhibit 7-1 states that Home Effects wants to hold at least $50.) Exhibit 7-6 also shows that Home Effects can repay the loan (ignoring interest) comfortably at the end of March. Home Effects's seasonal pattern of sales creates this short-term cash squeeze. Unless Home Effects can borrow, or otherwise raise additional cash, it cannot achieve its objectives for the three months.

So what will Home Effects's managers do now? They might borrow cash to tide the company over February and early March. They might reconsider their inventory policy, delaying purchases and consequently delaying the need for cash payments. They could also consider giving customers less time to pay their accounts, thus accelerating cash collections. But both policy changes would probably reduce sales.

The cash budget benefits the company because its managers know in advance that they will need additional cash. So the managers are more likely to be able to

**Exhibit 7-5  Cash Disbursements Budgets**

|  | January | February | March | Three-month Total |
|---|---|---|---|---|
| For merchandise, Exhibit 7-4 | $483 | $444 | $384 | $1,311 |
| Fixed costs requiring cash | 135 | 135 | 135 | 405 |
|  | $618 | $579 | $519 | $1,716 |

| Exhibit 7-6   Cash Budget | | | | |
|---|---|---|---|---|
| | January | February | March | Three-month Total |
| Beginning balance, Exhibit 7-1 | $ 80ᵃ | $ 52 | $ 50 | $    80 |
| Cash receipts, Exhibit 7-3 | 590 | 470 | 710 | 1,770 |
| Total available | $670 | $ 522 | $ 760 | $1,850 |
| Cash disbursements, Exhibit 7-5 | 618 | 579 | 519 | 1,716 |
| Indicated balance | $ 52 | $ (57) | $ 241 | $   134 |
| Borrow | | $ 107 | | $   107 |
| (Repay) | | | $(107) | (107) |
| Ending balance | $ 52 | $  50 | $ 134 | $   134 |

*a  From December 31, 20X3 balance sheet (Exhibit 7-1).*

find financing to carry the company over. The managers will be able to explain to potential lenders both (1) why the company needs the money and (2) how it will repay the loan. A company that doesn't seek a loan until its cash balance is precariously low will have to pay a higher interest rate—or might not get a loan on any terms.

Lenders want information to help decide whether a company's managers have plausible plans for repayment. A lender will want to see cash budgets and perhaps other pro forma statements at least each quarter. Later, managers (and lenders) can compare the actual balance sheets at March 31 with the pro forma ones to see whether operations are proceeding as planned. For example, suppose the sales forecast proves accurate but accounts receivable at March 31 are higher than budgeted. If customers are paying later than anticipated, Home Effects could still have a cash shortage. Increasing receivables might also be a sign that the company is extending credit to less worthy customers to meet its sales goals. In that case, bad debts might result, and the need for financing might increase as well.

At the end of March, Home Effects has a different concern. Cash will be much higher than the minimum required amount and the managers will want to find profitable uses for the cash. If budgets for subsequent periods show steady increases in cash, the company might invest in new fixed assets, pay dividends to stockholders, or invest in short-term securities. Having excess cash is not as serious a problem as having a cash deficiency, but idle cash earns little or no return and hoarding cash is poor financial policy. The accompanying Insight contains statements about financing from some well-known companies' annual reports or SEC filings.

## PRO FORMA BALANCE SHEET

A pro forma balance sheet for March 31 appears in Exhibit 7-7 on page 284. As we've already explained, the amounts shown for cash in the balance sheet comes from the revised cash budgets; the balance for inventory comes from the pur-

SIGHT

## How Companies Finance Operations

**Amazon.com's** 1997 annual report stated the following.

The Company believes that current cash and cash equivalent balances and short-term investments will be sufficient to meet its anticipated cash needs for at least 12 months. However, any projections of future cash needs and cash flows are subject to substantial uncertainty. If current cash and cash equivalents, the net proceeds of the offering of the Senior Discount Notes, . . . and cash generated from operations are insufficient to satisfy the Company's liquidity requirements, the Company may seek to sell additional equity or debt securities or to obtain a line of credit. The sale of additional equity or convertible debt securities could result in additional dilution to the Company's stockholders. There can be no assurance that financing will be available in amounts or on terms acceptable to the Company, if at all.

**Wal-Mart** has formal and informal lines of credit with 35 banks amounting to $4.35 billion. Wal-Mart uses these lines ". . . to finance seasonal buildups in inventory and interim financing requirements . . . ."

**Kodak** has a $3.5 billion revolving credit facility to ensure that it does not run out of cash. It also has authorization for $2.2 billion in additional debt.

**Dell Computer** has achieved such rapid inventory turnover that it seldom needs financing despite its extraordinary growth rate. Dell could even have a negative cash conversion cycle, the time it takes from paying suppliers to collecting from customers.

*Sources: Annual reports.*

chases budgets. The balances for accounts receivable and accounts payable are *derived* from the cash receipts budget and the cash disbursements budgets, respectively. The balances for fixed assets and stockholders' equity are derived from the pro forma income statements and the balance sheet at December 31, 20X3 (Exhibit 7-1). Overall, then, developing and understanding a pro forma balance sheet requires a thorough understanding of the accrual basis of accounting. The pro forma balance sheet serves as a snapshot of where the company is headed. It also serves as the basis for planning for the period after the balance sheet date. Very often, looking at a pro forma balance sheet provides information not readily apparent from a set of budgets, such as budgeted levels of receivables and inventories in relation to total current assets.

## CONCLUDING COMMENTS

At this point it is useful to return to the overview presented early in Chapter 6 of the relationships among the components of a comprehensive budget. For your

## Exhibit 7-7    Home Effects, Pro Forma Balance Sheet

| Assets | As of March 31, 20X4 |
|---|---|
| Cash (from cash budget, Exhibit 7-6 | $  134 |
| Accounts receivable (March sales x 30%) | 240 |
| Inventory (from purchases budget, Exhibit 7-2) | 780 |
| Fixed assets (beginning balance less $45 depreciation for 3 months) | 1,535 |
| **Total assets** | **$2,689** |
| Equities | |
| Accounts payable (March purchases x 40%) | $  144 |
| Stockholders's equity* | 2,545 |
| **Total equities** | **$2,689** |

*\* Beginning balance of $2,315 (Exhibit 7-1) plus income for three months of $230.*

CHAPTER 6

convenience, we reproduce the exhibit from Chapter 6 in Exhibit 7-8. As you've now seen, comprehensive budgeting combines basic ideas from both financial and managerial accounting. From financial accounting come the basic financial statements and the accrual concept; from managerial accounting come the emphasis on the future and the need to understand cost behavior. The result is an in-

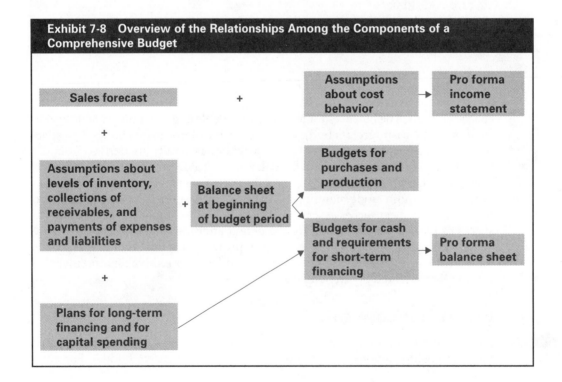

### Exhibit 7-8    Overview of the Relationships Among the Components of a Comprehensive Budget

tegrated set of schedules that reflects the expected outcomes of decisions made by managers for planning purposes. We now can point out some other advantages of budgeting and some important items that are missing from our illustration.

Our example is much simpler than is the case in practice. The most obvious item is that Home Effects will have to pay interest on the short-term loans it uses to finance operations. Home Effects will also have to pay income taxes. We ignored interest and income taxes because they do not change the fundamentals of cash budgeting, only the details. Most companies experience some bad debts, and their receipts budgets will reflect only the expected collections. A company could have other receipts, such as for interest or dividends on investments. Other cash-disbursement items are also likely, as when a company must make periodic interest payments, repayments of outstanding debt, and dividend payments. Payment schedules for expenses are likely to be far more complex than those in the example. (For example, fixed costs such as property taxes and insurance are usually paid quarterly or semiannually.)

Another commonly found item missing from our example is disbursements for new long-lived assets, which are often extremely large.

## MINIMUM CASH BALANCE POLICIES

For our illustration of budgeting cash for Home Effects we assumed a minimum cash balance of $50. Many companies adopt a policy of maintaining a **minimum cash balance** at all times, but most such policies are much more complicated. For instance, a policy might call for cash balances equal to budgeted cash disbursements for the next week or two weeks. Such a policy requires much more detailed budgeting than we show here.

Financial managers devote considerable attention to determining minimum levels of cash. As with most decisions, a trade-off exists between two conflicting objectives. On the one hand, a company certainly doesn't want to run out of cash. The lower the minimum required balance, the higher the probability of that happening, if for no other reason than that budgeting involves estimates. (Customers might pay more slowly than expected or cash outflows might be higher.) On the other hand, idle cash earns little or no return. The higher the minimum cash balance, the higher the opportunity cost of idle cash. The company could invest the cash elsewhere to earn additional income, save interest costs by retiring outstanding debt, or raise dividends. In deciding on a reasonable compromise, the financial manager must weigh carefully the conflicting objectives. Consider the balances of cash and short-term investments and, for comparison, sales in millions for some well-known companies shown below.

| Company | Cash and Marketable Securities | Annual Sales |
|---------|-------------------------------|--------------|
| **Yahoo Inc.** | $147 | $164 |
| **Merck** | $2,309 | $23,637 |
| **Coca-Cola** | $1,843 | $18,868 |

**Yahoo** needs an extremely high level of cash and equivalents because of its rocketing sales. The company needs plenty of cash because it is spending money to make money. The other two companies are growing, but not nearly as fast as Yahoo.

Financial managers practice some sophisticated techniques, as well as some generally accepted rules, in approaching cash policy. Financial management courses discuss such topics.

## CASH BUDGET FOR A MANUFACTURER

Home Effects, the company in the illustration, is a retailer. Chapter 6 showed that developing a budget for a manufacturer is more complex than for a nonmanufacturer, but that the principles are virtually the same. We showed that in Chapter 6 with the production budget for Brandon Company. If we know when costs of production are paid, we can easily compute cash requirements for production. Let us continue the example started on page 254 with Brandon showing a production budget (Exhibit 6-7) as follows.

| Month | Production |
|---|---|
| January | 210 |
| February | 285 |
| March | 320 |

Production costs are as follows: materials at $4 per unit, other variable costs at $4 per unit, and fixed costs of $1,900 per month.

Suppose Brandon is a JIT manufacturer and so acquires materials as it needs them and keeps no inventory of materials and components. Neither the JIT philosophy, nor having zero inventory, implies anything about the timing of payments for purchases. So, let us assume also that Brandon pays for materials in the month after purchase and pays other cash production costs in the month incurred. Assume further that December production was 300 units. The cash disbursements budget for manufacturing costs appears in Exhibit 7-9. The details of this schedule will become part of the company's overall cash disbursements budget, which will feed into Brandon's cash budget. The remainder of the budget package will be completed accordingly.

A quick glance back to the overview of the relationships among the components of a budget (Exhibit 7-8) confirms that there is no difference in principle be-

---

**Exhibit 7-9    Brandon Company, Cash Disbursements for Manufacturing Costs, January, February, and March 20X8**

|  | Jan. | Feb. | Mar. |
|---|---|---|---|
| Production* | 210 | 285 | 320 |
| Cash disbursements: |  |  |  |
| Materials ($4 × prior month's production) | $1,200 | $840 | $1,140 |
| Other variable costs ($4 × current production) | 840 | 1,140 | 1,280 |
| Fixed costs | 1,900 | 1,900 | 1,900 |
| Total | $3,940 | $3,880 | $4,320 |

\* *Exhibit 6-7 (page 254)*

tween the budgets for a retailer and for a manufacturer. In practice, the manufacturer's cash budget is more complicated. Individual production costs are likely to have different payment schedules, and the materials used for production may have to be purchased in advance of production needs. Normally, a separate materials-purchases budget, such as the one in Exhibit 6-8 (page 255), is the basis for determining cash disbursements for materials.

## ANNUAL AND LONG-TERM BUDGETS

To facilitate long-term planning, virtually all companies develop forecasts and budgeted financial statements one year in advance, and most companies do so for two, three, or even four years in the future. As we stated in Chapter 6, the usefulness of a company's forecasts for planning purposes is influenced not only by the abilities of its managers but also by characteristics of the company (including the industry or industries in which it operates).

Some industry characteristics critical to the company's ability to make useful forecasts are the rate of technological change, legal protections (e.g., patent laws, regulatory requirements), and product development times. For example, the average sales life of a model of personal computer is about six months, which affects the industry's ability to develop useful forecasts. Developers of software face similar problems because only a small proportion of new software packages is successful and competition demands upgrades of successful packages to maintain revenues. Patent laws enhance the reliability of forecasts by makers of prescription drugs, though product development times of up to 15 years complicate forecasts for products that might replace those whose protection is expiring.

Forecasting difficulties notwithstanding, companies do develop budgeted financial statements one or more years in advance. But for obvious reasons, such financial statements (1) are less detailed than those you've seen thus far and (2) do not involve detailed budgets of cash, production, and purchases. Rather, companies develop long-term budgets using techniques of financial statement analysis such as are presented in the introductory course in financial accounting. (Chapter 18 discusses such techniques in some detail.) Budgeted financial statements developed in this way are used to help managers plan the asset requirements for meeting long-term corporate goals and assess the company's need for long-term financing.

## ASSET REQUIREMENTS

We've shown how operating and financial budgets relate to each other in the short term. Using budgeted sales and expected relationships of certain assets to sales, we developed budgets of purchases and pro forma balance sheets showing budgeted amounts of cash, accounts receivable, and inventory. What was shown on the asset side of those balance sheets was essentially a statement of *asset requirements*—the amounts of various assets required to meet the company's goals of sales and income. We also said that a company might have to reconsider its sales and profit goals if it could not obtain the financing needed to carry its planned levels of assets.

Managers make similar analyses when developing **long-term budgets**. If the company forecasts increasing sales, it must also plan for the assets needed to support those planned levels of sales. Sales can seldom be increased significantly without providing additional production capacity and allowing receivables and inventory to increase. Moreover, the desired minimum cash balance probably will increase with higher sales volume.

In the long term, expected sales levels tend to dictate the necessary levels of assets. Hence, companies normally use *ratios* of various assets to sales to determine the required amounts of those assets. The ratios used will, of course, incorporate the objectives adopted by management, such as faster turnover of inventories. Recognize, however, that the analyses undertaken and numbers used for long-term budgeting are less precise than when budgeting for the shorter term. Moreover, there is more opportunity for circumstances to change. When developing long-term plans, managers try to allow for changes in general economic conditions, selling prices, purchase costs, and production methods. Such changes are extremely hard to predict over relatively long periods.

## FINANCING REQUIREMENTS

A company requires financing, in the form of liabilities or stockholders' equity, because it needs assets to generate sales. The need for assets creates *financing requirements*—the need for the items listed on the equity side of the balance sheet. (Items on the equity side of the balance sheet—liabilities and owners' equity—are often referred to as the sources of the assets.) As the need for assets increases because of increased sales, so does the need for sources to finance them. A few sources of financing are available almost automatically. For example, most companies buy merchandise on credit. A vendor who extends credit is, in effect, providing a short-term loan—a source of financing. Similarly, when a company earns income and does not distribute assets to its owners in an amount equal to net income, retained earnings increase. Increases in retained earnings are also sources of financing.

Few businesses can meet all of their financing needs through funds provided by operations and trade creditors. If a company uses short-term loans too liberally, and its current ratio (current assets/current liabilities) gets too low, trade creditors will become increasingly reluctant to extend credit. Thus, growing businesses need to seek long-term financing.

For long-term financing, companies issue stock or long-term debt. They can also lease assets, instead of buying them. We've already noted that a company not able to obtain the financing needed to support its short-term requirements might have to scale down its purchases of goods, and this in turn could reduce sales and profits. The same situation occurs in long-term budgeting—a company might not be able to obtain the long-term financing to support the asset levels necessary to reach the projected sales levels.

Managers know that obtaining short- and long-term financing requires planning. Potential providers of short-term loans consider the balance of current assets and current liabilities to be important. The focus of interest for potential long-term lenders is the balance between long-term debt and equity capital. Those lenders expect a borrower to maintain the ratio of long-term debt to equity (long-term liabilities/stockholders' equity) below some particular level, with that level depending on various characteristics of the borrower. Hence, a company must first study its long-term financing needs *as a whole*, and then pursue specific types and sources of long-term financing with those expectations in mind. The increasing globalization of business has multiplied the available sources of financing, both short term and long term, but has also complicated the decision about which sources to use. (See the accompanying Insight.) You will be introduced to the critical factors affecting international capital transactions in your course in financial management.

## ILLUSTRATIONS OF ANNUAL AND LONG-TERM BUDGETS

Companies often budget for longer periods by developing pro forma balance sheets for the future dates. We illustrate two levels of detail, one for an annual budget, and one for a three- to  five-year budget.

### ANNUAL BUDGETS

Northcote Industries, a major manufacturer of electrical equipment, had the following income statement for 20X3.

**SIGHT**

### Global Financing and Currency Risk

Choosing a financing source is more complicated when some of the sources are outside the boundaries of a company's home country, and even companies not doing business outside their home country often look at nondomestic sources of funds. A financial manager's choice is affected by additional factors such as expectations about exchange rates and inflation and willingness to take on risk.

For example, companies might seek financing in countries where interest rates are much higher than in the United States, but where high inflation will work to the borrower's advantage. Additionally, changes in currency exchange rates can work to the advantage or disadvantage of the borrower. Thus, we cannot say that it is always better to borrow in the United States at an 8 percent interest rate than in, say, Argentina at a 30 percent rate. Financial markets have developed instruments that balance the risks of engaging in transactions that involve more than one country's currency.

**IBM** "minimizes currency risk . . . by linking prices and contracts to U.S. dollars, by financing operations locally, and through foreign currency hedge contracts."

**Nike** also finances large parts of its operations overseas, and protects itself from currency fluctuations with forward exchange contracts. The company had about $1.7 billion in such contracts outstanding at year-end 1996.

**Merck** hedges against unfavorable moves in interest rates and in foreign currencies and performs sensitivity analyses to evaluate its positions. "If the U.S. dollar weakened by 10 percent against all currency exposures of the Company, income before taxes would decline by $10.9. The balance sheet hedging program has significantly reduced the volatility of U.S. dollar cash flows . . . ."

*Sources: Annual reports.*

Northcote Industries, Income Statement for 20X3, millions of dollars

| | |
|---|---|
| Sales | $500 |
| Variable costs at 60% | 300 |
| Contribution margin | $200 |
| Fixed costs | 140 |
| Income | $ 60 |

Northcote's balance sheet at the end of 20X3 follows. We include the percentages of current assets and current liabilities to sales of the same year because we will use them to develop the December 31, 20X4 pro forma balance sheet.

Northcote Industries, Balance Sheet at December 31, 20X3, millions of dollars

| Assets | | Percentage of Sales |
|---|---|---|
| Cash | $ 25 | 5.0 |
| Accounts receivable | 100 | 20.0 |
| Inventory | 50 | 10.0 |
| Total current assets | $175 | 35.0 |
| Plant and equipment, net | 400 | |
| Total assets | $575 | |

| Equities | | | Percentage of Sales |
|---|---|---|---|
| Current liabilities | | $ 50 | 10.0 |
| Long-term liabilities | | 80 | |
| Total liabilities | | 130 | |
| Common stock | $300 | | |
| Retained earnings | 145 | 445 | |
| Total equities | | $575 | |

Northcote's managers forecast a 20 percent increase in sales for 20X4. They expect current assets and current liabilities at the end of 20X4 to bear the same percentage relationships to sales that they did at the end of 20X3. They also expect variable costs to be the same percentage of sales as they were in 20X3 and total fixed costs to increase to $160 million. They budget net plant and equipment at $620 million at the end of 20X4. (The budgeted level of plant and equipment will consider acquisitions in Northcote's capital budget.) Northcote's managers do not expect to declare a dividend in 20X4.

We need the budgeted income statement for 20X4 to determine retained earnings, a significant source of financing, at the end of 20X4.

Northcote Industries, Budgeted Income Statement for 20X4, millions of dollars

| | |
|---|---|
| Sales ($500 × 120%) | $600 |
| Variable costs at 60% | 360 |
| Contribution margin | $240 |
| Fixed costs | 160 |
| Income | $ 80 |

We now determine asset requirements and equities available to support those asset requirements at the end of 20X4. Current assets are simply the percentages of sales from the 20X3 balance sheet multiplied by 20X4 budgeted sales. Of course, managers normally would adjust the percentages to reflect their expectations about changes in economic conditions and company practices. For example, a company moving into JIT operations would plan a lower level of inventory. Or perhaps the company will plan to have a larger amount of cash as part of a program to raise its cash reserves. Current liabilities are also at the same percentage of sales as they were in 20X3. Long-term liabilities and common stock are at their 20X3 levels. Retained earnings is the $145 million beginning balance plus the $80 million income budgeted for 20X4.

| Assets | | | Percentage of Sales |
|---|---:|---:|---:|
| Cash | | $ 30 | 5.0 |
| Accounts receivable | | 120 | 20.0 |
| Inventory | | 60 | 10.0 |
| Total current assets | | $210 | 35.0 |
| Plant and equipment, net | | 620 | |
| Total asset requirements | | $830 | |

| Equities Available | | | Percentage of Sales |
|---|---:|---:|---:|
| Current liabilities | | $ 60 | 10.0 |
| Long-term liabilities | | 80 | |
| Total liabilities | | $140 | |
| Common stock | $300 | | |
| Retained earnings | 225 | 525 | |
| Total available equities | | $665 | |

The $165 million difference between Northcote's asset requirements ($830 million) and its available equities ($665 million) is called its **financing gap**. What can Northcote do about the gap?

The managers have several options. With *no* plans to cover the gap, cash at the end of 20X4 will be a negative $135 million (the budgeted $30 million – the $165 million gap), but this cannot happen: the company would have to borrow money or reduce assets (thereby reducing sales and income) as cash drained away. The managers might plan to reduce current asset requirements. For example, they might change credit terms to require speedier payment of receivables, or they might try to reduce inventory levels. They might decide to pay current liabilities more slowly or postpone some capital expenditures. Or, most likely, the managers could decide to cover all or part of the financing gap by using additional financing, either debt or equity.

Each of these actions has potential problems. Reducing assets could hamper the company's ability to generate growth in sales and profits. Slower payment of liabilities could harm Northcote's credit rating. Obtaining additional financing could be costly if market conditions are unfavorable. Northcote's managers must evaluate all of the options and decide what risks they are willing to accept.

It is possible, of course, that an analysis of expectations and plans for asset requirements and available equities will reveal that available equities exceed asset requirements. In such cases, managers would plan how to use the excess cash. Some possibilities are paying (or increasing) dividends, reducing long-term debt, accelerating planned capital expenditures, making other investments, or buying back the company's stock.

## LONGER-TERM PLANNING

In the previous section we prepared a pro forma balance sheet to see whether Northcote could meet its objectives for the current year. Doing the same for a longer term usually involves preparing a series of schedules containing summary information about asset requirements and available financing. Once again, the long-term goals set by top managers will drive the asset requirements. Hence, as we stated earlier, planning for periods beyond the current year is mostly concerned with developing plans for expanding long-term debt and equity capital to meet financing requirements.

The choice between debt and equity can be critical. Most companies adopt policies about how much debt they will allow. A policy is often stated as a maximum percentage of long-term liabilities to stockholders' equity, or to total assets. You will study the advantages and disadvantages of particular kinds of financing in managerial finance and in Chapter 18. Here, we make only two points: (1) debt is risky because failing to meet periodic payments of principal and interest can cause bankruptcy; (2) equity financing is less risky but can lead to lower returns for stockholders.

CHAPTER
18

We illustrate long-term planning by using the following data, assumptions, and policies of QualCast, a multinational supplier of telecommunications equipment, in millions of dollars.

| Sales forecasts: | 20X4 | $800 |
|---|---|---|
| | 20X5 | $1,000 |
| | 20X6 | $1,300 |
| | 20X7 | $1,700 |
| | 20X8 | $2,100 |

Stockholders' equity at December 31, 20X3: $412

Current asset requirements are expected to be 30 percent of sales budgeted for the following year. Net fixed assets expected to be required to meet budgeted sales are 75 percent of sales budgeted for the following year. The company wants to maintain a current ratio of at least 3 to 1, so that current liabilities cannot exceed one-third of current assets.

QualCast does not want long-term liabilities to exceed 40 percent of total assets. QualCast wants to pay dividends equal to 40 percent of net income each year. The company expects net income to be 10 percent of sales.

These data are the bases of Exhibits 7-10 and 7-11, which determine year-by-year financing requirements. Exhibit 7-10 shows the analysis for 20X4 and 20X5 and how the numbers were derived. See if you can complete the rest of the table. (Answers appear in Exhibit 7-11.) Such a schedule gives the manager an idea of future financing needs.

QualCast's managers can now direct their efforts to devising a plan for obtaining the financing to satisfy line 9 in Exhibit 7-10 (Additional requirements). For several reasons, it is generally expensive and undesirable to seek equity financing frequently. Therefore, QualCast's managers might plan to obtain enough funds from issuing common stock in 20X4 to avoid taking on additional debt until 20X8. Funds received in excess of current needs might be invested or used to retire existing debt. As needs become more pressing, QualCast might issue additional debt up to the limit prescribed by the 40 percent debt ratio.

**Exhibit 7-10  Financing Requirements for QualCast (in thousands of dollars)**

|  |  | 20X4 | 20X5 | 20X6 |
|---|---|---|---|---|
|  | (1) Sales | $ 800 | $1,000 | $1,300 |
| (1) for next year × 30% | (2) Current assets required | $ 300 | $ 390 |  |
| (1) for next year × 75% | (3) Net fixed assets required | 750 | 975 |  |
|  | (4) Total assets required | $1,050 | $1,365 |  |
| (2)/3 | (5) Allowable current liabilities | $ 100 | $ 130 |  |
| (4) × 40% | (6) Allowable long-term debt | 420 | 546 |  |
| below | (7) Stockholders' equity | 460 | 520 |  |
|  | (8) Total available equities | $ 980 | $1,196 |  |
| (4) − (8) | (9) Additional requirements | $ 70 | $ 169 |  |

| Computation of stockholders' equity | 20X4 | 20X5 |
|---|---|---|
| Beginning stockholders' equity | $ 412 | $ 460 |
| Net income at 10% of sales | 80 | 100 |
| Dividends at 40% of net income | (32) | (40) |
| Ending stockholders' equity | $ 460 | $ 520 |

The purpose of the QualCast example was to illustrate techniques used for long-term planning. You should not assume that any of the policies and relationships are desirable, or even normal. (For example, the planned current asset

**Exhibit 7-11  Financing Requirements for QualCast (in thousands of dollars)**

|  |  | 20X6 | 20X7 | 20X8 |
|---|---|---|---|---|
|  | (1) Sales | $1,300 | $1,700 | $2,100 |
| (1) for next year × 30% | (2) Current assets required | $ 510 | $ 630 |  |
| (1) for next year × 75% | (3) Net fixed assets required | 1,275 | 1,575 |  |
|  | (4) Total assets required | $1,785 | $2,205 |  |
| (2)/3 | (5) Allowable current liabilities | $ 170 | $ 210 |  |
| (4) × 40% | (6) Allowable long-term debt | 714 | 882 |  |
| below | (7) Stockholders' equity | 598 | 700 |  |
|  | (8) Total available equities | $1,482 | $1,792 |  |
| (4) − (8) | (9) Additional requirements | $ 303 | $ 413 |  |

| Computation of stockholders' equity | 20X6 | 20X7 |
|---|---|---|
| Beginning stockholders' equity | $ 520 | $ 598 |
| Net income at 10% of sales | 130 | 170 |
| Dividends at 40% of net income | (52) | (68) |
| Ending stockholders' equity | $ 598 | $ 700 |

requirements and current ratio for QualCast do not reflect the widespread efforts of recent years to operate with low levels of inventory.)

## BUDGETING IN NOT-FOR-PROFIT ENTITIES

Not-for-profit (NFP) entities, especially governmental units, make extensive use of budgeting. But the budgeting process differs significantly from the type described earlier. First, such entities are likely to budget only for cash flows (receipts and expenditures), not for revenues and expenses. Second, the process is more likely to begin with expenditures rather than receipts. That is, in most cases, NFPs determine what receipts are required only after they've established the desired (budgeted) level of expenditures. We first suggested such an approach in Chapter 4, when we noted that some governmental units provide services they expect to operate on a break-even basis (e.g., municipal golf courses and swimming pools, and perhaps trash collection services, where users' fees are expected to cover costs).

Budgeting cash receipts for NFPs can be relatively simple or quite complex. Property taxes are the chief source of receipts for school districts and many towns and cities. Such taxes are levied on the basis of the assessed valuation of real property (land and buildings) in the area. Once the total assessed valuation is known, the entity can set the tax rate simply by dividing the desired tax revenues by the assessed valuation. If a school district needs $4,580,000 in tax receipts and the assessed valuation of property in the district is $54,000,000, the rate is 0.08482 ($4,580,000/$54,000,000), which is usually reported as $84.82 per $1,000 of assessed value. Because the desired receipts are determined on the basis of the budgeted expenditures, careful planning and monitoring of budgeted expenditures is especially important in NFPs. Some units of government face a legal requirement that limits the tax-rate increase in any year. Such a requirement can trigger the same reconsideration of plans forced on business enterprises whose asset requirements exceed available financing.

For government units that depend heavily on income and sales taxes, as do most states, determining required tax rates is more complex because estimating receipts requires estimates of total incomes subject to the income tax and of transactions subject to the sales tax. Forecasting methods such as those described in Chapter 6 may be used, and states have developed and used very sophisticated forecasting models.

To budget cash receipts, some NFPs use one or more of the methods already discussed to budget revenues. A not-for-profit private school might use forecasts of contributions and enrollments as a basis for setting tuition rates to cover budgeted costs. A not-for-profit hospital might forecast utilization of its various services to set charges that cover the costs of those services. Many NFPs also engage in activities similar to those of for-profit enterprises. For example, hospitals operate fitness centers for a profit, museums often operate on-site restaurants or gift shops, and cities operate gas, electric, and water companies. NFPs might use any of the methods introduced in Chapter 6 to forecast revenues from such enterprises. (Profit-making activities of an NFP are taxable if such activities are not related to the entity's principal purpose. Determining whether an activity is related to the entity's purpose is often very difficult for the NFP's managers because they know that paying income taxes will reduce the funds devoted to fulfilling the entity's purpose.)

Budget allowances for some cost categories at NFPs can be determined by activity analysis. For example, a university might budget faculty positions by applying some formula based on student enrollment and number of courses offered. Thus, an academic department might be given one position for each 300 credit hours of expected enrollment.

Budgets of government units such as towns, states, school districts, and the federal government usually require voter or legislative approval. Once adopted, such a budget must be strictly adhered to. (In some cases, overspending may even be illegal.) In addition, government units tend to practice **line-by-line approval** when authorizing budgets. That is, specific dollar amounts are authorized for specific categories of expenditures, such as salaries, equipment, supplies, travel, and postage. (The detail in such budgets can be overwhelming, with specified amounts for categories such as Grade II Data Entry Clerks and Grade IV Carpenters.) A budgeting process that includes a line-by-line approval procedure tends to have two major disadvantages in practice.

One problem is that a manager often has no discretion in using the total budgeted funds to achieve the desired objectives. This inflexibility can lead to actions inconsistent with the entity's objectives. For example, suppose that an accounting instructor in a public university is invited to a seminar on a contemporary accounting topic. The dean and faculty are in favor of the trip, but the travel budget is inadequate to cover the cost. Even if funds remain in the budget allowances for such items as supplies or secretarial help, the trip can't be authorized. The problem lies in focusing on individual budget items rather than on the objectives to be accomplished by the budget unit.

Another problem with line-by-line approval is that it encourages the setting of current budget allowances based on the prior year's (or an average of prior years') budget allowances or actual expenditures for each item. This approach is called **incremental budgeting**. Under this approach, each budget unit might be given a 5 percent increase (or decrease) in one or more of its line items. In a broader application of incremental budgeting, each budget unit might be given a 5 percent increase (or decrease) and allowed to spread the total increase (or decrease) over whatever line items are in the budget. Either variation implies that the increased (or decreased) benefits of changes in one segment of the total entity are equal to those of any other segment. Further, when the current budget allowance is based on prior expenditures, managers of budget units are inclined to spend the full allowance in order to avoid a reduction in the budget for the next period. With some regularity, the media have reported particularly interesting examples of such responses to incremental budgeting, as when some segment of government makes an end-of-year purchase of a five-year supply of toilet tissue or wastebaskets.

Neither line-item budgeting nor incremental budgeting is unique to NFPs. Many businesses also use these techniques, especially in areas of discretionary spending. What we referred to in Chapter 6 as "unwise adherence to budgets" includes some actions identified in this section. Indeed, all of the behavioral problems discussed in Chapter 6 apply as well to NFPs. The variety of nongovernmental NFPs rivals that of for-profit entities, with NFPs ranging from a local church or the PTA at a local school, through the local and national units of the YMCA and YWCA, to the American Association of Retired Persons and the national Muscular Dystrophy Association. Recent years have seen increasing attention focused on the activities of government and other NFPs. The next section discusses two alternative budgeting approaches, zero-based budgeting and program budgeting, which have been suggested as possible means of alleviating some of the problems.

## ZERO-BASED BUDGETING

Strictly interpreted, **zero-based budgeting** means that managers must justify every dollar they request in a budget proposal for a given year. Past budget allowances are considered irrelevant, and managers must start from scratch to convince higher-level managers that the current request is necessary. In a strict but practical application of the zero-based concept, each budget unit develops its budget request as a series of *decision packages*. The most basic of the unit's services constitutes the first package, and incremental packages represent higher levels of service and/or additional services. A critical aspect of the decision packages is that each is associated with a definable level or quantity of services.

For example, the basic package of the parks department for a city might cover a basic level of maintenance and repairs to keep existing parks open. A higher-level package might include on-site security personnel, its benefits associated with reducing repair costs from vandalism. At a much higher level, the department might propose a package for providing blooming plants throughout the year.

To evaluate and rank the packages from all units, higher-level managers perform cost-benefit analysis and exercise judgment about the entity's needs. The final budget might include the basic packages from all budget units, plus some incremental packages. This approach helps to circumvent one of the noted flaws of incremental budgeting—the assumption that increased (or decreased) expenditures in all units are equally beneficial (or harmful) to the entire organization. Moreover, forced managerial review of even the most basic functions of each budget unit might reveal budget units that have outlived their usefulness. That is, after reviewing all the decision packages and considering available resources, managers might conclude that the most basic service level of some budget units contributes less to achieving desired goals than do higher-than-basic service levels in other units.

Because a full review of each and every budget request every year is exceedingly time consuming, most organizations require such reviews only every few years. But the goals of these periodic reviews are the same as under the more strict application of the zero-based concept: to make sure of the need to spend money for a particular service. State-level *sunset laws*, which require that each program or regulatory agency created by the legislature receive a full, regular review and be dropped if it has served its purpose, are a variation of this second approach.

## PROGRAM BUDGETING

**Program budgeting** requires that a budget indicate not only how the requested funds are to be spent, but also why the funds are to be spent. A program budget emphasizes the desired results of the unit's efforts and normally provides the unit's manager with considerable discretion in shifting expenditures from one category to another as long as the shift will increase the likelihood of achieving the desired results. For instance, a traditional budget for a school district shows the objects of the expenditures, such as teachers' salaries, textbooks, and supplies.

A program budget for the district shows expenditures by such categories as reading, mathematics, remedial work, student activities, and support services. Similarly, a program budget for a police department might show amounts requested for crime prevention, juvenile work, and detection.

One beneficial feature of program budgeting, when implemented properly, is that managers making budget requests are expected to be able to state clearly what would happen if their requests were cut by, for example, 10 percent. Thus, the director of parks and recreation for a city should be in a position to say that such a cut would reduce the hours that a swimming pool would be open or require that grass be cut every ten days instead of once a week. In its result, this feature of program budgeting is similar to what can be accomplished with zero-based budgeting, in that different levels of service are associated with each level of requested funding.

The interest in and use of both program and zero-based budgeting probably owes much to the continually increasing public demand for accountability from NFPs. Taxpayers appear to have become dissatisfied with the performance of some government units, and donors to charitable causes have expressed concern about the proportion of contributed funds devoted to fund-raising and other costs not directly related to fulfilling the charitable objectives of the organization. Program budgets that specify goals allow people to see where their money is going and, eventually, to see whether it was spent effectively. (If a school district requests money "to raise the average reading levels of its pupils," board members can later see whether the levels rose.)

Both program and zero-based budgeting are applicable to business entities as well as NFPs. Corporate executives have, for example, adopted variations of these alternative budgeting approaches for all or some portions of their organizations because of an increasing concern with the productivity of research and development, general administration, and other such activities. In the typical business use, however, program budgets are developed in addition to, rather than as a substitute for, more traditional budgets.

## SUMMARY

Comprehensive budgeting brings together and coordinates the plans of many managers and many levels of management. A comprehensive budget is the most conspicuous process of communication within a firm, and facilitates the coordination of major functional areas—production, sales, finance, and administration.

Like operating budgets, financial budgets use forecasts and assumptions about the behavior of the various factors incorporated in them. Financial budgeting involves developing detailed budgets of cash receipts and cash disbursements and a pro forma balance sheet. Cash budgets use data from purchases and expense budgets and from the pro forma income statement. Hence, effective financial budgeting depends on good operational budgeting.

Completion of the tentative cash budget might reveal a need for additional financing and/or reconsideration of established policies. Knowing these needs in advance allows managers time to consider alternatives for meeting the needs.

Pro forma financial statements often are prepared one, two, or more years in advance. Such financial statements are less detailed than those prepared for the near term and result from planning relationships among financial statement items rather than from detailed budgets of cash and purchases. Though such budgets are less precise than those prepared for the short term, they can still assist managers in assessing long-term asset and financing requirements.

Not-for-profit entities, as well as for-profit businesses, budget. Although many of the same principles apply, there are some differences. The most significant difference is that not-for-profit entities normally budget receipts based on budgeted expenditures, while business entities budget expenditures based on budgeted receipts. Two additional budgeting approaches, program and zero-based budgeting, have been introduced for government units to help offset the tendency in not-for-profit budgeting to concentrate on detailed expenditures rather than on objectives. Businesses also use variations of these approaches.

## KEY TERMS

cash budget   *(278)*

financing gap   *(291)*

incremental budgeting   *(295)*

line-by-line approval   *(295)*

long-term budgets   *(287)*

minimum cash balance   *(285)*

pro forma balance sheet   *(278)*

program budgeting   *(296)*

zero-based budgeting   *(296)*

## REVIEW PROBLEM

This problem continues the review problem from Chapter 6. Using the following additional data, prepare a cash budget for January 20X4 and a pro forma balance sheet for January 31, 20X4. Prepare supporting budgets for cash receipts and cash disbursements.

### Harlow Stores, Balance Sheet at December 31, 20X3

| Assets | | Equities | |
|---|---|---|---|
| Cash | $ 20,000 | Accounts payable (for | |
| Accounts receivable | 30,000 | merchandise) | $ 12,000 |
| Inventory (8,000 units) | 48,000 | Common stock | 200,000 |
| Building and equipment, net | 200,000 | Retained earnings | 86,000 |
| Total | $298,000 | Total | $298,000 |

(a) Sales are collected 40% in month of sale, 60% in the following month.

(b) Purchases are paid 40% in month of purchase, 60% in the following month.

(c) All other expenses requiring cash are paid in the month incurred.

(d) The board of directors plans to declare a $3,000 dividend on January 10, payable on January 25.

(e) The following budgeted income statement and purchases budget from the solution in  6 are provided for convenience.

### Harlow Stores, Budgeted Income Statement for January 20X4

| | | |
|---|---|---|
| Sales | | $120,000 |
| Cost of sales (6,000 units at $6) | | 36,000 |
| Gross profit | | $ 84,000 |
| Other variable costs, commissions | | 12,000 |
| Contribution margin | | $ 72,000 |
| Fixed costs: | | |
| Depreciation | $ 2,000 | |
| Other operating expenses | 40,000 | 42,000 |
| Income | | $ 30,000 |

### Harlow Stores, Purchases Budget for January 20X4

| | Units | Dollars |
|---|---|---|
| Cost of sales | 6,000 | $ 36,000 |
| Desired ending inventory (8,000 × 150%) | 12,000 | 72,000 |
| Total requirements | 18,000 | $108,000 |
| Beginning inventory | 8,000 | 48,000 |
| Purchases | 10,000 | $ 60,000 |

## ANSWER TO REVIEW PROBLEM

### Harlow Stores, Cash Budget for January 20X4

| | |
|---|---|
| Beginning balance | $20,000 |
| Receipts (see below) | 78,000 |
| Cash available | $98,000 |
| Disbursements | 91,000 |
| Ending balance | $ 7,000 |

### Harlow Stores, Cash Receipts Budget for January 20X4

| | |
|---|---|
| Collection from December sales | $30,000 |
| Collection from January sales ($120,000 × 40%) | 48,000 |
| Total | $78,000 |

December sales will all be collected by the end of January. Because sales are collected in full by the end of the month following sale, all accounts receivable at the end of a month are expected to be collected in the coming month.

### Harlow Stores, Cash Disbursements Budget for January 20X4

| | |
|---|---|
| Merchandise [($60,000 × 40%) + $12,000] | $36,000 |
| Commissions | 12,000 |
| Fixed operating expenses | 40,000 |
| Dividend | 3,000 |
| Total | $91,000 |

### Harlow Stores, Pro Forma Balance Sheet as of January 31, 20X4

| Assets | | Equities | |
|---|---:|---|---:|
| Cash (cash budget) | $ 7,000 | Accounts payable[c] | $ 36,000 |
| Accounts receivable[a] | 72,000 | Common stock | 200,000 |
| Inventory (purchases budget) | 72,000 | Retained earnings[d] | 113,000 |
| Building and equipment[b] | 198,000 | | |
| Total | $349,000 | Total | $349,000 |

a  *60% of January sales of $120,000 (40% was collected in January).*
b  *$200,000 beginning balance less $2,000 depreciation expense.*
c  *60% of January purchases of $60,000 (40% was paid in January).*
d  *Beginning balance of $86,000 plus budgeted income of $30,000 minus dividend of $3,000.*

Notice that cash declined by $13,000 (from $20,000 to $7,000) even though income was $30,000. If Harlow's managers believe the budgeted cash balance of $7,000 is too low, they might begin to seek ways to increase that balance (e.g., a short-term bank loan).

## ASSIGNMENT MATERIAL

### INTERNET ACTIVITY

Find three to four annual reports and list the ways in which the companies expect to finance their operations. One such report should be that of **Dell Computer**, which has made cash management into a science.

### QUESTIONS FOR DISCUSSION

**7-1   Cash budgeting—effects of new information**   You are the controller of a large manufacturer and have recently completed the cash budget for the coming year. Knowledgeable managers have now given you new information. Considering each item independently, indicate (1) whether you expect it to influence your budgets for cash receipts, cash disbursements, or both, and (2) in which direction each budget would be affected. Explain your answers.

(a) The credit manager informs you that customers are not paying their bills as quickly as usual because of high interest rates.

(b) The sales manager informs you that sales should be higher than budgeted because of a strike at the factory of a major competitor.

(c) The purchasing manager informs you that suppliers who have been giving your company 45 days of credit are now requiring payment in 30 days.

(d) The vice presidents of production and marketing inform you that inventory policy is being changed from the carrying of the next two months' requirements to 80% of the next month's requirements because the company's JIT initiative appears to be working better than expected.

**7-2   Publication of budgets**   In financial accounting you learned that financial statements are distributed to persons outside the company. A comprehensive budgeting program involves the preparation of the same statements using budgeted data, but budgeted financial statements are not normally made available to people outside the organization. What do you see as the advantages and disadvantages of publishing these budgeted statements as part of a company's annual report?

**7-3   *Capital requirements***   In its 1997 annual report, **Eastman Chemical Company** listed as one of its principal strategies to reduce capital requirements, that is, long-term borrowings and common stock. The company planned "to accelerate cash receipts, reduce inventories, improve our credit payment policies with suppliers . . . ."

**Required**
Explain how the quoted actions will reduce capital requirements.

**7-4   *Philanthropy or business sense?***   Many public utilities offer "level-payment plans" for their customers. For example, households purchasing natural gas for heating purposes from **CMS Energy Corporation** in Michigan or purchasing electricity from **Texas Utilities** can elect to spread the payments for their purchases over the entire year. The normal plan is for a given month's payment to be 1/12 of the total cost of service provided in the 12 months ending with the current month. Discuss the reasons for a company to offer a level-payment plan.

**7-5   *Impact of policy changes on comprehensive budgets***   For many years, advertisements for **VanZandt Foods**, a grocery chain, have emphasized the high quality of its produce. The company's top managers have required that local store managers either trash day-old produce or sell it to the highest bidder in the local area. After studying a proposal submitted by the national council of community food banks, VanZandt's top managers decided that directing store managers to donate day-old produce to a local food bank would be in the company's best interests. What aspects of the company's comprehensive budget would be affected by this change in policy?

**7-6   *Relationships of profit and cash***   The financial vice presidents of two companies were talking about the performances of their respective companies in recent months.

*AceHigh Co's vice president:* We're making profits hand over fist because of rapid increases in monthly sales. We expected growth and have been keeping our inventories up to meet the increasing demand. But our cash balances have been a problem, and we've borrowed a lot of money lately.

*Tympanum's vice president:* Things haven't been going as well for us. We have entered our slow season, so sales have been falling. Of course, we knew this would happen and planned accordingly. We aren't making much profit, but do we have cash. Our balance has gone up every month.

**Required**
Explain why cash is going in the opposite direction from profit for each of these companies.

**7-7   *Speeding cash collections***   CableView has a franchise to provide cable TV services in a medium-sized city. The owner-president, Paul Fielding, tells you he can't budget cash receipts because he can't control when customers pay their bills. Give Mr. Fielding several ways the company can influence the timing of cash collections.

## EXERCISES

**7-8  Cash receipts budget (continuation of 6-9 and 6-10)**   Gentry Company collects 60% of its sales in the month of sale and 40% in the following month. Receivables at the end of April were $108,000.

**Required**
Prepare cash receipts budgets for May and June.

**7-9  Cash budget (continuation of 7-8)**   Gentry Company pays for its purchases in the month after purchase. Accounts payable for merchandise at the end of April were $180,000. Variable costs other than for cost of sales are paid as incurred, as are fixed costs requiring cash disbursement. The cash balance at the beginning of May is $30,000.

**Required**
1.  Prepare cash disbursements budgets for May and June.
2.  Prepare cash budgets for May and June.

**7-10  Cash receipts budget**   Jasica Company expects the following sales for the first five months of 20X7, in thousands of dollars.

|  | Jan. | Feb. | Mar. | Apr. | May |
|---|---|---|---|---|---|
| Budgeted sales | $1,100 | $1,400 | $1,700 | $1,300 | $900 |

Jasica typically collects 40% of its sales in the month of sale, 58% in the month after sale, with 2% bad debts never collected. Sales in December 20X6 were $1,200 thousand.

**Required**
Prepare a cash receipts budget for the five-month period ending May 31, 20X7, by month.

**7-11  Production and cash disbursements budgets**   ErgoChair has developed the following data.
(a) Sales forecast, January through April, 20X9 (in units): 2,300; 2,600; 3,100; and 3,400.
(b) Inventory policy: inventory is maintained at 10% of budgeted sales needs for the coming month.
(c) Cost data: materials, $4 per unit; direct labor, $8 per unit; and variable manufacturing overhead, $6 per unit. Monthly fixed manufacturing costs are $25,000, including $3,000 depreciation.
(d) ErgoChair uses some JIT principles. It purchases materials daily and pays for them as delivered; all other manufacturing costs requiring cash disbursements are also paid as incurred.
(e) The inventory of finished units at the beginning of January is 230.

**Required**
1.  Prepare a production budget for each of the first three months of 20X9.
2.  Prepare a schedule of budgeted cash disbursements for production costs for each of the first three months of 20X9.

**7-12 *Cash receipts and cash budget (continuation of 7-11)*** ErgoChair's product sells for $80 per unit. Sales are collected 25% in the month of sale, 75% in the month after sale. Receivables at December 31, 20X8, were $72,000.

The only variable selling cost is a 10% commission on sales, paid in the month after sale. Unpaid commissions were $9,800 at December 31, 20X8. Fixed selling and administrative costs requiring cash are $11,000 per month, paid as incurred. Depreciation on office and delivery equipment is $1,500 per month.

*Required*

1. Prepare a cash receipts budget for each of the first three months of 20X9.
2. Prepare a cash budget for each of the first three months of 20X9. Cash at January 1 is $35,000.

**7-13 *Cash budget (continuation of 6-11)*** Jordan Clothing owed its suppliers $31,000 at December 31 and Jordan's customers owed it $24,000. The company pays for its purchases 40% in the month of purchase and 60% in the following month. Jordan's customers pay for 60% of sales in the month of sale and 40% in the following month. All of its fixed costs require cash disbursements and are paid as incurred. Its cash balance at December 31, 20X8, was $20,000.

*Required*

1. Prepare a cash receipts budget for each of the first three months of 20X9 and for the quarter as a whole.
2. Prepare a cash disbursements budget for each of the first three months of 20X9 and for the quarter as a whole.
3. Prepare a cash budget for each of the first three months of 20X9 and for the quarter as a whole.

**7-14 *Pro forma balance sheet (continuation of 7-13)*** Jordan Clothing had the following balance sheet at December 31, 20X8.

| Assets | | Equities | |
|---|---|---|---|
| Cash | $ 20,000 | Accounts payable | $ 31,000 |
| Receivables | 24,000 | | |
| Inventory | 60,000 | Stockholders' equity | 73,000 |
| Total | $104,000 | Total | $104,000 |

Jordan rents all of its fixed assets.

*Required*

Prepare a pro forma balance sheet as of March 31, 20X9.

**7-15 *Cash budget (continuation of 6-12)*** Thomas Stationery pays for its purchases in the month after purchase. Its accounts payable at December 31, 20X3, were $30,000. It collects 20% of its sales in the month of sale and 80% in the following month. Receivables at December 31, 20X3, to be collected in January, were $64,000. Depreciation is $4,000 per month. All other costs require cash disbursements and are paid as incurred. The cash balance at December 31, 20X3, was $30,000.

*Required*

1. Prepare a cash receipts budget for each of the first three months of 20X4 and for the quarter as a whole.

2. Prepare a cash disbursements budget for each of the first three months of 20X4 and for the quarter as a whole.
3. Prepare a cash budget for each of the first three months of 20X4 and for the quarter as a whole.

**7-16  Pro forma balance sheet (continuation of 7-15)**    Thomas Stationery had the following balance sheet at December 31, 20X3.

| Assets | | Equities | |
|---|---|---|---|
| Cash | $ 30,000 | Accounts payable | $ 28,000 |
| Receivables | 64,000 | | |
| Inventory | 80,000 | | |
| Fixed assets, net | 150,000 | Stockholders' equity | 296,000 |
| Total | $324,000 | Total | $324,000 |

**Required**

Prepare a pro forma balance sheet as of March 31, 20X4.

**7-17  Cash budget and budgeted balance sheet for a manufacturer (continuation of 6-16, 6-17, and 6-18)**    Odell sells only on credit, collecting 70% in the month after sale and 30% the second month after sale. The company pays for its purchases of materials 60% in the month of purchase and 40% in the following month. It pays other cash manufacturing costs as incurred. Monthly fixed selling and administrative costs, all cash, are also paid as incurred, but sales commissions are paid in the month after the sale occurs. In December of 20X9 Odell declared a $220 dividend that it must pay in January of 20X0.

Following is Odell's balance sheet at December 31, 20X9.

Odell Company, Balance Sheet at December 31, 20X9

| Assets | | Liabilities and Owners' Equity | |
|---|---|---|---|
| Cash | $1,500 | Accounts payable, materials | $ 216 |
| Accounts receivable for: | | Accrued commissions payable | 360 |
| November sales | 660 | Dividend payable | 220 |
| December sales | 2,400 | | |
| Inventory, materials (34 lbs.) | 102 | Common stock | 5,000 |
| Building, net of depreciation | 1,680 | Retained earnings | 546 |
| Total | $6,342 | Total | $6,342 |

**Required**

1. Prepare a cash receipts budget for Odell for January 20X0.
2. Determine Odell's budgeted accounts receivable at January 31, 20X0.
3. Prepare a cash disbursements budget for Odell for January 20X0.
4. Determine Odell's budgeted accounts payable at January 31, 20X0, for materials purchases.
5. Prepare a cash budget for January 20X0.
6. Prepare Odell's budgeted balance sheet at January 31, 20X0.

**7-18  Cash budget—quarters**    Walton Company expects the following quarterly results in 20X4, in thousands of dollars.

| | 1 | 2 | 3 | 4 |
|---|---|---|---|---|
| Sales | $3,600 | $4,200 | $4,800 | $3,300 |
| Cash disbursements: | | | | |
|   Production costs | 2,900 | 3,400 | 3,300 | 2,400 |
|   Selling and administrative costs | 410 | 500 | 480 | 420 |
|   Acquisitions of fixed assets | 0 | 300 | 700 | 600 |
|   Dividends | 40 | 40 | 40 | 50 |

The beginning balance in accounts receivable is $1,700 thousand. Cash on hand at the beginning of the year is $200 thousand, which is also the desired minimum balance. Accounts receivable at the end of each quarter are two-thirds of sales for the quarter. Any borrowings are made in $10 thousand multiples and are repaid at the ends of quarters. Ignore interest.

### Required

1. Prepare a cash budget by quarters for the year.
2. What is the outstanding loan at the end of the year?

**7-19   *Pro forma balance sheet***   The controller of Lamb Industries is developing an analysis to see what financing requirements will be at the end of the current year. So far the controller has come up with the following data.

### Budgeted Income Statement for Year
#### (in thousands of dollars)

| | |
|---|---|
| Sales | $2,400 |
| Cost of sales | 1,600 |
| Gross profit | $ 800 |
| Operating expenses | 670 |
| Income | $ 130 |

### Outline of Pro Forma Balance Sheet
#### as of Year End (in thousands of dollars)

| Assets | | Equities | |
|---|---|---|---|
| Cash | $ 30 | Current liabilities | $ ? |
| Accounts receivable | ? | Long-term debt | 300 |
| Inventory | ? | | |
| Plant, net | 1,400 | Stockholders' equity | 1,300 |
| Total | $ ? | Total | $ ? |

Lamb's experience has been that accounts receivable are typically about 25% of sales and inventory about 30% of cost of sales. The company expects to have about the same income statement results for the next few years.

The controller would like to hold current liabilities to about one-half of current assets. The stockholders' equity figure given in the pro forma statement reflects expected profit and dividends for the year.

### Required

Determine total asset requirements, total available equities, and the financing gap.

## PROBLEMS

**7-20   *Comprehensive budgeting—selected elements***   Following is BLD Company's pro forma balance sheet at December 31, 20X3.

Pro Forma Balance Sheet as of December 31, 20X3

| Assets | | Equities | |
|---|---|---|---|
| Cash | $ 25,000 | Accounts payable | $ 12,000 |
| Receivables | 28,000 | Expenses payable | 5,000 |
| Inventory | 73,000 | Bank loan payable | 20,000 |
| Property, plant | | Common stock | 170,000 |
| and equipment, net | 125,000 | Retained earnings | 44,000 |
| Total | $251,000 | Total | $251,000 |

The following information is also available about BLD's plans and operations for 20X4.

(a) Budgeted sales for January through May are shown below.

| | Jan. | Feb. | Mar. | Apr. | May |
|---|---|---|---|---|---|
| Budgeted sales | $50,000 | $60,000 | $70,000 | $66,000 | $65,000 |

(b) All sales are on credit and collected 80% in the month of sale and 20% in the month after sale.

(c) Cost of sales is expected to be 60% of sales.

(d) BLD's policy is to maintain inventory equivalent to budgeted sales requirements for the following two months.

(e) Variable costs other than cost of sales are 15% of sales, with 40% paid in the month the costs are incurred and the remainder paid in the following month.

(f) Fixed costs are $8,000 per month, including depreciation of $2,000. Cash fixed costs are paid in the month they are incurred.

(g) BLD plans to declare a $1,500 cash dividend in January, to be paid in February.

(h) Purchases are all on credit and paid 80% in the month of purchase and 20% in the month after purchase.

(i) BLD plans to pay $2,200 to its bank on January 31, representing $2,000 of principal on its loan and $200 of interest for January. (Interest is paid monthly, based on the loan outstanding at the beginning of the month.)

### Required

1. What are BLD's budgeted cash receipts for January 20X4?
2. What are BLD's budgeted accounts receivable at January 31, 20X4?
3. What is BLD's budgeted inventory for January 31, 20X4?
4. What are BLD's budgeted purchases for January 20X4?
5. What is BLD's budgeted income for January 20X4?
6. What balance would BLD report for retained earnings in its pro forma balance sheet for January 31, 20X4?
7. List the purposes and budgeted amounts of all BLD's expected cash disbursements for January 20X4. (Give supporting computations, if any are necessary.)
8. List the names and budgeted amounts of all BLD's budgeted liabilities at January 31, 20X4. (Give supporting computations, if any are necessary.)

**7-21  Basic cash budget**  Before being called out of town on urgent company business, Sandy Banks, the controller of Zonar, Inc., developed the following information for the company's cash budget for the next few months.

| | Unit Sales | Unit Production | Materials Purchases |
|---|---|---|---|
| January | 900 | 1,200 | $160,000 *paid in Feb* |
| February | 1,300 | 1,600 | 180,000 |
| March | 1,700 | 1,500 | 130,000 |

Zonar's one product, a stereo unit, sells for $600. Customers pay 30% in the month of sale and 70% in the following month. Materials purchases are paid for in the month after purchase. Variable production costs, excluding materials, are $150 per unit of product. Fixed production costs are $150,000 per month, including $30,000 depreciation. Selling and administrative expenses are $50,000 per month, all cash, paid as incurred. Production costs other than those for materials are paid as incurred.

*150,000*
*−30,000*
*120,000*

At January 1, the company had $360,000 in accounts receivable from December sales and owed suppliers of materials $500,000. Cash at January 1 was $25,000.

*Required*
Prepare budgets of cash receipts and disbursements and a cash budget for January and for February. If you show a negative cash balance, assume borrowing to bring it to zero. Ignore interest and repayments.

**7-22  Comprehensive budget**  Borden Hardware Store is preparing its budgets for 20X7.

| Forecasted Sales | | Balance Sheet Data, December 31, 20X6 | |
|---|---|---|---|
| January | $60,000 | Cash | $ 8,000 |
| February | 80,000 | Accounts receivable | 24,000 |
| March | 70,000 | Inventory | 54,000 |
| April | 90,000 | Accounts payable (merchandise) | 42,000 |

Other data are as follows.
(a) Sales are on credit with 40% of sales collected in the month of sale and 60% in the month after sale.
(b) Cost of sales is 60% of sales.
(c) Other variable costs are 10% of sales, paid in the month incurred.
(d) Inventories are to be 150% of next month's budgeted sales requirements.
(e) Purchases are paid for in the month after purchase.
(f) Fixed expenses are $3,000 per month; all require cash.

*Required*
1. Prepare purchases budgets for each of the first three months of 20X7.
2. Prepare separate cash receipts and disbursements budgets and a cash budget for each of the first three months of 20X7.
3. Prepare a budgeted income statement for the three-month period ending March 31, 20X7.

**7-23  Understanding budgets**  Following are Blaisdel Company's balance sheet at December 31, 20X0, and information regarding Blaisdel's policies and past experiences.

### Blaisdel Company
### Balance Sheet at December 31, 20X0

| Assets | | Equities | |
|---|---|---|---|
| Cash | $ 33,000 | Accounts payable | $ 9,000 |
| Receivables | 31,000 | Income taxes payable | 8,000 |
| Inventory | 59,000 | Common stock | 180,000 |
| Fixed assets, net | 102,000 | Retained earnings | 28,000 |
| Total | $225,000 | Total | $225,000 |

Additional information:

(a) All sales are on credit and are collected 20% in the month of sale and 80% in the month after sale.

(b) Budgeted sales for the first five months of 20X1 are $50,000, $60,000, $70,000, $66,000, and $65,000, respectively.

(c) Inventory is maintained at budgeted sales requirements for the following two months.

(d) Purchases are all on credit and are paid 80% in the month of purchase and 20% in the month after purchase.

(e) Other variable costs are 20% of sales and are paid in the month incurred.

(f) Fixed costs are $6,000 per month, including $1,000 of depreciation. Cash fixed costs are paid in the month incurred.

(g) Blaisdel's income tax rate is 25%, with taxes being paid in the month after they are accrued.

(h) Cost of goods sold is expected to be 60% of sales.

### Required

1. What are budgeted cash receipts for January 20X1?
2. What is the budgeted inventory at January 31, 20X1?
3. What are budgeted purchases for January 20X1?
4. What is budgeted net income for January 20X1?
5. What is the budgeted cash balance at the end of January 20X1?
6. What are budgeted accounts receivable at February 28, 20X1?
7. What is the budgeted book value of fixed assets at March 31, 20X1?
8. What are budgeted accounts payable at March 31, 20X1?
9. If Blaisdel declared a cash dividend of $1,200 during January, payable in February, what balance would be reported for retained earnings in a pro forma balance sheet as of January 31, 20X1?
10. What amount would show as the liability for income taxes as of March 31, 20X1?

**7-24  Cash budget for a student**  Bo Phelps is a junior majoring in mathematics at a large university. Bo wants to develop a cash budget for the fall term, which runs from September 1 through November 30. He has collected the following information.

| | |
|---|---|
| Cash at September 1 | $1,250 |
| Tuition, due September 15 | 2,200 |
| Room rent, due September 15 (for entire term) | 800 |
| Cost of meals, per month | 300 |
| Clothing expenditures, per month | 50 |
| Textbook purchases, due September 15 | 280 |

Phelps has been awarded a scholarship of $2,000; the check should arrive by the end of the first week of September. He estimates that expenditures for dates and miscellaneous other items should total about $300 for the term, spread evenly over each month. He also expects that he can get a part-time job that pays $8 per hour. For the most part, Phelps will be able to set the hours he will work each month. His employer, a local business, must withhold 10% of his earnings for income and social security taxes.

**Required**

Determine how many hours Phelps must work each month to be able to maintain a $100 cash balance for emergencies.

**7-25   Cash budget—nursery school**   West Oak Community Church operates a nursery school on its premises from September through May. Parents can enroll a child for a morning or an afternoon class, but each class is limited to 20 children. The church's Board of Trustees sets the school's fees with the intention of breaking even.

The Board has the following report of cash receipts and disbursements for the school for the nine months ended May 31, 20X7.

| | | |
|---|---:|---:|
| Receipts | | $32,420 |
| Disbursements: | | |
| Teacher's salary | $19,000 | |
| Teacher's assistant ($400 per month) | 3,600 | |
| Payroll-related costs | 1,853 | |
| Supplies | 3,240 | |
| Food | 2,162 | |
| Equipment repair and replacement | 1,456 | |
| Licenses | 285 | |
| Miscellaneous | 1,226 | |
| Total | | 32,822 |
| Deficit | | $ (402) |

For the period covered by the report, the monthly fee was $90 per child and average enrollment per month was about 36 children.

In a letter accompanying the report, the teacher in charge of the school made the following comments about operations for the coming year.

(a) Costs for food and supplies are likely to increase 5%.
(b) Licensing fees will increase by $50.
(c) The need for a teacher's assistant continues because enrollment reaches 20 in one or both classes in several months.
(d) Payroll-related costs should continue at about the same percentage of payroll costs.
(e) Miscellaneous operating costs are likely to be about the same, but equipment-related costs will probably be about $1,650.

Based on the multitude of positive comments received about the school's teacher, the Board voted to increase the teacher's salary 15% and to accept the teacher's opinions about costs for the coming year.

**Required**

1. Prepare a cash disbursements budget for the coming year.
2. Determine what monthly fee per child the Board must set for the coming year to come within $100 of breaking even. Assume an average enrollment of 38 children per month.

**7-26    Pro forma financial statements and cash budget for a retailer**    The following is the expected balance sheet at December 31, 20X1, for Bob's Foods, a specialty retail food store in an affluent suburban area.

| Assets | | Liabilities and Owners' Equity | |
|---|---:|---|---:|
| Cash | $ 42,000 | Accounts payable | $ 48,000 |
| Accounts receivable | 4,500 | | |
| Inventory | 14,000 | Owners' equity | 142,000 |
| Equipment, net | 95,000 | | |
| Other | 34,500 | | |
| Total | $190,000 | Total | $190,000 |

Robert Granger, owner of Bob's, has regularly permitted about 4% of the customers to place orders on credit and pay for them in the following month. (These customers account for about 10% of dollar sales.) Late in 20X1, Granger decided to increase the number of customers permitted to order on credit. He made no formal analysis of the likely effects of the decision, but he believes that the store would benefit from expanding credit privileges to include a total of 15% of his customers who account for about 40% of the store's sales. Under Granger's new policy, sales would be 60% for cash and 40% on credit, with credit sales being collected in the month after sale.

Granger has developed or collected the following information to help him prepare a budget for the first quarter of 20X2.

(a) Estimated sales:

| | | | |
|---|---|---|---|
| January | $40,000 | March | $60,000 |
| February | 45,000 | April | 50,000 |

(b) Cost of sales is 70%. Vendors are paid in the month after purchase.
(c) Variable selling costs are 10% of sales.
(d) Administrative costs are fixed at $8,000 per month, including $2,500 depreciation.
(e) Cash operating costs other than for inventory items are paid in the month incurred.

Most suppliers of inventory items deliver at least weekly, but Granger wants to maintain his overall inventory at a 15-day supply (50% of the next month's sales needs). Because the new credit policy will have a fairly immediate impact on the store's cash balance, Granger is concerned that his cash balance may fall below the $20,000 he considers necessary.

**Required**
1. Prepare a budgeted income statement for the first quarter of 20X2.
2. Prepare a pro forma balance sheet as of March 31, 20X2.
3. Prepare the cash budget for the first quarter of 20X2. If you prepare a cash budget for each month, do not assume any borrowing should the cash balance fall below $20,000.
4. What time frame do you believe Bob's Foods should use to prepare its cash budget? Explain your answer.

**7-27    Comprehensive budget (adapted from a problem prepared by Professor Robert W. Koehler)**    The following data pertain to Elgin's, a specialty store in a large shopping mall.

### Sales Forecasts—20X8

| | |
|---|---|
| January | $ 80,000 |
| February | 90,000 |
| March | 110,000 |
| April | 120,000 |
| May | 100,000 |

### Balance Sheet at December 31, 20X7

| Assets | | Equities | |
|---|---|---|---|
| Cash | $ 15,000 | Accounts payable | $ 28,000 |
| Accounts receivable | 60,000 | Accrued sales commissions | 7,000 |
| Inventory | 102,000 | Common stock | 160,000 |
| Net fixed assets | 200,000 | Retained earnings | 182,000 |
| Total | $377,000 | Total | $377,000 |

Other data are as follows.

(a) All sales are on credit with 40% collected in the month of sale and 60% in the month after sale.

(b) Cost of sales is 60% of sales.

(c) The only other variable cost is a 7% commission to salespeople that is paid in the month after it is earned. All sales are subject to the commission.

(d) Inventory is kept equal to sales requirements for the next two months' budgeted sales.

(e) Purchases are paid for in the month after purchase.

(f) Fixed costs are $10,000 per month, including $4,000 depreciation.

**Required**

1. Prepare a budgeted income statement for the three-month period ending March 31, 20X8.
2. Prepare a cash budget for each of the first three months of 20X8 and all necessary supporting budgets.
3. Prepare a pro forma balance sheet as of March 31, 20X8.

**7-28  *Investing idle cash (continuation of 7-27; adapted from a problem prepared by Professor Robert W. Koehler)***  The president of Elgin's was pleased with the cash budget you prepared, but felt that the company might be able to invest some of its available cash and thereby earn an additional return. He knows that if the funds are invested in a money market fund the company will be able to earn 0.5% per month interest and can withdraw the money at any time. He believes that a $10,000 cash balance is sufficient and asks you to redo the cash budget to reflect the investing of excess cash at 0.5% per month. (Thus, you can invest $5,000 on January 1, because the $15,000 balance is $5,000 over the required minimum.) Assume that you invest at the end of months (except for January 1).

**Required**

Respond to the president's request.

**7-29  *Municipal budgeting—revenues***  The City of Wentworth is preparing its budget for 20X9. Total required revenues are $44,000,000. The city has two major sources of revenue, sales taxes and property taxes. The sales tax is 3.5% of taxable retail sales, which includes virtually all sales except for food and medicine. The assessed valuation of taxable property is $560,000,000. An economist hired by the city has forecast total taxable retail sales at $860,000,000 for 20X9.

**Required**

1. Determine the property tax rate needed to meet the city's revenue objective, assuming that the estimate of retail sales is correct.
2. The city council is considering a proposal to reduce property taxes on homes owned by people over 65 years of age. It is proposed that the rate on such homes be set at $20 per $1,000 assessed valuation. The total assessed valuation of homes owned by people over 65 is $45,000,000. Determine the rate that would have to be set on the remaining taxable property in order to meet the revenue objective if the proposal is adopted.

**7-30    *Manufacturer's cash budget—three months***    Tompkins Company produces a single product that sells for $15 per unit. Data are as follows.

(a) Variable manufacturing costs, all requiring cash, are $7 per unit.
(b) Variable selling and administrative expenses are $1 per unit.
(c) Fixed manufacturing costs requiring cash are $80,000 per month. Depreciation is $12,000 per month. Fixed selling and administrative expenses are $40,000 per month, all requiring cash.
(d) Tompkins maintains a supply of finished goods equal to 50% of the sales needs for the coming month. The beginning inventory (January 1) is 10,000 units.
(e) Tompkins has partially implemented JIT principles and therefore buys raw materials as needed, maintaining no inventory. The cost of raw materials is included in the variable manufacturing cost of $7.
(f) Tompkins makes all sales on credit, collecting 30% in the month of sale and 70% in the month after sale. The beginning balance in accounts receivable is $140,000.
(g) All cash manufacturing costs are paid for in the month of production.
(h) Tompkins pays 80% of selling and administrative expenses in the month of sale and 20% in the following month. At January 1 Tompkins owed $14,000 from December expenses.
(i) The minimum desired cash balance is $40,000, which is also the amount on hand at the beginning of January. If the company needs to borrow, it does so in multiples of $10,000. It borrows at the beginning of a month that indicates a deficiency and repays loans at the ends of months, if it has sufficient cash. The monthly interest rate is 1%, and Tompkins pays interest when it repays loans, whether in full or in part.
(j) The sales budget for the first six months is, in units, January, 20,000; February, 26,000; March, 30,000; April, 32,000; May, 30,000; June, 28,000.

**Required**

1. Prepare a cash budget and any necessary supporting schedules for the first three months of the year, by month and in total.
2. Given your results in requirement 1, does the company appear to be profitable? Explain.
3. Suppose that sales stabilize at 25,000 units per month. What will monthly cash collections be? What will monthly cash disbursements for manufacturing costs and for selling and administrative expenses be?

**7-31    *One-month cash budget—discounts***    Stony Acres Department Store makes about 20% of its sales for cash. Credit sales are collected 20%, 30%, and 45% in the month of sale, month after sale, and second month after sale, respectively. The remaining 5% become bad debts. The store tries to purchase enough goods each month to maintain its inventory at 2½ times the following month's budgeted sales needs. All purchases are subject to a 2% discount if paid within ten days and the store takes all discounts. Accounts payable are then equal to one-third of that month's net purchases. Cost of goods sold, without considering the 2% discount, is 60% of selling prices. The store records inventory net of the discount.

The general manager of the store has asked you to prepare a cash budget for August and you have gathered the following data.

| | |
|---|---:|
| Sales: | |
|    May (actual) | $220,000 |
|    June (actual) | 260,000 |
|    July (actual) | 300,000 |
|    August (budgeted) | 340,000 |
|    September (budgeted) | 300,000 |
| Inventory at July 31, net of discount | 455,700 |
| Cash at July 31 | 73,000 |
| Purchases in July (gross) | 210,000 |
| Selling, general, and administrative expenses | |
|    budgeted for August (including $21,000 depreciation) | 102,000 |

The store pays all of its other expenses in the month incurred.

**Required**
Prepare a cash budget for August.

**7-32   Long-range financial budget**   Millard Company has retained you to develop a financing plan for the next few years. You collect the following information about the firm's expectations, goals, and policies. All dollar amounts are in millions.

| Sales Forecasts | |
|---|---:|
| 20X4 | $  800 |
| 20X5 | 1,000 |
| 20X6 | 1,250 |
| 20X7 | 1,500 |

Millard expects a return on sales of 12%. The company's directors would like to maintain the policy of distributing dividends in an amount equal to 60% of net income each year. The directors would also like to have a current ratio of at least 2 to 1 and do not want long-term liabilities to exceed 30% of total assets.

Current asset requirements are 30% of expected sales in the coming year, and net fixed assets are 65% of budgeted sales for the coming year. At the end of 20X3, stockholders' equity is $400.

**Required**
Prepare a schedule showing financing requirements for year-end 20X4, 20X5, and 20X6. Round to the nearest $1 million.

**7-33   Budgeting equations (CMA adapted)**   Your firm has just acquired a new computer, and one of the first things the president wants to use it for is preparing the comprehensive budget. He assigns you the task of formulating a set of equations that can be used to write a program to perform the computations required for the budgets. You consult with the chief programmer, and the two of you decide that the following notation should be used, which will make it easy for the programmer to prepare the necessary programs.

| | |
|---|---|
| S0 | = sales in current month (units) |
| S1 | = sales in coming month (units) |
| S-1 | = sales in prior month (units) |
| S-2 | = sales in second prior month (units) |
| P | = selling price per unit |
| CGS | = cost of goods sold per unit (purchase price) |
| OVC | = other variable costs per unit |
| FC | = total fixed costs per month |
| FCC | = fixed costs per month requiring cash disbursements |
| PUR | = purchases in current month (units) |
| PUR-1 | = purchases in prior month (units) |

You examine the company's records and decide that the firm's policies or experienced relationships are as follows.

(a) Collections on sales are 30% in the month of sale, 50% in the month after sale, and 20% in the second month after sale.
(b) Inventory is maintained at twice the coming month's budgeted sales volume.
(c) Purchases are paid for 60% in the month after purchase and 40% in the month of purchase.
(d) All other costs are paid as incurred.

**Required**
Prepare equations that can be used to budget for the following.

1. Income for the current month.
2. Cash receipts in the current month.
3. Purchases in the current month in units.
4. Purchases in the current month in dollars.
5. Cash disbursements in the current month.

*7-34   Comprehensive budget (continuation of 6-48; adapted from a problem prepared by Professor Maurice L. Hirsch)*   The following additional information about Banana City is available.

(a) Sales of bananas are for cash only. Sales of nuts are on credit and are collected two months after sale.
(b) Banana City's suppliers give terms of 30 days for payment of accounts payable. Banana City takes full advantage of the 30-day payments. (Assume all months have 30 days.)
(c) The company must make quarterly payments on its income taxes. The payment for the first quarter of fiscal year 20X7 is due on January 15, 20X7. The liability for taxes payable shown on the balance sheet in item (e) is to be paid on October 15.
(d) Fixed expenses that require cash disbursement are paid as incurred with the following exceptions: (1) insurance premiums are all paid on November 1 in advance for the next 12 months and (2) interest payments are all made on January 1. The $156,000 "other fixed expenses" shown in item (f) of Problem 6-48 all require cash disbursements evenly over the year.
(e) The balance sheet at August 31, 20X6, is as follows.

| Assets | | Equities | |
|---|---:|---|---:|
| Cash | $ 15,000 | Accounts payable (merchandise) | $ 26,000 |
| Accounts receivable | 75,000 | Taxes payable | 31,000 |
| Inventories | 41,800 | Accrued interest | 4,000 |
| Prepaid insurance | 2,000 | Long-term debt, 6% | 100,000 |
| Land | 8,000 | Common stock | 150,000 |
| Equipment (net) | 210,000 | Retained earnings | 40,800 |
| Total | $351,800 | Total | $351,800 |

(f) Sales expected in the last part of fiscal year 20X6 are given as follows.

| | June | July | August |
|---|---:|---:|---:|
| Bananas | $31,000 | $34,000 | $32,500 |
| Nuts | 37,000 | 41,000 | 34,000 |

(g) The company plans to pay a dividend of $12,000 in October.

**Required**

1. Prepare budgets of cash receipts and disbursements for each of the first three months of fiscal year 20X7 and for the quarter as a whole.
2. Prepare a cash budget for the quarter, by month, and in total.
3. Prepare a pro forma balance sheet for November 30, 20X6.

**7-35  *Pro forma balance sheet and financing requirements***  Jill Eyre, treasurer of Caldwell Company, has collected the following information as part of her planning. She believes the company will have to issue long-term debt during the year, but she is unsure how much.

| Budgeted Income Statement for 20X6 | |
|---|---:|
| Sales | $300,000 |
| Cost of goods sold | 210,000 |
| Gross profit | $ 90,000 |
| Selling, general, and administrative expenses | 36,000 |
| Income before taxes | $ 54,000 |
| Income taxes (40% rate) | 21,600 |
| Net income | $ 32,400 |

| Balance Sheet Data at December 31, 20X5 | |
|---|---:|
| Plant and equipment—net | $150,000 |
| Common stock | 200,000 |
| Retained earnings | 83,000 |

| Known Asset Requirements, December 31, 20X6 | |
|---|---|
| Cash—minimum desired balance | $25,000 |
| Accounts receivable | 30% of sales |
| Inventory | 30% of cost of sales |
| Plant and equipment—net | $210,000 |

Jill also knows that accounts payable are normally 50% of inventory and that only half the income tax expense is paid before the end of the year. The company's annual dividend is $22,000 and is normally paid in October.

**Required**
Prepare a statement of asset requirements and available equities as of the end of 20X6. Determine the amount of long-term debt that Caldwell will need at the end of 20X6.

**7-36  Comprehensive budget**  Following are the balance sheet of your company, Arcon Industries, at December 31, 20X5, and its projected income statement for the first three months of 20X6.

### Balance Sheet at December 31, 20X5

| Assets | | Equities | |
|---|---:|---|---:|
| Cash | $ 5,000 | Accounts payable | $16,000 |
| Accounts receivable | 10,000 | Dividend payable | 2,000 |
| Inventory | 24,000 | Owners' equity | 61,000 |
| Plant and equipment, net of | | | |
| accumulated depreciation | 40,000 | | |
| Total | $79,000 | Total | $79,000 |

### Budgeted Income Statement for the Three Months Ending March 31, 20X6

| | | |
|---|---:|---:|
| Sales (10,000 units × $10) | | $100,000 |
| Cost of sales (10,000 units × $6) | | 60,000 |
| Gross profit | | $ 40,000 |
| Operating expenses: | | |
| Wages and salaries | $9,000 | |
| Rent | 3,000 | |
| Depreciation | 3,000 | |
| Other expenses | 1,500 | |
| Total operating expenses | | 16,500 |
| Income | | $ 23,500 |

You are quite happy with the projection, and gloat about it to your banker at lunch. The banker asks if you will need any cash to get through the first quarter. "Of course not" is your reply. Later, back at your office, the chief accountant informs you of the following.

(a) Sales are all on credit and are collected 50% in the month of sale and 50% in the month after sale.
(b) Company policy is to maintain inventory equal to the next two months' sales in units, but inventory at December 31, 20X5, does not conform to policy because of a recent dock strike.
(c) Arcon pays for purchases 50% in the month of purchase and 50% in the following month.
(d) Arcon is committed to paying the recorded cash dividend of $2,000 in March.
(e) All cash expenses are paid in the month incurred, except for purchases.
(f) A breakdown of projected sales by month is as follows:

| | | | | | |
|---|---|---|---|---|---|
| January | $20,000 | March | $50,000 | May | $20,000 |
| February | $30,000 | April | $20,000 | | |

(g) Maintaining a cash balance of at least $5,000 is necessary to accommodate emergencies and variations from estimates.

**Required**

Do you regret your reply to your banker? Explain by preparing the appropriate schedules. (If borrowings are necessary, assume that they are in $1,000 multiples at the beginning of the month and that repayments are at the end of months with 12% annual interest on the amount repaid.)

**7-37 Comprehensive budget (continuation of 6-38)** The managers and managerial accountants at Arctic Products have the following additional information.

(a) Sales should be collected 30% in the month of sale and 70% in the following month.
(b) Purchases are paid 40% in the month of purchase and 60% in the following month.
(c) Fixed manufacturing costs include $20,000 per month depreciation.
(d) Manufacturing costs that require cash disbursements are paid as incurred.
(e) Of selling and administrative expenses that require cash disbursements, 80% is paid as incurred; the remaining 20% is paid in the following month.

The balance sheet expected at December 31 appears below.

Arctic Products
Balance Sheet at December 31, 20X5

| Assets | |
|---|---|
| Cash | $ 75,000 |
| Accounts receivable | 280,000 |
| Finished goods (35,000 × $14) | 490,000 |
| Materials (66,000 × $8) | 528,000 |
| Plant and equipment, net | 1,200,000 |
| Total assets | $2,573,000 |

| Equities | |
|---|---|
| Accounts payable | $ 96,000 |
| Accrued expenses | 17,000* |
| Stockholders' equity | 2,460,000 |
| Total equities | $2,573,000 |

*$11,000 of the total relates to fixed costs.*

**Required**

1. Prepare cash budgets for January and February assuming the company desires a minimum cash balance of $60,000 at the end of each month. If projections show that borrowing is necessary to meet the minimum balance and cover a month's cash activity, such borrowings occur at the beginning of the month, in multiples of $10,000. Assume that repayments, in multiples of $10,000, are made at the end of the month, as soon as cash balances permit them. The bank charges interest at 1% per month, but interest payments need to be made only at the time a repayment occurs, and then only for the interest due on the amount being repaid.
2. Prepare a pro forma balance sheet as of the end of February.

**7-38 Cash budget (continuation of 6-47)** Spark Company collects its sales 30% in the month of sale, 30% in the next month, and 40% in the second month after sale. Fixed production costs not requiring cash are $40,000 per month. All selling, general, and administrative expenses require cash and are paid in the month incurred, except for sales commissions, which are paid in the month after incurrence.

All production costs requiring cash are paid 80% in the month of production and 20% in the month after production. This includes payments for materials, of which no inventory is kept since they are delivered daily.

Selected balance sheet data for Spark Company at May 31 are as follows.

| | | |
|---|---|---|
| Cash | $120,000 | (equals the desired minimum balance) |
| Accounts receivable: | | |
| From May sales | 336,000 | |
| From April sales | 120,000 | |
| Liabilities: | | |
| Sales commissions | 48,000 | |
| Production costs | 66,000 | |

### Required

Prepare a cash budget for Spark Company for the first three months of the fiscal year, by month. If the need arises, show borrowings, in multiples of $10,000, required to maintain the desired minimum balance of cash. Repayments are made at the end of months, and interest at 1% per month is paid when a repayment is made.

**7-39  Analysis of budgets of a manufacturing firm**  Budgets for Simpson Company appear as follows for the first three months of 20X6.

Budgeted Income Statements
for the Three Months Ending March 31, 20X6

| | | |
|---|---|---|
| Sales (10,000 units) | | $30,000 |
| Variable costs: | | |
| Production | $8,000 | |
| Selling and administrative | 7,500 | 15,500 |
| Contribution margin | | $14,500 |
| Fixed costs: | | |
| Production | $1,800 | |
| Selling and administrative | 2,400 | 4,200 |
| Income | | $10,300 |

Production Budget (in units)

| | January | February | March |
|---|---|---|---|
| Desired ending inventory | 4,500 | 7,500 | 6,000 |
| Units sold | 2,000 | 3,000 | 5,000 |
| Total requirements | 6,500 | 10,500 | 11,000 |
| Beginning inventory | 2,500 | 4,500 | 7,500 |
| Production | 4,000 | 6,000 | 3,500 |

Cash Receipts Budget

| | January | February | March |
|---|---|---|---|
| Collections: | | | |
| December sales | $ 750 | | |
| January sales | 1,500 | $4,500 | |
| February sales | | 2,250 | $ 6,750 |
| March sales | | | 3,750 |
| Total collections | $2,250 | $6,750 | $10,500 |

## Cash Disbursements Budget

|  | January | February | March |
|---|---|---|---|
| Production costs: |  |  |  |
| Variable | $3,200 | $4,800 | $2,800 |
| Fixed | 600 | 600 | 600 |
| Selling and administrative: |  |  |  |
| Variable—current month | 600 | 900 | 1,500 |
| —prior month | 150 | 900 | 1,350 |
| Fixed | 800 | 800 | 800 |
| Totals | $5,350 | $8,000 | $7,050 |

### Required

Answer the following questions about the assumptions and policies used in formulating the budgets.

1. What are variable manufacturing costs per unit?
2. What are monthly fixed manufacturing costs requiring cash disbursements?
3. What are the company's expectations about cash collections from receivables? (All sales are on account.)
4. What were sales in December 20X5?
5. What are accounts receivable at March 31, 20X6?
6. What proportion of variable selling and administrative expenses is paid in the month incurred, and what proportion is paid the following month? (Hint: Variable selling costs are 25% of sales.)
7. What are accrued expenses payable for selling and administrative expenses at March 31, 20X6?
8. How much cash does Simpson expect to have at March 31, 20X6? (The balance at January 1 is $1,800.)
9. If the company could sell 2,000 additional units in the three-month period, what would income be? (Ignore interest expense.)
10. Look at the production budget. From comparisons of inventories, sales, and so on, determine Simpson's inventory policy.
11. Does the beginning inventory for January reflect Simpson's policy? Show why or why not.
12. What are budgeted sales for April?

**7-40   Qualifying for a loan**   The president of Stern's Department Store has requested your assistance. He will be seeking a large bank loan in a couple of months for the purpose of opening a new store and has been told by his banker that the March 31, 20X8, balance sheet should look good if the loan is to be granted. The banker said specifically that working capital should be at least $500,000 and that the current ratio should be at least 2.5 to 1.

The end of January is now approaching and the president is becoming anxious. He asks you to prepare a cash budget for February and March and a pro forma balance sheet as of March 31. The balance sheet at the end of January is expected to be as follows, in thousands of dollars.

| Assets |  | Equities |  |
|---|---|---|---|
| Cash | $ 110 | Accounts payable (merchandise) | $ 410 |
| Accounts receivable | 240 | Notes payable | 40 |
| Inventory | 680 | Common stock | 2,000 |
| Building and equipment (net) | 1,830 | Retained earnings | 410 |
| Total | $2,860 | Total | $2,860 |

The sales forecasts for the months of February, March, April, and May are, respectively, $780,000, $650,000, $600,000, and $820,000. Cost of sales averages 60% of sales. Receivables are collected 60% in the month of sale, 40% in the following month. Inventory is normally maintained at budgeted sales requirements for the following two months. Purchases are paid for in 30 days.

The notes payable shown in the balance sheet are due on March 15. Although the company normally keeps a minimum cash balance of $80,000, the president asks you to disregard this for purposes of the budgets. He also informs you that monthly fixed costs are $265,000, of which $30,000 is depreciation. All fixed costs requiring cash are paid as incurred.

### Required

1. Prepare the cash budget and pro forma balance sheet that the president wants. Use thousands of dollars.
2. Determine whether the company will be likely to meet the criteria set by the bank.

**7-41   Variable minimum cash balance**   John Lock, chief financial officer of Bland Company, has asked for your help in preparing a cash budget. He plans to maintain a minimum balance based on the budgeted disbursements for the coming month and is unsure how to proceed. He tells you the following about his policy.

If the coming month's budgeted receipts are greater than budgeted disbursements, I want to hold a balance equal to 10% of budgeted disbursements and invest any excess cash in short-term government notes. If budgeted disbursements are greater than budgeted receipts, I want to have enough cash to make up the budgeted deficit and have 20% of budgeted disbursements on hand to begin the month. We will borrow if the indicated balance is less than required.

The budgets for sales and purchases in the coming months are as follows.

|           | April     | May       | June      | July      | August    |
|-----------|-----------|-----------|-----------|-----------|-----------|
| Sales     | $500,000  | $780,000  | $900,000  | $600,000  | $650,000  |
| Purchases | $470,000  | $550,000  | $560,000  | $480,000  | $600,000  |

Sales are collected 30% in the month of sale and 70% in the following month. Purchases are paid for 50% in the month of purchase and 50% in the following month. Sales in March were $450,000 and accounts payable for merchandise at March 31 were $185,000. Cash at March 31 was $140,000. Fixed expenses requiring cash disbursements are $110,000 per month.

### Required

1. Prepare a schedule by month for the April–July period indicating the amounts that would have to be borrowed, or would be available for investment, in each month. Borrowings would be repaid as soon as possible and are not included in the determination of disbursements for the purpose of setting the desired balance. Borrowings would be repaid before investments were made and investments would be sold before borrowings are made. Ignore interest.
2. Using the guidelines in Appendix A, write a memorandum to Mr. Lock describing the advantages and disadvantages of his policy in comparison with a policy of having a specific number of dollars as the minimum cash balance.

## CASES

**7-42   Financing requirements**   Larsen Company makes fertilizer in a midwestern state. The company has nearly completed a new plant that will produce twice as much as the old plant, which is being scrapped. Swen Larsen, the owner, has consulted you about his financing requirements for the coming year. He knows he will require additional financing because of the doubling of production, and he intends to obtain a loan as soon as possible. He is on good terms with local bankers and anticipates no difficulty in obtaining the loan, but he is anxious that the loan not be too large or too small.

The production process in the new plant is highly automated and can be carried out with a work force of the same size as that used last year in the old plant. The income statement for last year and the year-end balance sheet are as follows:

### Income Statement for 20X4

| | |
|---|---:|
| Sales | $1,600,000 |
| Cost of goods sold | 1,040,000 |
| Gross profit | $ 560,000 |
| Selling, general, and administrative expenses | 390,000 |
| Income | $ 170,000 |

### Balance Sheet at December 31, 20X4

| Assets | | Liabilities and Owners' Equity | |
|---|---:|---|---:|
| Cash | $ 40,000 | Accounts payable | $ 20,000 |
| Accounts receivable | 80,000 | Common stock | 900,000 |
| Inventory of materials | 250,000 | Retained earnings | 150,000 |
| Plant and equipment—old plant | 0 | | |
| —new plant | 700,000 | | |
| Total | $1,070,000 | Total | $1,070,000 |

You learn that depreciation expense on the old plant was $80,000 per year, all of which was included in cost of goods sold. The new plant will be depreciated at $120,000 per year. Wages paid last year to production workers were $280,000. Materials purchases were $400,000, which is also the amount of materials cost included in cost of goods sold (the beginning and ending inventories of materials were the same). Factory overhead, other than depreciation, was $280,000 last year and is expected to be $360,000 in the coming year.

Selling, general, and administrative expenses are expected to be $430,000 during the coming year. Sales will be only 120% of last year's sales because it will take some time to reach the full output of the new plant. Larsen expects to spend $250,000 buying new equipment to complete the plant. This expenditure will be made as soon as he obtains the new loan. The factory will be operating at full capacity the last few months of the year, so ending requirements for current assets should be double the beginning amounts.

Accounts payable are closely related to the amount of inventory carried. The company ships its products on completion, so all inventory is raw materials.

### Required

Prepare a budgeted income statement for 20X5 and a pro forma balance sheet (as far as possible) for December 31, 20X5. State any assumptions you have to make and indicate how much Mr. Larsen must borrow from the bank.

**7-43  *Growth financing***   Ronnon Inc. is a rapidly-growing maker of various infrastructure products for Internet Service Providers. Ronnon's board has set high targets, including 15% annual growth in sales. The controller wants you to help develop a plan for long-term financing. She gives you the following expectations and policies.

| Return on sales | 10% |
|---|---|
| Current asset requirements | 40% of next year budgeted sales |
| Net fixed assets | 110% of next year budgeted sales |
| Dividends | 40% of net income |
| Current ratio | 3-1 |
| Long-term liabilities | 30% of total assets |

Sales forecasts, in millions of dollars:

| 20X5 | $40.0 |
|---|---|
| 20X6 | $46.0 |
| 20X7 | $52.9 |
| 20X8 | $60.8 |

Stockholders' equity is $32.0 million at the beginning of 20X5.

*Required*

1. Prepare a schedule to show the treasurer the financing requirements that Ronnon needs from 20X5 through 20X7. Round to the nearest tenth of a million dollars.
2. As you and the controller review the schedule you prepared in requirement 1 you realize that, with the exception of the growth in sales, the assumptions and policies in the plan essentially preserve the status quo and ignore trends and conditions you've read about or observed in business. Identify which of the assumptions and policies—if they represent Ronnon's current circumstances—appear to ignore current trends and conditions, and explain your choices.

**7-44 Cash budgeting—a lender's viewpoint**  You are the chief assistant to Mr. Barnes, the loan officer of Metropolitan National Bank. In December 20X4 Mr. Barnes discussed a loan with Mr. Johnson, manager-owner of a local dry goods store. Mr. Johnson has requested a loan of $250,000 to be repaid at June 30, 20X5. He is expanding the store and needs additional inventory. From the proceeds of the loan, $200,000 will be spent on remodeling and new fixtures. The rest will be spent for additional inventory. At Mr. Barnes' request, Mr. Johnson submitted a budgeted income statement for the six months ending June 30, 20X5.

| | |
|---|---|
| Sales | $900,000 |
| Cost of goods sold | 360,000 |
| Gross profit | $540,000 |
| Selling and general expenses, including | |
| $15,000 interest | 310,000 |
| Income | $230,000 |

Mr. Johnson said that, since $50,000 in depreciation was included in selling and administrative expenses, his company would generate more than enough cash to repay the loan with $15,000 in interest (12% annual rate). Mr. Barnes asks you to check out the forecast with Mr. Johnson. From Mr. Johnson you obtain the following information:

(a) Sales are expected to be $100,000 in January, $140,000 in February, and $165,000 in each of the rest of the months of the entire year.
(b) Merchandise is held equal to two months' budgeted sales.
(c) Accounts payable are paid in 30 days.
(d) About half of sales are for cash. The rest are collected in the second month after sale (60 days).

(e) Cost of goods sold is variable, and 15% of sales is the variable portion of selling and general expenses. All selling and general expenses, except depreciation, are paid in the month incurred.
(f) At December 31, 20X4, the following balance sheet is expected.

Pro Forma Balance Sheet as of December 31, 20X4

| Assets | | Equities | |
|---|---|---|---|
| Cash (desired minimum) | $ 20,000 | Accounts payable | $ 30,000 |
| Accounts receivable | 40,000 | Common stock | 200,000 |
| Inventory | 60,000 | Retained earnings | 115,000 |
| Building and equipment | 375,000 | | |
| Accumulated depreciation | (150,000) | | |
| Total | $ 345,000 | Total | $345,000 |

**Required**

Using the guidelines in Appendix A, write a memorandum to Mr. Barnes giving and supporting your conclusions regarding the likelihood that Mr. Johnson's company can repay the loan and interest at the end of the first six months of 20X5.

**7-45  Budgeting from industry data**  Ralph Robertson is considering opening a menswear store in a new shopping center. He has had a great deal of experience in men's stores and is convinced that he can make a success of his own store. He plans to invest $10,000 of his own money in the business and has asked you to develop a plan he can take to a bank to obtain a loan to cover the remainder of the needed financing. He knows that a loan officer will be more receptive to an applicant who has made careful plans of his needs.

Ralph gives you the following data obtained from a trade association's study of stores of the kind and size he plans to open (1,200 square feet of selling space).

| | |
|---|---|
| Average sales per square foot | $90 per year |
| Average rent | $500/per month plus 5% of sales |
| Average gross profit | 55% of sales |
| Average annual operating expenses (excluding rent and depreciation): | |
| At $90,000 sales annually | $22,200 |
| At $120,000 sales annually | $26,700 |
| Inventory requirements | two-month supply |
| Investment in fixtures and equipment (useful life of five years) | $22,000 |

Ralph plans to sell for cash only. He will have to pay cash for his first purchase of inventory, but he expects to get 30-day credit from suppliers for further purchases. He will pay his other operating expenses, including rent, in the month incurred.

Ralph expects to have a steady growth in sales for the first four months of operation (January–April 20X8) and to reach the monthly average for the industry in May. His projections for the first four months are as follows: $5,000, $5,500, $6,200, and $7,100.

**Required**

Using the guidelines in Appendix A, write a memorandum to Mr. Robertson showing his financing requirements through April and a budgeted income statement for 20X8. Include in your memorandum brief comments about the assumptions you used to develop the financial data you are providing.

**7-46   Analyzing budgets**   TUV, Inc. has the following budgets for the first quarter of 20X9.

### Budgeted income statement

| | |
|---|---:|
| Sales ($70,000 + $70,000 + $90,000) | $230,000 |
| Cost of sales | 138,000 |
| Gross profit | $ 92,000 |
| Fixed costs ($14,000 x 3) | 42,000 |
| Income | $ 50,000 |

### Purchases budget

| | January | February | March | Total |
|---|---:|---:|---:|---:|
| Cost of sales | $ 42,000 | $ 42,000 | $ 54,000 | $138,000 |
| Desired ending inventory | 63,000 | 81,000 | 72,000 | 72,000 |
| Total requirements | $105,000 | $123,000 | $126,000 | $210,000 |
| Beginning inventory | 45,000 | 63,000 | 81,000 | 45,000 |
| Purchases | $ 60,000 | $ 60,000 | $ 45,000 | $165,000 |

### Cash receipts budget

| | January | February | March | Total |
|---|---:|---:|---:|---:|
| Collections from: | | | | |
| Current month | $42,000 | $42,000 | $54,000 | $138,000 |
| Prior month | 30,000 | 28,000 | 28,000 | 86,000 |
| Total | $72,000 | $70,000 | $82,000 | $224,000 |

### Cash disbursements budget

| | January | February | March | Total |
|---|---:|---:|---:|---:|
| Payments for purchases: | | | | |
| Current month | $24,000 | $24,000 | $18,000 | $66,000 |
| Prior month | 40,000 | 36,000 | 36,000 | 112,000 |
| Fixed costs | 10,000 | 10,000 | 10,000 | 30,000 |
| Total | $74,000 | $70,000 | $64,000 | $208,000 |

### Cash budget

| | January | February | March | Total |
|---|---:|---:|---:|---:|
| Beginning balance | $20,000 | $18,000 | $ 18,000 | $ 20,000 |
| Receipts | 72,000 | 70,000 | 82,000 | 224,000 |
| Available | $92,000 | $88,000 | $100,000 | $244,000 |
| Disbursements | 74,000 | 70,000 | 64,000 | 208,000 |
| Ending balance | $18,000 | $18,000 | $ 36,000 | $ 36,000 |

### Pro forma balance sheet as of March 31, 20X9

#### Assets

| | |
|---|---:|
| Cash (cash budget) | $ 36,000 |
| Accounts receivable | ? |
| Inventory | 72,000 |
| Fixed assets | 200,000 |
| Total assets | $344,000 |

#### Equities

| | |
|---|---:|
| Accounts payable | $ 27,000 |
| Stockholders' equity | 317,000 |
| Total equities | $344,000 |

1. How many days does TUV take to pay its suppliers?
2. What is the company's inventory policy?
3. How much would income change if the company could sell an additional $10,000?
4. What are budgeted accounts receivable at March 31?
5. What is monthly depreciation?
6. Construct the balance sheet from December 31, 20X8.
7. The president tells you that he cannot understand how the company could earn $50,000, while cash increased by only $16,000. The president also knows that depreciation does not require cash disbursement, so cash flow should be even higher than $50,000. Explain why cash increased so little given the income.

*Chapter Eight*

# CAPITAL BUDGETING DECISIONS—PART I

*LEARNING OBJECTIVES*

*After reading this chapter, you should be able to*

- *Explain the concepts of cost of capital and cutoff rates of return.*
- *Calculate cash flows from an investment, including the tax effects of depreciation.*
- *Use the net present value method to evaluate an investment.*
- *Use the internal rate of return method to evaluate an investment.*
- *Discuss qualitative reasons for making or not making particular investments.*
- *Use the payback method and accounting rate of return method.*
- *Understand why discounted cash flow methods are superior to non-discounting methods.*
- *Understand why investing in foreign countries poses special risks.*

*Anytime a company spends money now with the expectation of receiving more money back later, it is making an investment of the type that this chapter covers. A great deal of such investment is expenditures for land, buildings, production machinery and equipment, and other physical assets. This type of investment in the United States by U.S. companies alone is roughly $1.4 trillion per year. In addition, U.S. companies invest overseas, and foreign companies invest in the United States. We list below a few examples of spending from recent annual reports of multinational companies. All figures are in millions of dollars.*

| Company | Capital Expenditures | Sales |
|---|---|---|
| **General Electric** | *$2,191* | *$54,515* |
| **AT&T** | *$3,701* | *$67,156* |
| **Intel** | *$4,501* | *$25,070* |

*In early 1998, AT&T used $11 billion of its own stock to acquire **Teleport Communications Group, Inc.**, which provides local telephone service to businesses. The combined companies expected the following results in 2002.*

| | |
|---|---|
| Cost savings from sharing local network | $1.1 to $1.25 billion |
| Cost savings from sharing overhead | $.44 to $.50 billion |
| Additional revenues | $.66 to $.75 billion |
| Totals | $2.2 to $2.5 billion |

*Some analysts believed that the cost savings were relatively firm numbers but that the additional revenues were problematic, while others thought that the revenue estimates were very reasonable. AT&T also gained access to cable television, high-speed modem transfers, and perhaps even local telephone service, factors that, while difficult to quantify, impressed the market enough to send the stock price up 4% in one day.*

CHAPTER 5

*The size alone of capital investments makes them riskier than the types of decisions Chapter 5 discussed. Companies that make wise investment decisions will reap great rewards, but if they make poor decisions, they could go out of business. If **AT&T** achieves the gains it expects the decision will work out well, but if not the company could suffer a significant loss. How do companies make the decisions that result in such huge outlays? What do they expect to gain from these investments? What techniques do companies use and how does managerial accounting fit into the picture? Is it only profit-seeking companies that make such large expenditures and use managerial accounting techniques?*

Source: Peter Elstrom, "An $11 Billion Bargain," Business Week, January 26, 1998, 37.

CHAPTER 9

This and the following chapter require that you understand the principles of the time value of money. Before you begin this chapter, read Appendix B at the back of the book and work through the review problems to be sure that you understand these principles.

CHAPTER 7

Comprehensive budgets reflect the results expected from a wide variety of planning decisions, such as those about product mix, cost structure, and pricing. As you saw in Chapter 7, a comprehensive budget includes the expected results of decisions that involve long-term commitments, called **capital budgeting decisions** or **long-term decisions**. Expenditures for plant and equipment are often the largest items in the cash disbursements budget. Other types of spending are also capital budgeting in the sense that the company expects to gain a higher return in the future from spending cash now. Research and development is perhaps the most obvious example, but spending on employee training, information technology, and some types of marketing programs also fall into the category.

CHAPTER 5

We analyze capital budgeting decisions in much the same way we do short-term decisions, using differential revenues and costs. These concepts remain relevant to capital budgeting decisions. The difference between long-term and short-term decisions is that the former require considering the time value of money because of the lag between spending cash and receiving cash. Chapter 5 decisions did not entail significant waits between the expenditure and the receipt of cash.

CHAPTER 9

The analytical techniques we discuss in this and the following chapter help managers to decide whether to undertake long-term projects. The other aspect of such decisions, how we finance them, we cover only briefly. You will study in more detail the problems of selecting from among financing alternatives in managerial finance.

From Chapter 5, we know that a short-term action is desirable if incremental revenues exceed incremental costs. In capital budgeting decisions, the company must include as a relevant cost the **time value of money**, because capital budgeting decisions require investing money now to bring in more money in the future. The time value of money is an opportunity cost; by making a particular investment now, we give up the opportunity to make other investments.

## IMPORTANCE OF CAPITAL BUDGETING DECISIONS

Capital budgeting decisions commit companies to courses of action. The success or failure of a particular strategy, or even of the company itself, can hinge on one or a series of such decisions. And, for at least two reasons, capital budgeting decisions are generally riskier than short-term ones. First, the company expects to recoup its investment over a longer period. Much time expires between making the expenditure and receiving the cash. For example, **Intel's** 1994 annual report discussed a $1.3 billion plant the company began in 1994 that would not even start production until 1997. Because capital investments generate returns over several years, a company risks being caught in a business downturn that will reduce expected returns. Second, reversing a capital budgeting decision is much more difficult than reversing a short-term decision. A company that raises prices only to see sales and profits fall can usually just reinstate the lower prices. The company might suffer a decline in profits for a short time, but it can recover quickly once the managers see their error. But a company that buys land and constructs and equips a building to make a particular product is out of luck if the product fails. The plant might have little value in any other use (a low opportunity cost), so if the product is unsuccessful, the company will have made a large, nearly worthless investment. Annual reports are littered with the debris of such investments, sometimes under the heading of "write-offs" or "loss on discontinued business." A later Insight tells of some such losses.

## TYPES OF CAPITAL BUDGETING DECISIONS

Businesses and other economic entities make capital investments for a variety of reasons. The following is a representative list of the types of such decisions. The accompanying Insight describes some companies' investment priorities.

- *Investments mandated by law or policy*   This group includes investments made to comply with environmental, safety, and other laws and regulations. The group also includes investments made because company policy so dictates. In these cases, the organization must do something, so the only question is how to do it. For example, a company might have three alternatives that will reduce toxic emissions. The decision is which alternative to select.

- *Investments made to further strategic goals*   This group is composed of investments made for such purposes as securing global distribution of products, increasing quality, and reducing lead time. Companies need not make these investments, but probably will even if they do not meet normal profitability criteria (which we will discuss shortly).

- *Investments to increase capacity or reduce costs*   This group constitutes the bulk of investments that managers evaluate with the techniques covered in

SIGHT

### Variety of Capital Budgeting Decisions

Capital spending serves many purposes, with achieving lower costs (or higher productivity) and increasing capacity perhaps the most common and easiest to deal with quantitatively.

**Merck & Co.**, the giant pharmaceutical company, has made productivity gains one of its permanent strategies. Recent annual reports have discussed optimizing plants, reducing process costs, implementing research results more quickly, re-engineering manufacturing and administrative processes, and delayering the organization. Many annual reports will have similar statements. Companies in industries with large capital investment requirements have special problems. Such companies usually have high fixed operating costs and are often caught in price wars. **Cypress Semiconductor** described the difficulties that attended a sharp price decline in semiconductor prices in 1996 and stated that much of its investment would be directed toward reducing costs so as to mitigate future decreases.

Some capital spending goes toward consolidation and efficiency. **General Motors** suffered a $2 billion strike in July of 1998, partly because of its plans to build new factories that will use much less labor than its existing plants. GM is both the largest and the highest-cost automaker. Part of the reason is that it makes much more of its parts and components than do the others. The new plants will use more partly-assembled components, such as complete dashboards, provided by outside vendors. GM employees will do far less fabrication work and more assembly. GM employees earn about $40 per hour, including fringe benefits. The company will close some of its less efficient plants, reduce the number of engines it produces from ten to five, and reduce the number of models of car it makes. GM now loses $1,000 on each small car it makes, partly because of inefficient manufacturing. GM also announced that it was spinning off its $31 billion (sales) **Delphi Automotive Systems** unit, which made parts for GM.

**Intel** spent much of its capital budget in 1997 on increasing its capacity to produce microprocessors. The fabrication plants that the company operates can cost over a billion dollars to build and equip, and the useful life of the microprocessor produced therein could be only a few years.

**Ford Motor Company** is working with the U.S. government to develop lightweight, affordable, high-efficiency vehicles with very low emission levels. "We believe it's important to be at the forefront of alternative fuel vehicle development, wherever the most effective technology leads us. We want to be a world leader in all of our environmental efforts. Not only is it the right thing to do, we think it will give us a competitive advantage. . . .

Our Bridgend Engine Plant in the United Kingdom has just begun operating the largest solar power installation at any manufacturing site in Europe. Over a 30-year period its solar panels, which cover an area larger than five football fields, will reduce the amount of carbon dioxide emitted at the plant by more than 4,000 tons."

One reason **Gerber Childrenswear** bought **Auburn Hosiery Mills**, a large supplier of athletic socks to such companies as **Wilson Sporting Goods**, was simply to increase its buying power with cotton mills.

Time is money, but never more so than today. Companies now spend money to speed up their operating cycles, development time for new products, and construction time for capital investments. **Hewlett-Packard** now spends nine months developing a new product; the company once spent nearly six years doing so.

**Cisco Systems** spends to reduce manufacturing cycle times in order to remain competitive, because customers would cancel orders and ". . . not place future orders if shorter lead times are available from other manufacturers." Cisco probably has a difficult time in estimating the cash flows that it might lose because of customers' failure to place future orders, so the company would be likely to make cycle-time-reducing investments without favorable quantitative analyses.

**Caterpillar** undertook a six-year capital expenditure program devoted to making manufacturing more flexible. Caterpillar can now produce a wide product line without changing its assembly lines. The company reduced manufacturing times by 75 percent and inventories by 60 percent, while adding 220 new or upgraded products. Caterpillar also successfully leveraged its expertise in rubber track road-building machinery to farm equipment, which had historically run on wheels.

Sources: Annual reports from 1996 and 1997.
Rebecca Blumenstein, Robert L. Simison, and Joseph B. White, "GM Chairman Plans Sweeping Changes," The Wall Street Journal, *August 6, 1998, A3.*
Jim DuPlessis, "Selling Small Packages," Greenville News, *July 5, 1998, B14.*
Robert D. Hof, "Hewlett-Packard," Business Week, *February 13, 1995, 60.*
Peter Elstrom, "This Cat Keeps on Purring," Business Week, *January 20, 1997, 82–84.*

this chapter. Such decisions lend themselves to analytical treatment. These investments aim at increasing profitability.

- *Investments made for non-financial reasons*   A company might build a fitness center or cafeteria without much analysis of the potential benefits, simply because upper-level managers believe they should do so. Such decisions cannot show objective measures of profitability sufficient to justify them, though indirect, intangible benefits might be very high. The decision revolves around how to accomplish the desired result, for example, what equipment to purchase for the fitness center.

## CAPITAL BUDGETING FUNDAMENTALS

### COST OF CAPITAL AND CUTOFF RATES

Appendix B outlines the basic principles of time value of money, including the concept of a discount rate. For capital budgeting decisions, the theoretically correct discount rate is cost of capital. The study of cost of capital is the province of managerial finance. Briefly, **cost of capital** is the cost, expressed as a percentage, of obtaining the money needed to operate the company. Capital is obtained from two sources, creditors and owners, corresponding to the divisions of liabilities and owners' equity on the balance sheet. The cost of capital supplied by creditors is the effective interest rate on borrowings. For example, if the company makes annual interest payments of $80,000 to obtain $1,000,000 from a sale of bonds with that face value, the effective interest rate is 8 percent ($80,000/$1,000,000).[1]

The cost of equity capital is more difficult to determine, for it is based on how much investors expect the company to earn. In a *very* simple situation, we approximate the cost by dividing expected earnings by the market value of the stock. Thus, if a company is expected to earn $3 per share and the market price of the stock is $30 per share, the cost of equity capital is 10 percent ($3/$30).

Cost of capital is also the opportunity cost of investment. A company that invests in any particular project is tying up capital that it could invest elsewhere. The idea of cost of capital as an opportunity cost is illustrated by stock buy-backs that companies undertake from time to time. In a buy-back, the company buys its own shares on the open market, reflecting its view that the best investment available at that time is the company's own stock. Companies have been buying back huge amounts of their own stock, over $100 billion worth in a recent year. The 1997 annual report of **Coca-Cola** stated that it had bought back 20 million shares in 1997. The company has spent over $11 billion buying back shares since 1984. **Merck & Co**. has spent $9.7 billion buying back shares since 1988.

We are interested in cost of capital because it is the minimum acceptable rate of return on investment. But determining cost of capital is usually a complex task. Because of the practical difficulties of the task, managers might simply use their judgment to set a minimum acceptable rate, called a **cutoff rate**, **hurdle rate**, or **target rate**. Moreover, even if companies do have reasonable estimates of cost of capital, they might use a higher cutoff rate. Companies might use higher cutoff rates to provide a safety margin against unfavorable misestimates of cash flows. Remember that cash flows are estimates, some well out into the future, so safety margins are wise. Companies might also use a higher rate because productive investments must not only justify themselves, but must also cover indirect costs that might be missed in an incremental analysis. A large investment in machinery will require more workers, which will increase costs of payroll, personnel, and other support operations. Unless the company does an exhaustive ABC analysis, it will have only guesses of the extent to which such costs will increase. (A later Insight describes one company's use of ABC.) Using a higher cutoff rate accomplishes the objective of allowing for such costs.

## METHODS OF ANALYZING INVESTMENT DECISIONS

When making investment decisions, managers try to determine whether the rate of return associated with the investment is greater or less than the minimum acceptable rate. Two principal techniques are available: (1) find the rate of return associated with the project and compare that rate with the minimum acceptable

---

1 *You might recall the determination of bond prices in financial accounting. If bonds are issued at a premium or discount, the analysis is not so simple, but the refinements are not important to our discussion.*

rate, and (2) use the minimum acceptable rate to find the present value of the future returns and compare that value with the cost of the investment.

The first method is called the **internal rate of return (IRR)** method, the second the **net present value (NPV)** method. Using the NPV method, we compare the present value of future returns from an investment with the cost of obtaining those returns—the required investment. Both methods use the same basic principles. Later in this chapter, we consider two other commonly used techniques for analyzing long-term investments. These additional techniques are conceptually inferior to either the NPV or the IRR method because neither considers the time value of money.

In three of the four analytical approaches to capital budgeting decisions discussed in this chapter, returns are defined as **cash flows**, not as income. Given the emphasis on income in prior chapters, and probably in your first course in accounting, we will briefly explain why cash flows are so important in capital budgeting.

## CASH FLOWS AND BOOK INCOME

Analyses of the short-term decisions covered in Chapter 5 concentrated on whether the decision would increase income. We did not speak of cash flows in Chapter 5 because incremental revenues and incremental costs are the same as incremental cash inflows and incremental cash outflows in the short term. Thus, incremental profit is also incremental cash flow. In the short term, cash flows come in and go out within relatively short periods (during the year), so the time value of money is not significant. Income does not matter nearly as much as cash flow because without cash flow the company will not survive.

For long-term investments in depreciable assets, incomes and cash flows differ in the individual years of the life of the investment because of depreciation. Thus we cannot use income as a substitute for cash flow. The cash outflow for a depreciable asset occurs in the year of acquisition. Then, for accounting and tax purposes, the cost of that asset is depreciated over its useful life, so the incomes of those years are reduced by depreciation expense. But depreciation expense does not require a cash outlay. Therefore, the annual *income* from the investment will be less than the annual *cash flow* from the investment.

Depreciation *affects* cash flows because it is a legitimate deduction for income and tax purposes, and income taxes are a cash outflow. Hence, to determine the cash flow from an investment for a particular year, we must know the depreciation expense for that year. Later in this chapter we show how to deal with depreciation and income taxes.

Bear in mind one final and important point. As with all management decisions, the numbers used (for cash flows, useful lives, etc.) are estimates. They are almost never known with certainty at the time a manager decides on a course of action. Chapter 9 illustrates techniques managers use to allow for this uncertainty. The accompanying Insight describes some capital investments that did not pan out or were made obsolete by changes in conditions or strategies.

## CAPITAL BUDGETING METHODS

The relevant data for capital budgeting decisions are the incremental (or differential) cash flows expected from a decision and the discount rate. The following example illustrates the main points.

**SIGHT**

### Capital Disinvestments

**Coca-Cola** has for many years juggled its ownership of bottlers. Its business strategy does not include owning controlling interests in bottlers, but the company will take a controlling interest in a bottler to ". . . help focus . . . sales and marketing programs, assist in developing their business and information systems, and establish appropriate capital structure." As the company meets these objectives, it divests some of its interest.

Annual reports sometimes comment on failed investments in ways that stress larger strategic concerns. **Dole Food Companies** stated that it will ". . . reduce our involvement in business segments that require large investments with relatively low returns. . . ." Dole is committed to the food business but will "participate in the industry more selectively." Dole sold its juice business for $285 million because its top managers believed the company could not become a major factor in the industry.

**Quaker Oats** in 1995 cut loose businesses with sales of $1.6 billion. These included U.S. and European pet food operations, U.S. bean and chili, and Mexican chocolate makers. The businesses ". . . did not fit our grain-based food strategy and did not deliver adequate rates of return." In 1994, Quaker bought **Snapple** beverages for $1.9 billion. The 1995 annual report detailed some problems the company had already encountered with the Snapple supply chain. The problems continued and in 1997 Quaker threw in the towel and sold the brand at a $1.4 billion loss.

In 1997, **Hasbro** abandoned a five-year project to develop a virtual-reality game system for the mass market. The project had consumed $31 million.

*Sources: Annual reports.*

A company with a cutoff rate of 10 percent has an opportunity to introduce a new product. The best available estimates from marketing and production people are that the company will be able to sell 4,000 units per year for the next five years at $10 each. Variable costs should be $4 per unit. To make the product, the company will need machinery that costs $50,000, has a five-year life with no salvage value, and requires annual fixed cash operating costs of $8,000 for maintenance, insurance, and property taxes. (Notice that we have not included depreciation as a cost because it does not require a cash payment. We also ignore income taxes for now.)

Following are the annual incremental cash inflows.

|                                         | Annual Cash Flows Years 1–5 |
| --------------------------------------- | --------------------------- |
| Revenues ($10 × 4,000)                  | $40,000                     |
| Variable costs ($4 × 4,000)             | 16,000                      |
| Contribution margin ($6 × 4,000)        | $24,000                     |
| Cash fixed costs                        | 8,000                       |
| Net cash flow                           | $16,000                     |

Using this information, we analyze the proposed investment in two basic ways.

## NET PRESENT VALUE (NPV) METHOD

When using the NPV method we determine whether the present value of $16,000 per year to be received for five years is greater than the $50,000 outlay required today (which, obviously, has a present value of $50,000). The present value of the future cash flows of $16,000 minus the $50,000 required investment is called the NPV or the excess present value. If NPV is positive (present value of the future cash flows exceeds the required investment), the investment is desirable. If it is negative, the investment is undesirable. (As always, other factors might induce us to make investments that seem financially unwise.)

To find the present value of $16,000 per year for five years at 10 percent we go to Table B in Appendix B. We see that the factor for a series of payments of $1 for five years at 10 percent is 3.791. Multiplying this factor by $16,000 gives $60,656 as the present value of the future cash flows. This means that if you desire a 10 percent return and expect annual payments of $16,000 for five years, you would be willing to pay up to $60,656. Therefore, you are more than happy to pay only $50,000, and the investment is desirable. The NPV is $10,656 ($60,656 − $50,000). Following is a summary of the analysis.

| | |
|---|---|
| Present value of future cash flows ($16,000 × 3.791) | $60,656 |
| Investment required | 50,000 |
| Net present value | $10,656 |

## INTERNAL RATE OF RETURN (IRR) METHOD

Another approach to analyzing investment opportunities is to find the expected IRR. This method poses the question "What return are we earning if we invest $50,000 now and receive $16,000 annually for five years?" The investment is desirable if the IRR is higher than the cost of capital. The IRR is also called the **time-adjusted rate of return**. **Anheuser-Busch's** annual report states that it evaluates investments using the "discounted cash flow return on investment," which is the same as the IRR.

Financial calculators and spreadsheets calculate NPVs and IRRs. If net cash flows are equal in each year, the IRR is not difficult to find by hand. The rate equates the present value of the future cash flows with the amount to be invested now. Consider that the computation of the present value of the future flows is as follows:

$$\begin{array}{ccc} \textit{Present value of} \\ \textit{future flows} \end{array} = \begin{array}{c} \textit{Annual cash} \\ \textit{flows} \end{array} \times \begin{array}{c} \textit{Factor for the discount rate} \\ \textit{and the number of periods} \end{array}$$

To compute the IRR, we set the amount of the investment as the present value and try to determine the discount rate associated with the factor that, when multiplied by the annual flows, equals the cost of the investment. In effect, we are answering the question, "What discount rate gives the investment a net present value of zero?"

The first step is to find the factor related to both the discount rate and number of periods. Rearranging the preceding equation yields

$$\frac{Present\ value\ of\ future\ flows}{Annual\ cash\ flows} = \frac{Factor\ for\ the\ discount}{rate\ and\ the\ number\ of\ periods}$$

In our example,

$$\frac{\$50,000}{\$16,000} = 3.125$$

The second step is to relate this factor, 3.125, to the factor for the discount rate and five periods. We can find the discount rate by looking at the factors listed in the five-period row in Table B. In the five-period row under the 18 percent column, the factor is 3.127. Hence, the IRR on this project is just over 18 percent. (You should have been able to tell that the IRR on this project was greater than 10 percent because the NPV computed in the previous section is positive.)

Although we could use a financial calculator or spreadsheet to find the exact rate, we know it is about 18 percent and is higher than cost of capital. Hence, the investment is desirable. Because we are dealing with estimates of future cash flows, we do not need greater precision.

## GENERALITY OF THE ANALYSIS

Our example uses a new product, but the facts and numbers could just as well relate to an opportunity to expand productive capacity for an existing product, or to reduce costs. Companies responding to changes prompted by the new manufacturing environment are continually evaluating investments that they expect will reduce costs.

Suppose that instead of introducing a new product, the $50,000 investment is for machinery that will cut $6 from the per-unit variable production costs of an existing product through reductions in material waste and quicker processing. (The reduction in variable costs increases the contribution margin on the existing product by $6, which is equal to the contribution margin expected to result from the new product in the original example.) Assume further that the sales volume on the product is 4,000 units per year, and that the additional cash fixed costs for the new machinery are $8,000 (the same as in the original example). The incremental cash flows are then

| | |
|---|---:|
| Savings in variable costs ($6 × 4,000) | $24,000 |
| Less incremental cash fixed costs | 8,000 |
| Increase in annual net cash flows (savings) | $16,000 |

Thus, the pattern of analysis is the same whether the cash flows result from selling new products, expanding output of existing products, or saving on operating expenses. Find the incremental cash flows and then apply one of the methods described. How the cash flows come about is irrelevant.

Not-for-profit entities can also use the basic techniques. For example, a city might want to decide whether to build a new municipal building or convention center. Because cities are not subject to income taxes, the analysis we have already illustrated is adequate. As we noted earlier, however, managers in businesses must also consider the cash outflow for income taxes, which is affected by depreciation. The next section refines the analytical process to recognize the effects of taxes.

## TAXES AND DEPRECIATION

Calculating after-tax cash flows is slightly more complex. Continuing with the example of the new product, assume a 40 percent income tax rate and straight-line depreciation for income tax calculations.[2] The initial outlay is still $50,000, but the annual incremental cash flows are different because the income from the project is now subject to income taxes. The net incremental cash inflow for each of the five years is computed as follows.

| Net Incremental Cash Flow for Each Year | | |
|---|---|---|
| | Tax Computation | Cash Flow |
| Revenues | $40,000 | $40,000 |
| Cash expenses (variable and fixed) | 24,000 | 24,000 |
| Cash inflow before taxes | $16,000 | $16,000 |
| Depreciation ($50,000/5) | 10,000 | |
| Increase in taxable income | $ 6,000 | |
| Tax at 40% (cash outflow) | $ 2,400 | 2,400 |
| Increase in annual net cash inflow | | $13,600 |

The tax deduction for depreciation on the asset reduces taxes. Without the deduction, taxes would be $6,400 ($16,000 × 40%). Thus, the $10,000 in depreciation expense saves $4,000 (40% × $10,000). This important saving is called the **tax shield**, or **tax effect of depreciation**.

We do not show net income in the schedule because we want to emphasize that we are concerned with cash flows, not net income. However, you might find it easier, and more understandable, to develop an income statement and then add back depreciation to get net cash flow. (Accountants and financial managers frequently use this calculation.) The format is simple.

| | |
|---|---|
| Revenues (cash inflow) | $40,000 |
| Cash expenses | 24,000 |
| Cash inflow before taxes | $16,000 |
| Depreciation | 10,000 |
| Income before taxes | $ 6,000 |
| Tax at 40% | 2,400 |
| Increase in net income | $ 3,600 |
| Add back depreciation | 10,000 |
| Increase in annual net cash inflow | $13,600 |

This method of computing the increase in net annual cash flow is equivalent to the two-column approach used earlier. Using either approach, you must remem-

---

2  *We introduce income taxes at this stage to emphasize how they affect decisions. Accordingly, we do not yet consider the technical details of U.S. tax law. Chapter 9 introduces the Modified Accelerated Cost Recovery System and other tax issues.*

ber that taxes are determined by tax law, which does not always correspond to financial reporting principles. Chapter 9 discusses some of the differences.

Using either approach, annual incremental cash inflows are now $13,600 per year (rather than $16,000). We discount these flows at 10 percent.

| | |
|---|---:|
| Increase in annual net cash flow | $13,600 |
| Present value factor for 5 years at 10% | × 3.791 |
| Present value of future cash inflows | $51,558 |
| Investment | 50,000 |
| Net present value | $ 1,558 |

The flows have a present value of $51,558. The NPV is $1,558, so the investment is still desirable. To compute the IRR, we find the present value factor that, when multiplied by $13,600, equals $50,000. The factor is 3.677 ($50,000/$13,600). This factor falls between the factors for 10 and 12 percent. The IRR is therefore between 10 and 12 percent, but closer to 12 percent. (You should have expected an IRR greater than 10 percent, since the NPV is positive at a 10 percent cost of capital.) The actual IRR is 11.2 percent, from a Lotus 1-2-3® spreadsheet.

For the rest of the chapter, any comparisons with this basic example will refer to the analysis *with* taxes.

## UNEVEN CASH FLOWS

Our basic example had equal annual cash inflows, but it is not unusual for revenues or cash expenses, or both, to vary from year to year. For example, revenues from a new product might grow in the early years and decline in later years. Additionally, companies rarely use straight-line depreciation for income tax purposes. Accordingly, the cash outflow for taxes each year will vary. Or the investment might have a salvage value that increases cash flow in the last year. Uneven cash flows complicate the arithmetic of the analysis but do not affect the basic principles. We illustrate two situations involving uneven cash flows.

### SALVAGE VALUES

Many assets have salvage values at the ends of their useful lives. The simplest way to incorporate this factor into the analysis is to find the after-tax cash flow from the salvage value and discount it separately.

Suppose that the new asset purchased in the basic example has an expected salvage value of $5,000 at the end of its useful life. Your knowledge of financial accounting might lead you to expect the salvage value to change the depreciation of this asset. Such is not usually the case. Remember that the cash outflow for taxes depends on what is on the company's tax return, and tax law specifies that salvage values generally be ignored in computing annual depreciation. For this reason, any proceeds received from selling a depreciable asset at the end of its useful life probably will be taxed.

Using straight-line depreciation and incorporating the expected salvage value into the basic example, we get the following analysis.

### Incremental Cash Flows Years 1–5

| | Tax Computation | Cash Flow |
|---|---|---|
| Revenues | $40,000 | $40,000 |
| Cash expenses | 24,000 | 24,000 |
| Cash inflow before taxes | $16,000 | $16,000 |
| Depreciation ($50,000/5) | 10,000 | |
| Increase in taxable income | $ 6,000 | |
| Tax at 40% | 2,400 | 2,400 |
| Net cash inflow per year, as before | | $13,600 |

### Summary of Present Value of Investment

| | | |
|---|---|---|
| Annual cash flows ($13,600 × 3.791) | | $51,558 |
| Salvage value: | | |
|   Total salvage value | $5,000 | |
|   Tax on salvage value at 40% | 2,000 | |
|   After-tax cash inflow from salvage value | $3,000 | |
|   Times present value factor for 5 years | | |
|     hence at 10% | ×0.621 | |
|   Present value of salvage value | | 1,863 |
| Total present value | | $53,421 |
| Investment | | 50,000 |
| Net present value | | $ 3,421 |

NPV was $1,558 when taxes were first considered. The new NPV, $3,421, is higher by the $1,863 present value of the salvage value. We could use a financial calculator or spreadsheet to find the IRR. Note that we cannot simply look up a value in Table B because we no longer have equal cash flows in every year. We could use trial-and-error or interpolate to approximate the IRR. The IRR will be higher than before because the NPV is higher. It is 12.6 percent.

## VARIATIONS IN ANNUAL FLOWS

We said earlier that cash flows vary if sales vary during the life of a project. The uneven flows change the analysis only in that we need to discount the flows individually, instead of as an annuity.

To illustrate, let us return to our basic example of a new product. We assume no salvage value, but assume that sales are expected to be 3,000, 3,000, 4,000, 5,000, and 5,000 in years one through five, respectively. (The total is still 20,000 units for the five years.) Without making any calculations, can you tell whether the investment will be more or less desirable than it was when sales were spread evenly over the five years? That is, will NPV be higher or lower than the $1,558 determined earlier? If you decided that the investment will be less desirable (lower NPV) you are correct; sales occur later, so cash will be received later. The present value of a cash receipt declines the longer you must wait to receive it. (Of course, variable costs occur later too, but the inflow from sales exceeds the outflow from variable costs.)

The following schedule shows the calculations using the revised sales forecast. For brevity, we use the $6 per-unit contribution margin instead of showing both revenues and variable costs. As expected, NPV is now lower (negative $7 vs. $1,588), and the investment is not desirable because NPV is negative. However, the NPV is so small that even a minute error in estimating cash flows could make it positive. Notice that the totals are the same as they were before, which you can verify by multiplying the numbers in the previous schedule by five. Thus, total cash flow before taxes is $80,000 ($16,000 × 5), total income taxes are $12,000 ($2,400 × 5), and so on. The difference arises when the cash flows are converted to present values. The delay in the cash flows reduces the present value of those flows.

### Cash Flows and Present Values

| | Year | | | | | |
| --- | --- | --- | --- | --- | --- | --- |
| | 1 | 2 | 3 | 4 | 5 | Total |
| Unit sales | 3,000 | 3,000 | 4,000 | 5,000 | 5,000 | 20,000 |
| Contribution margin at $6 | $18,000 | $18,000 | $24,000 | $30,000 | $30,000 | $120,000 |
| Less cash fixed costs | 8,000 | 8,000 | 8,000 | 8,000 | 8,000 | 40,000 |
| Pretax cash inflow | $10,000 | $10,000 | $16,000 | $22,000 | $22,000 | $ 80,000 |
| Less depreciation | 10,000 | 10,000 | 10,000 | 10,000 | 10,000 | 50,000 |
| Income before taxes | $    0 | $    0 | $ 6,000 | $12,000 | $12,000 | $ 30,000 |
| Income taxes at 40% | 0 | 0 | 2,400 | 4,800 | 4,800 | 12,000 |
| Net income | $    0 | $    0 | $ 3,600 | $ 7,200 | $ 7,200 | $ 18,000 |
| Add depreciation | 10,000 | 10,000 | 10,000 | 10,000 | 10,000 | 50,000 |
| Net cash flow | $10,000 | $10,000 | $13,600 | $17,200 | $17,200 | $ 68,000 |
| Present value factor (Table A) | 0.909 | 0.826 | 0.751 | 0.683 | 0.621 | |
| Present value | $ 9,090 | $ 8,260 | $10,214 | $11,748 | $10,681 | $ 49,993 |
| Less investment | | | | | | 50,000 |
| Net present value | | | | | | $      (7) |

Finding the IRR by hand can be difficult when there are uneven cash flows. Spreadsheets and financial calculators make such calculations. Here the IRR is just below 10 percent because the NPV is negative, but tiny.

## DECISION RULES

Looking only at the quantitative aspects of an investment opportunity, the decision rules for the two methods of analysis we describe are simple. Under the NPV method, a project having a positive NPV should be accepted; others should be rejected. Under the IRR method, a project having an IRR greater than the company's cost of capital should be accepted. The relationship of the two criteria is as follows:

1.   If IRR is less than the discount rate, NPV is negative.
2.   If NPV is positive, IRR is greater than the discount rate.

When analyzing any single project for acceptance or rejection, both methods lead to the same decision. We discuss the problem of multiple investment opportunities in Chapter 9.

## STRATEGIC AND QUALITATIVE CONSIDERATIONS

Chapter 5 stated that qualitative, and hard-to-quantify, concerns often override quantitative analyses in short-term decisions. The same is true with capital budgeting decisions. Strategic considerations, which are qualitative, play an important part in major capital investment decisions. Companies usually commit themselves to following particular strategies and must be able to look past purely quantitative analyses to pursue those strategies. The accompanying Insight describes some decisions where cash flows were difficult to predict, but where strategic and qualitative concerns were critical.

Companies following cost leadership strategies will use activity-based costing to look for ways to reduce the levels of various drivers. And of course, companies following differentiation strategies are nonetheless concerned with costs. In the mid-1990s, **Procter & Gamble**, the consumer-products behemoth, began a program to pare down its product offerings, standardize its products, and reduce trade promotions and coupons. The company once offered 31 versions of Head & Shoulders shampoo and 52 varieties of Crest. P&G is "hacking away at layers of complexity in a drive to cut costs, serve customers better, and expand globally." The company found that reducing special price promotions caused the percentage of invoices that require manual correction to drop from 31 to 6 percent.[3]

Qualitative concerns are becoming increasingly important as companies adopt advanced manufacturing techniques. Some of the advantages of such techniques are difficult to quantify and might therefore be overlooked. For instance, while managers agree that increasing the quality of a product is desirable, the monetary effect is not easy to estimate. Similar considerations arise with such benefits as reducing cycle time. An early Insight mentioned companies that have invested in cutting cycle time or new product development time.

**Ford** has cut $11 billion from its new product budget for the next five years. It was able to do so because it has been reducing the number of "platforms," or basic cars. (For example, the Ford Taurus and Mercury Sable are built on the same platform.) Ford will use the same platform for more cars and will eliminate some platforms. Ford plans to go from its current 24 platforms to 16 in the year 2000. Ford expected to save $1 billion in 1996 by reducing "complexity, redundancy, and waste in its product-development effort."[4]

These improvements should increase cash flows and bring them in sooner, but managers will have a great deal of difficulty estimating the cash flow effects of such investments. However, while quantitative estimates of benefits of such improvements are difficult, managers cannot assume that doing nothing to improve

---

3 *Zachary Schiller, et. al., "Make It Simple,"* Business Week, *September 9, 1996, 96–104; "Quality: How to Make It Pay,"* Business Week, *August 8, 1994, 57.*
4 *Oscar Suris, "Ford Slashes $11 Billion Out of Budget for New Products Over Next Five Years,"* The Wall Street Journal, *February 29, 1996, A4.*

 **SIGHT**

### Qualitative Concerns in Capital Budgeting

**Toyota Motor Company** has an explicit qualitative goal that investments in plant automation should improve working conditions and make employees more comfortable and put them under less stress. The company expects these better conditions to reduce worker turnover, which in turn will save on training costs. However, the company is committed to such investments even if the tangible, quantifiable benefits are insufficient to justify the investment. Some automated operations now cost more than they would if people were still doing them.

After **CBS** lost the broadcast rights to National Football League games in 1994, eight affiliate stations jumped to other networks. CBS's highly-ranked show, *60 Minutes*, which aired after football games, suffered serious ratings declines. Some observers said that morale at the network suffered. In 1997, CBS outbid **NBC** for American Football Conference games, paying a price that many observers believed was economically unjustified. The losing bidder, NBC, then spent $900 million to keep its hit show, *ER*, in the fold, an amount that prompted one analyst to say that "There's no financial logic here, it's all strategic." NBC also offered Jerry Seinfeld, of *Seinfeld*, spectacular amounts, including **General Electric** shares (GE owns NBC), to keep the show on the air.

Major corporations have been buying sports franchises in recent years, sometimes paying what appear to be exhorbitant amounts. One observer stated that ". . . cash flows are generally low . . . but companies are not buying for value, . . . the payout is in the pipeline." The reference was to how baseball stadiums have increasingly become like theme parks, generating extensive revenues from off-field sources.

*Sources: Annual reports.*
*Alex Taylor III, "How Toyota Copes with Hard Times," Fortune, January 28, 1993, 78–81.*
*Mark Hyman, "How to Lose Fans and Get Richer," Business Week, January 26, 1998, 70.*
*Elizabeth Lesley Stevens and Ronald Grover, "Prime Time Emergency," Business Week, January 26, 1998, 40.*
*Roy S. Johnson, "Take Me Out to the Boardroom," Fortune, July 21, 1997, 44.*

product quality and reduce cycle time will permit the company to continue as it has. The company could well suffer as a result of not accepting such investments.

Having emphasized the importance of qualitative considerations, we must also point out that ignoring quantitative measures of profitability is also unwise. It is not correct to say that companies should relentlessly pursue objectives that entail large, unprofitable investments. At some point, reality must intrude and managers must pay attention to profitability or else the company could go under. Where qualitative factors are important, managers should still perform quantitative analyses so they will have a better idea of the cost to the company of accepting a particular qualitative goal as paramount.

# OTHER METHODS OF CAPITAL BUDGETING

Although the NPV and IRR methods are theoretically sound, some managers argue that they are not practical because of the many estimates involved (cost of capital, cash flows, useful lives, etc.). Interestingly, the methods advocated by these managers, payback and book rate of return, require most of the same estimates that NPV and IRR require.

## PAYBACK

One of the most commonly used methods of capital budgeting is the **payback** technique. This method poses the question "How long will it take to recover the investment?" If the annual cash inflows are equal, the payback period is

$$\frac{Payback}{period} = \frac{Investment}{Annual\ cash\ return}$$

Payback determines the rapidity of recovering an investment. In our basic example, the required investment of $50,000 generates annual net cash inflows of $13,600 and has a payback period of 3.7 years ($50,000/$13,600). Note that we automatically compute the payback period when we calculate the IRR on an investment with equal annual cash flows. The 3.7 (we used 3.677) payback period is also the present value factor we looked for in the five-year row of Table B.

The payback method requires a cutoff value above which you reject investments and below which you accept them. We are unaware of any analytical way to set such a cutoff (as cost of capital is an analytical way to set the discount rate). Managers simply state the acceptable limit to the payback period. Some companies impose an implicit payback period by discounting cash flows only up to some specified number of years, and ignoring any potential flows beyond that period. This practice compensates for rapid technological obsolescence that many companies face. **Eastman Chemical** stated that it ". . . will favor projects that require smaller initial investment and provide quicker returns." The company adopted that strategy because it established an overall goal of providing more rapid returns to its shareholders. The company still uses NPV, with a cutoff rate that is five percentage points higher than its cost of capital. Such a margin decreases risk.

### Advantages

The payback period is important to a company especially concerned about liquidity. Payback also serves as a rough screening device for investment proposals. A long payback period usually means a low rate of return, and an extremely short payback period often suggests a good investment. Some companies use payback as a measure of risk because the longer it takes to get your money back, the greater the risk that you won't get the money. As the time horizon lengthens, more uncertainties arise. Inflation might get worse; interest rates might rise or fall; new technology might make the investment obsolete. Because of the increased uncertainty, a manager might prefer a project that pays back its investment in two years to one that takes ten years, even if the one with the ten-year payback period has a higher expected NPV and IRR. Payback can therefore be helpful for companies investing in foreign countries, as we shall see shortly.

### Flaws of Payback

Payback has two very serious faults. The first is that it tells nothing about the profitability of the investment. Payback emphasizes the return of the investment but ignores the return *on* the investment.

Consider the following two investments.

|  | A | B |
|---|---|---|
| Investment | $10,000 | $10,000 |
| Useful life in years | 5 | 15 |
| Annual cash flows over the useful lives | $2,500 | $2,000 |

Investment A's payback period is four years ($10,000/$2,500); investment B's is five years ($10,000/$2,000). Using the payback criterion, investment A is better than investment B because its payback period is shorter. Yet it should be obvious that investment B is superior; the returns from A cease one year after the payback period, while B continues to return cash for ten more years.

The second serious fault of the payback method is that it ignores the timing of the expected future cash flows and so ignores the time value of money. This fault, like the method's failure to consider years after the payback period, can lead to poor decisions. Consider the following two investments.

|  | X | Y |
|---|---|---|
| Investment | $10,000 | $10,000 |
| Cash inflows by year: |  |  |
| 1 | $ 2,000 | $ 6,000 |
| 2 | 2,000 | 3,000 |
| 3 | 6,000 | 1,000 |
| 4–8 | 3,000 | 3,000 |

Both X and Y have payback periods of three years. They also show equal total returns. But the investment in Y will be recovered much more quickly than that in X and so the NPV of investment Y is higher than that of X, as is the IRR. (IRR on investment X is approximately 25 percent, whereas that on investment Y is about 32 percent.)

## BOOK RATE OF RETURN

Another commonly used capital budgeting method is the **book rate of return** technique. Under this method, the average annual expected book income is divided by the average book investment in the project. That is,

$$\textit{Average book rate of return} \; = \; \frac{\textit{Average annual expected book income}}{\textit{Average book investment}}$$

Consider again the $50,000 investment opportunity in our basic example. The book net income for each of the five years of the project's life is $3,600. The average book investment in this project is $25,000 ($50,000/2). With an annual net income of $3,600 and an average book investment of $25,000, the average book rate of return is 14.4 percent ($3,600/$25,000). This return is an average rate of return because we have used the average book investment. The book rate of return for each year will be different because the average book investment in the project will change with each year's depreciation. For example, using the average book investment in year one, the book rate of return is 8 percent ($3,600/$45,000); in the last year, the book rate of return is 72 percent ($3,600/$5,000).

Let us compare these results with those obtained using the IRR method. The IRR on this project is 11.2 percent. If the cutoff rate is above 14.4 percent, both the NPV and the IRR methods of analysis suggest that the investment should be rejected. Use of the book rate of return as the criterion for evaluating investments could mislead managers to accept this investment opportunity.

To emphasize the deficiencies of the book rate of return method, consider another simpler example. As shown in the following analysis, investments A and B require identical investments ($10,000) and produce identical total net incomes, identical average net incomes, and identical book rates of return of 26.7 percent. Investment A is clearly superior to investment B because its flows come in faster. (The IRR on investment A is about 23 percent, whereas that on investment B is only about 15 percent.)

|  | A | B |
|---|---|---|
| Pretax cash flows by year: |  |  |
| 1 | $10,000 | $ 2,000 |
| 2 | 5,000 | 5,000 |
| 3 | 1,666 | 9,666 |
| Totals | $16,666 | $16,666 |
| Depreciation | 10,000 | 10,000 |
| Income before taxes | $ 6,666 | $ 6,666 |
| Income taxes at 40% | 2,666 | 2,666 |
| Total net income | $ 4,000 | $ 4,000 |
| Average net income, $4,000/3 | $ 1,333 | $ 1,333 |
| Average book rate of return, $1,333/$5,000 | 26.7% | 26.7% |

The book rate of return method almost always misstates the internal rate of return because it ignores the timing of the cash flows and, therefore, the time value of money. This flaw makes it an unsatisfactory method of capital budgeting.

## SUMMARY EVALUATION OF METHODS

Again, qualitative factors can prevail over the decision rules for all of the methods. The critical difference between the NPV and IRR methods on the one hand, and the payback and book rate of return methods on the other hand, is the attention to the timing of the expected cash flows. The first two methods, called **discounted cash flow (DCF)** techniques, consider the timing of the cash flows; the last two methods do not. Their recognition of the time value of money makes DCF techniques conceptually superior, but payback is often used in conjunction with those techniques.

As stated earlier, some managers argue that DCF techniques are too complex or that they require too many estimates to make them useful in practice. We see little merit in these charges. All four methods require about the same estimates.

DCF methods require estimates of future cash flows and the timing of those flows. The book rate of return method requires estimates of future net incomes, which means making essentially the same estimates as those required to estimate cash flows. The payback method requires estimating cash flows but not useful lives. One point in favor of the payback method is that it emphasizes near-term cash flows, which are usually easier to predict than flows in later years. However, as we pointed out, unless consideration is given to useful life, the payback method could lead to very poor decisions.

The NPV, IRR, and book rate of return methods all require an estimate of the cost of capital, or at least a decision as to a minimum acceptable rate of return. The payback method requires a decision regarding the minimum acceptable payback period. Thus, DCF techniques are no less realistic or practical than the other two approaches. The conceptual superiority of DCF techniques argues strongly for their use, though the payback period should probably not be ignored.

## INVESTING DECISIONS AND FINANCING DECISIONS

You have probably noticed that none of our examples considered how the company will finance the project. That is, we did not say whether the company plans to issue debt, common stock, some combination of the two, or finance the investment using cash flows from existing operations. We did so because the financing of a project is irrelevant to its evaluation. The investing decision nearly always should be kept separate from the financing decision.

It might be tempting to argue that if the company plans to finance an investment with 7 percent debt, it should use 7 percent to discount the expected cash flows. Also, it might be tempting to subtract the interest payments as part of the cash flow computation. Resist these temptations!

A company should not accept projects that will return less than cost of capital, because the company must earn a satisfactory return for all investors—both creditors and stockholders. Both types of capital suppliers are concerned about the safety of their investments and therefore monitor company solvency by watching such factors as the ratio of debt to equity. A company that makes too liberal use of debt and earns returns that exceed the interest rate but not cost of capital will have to pay exorbitant rates to raise capital. (Stockholders will sell their stock, which reduces the price and thus raises the cost of equity capital. Lenders will insist on higher interest rates, thus raising the cost of debt capital.)

Including interest payments as part of the cash flow computation reflects a misunderstanding of the concept of discounting. The discount rate *automatically* provides for not only the recovery of the investment, but also for a return on the investment at least equal to the discount rate, which is cost of capital or a cutoff rate. Thus, subtracting interest payments to arrive at the net cash flow provides for the cost of debt twice—once by subtracting the interest payments, and again by using a discount rate that includes the cost of obtaining both the debt and equity capital.

## INTERNATIONAL ASPECTS OF CAPITAL BUDGETING

Investing in foreign countries entails special problems and opportunities. On the positive side, many countries eagerly seek foreign investment and will offer tax and other concessions to make them more attractive to foreign companies. When **Daewoo Electronics**, a large South Korean company, expanded its manufacturing operations in Europe, the governments gave the company cash grants, low-interest loans, plant sites, exemptions from taxes, and even discounts on electricity.[5] The U.S. is certainly amenable to foreign investment. Several states offered concessions to attract a **BMW** plant a few years ago. The plant went to South Carolina, which, along with some local governments, offered a package of tax abatement and other incentives reported to total $100 million.

In today's global economy, many once-closed nations are opening up for investment, particularly formerly communist nations. Russia and China are the most prominent and have attracted the most attention. Investing in such countries is not for the faint of heart. Investing in any new market is risky because the investor must deal with a new culture, with different customs, practices, and mores. China has offered many concessions in recent years, as have some of the formerly communist countries in Eastern Europe.

Capital budgeting for foreign operations is much more complicated and much less precise. Some factors that can be critical in making investments in foreign countries follow.

- The risk of nationalization (a country seizes the property of foreign companies with limited or no compensation) is very great in some countries.

- Instability in economic, social, and political conditions can cause serious losses. In emerging countries such as formerly communist countries, such risks are magnified.

- Astronomical inflation can wipe out the value of an investment.

- Restrictions on trade and on repatriation of cash can limit the company's ability to return its investment to its home country.

- Exchange rate fluctuations increase risk because overseas investments might be profitable in the local currency, but unprofitable when translated back to the home currency. Building plants and raising capital in foreign countries alleviates this risk.

- Failure to respect local customs and traditions could jeopardize investments.

The Russian and Asian financial meltdowns of 1998 soured many investors on the regions. These crises were yet more examples of the risks of doing business in countries without long traditions of economic and political stability. For some time companies doing business in China have found that its lack of protection for property rights created serious problems. Different companies have responded differently. **Chrysler** backed out of building minivans in China because the government required that the company turn over all of its technology for the van and allow China to sell the design to other Asian counties. **Mercedes-Benz** accepted those conditions and began building vehicles in China.

Brazil had been an economic backwater for many years, but began to get its house in order in the late 1970s. By the early 1990s, many U.S., European, and Japanese companies were investing heavily there. As Brazil instituted free-market reforms, its economy grew, its consumers became better-off, and the investment climate brightened.[6]

---

5  Worldbusiness, *Spring 1995, 20.*
6  *Ian Katz, "It's Carnival Time for Investors,"* Business Week, *March 13, 1995.*

## SUMMARY

Decisions to spend cash now and recoup the investment over a period longer than a year are capital budgeting decisions. Evaluating such decisions requires determining the investment and its resulting cash flows. Investments provide future cash flows through additional revenues and costs, and through cost savings. Critical to capital budgeting is that most, if not all, of the numbers used in the analyses are estimates. Depreciation, a noncash expense, affects income taxes and must therefore be recognized.

Capital budgeting decisions require recognizing the time value of money. The two approaches we recommend, called discounted cash flow techniques, are the net present value (NPV) and the internal rate of return (IRR) methods. Two other methods—payback and book rate of return—are often used, but are conceptually inferior because they fail to consider the time value of money. Nevertheless, such methods, particularly payback, might be useful as rough screening devices. The source of financing a particular investment is not relevant to analyzing it.

## KEY TERMS

book rate of return   *(343)*

capital budgeting decisions   *(327)*

cash flows   *(332)*

cost of capital   *(331)*

cutoff rate   *(331)*

discounted cash flow (DCF)   *(344)*

hurdle rate   *(331)*

internal rate of return (IRR)   *(332)*

long-term decisions   *(327)*

net present value (NPV)   *(332)*

payback   *(342)*

target rate   *(331)*

tax effect of depreciation   *(336)*

tax shield   *(336)*

time-adjusted rate of return   *(334)*

time value of money   *(328)*

## KEY FORMULAS

Present value of future flows = Annual cash flows × Present value factor

$$\text{Net present value} = \text{Present value of future flows} - \text{Required investment}$$

$$\text{Payback period} = \frac{\text{Investment required}}{\text{Annual cash returns}}$$

$$\text{Average book rate of return} = \frac{\text{Average annual expected book income}}{\text{Average book investment}}$$

## REVIEW PROBLEM

Belmont Maury Company has the opportunity to market a new product. The sales manager believes the company could sell 20,000 units per year at $10 per unit for five years. The product requires machinery that costs $200,000 and has a five-year life and no salvage value. Variable costs per unit are $4. The machinery has fixed operating costs requiring cash disbursements of $30,000 annually. Straight-line depreciation will be used for both book and tax purposes. The tax rate is 40% and the cutoff rate is 14%.

### Required

1. Determine the increase in annual net income and in annual cash inflows expected from the investment.
2. Determine the NPV of the investment.
3. Determine the payback period.
4. Determine the approximate IRR of the investment.
5. Determine the book rate of return on the average investment.
6. Suppose the machinery has salvage value of $5,000 at the end of its useful life, which is not considered in determining depreciation expense. The tax rate on the gain at the end of the asset's life is 40%. How will your answer to requirement 2 change?

### ANSWER TO REVIEW PROBLEM

1.

|  | Tax Computation | Cash Flow |
|---|---|---|
| Sales (20,000 × $10) | $200,000 | $200,000 |
| Variable cost (20,000 × $4) | 80,000 | 80,000 |
| Contribution margin (20,000 × $6) | $120,000 | $120,000 |
| Fixed cash operating costs | 30,000 | 30,000 |
| Cash inflow before taxes | $ 90,000 | $ 90,000 |
| Depreciation ($200,000/5) | 40,000 | |
| Increase in taxable income | $ 50,000 | |
| Income tax at 40% rate | 20,000 | 20,000 |
| Increase in net income | $ 30,000 | |
| Add depreciation | 40,000 | |
| Net cash inflow per year | $ 70,000 | $ 70,000 |

2. $40,310, calculated as follows:

| | |
|---|---|
| Net cash inflow per year | $ 70,000 |
| Present value factor, five-year annuity at 14% (Table B) | × 3.433 |
| Present value of future net cash flows | $240,310 |
| Less investment | 200,000 |
| Net present value | $ 40,310 |

3. The payback period is 2.857 years, which is $200,000 divided by $70,000.
4. IRR is just barely over 22%. The factor to seek is 2.857, which is the payback period calculated in requirement 3. The closest factor in the five-year row of Table B is 2.864, which is the 22% factor. Because 2.857 is less than 2.864, the rate is greater than 22%. (Remember, the higher the rate, the lower the factor.)
5. The book rate of return on the average investment is 30%, which is annual net income of $30,000 divided by the average investment of $100,000 ($200,000/2).
6. The only change required is the determination of the present value of the salvage value less tax on the gain.

| | |
|---|---|
| Salvage value | $ 5,000 |
| Tax at 40% | 2,000 |
| Net cash inflow, end of year 5 | $ 3,000 |
| Present value factor for single payment, 5 years at 14% (Table A) | × 0.519 |
| Present value of salvage value | $ 1,557 |
| Net present value from requirement 2 | 40,310 |
| Net present value | $41,867 |

Notice that we did not have to recompute annual net cash flows. The company still used $40,000 for depreciation expense. Therefore, at the end of five years, the machinery will have a book value of zero and the gain on disposal will equal the salvage value.

## ASSIGNMENT MATERIAL

### INTERNET ACTIVITY

Find an annual report of a company in a heavy manufacturing industry such as automobiles or farm equipment. Find a report of a company in the information technology field such as a software company or one that does business on the Internet. How much did these companies spend on capital investments in their most recent fiscal years? What do they say about their investments—do they state policies or strategies that guide investment? What differences do the companies exhibit?

### QUESTIONS FOR DISCUSSION

**8-1  Risk and capital investments**   What are some of the principal risks of each of the following decisions?

**Procter & Gamble**, the household and personal products giant, builds a new plant to increase its capacity to manufacture one of its major products.

**Merck & Co.**, the pharmaceutical giant, allocates several hundred million dollars to develop a new drug.

**8-2  Payback and risk**   Suppose you are a merchant in medieval Europe and are considering two investments, both of which require $1 million to buy a cargo of merchandise and ship it to a distant country. One voyage will take a year to complete, the other five years. The expected after-tax cash returns at the ends of the periods are $1,160,000 for the one-year voyage and $3,713,000 for the five-year voyage. The expected IRRs on the voyages are 16% and 30%, respectively and, when a cutoff rate of 10% is used, the NPVs are $54,545 and $1,305,481. Which investment would you take?

**8-3  Government actions and capital investment**   The federal government regulates many aspects of economic activity, and is especially concerned with encouraging production and investment to maintain high employment while not allowing excessive inflation. You are the controller of a large manufacturing company that employs a great many people. How will each of the following actions affect capital spending? Explain why.

1. The Federal Reserve Board lowers interest rates.
2. The federal government enacts tax legislation that allows companies to expense assets when purchased instead of depreciating them over their useful lives.
3. The federal government enacts legislation that will provide health care coverage for everyone. The cost will be financed by a tax on payroll. That is, for each dollar a company pays its employees, it will pay a tax to be determined annually. Your company now provides health insurance for its employees. You will no longer have to pay for insurance, but the payroll tax will greatly exceed the cost of insurance you now provide.
4. New trade legislation will reduce tariffs on foreign products entering the U.S. and on U.S. products entering other countries. Some segments of your company now compete with foreign companies for sales in the U.S.

**8-4  Boeing's new airplanes**  **Boeing** has announced two new versions of the 747 that it expects will require $4 to $5 billion in development costs. One will fly 430 passengers 8,500 miles without refueling (existing 747s are about 400 and 7,500, respectively), the other can carry 500 passengers 7,800 miles. **British Airways** wants to buy the 500-passenger version. **Air Korea** and **Singapore Airlines** are interested in the version that flies 8,500 miles non-stop.

**Required**
Why are the named airlines especially interested in the specific models? You might reason back from the characteristics of the aircraft to the types of flying the airlines do.

**8-5  Capital budgeting—effects of events**  You have evaluated a capital expenditure proposal for new machinery that will save labor costs and increase output of various of your products. How will each of the following events, not anticipated in the original analysis, affect the evaluation? That is, make it more attractive, less attractive, or have no effect? Consider each event independently.

1. Your company signs a new contract with its union. The negotiated wage rate for all categories of workers is higher than the prevailing rate.
2. Your company raises the selling prices of its products.
3. Your customers are companies in the auto industry. One of them announces that it expects its suppliers, such as your company, to reduce their prices over the next few years.

**8-6  Exceptions to decision rules**

**Required**
Answer the following questions independently.

1. Using its 14% target rate, Agro Inc., a farming company, determined that an investment in a tobacco farm had an NPV of $1,000,000. Suggest several reasons why Agro might reject the project despite its positive NPV.
2. The top managers of J&G Products, Inc., a manufacturer of high-quality electronic equipment, have established a minimum IRR for investment projects of 30%. The analysis of one project shows an IRR of 25%. Suggest some reasons why J&G might accept the project despite its failure to meet the 30% minimum IRR.

## EXERCISES

### 8-7   Discounting

**Required**

1. Find the approximate IRR for each of the following investments.
   (a) An investment of $30,000 with annual cash flows of $5,000 for 14 years.
   (b) An investment of $90,000 with a single return of $120,000 at the end of three years.
2. Find the NPVs of the following investments at a 12% discount rate.
   (a) Annual flows of $30,000 for ten years are produced by an investment of $160,000.
   (b) An investment of $30,000 with annual flows of $8,000 for four years and a single return of $4,000 at the end of the fifth year.

### 8-8   NPV and IRR methods   Jones Secretarial Service is thinking of buying some new word-processing equipment that promises to save $6,000 in cash operating costs per year. The equipment will cost $16,800. Its estimated useful life is four years. It will have no salvage value. (Ignore taxes.)

**Required**

1. Compute NPV if the minimum desired rate of return is 10%.
2. Determine the approximate IRR.

### 8-9   Discounting

**Required**

Solve each of the following problems independently.

1. Carol Conner starts college in one year. Her father wishes to set up a fund for her to use for the $15,400 she will need each year for four years. Carol will make withdrawals at the beginning of each school year. If Mr. Conner can invest at 9%, how much must he invest today to provide for Carol's college expenses?
2. Porter Gross is about to retire from his job. His pension benefits have accumulated to the point where he could receive a lump-sum payment of $500,000 or $70,000 per year for ten years, paid at the ends of years. Gross has no dependents and expects to live for ten years after he retires. If he can invest at 8%, which option should he take?
3. You have just won the $5,000,000 grand prize in a state lottery. The prize will be paid in $167,000 installments for 30 years. If your interest rate is 6%, how much would you take now, instead of accepting the annuity?

### 8-10   Time value of money relationships

**Required**

Answer the following questions.

1. A person received a single payment of $6,440 as a result of investing five years ago at an interest rate of 10%. How much did the person invest?
2. An investment of $2,000 returned a single payment of $5,400 at an interest rate of 18%. How many years elapsed between the investment and the return?
3. A person received seven annual payments of $1,000 from an investment. The interest rate was 12%. What was the amount of the investment?
4. An investment of $1,000 returned $343 annually for some years. The rate of interest was 14%. How many payments were received?

5. A $120,000 investment made today will provide a 12% return. The returns will be paid in equal amounts over 12 years. What is the amount of the annual payment?

**8-11    *Basic capital budgeting without taxes***    Nancy Vickrey owns Bytes, a popular restaurant in Silicon Valley. She has been thinking about acquiring a new, automated dishwasher, but is unsure whether it is a good idea. She asks for your advice and gives you the following information.

| | |
|---|---|
| Cost of dishwasher | $5,000 |
| Useful life | four years, no salvage value |
| Annual cash savings | $2,000 |

Ms. Vickrey tells you that she expects a 10% return on the business.

**Required**
1. Calculate the NPV of the investment.
2. Calculate the approximate IRR on the investment.
3. Determine the payback period for the investment.
4. Determine the book rate of return on the average investment.

**8-12    *Basic capital budgeting—taxes (continuation of 8-11)***

**Required**
Redo Exercise 8-11 with Vickrey now being subject to a 30% income tax rate.

**8-13    *Basic cost savings***    Grove City Pottery currently makes 400,000 large strawberry jars per year at a variable cost of $13.85. Equipment is available for $800,000 that will reduce variable costs by $2.25 per unit, while increasing cash fixed costs by $300,000. The equipment will have no salvage value at the end of its four-year life and will be depreciated using the straight-line method. Grove City faces a 40% income tax rate and a 12% cutoff rate.

**Required**
1. Determine the NPV of the investment.
2. Determine the change in NPV if the equipment has a $25,000 residual value.

**8-14    *Basic capital budgeting—services***    Carolina Consulting Group does political polling and market research. The company can buy automated telephone-dialing equipment and related software that should reduce its annual cash operating costs by $80,000. The equipment and software cost $240,000 and have a five-year life, with no salvage value. Cost of capital is 14%. Ignore taxes.

**Required**
1. Determine the NPV of the investment.
2. Determine the approximate IRR.
3. Determine the payback period.
4. Determine the book rate of return on the average investment.

**8-15    *Basic capital budgeting with taxes (continuation of 8-14)***

**Required**
Redo Exercise 8-14 with a 40% income tax rate.

**8-16   *Comparison of methods (continued in Chapter 9)*   Baltusrol Inc. has the following three investment opportunities.**

|  | A | B | C |
|---|---|---|---|
| Cost | $70,000 | $ 70,000 | $ 70,000 |
| Cash inflows by year: |  |  |  |
| Year 1 | $35,000 | $ 35,000 | $ 4,000 |
| Year 2 | 35,000 | 10,000 | 8,000 |
| Year 3 | 0 | 45,000 | 10,000 |
| Year 4 | 5,000 | 20,000 | 98,000 |
| Total | $75,000 | $110,000 | $120,000 |
| Average annual income | $ 1,250 | $ 10,000 | $ 12,500 |

**Required**
1. Rank the investment opportunities in order of desirability using (a) payback period, (b) average book rate of return (use average net book value of the investment as the denominator), and (c) NPV using a 16% discount rate.
2. Comment on the results.

**8-17   *NPV*   The owner-operator of Midway Driving Range recently talked to a salesperson from PickTech Co. PickTech has a machine that will pick up balls at an annual cash cost of $6,600 plus $0.10 per bucket. The machine costs $40,000 and has a five-year life. The range presently pays high school students $0.90 per bucket to pick up golf balls. Volume for the driving range is about 42,000 buckets per year. The combined state and federal tax rate is 30% and the appropriate discount rate is 16%.**

**Required**
Determine the NPV of the investment and identify one or more nonquantitative factors that might influence the decision.

**8-18   *Capital budgeting for a hospital*   Carter Memorial Hospital has the opportunity to acquire a two-year-old blood gas analyzer for $500,000. These analyzers usually last 12 years, so Carter will get ten years use from it. The analyzer will have no salvage value. Estimated revenue is $230,000 per year; estimated annual cash costs are $120,000. The hospital uses a 14% discount rate for capital budgeting decisions.**

**Required**
Determine (a) NPV, (b) payback period, and (c) approximate IRR.

**8-19   *Understanding IRR*   You want to withdraw $20,000 from a bank account at the end of each of the next three years. The interest rate is 10%.**

**Required**
1. How much must you have in the bank at the beginning of the first year to be able to make the subsequent $20,000 withdrawals?
2. Schedule the activity in the bank account for the three years. Set up columns for Beginning Balance, Interest, Withdrawal, and Ending Balance. Interest is earned at 10% of the beginning balance of each year.

**8-20   *NPV and IRR*   Boston Boots makes high-quality hiking boots. Its managers believe that the company can increase productivity by acquiring some new machinery but are unsure whether it would be profitable.**

The machinery costs $2,000,000, has a four-year life with no salvage value, and should save about $8 per pair in variable manufacturing costs. Annual volume is 100,000 pairs of boots. The company uses straight-line depreciation and has a 40% income tax rate and a 12% cost of capital.

**Required**
1. Calculate the NPV of the investment.
2. Calculate the approximate IRR.

**8-21  Relationships**

**Required**
Fill in the blanks for each of the following independent cases. In all cases the investment has a useful life of ten years and no salvage value.

|  | (a) Annual Net Cash Inflow | (b) Investment | (c) Cost of Capital | (d) Internal Rate of Return | (e) Net Present Value |
|---|---|---|---|---|---|
| 1. | $ 45,000 | $188,640 | 14% | ____ | $_____ |
| 2. | $ 75,000 | $_____ | 12% | 18% | $_____ |
| 3. | $_____ | $300,000 | ____ | 16% | $ 81,440 |
| 4. | $_____ | $450,000 | 12% | ____ | $115,000 |

## PROBLEMS

**8-22  Comparison of book return and NPV (continued in Chapter 9)**  Welton Company is introducing a product that will sell for $10 per unit. Annual volume for the next four years should be about 200,000 units. The company can use either a hand-fed or a semiautomatic machine to make the product. Data are as follows.

|  | Hand-fed Machine | Semiautomatic Machine |
|---|---|---|
| Per unit variable cost | $4 | $2 |
| Annual cash fixed cost | $725,000 | $850,000 |
| Cost of machine | $800,000 | $1,400,000 |

Both machines have four-year lives and no anticipated salvage value. Welton uses straight-line depreciation, has a 40% income tax rate, and has a 14% cost of capital.

**Required**
1. Determine which machine has the higher book rate of return on average investment.
2. Determine which machine has the higher NPV.
3. Determine which alternative has the higher IRR.

**8-23  Increasing volume**  Managers of Avenal Electric are pondering whether to increase capacity for one of their products, a car radio. Expanding capacity by 700,000 units will require equipment costing $20,000,000 and having a four-year life with no salvage value. The new machinery will increase annual cash fixed costs by $8.4 million. If they do increase capacity, they expect annual sales to increase by 500,000 units. The radio sells for $60. Unit variable costs are $25. These values will not change if Avenal goes ahead. Avenal has a 12% cost of capital and an income tax rate of 40%. Avenal uses straight-line depreciation.

**Required**

1. Determine the expected increase in future annual after-tax cash flows for this project.
2. Determine the NPV of the investment.
3. Determine the approximate IRR of the investment.
4. Suppose the equipment has a $1,000,000 salvage value. Avenal will still depreciate the full cost of the equipment, so there would be a tax on whatever proceeds are received from its sale. By how much and in what direction will the NPV of the project change because of the expected salvage value?

**8-24   *Investing in JIT***   Glenview Manufacturing Co. is implementing JIT throughout its several plants. The Morganton Plant is about to spend $4.5 million to rearrange the factory into manufacturing cells. The Internal Revenue Service has ruled that the company cannot deduct this cost immediately, but must amortize it over five years using the straight-line method. Walt Blinden, the factory manager, expects to save about $800,000 per year for the foreseeable future as a result of using cells. The tax rate is 40% and the cutoff rate is 10%.

**Required**

Determine the NPV of the investment. Use a 30-year period for the annual cost savings. It will be easier to discount the operating savings and tax shield separately.

**8-25   *Safety equipment***   RTP Corp. operates several factories, one of which was built some 50 years ago and is not in good condition. Because of safety concerns, that factory has workman's compensation premiums of $45,000 per year.

Recently, a state inspector recommended that the premium be increased to $93,000 per year. The inspector told the plant manager, Jane Strong, that new equipment costing $200,000 and with a 10-year life and no salvage value would be needed to continue the existing premium of $45,000 per year.

The company uses straight-line depreciation. The tax rate is 40% and the cutoff rate for investments is 14%.

**Required**

1. Determine the NPV of the investment using only the data provided.
2. Using the guidelines in Appendix A, write a memorandum to Ms. Strong making a recommendation. Include support for your recommendation and suggest relevant factors not mentioned.

**8-26   *Employment options***   Bob Keller is a college senior and an All-American basketball player. Drafted by the Middleton Brutes of the Tri-Continental League, he has been pondering two alternatives the team has offered. The first is that Bob receives $2,000,000 per year for ten years, the second is that he receives $1,200,000 per year for 30 years. Either way, Bob and the team both expect his playing career to be over in ten years. Under either alternative, he would get the prescribed amounts whether or not he plays.

Bob will face an income tax rate of 30%. The team has a 40% income tax rate. Bob believes that a 10% discount rate is appropriate. The team has a 14% cutoff rate.

**Required**

1. Which offer should Bob take?

2. Which offer is better for the owners of the team?
3. If your answers to requirements 1 and 2 differ, explain why. You need not make any calculations.

**8-27  Importance of depreciation period**   Your company has the opportunity to buy machinery for $100,000. It will last for five years, be depreciated using the straight-line method, and save $30,000 in cash operating costs per year. Cost of capital is 10% and the tax rate is 40%.

**Required**
1. Determine the NPV of the investment.
2. Suppose now that you could depreciate the machinery over two years for tax purposes instead of five years. Determine the NPV of the investment.

**8-28  Introducing a new product**   BDR is considering adding a new product with a selling price of $70 and variable cost of $18. It expects to sell 10,000 units per year. To make the product, BDR must acquire a new machine costing $800,000 and having a useful life of five years. The machine will have no residual value at the end of its life. Managers estimate cash fixed costs to make the product at $180,000 per year. BDR's cutoff rate is 14% and its tax rate is 30%. It uses straight-line depreciation for both financial reporting and tax purposes.

**Required**
1. What is the expected after-tax annual cash flow from the project?
2. What is the payback period for the project? (Round your answer to three decimal places.)
3. What is the IRR for the project?
4. What is the NPV for the project?
5. Assume BDR has determined that this project could be financed by an 11% loan from a bank. Explain your answer to each of the following.
   (a) Should BDR use 11%, instead of 14%, to compute the project's NPV?
   (b) Should BDR incorporate the annual interest payments on the note into its computation of the project's annual net cash flows?
6. Assume BDR could, for tax purposes only, depreciate the new machine using an accelerated method of depreciation such as double-declining balance. Explain your answers to each of the following.
   (a) Would BDR pay less total tax on the income from the project?
   (b) Would the project's payback period be different?

**8-29  Manufacturing cells, JIT**   Some of the plant managers of Emsworth Manufacturing Company are trying to switch to JIT manufacturing. The manager of the Seneca Plant has developed the following data on the effects of introducing JIT, mainly from talks with managers whose plants have adopted JIT principles.

(all amounts in thousands)

|  | Current Cost | Estimated JIT Cost |
| --- | --- | --- |
| Materials | $1,876.4 | $1,692.0 |
| Direct labor | 2,845.2 | 2,312.0 |
| Supervision | 434.6 | 88.3 |
| Maintenance | 493.2 | 23.6* |
| Inspection, incoming and outgoing | 256.3 | 32.8* |
| Other | 673.9 | 569.5 |
| Totals | $6,579.6 | $4,718.2 |

* Most costs of maintenance and inspection will be carried out by workers in their cells, thus greatly reducing the centrally administered amounts.

Moving to cellular manufacturing requires investments of $7.5 million for rearranging and for new machinery more suited to cellular manufacturing. All of these costs can be deducted for tax purposes over ten years. None of the depreciation and amortization of these costs is included in the figures. The company has a 40% tax rate and a 12% cost of capital. The horizon for discounting the after-tax savings in operating flows is 20 years.

### Required

Determine the NPV of the proposed change. You will find it easier to discount the two types of flows separately.

**8-30   Retirement options**   Jerry Waddlum will retire in a few months, on reaching his 65th birthday. His pension plan offers two options: (1) a lump-sum payment of $650,000 on the day of retirement and (2) annual payments of $75,000 per year beginning on the date of retirement and ending at death. Mr. Waddlum is not sure which option he should select and asks for your assistance. He tells you that he has no savings now, that he could earn a 12% return if he invested part of the lump-sum payment, and that he would like to spend $90,000 per year during his retirement. He has no relatives or other heirs and is not concerned about leaving an estate. He tells you that he could live on $75,000 per year but would much prefer to spend $90,000 and be more comfortable.

If he chooses the lump-sum payment, he will take out $90,000 to live on during the first year of retirement and invest the remainder. He will then draw $90,000 at the beginning of every year until the money runs out.

### Required

Determine how long Waddlum could afford to keep up a $90,000-per-year standard of living if he takes the lump-sum payment.

**8-31   Expanding a product line**   Kiernan Company makes office equipment of various sorts, such as tables, desks, chairs, and lamps. The sales manager is trying to decide whether to introduce a new model desk that will sell for $600 and have variable costs of $340. Kiernan expects volume to be 20,000 units per year for five years. To make the desks, the company will have to buy additional machinery that will cost $8,000,000 and have a five-year life with no salvage value. Straight-line depreciation will be used. Fixed cash operating costs will be $2,200,000 per year.

Kiernan is in the 40% tax bracket and its cutoff rate is 10%.

### Required

1. Use the NPV method to determine whether the new desk should be manufactured.
2. Compute the payback period.
3. Determine the approximate IRR on the investment.

**8-32   Buying air pumps**   Mighty Mart is a chain of convenience stores that sells food, beverages, household products, and gasoline. Its product development manager, Carolyn Schmidt, is trying to decide how to acquire coin-operated air pumps that customers can use to fill their tires. One choice is to lease pumps for $850 per year, renewable annually. The other is to buy them for $1,500. Pumps have a three-year life. For each pump, revenue should average $2,400 per year; operating costs, exclusive of lease payments or depreciation, should average $550 per year.

Mighty Mart is in the 40% tax bracket, has a 10% cutoff rate of return, and uses straight-line depreciation.

### Required

Using the guidelines in Appendix A, write a memorandum to Ms. Schmidt giving and supporting your recommendation about which acquisition method to select.

***8-33    Charitable donation***    Jan Williamson is a wealthy entrepreneur who wishes to make a substantial donation to her alma mater, Arkwright University. She is considering two alternatives, a $6,000,000 gift now or an equal annual amount in each of the next ten years.

From discussions with the president of Arkwright University, she has learned that the university, which pays no income taxes, earns a 10% return on its endowment fund. The president would be happy with either the $6,000,000 now or with equal annual amounts having a present value of $6,000,000. Mrs. Williamson is able to earn a 9% after-tax return investing in tax-free securities. She faces a combined state and federal tax rate of 35%.

**Required**

1. Determine the annuity that yields a $6,000,000 present value to the university.
2. Should Mrs. Williamson make the lump-sum donation or pay the annuity that you determined in requirement 1?

***8-34    Increasing capacity (continued in Chapter 9)***    Pitcairn Manufacturing has regularly been selling out its complete stock of its most popular style of men's socks, Heather. The production and marketing managers have investigated ways to increase capacity and have determined they could produce another 250,000 pairs annually if they bought equipment costing $1,200,000. The equipment has a five-year life with no salvage value. Pitcairn uses straight-line depreciation. The equipment would add $200,000 to annual cash fixed costs. The socks sell for $4 and have a variable cost of $1 per pair. The variable cost would not be affected by using the equipment. The managers are confident of selling 200,000 additional pairs annually. Cost of capital is 14% and the tax rate is 40%.

**Required**

1. Determine whether Pitcairn should acquire the equipment.
2. Suppose that additional volume is likely to be 250,000 pairs. Determine whether Pitcairn should acquire the equipment.

***8-35    Funding a pension plan***    Knowles Company has an agreement with the labor union that represents its workers. The agreement calls for Knowles to pay $25,000 per year for the next ten years into a pension fund. Payments would begin one year from now.

Knowles has excess cash on hand from the sale of some of its assets, so the treasurer approaches the head of the union and asks if it would be all right to make a single, lump-sum payment to discharge the ten-year obligation. Before receiving the union leader's reply, the treasurer decided to determine the maximum amount that Knowles could pay right now. The company is in the 40% tax bracket and has a cutoff rate of 16%. The annual payments are deductible for tax purposes in the years in which they were made and the single payment would be deductible in the current year.

**Required**

Determine the maximum amount that Knowles could pay in a lump-sum settlement of the obligation.

***8-36    Research and development investment***    Parker Pharmaceuticals is considering a major research project into human genomes. The project will have the following costs, in millions of dollars, in each of its first four years.

| Year | Cash Costs |
|------|-----------|
| 20X1 | $4.5 |
| 20X2 | 6.2 |
| 20X3 | 8.5 |
| 20X4 | 3.2 |

If all goes well, the project should provide cash inflows beginning in 20X5. The flows should begin at $7.0 million and increase $2 million per year through 20X8. Parker's managers are unwilling to forecast beyond that point. No depreciable assets are involved in the project.

The tax rate is 40% and all R&D costs are immediately deductible. Cost of capital is 12%.

**Required**

Determine whether Parker should undertake the project.

**8-37 Capital budgeting by a municipality** The City Council of Alton is considering constructing a convention center in the downtown area. The city has been losing employment to surrounding suburbs, and tax revenues have been falling. The proposed center would cost $22,000,000 to build, and the city would incur annual cash operating costs of $500,000. The city controller estimates that the annual receipts from the center will be approximately $1.8 million. He estimates the center's useful life at 30 years.

The controller's estimate of revenues is based on total annual convention attendance of 200,000 people. He reports that at 8% interest, the rate the city would have to pay on bonds to build the center, it would be a losing proposition. The present value of $1,300,000 ($1,800,000 − $500,000) annually for 30 years at 8% is $14,635,400, well below the cost of the center. (Assume this computation is correct.)

One member of the council comments that the rentals are not the only source of revenues to the city. To support this position, she offers studies showing that the average person attending a trade show or convention spends $500 in the city in which the event is being held. Because of the various taxes in effect, the city receives, on average, about 1% of all of the money spent in it.

**Required**

1. Prepare a new analysis, incorporating the additional tax receipts expected if the center is built.
2. Why is 8% used as the discount rate when it is the interest rate, not the cost of capital? (Is the interest rate the same as the cost of capital to a city?)

**8-38 Comparison of NPV and profit** Graham Auto Products is bringing out a new heavy-duty battery and has two choices with respect to the manufacturing process. No matter which choice it makes, it expects to sell 100,000 units per year for four years at $50 per unit. Data on the two processes are as follows:

| | Labor-Intensive Process | Capital-Intensive Process |
|---|---|---|
| Per-unit variable cost | $20 | $10 |
| Annual fixed cash operating costs | $400,000 | $600,000 |
| Investment in equipment | $4,000,000 | $6,000,000 |

Neither set of equipment is expected to have salvage value at the end of four years. The company uses straight-line depreciation. The cutoff rate is 16% and the tax rate is 40%.

**Required**
1. Which process will give the higher annual profit?
2. Which process will give the higher book rate of return on average investment?
3. Which process will give the higher NPV?
4. Using the guidelines in Appendix A, write a memorandum to Morton Brown, Graham's factory manager, giving and supporting your recommendation regarding which process should be selected.

**8-39  *Capital budgeting for a computer service company***  Compuservice, Inc., a computer service provider, has a high-speed machine that it rents from the manufacturer for $18,000 per month. The company is considering the purchase of a new machine, the M-80, that is the fastest machine of its type available. The old machine will be kept even if the M-80 is purchased. Cal Crandall, president of Compuservice, believes that a number of new customers will be attracted if the company acquires an M-80. He estimates additional revenues of $40,000 per month. Additional costs requiring cash would be $4,000 per month for maintenance and salaries for added operators. The new machine sells for $1,200,000 and has a useful physical life of about fifteen years. However, computer experts have estimated that it will probably be technologically obsolete in six years.

The company would use straight-line depreciation of $225,000 per year in order to depreciate the computer to its estimated salvage value of $300,000 at the end of four years. The company's tax rate is 40% and its cutoff rate is 16%.

**Required**
Using the guidelines in Appendix A, write a memorandum to Mr. Crandall giving and supporting your recommendation regarding the proposal.

**8-40  *Reevaluating an investment***  Ten years ago Kramer Company, of which you are controller, bought machinery at a cost of $250,000. The purchase was made at the insistence of the production manager. The machinery is now worthless, and the production manager believes that it should be replaced. He gives you the following analysis, which he says verifies the correctness of the decision to buy the machinery ten years ago. He bases his statement on the 21% return he calculated, which is higher than the 16% cutoff rate of return.

| | |
|---|---:|
| Annual cost savings: | |
|   Labor | $ 41,000 |
|   Overhead | 28,000 |
|   Total | $ 69,000 |
| Less straight-line depreciation ($250,000/10) | 25,000 |
| Increase in pretax income | $ 44,000 |
| Income taxes at 40% | 17,600 |
| Increase in net income | $ 26,400 |
| Average investment ($250,000/2) | $125,000 |
| Return on investment | 21% |

**Required**
Do you agree that the investment was wise? Why or why not?

**8-41   *Purchase commitment***   Ralston Company buys copper from a number of suppliers, including Boa Copper Company. The president of Boa has offered to sell Ralston up to 1,000,000 pounds of copper per year for five years at $0.80 per pound if Ralston will lend Boa $2,000,000 at 8% interest. The loan would be repaid at the end of five years; the interest would be paid annually.

Ralston uses at least 1,800,000 pounds of copper per year and expects the price to be $1.00 per pound over the next five years. The tax rate is 40% and Ralston's management considers the relevant discount rate to be 12%.

*Required*

1. Determine whether Ralston Company should accept the offer.
2. Determine the minimum price at which copper would have to sell, per pound, over the next five years to make accepting the offer worthwhile.

## CASES

**8-42   *New product—complementary effects***   Elmendorf Company makes a variety of cleaning products. The company's research and development department has recently come up with a new glass cleaner that is superior to all of the products on the market, including the one that Elmendorf currently makes. The new cleaner would be priced at $22 per case and have variable costs of $12 per case. Elmendorf would have to buy additional machinery costing $10,000,000 to make the new cleaner. The machinery has a ten-year life. Expected volume of the new cleaner is 800,000 cases per year for ten years. Cash fixed costs will increase $1,400,000 per year.

Elmendorf uses straight-line depreciation with no provision for salvage value. The machinery has about $100,000 expected salvage value at the end of ten years. The tax rate is 40% and the cutoff rate is 12%.

One disadvantage of making the investment is that sales of the firm's existing cleaner would be affected. Volume of the existing cleaner is expected to fall by 300,000 cases per year. A case of the existing cleaner sells for $15 and has variable costs of $9.

*Required*

Determine the NPV of the proposed investment.

**8-43   *Discounts and cash flows***   The managers of *PC Journal*, a magazine for computer users, are working on a campaign to get extended subscriptions. The magazine's base one-year rate is $28 for 12 issues. The managers tentatively set the two-year subscription rate at $50. Both amounts are payable in advance. The variable cost per subscription per year is $10. The cutoff rate is 12%. The company pays no income taxes.

*Required*

1. Suppose that all one-year subscribers will renew at the end of the year. Therefore, the company will either (a) collect $28 now and $28 in one year or (b) collect $50 now. Determine whether the magazine should offer the $50 rate for a two-year subscription.
2. Again, assuming that all subscribers taking one-year subscriptions would renew at the end of one year, determine the lowest two-year rate that the magazine should offer.
3. Suppose now there is a 40% attrition rate in subscriptions. That is, of every ten one-year subscribers, four will not renew next year. Determine whether the

magazine should offer the $50 rate. Assume that the variable costs are paid at the beginning of each year. You might find it convenient to work with a hypothetical batch of ten subscribers.

4. Using the facts from requirement 3, determine the lowest two-year rate that the magazine should offer.

**8-44  Quality improvement**   Shaffer Products is plagued by quality problems in its Fisherton Plant, which is relatively old. Technology has outstripped the plant's processes, leaving it severely outmoded. About 10% of output is spoiled and must be scrapped. The VP for manufacturing has been looking at new machinery and equipment that would reduce the rate of rejects to near zero. Retrofitting the plant will cost about $6.5 million. The new machines have five-year lives and no salvage value. The company uses straight-line depreciation. The existing machinery is fully depreciated and has no sales value.

The controller provided the following estimates, in millions of dollars.

|  | Current Processes |
| --- | --- |
| Total variable manufacturing costs | $58.0 |
| Total fixed manufacturing costs | 36.6 |
| Total manufacturing costs | $94.6 |

The manufacturing engineering department estimates that cash fixed operating costs will increase by about $2.2 million annually if the plant acquires the new machinery. The tax rate is 40% and cost of capital is 12%.

**Required**
1. Determine the NPV of reducing spoiled output to zero while maintaining the current level of good output.
2. Annual revenue under existing conditions is $117.8 million. Suppose that demand is far above capacity so that the plant could increase sales by 10% if it acquires the new equipment. Determine the NPV of the investment.

**8-45  Long-term special order**   Grayco makes connectors for TV satellite dishes. The connectors sell for $12 and have variable costs of $7. The company has been selling 200,000 units per year and expects to continue at that rate unless it accepts a special order from Acme Dishes. Acme wants to buy 40,000 units per year at $9, provided that Grayco agrees to make the sales for a five-year period. Acme will not take fewer than 40,000 units.

Grayco's capacity is 230,000 units per year. Capacity could be increased to 260,000 units per year if new equipment costing $100,000 were purchased. The equipment would have a useful life of five years, have no salvage value, and add $20,000 in annual fixed cash operating costs. Variable costs per unit would be unchanged.

Grayco would use straight-line depreciation for tax purposes. The tax rate is 40% and the cutoff rate is 14%.

**Required**
Using the guidelines in Appendix A, write a memorandum to Grayco's vice president of manufacturing, Bjorn Hansen, giving and supporting your recommendation about the best course of action.

**8-46  Analyzing a new product**   Jerry Burnside, controller of Pitts Industries, Inc., tells you about a meeting of several top managers of the firm. The topic discussed was the introduction of a new product that had been undergoing extensive research and development. Burnside had thought the product would be brought out in the coming year, but the managers decided to give it further study.

The product is expected to have a market life of ten years. Sales are expected to be 30,000 units annually at $90 per unit. The following unit costs were presented by Jamie Barker, manager of the division that would produce and sell the product.

| | |
|---|---|
| Materials | $10 |
| Direct labor | 17 |
| Overhead (manufacturing) | 30 |
| Selling and administrative expenses | 12 |
| Total costs | $69 |

Barker went on to point out that equipment costing $3,000,000 and having an expected salvage value of $100,000 at the end of ten years would have to be purchased. Adding the $900,000 that had already been spent on research and development brought the total outlay related to the new product to $3,900,000.

Depreciation of $300,000 per year would reduce taxes by $120,000 (40% rate). The $21 per-unit profit margin would produce $630,000 before taxes and $378,000 after taxes. The net return would then be $498,000 annually, which is a rate of return of about 4%, far below the 14% cutoff rate. Barker concluded that the product should not be brought out.

Burnside tells you that Barker is a strong believer in "having every product pay its way." The calculation of the manufacturing overhead cost per unit includes existing fixed costs of $600,000 allocated to the new product. Additional cash fixed costs are $200,000 per year. Selling and administrative expenses were also allocated to the product on the basis of relative sales revenue. Commissions of $4 per unit will be the only incremental selling and administrative expenses.

### Required

1. Prepare a new analysis.
2. Explain the fallacies in Barker's analysis.

# CAPITAL BUDGETING DECISIONS—PART II

## LEARNING OBJECTIVES

*After reading this chapter, you should be able to*

- *Analyze investments in working capital.*
- *Analyze replacement decisions using two approaches.*
- *Explain and apply sensitivity analysis.*
- *Describe and analyze mutually exclusive investments.*
- *Describe the Modified Accelerated Cost Recovery System and use it in evaluating investments.*
- *Explain how capital budgeting applies to not-for-profit entities and to social welfare.*

*Chapter 8 concentrated on investments in new plant and equipment, made mostly to reduce costs or increase capacity. Companies make other expenditures as well. Increasing capacity or introducing new products usually entails investments in accounts receivable and inventories, sometimes in amounts greater than the investment in physical assets.*

*As one investment expert puts it, "Say you're running a business with 60 days of inventory on hand, 45 days sales in receivables. . . . Incremental increases in sales will suck up cash, so an investor has to look not just at capital expenditures when a company expands, but also must consider the need to finance this negative working capital float. . . . The S&P 500 companies have effectively reduced their financing needs, as evidenced by the established long-term decline in inventory-to-sales ratios. The capital necessary to expand sales is thus reduced. . . . The earnings growth that results . . . is of a higher quality than that of a company that has to pour cash into receivables and inventories to facilitate growth. . . . Corporations are managing their supply chains better and have to tie up less cash in current assets. The less current assets you need to run your business, the more those current assets can be financed by current liabilities."*

*For some perspective on the amounts of investment in working capital, on the next page we show the combined total of receivables and inventories, and of plant assets, for several companies. All figures are in millions.*

|  | Receivables and Inventories | Plant Assets |
|---|---|---|
| **General Electric** | $14,163 | $11,118 |
| **Goodyear Tire** | 3,569 | 4,150 |
| **Cisco Systems** | 1,660 | 595 |

**General Electric** *is a diversified giant with a lot of manufacturing.* **Goodyear Tire** *is in a capital-intensive business, while* **Cisco** *outsources much of its manufacturing. For all three, the magnitudes of working capital investment are very large in relation to plant and equipment. Failure to consider investments in working capital can cause companies to make unwise capital budgeting decisions.*

*Sources: Annual reports.*
*Dale Wettlaufer,* The Motley Fool Evening News, *June 15, 1998.*

Chapter 8 treated decisions requiring new productive assets. This chapter considers more complicated decisions than those, but the basic principles remain the same. The analyses still concentrate on cash flows and the time value of money.

Capital budgeting decisions involve long periods and many estimates. Chapters 2 and 5 discussed sensitivity analysis, which is determining whether a decision is sensitive to a change in an important variable. We apply sensitivity analysis to capital budgeting decisions in this chapter. We also cover some aspects of income tax law that affect capital budgeting decisions. Finally, because budgets reflect planning decisions and many of those decisions have social consequences, we conclude the chapter (and Part Two) with a discussion of the social consequences of decision making and a brief look at the special problem of decision making in the public sector.

## INVESTMENTS IN WORKING CAPITAL

Virtually every business requires current assets. Businesses selling on credit have accounts receivable, while manufacturers and merchandisers have inventories. Even companies approaching the JIT ideal have some products in process. And, as Chapter 7 showed, businesses finance some of their current asset requirements with current liabilities. Together, current assets minus current liabilities equal **working capital**. Working capital is a significant part of many investments. Refer to the vignette at the beginning of the chapter to see the magnitude of working capital.

Tying up cash in working capital is as much an investment as is tying up cash in plant and equipment. Investment decisions must earn satisfactory returns on the entire investment, not just the plant and equipment portion. Projects aimed at increasing sales usually require an increase in working capital, as you saw in Chapters 6 and 7 when Home Effects's sales increased. Projects can also reduce working capital, and companies specifically target such investments, as we show in a later Insight. Changes in working capital are not difficult to incorporate within the capital budgeting framework. They have no tax effects because income taxes are based on accrual accounting. In the introductory analysis we present, such changes affect cash flows in the first and usually in the last years of the project. Because of differences in analyzing projects that require increases and decreases in working capital investment, we treat them separately, beginning with increases.

## INCREASES IN WORKING CAPITAL INVESTMENT

One difference between investments in working capital and in plant assets is important for our purposes. At the end of its useful life, a plant asset is almost always worth less than it cost. In contrast, working capital investments are typically recovered *in full*, or nearly so, because the higher receivables and inventory will be turned into cash during the final operating cycle in the life of the project. Remember the time lags, discussed in Chapters 6 and 7, between making a purchase and paying for it and between making a sale and collecting for it. In the final year of a project, the expectation of reduced sales reduces inventory, thereby reducing purchases, which in turn reduces the amount of cash needed to pay for purchases and *frees such cash for other uses*. Similarly, cash collections in that final year should exceed sales because of the delay in collecting for sales made in the previous year.[1]

Consider a new product with the following characteristics.

| | |
|---|---|
| Annual revenues | $30,000 |
| Annual cash costs | $12,000 |
| Investment | $50,000 in equipment and $35,000 in working capital |
| Life | 5 years |

The company uses straight-line depreciation, the equipment has no salvage value, cost of capital is 12 percent, and the tax rate is 40 percent. The cash flows and net present value (NPV) of the project appear below.

### Incremental Cash Flows Years 1–5

| | Tax Computation | Cash Flow |
|---|---|---|
| Revenues | $30,000 | $30,000 |
| Cash expenses | 12,000 | 12,000 |
| Pretax cash inflow | $18,000 | $18,000 |
| Depreciation ($50,000/5) | 10,000 | |
| Increase in taxable income | $ 8,000 | |
| Tax at 40% | $ 3,200 | 3,200 |
| Net cash inflow per year | | $14,800 |

---

1  *As a practical matter, the return of investments in accounts receivable might extend beyond the life of a project because the company will not collect sales made late in the final year until early the next year. Investments in inventory typically will be recovered late in the final year as the company gears down production as sales decline. Such minor timing differences are trivial when we are estimating cash flows years into the future.*

*Some companies anticipate recovering less than the full investment in working capital because they expect some overproduction in later years. In such cases, the recovery is less than the original investment and a tax effect also occurs.*

| End of Year 5 | |
| --- | --- |
| Recovery of working capital investment | $35,000 |

| Net Present Value of Investment | |
| --- | --- |
| Operating cash inflows ($14,800 × 3.605) | $ 53,354 |
| Recovery of working capital investment ($35,000 × 0.567)[2] | 19,845 |
| Total present value | $ 73,199 |
| Investment required ($50,000 + $35,000) | 85,000 |
| Net present value | $(11,801) |

The negative NPV tells us that the investment is undesirable. If only the machinery is considered, the investment appears desirable, showing a positive NPV of $3,354 ($53,354 – $50,000). Companies therefore strive to reduce working capital requirements to increase returns and, of course, companies also invest to reduce working capital.

## DECREASES IN WORKING CAPITAL INVESTMENT

Inventory is the most common target of investments that focus on reducing working capital. Companies that distribute products to retailers, such as **Procter & Gamble**, **Colgate**, and **Quaker Oats**, continually invest in projects to reduce inventories while providing the same levels of service to customers. Perhaps the most common of such investments occur in companies that are moving toward the JIT ideal of zero inventories.

A company embarking on an inventory-reduction project will draw down existing inventory the first year of the project. It will not manufacture or purchase as many units as it sells in the first year. Delaying production or purchases frees up cash for other purposes. Because the company is committed to the JIT philosophy, it does not expect to return to its prior inventory levels at the end of the project's life. The company therefore expects a cash saving in the first year of a project's life but does *not* expect a cash outflow in the final year. Accordingly, the analysis of an inventory-reducing decision includes only the cash saving from reducing inventory in the first year, with no offsetting outflow in the final year.

The accompanying Insight describes how some companies invest to reduce working capital, principally inventories, and the significance they place on inventory management and the logistics of getting products to customers quickly.

The second case we consider is the replacement decision, which requires different calculations to determine future cash flows.

## REPLACEMENT DECISIONS

Businesses frequently replace assets when economic or technological factors allow them to perform tasks at costs low enough to justify the additional investment. Typically, replacement decisions involve essential operations. The company must perform the function, such as attaching fenders to automobile bodies. The question is how to perform the operation.

2 *Some analysts prefer to subtract the present value of the recovery from the investment. The effect is the same.*

### Investing in Inventory Reduction

One of **Quaker Oats's** principal operating strategies is to enhance productivity in its supply chain. One element of the strategy is its program for continuous replenishment of customers' shelves. Quaker had about 35 percent of its customers on the program in 1997. Continuous replenishment is similar to JIT, featuring more rapid responses to changes in demand and more efficient order-filling. Quaker uses more rapid communications with customers to respond more quickly to changes in demand, which reduces the need to carry inventory buffers. Besides reducing investment in inventory, the program increases the freshness of products and boosts profits for the company and its customers.

**Compaq Computer's** ". . . highly innovative evolution from a "build-to-inventory" toward a "build-to-order" manufacturing and fulfillment environment has led to quality improvements across our product lines, market share gains and improved competitiveness while greatly reducing order cycle times—the time between when an order is placed and when it is fulfilled—and inventory costs." Compaq had been hurt in the past by high inventories, which had exposed the company to losses from price declines.

**Tiffany & Co.** is not a company one would expect to see pay a lot of attention to inventory because its profit margins are very high. Nonetheless, the company has paid considerable attention to inventory and logistics. Its newest distribution facility in Parsippany, New Jersey, can handle 50,000 units per day and operates less expensively than its older facilities. The new facility features ". . . advanced pick packing systems, including radio-frequency devices linked to inventory management, and improved process flow." By reducing the need to carry so much inventory in its stores, Tiffany increased its selling space to 60 percent of a new store, up from 40 percent, which also reduces store construction costs.

*Sources: Quaker Oats 1995, 1996, and 1997 annual reports.*
*Compaq Computer 1997 annual report.*
*Alex Schay, "Tiffany Sparkles," The Motley Fool Evening News, August 17, 1998.*

Determining cash flows for replacement decisions is more complex than for decisions about new assets because (1) depreciation on the replacement is likely to be different from that on the existing assets, and (2) determining the net cost to purchase the replacement requires more steps. We illustrate two methods for evaluating replacement decisions: the incremental approach and the total-project approach.

The **incremental approach** focuses on the *differences* between cash flows, given the alternatives of keeping or replacing the asset. The **total-project approach** compares the present values of operating each way. The two approaches give the same results, so selecting one or the other is a matter of computational convenience.

Suppose your company owns a machine for which it paid $100,000 five years ago. Other data relating to the machine are as follows:

| | |
|---|---|
| Remaining useful life | 5 years |
| Current book value | $50,000 |
| Annual depreciation | $10,000 |
| Expected sales value—now | $20,000 |
|             —in 5 yrs. | $0 |
| Annual cash operating costs | $30,000 |

If you sell the machine now, you will have a tax loss of $30,000 ($50,000 book value – $20,000 sales price). The tax rate is 40 percent, so the tax loss will save $12,000 ($30,000 × 40 percent).

Suppose a new machine comes on the market that sells for $60,000, has an estimated useful life of five years with no salvage value, and costs only $15,000 per year to operate. The new machine can be depreciated over five years using the straight-line method. Suppose further that the cutoff rate is 16 percent. Is it wise to replace the old machine now?

As with any capital project, the analysis must consider two things: the initial investment and the future cash flows. In a replacement decision, the computation of each of these is different from the computations we have made previously. First we determine the initial investment.

| | Tax Computation | Cash Flow |
|---|---|---|
| Purchase price of new asset | | $ 60,000 |
| Book value of old machine | $50,000 | |
| Sale price, which is a cash inflow | 20,000 | (20,000) |
| Loss for taxes, which can be offset against regular income | $30,000 | |
| Tax saved (40% × $30,000) | $12,000 | (12,000) |
| Net outlay for new asset | | $ 28,000 |

The book value or cost of an existing asset is sunk and irrelevant to decisions. However, book value *does* affect taxes if the asset is sold and so must be considered in determining those taxes.[3] The sale of the old asset reduces the outlay for the new one by $32,000, because the company will receive $20,000 from the sale and the loss on the sale produces a $12,000 saving in income taxes. Hence, a net outlay of only $28,000 is required to buy the new asset.

## INCREMENTAL APPROACH

On the next page is an analysis of the investment, using the incremental approach.

---

3 The tax basis *of the asset, its original cost less depreciation taken for tax purposes, is the relevant figure. The tax basis and book value will differ if the company uses one method for tax purposes and another for book purposes. Most companies do in fact use different methods for the two purposes.*

Annual Cash Savings Years 1–5

|  | | Tax Computation | Cash Flow |
|---|---|---|---|
| Pretax cash savings: | | | |
| Cash cost of using old asset | | $30,000 | $30,000 |
| Cash cost of using new asset | | 15,000 | 15,000 |
| Difference favoring replacement, inflow | (1) | $15,000 | $15,000 |
| Additional depreciation: | | | |
| Depreciation on new asset ($60,000/5) | | $12,000 | |
| Depreciation on old asset | | 10,000 | |
| Additional tax deduction for depreciation with replacement | (2) | $ 2,000 | |
| Increase in taxable income (1) – (2) = | (3) | $13,000 | |
| Additional tax ($13,000 × 40%), outflow | (4) | $ 5,200 | (5,200) |
| Additional net cash inflow favoring replacement (1) – (4) | | | $ 9,800 |
| Present value factor, 5 years, 16% | | | × 3.274 |
| Present value of savings | | | $32,085 |
| Investment | | | 28,000 |
| Net present value | | | $ 4,085 |

The NPV is positive, so the replacement is desirable.

## TOTAL-PROJECT APPROACH

In the total-project approach we calculate, separately, the present values of the future outflows using the existing asset and using the replacement asset. The decision rule, using the total-project approach, is to accept the alternative with the lower present value of future outflows. This is because the analysis of both alternatives deals with costs (cash outflows), not revenues (cash inflows); the alternative with the lower present value minimizes costs.

For the example just given, the present value of the total outflows if the existing machine is used is calculated as follows.

Decision–Operate Existing Machine

|  | Tax Computation | Cash Flow |
|---|---|---|
| Annual operating costs | $30,000 | $30,000 |
| Depreciation | 10,000 | |
| Total tax-deductible expenses | $40,000 | |
| Tax savings expected (40%) | $16,000 | 16,000 |
| Net cash outflow expected per year | | $14,000 |
| Present value factor for 5 years at 16% | | × 3.274 |
| Present value of future operating outflows | | $45,836 |

Now consider the present value of the total cash flows if the company buys the new machine.

| Decision–Sell Existing Machine, Buy New Machine | | |
| --- | --- | --- |
| | Tax Computation | Cash Flow |
| Annual operating costs | $15,000 | $15,000 |
| Depreciation | 12,000 | |
| Total tax-deductible expenses | $27,000 | |
| Tax savings expected (40%) | $10,800 | 10,800 |
| Net cash outflow expected per year | | $ 4,200 |
| Present value factor for 5 years at 16% | | × 3.274 |
| Present value of future operating outflows | | $13,751 |
| Net outlay required for the new machine | | 28,000 |
| Present value of total cash outflows of buying new machine | | $41,751 |

Comparing the two alternatives, we find

| | |
| --- | --- |
| Present value of using existing machine | $45,836 |
| Present value of buying and using new machine | 41,751 |
| Difference in favor of replacing machine | $ 4,085 |

The present value of the total outlays associated with using the existing machine is greater than that of the total outlays associated with acquiring and using the new machine. Note that the $4,085 difference equals the NPV we computed using the incremental approach. The two approaches give the same results, and the choice between them is a matter of convenience.

In the replacement decision considered here, it was possible to continue using the currently owned asset. The same two analytical approaches can be used if an essential asset has reached the end of its useful life and alternatives exist as possible replacements. For example, suppose that a company needs a new forklift truck because one of its existing trucks is about to be scrapped. Perhaps two different models are available as replacements, each with a different acquisition cost and associated annual operating costs. Because the firm is committed to replacing the old forklift, the decision becomes how to minimize the future costs, for which either the incremental or the total-project approach could be used.

## SENSITIVITY ANALYSIS

Chapter 5 emphasized that decision analysis involves many estimates, errors in which could lead to poor decisions. Because of the importance of estimates in decision making, managers analyze the sensitivity of decisions to changes in one or more variables. This testing of the estimates, called **sensitivity analysis**, involves finding out how much a particular factor can rise or fall before a different decision is indicated. Sensitivity analysis applies to all types of decisions but is especially beneficial when applied to capital budgeting decisions.

A misestimate of annual cash flow is magnified because it applies to several years and is multiplied by a present value factor. For a project with a ten-year life where the cutoff rate is 20 percent (present value factor of 4.192), a $1 drop in annual cash flow produces a drop of $4.192 in the present value of those flows. A capital budgeting decision also works out over an extended time, which is not true of short-term decisions, so a misestimate of useful life could be important.

Suppose an investment of $12,000 is expected to generate cash flows of $3,000 per year for ten years and that the discount rate is 12 percent. The project has a positive NPV. But considering the uncertainties surrounding estimates for years so far into the future, a manager might wonder just how long the investment must continue producing an annual flow of $3,000 to earn at least the required 12 percent return. Dividing the investment by the annual cash flow gives a present value factor (also the payback period) of 4 ($12,000/$3,000). Knowing the discount rate (12 percent) and the present value factor (4.0) we can consult Table B of Appendix B, look down the 12 percent column, and see that 3.605 is the factor for five years, 4.111 for six years. The project must yield annual flows of $3,000 for nearly six years in order to earn the required 12 percent return. In this case then, the estimated useful life of the project has to be in error by 40 percent (from ten to six years), a large error in the original estimate, before the decision changes; thus, the decision is not very sensitive to the estimate of useful life.

The outcome of analyzing a capital budgeting decision can also be affected significantly by differences in estimates of sales volumes, selling prices, and per-unit variable costs. (The effect of each such difference is magnified in the analysis, because each unit of volume is multiplied by contribution margin per unit.) For example, suppose a company with a cost of capital of 14 percent and a 40 percent tax rate can bring out a new product priced at $22. Managers estimate variable costs at $4 per unit, fixed costs requiring cash outlays at $100,000 annually, and 10,000 units annual sales volume. The product requires an investment of $200,000, all for depreciable assets with a five-year life and no salvage value. The company uses straight-line depreciation. The initial analysis for this decision follows.

|  | Tax | Cash Flow |
| --- | --- | --- |
| Expected contribution margin (10,000 × $18) | $180,000 | $ 180,000 |
| Fixed costs: |  |  |
|   Cash | $100,000 | (100,000) |
|   Depreciation | 40,000 |  |
|  | $140,000 |  |
| Increase in taxable income | $ 40,000 |  |
| Tax at 40% | $ 16,000 | (16,000) |
| Net cash inflow per year |  | $ 64,000 |
| Present value factor, 5-year annuity at 14% |  | ×    3.433 |
| Present value of annual cash inflows |  | $ 219,712 |
| Investment required |  | 200,000 |
| Net present value |  | $  19,712 |

Based on the available estimates, the project has a positive NPV and should be accepted. But the estimate of unit volume could be too optimistic. How far could annual volume fall before the investment becomes only marginally desirable?

Because NPV is now $19,712, we shall determine the decline in volume that will reduce NPV to zero or, equivalently, make the IRR just 14 percent. We can find the decrease in volume that will reduce NPV by $19,712 as follows.

| | |
|---|---|
| Net present value | $19,712 |
| Divided by 14% present value factor for 5 years | 3.433 |
| Equals decrease in annual net cash flows to make investment yield 14% | $ 5,742 |
| Divided by 1 minus the tax rate | 0.60 |
| Equals decrease in pretax cash flow for 14% IRR | $ 9,570 |
| Divided by contribution margin per unit | 18 |
| Decrease in sales to yield 14% IRR | 532 units |
| Volume required for 14% return (10,000 – 532) | 9,468 |

Note that a 5.32 percent decline in annual volume leads to a 9 percent ($19,712/$219,712) decline in the present value of the future cash flows. The managers might seek additional information, such as through test marketing, before embarking on the project.

Managers can perform sensitivity analysis with other variables such as selling price, unit variable cost, or total fixed costs. To test the sensitivity of selling price or unit variable cost, simply divide the allowable decrease in total pretax cash flow by unit volume to determine the allowable decrease in unit contribution margin. For our example, $9,570/10,000 = $0.957. A drop in selling price or increase in variable cost of $0.957 will bring the NPV to zero. We analyzed only one variable at a time, holding the others constant. There are ways of allowing several variables to change simultaneously, but these are beyond our scope.

Sensitivity analysis gives managers an idea about how unfavorable occurrences such as lower volumes, shorter useful lives, or higher costs affect the profitability of a project. It is used because of the uncertainty that prevails in almost any real-life situation.

## MUTUALLY EXCLUSIVE ALTERNATIVES

The decision rules presented in this and the preceding chapter classify investments as wise or unwise. They do not consider whether the company has enough money to make the investments. When resources are limited, all of the company's investment opportunities are *competing* for the available money. In some cases, the competition is even more specific, as when the company has two or more ways of accomplishing the same goal so that selecting one alternative precludes selecting the others. Such competing proposals are **mutually exclusive alternatives**.

Replacement decisions, such as the one just discussed, fit this definition. If the company keeps its present equipment, it doesn't need the newer model, and vice versa. Mutual exclusivity can also arise as a matter of policy. For example, a company might have a policy of introducing no more than one new product in any one year.

Whether exclusivity is inherent in the proposals or is the result of management policy, it is not unusual for competing alternatives to have unequal lives. Some analysts suggest that another evaluation technique, the profitability index, can be particularly useful in ranking and deciding among alternatives. These two special topics are discussed in the next sections.

## UNEQUAL LIVES

While both a conveyor belt and a forklift truck might meet the need to move semi-finished units from one place to another, the life of the conveyor is longer than that of the truck. To evaluate such alternative investments we need a way to make them comparable. A commonly used method of doing so is to assume a chain of replacements such that the analysis of each alternative covers the same number of years.

To illustrate this method, assume the following facts about two mutually exclusive investment opportunities involving a machine, versions Model G-40 and Model G-70, that is essential to the company's operations.

|  | Model G-40 | Model G-70 |
|---|---|---|
| Purchase price | $40,000 | $70,000 |
| Annual cash operating costs | $8,000 | $6,000 |
| Expected useful life | 4 years | 8 years |

Neither machine has any expected salvage value at the end of its useful life. The cutoff rate is 14 percent. To concentrate on the specific problem at hand—the unequal lives of the alternatives—we ignore income taxes and, therefore, need not be concerned with depreciation.

We select eight years as the time period for the evaluation because that is the lowest common denominator for the lives of the two investments. Evaluating first the alternative with the longer life (Model G-70), the present value of the expected cash outflows is $97,834.

| | |
|---|---:|
| Annual operating costs | $ 6,000 |
| Present value factor for 14% and 8 years | × 4.639 |
| Present value of operating costs | $27,834 |
| Investment required | 70,000 |
| Present value of total cash outflows for G-70 | $97,834 |

To provide comparable information about the alternative of using Model G-40, we assume replacement at the end of four years at a cost of $44,000 but no change in annual operating costs. The present value of total cash outflows assuming a choice of Model G-40 is $103,160.

| | |
|---|---:|
| Annual operating costs, years 1–8 | $ 8,000 |
| Present value factor for 14% and 8 years | × 4.639 |
| Present value of operating cash outflows, years 1–8 | $ 37,112 |
| Present value of purchase of replacement Model G-40 at the end of year 4 ($44,000 × 0.592) | 26,048 |
| Present value of future cash outlays | $ 63,160 |
| Investment required now | 40,000 |
| Present value of total cash outflows for G-40 | $103,160 |

Because we are dealing with cash *outflows* for the two alternatives, we want the one with the *lower* present value, which is Model G-70 ($97,834). However, the company's managers should consider how confident they are in the forecast of the replacement cost of the G-40 as well as the likelihood of a significant change in technology.

## RANKING INVESTMENT OPPORTUNITIES

In Chapter 8 we stated that the two discounted cash flow techniques (NPV and IRR) provide economic answers to accept/reject questions: should we invest in this project or not? However, DCF methods sometimes give conflicting answers to questions of ranking: which of two proposals is better? One proposal might have a higher NPV, but the other a higher IRR. If the proposals are mutually exclusive we have a conflict.

To deal with such situations, some accounting and finance personnel prefer a third discounted cash flow technique, the profitability index, which, they argue, is as useful as NPV and IRR in most situations but more useful than those approaches in evaluating mutually exclusive alternatives. The **profitability index (PI)** is the ratio of the present value of the future cash flows to the investment. In general terms,

$$\text{Profitability index} = \frac{\text{Present value of future cash flows}}{\text{Investment}}$$

Thus, a $100,000 investment with present value of future cash flows of $118,000 has a PI of 1.18.

The decision rule using PI is to accept projects with a PI greater than 1.0. In the case of acceptance/rejection decisions, the decision rule for using PI produces the same results as the rules for NPV and IRR. An investment with a positive NPV and an IRR greater than cost of capital also has a PI greater than 1.0. The advantage of PI is that it focuses on the present value of future cash flows generated per dollar of investment. The higher the PI, the higher the margin of safety offered by the investment. Consider the following two investments.

|  | A | B |
| --- | --- | --- |
| Present value of future flows | $10,100,000 | $500,000 |
| Investment | $10,000,000 | $400,000 |
| NPV | $100,000 | $100,000 |
| PI | 1.01 | 1.25 |

Investment A has little margin of safety, considering its size. If the present value of future flows falls only one percent, the NPV is wiped out. Investment B, however, requires a 25 percent drop in the present value of the future cash flows to wipe out the NPV. Most would argue that investment B is therefore safer than investment A.

Nonetheless, if the risk of decreases in future cash flows is not an issue, NPV is generally, preferable to either IRR or PI when it comes to ranking competing alternatives. Let us see how the three criteria perform in an example, and explain those special circumstances.

Following are data for two mutually exclusive investment opportunities confronting a company with a 10 percent cost of capital.

| | Investment Opportunities | |
|---|---|---|
| | X | Y |
| Investment required | $50,000 | $10,000 |
| Life of investment | 1 year | 1 year |
| Cash flows, end of year 1 | $55,991 | $11,403 |
| Present value of cash flows at 10% cost of capital (0.909 × cash flow) | $50,896 | $10,365 |
| Net present value of project | $896 | $365 |
| Internal rate of return | 12% | 14% |
| Profitability index: | | |
| $50,896/$50,000 | 1.018 | |
| $10,365/$10,000 | | 1.037 |

Project Y has both a higher IRR and a higher PI than does project X, which is higher using only the NPV criterion. However, provided that the 10 percent cost of capital is the rate at which other alternative investments can be made, project X should be selected. The simplest way to show this is as follows.

A company considering both opportunities X and Y must have at least $50,000 (the investment required for X) available for investment. If the company accepts project Y (outlay of $10,000), it will have $40,000 available for other projects. Project X returns 12 percent on the entire $50,000, so the question is whether the company can earn more than 12 percent on investment Y and whatever other investments it can make with the $40,000 available.

Now suppose another project, Z, is available that requires an investment of $40,000 and shows an expected return of 10.5 percent, slightly above the cost of capital but lower than the return on X. Z is acceptable using any criterion, but how much cash would the company have at the end of the year if it selected Y and invested the additional funds in Z? The cash position appears as follows:

| | | |
|---|---|---|
| Cash provided by investment in project Y | | $11,403 |
| Cash provided by investment in Z: | | |
| Investment returned | $40,000 | |
| Earnings on the investment (10.5%) | 4,200 | 44,200 |
| Total cash available to company at end of year | | $55,603 |

At the end of the year, the company has $55,603 from the two projects. But, had it invested the entire $50,000 in project X, the company would have had $55,991 at the end of the year. Thus, accepting project Y and using the excess funds for another project produces less cash than accepting only project X.

From the illustration we know that managers should exercise care when evaluating mutually exclusive investments that have different rankings under the three criteria (NPV, IRR, PI). If the opportunities competing for available funds include mutually exclusive projects, strict adherence to one criterion or another could lead to poor decisions.

## INCOME TAX COMPLICATIONS

Throughout this book we have assumed that a single tax rate applies to all of a company's revenues and expenses and that only revenues and expenses of the current year affect taxes. Neither of these assumptions is always true. Tax law is far too complex to be treated in depth in an introductory text in managerial accounting, so we therefore point out only a few aspects of the law that bear on capital budgeting decisions (and warn you at the outset that the details are subject to change virtually every time Congress meets).

First, no single tax rate applies to all incomes. Rates are graduated (progressively higher) and depend on whether the business is incorporated. Federal tax rates for corporations begin at 15 percent for income up to $50,000 and increase to 34 percent for income over $75,000. However, above $100,000, the corporation loses the benefit of the lower rates, so that the rate on some incremental income can be as high as 39 percent. The federal rates on incomes of unincorporated businesses depend on a variety of factors, including the incomes of their individual owners from sources other than the business. These rates are 15 percent, 28 percent, and 31 percent, though some can pay as much as 39.6 percent. Most states levy income taxes on individuals and on corporations, which further increases the rates. Nonetheless, because large and medium businesses are likely to be in the top brackets for both federal and state tax purposes, it is reasonable for them to use a single combined federal and state rate for analyzing capital budgeting decisions.

Second, income taxes do not depend solely on revenues and expenses for a given tax year. One feature of tax law, called the operating loss carryback/carryforward, allows businesses to offset losses in one year against profits in another. For example, if a company lost $200,000 in 20X4, then earns $50,000 in 20X5, it does not have to pay any taxes on the $50,000 because of the loss in 20X4. In fact, with some restrictions, the company does not have to pay income taxes until it earns over $200,000 cumulatively after 20X4.

The tax treatment of depreciation has changed periodically. Chapter 8 used straight-line depreciation, which is acceptable for tax purposes, but not usually optimal. Faster depreciation deductions are available under the provisions of the Modified Accelerated Cost Recovery System (MACRS).

## MACRS

For many years prior to 1981, business entities were allowed to use a different, and faster, depreciation method for tax purposes than was used for financial accounting purposes. The life over which an asset could be depreciated for tax purposes was called its Asset Depreciation Range (ADR) life. (ADR lives were developed by the Internal Revenue Service.) The schedule of ADR lives relieved a business from having to estimate useful lives for each of its assets for tax purposes.

The Economic Recovery Tax Act (ERTA) of 1981 continued to provide benefits from accelerated depreciation, but narrowed the options by introducing the **Accelerated Cost Recovery System (ACRS)**. ACRS specified much shorter depreciation periods than had previously been allowed. The Tax Reform Act of 1986 made some changes in ACRS and introduced **Modified Accelerated Cost Recovery System (MACRS)**. (Both acts allow businesses to use straight-line depreciation under the ADR lives, but that is usually less advantageous than MACRS.) Under MACRS, the business places individual assets into various classes according to their ADRs. For most industrial and service companies, four classes of property are important:

- 5-Year Class: This class includes automobiles, light trucks, typewriters, copiers, personal computers, and certain other enumerated items.
- 7-Year Class: This class includes office furniture and equipment, most types of machinery, and any property not designated by law as being in some other class.
- 10-Year Class: This class contains property with IRS-specified lives of at least 16 years and less than 20 years, including certain types of transportation equipment.
- 31.5-Year Class: This class includes nonresidential real property such as factory buildings.

Exhibit 9-1 gives the percentages (rounded to the nearest whole percent) of cost to be depreciated in each year for the three classes of most relevance to capital budgeting. Depreciation under MACRS for 3-, 5-, 7-, and 10-year classes reflects the 200 percent declining balance method, with a switch to straight-line depreciation when its deductions exceed those under the declining balance method. (The 150 percent declining balance method is used for other classes.) Companies need not recognize salvage value under MACRS, a further advantage. MACRS uses the half-year convention, which means that assets are assumed to be put in service halfway through the year. Its practical effect is that, as the exhibit shows, assets are depreciated over one year more than their class lives; that is, 5-year assets over six years, 7-year assets over eight years, and so on.

MACRS is usually advantageous because it concentrates depreciation deductions in the earlier years of an asset's life. MACRS class lives are much shorter than ADR lives, so write-offs are considerably faster than they were previously. Consequently tax payments in the early years are less than under the straight-line method. Payments in later years are higher, but remember that the present value of the tax payments is lower the later they are made. MACRS might not be advantageous if total taxes will be lower by postponing deductions now. A significant increase in the tax rate is one reason that taking a lower deduction now and higher deductions later might be advantageous.

**Exhibit 9-1    Percentages of Cost Depreciated Under MACRS**

| Year | 5-Year Class | 7-Year Class | 10-Year Class |
|------|--------------|--------------|---------------|
| 1 | 20% | 14% | 10% |
| 2 | 32 | 25 | 18 |
| 3 | 19 | 18 | 14 |
| 4 | 12 | 12 | 12 |
| 5 | 12 | 9 | 9 |
| 6 | 5 | 9 | 7 |
| 7 |  | 9 | 7 |
| 8 |  | 4 | 7 |
| 9 |  |  | 7 |
| 10 |  |  | 6 |
| 11 |  |  | 3 |

Calculating depreciation under MACRS can be tedious. Exhibit 9-2 provides a shortcut method for finding the present value of tax savings for 5- and 7-year property at various discount rates. To use the table, multiply the cost of the asset by the factor for the life and discount rate, then multiply by the tax rate.

Let's look at an example to see how the table works. Suppose a company expects pretax cash flows of $3,000 per year from an asset costing $10,000. The asset is in the 5-year class and, to reduce calculations, has a useful life of six years. The tax rate is 40 percent and cost of capital is 12 percent. A year-by-year analysis follows.

|  | \multicolumn{6}{c}{Year} |  |  |  |  |
|---|---|---|---|---|---|---|
|  | 1 | 2 | 3 | 4 | 5 | 6 |
| Pretax inflow | $ 3,000 | $3,000 | $3,000 | $3,000 | $3,000 | $3,000 |
| MACRS deduction[a] | 2,000 | 3,200 | 1,900 | 1,200 | 1,200 | 500 |
| Taxable income | $ 1,000 | $ (200) | $1,100 | $1,800 | $1,800 | $2,500 |
| Tax at 40% | 400 | (80) | 440 | 720 | 720 | 1,000 |
| Net cash inflow[b] | $ 2,600 | $3,080 | $2,560 | $2,280 | $2,280 | $2,000 |
| PV factors | × .893 | × .797 | × .712 | × .636 | × .567 | × .507 |
| Present values | $ 2,322 | $2,455 | $1,823 | $1,450 | $1,293 | $1,014 |
| Total present value | $10,357 |  |  |  |  |  |

a  *From the 5-year column of Exhibit 9-1.*
b  *Pretax inflows minus tax, year 1, $3,000 – $400 = $2,600.*

It is much easier to determine this present value of the operating inflows net of tax, and then to add the present value of the MACRS tax shield.

| | |
|---|---|
| Present value of operating flows | |
| $3,000 × (1 – 0.40) × 4.111 (from Table B) | $ 7,400 |
| Present value of MACRS shield | |
| $10,000 × 0.40 × 0.738 (from Exhibit 9-2) | 2,952 |
| Total present value (rounding difference) | $10,352 |

### Exhibit 9-2   Present Value of MACRS Tax Shields*

| Discount Rate | 5-Year Assets | 7-Year Assets |
|---|---|---|
| 0.08 | 0.811 | 0.766 |
| 0.10 | 0.774 | 0.722 |
| 0.12 | 0.738 | 0.681 |
| 0.14 | 0.706 | 0.645 |
| 0.16 | 0.675 | 0.611 |
| 0.18 | 0.647 | 0.580 |
| 0.20 | 0.621 | 0.552 |
| 0.22 | 0.597 | 0.526 |
| 0.24 | 0.574 | 0.502 |

a  *Factors in this table are the sums of the percentages of depreciation for each period multiplied by the present value factors. For example, the factor for 10% for a 5-year asset is .774 of (20% × 0.909) + (32% × 0.826) + (19% × 0.751) + (12% × 0.683) + (12% × 0.621) + (5% × 0.564). There is some rounding.*

We needed only two calculations. The operating flow, net of tax, is an annuity of $1,800 [$3,000 × (1 – 0.40)] for six years, and is discounted using the Table B factor for six years at 12 percent. Exhibit 9-2 gives the factor for a 5-year asset at 12 percent as 0.738, which, when multiplied by the cost of the asset and by the tax rate, gives the present value of the tax shield.

As noted earlier, the depreciation deductions mandated under MACRS are usually more advantageous than those under the straight-line method. The accompanying Insight describes some provisions of tax law that are especially important for economic activity. However, companies will not use the shorter lives for financial reporting purposes because the lives do not coincide with the useful lives. An important result of a difference between tax and financial reporting depreciation is that the tax basis of an asset (cost minus tax depreciation) does not equal its book value, and it is the tax basis we consider in calculating taxable gains and losses. For capital budgeting decisions involving replacements of existing assets, the analysis of both current cash outlay and cash inflow from salvage value requires calculating the tax basis of the asset at the time of disposition.

## CRITICISMS OF DCF METHODS

Chapter 8 cited companies that explicitly downplayed quantitative analyses because of overriding qualitative, or hard-to-quantify, concerns about particular in-

 SIGHT

### Tax Policy and Economic Activity

Congresses and presidents have used tax policy to further economic goals and objectives for many years. The text describes how changing the period over which a company can depreciate an asset can influence investment in the economy. As early as the Kennedy administration, taxpayers could use an Investment Tax Credit, which allowed companies to deduct a specific percentage of the cost of a qualifying asset from their tax bills. Tax credits are much more valuable than tax deductions because they reduce taxes by the amount of the credit, not by the tax rate times the amount, as is true with tax deductions. For some assets, the credit was 7 percent, meaning that if a company bought $100,000 of such assets, it could take an immediate credit against its tax bill of $7,000. If the tax were $50,000, the company paid $43,000. The reason for the tax credit was to stimulate investment, which creates jobs and increases economic activity. The investment tax credit went through a series of modifications and eventually was dropped. The credit favored capital-intensive industries such as automobiles and steel, some of which wound up paying no tax at all, a factor that helped lead to its demise.

In some countries, companies can deduct the entire purchase price of an asset in the year of acquisition, rather than depreciate it over future periods. This policy makes investments more desirable because the tax shield comes immediately, not over future years.

vestments. For instance, companies are much more likely to approve investments that enhance their ability to carry out their strategies than those with no such discernible effect.

Managers today know that they must modernize, automate, and move toward JIT and other advanced manufacturing techniques, but often the costs of investments directed at such results appear prohibitive, with the expected *objectively quantifiable* benefits not justifying the investments. For various reasons, high-tech investments often fail discounted cash flow tests. Yet such investments are clearly important. Management accountants are developing new ways of looking at such investments. For example, they are now estimating the effects of failing to adopt new technology, such as losing existing business. Accountants expected typical conventional investments to either increase business or serve existing business at a lower cost.

Many companies, especially those using JIT principles, include subjective factors in evaluating capital budgeting decisions. For example, projects that show negative NPVs are more likely to be accepted if they improve factors such as cycle time, product quality, competitive position, manufacturing flexibility, and delivery time. The accompanying Insight describes some investments with benefits that are extremely hard to quantify.

**IN** *SIGHT*

### Hard-to-Quantify Investment Decisions

**Perkin-Elmer**, a manufacturer of scientific instruments with $1.4 billion sales, has combined with the Institute for Genomic Research to embark on a project to map human DNA. They hope to decode the entire human genome by 2001. The federal government has such a project that it expects to complete in 2005. If the company succeeds, it will reap enormous rewards, but success is far from certain. The company's annual reports describe how it hopes to leverage its expertise in instrumentation to speeding up the decoding process. The company believes that the potential is enormous, but it is unlikely that the company uses carefully developed estimates of cash inflows. The uncertainty is too great.

Agricultural-biotechnology companies have suffered hard times for some years, enjoying very limited success. Finally, after huge investments, applications of biotechnology are finding their way into the mainstream of U.S. farming. The U.S. seed market seems to be ready for bio-engineered varieties. For instance, Bt corn, developed by **DeKalb** seed, is genetically engineered to resist the European corn borer. A relatively modest infestation of that insect can destroy 5 percent of a corn crop. Bt corn seed costs $7–$10 per acre more than other seeds, but the potential loss from corn borers is a minimum $18–$20 per acre. Similarly, **Monsanto's** Roundup Ready soybeans require only $18 per acre of herbicides compared to $25–$28 per acre for traditional soybeans.

*Sources: Annual reports.*
*Dale Wettlaufer,* The Motley Fool Evening News, *June 1, 1998.*

Some criticize the application of DCF methods because of too-high discount rates and the comparison of expected results against the status quo. They argue that these practices discriminate against high-tech investments. We leave the issue of discount rates to courses in finance. The question of comparison is whether the company will be able to maintain the status quo. Managers might erroneously believe that if they do nothing to increase quality or reduce cycle time they will continue selling as much as they do now. But in many cases the company that fails to invest in a product will lose sales to competitors who are investing in their products. The comparison should consider realistic sales expectations if the company falls behind its competitors. The accompanying Insight describes some of these types of investments.

Notwithstanding such criticisms, we should bear in mind that DCF techniques, supported by appropriate analyses such as ABC, do have a major role in capital budgeting decisions. The accompanying Insight on page 384 describes one such case.

## SOCIAL CONSEQUENCES OF DECISION MAKING

Throughout most of this book we have assumed that the consequences of an action were limited to the entity taking that action. But often the action of a single entity has many effects, desirable or detrimental, for other entities. We have referred to some of these implications in previous discussions of qualitative considerations of decision making. Costs that are not borne directly by the entity making a decision and taking an action are called **social costs**, or externalities.

For example, a company might find that using a machine that saves labor is justified on economic grounds. But the decision to use the machinery might put people out of work. The workers who lose their jobs will suffer if they cannot find other jobs fairly quickly. If they do not find work, they will receive unemployment compensation or some other type of payment that is borne by taxpayers. If they move away from the area to find work, they must incur moving costs, and might have problems in uprooting their families. The reduced payroll of the plant might adversely affect the community through declines in economic activity such as retail sales. Other jobs might be lost as a result of the layoffs.

**Social benefits** (also called externalities) are benefits not accruing directly to the entity making a decision. A company that hires workers who are currently unemployed (as opposed to hiring them away from other companies) provides benefits to the workers in the form of income and increased self-esteem, to the community in the form of increased economic activity and higher taxes, and to taxpayers in the form of reduced expenditures for unemployment compensation and other social services. The company does not benefit directly from these other benefits, even though its action caused them. Though business managers may not give direct and monetary recognition to externalities, they should at least try to recognize the existence of externalities as they study individual decisions.

Social benefits and costs are particularly critical in decisions made by government units such as municipalities, states, and the federal government. Decision making in these and other not-for-profit entities is, like that in businesses, based on estimates of discounted benefits and costs. There are several major differences between the analyses used by businesses and government units. One difference is that government units do not pay income taxes, which makes their decision mak-

**SIGHT**

## High-Tech Solutions and Investments

Throughout this book we have described how companies are rationalizing their operations, reducing inventory, concentrating on core competencies, and following strategies designed for long-term success. One manifestation of these trends is in investment that is not aimed at increasing sales or reducing manufacturing cost, but at freeing the company to work on its basic mission.

We have seen a surge of companies that aim at assisting companies in this way. Sophisticated supply chain management has blossomed, with companies such as **I2 Technologies** growing at nearly 200 percent per year. The company develops software products, advertising internal rates of return of 500 percent on the software investment. The company's statistics show that its products can help reduce inventories by 60 percent, order lead times by 10 percent, and late orders by 25 percent to 50 percent.

The most prominent high-tech area today is the Internet, where companies are investing enormous sums in both physical and intangible assets. **Yahoo!**, the Internet search engine company, spent $9,544,000 on product development in the first six months of 1998. The company reported that

> "Product development expenses consist primarily of employee compensation relating to developing and enhancing the features and functionality of Yahoo! online media properties. The increase in absolute dollars is primarily attributable to increases in the number of engineers that develop and enhance Yahoo! online media properties. To date, all internal product development costs have been expensed as incurred. The Company believes that significant investments in product development are required to remain competitive. Consequently, the Company expects to incur increased product development expenditures in absolute dollars in future periods. As a percentage of net revenues, the Company currently anticipates that product development expenses will approximate current levels during the remainder of 1998."

Pharmaceutical and bio-tech research has spawned the **Contract Research Organization (CRO)**, which does the work of taking drugs from the laboratory to the market. The CRO market has grown because pharmaceutical and biotech companies have decided to stick to their core competencies. CRO conducts "preclinical research, study design, clinical trial management, data collection, biostatistical analysis, and preparation of regulatory submissions. They get drugs to market more quickly and at a lower cost."

*Sources: Annual reports.*
*Louis Corrigan, Quintiles Seeks Envoy, Dominance,* The Motley Fool Evening News, *December 16, 1998.*

ing somewhat simpler than that of businesses. But other factors in the government decision-making process make decisions much more difficult. These special

**SIGHT**

### Using ABC in Evaluating Strategic Investments

A large company was about to invest $50 million in an interactive TV cybermall project, based primarily on strategic marketing criteria. The CFO argued that the company needed a detailed analysis of the cybermall business processes and activities before proceeding. The company used ABC to develop projections of cash flows that did not support the original, broad estimates. The company dropped the project.

The ABC analysis used data from public sources to estimate shopping frequency and the number of transactions. The analysts focused on the six processes that the cybermall required and determined the major activities of each process. (For example, one process was operations and some of its activities were processing orders [both manual and automated] and serving customers.) They then projected capital requirements based on the activities and determined that $50 million wouldn't do the job; the company would need to put up over $60 million.

*Source: Steve Coburn, Hugh Grove, and Tom Cook, "How ABC Was Used in Capital Budgeting,"* Management Accounting, *May 1997, 38–46.*

factors fall into three general categories: (1) measurement problems, (2) problems in determining whether a particular effect is a benefit or a cost, and (3) problems in the distribution of benefits and costs.

CHAPTER
4

Measurement problems arise in decisions of government units because, as mentioned in Chapter 4, not all benefits and costs are monetary. If an unemployed person obtains a job, the government benefits from additional taxes paid by the employed worker. But other benefits such as the worker's increased self-esteem are not readily measurable. Cleaner air is economically beneficial because of fewer deaths from respiratory ailments, less sickness, and reduced cleaning bills for clothing and buildings. But the monetary value of these benefits and of the increased pleasantness that accompanies cleaner air is not readily measurable.

The second factor, determining whether an effect is beneficial or costly, often depends on one's point of view. The government has sanctioned actions to reduce the populations of wolves and coyotes in sheep and cattle-raising states. These programs have been favorably received by ranchers but deplored by conservationists. Programs that result in growth in population of a particular area also receive mixed reviews. Some states and towns seek industrial development while others discourage it.

The problem of the distribution of benefits and costs has been a difficult social question since the beginning of government. Suppose a city or town is considering the construction of a municipal golf course and analyses show that the fees received will be insufficient to earn the minimum desired rate of return. If the project is accepted, taxpayers will subsidize those who use the golf course. The town government might still decide to build the golf course because it believes that the people who would use it deserve some inexpensive recreation, even if the general taxpayers must pay some of the costs. Similar reasoning applies to more widely used municipally owned facilities such as zoos, libraries, and parks.

The criterion that is most generally advocated for decision making by governmental units is the maximizing of "social welfare." Because of the many problems in identifying and quantifying social benefits and costs, this decision rule has often meant maximizing economic benefits—those subject to monetary estimates. To the extent that this can be done, the same general analytical approaches proposed for business decision making can be used in the public sector. And, like the business manager, the decision maker in the public sector must make an effort to at least identify and consider the unquantified but relevant factors before reaching a final decision.

## SUMMARY

Capital investments must earn returns on both working capital and plant investments. Investments that reduce inventories are especially desirable because the payoff is very high. Capital budgeting decisions involve many estimates, so managers perform sensitivity analysis to alert themselves to areas where they might face problems.

Mutually exclusive investment alternatives create special problems. A third DCF technique, the profitability index, might assist in choosing from among such alternatives. This technique can be useful, but the company's circumstances in terms of available funds and investment opportunities should be considered before selecting a single capital budgeting technique for general use.

Computations of cash flows for an investment opportunity require knowing the many special features of income tax laws, particularly the Modified Accelerated Cost Recovery System (MACRS).

Qualitative issues are associated with almost every investment opportunity. This is true in both the private and the public sectors. Decision makers in both sectors should make every effort to identify and quantify as many factors as possible and to consider factors that remain unquantified.

## KEY TERMS

Accelerated Cost Recovery System (ACRS) *(377)*
incremental approach *(368)*
Modified Accelerated Cost Recovery System (MACRS) *(377)*
mutually exclusive alternatives *(373)*

profitability index (PI) *(375)*
sensitivity analysis *(371)*
social benefits *(382)*
social costs *(382)*
total-project approach *(368)*
working capital *(365)*

## KEY FORMULAS

$$\text{Profitability index} = \frac{\text{Present value of future cash flows}}{\text{Investment}}$$

Working capital = Current assets − Current liabilities

## REVIEW PROBLEM—INVESTMENT IN WORKING CAPITAL

Parkman Co. wants to introduce a new product. The managers' best estimates appear below.

| | |
|---|---|
| Selling price | $20 |
| Variable costs | $12 |
| Sales volume | 30,000 units per year |

Bringing out the new product requires a $50,000 increase in working capital, as well as the purchase of new equipment costing $250,000 and having a five-year useful life with no salvage value. The new equipment has cash operating costs of $100,000 per year and will be depreciated using the straight-line method, ignoring the half-year convention. Parkman is in the 40% tax bracket and has 12% cost of capital.

**Required**
Determine the net present value of this investment opportunity.

### ANSWER TO REVIEW PROBLEM
The investment appears to be wise, as indicated by the following analysis.

#### Cash Flow, Years 1–5

| | Tax Computation | Cash Flow |
|---|---|---|
| Additional contribution margin (30,000 × $8) | $240,000 | $240,000 |
| Cash operating costs of new machine | 100,000 | 100,000 |
| Additional pretax cash flow | $140,000 | $140,000 |
| Depreciation ($250,000/5) | 50,000 | |
| Increase in taxable income | $ 90,000 | |
| Income taxes, at 40% | $ 36,000 | 36,000 |
| Net cash flow per year | | $104,000 |

#### Cash Flow, End of Year 5

| | |
|---|---|
| Recovery of working capital investment ($50,000 × 0.567) | $28,350 |

#### Summary of Net Present Value of Investment

| | |
|---|---|
| Operating cash flows, years 1-5 ($104,000 × 3.605) | $374,920 |
| Recovery of working capital investment, as above | 28,350 |
| Total present value of future cash flows | $403,270 |
| Investment ($250,000 machine + $50,000 working capital) | 300,000 |
| Net present value of investment | $103,270 |

Note that the analysis shows the $50,000 increase in working capital as part of the investment required for the project, and then includes the recovery of that investment at the end of the project's life as part of the future cash flows. Note also that there is no tax effect of the working capital increase in either part of the analysis.

## REVIEW PROBLEM—SENSITIVITY ANALYSIS

Refer to the facts in the first review problem.

### Required
1. Determine the annual unit volume required to give Parkman a 12% return.
2. With unit volume at 30,000, what selling price will give Parkman a 12% return?

### ANSWER TO REVIEW PROBLEM
1. Annual sales must be about 18,838 units. The previous Review Problem shows that the NPV of the investment is $103,270 with annual sales of 30,000 units and a 12% discount rate. We can solve the problem by determining the decline in annual volume that will reduce NPV of $103,270 to zero. That change is 5,968 units.

| | |
|---|---:|
| Change in NPV | $103,270 |
| Divided by the factor for an annuity of five years at 12% | 3.605 |
| Equals allowable decline in annual after-tax cash flow | $ 28,646 |
| Divided by 1 – 40% tax rate | 0.60 |
| Equals the allowable decline in annual before-tax cash flow, which is also the change in contribution margin | $ 47,743 |
| Divided by contribution margin per unit ($20 – $12) | 8 |
| Equals allowable decline in sales | 5,968 units |

Hence, the company could sell 5,968 units fewer than its original expectation of 30,000, or 24,032 units, and earn exactly 12% on its investment.
2. We can use the allowable decrease in total contribution margin calculated above.

| | |
|---|---:|
| Allowable decrease in annual total contribution margin | $47,743 |
| Divided by 22,000 unit volume | 30,000 |
| Allowable decrease in unit contribution margin | $ 1.59 |

A decrease in selling price or increase in unit variable cost of $1.59 will bring NPV to zero. Thus a price of $18.41 or variable cost of $13.59, or any combination that reduces unit contribution margin by $1.59, will give a 12% return.

## REVIEW PROBLEM—REPLACEMENT DECISION AND REDUCTION IN WORKING CAPITAL

Torkel Inc., which has a cutoff rate of 14% and a tax rate of 40%, owns a machine with the following characteristics.

| | |
|---|---:|
| Book value (and tax basis) | $40,000 |
| Current market value | $30,000 |
| Expected salvage value at end of its 5-year remaining life | $0 |
| Annual depreciation expense, straight-line method | $8,000 |
| Annual cash operating costs | $30,000 |

Torkel's managers look for opportunities consistent with their desire to create a JIT manufacturing environment. The managers believe that by replacing the old machine and rearranging part of the production area, the company could reduce its investment in inventory by $60,000 as well as save on operating costs. The replacement machine has the following characteristics.

| | |
|---|---|
| Purchase price | $100,000 |
| Useful life | 5 years |
| Expected salvage value | $0 |
| Annual cash operating costs | $12,000 |
| Annual straight-line depreciation expense | $20,000 |

Rearrangement costs are expected to be $12,000 and can be expensed immediately for both book and tax purposes. By the end of the life of the new machine, Verma's managers expect to be further advanced in their implementation of the JIT philosophy and so do not anticipate returning to the prior, higher level of inventory.

### Required

Determine whether Verma should purchase the new machine and undertake the plant rearrangement.

### ANSWER TO REVIEW PROBLEM

The project should be accepted. The NPV is $40,355.

#### Investment Required

| | Tax | Cash Flow |
|---|---|---|
| Purchase price of new machine | | $100,000 |
| Selling price of existing machine | $30,000 | (30,000) |
| Book value of existing machine | 40,000 | |
| Loss for tax purposes | $10,000 | |
| Tax saving at 40% | $ 4,000 | (4,000) |
| Cost of plant rearrangement | $12,000 | 12,000 |
| Tax savings at 40% | $ 4,800 | (4,800) |
| Reduction of working capital requirements | | (60,000) |
| Net required investment | | $ 13,200 |

Notice that the reduction in working capital is treated as a reduction of the required investment. Because the company does not expect to return to its prior inventory policies at the end of the life of this project, the calculation of cash flows from the project will not include a corresponding outflow in the project's final year. We calculate the annual cash flows and present values for this replacement decision using first the incremental approach and then the total-project approach.

#### Incremental Approach—Annual Cash Flows

| | Tax | Cash Flow |
|---|---|---|
| Savings in operating costs ($30,000 – $12,000) | $18,000 | $18,000 |
| Additional depreciation ($20,000 – $8,000) | 12,000 | |
| Increase in taxable income | $ 6,000 | |
| Increased tax at 40% | $ 2,400 | (2,400) |
| Net annual cash inflow | | $15,600 |
| Present value factor for 5-year annuity at 14% | | × 3.433 |
| Present value of annual cash inflows | | $53,555 |
| Required investment | | 13,200 |
| Net present value | | $40,355 |

## Total-Project Approach—Keep Existing Machine

|  | Tax | Cash Flow |
|---|---|---|
| Cash operating costs | $30,000 | $ 30,000 |
| Depreciation | 8,000 | |
| Total expenses | $38,000 | |
| Tax savings at 40% | $15,200 | (15,200) |
| Net cash outflow | | $ 14,800 |
| Present value factor for 5-year annuity at 14% | | × 3.433 |
| Present value of annual operating flows | | $ 50,808 |

## Buy New Machine

|  | Tax | Cash Flow |
|---|---|---|
| Cash operating costs | $12,000 | $12,000 |
| Depreciation | 20,000 | |
| Total expense | $32,000 | |
| Tax saving at 40% | $12,800 | 12,800 |
| Net cash inflow | | $ 800 |
| Present value factor for 5-year annuity at 14% | | × 3.433 |
| Present value of annual *inflows* | | $ 2,747 |
| Net outlay required for machine | | 13,200 |
| Net present value of future outflows | | $10,453 |

The existing machine has a present value of outflows of $50,808, while the new machine has a present value of outflows of $10,454. The NPV in favor of replacing the existing machine is $40,355 ($50,808 – $10,453), the same as we computed under the incremental approach.

Using the new machine will result in new annual cash inflows rather than outflows. This happens because depreciation is so high that the tax saving is greater than the annual cash operating costs. Do not conclude that if a replacement asset yields a positive cash flow, it is automatically a wise investment. In the example used here, if the project had not included the expectation of a reduction in inventory the replacement would not be wise.

## REVIEW PROBLEM—MACRS

Horner Company is considering a new machine that costs $100,000 and has an eight-year expected life with no salvage value. The machine is expected to save about $35,000 per year in cash operating costs and falls in the 7-year MACRS class. Cost of capital is 14% and the tax rate is 40%.

### Required
Determine the NPV of the investment, discounting the operating flows and the tax shield of depreciation separately. Use Exhibit 9-2 to find the present value of the tax shield.

### ANSWER TO REVIEW PROBLEM

| | |
|---|---|
| Operating flows $35,000 × (1 – 0.40) × 4.639 | $ 97,419 |
| Tax shield of depreciation ($100,000 × 0.40 × 0.645) | 25,800 |
| Total present value | $123,219 |
| Less investment | 100,000 |
| Net present value | $ 23,219 |

## ASSIGNMENT MATERIAL

### INTERNET ACTIVITY

Find annual reports of companies that are improving their management of working capital, especially inventory. Determine how they are doing so. Two industries where companies are undertaking such initiatives are consumer products (food, toiletries and personal care products, etc.) and high-tech, especially computer makers.

Find annual reports of Internet-related companies and determine how much they invest in physical assets and how much in intangible assets, such as product development.

### QUESTIONS FOR DISCUSSION

**9-1　Kinds of capital budgeting**　Microsoft, the giant software company, spent $656 million on plant and equipment and $2.5 billion on research and development in fiscal 1998. Can, and should, Microsoft use capital budgeting techniques to decide what research projects to pursue?

**9-2　Macroeconomic events and capital budgeting**　Governments frequently take actions that alter the economic climate. For each of the following events, state how it would change companies' capital spending—increase, decrease, or have no effect. Comment on what particular kinds of companies might be affected and how. Consider each independently.

1. Outlawed gasoline engines for automobiles; only electric cars are approved.
2. Discontinued long-standing price supports that have kept the price of cotton artificially high.
3. Levied high tariffs on foreign automobiles.
4. Raised the tax rate on corporate income.
5. Authorized cash grants for attending college to persons with low incomes.
6. Lengthened the period over which companies can depreciate assets.

**9-3　Capital budgeting—effects of events**　You have evaluated a proposal to acquire a new machine, based on information available at the time. How might each of the following events (not anticipated at the time the analysis was done) affect the analysis? Consider each event independently.

1. An increase in taxes on real property (land and buildings) is approved by the voters of the city in which the company has its manufacturing plant.
2. A new tax law provides for a credit against income taxes; the credit is a specified percentage of the investment in new long-lived assets.
3. *The Wall Street Journal* carries a report of a new product that is likely to be a good substitute for the product made by the machine being considered.

**9-4　Choosing depreciation methods**　When might a company use straight-line depreciation rather than MACRS?

### EXERCISES

**9-5　Comparison of methods (continuation of 8-16)**　Determine the profitability index for each opportunity in Exercise 8-16 and rank the investments based on these values.

**9-6  Basic investment analysis**  Athena Landscaping has an annual payroll of $500,000. The company can invest $200,000 in equipment that will reduce payroll by 10%. After its useful life of ten years, the equipment will have little or no salvage value. The tax rate is 40% and cost of capital is 14%. Athena uses straight-line depreciation.

**Required**
1. What is the NPV for the project?
2. What savings in annual cash operating costs make this project return exactly 14%?
3. Assuming that operating savings are $50,000, what useful life must the machine have to make the investment worthwhile?
4. Suppose the project is not really a new investment but rather a replacement for equipment that has a remaining life of ten years and a current book value of $66,000. The old machine can be sold now for $12,000 and will have no residual value if retained to the end of its useful life. Annual depreciation is $6,600. Should the company replace the old machine with the new one?

**9-7  Basic replacement decision**  WyTech manufactures gear assemblies. The production manager recently attended a trade show where she saw a new model lathe. The new lathe does the same work as one of the company's existing lathes, which has a book value of $30,000 and a market value of $18,000. It has an estimated remaining useful life of four years, at which time it will have no salvage value. The company uses straight-line depreciation of $7,500 per year on the lathe, and its annual cash operating costs are $83,000.

The new model costs $100,000 and has a four-year estimated life with no salvage value. Its annual cash operating costs are estimated at $32,000. The firm will use straight-line depreciation. The tax rate is 40% and cost of capital is 14%.

**Required**
1. Determine the investment required to obtain the new lathe.
2. Determine the present value of the net cash flows expected from the investment and the NPV of the investment.
3. Suppose that the new lathe has a salvage value of $5,000. The company will ignore the salvage value in determining annual depreciation and so will have a gain that will be taxed at 40%. Determine the NPV of the investment.

**9-8  Relationships**  A company invested $350,000 in depreciable assets and earned a 10% internal rate of return. The life of the investment, which had no salvage value, was four years.

**Required**
1. Determine the net cash flow that the company earned in each year, assuming that each year's flow was equal.
2. Assume that the tax rate is 40% and that the company used straight-line depreciation for the investment. Determine the annual pretax cash flow that the company earned.

**9-9  Working capital investment**  FidSound has developed a new high-performance videotape. They expect to sell 80,000 units annually for the next four years at $7 each. Variable costs are expected to be $2 per unit, annual cash fixed costs, $220,000. The product requires machinery costing $300,000 with a four-year life and no salvage value. DeCosmo uses straight-line depreciation. Additionally, accounts receivable will increase about $70,000, inventory about $50,000. These amounts will be returned in full at the end of the four years. The tax rate is 40% and cost of capital is 12%.

**Required**

Determine the NPV of the investment.

**9-10   *Replacement decision—working capital***   Bartle, Inc. has the opportunity to replace a large drill press. The replacement press costs $120,000, has a useful life of two years, and has annual cash operating costs of $40,000. Data on the existing press follow.

| Existing Press | |
| --- | --- |
| Current book value and tax basis | $30,000 |
| Annual cash operating costs | $110,000 |
| Current market value | $25,000 |
| Annual depreciation | $15,000 |
| Remaining useful life | 2 years |

The company uses straight-line depreciation. Neither press is expected to have salvage value at the end of its useful life. Using the proposed press will increase inventories by $40,000. The company has a 14% cutoff rate. The tax rate is 40%.

**Required**

Determine the NPV of the proposed investment.

**9-11   *Basic MACRS (continued in 9-25)***   ORM Company has the opportunity to buy a machine for $1,500,000. It is expected to save $400,000 annually in cash operating costs over its ten-year life. For tax purposes, the company will use a 5-year MACRS period. ORM has a 14% cost of capital and a 40% tax rate.

**Required**

Determine the NPV of the proposed investment.

**9-12   *Mutually exclusive alternatives (continuation of 8-22)***   In Problem 8-22, the company had a choice between a hand-fed machine and a semiautomatic machine to perform a function essential to bringing out a new product.

**Required**

1. Compute the PI for each alternative.
2. Using the guidelines in Appendix A, write a memorandum to J. Kratz, the production manager. Give and support your recommendation regarding which machine to acquire.

**9-13   *Investing to reduce inventory, JIT***   Park Mills manufactures several products in its relatively modern factory. Park maintains large inventories of materials, purchased components, and work in process as buffer stock to offset slow incoming deliveries and production bottlenecks.

Park's managers have been working on ways to reduce the investment in inventory. They have plans that include working with suppliers to have deliveries made right to the production areas instead of to an outside loading dock, revamping the flow of goods through the plant, and coordinating production activities better. Rearranging and outfitting the plant will cost about $9.5 million. The new assets have five-year lives and no salvage value. The company uses straight-line depreciation.

The best estimates are that cash operating costs will increase by about $0.90 million per year if the investment is made, while inventories will be reduced from about $33.7 million to about $3.2 million. The tax rate is 40% and cost of capital is 12%.

**Required**

Determine the NPV of the proposed investment.

**9-14   New product decision—sensitivity analysis**   Bee Company is considering adding a new product to its Big Bear line of pure honey products. The product will sell for $8 and have per-unit variable costs of $5 and annual cash fixed costs of $60,000. Equipment to make the product costs $210,000, is expected to last six years, and has no salvage value. Bee estimates annual sales of the product will be 50,000 units. Bee's income tax rate is 45% and its cost of capital is 14%. Straight-line depreciation would be used.

**Required**

1. What is the expected annual increase in future after-tax cash flows if the project is accepted?
2. What are (a) NPV, (b) IRR, and (c) PI for this project?
3. How much could annual cash fixed costs on the project be before the project would have an NPV of zero (IRR of 14%)?
4. Approximately how long must the life of the project be to earn an IRR of 16%?
5. How many units of the product must Bee sell each year to have an IRR equal to the 14% cost of capital?
6. How much could variable cost per unit be before the project would have IRR of 14%?

**9-15   Working capital**   The sales manager of Barnet Distribution has received an offer from an overseas company to buy 15,000 power saws for $20 per unit, well below the usual $42 price. Barnet's sales manager believes that no domestic sales would be lost if the offer is accepted. Unit variable cost of the saw is $18. The only drawback the sales manager sees is that, while Barnet must buy the units now and incur $270,000 ($18 × 15,000) in cash costs, the customer will pay for the saws one year from now because of restrictions on taking money out of the foreign country. Barnet's cost of capital is 16%. Ignore taxes.

**Required**

Determine whether Barnet should accept the order.

**9-16   Mutually exclusive investments**   Miro Manufacturing Company needs additional productive capacity to meet greater demand for its products. Two alternatives are available. The company can choose either one, but not both.

|  | Hand-fed Machine | Semiautomatic Machine |
|---|---|---|
| Required investment in depreciable assets | $1,000,000 | $2,000,000 |
| Annual cash operating costs | $1,450,000 | $1,230,000 |
| Useful life | 10 years | 10 years |

Under either alternative Miro expects additional revenues of $1,750,000. Additional variable costs are included in the cash costs given. Straight-line depreciation will be used for either investment. Neither is expected to have any salvage value. The tax rate is 40% and cost of capital is 10%.

**Required**

1. For each alternative, compute (a) NPV, (b) approximate IRR, and (c) PI.
2. Make a recommendation on which alternative should be chosen.

**9-17  Sensitivity analysis (continuation of 9-16)**  The cost behavior under each alternative in Exercise 9-16 is as follows:

|  | Hand-fed Machine | Semiautomatic Machine |
|---|---|---|
| Variable cost as percentage of revenue | 70% | 40% |
| Fixed cash operating costs | $225,000 | $530,000 |

**Required**
Determine the volume, in dollar sales, that will bring each alternative to an IRR of 10%. Does this new information affect the decision you made in Exercise 9-16?

**9-18  Basic MACRS**  Johnstone Manufacturing Company is considering a new machine that its managers expect will save $270,000 per year in scrap costs because of greater efficiency. The machine costs $1,000,000 and has a ten-year life with no expected salvage value. Johnstone has a 16% cost of capital and 40% tax rate.

**Required**
1. Determine the NPV of the investment using straight-line depreciation.
2. Determine the NPV of the investment using 7-year MACRS depreciation. Use Exhibit 9-2 to determine the present value of the MACRS tax shield.

## PROBLEMS

**9-19  Review of Chapters 8 and 9**  Bullmark Company is considering a new product that will sell for $11 per unit and have variable costs of $8 per unit and annual cash fixed costs of $90,000. Equipment required to produce the product costs $210,000 and is expected to last, and be depreciated on a straight-line basis, for six years, with no expected salvage value. Bullmark estimates that sales of the new product will be 60,000 units per year for six years. Bullmark's income tax rate is 40% and its cost of capital is 14%.

**Required**
1. What is the expected increase in future annual after-tax cash flows if the project is accepted?
2. What is the NPV of the project?
3. For this question only, suppose the project also involves an increase in inventories and receivables totaling $40,000. What is the NPV of the project?
4. What is the PI for the project? (Round to two decimal places.)
5. What is the payback period for the project? (Round to one decimal place.)
6. What is the approximate IRR for the project?
7. What annual unit volume must the company sell to earn a return just equal to the 14% cost of capital?
8. Approximately how long must the life of the project be to earn a return of 16%?

**9-20  Relationships**  Fill in the blanks for each of the following independent cases. There are no salvage values for the investments.

| | (a) | (b) | (c) | (d) | (e) | (f) | (g) |
|---|---|---|---|---|---|---|---|
| | | Annual | | | Internal | Net | |
| | Years of | After-tax | | | Rate of | Present | Profitability |
| | Project | Cash | Initial | Cutoff Rate | Rate of | Present | Profitability |
| Case | Life | Flows | Investment | of Return | Return | Value | Index |
| 1 | 15 | $40,000 | _____ | ___% | 14% | _____ | 1.109 |
| 2 | 8 | _____ | $448,470 | 16% | 18% | _____ | _____ |
| 3 | ___ | $80,000 | $361,600 | 12% | ___% | _____ | 1.25 |

**9-21  Review of Chapters 8 and 9**  Brockington Mills has the opportunity to acquire machinery that costs $282,000 and has a useful life of four years. The production manager believes that the machinery could reduce annual material and labor costs by $100,000. Brockington pays a 30% income tax rate and requires a 12% return. The company uses straight-line depreciation.

**Required**
1. What is the IRR of this project?
2. What is the NPV of this project?
3. What is the PI on this project?
4. What must annual savings be for the project to have a 12% IRR?
5. For this question only, assume that Brockington could depreciate the asset evenly over three years for tax purposes, though the life of the project and the asset are still four years. What would the NPV of this project be?
6. For this question only, assume that undertaking this project means Brockington must increase its working capital by $12,000. What effect would this new information have on the NPV of this project?
7. Assume that the asset in this project is actually a replacement for one now in use that has a remaining life of four years, a book value (and tax basis) of $25,000, and a current market value of $40,000. What is the NPV of the project?

**9-22  Asset acquisition and MACRS**  Peyton Company is considering a new asset that costs $800,000. Peyton's managers expect to reduce cash operating costs by $230,000 per year over its ten-year estimated life. The asset qualifies for 7-year recovery under MACRS. Cost of capital is 16% and the tax rate is 40%.

**Required**
Determine the NPV of the investment.

**9-23  Working capital investment (without income taxes)**  Alexander Company, a wholesaler of paper products, has been approached by Clark Paper Products. Clark has offered Alexander exclusive rights to distribute its products in the Denver area. The contract runs for three years, after which time either company can terminate the arrangement.

Alexander's managers expect revenue from Clark's products to be about $400,000 per month, with variable costs (all cost of goods sold) about 85% of revenue. Incremental monthly fixed costs should be about $36,000. Additionally, Rawson must carry inventory approximating a two-month supply and must give its customers 90 days credit. Alexander will pay cash on delivery of Clark's products. Cost of capital is 20%.

**Required**
Determine whether Alexander should accept Clark's offer.

**9-24   *Replacement decision***   Danube Locks manufactures security equipment. The company now uses a machine that has a book value of $60,000 and a market value of $35,000. The machine has three years of useful life and is depreciated $20,000 per year. Annual operating costs are $130,000. A newer machine is available that costs $270,000 and has a three-year life and annual operating costs of only $20,000. Danube uses straight-line depreciation, has an 18% cost of capital, and has a 40% income tax rate. Neither machine will have salvage value at the end of its useful life. If the company makes the replacement, it will finance the investment with debt bearing 10% interest.

**Required**

Determine the NPV of the proposed investment.

**9-25   *Sensitivity analysis and MACRS (continuation of 9-11)***   The managers of ORM Company are not sure of the annual savings in cash operating costs that the machine will generate. One manager has asked how low the savings could be and the company still earn the 14% target rate of return.

**Required**

Determine the annual cash operating savings that yield a 14% return.

**9-26   *Comparison of alternatives***   Stanley Company must choose between two machines that will perform an essential function. Machine A costs $40,000, has a ten-year life with no salvage value, and costs $12,000 per year to operate (cash costs). Machine B costs $80,000, has a ten-year life with no salvage value, and costs $3,000 per year to operate. The tax rate is 40% and cost of capital is 10%. Straight-line depreciation will be used for either machine.

**Required**

Using the guidelines in Appendix A, write a memorandum to Stanley's vice president of manufacturing, Frank Cousins, giving and explaining your recommendation regarding which machine should be purchased.

**9-27   *Unit costs***   High Flyer manufactures running shoes. Its managers are considering entering the low-priced market and are looking at several alternatives. The model they wish to introduce will, they believe, sell 200,000 pairs annually at $22. Estimates of unit costs for two alternative production methods are as follows:

|  | Use Existing Facilities | Buy New Machinery |
|---|---|---|
| Materials | $ 3.60 | $ 3.30 |
| Direct labor | 7.50 | 6.50 |
| Variable overhead | 2.40 | 2.25 |
| Fixed overhead | 3.75 | 4.25 |
| Total unit costs | $17.25 | $16.30 |

Company policy is to charge each product with both fixed and variable overhead. The basic charge for fixed overhead is $0.50 per direct labor dollar. The amount of fixed overhead shown for the new machinery includes $1.00 per unit for depreciation of $200,000 per year ($600,000 cost) on the new machinery, which has a three-year life. Thus, the $4.25 is $1.00 plus the normal overhead charge of $0.50 times $6.50 direct labor cost. One of the managers points out that the $0.95 difference in unit cost works out to $190,000 per year, a significant savings. He also points out that the after-tax savings is $114,000 (the tax rate is 40%), which gives a rate of return of 38% on the average investment of $300,000. Cost of capital is 18%.

**Required**

1. Determine the NPV of the investment.
2. Determine the approximate IRR on the investment.

**9-28 JIT, Inventory** Concord Industries' Williamston plant has been setting up manufacturing cells and smoothing the flow of work in an effort at implementing JIT principles. The plant must now make a multitude of changes related to reducing the number of vendors, ensuring the quality of the parts provided by the remaining vendors, opening walls so that trucks can make deliveries straight to the cell where the parts are used, and teaching new skills to workers.

All of these activities are estimated to cost about $6.7 million, of which $4.9 million can be expensed immediately for income tax purposes. The remaining $1.8 million is for changes in the physical plant that must be depreciated over the next ten years, using the straight-line method. The estimated annual cash savings before taxes over the next ten years are $600 thousand. Based on conversations with other plant managers, the plant manager expects inventory to fall to about $120 thousand from the current $2.7 million. The tax rate is 40% and cost of capital is 12%.

**Required**

Determine the NPV of the investment.

**9-29 Pollution control and capital budgeting** Craft Paper Company operates a plant that produces a great deal of air pollution. The local government has ordered that the polluting be stopped or the plant will be closed. Craft does not wish to close the plant and so has sought to find satisfactory ways to remove pollutants. Craft has found two alternatives, both of which will reduce the outflow of pollutants to levels satisfactory to the government. One, called Entrol, costs $1,000,000, has a ten-year life with no salvage value, and has annual cash operating costs of $180,000. The other, Polltrol, costs $2,000,000, has a ten-year life with no salvage value, and has cash operating costs of $210,000 annually. However, Polltrol compresses the particles it removes into solid blocks of material that can be sold to chemical companies. Annual sales of the material are estimated at $250,000.

Either device will be depreciated on a straight-line basis. Cost of capital is 16% and the tax rate is 40%.

**Required**

Using the guidelines in Appendix A, write a memorandum to Paula Graves, Craft's vice president of manufacturing, giving and explaining your recommendation about which device to acquire.

**9-30 Replacement decision and sensitivity analysis (without income taxes)** McCormick Associates is a market research consulting firm that is well-known for sophisticated statistical analysis. The firm owns a computer system that cost $80,000 five years ago and now has a book value of $40,000 and a market value of $18,000. The system costs $45,000 per year to operate and will have no value at the end of five more years. A new system will cost McCormick $65,000, will last five years with no salvage value, and cost $20,000 per year to operate.

The company has a cutoff rate of 14%.

**Required**

1. Determine whether the new equipment should be purchased.

2. Determine the approximate IRR on the investment.
3. Suppose the data processing manager knows that the new machine is more efficient than the old, but not how much more. What annual cash savings are necessary for the company to earn 14%?
4. Suppose that the estimate of annual cash flows is reliable, but that the useful life of the new equipment is in question. About how long must the new equipment last for the company to earn 14%?

**9-31  Alternative production process**   Noonan Statuary uses a labor-intensive manufacturing process. Existing equipment has a book value and tax basis of $20,000, a five-year remaining life, and a $25,000 market value. Annual depreciation is $4,000 and cash operating costs are $64,000. The proposed process requires machinery costing $100,000 with a useful life of five years and no salvage value. The new machinery requires $40,000 in annual cash costs. Straight-line depreciation will be used for tax purposes for the new machine. The tax rate is 40% and cost of capital is 12%.

**Required**
1. What is the net investment of the new equipment?
2. What is the NPV of the investment?

**9-32  Sensitivity analysis**   The managers of Boston Products Company have been trying to decide whether or not to introduce a new deluxe birdfeeder. They expect it to sell for $30 and to have unit variable costs of $14. Fixed costs requiring cash disbursements should be about $250,000 per year. The feeder also requires machinery costing $600,000 with a four-year life and no salvage value. The company uses straight-line depreciation. Cost of capital is 16%.
   The one point of which the managers are unsure is the annual unit volume. Estimates made by individual managers range from 30,000 to 55,000 units.

**Required**
1. Ignoring income taxes, determine the number of feeders per year the company must sell to make the investment yield just 16%.
2. Redo requirement 1 assuming a 40% income tax rate.

**9-33  Determining required cost savings**   A salesperson from Columbus Milling has shown the production manager of Van Ooteghem Products a machine that will reduce variable production costs of a product that sells 20,000 units annually. The machine costs $150,000, has no salvage value, and should last for five years. Annual fixed cash operating costs are $32,000. Cost of capital is 16%.

**Required**
1. Ignoring taxes, what reduction in unit variable production costs is necessary to make the investment desirable?
2. Answer requirement 1 assuming a tax rate of 40% and straight-line depreciation.
3. Suppose now that the machine will reduce unit variable production costs by $4, but that annual volume is in doubt. What annual volume is needed to make the investment desirable? Consider income taxes.

**9-34  Benefit-cost analysis**   The Department of Health has studied treatments for two diseases, a type of kidney disease and a type of heart disease. The following data have been assembled.

|  | Kidney Disease | Heart Disease |
|---|---|---|
| Cost to save one life | $100,000 | $150,000 |
| Average age of victim at death | 40 years | 50 years |
| Average annual income of victims | $15,000 | $25,000 |

The heart disease appears to be caused partly by stresses that affect higher-income people, which accounts in part for the difference in incomes between the two types of victims.

The department believes that a discount rate of 10% is appropriate. It also assumes that a person will work until age 70 (30 additional years for persons cured of kidney disease, 20 for those cured of heart disease).

### Required

1. Compute the NPV of saving a single life from each disease. The cost to save the life is incurred immediately, and the annual incomes are assumed to be received at the ends of years.
2. Suppose that a lack of trained personnel makes it impossible to pursue treatment for both diseases and that the same amount will be spent regardless of which disease is selected for treatment. Which disease do you prefer to see treated and why?

**9-35   When-to-sell decisions**   Glenburnie Scotch has a large quantity of Scotch whiskey that is approaching its sixth anniversary. When it reaches age six it can be sold for $700 per barrel. If it is held until it is ten years old it can be sold for $1,170 per barrel. Cost of capital is 12%.

### Required

1. Determine the IRR of holding the Scotch until it is ten years old.
2. The price of six-year-old Scotch is still $700 per barrel, but the projected price of ten-year-old Scotch in four years is in doubt. What is the minimum price per barrel that the company would have to receive four years hence to justify keeping the Scotch until it is ten years old?
3. Suppose now that the following schedule of prices is expected. Determine the point at which the Scotch should be sold using the criterion of highest IRR. (Assume that the cutoff rate of return is low enough so that all of the rates you compute would be acceptable. That is, the best decision is not to sell now.)

| Years of Age | Expected Price |
|---|---|
| 6 | $  700 |
| 7 | 800 |
| 8 | 950 |
| 9 | 1,200 |
| 10 | 1,400 |

4. Redo requirement 3 using the NPV criterion to make the decision.

**9-36   Increased sales and working capital**   Baker Company makes several labor-intensive products. The products average $4.50 in variable costs, of which labor is $2.25. Fixed costs are $100,000 annually. The company has had difficulty in expanding production to meet increased demand and is considering a large machine that will enable a production increase to 105,000 units with the same size work force.

Sales are currently 80,000 units at an $8 average selling price. The company expects to sell all its production at $7 per unit if the machine is bought.

Variable costs per unit other than labor will remain the same, and fixed costs will increase by the amount of depreciation on the new machine. The machine costs $80,000 and has a useful life of ten years. There will be increased working capital requirements of $80,000. Straight-line depreciation will be used for tax purposes. The tax rate is 40% and cost of capital is 14%.

**Required**

Determine whether Baker should buy the machine.

**9-37   Sensitivity analysis (continuation of 8-34)**   The managers of Pitcairn Manufacturing believe that volume will be 250,000 pairs, but are concerned about that estimate. They wish to know how many pairs of socks they must sell to earn an IRR of 14%.

**Required**

1. Determine the unit volume that will yield an IRR of 14%.
2. How does the calculation for requirement 1 change your attitude about the investment from your solution to Problem 8-34?

**9-38   Backing a play**   As a patron of the arts, you receive many proposals from authors and directors. Recently, Hayley Lane, the famous playwright, asked you to back his forthcoming play, Birds of a Feather. He has prepared the following analysis.

| | |
|---|---:|
| Investment: | |
| Sets and other depreciable assets (straight-line basis) | $  500,000 |
| Working capital | 200,000 |
| Total investment | $  700,000 |
| Annual gross receipts, expected to continue for 4 years | $1,500,000 |
| Annual salaries of actors and other personnel | $  600,000 |
| Rent, $20,000 + 5% of gross receipts | |
| Royalty to Clark, 10% of gross receipts | |
| Other annual cash expenses | $  140,000 |

You have a target rate of 20% and a tax rate of 40%.

**Required**

1. Should you back the play on the basis of the information given?
2. At what level of annual gross receipts does the play yield a 20% IRR?

**9-39   Replacement decision**   The management of Bettel Metals Inc. is considering a new machine. The new machine is more efficient than the one currently in use and would save the company $6,000 annually because of greater operating speed. To keep the old machine operating at the present level of efficiency requires immediate repairs costing $5,000. The repair cost is tax deductible this year. Annual depreciation on the old machine, which is expected to last ten years, is $1,800. No scrap value is expected at that time.

The new machine costs $37,300, including freight and installation charges. It has an expected useful life of ten years and no expected scrap value. Straight-line depreciation would be used on the new machine. The old machine has a book value of $18,000 and a market value of $12,000. The tax rate is 40%.

**Required**
1. Compute the net cash outlay if the new machine is purchased.
2. Evaluate the proposal, assuming a minimum required rate of return of 10%.

**9-40   *Valuing a football team***   Owners of athletic teams allocate a large portion of the purchase price to the value of the players' contracts. This amount can be amortized for income tax purposes. Some economists have argued that the principal value of a franchise is not the player contracts, but the monopoly right to operate and earn revenues from television, ticket sales, and so on. The amount allocated to the monopoly right is not amortizable for tax purposes, much as the cost of land is not depreciable.

Suppose you are in the 28% tax bracket and are considering buying the St. Paul Snowmen of the Transam Football League. You expect the operations of the team to generate pretax cash inflows of $4,000,000 annually. You also expect the league to fold in ten years, at which time your investment will be worthless. Your discount rate is 14%.

**Required**
1. Determine the maximum that you are willing to pay for the team assuming that the investment can be amortized evenly over ten years for tax purposes.
2. Determine the maximum that you are willing to pay for the team if you could not amortize the cost. (You then have a lump-sum tax deduction at the end of year 10 equal to your original investment.)

**9-41   *Investing in quality, JIT, declining base***   The Carterville Plant of Baldwin Industries is old and outmoded. The quality of the output is declining, and the plant is getting the reputation of being a low-quality producer. All this makes the managers believe that annual sales will fall about $1.5 million if they do nothing. Contribution margin is 60% of sales.   The manufacturing managers have been looking at new machinery and equipment that would increase quality to the point where the plant could regain its former reputation. They have also been looking at employing JIT principles. Outfitting the plant for the new machinery and to accommodate JIT will cost about $5.5 million. The entire investment can be depreciated over its ten-year useful life. It has no salvage value. The company uses straight-line depreciation. The new machinery will not affect variable costs, but will increase cash fixed costs by $0.7 million per year.

The managers also expect to reduce inventory by $4.8 million if they make the investment. The tax rate is 40% and cost of capital is 12%.

**Required**
Determine the NPV of the proposed investment.

**9-42   *Attracting industry***   Carboro is a small town with little industry and high unemployment. The mayor and members of the town council have been trying to interest businesses in locating factories in Carboro. Newman Industries has agreed to the following proposal of the town government. The town will build a $4.3 million plant to Newman's specifications and rent it to Newman for its estimated useful life of 20 years at $150,000 per year provided that Newman employs at least 600 currently unemployed citizens of Carboro.

The mayor expects some increases in the cost of town government to result from the additional employees that Newman would transfer to the new factory.

| | |
|---|---:|
| Additional fire and police protection | $ 35,000 |
| Additional school costs | 50,000 |
| Additional general governmental costs | 20,000 |
| Total additional annual costs | $105,000 |

An economist from the state university has projected the following annual results if the plant is built.

| | |
|---|---:|
| Increases in retail sales in Carboro | $6,000,000 |
| Increase in property tax base | $4,400,000 |

The town levies a 1% tax on all retail sales and taxes property at a rate of $80 per $1,000. The state spends about $2,000 per year in direct support for each unemployed person. The economist said that total unemployment is likely to fall by about 1,500 persons because the factory would help to create other jobs.

The council believes that the factory should be built provided that the benefits to the town government do not exceed the costs. The relevant discount rate is 9%.

### Required

1. Determine whether the additional receipts to the town, less the additional costs, justify the building of the factory.
2. Assuming that your answer to requirement 1 is no, list and discuss other factors that might be considered and other actions that might be taken.

**9-43 Dropping a product** Stracke Company makes a variety of products in several factories throughout the country. The sales manager is unhappy with the results shown by Quickclean, a spray cleaner for household use. Quickclean is made in only one factory. A typical income statement follows.

| | |
|---|---:|
| Sales | $4,500,000 |
| Variable costs | 3,800,000 |
| Contribution margin | $ 700,000 |
| Fixed costs | 880,000 |
| Loss | $ (180,000) |

The production manager tells the sales manager that about $580,000 of the fixed costs shown require cash disbursements. These are all avoidable. The remaining $300,000 in fixed costs consists of $100,000 in depreciation on equipment used only to make Quickclean and $200,000 in allocated costs. The equipment used to make Quickclean has a useful life of five more years, and no salvage value is expected at the end of five years. The book value is $500,000 and straight-line depreciation is being used.

Stracke has a 14% cutoff rate of return and a 40% tax rate.

### Required

1. Assume that the machinery used to make Quickclean has no resale value. If the product is dropped, the machinery will be scrapped. The loss is immediately tax deductible. Determine whether Quickclean should be dropped.
2. Assume that the machinery could be sold for $350,000. Redo requirement 1.

**9-44 *New product—complementary effects*** Beverly Hill, general manager of the McKeown Division of Standard Enterprises, Inc., is considering a new product. It will sell for $20 per unit and have variable costs of $9. Volume is estimated at 120,000 units per year. Fixed costs requiring cash disbursements will increase by $300,000 annually, mainly in connection with operating machinery that would be purchased for $2,000,000. The machinery has a useful life of ten years with no salvage value, and would be depreciated using the straight-line method.

The new product would be made in a section of the factory that is physically separate from the rest of the factory and is now leased to another firm for $120,000 per year. The lease expires this month, but the other company has expressed an interest in renewing the lease for an additional ten years.

Hill expects inventories to increase by $500,000 if the new product is introduced. She also expects customers to pay for their purchases two months after purchase, but she is uncertain how to consider these factors.

Cost of capital is 20% and the tax rate is 40%.

**Required**

1. Determine whether the new product should be introduced.
2. Suppose that if the new product is introduced, the sales of an existing product would increase by 30,000 units per year. The existing product sells for $10 and has variable costs of $6. The increase in sales of this product will lead to increases in inventories and receivables of $60,000. Determine whether the new product should be introduced.

**9-45 *Closing a plant—externalities*** Fisher Manufacturing Company operates a plant in Vesalia, a small city on the Platte River. The company has been notified that it must install pollution control equipment at the plant at a cost of $4,000,000, or else close the plant. The plant employs 400 people, virtually all of whom will lose their jobs if the plant closes. Fisher will make a lump-sum payment of $80,000 to the people put out of jobs if the plant closes.

A buyer is willing to purchase the plant for $400,000, which equals its book value. Fisher could shift production to the Montclair plant if it closed the Vesalia plant, with no increase in total cash production costs. (The increase in Montclair's cash production costs equals the cash operating costs of the Vesalia plant.) However, shipping costs will increase by $900,000 annually because the Montclair plant is much farther away from customers than the Vesalia plant.

The new equipment has a ten-year useful life with no salvage value. Straight-line depreciation is used for tax purposes. The tax rate is 40% and cost of capital is 14%.

**Required**

1. Considering only monetary factors, determine whether Fisher should install the pollution control equipment or close the plant.
2. What other factors might be considered by those interested in the decision?

## CASES

**9-46 *Modification of equipment*** Toll Company has equipment that it used to make a product that it has phased out of its operations. The equipment has a book value of $400,000 and remaining useful life of four years. Depreciation is being taken using the straight-line method at $100,000 per year. No salvage value is expected at the end of the useful life.

The existing equipment is worth $220,000 now on the open market. Or, at a cost of $300,000, the equipment can be modified to produce another product. The modifications will not affect the useful life or salvage value and will be depreciated using the straight-line method. If the company does not modify the existing equipment, it will have to buy new equipment at a cost of $800,000. The new equipment also has a useful life of four years with no salvage value, and would be depreciated using the straight-line method. The product to be made with the new equipment or modified existing equipment is essential to Toll's product line.

Cash operating costs of the new equipment will be $50,000 less than with the existing equipment. Cost of capital is 16% and the tax rate is 40%.

### Required

Using the guidelines in Appendix A, write a memorandum to the company's president, Grant Toll, giving and supporting your recommendation about which alternative should be selected.

**9-47    Mutually exclusive investments**    Seagle Company requires machinery for an essential task that will be carried out for the next ten years. Two available machines meet the company's needs.

|  | Rapidgo 350 | Rapidgo 600 |
|---|---|---|
| Purchase cost | $50,000 | $90,000 |
| Annual operating expenses, exclusive of depreciation | $12,000 | $15,000 |
| Useful life | 5 years | 10 years |

Either machine will be depreciated using the straight-line method. The firm expects to pay $60,000 to replace the Rapidgo 350 at the end of five years, if that machine is selected. The other data applicable to the Rapidgo 350 are applicable to the replacement model as well.

The cutoff rate is 16% and the tax rate is 40%.

### Required

Determine the course of action the company should take.

**9-48    Replacement decision, MACRS (CMA adapted)**    Lamb Company manufactures several lines of machine products. One valve stem requires special tools that must soon be replaced. The tools are fully depreciated and have no resale value. Management has decided that the only alternative to replacing these tools is to buy the stem from an outside supplier at $20 per unit.

Lamb has been using 80,000 stems over the past few years and this volume is expected to continue, although there could be some decline over the next few years. Cost records show the following at 80,000 units.

| | |
|---|---|
| Material | $ 3.80 |
| Labor | 3.70 |
| Variable overhead | 2.20 |
| Fixed overhead | 4.50 |
| Total unit cost | $14.20 |

Replacing the specialized tools will cost $2,500,000. The new tools have a life of eight years and $100,000 salvage value. Lamb will use MACRS. The tools qualify for a five-year recovery period. Cost of capital is 12% and the tax rate is 40%.

Lamb's managers have had discussions with the toolmaker's sales engineers and with another manufacturer that uses similar tools. Indications are that labor and variable overhead will drop, but that material cost will increase because the new tools require higher-quality material than the ones currently used. Their best estimates follow.

| | |
|---|---|
| Material | $ 4.50 |
| Labor | 3.00 |
| Variable overhead | 1.80 |
| Fixed overhead | 5.00 |
| Total unit cost | $14.30 |

Cash fixed costs associated with the new tools are $100,000 per year; with the existing tools these costs are $50,000 per year. There will be no such costs if Lamb buys the stem from the outside supplier.

**Required**
1. Determine whether Lamb should buy the stem or manufacture it using the new tools.
2. Lamb's managers are concerned about making such a large investment when there is a possibility that the volume of the part might drop. Determine the volume of parts that makes Lamb indifferent between making it and buying it.

**9-49 Evaluating an investment proposal** Your new assistant has just brought you the following analysis of an investment you are considering. The investment relates to a new manufacturing process for making one of the company's major products.

Required Investment

| | |
|---|---|
| New machinery (10-year life, no salvage value) | $350,000 |
| Research and development | 60,000 |
| Administrative time | 10,000 |
| Total investment | $420,000 |

Annual Cash Flows (10 Years)

| | |
|---|---|
| Savings in cost over old process: | |
| Labor | $ 75,000 |
| Materials | 80,000 |
| Variable overhead | 40,000 |
| Depreciation | (35,000) |
| Total operating savings | $160,000 |
| Less: Interest on debt to finance investment | 35,000 |
| Net savings before taxes | $125,000 |
| Less: Income taxes at 40% rate | 50,000 |
| Net cash flow after taxes | $ 75,000 |

Your assistant tells you that the new machinery would replace old machinery that has a ten-year remaining useful life with no salvage value. The old machinery will be scrapped if the new machinery is bought, and the salvage value equals the cost of having it removed. The old machinery has a book value of $110,000. The company uses straight-line depreciation for all machinery.

Your assistant also tells you that the listed costs for research and development and for administrative time relate solely to this project and contain no allocations. The costs have already been incurred, so their amounts are certain. The item in the analysis for interest on debt is for $350,000 at 10%, which will be borrowed if the new machinery is acquired.

Based on his analysis and the 16% cost of capital, he recommends that the project be rejected.

### Required

Determine whether you should make the investment.

**9-50    *Alternative uses of assets (AICPA adapted)*    Miller Manufacturing Company** has been producing toasters and blenders in its Syracuse plant for several years. The rent for the Syracuse factory building is $80,000 per year. Miller's directors have decided to cease operations at that location and scrap the equipment when the lease expires at the end of four years.

Blender production is approximately 50,000 per year and the company expects to continue production at that level. However, because of intense competition and price erosion, the company has decided to stop making toasters.

Two areas of the Syracuse plant, making up about 30% of the total floor space, are devoted to toasters. The equipment used to make toasters has a book value of $140,000 and is depreciated at $35,000 per year. The company has received an offer of $20,000 for all the equipment now used in toaster production, and the buyer is not interested in anything less than all of it. If the equipment were sold, the space now used for toaster production could be subleased for $12,000 per year.

Because the production of blenders is to be continued, the production manager, Hank Schrontz, was asked if he needed the space and/or equipment now devoted to toaster production. He said that though he had no need for additional productive capacity for tasks currently undertaken at the plant, he is interested in using the space and equipment to manufacture a blender part now being purchased from an outside company. The part is a blade assembly that the firm purchases for $5. The contract with the vendor runs for four more years and requires that Miller buy at least 5,000 assemblies per year.

Either of the two areas now used for toaster production could be converted to produce the blade assemblies. Schrontz estimates the variable cost to produce an assembly at $3.60; no additional fixed costs requiring cash would be incurred. However, the equipment now used has to be converted. He estimates the cost at $40,000 to convert enough of the equipment to make 35,000 assemblies per year and $80,000 to convert enough to make 60,000 assemblies. Because the prospective buyer of the equipment wants all or none of it, conversion of any of it means the company must forego the sale.

The company's tax rate is 40% and its cost of capital is 14%. Straight-line depreciation will be used on costs of converting equipment.

### Required

Use the guidelines in Appendix A to write a memorandum to Mr. Schrontz explaining your recommendation as to the best course of action.

**9-51    *Expanding a factory*    Fisher Company** needs more space and machinery to increase production. The production manager and president have been trying to decide which of two plans to accept.

|  | Plan A | Plan B |
|---|---|---|
| Investment required | $4,000,000 | $5,500,000 |
| Additional fixed cash operating costs per year | $600,000 | $800,000 |
| Additional capacity in machine hours per year | 200,000 | 280,000 |

The company uses straight-line depreciation. No salvage value is expected for either investment at the end of their ten-year useful lives.

The production manager prefers Plan B because the cost per machine hour and investment per machine hour are lower than those for Plan A. The president, E. J. Alvarez, is unsure about this and asks the sales manager whether the capacity would be fully utilized. The sales manager provides the following data.

| | Product | | |
| --- | --- | --- | --- |
| | 101-X | 201-X | 305-X |
| Potential increased sales, in units | 30,000 | 40,000 | 30,000 |
| Contribution margin per unit | $18 | $24 | $40 |
| Machine hours required per unit | 2 | 4 | 5 |

Fisher pays income taxes at a 40% rate and has cost of capital of 12%.

**Required**

Using the guidelines in Appendix A, write a memorandum to E. J. Alvarez giving and supporting your recommendation about expanding capacity and how the expanded capacity should be used.

# Part Three

## *control and performance evaluation*

Part Three concentrates on the management functions of control and performance evaluation. To perform these functions effectively, managers apply the principles and techniques of responsibility accounting. An essential step in the development of a responsibility accounting system is fixing responsibility for each cost. Fixing responsibility for costs is also important to derive the fullest advantage from comprehensive budgeting. In this part, the emphasis shifts from planning to control, and to evaluating actual results in relation to planned or budgeted results.

The major thrust of responsibility accounting is behavioral; the critical factor in its success is the extent to which the system encourages or discourages behavior consistent with the organization's best interests. Human behavior and the ways in which accounting methods encourage particular kinds of behavior are treated extensively in the three chapters in this part, including recent theories that cast doubt on traditional approaches.

## Chapter Ten

# RESPONSIBILITY ACCOUNTING

## LEARNING OBJECTIVES

*After reading this chapter, you should be able to*

- *Define goal congruence and explain its relationship to control and performance evaluation.*
- *Identify the types of responsibility centers and explain the differences among them.*
- *Determine the positive and negative aspects of specific criteria used for evaluating the performance of responsibility centers.*
- *Calculate contribution margin variances and explain their significance.*
- *Describe the pros and cons of including cost allocations in performance reports.*
- *Describe some approaches to allocating costs to responsibility centers.*
- *Explain how cost allocations can create ethical problems.*

---

The 1998 annual report for **Procter & Gamble** (P&G) presented the following goals for the organization:

1. To double their business in 10 years,
2. To grow market share in categories representing the majority of their volume, and
3. To remain consistently among the top third of their peer companies in Total Shareholder Return performance.

To achieve these goals, P&G made four changes in the way they are organized. First, they moved from being organized by regional business units to being organized by product-based, global business units. Second, they strengthened their country-based organizations to provide even deeper knowledge of local consumers and stronger partnerships with their customers. Third, P&G created a new Global Business Services organization to support the global business units and the local market organizations. This move brought together business services that were dispersed throughout the organization. Finally, P&G streamlined corporate staff. Many corporate resources were aligned with the business units.

Why do companies organize in particular ways? How do managers respond to different sets of responsibilities? Did P&G's regional business unit managers work in the company's best interests? How can companies motivate managers to work in the best interests of the company?

*Source: 1998 annual report for Procter & Gamble.*

Thus far we have concentrated on applying the concepts of managerial accounting to the management functions of planning and decision making. We now look more closely at managerial control, particularly performance evaluation. Managers exercise control through a management control system, a set of policies and procedures used to determine whether operations are going as planned and, if not, to suggest corrective action. Responsibility accounting is the gathering and reporting of information that is used to control operations and evaluate performance. The **responsibility accounting system** is the formal, financial communication system within the overall management control system. These systems use both financial and nonfinancial information.

Nonquantifiable factors are even more important for effective control and evaluation than they are for planning and decision making. The potential for accounting reports to influence the actions of managers is of particular concern. The problem of cost allocation introduced in Chapter 5 is also relevant here. There are good reasons for allocating cost—to encourage particular kinds of behavior and to assist in evaluating performance. But there are also good reasons not to allocate costs, so that the issue is less clear than it was in decision making, where allocation was virtually always undesirable.

*CHAPTER 5*

## GOAL CONGRUENCE AND MOTIVATION

Employees, including managers, work to achieve their own goals, which can include salary increases, promotion, and recognition. (When a company is downsizing, just keeping a job might be an important goal.) Much as students try to perform well on tasks that affect their grades, employees pursuing their goals try to perform well on the measures by which they are evaluated.

People do not need incentives to pursue their own goals. They might face ethical problems if such actions conflict with other personal values. For example, some companies, including CPA firms, evaluate people partly on how long they take to perform assigned tasks. Employees then have incentives to underreport time. Other companies evaluate people partly on how much billable time they generate: these employees have an incentive to overreport time.

Whether or not they seek profits, economic entities have goals. For any entity, the important question is whether employees are working toward achieving the *entity's* goals. A major objective of management control is to encourage **goal congruence**, which means that as people work to achieve their own goals, they also work to achieve the goals of the company. People must have incentives to work toward the company's goals. To accomplish that objective, managers must assign responsibilities and develop performance evaluation criteria that motivate employees to work toward the company's goals.

A responsibility accounting system generates reports to employees, including managers, about the performance of their assigned responsibilities. Because the reports influence behavior, they must be carefully designed and thoroughly understood both by the evaluators and those being evaluated. Most of the major problems in developing an effective responsibility accounting system are behavioral. Persons must trust the system; they must also believe that the system is fair. They must know the criteria used for evaluation and they must have a reasonable amount of control over their performance. Consider your response to learning, on the last day of class, that your clothing will be a factor in your grade. Or learning on the first day of class that your grade will be based partly on how well a randomly selected student performs on examinations. Evaluatees must also believe that the system reasonably depicts their performance with regard to the evaluation criteria, again, making controllability an important issue.

A management control system is most effective when it establishes evaluation criteria that encourage goal-congruent behavior and is implemented through a responsibility accounting system that employees trust to report their performance. The first step in implementing responsibility accounting is to establish responsibility centers.

## RESPONSIBILITY CENTERS

To be held accountable for performance, managers must have clearly defined areas of responsibility— activities they control. A **responsibility center** is an activity, such as a department, that a manager controls. You might think it is relatively easy to identify activities with specific managers. You might expect a plant manager to be responsible for producing budgeted quantities of specific products within budgeted cost limits, or a sales manager to be responsible for getting orders from customers. In the real world, a company's size, operating characteristics, and the philosophies of its upper-level managers influence the assignment of responsibility. Generalizing about the responsibilities of specific managers is unwise.

A factor that complicates the evaluation of performance in even the simplest of organizations is that the performance of one manager can affect the performance of others. For example, the best salespeople in the world will have difficulty selling poorly made products. By the same token, no production manager can minimize costs if production schedules change daily to accommodate rush orders. Such interdependencies cannot be eliminated entirely, but their effects can be minimized by careful selection of responsibility centers, appropriate use of rewards and penalties, and proper use of performance reports by managers who understand the information that they receive. For example, holding the production manager responsible for the quality of output as well as for production costs can reduce the potential for conflict between sales and production. Each situation where conflict might arise must be considered by itself and appropriate procedures and responsibilities assigned to the managers potentially in conflict; few general rules exist to which one can turn for guidance.

While most managers' responsibilities include meeting nonfinancial goals, responsibility centers are typically defined by financial responsibility. The four types of responsibility centers are cost centers, revenue centers, profit centers, and investment centers. The type of responsibility center depends on the breadth of control of the manager.

### COST CENTERS

A **cost center** is a segment whose manager is responsible for costs but not for revenues. A cost center can be relatively small, such as a manufacturing cell, the office of the chief executive, or the legal department. A cost center could also be quite large, such as a factory or the entire administrative area for a large firm. Large cost centers might be composed of smaller cost centers. For example, a factory might be segmented into many work stations, each of which is a cost center with several stations combined into departments that are also cost centers.

Identifying a responsibility center as a cost center doesn't mean that its manager is responsible only for controlling costs. A purchasing department manager is responsible for evaluating and selecting vendors, and is therefore responsible for the quality of materials and components the vendors supply.

## REVENUE CENTERS

**Revenue centers** are responsibility centers whose managers are held responsible for earning revenues, but not for the costs of generating revenues. Hospitals are the principal users of revenue centers, largely because of cost allocation issues and third-party reimbursers (such as Blue Cross, Medicare, and Medicaid). Some companies evaluate marketing managers by revenue, and ignore costs. But any center generates costs, if only the salary of its manager, so revenue centers exist because the organization chooses not to make the manager responsible for costs.

Again, managers of revenue centers might be held responsible for nonfinancial goals. Companies whose strategies include remaining only in markets where their products meet criteria such as specified market shares or rank will hold marketing managers responsible for such goals. **General Mills'** annual report lists the ranks of many of their products in their respective markets, and **General Electric's** strategy is to compete only where it is number one or two in sales.

## PROFIT CENTERS AND INVESTMENT CENTERS

A **profit center** is a segment whose manager is responsible for revenues as well as costs. For such a center, profit, defined in various ways, is used to measure performance. In some cases, the profit calculation includes only direct costs; in others the calculation includes some (or all) indirect costs.

An **investment center** is a segment whose manager is responsible not only for revenues and costs, but also for the investment required to generate profits. For such centers, companies calculate return on investment. Return on investment relates profit to the resources (plant and equipment, inventory, receivables) required to earn it. In both types of centers, the profit figure rarely reflects the generally accepted accounting principles (GAAP) that govern external reporting. The focus of internal responsibility accounting is the effectiveness and efficiency of the unit and its manager. The principle of controllability we discussed earlier argues against including such items as the annual audit fee in reports for profit and investment centers.

In practice, the term *profit center* often refers to both types of segments. Later in this chapter, and in parts of Chapter 11, we discuss various questions about how profit and investment might be measured. Of course, managers of profit and investment centers are also responsible for meeting nonfinancial performance goals such as market share, customer satisfaction, and employee development.

A major reason for using profit and investment centers is that profit and return on investment are more comprehensive measures of success than is cost alone. To survive, a company can't just control its costs. It must earn profits, and profitability is not necessarily a goal of managers whose responsibilities include only revenues or costs. The accompanying Insight illustrates how Caterpillar reorganized from being a functionally-based organization to a product-line–based organization.

CHAPTER
11

**SIGHT**

### Organizational Change at Caterpillar

Until 1990, **Caterpillar's** organizational structure focused on functional areas such as engineering, manufacturing, and accounting. The idea was that if each functional area achieved its goals and objectives, the customer would be happy and the corporation prosperous.

Then, in mid-1990, Caterpillar initiated the restructuring of its functional organization into one composed of 13 "profit center" divisions and four "service center" divisions. Product groups within the profit center divisions focus on serving the needs of the customers associated with a product line. Product group managers have direct control over engineering, manufacturing, and marketing.

*Source: James Hendricks, David Defreitas & Delores Walker, "Changing Performance Measures at Caterpillar,"* Management Accounting, *December 1996, 18-24.*

The idea that profit is a more comprehensive measure of performance than is cost has led some companies to create **artificial profit centers**, segments that deal with outsiders very little, if at all, but rather "sell" most of their goods or services to other segments within the company. The price that one center charges another center within the company is called a **transfer price**. (We discuss transfer prices in detail later in this chapter and in Chapter 11.) For example, a data processing department might charge the other departments that use its services. The department could then have an income statement, instead of just a statement of costs. The department's failure to show a profit—or to earn a satisfactory return on its investment—*might* indicate that it is inefficient. A loss might even indicate that the company would be better off to contract for the services from an outside company. With many companies now outsourcing ancillary functions to concentrate on their core businesses, efficiency measures of such functions are more important than ever. However, we say "might" because factors outside the control of the data processing manager could affect the results and cause the department to appear inefficient. A common example of such a confounding factor occurs when a growing company acquires more equipment and personnel than it currently needs because it expects higher use in the future. (Costs are now higher than necessary. But the decision to acquire higher capacity might be wise.)

Chapter 8 emphasized the need for investments to earn returns greater than the cost of the required capital. Companies that use investment centers recognize this principle by relating profits to the investment required to earn them. Managers responsible for both profit and investment have incentives to increase revenues, reduce costs, and reduce investment, all of which, taken by themselves, increase return on investment. Investment centers that fail to earn satisfactory returns might be candidates for elimination. Again, other factors might argue for keeping a center that appears to be performing poorly.

## PERFORMANCE EVALUATION CRITERIA

Selecting criteria to measure and evaluate performance is important because the criteria influence managers' actions. (How might a student's day-to-day actions be influenced by knowing that part of a course grade depended on appearance and punctuality?) The most common deficiencies in performance measurement are (1) using a single measure that emphasizes only one objective of the organization and (2) using measures that either misrepresent or fail to reflect the organization's objectives or the employee's responsibilities.

Managers want to use a single measure of performance. Such a measure would be objective because everyone would be measured the same way. It would be simpler to apply because there would be no question about how to weight several measures (such as examination scores, class contribution, and grades on projects). Unfortunately, such a measure is seldom found, and attempts to use a single measure often lead to unwanted results. Consider an example reported from the former Soviet Union. The government was unhappy with the output of nails and decided to evaluate managers of nail factories by the weight of the nails produced. The managers could produce much greater weight by making only large spikes, and they did. Once the government saw that its performance measure was not working, it changed the basis of evaluation to the number of nails produced, and the factories began to pour out carpet tacks and small brads. A single measure could be equally unsuccessful in other settings. For example, evaluating salespeople on total dollar sales fails to consider the profitability of the products sold. If, as seems probable, lower margin products are easier to sell than higher margin products, salespeople will concentrate on low margin products to the detriment of the company.

Failing to link performance measures to the entity's goals can also encourage dysfunctional actions. Imagine, if you will, a school district being offered the use of a distance education system that could reduce by 30 percent the time required for subliterate adults to complete an educational program. Because her budget is based on average daily attendance, and getting students through the program faster would reduce average attendance, the director of the program may turn down the offer. The director's action illustrates not only a poor choice of evaluation criteria, but also ethical blindness, since the people in the program would be served better by finishing faster.

Linking performance measures to the goals and objectives at a given time is important. For example, a young company in a rapidly growing industry does not need to be overly concerned with cost control because its early success depends on gaining customer acceptance and building a high market share. Prices and profit margins are usually high during the growth phase, so costs are not critical. But as the company and its industry mature, cost control becomes much more important. Many companies in the computer industry have begun to pay more attention to costs. Companies such as **Apple**, **Sun Microsystems**, and **Compaq** that used to achieve 70 percent gross margins now work hard to achieve 30 percent margins because of falling prices and cutthroat competition.

It is also important to consider the competitive strategy that is being used when choosing performance measures. As discussed in Chapter 1, two possible strategies for sustaining a competitive advantage are to be the lowest cost producer or to pursue a differentiation strategy. A company following a lowest cost producer strategy would be very concerned with measuring costs and expenditures and less concerned with market shares. A company pursuing a differentiation strategy would be more concerned about customer satisfaction measures and less concerned with costs.

Whether dealing with a cost, profit, or investment center, performance can be evaluated only by comparing actual results *with* something. The most common comparison is actual and budgeted results. Managers of production departments could be evaluated on producing budgeted quantities of product at budgeted costs. (Product quality expectations would, of course, be considered in establishing budgeted output and costs.) Managers of nonmanufacturing departments, such as a computer center or market research group, could be evaluated on whether they performed their assigned tasks and met budgeted costs. Managers of profit centers are evaluated by comparisons of actual and budgeted profit, and managers of investment centers might be evaluated on the basis of return on investment. (The special problems of evaluating investment centers are discussed in Chapter 11, but most of the comments on profit centers also apply to investment centers.)

CHAPTER 11

The legitimacy of evaluating a manager's performance by comparing budgeted and actual results depends on (1) how the budgeted amounts were determined and (2) the extent to which the comparisons consider the controllability of differences. As discussed in Chapters 6 and 7, managers are likely to try to achieve budgeted results that reflect currently attainable performance, or if they are convinced that stretch goals are necessary. We also noted that managers tend to react more favorably to an evaluation based on a budget they helped to set. But even with budgets that are agreed upon in advance, an uncontrollable change in conditions can influence results, and managers do not react favorably to a reporting and evaluation system that fails to allow for variations due to circumstances beyond their control.

CHAPTER 6

CHAPTER 7

Besides comparing budgeted and actual results, some companies evaluate managers on the basis of improvement over some prior period, or by comparison with other segments of the same company. Whatever the type of responsibility center, and whatever bases used to compare with actual results, evaluating a segment is different from evaluating its manager. A manager might be doing an excellent job even though the segment is performing poorly. For example, the manager of a segment doing business in a declining industry might be doing an excellent job if segment profits are steady or decline more slowly than those of the industry as a whole. Similarly, a segment operating in a growing market might look healthy even if its manager is not doing as good a job as another manager could. The question in both cases is the standard for comparison: what should the segment be able to accomplish? The performance of each segment is important to those corporate managers who are concerned with allocating resources to their best uses.

## USING MULTIPLE PERFORMANCE MEASURES: THE BALANCED SCORECARD

An approach known as the balanced scorecard has become popular recently. This approach extends performance evaluation from merely looking at financial results to formally incorporating measures that look at customer satisfaction, internal business processes, and the learning and growth potential of the organization.

The balanced scorecard asks four basic questions:

1.  How do customers see us? (the customer perspective)
2.  What must we excel at? (the internal business process perspective)
3.  Can we continue to improve and create value? (the learning and growth perspective)
4.  How do we look to stockholders? (the financial perspective)

This approach is called *balanced* for several reasons. First, a balance is maintained between external measures for shareholders and customers and internal measures of critical business processes, innovation, and learning and growth. Second, outcome measures of past results as well as measures that drive future performance are used. Third, objective, easily quantified outcome measures are balanced against subjective, somewhat judgmental, performance drivers of the outcome measures.

Measures in the customer perspective include a group of core measurements that are generic across all organizations, such as market share, customer retention, customer acquisition, customer satisfaction, and customer profitability. Additional measures are customized to reflect an organization's specific product/service attributes (such as functionality, quality, price, and time), the customer relationship, and the organization's image and reputation.

Measures for the internal business process perspective should be on those processes that will deliver the objectives established for customers and shareholders. The measures should reflect three distinct portions of the internal value chain: the innovation process, the operations process, and the post-sale process. The innovation process identifies current and future customers' needs and developing new solutions for those needs. The operations process delivers existing products and services to existing customers. Existing operations tend to be repetitive and can be scientifically measured with measures of process time, process quality, and process cost. Post-sale service is offering services after the sale that add to the value customers receive from the product and service offerings. What are the important aspects of service that occur after the delivery to the customer? By starting with shareholder and targeted customer expectations, you may find entirely new business processes at which you must excel.

The objectives of the financial, customer, and internal business process perspectives identify where an organization must excel to achieve breakthrough performance. The learning and growth perspective provides the infrastructure to enable the previous objectives to be reached. Three categories of measures include measures of employee capabilities such as employee satisfaction, which drives employee retention, and employee productivity; information system capabilities; and motivation, empowerment, and alignment. Specific measures may include a strategic job coverage ratio that tracks the number of employees qualified for specific strategic jobs relative to anticipated demands. This measure reveals gaps between future needs and present capabilities. Additional measures include strategic information availability that assesses the current availability of information relative to anticipated needs, the percentage of processes achieving targeted rates of improvement, and the percentage of key employees aligned to strategic balanced scorecard objectives. The accompanying Insight illustrates how the balanced scorecard has been used by various companies.

**IN** *SIGHT*

### Companies Using the Balanced Scorecard

**Allstate Corp** began to develop a balanced set of measures in mid-1994. In addition to competitive returns for shareholders, managers are now evaluated on customer satisfaction, employee effectiveness, process effectiveness, and innovation.

At **Tenneco Gas**, measures used to monitor customer satisfaction levels include the number of invoice adjustments incurred each month and four categories of survey results: data accuracy, corporate performance, reliability, and flexibility.

**AT&T Corp.'s Universal Card Services (UCS)**, gives receivables, the most critical driver of performance, special attention. The goal is to maximize the number of creditworthy customers that use the Universal Card. The key is to keep clients delighted with the service they get from UCS representatives. Receivables levels, the higher the better, are tallied daily along with quality and revenue metrics.

**Elf Atochem** installed new information systems that serve at least three purposes: to give more information to workers, to enhance decision-making information by managers, and to monitor a balanced set of measures for at least five levels in the organization. The new system merged the purchasing and payables processes. Buyers have the data to approve many purchases without a sign-off, finding buying terms, credit approval, delivery guidelines, expected quality, and other information right on their computer screen. The system then tracks vendor deliveries, price, and quality performance, feeding all that information into a scorecard on vendor performance.

If empowering employees, decentralizing decision-making authority, and putting everyone on teams to respond quickly to customers are important, measurement systems have to change. If the measurement systems do not, managers and employees will respond to the traditional measures, and strategy and behavior will not match.

*Source: Bill Birchard, "Making It Count: How Innovative Companies Really Use the New Metrics," CFO Magazine, October 1995.*

## RESPONSIBILITY REPORTING

### RESPONSIBILITY REPORTING FOR COST CENTERS

Exhibit 10-1 shows the interrelationships among reports for cost centers. Reports for a real company show more detail, more itemizations of individual costs. We restricted the number of items for simplicity.

The company whose reports are exhibited operates a factory that has three levels of supervision: (1) work stations, which are relatively small units under the control of supervisors; (2) departments, which are collections of work stations

## Exhibit 10-1    Responsibility Reports for Cost Centers

| | Current Month | | Year to Date | |
|---|---|---|---|---|
| | Budget | Over (Under) | Budget | Over (Under) |
| **Report to Supervisor of Work Station 106—Drill Press** | | | | |
| Materials | $   3,200 | $    (80) | $   12,760 | $   110 |
| Direct labor | 14,200 | 170 | 87,300 | 880 |
| Supervision | 1,100 | (50) | 4,140 | (78) |
| Power, supplies, miscellaneous | 910 | 24 | 3,420 | 92 |
| Totals | $ 19,410 | $     64 | $ 107,620 | $ 1,004 |
| | | | | |
| **Report to Supervisor of Fabrication Department** | | | | |
| Station 106—Drill Press | $ 19,410 | $     64 | $ 107,620 | $ 1,004 |
| Station 107—Grinding | 17,832 | 122 | 98,430 | (213) |
| Station 108—Cutting | 23,456 | 876 | 112,456 | 1,227 |
| Total work stations | $ 60,698 | $ 1,062 | $ 318,506 | $ 2,018 |
| Departmental costs (common to work stations): | | | | |
| General supervision | 12,634 | 0 | 71,234 | 0 |
| Cleaning | 6,125 | 324 | 32,415 | 762 |
| Other | 1,890 | (67) | 10,029 | (108) |
| Totals | $ 81,347 | $ 1,319 | $ 432,184 | $ 2,672 |
| | | | | |
| **Report to Manager of Factory** | | | | |
| Fabrication department | $ 81,347 | $ 1,319 | $ 432,184 | $ 2,672 |
| Milling department | 91,234 | (2,034) | 405,190 | (4,231) |
| Assembly department | 107,478 | 854 | 441,240 | 1,346 |
| Casting department | 78,245 | (433) | 367,110 | 689 |
| Total departments | $358,304 | $   (294) | $1,645,724 | $   476 |
| General factory costs (common to departments): | | | | |
| Engineering | 14,235 | 261 | 81,340 | 842 |
| Heat and light | 8,435 | 178 | 46,221 | 890 |
| Building depreciation | 3,400 | 0 | 20,400 | 0 |
| General administration (includes accounting, travel, plant manager's office, etc.) | 23,110 | 340 | 126,289 | 776 |
| Total factory costs | $407,484 | $   485 | $1,919,974 | $ 2,984 |

under the control of departmental supervisors; and (3) the factory as a whole, which is under the control of the factory manager. In addition, though not reflected in the reports, the factory manager is under the direction of the vice president of manufacturing. Two features of this set of sample reports are noteworthy and apply to all responsibility centers.

1.  The amount of detail in a report declines as the level of the manager receiving it rises.
2.  The reports are not necessarily *additive*.

The first feature is easy to understand. Managers are usually concerned most with the performance of those directly under their control. Routine reports to department managers do not detail all of the costs of each work station. Managers who want such detailed information can get it if they are particularly concerned.

The second feature, lack of additivity, requires further explanation. The total cost on the report to a manager is *not* the sum of the costs on the reports to the managers under her or his supervision. For example, Exhibit 10-1 shows that the total cost reported to the fabrication department supervisor is greater than the sum of the costs reported to the supervisors of the work stations. As we stated earlier, an important characteristic of good responsibility reporting is that reports separate controllable and uncontrollable costs (or omit uncontrollable costs entirely).

The company in Exhibit 10-1 omits uncontrollable costs. But all costs are controllable by *someone*. In the example company, the plant manager is responsible for some costs that the departmental supervisors are not: engineering, heat and light, building depreciation, and general administration. These costs are common to all of the departments and are therefore not controllable by any one departmental supervisor. Similarly, the department supervisors are responsible for some costs that the supervisors of work stations are not, and so on.

Lack of additivity also results from decisions not to hold particular managers responsible for costs they could control. In the preceding example, building depreciation is clearly not controllable by an individual department supervisor. However, the department managers can control the amount of electricity used to light their space by turning lights on and off as needed. The company simply does not consider it worthwhile to install separate meters in every department, so it does not try to hold the individual department managers responsible for the cost. Whether it is worthwhile to adopt procedures to assign responsibility for a particular cost to lower levels of management depends not only on the significance of the cost but also on the benefits to be gained by doing so. Benefits might include savings from lower-level managers using less of particular items (electricity, supplies, repair services, whatever). But the benefits must be weighed against the cost of obtaining the additional information (meters, time required to fill out more detailed requisition forms and to produce more detailed reports, etc.). In any case, the facts in a particular case determine whether a cost is controllable at a given level of management, and the responsibility reporting system should follow, as closely as possible, the principle of including only controllable items.

## RESPONSIBILITY REPORTING FOR PROFIT CENTERS

The principle of controllability also applies to responsibility reporting for profit centers (and for investment centers, which we consider in more detail in Chapter

11). Exhibit 10-2 provides sample reports for a company that organizes profit centers around product lines and geographical regions. Managers at the lowest level of profit centers are responsible for product lines. They are responsible to the managers of the geographical regions, who are in turn responsible to the executive vice president.

### Exhibit 10-2  Responsibility Reports for Profit Centers (thousands of dollars)

| | Current Month | | Year to Date | |
|---|---|---|---|---|
| | | Over | | Over |
| | Budget | (Under) | Budget | (Under) |
| **Report to Product Manager—** | | | | |
| **Appliances, European Region** | | | | |
| Sales | $122.0 | $ 1.5 | $ 387.0 | $ 3.2 |
| Variable costs: | | | | |
|   Production | $ 47.5 | $ 2.8 | $ 150.7 | $ 5.9 |
|   Selling and administrative | 12.2 | 1.8 | 38.7 | 1.9 |
| Total variable costs | $ 59.7 | $ 4.6 | $ 189.4 | $ 7.8 |
| Contribution margin | $ 62.3 | $ (3.1) | $ 197.6 | $ (4.6) |
| Direct fixed costs | 36.0 | (1.2) | 98.5 | (3.1) |
| Product margin | $ 26.3 | $ (1.9) | $   99.1 | $ (1.5) |
| | | | | |
| **Report to Manager—** | | | | |
| **European Region** | | | | |
| Product margins: | | | | |
|   Appliances | $ 26.3 | $ (1.9) | $   99.1 | $ (1.5) |
|   Industrial equipment | 37.4 | 3.2 | 134.5 | 7.3 |
|   Tools | 18.3 | 1.1 | 59.1 | (2.0) |
| Total product margins | $ 82.0 | $ 2.4 | $ 292.7 | $ 3.8 |
| Regional expenses (common | | | | |
|   to all product lines) | 18.5 | 0.8 | 61.2 | (1.3) |
| Regional margin | $ 63.5 | $ 1.6 | $ 231.5 | $ 5.1 |
| | | | | |
| **Report to Executive Vice President** | | | | |
| Regional margins: | | | | |
|   European | $ 63.5 | $ 1.6 | $ 231.5 | $ 5.1 |
|   Asian | 78.1 | (4.3) | 289.4 | (8.2) |
|   North American | 211.8 | (3.2) | 612.4 | (9.6) |
| Total regional margins | $353.4 | $ (5.9) | $1,133.3 | $(12.7) |
| Corporate expenses (common | | | | |
|   to all regions) | 87.1 | 1.4 | 268.5 | 3.1 |
| Corporate profit | $266.3 | $ (7.3) | $ 864.8 | $(15.8) |

Here again, the reports show decreasing detail to higher-level managers and are not additive. Unallocated costs—regional expenses common to product lines, or corporate expenses common to regions—include many items. For instance, regional expenses include the salaries of people at regional headquarters, including those in accounting, personnel, finance, and other functions administered from regional headquarters. These costs are not direct to product lines, and product managers cannot control them. In addition, image-building advertising not aimed at particular product lines could also be under the control of a regional manager. At the total-firm level there are similar kinds of common costs.

For simplicity, the sample report for the regional manager shows only product margins for each product group. In some companies, such managers receive more detail, such as sales, costs, contribution margin, and perhaps some expenses of special concern, such as advertising and promotion. Exhibit 10-3 shows an approach that provides more detail on individual components of the appliance segment in the European region and draws attention to costs that are common to the different categories of appliances. (To focus attention on the format, we have omitted budgeted figures.) The critical point in responsibility reporting is conveying the best information; the selection of the elements to include and the format are secondary. Notice that the amount of detail is greater in the alternative format and that some costs shown as direct to product lines in Exhibit 10-2 are shown as common to the individual products in the line in Exhibit 10-3.

In both Exhibit 10-2 and Exhibit 10-3, the sample reports to the manager of appliance sales for the European region include production costs. This report implies that the manager for the region can control, and is responsible for, production costs, but control of production is not necessary to justify this type of reporting. From earlier chapters you know that decisions about individual products or product lines are based on profitability. For decision-making purposes, then, regional sales managers must know the costs of manufacturing the products they sell.

**Exhibit 10-3   Alternative Responsibility Reporting Format Report to Product Manager—Appliances, European Region (thousands of dollars)**

|  | Small Home Appliances | Large Home Appliances | Commercial Appliances | Total |
|---|---|---|---|---|
| Sales | $39.0 | $34.2 | $48.8 | $122.0 |
| Variable costs: | | | | |
| Production | $12.1 | $ 9.4 | $26.0 | $ 47.5 |
| Selling and administrative | 3.9 | 3.4 | 4.9 | 12.2 |
| Total variable costs | $16.0 | $12.8 | $30.9 | $ 59.7 |
| Contribution margin | $23.0 | $21.4 | $17.9 | $ 62.3 |
| Direct fixed costs | 4.2 | 15.2 | 8.1 | 27.5 |
| Margin | $18.8 | $ 6.2 | $ 9.8 | $ 34.8 |
| Costs common to products in the appliance line | | | | 8.5 |
| Product margin | | | | $ 26.3 |

Accordingly, reports to managers who are responsible only for sales and regional selling costs often include a charge for the products, even though such reporting does not follow strictly the principle of controllability. (We discuss ways to bring such reporting more in line with the controllability principle later in the chapter.)

## ANALYZING CONTRIBUTION MARGIN VARIANCES

Profit depends on several factors, including selling prices, sales volumes, and costs. Budgeted and actual profits rarely coincide because prices, volume, and costs can (and do) vary from expectations. To plan and to evaluate previous decisions, managers need to know the sources of variances.

Our analytical approach concentrates on contribution margin variances that arise because of differences between (1) budgeted and actual sales volume and (2) budgeted and actual selling prices. We can also apply the same analysis to differences between actual and budgeted gross margins. Additionally, managers often use the same technique to explain differences between the actual results of two periods, such as the current and the prior month, or year. Of course, budgeted and actual contribution margin can differ because of changes in variable costs, but analyzing cost variances requires a full chapter, and we defer that topic until Chapter 12.

As an example, Horton Company expected to sell 20,000 units at $20 with unit variable costs of $12. Horton actually sold 21,000 units at $19. These results and the differences appear in Exhibit 10-4.

We want to explain the $13,000 unfavorable variance, the difference between budgeted and actual contribution margin. Total revenues were $1,000 less than budgeted, while total variable costs were $12,000 more than budgeted. But notice that actual variable cost per unit was $12 ($252,000/21,000), the same as budgeted. So the difference in *total* variable costs is due to the increase in volume, *not* to a difference between budgeted and actual per-unit variable cost.

Two factors caused the difference between total budgeted and total actual contribution margin: a variance in selling price and a variance in sales volume. To isolate the effect of each factor, we hold one factor constant and look at the effect of the other. One simple way to do this is to prepare a statement that shows what would have happened if the company had sold the actual volume at the budgeted price, as shown in Exhibit 10-5.

## SALES VOLUME VARIANCE

The **sales volume variance** is the difference between (1) the contribution margin the company would have earned selling the budgeted number of units at the bud-

| Exhibit 10-4    Horton Company, Planned and Actual Results | | | |
|---|---|---|---|
| | **Actual** | **Planned** | **Difference** |
| **Units sold** | 21,000 | 20,000 | 1,000 |
| **Sales** | $399,000 | $400,000 | $ 1,000 |
| **Variable costs** | 252,000 | 240,000 | 12,000 |
| **Contribution margin** | $147,000 | $160,000 | $13,000 |

---

**Exhibit 10-5   Horton Company, Expected Results at Planned Price and Actual Volume**

|  | Actual Results | Actual Volume at Planned Price | Planned Results |
|---|---|---|---|
| Units sold | 21,000 | 21,000 | 20,000 |
| Sales | $399,000 | $420,000 | $400,000 |
| Variable costs | 252,000 | 252,000 | 240,000 |
| Contribution margin | $147,000 | $168,000 | $160,000 |
| Differences | | $21,000 unfavorable | $8,000 favorable |
| Total difference | | $13,000 unfavorable | |

---

geted unit contribution margin and (2) the contribution margin it would have earned selling the actual number of units at the budgeted unit contribution margin. The $8,000 favorable difference in Exhibit 10-5 is Horton's sales volume variance. It resulted from Horton's selling 1,000 units more than budgeted at an $8 *budgeted* per-unit contribution margin. Thus, the sales volume variance can also be computed as

$$\text{Sales volume variance} = \frac{\text{budgeted contribution margin per unit}}{} \times \left(\text{actual unit sales} - \text{budgeted unit sales}\right)$$

$$\$8,000 = \$8 \times (21,000 - 20,000)$$

If a company sells more units than budgeted, as Horton did, the variance is favorable. If it sells fewer units than budgeted, the variance is unfavorable. Again, please notice that we are holding selling price and per-unit variable cost constant because we want to determine the effect on total contribution margin of selling more (or fewer) units than budgeted. Holding selling price and per-unit variable cost constant holds contribution margin per unit constant.

Even if unit variable cost changed, we still would use budgeted unit variable cost for this analysis, because we want to isolate the effects of sales volume apart from changes in variable costs or selling prices. Remember that we hold all factors but one constant; if we allow both volume and unit variable cost to vary we are confusing the analysis.

## SALES PRICE VARIANCE

A change in selling price changes unit contribution margin by the same amount and in the same direction. The **sales price variance** is the difference between (1) actual total contribution margin and (2) total contribution margin that would have been earned at the actual volume and budgeted unit contribution margin. Horton sold its product for $19, or $1 less than budgeted. The $21,000 difference between the $168,000 contribution margin that would have been earned selling 21,000 units at the $20 price (Exhibit 10-5) and the actual contribution margin of $147,000 is Horton's sales price variance. The variance is unfavorable because the actual selling price, and therefore actual contribution margin, was less than budgeted.

We can also calculate the sales price variance by multiplying the difference between the actual and budgeted prices by the actual unit volume.

$$\textit{Sales price variance} = \textit{units sold} \times (\textit{actual price} - \textit{budgeted price})$$
$$= 21{,}000 \times (\$19 - \$20) = -\$21{,}000$$

The $1 difference between the budgeted and actual selling prices is also the difference between budgeted and actual unit contribution margin, so we could also use contribution margin in the calculation.

$$-\$21{,}000 = 21{,}000 \times (\$7 - \$8)$$

A word of caution. An "unfavorable" variance, either sales price or sales volume, is not necessarily bad, nor is a "favorable" variance necessarily good. First, the two variances are often related. Managers often lower prices to increase volume, or increase prices realizing that volume will decline. The wisdom of such a decision depends on the *overall* results, including whether the changes are consistent with the company's strategy, not on either variance considered separately. To interpret variances managers also must know whether conditions were as expected when the original plans were developed. For instance, suppose that budgeted volume was based on forecasts of rapid growth for the industry, but that growth failed to materialize. The company probably could not meet its budgeted volume, but the managers are not at fault because they cannot control industry sales. (The managers are responsible for accepting the inaccurate forecast, however.) As mentioned earlier in the chapter, managers must also interpret variances in light of the company's strategic objectives.

## COST ALLOCATIONS ON RESPONSIBILITY REPORTS

A real-world fact that complicates responsibility accounting is that responsibility centers include both operating and service departments. **Operating departments** in a manufacturing company work directly on products. Operating departments in a retail company serve customers directly. Virtually all operating departments use services provided by other centers. **Service departments** or **service centers** provide such services to operating departments and to one another. Examples of service departments are human resources, accounting, building security, maintenance, and data processing.

A common reason to establish a service department is that having such a department can be cheaper than contracting for the service with an outside vendor or having each responsibility center perform or acquire the service on its own. For example, if there is no personnel department, each department must screen and hire its employees, maintain their records, and do all the other tasks that a personnel department performs—or contract with an outside company to handle these tasks. A company sometimes establishes a service department because its managers believe that a qualitative issue, such as a need for confidentiality, makes it wise to perform a particular service inside rather than have outsiders do it. For example, an auto company might prefer to have its own employees provide custodial services at research and development facilities.

Managers of centers using services cannot directly control the costs of those services. Managerial accountants often refer to such costs as *indirect*, and the emphasis in responsibility accounting on controllability suggests that such costs not be included in responsibility accounting reports. Yet because the departments receiving services benefit from those services, it seems natural that they should "pay" for those services. Moreover, users often can control the *amount* of the service they use, if not its cost. For example, the manager of a factory department can often use as much preventive maintenance service as she deems desirable. The manager of a product line can order as much market research as he thinks wise. Companies use two basic approaches to such payments, cost allocations and transfer prices.

You have encountered allocations before. In Chapter 2 you saw that a total cost per unit gives misleading information because it requires allocating fixed costs to units of product. In Chapter 5 you saw that the only costs relevant for decision making are incremental costs and that allocated costs are not incremental and therefore not relevant. But accountants and other managers disagree about whether to allocate indirect costs for control and performance evaluation. (And the allocation issue has become increasingly important because indirect costs of operating modern factories are growing rapidly as direct laborers are replaced by robots, creating a need for computer operators and maintenance workers.) Thus, while users unquestionably benefit from the activities of service departments, there are serious questions about whether to charge users for the services and, if so, how. The accompanying Insight discusses how **First Union** allocates some of its costs to various business segments.

**SIGHT**

### Allocations at First Union

**First Union** uses an internal performance reporting model to measure the results of four business segments: Consumer Bank, Capital Management, Commercial Bank, and Capital Markets. The model isolates the net income contribution and measures the return on capital for each business segment by allocating equity, funding credit and expense, and corporate expenses to each segment.

Various allocation bases are used. Equity is allocated based on the credit, market, and operational risks associated with each business segment. Operating capital is allocated based on the level of noninterest expense for each segment. General corporate expenses, with the exception of goodwill amortization, are allocated based on the direct and attributable indirect expenses for each segment.

*Source: First Union 1997 annual report.*

## REASONS FOR ALLOCATING COSTS

As we show in later chapters, the full-cost idea is important in product costing—determining the unit cost of products to determine inventory and cost of goods sold for financial reporting and income tax purposes. Because companies *must* allocate costs for financial reporting, some managers might be inclined to use them as well for internal reporting, arguing that failing to allocate understates the full cost of operating the service-using centers. But most proponents of allocation offer behavioral reasons.

A behavioral reason for allocation is to remind managers of the existence of indirect costs and the need to cover them. If the company as a whole is to make a profit, its revenues must cover not only the direct costs of its profit centers, but also its indirect costs. As an example of such a reminder, the Financial Services Department of **Weyerhaeuser**, a large integrated paper company, charges each department a fee for transactions related to each salaried employee (payroll checks, issuing tax forms, etc.). Managers of using departments who are considering adding salaried personnel therefore know what the costs will be.

Such allocations have some basis in cost behavior, for, as we discussed in several earlier chapters, fixed costs are not fixed forever at the same amounts. Step-variable costs (from Chapter 3) move up or down as activity changes by large amounts. Chapter 5 mentioned the need to consider incremental fixed costs. Moreover, arguing that allocations direct managers' attention to long-term survival is consistent with the view reflected in Chapter 3, that operating managers are apt to accept the soundness of allocations that are based on their use of activities that drive costs. A benefit of adopting JIT principles is that managerial accountants and other managers who find non-value-adding activities in the course of analyzing service departments will try to eliminate the activities and costs. Operating managers can then be more confident that they are not being charged with inefficiencies or with costs driven by activities irrelevant to their operations.

Proponents of allocations also argue that if indirect costs are not allocated, managers might overuse services because they view the services as "free." For example, if a company does not allocate its computer costs, managers might use more computer time than is economically justified, thus straining capacity and perhaps leading to an unwise purchase of additional capacity. Allocating computer costs could discourage overuse and help prevent incurring unnecessary costs. For a different example of using cost allocation to control costs, consider a sales manager who controls credit terms offered to customers and the level of inventory maintained. Sales managers normally want to carry a high inventory and offer liberal credit terms, with the company incurring costs to carry the investment in inventory and receivables. Sales managers are less likely to allow those assets to increase excessively if they are charged a financing fee based on the investments in those assets. (Note, however, that if the major objective of a relatively new company is to establish a strong demand for its products by getting as much market penetration as possible, allocating financing costs to the sales manager works against achieving the firm's objective.)

Some proponents of using cost allocations on performance reports offer a conflicting argument, also behavioral. They suggest that allocations are helpful when a service is underused. The reasoning behind this argument is that managers will use the service more because they are already paying for it through the cost allocation.

Another behavior-oriented reason for allocating indirect costs is that the managers to whom costs are allocated will encourage the managers of service departments to keep the cost of the service under control. For example, suppose the manager of computer services wants to buy newer, faster equipment. The manager must convince the users that it is economically sound for them. In the absence of allocations, users have no reason to object to decisions that increase computer costs.

Whatever the reasons for allocation, remember that virtually all allocations are arbitrary. By arbitrary we mean that there is no way to prove that one allocation method is better than another. Nevertheless, some allocation methods are more reasonable than others. Also, as stated earlier, different allocation methods might influence managers differently. We shall, therefore, discuss further how allocations are made and the potential behavioral effects of various allocation methods. The accompanying Insight describes a real case of behavior-influencing aspects of cost allocations.

## REASONS FOR NOT ALLOCATING COSTS

Accountants and other managers agree that allocating *variable* costs of a service center to service-using departments is reasonable because the managers of those departments can cause an increase in such costs. For example, a manager who orders 1,000 copies of a document from the Central Copying Center should pay for at least the variable cost of the copies. Note, however, that users cannot control the *per-unit* variable cost, so that allocating variable costs violates the principle of controllability. We shall see shortly how companies get around this difficulty.

Where managerial accountants disagree is on the matter of allocating indirect fixed costs. There are two principal arguments against allocating indirect fixed costs, both of which stress the potential for adverse behavioral consequences.

1. Because indirect fixed costs are not controllable by the users, allocating them violates the principle of controllability. Managers charged with costs they cannot control might come to distrust the whole system of control and evaluation. Worse, they might attempt to "beat the system" and so take actions inconsistent with the company's objectives. An example appears later in this chapter.

2. Including allocated costs on performance reports could lead to poor decisions because managers will treat the costs as differential. As shown in Chapter 5, making sound decisions requires using differential revenues and costs.

Companies can avoid these undesirable consequences by carefully selecting allocation methods and bases.

## ALLOCATION METHODS AND EFFECTS

Once managers have decided to allocate indirect costs, they have two decisions. One is to select the costs to be allocated, called **cost pools**. A cost pool often consists of the costs of a particular service department, but, as Chapter 4 described in

 **SIGHT**

### Allocations and Behavior

The Portables Group of **Tektronix Company** had been allocating overhead based on direct labor, but its design and process engineers had driven direct labor costs down to less than 7 percent of total manufacturing cost (just over 3 percent on some of its newer products). Because overhead costs were high and rising, the overhead allocation rate per direct labor hour was extremely high. Thus, though direct labor cost was fairly low, the high overhead cost allocated on the basis of direct labor made the total cost that seemed to be labor-related very high. Many managers interpreted the situation as encouraging efforts to further reduce direct labor, but labor-reducing efforts that also increased overhead simply raised the overhead allocation rate. Finally, the Group undertook an internal study that showed that costs related to materials and components—purchasing, receiving, inspecting, storage, and record keeping—constituted roughly half of overhead costs. Follow-up of this study showed that design and process engineers often recommended using more parts when their use reduced direct labor because, there being no overhead charge on parts, there was no incentive either to reduce the number of components or to standardize those in use.

After its study of overhead costs, the Portables Group began to allocate its material-related overhead based on the number of component parts needed and their annual use. A sample calculation of the two-step allocation process is as follows:

| | |
|---|---:|
| Total material-related overhead | $5,000,000 |
| Total number of parts needed, all types | 6,250 |
| Annual cost to carry a part | $800 |
| Cost per part (example): | |
|   Part A, annual use, 20,000 units | $800/20,000 = $0.04 |
|   Part B, annual use, 500 units | $800/500  = $1.60 |

The first step in the allocation process is to determine a cost per part, regardless of the annual volume of use of that part. The next step uses the annual volume of the part to determine a cost per unit, which is then allocated to the product based on the quantity of each part used in the product. Adopting the new cost allocation plan influenced behavior in three important ways. First, it encouraged engineers to reduce the number of parts in existing products. Second, it encouraged standardization of parts for use in several products. Third, it encouraged use of fewer, and more standardized, parts in new products.

*Source: John W. Jonez and Michael A. Wright, "Material Burdening,"* Management Accounting, *August 1987, 27–31.*

relation to ABC, cost pools can cut across departmental lines. The other decision is to select a basis, or bases, for making the allocations. The basis is usually some measure of activity or use of the service. For instance, some companies use the number of employees in each department as the basis for allocating the costs of its personnel department. Similarly, costs related to a building (such as depreciation, property taxes, and insurance) may be allocated on the basis of the space occupied by the departments.

The best allocation basis is the cost driver—the activity that reflects the causal relationship of use to cost. That is, if the users' actions cause the cost to increase, then the costs should be charged accordingly. The next best basis is one that reflects the benefits that the user receives. For instance, it is reasonable to allocate heating expense based on the space that each department occupies—a measure of the benefits received. Even if the managers of using departments cannot control heating expense, they must have heated space to operate.

When neither a use nor a benefit basis is available, allocations are often made on the basis of a department's "ability to bear" indirect costs. For example, there is no reasonable measure of how much each segment benefits from costs such as the salary of the president or the annual audit fee. Therefore such costs are often allocated based on sales or assets, with the idea that these measures reflect the segment's ability to bear them. (Or they might not be allocated at all.) Finally, sales volume is often used as the allocation basis when no measure of benefits received is available.

Assuming a decision to allocate on the basis of use, there are still several approaches to allocating indirect costs (both fixed and variable), and it is not easy to select a method that will work in the sense of accomplishing goal congruence. Using the following information, we shall illustrate some common methods.

Raleigh Company has one service department, Maintenance, and two operating departments, Fabrication and Assembly. Data for the departments follow.

| Operating Department | Hours of Maintenance Service Used | |
|---|---|---|
| | Budgeted | Actual |
| Fabrication | 20,000 | 20,000 |
| Assembly | 20,000 | 10,000 |
| Total | 40,000 | 30,000 |

| Maintenance Department Costs for Year | | | |
|---|---|---|---|
| | Budgeted Original | Flexible | Actual |
| Variable: | | | |
| $5 per hour | $200,000 | $150,000 | |
| $5.10 per hour | | | $153,000 |
| Fixed | 75,000 | 75,000 | 79,500 |
| Totals | $275,000 | $225,000 | $232,500 |

## ALLOCATING ACTUAL COSTS BASED ON ACTUAL USE

The simplest—and worst—allocation method is to allocate the actual total cost of the Maintenance Department based on the operating departments' relative use of the service. Using the actual per-hour cost of providing the service of $7.75 ($232,500 actual cost divided by 30,000 hours), the allocations are as follows:

| Fabrication (20,000 × $7.75) | $155,000 |
|---|---|
| Assembly (10,000 × $7.75) | 77,500 |
| Total maintenance cost allocated | $232,500 |

This method is flawed in two respects. First, it allocates actual costs rather than budgeted costs. The maintenance manager is responsible for controlling maintenance costs. Operating managers might be responsible for the use of the service, but cannot control the cost. Allocating actual costs passes the inefficiencies (or efficiencies) of the Maintenance Department on to the operating departments.

The second flaw of the method is that it allocates fixed costs based on use. This aspect too, allows the performance report of one manager to be affected by the actions of other managers. To see this, consider that each of Raleigh's operating departments budgeted 20,000 hours of maintenance for the year. The budgeted rate is $6.875, computed as follows:

| Variable rate | $5.000 |
|---|---|
| Fixed rate ($75,000/40,000) | 1.875 |
| Total rate (per hour) | $6.875 |

Budgeted total maintenance costs were $275,000 and each operating manager budgeted $137,500 in maintenance cost. Allocating on the basis of *actual* use, the manager of the Assembly Department looks good because $60,000 less than budget is charged ($137,500 budget minus the actual allocation of $77,500, as computed earlier). But the manager of Fabrication looks bad. The Fabrication Department is charged $155,000 (as previously computed), $17,500 over budget, even though it used exactly the budgeted amount for this service. The additional charge arose partly because the Maintenance Department was over *its* budget, but more importantly because *another* user—the Assembly Department—used less of the service than it had budgeted.

If an allocation is to be used in evaluation, the allocation to a given department should not be affected by the actions of other departments. In general, allocating fixed costs based on actual use encourages managers to underuse the service because the allocation depends not only on how much service a particular manager uses, but also on how much the other managers use.

## ALLOCATING BUDGETED COSTS USING DUAL RATES

A better allocation method is to allocate only *budgeted* costs. Using **dual rates**, a company allocates fixed costs and variable costs differently. The method allocates budgeted variable costs based on actual use of the service, and budgeted fixed costs based on expected long-term use.

Using dual rates overcomes the problems of allocating fixed costs based solely on actual use because each department's allocated fixed cost is a lump sum determined before the year begins. The idea supporting this approach is that service departments incur fixed costs to provide the capacity to serve, and the decisions that determined the capacity of the Maintenance Department were based on estimates made earlier by the managers of the operating departments. The argument is that if the manager of the Assembly Department has requested some amount of capacity, he or she should pay for it.

Suppose, for example, that the estimated long-term use is 60 percent for the Fabrication Department and 40 percent for the Assembly Department. We then have the following allocations, which assign variable costs at the budgeted rate of $5 per hour of use and fixed costs at the budgeted total of $75,000.

|  | Fixed | Variable | Total |
|---|---|---|---|
| Fabrication (60% × $75,000) | $45,000 | $100,000 | $145,000 |
| Assembly (40% × $75,000) | 30,000 | 50,000 | 80,000 |
| Total | $75,000 | $150,000 | $225,000 |

The dual rate method has several advantages. One is that operating managers do not absorb the inefficiencies of the Maintenance Department because only budgeted costs ($225,000) are allocated. The allocation to each department is not affected by the use of another department. Another advantage is that operating managers probably will not overuse the service because there is a charge for use. Moreover, because they know in advance that they will be charged the lump-sum as well as the charge based on use, managers probably will not underuse the service. Finally, operating managers are less likely to consider the allocated fixed costs in making decisions because the amount of allocated fixed cost is independent of the actual use of the service.

## ALLOCATING THROUGH TRANSFER PRICES

Early in the chapter we mentioned that some companies create artificial profit centers by having cost centers charge other centers a transfer price for their service. Transfer prices are not cost allocations in the strict sense of the term because the charge is not necessarily related to the costs of the service department. But using a transfer price accomplishes many of the goals sought through cost allocations, such as reminding managers of the need to cover indirect costs and encouraging goal-congruent behavior. Transfer prices can encourage less or more use of a service, whichever result upper-level management desires. It is probably easier to encourage or discourage use through transfer prices than through cost allocations.

Often, the transfer price approximates the market price for the services, which is the price that operating departments would have to pay to obtain the services from an outside company. Because the transfer price is set in advance, the using manager knows exactly how much will be charged to employ another ten hours of maintenance time. In this respect, the transfer price shares the advantage of the dual-rate method of allocation.

Suppose that in our example the transfer price for maintenance services was set at $8 per hour—a price management considered to be the best estimate of the cost to acquire maintenance services from another company. The amounts charged to each department are as follows:

| | |
|---|---|
| Fabrication (20,000 × $8) | $160,000 |
| Assembly (10,000 × $8) | 80,000 |
| Total maintenance cost charged | $240,000 |

Using a transfer price does not change the actual cost incurred anymore than does using a cost allocation. Actual total cost was $232,500. The report to the

Maintenance Department will show revenues of $240,000, actual costs of $232,500, and a profit of $7,500. Reports to the operating departments will show maintenance costs of $240,000. The Maintenance Department's $7,500 profit, netted against the $240,000 of cost, is $232,500, the actual cost Raleigh incurred.

Using transfer prices to create artificial profit centers is not a simple task, as evidenced by the experience of **Weyerhaeuser Company**. Weyerhaeuser requires all of its corporate-level service departments to charge for their services. The Financial Services Department provides general accounting and payroll services, and its charges are based on a variety of factors. For example, charges to account for receivables are based on invoice volume and number of customers and are adjusted for situations that require hand-processing. In developing its charges for general accounting work, the Department used separate rates for employees of three types: analytical, clerical, and systems. A critical factor in Weyerhaeuser's system is that users are free to acquire services from outside the company. Consistent with comments made earlier, one result of the transfer-pricing system (called "charge-backs" at Weyerhaeuser) was that service department managers became profit-conscious, seeking to provide better services to the company and seeking outside customers for their services. The accompanying Insight illustrates how **Teva Pharmaceutical Industries** used transfer prices based on activity-based costs.

Not all transfer-pricing systems include the freedom to purchase services from, or sell services to, outsiders. For example, upper-level managers might believe that a need for confidentiality overrides the benefits of permitting its segments to purchase secretarial services from outside. Permitting an artificial profit center to make outside sales can also create problems. Should the service department give preference to the needs of internal customers when time constraints exist? Might the "hard money" available from external customers prompt the manager to as-

---

**(IN) SIGHT**

### Activity-Based Transfer Prices

**Teva Pharmaceutical Industries** is an Israel-based maker of proprietary and generic drugs. Until the late 1980s, the marketing departments were treated as revenue centers. As such, they were evaluated on sales performance rather than profit performance. To be able to measure profits of each division, a transfer pricing system needed to be developed.

Teva decided to use an activity-based costing system to determine transfer prices. Prices are set using budgeted data for the coming year. Unit-level costs are based on actual quantities of each individual product that is transferred. Batch-level costs are charged based on the actual number of production and packaging batches of each product that is ordered. Product-specific and plant-level costs are charged to the marketing divisions annually.

*Source: Robert Kaplan, Dan Weiss, and Eyal Desheh, "Transfer Pricing with ABC,"* Management Accounting, *May 1997, 20–28.*

sign a lower priority to either anticipated or unanticipated needs of internal customers?

Determining a transfer price that approximates the outside cost for a service is often very difficult. But if reliable outside prices are available, there is a significant advantage to using that price as a transfer price and treating a service department as a profit center. A center consistently showing losses under such a pricing system alerts upper-level managers to the possibility that the company could benefit from shutting down the department and buying outside. Such a decision must consider the structure of fixed costs (avoidable and unavoidable) and would be analyzed along the lines described in Chapter 5 in connection with make-or-buy decisions. The accompanying Insight illustrates the use of transfer prices and profit centers in a value chain context.

The widespread efforts at cost-cutting in recent years have often resulted in companies going outside to purchase goods and services once produced internally. Responding to the same need to reduce costs, many companies have consolidated services once performed at individual units. And, as noted earlier, some companies have turned service centers into profit-seeking businesses that solicit outside and inside business. Some examples follow. **Geon Co.**, a $1 billion manufacturer of polyvinyl chloride, has stopped running its own trucks. It no longer writes its own checks, nor does it operate warehouses. **Xerox** has farmed out its computer needs to **Electronic Data Systems**. **IBM** changed its employee benefits operation into a separate business that seeks outside, as well as inside, business. **General Electric** replaced the accounting centers at its operating units with five regional accounting centers, then consolidated the regional centers into one.

 **SIGHT**

### Transfer Prices and the Value Chain

Recall our petroleum industry value chain example from Chapter 1. The overall value chain for the petroleum industry as a whole includes exploring for oil, developing an oil field, pumping the crude oil, piping and shipping the oil, and refining the crude into gasoline. The value chain would continue with pipelines for gasoline, terminal operations where the gas is transferred from pipelines to trucks, transportation of the gasoline, and the retail operation of a service station or convenience store. Recall also that very few companies compete in all segments of the value chain. An integrated company such as **Chevron** spans a wide portion of the petroleum value chain; **Apache** and **QuikTrip** operate only in narrow portions of the chain.

How do you evaluate profitability of each step of the value chain? By using a market-based transfer price, a company with operations that span wide areas of the value chain could assess each segment of the value chain as an independent (artificial) profit center.

*Source: John Shank, Eric Spiegel and Alfred Escher, "Strategic Value Analysis for Competitive Advantage: An Illustration from the Petroleum Industry,"* Strategy and Business, *First Quarter, 1998.*

**Johnson & Johnson** encourages its operating companies to share services such as finance, purchasing, and human resources administration. **Ryder** manages flows of parts and automobiles for **Saturn**.

## WHAT TO DO ABOUT ALLOCATIONS IN PERFORMANCE REPORTING

Virtually everyone agrees that managers should be charged with at least the incremental costs of carrying out their functions. If allocations are to be made, amounts allocated should be budgeted, rather than actual, costs. Charges should be for the quantity of the service at budgeted variable costs of providing the services. If fixed costs are allocated, the allocation should be budgeted fixed costs and should be based on the long-run percentages of the service capacity expected by each operating department. In any case, the allocation to a particular department should not be affected by the actions of other departments.

Compromises are possible. Performance reports can show controllable and allocated costs separately. If reports draw the attention of the higher-level managers who use the reports to the distinction, there is less likelihood of misunderstanding and complaining from the lower-level managers.

What all managers must understand is that allocations and their close relative, transfer prices, are *managerial accounting devices*, not economic activities. By themselves, neither allocations nor transfer prices can change a company's total income. Changes in income can occur only if a change in an allocation or transfer price induces managers to act differently.

## ETHICS AND ALLOCATIONS

When discussing why allocations might appear on performance reports we pointed out that allocations are needed for product costing. Some organizations must make allocations for other purposes. For example, public utilities must allocate some costs between classes of users (residential, commercial, industrial). Hospitals must allocate costs to determine their reimbursements under Medicare, Medicaid, and Blue Cross. Some federal grants to cities, counties, states, and universities require allocations to determine allowable costs.

Even though a grant, contract, GAAP, or a regulatory agency demands allocations, this does not make them correct. Indirect costs cannot be allocated "correctly," in the sense that one allocation is clearly right and all others clearly wrong. Nor do allocations change an entity's total costs. Yet allocations do have real-world consequences. We have seen that one reason for using allocations is to influence behavior, and changed behavior can change costs and revenues. Allocations can also influence profits by affecting revenues and taxes. In such circumstances, ethical problems can loom large.

Some governmental units, especially the Department of Defense, contract with businesses to do work on a cost-plus basis. Such contracts permit the company to be reimbursed for its costs, including an allocation of indirect costs, plus a specified profit. The temptation for a business involved in such contracts is to allocate as much cost as possible to government work. One way to do so is to include questionable costs in the pool of costs to be allocated. Government auditors probe allocation methods of some companies, but they do not audit every contract. Less than careful attention in determining the costs to be included in a pool had serious consequences for **Stanford University**, which does a great deal of research for agencies of the U.S. government. In an address to alumni, Stanford's then-president conceded that the cost pool allocated to government research had mistakenly included, among other things, the cost of flowers, furniture, and repairs for the president's house and the cost of a yacht.

State regulation of rates charged by public utilities presents another opportunity for allocations to affect revenues, because regulators are expected to approve rates that cover a utility's costs. Public utilities charge different rates for different classes of customers and must allocate costs to each class of customer to justify the rates. A major charge leading to the breakup of **AT&T** was that long-distance service was allocated so much cost that it heavily subsidized local service. That is, local rates were lower and long distance rates higher than they should have been. Moreover, utilities that operate nonregulated businesses are tempted to allocate large amounts of indirect costs to regulated services. They will receive increased revenues to pay for these costs.

Companies operating in more than one state and/or country often must allocate indirect costs among the jurisdictions where they operate. If income tax rates differ among those jurisdictions, the temptation is to assign higher costs to the jurisdictions with higher tax rates. Auditors of taxing authorities are aware of the temptation and give special attention to allocation methods. (Chapter 11 discusses this point further in connection with multinationals.)

In recent years, some charitable organizations have come under fire for questionable allocations. Donors naturally prefer charities that devote the bulk of their resources to charitable purposes and spend a relatively small portion of their money on fund-raising and administrative activities. A number of organizations have been accused of painting a false picture of their activities. In several cases, the false picture has been attributed to questionable cost allocations. For example, some charities spend money, quite legitimately, on public education, such as the benefits of sensible diets. But some charities have allocated significant amounts of the cost of fund-raising literature to their public education programs on the basis of including a few pieces of educational material in fund-raising brochures. Organizations that carry on both for-profit and not-for-profit activities (e.g., the **American Association of Retired Persons**) have come under scrutiny for similar reasons.

## SUMMARY

Managers use accounting information to control operations and evaluate their subordinates' performance. Those evaluated must be evaluated on bases that are consistent with the goals of the firm. Responsibility accounting should assist in achieving goal congruence and in motivating managers. No single responsibility accounting system is appropriate for all companies, or for the same company over its lifetime. The responsibility accounting system must parallel the structure of the organization. The structure of the organization depends on the nature of its operations and on the attitudes and management styles of top managers.

The reporting segments of a responsibility accounting system might be cost centers, revenue centers, natural or artificial profit centers, or investment centers.

Most companies use cost, profit, and investment centers. Whatever the plan for segmenting the company for reporting purposes, individual managers can be held responsible for only that which they can control. A number of companies are using a balanced scorecard approach to evaluate managers, balancing financial measures with nonfinancial measures of customer satisfaction, internal business processes, and learning and growth.

Cost allocations can be troublesome in responsibility accounting, as they have been shown to be in decision making. The principle of including on performance reports only items that a manager can control conflicts with management's desire to charge for benefits received and to use allocations to encourage goal-congruent behavior. Transfer prices can alleviate some of the problems of cost allocations. However, the pervasiveness of behavioral considerations in all aspects of responsibility accounting makes it difficult to draw general conclusions about the best or most useful approaches to follow.

## KEY TERMS

artificial profit center  *(415)*
cost center  *(413)*
cost pool  *(429)*
direct method  *(439)*
dual rates  *(432)*
goal congruence  *(412)*
investment center  *(414)*
operating department  *(426)*
profit center  *(414)*
reciprocal (simultaneous) method  *(441)*

responsibility accounting system  *(412)*
responsibility center  *(413)*
revenue center  *(414)*
sales price variance  *(425)*
sales volume variance  *(424)*
service center  *(426)*
service department  *(426)*
step-down allocation  *(439)*
step method  *(439)*
transfer price  *(415)*

## REVIEW PROBLEM

Scottso Enterprises services and repairs air conditioners and operates in three regions: the Northeast, Southeast, and Southwest. Data for 20X2 are as follows in thousands of dollars.

|  | Northeast | Southeast | Southwest |
|---|---|---|---|
| Service revenue | $2,400 | $5,600 | $3,800 |
| Variable cost of service | 1,220 | 2,200 | 1,700 |
| Variable selling costs | 170 | 330 | 240 |
| Direct fixed costs: |  |  |  |
| Service | 310 | 810 | 440 |
| Selling | 240 | 400 | 280 |
| Administrative | 320 | 440 | 380 |

Common fixed costs were $450,000 for administration and $110,000 for selling.

*Required*

Prepare a performance report by region, showing contribution margin and regional profit. Show common costs as lump-sum deductions in the total column.

**ANSWER TO REVIEW PROBLEM**

Scottso Enterprises
Performance Report for 20X2
(in thousands of dollars)

|  | Northeast | Southeast | Southwest | Total |
|---|---|---|---|---|
| Sales | $2,400 | $5,600 | $3,800 | $11,800 |
| Variable costs: |  |  |  |  |
| Production | $1,220 | $2,200 | $1,700 | $ 5,120 |
| Selling | 170 | 330 | 240 | 740 |
| Total variable costs | $1,390 | $2,530 | $1,940 | $ 5,860 |
| Contribution margin | $1,010 | $3,070 | $1,860 | $ 5,940 |
| Direct fixed costs: |  |  |  |  |
| Production | $ 310 | $ 810 | $ 440 | $ 1,560 |
| Selling | 240 | 400 | 280 | 920 |
| Administration | 320 | 440 | 380 | 1,140 |
| Total direct fixed costs | $ 870 | $1,650 | $1,100 | $ 3,620 |
| Regional profit | $ 140 | $1,420 | $ 760 | $ 2,320 |
| Common fixed costs: |  |  |  |  |
| Selling |  |  |  | $ 110 |
| Administration |  |  |  | 450 |
| Total common costs |  |  |  | $ 560 |
| Income |  |  |  | $ 1,760 |

## APPENDIX: OTHER ALLOCATION METHODS

As indicated in the chapter, common costs must be allocated for some purposes and allocations can be useful for influencing behavior. Allocation schemes are, therefore, of considerable interest. The chapter illustrated the direct method. The **direct method** ignores the services that service departments provide to other service departments. This appendix describes two techniques that many managerial accountants believe to be superior to the direct method: the step-down method and the reciprocal method.

### STEP-DOWN METHOD

Many companies and other organizations, particularly those that work with cost-reimbursement contracts, use a multistep allocation called the **step-down allocation**, the **step method**, or simply, step-down. It is seen in legislated or regulated methods for determining how much to reimburse hospitals for services performed for patients. State and local governments often receive reimbursements for indirect costs of programs that use the step method.

The principle of the step-down method is to recognize that service departments provide services for other service departments as well as for operating departments. We accomplish, partially, the objective of recognizing this service by allocating the costs of service departments one at a time. As a result, the costs of all service departments, except the first to be allocated, will reflect their shares of the costs of some of the other service departments. An example should make this idea clear.

Consider GNL Manufacturing Company, which has two operating departments and two service departments. The operating departments, Forging and Machining, receive services from Personnel and Administration. Personnel keeps all employee records and handles payrolls; Administration handles all other administrative tasks. Each service department provides services to the other service department as well as to the two operating departments. Data for the most recent month follow.

| Department | Direct Costs | Number of Employees |
|---|---|---|
| Personnel | $   200,000 | 10 |
| Administration | 500,000 | 30 |
| Forging | 1,800,000 | 100 |
| Machining | 3,000,000 | 300 |
| Totals | $5,500,000 | 440 |

As with any allocation, we must select the bases for making the allocations. Suppose that GNL's managers decide to allocate Administration costs based on the direct costs of the departments and Personnel costs based on the number of employees.

Because the step-down method allocates the costs of one service department at a time, we must decide which service department's costs to allocate first. Several guidelines are available. One is to start with the department that serves the most other service departments. Another is to order the departments based on the percentage of their services that go to other service departments. Suppose GNL's managers decide to allocate Administration costs first.

The following schedule shows the allocation of the $500,000 of Administration costs, using direct costs as the basis.

| | Personnel | Forging | Machining | Total |
|---|---|---|---|---|
| Direct costs | $200,000 | $1,800,000 | $3,000,000 | $5,000,000 |
| Percentage of total | 4% | 36% | 60% | 100% |
| Allocation of administrative costs | $  20,000 | $  180,000 | $  300,000 | $  500,000 |
| Direct costs | 200,000 | 1,800,000 | 3,000,000 | 5,000,000 |
| New total cost | $220,000 | $1,980,000 | $3,300,000 | $5,500,000 |

Total costs are still $5,500,000, the total direct costs before allocation. But the total is spread differently, with the $500,000 from Administration now in the other three departments.

We are now ready to allocate the costs for Personnel on the basis of the number of employees. Notice that we allocate $220,000, the new total of costs in

Personnel. Under the step-down method, a service department's costs build up through successive allocations to it. Note also that no Personnel costs are allocated to Administration. Once you allocate costs from a department, you do not allocate any back to the department. Following is the allocation of the Personnel costs and the final totals allocated to the operating departments.

|  | Forging | Machining | Total |
|---|---|---|---|
| Number of employees | 100 | 300 | 400 |
| Percentage of total | 25% | 75% | 100% |
| Allocation of personnel costs | $ 55,000 | $ 165,000 | $ 220,000 |
| Previous totals | 1,980,000 | 3,300,000 | 5,280,000 |
| New total cost | $2,035,000 | $3,465,000 | $5,500,000 |

By their nature, allocations are arbitrary no matter how sophisticated the method used to calculate them. The results are always influenced by the allocation basis chosen. Had we selected different bases for allocating the costs of either of the service departments, the final results would be different. Also, the results are influenced by the order in which allocations were made. That is, had we chosen to allocate Personnel first, the final total costs for each operating department would have been different. In summary, the allocation process succeeds in assigning the costs of service departments to the operating departments, but does not change the fact that the costs of service departments are common to the departments serviced. All of the reservations stated in the chapter about allocations and decision making apply regardless of the allocation scheme used. The 1997 annual report of **First Union** noted the allocation problem: "Because of the complexity of the corporation and the interrelationships of these business segments, we have used various estimates and allocation methodologies in the preparation of the Business Segments financial information. Restatements of various periods may occasionally occur because these estimates and methodologies could be refined over time."

The following schedule summarizes the procedures and explicitly shows the step-down feature as each department's costs are allocated.

|  | Administration | Personnel | Forging | Machining | Total |
|---|---|---|---|---|---|
| Direct costs | $ 500,000 | $ 200,000 | $1,800,000 | $3,000,000 | $5,500,000 |
| Administration | (500,000) | 20,000 | 180,000 | 300,000 | |
| Personnel | | (220,000) | 55,000 | 165,000 | |
| Total | $ 0 | $ 0 | $2,035,000 | $3,465,000 | $5,500,000 |

The total costs of the two operating departments ($5,500,000) are, of course, the same as the total costs of all departments before the allocation procedure began. As stated many times, allocations do not, by themselves, change total costs.

## RECIPROCAL METHOD

The **reciprocal**, or **simultaneous**, **method** of allocation fully recognizes the services that each service department renders to other service departments. This means, in terms of the example, that not only are Administration costs allocated to Personnel, but Personnel costs are also allocated to Administration. To accomplish this reciprocal allocation we first find the percentages that each service department receives from the other. The original data from the example are presented as follows, in somewhat modified form, to facilitate the calculations.

| Services Provided By | Services Provided To | | | | |
|---|---|---|---|---|---|
| | Personnel | Administration | Forging | Machining | Total |
| Administration: | | | | | |
| Direct costs | $200,000 | | $1,800,000 | $3,000,000 | $5,000,000 |
| Percentages | 4% | | 36% | 60% | 100% |
| Personnel: | | | | | |
| No. of employees | | 30 | 100 | 300 | 430 |
| Percentages | | 6.98% | 23.25% | 69.77% | 100% |

The next step in the reciprocal method is to calculate what are called the adjusted costs of the service departments, to recognize that the departments provide services to each other. We set up simultaneous equations, letting P = the adjusted costs for Personnel and A = the adjusted costs for Administration.

The equations are

$$P = \$200{,}000 + 0.04A$$
$$A = \$500{,}000 + 0.0698P$$

One way to solve these equations is to substitute the equation for A in that for P, as follows. (You could use other ways, of course.)

$$P = \$200{,}000 + 0.04 (\$500{,}000 + 0.0698P)$$

Simplifying and rearranging this equation yields

$$P = \$220{,}616$$

and substituting for P in the equation for A yields

$$A = \$515{,}399$$

The final step is to allocate these adjusted costs to the two operating departments using the percentages computed. (That is, we do not adjust the percentages as was done using the step-down method.)

| Service Departments | Operating Departments | | |
|---|---|---|---|
| | Forging | Machining | Total Costs |
| Allocations | | | |
| Personnel | | | |
| $220,616 × 23.25% | $ 51,293 | | |
| $220,616 × 69.77% | | $ 153,924 | |
| Administration | | | |
| $515,399 × 36% | 185,544 | | |
| $515,399 × 60% | | 309,239 | |
| Total allocated | $ 236,837 | $ 463,163 | $ 700,000 |
| Direct costs | 1,800,000 | 3,000,000 | 4,800,000 |
| Total cost | $2,036,837 | $3,463,163 | $5,500,000 |

Notice that the total costs allocated equal the direct costs of the two service departments ($500,000 for Administration and $200,000 for Personnel). The final total cost is still $5,500,000, the sum of the direct costs of the four departments, showing once again that the method of allocating costs does not, by itself, change the total cost incurred.

Those who favor the reciprocal method claim it is more accurate than other methods (including step-down) because it recognizes all reciprocal services. But the results still depend on the choice of an allocation basis for each department. Moreover, the method is subject to the same objection as is any other allocation method. It is arbitrary and so cannot be said to yield a "true" or "correct" cost for an operating department (especially if the costs of one or more of the service departments are largely fixed).

In this case, the choice between the step-down and reciprocal methods does not produce a significant difference in the total costs finally assigned to individual operating departments. (The difference is $1,837, which is less than 1 percent of the final total cost for each department.) In other cases, the difference could be much larger, and the need for managers to understand the potential impact of alternative allocation methods is much greater.

## ASSIGNMENT MATERIAL

### INTERNET ACTIVITY

Many companies offer consulting services to assist companies in developing and implementing a balanced scorecard approach to performance measurement. Find some of their Web sites. See how they view the balanced scorecard, what services they offer, what benefits they say they can provide. See if they offer examples of successful implementations. Be prepared to describe and discuss what you discovered. Take the viewpoint that your boss has asked you to make a preliminary survey to see whether it is feasible for your company to look into a balanced scorecard.

### QUESTIONS FOR DISCUSSION

**10-1   *Responsibility versus control***   The manager of a store of a large chain of supermarkets said the following to the controller of that chain.

> "My son is taking a managerial accounting course at CU, and he's been telling me about something called responsibility accounting and how it can help to motivate employees. How come we don't have responsibility accounting in our stores? I've got a meat manager who pretty much keeps that department in my store going. My son says the meat department would be a good candidate for what he calls a profit center."

***Required***
What do you think?

**10-2   *First Union's allocations***   The Appendix to this chapter quoted from **First Union's** 1997 annual report: "Because of the complexity of the corporation and the interrelationships of these business segments, we have used various estimates and allocation methodologies in the preparation of the Business Segments financial information. Restatements of various periods may occasionally occur because these estimates and methodologies could be refined over time."

**Required**
Explain the quotation.

**10-3    *Responsibility centers—universities*** What problems do you see in establishing and evaluating responsibility centers in the following: (a) universities, (b) colleges or schools within universities, and (c) departments within colleges?

**10-4    *Responsibility reporting*** The annual report of a major manufacturer carried the following paragraph (paraphrased).

"Specialization also continues within each marketing force as we increase the number of personnel. We are experiencing a steady rise in the number of customers as well as in the variety and complexity of products and equipment. As a result, an increasing proportion of our salespeople concentrate on just one or a few industries/or on certain product categories."

**Required**
Suppose that in the past, the salespeople sold all products to all kinds of customers in different industries. What effects will the new method of directing the efforts of the individual salespeople have on the responsibility reporting system?

**10-5    *Archer Daniels Midland operations*** An **Archer Daniels Midland** annual report stated that ADM had once been a "conglomeration of free-standing processing plants and free-standing elevators . . . some still operating as independent companies. . . ." Things have changed. "Our multi-purpose refineries now refine eight different kinds of vegetable oil. . . . Ships often carry five or more grains, oilseeds, and finished products. . . . The 150,000 tons processed each day are purchased mostly by the same purchasing organization, and many of the products manufactured in these plants are sold by one sales organization. . . . Our overhead is thus spread over this entire combination of activities." The report went on to say that management perceives ADM to be a one-purpose company and that it had become nearly impossible to determine how much ADM earned on any particular product.

**Required**
How would the changes in ADM's operations likely have influenced its organizational structure and its responsibility reporting?

**10-6    *Evaluating a performance measure*** The top-level administrators of Mid-State University announced that, henceforth, the major factor in evaluating the performance of a faculty member will be the number of students who enroll in classes taught by that faculty member.

**Required**
Discuss how the proposed performance evaluation measure does or does not (a) reflect application of the principle of controllability and (b) contribute to goal congruence.

**10-7    *Pricing, timing, allocations, and public relations*** For many years telephone companies did not charge for directory assistance (calling an operator to get a number). When they did begin to charge (usually 20 cents per request after three free requests per month), a commentator said, "This is ridiculous. They have operators on duty anyway, so there is no additional cost for their giving out a number. Ma Bell has just found another way to get into our pockets."

**Required**
Comment on the quotation.

**10-8   *Balanced scorecard in a not-for-profit organization*** The United Way of SouthEastern New England (UWSENE) operates in Rhode Island, Connecticut, and Massachusetts. In 1996, UWSENE developed a balanced scorecard approach to evaluate its performance. One major question addressed was whether the four perspectives normally found in a for-profit's scorecard are adequate and appropriate for UWSENE's scorecard.

**Required**
What types of measures might you find on UWSENE's balanced scorecard?

## EXERCISES

**10-9   *Alternative allocation bases*** The following data refer to the three departments of Andrews Legal Services.

| | Family Matters | Bankruptcy | Estate |
|---|---|---|---|
| Revenues | $400,000 | $900,000 | $700,000 |
| Square feet of space occupied | 6,000 | 9,000 | 15,000 |

Total common costs are $250,000.

**Required**
Allocate the common costs to the departments on the bases of (a) revenues and (b) square feet of space occupied.

**10-10   *Basic allocation methods*** Pro Mart Stores has three profit centers and one service center, a central purchasing department. Variable costs for central purchasing are related to the number of invoices processed. Data are as follows:

| | Profit Centers | | |
|---|---|---|---|
| | Groceries | Meat | Dairy |
| Budgeted invoices: current year | 4,000 | 2,500 | 3,500 |
| Actual invoices: current year | 4,200 | 2,625 | 3,675 |
| Long-term expected invoices | 4,500 | 4,500 | 6,000 |

Budgeted central purchasing costs were $400,000 fixed and $200,000 variable. Actual fixed costs were $390,000, and actual variable costs were $220,000.

**Required**
1. Allocate the actual central purchasing costs to the profit centers based on actual use of the services.

2. Allocate the variable central purchasing costs to the profit centers based on actual use of the services but using a budgeted variable rate and the budgeted fixed costs based on expected long-term use.
3. Which of the two methods do you prefer? Why?

**10-11  Performance report**  York Tool Company operates six departments in its main plant. Each department manager is responsible for materials, direct and indirect labor, supplies, small tools, and equipment maintenance. The factory manager is responsible for buying equipment and for all other costs. Last month, the manager of the Stamping Department received the following performance report. The costs of building occupancy have been allocated to the department.

|  | Budget | Actual | Over (Under) |
|---|---|---|---|
| Materials | $ 32,900 | $ 33,800 | $ 900 |
| Direct labor | 34,200 | 34,500 | 300 |
| Indirect labor | 15,250 | 14,220 | (1,030) |
| Supplies | 5,600 | 5,450 | (150) |
| Small tools | 4,200 | 4,340 | 140 |
| Equipment: |  |  |  |
| Depreciation | 12,800 | 12,800 | 0 |
| Maintenance | 5,700 | 4,950 | (750) |
| Building: |  |  |  |
| Depreciation | 2,200 | 2,200 | 0 |
| Maintenance | 980 | 950 | (30) |
| Property taxes | 760 | 770 | 10 |
| Total | $114,590 | $113,980 | $ (610) |

**Required**

Prepare a new performance report that shows only the costs for which the manager of the Stamping Department is responsible.

**10-12  Step-down allocation method (related to Appendix)**  Maple Leaf Engineering has two service departments, Personnel and Administration, and two operating departments, Architectural (ARCH) and Highway Design (HD). The following schedule shows the costs in each service department and the percentages of activity that each service department provides each of the other departments, both service and operating.

| Department Providing Service | Costs of Department | Department Receiving Service | | | |
|---|---|---|---|---|---|
|  |  | Personnel | Administration | ARCH | HD |
| Personnel | $400,000 | 0% | 60% | 10% | 30% |
| Administration | $600,000 | 30% | 0% | 50% | 20% |

A member of the controller's staff made the following allocations, rounded.

|  | ARCH | HD |
|---|---|---|
| Personnel: |  |  |
| $400,000 × (0.10/0.40) | $100,000 |  |
| $400,000 × (0.30/0.40) |  | $300,000 |
| Administration: |  |  |
| $600,000 × (0.50/0.70) | 428,600 |  |
| $600,000 × (0.20/0.70) |  | 171,400 |
| Totals | $528,600 | $471,400 |

The controller is wondering whether it would make any difference to use the step-down method, instead of the direct method shown.

**Required**

1. Allocate the service department costs using the step-down method, beginning with Personnel.
2. Explain why the controller should begin the step-down with Personnel.

**10-13  Reciprocal allocation (continuation of 10-12)**

**Required**

Perform the allocation in Exercise 10-12 using the reciprocal method.

**10-14  Allocations—*actual versus budgeted costs***   Merion Turf Products produces lawn fertilizers and grass seed. The company's Research Department, which works to improve both types of products, had budgeted costs of $450,000, virtually all fixed. These costs were to be allocated to the two product lines based on the relative amounts of time spent on each. All of the scientists keep time sheets showing which projects they work on each month.

At year-end the Research Department had actually spent $496,000 as a result of unanticipated cost increases and some inefficiencies in the department. The manager of the Fertilizer Department had budgeted $225,000 for allocated research costs but found that he was actually charged with $276,760. The final allocation was based on actual costs and actual relative time spent on work for his department. He was not happy with the situation, especially when he learned that the manager of the Grass Seed Department had canceled a major project, resulting in lower-than-budgeted research on grass seed.

**Required**

Suggest a way to allocate research costs that will not unduly penalize the managers of the Fertilizer and Grass Seed Departments.

**10-15  Assignment of responsibility**   Klee Company is organized by function: sales, production, finance, and administration. The production manager is upset about the following performance report. She contends that costs of $8,000 were incurred solely because the sales manager ordered changes in production for rush orders from customers.

**Performance Report—Production Department**

|  | Budget | Actual | Variance (Favorable) |
|---|---|---|---|
| Controllable costs: |  |  |  |
| Materials | $ 90,000 | $ 87,000 | $(3,000) |
| Direct labor | 150,000 | 153,000 | 3,000 |
| Other labor | 66,000 | 73,000 | 7,000 |
| Idle time* | 1,000 | 4,500 | 3,500 |
| Other production costs | 31,000 | 30,000 | (1,000) |
| Totals | $338,000 | $347,500 | $ 9,500 |

\* *Wages paid to workers while they are idle, as when machines are being reset because of a change from one product to another.*

The production manager argues that the $4,500 shown on the performance report as idle time was caused by changing the production process to meet special orders. In addition, she claims that about $8,000 in other labor was for costs incurred to make the necessary changes and for the overtime premium paid to workers to get the work finished in time to meet the deadlines given for rush orders.

**Required**
What is wrong and what do you recommend?

**10-16    Transfer prices and goal congruence**    The controller of Johnson Associates has set transfer prices for service departments, all of which had been cost centers. One is for stenographic services. The charge is $18 per hour, based on total budgeted hours of available service and total budgeted costs for the stenographic pool. The manager of one operating department, a profit center, has obtained a price of $15 per hour for stenographers' time from an outside agency for a task that will take about 50 hours. The manager informs the controller and the manager of the stenographic pool of the outside price and is told to take it if she wishes; the transfer price will not be lowered.

**Required**
Comment on the position taken by the controller and the manager of the steno-graphic pool. (Budgeted costs for the pool are about 90% fixed.) Make a recommendation.

**10-17    Basic variance analysis**    Tartan Mills expected to sell 40,000 of its Style 105 knit sweaters at $30 each. It actually sold 38,000 at $31. Variable cost is $14 per sweater.

**Required**
1. Determine the sales volume variance.
2. Determine the sales price variance.

**10-18    Relationships**    Palmeiri Prunes sold 11,000 cases of DeLight Prunes. Palmeiri had a $3,000 unfavorable sales volume variance and a $3,300 favorable sales price variance. It had a budgeted selling price of $18 and variable cost of $15.

**Required**
1. Determine the number of cases that Bruton had budgeted to sell.
2. Determine the actual price per case that Bruton received.
3. Determine Bruton's budgeted and actual contribution margins.

**10-19    Price and volume variances**    GarBage Company makes large plastic garbage cans. Budgeted results for March were as follows:

| | |
|---|---:|
| Sales (15,000 units) | $210,000 |
| Variable costs | 150,000 |
| Contribution margin | $ 60,000 |
| Actual results were as follows: | |
| Sales | $212,350 |
| Variable costs | 155,000 |
| Contribution margin | $ 57,350 |

Variable costs were incurred as expected, per unit.

*Required*

1. How many garbage cans did the company sell?
2. What was the actual selling price?
3. What were the volume variance and price variance?

**10-20  Development of performance report**  Stratton Company is organized by functional areas: sales, production, finance, and administration. The Sales Department has product managers who are responsible for a particular product and who are evaluated based on the following typical performance report.

Activity Report—Product Zee
May 20X4—Manager, J. Harrison

| | | |
|---|---:|---:|
| Sales | | $487,000 |
| Cost of goods sold | | 281,000 |
| Gross profit | | $206,000 |
| Other expenses: | | |
|   Advertising | $38,000 | |
|   Travel | 17,000 | |
|   Depreciation | 5,000 | |
|   Office expenses | 28,000 | |
|   Administrative expense | 25,000 | 113,000 |
| Product profit | | $ 93,000 |

The following additional information about the report is available.

(a) Because of problems in the production process, cost of goods sold is $19,000 higher than budgeted.
(b) Harrison authorized spending $26,000 on product advertising. The remainder of the advertising cost reported is an allocated share of general advertising costs incurred by the firm.
(c) Depreciation charges consist of the following: 20% on furniture and fixtures in Harrison's office and 80% for the product's share of depreciation on the building that houses all the firm's activities.
(d) Office expenses include $6,500 allocated from the expenses of the vice president for sales.
(e) Administrative expenses are allocated based on relative sales.

*Required*

Revise the performance report for product Zee to reflect the principle of controllability.

## PROBLEMS

**10-21  Cost allocation**  The following schedule shows the costs of the service departments of Salem Inc. and the percentages of service that the service departments provide to each other and to Salem's operating departments.

| Department Providing Service | Costs of Department | Department Receiving Service | | | |
|---|---|---|---|---|---|
| | | Purchasing | Administration | Trimming | Cutting |
| Purchasing | $300,000 | | 20% | 60% | 20% |
| Administration | $500,000 | 30% | | 20% | 50% |

**Required**
1. Use the direct method to allocate the service department costs to the operating departments. Exercise 10-12 shows how to calculate the percentages.
2. Use the step-down method to allocate the service department costs to the operating departments.
3. Use the reciprocal method to allocate the service department costs to the operating departments.

**10-22  Performance reporting and allocations**  Newton Company, a furniture outlet, allocates indirect costs to its two product lines based on sales. The income statement for 20X1 is as follows:

|  | Indoor Furniture | Outdoor Furniture | Total |
|---|---|---|---|
| Sales | $350,000 | $350,000 | $700,000 |
| Direct costs | 120,000 | 120,000 | 240,000 |
| Controllable profit | $230,000 | $230,000 | $460,000 |
| Indirect costs | 150,000 | 150,000 | 300,000 |
| Income | $ 80,000 | $ 80,000 | $160,000 |

In 20X2, price increases on indoor furniture increased sales of that line to $400,000, while unit sales remained constant. Prices of outdoor furniture were not changed, and their sales remained at $350,000. Direct costs of each line were again $120,000, and total indirect costs were again $300,000.

**Required**
1. Prepare a product-line income statement for 20X2, allocating indirect costs based on sales.
2. Comment on the results. (Are they logical? Did the manager of outdoor furniture do a better job in 20X2 than in 20X1?)

**10-23  Responsibility for rush orders**  Howard Company's sales manager, Ken Perrier, often requests rush orders from the production department. Howard's production process requires a great deal of setup time whenever changes in the production mix are made. The production manager, Brad Givens, has complained about these rush orders, arguing that costs are much lower when the process runs smoothly. Perrier argues that the paramount consideration is to keep the customer's goodwill and that, therefore, all sales orders should be made up as quickly as possible.

**Required**
1. Identify the issues creating the conflict.
2. Using the guidelines in Appendix A, write a memorandum to the two managers suggesting what steps might be taken to effect a satisfying solution.

**10-24  Performance measurement**  Eleanor Klein, the sales manager of Warner Company, is evaluated on the basis of total sales. Exceeding the sales budget is considered good performance. The sales budget and cost data for 20X3 follow.

|  | Product | | | |
|---|---|---|---|---|
|  | Alpha | Beta | Gamma | Total |
| Sales budget | $150,000 | $300,000 | $550,000 | $1,000,000 |
| Variable costs | 75,000 | 135,000 | 165,000 | 375,000 |
| Contribution margin | $ 75,000 | $165,000 | $385,000 | $ 625,000 |

Actual sales for the year were as follows:

| Alpha | Beta | Gamma | Total |
|-------|------|-------|-------|
| $500,000 | $400,000 | $200,000 | $1,100,000 |

Actual prices were equal to budgeted prices, and variable costs were incurred as budgeted (per unit).

**Required**

1. Did Klein perform well? Support your answer with calculations.
2. Using the guidelines in Appendix A, write a memorandum to Warner's controller, George Karpinski, explaining what the changes in the firm's performance evaluation might contribute to goal congruence.

**10-25  *Behavioral problem***  Watson Company recently bought a copier with a capacity of 10,000 copies per day. Annual fixed costs of the copier are $24,000; the variable cost is $0.01 per copy. Previously, Watson had leased a similar copier with annual fixed costs of $14,000 and variable costs of $0.06 per copy. Watson allocates the fixed costs of the copier based on expected long-term use of the copier and the variable costs based on actual use.

Total copying had run about 8,000 per day with the old machine. The new copier is nearly always running at capacity, and people have complained that they cannot get copies within a reasonable time. Some managers have been forced to send material to outside copying services, which charge about $0.08 per copy.

**Required**

What seems to be happening, and what do you recommend, if anything?

**10-26  *Hospital allocations and decisions***  Blake Memorial Hospital is a full-service hospital with several departments. Departments that perform services directly for patients are called revenue centers and include the Medical, Surgical, and Emergency Departments. Other departments, such as Admissions, Patient Records, Laundry, and Housekeeping, are called service centers. Costs of service centers are allocated to revenue centers. Following is a schedule showing the percentages of costs allocated from two service centers to two revenue centers, together with the direct costs of each of the service centers.

| Service Center | Costs | Revenue Center Medical | Revenue Center Surgical |
|----------------|-------|---------|----------|
| Admissions | $300,000 | 70% | 30% |
| Records | $400,000 | 20% | 80% |

The hospital receives reimbursements from Blue Cross, Medicaid, and other third parties for services performed for some patients. The reimbursement contracts typically allow recovery of both direct and indirect costs. Such reimbursements amount to about 30% of total Medical Department costs and about 90% of total Surgical Department costs. Thus, at the present time, the hospital is reimbursed for $144,000 of its Admissions costs, calculated as follows:

| | |
|---|---|
| Through medical reimbursements ($300,000 × 70% × 30%) | $ 63,000 |
| Through surgical reimbursements ($300,000 × 30% × 90%) | 81,000 |
| Total | $144,000 |

The hospital administrator is considering some different procedures that will increase the cost of Records by $10,000, while reducing Admissions costs by $6,000. Obviously, the change would increase total cost, but the administrator is well aware of the differing reimbursement rates.

**Required**

1. Calculate the total reimbursement that the hospital now receives for the indirect costs of Admissions and Records.
2. Calculate the total reimbursement that the hospital will receive if the new procedures are adopted.
3. Comment on the effects of the procedural changes beyond Blake Memorial.

**10-27    Allocations, expense reimbursement, and ethics**    You need to take a business trip from your office in Atlanta to a branch in Los Angeles sometime in the next few weeks. You have also planned to play in a golf tournament near San Francisco. You manage to combine the trips so that you fly to Los Angeles, finish your business, then go to the tournament. Some airfares are as follows:

| | |
|---|---|
| Atlanta–Los Angeles each way | $380 |
| Los Angeles–San Francisco each way | $105 |
| Atlanta–San Francisco each way | $420 |

Because you will be staying over a weekend, you get a special excursion ticket that allows you to make the entire trip for $740. You spend three days working, two days playing golf. Your company reimburses your business expenses.

**Required**

1. How much airfare will you show on your expense account?
2. Suppose that you were your boss. How much airfare would you allow the company to reimburse?

**10-28    Step-down allocation (related to Appendix)**    Walker Company has two operating departments—Machining and Assembly—and three service departments—Personnel, Data Processing, and General Administration. The controller wishes to allocate service department costs using the step-down method, beginning with Data Processing, then Personnel, and lastly, General Administration. She wants to use the following bases: Data Processing, number of transactions; Personnel, number of employees; and General Administration, total direct costs (before any allocation of service department costs).

The controller has assembled the following data.

| Department | Total Direct Costs | Number of Employees | Number of Data Processing Transactions |
|---|---|---|---|
| Data processing | $  300,000 | 20 | 0 |
| Personnel | 200,000 | 30 | 20,000 |
| General administration | 400,000 | 100 | 30,000 |
| Machining | 2,000,000 | 300 | 40,000 |
| Assembly | 3,000,000 | 600 | 10,000 |

**Required**

Prepare a step-down allocation.

**10-29  *Performance report for a cost center*** Dominic Porter, the manager of the Casting Department of Western Foundries, was disturbed by the report that he received last month.

### Monthly Cost Report—Casting Department
### July 20X1

| | |
|---|---:|
| Materials | $ 32,800 |
| Direct labor | 66,800 |
| Indirect labor | 2,380 |
| Power | 18,900 |
| Maintenance | 5,700 |
| Other | 9,350 |
| Total | $135,930 |

The factory manager had commented unfavorably to Porter about power and maintenance costs, both of which were higher than in previous months. Both costs are mixed. The variable portions are relatively controllable by the department managers, but the fixed portions are not controllable at the departmental level. The amounts shown are allocations based on the department's use of the services each month. The Casting Department used 9,500 kilowatt-hours of power and 800 hours of maintenance service in July. The budgeted monthly costs of the two services are as follows:

$$Power\ cost = \$130,000 + \$0.05\ per\ kilowatt\text{-}hour$$
$$Maintenance\ cost = \$24,000 + \$0.80\ per\ maintenance\text{-}hour$$

The Casting Department's long-term shares of the services are estimated at 10% for power and 15% for maintenance. All other costs on the report are controllable by the department manager.

### Required
Prepare a new performance report for the Casting Department that shows controllable costs and noncontrollable costs separately and allocates fixed power and maintenance costs based on the department's long-term use of those services.

**10-30  *Variances in a service business*** Earl Torgerson, the managing partner of Torgerson, Watts, and Gold, Management Consultants, is comparing budgeted and actual results for 20X2. Because all employees are on salary, there are no variable costs associated with chargeable hours (hours worked on client business).

| Employee Category | Budgeted Hourly Rate | Total Hours | Revenue | Actual Hourly Rate | Total Hours | Revenue |
|---|---|---|---|---|---|---|
| Junior staff | $40 | 30,000 | $1,200,000 | $38 | 26,000 | $ 988,000 |
| Senior staff | 80 | 12,000 | 960,000 | $84 | 15,000 | 1,260,000 |

### Required
For each category, determine the price (rate) and volume variances.

**10-31  *Performance report in a service company*** Louis Wardlaw heads the Tax Department at Bryan & Cummings, a large firm of certified public accountants. The firm also has an Audit Department and a Management Services Department. Wardlaw recently received the following performance report for his department.

|  | February | March |
|---|---|---|
| Revenues | $140,600 | $148,400 |
| Costs: | | |
| Staff salaries | $ 76,800 | $ 77,400 |
| Travel and supplies | 7,800 | 8,100 |
| Occupancy and utilities | 9,800 | 10,900 |
| General office expense | 15,400 | 21,800 |
| Total costs | $109,800 | $118,200 |
| Income | $ 30,800 | $ 30,200 |

Wardlaw thought that his department had done much better in March than in February and was surprised by the report. He talked to the firm's internal accountant, who had prepared the report, to gather additional information. Staff salaries, travel, and supplies are all direct to the department. Occupancy and utilities are allocated based on space occupied. In March, the lease on the firm's office expired and was renewed at a higher rent. General office expense is allocated to departments based on revenue. The Audit and Management Services Departments both experienced drops in revenue in March, resulting in a higher share going to the Tax Department.

**Required**

1. Revise the preceding report to show revenue, direct costs, controllable profit, allocated indirect costs, and income.
2. Did the Tax Department perform better in February than in March? Why or why not?

**10-32   *Product-line income statements*** The president of Oliver Tool Company has just received the firm's income statement for January 20X3. He is puzzled because you had told him last year, when working as a consultant to the firm, that sales of $500,000 should produce a profit of about $46,500 before income taxes.

Oliver Tool Company
Income Statement for January 20X3

| | | |
|---|---|---|
| Sales | | $500,000 |
| Cost of sales | | 307,500 |
| Gross profit | | $192,500 |
| Operating expenses: | | |
| Rent | $40,000 | |
| Salaries | 70,000 | |
| Shipping and delivery | 23,000 | |
| Other expenses | 30,000 | 163,000 |
| Income before taxes | | $ 29,500 |

The company sells three lines of power tools, and your analysis assumed the following sales mix in dollars: saws, 30%; drills, 20%; and sanders, 50%. The actual mix in dollars in January was 40%, 30%, 30%. The company does not manufacture its products. Cost of sales and shipping and delivery are variable costs. All others are fixed. Data per unit for each product follow.

|                      | Saws | Drills | Sanders |
|----------------------|------|--------|---------|
| Selling price        | $50  | $20    | $40     |
| Cost of sales        | $30  | $15    | $20     |
| Shipping and delivery| 2    | 1      | 2       |
| Total variable costs | $32  | $16    | $22     |
| Contribution margin  | $18  | $ 4    | $18     |

None of the fixed costs is directly associated with any particular product line. All costs were incurred as expected, per unit for variable costs, in total for fixed costs. Selling prices were as expected.

**Required**

1. Prepare a new income statement by product, based on actual results in January. Show both gross profit and contribution margin for each product.
2. Prepare an income statement by product for January, assuming that the expected sales mix had been achieved.
3. Explain the reasons for the differences between the two statements.

**10-33  Selecting an allocation base**   Amelia Strelcyzyk, controller of Carter Brothers Discount Mart, is considering allocating indirect costs to its departments. She proposes to allocate annual building rent of $2,000,000 based on the floor space that each department occupies. Jennifer Bynum, manager of the Children's Department, objects to this basis. She contends that the basis should be the relative value of the space. Her department is on the second floor. Comparable second floor space rents for about $10 per square foot, while first floor space rents for about $15 per square foot.

The Children's Department occupies 20,000 square feet of the total 100,000 square feet on the second floor. The first floor also has 100,000 square feet.

**Required**

1. Determine the amount of cost that the Children's Department would be allocated using the controller's method.
2. Determine the amount of cost that the Children's Department would be allocated using the department manager's method.
3. Using the guidelines in Appendix A, write a memorandum to Ms. Strelcyzyk, giving and supporting your recommendation about which allocation method to use.

**10-34  Allocations and decisions**   Cramer Company has several product lines, each controlled by a different manager. Each manager is evaluated partly on profit. The expenses charged to each line are the direct costs of the line plus 15% of sales. (The 15% covers costs not directly associated with the lines, such as salaries of the corporate staff, interest on corporate debt, and service functions such as personnel, building security, and cafeteria. These costs are virtually all fixed.) The president of the company estimated that 15% would cover these expenses at budgeted sales of $6,000,000 for the coming year. Each year the percentage is adjusted based on budgeted costs and budgeted sales for the entire company.

The manager of the small appliances line has the opportunity to sell 20,000 units to a chain store at $30 each. Per-unit variable costs are $27, ignoring the 15% charge. There would be no incremental fixed costs associated with the order, and there is sufficient capacity to make the additional units.

**Required**

1. Given the existing plan for evaluating performance, will the manager of small appliances accept the order? Why or why not?

2. Is it in the company's best interests for the manager to accept the order? Why or why not?

**10-35  Performance measures**  Following are five job titles and the measure by which performance in that job is judged. Comment on the usefulness of each in achieving goal congruence.

| Job or Job Title | Performance Measure |
|---|---|
| (a) Director of mental health program | Number of patients released from treatment |
| (b) Director of a program to reduce unemployment | Number of jobs found for unemployed people, as a percentage of total unemployed persons |
| (c) Director of a regional program to rehabilitate substandard housing | Number of homes now meeting local building codes that had previously been classified substandard |
| (d) Machine operator | Number of hours the machine runs |
| (e) Salesperson | Dollars of sales orders divided by number of customers visited |

**10-36  Evaluation of compensation plans (AICPA adapted)**  Gibson Company was established some years ago to bring several new products to the market. Its founder, Gilbert Wilson, believed that once customers tried their products, they would become well accepted. For the first several years, Gibson grew at a rate Wilson considered to be satisfactory. In recent years, some problems have developed both in the firm's profitability and in the morale of and harmonious relationships among the firm's salespeople. Since the company began, salespeople have been paid a base salary plus an 8% commission. The following data are available for two salespeople for the most recent year.

|  | Ronald McTavish | James Christy |
|---|---|---|
| Gross sales orders written | $270,000 | $200,000 |
| Commissions | 21,600 | 16,000 |
| Sales returns | 18,500 | 8,000 |
| Cost of goods sold—all variable | 139,500 | 68,400 |
| Discretionary expenses of salespersons (travel, entertainment, etc.) | 19,200 | 21,500 |

**Required**

1. Determine which salesperson contributed more to the company's profit by preparing a performance report for each.
2. Using the guidelines in Appendix A, write a memorandum to Mr. Wilson recommending (and supporting) changes in Gibson's method of compensating its salespeople.

**10-37  Allocations and ethics**  A slightly edited excerpt from an appeal for contributions from a charity is as follows:

"The Fund's expenses were $26,893,345. Of that amount, 21% was spent in support of research programs and 43% of expenses went in support of the Fund's public education programs in connection with fund-raising appeals.

Combined research and public education programs accounted for 64% of total expenses. Fund-raising expenses were 22% of total expenses and administrative expenses were 14% of total expenses."

The mailing included five health tips (such as cut down on fats, do not smoke, and exercise regularly) that occupied about 15% of the mailing.

**Required**
1. To which of the given categories do you think the charity allocated the costs of mailing? What sorts of costs might the charity have included as part of mailing costs?
2. With the information available, are you inclined to support the charity? Why or why not?

**10-38   *Revenue variances for an airline*** Big Sky Airline budgeted $22 million revenue in March, expecting a 60% load factor (percentage of seat-miles occupied). Actual revenue was $22.8 million. The load factor was 66%. Variable cost per seat-mile is negligible.

**Required**
Determine the difference between budgeted and actual revenue attributable to (a) price and (b) volume (load factor). Round to the nearest $100,000.

**10-39   *Performance reporting—alternative organizational structure (CMA adapted)***
Cranwell Company sells three products in a foreign market and a domestic market. An income statement for the first month of 20X2 shows the following.

| | | |
|---|---:|---:|
| Sales | | $1,300,000 |
| Cost of goods sold | | 1,010,000 |
| Gross profit | | $ 290,000 |
| Selling expenses | $105,000 | |
| Administrative expenses | 72,000 | 177,000 |
| Income | | $ 113,000 |

Data regarding the two markets and three products are as follows:

| | Products | | |
|---|---|---|---|
| | A | B | C |
| Sales: | | | |
| Domestic | $400,000 | $300,000 | $300,000 |
| Foreign | 100,000 | 100,000 | 100,000 |
| Total sales | $500,000 | $400,000 | $400,000 |
| Variable production costs (percentage of sales) | 60% | 70% | 60% |
| Variable selling costs (percentage of sales) | 3% | 2% | 2% |

Product A is made in a single factory that incurs fixed costs (included in cost of goods sold) of $48,000 per month. Products B and C are made in a single factory and require the same machinery. Monthly fixed production costs at that factory are $142,000.

Fixed selling expenses are joint to the three products, but $36,000 is direct to the domestic market and $38,000 to the foreign market. All administrative expenses are fixed. About $25,000 is traceable to the foreign market, $35,000 to the domestic market.

**Required**

1. Assume that Cranwell has separate managers responsible for each market. Prepare performance reports for the domestic and foreign markets.
2. Assume that Cranwell has separate managers responsible for each product. Prepare performance reports for the three products.

**10-40   *Cost allocations, transfer prices, and behavior***   Several top executives of Millard Company are discussing problems they perceive in the company's methods of cost allocation. For each of the following costs, indicate what changes will help accomplish the stated objectives.

(a) Computer cost, which is 95% fixed, is allocated using a transfer price of $100 per hour of use. The executives believe that lower-level managers do not use the computer enough.
(b) Maintenance costs, which are budgeted at $10 per hour variable and $200,000 per year fixed, are allocated by dividing total incurred cost by total maintenance hours worked and distributing the resulting per-hour cost to operating departments according to the number of hours of maintenance work done. The executives believe that operating managers request maintenance work only when machinery is about to break down. Production has halted while repairs were made on critical machines. Operating managers have complained that the per-hour cost is too high.
(c) Millard has a consulting department that advises operating managers on various aspects of production and marketing. The costs of the department are fixed but discretionary and have been rising in recent years because of heavy demand for its services. The costs are not allocated because it was felt that managers should be encouraged to use the service. One executive commented that operating managers call the department to find out where to go for lunch.

**10-41   *Allocations and behavior***   R. A. Shore is a large mail-order company dealing in men's and women's clothing and accessories. Shore operates its six regional distribution centers as profit centers. Until now, each distribution center handled its own trucking requirements. Shore has just acquired a fleet of trucks that are under the control of the traffic manager, who is based at central headquarters.

The traffic manager anticipates having to hire outside truckers because Shore's fleet is insufficient to meet peak demands. He wants the managers of the distribution centers to provide monthly estimates of their trucking needs, from which he will decide how much, if any, outside trucking to hire. For the following two reasons, costs will be higher than necessary if the estimates he receives are either too high or too low.

First, the typical agreement with an outside trucker provides for a payment of $1.20 per mile, but with a guarantee of 2,000 miles for a month. Thus, a trucker who drives 1,000 miles will be paid $2,400. The guarantees can add up to a substantial amount if the estimates are too high. Second, if the estimates are too low, the traffic manager must scramble to find additional truckers in the middle of the month, also adding to costs. Therefore, accurate estimates of trucking needs are desirable. The controller wants a cost allocation scheme that will encourage accuracy.

**Required**

1. Suppose the controller decides not to allocate trucking costs. Do you expect managers of the distribution centers to pay much attention to their monthly estimates of needs?

2. Answer the question in requirement 1 assuming that the controller decides to allocate all trucking costs, both for the owned fleet and for outsiders, based on mileage used by each center.
3. What would you do to encourage the managers of the distribution centers to act in Shore's best interests?

**10-42   Allocations and managers' bonuses**   Katherine Grove, the owner of GroveMart, wants to pay her department managers bonuses totaling $7,500. Grove wants the $7,500 allocated based on the profit each department earns. In the following income statement, all indirect costs are allocated based on sales.

|  | Dry Goods | Housewares | Total |
|---|---|---|---|
| Sales | $250,000 | $500,000 | $750,000 |
| Total direct costs | 166,000 | 437,000 | 603,000 |
| Controllable profit | $ 84,000 | $ 63,000 | $147,000 |
| Indirect costs (all fixed): |  |  |  |
| Sales salaries | $ 16,000 | $ 32,000 | $ 48,000 |
| Other | 8,000 | 16,000 | 24,000 |
| Total indirect costs | $ 24,000 | $ 48,000 | $ 72,000 |
| Profit | $ 60,000 | $ 15,000 | $ 75,000 |

Some salespeople work in one department or the other, while some cover both departments. The manager of Housewares argues that the allocation of indirect sales salaries is inappropriate. He believes that the allocation should be based on the relative direct sales salaries of $60,000 for Dry Goods and $20,000 for Housewares. (These amounts are included in direct costs.) He says that the work of the salespeople is related to the total sales effort.

**Required**
1. Compute each manager's bonus given the existing allocations.
2. Prepare a new income statement allocating indirect sales salaries as suggested by the manager of Housewares. Compute each manager's bonus.
3. Comment on the results. Which method of allocation gives the better result?
4. How might Grove distribute the $7,500 to the managers in a reasonable way without getting into arguments over allocations?

**10-43   Performance report**   Rudolf's Department Store has three major lines—housewares, clothing, and sporting goods. The controller is developing performance analyses for the managers of the lines and has prepared the following income statement, in thousands of dollars.

|  | Housewares | Clothing | Sporting Goods | Total |
|---|---|---|---|---|
| Sales | $900 | $1,200 | $400 | $2,500 |
| Cost of goods sold | 500 | 680 | 180 | 1,360 |
| Gross profit | $400 | $ 520 | $220 | $1,140 |
| Other expenses: |  |  |  |  |
| Salaries | $ 60 | $ 90 | $ 40 | $ 190 |
| Advertising | 45 | 60 | 20 | 125 |
| Rent | 40 | 40 | 20 | 100 |
| Depreciation | 20 | 16 | 12 | 48 |
| General and administrative | 90 | 120 | 40 | 250 |
| Miscellaneous | 60 | 85 | 32 | 177 |
| Total expenses | $315 | $ 411 | $164 | $ 890 |
| Profit | $ 85 | $ 109 | $ 56 | $ 250 |

You learn the following about the data in the income statement.

(a) Cost of goods sold is direct.

(b) Salaries expense includes allocated salaries of $75,000 for employees whose work takes them into different departments. The controller used relative sales to make the allocations.

(c) Advertising is partly allocated. Each department is charged at standard market rates for newspaper space, radio time, and television time that its manager requests. The $50,000 cost of general advertising ordered by the sales vice president was allocated based on sales dollars.

(d) The rent allocation is based on floor space occupied. The three departments occupy 100,000 square feet. Sporting Goods is in the basement, the others on the first floor. Similar property in the city rents for $1.05 per square foot for first floor space, $0.80 for basement space. Rent on space occupied by the administrative offices is included in general and administrative expenses.

(e) Depreciation is all for furniture and fixtures within the departments.

(f) General and administrative expenses are allocated based on sales dollars.

(g) Miscellaneous expenses are partly separable, partly allocated. The allocated amounts by department are as follows: Housewares, $28,000; Clothing, $36,000; and Sporting Goods, $16,000.

#### Required

Prepare a new performance report using the principle of controllability. Include a column for unallocated costs, as well as one for each department.

**10-44    *Transfer prices and behavior***    All operating departments of Genco Company are profit or investment centers, and some service departments are artificial profit centers. The Maintenance Department is an artificial profit center that charges $10 per hour for work it does for operating departments. The variable cost per hour is $4, and fixed costs are $40,000 per month.

The manager of Department A, an operating department, has just determined that some changes in the production process can be made. If the changes are made, maintenance requirements will drop from 2,100 hours per month to 1,600. However, the variable cost to produce a unit of product will increase from $6 to $7. Department A produces 4,000 units of product per month.

#### Required

1. Determine the change in monthly profit for Department A if the production process is changed.

2. Determine the change in profit of the Maintenance Department if Department A changes its production process.

3. Determine the effect of the change in Department A's production process on Genco's monthly profit.

4. Suppose that the manager of Department A is prompted to study possible changes in the production process because the transfer price for maintenance work is to be raised to $12 per hour. The Maintenance Department expects a $1 increase in variable cost per hour and approval of other expenditures that will raise fixed costs by $8,000 per month. For the last several months, the Maintenance Department has shown a profit of $8,000, and the proposed new transfer price was designed to maintain that profit level.

   (a) How many hours of maintenance work per month are currently done by the Maintenance Department?

   (b) If the manager of Department A makes the change in the production process, what profit will Maintenance show for a month?

**10-45   Cost allocation**   Danner Industries allocates indirect costs to departments and product lines using direct labor hours as the basis. The 20X5 allocations are based on 400,000 direct labor hours and $1,910,000 indirect costs. Data related to one product line, Cleaners, and to all others as a group for 20X5 follow.

| | Totals | Cleaners | All Others |
|---|---|---|---|
| Direct labor hours | 400,000 | 50,000 | 350,000 |

Danner's managers have become convinced that they need several bases to reflect the activities that drive their indirect costs. After careful study, the controller developed the following information regarding cost pools and activities that drive the pools.

| Cost Driver | Amount of Activity | Amount of Related Indirect Costs |
|---|---|---|
| Labor hours | 400,000 hours | $1,580,000 |
| Record keeping | 150,000 entries | 180,000 |
| Number of parts | 4,000 parts | 150,000 |
| Total indirect costs | | $1,910,000 |

Data related to one product line, Cleaners, and to all others as a group for 20X5 follow.

| | Totals | Cleaners | All Others |
|---|---|---|---|
| Direct labor hours | 400,000 | 50,000 | 350,000 |
| Record-keeping entries | 150,000 | 6,000 | 144,000 |
| Number of parts | 4,000 | 100 | 3,900 |

**Required**
1. Allocate the indirect costs to Cleaners and to the other products based on direct labor hours.
2. Allocate each group of costs separately to Cleaners and to the group of others using the separate bases.
3. Danner sells 30,000 cases of Cleaners annually. Its direct costs are $16.50 per unit. Separately calculate the total per-case costs using your results from requirements 1 and 2. Comment on the difference.

## CASES

**10-46   Cost allocations in a university**   Ed Cranston, the new dean of the School of Business at Midstate University, is concerned. It is only early February, and he has just received a report from the university's printing and duplicating service showing that the school has exceeded its budget for duplicating for the academic year. The report appears as follows:

Printing and Duplicating Department Statement of Budget and Charges for the School of Business, September–January

| Annual Budget | Actual Charges | Over (Under) |
|---|---|---|
| $4,200 | $4,350 | $150 |

An enclosed note states that Ed must either stop using the service or obtain approval of a supplemental budget request from the university's chief fiscal officer. Ed pulls out his latest statement, from December, and finds that actual charges at that time were $1,830. Since the school was on vacation during a good part of January, he wonders how $2,520 could have been incurred in January.

He finds out that costs for the Printing and Duplicating Department in January were $6,300, of which $700 was for paper, $2,000 for salaries, $2,000 for machine rentals, and $1,600 for general overhead (allocated share of all university utilities, depreciation, etc.). A total of 35,000 copies was made in January, a relatively low number because of the vacation. However, several faculty members in the School of Business had a substantial amount of printing done for scholarly papers that they were circulating to other professors throughout the country. The School of Business was responsible for 14,000 of the 35,000 copies. The $2,520 charge was computed by dividing total department costs for the month by the number of copies ($6,300/35,000) to arrive at a charge of $0.18 per copy. Ed also learned that during a typical month about $8,600 in cost is incurred and 150,000 copies are processed. Paper is the only variable cost.

## Required
Evaluate the cost allocation system used and recommend changes if you think any are necessary.

**10-47   Allocation of costs—distribution channels**   Weisner Company sells its products through wholesalers and retailers. Erica Stern is in charge of wholesale sales, and Ralph Pike manages retail sales. Florence Weisner, president of the firm, has ordered an analysis of the relative profitability of the two channels of distribution to determine where emphasis should be placed. The following data show the operations for the last six months.

|  | Wholesalers | Retailers |
|---|---|---|
| Sales | $2,000,000 | $3,000,000 |
| Cost of sales—all variable | $1,600,000 | $2,000,000 |
| Sales commissions (3% of sales) | 60,000 | 90,000 |
| Managers' salaries | 18,000 | 18,000 |
| Advertising (allocated as a percentage of sales dollars) | 12,000 | 18,000 |
| Selling expenses—salespeople's expenses, delivery, order processing, credit checking (allocated on the basis of number of orders from each group) | 80,000 | 160,000 |
| General expenses (allocated as a percentage of sales dollars) | 40,000 | 60,000 |
| Total expenses | $1,810,000 | $2,346,000 |
| Income | $ 190,000 | $ 654,000 |

The same products are sold to both wholesalers and retailers, but prices to wholesalers are about 20% less than those to retailers.

## Required
1. Comment on the reasonableness of the allocation methods used.
2. Recast the statement based on the principle of controllability.
3. What further information would help in assigning costs to the responsible managers?

**10-48 *Allocations and behavior*** Clifford Electronics operates a single plant. Clifford allocates indirect costs to departments and then to product lines based on their direct labor content. Each department concentrates on one product line. The cost of an average unit of one of its major lines, made in Department Z, follows. The data relate to a recent month when the company made 50,000 units of the product line.

| | |
|---|---:|
| Materials and components | $ 90 |
| Direct labor at $12 per hour | 24 |
| Indirect costs at 500% of direct labor | 120 |
| Total cost | $234 |

The indirect cost rate of 500% of direct labor cost is based on actual total indirect costs divided by the $4,000,000 total company-wide labor cost for the most recent month. Because of the high combined labor and indirect costs, the department manager urged the Design Engineering Department to work on reducing the labor time in the product. The engineers did a great deal of redesigning that resulted in a 25% reduction in labor time over a six-month period, largely by using costlier parts and components that required less time to assemble. The department manager was then surprised to see the following analysis for the sixth month of the program, when production was 50,000 units.

| | |
|---|---:|
| Materials and components | $ 95 |
| Direct labor at $12 | 18 |
| Indirect costs at 650% of direct labor | 117 |
| Total cost | $230 |

The manager was aghast at the results and could not understand why such a concentrated effort had shown so little payoff. The manager of engineering was also distressed at the results. The most disappointing aspect was the sharp increase in the indirect cost rate, and the manager decided to determine its cause. He learned that total labor hours for the company decreased about 10% over the six-month period because other departments were also trying to reduce labor costs.

**Required**
1. Determine total indirect costs allocated to the product line in each month.
2. What reasons might there be for the disappointing results?

**10-49 *Allocations and behavior (continuation of 10-48)*** Sarah Torg, controller of Clifford Electronics, was well aware of the problems created by the company's use of direct labor to allocate all indirect costs. She did considerable analysis and developed the following plantwide pools of average monthly indirect costs, as they related to particular cost drivers.

| Activity | Amount of Activity | Amount of Related Indirect Costs |
|---|---|---:|
| Labor cost | $3,480,000 | $ 9,880,000 |
| Record keeping | 2,400,000 entries | 840,000 |
| Materials | $48,000,000 cost of materials | 11,350,000 |
| Engineering hours | 4,000 hours | 770,000 |
| Total indirect costs | | $22,840,000 |

Torg noted that using direct labor cost to allocate the indirect costs gave a rate of about 650%, as Department Z experienced in a previous month. That is, $22,840,000/ $3,480,000 = 656%. She wanted to see how the allocations would change using these four bases, instead of just direct labor. She collected the following data for the line described in the preceding assignment.

| | |
|---|---|
| Labor cost | $900,000 |
| Record keeping | 400,000 entries |
| Cost of materials used | $4,750,000 |
| Engineering hours | 300   hours |

**Required**

1. Calculate the rate per unit of activity for each group of indirect costs.
2. Use the rates calculated in requirement 1 to allocate indirect costs to Department Z, and determine the unit cost of the average product in Z's line using the new allocation.
3. Using the guidelines in Appendix A, write a memorandum to Ms. Torg commenting on the differences between the alternative allocation schemes.

**10-50  *Performance measurement in an automobile dealership***  In automobile dealerships the sales managers of new and used cars are commonly evaluated according to the profits on sales of new and used cars, respectively. Complicating such evaluations is the interrelationship that often exists between the actions taken by the two segments.

A new-car sales agreement may include some allowance for a traded-in used car. The trade-in allowance is often based on what the used-car manager is willing to pay the new-car manager for the car. For example, suppose that a customer wants to buy a new car that has a list price of $12,000 and trade in a used car. If there were no trade-in, the price of the car would be $11,200. If the used-car manager will give $3,500 for the used car to be traded in, the new-car salesperson could allow up to $4,300 to the customer, because the net price would still be satisfactory. The $7,700 cash paid ($12,000 list price - $4,300 allowed on the old car) is the same as the difference between the $11,200 desired price and the $3,500 that the used-car manager will pay for the car.

Sometimes the used-car manager will offer lower prices than at other times, say, if the used-car lot is full and sales are slow. If the used-car manager will pay only $2,800 for the car, the salesperson could give only a $3,600 trade-in allowance to obtain $11,200.

**Required**

1. Assuming that each manager is evaluated on profits in his respective area, what is the disadvantage of the system to the new-car manager? Is there a disadvantage to the used-car manager?
2. Suppose the dealership's policy provides that the new-car manager can try to sell the car to another used-car dealer if he is unhappy with the price offered by the used-car manager. In the second example, suppose the new-car manager believed that the trade-in automobile could be sold to another used-car dealer for $3,500. The $11,200 deemed acceptable for the new car would be obtained ($7,700 from the customer plus $3,500 from selling the trade-in), so this deal for the new car would be accepted despite the lower bid from the used-car manager. Does the system encourage the managers to act in the best interests of the total firm?

**10-51  *Home office allocations and decisions***  Worcester Manufacturing Company has fourteen sales offices throughout the United States and Canada. Each sales office is a profit center, with the local manager able to set prices and offer special discounts to obtain customers. Many functions such as checking creditworthiness of customers, billing, and others are centralized in the home office. A few years ago, Martinique Nadeau, the president, decided to charge the sales offices for these functions. After some thought, she set the charge at 8% of revenue. Home office costs are almost all fixed.

The firm's factories bill the sales offices for goods at prices established annually. The charge includes both variable manufacturing costs and a margin to cover fixed costs. Variable manufacturing costs average about 40% of revenue at current prices.

Lee Holden, manager of the Miami office, has come to you for advice. She is considering a price reduction that she expects to add considerably to unit volume but is unsure of the effects on profit. She begins by showing you an income statement that reflects her expectations for the coming year without the price reduction.

| Miami Office Budgeted Income Statement for 20X2 | | |
|---|---|---|
| Sales | | $2,400,000 |
| Cost of sales | | 1,200,000 |
| Gross margin | | $1,200,000 |
| Salaries and commissions | $490,000 | |
| Rent, utilities, insurance | 86,000 | |
| Home office charge | 192,000 | 768,000 |
| Profit | | $  432,000 |

Holden believes that it is possible to obtain the following increases in unit volume given the associated decreases in selling prices.

| Decrease in Price | Increase in Unit Volume |
|---|---|
| 5% | 20% |
| 10% | 35% |

Holden tells you that the only variable costs of running the office are the 15% commissions that salespeople earn. Of course, her "cost of sales" is variable because it depends on unit volume, as is the home office charge because it depends on total revenue. Holden is evaluated on the profit that her office generates.

**Required**

1. Determine whether or not Holden should reduce prices, and if so, by how much.
2. Using the guidelines in Appendix A, write a memorandum to Ms. Holden giving and supporting your recommendation about which action (hold prices, reduce prices by 5%, reduce prices by 10%) is in Worcester's best interests.

**10-52   *Incurred costs and performance***   Weldon Oil Company operates a refinery in the northeastern United States. During the winter about 200 workers are employed as drivers of fuel-oil trucks to deliver oil for heating purposes. Drivers are paid $10 per hour. During the summer there is no need for their services as fuel-oil truck drivers, and they are given jobs in the refinery. These refinery jobs pay only $7 per hour. However, company policy is to pay the drivers their usual $10 rate.

The refinery manager is charged with the $10 wage paid to the drivers while they work in the refinery. The manager of fuel-oil distribution bears no charge except when the workers are delivering fuel oil. The refinery manager does not object to employing the drivers during the summer. Even with this addition to his regular work force he must hire students and other temporary employees in the summer. He does, however, object to the $10 charge in the summer, because he can obtain equally qualified (for those jobs) workers at $7 per hour and he must use the drivers as a matter of company policy.

### Required

Using the guidelines in Appendix A, write a memorandum to Ms. Cohen, Weldon's controller, pointing out the problems by the firm's present cost-assignment policies and recommending an alternative approach for assigning the charges for drivers' wages during the summer.

# DIVISIONAL PERFORMANCE MEASUREMENT

## LEARNING OBJECTIVES

*After reading this chapter, you should be able to*

- *Explain some of the advantages and disadvantages of decentralization.*
- *Describe the commonly used measures of evaluating the performance of investment centers and their managers.*
- *Describe how performance evaluation methods can encourage managers to act against the best interests of the company.*
- *Describe variations in measuring income and investment.*
- *Explain how evaluating a division is different from evaluating the manager of the division.*
- *Explain the problems in developing transfer pricing policies.*
- *Describe performance evaluation problems specific to multinational companies.*

In the 1997 annual report, Steve McMillan, president of **Sara Lee Corporation**, stated: "At Sara Lee, our decentralized management structure gives us a competitive advantage. It very clearly defines a culture in which highly motivated and talented people are given the authority to lead businesses—and are then held accountable for the performance of those businesses."

Sara Lee is organized into a large number of profit centers, each led by an operating executive with a high degree of authority. Executives are selected and developed based upon their ability to succeed in the entrepreneurial environment. Throughout the organization, division managers apply local talent and home-grown expertise in building brands such as Jimmy Dean, Hanes, and Bryan, and extending the reach of Douwe Egberts, Playtex, and Dim.

But with empowerment comes accountability, and at Sara Lee success is measured by performance. Given the right resources and strong incentives to succeed, managers understand that nonperforming businesses will be fixed, closed, or sold. For Sara Lee executives, "making plan" is not an option; it is an understood ethic.

**Georgia-Pacific Corporation** restructured in December 1997, creating The Timber Company, responsible for 5.4 million acres of timberland, and

> the Georgia-Pacific Group, responsible for manufacturing and distributing building products, pulp, and paper. By separating timberlands from manufacturing, managers of each unit are now responsible for maximizing the returns on their own business. The separation also provides increased financial and strategic flexibility, and more sharply defined incentives.
>
> Companies throughout the world are reorganizing, spreading responsibility, and loosening lines of authority. Such changes are often responses to the rapid pace of change that characterizes global competition. But how do companies control and evaluate managers and segments in these conditions?

*Sources: Sara Lee Corporation 1997 annual report.*
*Georgia-Pacific Corporation 1997 annual report.*

Chapter 10 introduced responsibility accounting systems and their task of providing information to help managers control operations and evaluate performance. This chapter focuses on control and evaluation in investment centers, though much of the discussion also applies to profit centers. Investment centers are often large enough to be divisions of a large company. Divisions are often relatively autonomous, which allows their managers to act almost as if they were chief executive officers of independent companies.

Investment centers control all the major components of financial performance: revenues, costs, and investments. They therefore can be evaluated by more comprehensive measures of performance than can cost centers or profit centers, which do not control all these elements. The more comprehensive the performance measure the better. The measures described in this chapter are more comprehensive than cost or profit measures.

## DECENTRALIZATION

In general terms, an organization is characterized as centralized or decentralized depending on the extent of the responsibilities granted to its managers. If employees, both managers and non-managers, have a good deal of responsibility and authority and can make many types of decisions without the approval of higher levels of management, **decentralization** exists. Where managers can act less freely, and decisions are made at the top, **centralization** exists. Profit and investment centers are more commonly associated with decentralization than are cost centers because managers of profit and investment centers have broader responsibility than do managers of cost centers. In visual terms, a centralized organizational structure tends to be hierarchical, or pyramid-like. Centralized organizations are usually organized by function: production, marketing, administration, etc. A decentralized organizational structure appears flatter, and is organized by product line, geographic area, or other non-functional basis.

Companies that use investment centers are usually highly decentralized. In highly decentralized companies, operating units (usually called *divisions* or **business units**) are almost autonomous; division managers are responsible for both production and marketing, as well as for functions such as personnel and accounting. Division managers also prepare and submit capital budgets to central headquarters for approval.

## BENEFITS OF DECENTRALIZATION

Proponents of decentralizing argue that it promotes better decision making. They believe that the managers closest to an operation make better decisions because they are better able to gather and evaluate information than are centrally located corporate managers. Managers at the scene can act more quickly because they need not report to headquarters and wait for approval of their proposed actions. **General Electric** uses a program called Work Out, which is based on the belief that people closest to the situation know best. Groups including shop floor workers, supervisors, and managers meet to solve problems.

Considerable evidence suggests that the broader responsibility accompanying decentralization increases motivation. Studies have shown that employees (including managers) tend to perform better as their responsibilities increase. In general, the least-motivated people are those who perform a single task repeatedly throughout the day. One effect of establishing manufacturing cells in companies using JIT is to broaden the responsibilities of workers that make up the cell. The term *job enlargement* describes giving increased responsibility. People who do much of the work on a product, as opposed to doing only one small operation, and managers who control most of the factors that affect profitability become more committed to their jobs and are more likely to view their jobs as sources of satisfaction, not just as sources of income. In recent years, work teams that manage themselves have become an important tool. Many companies use such teams.

Decentralization is particularly advantageous to companies that operate in different industries. As companies widen their range of products, the need to give broad responsibility to division managers increases. A company's president or other chief operating officer can't be thoroughly familiar with a great many product lines, such as textiles, furniture, appliances, automobile supplies, movies, and sporting goods. Similarly, increasing international operations has increased the need for knowledgeable on-site managers with decision-making authority. Managers of nearly autonomous divisions are also well prepared for higher positions. They appreciate all aspects of a company's operations. With such increased responsibility comes higher rewards, but greater risk. The accompanying Insight describes how **Boise Cascade** uses performance measures to compensate managers of decentralized units.

As a practical matter, it is impossible to operate a modern business of any complexity without delegating some authority to lower-level managers. The interdependence of functional areas and factors in the corporate culture make conflicts between managers inevitable. When the chief executive is the only manager whose span of responsibility includes the managers in conflict, arbitration and settlement of disputes must necessarily take place at the top. In most situations, decentralization allows conflicts among managers to be resolved at a lower level.

## PROBLEMS OF DECENTRALIZATION

Decentralization has its problems, the major one being that managers operating in nearly autonomous fashion might make decisions that harm the company. Indeed, perhaps the most formidable problem of decentralization is achieving goal congruence while at the same time promoting and maintaining divisional autonomy. **Magna International**, a leading auto parts supplier, decentralized to extremes in the early 1980s. The company rewarded plant managers almost solely on profits and gave them near-complete freedom. Unlike most companies, Magna

**IN** SIGHT

### Performance Measures at Boise Cascade

**Boise Cascade** adopted Economic Value Added as a key financial measure in 1994. Boise Cascade feels that the EVA measurement process encourages all employees to make business decisions that create economic value through improved operating efficiency, better asset utilization, and growth that generates returns which exceed the cost of capital. EVA is used to determine incentive compensation for management and other employees. The compensation of plan participants, including corporate officers, is tied directly to improvement in the EVA of their operations and the corporation as a whole.

George Harad, CEO of Boise Cascade, stated in the 1997 annual report, "We are moving rapidly to achieve fully competitive positions in all of our businesses and products and are focused on achieving our financial goals: To be profitable throughout the business cycle and to be EVA-positive over the cycle."

Source: 1997 Boise Cascade Annual Report.

permitted plant managers to borrow money, build new factories, and sign long-term contracts. The plant managers added huge amounts of debt until the burden almost sank Magna in 1990, as the recession hit the company's sales.

Decentralization can create other problems. In the early 1980s, **Levi Strauss** decentralized into divisions that each handled a product line. It reconsolidated because retailers were unhappy having to buy from several divisions instead of only one. Pressures from large customers who buy across product lines have prompted organizational changes at many other companies, whether the changes redefined segments; established segments to deal with such customers; or centralized ordering, distribution, billing, and other functions. For example, **Fieldcrest Cannon**, the home furnishings manufacturer, organized one of its units by type of customer: department and specialty stores, mass merchants, institutions, and international. This organization made the unit more responsive to the differing requirements of the customers.

Two managerial accounting issues are especially related to decentralization. First is the need to develop methods of evaluating performance that benefit the company as a whole. Second is a need to develop transfer prices that produce decisions in the best interests of the company. We turn first to the problem of selecting performance measures for divisions.

## MEASURES OF PERFORMANCE

Companies use three principal measures to evaluate divisions: income, return on investment, and residual income.

## INCOME

Net income for financial reporting purposes, computed under GAAP, is the most widely examined (and least understood) financial datum. For several reasons, income is unsatisfactory for measuring the performance of divisions.

- In calculating net income, companies subtract interest and taxes, neither of which is normally under the control of divisional managers and so are not typically shown in internal reports.

- A division's expenses usually include some charges (allocations) for services provided by central headquarters. For example, much of the payroll work for divisions of **Ford Motor Company** is done by an artificial profit center that bills divisions for its services.

- Factors that influence GAAP-based income do not necessarily apply to internal reports. For example, companies must expense research and development expenditures because of the importance of verifiability and objectivity in financial reporting. Because these qualities are less important in internal reporting, companies can capitalize and amortize R&D expenditures to reflect their long-term benefits.

- Income is not a comprehensive measure of success. A division that earns $10 million on a $200 million investment is far less successful than one earning $3 million on a $10 million investment. This objection applies not only to GAAP-based income, but to any other calculation such as we have made in earlier chapters, particularly Chapters 4 and 5.

Although income is not the most useful performance measure, neither is it irrelevant. Indeed, two of the three other widely used performance measures discussed in this chapter include income. But the importance of income is as a part of other measures rather than as a measure in itself.

## RETURN ON INVESTMENT

**Return on investment (ROI)** is the general term used to describe a ratio of *some measure of income to some measure of investment*. In financial accounting you might have seen the ratio net income divided by stockholders' equity, usually called *return on equity (ROE)*. ROE is one type of ROI. Another is *return on assets (ROA)*, usually measured as income before interest and taxes divided by total assets. Some companies use the term *return on capital employed*, or just return on capital, to designate the same ratio. For internal performance evaluation, managers generally use an ROI measure of the following form.

$$ROI = \frac{divisional\ income}{divisional\ investment}$$

Companies define and measure **divisional income** (also called *segment income* or *operating profit*) and **divisional investment** (also called *invested capital* or *identifiable assets*) in various ways. We examine some of these ways shortly.

ROI is the most frequently used criterion for divisional performance measurement, though the use of other measures is growing. ROI has a distinct advantage over income as a performance measure, because companies usually have divisions of different sizes. A division earning $300,000 on an investment of $1,000,000 is more efficient than one earning the same profit on an investment of $5,000,000. ROI makes it possible to compare the efficiency of different-size divisions by relating output (income) to input (investment).

Some managers find it helpful to restate the ROI formula when they are looking for ways to improve operating performance. The restatement, known as the **DuPont formula**, expands the basic formula (income ÷ investment) into two ratios.

$$ROI = \frac{income}{sales} \times \frac{sales}{investment}$$

The expanded version gives the same final answer because "sales" appears in the numerator of one factor and the denominator of the other and thus cancels out. But the expanded form helps to focus the manager's attention on the two components of ROI.

The first ratio, income ÷ sales, is the familiar **return on sales (ROS)** ratio introduced in Chapter 2, also called *profit margin* or just *margin*. The second, sales ÷ investment, is **investment turnover**, or just *turnover*. This expanded version clearly shows that an increase in sales, by itself, will not increase ROI because sales cancels out. But a decrease in investment, with other factors remaining the same, will increase ROI (as will an increase in income with other factors held constant).

With the expanded formula, a manager can readily determine the effect on ROI of a decision expected to change two factors. Suppose that ROS is now 15 percent and investment turnover is 2 times; ROI is 30 percent (15% × 2). A manager considering changing the product mix to items with lower margins and faster turnover, which will increase turnover to 2½ times while reducing ROS to 10 percent, can see that ROI will fall to 25 percent (10% × 2½).

The values of the two components of ROI often give clues to the strategies used by companies or divisions. For example, a single company might operate divisions that follow a differentiation strategy, and should therefore have high margins, as well as divisions that follow a cost leadership strategy, and should have high turnovers. The values can also offer clues as to why one division is outperforming another. The following data are for the 1997/1998 operations of high-tech companies **Rockwell** and **Dell Computer**. Amounts are in millions of dollars.

|  | Rockwell | Dell |
|---|---|---|
| Sales | $7,882 | $12,327 |
| Operating profit | $923 | $1,316 |
| Identifiable assets | $7,971 | $4,268 |
| Return on sales | 11.7% | 10.7% |
| Investment turnover | 0.99 | 2.89 |
| ROI | 11.6% | 30.8% |

Rockwell's profit margin is higher than Dell's, but Dell turns its investment over three times as fast as does Rockwell, giving Dell a wide lead in ROI. We cannot be sure why Dell has better results, but we can surmise that it manages its assets better. We should point out that these numbers come from annual reports that do not describe in detail how the numbers are calculated. The two companies might well calculate things differently, making comparisons less clear. Of course, a company doing these calculations for several of its divisions can be sure it defines numbers consistently.

While the advantages of ROI in considering relative sizes and alternative strategies are obvious, absolute size still matters in assessing a segment's contribution to the entity as a whole. Depending on the circumstances, a 12 percent ROI for a very large division might be making a greater contribution than a 40 percent ROI in another division. Recall from Chapter 8 that a company is wise to accept all proposed investments with expected returns greater than cost of capital. Residual income recognizes the same general principle in evaluating divisions.

## RESIDUAL INCOME

**Residual income (RI)** is the income a division produces in excess of the **minimum required (desired, target) rate of return**. Top management establishes the minimum rate of return, which should be greater than cost of capital, as described in Chapter 8. For one reason, the target ROI usually does not recognize income taxes because companies do not include income taxes in computing divisional income. Some companies set different minimum rates of return for different divisions to reflect differences in the risks associated with their businesses. A division in a risky industry such as fashion merchandise should earn higher returns than one in a more stable industry such as paper.

Residual income is computed as follows.

$$RI = income - (investment \times target\ ROI)$$

The parenthetical term is the profit that must be earned to satisfy the minimum requirement. It is the minimum required *dollar* return. Anything over that amount benefits the company. (Of course, *any* income benefits the company, but the minimum required ROI is needed simply to keep it going.) If the company earns less than investors demand, they will invest their capital elsewhere and the company will decline and perhaps go out of business. The most basic argument for using RI, in preference to ROI, for evaluating divisional performance is that RI explicitly recognizes the critical point that the capital invested in any division comes with a cost, as you know from Chapter 8. When the minimum ROI approximates cost of capital or the cutoff rate (pretax) for the company as a whole, RI measures the profit that the division provides to the company over and above the minimum profit required for the amount invested.

Proponents of RI argue that it reflects the contribution a division makes to the company better than does ROI. Suppose that Division A produces a $200,000 income on an investment of $1,000,000, an ROI of 20 percent, while Division B earns $1,500,000 on an investment of $10,000,000, an ROI of 15 percent. Depending on the required ROI for the company, the contributions of the divisions to the company as a whole will appear quite different. Consider two possibilities: (1) required ROI is 10 percent and (2) required ROI is 18 percent. The RIs for each division are as follows:

|  | 1<br>Required ROI is 10% | | 2<br>Required ROI is 18% | |
|---|---|---|---|---|
|  | Division A | Division B | Division A | Division B |
| Investment | $1,000,000 | $10,000,000 | $1,000,000 | $10,000,000 |
| Divisional income | $ 200,000 | $ 1,500,000 | $ 200,000 | $ 1,500,000 |
| Required minimum return<br>   (investment × minimum ROI) | 100,000 | 1,000,000 | 180,000 | 1,800,000 |
| Residual income | $ 100,000 | $ 500,000 | $ 20,000 | $ (300,000) |

If the minimum required ROI is 10 percent, Division B contributes more to the company than does Division A, despite Division B's lower ROI. In this situation we could say that Division B was more valuable to the company. On the other hand, if the company has an 18 percent minimum ROI, Division A contributes more and is more valuable under the RI criterion. The accompanying Insight describes a concept akin to RI that has become popular for evaluating both divisions and entire companies.

**IN** SIGHT

### Economic Value Added (EVA)

In recent years, well-known companies as diverse as **AT&T, Briggs & Stratton, Coca-Cola, Boise Cascade,** and **Quaker Oats** have adopted a performance measure called **EVA,** for **economic value added**. They use this measure not only for divisions, but for the company as a whole. *Fortune* publishes lists of companies ranked by EVA and many espouse it as an excellent performance measure for a company as a whole. The concepts of EVA and RI are very similar. EVA uses after-tax operating profit, which is RI's divisional profit less income taxes. EVA also uses cost of capital as the target ROI, while RI uses a pretax target return that is also higher than cost of capital. Those using RI often begin with a pretax cost of capital, then adjust the target return upward to allow for risk, indirect costs, investment, and other factors. We discussed this type of adjustment in Chapter 8. Suppose that the company in the example has a cost of capital of 11 percent and a 30 percent income tax rate. EVA for Division A is

| | |
|---|---:|
| Divisional profit | $200,000 |
| Less income taxes | 60,000 |
| After-tax profit | $140,000 |
| Less required minimum, $1,000,000 × 11% | 110,000 |
| EVA | $ 30,000 |

The CEO of Quaker Oats credits EVA with instilling an excellent attitude in managers, making them act as if they were owners. Quaker Oats calls EVA *controllable profit.* Coca-Cola increased EVA simply by moving some vending machines to higher-traffic locations. **International Multifoods Corporation's** 1998 annual report stated that "EVA is being used to drive the business changes required for maximum impact on profitable growth and value creation. It also serves as a catalyst for change—in the culture of the company and in the way work gets done and decisions are made. With EVA serving as a blueprint for strategic planning, decision-making, capital investments and compensation plans, International Multifoods is on the right track."

Because EVA recognizes that a division must cover cost of capital to thrive, it shares RI's advantage over ROI as a performance measure. The interest in

**SIGHT**                                                                    **(continued)**

EVA generated by the attention that *Fortune* and other publications have given it has encouraged companies to identify the investments of business units and to make more extensive use of investment centers. For example, before adopting EVA, Quaker Oats evaluated its divisions—and rewarded its managers—on income. Briggs & Stratton did not identify investment with any segments within its engine business. It has since organized those segments into five investment centers. Similarly, AT&T had only a few, very large investment centers before 1993. It reorganized one of those units into 40 investment centers.

Directing managers to thinking about both income *and* investment encourages them to think about ways to use capital more efficiently—to get more income from their existing capital or to reduce capital and hold income constant. Many of the profitable actions claimed as results of using EVA stem from directing managers' attention to *both* income and investment.

*Sources: Shawn Tully, "The Real Key to Creating Wealth,"* Fortune, *September 20, 1993, 38–50.*
*Coca-Cola brochure and annual reports.*
*International Multifoods annual report, 1998.*

Because numbers for divisional income and divisional investment are needed to compute both RI and ROI, the same questions arise as to how those numbers should be computed. These questions are discussed later in the chapter.

## BEHAVIORAL PROBLEMS

We pointed out in Chapter 10 that goal congruence is an important objective of a management control system. From Chapter 8 you know that, in the absence of some overriding qualitative issue, a company should accept an investment that will yield a positive net present value, or equivalently, that has an internal rate of return greater than cost of capital or the cutoff rate. Investment centers make significant capital investments, most of which must be approved by corporate headquarters. Divisional management must decide whether or not to seek approval for the investment opportunities it sees or to fund those for which it need not obtain corporate approval. A performance measure is dysfunctional if it encourages managers to make poor investment decisions. We can examine the performance measures so far discussed in relation to goal congruence.

### ROI VERSUS RI

Using ROI to evaluate divisions can encourage the divisions to reject good investments and accept poor investments.

#### Rejecting Valuable Investments—Division Q
Consider the manager of Division Q, who expects $300,000 income on a $1,000,000 investment for a 30 percent expected ROI. The manager has an oppor-

tunity offering a $75,000 incremental profit on an incremental investment of $300,000 (ROI of 25 percent on the additional investment). Suppose further that the company's minimum rate of return is 20 percent. From the company's viewpoint, the proposed investment should be undertaken because its 25 percent expected ROI exceeds the 20 percent required minimum. But if the performance of the division (and its manager) is evaluated on the basis of ROI, the manager will be inclined to reject the new investment because ROI (now 30 percent) will fall, as can be seen in the following computations.

| Divisional profit: | |
|---|---:|
| Current | $ 300,000 |
| From new project | 75,000 |
| Total divisional profit | $ 375,000 |
| | |
| Investment before new project | $1,000,000 |
| Additional investment for the project | 300,000 |
| Total investment | $1,300,000 |
| | |
| Divisional ROI after new investment ($375,000/$1,300,000) | 28.8% |

Using RI to evaluate performance encourages goal congruent behavior.

| | Without New Project | With New Project |
|---|---:|---:|
| Divisional investment | $1,000,000 | $1,300,000 |
| Minimum required ROI | 20% | 20% |
| Divisional profit | $ 300,000 | $ 375,000 |
| Less minimum required | 200,000 | 260,000 |
| Residual income | $ 100,000 | $ 115,000 |

A division manager evaluated on the basis of RI will undertake this project because performance improves. This should not be surprising because the 25 percent ROI exceeds the required 20 percent. The ROI criterion encourages maximizing the ratio of profit to investment. The RI criterion encourages maximizing total dollars of profit in excess of the minimum required dollar return. In fact, we could have said in advance that the project was desirable, and that it would increase RI by $15,000, which is the increase in income less the additional dollar return required [$75,000 – ($300,000 × 20%)].

### Accepting Value-Losing Opportunities—Division Z

Suppose that the manager of Division Z of the same company expects income of $200,000 on an investment of $2,000,000, for a 10 percent ROI. How would the manager respond to an opportunity to increase income $15,000 by investing $100,000? The investment is unwise for the company because it earns less than the 20 percent minimum. But the manager will accept the investment because divisional ROI increases to 10.2 percent.

$$\text{New ROI} = \frac{\$200,000 + \$15,000}{\$2,000,000 + \$100,000} = \frac{\$215,000}{\$2,100,000} = 10.2\%$$

Yet the proposed action actually generates negative residual income of $5,000 because a $100,000 investment requires income of $20,000 to meet the 20 percent minimum required rate of return. A manager evaluated on RI will reject the investment because the already negative RI of $200,000 [$200,000 – ($2,000,000 × 20%)] grows to $205,000 if the investment proposal is accepted.

In most companies, Division Z would not be able to make the undesirable investment because capital budgeting proposals must go to the corporation for approval. But that manager still might invest in receivables and inventory to increase income, investments which do not require headquarter approval.

## ROI AND RI

Because ROI and RI use book values, they can both encourage divisional managers to act against the company's best interests. Consider the following example. A manager is considering a project that requires a $100,000 investment and provides pretax cash flows of $40,000 per year for five years. The company requires a minimum pretax ROI of 25 percent. The present value of the $40,000 stream of payments discounted at 25 percent is $107,560 ($40,000 × 2.689). Under the decision rules developed in Chapter 8, the investment is desirable because it has a positive NPV of $7,560 ($107,560 – $100,000). The book rates of return and RIs for the first two years of the investment are as follows, using straight-line depreciation.

| Year | Additional Cash Flow | Additional Depreciation | Increase in Book Income | Average Additional Investment[a] | ROI on Additional Investment | RI[b] |
|------|------|------|------|------|------|------|
| 1 | $40,000 | $20,000 | $20,000 | $90,000 | 22.2% | $(2,500) |
| 2 | $40,000 | $20,000 | $20,000 | $70,000 | 28.6% | $2,500 |

a  Book value of investment at beginning of year plus book value at end of year, divided by two.
b  Book income of $20,000 minus 25 percent required return on average additional investment.

In the first year, ROI is below the 25 percent required minimum and RI is negative. The division manager, seeing that undertaking the project will penalize performance in the first year, is not encouraged to accept the project.

Because investment declines through depreciation, both ROI and RI rise over time unless income from the investment declines sharply. The pattern is more extreme if the company uses an accelerated method of depreciation. Even if cash flows, and therefore book income, decline, the pattern of increasing ROI is likely to occur.

The rise in ROI based on book values is even more pronounced in more realistic situations where returns do not begin immediately or do not reach their peaks in the early years. Ordinarily some lead time is required—to build a plant, install machinery, test the operation, remove bugs, and generally get the operation going. Heavy startup costs are common in the opening of a new plant or even the remodeling of an existing one. The returns are likely to increase over the first few years as the plant gains efficiency. If a new product is involved, its sales will usually begin low and rise over time, and so too will profits.

Thus, two factors work against the manager—lower income in early years and the natural tendency of ROI to rise as the book value of the investment falls because of depreciation charges. What can be done to encourage the manager to pursue worthwhile investments?

One way to avoid the first-year drop in ROI and thereby encourage managers to accept desirable investments is to leave the new investment out of the base for calculating ROI until the project is on-stream and running well. Of course, many major projects will take a relatively long time before they are running well. **Quaker Oats** allows units extra time to reach positive EVAs if they start out with especially large investments.

Another approach is to amortize the startup costs over several years instead of expensing them all in the first year of an investment's life. A third possibility, seldom observed in practice, is to base depreciation charges on budgeted income to be earned over several years; this results in lower depreciation in early years and higher charges in later years.

Essentially, the problem just described is a conflict between the long and the short terms. As stated several times in this book, many actions that can help meet short-term goals are harmful in the long run. Such actions could reduce profits, ROI, and RI in the long term, but by then the manager might have been promoted to another job. Conversely, a manager who takes actions that benefit the division and company in the long run, while hurting short-term performance, could be fired, not promoted, or otherwise penalized. The manager who takes over could well reap the benefits of the predecessor's good decisions. Something we said in Chapter 10 bears repeating here: evaluating managerial performance with a single quantitative measure is unwise. Managers should use other quantitative measures, as well as qualitative measures, to evaluate their subordinates. **AT&T** spends a good deal of money collecting and analyzing data from which it derives measures of customer satisfaction. The company uses this measure, as well as measures of employee satisfaction, in addition to EVA.

## PROBLEMS IN MEASUREMENT

Whether using ROI or RI as the evaluation criterion, a company must determine what revenues, costs, and investments are to be included in the calculations. The determinations should be made along the lines of responsibility, with controllability as the principal criterion for including costs and investments. A division manager who is held responsible for earning returns (income) on investment should control the elements of both income and investment.

### INCOME

To compute the income for which division managers are responsible, we must identify variable costs and direct fixed costs. As discussed in Chapter 10, some companies also allocate common indirect fixed costs for several reasons. If common fixed costs are allocated to divisions, they should be separated from direct fixed costs and clearly labeled as allocated. Companies using RI or EVA should exclude interest on corporate debt from the income calculation because cost of capital includes interest on debt. The accompanying Insight describes how several companies compute income by business unit for their annual reports.

### INVESTMENT

Opinions differ as to what to include in and how to measure divisional investment. Everyone includes assets that are used exclusively by a particular division.

 **SIGHT**

### Examples of Segment Reporting

Companies' annual reports do not necessarily list all investment centers. Companies refer to "segments" that might include several investment centers, so their annual reports might not reflect their internal reporting.

**Procter & Gamble** reports income after taxes when reporting for geographic segments, but uses revenues when reporting for product-line segments. The company reports "Identifiable Assets" for each segment with no reduction for liabilities. P&G does not allocate all corporate costs and investment to its segments. **Georgia-Pacific**, a worldwide maker of building products, pulp, and paper, excludes interest, income taxes, and unallocated corporate expenses from its calculations of segment income. The company also reports identifiable assets as those used by each segment in its operations. **Wal-Mart** allocates all corporate costs except interest and income taxes to its major segments. None of the real estate located in the United States is included in the identifiable assets. **American Standard** discloses revenues, earnings, and identifiable assets by geographic segment, as well as for product lines.

*Sources: Annual reports.*

Most assets can be readily identified with specific divisions. For financial reporting purposes, companies presenting segmented information often refer to *identifiable assets*. For example, virtually all plant and equipment (or fixed assets) falls under the control of specific divisions. Inventory and receivables, which are also investments, are under divisional control if the divisional manager controls production and credit terms. Divisional managers control some cash, but in many cases central headquarters receives payments directly from customers and pays bills submitted by the divisions. Centralizing the cash management function usually reduces costs for the company as a whole. Some assets are controlled only at the highest level of management. Central headquarters controls the headquarters building and equipment, cash and marketable securities (often called cash equivalents), long-term investments, and such intangible assets as goodwill and organization costs.

Suppose we have analyzed the revenues, costs, and assets of Bendan, Inc., and have identified these by divisions as shown in Exhibit 11-1. The company has three operating divisions, A, B, and C, and a central corporate office. The minimum required ROI is 10 percent.

From the data in Exhibit 11-1 we can compute ROI and RI for each division and for the company as a whole, as in Exhibit 11-2. The latter computation should be based on an investment defined as the total assets of the company. Note that no performance measurement is given for unallocated assets.

When a company does not allocate all costs and all investment to divisions, the company cannot earn the target ROI unless the divisions earn *more than* the target ROI. Although the company's ROI is 11.1 percent, only one division earns so low a rate. Note also that the combined RI of the divisions is partly consumed by

## Exhibit 11-1   Bendan, Inc. (in millions of dollars)

| | Division A | Division B | Division C | Unallocated | Total |
|---|---|---|---|---|---|
| **Investment** | | | | | |
| Cash | $ 20 | $ 30 | $ 60 | $ 30 | $ 140 |
| Accounts receivable, net | 60 | 80 | 90 | | 230 |
| Inventory | 100 | 180 | 240 | | 520 |
| Prepaid expenses | 10 | 10 | 20 | 20 | 60 |
| Plant and equipment— net of depreciation | 200 | 320 | 440 | 60 | 1,020 |
| Investments | 10 | — | — | 100 | 110 |
| Total assets | $400 | $620 | $850 | $210 | $2,080 |
| **Income** | | | | | |
| Sales | $100 | $400 | $700 | | $1,200 |
| Variable costs | 30 | 220 | 400 | | 650 |
| Contribution margin | $ 70 | $180 | $300 | | $ 550 |
| Direct fixed costs | 30 | 90 | 140 | | 260 |
| Divisional profit | $ 40 | $ 90 | $160 | | $ 290 |
| Common fixed costs | | | | | 60 |
| Income | | | | | $ 230 |

unallocated costs and assets, so that, although the divisions earn residual income of $103 million ($0 + $28 + $75), the company as a whole earns only $22 million in excess of a 10 percent return on total assets. Therefore, companies that do not allocate all costs and investment to divisions must set the target ROI for divisions higher than cost of capital to the *company as a whole*. If the company allocates all

## Exhibit 11-2   Bendan, Inc. (in millions of dollars)

| | A | B | C | Company as a Whole |
|---|---|---|---|---|
| **Computation of ROI:** | | | | |
| Profit of segment | $ 40 | $ 90 | $ 160 | $ 230 |
| Investment in segment | 400 | 620 | 850 | 2,080 |
| ROI (profit/investment) | 10% | 14.5% | 18.8% | 11.1% |
| **Computation of RI:** | | | | |
| Profit of segment | $ 40 | $ 90 | $ 160 | $ 230 |
| Required return (investment × minimum return of 10%) | 40 | 62 | 85 | 208 |
| RI (profit – required return) | $ 0 | $ 28 | $ 75 | $ 22 |

costs and investments to divisions, the target ROI for the divisions can be the cost of capital to the company.

Managers favoring complete allocation argue that divisional managers should be made aware of the substantial costs and investment involved in running the company as a whole, which each of the divisions must work to offset. This argument was explored in Chapter 10. Another, and perhaps more persuasive, justification for complete allocation is that corporate managers are interested in whether a division is earning returns comparable to those of independent companies in the same industry. If the division is to be treated more or less as an independent, autonomous entity, corporate managers argue that it should bear the costs and assets that a competing independent company must. An independent company will incur many costs, and maintain many assets, that a division often does not. For example, an independent company performs research and development, while a division often relies on a centralized R&D function. Similarly, an independent company must maintain more cash than a division that relies on a centralized cash management function. To make reasonable comparisons between the division and an outside company, then, corporate management might allocate central costs and assets to divisions.

Companies that allocate corporate costs to divisions do so in many ways. In some companies, central headquarters charges each division a management fee for services provided. For instance, divisions need financing, just as if they were separate companies; so the charge reflects that service. The fee might be a percentage of revenue, total investment in the division, or some other base. The desire to avoid having unallocated costs and investment has motivated top managers to use activity-based costing to study more closely the divisional activities that drive some of those costs and investments.

Efforts to make division managers realize that they must consider the performance of the entire company might be worthwhile, but allocating central costs and assets to divisions must be understood for what it is—allocation. Whatever the allocation methods used, managers at both the divisional and corporate levels must be aware that allocations in no way change the nature of the costs or assets as indirect to the divisions and not controllable by the divisional managers.

## LIABILITIES

Assigning liabilities to divisions increases their ROIs and RIs because it decreases investment. Some current liabilities (payables, accrued expenses) are readily associated with particular divisions. But assigning all liabilities to divisions is seldom possible without arbitrary allocations. As a rule, divisions cannot issue long-term debt, and their managers are not responsible for it. Long-term debt results from financing decisions made at the highest level of management on the basis of the organization's overall needs and goals. Companies do not usually allocate long-term liabilities to divisions. For performance measurement purposes, many companies include only those liabilities that are definitely (not arbitrarily) related to divisions, and define divisional investment as controlled assets minus divisional liabilities.

Exhibit 11-3 uses assumed values for liabilities to illustrate the computations of ROI and RI when a company uses liabilities in calculating investment.

As expected, both RI and ROI are higher for all divisions and for the company as a whole when liabilities are included in the computations.

## Exhibit 11-3    Bendan, Inc. (in millions of dollars)

|  | A | B | C | Company as a Whole |
|---|---|---|---|---|
| **Computation of ROI:** |  |  |  |  |
| Profit of the segment | $ 40 | $ 90 | $ 160 | $ 230 |
| Total assets | $400 | $ 620 | $ 850 | $2,080 |
| Divisional liabilities (assumed) | 60 | 170 | 310 | 540 |
| Divisional investment | $340 | $ 450 | $ 540 | $1,540 |
| Unallocated liabilities (assumed) |  |  |  | 730 |
| Total investment | $340 | $ 450 | $ 540 | $ 810 |
| ROI | 11.8% | 20.0% | 29.6% | 28.4% |
| **Computation of RI:** |  |  |  |  |
| Profit of the segment | $ 40 | $ 90 | $ 160 | $ 230 |
| Required return (investment × minimum return of 10%) | 34 | 45 | 54 | 81 |
| RI | $ 6 | $ 45 | $ 106 | $ 149 |

From a behavioral standpoint, the question of whether to include liabilities is undecided. In favor of their inclusion is that most current liabilities are related to the operating level of the division and provide financing to it and to the company. On the negative side, divisional managers could be encouraged to allow liabilities to rise too high in order to reduce investment and increase ROI. If divisional managers delay payments to suppliers, the credit rating of the company as a whole might suffer. A reasonable compromise might be a corporate policy that allows managers to carry, say, trade payables up to the length of time specified by suppliers. Then, if a division had 40 days' purchases in accounts payable and suppliers offered 30-day credit, the division could not deduct the extra 10 days' worth of liabilities to determine divisional investment. Under this policy, the manager has no incentive to allow payables to extend beyond the suppliers' credit terms. (Note that divisional managers have no opportunity for delaying payments if cash disbursements are handled at the central headquarters.)

## FIXED ASSETS

For all computations to this point, you have been given the amount of the investment in assets. In Exhibit 11-1, for example, the investments in cash, inventory, and fixed assets were given, but there was no mention of how these amounts were determined. There are many views about what values to use for fixed assets. Some of the valuation bases used are original (gross) cost, original cost less accumulated depreciation (often called net cost, or net book value), and current replacement cost. The basis used can have a significant effect on ROI and RI, and each basis has advantages and disadvantages.

The most popular basis by far is net book value. Its principal advantages are that it conforms to financial accounting practice and that it recognizes the decline in productivity that usually accompanies increasing age. Many believe it to be the most reasonable basis, given that the computation of divisional income includes a deduction for depreciation expense. The major disadvantage of net book value is that it gives, as shown earlier, rising ROI and RI over time. Using gross (original) cost for valuing fixed assets overcomes the objection about rising ROI and RI. **DuPont** believes that its managers should maintain facilities in excellent condition throughout the facilities' lives. The company also considers it inappropriate to hold operating managers responsible for earning a return on only net book values. Finally, the company pointed out that using net book values would relate returns to an ever-decreasing investment.

Yet virtually all assets lose productivity as they age, and continued use of gross cost ignores this decline. Moreover, the company's investment in a fixed asset declines over time, as the company recovers its investment through the cash flows that the asset produces.

Both gross and net book values suffer from the defect that they reflect costs the company has already incurred, perhaps many years ago. Managers who have older assets generally have lower investment bases (either gross or net) than managers using similar assets that are newer and, in all likelihood, costlier. For this reason, many accountants and managers advocate valuing investments at replacement cost.

There are at least three ways to define replacement cost.

1. The current cost of new assets just like those now in use.
2. The current cost of acquiring assets of the same age and condition as those being used.
3. The current cost of obtaining assets with similar productive capacity or service.

The third interpretation considers how the company would choose to accomplish a particular task today. For example, suppose a company has a fleet of forklift trucks to move materials within its factory, but would install a conveyor system if it were starting over today. Under the third interpretation, the replacement cost of the fleet is the cost of the conveyor system. Because managers should continuously evaluate the alternatives available for accomplishing tasks, we prefer the third interpretation (equivalent productive capacity) for evaluating divisional performance. However, much disagreement on this point exists.

Whatever definition of replacement cost is adopted, its use eliminates the problems of different depreciation methods and changes in prices of fixed assets. Thus, managers are not penalized or rewarded simply because of the depreciation methods used or the ages of their assets. The normal accounting system does not automatically provide information about current replacement costs, and the practical difficulties and costs of determining replacement costs continue to discourage their use. Despite the disadvantages, original cost less accumulated depreciation remains the most popular approach for valuing fixed assets.

## THE SUBJECT OF EVALUATION—DIVISION OR MANAGER

As we stated in Chapter 10, it is important to distinguish between evaluating a division and evaluating its manager. Evaluations of divisions are strategic. Should the company invest more in a particular division? Should it "milk" a division and use its cash flow to finance investments in other divisions? Should it allow the division to wither away, or should it be sold now? ROI and RI give clues to where the company might be wise to increase, maintain, or reduce investment; other things being equal, higher ROI and RI are desirable. However, for evaluating managers of divisions, both ROI and RI have drawbacks, depending on how the results for a division are interpreted. The critical issue is the standard used for comparison. With what should we compare a division's results? Several bases for comparison are available, including comparisons among divisions within the company, with historical results in the same division, with industry averages, and with budgets.

## INTERNAL RANKING

Ranking divisions within the company in terms of ROI and RI provides insight into the relative contributions of the divisions. But such a ranking should not be used to rank the managers of the respective divisions, because different kinds of divisions *should* have different ROIs. The expected ROI for a division should be based upon the strategic goals of the division. For example, ROI is generally higher for businesses (divisions or companies) operating in consumer markets than for those selling mostly to other industrial companies. Both ROI and RI should be higher for divisions taking on high risks. (For example, a division in plant genetics, a very risky field, should have a higher ROI than one making clothing.) The performance of a particular division manager must not be obscured by intracompany comparisons that ignore the nature of the division. A mediocre manager might be able to earn a respectable ROI in a division operating in a growing industry. On the other hand, an excellent manager might be doing a great job to maintain an ROI of 5 percent in a division operating in a declining industry. The responsibility of top managers is to decide which divisions the company should continue to operate and which it should fold or seek to sell. The critical concern here is how does the division fit into the overall strategic plan of the business.

## HISTORICAL COMPARISONS

Comparing current results with historical results in the same division overcomes differences in results stemming from divisions being in different industries. If there is a change in managers, the relative performance of two managers can also be compared. Historical comparisons also indicate relative improvement or decay. However, historical comparisons should be interpreted carefully. Historical experience can be good or bad and relative improvement might not be enough. A division now earning an 8 percent ROI is not doing well even if it has doubled ROI in the past few years. Conditions in the industry might change. If industry conditions improve, then a division should improve at more than its historical rate.

## INDUSTRY AVERAGES

Comparing divisional results with industry averages can be useful because differences among divisions resulting from differences in industry do not influence the comparison. A division (and its manager) can be seen as better or worse than the companies with which it competes. Such comparisons present their own problems, however, because, as noted earlier, a division should be expected to earn a higher ROI than an entire company operating in the same industry. A division benefits from being part of a larger organization. As the trend to diversification continues, it becomes increasingly difficult to find companies to which the performance of a single division can be compared.

## BUDGETS

Budgets developed with participation by divisional managers are valuable tools for assessing the performance of division managers. When managers participate and commit themselves to meeting budgeted goals, comparisons of actual and budgeted results are excellent comparisons for evaluation purposes. Exhibit 11-4 shows budgeted and actual statements of income and financial position for a division. Allocated costs are shown separately. The only assets shown are those controlled by the division's manager. The exhibit also shows why budgeted and actual ROI were not the same. The division earned more profit than budgeted, but its receivables and inventories climbed much higher than budgeted, resulting in a reduced ROI. This type of report gives more information than simple comparisons of ROI, RI, or both.

## TRANSFER PRICES

A great deal of intracompany buying and selling occurs in many companies, which necessitates setting transfer prices. A segment of **Anheuser-Busch** is the

---

### Exhibit 11-4   Divisional Performance Report (in millions of dollars)

|  | Budget | Actual | Variance |
|---|---|---|---|
| Sales | $573.0 | $591.0 | $18.0 |
| Variable costs (perhaps detailed) | 246.0 | 251.2 | 5.2 |
| Contribution margin | $327.0 | $339.8 | $12.8 |
| Direct fixed costs | 140.0 | 141.4 | 1.4 |
| Divisional profit | $187.0 | $198.4 | $11.4 |
| Allocated costs | 12.0 | 15.0 | 3.0 |
| Profit | $175.0 | $183.4 | $ 8.4 |
| Assets employed: |  |  |  |
| Cash | $ 15.5 | $ 17.0 | $ 1.5 |
| Receivables | 110.0 | 141.0 | 31.0 |
| Inventory | 90.0 | 122.5 | 32.5 |
| Fixed assets, net | 450.0 | 453.4 | 3.4 |
| Total assets employed | $665.5 | $733.9 | $68.4 |
| ROI | 26.3% | 25.0% | 12.3% |

third largest U.S. maker of aluminum cans, which it sells both internally and externally. **Georgia-Pacific** has a timberlands division that sells 80 percent of its output internally to the manufacturing divisions.

## PRICING POLICIES

Transfer prices are important because they are revenues to the selling division and costs to the buying division and therefore affect divisional performance. We know from Chapter 10 that changes in transfer prices do not, in themselves, affect total company profit. Total profit is affected only if individual managers change their operations because of a change in transfer prices. But because of their *potential* for encouraging actions that might not be in the interest of the total company, transfer prices are important factors in divisional performance measurement. The following examples explore some implications of several transfer-pricing policies.

1.  *Actual cost with or without a markup for the selling division.* We know from Chapter 10 that basing transfer prices on actual costs is unwise. The selling manager has no incentive to keep costs down. Worse, a price that is actual costs plus a percentage markup gives the selling manager more profit the higher costs go. The buying manager would naturally object that costs (and hence reported performance) are adversely affected.

2.  *Budgeted cost, with or without a markup.* This method does not reward the selling manager if costs go up and actually encourages the selling manager to keep costs down. If there is a markup, the selling division can earn a profit. The buying manager appreciates not having cost inefficiencies passed on from the selling division but prefers no markup at all. Thus, discussions center on budgeted cost and markup percentages.

3.  *Market-based prices.* This method is generally considered the best. It puts both the buying and selling managers on an independent basis, provided that they are free to buy or sell on the outside as well as within the company. One difficulty in using this policy is that outside market prices might not exist, or the prices that are available might not be representative. For example, available market prices might reflect relatively small transactions, whereas the divisions deal in very large quantities. Under such circumstances, buying managers might contend that they should pay less because of the quantities bought. The accompanying Insight discusses **Georgia-Pacific's** use of market prices for transfer prices.

    In many cases, the transfer price is less than the market price to reflect cost savings from dealing internally. For instance, suppose a division pays a 15 percent commission on outside sales and no commission on inside sales. The transfer price should be 85 percent of the market price to reflect that saving. Selling divisions will often accept less than market price when they are operating below capacity, just as Chapter 5 showed a company might accept a less-than-normal price on a special order.

4.  *Incremental cost.* Such prices are theoretically best *from the company's viewpoint when the selling division is operating below capacity.* The manager of the selling division will object to this price because it yields no profit to that division. Incremental cost can be as low as the variable cost of the goods or services, but might also include fixed costs that increase as a result of the transfer.

**SIGHT**

### Timber Pricing at Georgia Pacific

**Georgia-Pacific Corporation** is one of the world's leading manufacturers and distributors of building products, pulp, and paper. In December 1997 Georgia-Pacific separated its timber business into a new operating group called The Timber Company.

As an integrated forest products company, Georgia-Pacific faces the competing goals of maximizing the value of every tree and providing the lowest cost timber to the Corporation's plants and mills. Through a negotiated contract, The Timber Company is committed to supply 83 percent of its output to the manufacturing and distribution facilities in 1998, and up to 80 percent in the subsequent two years. The remaining output is available to the market through expansion of its customer base.

Timber pricing to the internal facilities will be based on an average of The Timber Company's outside sales and the facilties' own purchases from other suppliers. The creation of The Timber Company allows more accurate use of outside pricing data, imposing greater market discipline on the internal facilities.

*Source: 1997 Georgia-Pacific Corporation annual report.*

5. *Negotiated prices.* This method allows managers to bargain with each other and alleviates some problems that arise with other methods. A manager who is dissatisfied with the offered price can buy or sell in the outside market, if it exists. Some see as a disadvantage that managers with better negotiating skills will tend to prevail. Others contend that negotiating skills are part of effective management.

Despite our suggestion that market-based transfer prices are generally best, we hasten to point out that the autonomous division manager who is setting a transfer price must use judgment and *understand the information available.* Like the managers making decisions discussed in earlier chapters, division managers must understand the concepts of contribution margin and incremental cost, and the implications of those concepts in light of the available alternatives. For example, Chapter 5 presented the analysis underlying a decision whether to accept a special order at less than the normal selling price. Critical to that analysis was whether the company had an alternative use for the facilities and whether the additional contribution margin covered incremental fixed costs. The same principles apply when a division manager has to propose a selling price for an order from another division. When the selling division has excess capacity, its results (and the manager's reported performance) will be improved if the price is greater than variable costs and incremental fixed costs. When the division's capacity can be fully used without taking the order, the selling manager should demand the market price less any costs saved by dealing internally, such as commissions.

CHAPTER 5

In summary, if treated as heads of autonomous units, division managers should be free to offer transfer prices that reflect the cost structures of their divisions and the available alternatives. When the division is operating at full capacity, with sales to customers outside the company, a market-based transfer price is nearly always best. When the selling division is operating below capacity, a transfer price that falls between incremental cost and market price is usually best. Hence, division managers must understand the cost structures of their divisions and use that knowledge in setting transfer prices. If they have the freedom to negotiate prices, the resulting actions are likely to be in the company's best interests. To see why this is true, let us consider an example.

## ILLUSTRATIONS

Division A buys 6,000 units of a component for its major product from an outside supplier for $13 per unit. The component is very much like a product made by Division B, another division of the same company, and the manager of A has asked B to supply the item at $13. Division B now sells its output to outside customers at $15. The budgeted income statement for the coming year for Division B is as follows:

| Budgeted Income Statement, Division B | |
| --- | ---: |
| Sales, 10,000 × $15 | $150,000 |
| Variable costs, 10,000 × $7 | 70,000 |
| Contribution margin | $ 80,000 |
| Fixed costs | 30,000 |
| Income | $ 50,000 |

Let us assume, for simplicity, that Division B could make the component needed by A with no change in fixed costs and with the same variable cost per unit that it has now. How should the manager of B respond to the requested transfer price? What price serves the best interests of the divisions and of the company?

Suppose that Division B has capacity of 11,000 units, and cannot increase its outside sales above 10,000 units. If it accepts Division A's business, it loses 5,000 units of outside sales. (Capacity of 11,000 less 6,000 to Division A leaves 5,000 units available for sales to outsiders, a reduction of 5,000 from present sales of 10,000 units.) Following is a budgeted income statement for the division if a transfer takes place at $13, the price that A now pays to an outside supplier.

| Budgeted Income Statement, Division B (Component Sold Internally for $13) | |
| --- | ---: |
| Sales to outsiders, 5,000 × $15 | $ 75,000 |
| Sales to A, 6,000 × $13 | 78,000 |
| Total sales | $153,000 |
| Variable costs, 11,000 × $7 | 77,000 |
| Contribution margin | $ 76,000 |
| Fixed costs | 30,000 |
| Income | $ 46,000 |

Because Division A is already paying $13 to an outside supplier, purchasing the component internally for that price will not change Division A's income and its manager is indifferent to the source of supply. The manager of Division B will not accept the $13 price, because profit will decline by $4,000 (from $50,000 to $46,000). Is the manager's decision not to make the sale also in the best interest of the company as a whole?

From the standpoint of the company, the decision is a make-or-buy decision such as you studied in Chapter 5. That is, if Division B makes the component and sells it to Division A, the component is made by the company; alternatively, the component could be bought from an outside supplier. We can, therefore, look at the decision from the point of view of the company as we did in Chapter 5.

| | |
|---|---|
| Lost contribution margin from outside sales by Division B [5,000 × ($15 − $7)] | $40,000 |
| Savings of variable costs paid to outside supplier [6,000 × ($13 − $7)] | 36,000 |
| Loss to company | $ (4,000) |

The change in the company's income (a $4,000 decline) equals the combined changes in the incomes of its divisions (no change for A, a $4,000 decline for B).

Now suppose that Division B can produce 20,000 (rather than 11,000) units, and it can still sell only 10,000 units to outsiders. If fixed costs will not be affected by producing additional units for sale to Division A, Division B's results will improve by selling to A at any price greater than B's variable cost of $7 per unit. For example, a budgeted income statement for Division B if the transfer takes place at as little as $8 per unit follows.

| Budgeted Income Statement, Division B (Component Sold Internally for $8) | |
|---|---|
| Sales to outsiders, 10,000 × $15 | $150,000 |
| Sales to A, 6,000 × $8 | 48,000 |
| Total sales | $198,000 |
| Variable costs, 16,000 × $7 | 112,000 |
| Contribution margin | $ 86,000 |
| Fixed costs | 30,000 |
| Income | $ 56,000 |

The manager of Division A will be happy to accept an $8 price, for that division's income will increase by $30,000 [6,000 units × ($13 − $8)]. Division B's manager should accept the $8 price because that division's income will improve by $6,000, the $1 contribution margin ($8 − $7) on the 6,000 additional units. If you understood the previous example, you should see that the company's top managers also want the transfer to take place. The company's total income will increase by $36,000, the combined changes in the incomes of its divisions ($30,000 + $6,000). Analyzing the situation as a make-or-buy decision, the company saves $36,000 in variable costs [6,000 × ($13 − $7)] by making the unit rather than buying it outside.

It would be unfortunate if the manager of Division B didn't understand the division's cost structure and considered the $8 price to be unacceptable. For example, suppose the manager had reviewed the original budgeted income statement and concluded that the cost was $10 per unit (variable costs of $70,000 plus fixed costs of $30,000, divided by the 10,000 units of planned production). The decision not to sell at $8 would have been, as indicated earlier, detrimental to Division A, to the company, and to Division B.

As long as Division B has excess capacity, any price less than the market price of $13 and greater than B's variable costs of $7 is advantageous to both divisions and to the company as a whole. Division A acquires the component at a lower price than it would have to pay to an outside supplier. Division B gains some contribution margin. And the company benefits from having a lower total cost of the product (the $7 variable cost from Division B rather than the $13 outside price). Indeed, even a transfer price of $7 should be acceptable. Division B loses nothing and could gain by being able to retain good workers who might otherwise have left the area for other jobs, or by keeping good relations with suppliers who might be concerned about the low levels of B's orders for materials.

So long as the company gains from an internal exchange, the managers of the divisions should be able to agree on a price because they can both benefit from the exchange. The total gain to the company is also the total gain to the two divisions; the transfer price simply allocates the gain between the two divisions.

In summary, the major issue from the standpoint of the company as a whole is not the choice of a transfer price but whether the transfer should take place at all.

- The company faces a make-or-buy decision.
- For the buying division, the question is simply which supplier (sister division or outside company) offers the lower price (assuming equal quality, delivery schedules, etc.).

- The selling division faces a special-order decision, as in Chapter 5; the concern is whether the contribution margin from selling inside offsets the loss, if any, of contribution margin from lost outside sales.

If the transfer is profitable from the standpoint of the company as a whole, the best transfer-pricing system is one that prompts the managers to make a decision in the best interests of the company as a whole. Thus, setting transfer prices requires judgment and a full understanding of the circumstances and of the accounting information available.

## MULTINATIONAL COMPANIES—SPECIAL PROBLEMS

Companies that operate in several countries are called *multinationals*. Some multinationals operate divisions in foreign countries, others set up separate, legal corporations. Whether a division or a subsidiary corporation, a segment that operates in a particular country does business in the currency of that country, pays taxes in that currency, and reports its financial results in that currency. Many U.S. companies are multinationals, as are many foreign companies such as **British Petroleum**, **Toyota**, and **Unilever**. Multinationals face special problems related both to evaluating performance and to transfer pricing.

Multinational companies have more complicated reporting needs than domestic companies. Besides the currency translation problems discussed in earlier chapters, significant cultural and language barriers and little or no on-site supervision of operations by home-office managers present serious problems in evaluating performance. These factors contribute to a heavy reporting load. **Eastman Kodak** states that its managers receive 200 financial reports containing a total of 1,300 documents per year. Continuing advances in communications technology such as satellites and the Internet make reporting easier, but do not reduce its volume.

With respect to evaluation, multinationals must cope with changes in exchange rates, which are the relationships of foreign currencies to U.S. dollars. One problem for performance evaluation is that the local manager in the foreign country does business in the foreign currency, but the multinational cares about the results in its home currency (dollars for U.S. multinationals). The trouble is that the local manager and the division can look good or bad in U.S. dollars simply because of changes in exchange rates, over which the local manager has no control.

Consider the following division's monthly income statement in Xs, the currency of country X.

|                          | Division One |
|--------------------------|-------------:|
| Sales                    | X3,000       |
| Expenses                 | 2,000        |
| Income in local currency | X1,000       |

If an X was worth $10 during the month, the division would also show $10,000 income for the month. Suppose that next month the division does exactly the same business and has the same income statement, but that the value of an X drops to $8. The division then shows $8,000 income, a 20 percent drop from last month even though it did the same business. Evaluating the manager's (or the division's) performance on the basis of reports using the currency of the home country penalizes the division and the manager for a decline in the exchange rate (and gives undue credit when the rate rises). Of course, one factor that influences exchange rates is the relative inflation in the two countries and managers should consider inflation when making decisions. So the results do have some validity. A drop in the exchange rate for Xs from $10 to $8 suggests that X experienced, or anticipates, higher inflation than does the United States. If Division One could only maintain its position (sales of X3,000, profit of X1,000) during inflation, it is actually falling behind. The question of translating foreign currency also vexes financial accounting.

Evaluating the performance of foreign units (and their managers) can also be complicated by legal, cultural, and philosophical differences that direct attention to special areas or restrict a local manager's actions. For example, some Latin American countries limit staffing by foreigners, and Japanese companies are not inclined to employ foreign nationals in management positions. Some European countries virtually outlaw layoffs.

Transfer-pricing problems for multinationals are equally troublesome. In a recent study, **Ernst & Young**, a major international accounting and consulting firm, showed transfer-pricing issues to be the leading concern of multinationals. Because different countries have different income tax rates, multinationals want to show higher profits in low-tax countries and lower profits in high-tax countries. Doing so is sometimes termed *income shifting* and transfer prices are an ideal vehicle. For example, suppose that Division A buys a product from Division B. The divisions are in different countries, but both use the same currency, denoted as T. Data are as follows:

| | |
|---|---|
| Selling price of Division A's product | T100 |
| Variable cost, excluding transfer price | T20 |
| Tax rate in Division A's country | 20% |
| Variable cost of Division B's product | T30 |
| Tax rate in Division B's country | 60% |

The following income statements show the effects, including income taxes, of transferring 1,000 units of Division B's product at T30 and at T60.

| | Division A | Division B |
|---|---|---|
| Sales (1,000 × T100) | T100,000 | |
| (1,000 × T30) | | T30,000 |
| Variable cost [1,000 × (T20 + T30)] | 50,000 | |
| (1,000 × T30) | | 30,000 |
| Contribution margin | T 50,000 | T    0 |
| Income tax at 20% and 60% | T 10,000 | T    0 |

| | Division A | Division B |
|---|---|---|
| Sales (1,000 × T100) | T100,000 | |
| (1,000 × T60) | | T60,000 |
| Variable cost [1,000 × (T20 + T60)] | 80,000 | |
| (1,000 × T30) | | 30,000 |
| Contribution margin | T 20,000 | T30,000 |
| Income tax at 20% and 60% | T  4,000 | T18,000 |

Total income taxes are only T10,000 at the lower price, T22,000 at the higher price. (The corporation minimizes its total taxes if Division B gives the product to Division A, but the authorities in Division B's country would certainly not permit that.) If the company forces Division B to sell at a low price, it saves considerable taxes, but penalizes the performance of Division B and its manager and enhances the reported performance of Division A and its manager. Dictating transfer prices also reduces the sense of independence and autonomy that managers value.

The income-shifting potential of transfer prices is not limited to sales of product. As you know from Chapter 10, companies use transfer prices for services, and multinationals often charge foreign (and domestic) units a management fee or allocate some corporate costs to those units. A multinational could therefore shift income from a foreign country to the home country through such charges. Obviously, the temptation is to charge higher fees to units in high-tax countries and lower fees to those in low-tax countries. Here again, the performance of local managers is affected by a corporate decision.

Similar problems arise with import duties, or tariffs, which are typically based on values reported for incoming goods. If one division is transferring goods to another division located in a high-tariff country, a low transfer price reduces the tariff.

Besides the problems associated with portraying performance, some of the practices described are, if arbitrarily imposed, unethical and in some countries illegal. Various government authorities such as those responsible for collecting income taxes in the various countries will try to ensure that artificially high or low transfer prices are disallowed and that corporate charges actually reflect the ser-

CHAPTER
10

vices provided at the corporate level. Transfer prices and corporate fees are also of interest to the authorities in countries having significant currency restrictions. For example, for many years Brazil had severe restrictions on foreign companies taking out of the country profits made by local operating units (called *repatriation of profits*). Its extreme currency restriction policy, which permitted currency to leave the country only in payment for goods, might have been influenced by the ethically debatable efforts of some multinationals to repatriate profits through management fees or allocations of corporate costs.

Transfer pricing entered the public arena when politicians claimed that foreign-based multinationals were avoiding over $11 billion in annual taxes by manipulating transfer prices. Early in 1993 the IRS issued regulations that required companies to use pricing methods that accurately reflected business conditions, such as assets employed, functions performed, and risks taken by the subsidiaries or divisions. These regulations allowed more flexibility than older proposals that required that profits on intracompany business approximate profits on transactions with outsiders. Most authorities accept transfer prices that clearly represent arm's-length transactions, those that would be the same if the buyer and seller were unrelated companies.

## SUMMARY

Evaluating investment centers requires determining which revenues, costs, and investments the manager can control. Commonly used performance measures are return on investment (ROI) and residual income (RI), along with its variant, economic value added (EVA). ROI is the most popular measure, but RI is advantageous from a behavioral point of view. Use of either criterion requires answering difficult questions about which items to include in divisional income and investment and opinions differ about how some items should be measured.

Intracompany sales and purchases require transfer prices. Such prices can encourage managers to take actions that harm the company as a whole. However, managers who are free to negotiate transfer prices are likely to make decisions that benefit both the divisions and the company. Companies with divisions in countries using a different currency have special problems in evaluating the performance of those divisions. Such companies also have problems in setting transfer prices that take into consideration the different tax structures and currency restrictions of the countries in which their divisions operate.

## KEY TERMS

business units *(468)*
centralization *(468)*
decentralization *(468)*
divisional income *(471)*
divisional investment *(471)*
DuPont formula *(472)*
economic value added (EVA) *(474)*

investment turnover *(472)*
minimum required (desired, target) rate of return *(473)*
residual income (RI) *(473)*
return on investment (ROI) *(471)*
return on sales (ROS) *(472)*

## KEY FORMULAS

Return on investment (ROI) $= \dfrac{\text{divisional income}}{\text{divisional investment}}$

Return on investment (ROI) $= \dfrac{\text{income}}{\text{sales}} \times \dfrac{\text{sales}}{\text{investment}}$

Return on sales (ROS) $= \dfrac{\text{income}}{\text{sales}}$

Investment turnover $= \dfrac{\text{sales}}{\text{investment}}$

Residual income (RI) $= \text{income} - (\text{investment} \times \text{target ROI})$

## REVIEW PROBLEM

The manager of the Scooter Division of United Products Company has given you the following information related to budgeted operations for the coming year.

| | |
|---|---:|
| Sales (100,000 units at $5) | $500,000 |
| Variable costs at $2 per unit | 200,000 |
| Contribution margin at $3 per unit | 300,000 |
| Fixed costs | 120,000 |
| Divisional profit | $180,000 |
| Divisional investment | $800,000 |

The minimum required ROI is 20%.

### Required

Consider each part independently.

1. Determine the division's expected ROI using the DuPont formula.
2. Determine the division's expected RI.
3. The manager has the opportunity to sell an additional 10,000 units at $4.50. Variable cost per unit would be the same as budgeted, but fixed costs would increase by $10,000. Additional investment of $50,000 would also be required. If the manager accepts the special order, by how much and in what direction will RI change?
4. Scooter's budgeted volume includes 20,000 units that Scooter expects to sell to the Olympia Division of United Products. However, the manager of Olympia Division has received an offer from an outside company to supply the 20,000 units at $4.20. If Scooter Division does not meet the $4.20 price, Olympia will buy from the outside company. Scooter could save $25,000 in fixed costs if it dropped its volume from 100,000 to 80,000 units.
   (a) Determine Scooter's profit assuming that it meets the $4.20 price.
   (b) Determine Scooter's profit if it fails to meet the price and loses the sales.
   (c) Determine the effect on the company's total profit if Scooter meets the $4.20 price.
   (d) Determine the effect on the company's total profit if Scooter does not meet the price.

**ANSWER TO REVIEW PROBLEM**

1. 22.5%

$$\frac{income}{sales} \times \frac{sales}{investment} = \frac{\$180,000}{\$500,000} \times \frac{\$500,000}{\$800,000}$$

$$= 0.36 \times 0.625 = 0.225 = 22.5\%$$

2. $20,000

| | |
|---|---:|
| Profit budgeted | $180,000 |
| Minimum required return ($800,000 × 20%) | 160,000 |
| Residual income budgeted | $ 20,000 |

3. RI would increase by $5,000. This can be determined either by considering the changes in the variables or by preparing new data for total operations. Considering only the changes:

| | |
|---|---:|
| Increase in sales (10,000 × $4.50) | $45,000 |
| Increase in variable costs (10,000 × $2) | 20,000 |
| Increase in contribution margin | $25,000 |
| Increase in fixed costs | 10,000 |
| Increase in profit | $15,000 |
| Increase in minimum required return ($50,000 × 20%) | 10,000 |
| Increase in RI | $ 5,000 |

A new income statement and calculation of new total RI shows the following.

| | |
|---|---:|
| Sales ($500,000 + $45,000) | $545,000 |
| Variable costs (110,000 × $2) | 220,000 |
| Contribution margin | $325,000 |
| Fixed costs ($120,000 + $10,000) | 130,000 |
| Divisional profit | $195,000 |
| Minimum required return ($850,000 × 20%) | 170,000 |
| Residual income | $ 25,000 |

The new $25,000 RI is $5,000 more than RI based on budgeted operations without the special order.

4. (a) $164,000. If Scooter accepts the lower price, revenue (and hence contribution margin) will be reduced by $0.80 per unit for 20,000 units. With no change in fixed costs, the $16,000 drop in contribution margin means a similar drop in profit. An income statement under the new assumption would show the following.

| | |
|---|---:|
| Sales [($5 × 80,000) + ($4.20 × 20,000)] | $484,000 |
| Variable costs ($2 × 100,000) | 200,000 |
| Contribution margin | $284,000 |
| Fixed costs | 120,000 |
| Divisional profit | $164,000 |

(b) $145,000. If Scooter does not accept the lower price, the full contribution margin from sales to Olympia will be lost. The avoidable fixed costs will be saved. The contribution margin lost would be $60,000 (20,000 units at $3), and the fixed costs saved would be $25,000. Hence, divisional profit would drop $35,000 ($60,000 − $25,000) to $145,000 ($180,000 budgeted profit − $35,000).

The answer could also be arrived at by reference to the income statement prepared in (a). The contribution margin lost would be $44,000 (20,000 × the lower contribution margin of $2.20), with fixed costs savings of $25,000. The net decline in profits would be $19,000 ($44,000 − $25,000), which, when subtracted from the $164,000 total profit shown in the income statement in (a), equals $145,000.

A third, somewhat longer, approach to the problem would be to prepare an income statement assuming the sales to Olympia are not made. This approach, too, shows a new divisional profit of $145,000.

| | |
|---|---:|
| Sales ($5 × 80,000) | $400,000 |
| Variable costs ($2 × 80,000) | 160,000 |
| Contribution margin | $240,000 |
| Fixed costs ($120,000 − $25,000) | 95,000 |
| Divisional profit | $145,000 |

(c) If you concluded that the company's total profit would change as a result of the change in the transfer price, you have forgotten a very important point made in Chapter 10. Changes in transfer prices do not, in themselves, change total profit. Only if changes in transfer prices cause managers to change their operations and actions can total profit change. In this situation, the manager of Scooter Division had planned to sell to Olympia Division and the income statement was budgeted accordingly. If he accepts the lower price, he will still be selling to Olympia. Similarly, the manager of Olympia Division had planned to buy from Scooter Division. He will still buy from Scooter Division, but at a lower price. The only thing that has changed is the transfer price. The reduction in the profit of Scooter Division (because of the lower contribution margin) will be exactly offset by the increased profit of Olympia Division (because of that division's lower costs). Hence, the company's total profit will not change.

(d) The company will lose $19,000 if Olympia buys from an outside supplier. From the point of view of the company as a whole, the decision is a make-or-buy decision such as was discussed in Chapter 5. Consider, therefore, the two possible decisions, from the company's point of view.

| | Decision | |
|---|---|---|
| | Buy from Outside Supplier | Make Product Inside (Scooter) |
| Purchase price (20,000 × $4.20) | $84,000 | |
| Variable cost to produce (20,000 × $2) | | $40,000 |
| Avoidable fixed costs | | 25,000 |
| Costs of each decision | $84,000 | $65,000 |

As this analysis indicates, the decision to produce internally carries a $19,000 advantage.

Another approach to this problem is to consider the profits of the individual divisions and how those profits would differ from originally budgeted profits if a purchase were made from an outside supplier. If Olympia can buy at $4.20 from either source, its profits will increase $16,000 (20,000 units × $0.80 saved) over what has been budgeted with an original transfer price of $5.00. For this reason, the manager of Olympia would be eager to obtain the lower price. Now consider the position of the manager of Scooter Division, who has budgeted profits of $180,000. The profit of his division will decline $35,000 (budgeted profits of $180,000 − $145,000 profits, computed in (b)) if he does not get the order from Olympia. For this reason, Scooter's manager should not want to lose the order from Olympia. Putting these two changes in divisional profits together, we see that there will be a $19,000 loss (a $16,000 gain by Olympia and a $35,000 loss by Scooter).

The important factor in this second approach is that if each division's manager evaluates his own situation properly, each will make a decision consistent with the good of the company as a whole. The manager of Olympia Division will wisely seek the lower price because it will increase his profits. The manager of Scooter Division will wisely consider the lower price because failing to do so will decrease his profit.

## ASSIGNMENT MATERIAL

### INTERNET ACTIVITY

A number of companies offer consulting related to economic value added. Find some of their Web sites. See how they view the concept, what services they offer, what benefits they say they can provide. See if they offer examples of successful implementations. Be prepared to describe and discuss what you discovered. Take the viewpoint that your boss has asked you to make a preliminary survey to see whether it is feasible for your company to look into some form of EVA.

### QUESTIONS FOR DISCUSSION

**11-1  *Value menu***   McDonalds, Pizza Hut, and various other restaurant chains have announced some variant of the "value menu" idea, whereby consumers get more food value for their money. How will these programs likely affect the margins and turnovers of the restaurants? Can you tell how the programs will affect ROI?

**11-2  *Alternative accounting methods***   Explain how various inventory cost flow assumptions (last-in first-out, first-in first-out, weighted average) can affect the measurement of return on investment for a division.

**11-3  *Product-line reporting***   Financial analysts often express the desire that companies publish annual reports broken down by division or principal lines of activity. They have said they would like to see financial statements broken down by products, or perhaps separated into wholesale and retail business, or maybe separated into government and commercial business. What problems might arise from attempting to fulfill this desire for additional information? What recommendations might you make?

**11-4 Performance measures and bonuses** A 1998 *Fortune* magazine article stated "To make sure that managers' gray matter is as focused on the goal as their software, **Ford** has instituted a distinctive change in the way it pays top executives. Under the old bonus system, which had been in place since 1955, recipients got a percentage of the company's profits, adjusted for the capital employed. But the amount was secret until the end of the year and was only loosely tied to actual performance. Now the benchmarks have been changed to include such variables as customer satisfaction and warranty performance, and there are no more secrets. Each quarter, eligible managers—the top 5,200 of Ford's 364,000 employees—get reports on how they are progressing toward their targets." What effects on managerial behavior may occur under the new bonus plan that would have been missing under the old plan?

**11-5 Whirlpool's operating results** **Whirlpool's** annual report reveals that it sells 19% of its output to **Sears** under private label and the rest under the Whirlpool name. What effects might the Sears sales have on margin, turnover, and ROI?

# EXERCISES

**11-6 RI, ROI, and CVP analysis** The following data refer to the DJH division of MMC Corporation.

| | |
|---|---:|
| Average selling price | $10 |
| Average variable cost | $4 |
| Total fixed costs | $200,000 |
| Investment | $500,000 |

**Required**

Answer each of the following questions independently.

1. How many units must DJH sell to earn a 20% ROI?
2. If the division sells 60,000 units, what will ROI be?
3. The minimum desired ROI is 15%. If the division sells 60,000 units, what is RI?
4. The manager desires a 25% ROI and wishes to sell 50,000 units. What price must she charge?
5. The minimum desired ROI is 20% and RI is $30,000. What are sales, in units?

**11-7 Comparison of ROI and RI, investment decisions** The manager of Tejas Division of MacroWare, Inc. has developed the following schedule of investment opportunities. The schedule shows the amount to be invested and the expected annual profit. Currently, investment is $8,000,000 and profits are $2,000,000.

| Investment Opportunity | Amount of Investment | Annual Profit |
|:---:|---:|---:|
| A | $ 600,000 | $ 90,000 |
| B | 700,000 | 200,000 |
| C | 1,000,000 | 230,000 |
| D | 1,100,000 | 290,000 |
| E | 1,200,000 | 170,000 |

**Required**

1. The division manager wishes to maximize ROI. (a) Which projects will he select? (b) What ROI will he earn?
2. The manager wishes to maximize RI. Determine which projects he will select and the RI he will earn if the minimum desired ROI is (a) 15% and (b) 25%.
3. Assuming that the ROI on each project approximates the IRR discussed in this chapter and in Chapter 8, which policy (maximizing ROI or maximizing RI) is better for the company? Assume that the minimum desired ROI equals cost of capital.

**11-8  Basic transfer pricing**  Tuck Division of Horwood Industries manufactures furniture. Data on a sofa the division makes follows.

| | | |
|---|---|---|
| Selling price | | $800 |
| Variable costs: | | |
| Fabric | $150 | |
| Other variable costs | 350 | |
| Total variable costs | | 500 |
| Contribution margin | | $300 |
| Expected volume | | 2,000 units |

Tuck buys the fabric from an outside supplier. The manager of Tuck learns that Clearwater Division of Horwood makes a fabric that meets her requirements. Clearwater sells the fabric to outside customers for $180. Variable cost to Clearwater is $100. Tuck's manager offers to buy the fabric at $120.

**Required**

1. Clearwater has plenty of capacity to serve its outside customers and meet Tuck's needs. If Tuck buys 2,000 units from Clearwater at $120:
   (a)  What will happen to Clearwater's income?
   (b)  What will happen to Tuck's income?
   (c)  What will happen to Horwood Industries' income?
2. Redo requirement 1 assuming that Clearwater has no excess capacity and will lose outside sales if it supplies Tuck.

**11-9  Product-line evaluation**  "My division as a whole is evaluated on ROI and RI, so why shouldn't I use those measures to evaluate my product lines?" The speaker was Maria Rodriguez, manager of the Household Products Division of General Enterprises, Inc. Rodriguez provided the following data regarding the three major lines that the division handles.

| | Cleaners | Disinfectants | Insect Sprays |
|---|---|---|---|
| Margin | 20% | 18% | 25% |
| Turnover | 2.5 times | 2 times | 1.8 times |
| Annual sales, millions | $30 | $10 | $18 |

**Required**

1. For each product line, determine ROI, total investment, and annual profit.
2. The minimum required ROI is 30%. Determine RI for each product line.

**11-10  Basic transfer pricing**  The Games Division of Toys-and-Stuff Inc. uses 500,000 batteries per year for its products. Currently, Games buys the batteries from an outside supplier for $1.20 each. Power Division of Toys-and-Stuff makes batteries of the type used by Games Division and sells them at $1.30 each. Power's variable cost to produce each battery is $0.70. Power Division has ample manufacturing capacity to serve its regular customers and also meet the needs of Games Division.

**Required**

Answer each of the following questions independently.

1. If Power agrees to supply the batteries at $1.00, what will be the effect on the incomes of each of the divisions and on Toys-and-Stuff as a whole?
2. Why might Power's manager accept an offer as low as $0.70 per battery from Games?
3. Repeat requirement 1 assuming that Power has no excess capacity and so would lose outside sales if it supplies the batteries to Games, and then find the lowest per-battery price that Power's manager would accept for the 500,000 batteries.
4. Repeat requirement 1 assuming that Power has only 200,000 units of excess capacity and so would lose outside sales of 300,000 units if it supplied the 500,000 batteries needed by Games.
5. Power again has 200,000 units of excess capacity. What is the lowest price that Power can accept for 500,000 units without reducing its income?

**11-11   Procter & Gamble's ROI components**   The following information comes from a recent **Procter & Gamble** annual report.

|  | Laundry and Cleaning | Food and Beverages | Health Care |
|---|---|---|---|
| Sales | $10,224 | $6,507 | $3,025 |
| Operating profit | 1,695 | 736 | 360 |
| Identifiable assets | 5,375 | 5,511 | 3,321 |

**Required**

1. Compute ROI for each segment, using the ratios of ROS and investment turnover.
2. Assume each segment could increase its ROS by one percentage point with the same sales as are currently shown. Recompute ROI and comment on the differences between the results here and those in requirement 1.

**11-12   ROI, RI, and CVP analysis**   The following data refer to the operations of Becker Division of Ventura Enterprises.

| | |
|---|---|
| Selling price per unit | $30 |
| Variable cost per unit | $18 |
| Annual fixed costs | $300,000 |
| Investment | $900,000 |

**Required**

1. Determine the number of units that Becker must sell to achieve a 25% ROI.
2. Becker has been approached by a company wishing to buy 10,000 units per year at a reduced price. Current volume is 43,000 units. Accepting the special order will increase fixed costs by $30,000 and investment by $80,000.
   (a) Determine ROI without the special order.
   (b) Determine the lowest price at which Becker can sell the additional 10,000 units without reducing ROI.
3. Suppose that the minimum required ROI is 20%.

(a) Determine the change in RI that will occur if the special order is at the price you computed in requirement 2 (b).

(b) Determine the lowest price for the special order that will not reduce RI.

**11-13 ROI, RI, and EVA for Warner-Lambert** The Chewing Gum and Mint Division of **Warner-Lambert** had the following results, in millions of dollars.

| | |
|---|---|
| Profit | $264 |
| Investment | $872 |

**Required**

1. Determine ROI and RI if the minimum required return is 20%.
2. Warner-Lambert faced a 35% income tax rate. Cost of capital is 13%. Determine EVA.

**11-14 Basic RI relationships** Hughes Division had RI of $4 million, investment of $40 million, and asset turnover of 1.5 times. The minimum required ROI was 20%.

**Required**

1. Determine Hughes's sales, profit, and ROS.
2. Determine the ROS that Hughes needs to raise its RI to $5 million, holding sales and investment constant.
3. With the ROS calculated in requirement 1, determine the sales required to earn $5 million RI, holding investment constant.

**11-15 Transfer pricing—increased costs and sacrificed sales** Division A of ABC Inc. has a capacity of 100,000 units and expects the following annual results.

| | |
|---|---|
| Sales (80,000 units at $9) | $ 720,000 |
| Variable costs (at $4) | (320,000) |
| Fixed costs | (250,000) |
| Income | $ 150,000 |

Division B, another division of ABC, currently purchases 30,000 units of a part for one of its products from an outside supplier at $8 per unit. B's manager believes she could use a minor variation of A's product instead, and offers to buy the units from A at $7. The variation desired by B would cost A an additional $1 per unit and would increase A's annual fixed costs by $12,000. A's manager agrees to the deal offered by B's manager.

**Required**

Determine the amount and direction of the effect of the deal on the annual income for Division A, for Division B, and for ABC as a whole. If you see a problem, suggest a solution.

**11-16 Transfer prices and decisions** Montauk Inc. consists of two divisions, Carter and Devon. Carter makes only one product, a chemical compound, at a variable manufacturing cost of $2.50 per gallon. The division sells both to outsiders (at $5 per gallon) and to Devon (at $4 per gallon). Devon spends $2 per gallon converting what it buys from Carter into a product that it sells to outsiders at $9 per gallon. The budgeted income statements for Montauk and its divisions follow.

|                                    | Carter      | Devon     | Montauk     |
|------------------------------------|-------------|-----------|-------------|
| Sales to outsiders:                |             |           |             |
| Carter (200,000 × $5)              | $1,000,000  |           | $1,000,000  |
| Devon (60,000 × $9)                |             | $540,000  | 540,000     |
| Sales to Devon                     |             |           |             |
| 60,000 × $4                        | 240,000     |           | 240,000     |
| Total                              | $1,240,000  | $540,000  | $1,780,000  |
| Variable costs:                    |             |           |             |
| $2.50 per gallon × 260,000         | $ 650,000   |           | $ 650,000   |
| $4 paid to Carter × 60,000         |             | $240,000  | 240,000     |
| $2 per gallon × 60,000             |             | 120,000   | 120,000     |
| Total variable costs               | $ 650,000   | $360,000  | $1,010,000  |
| Contribution margin                | $ 590,000   | $180,000  | $ 770,000   |
| Direct fixed costs                 | 300,000     | 120,000   | 420,000     |
| Division profit                    | $ 290,000   | $ 60,000  | $ 350,000   |
| Common costs                       |             |           | 130,000     |
| Income                             |             |           | $ 220,000   |

An outside supplier has offered to sell Devon 60,000 gallons of the needed chemical compound at $3.50 per gallon. Neither the outsider supplier nor Carter is willing to supply anything less than Devon's total needs of 60,000 gallons.

**Required**

Answer each of the following questions independently.

1. If Carter reduces the transfer price to $3.50 and Devon continues to buy from Carter, what will happen to the incomes of each of the divisions and of Montauk Inc. as a whole?
2. If Carter refuses to reduce the transfer price and Devon buys outside, what will happen to the incomes of each of the divisions and of Montauk Inc. as a whole? (Assume Carter cannot increase its sales to outside customers.)
3. Assume that Carter's capacity is 260,000 gallons and that, if Devon doesn't buy from Carter, Carter can increase its outside sales by 45,000 gallons. Should Carter reduce its price to meet that offered by the outside supplier? (Consider the question from both Carter's and Montauk's points of view.)

**11-17  Range of transfer price**  Microtec Division of CR Industries makes a microchip that it presently sells only to outsiders. The Consumer Products Division of CR is bringing out a new oven that requires a sophisticated chip and has approached Microtec for a quotation. Microtec sells the chip for $38, incurs variable costs of $9, and has excess capacity. The Consumer Products Division can acquire a suitable chip from outside the company for $32.

**Required**

1. Determine the advantage to CR Industries as a whole for the Consumer Products Division to buy the chip from Microtec, as opposed to buying it outside.
2. Determine the minimum price that Microtec would accept for the chip.
3. Determine the maximum price that Consumer Products would pay Microtec for the chip.
4. How would your answers to each of the preceding items change if Microtec was working at capacity?

**11-18   Basic ROI relationships**   Peyton Division of National Motors had sales of $60 million, ROI of 20%, and asset turnover of 2 times.

**Required**
1. Determine Peyton's (a) investment, (b) profit, and (c) ROS. ·
2. Suppose that by reducing its investment, Peyton could increase its asset turnover to three times without affecting sales or income. What will its ROI be?

**11-19   ROI and RI relationships**   Fill in the blanks in the following schedule. Each case is independent of the others. In all cases, the minimum desired ROI is 20%.

| | Case | | | |
|---|---|---|---|---|
| | A | B | C | D |
| Sales | $  400 | $____ | $  700 | $  400 |
| Income | $____ | $____ | $   42 | $____ |
| Investment | $____ | $  300 | $____ | $____ |
| Margin | 15 % | 8 % | ____ % | 15% |
| Turnover | ____ times | 3 times | ____ times | ____ times |
| ROI | 30 % | ____ % | ____ % | 30% |
| RI | $____ | $____ | $   22 | $____ |

**11-20   Relationships**   Fill in the blanks for each of the following independent situations. In all cases the minimum required ROI is 20%.

| | (a) Income | (b) Investment | (c) ROI | (d) RI |
|---|---|---|---|---|
| 1. | $2,500 | $10,000 | ____ | ____ |
| 2. | $5,400 | ____ | 30% | ____ |
| 3. | ____ | $20,000 | 30% | ____ |
| 4. | $6,000 | ____ | ____ | $1,000 |
| 5. | ____ | ____ | 30% | $3,000 |

**11-21   Transfer prices—cost savings**   For several years, ABC Division of Slavic Corp. has been selling some (currently 8,000 units) of its product to XYZ Division of the same company at a price slightly below that charged to outside customers. Budgeted income statements for the two divisions follow.

| | ABC Division | XYZ Division |
|---|---|---|
| Sales of ABC: | | |
| To outsiders (80,000 at $6) | $480,000 | |
| To XYZ (8,000 at $5) | 40,000 | |
| Sales of XYZ: | | |
| To outsiders (8,000 at $70) | | $560,000 |
| Total sales | $520,000 | $560,000 |
| Variable costs: | | |
| ABC (88,000 at $2) | $176,000 | |
| XYZ (8,000 at $5) | | $ 40,000 |
| XYZ (8,000 at $35) | | 280,000 |
| Total variable costs | $176,000 | $320,000 |
| Contribution margin | $344,000 | $240,000 |
| Direct fixed costs | 250,000 | 95,000 |
| Divisional profit | $ 94,000 | $145,000 |

An outside supplier has offered to provide to XYZ, for $4.50 each, 8,000 units similar to those it currently purchases from ABC.

**Required**

1. Assume that ABC's manager refuses to meet the outside supplier's price, loses XYZ's business, and cannot increase sales to outsiders.
   - (a) How will ABC's profit be affected if XYZ buys the units from the outside supplier?
   - (b) How will total profit of Slavic Corp. be affected if XYZ buys the units from the outside supplier?
2. Assume that ABC's manager doesn't want to meet the price offered by the outside supplier because she believes that she's already giving XYZ a bargain. She says that meeting XYZ's needs is stretching her factory's capacity and that, while she couldn't make outside sales beyond the current level (80,000), her per-unit variable cost would drop to $1.85 for all units and her fixed costs would drop by $18,000 if she didn't sell to XYZ. How will total profit of Slavic Corp. be affected if XYZ accepts the offer from the outside supplier to provide 8,000 units at $4.50?

**11-22    *Transfer prices for service work***   The service department of an automobile dealership does two general kinds of work: (1) work on cars brought in by customers and (2) work on used cars purchased by the dealership for resale. The service manager is often evaluated on the basis of gross profit or some other dollar measure. Because of the evaluation measure, the prices to be charged to the used-car manager for reconditioning and repair work on cars bought for resale are particularly important. The used-car manager is also likely to be evaluated by his profits. Thus, he wants service work done as cheaply as possible. The service manager naturally wants the prices to be the same as those he charges outside customers.

**Required**

1. What possible transfer prices could be used, and what are their advantages and disadvantages?
2. What do you recommend?

**11-23    *Review of Chapters 10 and 11***   Selected information about the only two divisions of Major Corp. follows.

|  | Noble | Seneca |
|---|---|---|
| Sales | $6,400,000 | $9,600,000 |
| Income | 960,000 | 640,000 |
| Investment | 4,000,000 | 3,200,000 |

Unallocated costs common to the two divisions are $400,000 per year. Assets (net of liabilities) that are not associated with either division are $1,200,000.

**Required**

Answer the following questions. Note: The answers to most questions do not depend on the answers to previous questions.

1. What is ROS for Noble Division?
2. What is investment turnover for Noble Division?
3. What is ROI for Noble Division?
4. What is ROI for the company as a whole?
5. What is RI for Seneca Division if Major's minimum required ROI is 12%?
6. Suppose Major's top managers decide to allocate common costs to its divisions on the basis of divisional sales.
   - (a) Determine Seneca Division's ROI.

(b) Determine the ROI for the company as a whole.
7. If Major's top managers decide to allocate common costs on the basis of divisional investment, what will ROI be for the company as a whole?

## PROBLEMS

**11-24  Performance evaluation criteria**  Budgeted data for 20X2 for two of Hawthorne, Inc.'s divisions appear below. The company evaluates divisional managers based on ROI. Dollar amounts are in millions.

|                   | TDF    | Valco  |
|-------------------|--------|--------|
| Sales             | $ 60.0 | $ 30.0 |
| Expenses          | 30.0   | 20.0   |
| Divisional profit | $ 30.0 | $ 10.0 |
| Investment        | $120.0 | $100.0 |

An investment opportunity is available to both divisions that is expected to return $4 million annually for an investment of $20 million.

*Required*
1. Given that the divisional managers are evaluated based on ROI, which, if either, of the managers will accept the project? Explain.
2. Assume that the managers are evaluated on residual income. If the minimum required ROI is 18%, which, if either, of the managers will accept the project? Explain.
3. If the minimum required ROI is 18%, is it in Hawthorne's best interest for a division to accept the project? Explain.

**11-25  Components of ROI**  The managers of two divisions of Diversified Company were recently discussing their operations. Fran Margin commented, "I get a good return on sales, about 30%, but my investment is a drag. Turnover last year was only 0.50 times." Florence Turns said, "My problem is margins; turnover is about 4 times, but return on sales is only 3.75%."

*Required*
1. Compute ROI for each division.
2. (a) Assume that Margin's division will maintain the same ROS. Determine the investment turnover required to achieve a 20% ROI.
   (b) Assume that Turns' division will maintain its turnover. Determine the ROS required to achieve a 20% ROI.

**11-26  Appropriate transfer price**  Crandon Division of Wolfe expects the following results in 20X1 from selling only to outside customers.

| Sales (1,000,000 units at $8) | $8,000,000 |
|-------------------------------|------------|
| Variable costs at $4          | 4,000,000  |
| Contribution margin           | $4,000,000 |
| Fixed costs                   | 2,400,000  |
| Profit                        | $1,600,000 |

Early in 20X1, the manager of Wood Division of Wolfe asked the manager of Crandon to supply 300,000 units to Wood. Wood would modify the units at a variable cost of $5 and sell the resulting product for $11. Crandon Division has capacity of 1,200,000 units and will therefore lose 100,000 units in outside sales if it supplies the 300,000 to Wood. Crandon's fixed costs remain constant up to capacity.

**Required**

1. If Crandon transfers 300,000 units to Wood, which modifies and sells them as described, what will happen to the profit of Wolfe as a whole?
2. What is the minimum transfer price that Crandon will accept from Wood for the 300,000 units?
3. What is the maximum transfer price that Wood will pay?
4. Redo requirement 1 assuming that Crandon's capacity is 1,500,000 units and that Crandon cannot increase its outside sales beyond 1,000,000 units.

**11-27  ROI and RI on a special order**  The Appliance Division of TVM Industries has the opportunity to sell 250,000 units of one of its principal lines to a large chain store at $24 per unit. Selected data follow.

| | |
|---|---|
| Annual unit volume | 1,700,000 |
| Normal selling price | $40 |
| Unit variable cost | $18 |
| Annual fixed costs | $30,000,000 |
| Divisional investment | $25,000,000 |

The manager of the Appliance Division expects a 50,000 unit decline in sales at the normal price if she supplies the chain. She also expects fixed costs to increase by $100,000 and investment to increase by $1,200,000 if she accepts the order.

**Required**

1. Determine whether the manager of the Appliance Division should accept the order, assuming that she is evaluated based on ROI.
2. Determine whether the manager of the Appliance Division should accept the order, assuming that she is evaluated based on RI and that the minimum required ROI is 20%.

**11-28  Comprehensive review**  The following information relates to the Glove Division of Hand-and-Glove Company.

| | |
|---|---|
| Budgeted sales | 80,000 units |
| Selling price | $16 |
| Variable cost, per unit | $10 |
| Annual direct fixed costs, all unavoidable | $300,000 |
| Total divisional investment | $800,000 |
| Minimum required ROI | 20% |

**Required**

Answer each of the following questions independently.

1. What are Glove's budgeted ROI and RI?
2. How many units must Glove sell to earn $50,000 RI?
3. Assume that Glove expects to produce and sell 80,000 units but has the capacity to produce 100,000 units. The manager of Hand Division, which is currently buy-

ing 25,000 units of a similar product from an outside supplier for $13, offers to buy the units from Glove only if Glove will supply the full 25,000 units needed.
(a) What is the maximum price that Hand's manager is likely to offer for the units?
(b) What is the minimum price that Glove's manager is likely to accept on a sale of 25,000 units to Hand Division?
(c) If Hand's manager offers $12 per unit and Glove's manager accepts the offer, what will be the amount and direction of the effect on the total income of Hand-and-Glove?

**11-29 *Transfer prices and required profit margins*** Geri Roberts is the used-car manager of the Snappy Wheels automobile dealership. She is expected to earn a gross profit of 25% of sales in the used-car operation, and she is distressed by the company's transfer-pricing policy. Roberts is charged with the trade-in price she sets for a used car plus any reconditioning work. The charge for reconditioning is based on actual costs by the service department plus a one-third markup over cost (25% on sales). Roberts believes she is being unduly penalized by the one-third markup.

Ellen Black, the service manager, is held responsible for earning a 25% gross profit on sales. She argues that it would not be fair to force her to do reconditioning work any cheaper than the work she does on customers' cars.

Roberts has recently been approached by Joe Sharp, the owner of Sharp's Garage, an independent repair shop. Sharp offers to do reconditioning work for Roberts at 20% over cost: the work is to be done during Sharp's slack periods. The work will generally take about four days longer than work done by the service department, which has no excess capacity.

**Required**
Should Roberts take her reconditioning business to Sharp?

**11-30 *Make-or-buy and transfer pricing*** Barron Enterprises, Inc. has three divisions, A, B, and C. One of the company's products uses components made by A and B, with the final assembly done by C. One unit from A and one from B are required. Data for the product are as follows:

| | |
|---|---|
| Selling price (C division) | $110 |
| Variable costs: | |
|     A division | $ 36 |
|     B division | 20 |
|     C division | 16 |
| Total variable costs | $ 72 |
| Volume | 10,000 units |

Divisions A and B charge Division C $44 and $28, respectively, for each unit. Division C has been approached by an outside supplier who will sell the component now made by Division A at $40 per unit.

**Required**
1. Prepare partial income statements, down to contribution margin, for A, B, and C based on current operations.
2. Determine whether the offer from the outside supplier should be accepted. If A meets the outside price, C will continue to buy from A.
3. Suppose that A can sell its entire output of 10,000 units per year at $48 if it performs additional work on the component. The additional work will add $5 to vari-

able cost per unit; fixed costs will be unchanged. Capacity of Division A is 10,000 units. Should A meet the outside supplier's price or allow C to buy from the outside supplier? Support with calculations. Is A's decision good for the company?

**11-31  Goal congruence and motivation**  Roth Company manufactures furniture and related products. Tammie Bills, manager of the Redfern Division, has been seeking bids on a particular type of chair to be used in a new living room suite she wants to market. No division within the company can supply the chair.

The lowest outside bid is $140 from Thomas Chair Company. Wisner Chair Company has bid $150 and would buy some of the materials from the Ronson Upholstery Division of Roth Company. The Ronson Division has excess capacity, would incur variable costs of $35 for the amount of material needed for one chair, and would be paid $56 by Wisner. Bills has learned that Wisner would buy the materials from Ronson and that Thomas would not. Each division manager is evaluated on the basis of ROI.

**Required**

1. As manager of the Redfern Division, which bid would you accept, Thomas's or Wisner's?
2. As Roth's president, which bid do you want to see accepted? Explain.
3. Using the guidelines in Appendix A, write a memorandum to Jan Blane, Roth's president, giving and explaining your recommendations about how to handle this situation.

**11-32  Performance of international division**  CWK Industries is a division of Martek, Inc. CWK operates in Hungary, where the currency is the forint (F). The information CWK used to develop its operating budgets for the first quarter of 20X3 follow. The exchange rate is four forints per dollar.

| | |
|---|---|
| Unit sales | 100,000 |
| Unit price | F300 |
| Cost of sales percentage | 40% |
| Operating expenses | F13,000,000 per month |

**Required**

1. Prepare a budgeted income statement for the first quarter of 20X3, in forints.
2. Translate the budgeted income statement to dollars.

**11-33  Performance of international division (continuation of 11-32)**  CWK's actual results for the first quarter of 20X3 follow. After the budgets were prepared, the exchange rate quickly went to five forints per dollar and remained there over the quarter, during which sales were 104,400 units. Prices and costs were incurred as expected.

CWK Division
Income Statement
First Quarter, 20X3 (000s)

| | |
|---|---|
| Sales, 104,400 × F300 | F31,320 |
| Cost of sales | 12,528 |
| Gross profit | F18,792 |
| Operating expenses | 13,000 |
| Income | F 5,792 |

## Required

1. Translate the actual income statement to dollars.
2. Comment on the results. Did the managers of CWK perform well, badly, or about as expected?

**11-34  Divisional performance—interactions**   Acme Camera Company has two divisions, Film and Camera. The manager of the Film Division, John Kretzmar, has just received a report from his laboratory indicating a breakthrough in a new type of film that produces much clearer pictures. The film can only be used in the X-40, a low-priced camera made by the Camera Division. The film currently sold for the X-40 has a variable cost per roll of $0.90 and sells for $3.00 per roll. The film currently sells 2 million rolls per year.

Kretzmar is confident that if he devoted his efforts and facilities to the production and sale of the new film he could sell 2.5 million rolls at $2.80 each. He also believes, on the basis of several market research studies, that if the Camera Division sold 200,000 more X-40s per year, sales of the new film could reach 4.8 million rolls. The variable cost of the new film is $0.80 per roll, additional fixed costs to produce it are $250,000 per year, and additional required investment totals $600,000.

Samantha Brewer, manager of the Camera Division, is not happy with the proposal that she increase production of X-40s. She argues that the camera has a contribution margin of only $6 and that she would have to increase her investment by $4,000,000 and her fixed costs by $500,000 in order to increase production by 200,000 units. She is virtually certain, as is Kretzmar, that the extra units could be sold, but she is also well aware that Acme's minimum required ROI is 20%.

## Required

1. Compute the change in RI for the Camera Division if production and sales of X-40s are increased by 200,000 units to show why Brewer is not eager to expand its production.
2. If the manager of the Camera Division will not increase production, what is the best action for the Film Division?
3. What is the best action for the company as a whole?

**11-35  RI, ROI, CVP analysis, and effects of decisions**   The following data refer to the Pratt Division of Standard National Company.

| | |
|---|---|
| Selling price | $40 |
| Variable costs | $24 |
| Total fixed costs | $200,000 |
| Investment | $800,000 |
| Budgeted sales in 20X4 | 30,000 units |

## Required

Answer each of the following questions independently.

1. What is planned ROI for 20X4?
2. The minimum required ROI is 20% and the division manager wishes to maximize RI. A new customer wants to buy 10,000 units at $32 each. If the order is accepted, the division will incur additional fixed costs of $40,000 and will have to invest an additional $160,000 in various assets. Should Pratt accept the order?
3. The minimum desired ROI is 20% and the manager wishes to maximize RI. The division makes components for its product at a variable cost of $4. An outside supplier has offered to supply the 30,000 units needed at a cost of $5 per unit. The units that the supplier would provide are equivalent to the ones now being made and the supplier is reliable. If the component is purchased, fixed costs will decline

by $20,000 and investment will drop by $40,000. Should Pratt make or buy the component?

4. Again, minimum required ROI is 20% and the goal is maximizing RI. The manager is considering a new product. It will sell for $20, variable costs are $12, fixed costs will increase by $80,000, and sales are expected to be 15,000 units. What is the most additional investment that can be made without reducing RI?

5. Assume the same facts as in requirement 4 except that investment in the new product is $400,000 and introducing the product will increase sales of the existing product by 2,000 units. What increase in unit sales of the existing product is needed to justify introducing the new product?

**11-36   *Corporate charges and behavior***   MST Company charges its operating divisions a percentage of sales to cover corporate expenses, which are virtually all fixed. The percentage is based on budgeted sales and budgeted corporate expenses and is predetermined for each year. In 20X1 the charge is 3%. The charge is included in calculating the profit of each division and its ROI, which is the basis for evaluating the performance of divisional managers.

Calco Division makes electronic equipment and has some excess capacity. Its manager has found a customer who will pay $10 million for a batch of product that has variable costs of $8.8 million. No incremental fixed costs are associated with the order. Accepting the order will require increased investment in receivables and inventories of about $5.1 million. The 3% charge is not included in the $8.8 million.

The divisional manager expects to earn $15.5 million on an investment of $70.5 million without the order.

**Required**

1. Should the divisional manager accept the order, acting in her own best interests?
2. Assuming that the minimum required ROI is 20%, is it to the company's advantage to accept the order?

**11-37   *Performance measurement—athletic programs***   Point Lobos University is a medium-sized private university with a religious affiliation. Perhaps prompted by the prospect of declining college enrollment, a number of faculty members at Point Lobos have become increasingly concerned about the costs of the school's athletic program. The football program has been subjected to particular scrutiny. One professor assembled the following data and argues, based on these data, that football is clearly a drain on funds needed elsewhere in the university.

| 20X3 Football Program | |
|---|---:|
| Revenue from ticket sales | $300,000 |
| Revenue from concessions | 25,000 |
| Total revenue | $325,000 |
| Associated costs: | |
|   Tuition for players on scholarship | $120,000 |
|   Room rent in dormitories for players | 22,000 |
|   Board and incidentals for players | 110,000 |
|   Coaches' salaries | 90,000 |
|   Portion of salaries of athletic director, | |
|     ticket office personnel, attendants, etc. | 17,000 |
|   Uniforms, equipment, etc. | 10,000 |
| Total costs | $369,000 |
| Net loss on football program | $ (44,000) |

### Required

1. Comment on each item. Should it be included? If you are uncertain, state the conditions under which it should be included or excluded.
2. What other information do you want before reaching a decision on the desirability of the football program?

**11-38   Transfer prices**   Following is a budgeted income statement for Dreyfess of Midwest Products, Inc. The division sells both to outsiders and to a sister division.

| | Intercompany Sales to Thompson | Sales to Outsiders |
|---|---|---|
| Sales: | | |
| 100,000 units at $10 | | $1,000,000 |
| 50,000 units at $8 | $400,000 | |
| Variable costs ($4 per unit) | 200,000 | 400,000 |
| Contribution margin | $200,000 | $ 600,000 |
| Fixed costs ($300,000, allocated | | |
| at $2 per unit | 100,000 | 200,000 |
| Profit | $100,000 | $ 400,000 |

### Required

1. Thompson can buy all of its requirements from an outside supplier at $7 per unit and will do so unless Dreyfess meets the $7 price. Dreyfess' manager knows that if he loses the Thompson business he will not be able to increase sales to outsiders and fixed costs will not change. Should he meet the $7 price from the standpoint of (a) the company and (b) Dreyfess?
2. Dreyfess meets the $7 price. Dreyfess then is offered the opportunity to sell 60,000 units to a chain store at $7 each. The price of the 100,000 units now sold to outsiders will not be affected. However, Dreyfess has capacity of 190,000 units. If Dreyfess cannot fill all of the requirements of Thompson, then Thompson will have to buy all the units outside at $7. Should Dreyfess accept the order, considering (a) the company and (b) Dreyfess?
3. Suppose now that Thompson has received the offer from the outside supplier, who will provide as many units as Thompson wants to buy at $7. Dreyfess no longer has the opportunity to sell the 60,000 units to the chain store. The manager of Dreyfess believes that reducing prices to outsiders could increase those sales greatly. Best estimates are that reducing the price to $9.20 would yield sales of 120,000 units; to $8.40, 150,000 units; and to $7.80, 170,000 units. Capacity is 190,000 units. Dreyfess can sell any amount up to 50,000 units to Thompson. Thompson will buy units from the outside supplier as necessary. What should be done? How many units should Dreyfess sell to outsiders, and how many units should it sell to Thompson at $7?

**11-39   ROI, RI, and investment decisions**   The manager of Brandon Division of Greene Industries has been analyzing her investment opportunities. The division currently has profits of $1,250,000 and investment of $5,000,000.

| Investment Opportunity | Annual Profit | Amount of Investment |
|---|---|---|
| A | $300,000 | $ 900,000 |
| B | 300,000 | 1,600,000 |
| C | 240,000 | 1,200,000 |
| D | 280,000 | 800,000 |
| E | 260,000 | 1,000,000 |

### Required

1. The manager wants to earn the highest ROI possible. Determine which projects she will select and the ROI that she will earn.
2. The manager wants to maximize RI. Determine which projects she will select and the total RI she will earn if the minimum required return is (a) 20% and (b) 28%.
3. Assume that the ROI on each project approximates the IRR discussed in Chapter 8 and that the minimum desired ROI approximates cost of capital. Determine which policy is better for the company: maximizing ROI or maximizing RI.

**11-40   Transfer pricing**   MST Division of 3K Company expects the following results.

| | |
|---|---:|
| Sales (100,000 at $3) | $300,000 |
| Variable costs | 120,000 |
| Contribution margin | $180,000 |
| Fixed costs | 150,000 |
| Profit | $ 30,000 |

Sparkman Division of 3K Company wants to buy 30,000 units of MST's product. Sparkman will incur an additional $0.80 per unit and sell the resultant new product for $4.50. MST has capacity for 120,000 units.

### Required

1. What will happen to 3K's profit if the transfer of 30,000 units takes place at a price of $1.50?
2. What will happen to the profit of each division if the transaction takes place at the $1.50 transfer price?
3. What is the minimum transfer price MST will accept for the 30,000 units?

**11-41   Transfer prices and goal congruence (CMA adapted)**   A. R. Oma Company manufactures a line of men's perfumes and aftershave lotions. The manufacturing process is a series of mixing operations with the adding of aromatic and coloring ingredients. The finished product is bottled and packed in cases of six bottles each.

The bottles are made by one division, which was bought several years ago. Management believes that the appeal of the product is partly due to the attractiveness of the bottles and so has spent a great deal of time and effort developing new types of bottles and new processes for making them.

The bottle division has been selling all of its output to the manufacturing division at market-based transfer prices. The price has been determined by asking other bottle manufacturers for bids on bottles of the appropriate size and in the required quantities. At present, the company has the following bids.

| Quantity,<br>Cases of Six Bottles | Price per Case | Total Price |
|:---:|:---:|:---:|
| 2,000,000 | $2.00 | $ 4,000,000 |
| 4,000,000 | 1.75 | 7,000,000 |
| 6,000,000 | 1.6666 | 10,000,000 |

The bottle division has fixed costs of $1,200,000 per year and variable costs of $1 per case. Both divisions are investment centers, and their managers receive significant bonuses based on profitability, so the transfer price is of great interest to both of them.

The perfume manufacturing division has variable costs, excluding the cost of bottles, of $8 per case and fixed costs of $4,000,000 annually. The market research group has determined that the following price-volume relationships are likely to prevail during the coming year.

| Sales Volume in Cases | Selling Price per Case | Total Revenue |
|---|---|---|
| 2,000,000 | $12.50 | $25,000,000 |
| 4,000,000 | 11.40 | 45,600,000 |
| 6,000,000 | 10.65 | 63,900,000 |

The president, Miguel Enez, believes that the market-based transfer price should be used in pricing transfers. The bottle division has no outside sales potential because the company does not wish to supply its highly appealing bottles to competitors.

*Required*

1. Of the three levels of volume given, determine which will provide the highest profit to the (a) bottle division, (b) perfume division, and (c) company as a whole.
2. Do the results in requirement 1 contradict your understanding of the effectiveness of market-based transfer prices? Explain why or why not.
3. Using the guidelines in Appendix A, write a memorandum to Mr. Enez giving and supporting your recommendation about the course of action that should be selected.

**11-42   *Transfer pricing (CMA adapted)***   The manager of the Arjay Division of National Industries, Inc. has the opportunity to supply a brake assembly to an aircraft manufacturer for $50. The manager is willing to accept the order if he can break even on it because he has excess capacity and will be able to keep skilled workers busy who would otherwise have to be laid off. Additionally, he believes there is a good chance of getting more business from the same company at better prices.

Bradley Division of National Industries makes a part that is used in the brake assembly. Bradley is operating at capacity and producing the part at a variable cost of $4.25. Its selling price is $7.50 to outsiders. None of its output is currently being sold internally.

The manager of Arjay decides to offer Bradley a price that will result in breaking even on the order. He determines that the other costs involved in filling the order are as follows, per unit.

| | |
|---|---|
| Parts purchased outside | $23 |
| Other variable costs | 14 |
| Fixed overhead and administration | 8 |
| Total, before fitting | $45 |

He decides to offer the manager of Bradley $5 per fitting, which brings the total cost per unit to $50, the selling price of the assembly. The company is decentralized and the managers are evaluated based on ROI.

*Required*

1. Determine whether the manager of Bradley is likely to accept the $5 offer.
2. Determine whether it is to the company's advantage for Bradley to supply the part at $5.
3. As the controller of National Industries, what do you advise be done?

**11-43   Budgeted and actual results**   Managers of divisions of Wyandotte Company receive bonuses based on ROI. The bonuses constitute about 30% of total compensation of the average manager. Part of the bonus depends on whether the manager meets budgeted ROI.

F. C. Smith took over as general manager of the Whitefish Point Division six years ago. Budgeted and actual results for last year follow, in thousands of dollars.

|  | Budget | Actual |
|---|---|---|
| Sales | $ 2,500 | $ 2,480 |
| Cost of sales | (1,250) | (1,310) |
| Operating expenses | (750) | (610) |
| Profit | $  500 | $  560 |
| Investment |  |  |
| Current assets (50% of sales) | $ 1,250 | $ 1,240 |
| Current liabilities (40% of current assets) | (500) | (496) |
| Plant and equipment, net | 1,800 | 1,770 |
| Total investment | $ 2,550 | $ 2,514 |
| ROI | 19.6% | 22.3% |

Smith received a sizable bonus. Smith commented on the results by saying that once he saw sales would not meet budget, he began to cut costs, especially in discretionary areas such as maintenance, employee training, and engineering. (Engineers were responsible for improving the quality of products and methods of manufacturing.) He also held off payments to suppliers, letting them finance more of the division's asset requirements.

**Required**

Discuss Smith's performance. Include in your discussion the long-term implications of the specific actions mentioned and the ethical aspects of his actions.

**11-44   Divisional performance, cost allocations, and dropping a product line**   Sonya York is the manager in charge of two product lines for Pepin Company. She has just received the following income statement for the three months ended March 31. The statement shows York's two product lines and the total results for the company. The company has ten product lines.

|  | A | B | Pepin Co. |
|---|---|---|---|
| Sales | $100,000 | $200,000 | $2,000,000 |
| Cost of sales | $ 60,000 | $100,000 | $1,050,000 |
| Selling and general | 29,000 | 50,000 | 450,000 |
| Total separable expenses | $ 89,000 | $150,000 | $1,500,000 |
| Common costs (allocated on basis of sales dollars) | 15,000 | 30,000 | 300,000 |
| Total expenses | $104,000 | $180,000 | $1,800,000 |
| Income (loss) | $ (4,000) | $ 20,000 | $ 200,000 |

York is disturbed by the showing of product line A. She believes that the line is contributing to the common costs of the company and should be kept, but she is worried about the effect on her performance.

**Required**

1. Prepare an income statement assuming that product line A is dropped. Show the effects on both York's and the company's performance. All separable costs are avoidable. Be sure to reallocate common costs to product line B based on its relative percentage of the new sales for the company. Round to the nearest $500.
2. Comment on the results. Does York's performance look better if product line A is dropped? Is it better? Is the decision good for the company?

**11-45  Developing divisional performance data**  Dixon Company has three divisions: X, Y, and Z. The following data regarding operations and selected balance sheet elements have been prepared by the company's accountant (in thousands of dollars).

|  | X | Y | Z |
|---|---|---|---|
| Sales | $2,000 | $3,000 | $5,000 |
| Cost of goods sold | 1,000 | 1,400 | 3,300 |
| Gross profit | 1,000 | 1,600 | 1,700 |
| Selling and administrative expense | 400 | 900 | 800 |
| Income | $ 600 | $ 700 | $ 900 |
| Current assets | $ 400 | $ 700 | $ 600 |
| Current liabilities | $ 300 | $ 200 | $ 100 |
| Fixed assets (net) | $2,250 | $3,000 | $3,750 |

After determining costs and assets directly traceable to the divisions, the accountant allocated the remainder in the following way.

(a) Common cost of goods sold of $1,800 was allocated based on sales dollars.
(b) Common selling and administrative costs of $1,000 were allocated on the basis of relative sales dollars.
(c) Common fixed assets of $3,000 were allocated on the basis of relative shares of directly assignable fixed assets of $1,500, $2,000, and $2,500, for X, Y, and Z, respectively.
(d) All current assets except cash (which is held and managed by corporate headquarters) are directly assignable. Cash of $200 is allocated based on sales.

**Required**

1. On the basis of the data developed by the company, rank the divisions according to ROI on net assets and RI, with a 15% minimum required ROI.
2. Recast the statements, computing divisional profit and assets employed without allocations. Rank the divisions on the same bases as in requirement 1. Comment on the differences between your rankings.

## CASES

**11-46  Transfer pricing**  Westlake Division of Hatley Enterprises makes various electronic components, among which is a line of stereophonic speakers. The division sells speakers to companies that incorporate them in complete systems. The division can make 45,000 speakers per year and cannot increase production because of shortages of specialized skilled labor. Data for the speaker follow.

| | | |
|---|---:|---:|
| Selling price | | $80 |
| Variable manufacturing costs | $48 | |
| Variable selling costs | 8 | 56 |
| Contribution margin | | $24 |

Westlake has just lost a customer and its managers now project volume at 40,000 speakers per year for the next several years. Another division of Hatley, Valcourt Division, is interested in buying speakers from Westlake and putting them in sets to be sold through retail outlets. Valcourt now buys speakers of somewhat higher quality than those made by Westlake at $84 each. The speakers are of better quality than the rest of the components of the set, so the manager of Valcourt intends to reduce prices and predicts higher volume if she changes to the lower-quality speakers. Volume of the sets in which the speakers are to be used is currently 3,500 units per year. If the price were reduced from $680 to $600, volume is expected to be 4,500 units per year. Variable costs are currently $460 per set, including the $168 for two speakers now purchased outside. Valcourt Division wants 9,000 speakers per year from Westlake and has offered $62 per speaker. Valcourt will not accept fewer than 9,000 speakers. Westlake will not incur variable selling expenses on speakers sold to Valcourt.

### Required

1. Determine whether it is in the company's best interests if Westlake sold speakers to Valcourt.
2. At the suggested transfer price, is it in the interests of each of the managers to have Westlake sell to Valcourt?
3. Determine the limits on the transfer price—that is, the highest price that Valcourt would be willing to pay and the lowest price that Westlake will accept.

**11-47 Problems of market-based transfer prices** Lucrettia Division of Borgia Industries has developed an electronic measuring system that requires a sophisticated microprocessor. Medici Division makes such a microprocessor and currently sells it for $200 on the outside market. Medici incurs variable costs of $50 per unit. Medici has a lot of excess capacity. It now sells 30,000 units of the microprocessor per year and could make close to 40,000 units. However, increasing outside sales to 36,000 units would require reducing the selling price on all units to $160. Accordingly, Medici has been restricting output.

The manager of Lucrettia received a bid of $200, the current market price, from Medici for the microprocessor and then analyzed data regarding expected volume at different selling prices. He intended to set the price of the measuring system at either $600 or $550 based on the following.

| | Selling Price | |
|---|---:|---:|
| | $600 | $550 |
| Expected variable costs, per unit: | | |
| Materials | $ 90 | $ 90 |
| Microprocessor from Medici | 200 | 200 |
| Labor and variable overhead | 110 | 110 |
| Total variable costs | $400 | $400 |
| Contribution margin | $200 | $150 |
| Expected unit volume | 5,000 | 6,000 |

**Required**
1. At the $200 transfer price, what price will the manager of Lucrettia Division set for the measuring system?
2. From the standpoint of the company, which price is better, $600 or $550?
3. The manager of Medici Division knows that Lucrettia will buy 5,000 microprocessors at the $200 price. What is the minimum price he will accept for 6,000 units—the price that gives him the same total contribution margin he could earn selling 5,000 at $200?
4. Will the transfer price you calculated in requirement 3 induce the manager of the Lucrettia Division to try to sell 6,000 units of the measuring system at $550? Assume that the two managers have to agree on both the transfer price and the quantity to be taken. That is, the alternatives that the Lucrettia manager faces are to (1) buy 5,000 microprocessors at $200 and (2) buy 6,000 at $175.

**11-48   Divisional performance and accounting methods**   A division manager for Mykail Company has been criticized for allowing ROI to fall in the past two years. She has explained that the division made some large investments on which a 30% before-tax ROI is expected. She argues that the use of straight-line depreciation is hurting ROI, on which her performance is evaluated. Following are comparative income statements and other data for the past three years.

|  | 20X1 | 20X2 | 20X3 |
|---|---|---|---|
| Sales | $2,200 | $2,900 | $3,800 |
| Variable costs | 1,200 | 1,500 | 1,800 |
| Contribution margin | $1,000 | $1,400 | $2,000 |
| Total fixed costs | 600 | 950 | 1,400 |
| Divisional profit | $ 400 | $ 450 | $ 600 |
| Invested capital | | | |
| (mainly plant and equipment) | $1,000 | $1,600 | $2,400 |
| ROI | 40% | 28% | 25% |
| Capital expenditures | $200 | $900 | $1,500 |
| Depreciation included above | $300 | $450 | $600 |

**Required**
1. Explain why the falling ROI might not indicate poor performance.
2. What possible solutions are there?

**11-49   Capital budgeting and performance evaluation**   George Bailey, manager of the Potter Division of Bedford Enterprises, Inc., is considering an investment. He can save $10,000 in cash operating costs per year using a machine that costs $40,000 and has a ten-year life with no salvage value. Bailey calculates the ROI in the first year as 15% [($10,000 − $4,000 depreciation)/$40,000]. He decides that the machine is not a wise investment because his current ROI is 20% and he is evaluated based on ROI. (Current income is $40,000 and investment is $200,000.)

The seller of the machine offers to lease it at $8,500 per year if Bailey will accept a noncancellable lease for ten years. He asks your advice and specifically requests that you consider the effect of the lease on ROI. The company's minimum desired ROI before taxes is 12%, which approximates cost of capital.

**Required**
Using the guidelines in Appendix A, write a memorandum to Mr. Bailey explaining his choices and the effects of each alternative from his standpoint and that of the company.

**11-50   National Automobile Company—introduction of a new model**   National Auto Company consists of four relatively autonomous divisions. In the past each division has concentrated on a relatively limited range of models designed to appeal to a particular segment of the automobile market. The Yuma Division has been producing mid-sized cars for many years. They range in price (to dealers) from $14,000 to $25,300.

One day last August, Noel Mack, general manager of the Yuma Division, was studying some reports prepared by the company's market research department at central headquarters. Mack had been considering for some time the possibility of bringing out a stripped-down version of the division's most popular model, the Panther. He had been hesitant to do so because he feared that sales of the higher-priced Panthers would suffer. The market research indicated, however, that lost sales of higher-priced versions would be negligible if a new Panther were introduced and priced to sell to the customer for about $20,800. The lowest price at retail now charged for a Panther is $24,700.

Mack was pleased at the results of the study and instructed his production manager to determine the costs of producing 80,000 units of the new model per year—the number of units that the study indicated could be sold. Mack also asked for information about additional investment in equipment, inventories, and receivables necessitated by the higher volume.

A few days later Mack had the additional information. The production manager estimated the cost per unit to be $17,800, composed of the following basic categories.

| | |
|---|---|
| Variable costs | $13,800 |
| Fixed costs | 4,000 |
| Total | $17,800 |

The fixed cost per unit included $100 million in existing fixed costs that would be reallocated to the new model under a complicated formula used by the division's cost accounting department. The additional investment in equipment was $300 million and in receivables and inventories about $200 million.

Mack was reasonably certain that the information he had gathered was as accurate as estimates are likely to be. He consulted with several large dealers and concluded that the model could be priced at $18,100 to dealers. Any higher price would encourage the dealers to charge more than $20,800, with a consequent decline in volume below the 80,000 per year target.

Like the other divisional managers, Mack is evaluated based on the residual income earned by his division. The minimum required return is 18%. Income taxes are ignored in determining residual income for the divisions.

**Required**
Determine whether the new Panther should be brought out.

**11-51   National Automobile Company—interaction effects of decisions (continuation of 11-50)**   While mulling over his decision whether to introduce the new Panther model, Noel Mack was eating lunch with Debra Warren, general manager of the Tucson Division, which specializes in compact and subcompact cars. Mack told Warren about the study he had ordered and gave a general picture of the results, including the projection of 80,000 units of volume of the new model.

After lunch, Warren called Hanna Gregorich, the chief of market research for the firm, and requested more information about the study. Gregorich said that the study indicated a potential decline in volume of 30,000 units of one of the Tucson Division's best-selling higher-priced models if Yuma brought out the new lower-priced model. Warren asked why that information had not been included in the report given to Mack and was told that Mack had only asked for estimates in declines in volume of

Yuma Division cars. Warren then immediately telephoned her production manager and sales manager. She informed them of the situation and demanded that they quickly collect information.

Several days later, the production manager informed Warren that the model in question, which sold to retail dealers for $16,700, had unit costs of $16,400 at the division's current volume of 160,000 units per year. Fixed costs of $3,500 were included in the $16,400 figure. Warren asked what savings in fixed costs might be expected if volume were to fall by 30,000 units and was told that the fixed cost per unit would rise to about $4,000, even though some fixed costs could be eliminated. Conversations with other managers revealed that the division's investment could be reduced by about $100 million if volume fell as stated.

Warren was visibly distressed by what she had heard. She was concerned with her division's interests, but realized that Mack had the right to operate in accordance with his best interests. She pondered the possibility of going to the company's executive vice president for advice.

**Required**
1. Determine the effect on Tucson of the introduction of the new Panther.
2. Determine the effect on the company of the introduction of the new Panther.

**11-52   *ROI at Burlington Industries, Inc.***   Burlington Industries, Inc. is a very large and widely diversified manufacturer of textiles and associated products. The organization consists of several largely autonomous divisions, the performances of which have been evaluated using, among other measures, ROI and dollar profit. Profit measures are before tax but after a special deduction called the Use of Capital Charge (UOCC). The minimum required ROI for a division is the weighted average of the minimum required ROIs for three different types or classes of assets. The classes are (1) accounts receivable less accounts payable, (2) inventories, and (3) fixed assets.

The central managers at Burlington have stated that the use of different required ROIs recognizes the different risks of the different types of investment. They feel that fixed assets, which are committed for relatively long periods and lack liquidity, should earn a higher ROI than assets committed for a shorter time. Receivables, which are turned into cash more quickly than are inventories, require a lower ROI. The minimum required ROIs for the three classes are 7% for receivables less payables, 14% for inventories, and 22% for fixed assets. These minimums are based on estimates of cost of capital and of relative investment in each class of assets for the company as a whole.

The following data relate to a hypothetical division of Burlington, stated in thousands of dollars.

| | |
|---|---:|
| Sales | $23,450 |
| Cost of sales | 16,418 |
| Selling and administrative expense | 1,678 |
| Other expenses, not including UOCC | 1,025 |
| Accounts receivable less accounts payable | 2,540 |
| Inventories | 3,136 |
| Net fixed assets | 3,560 |

**Required**
1. Prepare an income statement for the hypothetical division. Use the same basis as is used by Burlington.
2. Compute ROI for the division and the weighted-average minimum required ROI.
3. Comment on the method used by Burlington. Does it seem to encourage desirable behavior on the part of managers? Is the use of different minimum ROIs a good idea?

## Chapter Twelve

# CONTROL AND EVALUATION OF COST CENTERS

### LEARNING OBJECTIVES

*After reading this chapter, you should be able to*

- *Develop standard variable costs for a product.*
- *Calculate direct labor, variable overhead, and materials variances.*
- *Discuss the advantages and disadvantages of approaches to setting standards.*
- *Describe new approaches to cost control and management, as described by proponents of JIT and other continuous improvement approaches.*

---

**Merrill-Continental Company, Inc.**, *a medium-sized process-based manufacturer, was profitable, except for one geographical region. The two plants in the region were modern and well-equipped. The work force was motivated and productive. Yet the region yielded a 2 percent return on sales compared with 20 percent for other regions. The only clue to the region's lack of profitability was that competitors operating strictly within the region produced parts of the company's product line using the same materials from the same suppliers and selling to the same customers. Yet, some of these competitors were very profitable. This region provided the impetus for developing a standard cost system.*

*One common way to develop performance standards is to have industrial engineers determine the standards. The company decided against this route because its managers believed that its shop floor people could perform the task in such ways as to prevent distrust and suspicion. The company was right. Employees accepted and used the performance standards. Profits increased dramatically. The bottom-up approach resulted in standards that gave the managers clear, achievable performance targets. The company could then determine whether actual operations were meeting the performance standards. Managers also learned which plants in the region manufactured particular products at the lowest cost. All of this new information enabled managers to determine which products were dragging down profits. The managers then raised prices, looked for cost-reduction opportunities, or dropped the products.*

Source: Thomas A. Faulhaber, Fred A. Coad, and Thomas J. Little, "Building a Process Cost Management System from the Bottom Up," Management Accounting, May 1988, 58–62.

The previous chapter applied the concepts of responsibility accounting to profit and investment centers. Chapter 12 does likewise with cost centers. The concepts are most highly developed and implemented in manufacturing companies, though they also apply to service providers. We describe how managers set performance standards and what behavioral problems they encounter in setting and using standards. We examine the use of standard costs in planning and control, with major emphases on developing standards for variable costs and interpreting variances from those standards. Finally, proponents of continuous improvement, such as those using JIT, and some advocates of emerging schools of managerial thought dispute the benefits of standard costs, and we consider their arguments and proposals.

## PRODUCTIVITY AND COST CONTROL

All companies must control costs and increase productivity because competition is now global. We laid the groundwork for this material in earlier chapters. Chapters 3 and 4 described cost management, including the management of the activities that drive costs. Chapter 6 described how companies use budgets to control costs while other chapters, especially Chapters 8 and 9, discussed increasing productivity through capital investment.

Cost control is critically important for companies following a cost leadership strategy, such as those in mature industries where total demand for the product is not growing. Such companies cannot usually raise prices, nor can they expect significantly higher volumes. Thus, they cannot increase profits unless they can reduce costs. The importance of cost control to three companies is described in the accompanying Insight.

## STANDARD COSTS AND VARIANCES

A **standard cost** is the per-unit cost a company should incur to make a unit of product. Companies develop and use standard costs for materials, direct labor, and overhead.

A standard cost has two components: a standard price, or rate, and a standard quantity. Both standards relate to the input factor (materials, direct labor, variable overhead). The standard price, or rate, is the amount that the company should pay for one unit of the input factor: $2 per pound of materials, $8 per hour of direct labor, and $4 variable overhead per machine hour. The standard quantity is the amount of the input factor that should be used to make a unit of product: three pounds of materials and 0.25 direct labor hours (DLH). Thus, a unit of product that requires 0.25 direct labor hours and the standard labor rate is $8 per hour has a standard direct labor cost of $2 (0.25 hours × $8).

## STANDARD COSTS AND BUDGET ALLOWANCES

Chapter 6 developed the principles of flexible budgets and flexible budget allowances. Recall that a flexible budget allowance is the amount of cost that should be incurred given the actual level of activity. In Chapter 6, activity could have been output (number of units produced) or input (number of labor or machine

### Cost-Conscious Companies

**Solectron** is a large provider of a wide variety of pre-manufacturing, manufacturing, and post-manufacturing services for electronics companies. The company competes at least partly on cost. Solectron's SEC filings state that it uses "advanced manufacturing technology, such as computer-aided manufacturing and testing, with manufacturing techniques including just-in-time manufacturing, total quality management, statistical process control and continuous flow manufacturing." The company also "uses sophisticated computer systems for material resource planning, shop floor control work-in-process tracking, statistical process control and activity-based product costing."

**Quaker Oats**, in a recent annual report, stated that one of its operating strategies (out of six) was to "enhance productivity and efficiency." The company took pride in reducing the unit cost of its foods, including Gatorade®. Cost control initiatives were significant factors in Quaker's improved profit margins. The company allotted 27 percent of its capital spending to cost-reduction projects. Concerns about cost control are not limited to manufacturers. **First Union's** annual reports in recent years have pointed to how it has held expenses to slower increases than have its competitors in the banking industry.

*Sources: SEC filings, annual reports.*

hours). Differences between the actual cost and the flexible budget allowance are variances.

The standard cost for a period's production is the flexible budget allowance for the *actual output of the period*. Thus, with the standard quantity of labor of 0.25 hours per unit of product and the standard labor rate of $8 per hour, the standard cost for labor is $2 per unit of product. If the company makes 20,000 units, the flexible budget allowance for labor is $40,000 ($2 × 20,000). [Notice also that the total standard time to make 20,000 units is 5,000 hours (0.25 hours per unit × 20,000 units). Multiplying 5,000 total standard hours by the $8 standard rate gives the same $40,000 flexible budget allowance.] If actual direct labor cost was $42,200, the variance is $2,200 ($42,200 minus the flexible budget allowance of $40,000).

Renfrew, Inc., a manufacturer of cleaning products, has determined that workers producing at normal efficiency need one-half hour per case of 10 gallons. Also, at normal efficiency, each case requires 10 gallons of ingredients. The company expects to pay direct laborers $16 per hour. Ingredients cost $0.80 per gallon. Renfrew estimates its variable overhead rate as $6 per direct labor hour. Using these data, we compute the standard variable cost of a case as shown in Exhibit 12-1. Actual results for a recent month also appear. While simplified, this example illustrates all of the principles of standard variable costs.

Almost any product requires several materials, perhaps several kinds of direct labor paid at different rates, and variable overhead driven by several factors.

## Exhibit 12-1   Renfrew, Inc.—Standard Variable Costs and Actual Results

|  | Standard Quantity | Standard Price | Standard Cost |
|---|---|---|---|
| Materials | 10.00 | $0.80 | $8.00 |
| Direct labor | 0.50 | 16.00 | 8.00 |
| Variable overhead | 0.50 | 6.00 | 3.00 |
| Total standard variable cost |  |  | $19.00 |

Actual results:

| Production | 1,000 units |
|---|---|
| Materials purchased, 11,000 gallons at $0.78 | $8,580 |
| Materials used | 10,200 gallons |
| Direct labor, 480 hours at $16.20 | $7,776 |
| Variable overhead incurred | $3,100 |

Many companies use activity-based rates. We use a single type of each factor to focus on the general concepts. We illustrate standards under an ABC system later.

The per-unit standard cost for each input factor consists of a price component and a quantity component. Therefore, variances arise when the actual price or quantity differs from the standard price or quantity. We therefore separate the total variance into price and quantity variances. Many terms are used to describe such variances. Price variances are sometimes called *rate, budget,* or *spending* variances. Quantity variances are sometimes called *use* or *efficiency* variances. The particular term you use is not important as long as you know which kind of variance is being referred to. We begin the illustration of variance analysis with direct labor costs. With a single exception, the analysis is the same for the other cost factors.

## LABOR VARIANCES

Given that the company produced 1,000 cases, what should direct labor cost be? The total standard direct labor cost, or flexible budget allowance, for 1,000 cases is $8,000, computed as follows from the data in Exhibit 12-1.

$$\text{Actual production (units)} \times \text{Standard direct labor cost per unit} = \text{Total standard direct labor cost}$$

$$1,000 \times \$8.00 = \$8,000$$

We could also compute the flexible budget allowance for 1,000 cases by multiplying the 1,000 cases by the 0.50 standard hours, giving 500 standard hours allowed, and then multiplying by the $16.00 standard rate. The calculation to be used is largely a matter of convenience. *Standard hours allowed* is the term for the number of direct labor hours that should have been used to produce 1,000 units.

Exhibit 12-1 shows that direct laborers actually worked 480 hours and earned $16.20 per hour, for $7,776 total actual cost. Actual costs were $224 less than standard (standard cost of $8,000 – $7,776 actual cost). But why? And who is responsible for the difference?

In the performance reports we presented earlier (as in Chapter 10, for example), we made no distinction between variances in prices paid and quantities used. However, it is likely that some managers control either prices or quantities, but not both. Most supervisors of manufacturing cost centers are responsible only for the quantities of labor and materials used, not for wage rates or material prices. These managers have no control over wage rates and material prices. Therefore, we want to isolate each type of variance so that we can identify the manager responsible for it. Here, we want to separate the $224 total variance into two components: (1) the difference due to price, or labor rate, and (2) the difference due to the quantity of labor used.

We shall illustrate two common approaches to separating a total variance into its components. The first deals with *total* costs. We hold one of the factors constant (either price or quantity) and see what portion of the total variance is due to the effect of the other factor. We can represent actual total labor cost as follows:

$$
\begin{array}{ccc}
\text{\textit{Actual input quantity}} & \times & \text{\textit{Actual rate for input factor}} & = & \text{\textit{Actual cost of input factor}} \\
\text{480 hours} & \times & \$16.20 & = & \$7{,}776 \\
\end{array}
$$

To separate the variances, we need a flexible budget allowance based on the actual quantity of our *input* factor, labor. That budget allowance is $7,680—the number of hours actually worked times the standard wage rate.

$$
\begin{array}{ccc}
\text{\textit{Actual input quantity}} & \times & \boxed{\text{\textit{Standard rate for input factor}}} & = & \text{\textit{Budget allowance for actual quantity of input factor}} \\
\text{480 hours} & \times & \$16 & = & \$7{,}680 \\
\end{array}
$$

The only difference between the two calculations is the rate used for the input factor. The input factor (circled in the calculations) is the same for both, 480 hours. Hence, the difference between the actual cost incurred ($7,776) and the flexible budget allowance ($7,680) is due to the difference between the standard wage rate and the actual wage rate. That $96 difference ($7,776 – $7,680) is the **labor rate variance**, and it is unfavorable because the actual cost is greater than the flexible budget allowance for that quantity of input (480 hours).

The variance due to quantity is calculated in much the same way. We previously calculated the flexible budget allowance *based on the actual output of 1,000 units* as $8,000. A slightly different, but equivalent, calculation follows.

$$
\begin{array}{ccc}
\text{\textit{Standard input quantity}} & \times & \boxed{\text{\textit{Standard rate for input factor}}} & = & \text{\textit{Budget allowance for actual quantity of output}} \\
\begin{array}{c}\text{1,000 units} \times \\ \text{½ hour per unit} \\ = \text{500 hours}\end{array} & \times & \$16 & = & \$8{,}000 \\
\end{array}
$$

Compare this formula with the one immediately preceding it, where a budget allowance was computed for the actual quantity of the input factor, labor hours. Note that both calculations use the $16 standard rate for the input factor (boxed in the calculations). The only difference between the two calculations is the quantity of input, labor hours. Hence, the $320 difference between the two budget allowances ($8,000 – $7,680) is due to the difference in the quantity of labor used. This difference is the **labor efficiency variance** or *direct labor efficiency variance* and is favorable because laborers worked fewer than the 500 standard hours allowed for 1,000 units of output. We can explain the $224 total variance as follows:

| | |
|---|---|
| Labor rate variance | $ 96 unfavorable |
| Labor efficiency variance | 320 favorable |
| Total labor variance | $224 favorable |

Exhibit 12-2 diagrams these relationships. The left-hand figure is actual cost, the middle figure is a flexible budget allowance based on input, and the right-hand figure is the budget allowance based on output. The chart can be used to determine the variance for any adjacent numbers: if the number to the right is larger than the one to the left, the variance is favorable; the variance is unfavorable if the opposite is true.

### Labor Efficiency and Idle Time

The labor efficiency variance should indicate how efficient direct laborers are *when they make product*. Hence, the labor hours used to compute that variance should not include **idle time**, the time when laborers do not have productive work. Idle time occurs for a variety of reasons having nothing to do with worker efficiency. For example, lack of orders for the finished product, unavailability of materials, or bottlenecks in earlier stages of production could idle workers.

Including idle time in the computation could mask problems in production scheduling or some other function, or could mislabel as labor inefficiency the cost of conscious decision or company policy not to lay off laborers. Moreover,

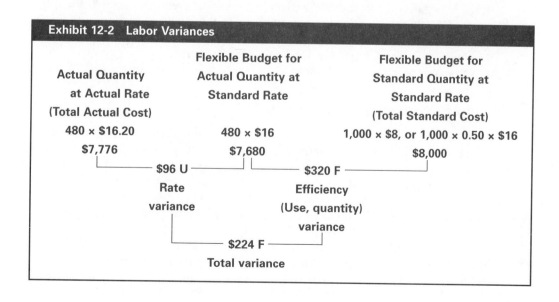

**Exhibit 12-2   Labor Variances**

| Actual Quantity at Actual Rate (Total Actual Cost) | Flexible Budget for Actual Quantity at Standard Rate | Flexible Budget for Standard Quantity at Standard Rate (Total Standard Cost) |
|---|---|---|
| 480 × $16.20 | 480 × $16 | 1,000 × $8, or 1,000 × 0.50 × $16 |
| $7,776 | $7,680 | $8,000 |

— $96 U —
Rate variance

— $320 F —
Efficiency (Use, quantity) variance

— $224 F —
Total variance

including idle time in the computation discourages goal congruence, because supervisors whose performance is evaluated in part by the efficiency variance might take actions that are not in the company's best interest. For example, the supervisor of laborers who would otherwise be idle might assign them to making unneeded product or components, so that the company will incur unnecessary costs for storage, financing, insurance, taxes, etc. until the units are needed. Such actions are obviously contrary to the efforts of manufacturing companies that are, as we have noted throughout this book, adopting JIT and other modern techniques that do not tolerate such production.

### Alternative Computation

We also can calculate variances by using the differences between the standard and actual figures for rate and quantity. We could compute the labor rate variance as follows:

$$\begin{matrix} Actual \\ hours \end{matrix} \times \left( \begin{matrix} Standard \\ rate \end{matrix} - \begin{matrix} Actual \\ rate \end{matrix} \right) = \begin{matrix} Labor\ rate \\ variance \end{matrix}$$

$$480 \times (\$16 - \$16.20) = -\$96$$

Direct laborers were paid $0.20 per hour more than standard (an unfavorable occurrence) and earned this amount over 480 hours.

Using the same approach to calculate the labor efficiency variance results in the following:

$$\begin{matrix} Standard \\ rate \end{matrix} \times \left( \begin{matrix} Standard \\ hours \end{matrix} - \begin{matrix} Actual \\ hours \end{matrix} \right) = \begin{matrix} Labor \\ efficiency \\ variance \end{matrix}$$

$$\$16 \times (500\ hours - 480\ hours) = \$320$$

Employees worked 20 fewer hours than the standard for producing 1,000 units (a favorable occurrence).

When the number inside the parentheses (using these alternative formulations) is negative, as in the rate variance, the variance is unfavorable. When the number inside the parentheses is positive, as in the efficiency variance, the variance is favorable. Do not memorize these relationships. Rather, think of favorable variances as those giving lower total cost and vice versa.

You may use either or both methods. They both give the same result.

### VARIABLE OVERHEAD VARIANCES

We used labor variances to illustrate the computations, but we could have used variable overhead. The computations are essentially the same.

As shown in Exhibit 12-1, variable overhead costs for the month are $3,100. What are the variable overhead variances? Total standard variable overhead cost for 1,000 units of output is $3,000 ($3 standard cost per case × 1,000 cases, or 500 standard direct labor hours at $6 standard rate per hour). So, the total variance is $100 unfavorable (actual cost of $3,100 compared with a standard of $3,000).

Exhibit 12-3 uses the diagrammatic approach to determining variable overhead variances. Note that actual direct labor hours are used to determine the middle term (the flexible budget based on the actual quantity of input), and that

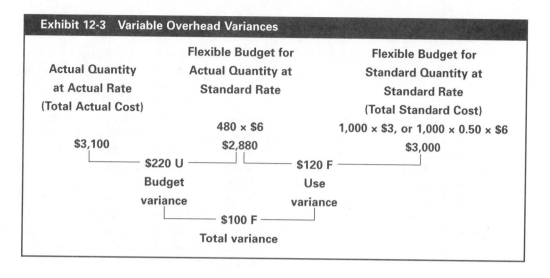

standard labor hours are used to determine the right-hand term. (The right-hand term is also given by $3 standard variable overhead per unit × 1,000 units.) Both variable overhead variances, the **variable overhead budget variance** (or **spending variance**) and the **variable overhead efficiency variance**, are calculated in the same way as labor variances. Exhibit 12-3 shows the calculations. If we based variable overhead on another activity, say machine hours, we would substitute actual and standard machine hours for actual and standard direct labor hours. We also could use more than one cost driver to assign variable overhead to a unit of product. An example appears later in the chapter.

Although the variable overhead budget variance is calculated in much the same way as the labor rate variance, it is not a rate variance in the sense of being the result of the prices paid for the input factor (overhead). For example, using more factory supplies than standard will show up in the variable overhead budget variance, not in the variable overhead efficiency variance. The variable overhead efficiency variance arises because of efficient or inefficient use of the driver—direct labor hours in this case. We cover this point in more detail shortly.

Both variable overhead variances can be computed using the alternative calculation method described earlier. The actual variable overhead rate is about $6.4583 ($3,100/480).

$$\text{Variable Overhead Budget Variance} = 480 \times (\$6 - \$6.4583) = \$220\ U$$

$$\text{Variable Overhead Efficiency Variance} = \$6 \times (500 - 480) = \$120\ F$$

## INTERPRETING VARIABLE OVERHEAD VARIANCES

No matter what drives variable overhead cost pools, variable overhead efficiency variances indicate efficient (or inefficient) use of the *drivers*, *not* of the factors making up variable overhead. Thus, for a pool of variable overhead that is related to machine time, the variable overhead efficiency variance will reflect the efficient or inefficient use of *machine hours*, not the use of power, lubricants, maintenance, and other elements of variable overhead driven by machine hours.

Of course, some elements of variable overhead might be related directly to the number of units produced, rather than to an input factor such as labor hours. For example, costs such as packaging materials (boxes, padding, lining) are directly related to units produced. Workers who pack the products should use standard quantities of these materials for each package even if they work more or less efficiently than standard (take more or less time to package the product). If variable overhead contains significant amounts of such cost elements, the conventional calculations of variable overhead efficiency and budget variances are not appropriate and are difficult for a manager to interpret.

It is important to identify the right cost drivers to achieve the best possible estimates of cost. If the number of components in a product drives a large portion of overhead cost, but the company uses direct labor hours as the driver, the company will have large, unexplainable budget variances because it is using the wrong driver. The reason is that, as we said earlier, use of overhead elements themselves is reflected in budget variances, while use of the driver is reflected in efficiency variances. If a company uses the wrong driver, it will compute the budget allowance based on input using the wrong driver. Such budget allowances will be well off the mark.

The choice of cost drivers for overhead is also important for behavioral reasons. Product designers, engineers, and other technical personnel whose responsibilities include cost reduction naturally will concentrate on high-cost factors. Recall that 80 percent or so of total product costs are designed into the products. The decisions made during the design phase reverberate throughout the life of the product. Thus, in a company using direct labor to assign variable overhead, these technical personnel will bend their efforts toward reducing labor time. Their efforts will be misplaced if direct labor does not drive significant amounts of overhead. The **Tektronix** example in Chapter 10 illustrates this point.

## MATERIALS VARIANCES

The **material use variance** is calculated the same as the labor and overhead efficiency variances. The **material price variance** differs from its counterparts in labor and variable overhead because materials, unlike labor, can be stored. (Of course, when we speak of materials, we also mean parts, components, and subassemblies.) Purchases made in one period are not necessarily used in that period, but the economic effect of paying more or less than standard prices for materials occurs at the time of purchase. So the material price variance is based on the quantity of materials purchased, not the quantity used. Moreover, the earlier that managers are aware of variances, the sooner they can take corrective action. Consequently, it makes sense to isolate the material price variance at the time of purchase rather than at the time the material is used.

Renfrew Inc. (see Exhibit 12-1) bought 11,000 gallons of ingredients for $8,580, an average price of $0.78 ($8,580/11,000). The standard price per gallons is $0.80 (also from Exhibit 12-1). In calculating the material price variance, the flexible budget allowance is based on what you expect to pay for the quantity purchased: $8,800 (11,000 gallons × $0.80 per gallon). The material price variance is diagramed in Exhibit 12-4.

We can also use the alternative formula as shown on the following page.

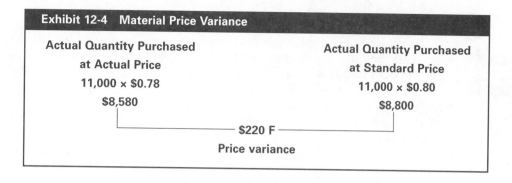

$$\begin{array}{ccccc}
\text{Material} & & \text{Actual} & & \\
\text{price} & = & \text{quantity} & \times & \left(\begin{array}{ccc}\text{Standard} & - & \text{Actual}\\ \text{price} & & \text{price}\end{array}\right)\\
\text{variance} & & \text{purchased} & & \\
\$220\ F & = & 11{,}000 & \times & (\$0.80\ -\ \$0.78)
\end{array}$$

The material use variance is calculated in the same way as the direct labor and variable overhead efficiency variances. Renfrew used 10,200 gallons to make 1,000 cases. The standard quantity is 10 gallons (see Exhibit 12-1), so the total standard quantity for 1,000 cases is 10,000 gallons. The standard cost for 1,000 cases is \$8,000 (10,000 gallons at \$0.80 per gallon, or 1,000 cases multiplied by the \$8 standard materials cost per case, as shown in Exhibit 12-1). The material use variance is diagramed in Exhibit 12-5.

Again, we can calculate the material use variance using the differences.

$$\begin{array}{ccccc}
\text{Material use} & = & \text{Standard} & \times & \left(\begin{array}{ccc}\text{Standard quantity} & - & \text{Actual}\\ \text{for actual output} & & \text{quantity}\end{array}\right)\\
\text{variance} & & \text{price} & & \\
\$160\ U & = & \$0.80 & \times & (10{,}000\ -\ 10{,}200)
\end{array}$$

Materials variances differ from the others because we have two actual quantities, one for materials purchased, the other for materials used. This is the only difference between materials variances and the other types of variances.

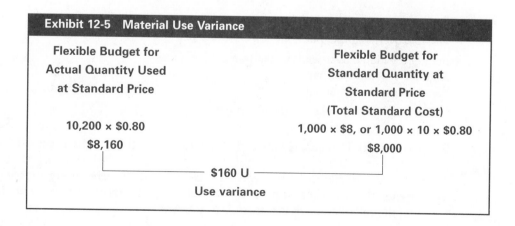

## STANDARDS IN MULTIPRODUCT COMPANIES

So far we have dealt with a company making a single product, but multiproduct companies also use standard costs. (As Chapters 14 and 15 will show, many multiproduct companies have no other choice than to use standard costs.) No conceptual problems are introduced simply because a company makes more than one product. But practical questions arise about the extent to which detailed information should be produced and the cost of obtaining the additional information.

Seldom does a multiproduct company encounter problems in developing standard costs. But isolating variances for each product is a different matter if products use the same facilities and the same workers, and the company cannot determine the actual use of materials, labor, and variable overhead drivers (such as machine time, setups, or production orders) for each product. The costs of materials, labor, and overhead are traceable to *production as a whole*. But under such circumstances it might be very costly (even impossible) to keep track of materials, direct labor time, and overhead drivers for each product.

Despite the difficulties of obtaining information about the actual costs of individual products, managers are interested in knowing such costs for planning and decision making. As a practical matter, a company might *periodically* track materials and labor by product as a check on standards. In addition, managers who suspect poor standards might investigate if efficiency variances fluctuate significantly as product mix changes. The overriding issue is whether the costs of keeping track of materials, direct labor, and overhead drivers by product is less than the benefits of having that information.

## STANDARD COSTS AND ACTIVITY-BASED COSTING

TGH Company has two principal variable overhead cost pools. One pool is driven by machine time and includes such costs as power, supplies, abrasive materials, and maintenance. The other pool is driven by the number of machine setups. These costs include wages of setup workers, supplies used in changeovers, and materials destroyed in testing machine settings and calibrations. The variable component of overhead related to machine hours is $6.00 per hour, and the variable component related to setups is $140 per setup. Data and calculations for a 1,000 unit batch of one of TGH's products are as follows:

| | | |
|---|---:|---:|
| Standard machine hours | | 1,500 |
| Variable overhead rate per hour | | $    6 |
| Standard variable overhead related to machine hours | | $ 9,000 |
| Number of setups per batch | 20 | |
| Variable overhead rate per setup | $140 | 2,800 |
| Total standard variable overhead per batch | | $11,800 |

Suppose that TGH made 10,000 units (10 batches) of this product using 14,000 machine hours. Actual machine-hour driven variable overhead was $85,000; setup-driven variable overhead was $27,500. Because of scheduling problems, TGH required 210 setups to achieve the output. A diagrammatic presentation showing the calculations of variances is as follows:

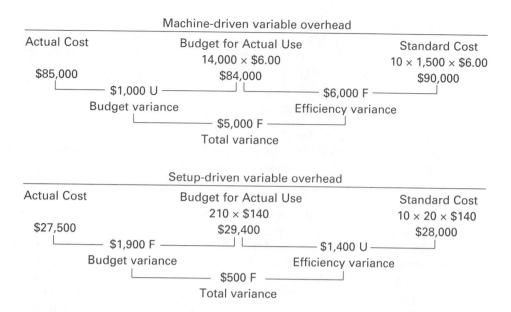

Of course, the company would also have materials and labor variances that it would calculate in the usual way.

## VARIANCES AND PERFORMANCE EVALUATION

Isolating price and quantity variances is the first step toward providing information for performance evaluation, but it does not identify causes of variances. Knowing that laborers worked more or fewer hours than standard does not explain *why* they did so. Interpreting variances is not a simple, mechanical process. Variances signal nonstandard performance only if they are based on up-to-date standards reflecting current production methods and current prices of input factors. A company that increases labor time to increase product quality, but does not adjust its standards, will have misleading unfavorable labor efficiency variances. These variances are not the fault of the managers responsible for using labor; the fault lies with the standard. Most companies continually seek to improve production methods. Developing new standards every time a change occurs is costly, and frequent revisions of standards might cause the standards to lose their meaning. Accordingly, the decision to revise standards must compare the cost of making the revision with the expected benefits in the form of better control and performance evaluation, and managers must interpret variances in the light of changes in manufacturing conditions not incorporated in standards. This point underlies the arguments of some proponents of continuous improvement that using standards stifles improvement because people will simply try to meet the standards, not improve continuously.

Moreover, variances are often interrelated, with one variance causing others. (We confronted a similar situation in Chapter 10, where the use of a particular cost-allocation scheme could cause one manager's actions to affect the reported performance of another.) For example, a purchasing manager could buy lower-quality materials at a favorable price. If the materials are hard to work with, labor time increases. Unfavorable labor and perhaps variable overhead efficiency variances (for the variable overhead that is driven by direct labor) in processing departments have the same cause as the favorable material price variance—the purchase of lower-quality materials. Thus, knowing that there was a variance for some element of cost (materials, labor, or overhead) is not the same as knowing why the variance occurred or which manager was responsible for it.

## INVESTIGATING VARIANCES

Once they have calculated variances, managers must decide whether to investigate them. As a general rule, managers should investigate a variance if they expect to be able to take corrective action that will reduce costs by an amount greater than the cost of the investigation. Because of the difficulty of estimating the relevant costs, many companies use rules of thumb, or rules derived from statistical analyses, to decide whether to investigate.

Because they want to investigate only significant variances, managers use two general criteria: absolute size of the variance and its percentage of standard cost. A variance of $5 is almost certainly not worth investigating, whereas a variance of $100 might be. If actual cost is $500 and standard cost is $400, the $100 variance is 25 percent of standard. This large variance percentage might well be worth investigating, whereas a $100 variance from a standard cost of $85,000 is almost certainly not. Thus, absolute size of a variance is probably less important than its percentage of standard cost.

The cost of investigating variances is difficult to determine. Managers with a fixed amount of time to spend on various tasks are wise to concentrate on variances that are likely to be correctable and whose correction may be expected to yield large savings. (There is a significant opportunity cost of managerial time.)

Many companies use **control charts** to decide when a particular variance should be investigated. These charts show past cost behavior patterns so that efforts will not be wasted investigating costs that normally show wide fluctuations. A control chart is shown in Exhibit 12-6.

The dots on the chart represent actual costs and outputs. The *dotted* lines represent the limits within which managers have decided not to investigate variances. Managers could set the lines closer to or farther away from total standard cost. The closer the limits, the more variances will be investigated, and vice versa.

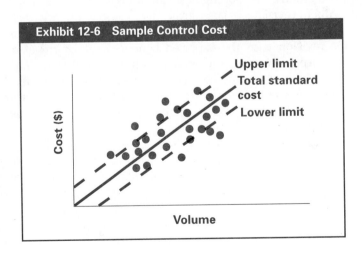

Exhibit 12-6   Sample Control Cost

The wide scattering of costs in a chart suggests high variances. A manager who believes that the production process is under adequate control and that the variances are unavoidable will set wide limits. A manager who thinks that most variances are caused by correctable factors will set narrow limits. Statistics courses cover sophisticated ways of developing control charts.

What should *not* be important in deciding whether to investigate a variance is whether the variance is favorable or unfavorable. As we pointed out in the previous section, variances are not necessarily independent; a favorable variance in one area of responsibility might have unfavorable effects on another area. Moreover, favorable variances can be caused by actions that could harm the company in the long run. For example, favorable variances in material prices or labor efficiency could stem from lessened concern for the quality of the finished products. When customers see reduced quality, the reputation and subsequent sales of the company will be hurt. Short-run profits might increase because of lower costs (favorable variances), but long-run profits will suffer.

Because, as we suggested early in the chapter, standards can be useful for planning, one of the most important reasons for investigating variances is to detect bad standards. Variances can occur because of out-of-date standards. Variances also can result if standards are set at levels that are either too tight or too loose. If standards are used for planning and decision making, they must reflect currently attainable performance.

## SETTING STANDARDS—BEHAVIORAL PROBLEMS

Companies use a variety of approaches to setting standards, and the approach used can influence how people respond to them.

### Engineering Methods

Some companies develop standard quantities for materials and labor by carefully examining production methods and determining how much of an input factor is necessary to obtain a finished unit. Time-and-motion study, a method developed in the early 20th century, is often used to set labor standards. Industrial engineers analyze the various movements necessary to perform each task. For example, a worker might have to reach into a bin, pick up a part, place it on the workbench, drill two holes in specified places, then place the part into another bin. Engineers time each movement. The total time required to perform the entire task becomes the standard time allowed. Similarly, industrial engineers study the characteristics of the product to determine how much material is required. Such studies also determine the materials wasted through cutting and trimming. One caution in applying engineering methods is that workers under observation might work much slower than usual, leading the company to set standards too low (standard costs too high).

Engineering methods also are used to set standards for some overhead items, such as maintenance. Industrial engineers develop a desirable maintenance program and estimate the costs of each component. A standard is then established that allows for specified maintenance expense per machine hour used, with allowance for other maintenance that occurs because parts break or wear out.

Although engineers can analyze some overhead items, they cannot usually analyze overhead by starting with a unit of product. Unlike materials and labor, most overhead costs are not directly related to single units of product. Rather, large amounts of overhead are related to large quantities of product, labor hours, machine hours or other cost drivers. Therefore, standards for elements of variable overhead are more often developed using the methods illustrated in Chapter 3: high-low, scatter diagram, and regression analysis.

## Managerial Estimates

Some companies rely on the judgment of managers closest to a task to determine quantities of input needed to produce a unit of product. Such managers understand current production conditions and specifications. This approach to setting standards is advantageous because, as we noted in Chapter 6, managers who participate in setting standards and budgets are more likely to commit to meeting them. There is, however, some reluctance to allow managers to set standards without guidance, because some higher-level managers believe—rightly or wrongly—that standards set in this way will include unnecessary slack (that is, standards will be too loose). Hence, standards initially determined by managerial estimates usually are carefully reviewed at higher levels of management.

Even companies that can carefully engineer standards rely on comments from managers because manufacturing managers understand that some factors are difficult to capture in engineering analyses. More important, as early as Chapter 6 we noted that managers who participate in setting goals (such as standards) are much more likely to commit themselves to achieving them.

The evidence is persuasive, but not conclusive, that performance also improves when *workers* participate in setting standards. The general idea of increasing employee involvement in managerial decisions extends to setting standards.

Product designers and managers developing standards should understand that cost reduction is not the only objective. Designing products that will be of high quality and relatively easy to manufacture are important as well. These facets of manufacturing have become even more important for U.S. companies that want to do business in the European Community. Companies that want to sell in the European Community must demonstrate that their products meet the standards established by the International Standards Organization (ISO) of Geneva. For example, ISO 9000 requires companies to document each step their workers perform that affects the quality of the product. Companies applying for ISO certification must meet stringent requirements in 20 functional areas, ranging from design to employee training. ISO dispatches independent auditors to verify that companies follow required procedures.

## Benchmarking and Best Practices

**Benchmarking** is a relatively recent development that companies use to determine whether their operations and costs compare favorably to those of world-class companies. Some use the term **best practices** as a synonym. The concept is not limited to costs of manufactured products. **L.L. Bean**, the mail-order retailer, has such an excellent order-filling system that companies from all over have gone to its headquarters to study its operations. Companies can also use published databases to make such comparisons.

Companies evaluating their operations can find all kinds of comparisons. For instance, one company investigating its accounting function found that it cost a world-class company $4.60 to prepare an invoice and $7.30 to process a payroll check.[1] In reengineering its accounts payable function, **ITT Automotive** used the **Hackett Group** database to evaluate the efficiency of various functions such as the number of invoices processed per person per year.[2]

The accompanying Insight describes an organization that assists companies in identifying and implementing best practices.

### What Standard—Ideal, Attainable, or Historical?

Perhaps the most critical issue of behavioral responses to standards is the level of performance of the standard. Should the standard be based on what people can do under the best possible conditions? Should it include allowances for waste, fatigue, and bottlenecks—that is, currently attainable performance? Should it be based on past performance, an historical measure?

**Ideal standards** can be attained only under perfect conditions. They assume that laborers continuously work at the peak of their abilities, that materials always arrive at work stations on time, that machines never break down, that maintenance on machinery never stops production, and that no one makes mistakes. In short, an ideal standard is not likely to be achieved under anything like normal working conditions. Using an ideal standard is sure to result in unfavorable variances.

Some argue that ideal standards are best because the resulting unfavorable variances alert managers to deviations from the ideal and motivate workers to do the best possible job. Whether ideal standards really do assist managers in these ways is questionable. Some evidence from the behavioral sciences suggests that

## SIGHT

### Benchmarking Resource

The **American Productivity & Quality Center** (APQC) is a not-for-profit education and research organization that helps companies improve processes and increase performance. APQC was founded in 1977 and works with organizations in manufacturing, service, health care, labor, government, and academia.

As APQC puts it, "Hundreds of leading enterprises rely on us for access to best practices, research services, benchmarking studies, networking, education programs, publications, events and more—enabling companies to break out of conventional thinking and excel with best practices."

APQC co-sponsored the White House Conference on Productivity that led to the creation of the Malcolm Baldrige National Quality Award.

*Source: APQC website.*

---

1  *Steve Coburn, Hugh Grove, and Cynthia Fukami, "Benchmarking with ABCM,"* Management Accounting, *January 1995, 58.*

2  *Richard J. Palmer, "Reengineering Payables at ITT Automotive,"* Management Accounting, *July 1994, 39.*

motivation is *reduced* rather than increased by the use of ideal standards. Being unattainable goals, ideal standards can foster discouragement, lack of commitment to the goal, and distrust of higher levels of management. Frustrated managers and workers might even ignore standards they know to be unattainable. However, we shall explain later in this chapter why some companies that focus on continuous improvement might set goals that appear to be ideal standards, but that such goals presume improvement in processes, not just worker efficiency. Our objections to ideal standards are based on applying them to existing processes and working conditions.

**Currently attainable standards** represent normal efficiency under current, normal working conditions. Such standards allow for losses of efficiency from typical recurring problems. But currently attainable standards are not lax. Performance requirements are high, but are attainable if everything goes reasonably well.

Research in the behavioral sciences indicates that managers and workers respond well to standards as goals when they have participated in setting the standards and when the standards are attainable. Such standards also can be useful for planning, whereas ideal standards cannot. Additionally, currently attainable standard costs are of more value than ideal standard costs for decision-making purposes. Acceptance of special orders, price reductions or increases, promotional campaigns, and other special decisions must be based on expected variable costs, not those that could be obtained only under ideal conditions.

**Historical standards** are based on experience. Using historical performance as a standard has serious drawbacks. Such standards perpetuate inefficiencies and ignore changes in product design and work methods that affect labor and materials requirements. Historical achievements have no particular significance except as they may aid in predicting the future. (Compare this reservation with those expressed earlier—particularly in Chapters 5, 6, 7, and 11—about the usefulness of historical information for predicting the future.) The accompanying Insight describes how one company has implemented ideal standards, while also taking steps to alleviate potential behavioral problems.

## STANDARD COSTS, PRODUCT LIFE CYCLE, AND STRATEGY

Some managerial tools work well in certain circumstances, poorly in others. Two factors affecting how well standard costs are likely to work are the life-cycle stage of the product and the strategy the company is following. Most products begin their lives with rapid sales growth, then mature into a stable phase, and finally decline. Some companies strive to be cost leaders, others try to differentiate their products through style, function, quality, customer service, or other factors.

Standard costs and variance analysis work best for mature, stable products (such as automobiles) and for undifferentiated commodities (such as paper and building products) where companies follow a cost leadership strategy. In the mature stage of product life, when price competition is important, cost control is a principal competitive weapon. Low costs allow a company to maintain its margins and to weather poor periods.

Products in growth stages often are highly differentiated and use rapidly changing technology. They compete more on style or function than on price. The critical success factors are increasing volume and achieving high market share. Margins tend to be high, so that being a low-cost producer contributes less to

**IN** *SIGHT*

**Six-Sigma at AlliedSignal**

**AlliedSignal** is a large, diversified manufacturer that has adopted Six-Sigma principles and goals. Six Sigma means 3.4 defective parts per million—a benchmark of quality. AlliedSignal has broadened Six Sigma to include all of its productivity efforts, both manufacturing and nonmanufacturing. The company credits the initiative with changing "people's mindset about their daily work. By providing them with unique training and new tools to effect change, it's expanded their thinking about our capacity for improvement."

The company realizes that

"Since participation by all our people is essential if we are to attain our ambitious objectives, the key to achieving our goals is an educated, satisfied and motivated work force. AlliedSignal employees average 40 hours of training per year in areas that will help the company prosper and help them develop their careers. And our senior leaders are required to commit 40 hours a year to teaching in our employee training programs.  To help alleviate the stresses of responsibility-rich and time-poor employees who are burdened by competing demands of their lives at work and at home, we provide, wherever practical, one-stop referral services, banking machines, child-care facilities, fitness centers and other on-site amenities. . . . Our ability to attract the best employees was enhanced by our inclusion in *Fortune's* list of "The 100 Best Companies To Work For" and in *USA Today's* list of the best employee savings plans."

*Source: Annual report.*

overall profitability than does volume. However, as previous Insights show, companies in high-tech industries do face severe pricing pressures for some products, yet must redesign their products so frequently that standards make little sense.

Standard costs do have a place with growing products, or differentiated products, so managers should not ignore costs in their quest for volume and high market share. The 1997 annual report of **Merck**, the giant maker of prescription drugs that are patented and therefore highly differentiated, lists as one of its three operating priorities, "preserve the profitability of our core pharmaceutical business through continuous improvements in productivity and organizational effectiveness."

## REPORTING VARIANCES

Managers of cost centers typically receive reports like the one in Exhibit 12-7. The "actual" costs reported to the manager on the sample report have been adjusted to eliminate price variances. That is, the amounts in the Actual column for materials, labor, and supplies are actual quantities multiplied by standard prices. This approach is used when the manager controls only the quantities of each factor used.

### Exhibit 12-7    Cost Center Report

```
REPORT NO. D476G88   PRODUCTION COST CENTER REPORT   FOUNDRY #60000
SITE: BARNESVILLE        PERIOD ENDING 10/31/20X3
```

| acct code | VARIABLE COSTS | CURRENT MONTH ACTUAL | CURRENT MONTH VARIANCE | YEAR TO DATE ACTUAL | YEAR TO DATE VARIANCE |
|---|---|---|---|---|---|
| 62001 | MATERIALS | 86,253 | 2,550 | 756,998 | 2,876 |
| 62101 | DIRECT LABOR | 21,232 | 2,677 | 232,678 | 10,209 |
| 62501 | UTILITIES | 9,875 | 1,239 | 102,334 | 8,928 |
| 62507 | SUPPLIES | 2,262 | 98 | 17,829 | 267 |
| 62550 | PACKAGING | 5,267 | (566) | 49,527 | (1,728) |
| | TOTAL VARIABLE | 124,889 | 5,998 | 1,159,366 | 20,552 |
| | CONTROLLABLE FIXED | | | | |
| 65101 | INDIRECT LABOR | 28,767 | (118) | 276,942 | (924) |
| 65220 | MAINTENANCE | 9,126 | 83 | 88,742 | 119 |
| 65322 | SUPERVISION | 18,298 | 222 | 167,153 | 348 |
| 65880 | TOOLS | 965 | (43) | 11,286 | (654) |
| | TOTAL CONTROLLABLE | 57,156 | 144 | 544,123 | (1,111) |
| | OTHER FIXED | | | | |
| 68102 | MAIN OFFICE—ALLOCATED | 2,862 | 0 | 28,620 | 0 |
| 68150 | PAYROLL OFFICE—ALLOCATED | 678 | 0 | 6,780 | 0 |
| 68160 | DEPRECIATION | 9,754 | 18 | 101,865 | 129 |
| | TOTAL OTHER FIXED | 13,294 | 18 | 137,265 | 129 |
| | TOTAL COSTS | 195,339 | 6,160 | 1,840,754 | 19,570 |

```
COMMENTS:
FAULTY MATERIALS CAUSED WASTE AND LABOR INEFFICIENCY
```

Because calculating a variance does not explain its cause, performance reports usually contain a section for comments and explanations of variances. The department manager can then concentrate on those variances that need explanation and, if the cause of the variance is in that department, comment on the prospects for improvement.

The sample performance report clearly labels some costs as noncontrollable and shows them separately. Chapter 10 pointed out reasons for doing this. In general, variable costs are controllable over short periods, whereas many fixed costs are not. Thus, depreciation on equipment in the machining department is direct to the department, but not controllable in the short run. Allocated costs are not controllable by the department to which they are allocated.

## CONTROL OF FIXED COSTS

From earlier discussions we know that the total cost per unit of product changes with a change in production because there is a fixed component in the total cost.

As we will discuss in Chapters 13 and 14, companies use per-unit fixed costs, including standard fixed costs, for product costing purposes. But for *control* purposes, the notion of a standard fixed cost *per unit* has little meaning. The total cost incurred for each element of fixed overhead is, however, relevant for planning and control.

Fixed overhead includes many components, such as depreciation, property taxes, supervisory and managerial salaries, and the fixed components of mixed costs, such as maintenance and power. Each item is budgeted separately for the department that controls it. There are two fixed cost variances. For cost control, only the budget variance is relevant. The other variance is described in Chapter 14.

## BUDGET VARIANCE

The **fixed overhead budget variance** is simply the difference between actual and budgeted fixed overhead. Companies compute the variance for each element of cost. Budget variances occur for many reasons. Since the company prepared the budget, there may have been changes in the prices for resources (a rise in salaries, an increase in property taxes); some discretionary costs, such as employee training or travel, might have increased or decreased by managerial action; and quantities of resources used might have been greater or less than budgeted, as when more or fewer industrial engineers were hired than were budgeted.

The major considerations in analyzing fixed cost budget variances are behavioral. Managers who are worried about exceeding their budgets might postpone discretionary costs (such as employee training). On the other hand, as we saw in Chapter 6, managers might incur unnecessary costs if they fear that being below budget this period will lead to a budget cut for the next period.

Managers can manipulate some discretionary costs to achieve low total budget variances (total fixed costs incurred less total fixed costs budgeted), so focusing only on totals can obscure critical problems. Managers who scrimp on employee training or maintenance are improving short-run performance to the detriment of long-run performance. This type of undesirable action might escape notice if managers look only at totals.

As you know from Chapter 6, managers hold different philosophies about budgeting fixed costs. Some advocate tight budgets, some loose budgets, and some prefer budgets based on currently attainable performance levels. Our preference is for the use of currently attainable budgets, with the persons whose budgets are being set participating in the determination of what is currently attainable. Likewise, the methods used in setting standard variable costs—historical analysis, engineering methods, and managerial judgment—can also be applied to the budgeting of fixed costs.

## FIXED COSTS ON PERFORMANCE REPORTS

Notice that the cost center performance report shown in Exhibit 12-7 distinguishes between controllable variable costs and controllable fixed costs. Whereas materials and direct labor are usually variable, the other controllable items could be variable, fixed, or mixed.

For planning, the manager wants to know whether a variance is likely to recur. It might be easier to plan for future variances if the fixed and variable controllable costs are separated. If a fixed cost is running $1,000 per month more or less than budgeted, and this variance is expected to continue, the manager can count on the variance being $1,000 per month. A direct labor efficiency variance of 10 percent of standard cost will be a different dollar amount in each month, depending on production. Thus, planning for future operations requires different analyses for the two kinds of costs—fixed and variable.

## A PROBLEM AREA—SEPARATING FIXED AND VARIABLE COSTS

Some companies cannot determine separate budget variances for variable overhead and fixed overhead because they cannot determine how much of the *actual* cost incurred is fixed and how much is variable. For example, a cost such as electricity usually has both a fixed and a variable component. But it might not be possible to determine how much of the actual cost relates to the fixed component and how much to the variable component.

Suppose that electricity is budgeted using the following formula: Total cost = $2,450 + ($0.80 × machine hours). The fixed portion is for lighting; the variable portion is for machinery that runs only during production. Assume that the standard and actual price per kilowatt-hour is $0.03. Any difference between actual electricity cost and the flexible budget amount must be caused by the quantity of electricity used.

Suppose that a product requires two standard machine hours, production was 4,000 units, 8,100 machine hours were used (100 hours over standard), and actual electricity cost was $9,210. The total standard hours allowed for production of 4,000 units are 8,000 (4,000 × 2). The total budgeted cost for electricity is $8,850 [$2,450 + ($0.80 × 8,000 standard machine hours)]. Because we cannot, in the absence of separate meters, analyze the actual cost into its fixed and variable components, we cannot calculate separately the budget variances for the fixed and variable elements. In such cases, companies calculate a single budget variance for the mixed cost as a whole. Using the data in our example, the budget variance is as follows:

$$\textit{Total budget variance} \;=\; \textit{Actual cost} \;-\; \textit{Flexible budget based on input}$$
$$=\; \$9,210 - [\$2,450 + (\$0.80 \times 8,100)]$$
$$=\; \$9,210 - \$8,930$$
$$=\; \$280 \textit{ unfavorable total budget variance}$$

The variance is unfavorable because actual cost exceeds the budget allowance. We also know that actual machine hours were 100 over standard, so we know there is an $80 unfavorable variable overhead efficiency variance (100 × $0.80).

Why might a company not isolate the fixed and variable components of the actual cost? Why, for example, would the company in the preceding example not install meters on its machines to determine how much electricity is related to machines and how much to lighting the factory? As stated earlier, especially in Chapter 10, the answer is usually that the cost to obtain the additional information exceeds the probable benefits. In this instance, the cost to install and maintain meters might exceed the savings that could be achieved through better control. Recall that a fundamental principle of managerial accounting is that obtaining additional information is desirable only if the benefits exceed the costs.

CHAPTER 10

## STANDARD COSTS, VARIANCES, AND CONTINUOUS IMPROVEMENT

Historically, conventional manufacturers paid great attention to labor variances because direct labor was a significant proportion of total manufacturing cost and also drove much overhead cost. Direct labor is less important in many of today's manufacturers, averaging 10 to 20 percent of total manufacturing cost. But direct labor can be as little as 3 to 5 percent of total cost in some operations. Nor does direct labor drive as much overhead cost as it once did. Accordingly, direct labor should receive correspondingly less attention.

As we noted earlier, including idle time in labor efficiency variances can encourage overproduction. Moreover, many managers believe that reporting labor efficiency variances, even excluding idle time, detracts from the main objective of rapid, smooth throughput of high-quality products. Managers committed to continuous improvement believe that the very idea of standards and standard costs conflicts with their philosophy. They argue that standards stifle improvement because people will strive to *meet*, but not beat, standards, which violates the principle of continuous improvement. They also argue that variances relate to cost centers, which typically are small units, when managers and workers should be concerned with the performance of the entire operation.

Advanced manufacturers emphasize developing worker skills and teamwork. Because many foreign countries have lower wage rates than the United States, U.S. companies will have to take measures to compete worldwide. **Levi Strauss**, maker of Levi's, now uses teams to produce an entire garment, replacing an assembly line where each worker did only a small part of the work. The company cut cycle time from six days to seven hours, so it can switch products quickly and respond better to customer needs. Defects also dropped when the workers took over production of the entire garment.[3]

Despite these reservations, some JIT companies and others seeking continuous improvement use standards (and analyze variances) much as do companies using conventional operations. Others use standards, but continually tighten them to encourage improvement. JIT companies that do *not* use standards compare current period actual costs with prior period actual costs (or an average of actual costs for the past few periods) to gauge their improvement. Such comparisons are similar to variance calculations, with the prior period costs acting as the "standard."

### KAIZEN COSTING AND TARGET COSTS

Japanese manufacturers have long used a technique called **kaizen**, or **kaizen costing**. Kaizen stresses continuous improvement, rather than simply meeting standards. Under kaizen, performance standards are continually raised, so the objective is to meet targeted *reductions*.

Previous chapters have discussed the importance of the product design stage of developing a product, where managers make decisions that commit perhaps 80 percent of total costs to make the product over its life. Kaizen comes in when products are being made and sold. It aims at achieving systematic, steady reductions through continuous improvement. Kaizen companies establish annual and

---

3 *"The Global Economy: Who Gets Hurt?"* Business Week, *August 10, 1992, 48.*

monthly target cost-reduction rates, which they then translate into amounts for individual cost elements and products. For instance, suppose a company has established a 5 percent target reduction rate beginning from a standard labor cost of $40 per unit. The first target is $38, 5 percent less than $40, or a reduction of $2; the next is $36.10, 5 percent less than $38, and so on. Companies adjust target rates and amounts for changes in manufacturing conditions such as design changes and changes in input factor costs (e.g., increase in labor rates).

We introduced target costs in Chapter 2 as costs determined by working from the market price of a product to the cost that will allow the company to earn a target profit. **Toyota**, among many other companies, uses kaizen and target costing principles in dealing with its suppliers. Toyota goes so far as to send its own engineers into potential suppliers' factories to help them increase quality and reduce costs even before they have become suppliers.[4]

Target costing is price-driven; market prices determine cost instead of vice versa. Companies reduce costs through systematic analyses of the features and functions deemed most important to customers. Much of target costing necessarily takes place during product design. Cross-functional teams usually do the work, and sometimes include customers and suppliers. Target costing also applies throughout the product life cycle. The following Insight describes target costing and continuous improvement.

## IN SIGHT

### Target Costing and Continuous Improvement

The **Consortium for Advanced Manufacturing—International** (CAM-I), **The University of Akron**, through **The Institute for Global Business**, and the **American Institute of Certified Public Accountants** (AICPA) are cooperating in an international study to identify and understand best practices in target costing. Their definition of target costing is "a strategic profit planning and cost management system that incorporates a strict focus on customer wants, needs and values, and translates them into delivered products and services."

CAM-I believes that "While this highly disciplined management system has been in practice in Japan for over fifteen years, companies in North America, Europe and other regions of the world are just beginning to understand and embrace this management process."

The objectives of the study include identifying the benefits and obstacles in implementing target costing, finding the best practices of target costing, determining resource requirements and key success factors. CAM-I anticipates developing a large database and network of experts that will enable interested companies to avoid re-inventing the wheel.

*Source: CAM-I website.*

4 Alex Taylor III, "How Toyota Defies Gravity," Fortune, December 8, 1997, 100–108.

One tool of target costing is **value engineering**, which refers to design and redesign that focuses on customer value. Cross-functional teams perform value engineering. Value engineering is redesigning products so that they will cost less, while delivering quality and functionality. Value engineering is an optimizing technique where people seek exactly what features the product needs, how to make it, what materials to use, and so on. One objective of value engineering is to make sure that products are not overdeveloped, with features that do not add value commensurate with their cost. Companies such as **Cypress Semiconductor** face annual price reductions ranging from 4.6 percent for data communications chips to 9.4 percent for programmable logic devices to 14.9 percent for static ram chips. In response, the company redesigns its chips so frequently (perhaps several times in one year) that standard costs make little sense. Instead, the company strives to continually reduce costs through better manufacturing processes.

## NONFINANCIAL MEASURES

Managers of JIT operations use many nonfinancial measures to evaluate performance. Measures used instead of, or along with, standard costs include the following:

1.  *Supplies of inventories* You already know that companies try to keep inventories low because they are costly to carry. Such measures as turnover and days' supply of inventory help managers judge how efficiently they are operating. Inventory supply is often expressed as turnover, which is the days' supply divided into 360 (or 365). Thus, a 10-day supply is the same as a turnover of 36 times. A company that can manufacture its products with only a 4-day supply of materials and components is doing better than one that requires a 12-day supply to keep its production lines running.

2.  *Cycle time* This is the total time a company takes from receiving a customer's order through making the product and shipping it to the customer. Time spent making the product is value-adding time, while the rest of the cycle time is non-value-adding. The closer cycle time is to manufacturing time, the greater is the value-adding time. Additionally, the shorter the cycle time, the higher customer satisfaction.

3.  *Setup time* This is the time it takes to change over from making one product to making another. It is a non-value-adding activity.

4.  *Percentage of deliveries to customers made on time* This indicates how well the company is meeting its commitments to customers.

5.  *Quality measures* We can assess and measure quality in many ways. Some common ways are the percentage of defective units, number of warranty claims or customer complaints, and number of units reworked.

6.  *Throughput measures* These indicate how much work a cell, a department, or an entire factory is doing. Measures of throughput include number of units finished, number of units finished divided by processing time available, and value-adding time divided by total time. These measures, as well as others, are consistent with the objectives of JIT manufacturing. They also can be used by conventional manufacturers. The accompanying Insight describes one company's use of such measures as well as data regarding the extent of use of some measures.

*SIGHT*

### Time of Ownership

**Quantum,** the disk drive supplier, uses time of ownership (TOO) to measure its efficiency. Quantum has had a close partnership with **Matsushita Kotobuke Electronics** (MKE) for many years. MKE manufactures products that Quantum designs, develops, markets, and sells. Quantum then customizes the drives for each customer. Quantum starts the clock when MKE invoices them for a disk drive and stops the clock when Quantum invoices the customer. Quantum takes interim measures when the drive arrives at Quantum, when the drive goes into processing, and when it moves to finished goods inventory. The length of time Quantum owns a disk drive is critical because of the competitive pressures in the personal computer industry. Because even very complicated customization does not take long, most of the time a drive spends at Quantum adds little value.

"Quantum measures TOO by tracking every disk drive through its serial number. One virtue of TOO is that it has helped Quantum to

"link various business processes together and to other important corporate measurements. . . . Establishing links between physical flow and financial metrics provided one of the major breakthroughs we achieved with TOO. That breakthrough was to show in a way convincing to non-logistics non-operations management the link between product complexity and supply chain costs. We made the connection by taking the cost of a day of ownership for a drive and then comparing the TOO of various products. We calculate the cost of a day of ownership by determining price erosion and several other time-sensitive costs. . . . When we measured TOO for various products, we found that more complex products take longer to go through our system, often significantly longer."

*Source: John Hamer, "Measuring Time of Ownership at Quantum," The Supply Chain Connection, Newsletter of the Stanford Global Supply Chain Forum, Vol. IV, No. III.*

## MATERIALS AND PURCHASING

World-class manufacturers do not evaluate their purchasing functions solely on the basis of the prices they pay for materials and components. **McKinsey & Co.,** a large consulting firm, reported a number of measures of performance for the purchasing function, some of which are as follows:

|  | Typical Company | World-class Company |
|---|---|---|
| Agents per $100 million purchases | 5.4 | 2.2 |
| Purchasing costs as percent of purchases | 3.3% | 0.8% |
| Time spent placing order, weeks | 6 | 0.001 |
| Percentage deliveries late | 33% | 2% |
| Percentage deliveries rejected | 1.5% | 0.0001% |
| Materials shortages, per year | 400 | 4 |

Some of these measures relate to the cost of the purchasing function, while others relate to the quality of suppliers. It is important that companies reduce lead time of their suppliers because that fosters the JIT objective of reducing cycle time and inventory. Of course, quality measures are especially important for JIT companies.[5]

A major study concluded that evaluating purchasing managers by material price variances is especially unwise for manufacturers that have embarked on supply chain management. Companies such as **Quantum**, described in the previous Insight, are developing long-term, strategic relationships with only a very few suppliers. Buyers give such suppliers large orders on long-term contracts in exchange for annual price decreases. Purchasing managers are also trying to reduce administrative costs of the purchasing function, which are non-value-adding and can run to millions of dollars annually.

The same study also found that competitive bidding is not always a good idea, either. Suppliers of Japanese automakers established factories close to auto plants, have face-to-face contact with customers (suppliers stationed engineers in customers' plants), and dedicated a considerable portion (about 22 percent) of assets to those customers, thus focused more on those customers, which increased product quality. U.S. suppliers are farther away from their customers and dedicate only 15 percent of assets to them. The study concludes that a tightly integrated production network with dedicated suppliers will outperform a loosely coupled one.[6]

**Cisco Systems**' annual report describes how the company has created "a single enterprise" by linking its suppliers through information sharing. The entire supply chain works from a single sales forecast. The company has saved $75 annually in reduced lead times, fewer engineering changes, and quicker product design.

The behavioral aspects of standards and variances extend to many areas of management. The accompanying Insight illustrates one.

## STANDARD COSTS FOR NONMANUFACTURING ACTIVITIES

Some companies have developed standard costs for nonmanufacturing activities. Such activities have certain traits that render the development of standard costs difficult. Most basically, measuring output in nonmanufacturing activities is difficult. Rarely do homogeneous physical units flow out of the work done by the product design, legal, accounting, marketing, and general administration departments. There is seldom a definable measure of output because there is no standard product.

Costs associated with administrative work also tend to be more fixed than those of manufacturing. Consequently, it might be impossible to develop standard variable costs per unit of output even if an appropriate unit of output could be found. Therefore, administrative activities usually are controlled by static budgets rather than by standard variable costs. Thus, the earlier discussion on control of fixed costs is applicable to nonmanufacturing activities, but the discussion on standard variable costs usually is not.

---

5 *"Quality,"* Business Week, *November 30, 1992, 72.*
6 *Jeffrey Dyer, "Dedicated Assets: Japan's Manufacturing Edge,"* Harvard Business Review, *November 1994.*

### Determining Responsibility for Variances

**Charles Machine Works** manufactures the Ditch Witch®, the well-known trenching equipment used to lay underground utility lines. In moving toward JIT and total quality management (TQM), the company used a tool called Socio-Technical Systems Analysis (STSA), which is especially useful for identifying variances that cause problems further down the production line. The company had found that some variances or quality problems were caused early in the process, but were not discovered until later. The worker who discovered the problem often scrapped the defective piece because to repair it would make his performance suffer.

For instance, at an early step, a worker could cause burrs in the barrel of a cylinder. These burrs would not show up until assembly, when the barrel would leak. The assembly worker who discovered the burrs simply tossed the defective barrels aside where they piled up until an engineer was notified. Additionally, the worker responsible for the burrs was not motivated to inspect and correct them because it would slow him down. "Someone else" would find them later. The task is to alleviate such problems through better teamwork and more coordination. The company used activity-based costing and standard costs to help TQM efforts by "focusing on activities that give 'the best return for the dollar.'"

*Sources: Michael F. Thomas and James T. Mackey, "Activity-Based Cost Variances for Just-in-Time,"* Management Accounting, *April 1994, 49–54.*

## SUMMARY

Standard costs are helpful in the planning, control, and evaluation of cost centers. Companies develop standards for each major element of product cost (materials, labor, and overhead). Standard costs consist of two components; one is the quantity of the input factor used in the product, the other is the price of a unit of that factor. The total variance between budgeted and actual cost has two components, one variance related to a difference in price and the other related to a difference in the quantity. Because different managers are usually responsible for acquiring (price and rate variances) and using (efficiency variances) resources, separating total variances into price and use components assists in assigning responsibility. The separation also is helpful in planning future operations.

Because managerial functions and activities of cost centers are interdependent, variances seemingly under the control of a particular manager do not automatically signal good or bad performance of that manager. The causes of variances are not always easy to determine and include poor management in the department showing the variance or poor management in an entirely different department. The cause also could be a bad standard.

Some advocates of continuous improvement methods, such as JIT, argue against the use of standards. Most JIT manufacturers use other measures to evaluate operations, whether or not they use standards.

## KEY TERMS

benchmarking *(534)*
best practices *(534)*
control chart *(532)*
currently attainable standard *(536)*
fixed overhead budget variance *(539)*
historical standard *(536)*
ideal standard *(535)*
idle time *(525)*
kaizen costing *(541)*
labor efficiency variance *(525)*

labor rate variance *(524)*
material price variance *(528)*
material use variance *(528)*
standard cost *(521)*
value engineering *(543)*
variable overhead budget (spending) variance *(527)*
variable overhead efficiency variance *(527)*

## KEY FORMULAS

$$\text{Total standard cost} = \text{Actual production} \times \begin{array}{c}\text{Standard quantity}\\\text{of input factor}\\\text{per unit of}\\\text{product}\end{array} \times \begin{array}{c}\text{Standard price}\\\text{(rate) for unit}\\\text{of input factor}\end{array}$$

$$\text{Price variance} = \begin{array}{c}\text{Actual quantity}\\\text{of input acquired}\end{array} \times \left(\begin{array}{c}\text{Standard price}\\\text{per unit of input}\end{array} - \begin{array}{c}\text{Actual price}\\\text{per unit of input}\end{array}\right)$$

$$\text{Quantity variance} = \begin{array}{c}\text{Standard price}\\\text{per unit of input}\end{array} \times \left(\begin{array}{c}\text{Total standard quantity}\\\text{of input}\end{array} - \begin{array}{c}\text{Actual quantity}\\\text{of input used}\end{array}\right)$$

## REVIEW PROBLEM

Baldwin Company makes stereo cabinets. The Deluxe model has the following requirements.

| | |
|---|---|
| Materials | 50 feet of wood at $1.40 per foot |
| Direct labor | 4 hours at $17 per hour |
| Variable overhead | $5 per direct labor hour |

During June 20X4, the company made 1,200 Deluxe cabinets. Operating results were as follows:

| | |
|---|---|
| Materials purchases (78,000 feet at $1.45) | $113,100 |
| Materials used | 63,200 feet |
| Direct labor (4,740 hours at $16.80) | $79,632 |
| Variable overhead | $25,500 |

**Required**

Compute the standard variable cost per Deluxe cabinet and the variances for June 20X4.

## ANSWER TO REVIEW PROBLEM

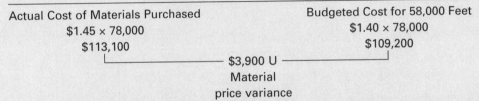

Standard Variable Cost

| | |
|---|---|
| Materials (50 feet of wood at $1.40) | $ 70 |
| Direct labor (4 hours at $17 per hour) | 68 |
| Variable overhead at $5 per direct labor hour | 20 |
| Total standard variable cost | $158 |

Materials Variances for June 20X4

Actual Cost of Materials Purchased
$1.45 × 78,000
$113,100

Budgeted Cost for 58,000 Feet
$1.40 × 78,000
$109,200

$3,900 U
Material
price variance

Alternatively, 78,000 × ($1.40 - $1.45) = $3,900 unfavorable.

Budgeted Cost
of Materials Used
63,000 × $1.40
$88,200

Budgeted Cost for 1,200 Units
1,200 x $70, or 1,200 × 50 x $1.40
$84,000

$4,200 U
Material
use variance

Alternatively, $1.40 × [(1,200 × 50) − 63,000] = $4,200 unfavorable.

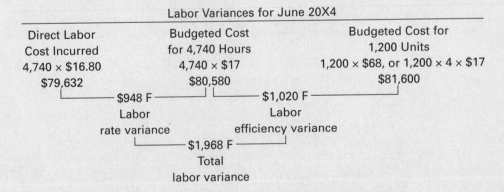

Labor Variances for June 20X4

Direct Labor
Cost Incurred
4,740 × $16.80
$79,632

Budgeted Cost
for 4,740 Hours
4,740 × $17
$80,580

Budgeted Cost for
1,200 Units
1,200 × $68, or 1,200 × 4 × $17
$81,600

$948 F
Labor
rate variance

$1,020 F
Labor
efficiency variance

$1,968 F
Total
labor variance

Alternatively, the labor rate variance is:

$$4,740 \times (\$17 - \$16.80) = \$948 \text{ favorable}$$

The labor efficiency variance is:

$$\$17 \times [(1,200 \times 4) - 4,740] = \$17 \times (4,800 - 4,740) = \$1,020 \text{ favorable}$$

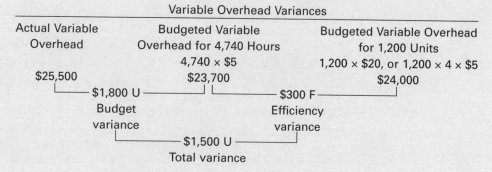

Variable Overhead Variances

| Actual Variable Overhead | Budgeted Variable Overhead for 4,740 Hours 4,740 × $5 | Budgeted Variable Overhead for 1,200 Units 1,200 × $20, or 1,200 × 4 × $5 |
|---|---|---|
| $25,500 | $23,700 | $24,000 |

$1,800 U — Budget variance

$300 F — Efficiency variance

$1,500 U — Total variance

Alternatively, we can compute the budget variance by calculating the actual rate of about $5.38 ($25,500/4,740), subtracting it from the standard rate of $5, then multiplying by 4,740 hours.

$$4,740 \times (\$5 - \$5.38) = -\$1,801 \text{ unfavorable (difference due to rounding)}$$

The efficiency variance is also given by $5 × (4,800 − 4,740) = $300 favorable.

## APPENDIX: VARIANCES AND QUALITY

Conventional variance calculations isolate the effects of price or rate differences, and of differences in efficiency. Sometimes efficiency variances can mask what is actually a quality problem. Consider the following example, which we limit to materials and direct labor to concentrate on the major points.

| | |
|---|---|
| Standard material cost, 5 pounds at $4 | $20 |
| Standard direct labor cost, 2 hours at $15 | 30 |
| Total standard cost | $50 |

The company produced 11,000 total units, of which 1,000 were rejected and scrapped. Costs were:

| | |
|---|---|
| Materials purchased and used, 54,000 pounds at $4 | $216,000 |
| Direct labor, 23,000 hours at $15 | 345,000 |

Conventional variance analyses follow. Note that we have no price or rate variances, again to highlight the major points.

Materials

| Actual Quantity at Standard Price 54,000 × $4 | Standard Quantity at Standard Price 10,000 × $20 |
|---|---|
| $216,000 | $200,000 |

$16,000 U — Material use variance

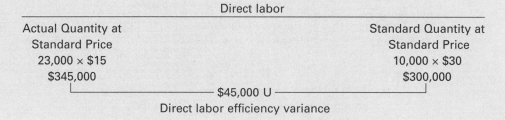

Direct labor

| Actual Quantity at Standard Price | | Standard Quantity at Standard Price |
|---|---|---|
| 23,000 × $15 | | 10,000 × $30 |
| $345,000 | | $300,000 |
| | $45,000 U<br>Direct labor efficiency variance | |

But these variances do not tell the real story. The company actually produced 11,000 units, but spoiled 1,000. Poor quality is a matter of effectiveness, not of efficiency. A better analysis focuses on the total output and on the amount spoiled and rejected.

Materials

| Actual Quantity at Standard Price | Standard Quantity for 11,000 units at Standard Price | Standard Quantity for 10,000 Good Units at Standard Price |
|---|---|---|
| 54,000 × $4 | 11,000 × $20 | 10,000 × $20 |
| $216,000 | $220,000 | $200,000 |
| $4,000 F<br>Material use variance | $20,000 U<br>Spoilage variance | |

The picture here is quite different. The company used materials efficiently, because the 11,000 units produced used 54,000 pounds, not 55,000. But the company worked ineffectively because it spoiled 1,000 units. The conventional calculation obscures this point, absorbing ineffectiveness into inefficiency. See if you can do the same analysis for direct labor before looking at the schedule below.

Direct labor

| Actual Quantity at Standard Price | Standard Quantity for 11,000 units at Standard Price | Standard Quantity for 10,000 units at Standard Price |
|---|---|---|
| 21,000 × $15 | 11,000 × $30 | 10,000 × $30 |
| $315,000 | $330,000 | $300,000 |
| $15,000 F<br>Direct labor efficiency variance | $30,000 U<br>Spoilage variance | |

Of course, we would also calculate price/rate variances as usual. The only difference here is that we calculate efficiency variances based on *total* units produced, not on good units, then calculate the cost (variance) of spoiled units. Managers need to know about both effectiveness and efficiency.

## ASSIGNMENT MATERIAL

### INTERNET ACTIVITY

Find the annual reports of three to four companies in different industries and compare their comments on productivity and cost control. At what stage of the value chain (design, manufacturing, distribution, etc.) do they concentrate their efforts? How do they accomplish productivity increases? What role does technology play?

## QUESTIONS FOR DISCUSSION

**12-1   *Outsourcing and standard costs***   Most toy companies outsource manufacturing and concentrate on their core competencies of designing and marketing. Short product cycles are the rule in the toy business, with very few toys lasting more than one season. **Mattel** has been using a strategy of rolling mix for its miniature car line, by which it changes the product offerings by 7%–8% every two weeks. Thus, it turns over its entire line-up twice a year. Mattel does not manufacture this line.

### *Required*

Do you think that the contract manufacturers who make toys for other companies use standard costs? Why or why not?

**12-2   *Predicting variances***   For each of the following situations, indicate what variances might be affected, and in what direction.

1. The economy is strong and wage rates are rising because the demand for workers is increasing.
2. To increase safety, the plant manager has reduced the speeds at which forklifts carrying materials and semifinished products can be driven.
3. Shortages of materials develop because of problems at suppliers.
4. The electric utility that supplies the company has been having difficulty with its generators. There are frequent blackouts and brownouts.
5. The company hires many part-time workers to meet increases in production.

**12-3   *Changes in automakers' operations***   Various publications have reported on how the major auto companies have changed their operations in recent years. (One of the best is Alex Taylor III, "The Auto Industry Meets the New Economy," *Fortune*, September 5, 1994, 52–60.) For each of the following items, indicate how costs, including standard costs, might be affected.

1. Companies have begun buying many components that they once made. The only parts that **BMW** will make for its new roadster to be produced in South Carolina are the engine, transmission, and suspension. American companies will supply all other parts.
2. Companies are reducing the number of suppliers, and requiring suppliers to do more design and development work. In the past, companies gave suppliers detailed specifications and awarded contracts to the low bidder. For instance, the 1994 Ford Tempo required over 700 suppliers, the 1995 Ford Contour only 227.
3. **Ford** and **General Motors** have centralized purchasing for their U.S. and European operations.
4. **Chrysler** involves its suppliers in product design, soliciting their ideas for parts and components.

**12-4   *Long-term contracts***   Annual reports of many companies describe long-term contracts they have with various suppliers. Some of these contracts obligate the company to buy a specified minimum quantity of the commodity or product.

### *Required*

What are the advantages and disadvantages of such arrangements to the buyers?

**12-5   Productivity gains**   The 1997 annual report of **General Mills** stated

"We generated continued productivity gains across the supply chain, from purchasing to manufacturing to distribution. This increased productivity enabled us to improve product quality, deliver record levels of customer service, reduce required order lead times, and partially offset increases in our input costs."

**Required**
Limit your attention to manufacturing and assume that the company did not change its standard costs as it generated its productivity gains. Which kinds of variances would have been favorable, and which unfavorable? Why?

**12-6   Responsibility for variances (CMA adapted)**   Phillips Company uses a standard cost system. Variances for each department are calculated and reported to the department manager. Reporting has two major purposes: evaluating performance and improving operations.

Jack Smith recently was appointed manager of the Assembly Department. He has complained that the system does not work properly and discriminates against his department because of the current practice of calculating a variance for rejected units. The procedures for making this calculation are as follows: (1) all units are inspected at the end of the assembly operation, (2) rejected units are examined to see if the cause of rejection can be assigned to a particular department, (3) units that are rejected but cannot be identified with a particular department are totaled, (4) the unidentifiable rejects are apportioned to each department on the basis of the identifiable rejects. Thus, if a department had 20% of the identified rejects, it will be charged with 20% of the unidentified rejects. The variance, then, is the sum of the identifiable rejects and the apportioned share of unidentified rejects.

**Required**
Write a memorandum to Henry Berger, Smith's supervisor, evaluating the validity of Smith's claim and making a recommendation for resolving the problem.

**12-7   Significance of variances**   Ginny Smith, controller of DavisCo, was recently told by several production managers that "as long as total costs do not exceed budgeted costs, based on standard prices and quantities, there is no reason to do any investigating or analysis."

**Required**
Comment critically on the statement. Cite at least two reasons why the policy is unwise.

## EXERCISES

**12-8   Basic material and labor variances**   The following are budgeted and actual results in December for Bayliss Blankets Co.

|                      | Budget | Actual |
|----------------------|--------|--------|
| Unit production      | 11,000 | 10,000 |
| Direct labor hours   | 22,000 | 20,200 |
| Materials used, yards| 44,000 | 39,700 |

The standard labor rate is $15 per hour; standard materials price is $4 per yard.

**Required**

Calculate the direct labor efficiency variance and the material use variance.

**12-9  *Comprehensive variance analysis***   CleenProd makes industrial cleaners. Standard costs for a gallon of Scumbegone are as follows, along with actual results for March.

| | |
|---|---:|
| Materials, 4 pounds at $5 per pound | $20 |
| Direct labor at $10 per hour | 5 |
| Variable overhead at $6 per DLH | 3 |
| Total standard variable cost | $28 |

Actual results for March:

(a) Production was 3,000 gallons.
(b) Material purchases were 11,200 pounds at $4.80 per pound.
(c) The company used 12,200 pounds of materials in production.
(d) Direct laborers worked 1,450 hours at $10.10, earning $14,645.
(e) Variable overhead was $9,100.

**Required**

Compute all variable cost variances.

**12-10  *Standard cost computations***   LeBeau, Inc. makes metal storage boxes. It has established the standard prices and quantities for a finished unit as follows:

| | |
|---|---|
| Materials | 8 pounds at $0.50 per pound |
| Direct labor | 3 hours at $16 per hour |
| Variable overhead | $6 per direct labor hour (DLH) |

LeBeau also has fixed overhead of $1,000,000 per year.

**Required**

Fill in the blanks in the following items.

1. The standard cost per unit of finished product is
   (a) _____ for materials.
   (b) _____ for direct labor.
   (c) _____ for variable overhead.
2. At 70,000 direct labor hours, total variable overhead cost should be _____.
3. At 90,000 direct labor hours, production should be _____ units.
4. If 400,000 pounds of materials are used, production should be _____ units.
5. At 120,000 direct labor hours, total materials used should be _____ pounds.
6. If 300,000 pounds of materials are used, total variable overhead cost should be _____ and total labor cost should be _____.

**12-11  *Fundamentals of standard costs and variances***   Hector Company manufactures large, ornate birdbaths. Each birdbath requires 10 pounds of special clay and 20 minutes of direct labor. The standard price of clay is $6 per pound. The standard direct labor rate is $12 per hour, and the standard variable overhead rate is $6 per direct labor hour.

During November, Hector manufactured 1,000 birdbaths. It bought 12,000 pounds of clay for $71,800 and used 10,800 pounds. Hector paid direct laborers $4,590 for 380 hours and incurred $2,350 in variable overhead.

**Required**
1. Determine the standard variable cost of a birdbath.
2. Determine all variable cost variances.

**12-12   Basic variance relationships—materials**   Fill in the following blanks. You can work them in order, but you do not have to.

| | |
|---|---:|
| Standard materials cost per unit of product | $10 |
| Material use variance | $1,200U |
| Standard material use for quantity produced, in pounds | 25,000 |
| Number of pounds of materials purchased | 30,000 |
| Material price variance | $2,000U |
| Standard price per pound of materials | $2 |
| Standard pounds of materials per unit of product | _____ |
| Units produced | _____ |
| Number of pounds of materials used | _____ |
| Amount paid for materials purchased | _____ |

**12-13   Ethics and overhead assignment**   Jill Roper, manager of a product line at Minars Industries, was complaining about the calculation of standard costs. "My line has only three products. They are very simple and require no machine setups, no special quality control, and little machine time. Only direct labor and three or four kinds of materials are required. But some of the other lines we carry have products that require all manner of setup time, extra record keeping, and more vendor analysis because they have many more materials and components. Most of them are also machine-intensive. It's just not fair for them to bear overhead based only on direct labor. I've talked to the controller, but he just tells me to do my job and he'll do his."

**Required**
Comment on Roper's complaints. Is the controller abiding by the IMA Standards reproduced in Exhibit 1-2? If not, why not?

**12-14   Spoilage variance (related to appendix)**   Following are the standard variable costs for one of Halsey Knitting's sweaters, the Highlander.

| | |
|---|---:|
| Materials, 3 pounds of yarn at $6 per pound | $18 |
| Labor, 2 hours of labor at $10 per hour | 20 |
| Variable overhead, $4 per labor hour | 8 |
| Total standard variable cost | $46 |

Actual results for March follow.

| Production | 1,800 good sweaters, 200 spoiled sweaters |
|---|---|
| Materials purchased | 7,000 pounds for $41,200 |
| Materials used | 6,200 pounds |
| Labor | 3,900 hours, $41,200 |
| Variable overhead incurred | $16,500 |

### Required
Compute all variable cost variances including variances related to spoiled units.

**12-15 *Evaluation in JIT manufacturing***   Baskin Products recently implemented JIT principles and its controller is having difficulty in analyzing performance. She has collected the following statistics and asks you to tell her how each could help evaluate performance in the two months.

|  | July | September |
|---|---|---|
| Average processing time, hours | 38 | 29 |
| Average cycle time, days | 25 | 19 |
| Production, units | 7,520 | 7,680 |
| Maximum capacity, units | 7,800 | 7,800 |
| Defective units | 96 | 72 |
| Inventory of materials, days' supply | 9 | 6 |
| Inventory of work in process goods, days' supply | 13 | 9 |
| Inventory of finished goods, days' supply | 3 | 4 |

### Required
Use the data to describe where Baskin is improving and where it is not. You might wish to calculate some ratios using these raw numbers.

**12-16 *Revising standard costs, target costs***   Chalmers Company manufactures various toys. One line consists of small cars, each of which requires the same quantities of materials and direct labor. The cars are packaged and sold in batches of 50. The standard variable cost of a batch is as follows:

| Materials | $18.00 |
|---|---|
| Direct labor (0.50 hours) | 10.00 |
| Variable overhead | 8.00 |
| Total standard variable cost | $36.00 |

The production supervisor is uncertain how to prepare the budget for the coming year. He tells you the following.

(a) Materials costs will average 10% higher because of price increases.
(b) Laborers will get an 8% raise at the beginning of the year.
(c) Increased efficiency will reduce direct labor hours by 10% and material use by 5%.
(d) The variable overhead rate will increase to $17 per direct labor hour.

### Required
1. Prepare revised standard variable costs.
2. How low must the company drive labor time to bring the new standard cost to the same $36 level as the current one?

**12-17   Relationships—labor variances** Each of the following independent situations relates to direct labor. Fill in the blanks.

|  | a | b | c | d |
|---|---|---|---|---|
| Units produced | 2,000 | ____ | 4,000 | ____ |
| Actual hours worked | 4,800 | 8,400 | ____ | ____ |
| Standard hours for production achieved | 5,000 | ____ | ____ | 6,000 |
| Standard hours per unit | ____ | 0.5 | 2 | 3 |
| Standard rate per hour | $12 | $10 | $12 | ____ |
| Actual labor cost | ____ | $83,600 | ____ | $24,500 |
| Rate variance | $650U | ____ | $600U | $300F |
| Efficiency variance | ____ | $2,000U | $1,200F | $800U |

**12-18   Variance analysis** Maxum Car Products makes automobile antifreeze. Maxum has developed the following formula for budgeting monthly factory overhead costs: Total overhead cost = $840,000 + ($11 × direct labor hours). Other data relating to the cost of a case of the product are as follows:

| | |
|---|---|
| Materials | 8 gallons at $1.10 per gallon |
| Direct labor | 10 minutes at $20 per hour |

Last month Maxum produced 200,000 cases and had the following costs.

| | |
|---|---|
| Materials purchased (1,800,000 gallons) | $2,108,000 |
| Materials used | 1,588,000 gallons |
| Direct labor, 32,200 hours | $645,750 |
| Overhead | $1,288,500 |

**Required**
Compute the price and quantity variances for materials and direct labor and the total variance for overhead.

**12-19   Performance reporting** Ted Woods, the president of your company, has asked you to investigate some unfavorable variances that occurred in one of the departments last month. You were given the following summary of the department's performance report.

|  | Budget | Actual | Variance |
|---|---|---|---|
| Production (in units) | 2,000 | 2,500 | 500F |
| Costs (based on budgeted production): | | | |
| Direct labor | $6,000 | $7,000 | $1,000U |
| Supplies | 400 | 650 | 250U |
| Repairs | 1,000 | 1,200 | 200U |
| Power | 800 | 1,100 | 300U |
| Total costs (all variable) | $8,200 | $9,950 | $1,750U |

**Required**
1. Was performance poor?

2. Write a memorandum to Mr. Woods recommending changes in the company's reporting. Use the guidelines in Appendix A.

**12-20   *Variances—relationships among costs***   Read the following in its entirety and then fill in the blanks.

1. Standard variable costs per unit:
   (a) Materials 4 pounds @ $____                                 $_____
   (b) Direct labor ____ hours @ $12.00                           $6.00
   (c) Variable overhead $8 per DLH                               $_____
2. Production                                                     8,000 units
3. Materials purchases, 32,000 pounds                             $62,000
4. Materials used at standard prices, 31,200 pounds              $_____
5. Direct labor, actual ____ hours                               $47,200
6. Material price variance                                       $2,000 U
7. Material use variance                                         $_____
8. Direct labor rate variance                                    $2,000 F
9. Direct labor efficiency variance                             $_____
10. Variable overhead spending variance                          $1,500 F
11. Variable overhead efficiency variance                        $_____
12. Actual variable overhead cost                                $_____

**12-21   *Standards—machine-hour basis***   Wilkens Company is highly automated and uses machine-hours to set standard variable costs. A unit of its product requires two pounds of material costing $8 per pound and 6 minutes of machine time. The standard variable overhead rate is $12 per machine hour. There is no direct labor; all workers are classified as indirect labor, and their wages are considered part of variable overhead.

During June, Wilkens produced 27,000 units using 2,840 machine hours. Variable overhead costs were $33,900. Purchases of materials were 53,000 pounds for $427,000 and 56,000 pounds were used.

**Required**

1. Compute the standard variable cost of a unit of product.
2. Compute the variances for June.

## PROBLEMS

**12-22   *Standards in a service function***   Graham Labs performs blood tests for local physicians. Dr. Graham, head of the company, has instituted a standard cost system to help control costs and measure employee efficiency. After extensive consultations with his employees, he developed the following standards for some high-volume tests.

| Test | Standard Time (in minutes) |
|------|----------------------------|
| Blood sugar | 11 |
| Cell count | 9 |
| Others | 6 |

The company's 15 lab technicians earn an average of $14 per hour, with a range of $10.25 to $18.50. During July, the first month the system was in effect, the lab had the following results.

| Test | Number Performed |
|------|------------------|
| Blood sugar | 4,100 |
| Cell count | 2,200 |
| Others | 4,900 |

Lab technicians earned $26,500 for 1,790 hours. The lab was open for 22 days during July and technicians work 7-hour days.

### Required
1. Determine the labor rate variance and labor efficiency variance.
2. In this instance, does the labor efficiency variance actually reflect technicians' inability to perform the tests in the standard times? Why or why not?

**12-23  Target costing**  Trapnell Company makes a variety of products, some of which compete with imports. Rises in the value of the dollar have made imports considerably cheaper than one of Trapnell's major products and the managers are seeking ways to stave off the competition. The standard cost of the product appears below.

| | |
|---|---|
| Materials | $20.35 |
| Direct labor, 0.40 hours at $15 | 6.00 |
| Variable overhead* | 3.00 |
| Total standard variable cost | $29.35 |

*\* Driven by labor time*

The production manager states that the product is over-engineered and has features that do not add value to most customers. "We could easily use some lower-cost materials. Moreover, by tweaking the assembly process we could knock something off the labor time. But remember that we have a 3% raise to direct laborers coming up next month."

The marketing manager took another tack. "We have a target contribution margin of about $15–$16 per unit. I don't see how we can compete unless we get the cost down below $24.50 or so because $40 is all we are ever going to be able to charge, what with the cheaper imports."

The head of design said she would look into using more common components and taking other steps to alleviate the problem. At the next meeting a few days later, the head of design said that she could cut materials requirements to $17.50 without compromising functionality.

### Required
Determine how much the production manager must reduce labor time to meet the $24.50 target price.

**12-24  Investigation of variances**  The production manager of ComPlast Company tells you that she exercises management by exception. She examines a performance report and calls for further analysis and investigation if a variance is greater than 10% of total standard cost or is more than $2,500. She is not responsible for rate or price variances and is therefore concerned only with efficiency variances. During April, the following occurred.

(a) Materials used, 4,880 gallons
(b) Direct labor hours, 7,780
(c) Production, 2,000 units

The standard cost of a unit is as follows:

| | |
|---|---|
| Materials (2 gallons at $4) | $ 8 |
| Direct labor (4 hours at $10) | 40 |
| Variable overhead ($6 per DLH) | 24 |
| Total standard variable cost | $72 |

**Required**

1. Compute the variances for which the production manager should be held responsible.
2. Determine which variances should be investigated according to her criteria.

**12-25  *Determining a base for cost standards***   The production manager of Rolland Company recently performed a study to see how many units of product could be made by a worker who had no interruptions, always had materials available as needed, made no errors, and worked at peak speed. He found that a worker could make 20 units in an hour under these ideal conditions. In the past, about 15 units per hour was the actual average output. However, new materials handling equipment had recently been purchased and the manager is confident that an average of 18 units per hour can be achieved by nearly all workers.

All workers earn $15 per hour. A month after the study was made, workers were paid $1,200,000 for 80,000 hours. Production was 1,410,000 units.

**Required**

1. Compute the standard labor cost per unit to the nearest $0.001 based on
   (a) historical performance
   (b) ideal performance
   (c) currently attainable performance
2. Compute the labor efficiency variance under each of the standards in requirement 1 and comment on the results.
3. Using the guidelines in Appendix A, write a short memo to Bonnie Gardella, the production manager, stating which method of setting the standard you prefer for planning purposes and for control purposes.

**12-26  *Kaizen costing***   Fordham Block Co. makes granite countertops. The company faces serious competition and wants to reduce its costs, which mostly involve cutting and polishing blocks of granite. The production manager has heard about kaizen costing and wonders if it applies to his operation. He gives you the following data for a batch of 50 of the company's most popular size countertop.

| | |
|---|---|
| Cutting time | 80 hours |
| Polishing time | 30 hours |

All workers earn $18 per hour. The production manager wants to reduce labor costs by 2% per quarter.

**Required**

Prepare a schedule showing target labor times for each type of work, and total labor costs (a) one quarter hence, (b) two quarters hence, and (c) three quarters hence. Round times to the nearest 1/10 of an hour.

**12-27   Determining standard costs**   Vernon Company makes its single product, Shine, by mixing the materials Dull and Buff in 500-pound batches in a 3:2 ratio (three pounds of Dull for each two pounds of Buff). The mixing is done by one laborer and takes two hours. The resulting mixture is boiled for four hours, which requires three workers. The mixture that comes out of the boiler yields four pounds of finished product for each five pounds of raw material, so that the 500 pounds of material mixed become 400 pounds of final product. (Evaporation during boiling reduces the volume.)

All laborers earn $12 per hour. Variable overhead is $4 per direct labor hour. Dull costs $3.20 per pound; Buff costs $4.40 per pound.

**Required**

Determine the standard variable cost per pound of Shine.

**12-28   Activity-based variances**   In the past, KC Valves, Inc. has used standard costs with all variable overhead being associated with direct labor. Some managers are unhappy with the results because direct labor is not the only cost driver. The managers have amassed the following data for a standard batch of 1,000 units of model GY-44.

| | |
|---|---:|
| Materials, various | $2,050 |
| Direct labor, 20 hours at $20 | 400 |
| Labor-driven variable overhead at $16 | 320 |
| Machine setups, 70 hours of setups at $20/hour | 1,400 |
| Laboratory tests, 5 at $60 | 300 |
| Total standard variable cost | $4,470 |

Actual results for March follow.

| | |
|---|---|
| Production | 10 batches |
| Direct labor hours | 190 |
| Labor-driven variable overhead | $3,250 |
| Setups | 820 hours, $16,500 |
| Laboratory tests | 47 tests, $2,870 |

The managers are unsure what variances to calculate, and how, aside from those related to direct labor.

**Required**

Determine all overhead variances that you can for March and explain your calculations.

**12-29   Standards and variances, two products**   Bascomb Company makes two coffee tables. Both go through the same processes. Standard cost data are as follows:

|  | Harcombe | Exeter |
|---|---|---|
| Materials: |  |  |
| 6 feet at $5 per foot | $30 |  |
| 8 feet at $5 per foot |  | $40 |
| Direct labor | 14 | 28 |
| Variable overhead | 8 | 16 |
| Total standard costs | $52 | $84 |

All direct laborers earn $14 per hour, and the variable overhead rate is $8 per direct labor hour. The same materials are used in both models.

During March, the company had the following results.

| Production | 2,000 Harcombe, 1,000 Exeter |
|---|---|
| Materials purchased | 22,000 feet at $4.90 per foot |
| Materials used | 19,900 feet |
| Direct labor | 4,200 hours at $14.20 per hour |
| Variable overhead | $31,500 |

**Required**

1. Compute all variable cost variances for production as a whole.
2. Can you compute variances for each model? If not, why not? What information would you need to be able to compute variances by model? Why might you want to compute variances for each product separately?

**12-30  Overhead rates, ABC, and pricing**  Paul Drake, the sales manager of Hassel Industries, was discussing a problem with Laura Hurlbut, the controller. The company's most recent operating results were disappointing because a downward trend in profit was accelerating, even though sales were remaining about the same. Drake said "Our major line is selling poorly because our competitors are undercutting our prices. I don't see how they do it! We have cut prices down to the bone. Fortunately, some of our minor lines are doing very well." Hurlbut replied that "The problem could be with our costs. Look at the standards for these representative products from the major line and one of the minor lines."

|  | Major Product | Minor Product |
|---|---|---|
| Materials | $ 35 | $ 65 |
| Direct labor at $12/hour | 36 | 36 |
| Variable overhead at $18/DLH | 54 | 54 |
| Total standard variable cost | $125 | $155 |
| Annual volume | 80,000 | 4,000 |
| Selling price | $135 | $200 |

Hurlbut continued, "We have been revising our overhead rate by looking at the requirements of each product. I have divided our variable overhead costs into three pools and developed variable rates for each. My chief accountant has collected data for each product." The data Hurlbut referred to follow.

| Driver for Cost Pool | Variable Rate | Major Product | Minor Product |
|---|---|---|---|
| Direct labor | $4.00/DLH | 3 DLH | 3 DLH |
| Machine setups | $9.00/setup | 1 setup | 8 setups |
| Number of parts | $0.50/part | 10 parts | 18 parts |

"Perhaps," Hurlbut went on, "we can get a better idea of our costs by incorporating this new information."

**Required**
1. Develop standard variable costs using the new information.
2. Write a memorandum to Ms. Hurlbut explaining the differences between your standard costs and the original standards as previously given. State why the company seems to be experiencing the results given previously. Follow the guidelines in Appendix A.
3. In general, do you expect that high-volume or low-volume products are more likely to show higher overhead costs under ABC than under labor-based assignment? Why?

**12-31   Input standards versus output standards**   Foelber Company manufactures a commercial solvent. Foelber budgets manufacturing costs based on direct labor hours. The production manager is unable to interpret the report he has just received and asks for your assistance. The report contains the following data.

|  | Actual Cost at 10,000 Direct Labor Hours | Budgeted Cost for 10,000 Hours |
|---|---|---|
| Materials used at standard prices | $ 26,700 | $ 24,000 |
| Direct labor | 69,200 | 68,000 |
| Indirect labor | 28,100 | 26,500 |
| Other variable overhead | 26,100 | 27,300 |
| Total variable costs | $150,100 | $145,800 |

Foelber budgeted 50,000 gallons of production. Actual production was 51,000 gallons, which requires 10,200 direct labor hours at standard performance.

**Required**
For each component of cost, determine the variance due to efficiency (or inefficiency) and that due to spending or price.

**12-32   Bases for standard costs and decisions**   Sewell Company uses very tight standards for determining standard costs. The production manager believes that the use of standards achievable only under ideal conditions helps to motivate employees by showing them how much improvement is possible and therefore giving them goals to achieve.

The sales manager has criticized the use of such high standards for performance and correspondingly low standard costs because it increases his difficulty in determining whether business at lower than normal prices should be accepted. In one specific instance, the sales manager was offered the opportunity to sell 4,000 units at $8.50, which is $4 below the normal selling price. He rejected the offer. The standard variable cost per unit of product is as follows:

| | |
|---|---|
| Materials (3 pounds at $0.50) | $1.50 |
| Direct labor (½ hour at $6 per hour) | 3.00 |
| Variable overhead ($4 per direct labor hour) | 2.00 |
| Total standard variable cost | $6.50 |

The sales manager was uncertain whether the order should have been accepted. He knew that the standards were never met. What bothered him was the extent to which they were not met. He asked his assistant to try to determine whether the order would have been profitable. The assistant developed the following information: material price and labor rate variances are negligible. However, during a normal month when 10,000 units are produced, the material use variance, direct labor efficiency variance, and total variable overhead variance are about $2,000, $6,000, and $5,200, respectively, all unfavorable.

### Required

1. Assuming that the experience of the month presented would have applied when the special order was being made up, should the order have been accepted?
2. Develop new standard variable costs based on currently attainable performance, assuming that the month described reflected currently attainable performance. Be sure to include both prices and quantities for each input factor.

**12-33  Multiple products**  Morgan Products manufactures three models of lawn benches. The standard material cost is $0.80 per pound, standard labor rate is $8.00 per hour, and standard variable overhead rate is $3.00 per direct labor hour. The standard quantities of each cost factor for each model are as follows:

|                     | Model 1 | Model 2 | Model 3 |
|---------------------|---------|---------|---------|
| Materials, pounds   | 24      | 24      | 42      |
| Direct labor hours  | 5       | 5       | 2       |

Actual results for March were as follows:

| | |
|---|---|
| Production: | |
| Model 1 | 12,000 |
| Model 2 | 16,000 |
| Model 3 | 14,000 |
| Materials purchased | 1,400,000 pounds at $0.78 |
| Materials used | 1,275,000 pounds |
| Direct labor | 173,000 hours for $1,365,200 |
| Variable overhead | $497,000 |

### Required

Determine the variable cost variances.

**12-34  Standards and idle time**  Prescott Textiles manufactures a single kind of cloth in its Petzel Mill. The standard labor cost per 100 yards of cloth is $14.00, which is two standard labor hours at $7 per hour. In August, orders were slow and the mill turned out only 1,200,000 yards, well below the usual volume. Workers were paid for 29,000 hours. The company guarantees a 40-hour work week to employees with five years of service. About 5,500 of the 29,000 hours were idle time, when eligible employees were paid but had no work to do.

### Required

1. Calculate the labor efficiency variance using the 29,000 hours actually worked.
2. Can you conclude from your answer to requirement 1 that the work force was inefficient in August? Why or why not? What do you recommend?

**12-35  Evaluation in JIT manufacturing**  Crystal Enterprises has been using JIT principles for a short time and has been developing a variety of performance measures. Sharon Fennell, the controller, recently received the following statistics and asks you to tell her how each could help evaluate performance.

| | |
|---|---|
| Production in units | 10,450 |
| Number of defectives | 180 |
| Percentage of orders shipped on time | 79% |
| Manufacturing interval (cycle time) | 36 hours |
| Supply of inventories | 15 days |
| Cost of scrap | $6,800 |
| Scrap as a percentage of output | 4% |
| Number of line disruptions | 8 |
| Percentage of people cross-trained | 45% |

**Required**

Write a memorandum to Ms. Fennell telling her how each measure can help her evaluate operations. Use the guidelines in Appendix A.

**12-36  Analyzing results—sales and cost variances**  Managers of Tirado Fashions were disappointed at the shortfall in profit for 20X7, as shown in the following income statements. Amounts shown are in millions.

| | Budgeted | Actual |
|---|---|---|
| Unit sales | 10.0 | 10.8 |
| Sales | $120.0 | $122.1 |
| Variable manufacturing costs: | | |
| Materials | $ 20.0 | $ 21.8 |
| Direct labor | 15.0 | 17.0 |
| Variable overhead | 5.0 | 5.2 |
| Total variable costs | $ 40.0 | $ 44.0 |
| Contribution margin | $ 80.0 | $ 78.1 |
| Fixed costs: | | |
| Manufacturing | $ 50.0 | $ 50.8 |
| Selling and administrative | 20.0 | 19.9 |
| Total fixed costs | $ 70.0 | $ 70.7 |
| Profit before taxes | $ 10.0 | $ 7.4 |

**Required**

The president wants an analysis showing why profit fell short of budget. He wants you to determine the effects of the difference between budgeted and actual unit volume, budgeted and actual selling prices, and budgeted and actual costs for the volume achieved. Production equalled sales. Prepare such an analysis and be sure that it fully accounts for the difference between budgeted and actual profit.

**12-37  Actual to actual comparisons—JIT**  Trivet Company operates a factory utilizing JIT operations. Results for two recent months follow.

| | June | May |
|---|---|---|
| Direct labor hours worked | 21,500 | 20,200 |
| Number of units produced | 11,000 | 10,300 |
| Rate paid to direct laborers | $7.20 per hour | $7.00 per hour |
| Price paid for materials | $0.96 per gallon | $0.98 per gallon |
| Materials purchased and used in production | 45,000 gallons | 41,000 gallons |
| Variable overhead incurred | $85,800 | $83,400 |
| Unit cost | $25.80 | $25.73 |

**Required**

The production manager wants to know if performance improved in June. Write a memorandum detailing the differences between May and June. Determine the differences in May and June costs resulting from changing input factory prices and changing efficiency.

**12-38   *Variance analysis—changed conditions*** Grimes, Inc. makes a warm-up outfit with the following standard costs.

| | |
|---|---|
| Materials (3 pounds at $4) | $12 |
| Direct labor (2 hours at $8) | 16 |
| Variable overhead ($4 per DLH) | 8 |
| Total standard variable cost | $36 |

The standards have proved to be currently attainable and are generally met within small variances each month. In August, the manufacturing vice president brought in a glowing report from the purchasing department. The company bought materials for $3.50 per pound. The new materials were different from the old but were of equal quality for the finished product. The materials bought during August were used in September with the following results.

| | |
|---|---|
| Production scheduled | 4,000 units |
| Actual production | 3,700 units |
| Direct labor (8,350 hours) | $66,100 |
| Variable overhead | $34,200 |
| Materials used | 12,300 pounds |

**Required**

1. Compute all of the variances that you can.
2. Why might the variances have occurred?
3. Assuming that the experience of September will continue, should the company continue buying the new materials?

**12-39   *Economic cost of labor inefficiency*** Columbia Windows makes high-quality bay windows for houses. It sells to wholesalers who in turn sell to building contractors or homeowners. Some months of the year the company has trouble keeping up with demand and loses sales because customers generally are unwilling to wait and buy from a competitor. Direct labor time is constrained by the production process, so that the company can obtain a maximum of 280,000 direct labor hours per month. The typical product mix results in an average standard labor time of 14 hours per unit. The standard labor rate is $10 per hour, and the standard variable overhead rate is $8 per direct labor hour. Average materials cost is $82 per unit; average selling price is $620 per unit. Results for two recent months follow. January is typically a slow month; June is a busy one with orders for over 22,000 units.

| | January | June |
|---|---|---|
| Units produced | 12,500 | 19,200 |
| Actual labor hours | 179,400 | 280,000 |

Materials costs were at standard. The actual labor rate equalled the standard rate, and variable overhead was incurred as budgeted for actual direct labor hours.

**Required**

1. Compute the labor efficiency variance and variable overhead efficiency variance for each month.
2. Do the variances for both months reflect the true cost to the company of labor inefficiency? Why or why not?

**12-40   Unit costs and total costs**   Wilton Matthews, the production manager of KRL Industries, was disturbed at the following results for November. Budgeted production was 90,000 units, and actual production was 100,000 units.

|  | Budget for 90,000 Units | Actual for 100,000 Units |
|---|---|---|
| Materials | $ 288,000 | $ 341,800 |
| Direct labor | 679,500 | 773,800 |
| Variable overhead | 339,750 | 391,300 |
| Fixed overhead | 850,000 | 860,700 |
| Total costs | $2,157,250 | $2,367,600 |
| Cost per unit | $23.969 | $23.676 |

Purchases of materials were about equal to use and were at 5% over standard prices. Labor rates were 2% over standard.

Matthews tells you that the 5% material price variance and 2% labor rate variance were the source of the unfavorable results, offering the following calculations to support his case.

| | |
|---|---|
| Adjust budgeted costs to 100,000 units ($2,157,250 × 100/90) | $2,396,944 |
| Material price variance ($288,000 × 100/90 × 0.05) | 16,000 |
| Labor rate variance ($679,500 × 100/90 × 0.02) | 15,100 |
| Total allowable costs | $2,428,044 |

"Look, these guys who prepare the reports can't hold me to a budget for 90,000 units when I put out 100,000. Besides, they charged me with variances that I am not responsible for, so I actually came in way under budget. Even with the stupid way they made up the report, you can see that my unit cost was below budget, but I should look even better."

**Required**

Matthews is responsible for materials and labor use and for all overhead costs. Determine whether his claim of good cost control is correct by calculating the total variances for which he is responsible. Calculate as many individual variances as you can.

**12-41   Design change variances**   Grogan Company manufactures machine tools and often changes the design of a tool during the year to make it more suitable for customers. Grogan does not change the standards when it changes the design, which has caused some grumbling by production managers. The controller wants to be able to reconcile the year's actual results with the original budget and argues that changing standards during the year makes it virtually impossible to do so.

As a compromise, a production manager has suggested dividing the efficiency variances into two parts, one that captures the effects of design changes, the other to reflect efficiency in meeting the standard created by the revised design. The total efficiency variance will still be the difference between actual inputs at standard prices and the original standard inputs at standard prices.

The following data are representative of design changes.

|  | Original | Redesigned |
|---|---|---|
| Materials: |  |  |
| 6 feet at $3 per foot | $18.00 |  |
| 7 feet at $3 per foot |  | $21.00 |
| Direct labor: |  |  |
| 0.60 hours at $10 per hour | 6.00 |  |
| 0.55 hours at $10 per hour |  | 5.50 |
| Variable overhead at $7 per DLH | 4.20 | 3.85 |
| Totals | $28.20 | $30.35 |

Production of the tool was 2,000 units, requiring 13,700 feet of materials and 1,180 direct labor hours.

**Required**
1. Determine the material, direct labor, and variable overhead efficiency variables, ignoring the redesign.
2. For each variance, determine how much resulted from the design change and how much from efficient or inefficient use of input factors.

**12-42  Use of unit costs**   The supervisor of the machining department of Glenmills Company has just received the following performance report, which was prepared by the new cost accountant.

|  | Costs per Unit | | |
|---|---|---|---|
|  | Budget | Actual | Variance |
| Materials | $ 3.00 | $ 2.96 | $(0.04) |
| Direct labor (1.5 standard hours) | 9.00 | 9.204 | 0.204 |
| Variable overhead: |  |  |  |
|   Indirect labor | 2.40 | 2.48 | 0.08 |
|   Power | 0.90 | 0.93 | 0.03 |
| Fixed overhead | 4.00 | 4.95[a] | 0.95 |
| Totals | $19.30 | $20.524 | $ 1.224 |

*a Actual cost incurred divided by actual production in units.*

Budgeted production was 12,000 units; actual production was 10,000 units. Budgeted fixed overhead per unit is based on budgeted production. You learn that actual materials cost in the report is based on standard prices and that all other actual cost figures are based on actual prices and quantities.

The supervisor is not responsible for direct labor rates, which were $5.90. He is also not responsible for variable overhead spending variances, but he is responsible for fixed overhead budget variances.

**Required**
Prepare a new report including only those items for which the supervisor is responsible. (You might wish to use a different type of presentation from that shown.)

**12-43  Analysis of income statement**   The controller of Taylors Company has given you the following income statement.

| | | |
|---|---:|---:|
| Sales (20,000 × $20) | | $400,000 |
| Standard variable cost of sales | | 240,000 |
| Standard variable manufacturing margin | | $160,000 |
| Variances: | | |
|   Materials | $ 6,000F | |
|   Direct labor | 4,000U | |
|   Variable overhead | 3,000U | 1,000U |
| Actual variable manufacturing margin | | $159,000 |
| Fixed costs: | | |
|   Budgeted manufacturing costs | $75,000 | |
|   Fixed cost budget variance | 2,000U | |
|   Selling and administrative expenses | 40,000 | 117,000 |
| Income before taxes | | $ 42,000 |

The controller gives you additional data. Production was 22,000 units. Materials purchased were all made at standard price. Direct laborers averaged 0.85 hours per unit, which was 0.05 hours above the standard time. Actual direct labor cost was $144,800. The standard variable overhead rate is $2 per direct labor hour.

*Required*
Answer the following questions.

1. What was the direct labor efficiency variance?
2. What was the direct labor rate variance?
3. What was the standard materials cost per unit?
4. What was actual total variable overhead?
5. What was the variable overhead efficiency variance?
6. What was the variable overhead budget variance?
7. What was actual total fixed manufacturing cost?
8. If the standard materials price is $2 per pound, how many pounds are needed at standard to make a unit of product?
9. How many pounds of materials did the company use?

**12-44  Forecasting income**  Robyn Company had the following income statement in 20X7.

| | | |
|---|---:|---:|
| Sales (110,000 × $20) | | $2,200,000 |
| Standard variable cost of sales | | 880,000 |
| Standard variable manufacturing margin | | $1,320,000 |
| Variances: | | |
|   Materials | $ 2,400U | |
|   Direct labor | 1,800F | |
|   Variable overhead | 1,600F | 1,000F |
| Actual variable manufacturing margin | | $1,321,000 |
| Fixed costs: | | |
|   Manufacturing | $560,000 | |
|   Selling and administrative | 470,000 | 1,030,000 |
| Income | | $ 291,000 |

The details of standard cost were as follows:

| | |
|---|---:|
| Materials (0.50 pounds at $4 per pound) | $2.00 |
| Direct labor (0.40 hours at $10 per hour) | 4.00 |
| Variable overhead at $5 per direct labor hour | 2.00 |
| Total standard variable cost | $8.00 |

The company's industrial engineers have redesigned the product so that (1) the materials requirement should be 0.45 pounds and (2) direct labor hours should be 0.35. The company expects to produce 120,000 units in 20X8 and to sell 115,000. Materials costs will increase to $4.20 per pound. Each element of fixed cost should increase by 5%.

 The managers and engineers expect to see materials use about 2% over the 0.45 pounds standard because it will take some time for workers to learn the new production methods. They also expect direct labor for the year to be about 6% above standard for the same reason. They do want to use the 0.45 pounds and 0.35 hours as the standards, however, because they expect workers to operate at standard by midyear. The standard variable overhead rate will increase by $0.20 per hour because of rising prices for input factors such as supplies and power. All elements not mentioned should be about the same as they were in 20X7.

### Required
1. Determine the standard cost for the product for 20X8.
2. Prepare an income statement for 20X8 reflecting the manager's expectations, using the same format as the one for 20X7.

**12-45  Relationships among data** Dempsey Company uses standard variable costs. Variable overhead rate is based on direct labor hours. The following data are available for operations during April 20X4.

| | |
|---|---:|
| Total production | _____ |
| Actual labor cost | $99,300 |
| Actual materials used | 7,700 pounds |
| Actual variable overhead | $37,150 |
| Standard labor cost per unit | $_____ |
| Standard materials cost per unit | $4.50 |
| Standard variable overhead cost per unit | $_____ |
| Materials purchased (8,200 pounds) | $12,800 |
| Material price variance | $500 U |
| Labor rate variance | $800 U |
| Variable overhead spending variance | $_____ F or U |
| Material use variance | $_____ F or U |
| Labor efficiency variance | $1,500 F |
| Variable overhead efficiency variance | $_____ F or U |
| Direct labor hours worked | 9,850 hours |
| Standard labor rate | $_____ |
| Standard direct labor hours per unit | 4 hours |
| Variable overhead rate per DLH | $4 |

**Required**

Fill in the blanks. (Hint: You cannot do the parts in the order given.)

**12-46  Standard costs—alternative raw materials**  Visodane, Inc. manufactures a household cleaner called Kleenall that is sold in 32-ounce (1/4 gallon) plastic bottles. The cleaner can be made using either of two basic raw materials: anaxohyde or ferodoxin. Their respective costs are $10 and $8 per pound. Whichever material is used is mixed with water and other chemical agents and is then cooked. The product is then bottled, and the bottles are packed into cartons of 20 bottles each.

Each batch is made with 1,200 gallons of water, costing $0.30 per 100 gallons. Chemical agents other than raw materials cost $120 per batch. If anaxohyde is used, 100 pounds are mixed with the water and chemical agents. If ferodoxin is used, 110 pounds are needed. Mixing takes three hours and requires three laborers.

The mixture is then cooked, for 80 minutes if anaxohyde is used and for 90 minutes if ferodoxin is used. One worker is needed for the cooking process. With either raw material, the output of the cooking process is 1,000 gallons because of evaporation. Bottling and packing requires one laborer working two hours.

All laborers are paid $6 per hour. Variable overhead is based on the time required in each process because the high degree of mechanization makes direct labor a poor measure of activity for variable overhead. Overhead per hour is $30 for the mixing process, $120 for the cooking process, and $60 for the bottling and packing process. Bottles cost $0.04 each and the cartons cost $0.20 each.

**Required**

1. Compute the standard cost of a carton of 20 bottles of Kleenall, assuming (a) anaxohyde is used and (b) ferodoxin is used.
2. Suppose that each carton sells for $20 and that cooking time available each month is 1,000 hours. Which material should be used?

## CASES

**12-47  Selecting a vendor**  Bill Nairn, controller of the Electronic Products division of Olesko, Inc., was trying to decide between two vendors for a valve for a product. Nairn gathered the following data regarding the two finalists. The data came from other divisions that do business with both companies. The division expects to use 1,000,000 valves per year.

|  | Capital Metals | Spartan Valve |
|---|---|---|
| Unit price | $3.90 | $4.40 |
| Discount for payment within 10 days | 2% | 1% |
| Normal lead time, purchase order to delivery | 27 days | 7 days |
| Percentage times missed delivery date | 18% | 4% |
| Reject rate | 5% | 1% |
| Technical support | good | excellent |

**Required**

State which vendor you would choose and why.

**12-48  Developing standard costs (CMA adapted)**  The controller of Berman Detergents has asked for your help in preparing standard variable costs for its major product, Sudsaway. Berman has never used standard costs, and the controller believes that better control will be achieved if standards are used. She wants the standards to be based on currently attainable performance.

The following data are available for operations in 20X6.

| | | |
|---|---:|---:|
| Materials used (1,350,000 gallons at $0.80 per gallon) | | $1,080,000 |
| Direct labor (160,000 hours at $5.50 per hour) | | 880,000 |
| Variable overhead: | | |
| Indirect labor | $240,000 | |
| Maintenance and repairs | 80,000 | |
| Packaging materials | 370,000 | |
| Other variable overhead | 480,000 | 1,170,000 |
| Total variable production costs | | $3,130,000 |

During 20X6, 740,000 cases of Sudsaway were produced. Each case contains 12 bottles of 16 ounces each, a total of 1.5 gallons per case. During 20X6 the company used an inferior raw material. During 20X7 the company expects to pay $0.90 per gallon for a better material. Even with the better material, some shrinkage will occur during production. The controller expects that output of Sudsaway in gallons will be 90% of the raw material put into process.

The company employed a number of inexperienced workers in 20X6. They worked about 48,000 of the total direct labor hours, which is about 12,000 more than standard hours. During 20X7 the controller expects all workers to be normally productive and to earn an average wage of $5.80.

According to the controller, variable overhead costs were under control during 20X6, given the excessive labor hours worked. Packaging materials were not affected by the excessive labor hours, being related to cases actually produced. Indirect laborers will receive a 10% wage increase early in 20X7.

### Required
Prepare standard variable costs, by category of cost, for a case of Sudsaway.

**12-49  *Standard costs, variances, and evaluation (CMA adapted)***  Bergen Company manufactures a single product. Standard variable cost of a unit is as follows:

| | |
|---|---:|
| Materials (1 pound plastic at $2) | $ 2.00 |
| Direct labor (1.6 hours at $4) | 6.40 |
| Variable overhead | 3.00 |
| Total standard variable cost | $11.40 |

The variable overhead cost is not related to direct labor hours, but rather to units of product because production is thought to be the causal factor in the incurrence of the variable overhead elements. The elements of variable overhead, based on a yearly volume of 60,000 units of production, are as follows:

| | |
|---|---:|
| Indirect labor (30,000 hours at $4) | $120,000 |
| Supplies, oil (60,000 gallons at $0.50) | 30,000 |
| Maintenance costs, variable portion (6,000 hours at $5 per hour) | 30,000 |
| Total budgeted variable overhead | $180,000 |

Fixed overhead is budgeted as follows, based on 60,000 units of product.

| | |
|---|---:|
| Supervision | $ 27,000 |
| Depreciation | 45,000 |
| Other fixed overhead (includes fixed maintenance costs of $12,000) | 45,000 |
| Total budgeted fixed overhead | $117,000 |

During November, 5,000 units were produced and actual costs were as follows:

| | |
|---|---:|
| Materials (5,300 pounds used at $2) | $10,600 |
| Direct labor (8,200 hours at $4.10) | 33,620 |
| Indirect labor (2,400 hours at $4.10) | 9,840 |
| Supplies (6,000 gallons of oil at $0.55) | 3,300 |
| Variable maintenance costs (490 hours at $5.30) | 2,597 |
| Supervision | 2,475 |
| Depreciation | 3,750 |
| Other fixed overhead (includes maintenance of $1,100) | 3,600 |
| Total | $69,782 |

Purchases of materials were 5,200 pounds at $2.10 per pound. The company has divided responsibilities so that the purchasing manager is responsible for price variances for materials and oil; the production manager is responsible for all quantities of materials, labor (direct and indirect), supplies, and maintenance. The personnel manager is responsible for wage rate variances, and the manager of the maintenance department is responsible for spending variances.

**Required**
1. Calculate the following variances.
    (a)  material price
    (b)  material use
    (c)  direct labor rate
    (d)  direct labor efficiency
    (e)  total variable overhead
    (f)  total fixed overhead

2. Prepare a report that details the overhead variances of each element by responsibility. (A convenient method is to list the managers across the top, and under each show the variances for which they are responsible.) You should account for all variable and fixed overhead variances. That is, the total of your answers to requirement 1 should be distributed to individual managers.

**12-50 Analyzing results (CMA adapted)** Aunt Molly's Old Fashioned Cookies bakes cookies for retail stores. The company's best-selling cookie is Chocolate Nut Supreme, which is marketed as a gourmet cookie and regularly sells for $8.00 per pound. The standard cost per pound of Chocolate Nut Supreme, based on Aunt Molly's normal monthly production of 400,000 pounds, is as follows:

| Cost Item | Quantity | Standard Unit Cost | Total Cost |
|---|---|---|---|
| Direct materials | | | |
| Cookie mix | 10 oz. | $0.02/oz. | $0.20 |
| Milk chocolate | 5 oz. | $0.15/oz. | 0.75 |
| Almonds | 1 oz. | $0.50/oz. | 0.50 |
| | | | $1.45 |
| Direct labor* | | | |
| Mixing | 1 min. | $14.40/hr. | $0.24 |
| Baking | 2 min. | $18.00/hr. | 0.60 |
| | | | $0.84 |
| Variable overhead** | 3 min. | $32.40/hr. | $1.62 |
| Total standard cost per pound | | | $3.91 |

\* *Direct labor rates include employee benefits.*
\*\* *Applied on the basis of direct labor hours.*

Aunt Molly's management accountant, Karen Blair, prepares monthly budget reports based on these standard costs. Following is April's contribution report that compares budgeted and actual performance.

### Contribution Report
### April

| | Budget | Actual | Variance |
|---|---|---|---|
| Units (in pounds) | 400,000 | 450,000 | 50,000F |
| Revenue | $3,200,000 | $3,555,000 | $355,000F |
| Direct material | $ 580,000 | $ 865,000 | $285,000U |
| Direct labor | 336,000 | 348,000 | 12,000U |
| Variable overhead | 648,000 | 750,000 | 102,000U |
| Total variable costs | $1,564,000 | $1,963,000 | $399,000U |
| Contribution margin | $1,636,000 | $1,592,000 | $ 44,000U |

Justine Molly, president of the company, is disappointed with the results. Despite a sizable increase in the number of cookies sold, the product's expected contribution to the overall profitability of the company decreased. Molly has asked Blair to identify the reasons why the contribution margin decreased. Blair has gathered the following information to help in her analysis of the decrease.

### Use Report
### April

| Cost Item | Quantity | Actual Cost |
|---|---|---|
| Direct materials | | |
| Cookie mix | 4,650,000 oz. | $ 93,000 |
| Milk chocolate | 2,660,000 oz. | 532,000 |
| Almonds | 480,000 oz. | 240,000 |
| Direct labor | | |
| Mixing | 450,000 min. | 108,000 |
| Baking | 800,000 min. | 240,000 |
| Variable overhead | | 750,000 |
| Total variable costs | | $1,963,000 |

**Required**

1. Prepare an explanation of the $44,000 unfavorable variance between budgeted and actual contribution margin for the Chocolate Nut Supreme cookie product line during April by calculating the following variances.
   - (a)  sales price variance
   - (b)  sales volume variance
   - (c)  material price variance (assume purchases of material equal use)
   - (d)  material quantity variance
   - (e)  labor efficiency variance
   - (f)  variable overhead efficiency variance
   - (g)  variable overhead spending variance
2. Explain the problems that might arise in using direct labor hours as the basis for allocating overhead.
3. How might activity-based costing solve the problems described in requirement 2?

# Part Four

# *product costing*

Part Four deals with product costing—determining unit costs of products. The emphasis is on manufacturing products, but the material applies to services as well. Knowledge of product costing is important to nonaccounting managers because they use reports that use the methods considered in Part Four. An understanding of cost behavior and of the significance of unit costs is particularly important in interpreting reports of manufacturers. Identifying cost drivers and developing activity-based costs is important because product costs are used for many managerial purposes such as pricing and evaluating the profitability of products and lines. Cost allocation is further considered together with some of its effects. The discussion of product costing methods also covers some behavioral problems. Thus, product costing has implications for control and performance evaluation.

## Chapter Thirteen

# INTRODUCTION TO PRODUCT COSTING

## LEARNING OBJECTIVES

*After reading this chapter, you should be able to*

- *Describe the flow of costs for manufacturers and service providers.*
- *Describe three types of manufacturing processes and their related costing requirements.*
- *Describe and illustrate job-order costing.*
- *Determine product costs under actual and normal costing systems.*
- *Analyze misapplied overhead into budget and volume variances.*
- *Develop ABC overhead rates and apply them to job-order companies.*
- *Discuss the role of overhead application in pursuing strategies.*

*Dell Computer, one of the world's largest sellers of personal computers, assembles each machine according to buyer specifications. When you graduate and send cards to friends and relatives, you may go to a print shop. Print shops make up business cards, wedding invitations, and other products to customer order. Valmont/ALS is a manufacturer of steel poles that range from 20 feet to over 200 feet. Each pole is made to customer specifications. The company maintains 6,500 part numbers and has 40 cost centers. Among other uses, the poles see service as street lights, traffic signal lights, sports lighting for stadiums, and cellular communications.*

*These companies, and others like them, are called job-order companies because they make products to customer order. (Of course, they often use common parts and components for different orders.) Job-order companies use job-order costing, which means that they track the cost of each job they do. Managers of job-order companies need to know how profitable each type of job is. For example, they need a good basis for pricing similar jobs in the future. We examine this type of company and its accounting in this chapter.*

Sources: Annual reports.
David S. Koziol, "How the Constraint Theory Improved a Job Shop Operation," Management Accounting, May 1988, 44–49.

Chapters 13 through 15 introduce the basic concepts and practices of product costing. Product costing focuses on determining the costs of manufactured products for reporting inventory and cost of goods sold in annual reports and other external financial statements. Because inventory and cost of goods sold are important for published financial statements, product costing is an important topic for financial reporting. Manufacturers must therefore adhere to GAAP for their published financial statements, but they are not required to do so for internal reporting and have complete flexibility in preparing financial statements to meet their needs for planning and control.

Product costing topics obviously relate to manufacturers, but much of the material is relevant to other kinds of companies and to not-for-profit organizations. While service and merchandising companies do not face the same GAAP requirements as manufacturers, they nonetheless have similar concerns regarding costs of products. Insurance companies and other financial service providers market a variety of policies and other products. Banks provide various checking account options and different types of loans. Such companies need to understand the costs of their various products. Professional services providers such as firms of CPAs, lawyers, engineers, and management consultants must determine the costs associated with specific kinds of business and specific clients.

Product costing presents many subtle and complex issues that only a competent cost accountant needs to understand. We discuss only basic product costing principles because managers of many types, from marketing through manufacturing, receive reports that use those principles. You are already familiar with the basic techniques of product costing, one of which is assigning overhead cost to products through drivers such as labor time, number of setups, or number of component parts for a product. While discussing ABC in prior chapters we included selling and administrative expenses in determining the costs associated with products because we were concerned with the overall long-term profitability of products, not just the margin of selling price over manufacturing cost. In this chapter, however, we are concerned only with product costs. *Selling and administrative expenses are expensed as incurred: they are not part of the cost of manufactured goods for determining inventories and cost of goods.*

The method that we use in this chapter is called **absorption costing**, or **full costing**, and is required for financial reporting and income tax purposes. Absorption costing simply means that inventory cost includes both fixed and variable manufacturing costs. We have pointed out on many occasions that calculating unit fixed costs is not always wise, especially for short-term decisions. Many authorities believe that absorption costing causes problems besides those we have pointed out and should not be used. We take up this issue in Chapter 14.

## COST FLOWS

As early as Chapter 3, we saw that manufacturers incur costs for materials and components, for the labor required to turn materials into finished product, for the facilities needed for the manufacturing process, and for selling and administrative efforts. Under GAAP, which governs product costing, selling and administrative costs are expensed in the period incurred and are called **period costs**. In general, manufacturing costs are expensed (as cost of goods sold) when the product is sold and are called **product costs**. The path through the company's accounts followed by a product cost, from the time it is incurred to the time it becomes an expense, is called the *flow of costs*. From your study of financial accounting you are familiar with the flow of product costs for a merchandising company. The cost of purchased products (including the purchase cost and freight-in) flows into inventory and then into cost of goods sold. For a manufacturing company, the flow is basically the same—costs flow into inventory and then to cost of goods sold. However, (1) manufacturers typically have three types of inventory and (2) the cost of manufacturers' inventories includes more than the purchase price of materials and components needed for the product. First, a typical manufacturer has three types of inventory.

1. **Materials and purchased parts/components inventory**, consisting of the various materials (steel, glass, wood) and components (items such as switches, valves, and handles purchased from other manufacturers). Merchandisers and service providers have no equivalent inventory. For brevity, we use the term *materials* to refer to both materials and purchased parts/components.

2. **Work in process inventory**, consisting of semifinished units (such as automobiles without windshields, doors, or engines). Reaching this semifinished state requires not only materials and purchased parts but also labor and machinery. This inventory has no equivalent in a merchandising concern. Service providers do have work in process, though not in physical form. The cost of work performed for a specific client for a specific job is work in process inventory to a law firm, CPA firm, or consulting firm.

3. **Finished goods inventory**, consisting of units that are ready for sale. This inventory is equivalent to a merchandiser's inventory. Service providers typically do not recognize finished goods, but rather, when they finish a job, bill the client and so have an account receivable.

The other factor is that manufactured inventories have three types of cost: materials, direct labor, and manufacturing overhead. Direct labor and overhead costs are necessary to transform materials into finished products, a principle we covered in Chapter 3. These costs all flow through inventory and eventually to cost of goods sold.

The flow of costs for a manufacturer is shown in Exhibit 13-1. The costs of materials are first collected in the Materials Inventory account.[1] As materials move into production, their costs flow to Work in Process Inventory.[2] The cost of labor is first collected in Direct Labor and then flows to Work in Process Inventory to show that work was done to transform materials to a semifinished state. Manufacturing overhead costs are collected in a temporary account called Manufacturing Overhead, and then flow to Work in Process Inventory to reflect the need for such items as supervision, power, and depreciation on factory equipment in transforming materials into finished product. Thus, Work in Process Inventory collects the costs of materials, labor, and manufacturing overhead. As goods are completed, their costs flow from Work in Process Inventory to Finished Goods Inventory. Finally, as goods are sold their costs flow from Finished Goods Inventory to Cost of Goods Sold. The approach to *accumulating* cost and production information differs depending on how the company operates.

---

1  *Terminology differs in practice. For example, some companies use the term "stores" for inventory of materials and purchased parts.*

2  *To facilitate the discussion, we capitalize the names of accounts and use lowercase to denote the things themselves. Thus, "Work in Process Inventory" refers to the account and "work in process inventory" refers to the physical, semifinished products.*

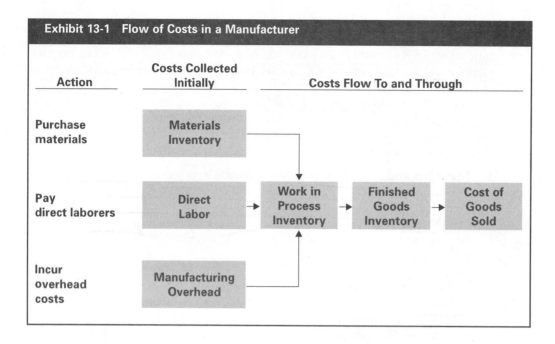

**Exhibit 13-1    Flow of Costs in a Manufacturer**

| Action | Costs Collected Initially | Costs Flow To and Through | | | |
|---|---|---|---|---|---|
| Purchase materials | Materials Inventory | | | | |
| Pay direct laborers | Direct Labor | Work in Process Inventory | Finished Goods Inventory | Cost of Goods Sold | |
| Incur overhead costs | Manufacturing Overhead | | | | |

## MANUFACTURING PROCESSES

Some factories make a single, homogeneous product in a more or less continuous process. Every pound of sugar or flour, gallon of tomato juice, or square yard of gypsum wallboard is virtually the same as any other made in the same plant. In such cases, we can calculate a unit cost by dividing total production costs by the number of units (pounds, gallons, etc.) produced.

$$\frac{Cost\ per}{unit\ of\ product} = \frac{Total\ production\ costs}{Total\ units\ processed}$$

Such factories use *process costing*, which we discuss in Chapter 15. Note that because such factories make only one product, they have no need for activity-based costing for *products* because *all* costs relate to that one product. As Chapter 4 discussed, such companies might still use ABC to analyze the profitability of other segments such as customers or geographical regions, but all products essentially cost the same. Many service providers operate similar processes as well. Banks have departments that process thousands of checks and insurance companies process thousands of claims. Some operations, such as payroll departments, perform their processing services within their specific organizations.

At the other end of the spectrum are companies or factories that rarely, if ever, make the same product twice. Construction companies never build exactly the same bridge, office building, or house twice. A printer might work on 50 different books in a month, each with a different number of pages, type of ink, and quality of paper. For either company, calculating an average cost using the previous equation is senseless, because the units are so different. Moreover, the managers of such companies are keenly interested in the cost of each unit or batch. For, while they might not make the same product (house, bridge, 300-page book) again, they will make similar ones—requiring similar amounts of materials, labor, and other resources—and will use the costs of current jobs to estimate costs of future jobs. Such companies use *job-order costing*, which we discuss later in this chapter. Most professional service providers fall into this class. Firms of lawyers, CPAs, and consultants do specific jobs for their clients, each requiring people of different levels doing different amounts of work. Job-order companies often use standard parts and standard operations, and therefore can do some standard cost and variance analysis.

Many hybrids lie along the spectrum: many modern companies and factories are *mass producers* or *repetitive manufacturers*. They make many products, so they cannot use the simple process costing formula for their total output. However, all of their products are relatively standard. An automobile assembly plant is a good example. It will assemble different models of cars, with different equipment options, but all of them are cars. Such companies typically use *standard costing*, which we introduced in Chapter 12 and continue in Chapter 14.

## JOB-ORDER COSTING

The essence of **job-order costing** is that you keep track of the cost of each job. You trace the materials and labor used on each job directly and then *allocate (apply, absorb,* or *assign)* manufacturing overhead to each job. Job-order operations have tended to be less efficient than processing or mass-production operations because of the costs of complexity. A job-order operation must have the capabilities to do various kinds of work. Managers must be able to track all jobs, meet demanding delivery requirements, schedule work at various stations, and do other things that a straightforward processing operation does not have to do. Additionally, recordkeeping costs of a job-order operation are high. Workers must record the materials used on every job. They must track their own time on jobs, and perhaps the time of various machines. Such recording adds no value to the product, so companies continually strive to reduce or eliminate such activities and their related costs. The accompanying Insight describes a few ways companies are seeking to reduce both complexity costs and recordkeeping costs.

As you know from Chapter 4, indirect manufacturing overhead costs—such as heat, light, power, and machinery depreciation—cannot be traced directly to specific jobs. Rather, overhead costs are applied (assigned) to jobs indirectly, by determining overhead rates of activities (drivers) with which overhead cost pools vary most closely. Chapter 10 called such activities *allocation bases*. Common bases are direct labor hours, direct labor cost, machine hours, number of machine setups, number of material moves, and cycle time. Managers use the techniques described in Chapter 3 to determine the activities with which overhead cost pools are most closely associated.

Historically, direct labor has been used more than any other base. Over time, companies with significant automation switched to machine hours. With the rise of activity-based costing, companies now use multiple bases. Of course, to apply overhead, the company must track how much of these resources each job requires, which brings up the benefit/cost issue. In Chapter 12, we examined this issue in the context of tracing electricity costs to machine use and to heating and

**SIGHT**

### Reducing Costs of Job-Order Operations

Technological developments such as bar coding have made gathering and recording data much less tedious and less costly. **Analytical Science Corporation** is one of a number of companies developing software to use with data-capturing technology. The company's software allows employees to use "bar coded and/or magnetic striped badges to activate the data capture terminals to track progress throughout the day." The company's products allow supervisors to track these changes by using a handheld portable unit. The company's products also allow managers to scan a job in or out at each workstation—from beginning to end. Customers asking about the status of their jobs can find out immediately where the job is and what it has yet to go through.

**Maxwell Business Systems** offers software that is especially aimed at defense contractors, who have very specific job-order requirements. Government contracts even require special forms such as one the contractor completes after producing each unit.

Electronic vision allows companies to perform tasks that were once too expensive. Inspections are a good example. Electronic eyes can detect defects too small for the human eye to see, and do it more cheaply than human beings. This advantage is not limited to job-order operations. But electronic eyes also allow much better quality on made-to-order items. **Foot-Joy**, the premier maker of golf shoes and gloves, is striving to custom-fit golf gloves, an item that retails for under $25. Clearly, custom-fitting such an inexpensive item using skilled workers is not feasible. **Mercedes-Benz** uses electronic eyes to inspect every SUV it makes in Alabama for the fits of body parts. The company once was able to inspect only 1 in 100 thoroughly because of time constraints.

*Sources: Analytical Sciences Corporation website.*
*Kathy Williams and James Hart, "Maxwell Business Systems High Flight,"* Management Accounting, *November 1996, 49–52.*
*Stuart F. Brown, "Vision Systems,"* Fortune, *February 16, 1998, 104B.*

lighting. Only if the benefits of more accurate information were greater than the costs should a company gather more information.

Chapter 4 introduced the concept of assigning overhead costs to one activity (e.g., customers) based on some other activity (e.g., number of deliveries). We applied the concept in Chapter 12, where we applied variable overhead through input factors such as labor time or machine time. We do the same in product costing.

Exhibit 13-2 contains the basic information for our example. (For now, ignore the lower part of the exhibit, which deals with budget information.) ZyCo manufactures electronic sensing devices to customer order. ZyCo worked on three jobs (J-1, J-2, and J-3) in July. The company uses machine hours to apply overhead. This basic example uses a single rate for simplicity. We cover multiple rates later in this chapter.

---

**Exhibit 13-2   ZyCo Data for July**

| | | | | |
|---|---|---|---|---|
| Total overhead costs | | | | $105,000 |
| Total machine hours | | | | 10,500 |

| | Job Number | | | |
|---|---|---|---|---|
| **Job Data** | **J-1** | **J-2** | **J-3** | **Totals** |
| Machine hours | 3,000 | 5,000 | 2,500 | 10,500 |
| Materials used | $20,000 | $15,000 | $10,000 | $45,000 |
| Direct labor cost | $10,000 | $20,000 | $15,000 | $45,000 |
| **Budgeted data for year:** | | | | |
| Machine hours | | | | 120,000 |
| Overhead costs, $600,000 + $4 per machine hour | | | | $1,080,000 |

**Other information:** Job J-1 was finished and sold for $110,000, job J-2 was finished, but not sold, and job J-3 was unfinished at the end of July.

---

Workers prepared forms that detailed the materials costs, direct labor costs, and machine hours in Exhibit 13-2. For overhead, companies use two methods: actual costing and normal costing. We shall illustrate both methods, and then discuss their effects on financial statements.

## ACTUAL COSTING

Under **actual costing**, all overhead cost for a period is applied to the jobs that the company worked on during the period. We calculate the actual overhead rate by dividing total actual overhead by the total amount of the input factor—machine hours here. We then multiply the rate by the number of units of the input factor used by each job. In general form,

$$Overhead\ rate\ =\ \frac{Total\ manufacturing\ overhead}{Total\ manufacturing\ activity}$$

In this situation,

$$Overhead\ rate\ =\ \frac{\$105,000}{10,500}$$
$$=\ \$10\ per\ machine\ hour$$

We can now determine the total costs on the three jobs.

| | Job Number | | | |
|---|---|---|---|---|
| | **J-1** | **J-2** | **J-3** | **Totals** |
| Overhead ($105,000): | | | | |
| 3,000 hrs. at $10 | $30,000 | | | |
| 5,000 hrs. at $10 | | $50,000 | | |
| 2,500 hrs. at $10 | | | $25,000 | $105,000 |
| Materials | 20,000 | 15,000 | 10,000 | 45,000 |
| Direct labor | 10,000 | 20,000 | 15,000 | 45,000 |
| Total cost of job | $60,000 | $85,000 | $50,000 | $195,000 |

CHAPTER
10

Notice that all $105,000 of overhead cost is allocated to the three jobs ($30,000 + $50,000 + $25,000 = $105,000). Under actual costing, total overhead incurred is assigned to individual jobs. Note that we could also allocate overhead the way we did in Chapter 10, by determining the percentage of the driver that each job used. Thus, J-1 used 3,000/10,500 of machine hours and so received 3,000/10,500 of $105,000, or $30,000. You might wish to verify the calculations for the other two jobs.

Let us move to the financial statements. Exhibit 13-2 states that job J-1 was sold in July, J-2 was finished, but not sold, and J-3 was not finished at the end of July. The cost of job J-1 appears in the July income statement as Cost of Goods Sold (as we shall show later). The cost of job J-2 appears in the July 31 balance sheet as Finished Goods Inventory and that of job J-3 appears on the balance sheet as Work in Process Inventory.

Actual job-order costing is simple, but it is not commonly used because it produces misleading results when overhead rates fluctuate significantly from month to month. Differences in monthly rates are related to fixed overhead costs and have two causes. First, activity (machine hours in our example) often differs from month to month. Second, fixed overhead costs can fluctuate—heating is an obvious example. Although heating costs are higher in winter, to say that products made in the winter "cost more" because overhead cost is higher is unwise. Customers will not pay more for products made in January just because the manufacturer had to heat its factory.

We use ZyCo data to illustrate the problem. Exhibit 13-2 shows that ZyCo's variable overhead cost is $4 per machine hour and that its fixed overhead averages $50,000 per month ($600,000 annual divided by 12 months). Suppose that in May its fixed overhead is $50,000, but in December, because of seasonal cost factors, it is $55,000. Machine hours are 10,000 in May and 5,000 in December, again because of seasonal factors. Variable overhead is incurred at $4 per machine hour in both months. Under actual job-order costing, the overhead rates for the two months are as follows:

|  | May | December |
|---|---|---|
| Total overhead costs: |  |  |
| $50,000 + (10,000 × $4) | $90,000 |  |
| $55,000 + (5,000 × $4) |  | $75,000 |
| Machine hours | 10,000 | 5,000 |
| Overhead rate per machine hour | $9 | $15 |

Suppose that ZyCo does two similar jobs in May and December, each requiring 100 machine hours, $500 in direct labor, and $300 in materials. Actual costing shows the following total costs of each job.

| | Job Done In | |
|---|---|---|
|  | May | December |
| Materials | $ 300 | $ 300 |
| Direct labor | 500 | 500 |
| Overhead, 100 hours at $9 and $15 | 900 | 1,500 |
| Totals | $1,700 | $2,300 |

Does the job done in December really cost $600 more than the one done in May? Will customers pay more for jobs just because they were made in a slow month? Actually, customers often pay lower, not higher, prices in slow months, because companies drop their prices to keep their workers busy. Yet the profitability of the two jobs will appear different if they were sold at the same price, and this appearance might mislead a manager trying to develop a price quotation on a similar job. Companies avoid this problem by using normal costing, which we consider in a moment.

Job-order companies are obvious candidates for extensive ABC analysis because their operations are complex and diverse. JIT and other world-class approaches are also useful in managing job shop operations. The accompanying Insight gives some clues about how such approaches can be especially helpful.

## NORMAL COSTING

Under **normal costing**, a company uses budgeted numbers to calculate an overhead rate at the beginning of a year, then uses this overhead rate all year. This procedure smooths the fluctuations of actual costing. The overhead rate is called a

 *SIGHT*

### World-Class Manufacturing for Job-Order Operations

**Valmont/ALS**, the steel fabricator introduced in the opening vignette, was experiencing serious profitability problems. Inventories were rising and the last week of every month required extensive overtime to meet shipping deadlines. The phenomenon of heavy, frantic activity late in each month (known as the hockey stick syndrome because the pattern of production looks like a hockey stick, with a long straight section, then one shooting off at an angle) is common to many manufacturing operations, especially job order. Shipments the last week of the month were often 40 percent of the total for the month. Personnel spend inordinate amounts of time resolving conflicts in scheduling jobs and expediting the flow of jobs through the plant. Inventories rose, storage space increased, and profitability fell.

The company's first step was to reduce the batch sizes of small parts that it made to provide buffer inventories. The result was much smoother flows because of less disruption from stockouts of such parts. The company went on to producing poles and parts *only* to meet customer orders, not to building up inventories of parts. The results were dramatic. Total operating costs declined while profits and return on investment soared, even though sales dropped 2 percent as a result of a recession. The company cut lead times and increased its on-time shipments.

*Source: David S. Koziol, "How the Constraint Theory Improved a Job Shop Operation,"* Management Accounting, *May 1988, 44–49.*

**predetermined overhead rate**, or a **normal overhead rate**. A predetermined overhead rate is based on budgeted results, not actual costs and activity. The calculation follows.

$$\text{Predetermined overhead rate} = \frac{\text{Budgeted manufacturing overhead for year}}{\text{Budgeted production activity for year}}$$

A company can use one rate or several rates. A company using more than one rate divides budgeted manufacturing overhead into specific cost pools and uses the corresponding drivers as the denominators. The activity measures (direct labor hours, number of setups, cycle time) used in normal costing are the same as those used in actual costing; the difference is in the use of budgeted rather than actual figures. We illustrate normal job-order costing using the budgeted data at the bottom of Exhibit 13-2. The budget formula for overhead costs has the same form we saw in earlier chapters.

$$\text{Budget allowance} = \text{Fixed costs} + \left( \text{Variable cost per unit of activity} \times \text{Amount of activity} \right)$$

Total budgeted overhead is $1,080,000, budgeted fixed overhead of $600,000 and budgeted variable overhead is $480,000 ($4 variable overhead per machine hour × 120,000 budgeted machine hours). The predetermined overhead rate is $9 per machine hour:

$$\text{Predetermined overhead rate} = \frac{\$600,000 + \$4 \times 120,000}{120,000}$$
$$= \$9$$

This rate, multiplied by the number of hours worked on each job, gives the overhead costs of the jobs. Overhead assigned to jobs is called **applied** (or **absorbed**) **overhead**.

|  | Job Number | | | |
|---|---|---|---|---|
|  | J-1 | J-2 | J-3 | Totals |
| Overhead |  |  |  |  |
| 3,000 hrs. at $9 | $27,000 |  |  |  |
| 5,000 hrs. at $9 |  | $45,000 |  |  |
| 2,500 hrs. at $9 |  |  | $22,500 | $94,500 |
| Materials | 20,000 | 15,000 | 10,000 | 45,000 |
| Direct labor | 10,000 | 20,000 | 15,000 | 45,000 |
| Total cost of job | $57,000 | $80,000 | $47,500 | $184,500 |

This schedule has several important points. First, materials costs and direct labor costs are the same as they were under actual costing. Only the overhead cost allocations are different. *The differences between actual costing and normal costing relate solely to differences in allocated overhead.* The following analysis should help you understand the different treatments of overhead under actual costing and normal costing. Under actual costing, the overhead cost assigned to a particular job is

$$\text{Overhead assigned to job} = \text{Actual hours worked on job} \times \frac{\text{Total actual overhead}}{\text{Total actual hours}}$$

Under normal costing, the overhead assigned to a job is

$$\text{Overhead assigned to job} = \text{Actual hours worked on job} \times \frac{\text{Total budgeted overhead}}{\text{Total budgeted hours}}$$

Thus, under actual costing, total actual overhead is spread over all jobs. But under normal costing, the total amount of overhead assigned to jobs will equal total actual overhead only if (1) total actual overhead equals total budgeted overhead and (2) total actual hours equal total budgeted hours. (Offsetting differences could make the assignment come out even, but that is very unlikely.)

Which set of costs, actual or normal, is "correct"? There is no answer to this question, much as there is no answer to the question of whether first-in first-out or last-in first-out is the "correct" inventory cost flow assumption. Normal costing has the advantage of minimizing the effects of fluctuations in the overhead rate, and is therefore more popular than actual costing. Earlier, we illustrated the wide range of costs that can occur under actual costing. Under normal costing, both jobs (the one done in May and the one done in December) would show $1,700 in total cost ($900 overhead plus $800 direct labor and materials). You should verify this calculation to check your understanding.

You might have noticed that under normal costing, we do not necessarily allocate all overhead to jobs. What happens to the rest? Differences between actual overhead and applied overhead under normal costing are called misapplied overhead.

## MISAPPLIED OVERHEAD

Let us look at the total overhead costs assigned under the two methods to jobs worked on in July.

|  | Overhead Applied to Jobs Using | |
| --- | --- | --- |
|  | Actual Costing | Normal Costing |
| Job J-1 | $ 30,000 | $27,000 |
| Job J-2 | 50,000 | 45,000 |
| Job J-3 | 25,000 | 22,500 |
| Total | $105,000 | $94,500 |

Misapplied overhead is $10,500 ($105,000 − $94,500). When actual overhead is greater than applied overhead, as above, the difference is called **underapplied** (or **underabsorbed**) **overhead**. When applied overhead is greater than actual overhead, we call the difference **overapplied** (or **overabsorbed**) **overhead**. So ZyCo has $10,500 of *underapplied* overhead. (Note that you can also calculate total applied overhead by multiplying the predetermined overhead rate of $9 by the 10,500 total machine hours: $9 × 10,500 = $94,500.) Please note also that applied overhead is *not* budgeted overhead, applied overhead is *not* the amount you expect to incur; overhead application is a product costing device. ZyCo budgets overhead as $50,000 per month plus $4 times machine hours, *not* as $9 per machine hour. *The $9 rate is for product costing, not for budgeting.*

CHAPTER 12
At first glance, misapplied overhead looks much like the variances we studied in Chapter 12. Applied overhead is similar to standard cost, and overapplication and underapplication are analogous to favorable and unfavorable cost variances. The forms are very similar, but the interpretations are not.

## OVERHEAD VARIANCES

Let us look more closely at ZyCo's July results. The budget formula for annual overhead cost is $600,000 fixed costs plus $4 per machine hour variable. With monthly fixed overhead budgeted at the average of $50,000 (one twelfth of the annual amount), we can compare July's actual costs with the flexible budget allowance based on 10,500 hours.

| | |
|---|---:|
| Actual costs, fixed and variable | $105,000 |
| Budgeted costs [$50,000 + ($4 × 10,500 hours)] | 92,000 |
| Budget variance, unfavorable | $ 13,000 |

ZyCo incurred $13,000 more overhead cost than budgeted, an unfavorable budget variance. We calculated **budget variances** in Chapter 12, so this calculation is not new with this chapter. In this case, we cannot determine how much of this variance relates to fixed cost and how much to variable cost because we do not know the actual amounts of fixed and variable costs. (We discussed this point in Chapter 12.) But we do know that $13,000 of the $10,500 underapplied overhead is an unfavorable budget variance because actual costs were higher than budgeted costs.

Activity is the other factor affecting the amount of overhead applied. We know (again from Exhibit 13-2) that ZyCo planned 120,000 machine hours for the year, for a monthly average of 10,000 hours. But ZyCo worked 10,500 hours of machine time in July and this difference affected applied overhead. The variance caused by a difference between actual machine hours and the budgeted hours used in the calculation of the predetermined rate is called the **volume variance**, or the **idle capacity variance**, and is the difference between budgeted overhead and applied overhead.

| | |
|---|---:|
| Budgeted overhead, as computed above | $92,000 |
| Applied overhead ($9 × 10,500 actual hours) | 94,500 |
| Volume variance, favorable | $ 2,500 |

When applied overhead exceeds budgeted overhead, the volume variance is favorable; when the opposite is true, the variance is unfavorable. We have now identified two variances that add up to the $10,500 difference between actual and applied overhead for the month. The meaning of a budget variance is clear and familiar from Chapter 12; ZyCo incurred $13,000 more overhead cost than budgeted. But what does the volume variance mean? Only that actual activity was different from budgeted activity—the level of activity used to set the predetermined overhead rate. What is the economic significance of the volume variance? Very little, if any. Whether it is favorable or unfavorable is not good or bad per se, because it relates solely to the smoothing of fixed overhead and arises only because actual hours do not equal the monthly average of budgeted hours. To demonstrate this point more clearly, let us look further at the $17 predetermined overhead rate.

The budgeted overhead cost used in calculating the $9 predetermined overhead rate has both a fixed and a variable component. The variable portion of the rate is $4 per hour, and the fixed portion is $5. (Budgeted fixed overhead is

$600,000 and budgeted hours are 120,000, giving a $5 fixed portion, or the $9 total rate consists of a $4 variable rate, and therefore a $5 fixed rate.) Now, look at the difference between actual hours (10,500) and the 10,000 monthly share of the hours budgeted for the year. The $2,500 volume variance is exactly that 500 hour difference multiplied by the $5 fixed overhead rate. Perhaps this point is more easily seen if you recast the calculation of the volume variance and separate budgeted and applied costs into their variable and fixed components, as follows:

|  | Variable Portion | Fixed Portion |
|---|---|---|
| Budgeted cost (10,500 hours × $4) | $42,000 | $50,000 |
| Applied cost: | | |
|   10,500 hours × $4 | 42,000 | |
|   10,500 hours × $5 | | 52,500 |
| Volume variance (500 hours × $5) | — | $ 2,500 |

The flexible budget allowance for variable costs depends on the actual level of activity. But because fixed costs do not change with the level of activity, the *budgeted* amount remains constant when more (or fewer) hours are worked. Thus, what produces the volume variance is the difference between budgeted and actual production activity, the 500 hours. We now have three different, but equivalent, formulas for calculating the volume variance.

$$\begin{aligned}
\frac{Volume}{variance} &= \frac{Total\ budgeted}{manufacturing\ overhead} - \frac{Total\ applied}{manufacturing\ overhead} \\[2mm]
&= \frac{Total\ budgeted\ fixed}{manufacturing\ overhead} - \frac{Total\ applied\ fixed}{manufacturing\ overhead} \\[2mm]
&= \frac{Predetermined\ overhead}{rate\ for\ fixed\ costs} \times \left(\begin{array}{c} Budgeted \\ production \\ activity \end{array} - \begin{array}{c} Actual \\ production \\ activity \end{array}\right)
\end{aligned}$$

You should use whichever formula is most convenient in a given situation; they all give the same answer. We can also use the graphical format shown in Chapter 12 to compute the overhead budget variance and volume variance.

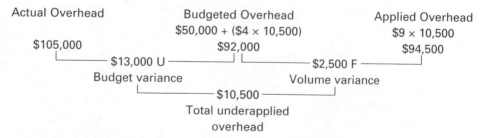

Before leaving this topic we want to remind you again that *applying overhead is an accounting device.* Managers do not expect to incur overhead at the rate used to apply it. Rather, they expect to incur overhead according to the budget formula. The accompanying Insight describes a company in the movie industry that uses normal costing.

## INSIGHT

### Job Costing for Visual Effects

**Buena Vista Visual Effects** creates visual effects for movies. Because of the complexity and difficulty of doing such effects, the company needs good cost data. Before the company takes a job, it determines exactly what it must do to produce each sequence the customer wants. It then develops a budget for the job and submits a bid to the filmmaker. Visual effects can cost $5–$10 million for a high-profile film.

Once the job begins, the company keeps careful track of the time spent by animators, artists, and editors (direct labor) on each job. The pay of creative people is the principal direct cost, so control is critical. Few of these people are full time; most are hired for specific projects. The company applies overhead at 65 percent of direct labor. The weekly cost summary of each job shows costs by category (effects editor, digital scanning, film processing, etc.). Costs appear for the past week and for the entire life of the job. The summary also shows budgeted information, including budget variances.

One managerial tool the company employs is a section on each job summary that shows "estimate to complete." This number is very important and serves as an early warning system that something could be going wrong. The company has found that spotting potential problems early makes them much easier to solve.

*Source: Ray Scalice, "Lights! Cameras! . . . Accountants," Management Accounting, June 1996, 42–46.*

## INCOME STATEMENTS, ACTUAL AND NORMAL COSTING

We now look at how the two methods affect the income statement. Exhibit 13-3 shows income statements for July under the two methods. We assume that ZyCo had $30,000 of selling and administrative expenses. Exhibit 13-2 tells us that job J-1 was completed and sold for $110,000. Costs accumulated on jobs J-2 and J-3 remain in inventory at the end of the month. In internal reports, many companies show additional detail about underapplied overhead, showing separately the budget and volume variances as computed earlier. The most obvious difference between the statements is the amount of income ($20,000 under actual costing and $12,500 under normal costing). What caused the $7,500 difference?

The difference between incomes under actual costing and normal costing lies in the treatment of overhead, not in the amount of overhead incurred, which is the same $105,000 regardless of the method used. The actual costing income statement shows actual overhead in a single amount; the normal costing income statement shows the actual overhead in two amounts, $94,500 assigned to jobs and $10,500 as a separate deduction.

If you look closely at the statements you will see that the $7,500 difference in incomes comes about from the $7,500 difference in the ending inventories. The cost of job J-2 is $5,000 greater and that of J-3 is $2,500 greater under actual cost-

## Exhibit 13-3  ZyCo Income Statements for July

| | | Normal Costing | Actual Costing |
|---|---|---|---|
| Sales | | $110,000 | $110,000 |
| Normal cost of sales | $57,000[a] | | |
| Plus underapplied overhead | 10,500 | | |
| Cost of sales | | 67,500 | 60,000[b] |
| Gross profit | | $42,500 | $ 50,000 |
| Selling and administrative expenses | | 30,000 | 30,000 |
| Profit | | $ 12,500 | $ 20,000 |
| Details of cost of sales: | | | |
| Beginning inventories | | $        0 | $        0 |
| Materials | | 45,000 | 45,000 |
| Direct labor | | 45,000 | 45,000 |
| Overhead | | 94,500 | 105,000 |
| Total costs | | $184,500 | $195,000 |
| Less ending inventories | | 127,500[c] | 135,000[d] |
| Normal cost of sales | | $ 57,000 | |
| Plus underapplied overhead | | 10,500 | |
| Cost of sales | | $ 67,500 | $ 60,000 |

a  Cost of J-1 from page 586.
b  Cost of J-1 from page 583.
c  Job J-2, $80,000 plus job J-3, $47,500, page 586.
d  Job J-2, $85,000 plus job J-3, $50,000, page 583.

ing than under normal costing. That difference occurs because more overhead is assigned to those jobs under actual costing. Remember that overhead was assigned at the actual rate ($10) under actual costing, but at the predetermined rate ($9) for normal costing, so that for a single period within the year such differences are very common. The difference in incomes, then, relates to the differences in overhead assigned to inventory.

We have shown underapplied overhead as an addition to normal cost of sales. Another possibility is to subtract normal cost of sales from sales, calling the result normal gross margin or normal gross profit, and then subtract underapplied overhead from normal gross margin. This approach gives the same income. The choice is a matter of preference. The income statement in Exhibit 13-4 shows the alternative format and also separates underapplied overhead into the budget variance and volume variance.

## ACTIVITY-BASED OVERHEAD RATES

Our example used a single overhead rate, which is fine if machine hours drive virtually all overhead cost, an unlikely situation for most manufacturers. As you know from previous chapters, companies using activity-based costing (ABC)

**Exhibit 13-4    ZyCo Normal Costing Income Statement for July**

| | | |
|---|---:|---:|
| Sales | | $110,000 |
| Normal cost of sales | | 57,000 |
| Normal gross profit | | $ 53,000 |
| Variances: | | |
| Unfavorable budget variance | $13,000 | |
| Favorable volume variance | 2,500 | 10,500 |
| Gross profit | | $ 42,500 |
| Selling and administrative expenses | | 30,000 |
| Profit | | $ 12,500 |

identify cost drivers for each pool of costs. Recall that, for product costing ABC does not assign selling and administrative expenses to jobs or units of product.

Cost pools might be costs of specific departments (such as engineering, maintenance, payroll), or costs related to such activities as materials use, number of setups, cycle time, or engineering changes. Some companies allocate such costs as purchasing, receiving, inspecting, and storing—costs associated with materials—to jobs based on the materials cost of each job.

As you know, using multiple ABC rates often provides better information than does a single plantwide rate. But it is costlier to operate a system where overhead is applied differently from department to department, or on multiple bases. For instance, it is necessary not only to identify cost drivers and pools, but to keep track of the amount of activity associated with each job, product, or other object of allocation. Keeping such records can be costly. Accordingly, using ABC rates is wise only when the expected benefits, in the form of better control and decision making, exceed the additional costs. It is no easy task to determine whether benefits exceed costs, for benefits are not usually quantifiable in dollar terms. Nonetheless, managers must make judgments about benefits.

Multiple rates are better than a single plantwide rate in two general cases. One is when overhead is related to more than one input factor. In our example, ZyCo applied overhead using machine hours, which reflects an automated, machine-intensive operation. However, a department with a low investment in machinery and many laborers could use labor hours to apply overhead. Another example of the same case is if some overhead is clearly related to materials and other overhead to labor or machine time; here again, ABC rates make sense. The other case is when the same input factor applies to all departments, but the overhead rates in the departments differ greatly from one to another. We now show how ABC overhead rates can improve pricing decisions. The following data relate to Tricomm Company, which makes electrical equipment.

| | Data for Cost Driver | | |
|---|---:|---:|---:|
| | Direct Labor | Machine Setups | Total |
| Budgeted overhead costs | $800,000 | $400,000 | $1,200,000 |
| Budgeted direct labor hours | 100,000 | | |
| Budgeted number of setups | | 2,000 | |
| Rates, $800,000/100,000; $400,000/2,000 | $8/hour | $200/setup | |

If Tricomm uses only direct labor to apply overhead, it will calculate a rate of $12 per direct labor hour, which is total overhead of $1,200,000 divided by 100,000 direct labor hours. The $12 rate does not capture the differences between the two types of overhead, and using it could lead to poor decisions. Suppose that Tricomm works on the following two jobs and sets prices at 150 percent of manufacturing costs, including overhead applied at the $12 rate.

|  | Job A | Job B |
|---|---|---|
| Direct labor hours | 800 | 200 |
| Materials cost | $10,000 | $10,000 |
| Direct labor cost at $10/hour | 8,000 | 2,000 |
| Overhead applied at $12/DLH | 9,600 | 2,400 |
| Total cost | $27,600 | $14,400 |
| Price at 150% of cost | $41,400 | $21,600 |

If job A requires two machine setups and job B requires 25 setups, the cost of each job using the activity-based rates is as follows:

|  | Job A | Job B |
|---|---|---|
| Materials cost | $10,000 | $10,000 |
| Direct labor cost at $10/hour | 8,000 | 2,000 |
| Overhead: |  |  |
|   Labor-related at $8/DLH | 6,400 | 1,600 |
|   Setup-related at $200/setup | 400 | 5,000 |
| Total cost | $24,800 | $18,600 |
| Price at 150% of cost | $37,200 | $27,900 |

Using the single, labor-based rate, Tricomm will charge lower prices for jobs requiring lots of setups (compare the prices on job B). If Tricomm has a competitor that has a similar cost structure and uses activity-based rates, Tricomm will bid higher than the competitor on labor-intensive jobs (like job A) and will lose much of that business to the competitor. Tricomm will obtain a great deal of setup-intensive business because it will underbid the competitor. The problem is that Tricomm's profitability will suffer if it bids so low on setup-intensive jobs. (Remember that Tricomm's prices must cover selling and administrative expenses as well as manufacturing costs.)

Determining cost drivers for JIT manufacturers is in some respects easier than for conventional manufacturers. Some costs that are indirect to departments in a conventional manufacturing environment are direct in a JIT environment. Activities such as materials handling, maintenance, and other support services are often carried out by centrally administered units in conventional manufacturing but are done by workers in each manufacturing cell of a JIT operation. The costs of these activities, which are direct to the output of a particular manufacturing cell, make product costing much simpler. We examine product costing in JIT environments in Chapter 15.

CHAPTER 15 ▶

Service organizations have become increasingly interested in cost analysis and especially in ABC. **Fireman's Fund**, the large property/casualty insurer, uses a technique it calls *cost sampling* to determine how much effort its people are directing toward specific types of activities such as screening policy applications, soliciting business, gathering information, negotiating price and coverage, and doing routine paperwork. The company uses various ways to sample people's efforts. One was for the people gathering the information to interrupt employees briefly and determine what type of work they were doing and on what product. The company also analyzed work by reference to type of policy and size of policy, which resulted in setting up a "fast-track" for smaller, routine policies to reduce processing costs.[3] The accompanying Insight describes how the Internal Revenue Service enhanced one of its operations.

## ETHICS IN PRODUCT COSTING

Ethical and legal questions arise in product costing, especially when a company works on a cost-plus basis (where the price is a multiple of cost, or cost plus a specified dollar amount). Such work is quite common in regulated companies, such as electric utilities, and in work done for governmental agencies, especially for the Department of Defense. The legal and ethical issues center on how much overhead is allocated to specific jobs or customers. Selecting drivers, classifying costs in pools, and setting bases for calculating rates can all create potential problems. Chapter 10 described the difficulties that Stanford University encountered because of costs it included in particular pools. Some of the widely publicized cost overruns on defense contracts could be traced at least partly to allocations.

CHAPTER 10

Companies that operate both regulated and non-regulated businesses, as do many communications companies, have incentives to load costs onto regulated businesses, where regulators typically allow cost recovery plus a reasonable profit. The more cost allocated to regulated businesses, the more total revenue the

---

**IN**SIGHT

### Cost Management at the IRS

The Internal Revenue Service operates a unit that handles field collections, such as collecting revenues from people who file returns but do not pay taxes due, or who do not file returns at all. In the past, each collection officer worked on 70–80 jobs at a time. The cases were quite different from one another, adding to the complexity of the job. A pilot study assigned work to teams that specialize in the five distinct types of work: classification, perfecting, and closing; complex cases; seizures and sales; technically complex collecting; and compliance. The results were much better and operations much more efficient.

*Source: John B. MacArthur, "Cost Management at the IRS," Management Accounting, November 1996, 42–48.*

---

3 *Michael Crane and John Meyer, "Focusing on True Costs in a Service Organization,"* Management Accounting, *February 1993, 41–45.*

company earns, and the higher its profit. Managers of not-for-profit entities also face difficult decisions about cost allocations because such entities often conduct both taxable and nontaxable activities. Paying taxes reduces cash available to the entity, so managers have incentives to allocate as much cost as possible to taxable activities. Management accountants are enjoined to perform allocations of overhead in objective ways by the Standards for Ethical Conduct, but gray areas require judgment.

## PRODUCT COSTS AND VALUE-CHAIN ANALYSIS

A company that wants to analyze its position in the value chain, perhaps to enter or leave a particular stage in the chain, must have good estimates of the costs of its products. As you now know, product costing, whether job-order or other, treats selling and administrative expenses as non-inventoriable, thus making product costs unsuitable for such analyses. In many companies selling and administrative expenses exceed manufacturing costs, so value-chain analysis (or any other analysis focusing on product profitability) must supplement product costing information with information about selling and administrative expenses. ABC and other techniques can assign some selling and administrative expenses to products for strategic analyses.

Companies are not only concerned with their own costs, but also with their competitors' costs. Many strategic analyses require determining whether you or your competitors have cost advantages.

## OVERHEAD APPLICATION, BEHAVIOR, AND STRATEGY

Allocating overhead to products, like other topics we have discussed, is fraught with behavioral problems, one of which is whether a particular approach will advance the company's pursuit of specific strategic goals. Chapter 10 introduced this question.

Perhaps the major source of problems is the choice of allocation bases, or drivers. As we said earlier, direct labor has been the principal basis for overhead application for many years. But as we noted several times, labor costs are dropping as a percentage of total costs, especially for companies adopting new manufacturing techniques such as just-in-time, flexible manufacturing, and computer-integrated manufacturing. In fact, because direct laborers also perform indirect, support functions such as maintenance, the distinction between direct labor and indirect labor is often blurry. At the same time, however, overhead costs have been rising, both in absolute dollars and as a percentage of total manufacturing cost. The rise in overhead is a natural consequence of changing the manufacturing environment to one that requires more brainwork. Support personnel such as industrial, mechanical, and electrical engineers; computer experts; and highly skilled maintenance workers are more in demand.

A company whose cost structure is moving toward less labor and more overhead (which also means more fixed cost and less variable cost) can make serious errors allocating overhead using direct labor hours or direct labor cost. When overhead is rising while direct labor hours and cost are falling, an overhead rate calculated using direct labor hours will become astronomically high. Careful studies of cost drivers led many companies to use activity-based rates to direct attention to areas where cost control was most needed. The accompanying Insight describes three cases of companies using overhead application bases to influence behavior, especially to lower costs.

## (IN) SIGHT

### Overhead Allocation and Behavior

The Portables Group of **Tektronix**, which we discussed briefly in Chapter 10, had based its overhead allocations on direct labor, but direct labor had declined to less than 7 percent of total manufacturing cost, and as low as 3 percent on newer products. Simultaneously, overhead costs were rising because the Group was introducing new manufacturing methods and operations had become increasingly technological. These two factors combined to make labor-based overhead rates extremely high. A serious consequence was that manufacturing people believed that reducing labor time was the best way to reduce total costs. While labor cost per se was low, when an hour of direct labor was loaded with a huge overhead charge, the total labor-related cost loomed very large. Design engineers drove labor time down by using special parts and other devices, but that did not have the desired effect. Overhead costs continued to rise.

As Chapter 10 reported, the Portables Group studied overhead costs and concluded that costs of activities such as purchasing, receiving, inspecting, storage, and recordkeeping were significant drivers. The Group changed its allocation procedures, using both materials and conversion activities (labor and machine time). The new allocation methods contributed to better understanding and to greater potential for cost reduction.

**Hitachi**, the giant electronics company, took a different view in one of its factories that manufactured VCRs. Upper-level management decided that lowering labor time was an essential component of a successful strategy. Accordingly, the factory applied overhead based on labor precisely to encourage designers and engineers to drive labor as low as possible.

**Peterson Ranch**, a world-class grower of nuts and fruits in the Sacramento Valley, uses overhead application to encourage desired behavior. Managers are responsible for individual fields and are charged for the labor and overhead they use. Peterson rates tractors and other equipment based on horsepower and so encourages managers to use smaller, less expensive equipment. The equipment fleet is actually dropping both in number of pieces and in size, cost, and complexity.

Sources: John W. Jonez and Michael A. Wright, "Material Burdening," Management Accounting, *August 1987*, 27–31.
T. Hiromoto, "Another Hidden Edge—Japanese Management Accounting," Harvard Business Review, *July–August 1988*, 22–24.
Donald E. Keller and Paul Krause, "'World Class' Down on the Farm," Management Accounting, *May 1990*, 39–45.

## SUMMARY

Product costing is determining costs of inventory and cost of goods sold for manufacturers. For financial reporting and income tax purposes, manufacturers must use absorption costing, which requires that all manufacturing costs, variable and fixed, be included in unit cost.

Manufacturing costs flow through inventory accounts to cost of goods sold. Companies accumulate cost data in several ways, depending on the type of manufacturing process. Factories that produce essentially identical products accumulate costs using process costing. Factories that seldom produce the same product accumulate costs using job-order costing.

Some companies compute product costs based on actual costs. Others use a normal costing system, under which they apply overhead to products using a predetermined overhead rate based on budgeted manufacturing overhead and budgeted production activity. Rates relate to input measures such as direct labor hours or machine hours. Predetermined overhead rates can be calculated for each department or for a factory as a whole.

Under normal costing, actual overhead will rarely equal applied overhead. The difference, called underapplied or overapplied overhead, can be reported in an income statement as an adjustment to either normal cost of sales or normal gross margin. Underapplied or overapplied overhead consists of a budget variance and a volume variance. The latter variance has little economic significance. Activity-based overhead rates are useful for many companies because they provide better information than a single plantwide rate or departmental rates based on labor or machine time. Companies using such rates have found that they improved decision making. An ABC system costs more to operate than a conventional system, so managers must weigh the benefits of an ABC system against the additional costs. The product-costing system can affect behavior and should encourage people to act in goal-congruent ways. In some organizations, choices related to cost allocation raise ethical and legal questions.

## KEY TERMS

absorption (full) costing  *(578)*
actual costing  *(583)*
applied (absorbed) overhead  *(586)*
budget variance  *(588)*
cost pools  *(592)*
finished goods inventory  *(579)*
idle capacity variance  *(588)*
job-order costing  *(581)*
materials and purchased parts/components inventory  *(579)*
normal costing  *(585)*

overapplied (overabsorbed) overhead  *(587)*
period costs  *(578)*
predetermined (normal) overhead rate  *(586)*
product costs  *(578)*
underapplied (underabsorbed) overhead  *(587)*
volume variance  *(588)*
work in process inventory  *(579)*

## KEY FORMULAS

$$\text{Predetermined overhead rate} = \frac{\text{Budgeted manufacturing overhead for year}}{\text{Budgeted production activity for year}}$$

$$\begin{matrix}\text{Overhead} \\ \text{budget variance}\end{matrix} = \begin{matrix}\text{Actual} \\ \text{overhead}\end{matrix} - \begin{matrix}\text{Flexible budget} \\ \text{allowance for actual} \\ \text{production activity}\end{matrix}$$

$$\begin{matrix}\text{Underapplied} \\ \text{(overapplied)} \\ \text{overhead}\end{matrix} = \begin{matrix}\text{Actual} \\ \text{manufacturing} \\ \text{overhead}\end{matrix} - \begin{matrix}\text{Applied} \\ \text{manufacturing} \\ \text{overhead}\end{matrix}$$

$$\text{Volume variance} = \begin{matrix}\text{Total budgeted fixed} \\ \text{manufacturing} \\ \text{overhead}\end{matrix} - \begin{matrix}\text{Total applied (fixed)} \\ \text{manufacturing} \\ \text{overhead}\end{matrix}$$

$$\text{Volume variance} = \begin{matrix}\text{Predetermined} \\ \text{overhead rate for} \\ \text{fixed costs}\end{matrix} \times \left( \begin{matrix}\text{Budgeted} \\ \text{production} \\ \text{activity}\end{matrix} - \begin{matrix}\text{Actual} \\ \text{production} \\ \text{activity}\end{matrix} \right)$$

## REVIEW PROBLEM

Kronzek Press makes large drill presses to customer order and uses job-order costing. The company began March with no inventories. During March, it worked on two jobs.

|  | Job #15 | Job #16 |
|---|---|---|
| Materials used | $69,000 | $45,000 |
| Direct labor at $10 per hour | $35,000 | $60,000 |

Kronzek incurred factory overhead costs of $209,000. Budgeted monthly factory overhead is:

$$\textit{\$150,000 + (\$5} \times \textit{direct labor hours)}$$

The company uses a predetermined overhead rate based on 10,000 direct labor hours per month. Activity does not usually fluctuate much from one month to another.

### Required
1. Calculate the predetermined overhead rate per direct labor hour.
2. Determine the amounts of overhead to apply to each job.
3. Determine the overhead budget variance and volume variance.
4. Suppose that job #15 was sold for $240,000 and job #16 remained in inventory. Selling and administrative expenses for March were $24,000. Prepare an income statement for March. Treat variances as adjustments to normal cost of sales.
5. Suppose now that the company used actual costing, allocating overhead to jobs based on the actual overhead rate per direct labor hour. Determine the amounts of overhead applied to each job and prepare an income statement assuming the relevant data from requirement 4.

**ANSWER TO REVIEW PROBLEM**

1. $20.00 per direct labor hour, calculated as follows.

$$\text{Predetermined rate} = \frac{\text{Total budgeted overhead}}{\text{Total budgeted activity}}$$

$$= \frac{\$150,000 + (\$5 \times 10,000)}{10,000}$$

$$= \$20$$

The rate consists of $15 fixed and $5 variable. Because there is no significant fluctuation in activity during the year, it is reasonable to use the monthly rather than the annual figures to calculate the rate. In fact, with annual fixed overhead of $1,800,000 ($150,000 × 12) and 120,000 direct labor hours (10,000 × 12), we would have exactly the same result.

2.

|  | Job #15 | Job #16 | Total |
|---|---|---|---|
| Direct labor hours: |  |  |  |
| $35,000/$10 | 3,500 |  |  |
| $60,000/$10 |  | 6,000 | 9,500 |

Overhead at $20 per hour: $70,000 + $120,000 = $190,000

3.

| Actual Overhead | Budgeted Overhead | Applied Overhead |
|---|---|---|
|  | $150,000 + ($5 × 9,500) | 9,500 × $20 |
| $209,000 | $197,500 | $190,000 |

└─────── $11,500 ───────┘ └─────── $7,500 ───────┘
Budget                          Volume
variance                        variance

└──────────── $19,000 ────────────┘
Total underapplied overhead

4.

| | |
|---|---|
| Sales | $240,000 |
| Cost of sales: | |
| Normal cost of sales[a] | $174,000 |
| Variances: | |
| Budget variance | 11,500U |
| Volume variance | 7,500U |
| Cost of sales | 193,000 |
| Gross profit | $47,000 |
| Selling and administrative expenses | 24,000 |
| Income | $23,000 |

a  *Job #15, materials + direct labor + applied overhead = $69,000 + $35,000 + $70,000 = $174,000.*

5. The problem here is simply to determine the actual overhead rate.

$$Actual\ rate = \frac{Actual\ overhead}{Actual\ activity}$$

$$= \frac{\$209,000}{9,500\ hours}$$

$$= \$22\ per\ hour$$

The applied amounts are as follows:

|  | Job #15 | Job #16 | Total |
|---|---|---|---|
| Direct labor hours | 3,500 | 6,000 | 9,500 |
| Overhead applied at $22 per hour | $77,000 | $132,000 | $209,000 |

All overhead goes to individual jobs, so there are no variances. The income statement shows the following, with job #15 costing $181,000 ($69,000 + $35,000 + $77,000).

| | |
|---|---|
| Sales | $240,000 |
| Cost of sales | 181,000 |
| Gross margin | $ 59,000 |
| Selling and administrative expense | 24,000 |
| Income | $ 35,000 |

The difference in incomes ($23,000 versus $35,000) arises from the differences in inventory. Under normal costing, as in requirement 2, overhead of $120,000 is applied to job #16, which is still in inventory. Under actual costing, as shown here, overhead of $132,000 is applied to job #16. The $12,000 difference in income under the two methods is explained by the $12,000 difference in the overhead assigned to the job remaining in inventory (job #16).

## ASSIGNMENT MATERIAL

### INTERNET ACTIVITY

Find annual reports or SEC filings of some construction/engineering companies. These are probably the best examples of job-order companies you can find. See what kinds of projects they undertake, such as fixed-fee or cost-plus. What do these companies see as the principal risks they face?

### QUESTIONS FOR DISCUSSION

**13-1   *FedEx's handling costs***   A recent annual report of **FedEx** stated,

"In fiscal 1994, our average daily U.S. domestic package volume rose 12%, or more than 196,000 packages per day. Our average cost for handling that volume declined, however, to an amount 1.5% lower than our fiscal 1993 per-package cost. Internationally, the high fixed costs of our world-wide network are steadily being offset by greater volume."

**Required**

1. Do you think FedEx's *total costs* for handling domestic packages rose or fell from 1993 to 1994? You might wish to work out an example using the figures given and an arbitrary per-package cost for 1993 of $10.
2. Explain the meaning of the last sentence in the quotation.

**13-2   *Overhead absorption*** Many companies set their overhead rates to allow them to absorb overhead costs at some specific percentage of capacity. For instance, **Trane Co**. uses rates that will absorb overhead at 85% of capacity. What does this statement mean?

**13-3   *Overhead application*** "Underapplied overhead is a bad sign because the more overhead you apply, the lower your fixed cost per unit." Discuss this statement critically.

**13-4   *Costing methods and inventories*** World-class manufacturers keep very little inventory. Suppose such a company begins and ends a year with no inventories. Will there be any difference between its income computed using actual costing and using normal costing? Why or why not?

**13-5   *"What's normal about it?"*** A student sitting near you in class just asked this question. The student does not see how you can apply overhead using a predetermined rate, and went on to say: "If overhead cost per hour is $15 in one month and $6 the next, that's the way it goes. All this 'applying' business is a bookkeeping trick, but it doesn't make any sense."

**Required**

Comment on the statements.

**13-6   *Are cost accountants the villains?*** Robert Fox, executive vice president of **Creative Output**, a management consulting firm in Connecticut, was quoted as arguing that allowing cost accounting "to dictate the way a factory floor is organized and run" is harmful. Fox was further quoted as saying that, "The cost accounting system assigns part of overall costs of running the factory to each step in the manufacturing process. Each hour a machine is running, for instance, may be costed at a given amount. A foreman will then try to get as much material as he can through that machine . . . to keep the costs assigned to his particular work stations as low as possible."

**Required**

Discuss the quotation. What does Mr. Fox mean and how must a company be applying overhead for the quotation to be correct?

## EXERCISES

**13-7   *Basic actual job-order costing*** StorTech manufactures ergonomic office furniture to customer order. The company uses actual job-order costing, applying overhead to jobs based on direct labor hours. StorTech worked on two orders in March.

|  | JO-8 | MK-11 |
|---|---|---|
| Direct labor hours | 10,000 | 9,000 |
| Material cost | $80,000 | $115,000 |
| Direct labor cost | $70,000 | $85,000 |

StorTech incurred $190,000 overhead cost in March.

### Required

1. Determine the actual overhead rate for March.
2. Determine the amount of overhead to be applied to each job.
3. Determine the total cost of each job.

**13-8  Basic normal job-order costing (continuation of 13-7)**  StorTech's president has heard about normal costing and wants you to illustrate how it works using March's results. You decide that $9 per direct labor hour is a reasonable predetermined overhead rate.

### Required

1. Determine the amount of overhead to be applied to each job.
2. Determine the total cost of each job.
3. Determine the amount of overapplied or underapplied overhead for March.
4. Suppose that StorTech developed the $9 rate based on 20,000 monthly budgeted direct labor hours and budgeted monthly overhead of $120,000 + ($3 × direct labor hours). What were the budget and volume variances?

**13-9  Job-order costing income statements (continuation of 13-7 and 13-8)**  StorTech's job JO-8 was incomplete at the end of March, while job MK-11 was sold for $550,000. Selling and administrative expenses were $180,000.

### Required

1. Prepare an income statement for March using the results from Exercise 13-7.
2. Prepare an income statement for March using the results from Exercise 13-8. Show any misapplied overhead as an adjustment to normal cost of sales.

**13-10  Job-order costing—income statement, service company**  Tyree Associates does market research and opinion polling. The company uses normal job-order costing. Its predetermined overhead rate is based on the following data.

| | |
|---|---|
| Variable overhead per professional hour | $3 |
| Total budgeted fixed overhead | $800,000 |
| Total budgeted professional hours | 200,000 |

The company began 20X5 with no jobs in process. A summary of direct expenses, professional salary cost, and professional hours for 20X5 is as follows:

| | Total | Jobs Finished and Billed | Jobs Unfinished and Unbilled |
|---|---|---|---|
| Direct expenses | $800,000 | $700,000 | $100,000 |
| Professional salary cost | $2,100,000 | $1,800,000 | $300,000 |
| Professional hours | 180,000 | 160,000 | 20,000 |

Direct expenses include travel, lodging, telephone, and other non-professional salary costs associated with a specific job.

Total sales were $5,500,000, selling and administrative expenses were $1,800,000, and total actual overhead was $1,180,000.

**Required**

1. Compute the predetermined overhead rate for 20X5.
2. Prepare an income statement for 20X5 with overapplied or underapplied overhead shown as an adjustment to cost of sales.

**13-11  Predetermined overhead rates**  For each of the following situations, fill in the missing data. The predetermined overhead rates are based on budgeted fixed costs and budgeted machine hours for the year. There is no variable overhead.

|     | (a) Fixed Overhead Rate | (b) Budgeted Fixed Overhead | (c) Budgeted Hours | (d) Actual Hours | (e) Fixed Overhead Applied |
|-----|-----|-----|-----|-----|-----|
| 1. |        | $180,000 | 30,000 | 31,000 |          |
| 2. | $8     |          | 20,000 | 22,000 |          |
| 3. |        | $70,000  |        | 11,000 | $77,000  |
| 4. | $5     | $160,000 |        |        | $175,000 |

**13-12  Ethics and overhead application**  Milton Machine does considerable work for the U.S. government on cost-plus contracts. The typical cost-plus contract provides that the government will pay for materials, direct labor, and overhead. The government requires that overhead assigned to jobs be reasonable and in conformity with the company's usual methods. An allowance for profit is then added to the total cost to determine the price.

Milton has been using machine hours to apply overhead but its controller believes that the company should shift to labor hours. He explains, "Our government business could be a lot more profitable if we used labor time to apply overhead. Government business is much more labor-intensive than commercial business and would therefore shoulder more overhead."

**Required**

Comment on the controller's proposal.

**13-13  Overhead relationships—variances**  Each of the following cases is independent. Fill in the blanks, being sure to indicate whether a variance is favorable or unfavorable. The amounts for "total budgeted overhead" are the flexible budget allowances for the actual level of activity for the period. In each case, the company uses a single rate to apply both fixed and variable overhead.

| Case | (a) Total Budgeted Overhead | (b) Total Actual Overhead | (c) Total Applied Overhead | (d) Budget Variance | (e) Volume Variance |
|------|-----|-----|-----|-----|-----|
| 1 | $400,000 | $405,000 | $398,000 |         |          |
| 2 | $200,000 |          | $195,000 | $3,000F |          |
| 3 | $700,000 |          |          | $3,000U | $15,000F |
| 4 |          | $310,000 |          | $6,000U | $18,000F |

**13-14  Job-order costing—assigning overhead**  Marquette Boatworks uses normal costing and its predetermined overhead rate is based on the following information. Monthly budgeted overhead = $800,000 + ($0.60 × direct labor cost). Monthly budgeted direct labor cost is $1,000,000. At the end of March, the following information was available.

| | Total | Jobs Sold | Jobs in Ending Inventory of Work in Process | Finished Goods |
|---|---|---|---|---|
| Materials cost | $630,000 | $500,000 | $70,000 | $60,000 |
| Direct labor cost | $1,210,000 | $920,000 | $150,000 | $140,000 |

Actual overhead for the month was $1,647,000.

**Required**
1. Compute the predetermined overhead rate based on direct labor cost.
2. Determine cost of goods sold for the month.
3. Determine ending inventory of work in process.
4. Determine ending inventory of finished goods.
5. Determine overapplied or underapplied overhead.
6. Determine the volume variance.
7. Determine the budget variance.

**13-15   Predetermined overhead rates—job-order costing**   Midus Communications uses predetermined rates for fixed overhead, based on machine hours. The following data relate to 20X5.

| | |
|---|---|
| Budgeted fixed factory overhead cost | $250,000 |
| Budgeted machine hours | 50,000 |
| Actual fixed factory overhead cost incurred | $248,000 |
| Actual machine hours used | 47,000 |

| Actual machine hours by job | |
|---|---|
| Job No. | Machine Hours Used on Job |
| 12 | 18,000 |
| 13 | 14,000 |
| 14 | 15,000 |

**Required**
1. Compute the predetermined overhead rate.
2. Determine the overhead to be applied to each job.
3. Determine the budget variance and the volume variance.

**13-16   Job-order costing—activity-based overhead rates**   Bondurant, Inc.'s manufacturing processes, and much of its overhead, are machine-driven, but the company also incurs a great deal of overhead in purchasing, receiving, storing, and issuing materials. The managers believe that simply using machine hours to allocate this overhead is inappropriate so Bondurant applies overhead to jobs using one overhead rate based on the number of parts used on each job, and another based on machine hours. Summary data for 20X5 follow.

| | Budget | Actual |
|---|---|---|
| Part-related overhead | $360,000 | $352,000 |
| Machine-related overhead | $900,000 | $960,000 |
| Cost of materials used on jobs | $1,400,000 | $1,422,000 |
| Direct labor cost | $632,000 | $656,000 |
| Machine hours | 150,000 | 158,000 |
| Number of parts | 800,000 | 820,000 |

Data related to jobs worked on in 20X5 follow.

| | Total | Jobs Sold | Jobs in Ending Inventory of Work in Process | Jobs in Ending Inventory of Finished Goods |
|---|---|---|---|---|
| Materials cost | $1,422,000 | $1,280,000 | $102,000 | $40,000 |
| Direct labor cost | $656,000 | $590,000 | $30,000 | $36,000 |
| Machine hours | 158,000 | 135,000 | 14,000 | 9,000 |
| Number of parts | 820,000 | 750,000 | 40,000 | 30,000 |

Sales were $4,240,000 and administrative expenses were $1,054,000.

**Required**

1. Compute the predetermined overhead rates for parts and for machine hours.
2. Determine the cost of jobs sold and the cost of ending inventories.
3. Prepare an income statement showing misapplied overhead as an adjustment to normal cost of sales.

**13-17   Basic job-order costing**   Tucker Machinery, Inc. manufactures large custom drills. It uses a predetermined overhead rate of $3.80 per machine hour. During August, Tucker worked on three jobs. Data are as follows:

| | Z-101 | K-221 | K-341 |
|---|---|---|---|
| Machine hours | 2,280 | 930 | 2,910 |
| Direct labor cost | $18,400 | $11,600 | $31,220 |
| Materials cost | $21,230 | $7,870 | $22,785 |

Job Z-101 was completed and sold. The other jobs were unfinished. Actual overhead for August was $22,110.

**Required**

1. Determine the overhead to be applied to each job.
2. Determine normal cost of sales and ending inventory.
3. Determine overapplied or underapplied overhead.

**13-18   Comparison of actual and normal costing**   Riopelle Company uses actual job-order costing, assigning overhead to jobs based on direct labor cost. During March, Riopelle had the following activity.

| | Jobs Worked on in March M-1 | Jobs Worked on in March M-2 | Jobs Worked on in March M-3 |
|---|---|---|---|
| Materials cost | $28,000 | $41,000 | $32,000 |
| Direct labor cost | $18,000 | $24,000 | $28,000 |

Total actual overhead was $217,000; selling and administrative expenses were $31,000. Job M-1 was sold for $160,000. Jobs M-2 and M-3 were incomplete at the end of March.

**Required**

1. Determine the actual overhead rate per direct labor dollar.
2. Determine the overhead assigned to each job and the total cost of each job.
3. Prepare an income statement for March.

4. Suppose now that Riopelle uses normal costing. Its predetermined overhead rate is based on $2,100,000 budgeted overhead and $700,000 budgeted direct labor cost for the year. Calculate the predetermined overhead rate and redo requirements 2 and 3 using normal costing. Show any misapplied overhead as an adjustment to normal gross margin.

**13-19  *Graphical analysis of overhead***  The following graph shows the budgeted manufacturing overhead for Minich Company.

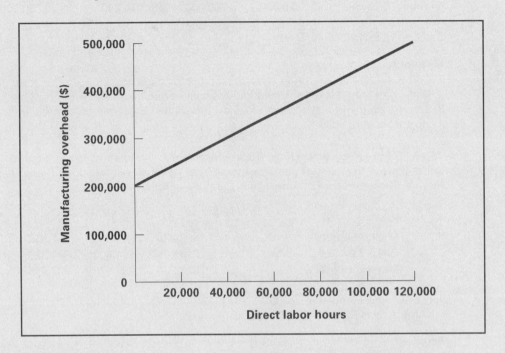

**Required**
1. Draw the line that represents applied overhead for each of the following two cases.
   (a)  The predetermined overhead rate is $5 per direct labor hour.
   (b)  The predetermined overhead rate is based on 100,000 direct labor hours.
2. Suppose that actual overhead equals budgeted overhead and that volume is 90,000 direct labor hours. What are the volume variances under each of the two cases from requirement 1?

**13-20  *Job-order costing for a service business***  D. J. Grimm Co. is an engineering consulting firm that specializes in mining work. The company uses a job-order cost system to accumulate costs for each job. Data on operations for August follow.

|                        | Grand Bay Gold | Big Butte Copper | Flake River |
|------------------------|----------------|------------------|-------------|
| Engineers' time, hours | 200            | 350              | 150         |
| Engineers' cost        | $5,000         | $8,300           | $3,600      |
| Other expenses         | $2,000         | $2,500           | $1,200      |

Other expenses include travel, lodging, auto rentals, meals and other items that are charged to clients. Grimm applies overhead to jobs using a predetermined overhead rate. The rate is based on $3,200,000 budgeted overhead cost and 100,000 budgeted engineering hours.

**Required**

1. Calculate the predetermined overhead rate.
2. Determine the cost of each job worked on in August.

**13-21  Basic job-order costing**  Kelton Company makes a wide variety of gear assemblies for industrial applications. The company uses normal costing, with a predetermined overhead rate of $3.70 per machine hour. During March 20X6, Kelton worked on the following jobs.

|  | Job Number | | |
| --- | --- | --- | --- |
|  | 311 | 312 | 313 |
| Materials used on job | $15,260 | $21,340 | $8,890 |
| Direct labor cost | $18,250 | $14,550 | $11,100 |
| Machine hours | 1,480 | 1,230 | 860 |

**Required**

1. Compute the amounts of overhead to be applied to each job and the total cost of each job.
2. Actual overhead for March was $12,980. What was overapplied or underapplied overhead?

**13-22  Overhead application**  The controller of Williams Company received the following budgeted data for manufacturing overhead costs of 20X7.

|  | Fixed Amount | Variable Cost per Direct Labor Hour |
| --- | --- | --- |
| Indirect labor | $ 47,800 | $0.40 |
| Supplies | 25,300 | 0.15 |
| Lubricants | 7,700 | 0.10 |
| Utilities | 46,400 | 0.48 |
| Repairs | 21,000 | 0.17 |
| Property taxes | 6,000 | 0 |
| Depreciation | 32,000 | 0 |
| Total | $186,200 | $1.30 |

The controller estimates that 70,000 direct labor hours will be worked in 20X7.

**Required**

1. Compute the predetermined fixed overhead rate per direct labor hour.
2. Assume that 67,000 direct labor hours are worked on jobs in 20X7.
   (a) How much fixed overhead will be applied?
   (b) How much variable overhead should be incurred? How much applied?
   (c) If actual overhead costs are $274,800, what are the budget and volume variances?

## PROBLEMS

**13-23  Overhead application**  VanMeter Company runs a highly automated operation that measures its activity by machine hours. Its managers have budgeted

300,000 machine hours for 20X2. They budget annual manufacturing overhead as total budgeted overhead = $600,000 + ($3 × machine hours). The company had no beginning inventories.

**Required**

1. Compute the predetermined overhead rate for 20X2.
2. At the end of 20X2, the controller collected the following information.

| | |
|---|---|
| Total manufacturing overhead incurred | $1,585,000 |
| Machine hours on jobs sold | 275,000 |
| Machine hours on jobs in ending inventories | 40,000 |

Determine the amounts of applied overhead in cost of goods sold and in ending inventories. Determine the amount of overapplied or underapplied overhead and break it down into the budget variance and volume variance.

**13-24  Job order costing—activity-based overhead rates**  Hughes Machines uses two rates to apply overhead to jobs. One rate is based on materials cost, the other on machine time. Hughes has relatively high overhead that is related to buying, receiving, storing, and issuing materials; hence the managers believe that applying this overhead through the relative materials cost of jobs is appropriate. The following data relate to 20X4.

| | Budget |
|---|---|
| Materials-related overhead | $640,000 |
| Machine-related overhead | $1,100,000 |
| Cost of materials used on jobs | $1,600,000 |
| Machine hours | 200,000 |

Data related to three jobs worked on in March follow.

| | Job XT-56 | Job XR-23 | Job XY-67 |
|---|---|---|---|
| Materials cost | $21,000 | $82,000 | $39,000 |
| Direct labor cost | $16,000 | $13,000 | $18,000 |
| Machine hours | 8,500 | 4,500 | 2,900 |

Actual material-related overhead was $59,200 and actual machine-related overhead was $92,800.

**Required**

1. Compute the predetermined overhead rates for materials and for machine hours.
2. Determine the amount of overhead to be applied to each job and the total cost of each job.
3. Determine overapplied or underapplied overhead for each type of overhead.

**13-25  Job-order costing—two departments**  WestCo makes industrial robots to customer order in two departments, Machining and Assembly. Machining is highly mechanized, and Assembly is labor-intensive. Accordingly, the company applies overhead using machine hours in the Machining Department and direct labor hours in the Assembly Department. Budgeted data for 20X6 are as follows:

|  | Machining Department | Assembly Department |
|---|---|---|
| Total budgeted overhead | $720,000 | $120,000 |
| Machine hours | 120,000 |  |
| Direct labor hours |  | 60,000 |

During March WestCo worked on two jobs.

|  | Job #1029 | Job #1030 |
|---|---|---|
| Materials used | $21,000 | $32,000 |
| Assembly Department direct labor at $12 per hour | $24,000 | $38,400 |
| Machine hours in Machining Department | 4,000 | 5,000 |

**Required**
1. Calculate the predetermined overhead rate for each department.
2. Calculate the overhead applied to each job and the total cost of each job.
3. Actual overhead in the Machining Department was $55,500, in the Assembly Department, $10,200. Calculate overapplied or underapplied overhead for each department.

**13-26  Basic job-order costing**  Walker Company manufactures precision optical instruments to customer order. Walker uses normal costing and sets its predetermined overhead rate based on machine hours. For 20X4, the rate is $11.40 per hour, based on $3,420,000 budgeted overhead and 300,000 budgeted hours. During January, the company worked on three jobs.

|  | Job Number | | |
|---|---|---|---|
|  | M-101 | R-12 | Z-610 |
| Materials used | $35,800 | $73,200 | $40,600 |
| Direct labor cost | $123,200 | $120,200 | $78,300 |
| Machine hours | 8,800 | 8,200 | 7,200 |

Job M-101 was completed and sold while the other two remained in inventory at the end of January. Actual overhead incurred in January was $271,300.

**Required**
1. Determine the amount of overhead that should be applied to each job.
2. Determine normal cost of goods sold for January and ending inventory.
3. Determine overapplied or underapplied overhead for January.

**13-27  Job costing in a service firm**  Barnes and DiLello form a partnership of architectural engineers operating in a single office in a medium-sized city. The firm charges clients for the time that each person on the staff spends on the client's business, using a rate of 2½ times the person's salary, based on an 1,800-hour working year. Thus, an architectural draftsperson earning a salary of $30,000 is charged out to clients at $42 per hour [($30,000/1,800) × 2.5 = $41.66, rounded to $42]. The rate is intended to cover all costs and to yield a profit.

|  | Budget for 20X9 |
|---|---|
| Salaries of professional staff | $  700,000 |
| Salaries of support personnel (clerks, typists, etc.) | 78,000 |
| Other costs | 680,000 |
| Total expected costs | $1,458,000 |

The listed costs do not include salaries for Barnes and DiLello. Each partner expects to work about 1,200 chargeable hours at a rate of $100 per hour. About 80% of the professional staff's time is chargeable to clients, as well as about 40% of the support personnel's time. Nonchargeable time is for general firm business, professional activities (attending seminars and continuing-education programs), and business development.

### Required

1. What total income will the partners earn if their estimates prove correct?
2. Suppose that two professional employees work on a design for a particular client. One earns $30,000 per year, the other $35,000, and each works 12 hours on this particular project. How much will the firm charge the client for the project assuming that neither the partners nor the support staff is involved in this project? (Round hourly rates to the nearest dollar.)

**13-28  Overhead costs and pricing policy**  HortonWorks is a medium-sized machine shop that does custom work for industrial customers. Business is seasonal, with about four busy months, three slack months, and the rest about average. HortonWorks uses an actual job-order costing system, assigning overhead to jobs at the end of each month based on the labor cost of each job. Rae Horton, the owner, sets prices using the following format, with typical data.

| | |
|---|---|
| Estimated material cost | $32.50 |
| Estimated labor cost | 16.80 |
| Subtotal | 49.30 |
| Allowance for overhead at 60% | 29.58 |
| Subtotal | $78.88 |
| Allowance for profit at 10% | 7.89 |
| Price | $86.77 |

Horton developed the formula based on experience and on the financial results of the past few years. Overhead has averaged about 60% of the sum of materials and labor costs, and a 10% profit is reasonable in the industry. Horton has found that similar jobs seem to be more or less profitable depending on the month in which they are done. This bothers her, and she has begun to wonder whether her pricing policy is sensible.

### Required

1. In which months, busy or slack, will jobs appear more profitable? Why?
2. Should Horton modify the pricing policy? What should Horton do?

**13-29  Job-order costing**  The following data pertain to the March operations of Covera Machine Tool Company. The company uses JIT principles and ships jobs as it completes them, keeping no inventory of finished goods.

| | |
|---|---|
| Jobs in beginning work in process: | |
| Materials | $237,670 |
| Direct labor | $322,200 |
| Factory overhead | $467,190 |
| Materials put into process in March: | |
| To jobs in ending inventory | $228,310 |
| To jobs finished and sold in March | $881,480 |
| Direct labor for March: | |
| To jobs in ending work in process | $452,400 |
| To jobs finished and sold in March | $892,880 |

The company uses normal costing and applies overhead at $1.50 per direct labor dollar. The materials and labor costs for jobs finished and sold include the cost to finish the beginning inventory of work in process. The company had March sales of $4,680,000 and selling and administrative expenses of $453,650.

**Required**

1. Determine the overhead cost in ending inventory of work in process and in cost of goods sold.
2. Overhead was overapplied by $18,430 in March. What was actual overhead?
3. Prepare an income statement for March, treating overapplied overhead as an adjustment to normal cost of sales.

**13-30  Job order costing—comparison of overhead rates**  Rubenstein Foundry uses a single overhead rate based on machine hours. One of its managers believes that the company could benefit from using two rates, one based on materials cost, the other on machine time. The manager believes that because Rubenstein has relatively high overhead related to buying, receiving, storing, and issuing materials, applying this overhead through the relative materials cost of jobs is appropriate. The following data relate to 20X4.

|  | Budget |
|---|---|
| Materials-related overhead | $  480,000 |
| Machine-related overhead | 1,300,000 |
| Total overhead | 1,780,000 |
| Cost of materials used on jobs | $1,600,000 |
| Machine hours | 200,000 |

Data related to three jobs worked on in March follow.

|  | Job XT-56 | Job XR-23 | Job XY-67 |
|---|---|---|---|
| Materials cost | $21,000 | $82,000 | $39,000 |
| Direct labor cost | $16,000 | $13,000 | $18,000 |
| Machine hours used | 8,500 | 4,500 | 2,900 |

Actual materials-related overhead was $39,800 and actual machine-related overhead was $105,800.

**Required**

1. Compute the predetermined overhead rate per machine hour assuming that Rubenstein uses only machine hours to apply overhead, as it has been doing.
2. Determine the amount of overhead to be applied to each job and the total cost of each job.
3. Redo requirements 1 and 2 using the two rates as suggested by the manager. Comment on the differences in job costs here and in requirement 2.

**13-31  Job-order costing for a service business**  D. J. Westlake Co. is a partnership of Certified Public Accountants specializing in tax work. The firm uses a job-order cost system to accumulate costs for each job it does for a particular client. Data on operations for June follow.

|  | Walton Estate Planning | GHK, Inc. Federal Return | All Other Jobs |
|---|---|---|---|
| Senior accountant time, hours | 40 | 20 | 3,000 |
| Junior accountant time, hours | 60 | 100 | 12,000 |

Westlake pays senior accountants an average of $60,000 per year for an expected 2,000-hour year. It pays juniors an average of $30,000 per year for the same expected hours. Westlake uses the average hourly pay to determine the cost of accountants' time on jobs. Westlake also charges an hourly amount to cover overhead costs and provide a profit. The client is charged for the time and the combined overhead/profit rate. This year, the rate is based on the following data.

| | |
|---|---:|
| Budgeted overhead cost | $8,200,000 |
| Budgeted profit | $600,000 |
| Budgeted hours | 200,000 |

### Required

1. Calculate the salary rates Westlake will use for senior accountants' and junior accountants' time.
2. Calculate the predetermined rate that Westlake must use to cover its overhead costs and meet its profit objective.
3. Determine the "cost" of each job worked on in June and the cost of "all other jobs."
4. How is Westlake's accounting different from that of a manufacturer? Does its method make sense?

**13-32  Job-order costing—beginning inventory**  Wisconsin Machinery Company makes large industrial machines. It uses a job-order costing system applying overhead at $15 per direct labor hour. Direct laborers earn $8 per hour. The following data relate to jobs worked on in March 20X4.

| | 4-22 | 4-23 | 4-24 | 4-25 |
|---|---:|---:|---:|---:|
| Costs in beginning inventory: | | | | |
| Materials | $ 34,000 | $10,000 | 0 | 0 |
| Direct labor | 48,000 | 8,000 | 0 | 0 |
| Overhead | 90,000 | 15,000 | 0 | 0 |
| Total | $172,000 | $33,000 | 0 | 0 |
| Costs incurred in March: | | | | |
| Materials | $11,000 | $46,000 | $60,000 | $9,000 |
| Direct labor | $16,000 | $32,000 | $52,000 | $12,000 |

Jobs 4-22, 4-23, and 4-24 were completed and sold. Job 4-25 was not finished at the end of March. Total overhead incurred during March was $212,000.

### Required

1. Compute the amounts of overhead to be applied to each job.
2. Compute the amount of overapplied or underapplied overhead for March.
3. Compute cost of goods sold for March and the inventory at March 31.
4. Revenue from the three jobs sold was $860,000. Selling and administrative expenses for March were $180,000. Prepare an income statement for March.

**13-33  CVP analysis for a job-order company**  Brill Optics manufactures special lenses to customer order. Kim Brill, the owner, is trying to develop a profit plan and has collected the following budgeted data for 20X7.

| Materials cost | $200,000 |
|---|---|
| Labor cost (40,000 hours at $9 per hour) | 360,000 |
| Variable overhead | 160,000 |
| Fixed overhead | 240,000 |
| Selling and administrative expenses, all fixed | 120,000 |

Brill has set a predetermined overhead rate of $10 per direct labor hour. The company sets prices at 120% of total manufacturing cost, including applied overhead.

**Required**
1. What profit will Brill earn if operations meet expectations?
2. Suppose that Brill is able to generate only 35,000 direct labor hours worth of work, a 12.5% decline. Materials and variable overhead also decline by 12.5%. Brill treats misapplied overhead as an adjustment to normal cost of sales. What will profit be, assuming prices were set using applied overhead?
3. What pricing policy, stated as a percentage of total manufacturing cost, will give a $100,000 profit at 40,000 direct labor hours?

**13-34   Costing and pricing in a hospital**   The controller of Prairie Memorial Hospital has recently decided to set prices for laboratory tests using a formula based on costs. She has analyzed each type of test as follows.

| Class of Test | Time Required (minutes) | Number Performed in Average Year |
|---|---|---|
| I | 12 | 38,000 |
| II | 15 | 17,000 |
| III | 30 | 9,000 |

Variable costs are negligible. The controller believes that because all lab technicians are salaried, it is best to treat their salaries as overhead costs. Total annual overhead costs are $960,000.

**Required**
1. Calculate a predetermined overhead rate per minute. Round to the nearest $0.001.
2. Determine the price for each class of test that will make the laboratory break even. Round prices to the nearest cent.
3. Suppose that the laboratory performs 37,000 Class I, 17,000 Class II, and 10,000 Class III tests. Total costs are $965,000. Determine profit or loss.

**13-35   Overhead application and pricing decisions**   Westminster Furniture, a high-quality manufacturer, has just received an offer from a large wholesaler for a single batch of goods. The offered price is $43,000, which is about $12,000 less than normal for similar work. Westminster has never done business with the wholesaler, and the sales manager wants to get a foot in the door. She is sure that existing sales would be unaffected by the special order and wants to accept the order if any profit can be made. The production manager provided the following estimates of cost for the order.

| Materials | $12,000 |
|---|---|
| Direct labor (3,000 hours) | 18,000 |
| Overhead | 15,000 |
| Total | $45,000 |

The production manager informed you that the overhead cost is based on the overhead application rate of $5 per direct labor hour. The rate includes both fixed and variable overhead and was based on 60,000 expected direct labor hours and $300,000 budgeted total overhead costs. The rate last year was $5.50, based on 50,000 direct labor hours and $275,000 total overhead costs. The production manager told you that the difference in rates is due to the difference in budgeted direct labor hours—the cost structure is the same this year as last year.

**Required**

1. Determine the incremental cost of the order. Should it be accepted?
2. What other factors should be considered in deciding whether to accept this special order?

**13-36    Overhead rates and cost analysis**    Walton Machinery Company has been operating well below capacity, and Frank Williams, the sales manager, has been trying to increase orders. He recently received an offer to bid on a large industrial press and submitted the specifications to Walton's cost estimators. Their estimate follows.

| | |
|---|---:|
| Materials | $29,600 |
| Direct labor at $9 per hour | 19,800 |
| Overhead at $12 per direct labor hour | 26,400 |
| Total manufacturing cost | $75,800 |
| Standard allowance for selling and administrative expenses, 10% of manufacturing cost | 7,580 |
| Total cost | $83,380 |
| Standard allowance for profit at 15% of total cost | 12,507 |
| Suggested price | $95,887 |

Williams told the executive vice president that the suggested price is not low enough to get the job. He said that the customer expected a price in the neighborhood of $75,000, which another company had already bid. The vice president called in the controller, who said that the overhead rate was about 60% variable, 40% fixed, and that variable selling and administrative expenses were negligible. The vice president was reluctant to meet the $75,000 price but agreed to think it over and get back to Williams.

**Required**

Write a memorandum to Mr. Williams indicating whether Walton should meet the $75,000 price.

**13-37    Pricing policy and profits**    Sumter Milling is a job-order company. It uses material supplied by its customers, so that virtually all of its manufacturing costs are direct labor and overhead. Jackie Wiggins, the controller, prepared the following data for use in establishing the company's pricing policy for the coming year.

| | |
|---|---:|
| Total budgeted direct labor hours | 240,000 |
| Total budgeted manufacturing costs | $4,800,000 |

Total budgeted manufacturing costs were developed using the following formula:

*Total manufacturing costs = $1,200,000 + ($15 × direct labor hours)*

Total selling and administrative expenses are budgeted as $800,000 + ($0.10 × revenue). The management of the company seeks an $880,000 profit.

**Required**
1. Determine the revenue Sumter must earn to achieve its profit objective.
2. Determine the price per direct labor hour Sumter must charge to achieve the objective.
3. Suppose that the company uses the pricing policy you developed and actually works 230,000 direct labor hours. What will its profit be?
4. Suppose that the company uses your pricing policy and works 250,000 hours. What will its profit be?

**13-38   Overhead rates, ABC, and pricing**   Jarod Kane, controller, and Renee Poston, sales manager of Hicks Furniture, were discussing the company's dismal operating results. Poston said "Some of the products in our high-volume lines just are not selling. Our competitors' prices are less than ours, but we are leaving almost no margin to cover selling and administrative expenses and provide a reasonable profit. However, some of our low-volume products are doing quite well, especially some of those we make in small jobs."

Kane had begun a study of the company's costs and thought that part of the problem might lie with the way it applied overhead to jobs.  "Look," he said, "an order of our high-volume chairs might be 200–300 units, while for some of the others, say an expensive sofa, a typical job size is more like 20.  There have to be significant costs of making up many such small batches instead of a few large ones. After all, we have to do a cost estimate and start some paperwork for each job, workers have to log in their time, we have to track the job through the plant, and so on. Plus, some of our costs are related to such activities as setting up machinery, moving materials and semifinished product, and packing up a shipment; they typically are made in large batches. My new assistant is completing the study I started and I expect to hear about the findings this afternoon."

You, the new assistant, have accumulated the following information that you believe is accurate enough for preliminary analysis.

Costs and activities under current procedures

|  | Model 807 Chair | Model 5052 Table |
|---|---|---|
| Number in typical order | 200 | 30 |
| Average cost per job: |  |  |
| Materials | $24,000 | $20,400 |
| Direct labor at $10/hour | 6,000 | 1,500 |
| Overhead at $25/DLH | 15,000 | 3,750 |
| Total cost | $45,000 | $25,650 |
| Price at 120% of manufacturing cost | $54,000 | $30,780 |

Activity-based data

| Driver for Cost Pool | Total Cost in Pool | Annual Activity of Driver |
|---|---|---|
| Direct labor | $4,800,000 | 300,000 |
| Machine setups | 1,200,000 | 5,000 |
| Number of parts/components | 900,000 | 450,000 |
| Number of recordkeeping transactions | 400,000 | 400,000 |

## Amounts of Cost Driver per Job

| Model 807 | Model 5052 |
|---|---|
| 600 DLH | 150 DLH |
| 1 setup | 12 setups |
| 400 parts | 800 parts |
| 200 transactions | 500 transactions |

### Required

1. Calculate overhead rates for each cost driver and determine the cost and price of each model.
2. Write a memorandum to Mr. Kane explaining the differences between your costs and the original costs. State why the company seems to be experiencing the operating results described by Poston. Use the guidelines in Appendix A.
3. In general, would you expect high-volume or low-volume products to show higher overhead costs under ABC than under labor-based assignment? Why?

**13-39 *Changing overhead rates*** Benson Electronics has been on a cost-cutting program designed to help it meet foreign competition. The cost of a typical unit of Benson's major product is as follows:

| | |
|---|---:|
| Materials and components | $180 |
| Direct labor | 44 |
| Overhead at 400% of direct labor | 176 |
| Total cost | $400 |

Overhead cost reflects actual overhead divided by actual labor hours at 50,000 units, the expected production level of the product. Benson's engineers did considerable redesigning of the product line to reduce labor cost. They introduced some custom-made components, which, though costlier than the existing components, were easier to assemble into the units. They also changed some job descriptions and rerouted product flow. The head of engineering understood that the changes would raise material/component costs by about $16, but would reduce labor cost by roughly $16 and therefore reduce overhead by about $64 at the 400% rate. The results in the first six months were not encouraging as the following unit cost calculation, which as before is based on actual overhead costs and direct labor for 50,000 units, shows.

| | |
|---|---:|
| Materials and components | $190 |
| Direct labor | 29 |
| Overhead at 600% of direct labor | 174 |
| Total cost | $393 |

The heads of production and engineering, as well as the controller, were not happy with the results. A great deal of work had resulted in little net decrease in unit cost. The most disappointing aspect was the sharp increase in the overhead rate occasioned by the drop in direct labor.

### Required

1. Determine total overhead before and after the cost-cutting program.
2. Suppose that the entire difference you found in requirement 1 is attributable to the component of overhead that varies with direct labor. Determine the variable

component of overhead, with respect to direct labor. Can you now explain why costs did not fall as much as one might have thought?
3. What do you recommend?

**13-40  Normal costing**  Boardman Company manufactures equipment used to cap bottles. The following data summarize 20X3 activities.

| | |
|---|---|
| Beginning inventories of work in process and finished goods | $  360,000 |
| Materials put into process | 2,240,000 |
| Direct labor | 1,780,000 |
| Manufacturing overhead incurred | 2,520,000 |
| Selling and administrative expenses | 880,000 |
| Sales | 7,960,000 |

The company uses an overhead application rate of $1.40 per direct labor dollar, based on budgeted direct labor cost of $1,800,000 and the following formula for budgeting manufacturing overhead: Manufacturing overhead = $1,440,000 + ($0.60 × direct labor cost). At the end of the year, the controller prepared the following analysis of costs.

| | Total | Jobs Sold | Incomplete Jobs | Finished Jobs |
|---|---|---|---|---|
| Materials | $2,240,000 | $1,890,000 | $120,000 | $230,000 |
| Direct labor | $1,780,000 | $1,480,000 | $100,000 | $200,000 |

**Required**
Prepare an income statement for the year, using normal costing and showing the budget variance and volume variance as separate adjustments to gross margin.

**13-41  Overhead rate behavior**  Ned Clinton, controller of Walcott Industries, has been puzzled by the behavior of overhead rates. The company has been engaged in a program to reduce costs and the focus has been on direct labor and associated overhead costs. Because the average wage rate is in the $16–$18 range and the average overhead rate around $55 per DLH, Clinton expected savings in the area of $71–$73 for reductions in DLH. Clinton has collected the following data for the past few quarters to track the progress of the program. Output was about the same in each quarter, so the decreased labor hours represent improved performance.

| Quarter | Actual Direct Labor Hours | Direct Labor Cost | Overhead Cost | Overhead per DLH |
|---|---|---|---|---|
| 3rd 20X1 | 61,900 | $1,051,500 | $3,429,300 | $55.40 |
| 4th 20X1 | 61,300 | 1,040,600 | 3,428,600 | 55.93 |
| 1st 20X2 | 61,100 | 1,042,450 | 3,430,700 | 56.15 |
| 2nd 20X2 | 57,600 | 993,200 | 3,428,200 | 59.52 |
| 3rd 20X2 | 55,400 | 939,400 | 3,428,000 | 61.88 |

Clinton was puzzled at the behavior of the overhead rate. He knew that overhead was not totally variable with direct labor, but thought that there surely should have been a considerable drop in overhead as direct labor hours declined.

**Required**
1. Using regression analysis, determine the variable component of overhead costs per direct labor hour.

2. State why you think Clinton might have been incorrect in his estimates of the effects of reducing labor time and what he might do now.

**13-42 Job-order costing and decisions** Last month, Marchmont Furniture Company began work on custom-made chairs ordered by a retail store. When the work was nearly complete, the retailer went bankrupt and was not able to pay for the chairs. The sales manager of Marchmont immediately called other stores in an effort to sell the chairs. The original price was $280,000, but the best price the sales manager could get if the chairs were finished according to the original specifications was $182,000. This offer was from the Z-Store chain. Randle Company, which also operates a chain of stores, offered $202,000 for the chairs provided that different upholstery and trim were used. The sales manager talked to the production manager about the order and got the following information.

|  | Costs Accumulated to Date |
|---|---|
| Materials | $ 31,500 |
| Direct labor (7,000 hours at $11) | 77,000 |
| Factory overhead at $10 per hour | 70,000 |
| Total accumulated costs | $178,500 |

The factory overhead rate includes $4 variable overhead and $6 fixed overhead. The additional work required to complete the chairs was estimated as follows by the production manager.

|  | Original Specifications | Randle's Specifications |
|---|---|---|
| Materials | $4,000 | $6,000 |
| Direct labor hours | 800 hours | 1,800 hours |

**Required**
1. Using the company's costing method, determine the total costs to be charged to the job assuming (a) the work is completed based on the original specifications and (b) the chairs are modified as required by Randle Company.
2. Determine which offer Marchmont should accept.

**13-43 Job-order costing—service business** CompuData Inc. develops computer programs for businesses, hospitals, local governments, and other organizations. The company has been having difficulty analyzing the profitability of jobs and estimating costs for use in bidding.

The company has hired you to develop a job-order costing system. So far, you have decided that production costs should include the following costs.

| | |
|---|---|
| Programmers' salaries | $480,000 |
| Supervisors' salaries | 120,000 |
| Other costs of programming | 240,000 |

You decide that the company should use normal costing, treating programmers' salaries as direct labor with each programmer having an hourly rate equaling his or her salary divided by the normal 2,000-hour working year. You also decide to treat the other two elements of cost as manufacturing overhead. You intend to use programming hours to set the predetermined overhead rate because programmers earn different salaries. Finally, you intend to treat the cost of idle programming time (actual salaries paid less salaries charged to jobs) and "excess cost" (amounts charged to jobs in excess of actual salaries paid) as part of overhead.

The president expects selling and administrative expenses to be $180,000. She also expects programmers to work about 24,000 hours, and you decide to use this figure to compute the predetermined overhead rate.

The president is interested in seeing how the system will operate and gives you the following information for a typical month. There was no beginning inventory and sales were $170,000. All costs incurred were one-twelfth of the estimated annual amounts given. Jobs sold had a total of 1,350 programming hours and jobs in process at the end of the month had 450 programming hours, so that actual charged hours for the month were 1,800 (1,350 + 450). Information on programmers' salaries follows.

| | |
|---|---|
| Salaries on jobs sold | $27,000 |
| Salaries in ending inventory | $9,200 |

Idle time was $3,800 ($40,000 incurred – $27,000 – $9,200).

**Required**

1. Calculate the predetermined overhead rate per hour of programmers' time.
2. Determine the cost of ending inventory of jobs in process.
3. Determine overapplied or underapplied overhead cost for the month, including idle time.
4. Prepare an income statement for the month showing overapplied or underapplied overhead as a separate expense or negative expense.

**13-44 *Comparing actual and normal costing—seasonal business*** Barnett Company has used actual job-order costing for several years. At the end of each month, a clerk divides total manufacturing overhead cost incurred during the month by total direct labor cost for the month to get an overhead rate per labor dollar. He then applies overhead at this rate to each job worked on during the month. Because the company uses actual costing, there is no underapplied or overapplied overhead.

The president has been unhappy with this method because it results in widely differing overhead costs in different months. The work is highly seasonal, with the summer months very heavy and the winter months light. The president has asked you to show how normal costing differs from actual costing and has given you the following data regarding two similar jobs done in the past year.

| | Job J-12 | Job A-16 |
|---|---|---|
| Materials cost | $10,410 | $10,310 |
| Direct labor | 16,900 | 16,400 |
| Overhead | 40,560 | 29,520 |
| Total | $67,870 | $56,230 |

Job J-12 was done in January, when total overhead was $528,000 and total labor cost was $220,000. Job A-16 was done in August, when total overhead was $1,179,000 and total labor cost was $655,000. The company budgets annual overhead using the formula Total annual overhead = $3,200,000 + ($1.20 × direct labor cost). Total budgeted labor cost for the current year is $4,000,000.

**Required**

1. Develop the predetermined overhead rate based on total budgeted overhead and labor cost.
2. Determine the costs of the two jobs using the rate calculated in requirement 1.
3. Comment on the advantages of using predetermined overhead rates.

**13-45    *Activity-based overhead rates***    Percan Industries has been using a single overhead rate, but its managers have become convinced that they need several rates to reflect the activities with which overhead costs are associated. After careful study, the controller developed the following budgeted information regarding cost pools and activities that drive the pools.

| Activity | Amount of Activity | Overhead Costs in Pool |
|---|---|---|
| Labor hours | 400,000 | $1,600,000 |
| Machine setups | 2,000 | $600,000 |
| Recordkeeping entries | 150,000 | $150,000 |

Data related to jobs worked on in 20X5 follow.

| | Totals | Jobs Sold | Jobs in Ending Inventories |
|---|---|---|---|
| Materials cost | $2,582,000 | $2,321,000 | $261,000 |
| Direct labor cost | $4,169,000 | $3,788,000 | $381,000 |
| Direct labor hours | 410,000 | 371,000 | 39,000 |
| Machine setups | 1,950 | 1,870 | 80 |
| Entries | 152,000 | 136,000 | 16,000 |

Actual overhead costs were, by pool: labor hour-based, $1,620,000; machine setup-based, $592,000; and recordkeeping, $148,000.

**Required**

1. Compute the predetermined overhead rate for each activity.
2. Determine the amount of each type of overhead to apply to jobs sold and jobs still in inventory.
3. Determine the total cost of jobs sold and the cost of ending inventory.
4. Determine the amount of misapplied overhead for each cost pool.

**13-46    *Effects of separate overhead rates (continuation of 13-45)***    One of the managers of Percan Industries says that the new system with its three overhead cost pools is more elaborate and costly than the company needs. He proposes to go back to the old basis, where all overhead was applied using labor hours. In trying to convince him of the wisdom of the separate rates, you pull out the following information about two products that the company manufactures regularly. The data are for typical-sized batches of each product. The company makes several models of each product, but they are all roughly the same. The company prices its products at 150% of total manufacturing cost.

| | Product XT-12 | Product JY-09 |
|---|---|---|
| Materials costs | $260 | $ 780 |
| Labor cost | 280 | 2,880 |
| Direct labor hours | 20 | 200 |
| Machine setups | 12 | 0 |
| Recordkeeping entries | 400 | 80 |

**Required**

1. Determine the cost and price of each product using the overhead rates you developed in the previous assignment.
2. Determine the cost and price of each product using a single overhead rate based on labor hours. Use the budgeted data from the previous assignment and remember to include all of the overhead cost, not just the labor-driven cost.
3. Comment on the results.

**13-47   *Analyzing overhead***   The president of your company has asked you some questions about overhead. You recently changed the accounting system from actual to normal costing, with some opposition from other managers who could not see the advantages. Although the president was not happy with the actual costing system, he is not convinced that normal costing is a significant improvement.

The specific questions he wants you to answer relate to determining whether or not costs are under control and what information he can get from the figures for underapplied and overapplied overhead. He gives you the following results from the most recent three months.

| | March | April | May |
|---|---|---|---|
| Machine hours | 14,000 | 8,000 | 5,000 |
| Total overhead incurred | $ 71,000 | $52,000 | $51,000 |
| Total overhead applied at $6 per hour | 84,000 | 48,000 | 30,000 |
| Underapplied (overapplied) overhead | $(13,000) | $ 4,000 | $21,000 |

The predetermined rate of $6 per machine hour was calculated using budgeted machine hours for the year of 120,000 and budgeted overhead of $480,000 fixed and $2.00 variable per machine hour. Budgeted fixed overhead is $40,000 for each of the three months.

**Required**

Making any calculations you consider relevant, tell the president what he can learn using the given data.

**13-48   *Departmental versus plantwide overhead rates***   PureVision, Inc. makes optical devices such as binoculars and telescopes. Because nearly all of its products are made to customer order, PureVision uses job-order costing. The company operates two departments, Grinding and Assembly. In the past, PureVision has used a single overhead application rate based on total budgeted direct labor hours and total budgeted overhead. The rate for 20X8 was computed using the following data.

| | Grinding Department | Assembly Department | Total |
|---|---|---|---|
| Total budgeted overhead | $1,200,000 | $800,000 | $2,000,000 |
| Budgeted direct labor hours | 200,000 | 50,000 | 250,000 |
| Rate ($2,000,000/250,000) | | | $8 |

Budgeted overhead was based on the following formulas.

*Grinding Department: $800,000 + ($2 × direct labor hours)*
*Assembly Department: $500,000 + ($6 × direct labor hours)*

The company bases its bid prices on total estimated cost including direct labor, materials, and overhead at $8 per direct labor hour. The controller has been thinking about changing to departmental rates and has collected the following data regarding two jobs recently completed. All direct laborers earn $10 per hour.

|  | Job 391 | Job 547 |
|---|---|---|
| Direct labor hours: | | |
| Grinding | 330 | 80 |
| Assembly | 30 | 180 |
| Materials cost | $3,000 | $2,500 |
| Direct labor cost | $3,600 | $2,600 |

The policy is to bid a price of 150% of total estimated manufacturing cost.

**Required**
1. Determine the overhead that the company will apply to each job using the $8 plantwide rate. Determine the total cost of each job. Assuming that the actual results for each job were also the estimated results that the company used to set the bid prices, determine the price that the company bid for each job.
2. Compute the predetermined overhead rate for each department.
3. Determine the amounts of overhead applied to each job, the total cost of each job, and the bid price for each job using the predetermined departmental overhead rates that you computed in requirement 2.
4. Comment on the differences in your results for the two jobs using the plantwide rate and departmental rates. Do you recommend that the company switch to departmental rates?

**13-49  CVP analysis in a job-order company**  Catherine Pitts, the president of Nutron Machine Works, tells you that her pricing policy is to charge the customer 150% of material cost plus a per-hour amount for direct labor. She wants to earn a profit of $180,000 before taxes in 20X8. Nutron manufactures industrial machinery, principally small cutting equipment. Virtually all machines are custom made and the company therefore uses job-order costing. Pitts has developed the following estimates for the coming year, 20X8.

| | |
|---|---|
| Materials cost | $400,000 |
| Fixed manufacturing overhead | $250,000 |
| Selling and administrative expenses | $80,000 |
| Direct labor hours | 20,000 |
| Direct labor wage rate | $15 per hour |
| Variable manufacturing overhead | 80% of direct labor cost |

**Required**
1. Determine the price per direct labor hour the company must charge to meet the target profit.
2. Suppose that the company adopts the per-hour charge you computed in requirement 1 and has the following results: material costs, $440,000; direct labor hours, 18,000. All overhead costs are incurred as expected (variable per unit of activity and fixed in total). Determine the profit that the company will earn.

**13-50  Overhead application and cost control**  Guinn Print Shop had the following results in three recent months.

| | April | May | June |
|---|---|---|---|
| Actual overhead costs | $25,000 | $28,000 | $34,000 |
| Applied overhead costs | 18,000 | 27,000 | 36,000 |

Arief Guinn, the owner, said that cost control was poor in April, better in May, and excellent in June. "We really need to overapply overhead because that reflects good cost control," he said.

Guinn budgets overhead as $2 variable per direct labor hour and $240,000 fixed per year. Monthly fixed overhead is budgeted at $20,000. Guinn uses 60,000 direct labor hours per year to set its predetermined overhead rate.

**Required**

1. Determine Guinn's predetermined overhead rate.
2. Determine the number of direct labor hours worked in each month.
3. Determine the budget variance for each month.
4. Explain to Mr. Guinn why his conclusions about cost control were, or were not, correct.

## CASES

**13-51   *Cost justification***   The following material is taken from a column by Rowland Evans and Robert Novak that appeared in the July 8, 1976, *Knickerbocker News* (Albany, New York). At that time, the federal election laws required that candidates for the presidency limit spending before their parties' conventions to $13 million.

When Treasury Secretary William Simon traveled to Raleigh, N.C., last Jan. 20 to address the state Chamber of Commerce and then a President Ford Committee (PFC) reception, the taxpayers' bill was $2,310. The reimbursement to Uncle Sam for the PFC for political expenses: $17.44. . . . The method used for Simon's Jan. 20 journey to North Carolina, an important primary state, is the model. The Air Force charged $2,310 for a Jetstar carrying Simon and seven others (including aides and Secret Service agents) to North Carolina. Since Simon occupied only one of eight seats, his share of the cost is $288.75. The 30 minutes spent at the PFC reception amounted to only 5 percent of the portal-to-portal time from Washington. So, 5 percent of $288.75 is $14.44. Add $3 for the share of meals, and the cost to the PFC is $17.44.

**Required**

1. Suppose that you had been engaged as a consultant to former President Ronald Reagan, who was President Ford's opponent in that campaign for the Republican nomination. What would you say about the method used to determine the cost billed to the PFC? What other information would you seek?
2. Suppose that you were engaged as a consultant to the PFC. How would you defend the $17.44 charge?

**13-52   *What is cost?—consumer action***   Easy Ed Johnson's Belchfire Auto Agency advertises that it will sell cars at $100 over cost and that anyone who can prove that Johnson is making more than $100 on a sale will get a $5,000 prize. Phyllis Henley decides to disprove Johnson's claim. She obtains the following information from a consumer magazine.

Cost Data from Consumer Scoop—
Belchfire 8 with Standard Equipment

| | |
|---|---:|
| Invoice cost to dealer | $13,400 |
| Commission to salesperson | 100 |
| Variable cost of make-ready (lubrication, washing, etc.) | 40 |
| Total cost to dealer | $13,540 |

Since Henley knows that Johnson has been selling this particular model for $14,190, she marches into the showroom and demands a $5,000 prize because she can "prove" that Johnson is selling this model at $650 over his cost. Johnson, with considerable aplomb, summons his accountant, who presents the following information to Henley.

| | |
|---|---:|
| Invoice cost to dealer | $13,400 |
| Commission to salesperson | 100 |
| Cost of make-ready services | 160 |
| General overhead | 430 |
| Total cost | $14,090 |

The accountant points out that Henley failed to consider the "real" costs of running a large automobile dealership. He states that the make-ready and general overhead costs are based on the total service department cost and total overhead costs divided by the number of cars sold last year (500). General overhead costs are virtually all fixed. Johnson pleasantly and politely offers his condolences to Henley for having failed to win the $5,000 and invites her back any time she wants to buy a car at $100 over cost. Henley is not at all happy with her reception at Johnson's or the data provided by his accountant, and she decides to sue for the $5,000.

### Required

Assume that Henley loses the case at the local level and appeals the decision to a higher court. The trial judge (original decision) agreed with the explanation of Easy Ed's accountant. Nevertheless, Henley argues that Easy Ed is defrauding the populace and owes her $5,000. Her lawyer has asked you to serve as an expert witness. What will your testimony be?

**13-53  Determining product costs**   Renata Tomato Company processes and cans tomato paste. The company has the capability to can whole tomatoes as well, but has not done so for about a year because of lack of profitability. The company has the capacity to process 5,000,000 pounds of tomatoes per month, whether for canning whole or making into paste.

The production manager and controller were recently discussing the production budget for the next several months. They agreed, on the basis of the information in the following schedule, that the company should continue to process only tomato paste.

| | Whole Tomatoes | Tomato Paste |
|---|:---:|:---:|
| Selling price per case | $ 6.00 | $5.80 |
| Variable costs: | | |
|    Tomatoes[a] | $ 3.10 | $2.00 |
|    Direct labor | 0.90 | 1.00 |
|    Variable overhead | 1.80 | 2.00 |
|    Packaging | 0.52 | 0.60 |
| Total variable costs | $ 6.32 | $5.60 |
| Contribution margin | $(0.32) | $0.20 |

[a]  *Whole tomatoes must be grade A tomatoes, which cost $0.155 per pound.*

Paste is made from grade B tomatoes, which cost $0.08 per pound. There are 20 pounds of tomatoes in a case of whole tomatoes, 25 pounds in a case of paste.

A few days after the decision had been made to process only paste, the president received a call from a large tomato grower who offered to sell Renata as many pounds of tomatoes as it could use for the next six months. The price was to be $0.095 per pound, and the batches would be mixed A and B grades. The grower guaranteed that at least 40% of the tomatoes would be grade A.

The president told the production manager about the offer. The latter replied that it should cost $0.005 per pound to sort the tomatoes into the two grades, but that there would be no other additional costs if the offer were accepted. The company's capacity to process 5,000,000 pounds per month would not be affected. The company can sell all it can produce of either product.

The production and sales managers decided to investigate the probable effects of taking the offer. They agreed that it was profitable to can whole tomatoes if the price were much less than the current $0.155 per pound, but they were uncertain of the effects on the contribution margin of paste. They agreed to ask the controller to prepare a new analysis of relative profitability of the two products. The controller's analysis showed that paste was now a losing proposition, while whole tomatoes were extremely profitable. For the cost of tomatoes, the controller used $0.10 per pound, the purchase price plus additional sorting costs.

|  | Whole Tomatoes | Tomato Paste |
|---|---|---|
| Selling price per case | $6.00 | $ 5.80 |
| Variable costs: | | |
| Tomatoes | $2.00 | $ 2.50 |
| Other variable costs | 3.22 | 3.60 |
| Total variable costs | $5.22 | $ 6.10 |
| Contribution margin | $0.78 | $(0.30) |

The production manager and sales manager wondered about the wisdom of using the $0.10 per pound cost of tomatoes for both products. "After all," said the sales manager, "aren't we paying more for the grade A tomatoes and less for the grade B? It seems unreasonable to say that they cost the same." The controller said that other methods were possible, suggesting that the costs could also be assigned based on the ratios of costs of buying tomatoes already sorted. "If we did it that way," he said, "buying 2,000,000 pounds of grade A tomatoes at $0.155 would cost $310,000. The 3,000,000 grade B tomatoes would cost $240,000 at $0.08. The total cost is $550,000. The cost of grade B is thus about 43.6% of the total. So we could assign $218,000 ($500,000 × 43.6%) to the grade B tomatoes in the package deal. That gives a cost per pound of $0.07267. Doing the same with the grade A produce gives $0.141 per pound."

At this point the president entered the room and commented that it seemed to her that the company was buying $240,000 worth of grade B tomatoes at $0.08 per pound and the rest of the purchase and sorting costs should be assigned to the grade A tomatoes. "That gives $260,000 to the grade A ($500,000 − $240,000), which is $0.13 per pound. Isn't that best?"

### Required

1. Determine whether the company should buy the unsorted tomatoes.
2. Discuss the appropriateness of the methods of determining the cost of tomatoes suggested by each of the managers and make a recommendation.

*Chapter Fourteen*

# STANDARD COSTING
# AND VARIABLE COSTING

CHAPTER
1

*Beginning with Chapter 1 we have pointed out that modern companies try to reduce inventories because inventories are costly, hide defects, and interrupt product flow. Why then do many companies continue to stock excess parts and product? One reason has to do with external reporting requirements. Absorption costing, which companies must use for GAAP, rewards inventory increases. As production increases, reported income increases. Conversely, when companies reduce inventories their incomes are lower. Additionally, some cost variances are more favorable, or less unfavorable, when production increases. Thus, the more you make, the higher the profit, even if you don't sell what you make. Lots of people believe this is a bad situation and have recommended ways to alleviate it. We present two techniques in this chapter, one that has been around for many years, another quite new, that avoid the problem.*

*One who has strongly criticized GAAP is Eli Goldratt, the developer of the Theory of Constraints. He and his associates have gone so far as to argue that cost accounting is the number one enemy of productivity. The Internet Activity at the end of this chapter asks you to explore Web sites devoted to Goldratt's ideas and how they relate to financial reporting.*

CHAPTER
12

CHAPTER
13

Chapter 12 showed how standards can be used to help manage costs. Chapter 13 introduced absorption costing—the product costing method required for external reporting under GAAP. This chapter shows how standard costs can be used in product costing and presents an alternative to absorption costing, called variable costing, or direct costing. Variable costing excludes fixed production costs from inventory and cost of goods sold calculations and uses the familiar contribution margin format of the income statement that we introduced in Chapter 2. Variable costing is acceptable, and widely used, for internal reporting purposes and for decision making. It can be used by job-order and process cost companies, and with actual, normal, or standard costing.

## STANDARD ABSORPTION COSTING

Under **standard costing** inventories appear at standard cost, not actual or normal cost, as Chapter 13 showed. Standard costing is much more widespread among manufacturing companies than actual or normal costing. The most important reason for the popularity of standard costing is that it is usually much simpler and more effective than the alternatives. Picture an automobile assembly plant that makes several models (2-door and 4-door sedans, 2-door coupes), with many options (manual and automatic transmissions, air conditioning, various trim packages). Such a plant cannot use the Chapter 13 formula, total costs divided by units produced, because the units are so different. The plant could use job-order costing, but might spend more money keeping records than making cars. Each worker would have to fill in a time report for each operation performed on each car. When a car got to the end of the line it would have hundreds of tags showing the times to install the windshield, put in the steering wheel, etc. Someone would have to assemble these tags, add the times, determine the wage rates for the workers, and so forth and so on. Such a situation is a recordkeeping nightmare and is clearly ridiculous. Even with bar coding and other technology, the cost to maintain such a system would be very high. Moreover, the information obtained would be of doubtful value. Ford cannot sell one car for more than another because its windshield required two more minutes to install. Instead, companies develop standards in the manner discussed in Chapter 12, then show inventories at the standard cost. Thus, a basic 2-door sedan has a standard cost, as does each possible option. So each car can be inventoried at the sum of its standard costs, basic plus options.

Another important reason for using standard costing is that it integrates standard costs and variances into the company's records, so it calculates variances as a normal part of recordkeeping with little or no additional cost. Capturing as much information as possible directly in the accounts is wise, because such information is very easy to retrieve and is more likely to be accurate.

Chapter 12 showed how to determine standards for variable production costs. Under standard absorption costing, manufacturers determine standard variable costs and also determine per-unit standard fixed overhead costs for each product. The resulting total standard cost per unit is used to calculate the cost of inventory and the cost of goods sold. Unfavorable variances are treated as expenses, favorable variances are treated as negative expenses, and both are reported in internal income statements. The development of a standard for fixed overhead follows from Chapter 13, which showed how to calculate and use a predetermined overhead rate. We begin with a simple, one-product company. Such a company can determine a standard fixed cost per unit simply by dividing total budgeted fixed manufacturing overhead by some number of units of its product.

Exhibit 14-1 presents data for SMP Company, which produces an automobile part. The company has standards for labor, materials, and variable overhead. To simplify the situation, we group all standard variable costs into a single per-unit variable cost. Because you already have learned to analyze variable cost variances, we will not give data to identify each variable cost variance, but will calculate only total variable cost variances. Notice that variable selling and administrative expenses are incurred based on units sold, not on units produced.

## CALCULATING A STANDARD FIXED COST

The standard fixed cost per unit depends, as did the predetermined overhead rate, on two things: (1) the choice of *a measure of activity* (e.g., direct labor hours, machine hours, setup time, etc.) and (2) *a level of activity* (budgeted hours in Chapter 13). Since we are dealing with a single-product company, the obvious measure of activity is units of product, but we must choose the level of activity.

In Chapter 13, under normal costing, we used budgeted activity to set the predetermined overhead rate. We could use that same level of activity, but we also could use other levels: normal activity (or normal capacity), practical capacity, and theoretical capacity. **Normal activity** is the average activity expected or budgeted over the coming two to five years. The objective in using this activity level is to develop a standard fixed cost that reflects the company's expected long-term per-unit costs, not the cost for a single year (as budgeted activity reflects).

**Practical capacity** is the maximum activity the company can achieve given the usual kinds of interruptions. (Events such as strikes or severe shortages of materials are not considered usual.) As with budgeted and normal activity, the measure of activity might be units of product, direct labor hours, or a set of activity-based measures. Standard costs based on practical capacity reflect the lowest reasonable long-term average fixed cost. **Theoretical capacity** is the absolute maximum that a plant can produce, with no interruptions or problems at all. Using practical capacity and theoretical capacity yields very low unit costs, costs that most companies can use as goals, but rarely reach. JIT factories that use standard costs often use practical capacity, or even theoretical capacity, *because* these levels give goals that the company can strive to reach.

| Exhibit 14-1   SMP Company, Operating Data 20X1 | |
|---|---:|
| Production in units | 110,000 |
| Sales in units, at $80 each | 90,000 |
| Ending inventory in units | 20,000 |
| Actual production costs: | |
|   Variable | $2,255,000 |
|   Fixed | $3,200,000 |
| Selling and administrative expenses: | |
|   Variable at $5 per unit | $450,000 |
|   Fixed | $1,400,000 |
| Standards and budgets: | |
|   Budgeted fixed production costs | $3,000,000 |
|   Standard variable production costs | $20 per unit |

Suppose that SMP's managers decide to set the standard per-unit fixed cost using normal capacity of 100,000 units. The standard is then $30 per unit, computed as follows:

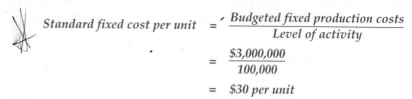

$$\text{Standard fixed cost per unit} = \frac{\text{Budgeted fixed production costs}}{\text{Level of activity}}$$

$$= \frac{\$3,000,000}{100,000}$$

$$= \$30 \text{ per unit}$$

The total standard cost per unit is $50, consisting of the $20 standard variable cost per unit and the $30 standard fixed cost per unit. We shall use this standard fixed cost per unit to determine variances and, if variances are not significant, the standard cost will also be used in external financial statements.

## VARIANCES

We first calculate variable manufacturing cost variances. From Exhibit 14-1 we know that actual production was 110,000 units, so total variable cost variances are $55,000 unfavorable, calculated as follows:

| | |
|---|---:|
| Total actual variable production costs (Exhibit 14-1) | $2,255,000 |
| Standard variable costs (110,000 × $20) | 2,200,000 |
| Unfavorable variable cost variances | $    55,000 |

CHAPTER 13

Fixed overhead variances follow the general pattern of Chapter 13. There is a budget variance and a volume variance.

The total fixed overhead variance (misapplied fixed overhead) is $100,000, computed as follows:

| | |
|---|---:|
| Total actual fixed overhead | $3,200,000 |
| Fixed overhead applied (110,000 × $30) | 3,300,000 |
| Overapplied overhead | $   100,000 |

The volume variance under standard costing is budgeted fixed overhead minus applied fixed overhead. (The volume variance under normal costing is calculated the same way, but applied overhead is based on inputs, not output.) The budget variance under standard costing is, just as under normal costing, actual fixed overhead ($3,200,000) minus budgeted fixed overhead ($3,000,000).

CHAPTER 12

Following is an analysis of fixed overhead variances using the diagram format introduced in Chapter 12. The budget variance is $200,000 unfavorable, and the volume variance is $300,000 favorable.

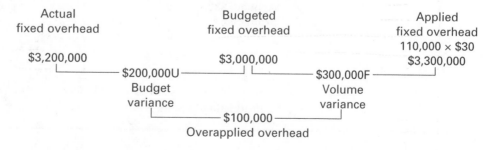

The unfavorable budget variance, as in the previous chapter, means that SMP incurred more fixed manufacturing overhead than it budgeted. The favorable volume variance, similar to the meaning in the previous chapter, means only that SMP worked more standard hours than it used to set the standard fixed cost.

Exhibit 14-2 provides a graphical analysis of SMP's results.

## INCOME STATEMENTS

Using the standard cost per unit and the operating data from Exhibit 14-1, we can prepare an income statement for SMP Company for 20X1. Exhibit 14-3 shows the statement. As you can see, the format is similar to those used for actual and normal absorption costing in Chapter 13, which in turn were based on the typical income statement presentation used in financial accounting. That is, cost of sales is computed by adding the standard production costs for the year to the beginning inventory and then subtracting the ending inventory.

Notice that the variable production costs and fixed production costs added to the beginning inventory are at standard cost per unit multiplied by unit production. Under standard costing, all amounts in the calculation of standard cost of sales (or standard cost of goods sold) are standard cost per unit multiplied by the number of units involved. This is true for the beginning inventory, applied fixed production costs, cost of goods available for sale, and ending inventory. Therefore, standard cost of sales is simply the per-unit standard cost multiplied by the num-

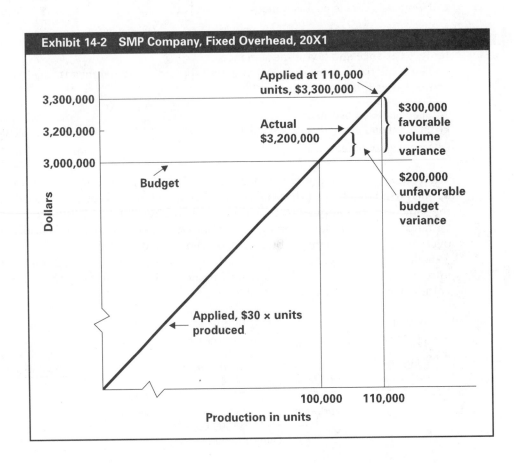

Exhibit 14-2   SMP Company, Fixed Overhead, 20X1

**Exhibit 14-3   SMP Company, Income Statement for 20X1**

| | | |
|---|---:|---:|
| Sales | | $7,200,000 |
| Standard cost of sales: | | |
| Beginning inventory | $          0 | |
| Standard variable production costs | | |
| (110,000 × $20) | 2,200,000 | |
| Applied fixed production costs (110,000 × $30) | 3,300,000 | |
| Cost of goods available for sale (110,000 × $50) | $5,500,000 | |
| Ending inventory (20,000 × $50) | 1,000,000 | |
| Standard cost of sales (90,000 × $50) | | 4,500,000 |
| Standard gross margin | | $2,700,000 |
| Variances: | | |
| Fixed manufacturing cost budget variance | $  200,000U | |
| Fixed manufacturing cost volume variance | 300,000F | |
| Variable manufacturing cost variances | 55,000U | 45,000F |
| Actual gross margin | | $2,745,000 |
| Selling and administrative expenses* | | 1,850,000 |
| Profit | | $  895,000 |

\* *Fixed costs of $1,400,000 plus variable costs of $450,000, 90,000 × $5*

ber of units sold. In such cases, we have no need to show the details of the section for the standard cost of sales, because it equals the number of units sold times the standard cost per unit. Thus, we can also prepare an income statement such as the one in Exhibit 14-4, which omits the details of the cost of sales section.

Exhibit 14-4 also shows variances as adjustments to standard cost of sales instead of as adjustments to standard gross margin. You should see that the final results for actual gross margin and income will be the same regardless of where the variances appear in the statement.

**Exhibit 14-4   SMP Company, Income Statement for 20X1 (Alternative format)**

| | | |
|---|---:|---:|
| Sales | | $7,200,000 |
| Cost of sales: | | |
| Standard cost of sales (90,000 × $50) | $4,500,000 | |
| Variances: | | |
| Fixed manufacturing cost budget variance | 200,000U | |
| Fixed manufacturing cost volume variance | 300,000F | |
| Variable manufacturing cost variances | 55,000U | |
| Cost of sales | | 4,455,000 |
| Gross margin | | $2,745,000 |
| Selling and administrative expenses* | | 1,850,000 |
| Profit | | $  895,000 |

\* *Fixed costs of $1,400,000 plus variable costs of $450,000, 90,000 × $5*

Finally, please remember that we do not expect to *incur* fixed overhead at the standard fixed cost per unit—we expect to incur total *budgeted* fixed overhead. *The application of fixed overhead to units of product is an accounting device used to avoid the fluctuating per-unit fixed costs that could result from using actual absorption costing.* Standard fixed costs are an extension of the predetermined overhead rates of Chapter 13.

Before we show how standards are used in a multiproduct company, complete the following review problem to make sure you understand the basics of standard costing.

## REVIEW PROBLEM

SMP continued to use the same standard costs for 20X2. Its operating data for 20X2 were as follows:

| | |
|---|---|
| Production, in units | 95,000 |
| Sales, in units, at $80 each | 100,000 |
| Ending inventory, in units | 15,000 |
| Actual production costs: | |
|   Variable | $1,881,000 |
|   Fixed | $2,950,000 |
| Selling and administrative expenses: | |
|   Variable at $5 per unit | $ 500,000 |
|   Fixed | $1,400,000 |
| Standard variable production cost | $20 per unit |
| Budgeted fixed production costs | $3,000,000 |

Prepare an income statement for 20X2. The solution that appears in Exhibit 14-5 uses a slightly different format from that in Exhibit 14-3. Here we show variances as an adjustment to standard cost of sales instead of as an adjustment to standard gross margin. Exhibits 14-3, 14-4, and 14-5 offer three possibilities for placement of variances, but all three eventually arrive at an actual gross margin figure.

## MULTIPLE PRODUCTS AND ACTIVITY-BASED COSTING

As we said earlier, standard costing is the overwhelming choice of repetitive manufacturers, companies that make many standard products. It also can be used by companies that make several products of different design. So long as the products are relatively standard, even a job-order company can use standard costing. Any company that can develop standards can use a standard costing system.

As early as Chapter 3 we began discussing the idea of activity-based costing (ABC), under which companies (and other organizations) associate overhead cost pools with their respective drivers and assign the costs in each overhead pool based on the relative use of drivers. Most recently, Chapters 12 and 13 used those concepts in applying overhead. ABC also applies to standard costing, especially for multiproduct companies. The idea behind activity-based costing—to associate as much cost as possible with activities, and subsequently with products, to determine how much resource use is traceable to the product—certainly applies to standard costing. The objective is to get better information about the costs and profitability of individual products. Companies that make a single product do not need ABC for products, but still might use it for identifying nonvalue-adding activities and for analyzing the profitability of customers or channels of distribution.

**Exhibit 14-5    SMP Company, Income Statement for 20X1**

| | | |
|---|---:|---:|
| Sales (100,000 × $80) | | $8,000,000 |
| Standard cost of sales: | | |
| Beginning inventory (Exhibit 14-3) | $1,000,000 | |
| Standard variable production costs (95,000 × $20) | 1,900,000 | |
| Applied fixed production costs (95,000 × $30) | 2,850,000 | |
| Cost of goods available for sale (115,000 × $50) | $5,750,000 | |
| Ending inventory (15,000 × $50) | 750,000 | |
| Standard cost of sales (100,000 × $50) | $5,000,000 | |
| Variances: | | |
| Fixed manufacturing cost budget variance | 50,000F | |
| Fixed manufacturing cost volume variance | 150,000U | |
| Variable manufacturing cost variances | 19,000F | |
| Cost of sales | | 5,081,000 |
| Gross margin | | $2,919,000 |
| Selling and administrative expenses* | | 1,900,000 |
| Profit | | $1,019,000 |

Variances:

Variable cost, $1,881,000 – ($20 × 95,000) = $19,000F

Fixed cost

| Actual fixed overhead | Budgeted fixed overhead | Applied fixed overhead (95,000 × $30) |
|---|---|---|
| $2,950,000 | $3,000,000 | $2,850,000 |

└── $50,000F ──┘  └── $150,000U ──┘
    budget              volume
    variance            variance
        └────── $100,000 ──────┘
        total fixed overhead variances

\* Fixed costs of $1,400,000 plus variable costs of $500,000, 100,000 × $5

Suppose that ARG Co. has two major types of fixed overhead. Overhead related to materials and component parts, such as purchasing, inspection, warehousing, and handling, is budgeted at $500,000. Overhead related to direct labor is $3,000,000 and the rate per direct labor hour is $4.00, based on 750,000 hours at normal activity. (You learned how to make that calculation in Chapter 13.) Material-related overhead is allocated based on the total number of component parts budgeted for use during a year. ARG makes two types of instruments. Data and calculations are as follows:

| | Portable Model | Table Model |
|---|---:|---:|
| Standard direct labor hours | 8 | 12 |
| Number of component parts | 100 | 200 |
| Budgeted production | 6,000 | 2,000 |
| Total budgeted use of components | 600,000 | 400,000 |
| Standard fixed overhead rate | | |
| per component $500,000/(600,000 + 400,000) = $0.50 | | |

We can calculate the standard overhead costs per unit as follows:

|  | Portable Model | Table Model |
|---|---|---|
| Material-related: |  |  |
| Portable model (100 × $0.50) | $50 |  |
| Table model (200 × $0.50) |  | $100 |
| Direct labor-related: |  |  |
| Portable model (8 hours × $4) | 32 |  |
| Table model (12 hours × $4) |  | 48 |
| Standard fixed overhead cost per unit | $82 | $148 |

The $50 and $100 for material-related overhead are treated just like any other overhead. The company will apply both types of overhead, just as we did in Chapter 13. It also will calculate misapplied overhead, budget variances, and volume variances separately for each pool of overhead. Let us illustrate for the material-related overhead. Assume the following results for the year.

| | |
|---|---|
| Actual material-related overhead | $510,000 |
| Actual production: | |
|   Portable model | 7,000 |
|   Table model | 2,000 |
| Standard use of components | 1,100,000* |
| Fixed overhead applied | $550,000* |

*The standard use of components is based on total production of each model, 7,000 × 100 plus 2,000 × 200 = 1,100,000 components, which, when multiplied by the $0.50 standard rate, gives $550,000 applied overhead.

Variances are as follows:

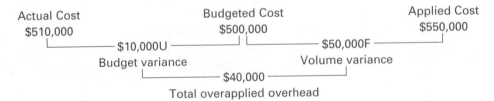

The calculations are the same no matter how many cost pools the plant uses. Manufacturers are interested not only in their own costs, but also in their competitors' costs. The accompanying Insight describes how one company uses techniques introduced in Chapter 12 to determine competitors' costs, including the structure of fixed and variable costs, for strategic purposes.

## COMPARISON OF STANDARD AND NORMAL COSTING

Although the normal costing concept of a predetermined overhead rate is related to the idea of a standard fixed cost per unit, the results reported under the two types of costing systems are not the same. Remember that, under normal costing, overhead is applied based on the actual level of the activity. Under standard costing, overhead is applied based on the number of units produced, or *standard* quantity of inputs used.

**IN SIGHT**

### Target Costs And Competitors' Costs

**ITT Automotive** is one of the world's largest auto parts manufacturers. It has used target costing for several years because it faces difficult competitive conditions. For instance, it expected the price it charges for an antilock braking system to drop from $200 in 1996 to $100 by 2000. The company uses value engineering extensively and performs discounted cash flow analyses to determine whether to accept new business.

ITT has no information about its competitors' prices or costs, but it sometimes estimates costs by tearing down a unit of a competitor's product and analyzing its content. Analysts are often able to estimate the competitor's cost structure, as well as the functionality of the component. From such analyses they are able to determine what processes the competitor used to make the component and how ITT might reduce its cost by using a different process.

ITT requires that a new product cover not only its direct manufacturing costs, but also promotion, service, and return on investment. The target costing team sets targets for each purchased component of the new product, as well as targets for labor and overhead. The company tracks the target and actual costs of the product from the early design stage until it drops the product. The attention the company pays to target costing is evidenced by the resources it devotes to the task.

*Source: George Schmelze, Rolf Geier, and Thomas E. Buttross, "Target Costing at ITT Automotive," *Management Accounting, *December 1996, 26–30.*

The two systems will always give the same budget variance, because the budget variance is simply actual cost minus budgeted cost. But unless standard hours equal actual hours, the volume variances will differ because different amounts of fixed overhead are *applied* under the two methods. The difference in volume variances serves to remind you of what we said when introducing the concept of a volume variance in Chapter 13: the variance has little or no economic significance and reflects only the effect of working at an activity level other than the level used to determine the overhead application rate.

We have presented several costing methods in this and previous chapters. The following table summarizes the similarities and differences among the three methods—actual costing, normal costing, and standard costing—by showing the basis for determining the inventoriable cost of a unit of product.

| Cost Element | Actual Costing | Normal Costing | Standard Costing |
|---|---|---|---|
| Materials | actual cost | actual cost | standard cost |
| Direct labor | actual cost | actual cost | standard cost |
| Overhead | actual cost | applied cost | standard cost |
|  | (actual **input** × actual rate) | (actual **input** × predetermined rate) | (actual **output** × standard cost) |

CHAPTER
13

The table shows that actual costing and normal costing differ only in the treatment of overhead, as explained in Chapter 13. Standard costing differs from both of the other methods by using standard costs for all input factors. The only difference between standard costing and normal costing with respect to overhead is that standard costing applies overhead based on *standard* quantities of the input factor (or, what amounts to the same thing, on actual unit production), while normal costing applies overhead based on *actual* quantities of input factors.

While standard costs for product costing are invaluable for many companies, their use in control and performance evaluation can create problems, some of which we introduced in Chapter 12.

CHAPTER
12

## VARIABLE COSTING

Thus far, we have discussed only absorption costing systems. Such systems are required for financial reporting and for income tax purposes and are often used, as we mentioned earlier, for internal purposes. However, throughout this book we have recommended internal reports using the contribution margin format, which treats all fixed costs as period costs. When this approach is applied to product costing the result is called variable costing (direct costing).

**Variable costing** excludes fixed production costs from the unit costs of inventories, and treats all fixed costs as expenses in the period incurred. It is possible—and we think preferable—to use variable costing for internal reports. The flow of manufacturing costs using variable costing can easily be shown by a slight variation of the cost flow figure presented in Chapter 13. Exhibit 14-6 depicts the difference in cost flows under variable and absorption costing systems.

CHAPTER
13

Exhibit 14-7 presents variable costing income statements using actual costing for SMP (the subject of our earlier example) for 20X1and Exhibit 14-8 shows an actual variable costing income statement for 20X2. Except when a company uses job-order costing, actual costing requires a cost flow assumption. We use FIFO.

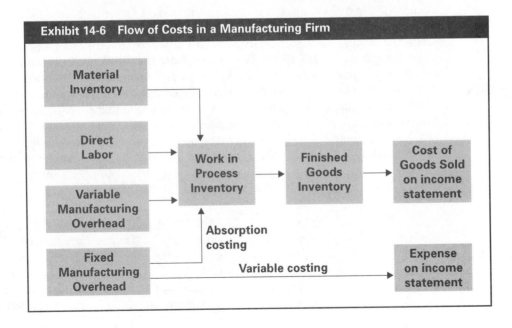

**Exhibit 14-6    Flow of Costs in a Manufacturing Firm**

**Exhibit 14-7 SMP Company, Income Statement for 20X1—Actual Variable Costing**

| | | |
|---|---:|---:|
| Sales | | $7,200,000 |
| Variable cost of sales: | | |
|   Beginning inventory | $ 0 | |
|   Actual variable production costs | 2,255,000 | |
|   Cost of goods available for sale | $2,255,000 | |
|   Ending inventory* | 410,000 | |
|   Variable cost of sales | | 1,845,000 |
| Variable manufacturing margin | | $5,355,000 |
| Variable selling and administrative expenses | | 450,000 |
| Contribution margin | | $4,905,000 |
| Actual fixed costs: | | |
|   Manufacturing | $3,200,000 | |
|   Selling and administrative | 1,400,000 | 4,600,000 |
| Profit | | $ 305,000 |

* $2,255,000/110,000 = $20.50 unit cost, 20,000 units times $20.50 = $410,000.

Variable costing can also be used with standard costs, as shown in Exhibits 14-9 and 14-10 for SMP for 20X1 and 20X2. We use the $20 per unit standard variable cost here. Note that there is no need to select a level of activity to calculate a pre-determined fixed overhead rate because variable costing does not include fixed costs in the calculation of inventory cost per unit. The variable cost variances are the same as they are under standard absorption costing, as is the fixed overhead budget variance. The volume variance does not appear under variable costing be-

**Exhibit 14-8 SMP Company, Income Statement for 20X2—Actual Variable Costing**

| | | |
|---|---:|---:|
| Sales | | $8,000,000 |
| Variable cost of sales: | | |
|   Beginning inventory | $ 410,000 | |
|   Actual variable production costs | 1,881,000 | |
|   Cost of goods available for sale | $2,291,000 | |
|   Ending inventory* | 297,000 | |
|   Variable cost of sales | | 1,994,000 |
| Variable manufacturing margin | | $6,006,000 |
| Variable selling and administrative expenses | | 500,000 |
| Contribution margin | | $5,506,000 |
| Actual fixed costs: | | |
|   Manufacturing | $2,950,000 | |
|   Selling and administrative | 1,400,000 | 4,350,000 |
| Profit | | $1,156,000 |

* $1,881,000/95,000 = $19.80 unit cost, 15,000 units times $19.80 = $297,000.

**Exhibit 14-9    SMP Company, Income Statement for 20X1—Standard Variable Costing**

| | | |
|---|---:|---:|
| Sales | | $7,200,000 |
| Standard cost of sales: | | |
| Beginning inventory | $        0 | |
| Standard variable production costs | | |
| (110,000 × $20) | 2,200,000 | |
| Cost of goods available for sale (110,000 × $20) | $2,200,000 | |
| Ending inventory (20,000 × $20) | 400,000 | |
| Standard variable cost of sales (90,000 × $20) | | 1,800,000 |
| Standard variable manufacturing margin | | $5,400,000 |
| Variable manufacturing cost variances | | 55,000U |
| Variable manufacturing margin | | $5,345,000 |
| Variable selling and administrative expenses | | |
| (90,000 × $5) | | 450,000 |
| Contribution margin | | $4,895,000 |
| Fixed costs: | | |
| Budgeted fixed manufacturing costs | $3,000,000 | |
| Fixed manufacturing cost budget variance | 200,000U | |
| Selling and administrative expenses | 1,400,000 | |
| Total fixed costs | | 4,600,000 |
| Profit | | $  295,000 |

**Exhibit 14-10    SMP Company, Income Statement for 20X2—Standard Variable Costing**

| | | |
|---|---:|---:|
| Sales | | $8,000,000 |
| Standard cost of sales: | | |
| Beginning inventory (20,000 × $20) | $  400,000 | |
| Standard variable production costs | | |
| (95,000 × $20) | 1,900,000 | |
| Cost of goods available for sale (115,000 × $20) | $2,300,000 | |
| Ending inventory (15,000 × $20) | 300,000 | |
| Standard variable cost of sales (100,000 × $20) | | 2,000,000 |
| Standard variable manufacturing margin | | $6,000,000 |
| Variable manufacturing cost variances | | 19,000F |
| Variable manufacturing margin | | $6,019,000 |
| Variable selling and administrative expenses | | |
| (100,000 × $5) | | 500,000 |
| Contribution margin | | $5,519,000 |
| Fixed costs: | | |
| Budgeted fixed manufacturing costs | $3,000,000 | |
| Fixed manufacturing cost budget variance | 50,000F | |
| Selling and administrative expenses | 1,400,000 | |
| Total fixed costs | | 4,350,000 |
| Profit | | $1,169,000 |

cause no fixed overhead is applied to products. Note that we show total budgeted fixed manufacturing costs and the fixed overhead budget variance separately. Recall from Chapter 12 that companies calculate fixed overhead budget variances because they are economically significant. (A variable costing company *recognizes* fixed costs—it just does not *inventory* them. It expenses them as they are incurred.)

Though it might seem otherwise, variable costing does not introduce new concepts. Suppose that at the end of Chapter 3 you were asked to prepare an income statement based on the following data.

| Sales | 90,000 units at $80 per unit |
| --- | --- |
| Variable costs per unit: | |
| Manufacturing | $20.50 |
| Selling and administrative | $5.00 |
| Total fixed costs: | |
| Manufacturing | $3,200,000 |
| Selling and administrative | $1,400,000 |

Your income statement would probably have looked like the one in Exhibit 14- 11.

The income statements in Exhibits 14-7 and 14-8 *appear* to be different from and more complex than statements you have seen in earlier chapters, but the only *real* difference is in the amount of detail on cost of sales. Whether you use the shortened format of Exhibit 14-11 or the expanded format of Exhibit 14-7, the income for the year is the same and reflects an expensing of fixed costs in the year incurred. Without knowing it, you have been preparing actual variable costing income statements since Chapter 3.

## COMPARING VARIABLE AND ABSORPTION COSTING RESULTS

Compare the 20X1 and 20X2 results under variable costing (Exhibits 14-9 and 14-10) with the results under absorption costing for the same economic activity (see Exhibits 14-3 and 14-5). *Absorption costing income is higher than variable costing income for 20X1 and lower for 20X2.* Absorption costing income in 20X1 is higher because absorption costing transfers some of the fixed costs of 20X1 into 20X2 as

| Exhibit 14-11    SMP Company Variable Costing Income Statement for 20X1 | | |
| --- | --- | --- |
| Sales (90,000 × $80) | | $7,200,000 |
| Variable costs: | | |
| Manufacturing (90,000 × $20.50) | $1,845,000 | |
| Selling and administrative (90,000 × $5) | 450,000 | 2,295,000 |
| Contribution margin | | $4,905,000 |
| Fixed costs: | | |
| Manufacturing | $3,200,000 | |
| Selling and administrative | 1,400,000 | 4,600,000 |
| Income | | $  305,000 |

part of the cost of the ending inventory of 20,000 units. Absorption costing income in 20X2 is lower because a similar shift of 20X2 costs (to 20X3) was smaller (fixed costs in an ending inventory of only 15,000 units) than the amount of fixed costs transferred in from 20X1.

In more general terms, the differences are traceable to the relationship between production and sales. Subject to a few technicalities, *when production exceeds sales* (so that ending inventory is greater than beginning inventory) *absorption costing gives a higher income than variable costing.* When sales exceed production, absorption costing gives a lower income than variable costing. The difference in incomes is due entirely to the fixed costs carried forward in inventory under absorption costing. Such costs are shown on the balance sheet as part of inventory and are expensed only when the goods are sold. Exhibit 14-12 shows the amounts of fixed production costs expensed in each year under the two approaches, along with a reconciliation of the incomes under standard costing.

If the standard fixed cost per unit does not change from year to year, the difference between absorption costing income and income under variable costing can be computed directly by multiplying the standard fixed cost per unit by the change in units in inventory. Thus, we could have made the reconciliation shown in Exhibit 14-12 simply by using the formula on the following page.

---

**Exhibit 14-12   Reconciliation of Incomes—Variable and Absorption Costing**

|  | 20X1 | 20X2 |
| --- | --- | --- |
| **Comparison of reported income:** | | |
| Variable costing (Exhibits 14-9 and 14-10) | $ 295,000 | $1,169,000 |
| Absorption costing (Exhibits 14-3 and 14-5) | 895,000 | 1,019,000 |
| Difference to be explained | $ (600,000) | $ 150,000 |
| **Explanation of income difference:** | | |
| Fixed production costs in beginning inventory | | |
| (transferred from prior year): | | |
| 0 units × $30 | $        0 | |
| 20,000 units × $30 | | $ 600,000 |
| Fixed production costs incurred during | | |
| the year | 3,200,000 | 2,950,000 |
|  | $3,200,000 | $3,550,000 |
| Less fixed production costs in ending inventory | | |
| (being transferred to a future year): | | |
| 20,000 units × $30 | 600,000 | |
| 15,000 units × $30 | | 450,000 |
| Total fixed costs expensed under absorption | | |
| costing for the year | $2,600,000 | $3,100,000 |
| Total fixed costs expensed under variable | | |
| costing—equal to total fixed costs incurred | 3,200,000 | 2,950,000 |
| Difference between fixed costs incurred and | | |
| expensed for the year | $ (600,000) | $ 150,000 |

$$
\begin{array}{ccc}
\begin{array}{c} \textit{Difference} \\ \textit{in} \\ \textit{incomes} \end{array}
&=&
\left( \begin{array}{c} \textit{Units in} \\ \textit{beginning} \\ \textit{inventory} \end{array} - \begin{array}{c} \textit{Units in} \\ \textit{ending} \\ \textit{inventory} \end{array} \right)
& \times &
\begin{array}{c} \textit{Standard} \\ \textit{fixed cost} \\ \textit{fixed cost} \end{array}
\end{array}
$$

$$
\begin{array}{llllllll}
\begin{array}{c} \textit{Difference} \\ \textit{20X1} \end{array} & = & (0 & - & 20{,}000) & \times & \$30 & = \$(600{,}000) \\[2mm]
\begin{array}{c} \textit{Difference} \\ \textit{20X2} \end{array} & = & (20{,}000 & - & 15{,}000) & \times & \$30 & = \$150{,}000
\end{array}
$$

## ABSORPTION COSTING, PRODUCTION, AND INCOME

Of more importance than reconciling incomes under the two methods is that *absorption costing income increases as production increases.* Absorption costing therefore encourages high production, because managers evaluated on income will show higher incomes the more they produce, regardless of whether they sell the output. Of course, production in excess of sales violates the principles of JIT and other advanced manufacturing techniques. Similarly, a manager following JIT principles who *reduces* inventory will suffer because reported income under absorption costing will be lower than it would be if she produced more. None of this holds for variable costing. Production does not affect variable costing income, which is a major reason many managers prefer it for internal purposes.

The accompanying Insight describes how volume variances affect companies' published income statements.

**IN** *SIGHT*

### Volume Variances in Annual Reports

**Acorn Corporation**, a manufacturer of lawn and garden tools, noted in its 1997 annual report, "The decrease in gross margin primarily was due to lower net sales of long handle tools and lower overhead absorption rates realized as the Company decreased production in response to sluggish demand, as well as additional promotional pricing in response to competitive pressures."

And from **Sunbeam's** 1997 annual report, "The Company continuously monitors future production plans at all of its facilities based on current inventory levels and anticipated new demand. The Company is currently evaluating whether to begin the second quarter season-end ramp down of production at its Neosho Outdoor Cooking products facility earlier than previously planned. If such action is taken, future operating results for the 1998 grill season would be adversely impacted due to unabsorbed fixed factory overhead during the second and third quarters and potential unanticipated inventory carrying costs."

It is important to note that neither company is talking about an increase in actual costs, rather they are discussing decreases in activity, which will lead to less overhead absorption, which will lead to lower inventory values and consequently lower reported income.

*Sources: Annual reports.*

## EVALUATION OF METHODS

We have already stated that we believe variable costing to be generally superior to absorption costing for internal reporting purposes. Not all managers, in accounting or elsewhere, agree with our position.

### EXTERNAL REPORTING

Although arguments about the suitability of either method for external reporting are not relevant to internal reporting, we mention some here to alert you to the principal justifications offered for absorption costing.[1]

The matching concept, which you studied in financial accounting, holds that costs must be matched against related revenues or against the revenues of the periods that have benefitted from the costs. As an example, the cost of a fixed asset is assigned, through depreciation, to the years of its life.

Fixed production costs "benefit" the company in the sense that, without them, few companies could produce anything at all. Thus, having a factory building and equipment entails depreciation, property taxes, some level of maintenance, and other fixed costs. Moreover, many supervisory personnel in a factory are salaried. Because these fixed costs are essential to the production of goods, one could argue that they should be expensed when the goods are sold, not when the goods are still in inventory. This argument is made by those favoring absorption costing.

Advocates of variable costing for financial reporting purposes counter by arguing that fixed production costs benefit production, but production as a whole, rather than any single unit of product. In other words, fixed costs provide the capacity to produce. Thus, once the company is in business and producing goods, fixed production costs have done their job; they are not needed for this or that unit, only for production as a whole. Accordingly, the argument continues, considering fixed costs on a per-unit basis is inappropriate because fixed costs cannot be identified with individual units; fixed costs are joint to all the units produced.

### INTERNAL REPORTING AND COST STRATEGY

Variable costing has important advantages for internal reporting. It presents information in the form that is most useful for managers—the form needed for CVP analysis—and its results do not depend on production.

Separating fixed and variable costs and reporting contribution margin enable managers to perform the CVP analysis that cannot be done working directly with absorption costing statements. Managers cannot predict income for future periods using an absorption costing income statement for two reasons: (1) they must predict not only sales for that future period, but also production, and (2) they must break down the cost figures into their fixed and variable components (i.e., managers must develop the information that is already provided by variable costing).

---

1 For income tax reporting, tax law, which can be extraordinarily complex, governs determination of inventory and cost of sales. In a growing economy, inventories will rise, so that companies will pay higher taxes under absorption costing than under variable costing.

As we stated earlier, production has no effect on income under variable costing. Managers can concentrate on the effects of changes in sales without having to allow for production. If sales fall from one period to another, variable costing income also will fall. Using absorption costing, income might well rise when sales fall if production is higher than sales. Most managers think of sales, not production, as the income-generating activity. Therefore, variable costing is more in tune with a manager's understanding of income than is absorption costing. Moreover, and perhaps most important, absorption costing encourages overproduction because reported income rises as production increases. Overproduction is at the root of many problems that JIT and other modern viewpoints try to solve.

Behavioral problems regarding costing methods extend to people's natural resistance to change. Overcoming top management's objections to changing accounting systems is critical, and often difficult. The controller of Martin Industries, a manufacturer of heating products, successfully introduced variable costing in part by securing the support of top management. The company benefitted from the use of variable costing as well as from other changes, but might have continued with its old system had the controller not been careful to seek support.[2]

Variable costing offers a significant strategic advantage because its income figure is not affected by production. Over the long run, production and sales for a given product will be about the same, so both absorption costing and variable costing will give the same total income. Variable costing income is an equilibrium figure because it shows what the company would earn over the long run if sales continued at the same level. Absorption costing income can be misleadingly high when production exceeds sales because the income cannot be maintained at the same level of sales. (A company cannot indefinitely produce in excess of current sales unless sales are rising.) Managers developing strategies for products are better served by incomes that represent equilibrium amounts, rather than by incomes influenced by inventory changes.

In summary, the information that managers need is provided much more directly by variable costing statements. Where absorption costing is used, a manager must recast statements to perform many of the analyses needed to plan, make decisions, control, and evaluate performance.

Advocates of absorption costing argue that variable costing might prompt managers to take a short-run approach to problems when a long-run approach is more desirable. Although they acknowledge the usefulness of variable costing information for specific short-run decisions, they argue that concentrating on variable costs can be harmful in the long run. Their objection is that managers who do not treat fixed costs as costs of product might set prices too low to cover fixed costs and earn profits. They argue that managers who become accustomed to reports prepared using variable costing could come to ignore the fixed costs that might be the great bulk of production costs. In short, advocates of absorption costing argue that it is useful because it alerts managers to the need to cover both fixed and variable costs.

Advocates of variable costing offer two counterarguments. One is that even absorption costing does not include all costs as product costs. Selling and administrative expenses are excluded from inventory under both costing methods. In many cases, these costs exceed production costs.

---

2 *Russell F. Briner, Michael D. Akers, James W. Truitt, and James D. Wilson, "Coping with Change at Martin Industries,"* Management Accounting, *July 1989, 45–49.*

The other counterargument is that it is unnecessary to allocate fixed costs to units in setting prices when the company faces competition and cannot charge any price it chooses. For example, suppose a company could analyze the expected volume-price relationships and select the best combination of price and expected volume. If a company has discretion over prices and can expect to sell about the same volume no matter what price is charged, there is no harm in using a total cost per unit to set prices. However, companies in these circumstances are much less common than those that face competition and therefore they cannot charge any price they wish.

A major study of pricing practices showed that 70 percent of manufacturers surveyed used full costs to set prices, 12 percent used variable costs, and 18 percent did not use costs, but rather prices based on their competitors' prices. The authors describe a similar study done in 1983 that found 82 percent using full costs, 17 percent using variable costs, and 1 percent "other." They concluded that full-cost pricing continues to be the norm, but with less dominance than before.

About half of those using full costs used full manufacturing costs, while the other half used manufacturing costs plus some selling and administrative expenses. About half of those using variable costs used only manufacturing costs, with the other half using some other variable costs as well. The authors attribute some of the strength of full-cost pricing to ABC, which better rationalizes individual product costs and eliminates much of the arbitrariness characteristic of older costing systems.[3]

Standard absorption costing is usually preferable to actual absorption costing. Companies that use standard absorption costing isolate the effect of actual production being different from the production level used to set the standard in the volume variance. (The volume variance tells us what the effect is, but is not helpful for control purposes.) Using standard fixed costs might alleviate the problem of a manager's changing prices at frequent intervals, if only because total cost per unit will not change as production changes.

## THROUGHPUT COSTING

CHAPTER 16

Throughput costing is an extreme form of variable costing. The method follows principles of the Theory of Constraints, which we introduce in Chapter 16. Throughput accounting is a radical departure from other methods in that it treats all costs except unused materials as expenses. Companies using throughput accounting inventory materials, just as do other companies. But throughput companies do not record work in process or finished goods inventories. Throughput accounting treats all direct labor and manufacturing overhead costs as period costs, expensing them as they are incurred. Cost of goods sold is the cost of materials *put into process.* A sample income statement appears shortly, along with absorption and variable costing income statements that reflect the same facts. This technique is being successfully used by a paper mill of **Champion International**, which we discuss in a later Insight, and by a British auto parts maker, among others.

The British company **AlliedSignal Limited, Turbochargers** faced a serious challenge when its European operations changed. The company had to manufacture

---

more product lines and make units in smaller batches. The company also had to make 3.5 percent reductions in cost under a contract with a major customer. Managers credit throughput accounting with helping the company by focusing managers' attention on turning materials into sales, not just into products. The right products to make are those that are sold; any products unsold are the wrong ones to have been made. The managers wanted to penalize overproduction and reward inventory reduction, which throughput costing does very well. The company considered ABC, but found it unhelpful because overhead costs were relatively low and increasing recordkeeping costs to obtain more accurate identification of overhead costs probably would not yield commensurate benefits. We shall use the following data to illustrate the technique.

| Example of Throughput Costing | |
| --- | --- |
| Units produced | 10,000 |
| Units sold at $20, 9,000 units | $180,000 |
| Cost of materials *used*, $5 per unit | $50,000 |
| Other variable manufacturing costs, $2 per unit | $20,000 |
| Fixed manufacturing costs | $30,000 |
| Selling and administrative expenses | $15,000 |

Standard fixed manufacturing cost (absorption costing), $3 based on 10,000 units at normal capacity; no beginning inventories; unit costs, variable costing, $7 per unit, $5 + $2; unit costs, absorption costing, $10 per unit, $5 + $2 + $3.

The income statements below show the differences between the methods. You are already familiar with the absorption costing and variable costing income statements. The following points regarding throughput costing are important.

| | Absorption Costing | Variable Costing | Throughput Costing |
| --- | --- | --- | --- |
| Sales | $180,000 | $180,000 | $180,000 |
| Cost of sales* | 90,000 | 63,000 | 50,000 |
| Gross margin | $ 90,000 | $117,000 | $130,000 |
| Other expenses: | | | |
| Other manufacturing costs** | | $ 30,000 | $ 50,000 |
| Selling and administrative | $ 15,000 | $ 15,000 | $ 15,000 |
| Total other expenses | $ 15,000 | $ 45,000 | $ 65,000 |
| Income | $ 75,000 | $ 72,000 | $ 65,000 |

* *9,000 × $10 = $90,000, 9,000 × $7 = $63,000, cost of materials used, $50,000*
** *Fixed manufacturing costs = $30,000, other variable manufacturing costs plus fixed manufacturing costs = $50,000*

The $7,000 difference between throughput income and variable costing income is the $7 variable manufacturing cost times 1,000 units in inventory. Notice that throughput costing results in even lower income than does variable costing when production exceeds sales. Throughput costing will also show higher incomes than does variable costing when sales exceed production. So while variable costing neither rewards nor penalizes production that is higher or lower than sales, *throughput costing penalizes high production and rewards low production.* Throughput costing is therefore very much in tune with JIT and other philosophies that seek lower inventories.

---

 **SIGHT**

### Throughput Costing in a Paper Mill

The Hamilton, Ohio, mill of **Champion International**, the giant paper company, generates over $250 million revenues per year. Demand for paper is very cyclical and prices fluctuate considerably, creating a feast-or-famine environment. The industry suffers from chronic overcapacity as companies add capacity in good times, only to see paper go unsold in poor times. Historically, paper mills have stressed high levels of production, even if prices were too low to enable the mills to make profits. Mills emphasized production partly because of extremely high fixed costs and huge capital investment. A single paper-making machine can cost $400 million and managers did not like to see such expensive machines lying idle. The problem was that mills produced too much paper, with too much waste, at too great a cost. One reason for such situations is that product costing methods can encourage overproduction, as we have seen in the chapter.

The Hamilton mill took a new approach, focusing on customer satisfaction, reduction of inventory, and reduction of waste. To bring its performance evaluation into congruence with its new strategy, the mill scrapped its existing cost system and installed throughput accounting because it penalizes increasing inventory and rewards reducing it, which focuses the attention of mill managers. Variable costing does not reward overproduction, but does not penalize it either.

*Source: Kim Constantinides and John K. Shank, "Matching Accounting to Strategy: One Mill's Experience,"* Management Accounting, *September 1994, 32–36.*

---

## SUMMARY

Standard costing uses standard costs instead of actual or normal costs to determine inventory and cost of goods sold. Standard costing ties the accounting records to the calculations of the variances used for control purposes, so that variances are integrated into the system. Standard costing also greatly simplifies recordkeeping for a company that makes several products; for some companies it is the only sensible choice.

Standard absorption costing uses a standard fixed cost per unit. Like normal costing, standard absorption costing yields a fixed overhead volume variance as well as a fixed overhead budget variance. But the volume variance is of little economic significance. The most common levels of activity used to set standard fixed overhead rates are normal activity and practical capacity. The size of the volume variance depends on the activity level.

For internal managerial purposes, some companies use standard variable costing or actual variable costing, which consider only variable production costs as product costs and treat fixed manufacturing costs as expenses in the period in which they are incurred. Variable costing is compatible with both CVP analysis and the contribution margin format of the income statement. Throughput costing is an extreme form of variable costing, in which only materials costs are inventoried. Throughput accounting is related to Theory of Constraints, which we discuss in Chapter 16.

## KEY TERMS

normal activity (normal capacity)  
  *(628)*  
practical capacity   *(628)*  
standard costing   *(627)*  

standard fixed cost per unit   *(628)*  
theoretical capacity   *(628)*  
throughput costing   *(644)*  
variable (direct) costing   *(636)*  

## KEY FORMULA

$$\text{Volume variance—standard costing} = \left(\begin{array}{c}\text{Actual} \\ \text{units} \\ \text{produced}\end{array} - \begin{array}{c}\text{Units at} \\ \text{selected} \\ \text{activity}\end{array}\right) \times \begin{array}{c}\text{Standard} \\ \text{fixed cost} \\ \text{per unit}\end{array}$$

## REVIEW PROBLEM

In 20X3, SMP Company again used a $20 standard variable cost and $30 standard fixed cost based on $3,000,000 and 100,000 units. SMP produced 112,000 units and sold 102,000. It incurred all manufacturing costs as expected. Selling and administrative expenses were again $5 variable per unit and $1,400,000 fixed.

### Required
1. Prepare an income statement using absorption costing.
2. Prepare an income statement using variable costing.
3. Suppose that $8 of the $20 standard variable cost is for materials. Prepare an income statement using throughput costing.

## ANSWER TO REVIEW PROBLEM

1. ___SMP Company, 20X3 Income Statement—Absorption Costing___

| | | |
|---|---:|---:|
| Sales (102,000 × $80) | | $8,160,000 |
| Standard cost of sales: | | |
| Beginning inventory (15,000 × $50) | $ 750,000 | |
| Variable production costs (112,000 × $20) | 2,240,000 | |
| Fixed production costs (112,000 × $30) | 3,360,000 | |
| Cost of goods available (127,000 × $50) | $6,350,000 | |
| Ending inventory (25,000 × $50) | 1,250,000 | |
| Standard cost of goods sold (102,000 × $50) | | 5,100,000 |
| Standard gross margin | | $3,060,000 |
| Fixed cost volume variance, favorable | | 360,000 |
| Actual gross margin | | $3,420,000 |
| Selling and administrative expenses | | 1,910,000 |
| Profit | | $1,510,000 |

The volume variance can be computed in either of two ways. It is the difference between budgeted fixed production costs of $3,000,000 and applied fixed production costs of $3,360,000. Because applied costs exceeded budgeted costs, the variance is favorable. Volume variance is also the difference between the 112,000 units produced and the 100,000 units used to set the standard fixed cost, multiplied by the standard fixed cost (12,000 units × $30 = $360,000).

2. ___SMP Company, 20X3 Income Statement—Variable Costing___

| | | |
|---|---:|---:|
| Sales (102,000 × $80) | | $8,160,000 |
| Standard variable cost of sales: | | |
| Beginning inventory (15,000 × $20) | $ 300,000 | |
| Variable production costs (112,000 × $20) | 2,240,000 | |
| Cost of goods available (127,000 × $20) | $2,540,000 | |
| Ending inventory (25,000 × $20) | 500,000 | |
| Standard variable cost of sales (102,000 × $20) | | 2,040,000 |
| Standard variable manufacturing margin | | $6,120,000 |
| Variable selling and administrative expenses | | 510,000 |
| Contribution margin | | $5,610,000 |
| Fixed costs: | | |
| Production | $3,000,000 | |
| Selling and administrative expenses | 1,400,000 | 4,400,000 |
| Profit | | $1,210,000 |

As explained in the chapter, the $300,000 difference in income under the two methods results because of the fixed overhead costs in the beginning and ending inventories under absorption costing. The beginning inventory of 15,000 units included fixed overhead costs of $450,000 (15,000 × $30 standard fixed cost per unit) carried forward from 20X2. The ending inventory of 25,000 units includes fixed overhead costs of $750,000 (25,000 × $30) being carried forward to 20X4. The $300,000 difference in income occurs because the fixed costs being carried forward from 20X3 ($750,000) are greater than those carried forward to 20X3 ($400,000). That is, the income difference results from the increase in inventory or, described another way, because 20X3 production (112,000 units) was greater than 20X3 sales (102,000 units).

3.   SMP Company, 20X3 Income Statement—Throughput Costing

| | |
|---|---:|
| Sales (102,000 × $80) | $8,160,000 |
| Standard throughput cost of sales, 112,000 × $8* | 896,000 |
| Throughput | $7,264,000 |
| Other manufacturing costs** | 4,344,000 |
| Manufacturing margin | $2,920,000 |
| Selling and administrative expenses | 1,910,000 |
| Profit | $1,010,000 |

*$8 material cost per unit times units produced.
** $12 non-material variable manufacturing costs times 112,000 units, plus $3,000,000 fixed manufacturing costs.

The $200,000 difference between variable costing income ($1,210,000) and throughput income ($1,010,000) is the $20 total variable manufacturing cost multiplied by the 10,000 units produced, but not sold.

## ASSIGNMENT MATERIAL

### INTERNET ACTIVITY

Visit Web sites devoted to Theory of Constraints to see what they say about cost accounting.  Do not be concerned with the rest of the theory, Chapter 16 will cover it.  You should nonetheless be able to assess the arguments against absorption costing and activity-based costing.

### QUESTIONS FOR DISCUSSION

**14-1  JIT and costing methods**  Which of the three choices, absorption costing, variable costing, or throughput costing, is most compatible with JIT? Why?

**14-2   Use of costing methods**  Which of the following companies is least likely to use standard costing? Why?
• an automaker
• a construction company
• a processor of flour

**14-3   Product cost—period cost**  The distinction between product costs and period costs is important for financial reporting. Is the distinction important for decision making?

**14-4   Costing methods and zero inventories**  Suppose a manufacturer achieves the JIT ideal of zero inventories. What will the relationships of income be under the three methods, absorption, variable, or throughput costing? For example, will one method give consistently higher or lower incomes?

EXERCISES

**14-5   Fundamentals of absorption and variable costing**   Bentham Manufacturing produces theater seats. Data for March 20X3 follow.

| | |
|---|---|
| Production | 10,000 units |
| Sales, 9,000 units at $100 | $900,000 |
| Variable production costs | $400,000 |
| Fixed production costs | $300,000 |
| Fixed selling and administrative expenses | $200,000 |

Standard variable production cost is $40 per unit; standard absorption cost is $30 per unit based on 10,000 units. Bentham had no beginning inventories.

**Required**
1. Prepare an income statement using standard absorption costing.
2. Prepare an income statement using standard variable costing.

**14-6   Fundamentals of absorption and variable costing (continuation of 14-5)**   In the following month, April, Bentham continued its operations. Results follow.

| | |
|---|---|
| Production | 10,000 units |
| Sales, 11,000 units at $100 | $1,100,000 |
| Variable production costs | $400,000 |
| Fixed production costs | $300,000 |
| Fixed selling and administrative expenses | $200,000 |

**Required**
1. Prepare an income statement using standard absorption costing.
2. Prepare an income statement using standard variable costing.

**14-7   Basic standard costing—absorption and variable**   Wiskaway is a household cleaning product made by B&Y. Wiskaway sells for $7 per case; its standard variable manufacturing cost is $3 per case. Fixed production costs are $300,000 per month; fixed selling and administrative expenses are $60,000 per month. The company began March 20X1 with no inventories and had the following activity in March and April.

| | March | April |
|---|---|---|
| Production in cases | 130,000 | 90,000 |
| Sales in cases | 100,000 | 100,000 |

The president wants two sets of monthly income statements: one showing monthly income using variable costing, the other showing monthly income using absorption costing. Use practical capacity of 150,000 cases per month to set the standard fixed cost.

**Required**

1. Prepare income statements by month as the president requested. Use the format that shows the details of beginning and ending inventories and of production costs in the cost of goods sold section.
2. If the company could sell 100,000 per month from now on, at the same price, and could maintain the same cost structure ($3 per case, $360,000 total fixed costs), how much income would it average per month?

**14-8   Actual costing income statements**   Corcoran, Inc. expects the following unit sales and production for the first two months of 20X2.

|  | January | February |
|---|---|---|
| Production | 10,000 | 10,000 |
| Sales | 8,000 | 12,000 |

The selling price is $25 per unit, variable manufacturing cost is $5 per unit, fixed manufacturing costs are $100,000 per month. Selling and administrative expenses are $12,000 per month.  Lindsey had no inventories at the beginning of January.

**Required**

1. Prepare income statements for each month using actual absorption costing.
2. Prepare income statements for each month using actual variable costing.

**14-9   Absorption costing**   Logomatic Inc. makes network connectors that sell for $400. Standard variable manufacturing cost is $100 and the standard fixed manufacturing cost is $150, based on budgeted fixed costs of $15,000,000 and budgeted production of 100,000 units. During 20X1, the company produced 96,000 units and sold 90,000. Actual fixed manufacturing costs were $14,870,000; actual variable manufacturing costs were $9,550,000. Selling and administrative expenses were $10,550,000, all fixed. There were no beginning inventories.

**Required**

Prepare a standard absorption costing income statement.

**14-10   Variable costing (continuation of 14-9)**   Prepare an income statement for Logomatic using standard variable costing.

**14-11   Standard fixed cost and volume variance**   Anderson Products had the following results in 20X3.

| | |
|---|---|
| Normal capacity | 225,000 units |
| Practical capacity | 300,000 units |
| Actual production | 240,000 units |
| Fixed costs—budgeted and actual | $900,000 |

**Required**

1. Compute the standard fixed cost per unit based on (a) normal capacity and (b) practical capacity.
2. Compute the volume variances for each of the methods given in requirement 1.

**14-12   Relationships**   For each of the following independent situations, fill in the missing data. In all cases, the standard fixed cost per unit is based on normal capacity of 10,000 units.

| | (a) Standard Fixed Cost per Unit | (b) Total Budgeted Fixed Costs | (c) Actual Production | (d) Volume Variance (Favorable) |
|---|---|---|---|---|
| 1. | $_____ | $_____ | 9,000 | $ 6,000 |
| 2. | $    6 | $_____ | _____ | $(1,500) |
| 3. | $_____ | $80,000 | 9,000 | $ _____ |
| 4. | $_____ | $30,000 | _____ | $(7,500) |

**14-13   Effects of changes in production—standard variable costing**   The following data relate to Mr Charles best-selling aftershave lotion.

| | |
|---|---|
| Sales, 40,000 cases at $10 per case | $400,000 |
| Production costs: | |
|    Variable costs, standard and actual | $3 per case |
|    Fixed, budgeted and actual | $200,000 |

Mr. Charles had no beginning inventories and no selling and administrative expenses.

**Required**

Prepare income statements using standard variable costing assuming the company produced (a) 40,000 cases and (b) 41,000 cases. Show the details of the cost of sales section of the income statements.

**14-14   Effects of change in production—standard absorption costing (continuation of 14-13)**   Assume that Mr. Charles uses standard absorption costing with a standard fixed cost per case of $5 based on normal activity of 40,000 cases.

**Required**

Prepare income statements assuming that production is (a) 40,000 cases and (b) 41,000 cases. Show details of cost of sales.

**14-15   "Now wait a minute here."**   The title of this problem is the statement your boss made when you showed him the results of completing requirement 1 of this assignment.

Hownet makes panes for greenhouse windows, selling them for $10 each. Standard variable manufacturing cost is $1 and total fixed manufacturing costs are $60,000. Normal volume is 10,000 units, so the standard fixed cost per unit is $6. Your boss asked you to determine the company's gross profit (after any production variances) from selling 10,000 units. The company treats all variances as adjustments to standard gross margin. Being conscientious, you decided to check your results by preparing income statements down to actual gross margin under each of the following cases. There are no beginning inventories.

(a) Sales are 10,000 units, production is 10,000 units.
(b) Sales are 10,000 units, production is 10,001 units.
(c) Sales are 10,001 units, production is 10,001 units.
(d) Sales are 9,999 units, production is 10,001 units.

**Required**

1. Prepare the income statements.
2. Explain why your boss gave the response he did.
3. Tell your boss why the results came out as they did.

**14-16   All fixed cost company**   Fixed Company began operations January 1, 20X2. The balance sheet at that time showed plant and equipment of $2,500,000 and common stock of $2,500,000. The plant is completely automated and makes its one product from air. Its only cost is $500,000 depreciation, based on a five-year life and the straight-line method. During the first two years of operation the company had the following results.

|                | 20X2    | 20X3    |
|----------------|---------|---------|
| Units produced | 150,000 | 90,000  |
| Units sold     | 120,000 | 120,000 |

All sales were at $6 per unit and were for cash. The company uses a standard fixed cost of $4 per unit based on normal volume of 125,000 units. There were no cash disbursements in either year so that cash at the end of each year was $6 multiplied by cumulative sales.

**Required**
1. Prepare income statements for each year.
2. Prepare a balance sheet as of the end of each year.
3. Repeat requirements 1 and 2 using variable costing.

## PROBLEMS

**14-17   Basic absorption costing**   Jasper Storage manufactures disk drives for microcomputers. Data related to its best-selling model, which is the only one made in its Richmond plant, follow.

| | |
|---|---|
| Production: | |
| April | 12,000 units |
| May | 9,000 units |
| Sales: | |
| April | 9,000 units |
| May | 11,000 units |
| Standard variable manufacturing cost ~materials, labor~ | $25 |
| Standard fixed manufacturing cost ~overhead~ | 40   ( 400,000/10,000 |
| Total standard manufacturing cost | $65 |

Jasper has set its standard fixed manufacturing cost based on normal activity of 10,000 drives per month and budgeted fixed manufacturing costs of $400,000 per month. There was no inventory at the beginning of April. The drive sells for $100. Selling and administrative expenses are $280,000 per month. All manufacturing costs were incurred as expected (variable per unit and total fixed) in both months.

**Required**
Prepare standard absorption costing income statements for April and May.

**14-18   Basic variable costing (continuation of 14-17)**

**Required**
1. Using the data in the previous assignment, prepare standard variable costing income statements for Jasper Storage for April and May.

2. Suppose that Jasper could sell 11,000 units per month for the foreseeable future, at the same price. The company could also keep its current cost structure (variable per unit, total fixed) in place. How much income would the company average per month?

**14-19  Throughput costing  (continuation of 14-17)**   Of the $25 standard variable manufacturing cost, $15 is for materials.

**Required**
Prepare throughput costing income statements for April and May.

**14-20  Effect of measure of activity (continuation of 14-17)**   The president of Jasper Storage has heard that some companies use practical capacity as the basis for determining standard fixed manufacturing costs. He asks you to show him how using Jasper's practical capacity of 20,000 drives per month would affect the income statements you prepared in Exercise 14-17.

**Required**
Prepare the income statements that the president wants. Comment on the differences between these statements and the ones you prepared in Exercise 14-17.

**14-21  Interpreting results**   Linda Dayhuff, president of Coker Candies, has been reviewing the income statements of the two most recent months. She is puzzled because sales rose significantly and profits rose only slightly in March, and she asks you, the controller, to explain.  She knows that production in February is very high to meet anticipated high demand in March, and that production falls sharply in March because April is a relatively slow month.

|  | February | March |
|---|---|---|
| Sales ($20 per case) | $ 480,000 | $ 680,000 |
| Standard cost of sales | 192,000 | 272,000 |
| Standard gross profit | $ 288,000 | $ 408,000 |
| Volume variance | 60,000 | (54,000) |
| Selling and administrative expenses | (120,000) | (120,000) |
| Income | $ 228,000 | $ 234,000 |

The standard fixed cost per case is $6, based on normal capacity of 25,000 cases per month.

**Required**
1. Determine production in each month.
2. Explain the results to the president.
3. Prepare income statements using variable costing.

**14-22  Income determination—absorption costing**   The following data apply to Craft Company's 20X1 operations.  Craft had no beginning inventories.

| | |
|---|---|
| Sales (90,000 units) | $2,700,000 |
| Production | 110,000 units |
| Variable costs of production, standard and actual | $880,000 |
| Fixed production costs, budgeted and actual | $960,000 |
| Selling and administrative expenses | $250,000 |

**Required**
Prepare income statements for 20X1 using standard absorption costing with (1) 80,000 units and (2) 120,000 units used to set the standard fixed cost.

**14-23  Income determination—variable costing (continuation of 14-22)**  Prepare an income statement for Craft for 20X1, using standard variable costing.

**14-24  Relationships**  Fill in the blanks for each of the following independent situations. In all situations, selling price is $10, standard and actual variable manufacturing cost is $4, fixed production costs—budgeted and actual—are $240,000, and the volume used to set the standard fixed cost per unit is 80,000 units. There are no selling and administrative expenses.

| | (a) | (b) | (c) | (d) |
| | | | Income— | Income— |
| | Unit | Unit | Variable | Absorption |
| Case | Sales | Production | Costing | Costing |
|---|---|---|---|---|
| 1 | 80,000 | _____ | $_____ | $210,000 |
| 2 | _____ | _____ | $60,000 | $120,000 |
| 3 | 60,000 | 55,000 | $_____ | $_____ |

**14-25  All fixed company**  Earthcare, Inc. manufactures a single product from garbage. It sells for $5 per unit. The production process is automated and there are no variable costs. Earthcare's production costs are $20,000 per month. Normal activity is 10,000 units per month, and the standard fixed cost per unit is $2. Earthcare has no selling and administrative expenses. Earthcare began May with no inventory. Its activity for May, June, and July is summarized as follows, in units.

| | May | June | July |
|---|---|---|---|
| Production | 11,000 | 10,000 | 9,000 |
| Sales | 9,000 | 10,000 | 11,000 |

**Required**

1. Prepare income statements for each of the three months using standard absorption costing. Show the details of the cost of sales calculations.
2. Prepare income statements for each of the three months using standard variable costing.

**14-26  Standard costing—absorption and variable**  Testeron Company makes shaving lotion and uses standard absorption costing. Standard labor and materials per case are as follows:

| | |
|---|---|
| Materials (3 gallons at $5 per gallon) | $15 |
| Direct labor (0.50 hour at $12 per hour) | 6 |

Total annual manufacturing overhead is budgeted according to the formula $500,000 + ($2 × direct labor hours). The company uses normal capacity of 25,000 direct labor hours (50,000 cases) to set the standard fixed cost.

Testeron began 20X2 with no inventories. It produced 45,000 cases and sold 40,000 at $40 each. Selling and administrative expenses were $200,000. There were no variable cost variances, and fixed production costs were incurred as budgeted ($500,000).

**Required**

1. Determine the total standard cost per case.
2. Prepare an income statement for 20X2.
3. Prepare an income statement for 20X2 using variable costing.

**14-27   Absorption costing and variable costing**   Gordon Soups, Inc. makes a variety of soups. Data related to its chicken gumbo follow.

| | |
|---|---|
| Selling price per case | $90 |
| Variable manufacturing costs per case | $25 |
| Fixed manufacturing costs per month | $600,000 |
| Selling and administrative expenses, all fixed, per month | $160,000 |

Gordon uses standard absorption costing, basing its unit fixed cost on normal activity of 15,000 cases per month. In July, Gordon produced 16,000 cases and sold 14,000. There were 3,000 cases in beginning inventory at standard cost. All costs were incurred as expected.

**Required**
1. Determine the standard fixed cost per unit.
2. Prepare an income statement for July. Use the short form of the income statement but calculate cost of goods sold separately.
3. Prepare an income statement for July assuming that Gordon uses variable costing. Remember that inventory at the beginning of July will be at standard variable cost.

**14-28   Absorption costing and variable costing—variances**   VCX Company uses standard absorption costing, basing its standard fixed cost on 300,000 units of product per year and $900,000 annual budgeted fixed manufacturing overhead. Standard variable manufacturing cost is $6 per unit. Results for 20X1 follow. There were no beginning inventories.

| | |
|---|---|
| Unit production | 290,000 |
| Unit sales (at $20 per unit) | 270,000 |
| Actual variable manufacturing costs | $1,715,000 |
| Actual fixed manufacturing costs | $910,000 |
| Actual selling and administrative expenses, all fixed | $800,000 |

**Required**
1. Determine the standard fixed cost per unit and the total standard cost per unit.
2. Compute all variances.
3. Prepare an income statement for 20X1. Show any variances as adjustments to standard cost of sales.
4. Prepare an income statement using variable costing.

**14-29   Budgeted income statements**   Morrison WinterSports manufactures several lines of skiing equipment. Its Riverdale Plant makes a single model, the M-80 ski. Budgeted data for 20X3 follow.

| | |
|---|---|
| Sales (37,000 pairs at $70) | $2,590,000 |
| Production | 39,000 pairs |
| Standard variable cost | $15 |
| Standard fixed cost | 25 |
| Total standard cost | $40 |
| Selling and administrative expenses: | |
|  Fixed | $600,000 |
|  Variable | $8 per pair |

Morrison uses normal activity of 40,000 pairs per year and budgeted fixed manufacturing costs of $1,000,000 to set its standard fixed cost. There were no beginning inventories.

**Required**
1. Prepare a budgeted income statement using standard absorption costing.
2. Prepare a budgeted income statement using standard variable costing.

**14-30   Analysis of results (continuation of 14-29)**   The Riverdale Plant of Morrison WinterSports actually produced 41,000 pairs and sold 40,000. All costs were incurred as expected—fixed in total and variable per unit.

**Required**
1. Prepare an income statement using standard absorption costing.
2. Prepare an income statement using standard variable costing.
3. Which set of statements (standard absorption costing or variable absorption costing) from this and the previous assignment gives better information for analyzing results?

**14-31   Analysis of income statement—standard costs**   The income statement for Bourque Manufacturing Company for 20X2 follows. The company has established the following standards for a unit of finished product.

| | |
|---|---:|
| Materials (16 pounds at $0.50) | $ 8 |
| Direct labor (2 hours at $12) | 24 |
| Variable overhead ($1 per direct labor hour) | 2 |
| Fixed overhead | 2 |
| Total | $36 |

The fixed overhead standard is based on normal capacity of 20,000 units. During 20X2, 47,000 direct labor hours were worked and 370,000 pounds of materials were used.

Bourque Manufacturing Company,
Income Statement for 20X2

| | | |
|---|---:|---:|
| Sales (20,000 units at $50) | | $1,000,000 |
| Cost of goods sold—at standard | | 720,000 |
| Standard gross profit | | $ 280,000 |
| Variances: | | |
| Materials | $3,000U | |
| Labor | 4,000F | |
| Variable overhead | 2,000U | |
| Fixed overhead: | | |
| Spending variance | 3,000F | |
| Volume variance | 8,000F | 10,000F |
| Gross profit | | $ 290,000 |
| Selling and administrative expenses | | 230,000 |
| Income | | $   60,000 |

**Required**
1. Based on the information provided, determine the following:
   (a) number of units produced

   (b) material use variance
   (c) material price variance
   (d) direct labor efficiency variance
   (e) direct labor rate variance
   (f) variable overhead efficiency variance
   (g) variable overhead spending variance
   (h) fixed overhead incurred
2. Prepare an income statement using standard variable costing.

**14-32   Conversion of absorption costing income statement from normal to practical capacity (continuation of 14-31)**   The standard costs and the income statement for Bourque Manufacturing Company use a standard fixed cost per unit based on normal capacity of 20,000 units. Assume, instead, that Bourque bases its standard fixed cost per unit on its practical capacity of 25,000 units.

**Required**
1. Determine the standard fixed cost per unit.
2. Prepare an income statement for 20X2.

**14-33   Reconciling incomes—absorption costing**   Glaab Products Co. had the following budgeted income statement for July 20X1 (thousands of dollars).

| | |
|---|---:|
| Sales | $4,230.0 |
| Standard cost of sales | 1,903.5 |
| Standard gross margin | $2,326.5 |
| Operating expenses (all fixed) | 1,800.0 |
| Income | $ 526.5 |

Budgeted volume was 211.5 thousand units at a selling price of $20. Standard cost of sales was $9, of which $5 was fixed. The assistant who prepared the statement had no information about budgeted production, so assumed that it would be equal to normal activity of 220 thousand units per month, eliminating the volume variance.
   Glaab actually sold 214 thousand units and produced 210 thousand. Actual fixed production costs were $1,100 thousand, actual variable production costs were $840 thousand. Selling and administrative expenses were as budgeted.

**Required**
1. Prepare an income statement reflecting the actual results.
2. Does it make sense that actual income is less than budgeted income when actual sales were higher than budgeted sales? Write a memorandum to Lynn Maffett, Glaab's president, explaining why the actual results were different from budget. Use the guidelines in Appendix A.

**14-34   Reconciling incomes—variable costing (continuation of 14-33)**

**Required**
1. Use the information from the previous assignment to prepare budgeted and actual income statements for Glaab Co. using variable costing.
2. Explain the difference between budgeted and actual income.

**14-35   Analyzing income statements**   Your boss, the president of Taylor Industries, has asked you to explain the difference between the two income statements prepared for her consideration. One was prepared by the controller, the other by the sales manager. Both used the same data from last year's operations. Taylor had no beginning inventories.

|  | Statement A | Statement B |
| --- | --- | --- |
| Sales (20,000 units) | $3,000,000 | $3,000,000 |
| Cost of goods sold: | | |
|   Production costs | 1,800,000 | 2,700,000 |
|   Ending inventory | (600,000) | (900,000) |
| Cost of goods sold | $1,200,000 | $1,800,000 |
| Gross profit | $1,800,000 | $1,200,000 |
| Other costs | 1,200,000 | 300,000 |
| Income | $  600,000 | $  900,000 |

Variable costs of production, the only variable costs, are $60 per unit.

**Required**

1. Determine which statement was prepared using variable costing and which was prepared using absorption costing.
2. Determine (a) fixed production costs, (b) selling and administrative expenses, (c) production in units, and (d) cost per unit of inventory for both statements.
3. Which statement do you think was prepared by which manager and why do you think so?

**14-36  Conversion of income statement**  The manager of the Morgan Division of Rorshoot Industries has been on the job only a short time. The following income statement, for the third quarter of 20X3, is the first report she has received. She is having some difficulty understanding it because she is familiar only with variable costing, and she has asked you to convert the statement to a variable costing basis.

| | | |
| --- | --- | --- |
| Sales | | $1,324,000 |
| Cost of sales | | 893,700 |
| Gross profit | | $  430,300 |
| Operating expenses: | | |
|   Selling and administrative | $276,300 | |
|   Unabsorbed fixed overhead | 21,600 | 297,900 |
| Income | | $  132,400 |

From reviewing internal records you have determined the following:
(a) Selling and administrative costs are all fixed.
(b) The division sells its one product at $40 per unit.
(c) Fixed manufacturing overhead is applied at $12 per unit.
(d) There was no fixed overhead budget variance.
(e) Production during the quarter was 38,200 units.

**Required**

Prepare an income statement using standard variable costing.

**14-37  Effects of costing methods on balance sheet**  McPherson Company has a loan with a large bank. Among the provisions of the loan agreement are (a) the current ratio must be at least 3 to 1 and (b) the ratio of debt to stockholders' equity must be no higher than 75%. The balance sheet at December 31, 20X1 follows.

| Assets | | Equities | |
|---|---|---|---|
| Cash and receivables | $ 460,000 | Current liabilities | $ 200,000 |
| Inventory (40,000 units | | | |
|   at variable cost) | 200,000 | Long-term bank loan | 300,000 |
| Total current assets | $ 660,000 | Stockholders' equity | 760,000 |
| Fixed assets (net) | 600,000 | | |
| Total assets | $1,260,000 | Total equities | $1,260,000 |

Current ratio: $660,000/$200,000 = 3.3/1
Debt/stockholders' equity: $500,000/$760,000 = 66%
The budgeted income statement for 20X2 follows.

| | | |
|---|---|---|
| Sales (100,000 units) | | $1,000,000 |
| Variable cost of sales | | 500,000 |
| Variable manufacturing margin | | $ 500,000 |
| Other variable costs (variable with sales) | | 50,000 |
| Contribution margin | | $ 450,000 |
| Fixed costs: | | |
|   Manufacturing | $300,000 | |
|   Other | 50,000 | 350,000 |
| Income | | $ 100,000 |

Budgeted production is 100,000 units. The company's president foresees substantial expenditures for fixed assets and intends to obtain a loan to finance these expenditures. He projects the following pro forma balance sheet for December 31, 20X2.

| Assets | | Equities | |
|---|---|---|---|
| Cash and receivables | $ 400,000 | Current liabilities | $ 240,000 |
| Inventory (40,000 units | | | |
|   at variable cost) | 200,000 | Long-term bank loan | 460,000 |
| Total current assets | $ 600,000 | Stockholders' equity | 860,000 |
| Fixed assets (net) | 960,000 | | |
| Total assets | $1,560,000 | Total equities | $1,560,000 |

He sees that the company will be in default on both provisions of the loan agreement. (Compute the current ratio and debt/stockholders' equity ratio to verify his finding.) Trying to resolve the problem, he lists the following points.

(a) Practical capacity is 150,000 units.
(b) The company might benefit by using absorption costing.

### Required

1. Prepare the income statement and balance sheet using standard absorption costing, with production of 150,000 units used to set the standard fixed cost. Also assume production of 150,000 units. Assume that all increased production costs are paid in cash.
2. Is the company safely within the limits of the loan agreement?
3. Is the company better off using absorption costing?

**14-38 CVP analysis and absorption costing** The Baltic Division of Samar Industries manufactures large drill bits. The division had the following plans for the first quarter of 20X3.

| | |
|---|---|
| Unit sales | 80,000 |
| Selling price | $40 |
| Variable cost | $24 |
| Fixed costs | $800,000 |

The divisional manager expected profit of $480,000 from these results. The actual income statement for the quarter follows. The divisional manager was surprised to see that the targets for volume, price, and costs were met or exceeded, but that profit was less than anticipated.

| | |
|---|---|
| Sales (82,000 units at $40) | $3,280,000 |
| Standard cost of sales at $30 | 2,460,000 |
| Standard gross margin | $ 820,000 |
| Production variances | (180,000) |
| Actual gross margin | $ 640,000 |
| Selling and administrative expenses | 200,000 |
| Profit | $ 440,000 |

The divisional manager was informed that all variable costs and 75% of fixed costs were for manufacturing. The division uses standard costing, with practical capacity of 100,000 units per quarter used to set the standard. Actual production was only 70,000 units in the first quarter of 20X3 because of a large supply of inventory left over from the previous period.

### Required
1. Prepare an income statement using variable costing.
2. Tell the divisional manager how your income statement would be of more help to her than the one shown above.

**14-39 *Standard costing—activity-based overhead rates*** Cannon Industries applies overhead to products using two rates—one based on machine hours, the other on the number of component parts. The latter rate is used because of the high amounts of overhead associated with purchasing, receiving, storing, and issuing parts. The company does not classify any employees as direct labor because production is highly automated. Summary data for 20X2 follow.

| | Budget |
|---|---|
| Parts-related overhead | $1,200,000 |
| Machine-related overhead | $6,480,000 |
| Machine hours | 100,000 |
| Total number of parts to be used | 8,000,000 |

The overhead costs are largely fixed with respect to output. Data for product GT-1029 follow.

| | |
|---|---|
| Component parts, 11 parts at average $2.50 price | $27.50 |
| Machine time | 0.15 hours |

During March 20X3, the company made 60,000 units of product GT-1029, and no other products. Parts-related overhead was $105,300; machine-related overhead was

$542,230. The managers expect both of these categories of cost to be incurred evenly throughout the year. Use of parts was at standard.

**Required**
1. Calculate the predetermined overhead rates for parts and for machine hours.
2. Determine the standard cost of product GT-1029.
3. Determine whatever variances you can.

**14-40   Preparing income statements**   Bob Cransk, president of BC Company, has been receiving monthly reports like the one which follows since he founded the company ten years ago. As BC's newly hired controller, you have been discussing the reports with Cransk, trying to decide whether to make any changes. (All numbers are in thousands of dollars.)

|  | March | February |
|---|---|---|
| Sales | $1,256.8 | $1,452.4 |
| Standard cost of sales | $ 769.3 | $ 879.7 |
| Production variances | 7.3U | 29.8U |
| Cost of sales | $ 776.6 | $ 909.5 |
| Gross margin | $ 480.2 | $ 542.9 |
| Selling and administrative expenses | 406.4 | 412.6 |
| Profit before taxes | $ 73.8 | $ 130.3 |
| Summary of variances: | | |
|   Materials | $   8.4U | $   7.1U |
|   Direct labor | 7.8U | 6.9U |
|   Overhead | 8.9F | 15.8U |
| Total | $   7.3U | $  29.8U |

Cransk has told you that he is generally satisfied with the reports, but he is sometimes surprised because they seem to contradict what he believes from his knowledge of operations. He attributes some of his surprise to his lack of understanding of accounting principles.

"For example," he said, "February is a good month. March starts our slow season. I expected February to be a little better than it was, but it seemed okay. March showed better than I had thought it would. I know that our production affects income, so I sort of make mental adjustments for it, but I'd rather not have to."

A review of the records reveals that standard variable cost of sales was $580.5 in February and $510.3 in March. Total fixed manufacturing overhead was $305.2 in February and $299.8 in March. Budgeted fixed manufacturing overhead was $304.5 in both months. Variable overhead variances were $3.2 unfavorable in February, $2.3 unfavorable in March. Although there is some variation in selling and administrative expenses, they can be considered fixed.

**Required**
1. Prepare income statements for February and March using standard variable costing.
2. Tell Cransk how much of the variances in the income statements are attributable to the use of absorption costing.

**14-41   Incorporating variances into budgets**   Viner Company is developing its budgets for the coming year. The company uses the following standard costs for its final product.

| | |
|---|---:|
| Materials (3 gallons at $3) | $ 9 |
| Labor (2 hours at $10) | 20 |
| Variable overhead ($12 per DLH) | 24 |
| Total standard variable cost | $53 |

Budgeted fixed manufacturing costs are $300,000. Selling and administrative expenses, all fixed, are budgeted at $400,000. Generally, there is about a 10% variance over standard quantity for materials, but the materials usually cost 5% less than the standard price. Direct laborers will receive a 6% wage increase at the beginning of the year, and labor efficiency is expected to be 4% better than standard. An unfavorable variable overhead spending variance of 5% is expected. Sales for the year are budgeted at 20,000 units at $100; production schedules indicate planned production of 24,000 units. There are no beginning inventories. Purchases of materials are budgeted to be equal to expected materials use.

### Required

1. Determine the expected variable cost variances for the year.
2. Prepare a budgeted income statement for the coming year using standard variable costing.

**14-42   Costs and decisions**   "You're fired!!" was the way your boss, the controller of Saran Bathing Suit Company, greeted you this morning. His ire was based on the following two income statements. A few months ago you recommended accepting an offer from a national chain for 10,000 suits at $12 each. At that time, inventories were rising because of slow sales. Things have not improved noticeably since then. Your recommendation was based on the variable production costs of $10 per unit, which are the only variable costs. The total standard cost of $16 per suit includes $6 in fixed costs, based on normal production of 130,000 units.

| Income Statements for 20X4 | | |
|---|---:|---:|
| | If Special Order Had Not Been Accepted | Actual, with Special Order |
| Sales: 100,000 × $25 | $2,500,000 | $2,500,000 |
| 10,000 × $12 | | 120,000 |
| Total sales | $2,500,000 | $2,620,000 |
| Cost of sales at $16 standard cost | 1,600,000 | 1,760,000 |
| Standard gross profit | $ 900,000 | $ 860,000 |
| Volume variance (20,000 × $6) | 120,000U | 120,000U |
| Actual gross profit | $ 780,000 | $ 740,000 |
| Selling and administrative expenses | 710,000 | 710,000 |
| Income | $ 70,000 | $ 30,000 |

"Your recommendation cost us $40,000! Now clean out your desk and leave."

### Required

Write a memorandum to your boss, Mr. Beatty, that will get your job back. Use the guidelines in Appendix A.

**14-43   Actual versus standard costs—multiple products**   Brennan Company makes luggage. For some time, its managers have been dissatisfied with the company's cost information. Unit costs have fluctuated greatly and have not been useful for planning and control purposes.

Under the present system, unit costs are computed at the end of each month. The costs are determined by allocating all actual production costs for the month to the various models produced, with the allocation based on the relative materials costs of the various models.

The controller has decided to develop standard costs for product costing purposes. She has analyzed the materials and labor requirements for each model, based on what she believes to be currently attainable performance. The results of her analysis follow. (For simplicity, the problem is limited to three models.)

|  | Briefcase #108 | Cosmetic Case #380 | Two-Suiter #460 |
|---|---|---|---|
| Materials costs | $12.00 | $14.00 | $18.00 |
| Labor hours required | 0.5 | 0.8 | 1.5 |

Workers all earn $8 per hour, and the company usually works about 6,000 labor hours per month. The controller intends to use 6,000 hours to set the standard fixed cost per unit. Her analysis of monthly manufacturing overhead yielded the formula $90,000 + ($7 × direct labor hours).

During April the company had the following results. There were no inventories at April 1.

|  | Briefcase #108 | Cosmetic Case #380 | Two-Suiter #460 |
|---|---|---|---|
| Production in units | 3,000 | 2,500 | 1,200 |
| Sales in units | 2,400 | 1,800 | 1,000 |
| Sales in dollars | $84,000 | $90,000 | $85,000 |

There were no variable cost variances and fixed production costs were $92,000.

### Required

1. Compute the standard cost for each model.
2. Compute the ending inventory of finished goods.
3. Prepare an income statement for April. Selling and administrative expenses were $28,000.

**14-44  *Interim results, costing methods, and evaluation of performance***  Kleffman Company sells a product with a highly seasonal demand. The budgeted income statement for 20X1 is as follows:

| | | |
|---|---|---|
| Sales (240,000 units) | | $2,400,000 |
| Cost of goods sold—at standard: | | |
| Materials | $420,000 | |
| Direct labor | 540,000 | |
| Manufacturing overhead | 600,000 | 1,560,000 |
| Gross profit—at standard | | $ 840,000 |
| Selling and administrative expenses | | 420,000 |
| Income before taxes | | $ 420,000 |

Budgeted production is 240,000 units, the number used to set the standard fixed cost per unit. The controller has determined that materials, labor, 40% of manufacturing overhead ($240,000), and $120,000 of the selling and administrative expenses are variable. All fixed costs are incurred evenly throughout the year.

January and February are relatively slow months, each with only about 5% of annual sales. March is the first month of a busy period, and production in February is generally high in order to stock up for the anticipated increase in demand. The actual income statements for January and February 20X1 are as follows:

| | January | February |
|---|---|---|
| Sales (12,000 units) | $120,000 | $120,000 |
| Cost of goods sold—at standard | 78,000 | 78,000 |
| Gross profit—at standard | $ 42,000 | $ 42,000 |
| Manufacturing variances: | | |
| Variable costs | 3,000F | 4,000U |
| Fixed cost—budget | 2,000F | 3,000U |
| Fixed cost—volume | 9,000U | 7,500F |
| Gross profit—actual | $ 38,000 | $ 42,500 |
| Selling and administrative expenses | 31,000 | 31,000 |
| Income | $  7,000 | $ 11,500 |

Although the president is pleased that performance improved in February, she has asked the controller why the two months showed different profits, since sales were the same. She also wonders why profits were not about 5% of the $420,000 budget, as each month's sales were 5% of the annual budget.

**Required**

1. Explain to the president why profits in January and February would be less than 5% of the budgeted annual profit, even though each month's sales were 5% of the budgeted annual amount.
2. Explain to the president why profits differed in the two months. Comment on the president's being pleased that "performance improved in February."

**14-45   *Income statements and balance sheets***   MicroCook makes a single product, a microwave oven that sells for $300. Standard variable cost of production is $180 per unit, and the only other variable cost is a 10% sales commission. Fixed production costs are $3,600,000 per year, incurred evenly throughout the year. Of that amount, $800,000 is depreciation and the remainder all require cash disbursements. Fixed selling and administrative expenses of $200,000 per month all require cash disbursements.

For inventory costing MicroCook uses a standard fixed cost of $45 per unit, based on expected annual production of 80,000 units. However, during 20X3 the company experienced the following results, by six-month periods.

| | January–June | July–December |
|---|---|---|
| Sales in units | 30,000 | 40,000 |
| Production in units | 32,000 | 42,000 |

The company sells for cash only and pays all of its obligations as they are incurred. Its balance sheet at December 31, 20X2, in thousands of dollars, was as follows:

| Assets | | Equities | |
|---|---|---|---|
| Cash | $400 | | |
| Inventory (1,000 units) | 225 | Common stock | $3,000 |
| Plant and equipment (net) | 3,000 | Retained earnings | 625 |
| Total assets | $3,625 | Total equities | $3,625 |

During 20X3, all costs were incurred as expected (variable costs per unit and fixed costs in total).

**Required**

1. Prepare income statements (in thousands of dollars) for each of the two six-month periods and the year as a whole.
2. Prepare balance sheets as of June 30 and December 31, 20X3, in thousands of dollars.

**14-46  Pricing dispute**  Calligeris Company manufactures brake linings for automobiles. Late in 20X2 the company received an offer for 10,000 linings from Phelan Company. Phelan was unwilling to pay the usual price of $5 per lining but offered to buy at a price that would give Calligeris a $0.50 gross profit per lining.

Without consideration of the order, Calligeris expected the following income statement for the year.

| | | |
|---|---:|---:|
| Sales (100,000 linings at $5) | | $500,000 |
| Cost of goods sold at standard: | | |
| Beginning inventory (20,000 at $4) | $ 80,000 | |
| Variable production costs (100,000 units at $2.50) | 250,000 | |
| Fixed production costs at $1.50 per unit | 150,000 | |
| Cost of goods available for sale | $480,000 | |
| Ending inventory (20,000 at $4) | 80,000 | |
| Cost of goods sold at standard | | 400,000 |
| Standard gross profit | | $100,000 |
| Volume variance (20,000 at $1.50) | 30,000F | |
| Selling and administrative expenses | 50,000 | 20,000 |
| Income | | $80,000 |

The production manager decided that the order could be filled from inventory, so no additional production was planned. The company shipped 10,000 linings to Phelan Company, billing that company for 10,000 units at $4.50 per lining. No additional costs were incurred in connection with this order.

**Required**

1. Prepare an income statement for 20X2 assuming that the actual results for the year were as planned except that the additional sale was made to Phelan company. Do the results show that the company earned the agreed gross profit?
2. Suppose that you were the controller of Phelan Company. Would you dispute the $4.50 price? If so, why? What price would you propose and why?

**14-47  Predetermined overhead rates—multiple products**  The controller of Salmon Company has been developing a new costing system. He believes that the use of standard costs would reduce the cost of recordkeeping and simplify the company's internal reporting to managers. He has asked your assistance and you have collected the following information relating to the company's three products.

| | Model 84 | Model 204 | Model 340 |
|---|---:|---:|---:|
| Variable production costs | $4.00 | $7.00 | $11.00 |
| Direct labor hours required | 0.50 | 0.80 | 1.50 |

The company works 50,000 direct labor hours per year at its normal operating level, and the controller uses that figure to set the predetermined overhead rate. Budgeted fixed production costs are $300,000. Operating results for 20X1 follow. There were no beginning inventories.

| | Production in Units | Sales in Units | Sales in Dollars |
|---|---|---|---|
| Model 84 | 30,000 | 25,000 | $250,000 |
| Model 204 | 24,000 | 20,000 | $280,000 |
| Model 340 | 20,000 | 18,000 | $450,000 |

All production costs were incurred as expected, including variable costs per unit and total fixed costs. Selling and administrative expenses were $140,000.

### Required
1. Compute standard fixed costs per unit for each model.
2. Compute the ending inventory in dollars for each model.
3. Prepare an income statement for 20X1.

**14-48  Comprehensive review, budgeting, overhead application**  Ruland Company makes and sells a single product. The product sells for $20 and Ruland expects sales of 880,000 units in 20X5. The distribution of sales by quarters is expected to be 20%, 25%, 25%, and 30%. The company expects the following costs in 20X6.

#### Manufacturing Costs

| | Fixed | Variable per Unit |
|---|---|---|
| Materials (4 pounds at $0.80) | — | $3.20 |
| Direct labor (0.1 hour at $20) | — | 2.00 |
| Maintenance | $    46,000 | 0.20 |
| Indirect labor | 422,000 | 0.40 |
| Supplies | 316,000 | 0.55 |
| Power | 186,000 | 0.10 |
| Depreciation | 1,900,000 | — |
| Supervision | 310,000 | — |
| Miscellaneous | 320,000 | 0.05 |
| Totals | $3,500,000 | $6.50 |

#### Selling, General, and Administrative Expenses

| | Fixed | Variable per Unit |
|---|---|---|
| Sales commissions | — | $2.00 |
| Salaries and wages | $1,200,000 | — |
| Other expenses, including interest | 4,350,000 | — |
| Total | $5,550,000 | $2.00 |

Budgeted production and purchases are as follows:

| Quarter | Production (units) | Material Purchases (pounds) |
|---|---|---|
| 1 | 210,000 | 733,000 |
| 2 | 220,000 | 950,000 |
| 3 | 260,000 | 904,000 |
| 4 | 210,000 | 795,000 |
| Total | 900,000 | 3,382,000 |

Other information relating to Ruland's operation follows.

(a) The company uses a standard fixed cost of $3.50 per unit.
(b) Sales are collected 60 days after sale.
(c) Purchases of raw materials are paid for in the month after purchase.
(d) Direct labor costs unpaid at the end of a quarter are about 10% of the cost incurred in that quarter. All other manufacturing costs requiring cash disbursements (all but depreciation) are paid as incurred, except for raw material purchases.
(e) All selling and administrative expenses require cash disbursements and are paid as incurred except for salespersons' commissions. These are paid in the month after incurrence.
(f) The company has a 40% income tax rate. At year end, the amount of unpaid taxes is about 25% of the total expense for the year.
(g) A dividend of $300,000 will be paid in 20X5.
(h) Purchases of plant assets, all for cash, will total $2,100,000 in 20X5.
(i) Assume that sales, production, and purchases of raw materials are spread evenly over the months of each quarter (one-third of the quarter in each month of the quarter).

The balance sheet at the end of 20X4 appears as follows, in thousands of dollars.

| Assets | | Equities | |
|---|---:|---|---:|
| Cash | $    840 | Accounts payable (materials) | $    240 |
| Accounts receivable | 2,800 | Accrued commissions | 120 |
| Inventory—finished goods | | Accrued payroll (direct labor) | 64 |
| (146,000 units) | 1,460 | Income taxes payable | 80 |
| Inventory—materials | | | |
| (530,000 pounds) | 424 | Long-term debt | 4,000 |
| Plant and equipment | 16,200 | Common stock | 7,000 |
| Accumulated depreciation | (8,400) | Retained earnings | 1,820 |
| Total | $13,324 | Total | $13,324 |

### Required

1. Prepare a budgeted income statement for 20X5.
2. Prepare a cash budget for 20X5 for the year as a whole, not by quarter.
3. Prepare a pro forma balance sheet for the end of 20X5.
4. Without preparing new statements, describe the differences that would occur in your prepared statements if the company were using variable costing.

## CASES

**14-49  Standard costs and pricing**   The controller of Carolina Mills has been discussing costs and prices with the treasurer. The controller wants to use 2,400,000 machine hours to set standard fixed costs, while the treasurer prefers to use 3,000,000 hours. The controller feels that the lower base will make it easier for the company to absorb its fixed overhead, but the treasurer is concerned that the company might set its prices too high to be competitive with other companies.

"Look," the treasurer said, "suppose we use our formula for budgeting total manufacturing costs, materials, labor, and overhead."

*Total manufacturing cost = $7,680,000 + $4.25 per machine hour*

"Now," she went on, "if we use your basis of 2,400,000 hours and our usual pricing formula, setting prices at 150% of total manufacturing cost, we will have higher prices than competition will permit, with consequent loss of volume."

The controller replied, "I can't agree with you. Your basis of 3,000,000 hours is very close to practical capacity, and we'd be taking the risk of having a significant amount of underabsorbed overhead that would really hurt our profits."

**Required**
1. Suppose that selling and administrative expenses are $6,200,000, all fixed. What profit will the company earn if it uses 2,400,000 hours to set standard fixed costs, sets prices using the given formula, and sells output requiring 2,400,000 machine hours? (Assume no inventories.)
2. Repeat requirement 1 substituting 3,000,000 machine hours for 2,400,000 hours.
3. Is the real issue here the selection of the base for applying fixed overhead? Why or why not? If not, what is the real concern?

**14-50   Product costing methods and CVP analysis**   Tollgate Company expects to produce 190,000 units in 20X3. The company uses a predetermined overhead rate for fixed overhead based on 210,000 units, which is normal capacity. Overabsorbed or underabsorbed overhead is shown separately in the income statement. The selling price is $16 per unit. At the expected level of production Tollgate expects the following costs.

| | |
|---|---|
| Variable production costs | $1,330,000 |
| Fixed production costs | 630,000 |
| Fixed selling and administrative costs | 434,000 |

In addition, there are variable selling costs of $2 per unit. The company had no inventory at the end of 20X2.

**Required**
1. Determine the break-even point assuming that variable costing is used.
2. Determine the number of units that must be sold to break even given that production will be 190,000 units. Assume absorption costing.
3. If your answers to the first two requirements differ, explain the difference, showing calculations.
4. Would your answer to requirement 2 be different if the company had a beginning inventory of 10,000 units costed at the same per-unit amount that the company will use in 20X3? Explain why or why not, with calculations.

**14-51   Costing methods and evaluation of performance**   Donita Boroff is the manager of the Wallace Division of Fizer Industries, Inc. She is one of several managers being considered for the presidency of the company, as the current president is retiring in a year.

All divisions use standard absorption costing; normal capacity is the basis for application of fixed overhead. Normal capacity in the Wallace Division is 40,000 units per quarter, and quarterly fixed overhead is $500,000. Variable production cost is $50 per unit. Boroff has been looking at the report for the first three months of the year and is not happy with the results.

## Wallace Division Income Statement for First Quarter

| | | |
|---|---:|---:|
| Sales (25,000 units) | | $2,500,000 |
| Cost of goods sold: | | |
|   Beginning inventory (10,000 units) | $ 625,000 | |
|   Production costs applied | 1,562,500 | |
|   Total | $2,187,500 | |
|   Less ending inventory | 625,000 | 1,562,500 |
| Gross profit | | $ 937,500 |
| Volume variance | | (187,500) |
| Selling and general expenses | | (500,000) |
| Income | | $ 250,000 |

The sales forecast for the second quarter is 25,000 units. Boroff had budgeted second quarter production at 25,000 units but changes it to 50,000 units, which is practical capacity for a quarter. The sales forecasts for each of the last two quarters of the year are also 25,000 units. Costs incurred in the second quarter are the same as budgeted, based on 50,000 units of production.

### Required

1. Prepare an income statement for the second quarter.
2. Does the statement for the second quarter reflect Boroff's performance better than that for the first quarter? Can you make any suggestions for reporting in the future? Do you think Boroff should be seriously considered for the presidency? Why or why not?

**14-52  *Costing methods and performance evaluation*** Warren Progman, the new manager of the Oliver Division of General Products Company, was greatly displeased at the income statements that his controller, Hal Gannon, had been giving him. Progman recently had been placed in charge of the division because it had not been showing satisfactory results. Progman was upset because, although sales had risen in each of the last two months, profits had not kept pace. Income statements for the last three months are as follows:

| | March | April | May |
|---|---:|---:|---:|
| Sales | $360,000 | $440,000 | $560,000 |
| Cost of sales | 198,000 | 264,000 | 381,000 |
| Gross profit | $162,000 | $176,000 | $179,000 |
| Other expenses | 142,000 | 150,000 | 162,000 |
| Profit before taxes | $ 20,000 | $ 26,000 | $ 17,000 |

Progman asked Gannon why profits had declined when sales had increased and why a substantial increase in sales from March to April had produced only a small increase in profits. Gannon's reply was simply that operations had gone according to plans that Progman had set, and that the problems that Progman wanted to know about were due to the method of accounting for product costs and the relationships of sales to production.

Progman was unimpressed with this explanation and rather testily pointed out that he had been put in charge of the division to "turn it around." He was not about to let accounting conventions give corporate management second thoughts about placing him in charge. Gannon, who was fully aware of the claims Progman had made when being considered for the manager's job, had not liked Progman from the start. To the suggestion that accounting conventions were standing in the way of Progman's performance, Gannon replied only that the reports for all divisions were prepared from the same uniform accounting system and in the form required for corporate reporting. He told Progman that the reports were prepared using GAAP, which was necessary because the corporation was publicly held and had to issue reports to shareholders. He did not tell Progman that he believed the methods used by the company for external reporting were inappropriate for internal purposes.

Later, at lunch with Theodora Holloway, the division's sales manager, Gannon related the conversation that he had had with Progman. Holloway, who had also wondered about the company's accounting methods, asked Gannon why he didn't just explain the statements to Progman. "Not on your life," said Gannon. "I see no reason to help that braggart. Let him explain to the top brass why things aren't going the way he said they would if he were put in charge instead of me."

"Actually," Gannon continued, "what he's worried about just isn't a difficult problem. Cost of sales included both standard cost and the adjustment needed when production for the month did not equal the 25,000-unit volume that was used to set the standard fixed cost of $9 per unit. In fact, things have gone very well. We had no variances at all except for volume. Selling prices held very well at $20 per unit, and the division is doing much better now. But would I like to be there when the brass asks Progman why things are not going so well! Why, even production in April was right on target at 25,000 units budgeted."

**Required**

1. Explain the results in the three-month period. You may wish to compute standard fixed costs per unit and production in each month.
2. Prepare income statements for the three months using variable costing.

**14-53  *Costing methods and product profitability***   At a recent meeting, several of the managers of Cornwall Valve Company were discussing the company's costing and pricing methods. Although there was general agreement that the methods should be helpful to managers in determining which products to emphasize, there was considerably less agreement on which methods would accomplish this.

The sales manager, Bill Namura, expressed his preference for product costs based on variable costs only. "I see no reason to charge a product with fixed costs. Contribution margin is, after all, the critical question in selecting the products to push."

"I just can't agree with you," said Perrie Emerson, the production manager. "If you'd just take a walk through the plant you'd be reminded that people and materials aren't the only things needed to produce one of our valves. There are tons of machinery that cost money too. Ignoring those costs can only get you into trouble, and it sure isn't very realistic anyway. You've got to consider the machine time required for each product, and that can only be accomplished by allocating the fixed production costs to products. Machine time is critical, and production costs should be allocated on a machine-hour basis."

To make this point, Emerson put an example on the conference room blackboard. "Look, let me show you. Let's take just three of our basic products that require time in the grinding department. That department has a capacity of 1,000 machine hours a month, and the monthly fixed costs of the department are $10,000." Following is the schedule Emerson put on the board.

|  | 101-27 | 101-34 | 101-56 |
|---|---|---|---|
| Selling price | $9.00 | $12.00 | $17.40 |
| Variable costs | 5.00 | 6.00 | 8.40 |
| Contribution margin | $4.00 | $ 6.00 | $ 9.00 |
| Fixed costs | 1.00 | 1.25 | 2.50 |
| Profit per unit | $3.00 | $ 4.75 | $ 6.50 |
| Number of valves processed per hour | 10 | 8 | 4 |

Emerson continued, "Now what I've done is compute a fixed cost per unit by dividing the $10 per-hour fixed cost by the number of valves of each type that we can process in one hour. You can see that what I use the grinding machinery for does make a difference. It seems to me that this approach is much better at showing which products to emphasize. This shows that the 56 is the best bet and the 27 is the worst."

"But Perrie," said Namura, "we don't disagree. The 56 is a winner because it has the highest contribution margin, and we wouldn't push the 27 because it contributes the least. What are we arguing about?"

Emerson was not too happy about having her own example used to counter her argument. She admitted that, in the case she used, the relative rankings of the products were the same as they would be using the contribution margin approach. But she still felt that her method would be more valuable to the sales manager than a simple contribution margin approach, and she looked around the room for support.

"Well, now, it's nice to hear that you two are so interested in the information my staff has to offer," commented Joe Anderson, the controller. "But if you want to be realistic, let's consider something else. We're committed to making some of each of these valves, though not nearly enough to keep the grinding department operating at capacity. So the big decision isn't really which valve to produce and sell. What we really need to know is which one to produce after we've met the commitments we made. And the kicker is that we could probably sell all of whatever we produce. The way I see it, we have about 600 hours of grinding time available for discretionary production. So what do we do?"

Emerson continued to argue for her approach, and she specifically attacked the question of pricing. "The way we price our products just isn't rational; I know we could do better if we considered the fixed costs the way I said. We should be selling the 27s for $12.50 if we want to make them as profitable as the 56s, and we'd have to jack up the price of 34s by $1.75 to equal the profit on the 56s. Okay, okay, I can see you're getting upset about the idea of such increases, Bill. I know the customers would be unhappy. But if we cater to their needs by producing these models, we ought to get a fair return for doing it."

### Required

Determine which valve should be produced once the committed demand is satisfied. Criticize the analyses of the sales manager and the production manager, including their comments about pricing.

**14-54 Budgeting, cash flow, product costing, motivation** After almost two decades of profitable operations, Pennywise Company experienced its first loss in 20X1, and all internal reports during the first 11 months of 20X2 indicated a second losing year. At the meeting of the board of directors at the end of December 20X2, the members were given the first draft of the basic operating data for 20X2. (Exhibit 1 shows the basic data available to the directors at the meeting.) Public announcement of the data is made shortly after the directors' meeting.

Exhibit 1  Pennywise Company—Operating Data for 20X2

Part A:  Condensed Statement of Income

| | |
|---|---|
| Sales (1,200,000 units at $12 per unit) | $14,400,000 |
| Cost of goods sold | 11,760,000 |
| Gross margin on sales | $ 2,640,000 |
| Selling and administrative expenses | 3,630,000 |
| Net operating loss for the year 20X7 | $  (990,000) |

## Part B: Miscellaneous Operating Data

| | |
|---|---:|
| Normal operating capacity, in units | 1,875,000 |
| Fixed costs: | |
|   Manufacturing | $6,000,000 |
|   Selling and administrative | $750,000 |
| Variable costs, per unit: | |
|   Manufacturing | $4.80 |
|   Selling and administrative | $2.40 |

The directors had maintained the dividend so as not to antagonize the stockholders or give the impression that the recent losses were any more than a temporary setback. Most of the directors had come to realize, by the end of 20X2, that future dividends were advisable only if the company returned to profitable operations. Consequently, the board members were willing to consider any plans that might help minimize inefficiencies, reduce costs, and build a profitable operation once again.

The chair of the board (and principal stockholder), Mr. Ira Hayes, had recently attended a conference sponsored by the National Association of Manufacturers on motivating personnel to better performance. Mr. Hayes was not particularly impressed with most of the discussions. He told the personnel manager, Ms. Gray: "Those speakers all seemed to concentrate on qualitative and nonquantifiable issues like working conditions and improving the general atmosphere to promote creativity and individuality. There was the usual noise about implementing methods of 'participatory management,' and the like, and coordinating the efforts of the management team. But really, there wasn't much in the way of concrete suggestions."

Having been closely associated with the company since its founding by Mr. Hayes sixteen years before, Ms. Gray was well acquainted with Mr. Hayes' feelings on the matter of motivation. As Mr. Hayes had said on many occasions, he was convinced that the surest (and easiest) way to motivate people was to provide monetary incentives of some kind and then let them know exactly what measures would be used to assess their performance. In keeping with this philosophy, Mr. Hayes proposed, at the first board meeting in 20X3, that the company adopt a profit-sharing plan in which all employees could participate. The other members of the board were receptive to the idea and a committee was appointed to draw up a plan.

According to the plan devised by the committee, the company would set aside cash equal to a certain percentage of before-tax profits. The cash would be distributed to all employees on the basis of a preestablished formula. Or, more correctly, a set of such formulas was needed because the performances of employees in different areas of the company had to be measured in different ways. Ira Hayes Jr., the president, wanted to provide his own incentives to encourage better performance by sales and production personnel. He gave the sales and production manager, individually, several long and enthusiastic pep talks on expanding their respective areas to higher levels. He further authorized an expenditure for $450,000 on a national advertising program.

Production in the plant reached the normal capacity of 1,875,000 units for the year 20X3. At the board meeting in early 20X4, the president remarked: "Back in the black again. The field people did a great job pushing sales up by almost 17%." (Exhibit 2 shows the data presented to the board at that meeting.)

The board was pleased with the results of their new plan and with its apparent immediate effectiveness. There was, in fact, much optimistic talk at the meeting about the effect that the new plan would have on 20X4 operations, especially because the special sales campaign would probably not be repeated regularly. The board voted to continue the plan for at least one more year. After the vote, Mr. Hayes, Jr. suggested that it probably would be good for employee relations if the board would an-

### Exhibit 2 Pennywise Company—Operating Data for 20X3

| | | |
|---|---:|---:|
| Sales (1,406,250 units at $12) | | $16,875,000 |
| Cost of goods sold: | | |
| Fixed costs | $ 6,000,000 | |
| Variable costs (1,875,000 @ $4.80) | 9,000,000 | |
| | $15,000,000 | |
| Less: Ending inventory (468,750 units @ $8.00) | 3,750,000 | 11,250,000 |
| Gross margin on sales | | $ 5,625,000 |
| Selling and administrative expenses: | | |
| Fixed costs | $ 1,200,000 | |
| Variable costs (1,406,250 @ $2.40) | 3,375,000 | 4,575,000 |
| Operating profit before taxes and allowance for profit-sharing pool | | $ 1,050,000 |
| Provision for profit-sharing pool | | 210,000 |
| Operating profit before taxes | | $   840,000 |
| Provision for federal income taxes | | 420,000 |
| Net income for the year 20X3 | | $   420,000 |
| Dividends to common stockholders ($0.20 per share) | | $   200,000 |

nounce soon when the pool for profit sharing would be distributed in cash to the employees because the dividend announcement had already been widely publicized. In an outer room, the sales manager, the production manager, and the controller were discussing the advantages and disadvantages of nepotism and of nonoperating management on the board of directors.

### Required

The questions following this paragraph are not designed to limit your discussion or specifically direct your analysis. Nor is there any particular significance to the order in which they are listed. You will find it worthwhile to answer the first one first because it might provide some clue as to how you might proceed. It is probably inefficient to answer each of the questions in order because some are interrelated, but you might want to incorporate some comments about each of them in your answer.

1. What is the company's break-even point?
2. What is the company's system for implementing the management functions of planning and control?
3. Are profits likely to continue?
4. Has the profit-sharing plan contributed to efficiency? to cost reduction? to a return to profitable operations?
5. Should the board announce a cash distribution to employees relatively soon?

## Chapter Fifteen

# PROCESS COSTING AND THE COST ACCOUNTING CYCLE

## *LEARNING OBJECTIVES*

*After reading this chapter, you should be able to*

- *Determine when process costing is appropriate.*
- *Explain the concept of equivalent unit production.*
- *Determine unit costs, inventories, and costs transferred.*
- *Use the backflush costing method.*
- *Describe and apply the cost accounting cycle for manufacturers.*

*The movie industry shares risks by offering profit-sharing contracts in lieu of salaries or fees. Big-name stars, producers, and directors often have gross participation* contracts, *in which they receive a percentage of revenues (to the studio, not to the movie house). Lesser name stars, writers, and others often share in profits through* net profit participation *contracts. A net profit participation contract relies on the studio's definition of the cost of its product, a movie. Net profit participants often receive nothing, even on such hits as* Coming to America, *as we describe below.*

*Net profit typically means revenues less the cost of the film, which includes distribution fees, some direct distribution expenses, production costs of the film, payouts to gross participants, and interest on unrecovered costs. Some of these costs are direct while others are indirect, and some, such as the interest on unrecovered cost, are imputed.*

*Direct costs include some direct distribution costs including the cost of prints, reprints, dubbing, advertising, taxes, and union fees. Direct production costs include the cost of personnel, film, equipment rental, costumes, and other production expenses. Both of these categories include percentage charges for overhead. Payouts to gross participants are also direct costs.*

*Distribution fees are probably the most controversial item. They are charged as a percentage of revenues (30 to 50 percent) and bear no necessary relationship to the studio's overhead associated with distributing the film. In one court case, writer Art Buchwald showed that distribution fees charged to* Coming to America *"more than covered the cost of* **Paramount's** *worldwide distribution network for an entire year." In that year, the studio charged movies for distribution fees that exceeded its*

> distribution costs by $63 million. So net profit participants had to wait for Paramount to earn $63 million over its costs before they received any payout.
>
> The interest charge is an imputed cost, similar to the minimum required ROI used in calculating residual income. Interest is based on all costs of the film, both direct and indirect, and continues until the film breaks even for participation purposes. The amount of interest, too, is not necessarily related to costs that the studio actually incurs.
>
> As we said at the top, the typical arrangement finds net profit participants getting little, if anything, because films typically show losses after all of the deductions. Only 5 percent show profits. Some net participants have sued, claiming fraud, but have usually lost.

*Source: Ross Bengel and Bruce Ikawa, "Where's the Profit?" Management Accounting, January 1997, 40–47.*

Chapter 13 introduced product costing—determining the cost of manufactured products for inventory and cost of goods sold. While Chapter 13 emphasized job-order costing, the concepts (such as cost flows and application of overhead) apply to all types of manufacturing. As Chapter 13 noted, companies producing non-standard products use job-order costing, while companies making a single, homogeneous product use a cost accumulation method called process costing. Some examples of companies that can use process costing are makers of sugar, bricks, cement, and bulk chemicals. The first part of this chapter discusses process costing and includes an example describing how a service business, a bank, uses process costing concepts.

We complete our study of product costing by illustrating the cost accounting cycle in the three principal types of cost accumulation systems: job-order costing, process costing, and standard costing. Because they keep low inventories, ideally none, advanced manufacturers have fewer problems with product costing. We illustrate one way that they account for product costs.

## PROCESS COSTING

The essence of **process costing** is the accumulation of costs by process, or department, for a period of time. The company calculates per-unit costs for goods passing through a process by dividing costs for the process by production for the period. For internal reporting, a process costing factory, like a job-order factory, can use either variable or absorption costing, as described in Chapter 14. We concentrate on absorption costing in this chapter. A process coster can also use actual costing, normal costing, or standard costing.

Because process costers manufacture a single, homogeneous product, they can use the basic formula we described in Chapter 13.

$$Unit\ cost = \frac{Production\ costs}{Production}$$

The unit cost is then applied to inventories and cost of goods sold. The key to process costing is determining production. Look at the data for our illustration in

Exhibit 15-1. The company finished 50,000 units in May, and also did 60 percent of the work on 10,000 units. What is production for the period? The 50,000 units finished? No, because the company also worked on the 10,000 units. To account for such work, we calculate equivalent unit production (or equivalent production) for use in the denominator. First, however, we must select a cost flow assumption, either first-in first-out or weighted average. We shall use the weighted-average method in this chapter. (We describe the FIFO method in the Appendix at the end of this chapter.)

Recall from financial accounting that the **weighted-average inventory method** applied to a merchandiser combines the cost of the beginning inventory with the costs incurred during the period and also combines the units in the beginning inventory with those purchased during the period. The principle is the same for manufactured products.

## EQUIVALENT UNIT PRODUCTION AND UNIT COST

Under the weighted-average method, **equivalent unit production** is the sum of (1) the units finished during the period and (2) the equivalent units in the ending inventory of work in process.

$$\frac{Equivalent}{production} = \frac{Units}{completed} + \left( \frac{Units\ in}{ending\ inventory} \times \frac{Percentage}{complete} \right)$$

In our example, the 10,000 units in process at the end of May are *equivalent* to 6,000 complete units (10,000 × 60%). Thus, at the end of May the company had 6,000 equivalent units and at the end of June had 8,000 equivalent units (20,000 × 40%).

Equivalent unit production for May is as follows:

| | |
|---|---|
| Units completed | 50,000 |
| Equivalent units in ending inventory, 10,000 × 60% | 6,000 |
| Weighted-average equivalent unit production | 56,000 |

The weighted-average unit cost formula is as follows:

$$Unit\ cost = \frac{Cost\ of\ beginning\ inventory\ +\ Current\ period\ cost}{Weighted\text{-}average\ equivalent\ unit\ production}$$

| **Exhibit 15-1   Data for Kelco Company** | | |
|---|---|---|
| | **May** | **June** |
| **Production costs** | $112,000 | $128,400 |
| **Unit data:** | | |
| Units in beginning work in process | 0 | 10,000 |
| Units completed during month | 50,000 | 70,000 |
| Units in ending work in process | 10,000 | 20,000 |
| Percentage of completion of work in process | 60% | 40% |

Because there is no beginning inventory for May, the numerator is just May production costs. The unit cost for May is therefore $2.00.

$$\$112,000/56,000 \ = \ \$2.00$$

## ENDING INVENTORY AND TRANSFERS

We use the $2 unit cost both for the units completed and those in the ending inventory of work in process. Thus, we transfer $100,000 to Finished Goods Inventory (50,000 × $2) and leave $12,000 in Work in Process Inventory (10,000 × 60% × $2). Notice especially that Work in Process Inventory reflects equivalent whole units. That is, we do not multiply the 10,000 *physical units* in process by the $2 unit cost because those 10,000 units are only 60 percent complete.

We encourage you to account for total production costs as we do in the following schedule. This schedule offers a check on your work. If the total costs accounted for as either transferred out or still in process do not equal the beginning inventory plus current period cost (with due regard for rounding errors), you have made an error. In May, there is no beginning work in process, so we account for only the $112,000 May production costs.

| | |
|---|---:|
| Cost of finished units transferred to finished goods (50,000 × $2 per unit) | $100,000 |
| Cost of ending inventory (10,000 units × 60% × $2 per unit) | 12,000 |
| Total production costs accounted for | $112,000 |

## EFFECTS OF BEGINNING INVENTORY

As we just calculated, Kelco began June with 6,000 equivalent units of work in process with a cost of $12,000. As the formula showed, these units do not affect the denominator of the unit cost calculation for June, but the $12,000 cost does. June equivalent production is as follows:

| | |
|---|---:|
| Units completed | 70,000 |
| Equivalent units in ending inventory, 20,000 × 40% | 8,000 |
| Weighted-average equivalent unit production | 78,000 |

Unit cost is $1.80.

$$\frac{\$12,000 \ + \ \$128,400}{78,000} \ = \ \frac{\$140,400}{78,000} \ = \ \$1.80$$

The weighted-average unit cost is $1.80. The disposition of the costs follows.

| | |
|---|---:|
| Ending inventory of work in process 20,000 × 40% × $1.80 | $ 14,400 |
| To finished goods inventory, 70,000 × $1.80 | 126,000 |
| Total | $140,400 |

The sum of the cost of the beginning inventory and June production costs is $140,400. Therefore, the $140,400 cost in ending inventory and transferred to finished goods inventory accounts for those costs.

Process costing has no other conceptual problems. It does have some refinements that arise in practice. We consider the two most common. The first is when units in work in process are not equally complete with respect to all components of manufacturing cost (materials, labor or machine time, and overhead). The second situation is when—as is true in most manufacturing companies—units pass through more than one department or process. The next two sections discuss these refinements.

## MATERIALS AND CONVERSION COSTS

In the Kelco example the same percentage-of-completion figure applied to all productive factors—materials, labor or machine time, and overhead. This situation is unlikely because materials usually go into process at an early stage. (Obviously, *some* materials must go into process immediately because you cannot work on nothing.) Labor and overhead are usually added more or less continuously throughout the process. Thus, work in process inventories usually include all (or nearly all) materials, but *always* less than the necessary labor and overhead (or else the units would be finished). A company that grinds wheat into flour will, at any given time, have all of the wheat in process. The flour is 100 percent complete with regard to materials: the wheat must be in process before any work is done. But grinding wheat into flour takes time, so that in-process flour is not complete with regard to labor and overhead.

Converting raw materials into finished product requires labor and overhead—power, supplies, maintenance, and so on. Labor and overhead together are called **conversion costs** and generally have the same completion percentage. In a machine-driven department where labor is insignificant, there might be only materials and overhead—no direct labor cost at all.

Differing degrees of completion for materials and conversion costs do not change the general formula for computing unit costs; they only require calculating costs separately for materials and conversion costs. We shall illustrate the computations using the data and computations of unit cost for Kray Company in Exhibit 15-2.

As before, we use these unit costs to determine the cost of the ending inventory of work in process and the cost of the units transferred to finished goods inventory.

Ending inventory:

| | |
|---|---:|
| Materials cost (15,000 units × 100% × $1.10) | $16,500 |
| Conversion cost (15,000 units × 40% × $0.90) | 5,400 |
| Total cost of ending work in process inventory | $21,900 |

Transferred to finished goods:

| | |
|---|---:|
| Materials cost (45,000 units × $1.10) | $49,500 |
| Conversion cost (45,000 units × $0.90) | 40,500 |
| Total cost transferred to finished goods | $90,000 |

Taking advantage of the checkpoint presented in earlier sections, we can see that the total costs are fully accounted for through the transfer of completed units and the costs assigned to the ending inventory.

## Exhibit 15-2    Data for Kray Company

|  | Materials | Conversion Costs |
|---|---|---|
| Costs of beginning inventory | $8,000 | $4,900 |
| Production costs for May | $58,000 | $41,000 |
| Unit data: |  |  |
| Units completed during month 45,000 |  |  |
| Units in ending work in process 15,000 |  |  |
| Percentage of completion |  |  |
| of work in process | 100% | 60% |
| Equivalent production: |  |  |
| Units completed | 45,000 | 45,000 |
| Equivalent production in |  |  |
| ending inventory |  |  |
| 15,000 × 100% | 15,000 |  |
| 15,000 × 40% | _____ | 6,000 |
| Equivalent unit production | 60,000 | 51,000 |
| Unit costs | $8,000 + $58,000 | $4,900 + $41,000 |
|  | 60,000 | 51,000 |
|  | $1.10 | $0.90 |

| Total costs to be accounted for: |  |
|---|---|
| Costs in beginning inventory ($8,000 + $4,900) | $ 12,900 |
| Costs for current month ($58,000 + $41,000) | 99,000 |
| Total | $111,900 |

| Total costs accounted for as: |  |
|---|---|
| Cost of finished units transferred to finished goods | $ 90,000 |
| Cost of ending inventory | 21,900 |
| Total | $111,900 |

Thus, the different percentages of completion for materials and conversion costs require only that we compute different amounts of equivalent production and separate total costs by type. No new concepts are involved. The accompanying Insight discusses how one major company's cost structure is changing.

### MULTIPLE PROCESSES

The cost of a product that passes through several processes obviously must include the costs of all the processes. Suppose that Kray's manufacturing process includes a cutting operation (cutting large blocks of raw material into smaller blocks) and a sanding operation (refining the shapes to common specifications). The data in Exhibit 15-2 relate to the cutting operation, and the 45,000 units that the Cutting Department finished were transferred to the Sanding Department.

**SIGHT**

### Composition of Product Costs

Earlier chapters discussed how direct labor costs are decreasing while overhead costs are increasing. Another trend in product costs is that for many manufacturers the relative costs of materials and components are increasing as they outsource more and more work. **General Motors**, once the most vertically integrated auto manufacturer, has increased the amount of work its suppliers do. Suppliers now make large modules such as doors and chassis. GM then assembles these modules. In the past GM had fabricated many of these components itself.

GM's suppliers have begun to locate near its plants, thus reducing freight charges and bringing JIT production closer to reality. For instance, GM has invested $900 million in two areas of Mexico to build cars and trucks for the Mexican market. Its suppliers have invested $445 million in the same areas. Because GM will be assembling larger chunks, its labor costs, and probably some overhead cost, will decline, while the materials/components portion will rise.

Source: Jonathan Freidland and Joseph B. White, "GM Is Leading an Investment Boom in Mexico," The Wall Street Journal, *December 24, 1998, A4.*

The cost of a unit transferred from Sanding to finished goods must include the cost of both the forming and the sanding processes. The cost of a unit in process in the Sanding Department must include not only the cost of that operation but also the cost of the Cutting Department. The Sanding Department adds no materials, so all costs it incurs are for conversion. Operating data for May for the sanding process follow.

| Unit Data: | |
|---|---|
| Units on hand at beginning of June | 0 |
| Transferred in from Cutting Department | 45,000 |
| Completed and transferred to finished goods | 40,000 |
| On hand at end of period (80% complete) | 5,000 |
| Cost Data: | |
| Beginning inventory | $0 |
| Transferred in from Cutting Department | $90,000 |
| Sanding Department conversion costs for June | $132,000 |

The first step, of course, is to calculate the equivalent production for the sanding process.

| | |
|---|---|
| Units completed | 40,000 |
| Equivalent units in ending inventory, 5,000 × 80% | 4,000 |
| Weighted-average equivalent unit production | 44,000 |

So unit cost for the Sanding Department is $3.00.

$$\frac{\$0 + \$132,000}{44,000} = \$3.00$$

The cost of a unit transferred from Sanding to finished goods is the $2.00 from the Cutting Department plus $3.00 from the Sanding Department, a total of $5.00. Finding the cost of the Sanding Department's ending work in process inventory requires two steps because the units have had all of the work done by the prior department, but only 80 percent of the work of the Sanding Department.

Ending work in process:
Cost from prior department, 5,000 × 100% × $2.00 .......... $10,000
Sanding Department conversion costs,
  5,000 × 80% × $3.00 .......... 12,000
Ending work in process .......... $22,000

The total cost to be accounted for by the Sanding Department consists of the costs transferred in ($90,000), the costs in the beginning inventory (none), and the current month production costs ($132,000), or $222,000. We account for that total as follows:

Transferred to finished goods, 40,000 × $5.00 .......... $200,000
Ending inventory of work in process, above .......... 22,000
  Total .......... $222,000

## THE COST ACCOUNTING CYCLE

Chapter 13 presented an overview of the flow of manufacturing costs (Exhibit 13-1), noting that costs are first accumulated by object (materials, labor, and overhead) and are then passed on to Work in Process, then to Finished Goods and, ultimately, to Cost of Goods Sold.[1] Using journal entries and T-accounts, we show how these costs flow through the accounting records. We shall concentrate our discussion of accounting entries on those relevant to absorption costing, but the application to variable costing, or throughput accounting for that matter, should follow naturally.

The two principal cost accumulation systems are process and job-order costing. Actual or normal costing can be used under either system, and standard costs can always be used by process manufacturers and sometimes by job-order manufacturers. Despite the differences among the various combinations available, the journal entries to record the flow of costs differ little from one system to another because there is a limited number of places for costs to be collected or transferred. Our first illustration is for actual process costing, the second is a job-order company using normal costing. We also illustrate standard costing in a simple setting to concentrate on the accounting issues specific to standard costing.

### ILLUSTRATION OF ACTUAL PROCESS COSTING

Bryan Company produces a plywood countertop backing. The manufacturing process requires sequential applications of layers of wood until the plywood reaches the required thickness.

---

1 Following the pattern in Chapter 13, we capitalize the names of accounts and use lowercase to designate the objects themselves. Thus "work in process" refers to physical, semifinished products, while "Work in Process" refers to the account.

Bryan had no beginning inventories of work in process. (The implications of beginning work in process inventories for the calculation of equivalent production were discussed on page 678.) Bryan had the following transactions in 20X5. (We omit explanations of the journal entries because the descriptions of the transactions serve the same purpose.)

Purchase of materials: Bryan bought 1,400,000 feet of wood at $0.095 per foot.

| | | |
|---|---|---|
| 1. Materials Inventory (1,400,000 × $0.095) | $133,000 | |
|     Cash or Accounts Payable | | $133,000 |

Materials put into process: Bryan used 1,300,000 feet of wood.

| | | |
|---|---|---|
| 2. Work in Process (1,300,000 × $0.095) | $123,500 | |
|     Materials Inventory | | $123,500 |

Direct labor: Direct laborers earned $344,400 for 41,000 hours of work at $8.40 per hour.

| | | |
|---|---|---|
| 3a. Direct Labor | $344,400 | |
|     Cash or Accrued Payroll | | $344,400 |
| 3b. Work in Process Inventory | $344,400 | |
|     Direct Labor | | $344,400 |

Overhead costs incurred: Bryan incurred various overhead costs. We record them in a single control account and subsidiary accounts show the details (utilities, indirect labor, depreciation, and so on). We use accounts for both fixed and variable overhead, but some companies use a single account for both types of cost.

| | | |
|---|---|---|
| 4. Variable Manufacturing Overhead | $251,300 | |
|     Fixed Manufacturing Overhead | 461,000 | |
|       Various, Cash, Accrued Expenses, | | |
|       Accumulated Depreciation | | $712,300 |

The manufacturing overhead accounts are for convenience and are especially helpful when standard costing is used, as we shall show shortly. The amounts put into the manufacturing overhead accounts are now transferred to Work in Process Inventory.

| | | |
|---|---|---|
| 5. Work in Process Inventory | $251,300 | |
|     Variable Manufacturing Overhead | | $251,300 |
|     Work in Process Inventory | $461,000 | |
|       Fixed Manufacturing Overhead | | $461,000 |

Production: Bryan finished 40,000 square yards of plywood. Another 3,000 square yards were still in process at the end of 20X5. These 3,000 square yards were two-thirds finished for both materials and conversion costs.

To transfer the cost of finished units to Finished Goods Inventory, we need the per-unit cost of production. Therefore, we need equivalent production, which is calculated as follows:

$$Equivalent \ = \ 40,000 \ + \ (3,000 \times 2/3) \ = \ 42,000 \ square \ yards \ production$$

The 42,000 equivalent production is used to determine the cost per unit. At this point we have $1,180,200 in Work in Process Inventory, composed of the following costs. The numbers in parentheses refer to journal entries.

| Materials (2) | $  123,500 |
| Direct labor (3b) | 344,400 |
| Variable overhead (5) | 251,300 |
| Fixed overhead (5) | 461,000 |
| Total | $1,180,200 |
| Divided by equivalent production | 42,000 |
| Equals cost per unit | $     28.10 |

The $28.10 cost per unit is used to transfer to Finished Goods Inventory.

    6.  Finished Goods Inventory (40,000 × $28.10)    $1,124,000
            Work in Process Inventory                              $1,124,000

Sales: Bryan sold 35,000 square yards at $40 each.

    7a. Cash or Accounts Receivable (35,000 × $40)    $1,400,000
            Sales                                                     $1,400,000
    7b. Cost of Goods Sold (35,000 × $28.10)    $983,500
            Finished Goods Inventory                          $983,500

Selling and administrative expenses: The company incurred $340,000 in selling and administrative expenses.

    8.  Selling and Administrative Expenses    $340,000
            Cash, Accrued Expenses                      $340,000

At this point the accounts for direct labor, variable overhead, and fixed overhead all have zero balances. The other key accounts show the following:

**Work in Process Inventory**

| (2) | $   123,500 | | |
| (3b) | 344,400 | | |
| (5) | 251,300 | $1,124,000 | (6) |
| (5) | 461,000 | | |
| | 1,180,200 | 1,124,000 | |
| Bal. | $    56,200 | | |

**Finished Goods Inventory**

| (6) | $1,124,000 | $983,500 | (7b) |
| Bal. | $  140,500 | | |

**Cost of Goods Sold**

| (7b) | $983,500 | |

An income statement for Bryan Company appears in Exhibit 15-3.

We said earlier that non-manufacturing organizations use the techniques of product costing. The accompanying Insight describes a bank's use of process costing concepts.

**Exhibit 15-3   Income Statement for Bryan Company, Actual Process Costing**

| | |
|---|---|
| Sales (7a)* | $1,400,000 |
| Cost of goods sold (7b) | 983,500 |
| Gross profit | $  416,500 |
| Selling and administrative expenses (8) | 340,000 |
| Income | $    76,500 |

* Figures in parentheses indicate journal entry numbers from the earlier illustrations.

 **SIGHT**

### Process Costing in a Bank

Banks, as well as other types of companies, operate telephone service centers for customers. Some banks have a center for each large department, such as the mortgage department, and offer different services within those departments. Mortgage departments offer both fixed and adjustable rate mortgages, so managers must determine the costs of servicing each type for pricing and for analyzing profitability. The traditional way that banks developed such costs was a simple process costing calculation:

$$Unit\ cost\ of\ call\ \ =\ \ Total\ cost\ of\ center/Total\ number\ of\ calls$$

Banks then allocated costs to each type of mortgage based on the number of calls related to each type.

Managers of a regional bank believed that this simple approach failed to recognize that some types of calls require considerably more time than others. The three basic types of calls are inquiries about rates and terms, inquiries about the status of mortgage applications, and problem solving/other. Inquiries about the status of applications took about the same time whether the application was for a fixed or adjustable rate mortgage. But problem-solving calls regarding adjustable rate mortgages took over twice the time as those regarding fixed rate mortgages. The bank incorporated the average time per call into the cost calculation to develop a cost per minute.

The bank actually developed three cost-per-minute figures. The first is based on historical costs. The second is based on practical capacity, which gives the lowest possible cost and serves as a target. The third is based on expected activity over five years and is used to estimate costs over the planning period.

*Source: Gilbert Y. Yang and Roger C. Wu, "Strategic Costing and ABC,"* Management Accounting, *May 1993, 33–37.*

## ILLUSTRATION OF JOB-ORDER COSTING

Portland Mill Works makes industrial products in a highly mechanized environment. The company uses activity-based costing. For simplicity, we limit the activities to machine hours and setup time.

The company has established the following predetermined overhead rates.

|  | Machine-Related | Setup-Related |
| --- | --- | --- |
| Total budgeted overhead | $600,000 | $250,000 |
| Divided by budgeted levels of activity | 100,000 MH | 10,000 setup hours |
| Equals predetermined overhead rates | $6 per MH | $25 per setup hour |

Exhibit 15-4 presents the actual results for the year, including the overhead applied for each activity.

We can calculate misapplied overhead as follows:

| | |
|---|---:|
| Total applied overhead ($660,000 + $225,000) | $885,000 |
| Total actual overhead ($645,000 + $235,000) | 880,000 |
| Total overapplied overhead | $  5,000 |

The journal entries and accounts of a job-order company are similar to those of a process costing company (or one that uses standard costs). Job-order costing is a specific identification method, so that transfers from Work in Process Inventory to Finished Goods Inventory and to Cost of Goods Sold are based on the particular jobs finished and sold and do not require a cost flow assumption. The following entries summarize Portland's flows. All of the information comes from Exhibit 15-4.

Materials purchased

| | | |
|---|---:|---:|
| 1. Materials Inventory | $720,000 | |
|    Cash, Accounts Payable | | $720,000 |

Materials used

| | | |
|---|---:|---:|
| 2. Work in Process Inventory | $650,000 | |
|    Materials Inventory | | $650,000 |

Direct labor

| | | |
|---|---:|---:|
| 3a. Direct Labor | $800,000 | |
|     Cash or Accrued Payroll | | $800,000 |

### Exhibit 15-4    Portland Mill Works, Results for 20X6

| Activity Data | Totals | Jobs Sold | Jobs in Ending Work in Process Inventory | Jobs in Ending Finished Goods Inventory |
|---|---:|---:|---:|---:|
| Machine hours | 110,000 | 100,000 | 3,000 | 7,000 |
| Setup hours | 9,000 | 8,000 | 200 | 800 |
| **Cost Data** | | | | |
| Materials used | $ 650,000 | $ 580,000 | $30,000 | $ 40,000 |
| Direct labor | 800,000 | 720,000 | 20,000 | 60,000 |
| Applied overhead at $6/MH | 660,000 | 600,000 | 18,000 | 42,000 |
| Applied overhead at $25/setup hour | 225,000 | 200,000 | 5,000 | 20,000 |
| Total costs | $2,335,000 | $2,100,000 | $73,000 | $162,000 |

Portland purchased materials and components for $720,000 during the year.
Actual overhead, machine-related $645,000, setup-related $235,000.

3b. Work in Process Inventory $800,000

    Direct Labor $800,000

Overhead incurrence and application. We omit fixed and variable categories.

4a. Factory Overhead—machine-related $645,000

    Factory Overhead—setup related 235,000

      Various Credits, Cash, Accrued

      Expenses, Accumulated Depreciation $880,000

4b. Work in Process Inventory $885,000

    Factory Overhead—machine-related $660,000

    Factory Overhead—setup-related 225,000

Completion of jobs

5.  Finished Goods Inventory $2,262,000

    Work in Process Inventory $2,262,000

This entry is the total cost of all jobs completed during the year, which consists of the $2,100,000 cost of jobs sold plus the $162,000 cost of jobs still in Finished Goods Inventory at year end.

Cost of sales

6.  Cost of Goods Sold $2,100,000

    Finished Goods Inventory $2,100,000

At this point, the various manufacturing overhead and inventory accounts appear as follows:

| Factory Overhead—machine-related | | | |
|---|---|---|---|
| (4a) | $645,000 | $660,000 | (4b) |
| Bal. | | $ 15,000 | |

| Factory Overhead—setup-related | | | |
|---|---|---|---|
| (4a) | $235,000 | $225,000 | (4b) |
| Bal. | $ 10,000 | | |

| Work in Process Inventory | | | |
|---|---|---|---|
| (2) | $ 650,000 | | |
| (3b) | 800,000 | | |
| (4b) | 885,000 | $2,262,000 | (5) |
| | 2,335,000 | 2,262,000 | |
| Bal. | $ 73,000 | | |

| Finished Goods Inventory | | | |
|---|---|---|---|
| (5) | $2,262,000 | $2,100,000 | (6) |
| Bal. | $ 162,000 | | |

| Cost of Goods Sold | |
|---|---|
| (6) | $2,100,000 |

The amounts shown as ending balances in Cost of Goods Sold and the two inventory accounts agree with the amounts shown in Exhibit 15-4. The balances of the factory overhead accounts represent the overapplied or underapplied overhead for the departments. The net overapplied overhead of $5,000 ($15,000 overapplied machine-related overhead minus $10,000 underapplied setup-related overhead) agrees with the misapplied overhead computed on page 686.

    What happens to the balances in the overhead accounts, overapplied and underapplied overhead? As Chapter 13 stated, the $5,000 can be shown in the income statement as an adjustment either to cost of goods sold or to gross margin. For financial reporting purposes, if misapplied overhead is material, the company

CHAPTER 13

must convert to an actual costing basis. Doing so requires allocating misapplied overhead to cost of sales and ending inventories based on the amounts of applied overhead in each account.

## ILLUSTRATION OF STANDARD COSTING

Our final illustration of the cost accounting cycle is of a standard costing system. Virtually all such systems require that transfers of costs from Work in Process Inventory to Finished Goods Inventory be made at the total standard cost of units completed. But costs can be put into Work in Process Inventory in two ways: (1) put in actual quantities of inputs at standard prices or (2) put in standard quantities of inputs at standard prices. We shall illustrate the latter technique. We also note that standard product costing can be used without using standard costs and variances to evaluate performance. As Chapter 12 stated, some companies do not use standards because they believe standards limit performance and stifle continuous improvement. Such companies can still benefit from using standard product costing because it is probably cheaper and simpler than actual or normal costing. They can do so without using standards and variances to evaluate performance. The accompanying Insight describes two companies' different attitudes about their standard cost systems.

**(IN)** *SIGHT*

### How Precise Should Your System Be?

The standard cost system used by **Trane Company**, a major producer of air conditioning systems and fixtures for home and commercial use, tries to get costs "close enough." The company does not expect precision in developing its products' costs; rather, its cost system is designed to support Trane's overriding objectives of on-time delivery of quality products. Simplicity and lowest total cost are part of the company's philosophy. The company applies the principle of simplicity to its accounting as well as to its operations, paying little attention to immaterial elements of cost. For example, because labor cost is less than 5 percent of total cost, Trane does no detailed reporting of labor productivity. The company expenses low-cost parts such as screws and nuts.

In contrast, **Sally Industries**, a manufacturer of entertainment robots for theme parks, pays very close attention to labor cost and productivity because labor is a high percentage of total cost. Moreover, Sally even keeps track of *which* workers perform *which* tasks because rates of pay vary considerably. Sally's system makes workers much more conscious of how they use their time and reduces non-value-adding work.

*Sources: Ronald B. Clements and Charlene W. Spoede, "Trane's SOUP Accounting,"* Management Accounting, *June 1992, 46–52.*
*Thomas L. Barton and Frederick M. Cole, "Accounting for Magic,"* Management Accounting, *January 1991, 27–31.*

Data for one of Kosto Company's products appear in Exhibit 15-5. For simplicity, we assume that the company has no inventories of work in process—that it finishes the units it starts each day. With the information given, we can calculate variances as we make the entries.

One objective of a standard costing system is to isolate variances in the accounts as quickly as possible, instead of making separate calculations outside of the accounting system. Timely determination of variances helps in control because the sooner that managers know about variances, the sooner they can decide whether or not to investigate and possibly act.

The journal entries describing the events of March isolate price variances when the cost is incurred, which is when the variance first becomes known. They isolate quantity variances when costs go into process. Thus, the entries putting costs into process are made at the end of the period, when production is known, because you must know production to determine efficiency variances and the fixed overhead volume variance. As we have said, there are other possible patterns, but they all share the essential characteristic of standard costing: all inventories appear at standard cost at the ends of periods.

Materials purchases

| | | | |
|---|---|---:|---:|
| 1. | Materials Inventory (20,000 pounds × $5.00) | $100,000 | |
| | Material Price Variance | 4,000 | |
| | Cash or Accounts Payable | | $104,000 |

Materials use

| | | | |
|---|---|---:|---:|
| 2. | Work in Process Inventory (18,000 pounds × $5) | $90,000 | |
| | Material Use Variance | | $ 1,000 |
| | Materials Inventory (17,800 pounds × $5) | | 89,000 |

---

**Exhibit 15-5   Kosto Company, Data for Illustration**

**Standard Costs**

| | |
|---|---:|
| Materials, 2 pounds at $5 | $10 |
| Direct labor, ½ hour at $16 | 8 |
| Variable overhead at $12 per DLH | 6 |
| Fixed overhead at $20 per DLH* | 10 |
| Total standard cost | $34 |

**Results for March 20X2**

| | |
|---|---:|
| Beginning inventory, finished goods, 1,000 units at $34 | $34,000 |
| Units produced | 9,000 |
| Units sold | 8,000 |
| Ending inventory, finished goods | 2,000 |
| Material purchases, 20,000 lbs. at $5.20 | $104,000 |
| Material use | 17,800 pounds |
| Direct labor, 4,700 hours at $15.50 | $72,850 |
| Variable overhead | $59,000 |
| Fixed overhead | $98,000 |

* *Based on budgeted fixed overhead of $100,000 per month and monthly normal activity of 5,000 direct labor hours*

Direct labor

| | | | |
|---|---|---:|---:|
| 3a. | Direct Labor (4,700 × $16) | $75,200 | |
| | Cash or Accrued Payroll | | $72,850 |
| | Direct Labor Rate Variance | | 2,350 |
| 3b. | Work in Process Inventory (4,500 × $16) | $72,000 | |
| | Direct Labor Efficiency Variance | 3,200 | |
| | Direct Labor | | $75,200 |

Variable overhead

| | | | |
|---|---|---:|---:|
| 4a. | Variable Manufacturing Overhead (4,700 × $12) | $56,400 | |
| | Variable Overhead Spending Variance | 2,600 | |
| | Various Credits, Cash, Accrued Expenses | | $59,000 |
| 4b. | Work in Process Inventory (4,500 × $12) | $54,000 | |
| | Variable Overhead Efficiency Variance | 2,400 | |
| | Variable Manufacturing Overhead | | $56,400 |

Fixed overhead

| | | | |
|---|---|---:|---:|
| 5a. | Fixed Manufacturing Overhead | $100,000 | |
| | Fixed Overhead Budget Variance | | $ 2,000 |
| | Various Credits, Cash, Accumulated Depreciation | | 98,000 |
| 5b. | Work in Process Inventory (9,000 × $10) | $90,000 | |
| | Fixed Overhead Volume Variance | 10,000 | |
| | Fixed Manufacturing Overhead | | $100,000 |

Completion of goods

| | | | |
|---|---|---:|---:|
| 6. | Finished Goods Inventory (9,000 × $34) | $306,000 | |
| | Work in Process Inventory | | $306,000 |

Cost of sales

| | | | |
|---|---|---:|---:|
| 7. | Cost of Goods Sold (8,000 × $34) | $272,000 | |
| | Finished Goods Inventory | | $272,000 |

The T-accounts for each type of inventory and for Cost of Goods Sold follow. The beginning balance in Finished Goods Inventory is the standard cost of the 1,000 units on hand at the beginning of March (from Exhibit 15-5). The ending balance reflects the standard cost of the remaining 2,000 units (2,000 × $34 = $68,000). Materials Inventory shows the standard price of the 2,200 pounds in the ending inventory, which is the 20,000 pounds bought less the 17,800 used.

| Work in Process Inventory | | | | | Finished Goods Inventory | | | |
|---|---|---|---|---|---|---|---|---|
| (2) | $ 90,000 | | | 3-1 Bal. | $ 34,000 | | | |
| (3b) | 72,000 | | | (6) | 306,000 | $272,000 | (7) | |
| (4b) | 54,000 | | | | 340,000 | 272,000 | | |
| (5b) | 90,000 | $306,000 | (6) | 3-31 Bal. | $ 68,000 | | | |
| | $306,000 | $306,000 | | | | | | |

| Materials Inventory | | | | | Cost of Goods Sold | |
|---|---|---|---|---|---|---|
| (1) | $100,000 | $89,000 | (2) | (7) | $272,000 | |
| 3-31 Bal. | $ 11,000 | | | | | |

As with misapplied overhead, we have two alternatives for treating variances: we can carry variances to the income statement as adjustments to either standard cost of goods sold or to standard gross margin, or we can prorate them among Cost of Goods Sold, Finished Goods Inventory, and Work in Process Inventory. The proration of a material price variance also includes Materials Inventory if materials were still on hand. As stated earlier, the need for proration depends on the magnitude of the variances and the ending inventories, since GAAP accepts standard costs for financial reporting purposes as long as the income statement results of using such costs do not differ *materially* from the results under actual costing. However, what constitutes a "material" difference is a matter of continuing debate.

Besides financial reporting and income taxation, product costing is important in many legal settings, for example, in complying with provisions of government contracts or international trade agreements. The opening vignette described how movie studios do product costing, and how their practices are often deemed unreasonable by net profit participants.

## PRODUCT COSTING IN AN ADVANCED MANUFACTURING ENVIRONMENT

Advanced manufacturers usually have no significant work in process inventory and so have relatively few problems in accounting for that type of inventory. Such operations might have significant finished goods inventories, in which case product costing is still a concern. One technique used by such companies is backflushing, or backflush costing.

**Backflushing** concentrates on completed units, rather than on units making their way through work in process. Backflushing requires relatively few entries. Backflushers do not try to maintain Materials Inventory, Work in Process Inventory, or Finished Goods Inventory at their correct balances. Rather, companies using this technique maintain two inventory accounts, one for finished goods and the other for both materials and work in process.

Terminology and procedures vary, but the fundamentals are straightforward. The following example shows one way to record events using a backflush system. Data for the example follow.

| | |
|---|---:|
| Beginning inventories | None |
| Materials and components purchased and put into process | $250,000 |
| Labor and overhead costs incurred | $180,000 |
| Units completed | 40,000 |
| Units sold | 35,000 |

Because materials are put into process almost immediately after being received, backflushing factories do not need two separate accounts for materials and for work in process. They might record material purchases in the following manner.

| | | |
|---|---:|---:|
| Materials and Work In Process Inventory | $250,000 | |
|     Cash or Accounts Payable | | $250,000 |

Conversion costs are collected in a single account as follows:

| | | |
|---|---:|---:|
| Conversion Costs | $180,000 | |
|     Cash, Accounts Payable, Accumulated Depreciation, etc. | | $180,000 |

Entries for transactions like these are made throughout the period as events require.

At the end of the period, the company records the cost of the ending inventory of finished units and the cost of units sold. Average cost of production for the period is $10.75 [($250,000 + $180,000)/40,000].

| | | |
|---|---|---|
| Cost of Sales (35,000 × $10.75) | $376,250 | |
| Finished Goods Inventory (5,000 × $10.75) | 53,750 | |
|     Materials and Work In Process Inventory | | $250,000 |
|     Conversion Costs | | 180,000 |

The entry could also be made using standard costs, though JIT operations typically use actual rather than standard costs.

The pattern of entries shown is not the only possibility. Some companies charge all costs to Finished Goods Inventory on the basis of reports of the number of units completed, and make a transfer of Cost of Sales only at month-end. Because backflush costing has the potential for reducing the information provided to managers during each period, it is best suited to a company with relatively stable levels of production activity and little work in process.

**Trane Co.**, which we described in an earlier Insight, uses a backflushing system along with standard costs. The company accounts for materials and conversion costs only when it finishes units. Using standard costs simplifies Trane's record-keeping.

Backflushing is an instance of accountants reducing non-value-adding costs by reducing recordkeeping. Much of the analysis and work that management accountants have performed in recordkeeping has to do with reducing the volume of transactions by eliminating recording that is non-value-adding, while preserving information needed for managing operations. The accompanying Insight describes how one company's reduction of complexity has reduced costs.

## FINAL COMPARATIVE COMMENTS

We have illustrated the cost accounting cycle in four situations. We showed a processing company using actual costing, a job-order company using normal costing, an operation using standard costs, and finally, a JIT operation. At this point we pause to review briefly the many topics covered as part of our three-chapter discussion of product costing.

Any cost accounting system uses either variable costing or absorption costing, the difference being that only the latter assigns fixed manufacturing overhead to units of product. Any system must use either actual, normal, or standard costs. The nature of the manufacturing operation separates cost accumulation systems into job-order and process. Both types of manufacturers can use either absorption or variable costing, and actual, normal, or standard costs. (Job-order cost systems are least likely to use standard costs because of the uniqueness of the products made on the various jobs.)

Yet, with all these possibilities, the only real differences among the various methods and systems lie in the valuation of inventories. That is, total fixed and variable manufacturing costs incurred in a particular period are facts that do not depend on the costing system, so the choice of a cost system does not change *actual* costs. The different techniques are simply different ways of *assigning those costs to cost of goods sold and to inventories. If a company has no inventories, every one of the various approaches will give the same income on the income statement.*

SIGHT

### Quality and Complexity

Automakers have been reducing complexity for some time, and one payoff has been increased quality and value for customers. All companies are offering more standard equipment on subcompacts. For example, **Chrysler's** steps in this direction have reduced the number of possible combinations of its Neon model from 50,564 versions to 2,792. The company's assembly costs also fell as a result of less complexity. Moreover, investment required to bring out the new Neon was $703 million, down from $1.3 billion for its predecessor. The company will soon be using the same platform to build all of its Neons.

Automakers must sell considerable numbers of subcompacts because of federal regulations on fleet gas consumption, the weighted-average consumption of all models. Failing to reach federal mandates on gas mileage carries severe penalties. Subcompacts are less profitable than other offerings and the companies hope that upgrading them will increase their sales and profitability.

*Source: Gregory L. White, "A Gussied-Up Neon: Detroit's Answer to Cheap Chic,"* The Wall Street Journal, *December 30, 1998, B1.*

Thus, managers who must use accounting reports to help them in decision making must know the basis used for those reports and must understand the effects that any given method has on those reports.

## SUMMARY

In process costing, partially completed units in work in process inventory complicate the calculation of unit costs. Equivalent production resolves this complication. Process costing, unlike job-order costing, requires a cost flow assumption (weighted-average or first-in first-out).

Manufacturing companies account for their flows of costs in several ways regardless of whether they use job-order or process costing. Such a company can use either actual or normal costing in the assignment of manufacturing overhead, or it can use standard costs. (In addition, a company could use either variable or absorption costing, but the latter is required for external reporting.)

The journal entries to record cost flows are similar for all costing systems. They are more complex when standard costs are used, because entries under standard costing isolate variances into separate accounts.

JIT operations, or others where work in process inventories are negligible or constant, can use simpler methods such as backflushing, which records far fewer transactions than conventional systems and therefore costs much less to operate.

## KEY TERMS

backflushing (or backflush costing) *(691)*

conversion costs *(679)*

equivalent unit production *(677)*

process costing *(676)*

weighted-average inventory method *(677)*

## KEY FORMULAS

$$\text{Equivalent production—weighted average} = \text{Units completed} + \left(\text{Units in ending inventory} \times \text{Percentage complete}\right)$$

$$\text{Cost per unit—weighted average} = \frac{\text{Cost of beginning inventory} + \text{Current period cost}}{\text{Equivalent unit production—weighted average}}$$

## REVIEW PROBLEM—PROCESS COSTING

Lahti Manufacturing Company makes a chemical solvent and uses weighted-average process costing. Data for February 20X8 follow.

| | |
|---|---|
| Beginning inventory of work in process | $12,000 |
| Materials used | $479,000 |
| Direct labor | $221,000 |
| Overhead | $422,000 |
| Gallons completed and sent to finished goods | 610,000 |
| Gallons in ending inventory (40% complete) | 50,000 |

### Required

1. Determine equivalent production and cost per unit.
2. Determine the cost of the ending inventory of work in process.
3. Prepare a T-account for Work in Process Inventory. Check the ending balance with your answer to requirement 2.
4. There was no inventory of finished product at the beginning of February. During February, 580,000 gallons were sold and 30,000 gallons remained in ending finished goods inventory. Determine cost of goods sold and the cost of the ending inventory of finished product.

### ANSWER TO REVIEW PROBLEM

1. Equivalent production and cost per unit.

| | |
|---|---|
| Equivalent production: | |
| Gallons completed | 610,000 |
| Equivalent production in ending inventory (50,000 × 40%) | 20,000 |
| Equivalent production for February | 630,000 |

| Cost per unit—weighted average: | |
|---|---|
| Beginning inventory of work in process | $ 12,000 |
| Costs incurred: | |
| Materials | 479,000 |
| Direct labor | 221,000 |
| Overhead | 422,000 |
| Total | $1,134,000 |
| Divided by equivalent production | 630,000 |
| Equals cost per unit | $ 1.80 |

2. Ending inventory of work in process is $36,000 (20,000 equivalent units × $1.80).
3.

| Work in Process Inventory | | | |
|---|---|---|---|
| Beginning balance | $ 12,000 | | |
| Materials | 479,000 | | |
| Direct labor | 221,000 | | |
| Overhead | 422,000 | $1,098,000 transferred out (610,000 × $1.80) | |
| | 1,134,000 | 1,098,000 | |
| Ending balance | $ 36,000 | | |

The $36,000 balance equals the answer to requirement 2.

4. Cost of goods sold is $1,044,000, 580,000 gallons multiplied by $1.80. Ending inventory of finished goods is $54,000, which is 30,000 gallons (610,000 – 580,000) multiplied by $1.80.

## REVIEW PROBLEM—STANDARD COSTING

Bryan Company, whose actual operations were accounted for in the chapter, has changed to standard costing. It developed the following standards per square yard of plywood.

| | |
|---|---|
| Materials (30 feet of wood at $0.10 per foot) | $ 3 |
| Direct labor (1 hour at $8 per hour) | 8 |
| Variable overhead ($6 per direct labor hour) | 6 |
| Fixed overhead* | 9 |
| Total standard cost | $26 |

*\* Based on budgeted fixed overhead of $450,000 and normal capacity of 50,000 square yards ($450,000/50,000 = $9 per square yard).*

### Required

1. Prepare journal entries to record the events, isolating variances at the earliest point.
2. Prepare T-accounts for Work in Process Inventory, Finished Goods Inventory, Materials Inventory, and Cost of Goods Sold at standard.
3. Prepare an income statement for the year and contrast it with the one shown in Exhibit 15-3 that uses actual costing.

**ANSWER TO REVIEW PROBLEM**

1.

| | | | |
|---|---|---|---|
| 1. | Materials Inventory (1,400,000 × $0.10) | $140,000 | |
| | Material Price Variance | | $  7,000 |
| | Cash or Accounts Payable | | 133,000 |
| 2. | Work in Process Inventory (1,260,000 × $0.10) | $126,000 | |
| | Material Use Variance | 4,000 | |
| | Materials Inventory | | $130,000 |
| 3a. | Direct Labor (41,000 × $8) | $328,000 | |
| | Direct Labor Rate Variance | 16,400 | |
| | Cash | | $344,400 |
| 3b. | Work in Process Inventory (42,000 × 1 × $8) | $336,000 | |
| | Direct Labor Efficiency Variance | | $  8,000 |
| | Direct Labor | | 328,000 |
| 4a. | Variable Manufacturing Overhead | | |
| | (41,000 hours × $6) | $246,000 | |
| | Variable Overhead Spending Variance | 5,300 | |
| | Cash, Accrued Expenses | | $251,300 |
| 4b. | Fixed Manufacturing Overhead | $450,000 | |
| | Fixed Overhead Budget Variance | 11,000 | |
| | Accumulated Depreciation | | $ 96,000 |
| | Cash, Accrued Expenses | | 365,000 |
| 5a. | Work in Process Inventory (42,000 × $6) | $252,000 | |
| | Variable Overhead Efficiency Variance | | $  6,000 |
| | Variable Manufacturing Overhead | | 246,000 |
| 5b. | Work in Process Inventory (42,000 × $9) | $378,000 | |
| | Fixed Overhead Volume Variance (8,000 × $9) | 72,000 | |
| | Fixed Manufacturing Overhead | | $450,000 |
| 6. | Finished Goods Inventory (40,000 × $26) | $1,040,000 | |
| | Work in Process Inventory | | $1,040,000 |
| 7a. | Cash or Accounts Receivable (35,000 × $40) | $1,400,000 | |
| | Sales | | $1,400,000 |
| 7b. | Cost of Goods Sold (35,000 × $26) | $910,000 | |
| | Finished Goods Inventory | | $910,000 |
| 8. | Selling and Administrative Expenses | $340,000 | |
| | Cash, Accrued Expenses | | $340,000 |

2.

| Work in Process Inventory | | | |
|---|---|---|---|
| (2) | $   126,000 | | |
| (3b) | 336,000 | | |
| (5a) | 252,000 | | |
| (5b) | 378,000 | $1,040,000 | (6) |
| | 1,092,000 | 1,040,000 | |
| Bal. | $     52,000 | | |

| Finished Goods Inventory | | | |
|---|---|---|---|
| (6) | $1,040,000 | $910,000 | (7b) |
| Bal. | $   130,000 | | |

| Materials Inventory | | | |
|---|---|---|---|
| (1) | $140,000 | $130,000 | (2) |
| Bal. | $  10,000 | | |

| Cost of Goods Sold | | |
|---|---|---|
| (7b) | $910,000 | |

3.                   Income Statements for Bryan Company

|  | Actual Costing | Standard Costing |
|---|---|---|
| Sales (7a) | $1,400,000 | $1,400,000 |
| Cost of goods sold (7b) | 983,500 | 910,000 |
| Gross profit | $ 416,500 | 490,000 |
| Manufacturing variances |  | 87,700U* |
| Gross profit |  | $ 402,300 |
| Selling and administrative expenses (8) | 340,000 | 340,000 |
| Income | $ 76,500 | $ 62,300 |

\* *The sum of variances is $87,700 unfavorable.*

## APPENDIX: PROCESS COSTING—THE FIFO METHOD

The illustration in the chapter used the weighted-average method. The other commonly used method is first-in-first-out (FIFO). Under FIFO, you calculate the cost of the current period production, not a weighted average of current period and prior period. The numerator includes only the production costs of the current period, and the denominator includes only the work done during the current period.

### ILLUSTRATION OF FIFO

To illustrate FIFO, let us return to the data used in this chapter to illustrate the weighted-average method. For your convenience, the data in Exhibit 15-1 are reproduced in Exhibit 15-6.

The company starts the month of May with no units in process. Hence, there is no need to know the cost flow assumption. FIFO gives the same result as does the weighted-average method.

The situation in June is different. In June, 70,000 units were completed and 20,000 were on hand, 40 percent complete. But of the 70,000 units completed, 10,000 units were 60 percent complete at the beginning of the period, so that the production costs for June apply to those beginning inventory units only to the extent of the 40 percent of the work done in June. Therefore, we calculate the cost of processing a unit of product in June by using only June's costs and an equivalent production figure that reflects only June's work. We already know that produc-

### Exhibit 15-6   Data for Kelco Company

|  | May | June |
|---|---|---|
| Production costs | $112,000 | $128,400 |
| Unit data: |  |  |
| Units in beginning work in process | 0 | 10,000 |
| Units completed during month | 50,000 | 70,000 |
| Units in ending work in process | 10,000 | 20,000 |
| Percentage of completion of work in process | 60% | 40% |

tion costs in June were $128,400, so the task is to calculate equivalent production related only to the June work. The easiest approach is to calculate weighted-average equivalent unit production (EUP), then subtract the work done in May. Thus, the calculation of equivalent production for June using the FIFO method follows.

| | |
|---|---:|
| Units completed in June | 70,000 |
| Work done on June work in process, 20,000 × 40% | 8,000 |
| Weighted-average equivalent production | 78,000 |
| Less work done in May on units completed in June | |
| EUP in beginning inventory, (10,000 units × 60%) | 6,000 |
| Equivalent production, FIFO | 72,000 |

We can generalize this calculation in this way.

$$\begin{array}{c} \text{Equivalent} \\ \text{production} \\ \text{—first-in} \\ \text{first-out} \end{array} = \begin{array}{c} \text{Units} \\ \text{completed} \end{array} + \left( \begin{array}{c} \text{Units in} \\ \text{ending} \\ \text{inventory} \end{array} \times \begin{array}{c} \text{Percent} \\ \text{complete} \end{array} \right) - \left( \begin{array}{c} \text{Units in} \\ \text{beginning} \\ \text{inventory} \end{array} \times \begin{array}{c} \text{Percent} \\ \text{complete} \end{array} \right)$$

Under FIFO, equivalent production reflects only work done during the current period. Thus, the calculation of FIFO unit cost uses only the production costs for the period. The formula under FIFO is as follows:

$$\text{Unit cost—FIFO} = \frac{\text{Current period production costs}}{\text{Equivalent production—FIFO}}$$

In our example, $128,400/72,000 = $1.7833.
    The reconciliation follows.

| | |
|---|---:|
| Costs of beginning inventory (10,000 units × 60% × $2) | $ 12,000 |
| Production costs for June | 128,400 |
| Total cost to be accounted for | $140,400 |

These costs either have been transferred to finished goods (for the completed units) or are associated with the units still in process. Under FIFO, the cost of the units in process at the end of the period is the unit cost for work done in June, or $1.7833 per equivalent unit. The cost assigned to the ending inventory of 20,000 units that are 40 percent complete is $14,267 (20,000 × 40% × $1.7833).
    The costs transferred to finished goods can be determined by analyzing the units transferred.

| | |
|---|---:|
| Transfer of units in process at the beginning of the month: | |
| Cost from prior period, beginning inventory | $ 12,000 |
| Completion costs (10,000 × 40% × $1.7833) | 7,133 |
| Transfer of units started and completed in June | |
| [(70,000 − 10,000) × $1.7833] rounded | 107,000 |
| Total | $126,133 |

Thus, the total cost of $140,400 can be accounted for as follows:

| | |
|---|---:|
| Costs transferred to finished goods | $126,133 |
| Costs in ending inventory | 14,267 |
| Total cost accounted for | $140,400 |

If you compare the FIFO results with the weighted-average results shown in the chapter, you will see that the unit cost for June under FIFO ($1.7833) is slightly lower than that under weighted average ($1.80). Hence, the total cost of the ending work in process under FIFO ($14,267) is slightly lower than that under weighted average ($14,400). The magnitude of the difference is a function of the illustrative data; you should not assume that the difference will always be so small.

## ADVANTAGES OF FIFO

FIFO supports a manager's interest in controlling costs. The weighted-average per-unit cost is not suitable for control purposes because it mixes performance of the current period with performance in prior periods.

Because the unit cost calculation under FIFO uses (1) equivalent production that includes only current work and (2) only the current period production costs, managers obtain performance data related to the current period, not to current and prior periods. Additionally, a processing company using standard costing must compute FIFO equivalent unit production to be able to determine variances, which depend on work done in the current period.

## ASSIGNMENT MATERIAL

### INTERNET ACTIVITY

Go to Web sites for a couple of manufacturing companies in different industries. Select one or two companies in basic industries such as autos, tires, or steel, and one or two in a newer industry such as computer chips or communications equipment. Determine the percentages that cost of goods sold bear to sales. Why do you think the percentages differ? What management strategy is implied by a low ratio of cost of sales to sales? By a high ratio?

### QUESTIONS FOR DISCUSSION

**15-1   *Dell Computer's costing methods*   Dell Computer** makes each computer to customer order, though from stock parts. That is, the company offers various combinations of disk drives, memory, monitors, etc. The company maintains less than one week's supply of parts inventory and fills orders overnight. What costing method do you think the company uses? Why does Dell strive to keep low inventories?

**15-2   *Strategic uses of overhead allocation*   Some management accountants have advocated allocating overhead using cycle times of products, the times from order to manufacture to shipment to customer, instead of labor time or machine time. Thus, products that stay in the system longer receive higher allocations than those that move through quickly. What advantages do you see in this practice? You might recall the **Tektronix** example from Chapter 10.

**15-3   *Cost of accounting systems***   Which of the following systems do you think is the costliest to operate and which is the cheapest, so far as recordkeeping costs are concerned: job-order costing, actual process costing, standard costing, backflush costing?

**15-4   *Cost/benefit of accounting system***   Following are sales, cost of goods sold, and inventory figures for **Cisco Systems**, the networking giant, and for **Lincoln Electric**, one of the world's largest manufacturers of cutting and welding equipment. All amounts in millions of dollars.

|  | Cisco Systems | Lincoln Electric |
|---|---|---|
| Sales | $6,440 | $1,159 |
| Cost of sales | 2,241 | 718 |
| Inventories | 255 | 179 |

**Required**
Given the choice between two cost systems, one very accurate but expensive, the other less accurate, but relatively cheap, which company do you think would be more likely to pick the more accurate, costlier system? Explain.

## EXERCISES

**15-5   *Basic process costing***   Golden Compost uses weighted-average process costing. The company acquires its raw materials from the local landfill and so has no material costs. The following data relate to July.

| | |
|---|---|
| Beginning inventory, 8,000 units, 70% complete | $8,200 |
| Units completed in July | 50,000 units |
| Units in ending work in process, 60% complete | 6,000 units |
| July conversion costs | $77,560 |

**Required**
1. Determine equivalent production for July.
2. Determine the unit cost.
3. Determine the cost of the ending inventory of work in process.
4. Determine the cost of goods transferred to finished goods.
5. Prepare journal entries for the month. Use the account, Conversion Costs, to record the costs incurred.

**15-6   *Job-order costing—journal entries***   Fortune Foundry, a job-order company, had the following activity in March. The company had no inventories at the beginning of the month.

(a) Used $4,960 in materials on jobs.
(b) Direct labor was $7,280.

(c) Factory overhead was $4,710.

(d) Cost of jobs finished was $12,500.

(e) Cost of jobs sold was $9,600.

**Required**

Prepare journal entries to record these events. Prepare a T-account for Work in Process Inventory.

**15-7   Basic process costing—weighted average**   The following data relate to the operations of Walton Milling, Inc. for March. The company puts materials, labor, and overhead into process evenly throughout.

| | |
|---|---|
| Beginning inventory, (15,000 units, 20% complete) | $6,600 |
| Units completed in March | 80,000 units |
| Ending inventory, 40% complete | 10,000 units |

Production costs incurred in March were $291,600. The company uses the weighted-average method.

**Required**

1. Compute equivalent production.
2. Compute unit cost.
3. Compute the cost of the ending inventory.
4. Compute the cost of units finished and transferred to finished goods inventory.

**15-8   Basic process costing—FIFO (continuation of 15-7, related to Appendix)**   Redo the previous assignment using the first-in first-out method.

**15-9   Journal entries (continuation of 15-7)**   Additional information about Walton's March operations follows.

| | |
|---|---|
| Materials purchases, on account | $71,000 |
| Materials use | $55,000 |
| Conversion costs: | |
| Direct labor | $54,500 |
| Overhead | $182,100 |

**Required**

Prepare journal entries to account for Walton's March operations using the weighted-average method and show a T-account for Work in Process Inventory.

**15-10   Journal entries (continuation of 15-8 and 15-9)**   Refer to 15-8 and to the additional information in 15-9.

**Required**

Prepare journal entries to account for Walton's March operations using FIFO and show a T-account for Work in Process Inventory.

**15-11   Relationships—income, production, and volume variance**   Hoskin, Inc. sells a single product at $40 per unit. There are no variable manufacturing costs, and fixed manufacturing costs are budgeted at $600,000. In 20X5 the company had a standard gross profit of $320,000 and income of $190,000 on sales of 20,000 units. Selling and administrative expenses were $112,000, and fixed manufacturing costs were incurred as budgeted.

**Required**
1. Compute the standard fixed cost per unit.
2. Compute the volume variance for 20X5.
3. Determine how many units were produced in 20X5.
4. Determine what income Hoskin would have earned using variable costing.

**15-12  Relationships—income, sales, and volume variance**  In 20X3, Bishop Company sold 98,000 units of product. Variable cost per unit was $4, both standard and actual. Standard fixed manufacturing cost per unit is $10 and selling and administrative expenses were $250,000. Fixed manufacturing costs were incurred as budgeted. Income for 20X3 was $172,000 after considering a favorable volume variance of $30,000. Beginning and ending inventories were the same.

**Required**
1. Determine the selling price of a unit of product.
2. Determine the level of volume used to set the standard fixed cost per unit.
3. Determine budgeted fixed manufacturing costs.

**15-13  Process costing—T-account**  Valley Manufacturing Company uses a process costing system. The following data apply to July 20X9. Percentages of completion are the same for materials and for conversion costs.

| | |
|---|---:|
| Units: | |
| Beginning inventory, 20% complete | 10,000 |
| Finished during July | 45,000 |
| Ending inventory, 60% complete | 5,000 |
| Production costs: | |
| Cost in beginning inventory | $26,600 |
| Incurred during July | $943,000 |

**Required**
1. Compute the cost per unit of the units finished during the period, using the weighted-average method.
2. Compute the amount of ending work in process inventory and transfers to finished goods.
3. Prepare a T-account for Work in Process Inventory.

**15-14  Process costing (continuation of 15-13, related to Appendix)**  Redo 15-13, using the first-in first-out method.

**15-15  Backflush costing**  Timmins Company has completed the transition to just-in-time manufacturing and is attempting to simplify its recordkeeping. The controller has given you the following data for January and asked what is the simplest, most direct way to record the events.

| | |
|---|---:|
| Beginning inventories | None |
| Units finished | 100,000 |
| Units sold | 90,000 |
| Materials purchased and used | $410,000 |
| Direct labor and manufacturing overhead | $350,000 |

There was no ending inventory of materials or of work in process.

**Required**
Determine ending inventory and cost of goods sold.

**15-16   Backflush costing, journal entries (continuation of 15-15)**

**Required**
Prepare journal entries for Timmins Company's January activity.

**15-17   Backflush costing with standards (continuation of 15-15)**   Suppose that Timmins uses the following standard costs.

| | |
|---|---|
| Materials | $4.00 |
| Direct labor and overhead | 3.20 |
| Total standard cost | $7.20 |

**Required**
Repeat Exercise 15-15 using standard costs to value inventory. Show variances as adjustments to standard cost of sales.

**15-18   Process costing—two departments**   The Westminister Plant of Byron Chemicals makes an industrial cleaner called Argot. The product requires two processes, mixing and distilling. The following data apply to May 20X7. There were no beginning inventories. Percentages of completion are the same for materials and for conversion costs.

| | Mixing | Distilling |
|---|---|---|
| Barrels completed during May | 80,000 | 80,000 |
| Barrels on hand at May 31, 60% complete | 9,000 | 0 |
| Production costs incurred | $25,620 | $60,000 |

**Required**
1. Compute the cost per barrel for each process.
2. Compute the amount of ending work in process inventory in the Mixing Department.
3. The company had no finished product on hand at the beginning of May. Of the 80,000 gallons finished during May, 65,000 were sold. Compute cost of goods sold and ending inventory of finished goods.

**15-19   Process costing**   Hittite Company makes a water-soluble paint. All materials are put into process and are then mixed for several hours. Data for July follow.

| | |
|---|---|
| Unit data: | |
|     Gallons completed in July | 180,000 |
|     Gallons in ending inventory | 30,000 |
|     Percentage complete: | |
|       Materials | 100% |
|       Conversion costs | 80% |

Cost data:

|  | Materials | Conversion Costs |
|---|---|---|
| Beginning inventory | $3,240 | $9,620 |
| Incurred during July | $42,960 | $127,060 |

### Required

1. Using the weighted-average method, compute equivalent production for (a) materials and (b) conversion costs for the month of July.
2. Compute unit costs for each cost factor using the weighted-average method.
3. Prepare the journal entry to transfer the cost of finished gallons to Finished Goods Inventory.
4. Prepare a T-account for Work in Process Inventory.
5. Prove that your ending balance in Work in Process, from requirement 4, is correct.

## PROBLEMS

**15-20   Equivalent production and unit costs**   VanDoerr Company manufactures fertilizer in a single process. Data for April are as follows:

| | |
|---|---|
| Beginning inventory of work in process | 5,000 pounds |
| Completed in April | 150,000 pounds |
| Ending inventory of work in process | 20,000 pounds |
| Cost of materials used in production | $366,150 |
| Conversion costs incurred | $571,900 |
| Costs in beginning inventory: | |
| Materials | $14,650 |
| Conversion costs | $19,400 |

The inventories were 100% complete for materials. The beginning inventory was 75% complete for conversion costs, and the ending inventory was 60% complete. VanDoerr uses the weighted-average method.

### Required

1. Determine equivalent production for materials and for conversion costs.
2. Determine unit costs for materials and for conversion costs.
3. Determine the cost of the ending inventory of work in process and the cost transferred to finished goods inventory.

**15-21   Equivalent units and standard costs (related to Appendix)**   The production manager of Knox Company has just received his performance report for June 20X1. Among the data included are the following:

| | Costs | | |
|---|---|---|---|
| | Budget | Actual | Variance |
| Materials | $10,000 | $11,400 | $1,400U |
| Direct labor | 20,000 | 21,500 | 1,500U |
| Variable overhead | 15,000 | 15,400 | 400U |
| Fixed overhead | 18,000 | 18,800 | 800U |
| Total | $63,000 | $67,100 | $4,100U |

The budgeted amounts are based on 2,000 units, the number actually completed during June. The production manager is upset because 600 units 75% complete are still in process at the end of June and are not counted as part of production for the month. However, at the beginning of June, 300 units were one-half complete.

**Required**

1. Compute equivalent unit production on a first-in first-out basis.
2. Prepare a new performance report.

**15-22 *Costing methods and pricing*** The sales manager and the controller of Emerson Company were discussing the price to be set for a new product. They had accumulated the following data.

| | |
|---|---|
| Variable costs | $8 per unit |
| Fixed costs | $160,000 per year |

The sales manager had set a target volume of 20,000 units per year. He determined average fixed cost to be $8 per unit, bringing average total cost per unit to $16. The company follows a policy of setting prices at 200% of cost, so the sales manager stated that the price should be $32 per unit.

The controller said that $32 seemed high, especially as competitors were charging only $30 for essentially the same product. The sales manager agreed, stating that perhaps only 18,000 units per year could be sold at $32. However, he was convinced that the price should be set at 200% of cost. He added that it was unfortunate that fixed costs were so high, because he thought that 20,000 units could definitely be sold if the price were $30, and probably 24,000 at $28. However, it would not be possible to achieve the desired markup at those prices.

**Required**

1. Point out the fallacies in the reasoning of the sales manager. (You might wish to show what would happen at the $32 price. Would the company achieve the desired markup?)
2. Determine which price ($32, $30, $28) will give the highest profit.

**15-23 *Overhead rates, standard cost income statement*** The following data pertain to the operations of Dickson Company for 20X5.

| | |
|---|---|
| Budgeted production | 100,000 units |
| Actual production | 90,000 units |
| Budgeted costs for 100,000 units: | |
| Materials | $400,000 |
| Direct labor | $300,000 |
| Variable overhead | $200,000 |
| Fixed overhead | $300,000 |
| Actual costs: | |
| Materials | $350,000 |
| Direct labor | $280,000 |
| Variable overhead | $190,000 |
| Fixed overhead | $320,000 |
| Administrative | $400,000 |
| Actual sales (80,000 units) | $1,600,000 |

There were no beginning inventories. Dickson uses a standard fixed cost based on budgeted production.

**Required**

Prepare a standard cost income statement. Show variances separately for each category of manufacturing cost.

**15-24  Standard cost system—journal entries**  Watson Company makes a single product. Its standard cost is as follows:

| | |
|---|---:|
| Materials (2 pounds at $4) | $ 8 |
| Direct labor (3 hours at $10) | 30 |
| Variable overhead ($6 per direct labor hour) | 18 |
| Fixed overhead (based on normal capacity of 50,000 units) | 10 |
| Total standard cost | $66 |

At the beginning of 20X9 there were no inventories. During 20X9 the following events occurred.

(a) Materials purchases were 120,000 pounds for $455,000.
(b) Direct laborers were paid $1,490,000 for 151,000 hours of work.
(c) Variable overhead of $895,000 was incurred.
(d) Fixed overhead incurred was $490,000.
(e) Materials used were 95,000 pounds.
(f) Production was 48,000 units. All units started were finished.
(g) Sales were 45,000 units at $100 each.

**Required**

Prepare journal entries to record these events. Isolate variances as early as possible.

**15-25  Process costing—journal entries**  Swanson Company makes a single type of pump on an assembly line. The company uses process costing and applies manufacturing overhead at the rate of $12 per direct labor hour. Inventories at the beginning of 20X6 were as follows:

| | |
|---|---:|
| Raw materials | $ 34,000 |
| Work in process | 67,000 |
| Finished goods | 125,000 |

During 20X6 the following transactions took place.

(a) Materials purchases were $286,000.
(b) Wages earned by direct laborers for 35,000 hours were $289,000.
(c) Raw materials costing $271,000 were put into process.
(d) Other manufacturing costs incurred were
  (1) Indirect labor, $46,000
  (2) Supervision and other salaries, $182,000
  (3) Utilities and insurance, $23,500
  (4) Depreciation, $72,000
  (5) Other miscellaneous costs, $112,000
(e) Transfers from Work in Process to Finished Goods were $863,000.
(f) Sales were $1,314,000.
(g) Cost of goods sold was $818,000.
(h) Selling and administrative expenses were $387,000.

**Required**

1. Prepare journal entries to record these events.

2. Determine the ending balance in each inventory account.
3. Prepare an income statement for 20X6.

**15-26   Product costing and CVP analysis**   The president of Landry Company asked for your assistance in analyzing the firm's revenue and cost behavior. You gathered the following data relating to the firm's only product.

| | | |
|---|---|---|
| Selling price | | $10 |
| Variable costs: | | |
| Production | $4 | |
| Selling | 2 | 6 |
| Contribution margin | | $ 4 |
| Fixed production costs | $120,000 per month | |
| Fixed selling and administrative expenses | $30,000 per month | |

You calculated the monthly break-even point as 37,500 units and the monthly sales required to earn the president's $8,000 target profit as 39,500 units.

Three months after you provided the analysis, the president called you. On your arrival at her office she gave you the following income statements.

| | April | May | June |
|---|---|---|---|
| Sales | $380,000 | $395,000 | $420,000 |
| Cost of goods sold | 243,200 | 269,300 | 316,125 |
| Gross profit | $136,800 | $125,700 | $103,875 |
| Selling and administrative costs | 106,000 | 109,000 | 114,000 |
| Profit (loss) before taxes | $ 30,800 | $ 16,700 | $ (10,125) |

The president is extremely upset. She asks why your analysis did not work, particularly because the production manager assured her that variable costs per unit and fixed costs in total were incurred as budgeted during the three months. The sales manager has also assured the president that selling prices were as expected.

After a few minutes you talk to the controller, who tells you the company uses actual absorption costing and produced the following quantities of product during the three months: April, 50,000 units; May, 40,000 units; June, 32,000 units. There were no inventories on hand at the beginning of April.

**Required**
Explain the results to the president. Show calculations of the determination of cost of goods sold for each month.

**15-27   Process costing**   Stockton Company makes a chemical spray that goes through two processes. Data for February are as follows:

| | Mixing Department | Boiling Department |
|---|---|---|
| Gallons transferred to Boiling Department | 75,000 | |
| Gallons transferred to finished goods | | 68,000 |
| Gallons on hand at end of month | 9,000 | 15,000 |
| Percent complete: | | |
| Prior department costs | — | 100% |
| Materials | 100% | —[a] |
| Labor and overhead | 60% | 40% |

|  | Mixing Department | Boiling Department |
|---|---|---|
| Costs incurred during February: | | |
| Materials | $18,480 | — |
| Labor and overhead | $32,160 | $25,900 |
| Beginning inventories: | | |
| Gallons | 8,000 | 8,000 |
| Costs: | | |
| Materials | $1,680 | — |
| Prior department costs | — | $6,350 |
| Labor and overhead | $4,020 | $2,220 |

*a  No material is added in this department.*

### Required

1. Determine the weighted-average equivalent production by cost category for each department.
2. Determine the per-unit cost by cost category for the Mixing Department.
3. Prepare the journal entry to record the transfer from the Mixing Department to the Boiling Department.
4. Determine the per-unit cost by cost category for the Boiling Department.
5. Prepare the journal entry to record the transfer of product from the Boiling Department to Finished Goods.
6. Prepare the T-accounts for Work in Process Inventory for each department. Verify the ending inventory balances.

**15-28  *Process costing (continuation of 15-27, related to Appendix)*** Assume that Stockton Company uses FIFO and that the beginning inventory in the Mixing Department was 60% complete as to materials and 70% complete as to conversion costs.

### Required

1. Determine the FIFO equivalent production by cost category for the Mixing Department and the unit cost for each category.
2. Determine the total cost to be transferred to the Boiling Department.
3. Prepare a T-account for Work in Process in the Mixing Department and verify the ending inventory balance.

**15-29  *Standard costs—performance evaluation*** Arnold Company is opening a new division to make and sell a single product. The product is to be made in a factory with practical capacity of 150,000 units. Production is expected to average 120,000 units after the first two years of operation. During the first two years, sales are expected to be 80,000 and 100,000, respectively, with production being 100,000 and 110,000 in those years.

The product is to sell for $20, with standard variable manufacturing costs of $8. Fixed production costs are expected to be $360,000 annually for the first several years. Selling and administrative costs, all fixed, are budgeted at $300,000 annually.

Dee Yost, controller of Arnold Company, has suggested that the normal capacity of 120,000 units be used to set the standard fixed cost per unit. The other managers agree that Yost's idea is sound, and Bill Van Der Meer, the controller of the new division, is given the task of developing budgeted income statements based on the data given.

The operations of the first year are summarized as follows:

| Sales (77,000 units) | $1,540,000 |
|---|---|
| Production | 118,000 units |
| Costs incurred: | |
| Variable production costs | $954,000 |
| Fixed production costs | $370,000 |
| Selling and administrative expenses | $300,000 |

**Required**

1. Prepare a budgeted income statement based on the expected results in the first year of operations.
2. Prepare an income statement based on actual results.
3. Comment on the results. Was performance better than expected or worse? Explain.

**15-30   Standard cost income statement—relationships and variances**   The income statement for Rider Company for 20X6 follows.

| Sales (200,000 units) | | | $2,000,000 |
|---|---|---|---|
| Cost of sales: | | | |
| Materials | $300,000 | | |
| Direct labor | 400,000 | | |
| Overhead | 600,000 | 1,300,000 | |
| Standard gross profit | | | $ 700,000 |
| Manufacturing variances: | | | |
| Materials | $ 12,000U | | |
| Direct labor | 18,000F | | |
| Variable overhead spending | 4,000U | | |
| Variable overhead efficiency | 8,000F | | |
| Fixed overhead budget | 7,000F | | |
| Other underabsorbed overhead | 20,000U | 3,000U | |
| Actual gross profit | | | $ 697,000 |
| Selling and administrative expenses | | | 600,000 |
| Income | | | $ 97,000 |

Other data are as follows:

(a) There were no beginning inventories.
(b) Fixed overhead absorbed per unit is $2, based on budgeted production of 200,000 units and budgeted fixed costs of $500,000.
(c) The standard direct labor rate is $4 per hour.
(d) Variable overhead standard cost is based on a rate of $2 per direct labor hour.
(e) Direct laborers worked 116,000 hours.
(f) The standard price for materials is $0.50 per pound.
(g) Materials purchases were 800,000 pounds at $3,000 over standard price.

**Required**

Determine the following:

1. Standard cost per unit, including standard prices and quantities for each element of cost.

2. Standard variable cost per unit.
3. Production for the year.
4. Ending inventory at standard cost.
5. Fixed overhead costs incurred.
6. Cost of materials purchased.
7. Material use variance.
8. Pounds of materials used in production.
9. Direct labor efficiency variance.
10. Direct labor rate variance.
11. Direct labor costs incurred.
12. Variable overhead costs incurred.
13. Amount by which income would have increased if one more unit had been sold, no more produced.
14. Amount by which income would have increased had one more unit been produced and sold.

**15-31  Interpretation of standard cost statement**  The following income statement represents the operations of c-Trin Company for June. Variable manufacturing costs at standard are 50% of total standard manufacturing cost. Standard fixed cost per unit is based on normal activity of 30,000 units per month.

c-Trin Company
Income Statement for June 20X4

| | | |
|---|---:|---:|
| Sales (20,000 units) | | $200,000 |
| Standard cost of sales | | 120,000 |
| Standard gross profit | | $ 80,000 |
| Manufacturing variances: | | |
| Materials | $2,000U | |
| Direct labor | 1,000F | |
| Overhead budget | 1,000U | 2,000U |
| | | $ 78,000 |
| Volume variance | | 24,000U |
| Gross profit, actual | | $ 54,000 |
| Selling and administrative costs | | 48,000 |
| Income | | $  6,000 |

**Required**
Answer the following questions.

1. What are fixed and variable standard costs per unit?
2. What are monthly fixed manufacturing costs?
3. How many units were produced in June?
4. If beginning inventory of finished goods was $60,000 at standard cost, how much is ending inventory at standard cost? (Hint: Prepare an expanded cost of goods sold section.)

**15-32  Income statement for standard costing, practical capacity (continuation of 15-31)**  Assume the same facts as in problem 15-31, except for the following.

(a) Production is 22,000 units.
(b) Total fixed production costs are $90,000.
(c) c-Trin bases its standard fixed cost per unit on its practical capacity of 40,000 units per month.
(d) There were no beginning inventories.

**Required**

Prepare a new income statement. (Hint: The standard fixed cost per unit will not be the same as in 15-31.)

**15-33   Standard costs, budgets, variances, journal entries**   The following data relate to the operations of Warner Company for 20X2.

| | |
|---|---|
| Budgeted sales (100,000 units) | $1,000,000 |
| Budgeted production | 140,000 units |
| Budgeted costs: | |
| Materials (2 pounds per unit) | $210,000 |
| Direct labor (1 hour per unit) | $420,000 |
| Variable overhead ($1 per direct labor hour) | $140,000 |
| Fixed overhead—manufacturing | $300,000 |
| Selling and administrative (all fixed) | $180,000 |

The company uses a standard cost system; the preceding production costs are based on standard cost per unit. Standard fixed cost per unit is based on 150,000 units of production at practical capacity. The inventory of finished goods at December 31, 20X1, is 13,000 units. There were no other inventories at December 31, 20X1.

Actual results for 20X2 follow:

| | |
|---|---|
| Sales (95,000 units) | $950,000 |
| Production | 130,000 units |
| Materials purchased (250,000 pounds) | $192,500 |
| Materials used | 236,000 pounds |
| Direct labor (133,000 hours) | $402,000 |
| Variable overhead | $128,000 |
| Fixed overhead | $285,000 |
| Selling and administrative expenses | $175,000 |

**Required**

1. Prepare a budgeted income statement for 20X2.
2. Prepare all necessary journal entries to record events in 20X2. The production manager is responsible for all variances except material price and labor rate.
3. Prepare an income statement for 20X2.

**15-34   Actual process costing, journal entries, and income statement**   Pawtucket Manufacturing uses actual process costing. The following data relate to its operations in July 20X7. There were no beginning inventories.

(a) Materials purchases were $39,600 for 12,000 pounds ($3.30 per pound).
(b) Payments to direct laborers were $28,850 for 1,700 hours of work.
(c) Variable overhead costs incurred were $15,690.
(d) Fixed overhead costs incurred were $23,500.
(e) Materials use was 11,000 pounds.
(f) Units completed totaled 7,200. At the end of July 20X7, units in process totaled 500 and were 40% complete.
(g) Sales were 6,500 units at $50 per unit.
(h) Selling and administrative expenses were $106,000.

**Required**

1. Prepare journal entries for July.
2. Prepare an income statement for July.

**15-35   Standard process costing, journal entries, and income statement (continuation of 15-34)**   The president of Pawtucket needs your assistance. She wants to know whether her company could use standard costing and how it works. She believes that the following standards are appropriate.

| | |
|---|---:|
| Materials (1.5 pounds at $3.20) | $ 4.80 |
| Direct labor (0.25 hour at $16) | 4.00 |
| Variable overhead at $8 per direct labor hour | 2.00 |
| Fixed overhead at $12 per direct labor hour | 3.00 |
| Total standard cost | $13.80 |

The president tells you that the $12 fixed overhead rate is based on normal capacity of 2,000 direct labor hours per month.

**Required**
1. Prepare journal entries for July using standard process costing.
2. Prepare an income statement for July using standard process costing.

**15-36   Special order**   Western Corn Oil Company has found that its sales forecast for 20X6 was too high by about 40,000 cases of oil. Because the production budget was not revised, inventory is expected to be about 40,000 cases above normal at year end. In early December the sales manager was offered the opportunity to sell 25,000 cases at $4.80, well below the normal price of $8. Regular sales would not be affected by the order. He asked the controller for an analysis of the order and was given the following partial income statement. The controller said that because general and administrative expenses would not be affected, it was only necessary to determine the effect on gross profit.

Expected Income Statements

| | Without Order | With Order |
|---|---:|---:|
| Sales | $2,400,000 | $2,520,000 |
| Standard costs of sales, $6 per case | 1,800,000 | 1,950,000 |
| Standard gross profit | $ 600,000 | $ 570,000 |
| Volume variance | (120,000) | (120,000) |
| Actual gross profit | $ 480,000 | $ 450,000 |

The sales manager was puzzled and asked the controller about the volume variance. The controller replied that the volume variance related to production, not sales, and that production would not be increased because inventory was already too high. She said that the volume variance resulted because the company used 400,000 cases on which to base the standard fixed cost, and actual production was expected to be only 340,000 cases.

**Required**
1. Determine whether the order should be accepted.
2. Prepare new partial income statements, using variable costing.
3. Prepare a new partial income statement assuming that production would be increased by 25,000 cases if the order were accepted.

**15-37 Job-order costing—standards and variances** Carlson Company makes a variety of furniture. The company has established the following standard variable costs for some of its high-volume models.

| | Chair<br>Model 803 | Sofa<br>Model 407 |
|---|---|---|
| Materials: | | |
| Wood | $ 24 | $ 58 |
| Fabric | 46 | 92 |
| Other | 13 | 21 |
| Total materials | $ 83 | $171 |
| Direct labor at $5 standard rate per hour | 65 | 90 |
| Variable overhead at $8 per direct labor hour | 104 | 144 |
| Total standard variable cost | $252 | $405 |

During June the company worked on two jobs. Order 82 was for 80 units of Model 803, and order 83 was for 50 units of Model 407. Both jobs were finished and sold for a total of $97,000.

Cost data are as follows:

| | |
|---|---|
| Materials used, at standard prices: | |
| Wood | $ 4,855 |
| Fabric | 8,360 |
| Other | 2,090 |
| Direct labor (2,050 hours × $5 per hour) | 10,250 |
| Variable overhead incurred | 16,850 |

Fixed production costs were incurred as budgeted, $24,600. Selling and administrative expenses were $18,700. There were no material price variances.

**Required**

1. Determine the standard cost of each job order, by individual cost category.
2. Determine the following variances: material use, by type of material; direct labor efficiency; variable overhead spending; variable overhead efficiency.
3. Prepare an income statement for June using standard variable costing. Show the variances calculated in requirement 2 as a lump sum.

**15-38 Comprehensive problem on costing methods** The following data relate to Gagner Company operations for 20X5.

| | Budgeted | Actual |
|---|---|---|
| Production (units) | 200,000 | 180,000 |
| Sales (units) | 190,000 | 160,000 |
| Direct materials | $400,000 | $375,000 |
| Direct labor | $600,000 | $580,000 |
| Variable overhead | $400,000 | $395,000 |
| Fixed overhead | $200,000 | $208,000 |
| Selling and administrative expenses | $700,000 | $700,000 |

There were no beginning inventories; sales prices averaged $15 per unit; practical capacity is 250,000 units.

**Required**
1. Prepare income statements based on the following costing methods:
   (a) actual absorption costing.
   (b) standard absorption costing—fixed overhead based on budgeted production (show the total variance for each element of cost).
   (c) standard absorption costing using practical capacity as the fixed overhead allocation base.
   (d) standard variable costing.
   (e) actual variable costing.
2. Compare and contrast the results obtained in requirement 1.

**15-39 Comprehensive problem on costing methods (continuation of 15-38)** Gagner Company now has data regarding operations for 20X6, during which selling prices again averaged $15 per unit. The following data relate to 20X6 activity.

|  | Budgeted | Actual |
|---|---|---|
| Production (units) | 150,000 | 190,000 |
| Sales (units) | 140,000 | 200,000 |
| Direct materials | $300,000 | $400,000 |
| Direct labor | $450,000 | $590,000 |
| Variable manufacturing overhead | $300,000 | $410,000 |
| Fixed manufacturing overhead | $200,000 | $215,000 |
| Selling and administrative expenses | $700,000 | $720,000 |

**Required**
Prepare income statements for 20X6, using each of the methods listed in the previous assignment.

**15-40 Standard costs and product profitability** Tucumcary Office Products Company makes three sizes of file folders. The company has practical capacity of 50,000 machine hours per year and uses that figure to set standard fixed costs for each size of folder. At the beginning of 20X6 the controller had prepared the following data regarding the three sizes of folders (all data per carton of 50 folders).

|  | Two-Inch | Three-Inch | Four-Inch |
|---|---|---|---|
| Selling price | $17.00 | $24.00 | $31.00 |
| Standard variable costs | $ 8.00 | $11.00 | $16.00 |
| Standard fixed costs | 4.80 | 6.40 | 9.60 |
| Total standard cost | $12.80 | $17.40 | $25.60 |
| Standard gross profit | $ 4.20 | $ 6.60 | $ 5.40 |
| Expected sales in cartons | 44,000 | 25,000 | 30,000 |
| Machine hours required per carton | 0.3 | 0.4 | 0.6 |

The sales manager has informed the controller that he has been approached by a large office supplies chain. The chain wants to buy 24,000 cartons of a six-inch folder and is willing to pay $40 per carton. The sales manager discussed the offer with the production manager, who stated that the folders could be made using the existing equipment. Variable costs per carton should be $19, and 0.8 machine hours should be required per carton.

Because the chain will take not fewer than 24,000 cartons, the sales manager was fairly sure that the company did not have the capacity to fill the special order and still manufacture its other products in the volumes required by the expected sales. He therefore asked the controller to develop data on the proposed order and to decide which of the existing products should be partially curtailed. The controller then prepared the following analysis, which is incomplete because he was called away before finishing it. The sales manager was not sure how to proceed from this point and asked you to help him make the decision.

|  | Six-Inch Folder |
| --- | --- |
| Selling price | $40.00 |
| Standard variable cost | $19.00 |
| Standard fixed cost | 12.80 |
| Total standard cost | $31.80 |
| Standard gross profit | $ 8.20 |

The controller also prepared the following analysis of budgeted profit for the year.

|  | Two-Inch | Three-Inch | Four-Inch | Total |
| --- | --- | --- | --- | --- |
| Standard gross profit per carton | $  4.20 | $  6.60 | $  5.40 | |
| Expected volume | × 44,000 | × 25,000 | × 30,000 | |
| Expected gross profit—standard | $184,800 | $165,000 | $162,000 | $511,800 |
| Expected volume variance | | | | 140,800 |
| Expected actual gross profit | | | | $371,000 |
| Budgeted selling and administrative expenses, all fixed | | | | 327,000 |
| Budgeted profit before taxes | | | | $ 44,000 |

The company generally manufactures about as many cartons of each size of folder as it sells. Because it rarely experiences differences between standard and actual machine hours for given levels of production, it computes its volume variance based on the difference between 50,000 hours and actual hours worked.

**Required**

Prepare an analysis for the sales manager showing him whether the special order should be accepted and for which products, if any, production and sales should be reduced.

**15-41   *Review problem***   Sally Ann Frocks is a manufacturer of dresses. Its relevant range is 1,500 to 5,000 dresses per month. For the month of May 20X5, it has prepared the following forecast.

---

Sales, 2,500 dresses @ $30 each
Variable manufacturing costs per dress:
  Materials, 3 yards @ $2 per yard
  Direct labor, 2 hours @ $0.50 per hour
  Variable overhead, $1 per DLH
Fixed manufacturing overhead, $3,000
Variable selling expenses, commissions at 10% of sales
Fixed selling and administrative costs, $6,000
Inventories:
  May 1, 20X5 none
  May 31, 20X5 materials, 500 yards; finished dresses, 500

---

Normal capacity is 3,000 dresses per month, which is the basis for overhead application.

**Required**

Answer the following questions.

1. What is practical capacity?
2. What is budgeted production for May?
3. How many yards of materials should be purchased during May?
4. How many hours does it take to produce a dress?
5. What are total variable manufacturing costs per dress?
6. What are total manufacturing costs per dress?
7. What is contribution margin per dress?
8. What is the cost per dress if variable costing is used?
9. What is the cost per dress if actual absorption costing is used?
10. What is the cost to produce one additional dress?
11. What is the cost to produce and sell an additional dress?
12. What is the predetermined fixed overhead rate per direct labor hour?
13. What are total budgeted manufacturing costs for May?
14. Give a formula for total manufacturing costs in the range of 1,500 to 5,000 dresses per month.
15. What would the predetermined fixed overhead rate be per direct labor hour if practical capacity were used as the base?
16. What is budgeted income for May?
17. What is the break-even point in dresses?
18. By how much could budgeted sales fall before a loss was incurred?
19. By how much would income increase for each unit sold above budgeted volume?

**15-42  Process costing, second department (continuation of 15-27 and 15-28, related to Appendix)**  The beginning inventory in the Boiling Department of Stockton Company was 50% complete as to conversion costs.

**Required**

Using the data from Problems 15-27 and 15-28 and the above information, do the following.

1. Determine the FIFO equivalent production for conversion costs in the Boiling Department and the per-unit conversion cost.
2. Determine the total cost to be transferred from the Boiling Department to Finished Goods Inventory
3. Prepare a T-account for Work in Process Inventory in the Boiling Department and verify the ending inventory balance.

**15-43  Review of Chapters 12, 13, 14, and 15**  ARC Industries makes fiberglass insulation, selling it for $20 per roll. The standard variable cost per roll is as follows:

| | |
|---|---|
| Materials (25 pounds at $0.20 per pound) | $5 |
| Direct labor (0.20 hour at $10 per hour) | 2 |
| Variable overhead at $5 per direct labor hour | 1 |
| Total standard variable cost per roll | $8 |

Budgeted fixed production costs are $1,500,000 per year.
ARC began 20X3 with no inventories. Actual results for 20X3 follow.

| Sales (230,000 rolls) | $4,600,000 |
| Production | 260,000 rolls |
| Production costs: | |
|    Materials purchased (7,000,000 pounds) | $1,425,000 |
|    Materials used | 6,450,000 pounds |
|    Direct labor (53,000 hours) | $520,000 |
|    Variable manufacturing overhead | $270,000 |
|    Fixed production overhead | $1,480,000 |
| Selling and administrative costs, all fixed | $800,000 |

The company uses actual absorption costing for most purposes, though it has established standard variable production costs. The treasurer wants to see how standard costing works for income determination and asks you to prepare income statements using the two approaches. One statement is to be a standard variable costing statement, the other a standard absorption costing statement, with 250,000 rolls used to set the standard fixed cost.

**Required**

1. Determine all variances from standard costs, including the fixed overhead budget and volume variances.
2. Prepare the income statements that the treasurer requested. On each, show the variances as a lump sum subtracted from the standard gross margin or contribution margin.

**15-44    Review of Chapters 12, 13, 14, and 15 (continuation of 15-43)**    During 20X4, ARC Industries produced 240,000 rolls and sold 250,000. The same standards and budgets in effect in 20X3 applied to 20X4, and the selling price remained at $20 per roll. Actual costs follow.

| Materials purchased (6,200,000 pounds) | $1,210,000 |
| Materials used | 5,900,000 pounds |
| Direct labor (47,000 hours) | $475,000 |
| Variable overhead | $240,000 |
| Fixed production overhead | $1,510,000 |
| Selling and administrative costs | $810,000 |

**Required**

Prepare income statements using the same bases as for Problem 15-43. Again, calculate all variances and show the appropriate total as a lump sum on each statement.

## CASES

**15-45    Unit costs (CMA adapted)**    Wood Glow Manufacturing Co. produces a single product, a wood refinishing kit that sells for $17.95. The final processing of the kits occurs in the Packaging Department. An internal quilted wrap is applied at the beginning of the packaging process. A compartmented outside box printed with instructions and the company's name and logo is added when units are 60% through the process. Conversion costs, consisting of direct labor and applied overhead, occur evenly throughout the packaging process. Conversion activities after the addition of the box involve package sealing, testing for leakage, and final inspection. The following data pertain to the activities of the Packaging Department during the month of October.

| | |
|---|---|
| Beginning work in process inventory | 10,000 units, 40% complete |
| Units started and completed in October | 30,000 units |
| Ending work in process | 10,000 units, 80% complete |

The Packaging Department's October costs were as follows:

| | |
|---|---|
| Quilted wrap | $80,000 |
| Outside boxes | 50,000 |
| Direct labor | 22,000 |
| Applied overhead | 66,000 ($3.00/per direct labor dollar) |

Costs transferred in from prior processing were $3.00 per unit. Cost of goods sold for the month was $240,000, and the ending finished goods inventory was $84,000. Wood Glow uses the first-in first-out method of inventory valuation. Wood Glow's controller, Mark Brandon, has been asked to analyze the activities of the Packaging Department for the month of October. Brandon knows that in order to properly determine the department's unit cost of production, he must first calculate the equivalent units of production.

### Required

1. Determine equivalent units of production for the October activity in the Packaging Department. Be sure to account for the beginning work in process inventory, the units started and completed during the month, and the ending work in process inventory.
2. Determine the cost per equivalent unit of the October production.
3. Actual overhead incurred during October was $5,000 more than the overhead applied. Describe two ways the company could account for this amount.

**15-46  Cost of rejected units**   Pacific Compressors manufactures a variety of industrial equipment, but its Redwood Plant specializes in a single type of valve. The company uses the following standard variable costs.

| | |
|---|---|
| Materials | $22 |
| Conversion costs at $18 per machine hour | 36 |
| Total standard cost | $58 |

During March the plant produced 20,000 units, of which 19,000 passed inspection. The remaining 1,000 were scrapped. The variance report showed the following. The figures shown for "actual cost" are actual quantities at standard rates, so all variances are efficiency variances.

| | Actual Cost | Standard Cost | Variance |
|---|---|---|---|
| Materials | $ 451,000 | $ 418,000 | $33,000U |
| Conversion costs | 712,000 | 684,000 | 28,000U |
| Totals | $1,163,000 | $1,102,000 | $61,000U |

The production manager and controller had never been satisfied with the variance report because a manager could not tell from the report whether variances related to efficiency or to rejected units.

**Required**

1. How many units were used in calculating the total standard costs for March?
2. Devise a variance analysis that shows separately the cost of rejected units and the efficiency or inefficiency with which the plant operated. How does your analysis improve matters?

# Part Five

# special topics

The last part of this book covers three topics that are often treated in managerial accounting courses, but that are also frequently included as parts of other courses. Chapter 16 introduces several quantitative decision-making techniques that are commonly employed in approaching real-world problems. Chapter 17 covers the cash flow statement. Chapter 18 introduces financial statement analysis and is geared primarily to the uses of financial statements by managers, creditors, and stockholders.

## Chapter Sixteen

# QUALITY COSTS, THEORY OF CONSTRAINTS, AND LEARNING CURVES

## LEARNING OBJECTIVES

*After reading this chapter, you should be able to*

- *Describe and illustrate four categories of quality costs.*
- *Understand the difficulties in determining quality costs.*
- *Explain what is meant by a constraint, either internal or external.*
- *Apply the five focusing steps to a decision setting.*
- *Describe several approaches to managing constraints.*
- *Discuss how Theory of Constraints affects managerial accounting.*
- *Describe and illustrate learning curves.*

*"Find your main bottleneck and attack it relentlessly," said Fred Wenninger, CEO of* **Iomega**, *a high-tech manufacturer. Wenninger believes that reducing cycle time is the best way for a small company to increase quality. Low cycle times mean that inventories cannot pile up and therefore defects appear immediately. Workers can then isolate the cause of the defective units. Wenninger pointed out that "When your cycle is 28 days and you spot a defect at the end of the line, you can imagine how hard it is to isolate the problem."*

*    **Bombardier**, the Canadian maker of airplanes, railcars, snowmobiles, and personal watercraft, has undertaken a "Six-Sigma Initiative." This initiative is based on the principle that the best way to reduce costs, improve cycle time, and improve customer satisfaction is to reduce and eventually eliminate defects the first time around in engineering, production, and administrative systems. A system with Six-Sigma quality will have only 3.4 defects per million opportunities. At Bombardier Aerospace, a Six-Sigma project objective was to reduce documentation errors by 80 percent. Actual improvements to date are in the order of 90 percent, and savings are expected to approximate $200,000 per year.*

Sources: "Quality," Business Week, *November 30, 1992, 67–70.*
Bombardier 1998 annual report, 31.

Earlier chapters have stressed the importance of quality and continuous improvement. This chapter discusses the costs of quality, including two competing views of the behavior of those costs. The chapter then discusses the approach to continuous improvement known as the Theory of Constraints. The chapter concludes with a discussion of learning curves.

## COST OF QUALITY

The modern company's emphasis on quality that we have discussed throughout this book has caused accountants and other managers to rethink many ideas about the cost of increasing quality. At various places throughout this book we have described companies' efforts at increasing quality and have described some benefits and costs. We now take a more systematic look at determining how much quality, or the lack thereof, costs. Such costs are substantial. Experts have estimated the cost of quality for American businesses in the range of 10 to 30 percent of sales. Definitions of **cost of quality** vary, but one simple and effective definition is that of the president of **Kodak**, who, in a recent annual report, said "It's basically the sum of all costs that would disappear if we did everything right the first time."

We can analyze and categorize quality costs in several ways. The most common is a four-way classification.

1.  Prevention costs, incurred to avoid defects, which are units that do not meet specifications.
2.  Appraisal costs, incurred to monitor and find defective units before they leave the plant.
3.  Internal failure costs, incurred when a unit is found to be defective before it leaves the plant.
4.  External failure costs, incurred when customers find defective units.

Examples of each appear in Exhibit 16-1.

Some people refer to the first two as costs of conformance to quality standards and the latter two as costs of nonconformance. Companies incur the first two types to bring as much product as possible into conformance with their quality standards. They incur the last two as a consequence of not achieving such standards. We can also classify quality costs as voluntary and involuntary, with prevention and appraisal costs being voluntary and internal and external failure costs being involuntary.[1] The advantage of this classification is that it focuses on what the organization can do and the consequences of its inability to eliminate failure. The basic four categories are generally acknowledged as capturing the relevant elements.

### MEASURING QUALITY COSTS

Measuring and reporting the total cost of quality is extremely difficult. A glance at external failure costs reveals that some, and probably by far the most in dollar

---

1 *Lawrence P. Carr and Thomas Tyson, "Planning Quality Cost Expenditures,"* Management Accounting, *October 1992, 52–56.*

---

**Exhibit 16-1    Quality Costs**

**Prevention costs, incurred to increase the likelihood that products will meet quality standards**

- design costs
- costs of improving production processes and methods
- costs of upgrading worker skills and instilling in them the importance of quality
- higher wages paid to workers who produce higher quality work
- preventative maintenance

**Appraisal costs, incurred to determine whether particular units of product meet quality standards**

- inspection costs for materials, semifinished units, and finished units
- costs of automated monitoring of processes and products, such as lasers that scan products for defects
- cost of maintaining a laboratory to test for conformance to specifications

**Internal failure costs, incurred when company determines that specific units do not meet quality standards**

- lost contribution margin on lost output
- cost to repair or rework defective units
- cost to produce defective units that must be scrapped
- cost of downtime on machinery while rework is done
- cost to readjust malfunctioning machinery

**External failure costs, incurred when a unit of product fails to perform to customers' expectations**

- cost to repair or replace returned units
- cost of processing customer complaints
- cost to send servicepeople to customer's premises
- ill-will of customers who might not buy from you again, and might inform others of problems with your products

---

amount, are opportunity costs and cannot be known, only estimated. How can a company determine the cost of losing future sales to dissatisfied customers, let alone the cost of those customers telling other people of their bad experiences? One analysis suggests that opportunity costs are three to four times the out-of-pocket costs of failure.[2] Some observers in the automobile industry believe that satisfied customers tell 8 people about their cars, while dissatisfied customers tell 22 others.[3] They hesitate to suggest how many of the 22 are deterred from buying a particular company's cars, so they are still a step away from estimating the cost

---

2 *Francis X. Brown and Roger W. Kane, "Quality Cost and Profit Performance," in* Quality Costs: Ideas and Applications, *Milwaukee, WI: American Society for Quality Control, 1984, 203–9.*
3 *Carr and Tyson, 53.*

of having a dissatisfied customer. Exhibit 16-2 is a sample cost of quality (COQ) report.

Serious difficulties work against determining whether some costs relate to quality at all, and if so, whether they might belong to one category or another. Do all training costs advance quality? Some are aimed at more efficient use of available technology, which might or might not increase quality. How about worker safety programs? Such costs have some relationship to quality, but serious allocation problems arise with many costs that are common to several purposes. Determining quality costs thus involves ABC and ABM, since many activities include some components related to quality. As always, cost/benefit concerns are important. Trying to analyze costs too finely can be counterproductive because the costs to obtain the information outweigh the benefits of better information. Nonetheless, activity analyses can yield important insights.

Additionally, capital expenditures often have a quality dimension. For instance, **West Point Stevens**, a large manufacturer of home furnishings, replaced its shuttle looms with air jet and projectile looms. The company's annual report noted that the new looms produce at higher speeds, yield fewer defects, require less maintenance, and provide cleaner and safer working environments. The company also installed open-end spinning machines that use computerized monitors and sensors to detect defects immediately and therefore improve yarn quality. How much of the cost associated with new investment is cost of quality? The company must have looms and spinning machines to produce at all, and the advanced equipment provides benefits not directly related to quality, so teasing out quality costs is not a simple matter.

### Exhibit 16-2    Cost of Quality Report

**GWE Enterprises**
**April 20X2**
**Thousands of dollars**

| | | |
|---|---:|---:|
| **Prevention costs:** | | |
| Quality training | $22.5 | |
| Process engineering | 16.8 | $ 39.3 |
| **Appraisal costs:** | | |
| Materials inspection | $ 3.6 | |
| Process monitoring | 13.8 | |
| Laboratory | 18.6 | 36.0 |
| **Internal failure costs:** | | |
| Rework | $11.2 | |
| Scrapped units | 14.6 | 25.8 |
| **External failure costs:** | | |
| Warranty costs | $28.9 | |
| Field engineering | 34.7 | 63.6 |
| Total | | $164.7 |

## TRADITIONAL VIEW

The traditional view of quality held that workers were principally responsible for defectives and that quality could be inspected into products by careful placement of inspection stations at key points along the production process. Additionally, some level of defectives was "optimal," beyond which you should not go. You could spend too much on quality as well as too little.

Under this view, for many years managers believed that total quality costs plotted against the number or percentage of defective units (or of good units) was a saucer-shaped curve, such as that depicted in Panel A of Exhibit 16-3. Prevention and appraisal costs increase as the company produces a higher percentage of good units, while failure costs, both internal and external, fall. Thus, for a while, as the percentage of good units rises (or of defective units goes down) total quality costs decline, but then begin to rise because the costs of preventing defectives at some point exceed the costs of producing defectives. Using this model, the idea was to find the optimal percentage of defectives, where total costs were lowest. This view accepts some percentage of defectives as normal and regards the pursuit of zero defects as not cost-effective.

Part of the reason for the traditional view might have to do with the status of marketing. The years after World War II saw a proliferation of products and variations, styles, colors, features, and designs—something for everyone. In such an environment, designing for manufacturability did not exist. Production managers were responsible for volume, and getting product out was the major objective. "Fix it later" might have been the mantra; finding defectives, instead of preventing them, was the objective.

Statistics courses for many years paid a great deal of attention to determining whether to accept a shipment of parts given that a sample revealed that some were defective. The question was whether the shipment was likely to contain a higher than acceptable percentage of defectives. Similarly, managers concentrated on determining how often to inspect and when to inspect.

## THE TOTAL QUALITY VIEW

The saucer-shaped curve and approach to finding the optimal percentage of defects is now in disrepute. Many managers now believe that total quality costs continually decline as defects decline. One major reason for the new way of thinking is the more comprehensive view of costs that now prevails. Many managers believe that the costs of defectives rise so fast that the total cost curve never goes up regardless of expenditures on prevention and appraisal. Such a curve is depicted in Panel B of Exhibit 16-3.

As we stated above, the traditional view of quality included the ideas that workers were responsible for defects, that periodic inspection was the way to catch defects, and that an "acceptable level" of quality existed that the company should try to achieve, but not exceed. The more modern view is that management is responsible for quality, especially by ensuring that quality is designed into products to begin with, not added on later. Under this view, the evaluation of design engineers should include how manufacturable and how prone to failure their designs are. Recall the **Tektronix** case from Chapters 10 and 13. Design engineers were evaluated on how much labor time they could cut from products, which led them to use non-standard parts that were easier for workers to install.

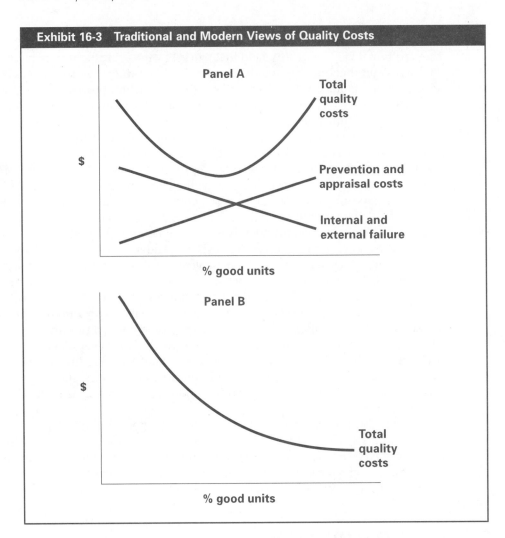

**Exhibit 16-3   Traditional and Modern Views of Quality Costs**

Using non-standard parts probably reduces quality and reliability because of the increased complexity.

Quality experts today are more likely to monitor production processes, rather than inspect units of product. If the process is well-designed, and is working as specified, it should be producing good units.

Of course, some now assert that increasing quality decreases total costs, expressed by one expert as "quality is free." Reducing quality costs requires work both inside and outside the company. The entire value chain is involved because both suppliers and customers influence quality. Companies now are viewing quality in relation to customer needs, not just to whether a product performs as specified. Customers determine the levels of quality they require, and are willing to pay for. **GE's** Six-Sigma program focuses not just on internal quality, but also on improving customers' businesses.

Suppliers obviously affect appraisal costs by the quality of their parts and components. As Chapter 12 stated, companies evaluate suppliers based on factors other than price, of which quality is perhaps the major factor. Companies now try to determine the total cost of dealing with a particular supplier, which includes appraisal costs and possibly some costs of internal and external failure. Quality is thus a matter of strategic partnerships with suppliers, including sharing information, so that the entire value chain runs as smoothly as possible. Companies today emphasize relationships all along the value chain. **Motorola**, which developed Six-Sigma, believes that quality is a matter of corporate culture. From a recent annual report,

> "Quality is the universal language of a global company, and our employees learn the fundamentals of Motorola's Six-Sigma quality culture—a culture that strives to achieve perfection. Motorola's selected key suppliers, customers and distributors are part of the process, and receive training in quality and cycle-time management. Our training has resulted in improved quality in the goods received from our vendors, and, in turn, in our own products."

Motorola has reduced defects to 1/250 of their levels 10 years ago, and has increased productivity at a 13.2 percent annual rate. The company believes that its quality initiative, much of which is directed toward increasing the value of products to Motorola's customers, has been a strategic success.

The accompanying Insight describes **Xerox's** experience with evaluating quality costs in a support function as well as an initiative **Ford Motor Company** uses as part of its view that quality is an important strategic weapon.

## INTERNATIONAL ORGANIZATION FOR STANDARDIZATION (ISO)

This international organization has issued several statements about quality, the most prominent of which is ISO 9000. Companies selling in the European Community need ISO 9000 certification. Essentially, obtaining certification requires a demonstration of adherence to quality standards. The standards apply not to products, but to processes. Such processes include those by which the company makes and tests its products, trains employees, finds and fixes defects, and deals with customer complaints.

Obtaining certification can take a year or more, and cost $200,000. Going through the process can yield many benefits besides certification. Companies have found that the process identifies areas for improvement and cost savings and thus might pay for itself. Many companies, **GE** and **Motorola** among them, are encouraging their suppliers to obtain certification. Even small companies seek certification. A small manufacturer, under 80 employees, near the home of one of this book's authors displayed for several months a banner proclaiming its certification.

Monitoring quality is an important step in the continuous improvement process. Another step in the continuous improvement process is to identify the bottlenecks that limit production. The next section discusses an approach to identifying bottlenecks known as the Theory of Constraints.

## THEORY OF CONSTRAINTS

The **Theory of Constraints (TOC)** is a set of techniques developed by Eli Goldratt and his associates, popularized in his novel, *The Goal*.[4] These techniques address

---

4 *Eliyahu Goldratt and Jeff Cox,* The Goal, *Croton-on-Hudson: North River Press, 1984. See also E. Goldratt,* It's Not Luck, *1994 and E. Goldratt,* Critical Chain, *1997.*

**IN SIGHT**

## Quality in Non-Manufacturing Situations

Some companies have found that concentrating on quality actually reduces costs, which accords with the view of many experts in the field. **Xerox Corporation** is a good example, having saved considerable amounts of money by increasing the quality of its business processes, as well as its products. The U.S. Customer Operations group (USCO), a service business, applied cost of quality (COQ) principles and saved the company $200 million in four years. USCO set up various projects using multifunctional teams to find areas of the business process that were not working well.

One project involved reducing the $22 million annual cost (7.3 percent of revenues) of excess and obsolete spare parts. The team of experts from several areas of the business met weekly until the solution was implemented. They first established a benchmark of 2.1 percent of sales, then studied the problems. One of their findings was that no end-of-life strategy existed. No one told anyone else when the need for a part ceased, leading to unexpectedly high inventories at phase-out time. The team recommended a communication network between product planners and parts planners. Another finding was that spare parts failed at too high a rate based on engineering standards. They recommended making engineering responsible for the failure rate so that it had incentives to design in quality.

USCO ran into apathy as projects were completed and improvements made. One response was to report on quality costs quarterly to maintain the focus of managers.

**Ford Motor Company** has long accepted quality as a strategic imperative. Its advertising stresses that it considers quality Job 1. Ford also operates, as do other auto manufacturers, a Customer Assistance Center, where from 120 to 140 people answer customers' questions and register their complaints. Service representatives are college graduates destined for the marketing department, or temporaries hired from an agency. All get four and a half weeks of training, including two days spent learning how to handle irate customers.

A large screen in the Center continuously flashes the number of callers waiting for a live representative. An average call takes two minutes. Calls range from customers who want refunds on alleged lemons to those wanting to know how to set the clock, a popular topic when time changes go into effect.

Representatives will not recommend specific dealers because Ford's franchising agreements with its dealers preclude it, but the representative will divulge the names of dealers cited as Chairman's Award winners. Ford recognizes these dealers for outstanding customer service.

How would you classify the cost of maintaining the Center? Is it appraisal cost, or perhaps external failure cost? Not a quality cost at all? The cost is common to several functions, including marketing, as well as quality. Many of the calls do not relate to quality, for example, the ones about setting the clock. Some might argue, however, that people make such calls because it is too difficult to read the owners's manual, which most would consider a quality defect.

Source: Lawrence P. Carr, "How Xerox Sustains the Cost of Quality," Management Accounting, *August 1995*, 26–37.

the fundamental question, "What is the goal of the enterprise?" For a profit-making enterprise the goal is assumed to be "To make money, now and in the future." The follow-up question is then "What keeps us from achieving our goal?"

In TOC, a **constraint** limits a system from achieving higher performance relative to its goal. A constraint can be external, such as market demand or vendor quality, or internal, such as labor or machine capacity, behavior of managers or workers, logistics, or policy. Notice that internal constraints can be either physical, such as capacity, or nonphysical, such as a manager's behavior or policy. TOC holds that, at any one point in time, some constraint exists. If there were no constraints, the company could make and sell an infinite number of units. Furthermore, TOC holds that, although there may be several constraints, only one is binding, preventing the system from achieving its goal. Management's concern, then, is to identify the constraint and to determine a course of action. Managers must seek solutions that address the constraint, not another (nonconstraining) element within the system. Overcoming the constraint and thus improving the system's performance results only from solving the right problem.

The TOC approach is iterative and continuous—a process of ongoing improvement. The basic steps, called the five focusing steps, are as follows:

1. Identify the constraint. Determine what limits the system's performance.
2. Decide how to exploit the constraint. Develop a logical plan for overcoming the limitation.
3. Subordinate everything else to the plan in step 2. Make effective management of the existing constraint the top priority. Measure performance by reference to meeting the plan, not by reference to meeting local objectives.
4. Elevate the constraint. Inject improvement into the system to break the constraint.
5. If, in the previous steps, you break the constraint, go back to step 1, but do not allow inertia to become the new constraint. Go back and find the new weakest link that limits system performance.

The five focusing steps are illustrated in Exhibit 16-4. These steps are followed whether the constraint is an internal constraint or an external constraint.

Proponents of TOC argue that only three financial measurements are needed. These measurements differ from the traditional, cost-based, accounting measurements and use familiar terminology in different ways. **Throughput** is defined as sales revenue less all truly variable costs.[5] Many TOC proponents claim that material costs are the only costs that are truly variable; others hold that labor and overhead may also be variable. We will consider this point in more detail later in this chapter. **Inventory** is the amount of money tied up in materials and purchased parts.[6] **Operating expenses** includes all of the money spent by the system except for truly variable costs.[7] These measures emphasize that the goal of the enterprise will be met only by selling more product, not by simply producing more product.

5 *Mokshagundam Srikanth and Michael Umble,* Synchronous Management: Profit-Based Manufacturing for the 21st Century, *Volume One, Guilford, CT: Spectrum Publishing, 1997, 56.*
6 *Ibid, 57.*
7 *Ibid, 57.*

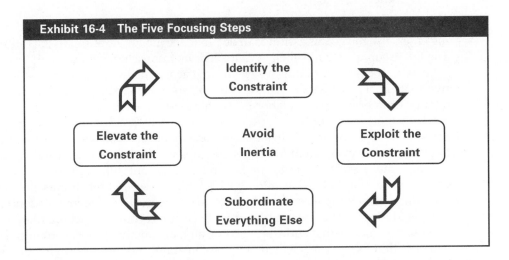

**Exhibit 16-4    The Five Focusing Steps**

## INTERNAL CONSTRAINT: PRODUCTION CONSTRAINTS

Production constraints are physical and relatively easy to recognize. Examples of production constraints include machine capacity or capability, labor availability or capacity, space availability, and quality of production (or lack of it). Production constraints are essentially constraints on capacity; they limit the ability of the organization to meet the demands of the marketplace.

Consider the following example. Acme Corporation has a machine shop that produces four products (A, B, C, and D). The details of the market demand, selling prices, materials costs, and production times are given in Exhibit 16-5. The first step is to identify the constraint. The time demanded of each process is as follows:

*Milling:*    $A (60 \times 20) + B (30 \times 10) + C (50 \times 10) + D (30 \times 20) = 2,600 \text{ minutes}$

*Grinding:*    $A (60 \times 10) + B (30 \times 20) + C (50 \times 10) + D (30 \times 10) = 2,000 \text{ minutes}$

*Assembly:*    $A (60 \times 5)\ \ + B (30 \times 5)\ \ + C (50 \times 20) + D (30 \times 10) = 1,750 \text{ minutes}$

*Finishing:*    $A (60 \times 15) + B (30 \times 15) + C (50 \times 0)\ \ + D (30 \times 10) = 1,650 \text{ minutes}$

Since there is a total of 2,400 minutes available at each process, the constraint is the Milling process. Grinding, Assembly, and Finishing all have excess capacity. The **load factor** of each process is a useful calculation.

$$\text{Load Factor} \ = \ \frac{\text{Time required at a process}}{\text{Time available at a process}}$$

If a load factor is greater than 1.00, there is insufficient capacity to process all units demanded by the marketplace. In our example, Milling has a load factor of 2,600 ÷ 2,400 = 1.083, while the other three processes would have load factors of 0.833 for Grinding, 0.729 for Assembly, and 0.688 for Finishing.

The second step is to decide how to exploit the constraint. According to Chapter 5, the basic rule is to rank the products according to the contribution margin per unit of scarce resource. Notice that TOC uses the term "throughput" rather than "contribution margin." The difference between the terms is which

---

**Exhibit 16-5   Acme Corporation**

| | Market | Time on Machine (minutes) | | | |
|---|---|---|---|---|---|
| **Product** | **Demand** | **Milling** | **Grinding** | **Assembly** | **Finishing** |
| A | 60 | 20 | 10 | 5 | 15 |
| B | 30 | 10 | 20 | 5 | 15 |
| C | 50 | 10 | 10 | 20 | 0 |
| D | 30 | 20 | 10 | 10 | 10 |
| **Time available per week** | | 2,400 | 2,400 | 2,400 | 2,400 |

| **Product** | **Selling Price** | **Material Cost** |
|---|---|---|
| A | $100 | $35 |
| B | 50 | 10 |
| C | 40 | 15 |
| D | 25 | 10 |

---

costs are considered variable. In our example, Product A has a throughput of $100 − 35 = $65; B $50 − 10 = $40; C $40 − 15 = $25; and D $25 − 10 = $15. Since Milling is the constraint, we divide the throughput for each product by the time required in the Milling process.

$$A:\quad \$65 \div 20 \text{ minutes} = \$3.25 \text{ per minute}$$
$$B:\quad \$40 \div 10 \text{ minutes} = \$4.00 \text{ per minute}$$
$$C:\quad \$25 \div 10 \text{ minutes} = \$2.50 \text{ per minute}$$
$$D:\quad \$15 \div 20 \text{ minutes} = \$0.75 \text{ per minute}$$

The Milling process should produce product B first, followed by product A, product C, and finally, if there is sufficient time, product D. The quantities that should be produced can be calculated as follows:

| Product | Time Required | Time Remaining |
|---|---|---|
| | | 2,400 |
| B | 30 × 10 = 300 | 2,100 |
| A | 60 × 20 = 1,200 | 900 |
| C | 50 × 10 = 500 | 400 |

Since only 400 minutes remain, Acme can produce 20 units of product D (400 ÷ 20).

The third of the five focusing steps is to subordinate everything else to the plan in step 2. For Acme Corporation, this means that the Grinding, Assembly, and Finishing processes will be operating at much less than full capacity. Exhibit 16-6 presents a summary of the time each process is producing saleable product. If each process were being evaluated on its efficiency, only Milling would have favorable results. The efficiencies would be as follows:

Milling:    *2,400 minutes worked ÷ 2,400 minutes available = 100%*

Grinding:   *1,900 ÷ 2,400 = 79.17%*

Assembly:  *1,650 ÷ 2,400 = 68.75%*

Finishing:  *1,550 ÷ 2,400 = 64.58%*

Efficiencies are a measure of the use of each process individually (a local objective); a more important efficiency is how fully the constraint is being utilized (a measure of the global objective of maximizing throughput). In TOC, only global measures make sense. Local measures of success, such as standard cost variances, encourage managers to take unwise actions. We shall say more about some of these issues later.

The fourth step is to elevate the constraint. How can we put more product through the constraining process? Several possibilities include eliminating periods of idle time (such as coffee or lunch breaks), reducing either setup time or run time, improving quality of the product entering the constraint, determining the root cause of quality problems after the constraint, reducing the workload at the constraining process, or acquiring additional capacity. In our example, the value of additional capacity would be the opportunity cost of not producing the unfilled market demand of 10 units of D. Since product D has a throughput of $15, the opportunity cost is $0.75 per minute of Milling process time. If the constraint is elevated, some other factor will become the constraint. For Acme, the constraint will become external: the market demand for each of the products. The entire process will repeat itself, with the concern now being to address the market constraint.

## INTERNAL CONSTRAINT: POLICY CONSTRAINTS

Policy constraints arise when managers within the enterprise limit or constrain operations. Policy constraints take three forms: mindset constraints, measures constraints, and methods constraints.[8] Mindset refers to the way management thinks, or the organization's culture. A company's mindset often limits whether change can be made or not. An example of a mindset is a "keep busy" attitude by production supervisors. A company's mindset is often the result of traditions.

### Exhibit 16-6   Production Times

| Product | Units Produced | Milling | Grinding | Assembly | Finishing |
|---------|---------------|---------|----------|----------|-----------|
|         |               | *Time on Machine (minutes)* | | | |
| B | 30 | 300 | 600 | 150 | 450 |
| A | 60 | 1,200 | 600 | 300 | 900 |
| C | 50 | 500 | 500 | 1,000 | 0 |
| D | 20 | 400 | 200 | 200 | 200 |
|   |    | 2,400 | 1,900 | 1,650 | 1,550 |

8 *Srikanth and Umble, 135–7.*

Measures often create constraints by encouraging dysfunctional behavior, a point we have made throughout this book. For example, a purchasing agent rewarded for favorable material price variances has an incentive to purchase large quantities of materials at favorable prices, whether they are needed or not and regardless of storage costs.

Finally, *methods* refers to the way that work is performed. A company's policy might be to use large production batches to make efficient use of long setup times. This might cause reduced throughput by creating excessively long lead times.

Policy constraints usually manifest themselves as reduced throughput potential of the production line. Thus, even though the constraint appears to be a production constraint, the underlying root of the problem is the misguided policy. Identifying these constraints is difficult because they lurk below the surface of physical constraints. Managers must perform logical, cause-and-effect analysis to link the undesirable effects with the underlying root core problems. The accompanying Insight describes how one company applied TOC concepts.

## EXTERNAL CONSTRAINT: MATERIALS CONSTRAINTS

Some constraints are not found within the company but are rather imposed by external forces. A shortage of purchased materials could be the constraining factor. In this case, the opportunity cost of the constraining material is equal to the purchase price plus the throughput value of the finished product that uses the material. The opportunity cost of a nonconstraining material is simply the purchase price.

Material shortages also arise from internal factors such as poor scheduling, excessive scrap at a production process, or breakdowns in earlier processes. It might be prudent to maintain an inventory buffer before an internal constraint because any downtime on an internal constraint is lost forever.

## EXTERNAL CONSTRAINT: MARKET CONSTRAINTS

Insufficient demand for a company's products is the most common market constraint. This form of a market constraint is truly external to the company. A market constraint might also result from internal actions that lead to the company being uncompetitive. Examples include inability to meet lead times, lead times that are longer than the competition, pricing, reliability of delivery, and quality standards.[9] The company might also have done a poor job of finding ways to expand into new markets. The Insight on page 737 describes how one company used TOC to increase throughput.

## THEORY OF CONSTRAINTS AND PRODUCTION SCHEDULING

Recall that the third focusing step was to subordinate everything to the plan developed in step 2. One approach to subordinating everything else to the plan is through production scheduling. The Theory of Constraints has developed a scheduling approach known as **drum-buffer-rope**. Just as a drum serves as the pacing mechanism in a marching band, the constraining resource should set the pace for the production schedule. Materials should be released to the production

---

9 *Ibid, 133.*

**SIGHT**

### Breaking a Policy Constraint

The Stanleytown factory of **Stanley Furniture Company** was quoting lead times of 45 days, even though 95 percent of its sales were standard, made-to-stock items. Of the 45 days, 25 were for manufacturing and 20 were for administrative/distribution activities including order processing, credit approval, and shipping. The company suffered from the "hockey stick" production pattern, where output was relatively low until month-end, when it shot upward to meet monthly sales targets. The rush of production increased overtime and generated expediting costs. Management wanted to reduce the lead time to provide better service. It first made several improvements to the manufacturing process, then turned its attention to administrative/distribution activities.

Order processing went as follows. Sales representatives sent orders to headquarters, where clerks entered them into a sales order system. Other employees approved credit for the customer. Only after credit approval was the order placed on the production schedule. The traffic department then consolidated orders into groups and scheduled deliveries.

The team applying the focusing steps found, in step 1, that credit approval was the bottleneck. Work piled up in this operation because its employees reviewed each customer's credit history and had different procedures for different-size orders. In step 2, the company reduced the steps required to approve orders from customers with good credit. The result was a drop in the backlog at each station and a reduction in the administrative lead time.

In step 3, the team subordinated all other activities to credit approval, and management de-emphasized other departments' goals and objectives.

In step 4, the company eliminated the constraint by changing the flow. Instead of waiting for credit approval before allocating inventory for an order, the company allowed the warehouse to allocate inventory before final credit approval. The company was able to do this without disrupting its production schedules, fear of which was one reason it had not taken the step earlier.

In step 5, the team determined that the constraint had been broken and turned its attention to the shipping function, starting again with step 1.

*Source: Michael S. Spencer and Samuel Wathen, "Applying the Theory of Constraints Process Management Technique,"* National Productivity Review, *Summer 1994, 381–3.*

process at the same pace that the constraint utilizes the materials. In essence, the constraint and the first process are "roped" together. Finally, there should be a buffer of inventory immediately before the constraint to ensure that the constraining process is never starved for work to perform. Recall that a unit lost at the constraint (either a unit of product or a unit of time) is lost forever and cannot be recovered.

Such buffers are one area where TOC departs from other philosophies of continuous improvement, most obviously JIT, which does not support the idea of buffer inventories.

SIGHT

### Implementing TOC at LucasVarity

**LucasVarity plc** designs, manufactures, and supplies advanced technology systems, products, and services in the world's automotive and aerospace industries. At LucasVarity's Detroit plant, using TOC resulted in:

- Improved machine uptime at the constraint by over 15%
- Increased line output by 76%
- Reduced cycle time at the constraint by 24%
- Increased first-run yield by more than 4%

The Fowlerville, Michigan, Anti-Lock Brake System plant reported improvements including:

- Increased line output by 135%
- Reduced scrap cost per unit by 68%

These improvements in line output allowed the corporation to delay a major (6 million dollar) investment one year with no negative impact to customers.

At the Detroit plant, constraint capacity was increased two different ways. One way was through cycle time reduction. A thorough review of the various process steps that occurred within the constraint uncovered changes that eventually led to a 9 second reduction in cycle time (from 37 to 28 seconds). The process analysis was performed not only to uncover cycle time reductions but also to reveal the root causes of a number of machine faults. Secondly, usable capacity was created by reducing the amount of machine downtime. Reducing unplanned machine downtime resulted in an increase in net capacity.

*Source: Avraham Y. Goldratt Institute.*

## ACCOUNTING ISSUES

CHAPTER
2

We should consider several accounting issues relative to the theory of constraints. First, what costs are "truly variable costs"? The accountant normally treats contribution margin as selling price less the variable costs of materials, labor, and variable overhead. In Chapter 2, variable costs were defined as those costs that changed (in total) as the level of activity changed. TOC proponents generally argue that only material costs are variable, that labor and overhead are "operating expenses" and are fixed. This question is specific to each situation: in some cases labor is variable, in others it is fixed over short periods of time. If production increases, will labor increase? If a large increase in production is considered, labor will probably also increase. But if a smaller production increase is considered the answer is not quite as simple. Labor very likely follows a step-variable cost pattern: for small changes in volume labor cost does not change; for larger changes in volume the labor cost will change. The same logic also applies to variable overhead. The accompanying Insight illustrates how two companies have classified their costs as fixed or variable.

A second issue is what costs will be relevant for particular decisions? The relevant costs in a make-or-buy decision, for example, depend upon whether the product will utilize the constraint or not. If the constraint is necessary for production, the relevant costs include the opportunity cost of the units not being produced. If the constraint is not necessary for the production, the opportunity cost is zero.

A third accounting issue is how to measure performance. Traditional absorption cost accounting as presented in Chapter 14 includes all of the costs of producing a product with overhead rates based on an assumed capacity level. The cost of a product will vary depending upon what level of capacity is assumed. A portion of fixed overhead will be assigned to the inventory value of any unsold product. TOC measures include only the materials and purchased parts as inventory, considering all other expenditures as operating expense. Thus, TOC favors throughput accounting, an extreme form of variable costing.

## **IN** SIGHT

### Are Costs Fixed or Variable?

In implementing TOC, companies differ in how they have defined costs as fixed or variable. The following illustrations show how the specific circumstances each company faces will determine whether a cost is variable or not.

**Bertch Cabinet Mfg., Inc.** is a Midwestern manufacturer of wood cabinets and their accessories. Theory of Constraints concepts were applied to production in 1993; the accounting system was formally modified to measure throughput margin in 1995. Bertch uses the modified accounting information to evaluate the profit performance of each division, for pricing decisions, to establish bids on new contract opportunities, and for product mix decisions.

Direct labor workers at Bertch are paid an hourly wage. Management has classified about 30 percent of the direct labor as nonvariable to units produced; the remaining 70 percent is added to direct material costs as unit-level variable costs. The high percentage (22 percent) of total costs represented by labor justified its inclusion in the throughput calculations.

**Foldcraft Company** is a $25 million, employee-owned company specializing in restaurant and institutional furniture. The company adopted a TOC performance measurement system in 1995. Foldcraft treats labor costs as fixed when evaluating incremental business because management has a policy of no layoffs. The actual costs of labor and general overhead are basically fixed at the predetermined throughput levels.

*Sources: John MacArthur, "From Activity-Based Costing to Throughput Accounting,"* Management Accounting, *April 1996, 30–38.*
*Douglas Westra, M.L. Srikanth, and Michael Kane, "Measuring Operational Performance in a Throughput World,"* Management Accounting, *April 1996, 41–47.*

## LEARNING CURVES

Even before they faced serious competition from overseas companies, U.S. companies paid a great deal of attention to improving employee productivity and recognized that people generally need less time to do a task as they become more familiar with the task. For instance, airplane manufacturers long ago determined that the labor time required for each airplane of a given model declines as the workers learn.

The **learning curve** is a measure of increases in efficiency. The rate of performance improvement, expressed as a percentage, is called the learning rate. The most common form of the learning curve is expressed as follows: as output doubles, the average time to make a unit or batch of units drops to the learning rate percentage multiplied by the average time at the previous point. An example will clarify this relationship.

Midwestern Manufacturing is about to begin making a new product. The expected labor time for the first batch is 10 hours, and the expected learning rate is 80 percent. Exhibit 16-7 illustrates the learning curve for Midwestern. The exhibit shows, for selected numbers of batches, both the average time per batch and the total time.

Notice that the exhibit shows results only at doubling points (2 is double 1, 4 is double 2, 8 is double 4). To determine the average time for some other number of batches, we can use the following formula.

$$Y = aX^b$$

where

$Y$ = average time for X number of batches
$a$ = the time required for the first batch (or unit)
$X$ = total output (number of batches)
$b$ = the learning exponent

The value of $b$ is the logarithm of the learning rate (expressed as a decimal) divided by the logarithm of 2. With the formula you can find the average time for any output level. For instance, in the example, the value of $b$ is about −0.322. Thus, the per-batch average time for seven batches is

$$
\begin{aligned}
Y &= 10 \times 7^{-0.322} \\
&= 10 \times 0.5344 \\
&= 5.344
\end{aligned}
$$

---

**Exhibit 16-7   Examples of Expected Average and Total Times—80% Learning Curve**

| Total Output in Batches | Expected Average Time per Batch (hours) | Expected Total Time (hours)[a] |
|---|---|---|
| 1 | 10   (given) | 10 |
| 2 | 8   (10 × 80%) | 16   (2 × 8) |
| 4 | 6.4  (8 × 80%) | 25.6  (4 × 6.4) |
| 8 | 5.12 (6.4 × 80%) | 40.96 (8 × 5.12) |

*a Number of batches × average time per batch.*

We stress that the learning curve is expressed in terms of the per-batch average time for some total number of batches, not the incremental time to produce some number of additional batches. Thus, if we refer to Exhibit 16-7, the second batch does not require eight hours; rather eight hours is the per-batch average time to produce both of the first two batches. To find the incremental time for a batch, you must first find the total times for that number of batches and for one batch fewer. For Midwestern, we know from Exhibit 16-7 that eight batches require 40.96 hours. Seven batches require 37.408 hours ($7 \times 5.344$, the average time computed above using the formula). Hence, the eighth batch requires 3.552 hours (40.96 − 37.408).

You can also apply the learning curve directly to cost, rather than to time. For example, we could have said that labor and labor-related variable overhead costs were $10 for the first batch. In that case, the answers derived in the exhibit or from the formula would be expressed in dollars.

The learning curve is useful in planning and controlling. Managers can estimate labor time, and therefore labor and labor-related variable overhead costs, for specific quantities of output. They can then determine, by comparing actual time or cost with the estimated values, whether learning is as expected. The accompanying Insight describes how learning curves can be included in the analysis of emerging technologies.

Suppose that Western Semiconductor is considering a customer's offer to buy eight batches of a specialized microprocessor. (A batch could be 500, 1,000, or any other number of units, so long as all batches are the same size.) The customer has offered to pay $80,000 for the entire order. No incremental fixed costs are associated with the order. Materials and purchased components will cost $3,500 for each batch. (This portion of the cost is not subject to learning.) Western estimates

## INSIGHT

### Learning Curves and Emerging Technologies

Proponents of photovoltaic technology argue that expected cost reductions will make the technology more and more competitive as time goes on. This expectation is based on the observation that the unit costs of a manufactured product progressively decrease as more units are manufactured. The pattern of this reduction among many different types of technology has been remarkably consistent, following an exponential reduction variously named a learning curve, progress curve, or experience curve.

The rate of reduction in an experience curve can be defined by the percentage reduction in the unit cost with successive doubling of the quantity manufactured. Experience in producing photovoltaics between 1976 and 1992 demonstrates an 82 percent experience curve.

*Source: "Down the learning curve with emerging technologies,"* The International Energy Agency ETSAP Newsletter, *July 1998.*

the cost of direct labor and labor-related variable overhead for the first batch at $3,000 and has usually experienced an 80 percent learning rate.

Suppose Western's managers have decided not to accept the order unless they expect more than the $35,000 in contribution margin which the company could earn doing other business if the order is rejected. If the managers ignore the potential for lower costs because of learning, they would reject the order on the basis of the following analysis.

| | | |
|---|---:|---:|
| Revenues | | $80,000 |
| Variable costs: | | |
| Materials and components (8 × $3,500) | $28,000 | |
| Labor and labor-related overhead (8 × $3,000) | 24,000 | 52,000 |
| Expected contribution margin | | $28,000 |

However, the order does have the desired profit potential if the learning factor is considered. The following schedule shows the expected costs of labor and labor-related variable overhead, based on the 80 percent learning rate and expected costs of the first batch.

| Total Output in Batches | Expected Average Cost per Batch | Expected Total Cost[a] |
|:---:|:---:|:---|
| 1 | $3,000 (given) | $ 3,000 |
| 2 | 2,400 ($3,000 × 80%) | 4,800 (2 × $2,400) |
| 4 | 1,920 ($2,400 × 80%) | 7,680 (4 × $1,920) |
| 8 | 1,536 ($1,920 × 80%) | 12,288 (8 × $1,536) |

a  *Number of batches × average cost per batch.*

With this cost information, the order shows higher profit.

| | | |
|---|---:|---:|
| Revenues | | $80,000 |
| Variable costs: | | |
| Materials and components (8 × $3,500) | $28,000 | |
| Labor and labor-related overhead, previously given | 12,288 | 40,288 |
| Expected contribution margin | | $39,712 |

Total expected contribution margin from the order is nearly $12,000 more than that shown by the analysis that ignores the cost reduction expected to result from learning and the order is more profitable than the available alternative (contribution margin of $35,000). The lesson here is that managers must study their companies' experiences for evidence of potential cost reductions as a result of learning and, where it exists, incorporate that potential into decision making.

## SUMMARY

Quality costs are an important component of operations. Companies striving to improve quality can use the four categories of quality cost to assist in their analysis. The traditional view of quality accepts some percentage of defectives as normal; the total quality view holds that total quality costs continually decline as defects decline.

Theory of Constraints is a management approach that focuses a manager's attention on what it is that keeps the company from reaching its goal. These constraints may be internal or external. A five-step process is used to identify and manage the constraints.

Accounting implications of TOC include what costs are truly variable and should be considered relevant to a decision. A cost would be relevant to a decision only where a constraint is involved. TOC uses a form of variable costing rather than absorption costing when considering the financial results of a decision.

The learning curve claims that as output doubles, the average cost will decrease. This is due to workers "learning" how to perform their tasks more efficiently.

## KEY TERMS

constraint   *(731)*
cost of quality   *(724)*
drum-buffer-rope   *(735)*
inventory   *(731)*
learning curve   *(739)*

load factor   *(732)*
operating expenses   *(731)*
Theory of Constraints   *(729)*
throughput   *(731)*

## REVIEW PROBLEM

Bloomer Industries has the following accounts and costs pertaining to quality.

|  | 20X1 | 20X2 |
| --- | --- | --- |
| Engineering changes | $16,000 | $ 6,000 |
| Final product inspection | 45,000 | 33,000 |
| Incoming materials inspection | 7,500 | 4,000 |
| Preventive maintenance | 8,000 | 15,500 |
| Product returns | 30,000 | 27,000 |
| Quality reporting | 1,250 | 6,600 |
| Reinspection | 31,500 | 28,800 |
| Rework | 66,200 | 48,900 |
| Scrap | 53,700 | 36,500 |
| Training | 800 | 12,100 |
| Warranty expense | 75,000 | 80,000 |

### Required

1. Categorize the costs into the four cost of quality categories.
2. If sales were $1,500,000 in 20X1 and $2,400,000 in 20X2, show the costs of quality as a percentage of sales for each category and in total for each year.

## ANSWER TO REVIEW PROBLEM

1.

| | 20X1 | 20X2 |
|---|---|---|
| **Prevention costs:** | | |
| Engineering changes | $ 16,000 | $ 6,000 |
| Preventive maintenance | 8,000 | 15,500 |
| Training | 800 | 12,100 |
| Total prevention costs | $ 24,800 | $ 33,600 |
| | | |
| **Appraisal costs:** | | |
| Final product inspection | $ 45,000 | $ 33,000 |
| Incoming materials inspection | 7,500 | 4,000 |
| Quality reporting | 1,250 | 6,600 |
| Total appraisal costs | $ 53,750 | $ 43,600 |
| | | |
| **Internal failure costs:** | | |
| Reinspection | $ 31,500 | $ 28,800 |
| Rework | 66,200 | 48,900 |
| Scrap | 53,700 | 36,500 |
| Total internal failure costs | $151,400 | $114,200 |
| | | |
| **External failure costs:** | | |
| Product returns | $ 30,000 | $ 27,000 |
| Warranty expense | 75,000 | 80,000 |
| Total external failure costs | $105,000 | $107,000 |

2.

| | 20X1 | 20X2 |
|---|---|---|
| **Prevention:** | | |
| $24,800 ÷ $1,500,000 | 1.7% | |
| $33,600 ÷ $2,400,000 | | 1.4% |
| **Appraisal:** | | |
| $53,750 ÷ $1,500,000 | 3.6% | |
| $43,600 ÷ $2,400,000 | | 1.8% |
| **Internal failure:** | | |
| $151,400 ÷ $1,500,000 | 10.1% | |
| $114,200 ÷ $2,400,000 | | 4.8% |
| **External failure:** | | |
| $105,000 ÷ $1,500,000 | 7.0% | |
| $107,000 ÷ $2,400,000 | | 4.5% |

## ASSIGNMENT MATERIAL

### INTERNET ACTIVITY

A number of companies offer consulting or educational services related to Theory of Constraints. Find some of their Web sites. See how they view the concept, what services they offer, what benefits they say they can provide. See if they offer examples of successful implementations. Be prepared to describe and discuss what you discovered. Take the viewpoint that your boss has asked you to make a preliminary survey to see whether it is feasible for your company to consider TOC.

## QUESTIONS FOR DISCUSSION

*16-1    Quality costs*    Of the four categories of quality costs, which is the hardest to estimate? Why?

*16-2    Learning curves*    Which of the following operations of companies do you think experience significant learning effects?

1. **General Motors'** automobile assembly plants.
2. **Pillsbury's** flour mills.
3. **Colgate-Palmolive's** toothpaste plants.
4. **Boeing's** aircraft plants.

*16-3    Classifying quality costs*    Classify each of the following costs as prevention, appraisal, internal failure, external failure, or as not a cost of quality. State any assumptions you make.

1. Training new workers.
2. Upgrading skills of existing workers.
3. Inspecting purchased components.
4. Reworking defective units.
5. Routine maintenance on machinery.
6. Salaries of field engineers who assist customers with problems and service products in the field.
7. Sales returns.

*16-4    Comparison of costing methods*    Chapter 14 described absorption, variable, and throughput costing. Why do you believe TOC advocates throughput costing? Recall that throughput costing is an extreme version of variable costing in which only materials costs are inventoried.

*16-5    Theory of Constraints*    Suppose you work with a team of people assembling small engines. All of you have about equal ability except for Bob, who is considerably slower than everyone else. What would you do to maximize the output of the group?

## EXERCISES

*16-6    Bottlenecks*    Creative Mailing Services provides custom mailing services to small businesses. A typical job consists of 20 letters and contains the following steps and times to complete each step:

| Step | Time to Complete |
| --- | --- |
| Type | 14 minutes |
| Proofread | 5 minutes |
| Address envelopes | 6 minutes |
| Stuff and stamp envelopes | 3 minutes |

**Required**

1. Under normal circumstances, how long will it take to complete a batch of 20 letters?
2. Which step is the bottleneck?

**16-7  Basic learning curve**  Industrial engineers at Kvam Inc., a manufacturer of industrial presses, expect the first unit of a new model, the TN-22, to require 1,000 direct labor hours. They also expect an 85% learning curve.

**Required**

1. Determine the average direct labor time and the total direct labor time to make four units of the TN-22.
2. Determine the average direct labor time and the total direct labor time to make eight units of the TN-22.

**16-8  TOC**  Sandy Company has the following products and costs:

|  | A | B | C |
|---|---|---|---|
| Unit sales | 10,000 | 4,000 | 2,000 |
| Selling price | $20.00 | $30.00 | $50.00 |
| Materials | 8.00 | 7.00 | 10.00 |
| Labor | 2.00 | 4.00 | 8.00 |
| Variable overhead | 2.00 | 4.00 | 8.00 |
| Variable selling | 3.00 | 3.00 | 5.00 |

The labor wage rate is $8.00 per hour. Overhead is applied based on direct labor dollars.

**Required**

1. Sandy currently has 7,000 labor hours available. If 100 more units of any one product can be sold, how many units of which product should Sandy produce and sell?
2. Suppose that Sandy has only 6,000 labor hours available next month. If next month's demand will be the same as this month's demand, how many of each product should be produced and sold?

**16-9  TOC**  Preston Co. assembles a variety of pressure gauges to customer order. Preston buys steel and brass fittings, plungers, and electrical connections. It then assembles and tests them. The testing operation is necessary because current technology does not permit zero defects. Data on the two operations appear below.

|  | Assembly | Testing |
|---|---|---|
| Monthly capacity in units | 300,000 | 250,000 |

The average gauge sells for $22 and has total variable costs of $18. Preston could sell 300,000 gauges per month if it could supply them.

**Required**

1. Preston can acquire machinery that will allow it to increase testing capacity by 40,000 units per month. The machinery, which Preston will lease, will add $70,000 to monthly costs. Should Preston acquire the equipment?
2. Preston can also acquire equipment that will increase capacity in the assembly operation by 30,000 units per month. The equipment will add $60,000 to monthly costs. Should Preston acquire this equipment?

**16-10    *Quality costs and TOC*** Harnish Industries operates a plant with three departments. The machining department has 100,000 hours available per month.
Output of the department ordinarily contains about 10% defectives, or about 10,000
hours worth of work. The company can make some changes that will cost about
$25,000 per month, but will reduce defective production to about 3,000 hours worth
of output. The variable cost of output scrapped is about $30,000 for 10,000 hours
worth; the contribution margin on that much output is about $60,000.

***Required***
1. If the machining department is not a bottleneck (the company cannot sell any
   more than the department now produces), should the company make the improvement?
2. If the machining department is a bottleneck, should the company make the improvement?

**16-11    *Learning curve*** GenCo Industries is bidding on a contract to make eight
batches of landing gear assemblies for an aircraft company. GenCo's engineers expect direct labor and variable overhead for the first batch to be $80,000. Variable
overhead is related to direct labor. GenCo usually achieves an 80% learning rate.

***Required***
1. Determine the expected average cost for direct labor and variable overhead for
   the eight batches.
2. Determine the expected total cost for direct labor and variable overhead for the
   eight batches.

**16-12    *Learning curve (continuation of 16-11)*** GenCo's managers expect the cost
of materials and purchased components to be $25,000 per batch (not subject to
learning). They also want an average contribution margin of $15,000 per batch.

***Required***
1. Determine the price that GenCo must bid to earn $15,000 average contribution
   margin per batch for eight batches.
2. Suppose now that the contract is for 16 batches. Redo requirement 1.
3. Suppose that the contract is still for eight batches, but that GenCo's managers believe that the learning rate will actually be 85%. Redo requirement 1.

**16-13    *Quality costs*** Acme Corporation is considering adding an additional inspection point into its production process. The inspection will occur immediately
prior to packaging and will cost $10 per unit. The inspection has a 95% probability
of detecting a defective product. Past history has shown that 8% of products produced are defective and require on-site servicing. It costs Acme $300 to repair a unit
in the field. Correcting the defects in a unit would cost $50 if the repair was made
before the unit left the factory. Assume 1,000 units are produced and sold each
month.

***Required***
1. How should Acme classify each of the costs?
2. Should Acme Corporation institute the additional inspection?

**16-14    *Classifying quality costs*** Annandale Corporation has the following financial
data related to its quality initiatives:

| | |
|---|---:|
| Incoming materials inspection | $ 120,000 |
| Product inspection | 150,000 |
| Product warranty | 950,000 |
| Quality training | 65,000 |
| Rework | 650,000 |
| Scrap | 375,000 |
| Total | $2,310,000 |

**Required**

Classify the costs as prevention, appraisal, internal failure, or external failure.

**16-15   *Quality improvements and the learning curve***   Wheeler Industries is considering bidding on a contract to produce 16 units of a custom injector molding machine. To prepare the bid, Wheeler produced a prototype with the following costs:

| | |
|---|---:|
| Materials | $100,000 |
| Direct labor | 120,000 |
| Variable overhead | 80,000 |

Wheeler has experienced labor and variable overhead following an 80% learning curve. Wheeler has also experienced a rapid quality improvement with respect to materials. The materials improvement has been observed to follow a 60% learning curve.

**Required**

1. Determine the expected total cost for materials for the 16 units. Assume that the prototype can be used as the first unit.
2. Determine the expected total cost for direct labor and variable overhead for the 16 units.
3. If Wheeler wants a 25% contribution margin, what bid price should be set for the 16 units?

## PROBLEMS

**16-16   *Quality costs***   RST Company has the following costs, among others.

| | |
|---|---:|
| Inspection of outgoing shipments | $ 70,000 |
| Employee training | 50,000 |
| Salaries of laboratory personnel who test samples of product | 150,000 |
| Rework of defective units | 40,000 |
| Salaries of customer service personnel, who spend 40% of their time fixing products, 60% taking orders | 200,000 |
| Product design | 250,000 |
| Vendor certification, principally determining whether vendors' quality controls are adequate | 80,000 |
| Inspection of incoming shipments | 40,000 |

**Required**

1. Determine the total amounts the company is spending on each of the four quality cost categories.
2. Do these costs capture all of the costs of quality the company incurs? Assume that all costs are recorded correctly.

**16-17 *TOC and quality*** Winston Company manufactures small motors. Each motor goes through a fabrication process and an assembly operation. The average motor sells for $42 and has $8 in material costs. The company rejects 10% of the motors that come through fabrication and scraps the rejects. The company identifies rejects before they enter the assembly process.

|  | Fabrication | Assembly |
|---|---|---|
| Monthly output | 20,000 | 18,000 |
| Unit variable cost of process, labor and variable overhead | $12 | $10 |
| Monthly fixed costs | $200,000 | $90,000 |

**Required**

1. Suppose that Winston cannot sell more than 18,000 motors per month. What is the monthly cost of making defective motors?
2. Suppose that Winston can sell all of the motors it can make and that the fabrication process cannot produce more than 20,000 motors (good and defective) per month. What is the amount of monthly profit Winston loses by making defective motors?

**16-18  *Learning curve in administrative work*** The Dean of Admissions at Midland University needs student help to process 6,400 application forms. She has found that a new student helper can process 40 forms the first day. The helpers usually achieve an 85% learning rate. The Dean plans to hire ten helpers, so each will process 640 forms. You may consider 40 forms to be a batch.

**Required**

Determine how many days it will take ten new helpers to process the 6,400 forms.

**16-19  *Learning curve in administrative work (continuation of 16-18)*** The Dean of Admissions at Midland University believes that the student workers can learn at a faster pace than previously considered. Assume that the student helpers can achieve a 70% learning rate. Also assume that a batch consists of 10 forms.

**Required**

Determine how many days it will now take the ten new helpers to process the 6,400 forms.

**16-20  *Quality costs in a law firm*** Quality costs can be as much as 30% of a service firm's operating budget. Following is a listing of activities of the law firm Dancer, Donner & Blitzen.

1. Bad debt write-offs
2. Billing or payroll errors
3. Computer downtime
4. Employee turnover
5. Frequent budget revisions
6. Overstaffing

7. Overtime
8. Unplanned revision of documents
9. Premiums for malpractice insurance
10. Review time by partners
11. Revising or recopying of documents to correct errors
12. Settlements paid out by the firm
13. Time devoted to addressing client complaints
14. Time spent defending lawsuits filed by other parties against the firm
15. Travel to continuing legal education
16. Underutilization of office equipment
17. Unproductive meeting time

### Required

Classify each of the activities into one of the four categories of quality costs.

**16-21    Production and market constraints**    Gamma Company manufactures two products, alpha and beta, in a single plant. Gamma can sell 50 alphas each week for $180 and 25 betas each week for $180. Each unit of alpha is comprised of one component A and one component B. Each unit of beta is comprised of one component B and one component C.

A single unit of component A is produced by machining raw material #1 for 30 minutes on machine 1 followed by 20 minutes on machine 3. A single unit of component B is produced by machining raw material #2 for 30 minutes on machine 2 followed by 10 minutes on machine 3. A single unit of component C is produced by machining raw material #3 for 20 minutes on machine 1 followed by 30 minutes on machine 2.

A unit of alpha is completed by fastening one component A to one component B using machine 4. This process takes 20 minutes. A unit of beta is completed by fastening one component B to one component C using machine 4. This process takes 10 minutes.

Raw material #1 costs $40 per unit; raw material #2 costs $50 per unit; raw material #3 costs $30 per unit. There are 40 hours available each week for each machine. Assume no idle time nor any machine breakdowns. Fixed costs, including labor, are $5,000 per week.

### Required

1. What is the net profit per week if there were no constraints on the production?
2. What are the load factors for each of the machines? Where is the production constraint?
3. How many units of alpha and beta should be produced each week?

**16-22    Production and market constraints with changing conditions (continuation of 16-21)**    Gamma Company is considering several different marketing and production options.

*Option 1:* The production engineer has determined that if raw material #2 were replaced with an alternative material, production time on machine 3 would be cut by 20%. However, the time to assemble on machine 4 would increase by 1 minute for either alpha or beta. The alternative material would cost $55 per unit.

*Option 2:* The marketing manager has estimated that additional weekly advertising, coupled with price changes, would have an impact on the market demand for each product. The advertising campaign would cost $200 per week. If the price of alpha were cut by $15, demand would increase by 10%. If the price of beta were increased by $20, demand would only drop by 2 units.

*Option 3:* The quality manager has estimated that some of the work performed by machine 2 could be completed on machine 3 with no loss of quality. A process that currently takes 30 minutes on machine 2 to complete could be replaced with 20 minutes on machine 2 followed immediately by an additional 25 minutes on machine 3.

**Required**
1. What is the revised net profit per week under each of the options? Assume all other costs and conditions remain the same.
2. Which option is most desirable?

**16-23   *Learning curve in make-or-buy decision***   Oxwright Company currently buys a component for one of its products at $22 per unit. Oxwright needs 32,000 units of the component in the coming year. The product will be redesigned, so that the component will not be needed beyond the coming year. The production manager believes that Oxwright could make the component with the following costs for the first batch of 1,000 units.

| | |
|---|---:|
| Materials | $13,000 |
| Direct labor and variable overhead | 15,000 |
| Total variable cost | $28,000 |

Making the component involves no incremental fixed costs because Oxwright could use existing equipment. The production manager expects an 85% learning rate on direct labor and variable overhead. Consider a batch to be 1,000 units.

**Required**
Determine whether Oxwright should make or buy the component.

## CASES

**16-24   *Categorizing quality costs***   Tejas Components is considering implementing a cost of quality reporting system. An initial analysis of quality variables resulted in the following 17 variables:

Design analysis
Design engineering
Equipment repair/maintenance
Liability claims
Manufacturing inspection
Manufacturing process/engineering
Marketing
Product acceptance
Quality engineering
Quality scrap
Quality testing
Quality training
Receiving inspection
Returned merchandise cost
Repair
Rework
Travel

**Required**

Categorize the quality variables into the four quality cost categories. Some of the variables will appear in more than one category.

**16-25   Product mix with production constraints**   The manager of Colfax Company, Lars Anderson, is faced with developing a production schedule for the coming weeks. Colfax Company produces two products in a single plant. Product X has a weekly demand of 40 and is sold for $180. Product Y has a weekly demand of 80 and is sold for $240. There are three raw materials: RM 1 costs $30, RM 2 costs $35, and RM 3 costs $30.

The production process consists of 5 different workstations, each operated by a single employee. Weekly capacity at each workstation is 40 hours. All costs (other than materials) including labor are fixed at $9,800 per week.

Both products X and Y consist of two different subcomponents. Subcomponent ZT-15 is initiated by processing one unit of RM 1 at workstation B for 4 minutes. One unit of RM 2 is processed at workstation B for 5 minutes. The two parts are fastened at workstation E in a procedure that takes 8 minutes, resulting in a completed ZT-15. Subcomponent XP-75 is produced by processing one unit of RM 3 at station C for 9 minutes followed by 18 minutes at station D and 28 minutes at station A, resulting in a completed XP-75.

Product X is manufactured by processing one subcomponent ZT-15 at workstation B for 15 minutes. This is followed by 15 minutes at station C, 20 minutes at station D, and finally 18 more minutes at station C.

Product Y is manufactured by processing one subcomponent ZT-15 at station A for 6 minutes. This is fastened to one subcomponent XP-75 at station E in an 8-minute process. The resulting unit is processed at station E for 9 minutes followed by 6 minutes at station C.

**Required**

1. How many units of product X and product Y should be produced and sold each week?
2. Which workstations should be the "drum" for the plant? Where should buffers be maintained?

## Chapter Seventeen

# STATEMENT OF CASH FLOWS

### LEARNING OBJECTIVES

*After reading this chapter, you should be able to*

- *Explain why investors and others are interested in cash flows.*
- *State the three types of activities reported in a cash flow statement, and classify cash flows by type of activity.*
- *Describe the supplementary information disclosed in a cash flow statement.*
- *Develop cash flow statements.*

In its 1998 annual report, **Microsoft** discussed its cash position, cash flow, and plans for its cash. The report contained the following quotations. "Microsoft's cash and short-term investment portfolio totaled $13.93 billion at June 30, 1998. The portfolio is diversified among security types, industries, and individual issuers. . . . The portfolio is primarily invested in short-term securities to minimize interest rate risk and facilitate rapid deployment in the event of immediate cash needs. Microsoft also invests in equities . . . During 1997 Microsoft invested $1.0 billion in **ComCast Corporation**."

The company said it would also ". . . continue to invest in sales, marketing, and product support infrastructure. Additionally, research and development activities will include investments in existing and advanced areas of technology, including using cash to acquire technology and to fund ventures and other strategic opportunities. Additions to property and equipment will continue, including new facilities and computer systems for research and development, sales and marketing, support, and administrative staff. Commitments for constructing new buildings were $420 million on June 30, 1998." Additionally, "Microsoft's cash and short-term investments are available for strategic investments, mergers and acquisitions, other potential large-scale cash needs that may arise, and to fund an increased stock buyback program . . ."

All of these items evidence significant needs for cash, lots of cash. Where does Microsoft get its cash? The annual report tells us that "Management believes existing cash and short-term investments together with funds generated from operations will be sufficient to meet operating requirements for the next 12 months." Were cash generated by operations insufficient to meet the company's needs, it would have to take other steps, such as we outlined in Chapter 7.

CHAPTER
7

Financial analysts now devote much more attention to cash flow than they once did. Part of the reason is that accrual accounting can conceal problems, as Chapter 14 showed with regard to absorption costing. GAAP have for some years required that companies prepare a cash flow statement to meet investors' needs. Although the cash flow statement is similar to the internally used cash budget introduced in Chapter 7, because the statement is part of the annual report, it is subject to GAAP.[1]

Many users of financial statements misunderstand the cash flow statement and how it relates to the other financial statements. Although this chapter takes the perspective of financial reporting, you should recognize that, as various chapters have pointed out, much of the information in annual reports is also used by internal managers.

## IMPORTANCE OF CASH FLOWS

While profitability is essential to the health of a business, it is not the only important factor. Cash flows are critical to survival and growth. From Chapter 7 we know that managers develop cash budgets to anticipate shortages of cash. Their concern is that cash be available for operations, capital expenditures, debt service, and dividends. From Chapters 8 and 9 we know that cash flows are the critical factor in making investment decisions. You cannot eat income, you can only eat cash flow. Until a company can convert its inventory and receivables into cash, it cannot reinvest to earn more cash.

Managers plan how and when to obtain and use cash. When budgeted cash outflows exceed budgeted inflows, managers face a problem. Sometimes they obtain financing (through borrowing or issuing stock) or sell an existing investment (perhaps securities, or perhaps an entire segment of the business). Sometimes they curtail activities by revising plans for operations (e.g., dropping a special advertising campaign), new investments (e.g., delaying acquisition of new machinery), or payments to financing sources (e.g., delay debt repayment or reduce dividends). Whatever they do, the managers' goal is to balance the cash available and the needs for cash.

Creditors, stockholders, suppliers, and other outsiders also understand the importance of planning and of decisions for balancing available cash and cash needs. They know that cash flows into the company from operations, issuing debt and equity, and sales of assets. They know that companies use cash for operations, dividends, repaying debt, and expansion. They are interested in cash flows because these flows reflect the company's decisions for implementing its short-term and long-term plans for operations, investment, and financing. Stated more generally, outsiders are interested in information about the company's **operating, investing,** and **financing activities** and the cash flows those activities generate. The cash flow statement provides information to assess managerial decisions and performance, prospects for future profit, payments to financing sources, and growth.

For instance, in fiscal 1997, **General Electric** generated enough cash flow from operations to enable it to repurchase $2.8 billion of its own stock, reduce long-

---

1 *The official pronouncement governing cash flow statements is Statement of Financial Accounting Standards Board, No. 95 (Stamford, Conn.: Financial Accounting Standards Board, 1987).*

term debt by $2.5 billion, make $5.2 billion investments in other companies, and add $8.4 billion to its own plant and equipment. Had the company not generated so much cash it would have had to borrow or issue stock, or forego some of its initiatives.

## CASH FLOW STATEMENT

As you might have guessed from the preceding discussion, the **cash flow statement** has three basic parts, which classify cash inflows and outflows as related to operating, investing, or financing activities. Examples follow.

> *Operating flows:* Operating inflows include cash received from customers and from interest and dividends on investments. Outflows include cash paid for inventory, salaries and wages, interest, taxes, and other expenses.
>
> *Investing flows:* Investing inflows include receipts from sales of long-lived assets, such as property, plant, equipment, and patents and from sales of investments. Cash outlays to acquire these same types of assets, or to lend to others, are examples of investing outflows.
>
> *Financing flows:* Financing inflows include cash received from long-term or short-term borrowing, from issuing common or preferred stock, and from selling treasury stock. Dividends, purchases of treasury stock, retirements of bonds, and repayments of other long-term loans are examples of financing outflows.[2]

Beyond the basic classification scheme, a few other considerations affect the content and format of a cash flow statement. Before we present an example of a typical statement and illustrate its development, we discuss the three most important considerations.

### DEFINING CASH

For purposes of the cash flow statement, *cash* includes both cash and **cash equivalents**, which are highly liquid securities such as government notes. This definition recognizes that companies temporarily invest excess cash in such securities. In this chapter, therefore, we use the term *cash* to refer to both cash and cash equivalents.

### OPERATING CASH FLOWS

Reread the examples of operating cash flows provided earlier. Does the income statement report these inflows and outflows? Does net income equal net cash flow from operating activities? The answer to both questions is "no." From your study of financial accounting and of Chapter 7 you know that the income state-

---

2  *Note that interest payments are operating items while dividends are financing items even though both are payments to suppliers of financing. The FASB requires these classifications. The FASB apparently classified interest as an operating item because it is included on the income statement, while dividends are not. The FASB also requires disclosure of total interest payments. The same reasoning appears to apply to interest and dividend revenues, which are cash inflows from investing activities. However, the FASB required separate disclosure of such revenues only if a company presents its operating cash flows using the "direct method," which is discussed later in the chapter.*

ment uses the accrual basis of accounting and does not necessarily reflect cash transactions. For this reason, information about **cash flows from operations** is not directly available from an income statement. Exhibit 17-1 shows the net income and net cash flow from operations reported for four companies. The net cash provided (or used) by operations can be higher or lower than net income, and of course the change in cash over the year differs from both of those amounts. Notice especially **Amazon.com's** figures. The company lost $28 million, yet its operations generated $4 million cash and the company wound up the year with $104 million more than it had to start. All of the companies generated more cash than income, typically because of significant noncash expenses, as we show later.

The FASB permits two reporting methods for operating cash flows. The first, called the **direct method**, reports operating cash inflows and outflows such as collections from customers and payments to employees, suppliers of goods, and other vendors such as utilities. A reporting of operating cash flows under this method resembles a cash budget showing receipts and disbursements for operations.

The second approach, called the **indirect method**, reports the same value for net cash flow from operations as does the direct method, but does so by starting with net income and then adjusting that amount for the effects of noncash items that affected net income. (At least one large company starts with income before taxes, as we describe in a later Insight.) The indirect approach *reconciles* the differences between net income and net cash flow from operations. While terminology varies, most companies call this section of the cash flow statement something like "Adjustments to reconcile net income and net cash flow from operations." Users are so interested in why income differs from net operating cash flow that a company using the direct method must still provide a reconciliation.

Companies that use the indirect method must supplement their statements with disclosures of two specific cash flows. The first is cash paid for interest. The second is cash paid for income taxes.

We use the indirect method in the sample format and illustration because (1) it is the method most often used in practice and (2) you will have to understand the reconciliation approach whether or not the cash flow statement uses that method of presentation.

## NONCASH TRANSACTIONS

Some important operating, investing, and financing activities do not affect cash. For example, during recent fiscal years, **First Union Corporation** reported that it

**Exhibit 17-1   Net Income and Operating Cash Flow, Selected Companies (in millions of dollars)**

|  | Net Income (Loss) | Net Cash Provided by Operations | Net Increase (Decrease) in Cash |
|---|---|---|---|
| Kmart | $ (220) | $    738 | $ (677) |
| DuPont | 2,405 | 6,984 | (62) |
| General Electric | 8,203 | 14,240 | 1,670 |
| Amazon.com | (28) | 4 | 104 |

acquired assets by issuing debt. Acquiring property is an investing activity and taking on debt is a financing activity, but no current cash flow reflects these activities. As another example, First Union reported the conversion of preferred stock into common stock. Both retiring preferred stock and issuing common stock are financing activities, but no cash changed hands.

Significant activities not involving cash must also be reported, either in a supplementary schedule or in narrative form. Whichever alternative is adopted, noncash transactions must be reported in a way that clearly distinguishes them from the cash flows for each of the three major types of activities. For simplicity, we use the supplementary schedule approach in the sample format and basic illustration.

## CASH FLOW STATEMENT FORMAT

Exhibit 17-2 shows the cash flow statement of **Clorox**, which sells everything from bleach to barbeque sauce (K.C. Masterpiece brand), but is mostly in the household cleaner business. The statement uses the indirect method of presenting operating cash flows and reports important noncash transactions and other required disclosures in a supplementary schedule. Notice that Clorox reports both additions to, and reductions of, long-term debt. From the beginning-of-year and end-of-year balance sheets we could determine the net change in long-term debt, but not the separate amounts of new debt and repayments of existing debt. Another noteworthy point in the statement is that, as required by GAAP, it combines the net change in cash with the cash balance at the beginning of the year to produce the end-of-year cash balance. This calculation ties the cash flow statement to the balance sheet, just as starting the operating activities section with net income ties the statement to the income statement. Some companies show the beginning cash balance at the end of the schedule, after the change in cash.

Also notice the description of the net cash flow in each of the three major sections. Depending on the transactions during the year, the net flow in any section could be an inflow or an outflow and the description would be worded accordingly. A few companies simply give a total for each classification, but most use descriptive titles. Note also that the statement provides the required supplementary disclosures for interest and income taxes.

## ILLUSTRATION OF CASH FLOW STATEMENT

The subject of our illustration is VyTrol Corporation, a retailer whose income statement and balance sheets appear in Exhibits 17-3 (page 758) and 17-4 (page 759). Exhibit 17-4 also includes information about some VyTrol activities in 20X5. For convenience, Exhibit 17-4 also shows the increase or decrease in each balance sheet item.

The comparative balance sheets show that VyTrol's cash decreased $190 and that there are no short-term investments that might qualify as cash equivalents. Our objective, then, is to develop a statement that shows how VyTrol's operating, investing, and financing activities combined to produce that decrease. If the net result of all such activities during the current year was to decrease cash by $190, the changes in the other items in the balance sheet must offset the change in cash. We will refer to these other changes as we develop the cash flow statement. When

## Exhibit 17-2   Clorox Company Statement of Cash Flows (thousands of dollars)

| | 1998 | 1997 |
|---|---|---|
| **Operations** | | |
| Net earnings | $ 297,960 | $ 249,442 |
| Adjustments to reconcile to net | | |
| cash provided by operations | | |
| Depreciation and amortization | 137,559 | 126,386 |
| Deferred income taxes | 32,223 | 2,120 |
| Other | 2,699 | (3,864) |
| Effects of changes in | | |
| Accounts receivable | (69,896) | (1,706) |
| Inventories | (38,944) | (24,299) |
| Prepaid expenses | 2,321 | (4,458) |
| Accounts payable | 8,285 | (26,024) |
| Accrued liabilities | (52,940) | 37,866 |
| Income taxes payable | (6,600) | 6,625 |
| Net cash provided by operations | 312,667 | 362,088 |
| **Investing Activities** | | |
| Property, plant, and equipment | (98,979) | (95,188) |
| Businesses purchased | (148,374) | (469,701) |
| Disposal of property, plant, and equipment | 10,461 | 6,116 |
| Other | (73,318) | (13,871) |
| Net cash used for investment | (310,210) | (572,644) |
| **Financing Activities** | | |
| Long-term borrowings | 3,279 | 199,077 |
| Long-term debt and other repayments | (65,390) | (22,678) |
| Short-term borrowings | 201,450 | 193,926 |
| Cash dividends | (132,382) | (119,963) |
| Treasury stock acquired | (83,329) | (54,063) |
| Employee stock plans and other | 62,550 | 24,475 |
| Net cash provided by (used for) financing | (13,822) | 220,774 |
| Net increase (decrease) in cash and | | |
| short-term investments | (11,365) | 10,218 |
| Cash and short-term investments | | |
| Beginning of year | 101,046 | 90,828 |
| End of year | $  89,681 | $ 101,046 |
| **Supplemental Disclosure** | | |
| Cash paid for | | |
| Interest (net of amounts capitalized) | $  71,893 | $  51,813 |
| Income taxes | 96,504 | 120,223 |
| Noncash transactions: | | |
| Liabilities assumed with businesses purchased | $  28,115 | $ 107,227 |
| Share repurchase and other obligations | 79,179 | — |

**Exhibit 17-3    VyTrol Corporation, Combined Income Statement and Statement of Retained Earnings for 20X5**

| | |
|---|---|
| Sales | $1,180 |
| Cost of goods sold | 585 |
| Gross profit | $ 595 |
| Expenses: | |
| Depreciation | $ 178 |
| Interest | 65 |
| Income taxes | 125 |
| Other | 52 |
| Total expenses | $ 420 |
| Net income | $ 175 |
| Retained earnings, beginning of year | 145 |
| | $ 320 |
| Dividends | 90 |
| Retained earning, end of year | $ 230 |

we have explained all of those changes, the cash flow statement will be complete except for some required supplementary disclosures. Let us begin by determining cash flow from operations.

## CASH FROM OPERATIONS

Using the indirect method, we begin with net income of $175. (Note that in starting with net income we are actually dealing with one of the two factors that explain the net change in Retained Earnings. Dividends is the other factor.) Deriving net operating cash flow from net income is not difficult if you keep in mind the makeup of the income statement and the balance sheet. Look at Exhibit 17-3 and ask yourself the following questions.

- Why might revenues on the income statement differ from cash collected from customers?
- Why might cost of goods sold differ from the cash paid to purchase merchandise for sale?
- Why might the amounts reported as expenses not equal the cash paid for those items?

The answers to these questions give the content of the "Adjustments" section of the cash flow statement and come from your understanding of accrual accounting.

### Revenues Versus Cash Inflows

Sales and cash receipts rarely coincide. First, early in the year a company receives cash from customers for sales made last year and included in last year's income statement. (This amount was the amount of accounts receivable at the start of the

### Exhibit 17-4   VyTrol Corporation Balance Sheets as of December 31

| | 20X5 | 20X4 | Increase (Decrease) |
|---|---|---|---|
| **Assets** | | | |
| Current assets | | | |
| Cash and equivalents | $ 130 | $ 320 | $(190) |
| Accounts receivable | 565 | 475 | 90 |
| Inventory | 355 | 285 | 70 |
| Prepayments | 45 | 35 | 10 |
| Total current assets | $1,095 | $1,115 | |
| Noncurrent assets | | | |
| Plant and equipment, at cost | 1,450 | 1,120 | 330 |
| Accumulated depreciation | 455 | 280 | 175 |
| Net | $ 995 | $ 840 | |
| Total assets | $2,090 | $1,955 | |
| **Equities** | | | |
| Current liabilities | | | |
| Accounts payable | $ 200 | $ 145 | $ 55 |
| Short-term loans | 200 | 250 | (50) |
| Accrued income taxes | 35 | 25 | 10 |
| Accrued expenses | 25 | 20 | 5 |
| Total current liabilities | $ 460 | $ 440 | |
| Bonds payable, due 20X9 | 800 | 800 | |
| Total liabilities | $1,260 | $1,240 | |
| Owners' equity | | | |
| Common stock | $ 600 | $ 570 | 30 |
| Retained earnings | 230 | 145 | 85 |
| Total owners' equity | $ 830 | $ 715 | |
| Total equities | $2,090 | $1,955 | |

*Additional information:*
*During the year, VyTrol*
*(a) issued common stock for $20 cash and issued additional stock of $10 for new equipment.*
*(b) obtained a new short-term bank loan for $80 and paid off a total of $130 on that and previous loans.*
*(c) bought new plant and equipment for $328 cash (in addition to that acquired by issuing stock).*
*(d) received $5 cash on the sale of equipment that had cost $8 and had accumulated depreciation of $3.*

year.) Second, for some sales made late in the year, cash will not be collected until next year. (Amounts due at year-end are accounts receivable at the end of the year.) Thus, net income reflects sales made this year regardless of the period in which cash was collected, while cash receipts reflect cash collected this year regardless of the period in which the sales were made.

To move from the amount of net income to the cash flow for the year, we must (1) add the accounts receivable at the beginning of the year and (2) subtract the accounts receivable at the end of the year. In VyTrol's case, we add $475 and subtract $565, giving us the $90 negative adjustment, Increase in Accounts Receivable. This is the second of the items in the Adjustments section of the cash flow statement's section on operating activities. (You might want to look briefly now at the completed statement shown in Exhibit 17-5.)

### Cost of Sales Versus Cash Outflows

Consider next why there is a difference between cost of goods sold ($585) on the income statement and the amount of cash actually paid for merchandise. Two factors create a difference.

First, the beginning and ending inventories affect cost of goods sold for the year regardless of the year in which the company pays for inventory. The beginning inventory increased cost of goods sold and so decreased net income; the ending inventory decreased cost of goods sold and so increased net income. Thus, net income includes the effects of inventories, while cash payments for merchandise do not. To remove from net income the effect of inventories, we must (1) add the beginning inventory and (2) subtract the ending inventory. In VyTrol's case, we add $285 and subtract $355, to obtain $70. This is the third adjustment in the statement in Exhibit 17-5.

The second reason for a difference between cost of goods sold and cash outflows for merchandise is that cost of goods sold shows the merchandise purchases made this year regardless of when the purchased merchandise was paid for. From your knowledge of financial accounting you know two things. First, early in the year the company pays cash for some of the purchases made in the prior year. (This amount was the beginning balance in accounts payable.) Second, some purchases made late in the year will not be paid for until the next year. (Unpaid amounts at year end are the ending balance in accounts payable.) Thus, the amount shown as cost of goods sold in this year's income statement can be higher or lower than cash payments for merchandise, depending on the relationship between the beginning and ending balance in Accounts Payable. To move from net income to the cash flow for the year, we must (1) subtract the accounts payable at the beginning of the year and (2) add the accounts payable at the end of the year. In the case of VyTrol, we subtract $145 and add $200, obtaining the $55 increase in Accounts Payable. This is the fourth adjustment in Exhibit 17-5.

### Operating Expenses and Cash Outflows

Finally, let us consider why other expenses shown on the income statement might not equal cash disbursements. One reason for a difference is well known to you. The first expense listed, depreciation, requires no current disbursement of cash. Depreciation expense reduced net income without having any effect on cash flows this period. Hence, to remove from net income the effect of depreciation expense, we must add depreciation (in VyTrol's case, $178) to net income. This is the first adjustment in Exhibit 17-5. It is typically shown first on published statements.

There are two other reasons for the difference between the amounts shown in the income statement for various expenses and the cash payments for such expenses: accruals and prepayments. Let us consider accruals first.

Early in the year cash is paid to liquidate liabilities for expenses of the prior year (accrued expenses at the beginning of the year); in the latter part of the year expenses are incurred for which cash will not be paid until the next year (the ending balance of accrued expenses). Thus, the current year's income is reduced by

## Exhibit 17-5   VyTrol Corporation, Statement of Cash Flows for 20X5

| | | |
|---|---:|---:|
| **Cash flow from operating activities:** | | |
| Net income | | $ 175 |
| Adjustments for noncash expenses, revenues, | | |
| losses, and gains included in income: | | |
| Depreciation | $ 178 | |
| Increase in accounts receivable | (90) | |
| Increase in inventory | (70) | |
| Increase in accounts payable | 55 | |
| Increase in accrued taxes | 10 | |
| Increase in accrued expenses | 5 | |
| Increase in prepaid expenses | (10) | |
| Total adjustments | | 78 |
| **Net cash flow from operating activities** | | $ 253 |
| **Cash flows from investing activities:** | | |
| Purchase of plant and equipment | $(328) | |
| Sale of equipment | 5 | |
| Net cash (used) by investing activities | | (323) |
| **Cash flows from financing activities:** | | |
| New short-term borrowing | $ 80 | |
| Repayment of short-term debt | (130) | |
| Proceeds from issuing common stock | 20 | |
| Dividends paid on common stock | (90) | |
| Net cash (used) by financing activities | | (120) |
| Net change (decrease) in cash | | $(190) |
| Cash balance, beginning of year | | 320 |
| Cash balance, end of year | | $ 130 |
| | | |
| **Supplementary Disclosures:** | | |
| Interest paid | | $ 65 |
| Income taxes paid | | $ 115 |
| Issuance of common stock to acquire new equipment | | $ 10 |

this year's expenses regardless of the year in which the payments were made. To move from net income to cash flow, we must (1) subtract accrued expenses at the beginning of the year and (2) add accrued expenses at the end of the year. In the case of VyTrol, we subtract $25 and $20, the beginning balances in the two accrued expense accounts (for taxes and wages); then we add $35 and $25, the ending balances of the same two accruals. For simplicity, we will add $10 and $5, the increases in the two accounts. These are the fifth and sixth adjustments in the cash flow statement.

Prepayments of expenses are similar to expense accruals in that the year in which cash is paid is not the year in which the expense affects net income. For prepayments, however, the cash flow occurs before the item appears in the income statement. Thus, the current year's income was reduced by some expenses paid for in the previous year (the beginning balance of prepaid expenses), but cash was paid this year for expenses that will not reduce income until next year (the ending balance of prepaid expenses). To move from net income to the cash flow for the year, we must (1) add the beginning-of-year prepayments and (2) subtract the end-of-year prepayments. VyTrol will add $35 and subtract $45, or simply subtract the $10 increase in Prepaid Expenses. This is the seventh and final adjustment in the cash flow statement and completes the reconciliation of the difference between VyTrol's net income and its cash flow from operations. **Iomega's** annual report explicitly discussed the role of current assets and liabilities. "The primary sources of cash provided by operating activities were net income and increases in accounts payable and accrued liabilities. These sources of cash were partially offset by increases in trade receivables and inventories."

The accompanying Insight shows two alternative ways to present cash flow from operating activities.

 *SIGHT*

### Presentation of Cash Flow

**Dell Computer** abbreviates its presentation of changes in current accounts, lumping all changes in current accounts together as "operating working capital."

DELL COMPUTER CORPORATION
CONSOLIDATED STATEMENT OF CASH FLOWS
(IN MILLIONS)

| | February 1, 1998 | February 1, 1997 | January 28, 1996 |
|---|---|---|---|
| Cash flows from operating activities: | | | |
| Net income | $ 944 | $ 518 | $ 272 |
| Adjustments to reconcile net income to net cash provided by operating activities: | | | |
| Depreciation and amortization | 67 | 47 | 38 |
| Other | 24 | 29 | 22 |
| Changes in: | | | |
| Operating working capital | 529 | 659 | (195) |
| Non-current assets and liabilities | 28 | 109 | 38 |
| Net cash provided by operating activities | $1,592 | $1,362 | $ 175 |

Fiscal Year Ended

## IN SIGHT (continued)

**Merck & Co.** starts its statement with income before taxes and subtracts income taxes later to arrive at net cash flow provided by operations.

Consolidated Statement of Cash Flows
Merck & Co., Inc. and Subsidiaries
Years Ended December 31
($ in millions)

|  | 1997 | 1996 | 1995 |
|---|---|---|---|
| Cash Flows from Operating Activities |  |  |  |
| Income before taxes | $ 6,462.3 | $ 5,540.8 | $ 4,797.2 |
| Adjustments to reconcile income before taxes to cash provided from operations before taxes: |  |  |  |
| Gains on sales of businesses | (213.4) | — | (682.9) |
| Depreciation and amortization | 837.1 | 730.9 | 667.2 |
| Other | 528.4 | 175.1 | 630.1 |
| Net changes in assets and liabilities: |  |  |  |
| Accounts receivable | (271.7) | (224.7) | (244.1) |
| Inventories | (53.5) | (267.6) | (271.8) |
| Accounts payable and accrued liabilities | 321.8 | 414.2 | 383.1 |
| Noncurrent liabilities | 20.4 | 143.0 | (262.0) |
| Other | (19.9) | 10.4 | (43.0) |
| Cash Provided by Operating Activities |  |  |  |
| Before Taxes | 7,611.5 | 6,522.1 | 4,973.8 |
| Income Taxes Paid | (1,294.9) | (1,094.4) | (2,029.6) |
| Net Cash Provided by Operating Activities | $ 6,316.6 | $ 5,427.7 | $ 2,944.2 |

## INVESTING AND FINANCING ACTIVITIES

Look again at the comparative balance sheets in Exhibit 17-4. Every item on the balance sheet, except Bonds Payable, shows a change over the year. We know already that the changes in Accounts Receivable, Inventory, Prepaid Expenses, Accounts Payable, the two expense accruals, and part of the changes in Accumulated Depreciation and Retained Earnings relate to operating activities. What brought about the other changes? Unless our investigation of these changes reveals some way in which they affected net income, they must be related to financing and investing activities.

From the combined statement of income and retained earnings (Exhibit 17-3) we know that VyTrol paid $90 in dividends, which is a financing activity, and the change in Retained Earnings is now fully explained. The additional information in Exhibit 17-4 explains the other changes in the balance sheet. The stock issued for cash (additional information item a) is a financing activity; the stock issued for new equipment is a significant noncash activity to be shown in the schedule of supplementary disclosures. Taking on a new bank loan and repaying old loans (item b) are also financing activities. Items c and d describe the acquisition and sale of property, two types of investing activities.[3]

The cash flow statement is now complete except for the required disclosures of payments for interest and for income taxes. Because the balance sheet shows no accrued interest at either the beginning or the end of the year, the $65 interest expense on the income statement is also the cash paid. Deriving the cash paid for income taxes involves using the same type of reasoning needed to derive the adjustments to net income. The $125 tax expense is not the cash paid because (1) early in the year VyTrol paid $25 for taxes of the prior year (the beginning balance of accrued taxes) and (2) $35 of the tax for the current year will not be paid until next year (the ending balance of accrued taxes). To find the cash paid this year, we must add the $25 and subtract the $35 from the reported expense of $125. The result, $115, is the supplementary disclosure.

To summarize briefly, we started with comparative balance sheets for VyTrol and noted that cash had decreased by $190. To explain that change, we analyzed the changes in all the other items on the balance sheet. The results of that analysis appear in the cash flow statement shown in Exhibit 17-5, which is further discussed in the next section.

## CASH FLOW STATEMENT

Consider first VyTrol's adjustments to net income. If you reflect for a moment about the adjustments, you will recognize that the first, for depreciation, is quite different from the others.

The depreciation adjustment, required because depreciation expense appears on the income statement, has no relation to the operating cash inflows or outflows for the current period. The other six adjustments are needed because of short-term timing differences between cash flows and appearance on the income statement. Once you understand the reasoning for the treatment of these other adjustments, you may find the following rules helpful.

1. Add to net income a decrease in an asset (or an increase in a liability) resulting from operations.
2. Subtract from net income an increase in an asset (or a decrease in a liability) resulting from operations.

Note that the net change in cash, a decrease of $190,000, agrees with the decrease shown in the comparative balance sheets in Exhibit 17-4. The two statements are thus linked, with the cash flow statement describing the cash inflows and out-

---

3 Completing the cash flow statement without some of the additional information in Exhibit 17-4 would be difficult. It is sometimes possible to study the information available within the financial statements, deduce what transactions might have occurred, and then ask questions about such transactions. For example, because accumulated depreciation increased by $175 when depreciation expense was $178, we could infer a sale of some asset(s) with accumulated depreciation of $3 and know that the $330 increase in plant and equipment was a combination of the sale and some acquisitions. Similarly, the $30 increase in common stock would prompt a question about what the company received when the new stock was issued. The availability of the cash flow statement to interested parties outside a company eliminates the need for the parties to make and pursue such inferences, though that approach might be necessary when a statement is not available for some reason.

flows that contributed to the decline in cash, a balance sheet item. The link with the income statement is provided by using the indirect method to present cash flow from operations.

As we have shown, we develop the information for a cash flow statement by analyzing the other financial statements and gathering some other information. Because the company's managers have access to information about its actual cash flows, their task is relatively easy. Without access to information about actual flows, the task is more difficult. But for anyone—manager, stockholder, or creditor—presented with a cash flow statement, what is important is to understand its contents and implications; and that understanding begins with an understanding of how the statement is developed. The accompanying Insight describes how some companies discuss their cash flows in annual reports.

## OPERATING FLOWS—SPECIAL CONSIDERATIONS

In developing VyTrol's cash flow statement, we used the indirect method of presenting operating cash flows. We also used fairly common transactions. In this section we discuss and illustrate two important variations of these basic circumstances.

**SIGHT**

### Discussions of Cash Flow

**Sara Lee Corporation** noted that "Our current goal for financial strength is to maintain a total-debt-to-total-capital ratio of no more than 40% . . . strong cash flow from operations allowed us to maintain a 33.4% leverage ratio despite additional financial requirements for acquisitions, internal growth projects, dividend payments, and the repurchase of almost $400 million of common stock."

**Kmart** pointed to ". . . cash generated by holiday business between Thanksgiving and December 15 was sufficient to pay down the [revolving line of credit]." Kmart owed over $1 billion before Thanksgiving. The company's cash flow was also enough to ". . . retire a $1.2 billion term loan two years ahead of schedule."

**Disney** used its cash flow from operations of over $15 billion during a five-year period to " . . . reinvest in the company's core businesses, in acquisitions and new initiatives, and in selected share repurchase."

**General Electric** told its shareholders that "operating activities are the principal source of GE's cash flows. Over the past three years, operating activities have provided more than $24 billion of cash. The principal application of this cash was distributions of more than $19 billion to share owners, both through payments of dividends ($9.2 billion) and through the share repurchase program ($9.9 billion). . . ."

## DIRECT METHOD, INFLOWS AND OUTFLOWS

Although the indirect method of reporting the cash flow from operating activities is acceptable and most widely used, the FASB and many financial statement users prefer the direct method. Supporters of the direct method stress its separate disclosure of inflows and outflows. Of course, the *net* operating cash flow is the same regardless of the method used. Hence, the same items that reconcile net income with net operating cash flow under the indirect method also explain the differences between cash inflows and outflows for specific items included in the income statement.

Consider the three income statement categories that affected net income for VyTrol Corporation: sales, cost of goods sold, and other expenses. What is the difference between sales reported in the year's income statement and cash received during the year from customers? You answered that question already: the beginning and ending balances in Accounts Receivable. What is the difference between reported cost of goods sold and cash payments to acquire merchandise? You already answered that question, too: the beginning and ending balances in Inventory and Accounts Payable. Finally, why are the expenses shown on the income statement different from the year's cash payments for operating expenses? The answer you already know is that accruals, prepayments, and the noncash expense of depreciation explain the difference.

Thus, the same type of analysis that produced the information needed to reconcile net income with net operating cash flow provides the information needed to present net operating cash flow under the direct method. The only difference is that, to develop the information about inflows and outflows separately, we must adjust individual items in the income statement rather than the net result of those items (net income). Let us determine the separate operating cash flows for VyTrol using the information developed earlier. In each case we begin with the amount shown on the income statement (see Exhibit 17-3) and compute the cash flow for that item.

### Cash Receipts from Customers

Reported sales were $1,180,000, but Accounts Receivable increased by $90,000. We can compute the cash received from customers as follows:

| | | |
|---|---:|---:|
| Sales | | $1,180 |
| Add Accounts Receivable, beginning of year (additional current cash collections) | $ 475 | |
| Deduct Accounts Receivable, end of year (uncollected sales) | (565) | |
| Increase in Accounts Receivable | | (90) |
| Cash receipts from customers | | $1,090 |

### Cash Payments to Merchandise Suppliers

Cost of goods sold was $585, but we know that this amount differed from cash payments to suppliers because of changes in Inventory and in Accounts Payable. To convert Cost of Goods Sold to cash payments to suppliers, we adjust for changes in these two balance sheet items, as follows.

| | | |
|---|---:|---:|
| Cost of goods sold | | $585 |
| Add Inventory, end of year | $ 355 | |
| Deduct Inventory, beginning of year | (285) | |
| Increase in Inventory | | 70 |
| Add Accounts Payable, beginning of year | $ 145 | |
| Deduct Accounts Payable, end of year | (200) | |
| Increase in Accounts Payable | | (55) |
| Cash payments to merchandise suppliers | | $600 |

If you have trouble seeing why an increase in Inventory should be added to cost of goods sold to arrive at cash payments while an increase in Accounts Payable is subtracted, consider again how these items affect cost of goods sold and review our earlier explanation.

### Cash Payments for Expenses

From the earlier analysis we know that depreciation and the changes in Prepaid Expenses and the two accrued expense accounts explain the difference between reported expenses and the cash flows for expenses. As stated earlier, the FASB requires separate disclosure of the cash paid for two expense items, interest and income taxes, regardless of which method is used to present operating cash flows. Hence, although the same calculations apply to all the expenses, we separated these two items from other expenses. Accordingly, we calculate the cash payments for expenses below. We leave depreciation out because we know it does not affect cash flow.

| | Interest | Income Taxes | Other |
|---|---:|---:|---:|
| Expenses for the year | $65 | $125 | $ 52 |
| Eliminate effect of change in prepaid expenses: | | | |
| Deduct beginning prepaid expenses | | | (35) |
| Add ending prepaid expenses | | | 45 |
| Eliminate effect of change in accrued expenses: | | | |
| Add total beginning accrued expenses, $25 + $20 | | 25 | 20 |
| Deduct ending accrued expenses, $35 + $25 | | (35) | (25) |
| Cash payments for expenses | $65 | $115 | $ 57 |

As you can see, the $115 calculated as payments for income taxes agrees with the amount computed and disclosed earlier.

### Direct Method Statement

Exhibit 17-6 shows the cash flow statement for VyTrol Corporation using the direct method. As you can see, net cash flow from operations is the same as that shown in Exhibit 17-5 under the indirect method. Note that, with the use of the direct method, the details of the computations (i.e., the descriptions of the adjustments) are not part of the presentation. Remember, however, that a reconciliation of net income and net cash flow from operations must also be provided.

Companies using the direct method differ in the number and types of items reported separately as operating flows. For example, some highlight amounts paid for wages and fringe benefits, rent, or some other major expense. In the next section we discuss a common circumstance that affects both the computation and reporting of operating cash flows regardless of which reporting approach is followed.

## NONOPERATING GAINS AND LOSSES

One transaction included in the example is unrealistic: the sale of plant and equipment at book value. Because there was no gain or loss on the sale to appear in the income statement, VyTrol had only to report the proceeds as an inflow from investing activities. It is highly unlikely that a company will sell a noncurrent asset for its book value. Rather, the company will almost always have a gain or loss on the sale. The gain or loss appears on the income statement. Reporting a gain or loss in no way changes the fact that the *sale* is an investing activity. The

| Exhibit 17-6    VyTrol Corporation, Statement of Cash Flows for 20X5 | | |
|---|---|---|
| **Cash flow from operating activities:** | | |
| Cash receipts from customers | $1,090 | |
| Cash payments to merchandise suppliers | (600) | |
| Interest paid | (65) | |
| Income taxes paid | (115) | |
| Cash paid for other operating costs | (57) | |
| Net cash flow from operating activities | | $ 253 |
| Cash flows from investing activities: | | |
| Purchase of plant and equipment | (328) | |
| Sale of equipment | 5 | |
| Net cash (used) by investing activities | | (323) |
| Cash flows from financing activities: | | |
| New short-term borrowing | 80 | |
| Repayment of short-term debt | (130) | |
| Proceeds from issuing common stock | 20 | |
| Dividends paid on common stock | (90) | |
| Net cash (used) by financing activities | | (120) |
| Net change (decrease) in cash | | (190) |
| Cash balance, beginning of year | | 320 |
| Cash balance, end of year | | $ 130 |
| | | |
| **Supplementary Disclosure:** | | |
| Issuance of common stock to acquire new equipment | | $   10 |

proceeds from the sale are still an inflow to be reported under investing activities. The complication presented by such sales is that gains and losses are not cash flows from operating activities.

For example, suppose a long-term investment that cost $30,000 is sold for $45,000. The sale provides $45,000 cash, and the cash inflow should appear on the cash flow statement as an investing activity. But the income statement includes the $15,000 gain on the sale. Hence, net income was increased by $15,000 as a result of a nonoperating activity. Under either the direct or the indirect method of presenting operating cash flows, the $15,000 income effect of the sale has to be eliminated. (If the book value of the investment had been $60,000, so that a $15,000 loss, rather than a $15,000 gain, occurred on the sale, the cash inflow would still be $45,000, and the $15,000 loss on the sale would also have to be eliminated to arrive at the cash flow from operating activities.)

Thus, gains and losses from investing activities are adjustments in deriving operating cash flows from amounts reported in an income statement. In a cash flow statement that uses the indirect method of reporting flow from operating activities, losses appear as additions to net income and gains as subtractions.

Let's look at the logic of why gains and losses on sales of noncurrent assets do not directly affect cash. Suppose a company sells a plant asset that cost $50,000 and has accumulated depreciation of $30,000 (book value of $20,000). First, suppose the sale is for $24,000, giving a $4,000 gain; then suppose the sale is for $15,000, giving a $5,000 loss. In journal entry form, the sales would show as follows:

| | | |
|---|---|---|
| Sale for $24,000: | | |
| Cash | $24,000 | |
| Accumulated Depreciation | 30,000 | |
| Plant and Equipment | | $50,000 |
| Gain on Sale of Equipment | | 4,000 |
| Sale for $15,000: | | |
| Cash | $15,000 | |
| Accumulated Depreciation | 30,000 | |
| Loss on Sale of Equipment | 5,000 | |
| Plant and Equipment | | $50,000 |

In both cases, the cash flow is the amount of cash received. The gain or loss is reported on the income statement. Because the gain or loss is not a cash flow and the sale of a noncurrent asset is not an operating activity, the gain or loss must be removed to determine cash provided by operations using the indirect method. Using the direct method, the gain or loss is simply not reported and no adjustment is needed.

## CONCLUDING COMMENTS

Over the years, a common misconception has arisen that depreciation and similar expenses are inflows of cash. This misconception is understandable if we recognize that the indirect method of computing operating cash flows has predominated in practice and that under that method depreciation is added to net income to arrive at cash flow from operations. As you know, depreciation neither increases nor decreases cash. Depreciation requires no current outlay of cash; rather, a cash outflow occurs at the time the asset is acquired, and that outflow is reported as an investing activity.

In one sense, however, depreciation influences cash flows. Because depreciation is deductible for tax purposes, a company's income tax payment— which *is* an operating cash flow—is lower than it would have been had there been no depreciation to deduct. Hence, net cash inflow from operations is higher than would be the case had there been no depreciation.

We should also point out that the cash flow statement provides information beyond a classified listing of the company's cash flows. As we note in the next chapter, an understanding and evaluation of a company's activities requires study of more than one year's financial statements. At this point we comment only briefly on insights that might be provided by review of the cash flow statements.

Consider VyTrol, the company whose cash flow statements we developed. Exhibit 17-5 (and Exhibit 17-6) shows that VyTrol's net cash expenditure for plant assets ($323,000) was more than the cash made available from normal operations ($253,000) and traditional sources of long-term financing sources ($20,000 from new common stock issued for cash). Is this a good or bad sign? As you might expect, the answer is that it depends. A substantial net new investment in plant and equipment suggests expansion and the potential for growth in earnings. True, normal operating activities and financing sources didn't provide enough cash for VyTrol's new investment. But VyTrol's cash balance at the beginning of 20X5 was relatively large (about 17 percent of total assets), which might indicate that VyTrol obtained significant new financing in the preceding year. (Remember that managers plan in advance to meet cash needs for planned capital expenditures.) Thus, a reader should review VyTrol's prior year's financial statements, particularly the cash flow statement, before drawing any conclusions. To return to the ideas presented at the beginning of this chapter, perhaps the primary value of a cash flow statement is that it shows managers' current responses to planned short-term and long-term needs for cash. The accompanying Insight describes how one financial commentator views the cash flow statement.

## SUMMARY

Information about flows of cash is important to both managers and external parties. Generally accepted accounting principles require a cash flow statement as part of the financial statement package. *Cash* means both cash and cash equivalents such as highly liquid short-term investments.

Activities affecting cash are operating, investing, or financing activities. A cash flow statement reports the amount of cash provided or used by these three categories. Significant activities having no effect on cash flows are also reported, either in narrative form or in a separate schedule of the cash flow statement.

Companies can report cash flows from operating activities in two ways. The indirect method reconciles net income with the net cash flow from operations. The indirect method does not report operating inflows and outflows separately. The direct method reports inflows and outflows separately but does not offer a direct

 **SIGHT**

## Importance of Operating Flows

When some analysts quoted in *The Wall Street Journal* questioned the high stock price of **Amazon.com**, one commentator pointed out that Amazon's cash flows were one ingredient in its lofty price. (The stock was then selling for over $100 per share and the company had yet to show a profit.) He presented the following schedule, which depicts the excess or deficiency of each company's net cash flows from operating activities over their capital spending. In other words, how much financing do the companies have to acquire to support their building infrastructure to operate on the Internet and their other capital requirements. The less cash companies must raise on the market, the higher the returns their stockholders will earn. (Companies that borrow must pay interest, those that issue stock dilute the ownership interest of existing stockholders. Chapter 18 deals with such matters.)

Net Cash Flows from Operating Activities Less
Cash Used for Capital Expenditures and Acquisitions
($ in millions)

|  | 1997 | 1996 | 1995 |
|---|---|---|---|
| **Barnes & Noble** | $ 47.3 | $(52.3) | $(211.8) |
| **Borders** | (28.0) | 4.0 | (104.3) |
| **Amazon.com** | (3.7) | (2.9) | (0.3) |

Even though Amazon was growing at sensational rates, with sales in fiscal 1997 up 838 percent from 1996, the company did not consume cash the way the other book retailers did. Amazon used payables to finance much of its operations, but its growth is cheaper to finance than that of the others. Moreover, Amazon's cash outflows necessary to finance growth are comparatively very small. The commentator concluded "It's all about how much of the shareholders' cash the company has to spend to grow. Period. With that in mind, investors can forget the flabby theories on retail investors' buying influence and whatever else. What you need to know is on the cash flow statement."

*Source: Dale Wettlaufer, "Wall Street Journal Takes on Amazon," The Motley Fool, July 8, 1998.*

link between the cash flow statement and reported net income. To provide that link, companies using the direct method must also provide a reconciliation of net income to net cash flow from operations. Cash flow statements prepared using either the direct or the indirect method will report the same net cash flow from operations, the same cash flows relating to investing and financing activities, and the same net change for cash, and will disclose the cash paid for interest and for income taxes.

## KEY TERMS

cash equivalents   *(754)*              financing activities   *(753)*
cash flow from operations   *(755)*     indirect method   *(755)*
cash flow statement   *(754)*           investing activities   *(753)*
direct method   *(755)*                 operating activities   *(753)*

## REVIEW PROBLEM

Comparative balance sheets and a combined statement of income and retained earnings for Quadro Company appear in Exhibits 17-7 and 17-8.

### Exhibit 17-7   Quadro Company, Balance Sheets as of December 31

|                                  | 20X7   | 20X6   |
|----------------------------------|--------|--------|
| **Assets**                       |        |        |
| **Current assets**               |        |        |
| Cash and equivalents             | $   90 | $  115 |
| Accounts receivable              | 225    | 210    |
| Inventory                        | 180    | 220    |
| Prepayments                      | 20     | 5      |
| Total current assets             | $  515 | $  550 |
| **Noncurrent assets**            |        |        |
| Plant and equipment, at cost     | $1,200 | $  950 |
| Accumulated depreciation         | 600    | 480    |
| Net                              | $  600 | $  470 |
| Total assets                     | $1,115 | $1,020 |
| **Equities**                     |        |        |
| **Current liabilities**          |        |        |
| Accounts payable                 | $  110 | $   80 |
| Accrued income taxes             | 20     | 30     |
| Accrued expenses                 | 15     | 30     |
| Total current liabilities        | $  145 | $  140 |
| Bonds payable, due 20X9          | 260    | 330    |
| Total liabilities                | $  405 | $  470 |
| **Owners' equity**               |        |        |
| Common stock                     | $  430 | $  380 |
| Retained earnings                | 280    | 170    |
| Total owners' equity             | $  710 | $  550 |
| Total equities                   | $1,115 | $1,020 |

### Exhibit 17-8   Quadro Company, Income Statement and Statement of Retained Earnings for 20X7

| | | |
|---|---:|---:|
| Sales | | $975 |
| Cost of goods sold | | 455 |
| Gross profit | | $520 |
| Operating expenses: | | |
| Depreciation | $130 | |
| Interest | 40 | |
| Other | 50 | |
| Total | | 220 |
| Operating income | | $300 |
| Gain on sale of plant assets | | 15 |
| Income before taxes | | $315 |
| Income taxes | | 95 |
| Net income | | $220 |
| Retained earnings, beginning of year | | 170 |
| | | $390 |
| Dividends | | 110 |
| Retained earnings, end of year | | $280 |

The following additional information is also available.

(a) The company issued common stock for $50 cash.

(b) The company sold equipment for $30. The equipment cost $25 and had accumulated depreciation of $10.

**Required**

1. Determine cash flow from operations using the indirect method.
2. Prepare a cash flow statement for 20X7.
3. Show the cash flow from operations using the direct method. Show separately the cash inflow from sales and the cash outflows for merchandise purchases, operating expenses, interest, and income taxes.

## ANSWER TO REVIEW PROBLEM

1. To compute cash flow from operations we must determine the adjustments to net income. The income statement reveals the need for two adjustments:

   (a) Depreciation is a noncash expense.

   (b) The sale of a long-term investment, a nonoperating transaction, has increased income.

   We can then turn to the comparative balance sheets. They reveal the need for three additional adjustments:

   (c) The increase in Accounts Receivable means that cash collections from customers were less than sales.

   (d) The change in Inventory means that purchases were greater than cost of sales.

   (e) The increase in Prepayments means that payments for expenses were greater than the expenses.

(f)  The increase in Accounts Payable means there is a difference between cash outflows for operations and purchases of goods. In conjunction with the change in Inventory, this change means that cash paid for merchandise exceeded cost of goods sold.

(g)  The changes in the two types of accrued expenses means that there are differences between operating cash outflows for expenses and reported operating expenses and taxes.

Changes in the other balance sheet items, though they may have affected cash, would not have given rise to operating cash flows. If such changes affected net income, their effects should be eliminated from net income as we compute the cash flow from operating activities. Let us look at the other balance sheet changes.

The changes in long-term debt and common stock, whatever their causes, give rise to financing flows. Again, there is no evidence (such as a gain from retirement of debt) in the income statement that financing activities affected net income. The change in Retained Earnings is explained by net income, which we have already considered, and the payment of dividends, which is a financing activity.

Thus, we can compute the cash flow from operations by starting with net income and making the adjustments (a) through (g).

| Reconciliation of Net Income and Cash from Operations | | |
|---|---|---|
| Net income | | $220 |
| Adjustments to reconcile net income and net cash provided by operating activities: | | |
| (a) Depreciation | $130 | |
| (b) Gain on sale of plant assets | (15) | |
| (c) Increase in accounts receivable | (15) | |
| (d) Decrease in inventory | 40 | |
| (e) Increase in prepayments | (15) | |
| (f) Increase in accounts payable | 30 | |
| (g) Decrease in accrued income taxes | (10) | |
| (g) Decrease in accrued expenses | (15) | |
| | | 130 |
| Net cash flow from operating activities | | $350 |

2.  In requirement 1, the information needed for one section of the statement, cash flow from operations, was developed. Our objective now is to find any nonoperating inflows or outflows of cash. For this information we refer again to the balance sheet changes that did not affect cash flow from operations. The changes, already discussed briefly, are summarized as follows:

| Item | Change Increase (Decrease) | Change Already Explained Increase (Decrease) |
|---|---|---|
| Plant and equipment | $250 | $(25) |
| Accumulated depreciation | 120 | 130 |
| Long-term debt | (70) | |
| Common stock | 50 | |
| Retained earnings | 110 | 205 |

Let us examine each of these changes.

The normal reason for an increase in Plant and Equipment is purchases of new equipment. But, we already know that during the year the company sold equipment that originally cost $25, reducing Plant and Equipment by $25. Thus, the purchases of new plant and equipment must have been enough to offset this decrease and produce a net increase in Plant and Equipment of $250, or $275 ($250 + $25). So we have two transactions: sale of equipment and purchase of equipment, both of which involve investing cash flows. The old equipment was sold for $30, and this amount should be reported as an investing cash inflow. The new equipment must have cost $275 and should be reported as an investing use of cash.

As we know, depreciation neither produces nor uses cash. Hence, the change in Accumulated Depreciation is not a cash inflow or outflow. Accumulated Depreciation increased by $130 because of the current year's depreciation expense, as shown on the income statement. Accumulated Depreciation decreased by $10 because an asset on which depreciation of $10 had accumulated was sold. The net change is an increase of $120 (an increase of $130 offset by a decrease of $10). In our analysis of Plant and Equipment, we determined that an investing cash inflow of $30 should be reported in connection with the sale of equipment.

The normal reason for a decline in long-term debt is that some of the debt was repaid. Such a repayment is a financing outflow. Since we have no evidence to indicate some other reason for the decrease, we shall report the decline as a financing outflow in the amount of $70.

Common Stock increased by $50; the usual explanation for such an increase is that the company issued additional shares of stock. This conclusion is confirmed by the information at the beginning of the problem, and so we include among the financing inflows of cash the issuance of additional stock for $50.

The lower portion of Exhibit 17-8 reports that the net change in Retained Earnings resulted from an increase because of net income and a decrease because of dividends. Net income is an operating source of cash, and we have already dealt with cash from operations. The payment of dividends should be reported on our statement as a $95 financing outflow of cash.

The completed cash flow statement appears in Exhibit 17-9 on pages 776-777.

3. Calculating cash flow from operations under the direct method requires using the adjustments determined in requirement 1. Following are the calculations of specific operating cash inflows and outflows. We already know that the only other item to affect net income, the gain on sale of plant assets, resulted from an investing, rather than an operating, activity. Hence, neither the gains nor the proceeds from the sale are reported as a part of the cash flow from operations. If Quadro used the direct method of reporting its cash flow from operations, that segment of its cash flow statement would appear as follows:

| Net cash flow from operating activities: | |
|---|---:|
| Cash receipts from customers | $ 960 |
| Cash payments to merchandise suppliers | (385) |
| Cash paid for interest | (40) |
| Cash paid for income taxes | (105) |
| Cash payments for operating expenses | (80) |
| Net cash provided by operating activities | $ 350 |

Note that the $335 cash provided by operating activities agrees with the amount shown in Exhibit 17-9, where the indirect method was used.

**Exhibit 17-9    Quadro Company Statement of Cash Flow for 20X7**

| | | |
|---|---:|---:|
| **Net cash flow from operating activities:** | | |
| Net income | | $ 220 |
| Depreciation | $ 130 | |
| Gain on sale of plant assets | (15) | |
| Increase in accounts receivable | (15) | |
| Decrease in inventory | 40 | |
| Increase in prepayments | (15) | |
| Increase in accounts payable | 30 | |
| Decrease in accrued income taxes | (10) | |
| Decrease in accrued expenses | (15) | |
| Total adjustments | | 130 |
| Net cash flow from operating activities | | $ 350 |
| **Cash flows from investing activities:** | | |
| Acquisition of plant and equipment | $(275) | |
| Sale of equipment | 30 | |
| Net cash used in investing activities | | (245) |
| **Cash flows from financing activities:** | | |
| Issues of common stock | $  50 | |
| Repayments of long-term debt | (70) | |
| Dividends | (110) | |
| Net cash used in financing activities | | (130) |
| Net decrease in cash | | $ (25) |
| Cash balance, beginning of year | | 115 |
| Cash balance, end of year | | $  90 |
| | | |
| **Supplemental disclosure:** | | |
| Cash paid for interest | | $  40 |
| Cash paid for income taxes | | $ 105 |
| | | |
| **Cash receipts from customers:** | | |
| Sales | | $ 975 |
| Add accounts receivable, beginning of year | $ 210 | |
| Less accounts receivable, end of year | (225) | |
| Increase in accounts receivable | | (15) |
| Cash collections from customers | | $ 960 |
| | | |
| **Cash payments for merchandise:** | | |
| Cost of goods sold | | $ 455 |
| Add ending inventory | $ 180 | |
| Less beginning inventory | (220) | |
| Decrease in inventory | | (40) |
| Add beginning accounts payable | $  80 | |
| Less ending accounts payable | (110) | |
| Increase in accounts payable | | (30) |
| Cash paid for merchandise | | $ 385 |

---

**Exhibit 17-9   Quadro Company Statement of Cash Flow for 20X7** *(continued)*

Cash payments for operating expenses:

| | Interest | Taxes | Other |
|---|---|---|---|
| Expenses for the year | $40 | $ 95 | $ 50 |
| Add prepayments, end of year | | | 20 |
| Less prepayments, beginning of year | | | (5) |
| Add accruals, beginning of year | | 30 | 30 |
| Less accruals, end of year | | (20) | (15) |
| Cash paid for operating expenses | $40 | $105 | $ 80 |

---

## ASSIGNMENT MATERIAL

### INTERNET ACTIVITY

Find cash flow statements of two companies in traditional industries such as autos, steel, or paper, and two in newer industries such as telecommunications equipment, computers, or internet commerce. What are the principal differences in cash flows for these two types of companies? For example, which group generates relatively more of its cash flows from operating activities? What are the major uses of cash for each group?

### QUESTIONS FOR DISCUSSION

**17-1   *Depreciation provides cash?*** One frequently hears businesspeople say that depreciation is a major source of cash. Explain why this statement is or is not true.

**17-2   *Net income and cash flow*** Hank Rogers started Rogers Metals five years ago. The shop has been profitable and Mr. Rogers has been withdrawing cash in an amount equal to net income each year. He has taken out an amount equal to nearly half of his original investment of $80,000, most of which was used originally to purchase machinery. Mr. Rogers' customers pay cash on completion of work. He keeps very little inventory and pays his bills promptly, and he is puzzled because the cash balance keeps growing despite his withdrawals. Can you explain the increase in cash?

**17-3   *Relationship of net income and cash flow*** Suppose that a large, rapidly growing retail chain and a mature steel company earned the same income. Which company would you expect to show the higher cash provided by operations? Explain your answer.

**17-4   *Explanation of a cash flow statement*** You have provided the president of Pecknell Company with a full set of financial statements, including a statement of cash flows. He understands everything except some of the adjustments in the operations section of the statement. He has three specific questions.

1. "Why do you subtract the increase in accounts receivable? We don't pay out cash for our accounts receivable, we collect it."

2. "You show the decrease in inventory as an addition. We sure didn't get any cash because our inventory decreased. In fact, the decrease means that we have less to sell next year and will have to spend more cash to replenish our supply. So why add it back to net income?"

3. "Our accrued expenses increased, and you showed this as an addition? Look, we had especially heavy payroll costs at the end of the year, and we paid them the third day of the new year. So it seems to me that we had to use more cash because of the increase, not less."

**Required**
Explain each of the items to the president.

**17-5   Clorox's cash flow statements**   Refer to the **Clorox** cash flow statements in Exhibit 17-2 on page 757. Answer the following questions.

1. What was the difference between Clorox's sales and its cash receipts from customers in 1998?
2. Did Clorox pay its suppliers more or less than the amount of its purchases in 1998? How much more or less?
3. Did any of Clorox's current assets and current liabilities increase in both 1997 and 1998? Decrease in both 1997 and 1998?
4. Did any current asset decrease in 1998?
5. Did Clorox add to or reduce its debt, other than payables and accruals, in 1998?
6. Was Clorox's operating cash flow sufficient to cover its investing activities in 1998? In 1997?

## EXERCISES

**17-6   Cash flow from operations**   Use the following information to prepare the operations section of a cash flow statement for Steiner Co. for 20X6.

| | |
|---|---|
| Net income | $250,000 |
| Increase in inventory | 40,000 |
| Increase in accounts payable | 25,000 |
| Depreciation expense | 70,000 |
| Increase in accounts receivable | 20,000 |
| Gain on sale of land | 30,000 |

**17-7   Basic cash flow statement**   Use the information below to prepare a statement of cash flows for Grina Corporation for 20X8.

| | |
|---|---|
| Depreciation expense | $110,000 |
| Decrease in inventory | 20,000 |
| Increase in accounts payable | 12,000 |
| Purchases of plant and equipment | 500,000 |
| Increase in accounts receivable | 40,000 |
| Dividends paid to shareholders | 60,000 |
| Net income | 170,000 |
| Issuance of common stock for cash | 400,000 |
| Retirement of long-term bonds | 70,000 |

**17-8    Cash receipts from customers**    Fill in the blanks in the following schedule.

| | Case A | Case B | Case C | Case D |
|---|---|---|---|---|
| Sales for 20X8 | $800,000 | $1,000,000 | $_____ | $650,000 |
| Accounts receivable: | | | | |
| At beginning of 20X8 | 42,000 | 37,000 | 28,000 | 31,000 |
| At end of 20X8 | 25,000 | 45,000 | 45,000 | _____ |
| Cash collected from | | | | |
| customers in 20X8 | $_____ | $_____ | $853,000 | $625,000 |

**17-9    Cash payments to merchandise suppliers**    For each of the following cases, compute the cash paid in 20X7 to merchandise suppliers.

| | Case A | Case B |
|---|---|---|
| Cost of goods sold in 20X7 | $431,000 | $845,000 |
| Merchandise inventory: | | |
| Beginning of 20X7 | 105,000 | 167,000 |
| End of 20X7 | 83,000 | 116,000 |
| Accounts payable: | | |
| Beginning of 20X7 | 31,000 | 37,000 |
| End of 20X7 | 42,000 | 33,000 |
| Cash paid to merchandise | | |
| suppliers in 20X7 | $_____ | $_____ |

**17-10    Relationships**    Fill in the blanks in the following schedule.

| | Case A | Case B | Case C |
|---|---|---|---|
| Cost of goods sold in 20X3 | $649,000 | $621,000 | $_____ |
| Merchandise inventory: | | | |
| Beginning of 20X3 | 91,000 | 57,000 | 262,000 |
| End of 20X3 | 84,000 | 71,000 | 245,000 |
| Accounts payable: | | | |
| Beginning of 20X3 | 42,000 | 68,000 | 93,000 |
| End of 20X3 | 51,000 | _____ | 85,000 |
| Cash paid to merchandise | | | |
| suppliers in 20X3 | $_____ | $623,000 | $2,824,000 |

**17-11    Components of cash flow from operating activities**    Which of the following items appears in the operations section of the cash flow statement for Washburn Company? Washburn uses the indirect method.

1. Depreciation expense.
2. Increase in Dividends Payable.
3. Decrease in Income Taxes Payable.
4. Loss from sale of long-term investments.
5. Decrease in Prepaid Insurance.
6. Increase in Inventory.
7. Proceeds from sale of long-term investments.
8. Increase in Accounts Receivable.
9. Amortization of patents covering Washburn's major product.
10. Payment for machinery to be used to produce Washburn's major product.

**17-12   *Classifying activities***   Classify each of the following transactions as an operating, investing, or financing activity.

1. Sale of merchandise for cash.
2. Sale of merchandise on account.
3. Sale of a fully depreciated machine for cash.
4. Declaration of a cash dividend on common stock.
5. Payment of a previously declared cash dividend on common stock.
6. Purchase of merchandise on credit.
7. Payment of cash for purchase made in item 6.
8. Payment of the premium on a three-year policy for theft insurance on the company's inventory.
9. Acquisition of land by issuing a long-term note payable.
10. Payment of wages.
11. Purchase of 10,000 shares of the company's common stock from some of its stockholders. The price paid is less than that at which the shares were originally issued.
12. Sale of 5,000 shares of treasury stock at a price in excess of that paid to acquire that stock.
13. Accrual of interest due on a 20-year mortgage note payable.
14. Payment of previously accrued wages and salaries for employees.

**17-13   *Reconciliation of net income and cash from operations***   Prepare a reconciliation of net income and net cash flow from operations using the relevant items from the following list.

| | |
|---|---:|
| Increase in land | $ 76,000 |
| Increase in accounts receivable | 62,000 |
| Increase in accrued expenses payable | 6,800 |
| Decrease in inventory | 35,000 |
| Decrease in accounts payable | 48,000 |
| Decrease in prepaid insurance | 1,500 |
| Increase in common stock | 365,000 |
| Loss on sale of long-term investment | 53,000 |
| Net income | 284,000 |
| Depreciation expense | 61,000 |
| Decrease in cash | 14,000 |
| Cash received from sale of long-term investment | 156,300 |
| Cash provided by operations | 331,300 |

**17-14   *Cash payments for operating expenses***   For each of the following three cases, compute the cash paid in 20X7 for operating expenses.

| | Case A | Case B | Case C |
|---|---:|---:|---:|
| Operating expenses in 20X7 | $476,900 | $ 71,425 | $4,150,000 |
| Prepaid expenses: | | | |
|   Beginning of 20X7 | 32,000 | 1,063 | 97,100 |
|   End of 20X7 | 29,300 | 741 | 105,400 |
| Accrued expenses payable: | | | |
|   Beginning of 20X7 | 11,200 | 2,460 | 57,800 |
|   End of 20X7 | 15,100 | 1,245 | 53,400 |
| Cash paid in 20X7 for operating expenses | $_____ | $_____ | $_____ |

**17-15   *Relationships*   Fill in the blanks in the following schedule.**

|  | Case A | Case B | Case C |
|---|---|---|---|
| Operating expenses in 20X7 | $827,400 | $223,800 | $_____ |
| Prepaid expenses: |  |  |  |
|   Beginning of 20X7 | 25,400 | 15,500 | 103,000 |
|   End of 20X7 | 19,300 | _____ | 81,000 |
| Accrued expenses payable: |  |  |  |
|   Beginning of 20X7 | 48,800 | 11,400 | 193,000 |
|   End of 20X7 | 51,100 | 14,300 | 242,000 |
| Cash paid in 20X7 for operating |  |  |  |
|   expenses | $_____ | $218,400 | $4,250,000 |

**17-16   *Cash from operations*   In 20X9, Drew Company reported net income of $33,000. You also have the following information about 20X9.**

1. Depreciation expense for the year was $132,000.
2. Accounts Receivable increased by $17,000.
3. Inventory declined by $7,000.
4. Accounts Payable decreased by $12,000.
5. Accrued Expenses increased by $6,000.

**Required**

Determine cash flow from operations.

**17-17   *Effects of transactions*   Determine the effect, if any, of each of the following transactions on (a) net income and (b) cash. Show the amount of the change and its direction (+ or −).**

1. Common stock with a market value of $700,000 was issued in exchange for equipment.
2. A cash dividend of $200,000 was declared, but not paid.
3. The dividend in item 2 was paid.
4. An account receivable of $12,000 was written off against the Allowance for Doubtful Accounts.
5. A customer who owed the company $22,000 on account gave the company equipment with a fair market value of $22,000 in settlement of the receivable.
6. Interest payable was accrued in the amount of $14,000.
7. The interest payable in item 6 was paid.
8. The company bought 100 shares of its own stock for the treasury. The cost was $4,600, paid in cash.
9. Inventory with a cost of $18,000 was written off as obsolete.
10. Plant assets that had cost $45,000 and were one-third depreciated were sold for $12,000 cash.

**17-18   *Classifying activities*   Indicate whether each of the following transactions is an operating, investing, or financing activity.**

1. Cash collected on previously recorded credit sale of merchandise.
2. Sale of factory machinery for an amount of cash that exceeds the machine's book value.
3. Sale of factory machinery for an amount of cash that is less than the machine's book value.
4. Payment of cash for a previously recorded credit purchase.
5. Payment of the premium on a three-year policy for theft insurance on the company's inventory.

6. Acquisition of land by issuing common stock having a market value in excess of par.
7. Payment of wages.
8. Purchase of 10,000 shares of the company's common stock from some of its stockholders. The price paid is in excess of the price at which the shares were originally issued.
9. Sale of 5,000 shares of treasury stock at a price in excess of that paid to acquire the stock.
10. Payment of previously accrued interest on a 5-year note payable.
11. Receipt of insurance proceeds as a result of destruction of the company's factory buildings and machinery because of an earthquake. (The proceeds exceeded the book value of buildings and machinery destroyed.)

**17-19   *Analysis of noncurrent accounts*** The following data were taken from the records of Miller Mining Company.

|  | End of Year | |
|---|---|---|
|  | 20X6 | 20X5 |
| Plant and equipment | $ 5,240,000 | $4,980,000 |
| Accumulated depreciation | (1,080,000) | (840,000) |
| Mineral properties, net of depletion | 6,750,000 | 5,950,000 |

You have also determined that plant and equipment costing $350,000 and with accumulated depreciation of $110,000 was sold for $60,000 and that depletion expense related to mineral properties was $440,000. The only other transactions affecting the accounts shown were depreciation expense, purchases of plant and equipment, and purchases of mineral properties.

**Required**

1. Determine the amount of cash provided by sales of plant and equipment.
2. Determine the gain or loss to be added or subtracted in the reconciliation of net income to cash flow from operations.
3. Determine the amount of depreciation expense to be added to net income in the reconciliation of net income to cash flow from operations.
4. Determine the amount of cash paid to buy plant and equipment.
5. Determine the amount of cash paid to buy mineral properties.

**17-20   *Cash flow from operations—special situations (continuation of 17-16)*** After more careful study of Drew Company's income statement for 20X9, you determine that the following items also affected net income.

1. Amortization of intangible assets, $22,000.
2. Loss on sale of plant assets, $3,000.
3. On one sale of merchandise, for $24,000, the customer gave Drew a 5-year note bearing interest at 9%.

**Required**
Recompute cash provided by operations.

## PROBLEMS

**17-21   *Statement preparation*** Following is a list of items for the cash flow statement for Cryton, Inc. for the year 20X8.

| | |
|---|---:|
| Net income | $430,000 |
| Dividends paid | 210,000 |
| Proceeds from sale of a 10-year bond | 650,000 |
| Amortization of patents | 42,000 |
| Depreciation expense | 158,000 |
| Decrease in inventory | 17,000 |
| Increase in accounts receivable | 104,000 |
| Decrease in accrued expenses | 2,000 |
| Cash purchase of new equipment | 510,000 |
| Cash purchase of a long-term investment | 265,000 |
| Increase in income taxes payable | 6,000 |
| Decrease in accounts payable | 48,000 |
| Purchase of land and buildings by giving a 10-year note | 350,000 |

**Required**

Prepare a cash flow statement for 20X8. You should use all the items given and find that cash increased by $164,000.

**17-22   *Converting cash flow to income***   Boyd Company uses the direct method of reporting cash flow from operations. Following is the operations section of its cash flow statement for 20X7.

| | | |
|---|---:|---:|
| Cash receipts from customers | | $980,000 |
| Cash payments for: | | |
|   Merchandise | $496,000 | |
|   Wages and salaries | 220,000 | |
|   Income taxes | 35,000 | |
|   Other operating expenses | 140,000 | |
|     Total cash payments for operating activities | | 891,000 |
| Cash provided by operations | | $ 89,000 |

Other data taken from Boyd's records for 20X7 show the following.

(a) Accounts receivable increased by $30,000.
(b) Accounts payable decreased by $2,000.
(c) Inventory remained constant at $150,000.
(d) Accrued wages and salaries (the only accrued expense) increased by $4,000.
(e) Depreciation expense was $72,000.

**Required**

Determine Boyd Company's net income for 20X7.

**17-23   *Reconciliation of net income and cash flow from operations (continuation of 17-22)***   Using the data provided in Problem 17-22 prepare a reconciliation of net income and cash flow from operations.

**17-24   *Cash flow statement from comparative balance sheets***   Following are balance sheets for Belmarle Company at December 31, 20X5 and 20X6, in thousands.

|  | December 31 | |
| --- | --- | --- |
|  | 20X5 | 20X6 |
| Cash | $ 2,000 | $ 3,000 |
| Accounts receivable, net | 13,000 | 16,000 |
| Inventory | 20,000 | 23,000 |
| Property, plant, and equipment, net | 50,000 | 57,000 |
| Total assets | $85,000 | $99,000 |
| Accounts payable | $ 5,000 | $ 4,000 |
| Notes payable, due in one year | 6,000 | 5,000 |
| Long-term notes payable | 10,000 | 16,000 |
| Common stock | 60,000 | 67,000 |
| Retained earnings | 4,000 | 7,000 |
| Total equities | $85,000 | $99,000 |

The following information is also available about the company's transactions in 20X6.

(a) Net income was $12,000.
(b) Depreciation on plant and equipment was $6,000.
(c) Property, plant, and equipment costing $7,000 was purchased for cash.
(d) Dividends of $9,000 were declared and paid.
(e) Equipment was purchased by giving a $6,000 long-term note.

**Required**
Prepare a cash flow statement for 20X6. Use the indirect method to present operating cash flows.

**17-25  Determining cash flow from operations**  Use the information provided to determine cash flow from operations.

| | |
| --- | --- |
| From the income statement: | |
| Sales | $1,850,000 |
| Cost of goods sold | 925,000 |
| Operating expenses | 683,000 |
| Depreciation (included in operating expenses) | 73,000 |
| From the balance sheet: | |
| Increase in Accounts Receivable | 25,000 |
| Decrease in Prepaid Expenses | 12,000 |
| Decrease in Inventory | 37,000 |
| Decrease in Accounts Payable | 68,000 |
| Increase in Accrued Expenses | 17,000 |

**17-26  Cash from operations—direct method (continuation of 17-25)**  Use your results from Problem 17-25 to prepare the operations section of the cash flow statement using the direct method of presenting operating cash flows.

**17-27  Distinguishing operating cash flows**  In 20X5, Bard Company's net income was $233,000. The following facts are also known about the year's activities.

| | |
|---|---:|
| Increase in Inventory | $15,000 |
| Decrease in Prepaid Expenses | 1,500 |
| Depreciation expense | 38,000 |
| Increase in Accounts Receivable | 13,000 |
| New short-term bank borrowings | 25,000 |
| Decrease in Dividends Payable | 32,000 |
| Amortization expense—patents | 11,000 |
| Decrease in Accounts Payable | 4,000 |

**Required**
1. Compute cash flow from operations for 20X5.
2. Explain how your answer to requirement 1 would change if you also knew that during 20X5 Bard sold some machinery for $2,800 cash, incurring a loss of $1,300 that was included in the $233,000 net income.

**17-28   Selecting relevant information**   Use the following information as necessary to compute cash flow from operations.

| | |
|---|---:|
| Net income | $130 |
| Dividends paid | 72 |
| Increase in Accounts Receivable | 22 |
| Increase in Inventory | 52 |
| Decrease in Accrued Interest Receivable | 3 |
| Increase in Long-term Investments | 135 |
| Depreciation and amortization expense | 91 |
| Loss on sale of machinery and equipment | 17 |
| Proceeds from sale of machinery and equipment | 198 |
| Increase in Accounts Payable | 14 |

**17-29   Cash flow statement from transactions**   DLW, Inc. began 20X4 with $18,000 cash. The following information is available for 20X4 activities.

(a) Net income was $115,000.
(b) Depreciation expense was $70,000.
(c) DLW retired bonds payable that were due in 20X9. The cash paid to retire the bonds was equal to their $60,000 book value.
(d) DLW paid $90,000 cash for new plant and equipment.
(e) DLW declared dividends of $18,000 to be paid in January of 20X5. Dividends payable at the end of 20X3 were $3,000.
(f) One of DLW's long-term investments in stock was written off as a loss in 20X4 because the company in which DLW had invested went bankrupt. The book value of the investment was $30,000.
(g) Accounts Receivable increased by $15,000 during the year.
(h) Inventory increased by $26,000 during the year.
(i) Prepaid Expenses decreased by $8,000 during the year.
(j) During 20X4 DLW sold, for $54,000 cash, a patent with a $38,000 book value.

**Required**
Prepare a cash flow statement for DLW, Inc. for 20X4.

**17-30  *Cash flows from transactions*** Transactions of Martin Company for 20X6 and other selected data are as follows:

(a) Sales, all on account, were $800,000.
(b) Cost of goods sold was $360,000.
(c) Depreciation expense was $60,000.
(d) Other operating expenses, all paid in cash, were $210,000.
(e) Equipment was purchased for $220,000 cash.
(f) Long-term investments were sold at an $8,000 gain. They had cost $57,000.
(g) Common stock was issued for cash of $150,000.
(h) A building that had cost $80,000 and had accumulated depreciation of $72,000 was destroyed by fire. There was no insurance coverage.
(i) Over the year, the following changes occurred in the current accounts.

| | |
|---|---|
| Cash | +$ 17,000 |
| Accounts receivable, net | + 128,000 |
| Prepaid expenses | + 12,000 |
| Inventory | + 82,000 |
| Accounts payable | + 14,000 |

**Required**
1. Determine net income for 20X6.
2. Prepare a cash flow statement for 20X6.

**17-31  *Effects of transactions*** Explain how each of the following affects the 20X9 cash flow statement of Gray Company.

1. A long-term investment in the common stock of Black Company was sold for $183,000, which was $42,000 less than its book value at the date of sale.
2. At the beginning of 20X9, Gray had a patent with a book value of $180,000. On November 15, 20X9, Gray sold the patent for $98,000. Amortization expense (for 20X9) to the date of sale was $45,000.
3. On October 31, 20X9, Gray sold some of its equipment for $18,000. The book value of the equipment at the beginning of 20X9 was $13,000, and 20X9 depreciation on the equipment to the date of sale was $2,200.
4. On July 3, 20X9, when the market value of its common stock was $28 per share, Gray declared a 10% stock dividend on its 100,000 shares of outstanding $20 par-value stock. The dividend was distributed on October 1, 20X9.
5. On April 1, 20X9, Gray retired an outstanding issue of bonds, paying $103,500 in cash. The bonds had a book value at the date of retirement of $98,300. Amortization of discount on these bonds between January 1 and April 1 of 20X9 was $200.
6. On March 19, 20X9, Gray acquired new machinery valued at $460,000. Gray paid $85,000 in cash for this machinery and gave a 5-year, 10% note for the difference.

**17-32  *Cash flow statement from comparative trial balances*** At the top of the next page are the beginning and ending balances of the balance sheet accounts for Truitt Company for 20X3.

The following information is also available about the company's activities in 20X3.

(a) Net income was $14,000.
(b) Dividends of $8,000 were declared and paid.
(c) A stock dividend was declared and distributed, and for this reason $20,000 was charged to Retained Earnings, which represented the par and market value of the stock issued in connection with the dividend.

| | Beginning of Year | | End of Year | |
|---|---|---|---|---|
| | Dr. | Cr. | Dr. | Cr. |
| Cash | $ 36,000 | | $ 26,000 | |
| Accounts receivable | 50,000 | | 60,000 | |
| Allowance for bad debts | | $ 10,000 | | $ 12,000 |
| Inventory | 70,000 | | 85,000 | |
| Buildings and equipment | 190,000 | | 240,000 | |
| Patents | 26,000 | | 20,000 | |
| Accounts payable | | 30,000 | | 40,000 |
| Accrued wages payable | | 4,000 | | 5,000 |
| Accumulated depreciation on buildings and equipment | | 96,000 | | 100,000 |
| 10-year bonds payable | | 80,000 | | 104,000 |
| Premium on bonds payable | | — | | 1,000 |
| Treasury stock | | — | 4,000 | |
| Common stock | | 100,000 | | 135,000 |
| Retained earnings | | 52,000 | | 38,000 |
| Totals | $372,000 | $372,000 | $435,000 | $435,000 |

(d) Depreciation in the amount of $8,000 was recorded as an expense this year.

(e) Machinery costing $6,000 and having a book value of $2,000 was sold for $3,000 cash in 20X3.

**Required**

Prepare a cash flow statement for Truitt Company for 20X3. You may assume that any changes other than those described are attributable to reasonable transactions with which you should be familiar.

**17-33 Treatment of transactions** Explain how each of the following transactions is reflected on a cash flow statement. Be specific.

1. Depreciation expense was $660,000.
2. A $200,000 dividend was declared late in the year and will be paid early next year.
3. Fixed assets costing $980,000 with accumulated depreciation of $770,000 were sold for $90,000 cash.
4. Long-term investments were written off because the companies issuing the securities were bankrupt. The write-off was $650,000.
5. The company issued long-term debt in exchange for land. The value of the land was $640,000, which equaled the value of the debt.
6. Near the end of the year the company sold a parcel of land for $300,000, which was $60,000 more than its cost. The buyer gave the company a 5-year, 8% note for $300,000.
7. The company paid $50,000 in settlement of a dispute relating to its income tax return of three years ago. The company debited Retained Earnings for $50,000.

**17-34 Statements from limited data** The following changes in the balance sheet accounts for Rohmer Company occurred during 20X8.

|  | Change | |
| --- | --- | --- |
|  | Debit | Credit |
| Cash | $120 | |
| Accounts receivable, net | | $180 |
| Inventory | 120 | |
| Plant and equipment | 350 | |
| Accumulated depreciation | | 90 |
| Accounts payable | 80 | |
| Accrued expenses | | 30 |
| Long-term debt | 15 | |
| Common stock | | 200 |
| Retained earnings | | 185 |
| Totals | $685 | $685 |

The company had net income of $225 and paid dividends of $40. No plant assets were sold or retired.

**Required**

Prepare a cash flow statement. In the absence of information, make the most reasonable assumption about the cause of a change.

**17-35    Classification of items in cash flow statements**    A list of items follows, most of which appear on a cash flow statement for Brillan Company for 20X8. During the current year, cash increased by $101,000.

(a) Dividends declared during the year were $125,000, but dividends actually paid in cash were $103,000.

(b) An issue of 10-year bonds payable was sold for $275,000 cash.

(c) Amortization of the company's franchise cost was $6,000.

(d) Depreciation on the company's tangible fixed assets was $159,000.

(e) Land was sold at a loss of $14,000; cash received for the sale was $74,000.

(f) Decrease in Inventory was $6,000.

(g) Increase in Accounts Receivable was $81,000.

(h) Increase in Accrued Expenses Payable was $11,000.

(i) Decrease in Income Taxes Payable was $24,000.

(j) Increase in Accounts Payable was $51,000.

(k) Decrease in Prepaid Expenses was $1,000.

(l) Increase in Allowance to Reduce Short-term Investments to Lower-of-Cost-or-Market was $3,000.

(m)Decrease in short-term bank borrowings (debt) was $13,000.

(n) Cash paid for new equipment was $500,000.

(o) Cash paid for a long-term investment was $158,000.

(p) A 10-year note payable for $200,000 was given to acquire land and buildings.

(q) Amortization of discount on the 10-year bond issue mentioned in item (b) was $2,000.

(r) Cash received as dividends on stock held as a long-term investment and accounted for on the equity basis was $25,000.

(s) Amortization of discount on a long-term investment in bonds was $3,000.

(t) Cash received from sale of treasury stock was $6,000; the stock cost the company $4,000.

(u) Increase in the credit balance of the Deferred Taxes was $4,000.

(v) Brillan's portion of net income of the company whose stock is mentioned in item (r) was $56,000.

(w) Net income for the year was $402,000.

**Required**
Prepare Brillan's cash flow statement for 20X8.

*look at 761*

**17-36   Comprehensive problem**   Comparative balance sheets and an income statement for RJM Company follow. All data are in millions of dollars.

RJM Company, Balance Sheets as of June 30

|  | current 20X7 | 20X6 previous |
|---|---|---|
| **Assets** | | |
| Cash | $  9.5 | $  28.7 |
| Accounts receivable, net | 125.8 | 88.6 |
| Inventories | 311.4 | 307.0 |
| Prepayments | 12.6 | 11.4 |
| Total current assets | $ 459.3 | $ 435.7 |
| Investments | 68.3 | 71.8 |
| Plant and equipment | 1,313.9 | 1,240.6 |
| Accumulated depreciation | (753.1) | (687.4) |
| Intangible assets | 42.5 | 46.2 |
| Total assets | $1,130.9 | $1,106.9 |
| **Equities** | | |
| Accounts payable | $  62.6 | $  59.8 |
| Taxes payable | 32.4 | 29.6 |
| Accrued expenses | 38.9 | 52.6 |
| Total current liabilities | $ 133.9 | $ 142.0 |
| Long-term debt | 505.3 | 496.2 |
| Common stock, no par value | 384.2 | 377.4 |
| Retained earnings | 107.5 | 91.3 |
| Total equities | $1,130.9 | $1,106.9 |

RJM Company, Income Statement for 20X7

| | |
|---|---|
| Sales and other revenues | $896.3 |
| Expenses: | |
| Cost of goods sold | $493.2 |
| Depreciation | 69.3 |
| Amortization | 3.7 |
| Income taxes | 85.0 |
| Other expenses | 203.5 |
| Total expenses | 854.7 |
| Net income | $ 41.6 |

$28.7 million to $9.5 million

Sales and other revenue includes a gain of $0.8 million on sale of investments. Amortization expense is related to intangible assets. Other expenses include losses of $1.3 million on sales and other disposals of equipment. These assets had cost $9.6 million and had accumulated depreciation of $3.6 million. Long-term debt and common stock were issued for cash. *(so they will fit into cash flow statement)*

**Required**
Prepare a cash flow statement for the year ended June 30, 20X7.

**17-37   *Cash flow statement from comparative trial balances—comprehensive problem*** Following are the trial balances for Voltan Company at the beginning and the end of 20X5.

| | Beginning of Year | | End of Year | |
| --- | --- | --- | --- | --- |
| | Dr. | Cr. | Dr. | Cr. |
| Cash | $ 50,000 | | $ 60,000 | |
| Accounts receivable | 150,000 | | 200,000 | |
| Inventory | 250,000 | | 270,000 | |
| Prepaid expenses | 50,000 | | 70,000 | |
| Land | 250,000 | | 307,000 | |
| Buildings and equipment | 700,000 | | 838,000 | |
| Bond discount—5% bonds | — | | 8,000 | |
| Allowance for bad debts | | $ 25,000 | | $ 35,000 |
| Accumulated depreciation | | 300,000 | | 421,000 |
| Accounts payable | | 170,000 | | 220,000 |
| Accrued expenses | | 105,000 | | 115,000 |
| Bonds payable: 5% bonds | | — | | 200,000 |
| 6% bonds | | 175,000 | | — |
| Bonds premium—6% bonds | | 4,000 | | — |
| Long-term notes payable | | — | | 80,000 |
| Capital stock—par value | | 450,000 | | 475,000 |
| Paid-in capital in excess of par | | 81,000 | | 83,500 |
| Retained earnings | | 140,000 | | 123,500 |
| Totals | $1,450,000 | $1,450,000 | $1,753,000 | $1,753,000 |

The following data are available regarding Voltan Company's 20X5 activities.

(a) Net income was $70,000, including gains and losses on transactions relating to fixed assets and bond retirements.

(b) Land costing $100,000 was purchased, paying 20% in cash and giving long-term notes payable for the remainder of the purchase price. The only other transaction related to land was a sale that produced a gain of $12,000.

(c) Equipment that had originally cost $82,000 and had a book value of $23,000 was sold for $8,000 cash. Additional equipment was purchased for cash.

(d) At the beginning of the year, bonds payable carrying an interest rate of 5% and a maturity value of $200,000 were sold for $190,000 cash. Very shortly thereafter, the 6% bonds were purchased on the open market for $159,000 and retired.

(e) During the year, a stock dividend was declared and issued and was accounted for by a charge against Retained Earnings for $27,500, the market value of the stock distributed in connection with the dividend. The market value was 10% higher than the par value for the shares issued. Cash dividends were declared and paid as usual.

**Required**
Prepare a cash flow statement for 20X5.

## CASES

**17-38   *Explaining cash flow*** You have been hired as a trainee in the finance department of Metrigo Company, a growing provider of electronic switches and circuits. While you were in the cafeteria one day, the president walked in and introduced herself. Upon learning that you were in the finance department, she said that she was disturbed at the latest financial statements and wanted your help. She explained that the company was faced with a serious shortage of cash even though profits were high and working capital increased. She showed you the following condensed financial statements. (All data are in thousands of dollars.)

| Metrigo Company, Income Statement for 20X7 | |
| --- | --- |
| Sales | $7,220 |
| Cost of sales | 4,150 |
| Gross profit | $3,070 |
| Operating expenses | 2,290 |
| Net income | $ 780 |

| Metrigo Company, Balance Sheets as of December 31 | | | |
| --- | --- | --- | --- |
| | 20X7 | 20X6 | Change |
| **Assets** | | | |
| Cash | $ 20 | $ 360 | $(340) |
| Accounts receivable, net | 880 | 740 | 140 |
| Inventory | 1,450 | 1,200 | 250 |
| Plant and equipment, net | 3,850 | 3,370 | 480 |
| Totals | $6,200 | $5,670 | |
| **Equities** | | | |
| Accounts payable | $ 140 | $ 210 | (70) |
| Accrued expenses | 170 | 230 | (60) |
| Long-term debt | 2,500 | 2,450 | 50 |
| Common stock | 2,140 | 2,140 | — |
| Retained earnings | 1,250 | 640 | 610 |
| Totals | $6,200 | $5,670 | |

The president told you that it had been touch-and-go whether the company would have enough cash to pay a $170 thousand dividend that had been declared when the directors realized that the company was having an excellent year. To pay the dividend, the company had to increase its long-term borrowings. "We made $780 K, our best year ever, and had depreciation expense of $190 K. We did buy $670 K worth of plant assets, but I figured that our cash would stay about the same as it was last year. Look at this stuff and tell me what happened."

**Required**
Prepare a memorandum that explains the results to the president.

**17-39   Lands' End's cash flow statements**   Cash flow statements for **Lands' End**, the catalog retailer, appear on page 792.

**Required**
Answer the following questions.

1. Was Lands' End profitable in 1998?
2. Did Lands' End add to or reduce its cash over the three-year period?
3. Did Lands' End's customers owe more or less to the company at the end of 1998 than at the beginning of 1998?

## Consolidated Statements of Cash Flows
### Lands' End, Inc. & Subsidiaries for the Period Ended (in thousands)

| | 1998 | 1997 | 1996 |
|---|---|---|---|
| Cash flows from operating activities: | | | |
| Net income | $ 64,150 | $ 50,952 | $ 30,555 |
| Adjustments to reconcile net income to net cash flows from operating activities— | | | |
| Depreciation and amortization | 15,127 | 13,558 | 12,456 |
| Deferred compensation expense | 323 | 317 | 228 |
| Deferred income taxes | (1,158) | 994 | (669) |
| Pre-tax gain on sale of subsidiary | (7,805) | — | — |
| Loss on disposal of fixed assets | 1,127 | 325 | 1,544 |
| Changes in assets and liabilities excluding the effects of acquisitions and divestitures: | | | |
| Receivables | (7,019) | (675) | (4,888) |
| Inventory | (104,545) | 22,371 | 1,423 |
| Prepaid advertising | (7,447) | 4,758 | (8,318) |
| Other prepaid expenses | (1,366) | (145) | (1,611) |
| Accounts payable | 11,616 | 14,205 | 9,618 |
| Reserve for returns | 944 | 629 | (456) |
| Accrued liabilities | 8,755 | 4,390 | (2,208) |
| Accrued profit sharing | 1,349 | 1,454 | (196) |
| Income taxes payable | (1,047) | 8,268 | 3,877 |
| Other | 64 | 394 | 37 |
| Net cash flows from (used for) operating activities | (26,932) | 121,795 | 41,392 |
| Cash flows from (used for) investing activities: | | | |
| Cash paid for capital additions | (47,659) | (18,481) | (13,904) |
| Proceeds from sale of subsidiaries | 12,350 | — | 1,665 |
| Net cash flows used for investing activities | (35,309) | (18,481) | (12,239) |
| Cash flows from (used for) financing activities: | | | |
| Proceeds from short-term borrowings | 21,242 | 1,876 | 1,780 |
| Payment of long-term debt | — | — | (40) |
| Purchases of treasury stock | (45,899) | (30,143) | (20,001) |
| Issuance of treasury stock | 409 | 604 | 858 |
| Net cash flows used for financing activities | (24,248) | (27,663) | (17,403) |
| Net increase (decrease) in cash and cash equivalents | (86,489) | 75,651 | 11,750 |
| Beginning cash and cash equivalents | 92,827 | 17,176 | 5,426 |
| Ending cash and cash equivalents | $ 6,338 | $ 92,827 | $ 17,176 |
| Supplemental cash flow disclosures: | | | |
| Interest paid | $ 1,995 | $ 517 | $ 2,833 |
| Income taxes paid | 39,337 | 25,261 | 16,896 |

4. Did accounts payable increase or decrease in 1998?

5. The operating activities section shows a $7,805 gain on sale of a subsidiary as a *negative* adjustment. How can the company lose cash by selling a subsidiary at a profit? How much did the company receive for selling the subsidiary? What was the book value of the subsidiary?

6. Cash amounts paid for interest and for income taxes are highlighted at the bottom of the statement. Why aren't these items added back to net income in the operations section?

7. In 1996 and 1997 cash provided by operations was much greater than net income. Then in 1998 cash provided by operations was much less than net income. What is the biggest reason for Lands' End's 1998 cash flow from operations being so much lower than its net income?

8. Is Lands' End using its suppliers to finance its inventories? Has it done so over the three-year period?

9. What were the company's major uses of cash in 1998, aside from operations? Where did the company get the money for those uses?

10. Did the company pay dividends in any of the latest three years?

11. What has happened to Lands' End's long-term debt over the three-year period?

12. Did the company spend more or less on advertising in 1998 than it recognized as expense? How much more or less?

## Chapter Eighteen

# ANALYZING FINANCIAL STATEMENTS

## LEARNING OBJECTIVES

*After reading this chapter, you should be able to*

- *Explain why financial analysts use ratios to evaluate companies.*
- *Explain liquidity and show how ratios can measure a company's liquidity.*
- *Explain profitability and show how ratios can measure a company's profitability.*
- *Explain solvency and show how ratios can measure a company's solvency.*
- *Describe leverage and show how it changes returns to stockholders.*
- *Explain some limitations of ratio analysis.*

*The financial performance of a company is of major interest to its employees and shareholders, among others. A company's goals are often stated in terms of financial results. For example:*

*__Minnesota Mining & Manufacturing__ (3M) has stated its financial goals as follows: "We strive to maximize shareholder value through solid, profitable growth and effective use of capital. Specific financial goals are to achieve (1) at least 30 percent of sales from products introduced during the past four years; (2) growth in earnings per share of more than 10 percent a year, on average; (3) growth in economic profit exceeding earnings per share growth, and return on invested capital among the highest of industrial companies."*

*__Walt Disney Company__ has stated: "The company's primary financial objective remains 20% compound annual earnings per share growth over future five-year periods and, secondarily, steady improvement in return on equity."*

*__Boise Cascade__ has stated: "We are moving rapidly to achieve fully competitive positions in all of our businesses and products and are focused on achieving our financial goals: To be profitable throughout the business cycle and to be EVA-positive over the cycle."*

*Sources: 3M 1997 annual report.*
*Walt Disney Company 1997 Factbook.*
*Boise Cascade 1997 annual report.*

Throughout this book we have stressed the importance of expectations and the ways that accounting and other information help managers form reasonable expectations. We have also used ratios among financial statement elements. Chapter 2 showed that managers often express target profits as a ratio of income to sales (return on sales). In Chapter 11 you saw that managers commonly use the ratio of income to total assets (or some other measure of return on investment) to measure divisional performance. Chapter 7 illustrated the cash squeeze that can accompany buildups of inventories and receivables, as well as how managers use ratios when developing long-term plans. This chapter addresses the analysis of financial statements, including the calculation, interpretation, and evaluation of financial ratios.

Many people and organizations outside a company, such as suppliers and investors in debt or equity securities, are interested in the company's activities. Banks that provide short-term loans, insurance companies that buy long-term bonds, brokerage firms that give (or sell) investment advice to their customers, mutual funds that buy stocks or bonds—all of these, and many other institutions, employ financial analysts to help make decisions about individual companies. Individual investors also perform financial analyses. Our approach to analyzing financial statements is that of a financial analyst, who makes recommendations to investors after studying financial statements and other sources of information about a business. Because an analyst's recommendations can affect a company's ability to obtain credit, sell stock, and secure new contracts, internal managers must also be aware of what concerns financial analysts.

## EXPECTATIONS AND PERFORMANCE

Like a company's managers, financial analysts base their decisions on expectations about the future. Just as managers focus on forecasts, financial analysts concentrate on what the future holds. Analysts want to know what to expect from a company—whether it will be able to pay its employees and suppliers, repay its loans, pay dividends on its stock, and expand into new areas. As with company managers, financial analysts also are concerned with the past only insofar as they can use the past as a reliable guide to the future. For example, an impressive history of growth in net income, sales, financial stability, and capable management is overshadowed if the company's major product is determined to be harmful in some way (e.g., tobacco, leaded gasoline), or becomes illegal (e.g., asbestos, the insecticide DDT) or obsolete (e.g., early types of computers and calculators). Nevertheless, analysts assume that what has held true in the past is likely to continue unless they have information that indicates otherwise, much as managers use a cost prediction formula developed on the basis of past experience. Hence, both analysts and a company's managers must be continually alert for signs that the future will differ from the past. In addition to focusing on the future, managers and financial analysts use many of the same analytical approaches.

## METHODS OF ANALYSIS

Financial analysis consists of a number of interrelated activities. Among the most important are considerations of ratios and trends and the comparison of ratios and trends against some norms. (A *norm* is a standard for comparison, which could be an average value for a particular industry or for all companies in the economy.) Trends are of interest as clues to the future.

Ratios can take three different forms. Some ratios are comparisons of an income statement element with another income statement element. Other ratios are comparisons of balance sheet elements with other balance sheet elements. Still others compare an income statement element such as sales or cost of goods sold, with a balance sheet element such as accounts receivable or total assets. In this last set of ratios we could use either average assets or assets at year end. Analysts use both versions, depending on circumstances and preferences. We shall illustrate this point a few times as we proceed through the ratios. You should keep in mind that no one version is "right" and another "wrong." Analysts simply have differing views.

## AREAS OF ANALYSIS

Different types of investors are interested in different aspects of a company. Short-term creditors, such as suppliers and banks considering loans of relatively short duration (90 days or six months), are concerned primarily with a company's short-term prospects. They want to know whether a company will be able to pay its obligations in the near future. Banks, insurance companies, pension funds, and other investors considering relatively long-term commitments (e.g., ten-year loans) cannot ignore short-term prospects, but are more concerned with the long-term outlook. Even if such investors are satisfied that a company has no short-term problems, they want to be reasonably sure that it has good prospects for long-term financial stability and can be expected to repay its longer-term loans with interest.

Stockholders, current and potential, are also interested in both the short-term and long-term prospects of the company. But their interest goes beyond the company's ability to repay loans and make interest payments. Their concern is with profitability—the ability to earn satisfactory profits and pay dividends—and the likelihood that the market price of the stock will increase.

We have divided the discussion of these aspects of a company's prospects into three major areas: liquidity, solvency, and profitability. For the most part we work with ratios. Apart from expressing relationships between two factors, ratios are useful because they facilitate comparisons among companies of different sizes.

## ILLUSTRATION

We shall use the comparative financial statements and the additional financial information about Burke Company shown in Exhibit 18-1.

The analysis has actually begun in the exhibit because it shows the percentages of sales for each item on the income statement and the percentage of total assets or total equities for each balance sheet item. These percentage statements, or **common-size statements**, can help an analyst to spot trends.

Two of the more important percentages on the income statement are the gross profit ratio, which is gross profit divided by sales, and return on sales (ROS), which is net income divided by sales. These ratios for Burke in 20X2 are 38.5 and 7.9 percent, respectively. The gross profit ratio improved in 20X2 over 20X1, but ROS declined.

## Exhibit 18-1  Burke Company, Balance Sheets as of December 31

|  | 20X2 | | 20X1 | |
|---|---|---|---|---|
|  | Dollars | Percent | Dollars | Percent |
| **Current assets:** | | | | |
| Cash | $ 80,000 | 5.2% | $ 50,000 | 3.6% |
| Accounts receivable, net | 180,000 | 11.6 | 120,000 | 8.7 |
| Inventory | 190,000 | 12.2 | 230,000 | 16.7 |
| Total current assets | $ 450,000 | 29.0 | $ 400,000 | 29.0 |
| Plant and equipment—cost | $1,350,000 | 87.1 | $1,150,000 | 83.3 |
| Accumulated depreciation | (340,000) | (21.9) | (250,000) | (18.1) |
| Net plant and equipment | $1,010,000 | 65.2 | $ 900,000 | 65.2 |
| Other assets | $ 90,000 | 5.8 | $ 80,000 | 5.8 |
| Total assets | $1,550,000 | 100.0% | $1,380,000 | 100.0% |
| **Current liabilities:** | | | | |
| Accounts payable | $ 110,000 | 7.1% | $ 105,000 | 7.6% |
| Accrued expenses | 40,000 | 2.6 | 15,000 | 1.1 |
| Total current liabilities | $ 150,000 | 9.7 | $ 120,000 | 8.7 |
| Long-term debt | 600,000 | 38.7 | 490,000 | 35.5 |
| Total liabilities | $ 750,000 | 48.4 | $ 610,000 | 44.2 |
| **Common stock, 22,000** | | | | |
| shares | $ 220,000 | 14.2 | $ 220,000 | 15.9 |
| Paid-in capital | 350,000 | 22.6 | 350,000 | 25.4 |
| Retained earnings | 230,000 | 14.8 | 200,000 | 14.5 |
| Total stockholders' equity | $ 800,000 | 51.6 | $ 770,000 | 55.8 |
| Total equities | $1,550,000 | 100.0% | $1,380,000 | 100.0% |

### Burke Company, Income Statements for the Years Ended December 31

|  | 20X2 | | 20X1 | |
|---|---|---|---|---|
|  | Dollars | Percent | Dollars | Percent |
| Sales | $1,300,000 | 100.0% | $1,080,000 | 100.0% |
| Cost of goods sold | 800,000 | 61.5 | 670,000 | 62.0 |
| Gross profit | $ 500,000 | 38.5 | $ 410,000 | 38.0 |
| Operating expenses[a] | 280,000 | 21.6 | 210,000 | 19.4 |
| Income before interest | | | | |
| and taxes | $ 220,000 | 16.9 | $ 200,000 | 18.6 |
| Interest expense | 48,000 | 3.7 | 42,000 | 3.9 |
| Income before taxes | $ 172,000 | 13.2 | $ 158,000 | 14.7 |
| Income taxes at 40% rate | 68,800 | 5.3 | 63,200 | 5.9 |
| Net income | $ 103,200 | 7.9% | $ 94,800 | 8.8% |

*a  Including depreciation of $90,000 in 20X2 and $75,000 in 20X1*

Both financial analysts and internal managers are interested in ROS and the gross profit ratio because these ratios indicate how valuable a dollar of sales is to the company. (These ratios are not the same as the contribution margin ratio, but they do give a rough idea of the profit/sales relationship.) A relatively low ROS, combined with a gross profit ratio that is normal for the industry, could indicate that operating expenses are higher than those of other companies. Similarly, a decline in ROS or the gross profit ratio could suggest weakening prices, which could be very serious. Stocks of many manufacturers of computer chips fall sharply because of concerns over softening prices, reflected in falling margins. **3Com** stated that its margins declined in late 1997 due to reducing selling prices by as much as 40 percent in order to remain competitive. As we mention several times in this chapter, ratios provide clues or indicators, but they do not tell you whether a company's managers are acting wisely or unwisely.

Balance sheet ratios show whether the proportions of particular assets or liabilities are increasing or decreasing, and whether they are within reasonable bounds. We explore balance sheet ratios in more detail later in the chapter.

## LIQUIDITY

**Liquidity** is a company's ability to meet obligations due in the near future. The more liquid the company, the more likely it will be able to pay its employees, suppliers, and holders of its short-term notes payable. A company with excellent long-term prospects could fail to realize them because it was forced into bankruptcy when it could not pay its debts in the near term. Hence, while liquidity is most important to short-term creditors, it also interests long-term creditors and stockholders.

### WORKING CAPITAL AND THE CURRENT RATIO

**Working capital**, the difference between current assets and current liabilities, is a very rough measure of liquidity. Burke had the following amounts of working capital at the end of 20X1 and 20X2.

|                     | 20X2      | 20X1      |
|---------------------|-----------|-----------|
| Current assets      | $450,000  | $400,000  |
| Current liabilities | 150,000   | 120,000   |
| Working capital     | $300,000  | $280,000  |

Working capital is positive and has increased. But this does not necessarily mean that Burke has adequate liquidity or became more liquid. Most analysts consider changes in working capital as only a very rough indication of changes in liquidity and supplement their analysis with several other calculations. Working capital is stated in absolute dollar terms and hence is greatly influenced by the size of the company.

The current ratio is a measure of relative liquidity that takes into account differences in absolute size. It is used to compare companies with different total current assets and liabilities as well as to compare the same company's liquidity from year to year.

$$Current\ ratio\ =\ \frac{current\ assets}{current\ liabilities}$$

Burke has current ratios of 3.33 to 1 in 20X1 ($400,000/$120,000) and 3 to 1 in 20X2 ($450,000/$150,000). On the basis of the current ratio, we would say that the company seemed to be less liquid at the end of 20X2. With good reason we said "seemed to be less liquid." One major problem that arises with any ratio, but especially the current ratio, is that of composition. The **composition problem** arises when one uses a total, such as total current assets (or current liabilities), that might mask information about the individual components. How soon will the current assets be converted into cash so that they can be used to pay current liabilities? How soon are the current liabilities due for payment? You already know that current assets normally are listed in order of liquidity from cash, the most liquid, to prepaid expenses. The analyst obtains a general idea of the magnitude of the composition problem by reviewing the common-size balance sheet to see how much of current assets consists of relatively liquid items.

## QUICK RATIO (ACID-TEST RATIO)

The quick ratio, or acid-test ratio, is cash plus marketable securities plus accounts receivable divided by current liabilities. It is similar to the current ratio, but includes only those assets that are cash or "near cash" (called **quick assets**). Hence, the ratio gives a stricter indication of short-term debt-paying ability than does the current ratio.

$$Quick\ ratio\ =\ \frac{cash\ +\ marketable\ securities\ +\ accounts\ receivable}{current\ liabilities}$$

Burke had no marketable securities at the end of either year, so its quick ratios are as follows:

$$20X1\qquad \frac{\$50,000\ +\ \$120,000}{\$120,000}\ =\ 1.42$$

$$20X2\qquad \frac{\$80,000\ +\ \$180,000}{\$150,000}\ =\ 1.73$$

Burke seems to have increased its liquidity because its quick ratio increased. We could say that the company was better able to meet current liabilities at the end of 20X2; but we would still like to know how soon its current liabilities have to be paid and how rapidly it can expect to turn its receivables and inventory into cash. The next section presents ratios that measure the liquidity of current assets.

## WORKING CAPITAL ACTIVITY RATIOS

Two commonly used ratios provide information about the time within which a company should realize cash from its receivables and inventories. And, although we cannot tell the time within which the company must pay its various current liabilities simply by examining the financial statements, one commonly used ratio offers some insight into the company's bill-paying practices.

## Accounts Receivable Turnover

Accounts receivable turnover measures how rapidly a company collects its receivables; in general, the higher the turnover the better.

$$Accounts\ receivable\ turnover\ =\ \frac{sales}{accounts\ receivable}$$

*Average receivables* is defined as the beginning accounts receivable balance plus the ending balance, divided by 2. The year-end balance also may be used. The simple averaging procedure is satisfactory so long as there are no extremely high or low points during the year (including the end of the year). If a company's receivables fluctuate widely, using a monthly average for receivables is better. Again, many analysts simply use the year-end value.

Some analysts prefer to use credit sales for the calculation, instead of total sales, but outsiders typically cannot determine how much of total sales are on credit or for cash. Internal managers can determine credit sales and thus can compute the turnover of credit sales, as well as of total sales.

Because we do not have the beginning balance for 20X1, we can only calculate the turnover of *average* receivables for 20X2 for Burke Company. (We can compute 20X1 turnover using the end of year value.)

$$\frac{\$1,300,000}{(\$120,000\ +\ \$180,000)/2}\ =\ \frac{\$1,300,000}{\$150,000}\ =\ 8.67\ times$$

The 20X1 turnover using the ending balance is

$$\$1,080,000/\$120,000\ =\ 9\ times$$

Some analysts make a related calculation called number of days' sales in accounts receivable. This figure indicates the average age of ending accounts receivable.

$$Days'\ sales\ in\ accounts\ receivable\ =\ \frac{ending\ accounts\ receivable}{average\ daily\ sales}$$

Average daily sales is simply sales for the year divided by 365. For Burke Company, we have average daily sales of about $2,959 ($1,080,000/365) for 20X1 and about $3,562 ($1,300,000/365) for 20X2. Hence, days' sales in accounts receivable are

$$20X1\qquad \frac{\$120,000}{\$2,959}\ =\ 41\ days$$

$$20X2\qquad \frac{\$180,000}{\$3,563}\ =\ 51\ days$$

On average, then, Burke's accounts receivable were 41 days old at the end of 20X1 and 51 days old at the end of 20X2. The collection period has lengthened considerably in one year, but the period must be interpreted in light of the credit terms offered to customers. The faster customers pay, the better, but there are always trade-offs. If a company loses sales because of tight credit policies, the advantage of faster collection might be more than offset by the loss of profits from lower total sales. The increase in the average collection period might well be the result of a management decision to offer more liberal terms to stimulate sales.

### Inventory Turnover

The type of analysis discussed in connection with receivables also applies to the company's inventory. Inventory turnover is calculated as follows:

$$Inventory\ turnover\ =\ \frac{cost\ of\ goods\ sold}{inventory}$$

Again, most analysts use an average value, the sum of the beginning and ending balances divided by 2, unless the company has much higher and lower inventories for significant portions of the year because of seasonal business. It is then better to use monthly figures to determine the average. And, again, many analysts simply use the year-end value for inventory.

Burke's inventory turnover for 20X2 is about 3.8 times, calculated as follows:

$$\frac{\$800,000}{(\$230,000\ +\ \$190,000)/2}\ =\ \frac{\$800,000}{\$210,000}\ =\ 3.8\ times$$

Using only the year-end inventory for 20X1, turnover is 2.9 times ($670,000/$230,000).

Inventory turnover indicates the efficiency with which a company uses its inventory. High inventory turnover is critical for many businesses, especially those that sell at a relatively low markup (ratio of gross profit to sales) and depend on high sales volumes to earn satisfactory profits. For example, discount stores and food stores rely on quick turnover for profitability. Companies with very high markups, such as jewelry stores, do not need such rapid turnovers to be profitable.

As discussed in Chapters 1, 6, and 9, maintaining inventory can be very expensive. Some costs—insurance, personal property taxes, interest on the funds tied up in inventory, and obsolescence—can be very high. Therefore, managers prefer to keep inventory as low as possible. The problem is that if inventory is too low, particularly in retail stores, sales might be lost because customers cannot find what they want.

Analysts sometimes calculate the number of days' sales in inventory, which is a measure of the supply that the company maintains.

$$Days'\ sales\ in\ inventory\ =\ \frac{ending\ inventory}{average\ daily\ cost\ of\ goods\ sold}$$

Average daily cost of goods sold is simply cost of goods sold for the year divided by 365. For Burke, this is $1,836 ($670,000/365) for 20X1 and $2,192 ($800,000/365) for 20X2. Days' sales in inventory are as follows:

$$20X1\quad \frac{\$230,000}{\$1,836}\ =\ 125\ days$$

$$20X2\quad \frac{\$190,000}{\$2,192}\ =\ 87\ days$$

The decline in days' sales in Burke's inventory could indicate a deliberate change in inventory policy, or perhaps just a temporary reduction of inventory because of heavier than expected sales near the end of the year. The accompanying Insight illustrates how **Dell Computer Corporation** manages working capital to achieve a strategic advantage.

As you may remember from your study of financial accounting, generally accepted accounting principles (GAAP) allow several formats for the income statement. Some formats do not show cost of goods sold, so that an outside analyst cannot compute inventory turnover using the approach just presented. In such cases, the analyst will use sales as a substitute for cost of goods sold, even though sales and inventory are not measured in the same way. (Sales is measured in selling prices, while inventory is measured in cost prices.) The inventory turnover so derived is *overstated*—a unit costing $1 and sold for $2 will reflect two inventory turnovers when only one unit has been sold. If analysts recognize the overstatement in the calculation, they will not be misled by the results.

## PROFITABILITY

Profitability can be measured in absolute dollar terms, such as net income, or by ratios. The most commonly used measures of profitability fall under the general

---

 **SIGHT**

### Working Capital Ratios at Dell Computer

**Dell Computer Corporation's** business strategy is to sell computers to corporations and consumers through a direct sales approach. This allows Dell to carry little or no finished goods inventory and to use the latest components. In the computer industry, using the latest components also provides the highest profit margins. It also protects the company against price changes in components.

The company focuses on the cash conversion cycle, which consists of inventory, payables, receivables, and cash flow from operations. A recent annual report presented the following ratios:

|  | 1998 | 1997 | 1996 |
|---|---|---|---|
| Days of Sales in Accounts Receivable | 36 | 37 | 42 |
| Days of Supply in Inventory | 7 | 13 | 31 |
| Days in Accounts Payable | 51 | 54 | 33 |

In a business where inventory prices drop by 1 percent a week, inventory is risk. While Dell had 13 days of inventory in 1997, a typical competitor that did not sell directly had 30, with another 40 in the distribution channel. "That's a difference of 58 days," Mr. Dell said. "In 58 days, the cost of materials will decline about 6 percent."

---

*Sources: Dell Computer Corporation 1998 annual report.*
*Andy Serwer, "Michael Dell Rocks,"* Fortune, *May 11, 1998, 58–70.*
*Lawrence Fisher, "Inside Dell Computer Corporation: Managing Working Capital,"* Strategy and Business, *First Quarter, 1998, 68–75.*

heading of return on investment (ROI). As described in Chapter 11, ROI is actually a family of ratios having the general form

$$\text{Return on investment} = \frac{income}{investment}$$

External investors, especially stockholders and potential stockholders, are interested in the return that they can expect from their investments. A company's managers want to earn satisfactory returns on the investments that they control. As a practical matter, then, different analysts and managers will define both income and investment differently when trying to measure the same basic relationships. In this section, we present some of the most often used alternative ways of looking at this basic relationship of accomplishment (return, income) to effort (investment).

## RETURN ON ASSETS (ROA)

ROA measures operating efficiency—how well managers have used the assets under their control to generate income. The following ratio is one way to make the calculation.

$$\text{Return on assets} = \frac{net\ income + interest + income\ taxes}{total\ assets}$$

The familiar alternatives, averages or year-end values, apply here as well. For Burke, ROA was about 15 percent for 20X2, calculated as follows:

$$\frac{\$103{,}200 + \$48{,}000 + \$68{,}800}{(\$1{,}380{,}000 + \$1{,}550{,}000)/2} = \frac{\$220{,}000}{\$1{,}465{,}000} = 15.0\%$$

Adding interest and income taxes back to net income is equivalent to using income before interest and income taxes. Remember that we are concerned with operations: Interest and, to some extent, income taxes depend on how the company finances its assets—how much debt it uses. Moreover, income taxes are affected by many matters not related to operations, which is another reason for adding them back. (Some of these nonoperating factors are the company's investments in securities and its use of tax benefits such as percentage depletion.) Some analysts add back only interest; others add back only the after-tax effect of interest. There are arguments to support several measures of the numerator in the ROA calculation. Choosing one alternative over another is a matter of both personal preference and of the particular objective.

Some analysts use end-of-year assets in the denominator, some use beginning-of-year amounts, and still others use total assets minus current liabilities. (Analysts in the latter group argue that current liabilities are operating sources, rather than financing sources.) In this chapter, we use average total assets, or total year-end assets, with no consideration of current liabilities, but we caution you that this is a matter of choice and preference.

Both internal and external analysts can obtain the information for this ratio directly from publicly available financial statements, and can make direct comparisons with companies in the same industry.

## RETURN ON COMMON EQUITY (ROE)

ROA is a measure of operating efficiency. Common stockholders are also concerned with the return on their investment, which is affected not only by operations but also by the amount of debt and preferred stock in the company's capital structure.

ROE is computed as follows.

$$\textit{Return on common equity} \; = \; \frac{\textit{net income} - \textit{dividends on preferred stock}}{\textit{common stockholders' equity}}$$

If there is preferred stock, preferred dividends must be subtracted from net income in the numerator, and the amount of total stockholders' equity attributable to preferred stock is subtracted in the denominator to obtain common stockholders' equity.

Burke Company has no preferred stock, but it does have debt. ROE for Burke in 20X2 is a bit over 13 percent.

$$\frac{\$103,200}{(\$770,000 + \$800,000)/2} = \frac{\$103,200}{\$785,000} = 13.1\%$$

Notice that Burke's ROE is less than its ROA. If a company finances its assets solely with common stock, such a relationship will hold between ROE and ROA because ROE is computed using after-tax income. But debt holders do not participate in the earnings of the company; they receive a stipulated, constant amount of interest. Hence, the company can increase its ROE if it uses debt, provided that ROA is greater than the interest rate it must pay to debt holders. This method of using debt (or preferred stock) to increase ROE is called **leverage** or **trading on the equity** (sometimes financial leverage). Leverage increases both risk and the potential for greater return.

## THE EFFECTS OF LEVERAGE

Suppose that a company with a 40 percent tax rate requires total assets of $1,000,000 to earn $180,000 per year before interest and income taxes, for an ROA of 18 percent. Three possible financing alternatives are (1) all common stock, (2) $400,000 common stock and $600,000 in 7 percent bonds (interest expense of $42,000), and (3) $400,000 in common stock and $600,000 in 8 percent preferred stock (dividends of $48,000). The following schedule shows the differing effects of the three alternatives on ROE.

|  | (1) All Common Stock | (2) Debt and Common Stock | (3) Preferred Stock and Common Stock |
|---|---|---|---|
| Income before interest and taxes | $ 180,000 | $180,000 | $180,000 |
| Interest expense at 7% | 0 | 42,000 | 0 |
| Income before taxes | $ 180,000 | $138,000 | $180,000 |
| Income taxes at 40% | 72,000 | 55,200 | 72,000 |
| Net income | $ 108,000 | $ 82,800 | $108,000 |
| Less preferred stock dividends | 0 | 0 | 48,000 |
| Earnings available for common stock | $ 108,000 | $ 82,800 | $ 60,000 |
| Divided by common equity invested | 1,000,000 | 400,000 | 400,000 |
| Equals return on common equity | 10.8% | 20.7% | 15.0% |

Note that dividends on preferred stock must be subtracted from net income to reach earnings *available for common stockholders* (because the claim of preferred stockholders on company earnings comes before the claim of common stockholders). Note also that, although the plans that include debt or preferred stock both result in lower earnings available for common equity, both produce a higher ROE than the company would achieve if it used all common equity. That is, these two plans provide the benefits of leverage.

However, leverage works both ways. It is good for the common stockholder when earnings are high and bad when they are low. If in one year the company earns only $60,000 before interest and taxes, it has the following results.

|  | (1)<br>All<br>Common | (2)<br>$600,000<br>Debt | (3)<br>$600,000<br>Preferred |
|---|---|---|---|
| Income before interest and taxes | $ 60,000 | $ 60,000 | $ 60,000 |
| Interest expense at 7% | 0 | 42,000 | 0 |
| Income before taxes | $ 60,000 | $ 18,000 | $ 60,000 |
| Income taxes at 40% | 24,000 | 7,200 | 24,000 |
| Net income | $ 36,000 | $ 10,800 | $ 36,000 |
| Less preferred stock dividends | 0 | 0 | 42,000 |
| Earnings available for common stock | $ 36,000 | $ 10,800 | $ (6,000) |
| Divided by common equity invested | 1,000,000 | 400,000 | 400,000 |
| Equals return on common equity | 3.6% | 2.7% | negative |

As you can see, ROE is highest if all common equity is used, but the return is very low. Companies having relatively stable revenues and expenses, such as public utilities, can use considerable leverage. Leverage is very risky for companies in cyclical industries such as automobile and aircraft manufacturing, and construction, where income fluctuates greatly from year to year. A couple of bad years in a row could bring a heavily leveraged company into bankruptcy. During the 1980s, leverage was so important in the acquisition of entire companies that the term *leveraged buyout* (LBO) became a standard part of financial discussions. Often such acquisitions were financed with high-yield bonds, called junk bonds because of their high risk.

## EARNINGS PER SHARE (EPS)

Investors in common stock are less concerned with a company's total income than with their share of that income as expressed by the company's earnings per share (EPS). EPS is the most widely cited statistic in the financial press, the business section of newspapers, and recommendations by brokerage firms and other investment advisers. In simple cases, EPS is calculated as follows:

$$\text{Earnings per share (EPS)} = \frac{\text{net income} - \text{dividends on preferred stock}}{\text{weighted average common shares outstanding}}$$

The weighted average of common shares outstanding is the best measure of the shares outstanding throughout the period when the income is earned. If Burke has 22,000 shares outstanding all through 20X1 and 20X2, as well as at the ends of those years, its EPS figures are

$$20X1 \quad \frac{\$94,800 - \$0}{22,000} = \frac{\$94,800}{22,000} = \$4.31$$

$$20X2 \quad \frac{\$103,200 - \$0}{22,000} = \frac{\$103,200}{22,000} = \$4.69$$

EPS in 20X2 was $0.38 higher than in 20X1. This is an 8.8 percent growth rate, which we calculate as follows:

$$Growth\ rate\ of\ EPS \quad = \quad \frac{EPS\ current\ year\ -\ EPS\ prior\ year}{EPS\ prior\ year}$$

The greater the growth that investors expect, the more they are willing to pay for the common stock. Of course, an increase in EPS from one year to the next does not always mean that the company is growing; it might simply reflect a rebound from a particularly poor year. EPS could also increase (or decrease) because of an unusual event that is unlikely to recur frequently. (Financial accounting refers to such events as extraordinary items.) Many analysts compare EPS numbers without the effects of extraordinary items and other one-time events such as the discontinuance of a major segment of the business or a change in accounting principle used to prepare financial statements, such as a change from FIFO to LIFO. GAAP accommodates that practice by requiring the reporting of an EPS number before extraordinary items, gains or losses on discontinued operations, and changes in accounting principle. In any case, growth rates should be calculated over a number of years, rather than for a single year as we have done here. The accompanying Insight explores the growth rates of selected companies.

Some companies issue **convertible securities**, bonds and preferred stock that can be converted into common stock at the option of the owner. Conversion poses the problem of potential **dilution** (decreases) in EPS, because earnings have to be spread over a greater number of shares.[1] Calculating EPS when dilution is possible can be extremely complex. We shall show a single, relatively simple, illustration. Assume that a company has net income of $200,000, 80,000 common shares outstanding, and an issue of convertible preferred stock. The preferred stock pays dividends of $20,000 and is convertible into 30,000 common shares. Using the basic formula, EPS is $2.25.

$$\frac{\$200,000 - \$20,000}{80,000} = \frac{\$180,000}{80,000} = \$2.25$$

The company will show the $2.25 as *basic earnings per share* on the income statement. Then the income statement will report another EPS number, called *diluted earnings per share*. Diluted EPS is a pro forma calculation that shows what EPS would have been if convertible securities had actually been converted into common stock at the beginning of the year. Had the conversion occurred, there would have been no preferred dividends, but an additional 30,000 common shares would have been outstanding for the entire year. We calculate diluted EPS by adding back the preferred dividends on the convertible stock to the $180,000 earnings available for common stock and adding 30,000 shares to the denominator.

---

1 *The computation of EPS is governed by Statement of Financial Accounting Standards No. 128 (Stamford, CT: Financial Accounting Standards Board, 1997).*

SIGHT

## High-Growth Companies

Many investors, called growth investors, seek out stocks with rapidly increasing profits, and such stocks can be very volatile. *Fortune* magazine publishes an annual listing of America's fastest growing companies. Some of these companies will be stellar investments (**Dell Computer's** stock price grew from a stock-adjusted 1990 price of $0.23 to a 1998 high of $128.63, a 55,826 percent gain). Other companies on this list will be losers. The challenge of investing in growth stocks is to be able to tell which stock will be in which group.

A sampling of the 1998 list is as follows:

| | Average EPS growth (3-year average) | Annual revenue growth | Estimated P/E |
|---|---|---|---|
| **Noble Drilling** | 394% | 36% | 10 |
| **Vitesse Semiconductor** | 227% | 55% | 49 |
| **Rainforest Café** | 113% | 175% | 13 |
| **Dell Computer** | 90% | 53% | 57 |

*Source:* Fortune, *September 28, 1998.*

$$\frac{\$180,000 + \$20,000}{80,000 + 30,000} = \frac{\$200,000}{110,000} = \$1.82 \ diluted \ EPS$$

## PRICE-EARNINGS RATIO (PE)

The PE ratio is the ratio of the market price of a share of common stock to its EPS. The ratio indicates the amount investors are paying to buy a dollar of earnings. PE ratios of high-growth potential companies are often very high; those of low-growth potential or declining companies tend to be low. Assume that Burke's common stock sold at $60 per share at the end of 20X1 and $70 at the end of 20X2. The PE ratios are

$$Price\text{-}earnings \ ratio \ = \ \frac{market \ price \ per \ share}{earnings \ per \ share}$$

$$20X1 \ = \ \frac{\$60.00}{\$4.31} \ = \ 13.9$$

$$20X2 \ = \ \frac{\$70.00}{\$4.69} \ = \ 14.9$$

The increase in the PE ratio from 20X1 to 20X2 could have happened because EPS had been growing rather slowly until 20X2 and investors believed the growth rate would increase in the future. Such a situation justifies a higher PE ratio. Or perhaps PE ratios throughout the economy increased because of good economic news and expectations of good business conditions.

## DIVIDEND YIELD AND PAYOUT RATIO

We have been viewing earnings available for common stockholders as the major return accruing to owners of common stock. But investors do not "get" EPS. They receive dividends and, they hope, increases in the market value of their shares. The dividend yield is a measure of the current cash income that an investor can obtain per dollar of investment.

$$Dividend\ yield \ = \ \frac{dividend\ per\ share}{market\ price\ per\ share}$$

Burke declared and paid dividends of $63,000 in 20X1 and $73,200 in 20X2 on 22,000 shares, giving dividends per share of $2.86 and $3.33 for 20X1 and 20X2, respectively. Given per-share market prices of $60 and $70 at the ends of 20X1 and 20X2, dividend yields are

$$20X1 \quad \frac{\$2.86}{\$60.00} \ = \ 4.77\%$$

$$20X2 \quad \frac{\$3.33}{\$70.00} \ = \ 4.76\%$$

The payout ratio is the ratio of dividends per share to EPS. For Burke, the payout ratio in 20X2 is 71 percent ($3.33/$4.69) and in 20X1 was 66 percent ($2.86/$4.31). In general, companies with high growth rates have relatively low dividend yields and payout ratios. Such companies are investing the cash they could use for dividends. Investors who favor high-growth companies are not looking for dividends so much as for increases in the market price of the common stock. Because such hoped-for increases might or might not occur, investing in high-growth companies is generally riskier than investing in companies that pay relatively high, stable dividends.

## ECONOMIC VALUE ADDED (EVA)

Chapter 11 referred to EVA in the context of divisional performance evaluation and compared it with residual income. The proponents of EVA argue that it is the best measure of the success of a company as a whole. EVA is computed as

$$EVA \ = \ After\text{-}tax\ operating\ income \ - \ (cost\ of\ capital \ \times \ investment)$$

After-tax operating income is income before interest and taxes multiplied by one minus the tax rate. EVA proponents define investment differently from GAAP. Some explanations of EVA give investment as total assets less current liabilities, plus expenditures made for long-term purposes. Expenditures for research and development and for employee training are common examples. They advocate amortizing such investments over five years. Suppose Burke's cost of capital is 9 percent and that it has no investments we need to add back. Its EVA for 20X2 is

$$EVA = \$220,000 \times (1 - 40\%) - [9\% \times (\$1,550,000 - \$150,000)]$$
$$= \$132,000 - 9\% \times \$1,400,000$$
$$= \$6,000$$

The $6,000 EVA says that Burke is covering its cost of capital and providing additional economic value to its shareholders. The accompanying Insight illustrates how companies set financial goals using EVA.

## SOLVENCY

**Solvency** refers to long-term safety, the likelihood that the company will be able to pay its long-term liabilities. Solvency is similar to liquidity but has a much longer time horizon. Both long-term creditors and stockholders are interested in solvency—long-term creditors because of a concern about receiving interest payments and a return of principal, stockholders because they cannot receive dividends and benefit from increased market prices unless the company survives.

### DEBT RATIO

One common measure of solvency is the debt ratio, which is calculated as shown on the following page.

 **SIGHT**

### Economic Value Added Goals at Champion International

"When we announced a new strategic direction for **Champion** on October 8, 1997, we committed the company to a goal of maximizing total shareholder return. To do this, we will focus on those businesses that have the greatest opportunity for us to earn an economic profit; we will significantly improve our profitability; and we will exercise strong financial discipline in all our spending. Improving the way we serve our customers will help us achieve a sustainable competitive advantage. In the course of implementing this new strategic direction, we will help to build a different Champion. Our governing objective is clear—to maximize total shareholder return. To accomplish this objective, we must create economic profit in all of our businesses by earning at a level that is in excess of our capital charge. Our ambitious goal is to earn an 11 percent return on capital employed and perform in the top quartile of our industry. Incentive compensation for key managers has been tied to shareholder return through a performance share plan. This plan will pay out only if, at any time within three years from inception, the total return to our shareholders has increased at a rate that is equivalent to approximately 15 percent per annum compounded for three years."

*Source: Letter to Shareholders, 1997 annual report.*

$$Debt\ ratio\ =\ \frac{total\ liabilities}{total\ assets}$$

This ratio measures the proportion of debt in a company's capital structure. It is also called the debt-to-assets ratio. As with other ratios, variations provide much the same information. For example, some analysts calculate a debt-to-equity ratio, dividing total liabilities by stockholders' equity; others calculate a ratio of long-term liabilities to total assets or of long-term liabilities to long-lived assets, such as property, plant, and equipment. All of these variations have the same basic objective: to determine the company's degree of debt. The higher the proportion of debt in the capital structure, the riskier the company. Companies in different industries can handle different percentages of debt. For example, public utilities typically have very high percentages of debt because they have stable cash flows, manufacturers somewhat lower.

The debt ratios for Burke Company for 20X1 and 20X2 are

$$20X1\ =\ \frac{\$610,000}{\$1,380,000}\ =\ 44.2\%$$

$$20X2\ =\ \frac{\$750,000}{\$1,550,000}\ =\ 48.4\%$$

Notice that if we subtract the debt ratio from 100 percent, we get the proportion of stockholders' equity in the capital structure. This is usually called the *equity ratio*. Like the debt ratio, it is a way of measuring solvency, but from a different standpoint.

Burke's debt ratio increased from 20X1 to 20X2, but we cannot tell whether it is near a dangerous level without knowing a good deal more. We can obtain some additional information by calculating the burden that interest expense places on the company.

## TIMES INTEREST EARNED

Times interest earned, or interest coverage, measures the extent to which operations cover interest expense. The higher the ratio, the more likely the company will be able to continue meeting the interest payments.

$$Times\ interest\ earned\ =\ \frac{income\ before\ interest\ and\ taxes}{interest\ expense}$$

Burke had interest coverage of 4.8 times in 20X1, but slipped to 4.6 times in 20X2.

$$20X1\quad \frac{\$200,000}{\$42,000}\ =\ 4.8\ times$$

$$20X2\quad \frac{\$220,000}{\$48,000}\ =\ 4.6\ times$$

We use income before interest and taxes because interest is a tax-deductible expense. Some analysts also add depreciation in the numerator. Reasoning that depreciation does not require cash payments, these analysts believe that the numerator in their ratio approximates the total amount of cash available to pay interest.

## CASH FLOW TO TOTAL DEBT

A classic study of ratios computed for actual companies showed that the single best ratio for predicting a company's failure was the ratio of **cash flow to total debt**.[2] In that study, cash flow was defined as net income plus depreciation, amortization, and depletion, and total debt was defined as total liabilities plus preferred stock.

$$\text{Cash flow to total debt} = \frac{net\ income\ +\ depreciation\ +\ amortization\ +\ depletion}{total\ liabilities\ +\ preferred\ stock}$$

Burke has no amortization or depletion and no preferred stock. Therefore, the values of the ratio are

$$20X1 \quad \frac{\$94,800\ +\ \$75,000}{\$610,000} = \frac{\$169,800}{\$610,000} = 27.8\%$$

$$20X2 \quad \frac{\$103,200\ +\ \$90,000}{\$750,000} = \frac{\$193,200}{\$750,000} = 25.8\%$$

The research study drawing attention to this ratio was conducted before companies were required to provide a cash flow statement as part of the financial statement package. Using the operating cash flow taken *directly* from Burke's cash flow statement, the ratios are

$$20X1 \quad \frac{\$177,600}{\$610,000} = 29.1\%$$

$$20X2 \quad \frac{\$203,200}{\$750,000} = 27.1\%$$

Though both versions of this solvency ratio show a decline, the decline does not seem serious. Nevertheless, comparison of the ratio with the industry average might indicate a potential problem.

Other uses of cash flow ratios have become popular, especially now that GAAP requires virtually every publicly traded company to publish its cash flow statement. A number of different forms of cash flow ratios can be computed.[3] Analysts use ratios to assess the adequacy of a company's cash flow for financing operations and its growth. The accompanying Insight describes how cash ratios can provide information other balance sheet ratios cannot.

## RATIOS AND EVALUATION

Calculating ratios for the current year is only the starting point in analyzing a company's operations and prospects. Comparisons are critical and many factors besides the magnitudes of the ratios must be considered.

---

2 See William H. Beaver, "Financial Ratios as Predictors of Failure," *Empirical Research in Accounting, Selected Studies, 1966,* Journal of Accounting Research, *1967, 71–111.*
3 *For an excellent discussion of cash flow ratios, see John Mills and Jeanne Yamamura, "The Power of Cash Flow Ratios,"* Journal of Accountancy, *October 1998, 53–61.*

### Cash Flow Ratios

**Boomtown** was a Nevada casino company that went public in 1992. By 1996, Boomtown had four properties in three different states. Total assets increased over this time period from $56 million in 1992 to $206 million in 1996. The current ratio and the quick ratio for the 5-year period would lead an analyst to believe Boomtown was a strong company financially.

Cash flow ratios pointed out severe problems. Boomtown's growth was funded almost exclusively through outside funds. In 1997, Boomtown ran out of cash and was acquired by **Hollywood Park, Inc.**

Source: John Mills and Jeanne Yamamura, "Case Study: Running a Casino Is Not a Game," Journal of Accountancy, October 1998, 54–55.

Analysts should compare ratios with those from prior years, evaluate trends, and explore related ratios. (Is the company becoming more or less liquid? More or less profitable? Were changes in sales and ROA consistent with changes in turnovers of receivables and inventory?) Whenever possible, analysts also compare a company's ratios with those of similar companies and with those for the industry as a whole. (Are the company's ratios consistent with, and moving in the same direction as, those for the industry? Are out-of-line ratios or trends explainable?)

Several factors make both inter-company and industry comparisons difficult. Comparisons become more difficult as more and more companies diversify their operations. Highly diversified companies might operate in fifteen or more different industries. A welcome trend in financial reporting is increased disclosure of data about the major segments of diversified companies. Such additional disclosure allows analysts to make comparisons that were not possible when only overall results were available.

Even comparisons with fairly similar companies must be made with care, because ratios can differ considerably when companies use different accounting methods. For example, differences in the accounting methods used to value inventory (e.g., FIFO and LIFO) can influence many ratios. If purchase prices have generally been rising, a company using LIFO will show a lower inventory, current ratio, ROS, and EPS, and a higher inventory turnover than a company using FIFO. The longer the price trend has continued and the longer the company has used LIFO, the more marked the effects of the difference in inventory method. Consider too the effects of different depreciation methods on ratios. A business using the sum-of-the-years'-digits method will show lower book values for its plant assets than one using the straight-line method; the differences will affect all ratios involving total assets, net income, or both.

Even comparisons among similar companies using similar accounting methods can be misleading in the sense that one business could show up better than another in several measures of liquidity, profitability, or solvency and still not be better managed, more successful, or stronger than the other. For example, a company might be *too* liquid. Too much cash is not as bad as too little cash, but having excessive cash is unwise, because cash does not earn profits unless it is used for something. Faster turnover of inventory could be the result of unnecessarily low selling prices. A shorter collection period on receivables could result from highly restrictive credit policies. Hence, turnovers must be studied in relation to ROS and gross profit ratios, and to trends in the industry. In short, no single ratio, or group of ratios, should be considered in a vacuum.

Another factor to consider in evaluating a company is the extent to which one or more ratios can be affected by a single transaction. For example, consider the effects of a large cash payment for a current liability. Such a payment reduces both cash and current liabilities, and has no effect on total working capital. Yet it can improve the current ratio. To illustrate, look at the ratios for Burke Company for 20X2 and assume that it paid current liabilities of $30,000 just before the end of that year. Its current assets before the payment would have been $480,000 ($450,000 + $30,000), and its current liabilities would have been $180,000 ($150,000 + $30,000), giving a current ratio of 2.67 to 1. This ratio is lower than the 3 to 1 we calculated earlier. Before the payment the acid-test ratio would have been 1.6 to 1 [($80,000 + $180,000 + $30,000)/($150,000 + $30,000)]. This is also lower than the ratio calculated earlier (1.73 to 1). Taking actions to improve ratios is called **window dressing**. This type of window dressing is possible if the current ratio and acid-test ratio are greater than 1 to 1. If those ratios are less than 1 to 1, paying a current liability will reduce them, but window dressing is then possible by delaying payments of current liabilities.

Any evaluation based on ratios and comparisons of them must recognize the relative importance of the ratio to the particular industry. The nature of the product and of the production process, the degree of competition in the industry, and many other industry-related factors are relevant in interpreting a particular company's liquidity, profitability, and solvency ratios. For example, consider the utility industry. Because a utility is a monopoly, the government unit granting the monopoly right also regulates many of the utility's actions. In most cases, the regulating authority both ensures and limits the utility's profitability. Utilities seldom have liquidity problems, because their cash flows are relatively stable, because selling a service means they need not maintain inventories, and because their ability to shut off the service minimizes problems in collecting their receivables. For the same reasons, the investing public tolerates more leverage and a lower, but more stable, level of profitability in a utility.

All of the preceding considerations point out the need for understanding (1) the company being analyzed and (2) the industry in which the company operates. That a company's ratios differ from those in the past, or are in-line or out-of-line with those of other companies in the industry, is not good or bad in itself. (In the 1980s, **Chrysler Corporation** improved its liquidity, profitability, and prospects for solvency, in relation to both its prior performance and to the average for the industry. Nevertheless, the entire industry performed poorly during that period.) Finally, financial statements do not tell analysts all they want to know.

## SUMMARY

Ratio analysis is used in making investment decisions. Analysts are concerned with trends in ratios and with whether a company's ratios are in line with those of other companies in the same industry. Ratios can be classified into three major types: liquidity, profitability, and solvency.

Which ratios to use and which to emphasize depend on the type of decision to be made. Short-term creditors look primarily at liquidity. Long-term creditors are concerned more with solvency than with liquidity and profitability, but the latter aspects are still important. Current and potential holders of common stock are most interested in profitability, but liquidity and solvency are still significant.

Ratio analysis must be used with care. Ratios provide information only in the context of a comparison. Comparisons must be made with other companies and with norms for the industry. Different accounting methods, such as LIFO and FIFO, sum-of-the-years'-digits depreciation and straight-line depreciation, can cause similar companies to show quite different ratios.

## KEY TERMS

cash flow to total debt  *(811)*
common-size statements  *(796)*
composition problem  *(799)*
convertible securities  *(806)*
dilution (of earnings per share)  *(806)*
leverage (trading on the equity)  *(804)*

liquidity  *(798)*
quick assets  *(799)*
solvency  *(809)*
window dressing  *(813)*
working capital  *(798)*

## KEY FORMULAS

### Liquidity Ratios

$$\text{Accounts receivable turnover} = \frac{\text{sales}}{\text{accounts receivable}}$$

$$\text{Current ratio} = \frac{\text{current assets}}{\text{current liabilities}}$$

$$\text{Days' sales in accounts receivable} = \frac{\text{ending accounts receivable}}{\text{average daily sales}}$$

$$\text{Days' sales in inventory} = \frac{\text{ending inventory}}{\text{average daily cost of goods sold}}$$

$$\text{Inventory turnover} = \frac{\text{cost of goods sold}}{\text{inventory}}$$

$$\text{Quick ratio} = \frac{\text{cash + marketable securities + accounts receivable}}{\text{current liabilities}}$$

### Profitability Ratios

$$\text{Dividend yield} = \frac{\text{dividend per share}}{\text{market price per share}}$$

$$\text{Earnings per share (EPS)} = \frac{\text{net income} - \text{dividends on preferred stock}}{\text{weighted average common shares outstanding}}$$

$$\text{EVA} = \text{After-tax operating profit} - (\text{cost of capital} \times \text{investment})$$

Gross profit ratio $= \dfrac{\text{gross profit}}{\text{sales}}$

Payout ratio $= \dfrac{\text{dividend per share}}{\text{earnings per share}}$

Price-earnings ratio (PE) $= \dfrac{\text{market price per share}}{\text{earnings per share}}$

Return on assets (ROA) $= \dfrac{\text{net income + interest + income taxes}}{\text{total assets}}$

Return on common equity (ROE) $= \dfrac{\text{net income − dividends on preferred stock}}{\text{common stockholders' equity}}$

Return on sales (ROS) $= \dfrac{\text{net income}}{\text{sales}}$

**Solvency Ratios**

Debt ratio $= \dfrac{\text{total liabilities}}{\text{total assets}}$

Times interest earnings $= \dfrac{\text{income before interest and taxes}}{\text{interest expense}}$

Cash flow to total debt $= \dfrac{\text{net income + depreciation + amortization + depletion}}{\text{total liabilities + preferred stock}}$

## REVIEW PROBLEM

Financial statements for Q-Comm Company follow.

### Q-Comm Company, Balance Sheets at December 31

|  | 20X3 | 20X2 |
|---|---|---|
| **Assets** | | |
| Cash | $ 180,000 | $ 200,000 |
| Accounts receivable, net | 850,000 | 830,000 |
| Inventory | 620,000 | 560,000 |
| Total current assets | $ 1,650,000 | $ 1,590,000 |
| Plant and equipment | 7,540,000 | 6,650,000 |
| Accumulated depreciation | (1,920,000) | (1,500,000) |
| Total assets | $ 7,270,000 | $ 6,740,000 |
| **Equities** | | |
| Accounts payable | $ 220,000 | $ 190,000 |
| Accrued expenses | 450,000 | 440,000 |
| Total current liabilities | $ 670,000 | $ 630,000 |
| Long-term debt | 1,000,000 | 950,000 |
| Total liabilities | $ 1,670,000 | $ 1,580,000 |
| Common stock, no par value | 4,000,000 | 4,000,000 |
| Retained earnings | 1,600,000 | 1,160,000 |
| Total equities | $ 7,270,000 | $ 6,740,000 |

### Q-Comm Company, Income Statement for 20X3

| | | |
|---|---|---|
| Sales | | $8,650,000 |
| Cost of goods sold | | 4,825,000 |
| Gross profit | | $3,825,000 |
| Operating expenses: | | |
| Depreciation | $ 420,000 | |
| Other | 2,135,000 | |
| Total | | 2,555,000 |
| Income before interest and taxes | | $1,270,000 |
| Interest expense | | 70,000 |
| Income before taxes | | $1,200,000 |
| Income taxes at 30% | | 360,000 |
| Net income | | $  840,000 |

### Q-Comm Company, Cash Flow Statement for 20X3

| | | |
|---|---|---|
| Net cash flow from operating activities: | | |
| Collections from customers | | $ 8,630,000 |
| Payments to suppliers | | (4,855,000) |
| Payments for operating expenses | | (2,163,000) |
| Interest paid | | (72,000) |
| Taxes paid | | (320,000) |
| Net cash provided by operations | | $ 1,220,000 |
| Cash flows for investing activities—purchase | | |
| of plant and equipment | | (890,000) |
| Cash flows for financing activities: | | |
| Payment of dividends | $(400,000) | |
| Proceeds from new long-term debt issue | 50,000 | |
| Net cash for financing activities | | (350,000) |
| Change in cash (decrease) | | $   (20,000) |
| Cash balance, beginning of year | | 200,000 |
| Cash balance, end of year | | $   180,000 |

Q-Comm had 200,000 shares of common stock outstanding throughout the year. The market price of the stock at year end was $65 per share. All sales are on credit.

**Required**

Compute the following ratios as of the end of 20X3 or for the year ended December 31, 20X3, whichever is appropriate.

1. Current ratio.
2. Quick ratio.
3. Accounts receivable turnover.
4. Days' sales in accounts receivable.
5. Inventory turnover.
6. Days' sales in inventory.
7. Gross profit ratio.
8. Return on sales (ROS).
9. Return on assets (ROA).
10. Return on equity (ROE).

11. Earnings per share (EPS).
12. Price-earnings ratio (PE).
13. Dividend yield.
14. Payout ratio.
15. EVA, assuming cost of capital is 12%.
16. Debt ratio.
17. Times interest earned.
18. Cash flow to total debt.

## ANSWER TO REVIEW PROBLEM

1. Current ratio

$$\frac{\$1,650,000}{\$670,000} = 2.46 \text{ to } 1$$

2. Quick ratio

$$\frac{\$180,000 + \$850,000}{\$670,000} = 1.54 \text{ to } 1$$

3. Accounts receivable turnover

$$\frac{\$8,650,000}{(\$850,000 + \$830,000)/2} = 10.3 \text{ times}$$

4. Days' sales in accounts receivable

$$\frac{\$850,000}{\$8,650,000/365} = 36 \text{ days}$$

5. Inventory turnover

$$\frac{\$4,825,000}{(\$620,000 + \$560,000)/2} = 8.2 \text{ times}$$

6. Days' sales in inventory

$$\frac{\$620,000}{\$4,825,000/365} = 47 \text{ days}$$

7. Gross profit ratio

$$\frac{\$3,825,000}{\$8,650,000} = 44.2\%$$

8. ROS

$$\frac{\$840,000}{\$8,650,000} = 9.7\%$$

9. ROA

$$\frac{\$840,000 + \$70,000 + \$360,000}{(\$7,270,000 + \$6,740,000)/2} = 18.1\%$$

10. ROE

$$\frac{\$840,000}{(\$5,600,000 + \$5,160,000)/2} = 15.6\%$$

11. EPS

$$\frac{\$840,000}{200,000} = \$4.20$$

12. PE ratio

$$\frac{\$65.00}{\$4.20} = 15.5 \text{ times}$$

13. Dividend yield

$$\frac{\$2}{\$65} = 3.1\%$$

14. Payout ratio

$$\frac{\$2.00}{\$4.20} = 47.6\%$$

15. EVA

$$\$1,270,000 \times (1 - 30\%) - [12\% \times (\$7,270,000 - \$670,000)] = \$97,000$$

16. Debt ratio

$$\frac{\$1,670,000}{\$7,270,000} = 23.0\%$$

17. Times interest earned

$$\frac{\$1,270,000}{\$70,000} = 18 \text{ times}$$

18. Cash flow to total debt

$$\frac{\$840,000 + \$420,000}{\$1,670,000} = 75.4\%$$

## ASSIGNMENT MATERIAL

### INTERNET ACTIVITY

The Association for Investment Management and Research (AIMR) sponsors a certification for financial analysts known as Chartered Financial Analyst (CFA). Use a Web search engine such as Yahoo to find the AIMR Web site. Search this site to find out about the CFA examination. Be prepared to describe and discuss what you discovered.

### QUESTIONS FOR DISCUSSION

**18-1   Dividend yield**   Your friend bought stock in Acme Corporation five years ago for $25 per share. Acme is now paying a $5 dividend per share and the stock sells for $165. He says that the 20% dividend yield is an excellent return. How did he calculate the dividend yield? Is he correct?

**18-2   Ratios and accounting methods**   LIFO Company uses the last-in first-out method of inventory determination; FIFO Company uses first-in first-out. They have virtually identical operations, physical quantities of inventory, sales, and fixed assets. What differences would you expect to find in the ratios of the companies?

**18-3  Ratios and operating decisions**  Bronson Company and Corman Company are in the same industry and have virtually identical operations. The only difference between them is that Bronson rents 60% of its plant and equipment on short-term leases, while Corman owns all of its fixed assets. Corman has long-term debt of 60% of the book value of its fixed assets, Bronson has none. The two companies show the same net income because Bronson's rent and depreciation are the same as Corman's depreciation and interest. What differences would you expect to find in the ratios of the two companies?

**18-4  Foreign exchange risk**  Coca-Cola gains about 82% of its operating profit outside the United States. It makes most of the product it sells overseas in the host countries. If the dollar strengthens against foreign currencies (a dollar buys more units of foreign currency), will that help or hurt the company? Why?

**18-5  Liquidity**  You are the chief loan officer of a medium-size bank. Two companies have applied for short-term loans, but you can grant only one because of limited funds. Both companies have the same working capital and the same current ratio. They are in the same industry and their current ratios are well above the industry average. What additional information about their current positions would you seek?

**18-6  Seasonality and ratios**
1. At December 31, 1997, **Hasbro, Inc.**, the toy company, had $783 million accounts receivable. Sales for 1997 were $3,189 million. What are days' sales in accounts receivable? Why might Hasbro's days' sales in receivables seem high at December 31?
2. Hasbro's inventories at December 31, 1997 were $243 million and its cost of sales for 1997 was $1,359 million. What was its inventory turnover? Do you think the figure reflects what Hasbro experiences throughout the year?

**18-7  Price-earnings ratio**  Your friend says that his investment strategy is simple. He buys stocks with very low PE ratios. He reasons that he is getting the most for his money that way. Do you agree that this is a good strategy?

**18-8  Relevance of ratios to industry**  The 1997 annual report of **Bangor Hydro-Electric Company**, a regional electric utility, contained the usual set of financial statements. A condensed balance sheet follows, in thousands of dollars.

|  | December 31 | |
| --- | --- | --- |
|  | 1997 | 1996 |
| **Assets** | | |
| Utility plant | $288,754 | $279,801 |
| Current assets | 33,443 | 37,060 |
| Deferred debits and other assets | 278,386 | 239,768 |
| Total assets | $600,583 | $556,629 |
| **Capitalization and Liabilities** | | |
| Stockholders' equity | $106,558 | $108,321 |
| Preferred stock | 13,871 | 15,404 |
| Long-term debt | 221,643 | 274,221 |
| Current liabilities | 105,213 | 68,155 |
| Deferred credits | 153,298 | 90,528 |
| Total capitalization and liabilities | $600,583 | $556,629 |

**Required**

Discuss the relevance of the three ratio groups to the analysis of a company such as Bangor Hydro-Electric.

**18-9    *Ratio variation***    The Financial Highlights section of an annual report of **Motorola Inc.** included the values of the following ratios.

1. Return on average invested capital (stockholders' equity) plus long-term and short-term debt, net of marketable securities.
2. Percent of total debt less marketable securities to total debt less marketable securities plus equity.

To which of the three general categories of ratios does each of these ratios belong? How would you explain why the components of these ratios differ from those given in the chapter?

## EXERCISES

**18-10    *Effects of transactions***    Indicate the effects of each of the following transactions on the company's (a) current ratio and (b) acid-test ratio. There are three possible answers: (+) increase, (−) decrease, and (0) no effect. Before each transaction takes place, both ratios are greater than 1 to 1.

|  | Effects on | |
|---|---|---|
|  | (a)<br>Current<br>Ratio | (b)<br>Acid-Test<br>Ratio |
| Transaction |  |  |
| Example: Sell merchandise for cash | + | + |
| 1. Buy inventory for cash. | \_\_\_\_\_ | \_\_\_\_\_ |
| 2. Pay an account payable. | \_\_\_\_\_ | \_\_\_\_\_ |
| 3. Borrow cash on a short-term loan. | \_\_\_\_\_ | \_\_\_\_\_ |
| 4. Purchase plant assets for cash. | \_\_\_\_\_ | \_\_\_\_\_ |
| 5. Issue long-term bonds payable. | \_\_\_\_\_ | \_\_\_\_\_ |
| 6. Collect an account receivable. | \_\_\_\_\_ | \_\_\_\_\_ |
| 7. Record accrued expenses payable. | \_\_\_\_\_ | \_\_\_\_\_ |
| 8. Sell a plant asset for cash at a profit. | \_\_\_\_\_ | \_\_\_\_\_ |
| 9. Sell a plant asset for cash at a loss. | \_\_\_\_\_ | \_\_\_\_\_ |
| 10. Buy marketable securities, for cash, as a<br>    short-term investment. | \_\_\_\_\_ | \_\_\_\_\_ |

**18-11    *Relationships***    Answer the questions for each of the following independent situations.

1. The current ratio is 2.5 to 1. Current liabilities are $200,000. What are current assets?
2. ROA is 18%. ROE is 10%. There is no preferred stock. Net income is $4 million and average total assets are $30 million. What is average stockholders' equity?
3. The current ratio is 2.5 to 1; the acid-test ratio is 0.9 to 1; cash and receivables are $270,000. The only current assets are cash, receivables, and inventory. (a) What are current liabilities? (b) What is inventory?
4. Accounts receivable turnover is 5 times; inventory turnover is 4 times. The company recently bought inventory. (a) On the average, how long will it be before the

new inventory is sold? (b) On the average, how long after the inventory is sold will cash be collected?

5. A company had current assets of $600,000. It then paid a current liability of $90,000. After the payment, the current ratio was 2 to 1. What were current liabilities before the payment was made?

6. Accounts receivable equal 45 days' credit sales. The coming year should see sales of $900,000 spread evenly over the year. What should accounts receivable be at the end of the year?

**18-12   Leverage**   Balance Company is considering the retirement of $500,000 in 10% bonds. These bonds are the company's only interest-bearing debt. The retirement plan calls for the company to issue 10,000 shares of common stock at a total price of $500,000 and use the proceeds to buy back the bonds. Stockholders' equity is now $1,000,000, with 40,000 shares of common stock outstanding (no preferred stock). The company expects to earn $400,000 before interest and taxes in the coming year. The tax rate is 40%.

**Required**

1. Determine net income, EPS, and ROE for the coming year, assuming that the bonds are retired before the beginning of the coming year.
2. Determine net income, EPS, and ROE for the coming year, assuming that the bonds are not retired.
3. Is the proposed retirement wise? Why or why not?

**18-13   Return on assets and return on equity**   Z-Way Corporation had ROS of 5% and sales of $24 million. Interest expense is $0.3 million; total assets are $16 million; the debt ratio is 40%. There is no preferred stock. Ignore taxes.

**Required**

1. Determine income, ROA, and ROE.
2. Suppose the company could increase its ROS to 6% and keep the same level of sales. What would net income, ROA, and ROE be?
3. Suppose that the company reduced its debt ratio to 20% by retiring debt. New common stock was issued to finance the retirement, keeping total assets at $16 million. Net income is $1.35 million because of lower interest expense that now totals $0.15 million. What are ROA and ROE?

**18-14   Financing alternatives**   The founders of Marmex Company are trying to decide how to finance the company. They have three choices:

(a) Issue $8,000,000 in common stock.
(b) Issue $4,800,000 in common stock and $3,200,000 in 10% bonds.
(c) Issue $4,800,000 in common stock and $3,200,000 in 12% preferred stock. Income before interest and taxes is expected to be $2,000,000. The tax rate is 40%.

**Required**

1. Compute net income, earnings available for common stock, and ROE for each financing choice.
2. Suppose that the tax rate increases to 60%. Redo requirement 1. Can you draw any conclusions about the effects of tax rates on the relative desirability of the three choices?

**18-15   Turnovers and ratios for computer companies**   The following amounts have been collected from the annual reports for selected computer companies for 1996 and 1997.

|  | Dell | | Compaq | | Gateway | |
|---|---|---|---|---|---|---|
|  | 1997 | 1996 | 1997 | 1996 | 1997 | 1996 |
| Sales | 12,327 | 7,759 | 24,584 | 20,009 | 6,293 | 5,035 |
| Cost of sales | 9,605 | 6,093 | 17,833 | 14,855 | 5,217 | 4,099 |
| Interest expense | 3 | 7 | 168 | 106 | 164 | 102 |
| Taxes | 424 | 216 | 903 | 565 | 94 | 132 |
| Net income | 944 | 518 | 1,855 | 1,318 | 110 | 251 |
|  |  |  |  |  |  |  |
| Accounts receivable | 1,486 | 903 | 2,891 | 3,718 | 511 | 450 |
| Inventories | 233 | 251 | 1,570 | 1,267 | 249 | 278 |
| Total assets | 4,268 | 2,993 | 14,631 | 12,331 | 2,039 | 1,673 |

**Required**
1. Calculate the return on sales and return on assets for each company for both 1996 and 1997. Use year-end balance sheet values. What can you conclude from these ratios?
2. Calculate the accounts receivable turnover and the inventory turnover for each company for both 1996 and 1997. Use year-end balance sheet values. What can you conclude from these ratios?

**18-16 Return on assets and equity** Randolph Company has total assets of $12,000,000 and a debt ratio of 30%. Interest expense is $360,000, and return on average total assets is 12%. The company has no preferred stock. Ignore taxes.

**Required**
1. Determine income, average stockholders' equity, and ROE.
2. Suppose that sales have been $10,800,000 annually and are expected to continue at this level. If the company could increase its ROS by one percentage point, what would be its income, ROA, and ROE?
3. Refer to the original data and your answers to requirement 1. Suppose that Randolph retires $1,800,000 in debt and therefore saves interest expense of $180,000 annually. The company would issue additional common stock in the amount of $1,800,000 to finance the retirement. Total assets would remain at $12,000,000. What would be the income, ROA, and ROE?

**18-17 Effects of transactions—returns ratios** Indicate the effects of each of the following transactions on the company's (a) ROS, (b) ROA, and (c) EPS. There are three possible answers: (+) increase, (−) decrease, and (0) no effect. Before each transaction takes place, the ratios are as follows: (a) ROS, 10%; (b) ROA, 5%; (c) EPS, $0.25.

|  | Effects on | | |
|---|---|---|---|
|  | (a) ROS | (b) ROA | (c) EPS |
| 1. Sell a plant asset for cash, at twice the asset's book value. | ___ | ___ | ___ |
| 2. Declare and issue a stock dividend. | ___ | ___ | ___ |
| 3. Purchase inventory on account. | ___ | ___ | ___ |
| 4. Purchase treasury stock for cash. | ___ | ___ | ___ |
| 5. Acquire land by issuing common stock. | ___ | ___ | ___ |

**18-18 Ratios** The financial statements for Massin Company, a merchandising company, follow (in thousands of dollars). Massin has 1,000,000 common shares outstanding. The price of the stock is $8. Massin declared dividends of $0.10 per share. The balance sheet at the end of 20X1 showed approximately the same amounts as that at the end of 20X2.

| Massin Company, Income Statement for 20X2 | | |
|---|---|---|
| Sales | | $4,700 |
| Cost of goods sold | | 2,300 |
| Gross profit | | $2,400 |
| Operating expenses: | | |
| Depreciation | $ 320 | |
| Other | 1,230 | |
| Total | | 1,550 |
| Income before interest and taxes | | $ 850 |
| Interest expense | | 150 |
| Income before taxes | | $ 700 |
| Income taxes | | 280 |
| Net income | | $ 420 |

| Massin Company, Balance Sheet at December 31, 20X2 | | | |
|---|---|---|---|
| Assets | | Equities | |
| Cash | $ 220 | Accounts payable | $ 190 |
| Accounts receivable | 440 | Accrued expenses | 180 |
| Inventory | 410 | Total current liabilities | $ 370 |
| Total current assets | $ 1,070 | Long-term debt | 1,960 |
| Plant and equipment | 5,600 | Common stock | 1,810 |
| Accumulated depreciation | (2,100) | Retained earnings | 430 |
| Total assets | $ 4,570 | Total equities | $4,570 |

**Required**
Calculate the following ratios.

1. Current ratio.
2. Acid-test ratio.
3. Accounts receivable turnover.
4. Inventory turnover.
5. Gross profit ratio.
6. ROS.
7. ROA.
8. ROE.
9. EPS.
10. PE ratio.
11. Dividend yield.
12. Payout ratio.
13. EVA, assuming a 10% cost of capital.
14. Debt ratio.
15. Times interest earned.
16. Cash flow to total debt.

## PROBLEMS

**18-19   *Analyzing ROE (adapted from a paper by Professor William E. Ferrara)***
Chapter 11 introduced the idea of separating the components of ROI as follows:

$$ROI = \frac{net\ income}{sales} \times \frac{sales}{investment}$$

Applying this separation to the calculation of return on stockholders' equity, we could express ROE as

$$ROE = \frac{net\ income}{sales} \times \frac{sales}{stockholders'\ equity}$$

This separation is less enlightening than it might be, however, because net income combines the effects of financing choices (leverage) with the operating results. Letting total assets/stockholders' equity stand as a measure of financial leverage, we can also express return on stockholders' equity as follows:

$$ROE = \frac{net\ income}{sales} \times \frac{sales}{total\ assets} \times \frac{total\ assets}{stockholders'\ equity}$$

Sales and total assets cancel out, leaving the ratio net income/stockholders' equity. The three-factor expression allows the analyst to look at operations (margin × turnover, the first two terms) separately from financing (the last term).

The separation is not perfect because interest (financing expense) is included in calculating net income, but the expansion is adequate for many purposes. Thus, the product of the first two terms is a measure of operating efficiency, while the third is a measure of leverage and therefore of financial risk.

The following data summarize results for three companies.

### Company Results (in thousands of dollars)

|                       | A       | B       | C       |
| --------------------- | ------- | ------- | ------- |
| Sales                 | $4,500  | $6,000  | $5,000  |
| Net income            | $450    | $400    | $480    |
| Total assets          | $4,500  | $4,500  | $4,400  |
| Stockholders' equity  | $3,000  | $2,000  | $4,000  |
| ROE                   | 15%     | 20%     | 12%     |

**Required**
Calculate ROE for each company using the three-factor expression and comment on the results. You should be able to draw tentative conclusions about the relative operating and financing results of the companies.

**18-20   *Current asset activity***   The treasurer of Billingsgate Company has asked for your assistance in analyzing the company's liquidity. She provides the following data, in millions of dollars.

|                                  | 20X3  | 20X2  | 20X1  |
| -------------------------------- | ----- | ----- | ----- |
| Total sales                      | $481  | $440  | $395  |
| Cost of goods sold               | 322   | 290   | 245   |
| Accounts receivable at year end  | 64    | 48    | 31    |
| Inventory at year end            | 51    | 44    | 38    |
| Accounts payable at year end     | 36    | 29    | 28    |

**Required**
1. Compute accounts receivable turnover for 20X2 and 20X3.
2. Compute days' sales in accounts receivable at the end of 20X2 and 20X3.
3. Compute inventory turnover for 20X2 and 20X3.
4. Compute days' sales in inventory at the end of 20X2 and 20X3.
5. Comment on the trends in the ratios. Do the trends seem to be favorable or unfavorable?

**18-21   Constructing financial statements from ratios**   The following information is available concerning Warnock Company's expected results in 20X2 (in thousands of dollars). Turnovers are based on year-end values.

**Required**
Fill in the blanks.

| | |
|---|---|
| Return on sales | 6% |
| Gross profit percentage | 40% |
| Inventory turnover | 4 times |
| Receivables turnover | 5 times |
| Current ratio | 3 to 1 |
| Ratio of total debt to total assets | 40% |

| Condensed Income Statement | |
|---|---|
| Sales | $ 900 |
| Cost of sales | _____ |
| Gross profit | _____ |
| Operating expenses | _____ |
| Net income | $_____ |

| Condensed Balance Sheet | | | |
|---|---|---|---|
| Cash | $    30 | Current liabilities | $_____ |
| Receivables | $_____ | Long-term debt | _____ |
| Inventory | _____ | Stockholders' equity | _____ |
| Plant and equipment | 670 | | |
| Total | $_____ | Total | $_____ |

**18-22   Effects of transactions on ratios**   Indicate the effects of each of the following transactions on the company's current ratio, acid-test ratio, and debt ratio. There are three possible answers: increase (+), decrease (−), and no effect (0). Before each transaction takes place, the current ratio is greater than 1 to 1 and the acid-test ratio is less than 1 to 1.

| | Effects on | | |
|---|---|---|---|
| | Current Ratio | Acid-Test Ratio | Debt Ratio |
| Example: An account payable is paid. | + | − | − |
| 1. Bought inventory for cash. | _____ | _____ | _____ |
| 2. A sale is made on account; cost of sales is less than selling price. | _____ | _____ | _____ |
| 3. Issued long-term bonds for cash. | _____ | _____ | _____ |
| 4. Sold land for cash at its book value. | _____ | _____ | _____ |

| | Effects on | | |
|---|---|---|---|
| | Current Ratio | Acid-Test Ratio | Debt Ratio |
| 5. Marketable securities held as temporary investments are sold at a gain. | _____ | _____ | _____ |
| 6. Issued common stock in exchange for plant assets. | _____ | _____ | _____ |
| 7. Collected an account receivable. Issued long-term debt for plant assets. | _____ | _____ | _____ |
| 9. Declared, but did not pay, a cash dividend. | _____ | _____ | _____ |
| 10. Paid the dividend in item 9. | _____ | _____ | _____ |
| 11. Paid a short-term bank loan. | _____ | _____ | _____ |
| 12. Recorded depreciation expense. | _____ | _____ | _____ |

**18-23  Comparisons of companies**  Condensed financial statements for Genco Company and Rella Company appear on the bottom of the following page (in thousands of dollars). Both companies are in the same industry and use the same accounting methods. Balance sheet data for both companies were the same at the end of 20X1 as at the end of 20X2.

**Required**

On the basis of the data given, answer the following questions. Support your answers with whatever calculations you believe appropriate.

1. Which company seems to be more liquid?
2. Which company seems to be more profitable? Suppose cost of capital is 12% for both companies.
3. Which company seems to be more solvent?
4. Which stock seems to be a better buy?

**18-24  Effects of transactions—selected ratios**  In the following exhibit, several transactions or events are listed in the left-hand column and the names of various ratios and the value of that ratio before the associated transaction are listed in the right-hand column. Indicate the effect of the transaction on the specified ratio. There are three possible answers: (+) increase, (−) decrease, and (0) no effect.

| Transaction | | Effect on Ratio |
|---|---|---|
| 1. Write off an uncollectible account receivable. | _____ | Current ratio of 3 to 1 |
| 2. Sell merchandise on account, at less than normal price. | _____ | 42 days' sales in accounts receivable |
| 3. Borrow cash on a short-term loan. | _____ | Acid-test ratio of 0.9 to 1 |
| 4. Write off an uncollectible account receivable. | _____ | Return on sales of 18% |
| 5. Sell treasury stock at a price greater than its cost. | _____ | Return on equity of 20% |
| 6. Acquire plant asset by issuing long-term note. | _____ | Debt ratio of 40% |
| 7. Record accrued salaries payable. | _____ | Times interest earned of 3.2 |

| Transaction | Effect on Ratio | |
|---|---|---|
| 8. Record depreciation on plant assets. | _____ | Cash flow to debt ratio of 60% |
| 9. Return inventory items to supplier for credit. | _____ | Inventory turnover of 8 times |
| 10. Acquire plant assets by issuing common stock. | _____ | Debt ratio of 60% |

### Balance Sheets, End of 20X2

|  | Genco Company | Rella Company |
|---|---|---|
| **Assets** | | |
| Cash | $ 185 | $ 90 |
| Accounts receivable | 215 | 170 |
| Inventory | 340 | 220 |
| Plant and equipment (net) | 850 | 810 |
| Total assets | $1,590 | $1,290 |
| **Equities** | | |
| Accounts payable | $ 150 | $ 140 |
| Other current liabilities | 80 | 90 |
| Long-term debt | 300 | 500 |
| Common stock | 700 | 300 |
| Retained earnings | 360 | 260 |
| Total equities | $1,590 | $1,290 |

### Income Statements for 20X2

|  | Genco Company | Rella Company |
|---|---|---|
| Sales | $3,050 | $2,800 |
| Cost of goods sold | 1,400 | 1,350 |
| Gross profit | $1,650 | $1,450 |
| Operations expenses: | | |
|   Depreciation | $ 280 | $ 240 |
|   Other | 1,040 | 900 |
| Total | $1,320 | $1,140 |
| Income before interest and taxes | $ 330 | $ 310 |
| Interest expense | 30 | 55 |
| Income before taxes | $ 300 | $ 255 |
| Income taxes at 40% | 120 | 102 |
| Net income | $ 180 | $ 153 |
| Earnings per share | $0.90 | $0.77 |
| Dividends per share | $0.40 | $0.20 |
| Market price of common stock | $12.00 | $11.50 |

**18-25  Constructing financial statements using ratios**  The following data are available for Wasserman Pharmaceutical Company as of December 31, 20X2 and for the year ended.

| | |
|---|---|
| Current ratio | 2.5 to 1 |
| Days' sales in accounts receivable | 55 days |
| Inventory turnover | 4 times |
| Debt ratio | 40% |
| Current liabilities | $450,000 |
| Stockholders' equity | $1,500,000 |
| Return on sales | 10% |
| Return on common equity | 20% |
| Gross profit ratio | 40% |

Wasserman has no preferred stock, no marketable securities, and no prepaid expenses. Beginning-of-year balance sheet figures are the same as end-of-year figures. The only noncurrent assets are plant and equipment.

**Required**
Prepare a balance sheet as of December 31, 20X2 and an income statement for 20X2 in as much detail as you can with the available information. Round all figures to the nearest $1,000.

**18-26  Dilution of EPS**  Boston Tarrier Company has been very successful in recent years, as shown by the following data.

| | 20X2 | 20X3 |
|---|---|---|
| Net income | $6,200,000 | $8,600,000 |
| Preferred stock dividends | 800,000 | 800,000 |
| Earnings available for common stock | $5,400,000 | $7,800,000 |

The treasurer of the company is concerned because he expects holders of the company's convertible preferred stock to exchange their shares for common shares early in the coming year. All of the company's preferred stock is convertible, and the number of common shares issuable on conversion is 400,000. Throughout 20X2 and 20X3 the company had 600,000 shares of common stock outstanding.

**Required**
1. Compute basic EPS for 20X2 and 20X3.
2. Compute diluted EPS for 20X2 and 20X3.

**18-27  Inventory turnover and return on equity**  Timmons Company is presently earning net income of $400,000 per year, which gives a 10% ROE. The president believes that inventory can be reduced with tighter controls on buying. Any reduction of inventory frees cash, which would be used to pay a dividend to stockholders. Thus, stockholders' equity would drop by the same amount as inventory.

Inventory turnover is 3 times per year. Cost of goods sold is running at $3,600,000 annually. The president believes that careful management can increase turnover to 5 times. He also believes that sales, cost of goods sold, and net income will remain at their current levels.

**Required**
1. Determine Timmons's average inventory.

2. Determine Timmons's average inventory if turnover could be increased to 5 times per year.
3. Determine ROE if Timmons can increase turnover and reduce stockholders' equity by the amount of the reduction in investment in inventory.

**18-28  Ratios—industry averages**   The president of Brewster Company has been concerned about its operating performance and financial strength. She has obtained, from a trade association, the averages of certain ratios for the industry. She gives you these ratios and the company's most recent financial statements (in thousands of dollars). The balance sheet amounts were about the same at the beginning of the year as they are now.

Brewster Company, Balance Sheet as of December 31, 20X1

| Assets | | Equities | |
|---|---|---|---|
| Cash | $    860 | Accounts payable | $    975 |
| Accounts receivable | 3,210 | Accrued expenses | 120 |
| Inventory | 2,840 | Taxes payable | 468 |
| Total current assets | $ 6,910 | Total current liabilities | $ 1,563 |
| Plant and equipment, net | 7,090 | Bonds payable, due 19X9 | 6,300 |
| | | Common stock, no par | 4,287 |
| | | Retained earnings | 1,850 |
| Total assets | $14,000 | Total equities | $14,000 |

Brewster Company, Income Statement for 20X1

| | |
|---|---|
| Sales | $11,800 |
| Cost of goods sold | 7,350 |
| Gross profit | $ 4,450 |
| Operating expenses, including $650 depreciation | 2,110 |
| Operating profit | $ 2,340 |
| Interest expense | 485 |
| Income before taxes | $ 1,855 |
| Income taxes at 40% | 742 |
| Net income | $ 1,113 |

Brewster has 95,000 shares of common stock outstanding, which gives earnings per share of $11.72 ($1,113,000/95,000). Dividends are $5 per share and the market price of the stock is $120. Average ratios for the industry are as follows:

| | | | |
|---|---|---|---|
| Current ratio | 3.8 to 1 | Return on equity | 17.5% |
| Quick ratio | 1.9 to 1 | Price-earnings ratio | 12.3 |
| Accounts receivable turnover | 4.8 times | Dividend yield | 3.9% |
| Inventory turnover | 3.6 times | Payout ratio | 38.0% |
| Return on sales | 7.6% | Debt ratio | 50.0% |
| Return on assets | 17.6% | Times interest earned | 6 times |
| Cash flow to total debt | 25.0% | | |

**Required**
1. Compute the ratios shown above for Brewster Company.

2. Prepare comments to the president indicating areas of apparent strength and weakness for Brewster Company in relation to the industry.

**18-29  *Generating cash flows***  Humbert Company must make a $900,000 payment on a bank loan at the end of March 20X2. At December 31, 20X1, Humbert had cash of $125,000 and accounts receivable of $632,000. Estimated cash payments required during the first three months of 20X2, exclusive of the payment to the bank, are $645,000. Humbert expects sales to be $1,200,000 in the three-month period, all on credit. Accounts receivable normally equal about 45 days' sales.

**Required**
1. Determine the expected balance in accounts receivable at the end of March 20X2.
2. Determine whether the company will have enough cash to pay the bank loan on March 31, 20X2.

## CASES

**18-30  *Evaluation of trends and comparison with industry***  Comparative balance sheets and income statements for Marcus Manufacturing Company appear on the following page (in thousands of dollars). Your boss, the chief financial analyst for Hanmattan Bank, has asked you to analyze trends in the company's operations and financing and to make some comparisons with the averages for the same industry. The bank is considering the purchase of some shares of Marcus for one of its trust funds.

Selected data from the 20X2 balance sheet (in thousands of dollars) include the following:

| | |
|---|---:|
| Accounts receivable | $  510 |
| Inventory (all finished goods) | 620 |
| Total assets | 2,940 |
| Stockholders' equity | 1,320 |

The following are averages for Marcus's industry.

| | | | |
|---|---|---|---:|
| Current ratio | 2.7 to 1 | Receivables turnover | 8.5 times |
| Quick ratio | 1.4 to 1 | Inventory turnover | 4.2 times |
| Debt ratio | 52% | Return on assets | 15.0% |
| Price-earnings ratio | 11.5 | Return on equity | 13.5% |
| Dividend yield | 4.5% | Return on sales | 5.0% |
| Payout ratio | 48.0% | | |

**Required**
Compute the above ratios for Marcus for 20X3 and 20X4 and comment on the trends in the ratios and on relationships to industry averages.

**18-31  *Trends in ratios***  As the chief investment officer of a large pension fund, you must make many investing decisions. One of your assistants has prepared the following ratios for MBI Corporation, a large multinational manufacturer.

## Marcus Manufacturing Company, Balance Sheets as of December 31

| | 20X4 | 20X3 |
|---|---|---|
| **Assets** | | |
| Cash | $ 170 | $ 180 |
| Accounts receivable | 850 | 580 |
| Inventory (all finished goods) | 900 | 760 |
| Total current assets | $1,920 | $1,520 |
| Plant and equipment, net | 2,050 | 1,800 |
| Total assets | $3,970 | $3,320 |
| **Equities** | | |
| Current liabilities | $ 812 | $ 620 |
| Long-term debt | 1,640 | 1,300 |
| Common stock | 1,000 | 1,000 |
| Retained earnings | 518 | 400 |
| Total equities | $3,970 | $3,320 |

## Marcus Manufacturing Company, Income Statements

| | 20X4 | 20X3 |
|---|---|---|
| Sales | $4,700 | $4,350 |
| Cost of goods sold | 2,670 | 2,460 |
| Gross profit | $2,030 | $1,890 |
| Operating expenses | 1,470 | 1,440 |
| Income before interest and taxes | $ 560 | $ 450 |
| Interest expense | 130 | 100 |
| Income before taxes | $ 430 | $ 350 |
| Income taxes at 40% | 172 | 140 |
| Net income | $ 258 | $ 210 |
| Earnings per share | $2.58 | $2.10 |
| Market price of stock at year end | $32.00 | $28.00 |
| Dividends per share | $0.96 | $0.80 |

| | Industry Average All Years | 20X3 | 20X2 | 20X1 |
|---|---|---|---|---|
| Current ratio | 2.4 | 2.6 | 2.4 | 2.5 |
| Quick ratio | 1.6 | 1.55 | 1.6 | 1.65 |
| Receivable turnover | 8.1 | 7.5 | 7.9 | 8.3 |
| Inventory turnover | 4.0 | 4.3 | 4.2 | 4.0 |
| Debt ratio | 43.0% | 38.0% | 41.3% | 44.6% |
| Return on assets | 17.8% | 19.1% | 19.4% | 19.5% |
| Return on equity | 15.3% | 15.1% | 15.6% | 15.9% |
| Price-earnings ratio | 14.3 | 13.5 | 13.3 | 13.4 |
| Times interest earned | 8.3 | 9.7 | 9.5 | 8.9 |
| Earnings per share growth rate | 8.4% | 7.1% | 6.9% | 7.0% |

### Required

What is your decision in the following cases? Give your reasons.

1. Granting a short-term loan to MBI.
2. Buying long-term bonds of MBI on the open market. The bonds yield 7%, which is slightly less than the average for bonds in the industry.
3. Buying MBI common stock.

**18-32　Financial planning with ratios**　The treasurer of SmartStore, Inc., a large chain of convenience stores, has been trying to develop a financial plan. In conjunction with other managers, she has developed the following estimates, in millions of dollars.

|  | 20X1 | 20X2 | 20X3 | 20X4 |
|---|---|---|---|---|
| Sales | $100 | $120 | $150 | $210 |
| Plant assets, net | 80 | 95 | 110 | 125 |

In addition, for planning purposes she is willing to make the following estimates and assumptions about other results.

| | |
|---|---|
| Cost of goods sold as a percentage of sales | 55% |
| Return on sales | 15% |
| Dividend payout ratio | 20% |
| Turnovers based on year-end values: | |
|   Cash and accounts receivable | 5 times |
|   Inventory | 4 times |
| Required current ratio | 3 to 1 |
| Required ratio of long-term debt to stockholders' equity | 50% |

At the beginning of 20X1 the treasurer expects stockholders' equity to be $60 million and long-term debt to be $30 million.

### Required

Prepare pro forma balance sheets and any supporting schedules you need for the end of each of the next four years. Determine how much additional common stock, if any, the company will have to issue each year if the treasurer's estimates and assumptions are correct.

**18-33　Leverage**　Mr. Harmon, treasurer of Stokes Company, has been considering two plans for raising $2,000,000 for plant expansion and modernization. One choice is to issue 9% bonds. The other is to issue 25,000 shares of common stock at $80 per share. The modernization and expansion is expected to increase operating profit, before interest and taxes, by $320,000 annually. Depreciation of $200,000 is included in the $320,000. Condensed financial statements for 20X2 follow (in thousands of dollars).

**Stokes Company, Balance Sheet as of December 31, 20X2**

| Assets | | Equities | |
|---|---|---|---|
| Current assets | $ 3,200 | Current liabilities | $ 1,200 |
| Plant and equipment, net | 7,420 | Long-term debt, 7% | 3,000 |
| Other assets | 870 | Stockholders' equity | 7,290 |
| Total assets | $11,490 | Total equities | $11,490 |

### Stokes Company, Income Statement for 20X2

| | | |
|---|---:|---:|
| Sales | | $8,310 |
| Cost of sales | $5,800 | |
| Operating expenses | 1,200 | |
| Total | | 7,000 |
| Operating profit | | $1,310 |
| Interest expense | | 210 |
| Income before taxes | | $1,100 |
| Income taxes at 40% | | 440 |
| Net income | | $ 660 |
| Earnings per share* | | $6.60 |
| Dividends per share | | $3.30 |

*\* Based on 100,000 outstanding shares*

Mr. Harmon is concerned about the effects of issuing debt. The average debt ratio for companies in the industry is 42%. He believes that if this ratio is exceeded, the PE ratio of the stock will fall to 11 because of the potentially greater risk. If Stokes increases its common equity substantially by issuing new shares, he expects the PE ratio to increase to 12.5. He also wonders what will happen to the dividend yield under each plan. The company follows the practice of paying dividends equal to 50% of net income.

### Required

1. For each financing plan, calculate the debt ratio that the company would have after the securities (bonds or stocks) are issued.
2. For each financing plan, determine the expected net income in 20X3, expected EPS, and the expected market price of the common stock.
3. Calculate, for each financing plan, the dividend per share that Stokes would pay following its usual practice and the yield that would be obtained at the market prices from your answer to requirement 2.
4. Suppose that you now own 100 shares of Stokes Company. Which alternative would you prefer the company to use? Why?

# GUIDELINES FOR PREPARING MEMORANDA

Some assignments require you to write a memorandum about a specific problem. In most cases, such memoranda should be short and focus on a few points. The general guidelines in this appendix regarding names, headings, supporting schedules, and jargon apply to memoranda. In addition, other things to consider include:

1.  Use proper format, including a heading, to whom the memorandum is addressed, who wrote the memorandum, the date, and the subject, as the following illustrates.
2.  Be direct and to the point. Use the active voice: "We have concluded that . . ." not, "It was concluded . . ." Do not use fancy words and avoid jargon as much as possible. Know your audience and make sure that you provide information in an understandable way. Take the viewpoint of the reader. What would you like to see if you were the reader?
3.  Make your purpose clear. Executives are busy. If you do not grab their attention and hold it, they will scan your report with little interest or not read it at all. Make clear what response you would like from the reader.
4.  Use the opening of your memorandum to establish a link between what you have been asked to do and your recommendations/conclusions. See the

---

**Illustration of Memorandum Format**

```
                        MEMORANDUM

To:        John Jones, Controller
From:      Mary Smith, Smith & Co. Certified Public Accountants
Date:      January 19, 20X2
Subject:   Analysis of Plant Location

At your request, we evaluated alternative plant locations. We
have concluded that the Middleton location best suits your
needs. Only the question of transportation charges remains. We
used the net present value of the cost savings from each alter-
native location to develop our analysis (exhibit attached).
```

previous illustration. At the end of the memorandum tie things together. Also, end in such a way that the reader understands what you have done and is satisfied with your analysis.

## GENERAL GUIDELINES

Some guidelines for writing any report or memorandum follow. Some might not apply to a particular assignment, but they are generally useful.

## AUDIENCE ANALYSIS

No writing assignment can be successful without your defining and analyzing your audience. Ask yourself these questions: Who will be reading this? What is their level of sophistication and understanding of technical terms? What is my relationship with the readers? What do my readers know about the subject? Do my readers have strong feelings about this subject? Answering these questions will help you develop an audience profile to shape what you say and how you say it.

## ANALYSIS VERSUS RESTATEMENT

Many people confuse analysis with restatement. A restatement is a summary of the facts. An analysis involves critical thinking and requires that you go beyond the facts to answer the following questions: What are the implications of this information? How does this information affect the present or future situation? What effect does this information have on my audience? By answering these questions, you are performing an analysis. All memoranda and cases require analysis; restatement is insufficient.

## NAMES AND ABBREVIATIONS

In general, the first time you use names of individuals and companies, you should not abbreviate them. For instance, do not substitute Co. for Company or make any change in the name of a company. Define your abbreviations. For example, you could state, "In 1999, the situation at Federal Paper, Inc. (Federal) involved . . . ." From that point, you could refer to the company as Federal. Once you have defined an abbreviation, use it consistently. If you want to abbreviate an individual's name, use the last name (e.g., Smith for Robin Smith) or use Ms. Smith. Your perspective will dictate how formal or informal to be with names.

Of course, if you are writing to the controller, you can use abbreviations such as CVP or NPV because all controllers recognize such terms instantly.

## SUPPORTING SCHEDULES

You must label all supporting schedules, exhibits, graphs, and tables. Supporting materials can be called exhibits or tables and should be numbered in the order that they are referred to in the memorandum. All exhibits must have headings that describe their content.

We encourage you to generate material for exhibits and/or figures using programs such as Microsoft Excel. You will use such programs in your working career.  However, be selective in what you include in exhibits.  Consider your audience, role, and task; carefully format your exhibits, make sure they are properly titled, and provide appropriate references to sources.

## USE OF JARGON

Avoid using jargon (topic or industry-specific terminology).  You should be able to present your analyses without jargon, buzzwords, and cliches.

## ASSIGNMENTS

The assignments are glimpses of situations, some real, some not.  Your knowledge is limited.  The issues might or might not be clear.  Ambiguity and uncertainty are characteristic of the real world.  Nevertheless, you can see what problems are emerging and the kinds of decisions needed to solve them.  Lack of information is not an excuse to avoid dealing with the issues.

## READING THE ASSIGNMENT

Carefully read and reread the assignment.  Get an overall understanding of the situation and supporting facts.  When you reread the assignment, take notes about key facts, assumptions, and issues.  Outline appropriate analytical techniques to help you gain additional information (e.g., cost-volume-profit analysis, discounted cash flow analysis, transfer pricing).  Examine the quantitative information for clues.  Look at the assignment's questions for hints on how to approach your analysis.

First, avoid rushing to conclusions.  You might overlook important information or distort it to fit a preconceived idea.  Second, be sure that you fully understand the assignment before you try numerical analysis.  Third, differentiate between facts, estimates, and assumptions or suppositions. As you read, ask yourself a range of questions: What are the problems and opportunities here?  What information do I have that will aid in solving these problems? What information is lacking? What is happening among the people in this organization?  When you use an appropriate analytical technique, what will you learn?  How sensitive is your analysis to changes?  How probable are these changes?  What assumptions and/or estimates do you have to make?

You should be very careful not to confuse the basic problem with its symptoms.  For example, a decline in sales is probably a symptom of a problem, not the problem per se.  Make sure you understand what background information is needed.  Depending on the assignment, you might have to discuss factors inside the organization (management, marketing issues, finances, etc.) and outside the organization (industry makeup, foreign competition, economic conditions, government regulations, etc.).  The more a problem relates to strategic planning issues, the more important it is to identify the strengths and weaknesses of the company in relation to its internal and external environment.

In analyzing and planning how to respond to an assignment, do not be limited by the specific questions asked.  Do not feel bound to address specific questions in lockstep, though your answer should cover all of them.  Remember that an assignment should be used as a springboard for any relevant issues that can usefully be brought into the analysis.  Also, remember that you will write this response after having done all the supporting analysis. Thus you should integrate your presentation. For example, if there are four sequential parts to an assignment, your answers to part 1 should not be presented as if you had not read and analyzed parts 2, 3, and 4.

Because an assignment extends the text in many instances, do not expect to always find specific text references or techniques for your analysis or solution. You might have to draw on ideas and/or techniques from several sources.

## PERSPECTIVE OF WRITER AND READER

Take the detached role of a person observing the information and problem(s) who is analyzing and commenting. Your audience is another person who is less detached from the situation. Instructions should be clear about how much information your audience requires (how much background information is known and how much you should explain and/or summarize). If you are writing from the perspective of an outside consultant hired by a company or a member of management of a company, you are working with management. The assignment instructions or specific instructions from your instructor will let you know what perspective to take and for what audience. Knowing your audience should help you decide how much background information or explanation is appropriate.

## HEADINGS

Headings provide transitions between sections and help the reader know where you are going. In addition, they provide a framework for your analysis and can help you write a more organized memorandum. They are valuable and you should use them whenever you change from one principal topic to another.

## GENERAL WRITING GUIDELINES

The following guidelines for memoranda should be amended depending on your instructor and your assigned perspective (neutral, consultant, member of management).

### Beginning/Introduction

The introduction to your analysis should include a statement of the problem(s) you have identified. You should state how you approached the analysis and solution to the problems and what courses of action you have identified. List the decisions you need to make. If you have made assumptions and/or estimates, state them clearly and justify them. If there is additional information that you could use to make a more informed decision, state what it is. Finally, include a brief summary of your conclusions (including actions recommended). Make sure that you use the specific evidence in the assignment to support your position.

The introduction sets the tone. Make sure that you build a sufficient foundation regarding the problems or issues, the facts, your approaches, etc. Make sure it is clear to the reader what you are doing and why.

### Middle/Analysis

This is the heart of the memorandum, where you present your analyses and bases for your conclusions. What criteria are you using to select a course of action? What are the results of your analysis? Make sure to support your analysis. Do not make assertions without evidence or argument. Here is where you need to spend the greatest amount of time and space. Your conclusions and recommendations should be clear and should logically follow your analysis. Finally, there must be a way to measure the consequences of your recommendations. Therefore, this section should:

1.  Identify and explain courses of action open to the organization. Not all such courses of action are necessarily delineated in the assignment.
2.  Clearly explain the criteria used to select the final course of action (increase profits, reduce risk, report only controllable costs). If criteria are mentioned in the assignment, you should evaluate them and justify their use. If no criteria are presented, you should develop realistic and applicable criteria through your analysis of the assignment's information and your knowledge from the course and from other courses.
3.  Select a course of action. If appropriate, indicate how to implement your proposal.
4.  Discuss means to measure the consequences of your recommendation(s). Establish standards by which the success or failure of your proposed course of action should be judged.

You should build a logical, integrated presentation, developing the ideas and issues within this section. Organization and the use of headings is very important. Everything should flow in a logical order; it should be clear how you have come to your conclusions and why you have made particular choices.

### End/Conclusion

Your ending section should summarize your solutions. If there are unanswered questions, state them and indicate what you would do to resolve them. Give whatever recommendations you have. This final section should bring everything together in a natural end to the paper. There should be no surprises or new material; everything should continue logically from the previous sections and must be fully supported by discussion and facts presented earlier.

# TIME VALUE OF MONEY

Suppose you had the choice between receiving $10,000 either now or at the end of one year. Suppose you are absolutely sure to receive $10,000 at either time. Virtually everyone would choose the first alternative. A dollar now is worth more than a dollar to be received in one year, or at any later date. This statement sums up the important principle that *money has a time value.* The reason that a dollar now is worth more than a dollar to be received in the future is that you could invest the dollar now and have more than a dollar at the later date. It does not matter whether you expect inflation or deflation to change the purchasing power of money; you always prefer money now to the promise of the same amount of money later.

Many economic decisions involve investing money now in the hope of receiving more money later on. Any analysis of such decisions should consider the **time value of money**. Suppose you can invest $10,000 today with a promise that you will receive $10,800 at the end of one year. Should you make the investment? You know that to justify waiting for the money, the amount to be received should be larger than the amount available to you now. But how much larger? It depends on what else you could do with the cash you have to invest—the opportunities that are available.

Suppose your best alternative investment would earn 10 percent interest per year. If you invest $10,000 at 10 percent per year, you have $11,000 at the end of one year [$10,000 + ($10,000 × 10%)]. Comparing the two alternatives, you could have $11,000 at the end of the year as a result of a $10,000 investment now, or you could have $10,800 at the end of the year for a $10,000 investment now. You should choose the first alternative.

What happens when the time horizon is extended beyond one period? Suppose you can invest $10,000 today and receive $12,500 at the end of two years. Should you make the investment if the interest rate on another alternative is 10 percent? First determine how much you would have at the end of two years if you invested at a rate of 10 percent, as follows.

| | |
|---|---|
| Now | You have $10,000 |
| At the end of year 1 | You have $11,000 [$10,000 + ($10,000 × 10%)] |
| At the end of year 2 | You have $12,100 [$11,000 + ($11,000 × 10%)] |

The interest earned in the second year is 10 percent of the total amount you have at the end of the first year, not 10 percent of the $10,000 you originally invested. This calculation reflects **compound interest**: you earn the quoted interest rate both on the original amount invested and on the interest that you subsequently earn. The $12,100 you have at the end of two years is the **future value** of the $10,000 at a 10 percent interest rate. The $10,000 is the **present value** of $12,100 at a 10 percent interest rate.

By comparing the values of each available alternative at the end of the two years, you can see that you are better off investing $10,000 now to receive $12,500 at the end of the two years. You would have only $12,100 by investing elsewhere. We show this by comparing the two values at the end of the investment term. The practice of comparing present values is more common than that of comparing future values.

## PRESENT VALUE OF A SINGLE AMOUNT

To evaluate an opportunity to receive a single payment at some date in the future at some interest rate, we determine the present value of that choice. Instead of determining how much we would have at some future date if we invested $1 now, we want to know how much we would have to invest now to receive $1 at some future date. The preceding example showed that, at a 10 percent interest rate, an investment of $10,000 will accumulate to $12,100 at the end of two years. The present value of $12,100 two years from now at 10 percent is thus $10,000. The procedure used to determine present values is called **discounting**, and the interest rate used is called the **discount rate**. The amount of money to be received later is always a combination of the original investment (sometimes called *principal*) and the interest on that investment.

Formulas are available for determining the present value of a sum of money to be received in the future. Computer spreadsheets and many calculators have functions to find present and future values. You can also use tables to determine present values without the formulas. Suppose we want to find the present value of $1.21 to be received two years from now when we know that the interest rate is 10 percent. (We know already that the present value is $1, and this is the answer the table should give us.) Table A on page 851 shows the present value of $1 to be received at various times in the future and at various interest rates. Referring to the 10% column and the row for two periods, we find the factor .826. This means that the present value of $1 to be received two years from now is $0.826 when the interest rate is 10 percent. Because we expect to get $1.21 we multiply the factor by $1.21. This multiplication produces a present value of $0.99946, which is not significantly different from $1. (The slight difference is due to rounding in preparing the table.) The factors in Table A are generated by the following formula.

$$(1 + i)^{-n}$$

where
  $i$ = the interest rate
  $n$ = the number of periods

Notice two things about Table A. First, as you move down any column in Table A, the factors become smaller. You should expect this because the longer you must wait for a payment, the less it is worth now. If a dollar now is worth more than a dollar to be received in one year, then surely a dollar to be received in one year is worth more than one to come in two years. Second, the factors become smaller as you move across the table in any row. As the interest rate increases, the present value of the amount to be received in the future decreases. You should also expect this. The higher the interest rate you can expect to earn on the sum invested now, the less you need to invest now to accumulate a given amount at the end of some number of years. In summary, the longer you have to wait for your money and the higher the interest rate you can earn, the less it is worth to you now to receive some specified amount at a future date.

## PRESENT VALUE OF A STREAM OF EQUAL RECEIPTS

Sometimes it is necessary to compute the present value of a series of equal amounts to be received at the ends of a series of years. Such a stream is an **annuity**. Annuities abound in the world of finance. Bond interest is a common example. Payments to lottery winners are another. You can find the present value of an annuity by finding the present values of each component of the stream and adding them. For example, what is the present value of an annuity of $1 per year for four years at 10 percent?

| Received at End of Year | Amount to Be Received | Present Value Factor (from Table A) | Present Value of Future Receipt |
|:---:|:---:|:---:|:---:|
| 1 | $1 | .909 | $0.909 |
| 2 | $1 | .826 | 0.826 |
| 3 | $1 | .751 | 0.751 |
| 4 | $1 | .683 | 0.683 |
| Present value of annuity | | | $3.169 |

This procedure is cumbersome, especially if the annuity lasts for many years. You are multiplying the same number ($1) by several different numbers (the present value factors). It is much simpler to add the present value factors (3.169) and multiply the sum by $1. This procedure gives the same answer. (You can verify this at a glance because we are using an annuity of $1.)

Many practical situations deal with a series of equal receipts over several periods. These could be analyzed by using Table A and the lengthy procedure described above. But the task is made simpler by using a table like Table B on page 852, which adds the present value factors for you. Look at Table B in the column for 10% and the row for four periods. The factor is 3.170. This is the present value of a series of four $1 receipts when the interest rate is 10 percent. (The factor, 3.170, is rounded up from the sum of the factors given in Table A.)

The values shown in Table B are the cumulative sums of the factors from Table A (with an occasional rounding difference). The factor for an annuity for one period in Table B is the same as the factor for a single receipt in Table A at the same interest rate. Try adding down Table A and checking each successive sum with the factor in Table B. The factors are generated by the following formula.

$$\frac{1 - (1 + i)^{-n}}{i}$$

All the factors in both tables relate to future receipts (or payments) of $1. When dealing with amounts other than $1, you multiply the factor by the number of dollars involved to compute the present value. But remember that you can use Table B only when all payments in the stream are equal.

## STREAMS OF UNEQUAL AMOUNTS

What if the payments to be received in the future are not equal? You could use the factors from Table A, but that can be cumbersome.  If most of the payments are equal, you can find the present value of the equal portions of each payment using Table B, then discount the remainder separately. We shall illustrate this method by modifying the previous example. Instead of receiving $1 per year for four years, you will receive $1 at the end of each of the first three years and $2 at the end of the fourth year.

From Table B we know that $1 per year for four years has a present value of $3.170 at 10 percent. That is the present value of the stream except for the extra $1 to be received at the end of year 4. Looking in Table A (for the present value of $1 to be received at the end of four years) we find that the extra $1 has a present value of $0.683. Adding the $0.683 to the $3.170, we obtain $3.853. We can check this by discounting each receipt separately.

| Received at End of Year | Amount to Be Received | Present Value Factor (from Table A) | Present Value of Future Receipt |
|:---:|:---:|:---:|:---:|
| 1 | $1 | .909 | $0.909 |
| 2 | $1 | .826 | 0.826 |
| 3 | $1 | .751 | 0.751 |
| 4 | $2 | .683 | 1.366 |
| Present value of this series of payments | | | $3.852* |

*The difference ($0.001) is due to rounding.*

Suppose that only $0.60 is to be received at the end of the fourth year. We now have a stream of equal payments of $1 for three years, then a $0.60 payment at the end of the fourth year. Use Table B to find the present value of a stream of $1 payments for three years, then add to it the present value of $0.60 to be received at the end of four years (from Table A). The solution is as follows.

| | |
|:---|---:|
| Present value of $1 per year for 3 years at 10% ($1 × 2.487) | $2.4870 |
| Present value of $0.60 at end of year 4 at 10% ($0.60 × .683) | 0.4098 |
| Present value of this series of payments | $2.8968 |

## COMPUTATIONS FOR PERIODS OTHER THAN YEARS

It is a common practice to quote an annual interest rate. Nevertheless, many investments make payments more than once a year. For example, a savings bank might credit interest quarterly or even daily, and interest on most bonds is paid semiannually.

If interest is compounded more often than annually, the rate of interest actually earned is higher than the quoted interest rate. Suppose a savings bank pays 6 percent annual interest compounded semiannually. How much will you have at the end of a year if you deposit $1,000 today? You earn $30 for the first six months ($1,000 × 0.06 × 1/2). For the second six months, you earn interest on $1,030 ($1,000 + $30) and the interest earned is $30.90 ($1,030 × 0.06 × 1/2). Hence, at the end of the year you have $1,060.90. In effect, you earned at the rate of 6.09 percent per year, because the interest of $60.90 for one year is 6.09 percent of the $1,000 investment. The 6.09 percent is called the **effective interest rate** and must be distinguished from the quoted, or **nominal interest rate**, of 6 percent. We could say that the investment is earning 3 percent per period (6 percent divided by the two compoundings per year). You are earning 3 percent on the investment at the beginning of each period. For any given nominal interest rate, the effective interest rate rises as the number of compoundings per year increases.

Compound interest tables such as Tables A and B are constructed on the basis of an interest rate per period. Therefore, you must be careful to determine the interest rate you should use in any given situation. If you want the present value of an amount to be received ten years from now using an effective rate of 10 percent, you look in Table A in the 10% column and the row for 10 periods. (Remember that an effective rate is a rate per year.) If, on the other hand, you want the present value of an amount to be received ten years from now using a nominal interest rate of 10 percent compounded semiannually, you look in Table A in the 5% column (10% divided by the number of compoundings per year) and the row for 20 periods (10 years × the number of compoundings per year).

In most situations you know the nominal interest rate. Therefore, to complete the desired computation you convert the nominal rate to a rate per compounding period and revise the number of periods to take into account the compoundings. *When consulting the tables, the number of periods is the number of years times the number of compoundings per year, and the interest rate is the nominal annual rate divided by the number of compoundings per year. Doing this you are stating the interest rate per compounding period.*

One practical example involves applying almost every technique in this appendix. Suppose you can buy a bond that will mature in ten years. The bond carries a nominal interest rate of 6 percent, and interest is paid semiannually. You want to earn 10 percent compounded semiannually. How much would you be willing to pay for a bond with a face (maturity) value of $10,000?

First, you must recognize that your investment has two components. If you buy the bond you contract to receive (1) $10,000 ten years from now and (2) payments of $300 ($10,000 × 0.06 × 1/2) every six months for ten years. What is each of these components worth to you now? The price you would be willing to pay for the bond is the sum of the present values of the components.

To compute the price you would pay for the bond, you need the following.

1. The present value of $10,000 to be received ten years from now. You want to earn 10 percent compounded semiannually, so you refer to Table A for the present value factor for 20 periods (10 years × 2 compoundings) at 5 percent (10 percent divided by 2 compoundings). The factor is .377, so the present value you are looking for is $3,770 ($10,000 × .377).

2. The present value of an annuity of $300 to be received every six months for ten years. You want to earn 10 percent compounded semiannually, so you refer to Table B for the present value factor for 20 periods (10 years × 2 compoundings) at 5 percent (10 percent divided by 2 compoundings). The factor is 12.462, so the present value you are looking for is $3,739 ($300 × 12.462).

Thus, the price you would pay for this $10,000, 6 percent bond is $7,509 ($3,770 + $3,739). Note that the interest rate per period (5 percent) and the number of periods (20) are the same for both calculations. The bond is a single investment and earns a single rate of interest even though it provides both a single payment and an annuity.

## USES AND SIGNIFICANCE OF PRESENT VALUES

Should you invest a sum of money now in order to receive a larger amount later (whether the amount comes in a single payment, a stream of payments, or both)? Your decision should be based on the amount of the cash to be invested and received later, the length of time over which the inflows are received, and the interest rate.

When the dollars to be received in the future are known, you can refer to the tables for an appropriate factor, multiply by the number of dollars to be received in the future, and compare that amount with the money that must be invested now to receive the amount or amounts in the future. If the result of the multiplication is greater than the amount to be invested now, the present value of the future returns is greater than the investment and the investment is desirable. Such an investment has a positive **net present value (NPV)**. If the result of the multiplication is smaller than the required investment, the opportunity is not desirable. (It has a negative NPV.)

The most common use of present value is to find values of future payments. In some situations, however, you want to find the interest rate earned by investing so many dollars now and receiving so many in the future. The procedures are discussed in the next section.

## DETERMINING INTEREST RATES

When you wish to know the interest rate on an investment with known future receipts, you also use present value tables. The interest rate is also called the discount rate, the **time-adjusted rate of return**, or the **internal rate of return (IRR)**. The last term is the most common.

To find the present value of a stream of equal future receipts (annuity), you multiplied the annuity by a factor that incorporated both the length of the series of receipts and the interest rate being earned. This can be shown mathematically.

$$\begin{array}{c} \textit{Present value of} \\ \textit{future receipt(s)} \end{array} = \begin{array}{c} \textit{amount of each} \\ \textit{future receipt} \end{array} \times \begin{array}{c} \textit{factor for discount} \\ \textit{rate and waiting period} \\ \textit{(present value factor)} \end{array}$$

In previous examples, you were looking for the value to the left of the equal sign. In trying to find the interest rate on a given investment when you know the future receipts, you look for the interest rate that equates the present value of the future receipts with the investment required to produce those receipts. Using the preceding equation, you state that the value to the left of the equal sign is the investment required now. You know the amount of the future receipts, and you know one element in determining the factor required—the waiting period. You want the missing element in our equation—the interest rate, or IRR.

Suppose you can invest $3,791 today and receive $1,000 per year for five years beginning one year from now, and you want to know the interest rate you would be earning. Substituting in the preceding equation yields

$$\$3{,}791 \ = \ \$1{,}000 \ \times \ \textit{(the factor for the interest rate for five periods)}$$

The factor is 3.791, which is obtained by rearranging the equation to show

$$\textit{Present value factor for five periods} \ = \ \$3{,}791/\$1{,}000 \ = \ 3.791$$

The $1,000 payments are an annuity, so you can look in Table B for the factor in the five-period row that is closest to 3.791. That exact factor is found in the 10% column, so the investment yields a rate of return of 10 percent. (We can check this by multiplying $1,000 by 3.791, giving $3,791 as the present value.) In general terms, this basic equation can also be shown as

$$\textit{Present value factor} \ = \ \frac{\textit{present value of receipts (required investment)}}{\textit{periodic receipts}}$$

The basic formula can also be used with a single payment. Suppose you could receive $1,450 at the end of four years if you invested $1,000 today. The factor to look for in Table A is .690 (rounded), which is $1,000/$1,450. Looking across the four-period row in Table A, we come to .683 in the 10% column. The rate of return is therefore a bit less than 10 percent.

You can also use this modification of the basic equation if you know the receipts, the amount of investment (which is the present value), and the interest rate, but you want to know the length of time. Suppose you could invest $1,000 now and receive $300 per year, but the number of years is uncertain. If you want a 14 percent rate of return, you can compute the number of years over which you would have to receive the $300 payments.

$$\textit{Present value factor} \ = \ \frac{\$1{,}000}{\$300} \ = \ 3.333$$

This factor is for 14 percent and an unknown number of years. Therefore you look down the 14% column in Table B and find that 3.433 is the factor for five years. If you received five $300 annual payments you would earn slightly more than the desired 14 percent.

## DETERMINING REQUIRED RECEIPTS

For some decisions you want to know the receipts, either single payment or annuity, needed to earn a particular interest rate (or IRR) given the necessary investment and the life of the receipts. The basic formula can be rearranged as follows.

$$\textit{Periodic receipt} \ = \ \frac{\textit{present value of receipts (required investment)}}{\textit{present value factor}}$$

Suppose you can invest $10,000 now expecting to receive $3,000 per year for six years. You would like to earn a 12 percent return. If you do receive $3,000 per year, your rate of return will be about 20 percent ($10,000/$3,000 = 3.33, which is close to the factor for 20 percent and six years). However, you are uncertain whether you will actually receive $3,000 and want to know the minimum annual receipt for six years that will give a 12 percent return.

$$Periodic\ receipt\ =\ \frac{\$10,000}{4.111\ (the\ factor\ for\ six\ years\ and\ 12\%)}\ =\ \$2,432$$

Thus, if you receive at least $2,432 each year for the next six years you will earn at least a 12 percent return.

This method can also be applied to single payments; the only difference is the table to be used. Suppose you can invest $1,000 and receive a single payment at the end of five years. If you wish to earn a 14 percent return, you would have to receive $1,927 (rounded), which is $1,000/.519, the factor for a single payment at 14 percent at the end of five periods.

## SUMMARY

Many decisions involve cash inflows and outflows at different times. Such situations require recognizing the time value of money. To evaluate a situation that involves cash flows occurring at different times, it is necessary to use the values of those flows at the same point in time.

Almost all managerial accounting decisions involving cash flows at different times use the present value of those flows as the point of analysis. The present value of a single cash flow at some time in the future can be computed manually or determined with the help of tables such as Table A. When several future cash flows are involved, it is usually easier to compute their present value by using tables such as Table B. Although tables such as Table B apply only when the individual amounts in the series of cash flows are equal, it is possible to deal with uneven cash flows by using Tables A and B.

The present value of a future cash flow (or a series of future cash flows) depends on the amount of the flow(s), the interest (discount) rate, and the length of the waiting period. Sometimes the present value is known, but one of the other elements is not. The tables can also be used to determine the value of the unknown element.

Applications of the concept of present values include the computation of bond prices and the evaluation of other long-term investment opportunities. Chapters 8 and 9 of this book include managerial decisions that must be analyzed using present values. The use of present values is not limited to accounting. You may apply your knowledge of present values in the study of economics, finance, and statistics.

## KEY TERMS

annuity  *(841)*                          discounting  *(840)*
compound interest  *(839)*                discount rate  *(840)*

effective interest rate   *(843)*                 nominal interest rate   *(843)*
future value   *(840)*                            present value   *(840)*
internal rate of return (IRR)   *(844)*           time-adjusted rate of return   *(844)*
net present value (NPV)   *(844)*                  time value of money   *(839)*

## KEY FORMULAS

$$\text{Present value of future receipt(s)} = \text{amount of each future receipt} \times \begin{array}{c}\text{factor for discount rate} \\ \text{and waiting period} \\ \text{(present value factor)}\end{array}$$

$$\text{Present value factor} = \frac{\text{present value of receipts (required investment)}}{\text{periodic receipts}}$$

$$\text{Periodic receipt} = \frac{\text{present value of receipts (required investment)}}{\text{present value factor}}$$

## REVIEW PROBLEM

1. Find the present value of the following sets of payments if the discount rate is (a) 10% and (b) 16%.

| Received at End of Year | Amount | | | |
|---|---|---|---|---|
| | i | ii | iii | iv |
| 1 | $1,000 | $2,000 | $1,500 | $    0 |
| 2 | 1,000 | 2,000 | 2,000 | 3,000 |
| 3 | 1,000 | 2,000 | 2,000 | 3,000 |
| 4 | 1,000 | 2,000 | 2,000 | 3,000 |
| 5 | | 5,000 | | 4,000 |

2. Find the discount rates for the following situations.

| Case | Investment Required Now | Periodic Receipts | Number of Years for Receipts |
|---|---|---|---|
| i | $3,605 | $1,000 | 5 |
| ii | $12,300 | $2,000 | 10 |
| iii | $9,380 | $3,000 | 5 |

3. Fill in the blanks for each of the following situations. All involve a single payment to be received at the end of the number of years given.

| Case | Investment | Year in Which Payment to Be Received | Payment to Be Received | Interest Rate |
|---|---|---|---|---|
| i | $____ | 4 | $4,000 | 14% |
| ii | $1,000 | 5 | $1,464 | ____ |
| iii | $3,000 | __ | $5,290 | 10% |
| iv | $5,000 | 7 | $____ | 14% |

4. Fill in the blanks for each of the following situations. All involve streams of equal annual payments. Round dollar calculations to the nearest $1.

| Case | Investment | Annual Cash Payments | Number of Years Payments to Be Received | Interest Rate |
|---|---|---|---|---|
| i | $_____ | $1,000 | 10 | 14% |
| ii | $10,000 | $_____ | 8 | 10% |
| iii | $20,000 | $5,000 | — | 8% |
| iv | $10,000 | $2,000 | 8 | _____ |

## ANSWER TO REVIEW PROBLEM

1. i.   Stream of equal payments of $1,000 per year for four years.
   (a) At 10%—3.170 × $1,000 = $3,170
   (b) At 16%—2.798 × $1,000 = $2,798

   ii.   Stream of four equal payments and larger amount at end of fifth year. We will discount the four equal payments and add the present value of the fifth one.

   (a) At 10%—3.170 × $2,000                         $6,340
       (Table A, five years, 10%) .621 × $5,000       3,105
                                                      $9,445

   (b) At 16%—2.798 × $2,000                         $5,596
       (Table A, five years, 16%) .476 × $5,000       2,380
                                                      $7,976

   iii.   Stream of unequal payments for four years. The easiest method is to find the present value of a $2,000 stream of payments for four years and subtract the present value of $500 at the end of one year.

   (a) 10%—3.170 × $2,000                            $6,340.00
       (Table A, one year, 10%) .909 × $500           (454.50)
                                                      $5,885.50

   (b) At 16%—2.798 × $2,000                         $5,596.00
       (Table A, one year, 16%) .862 × $500           (431.00)
                                                      $5,165.00

   iv.   Stream of unequal payments beginning at the end of year two. Although there are shortcuts, it is probably simplest to discount separately.
   (a) At 10%

| Received at End of Year | Amount to Be Received | Present Value Factor (from Table A) | Present Value of Future Receipt |
|---|---|---|---|
| 1 | $0 | | |
| 2 | $3,000 | .826 | $2,478 |
| 3 | $3,000 | .751 | 2,253 |
| 4 | $3,000 | .683 | 2,049 |
| 5 | $4,000 | .621 | 2,484 |
| Present value of this series | | | $9,264 |

(b) At 16% the present value is $7,712. Computations are similar to those for (a), except that the factors for 16% are used.

2. All of these problems require the use of Table B.

$$\frac{Investment\ required}{periodic\ receipt} = the\ factor$$

i.

$$\frac{\$3,605}{\$1,000} = 3.605\ for\ five\ years\ =\ 12\%$$

ii.

$$\frac{\$12,300}{\$2,000} = 6.15\ for\ ten\ years;\ 6.145\ for\ 10\%\ is\ the\ closest\ factor$$

iii.

$$\frac{\$9,380}{\$3,000} = 3.126\ for\ five\ years;\ closest\ factor\ is\ 3.127\ for\ 18\%$$

3. All of these problems require the use of Table A.
   i. $2,368. $4,000 × .592 (the factor for 14% for four years)
   ii. About 8%. $1,000/$1,464 = .683, which is very close to .681, the factor for a single payment in five years at 8%.
   iii. About six years. $3,000/$5,290 = .567, which is very close to the six-year factor at 10% (.564). In this case, you know the interest rate, so you are looking for the column with a factor that is closest to .567.
   iv. $12,500. $5,000/.400 (the factor for seven years at 14%)

4. All of these problems are solved by using Table B and the equation

*Present value = annual payment × present value factor*

The present value, in each case, is the amount of the investment.
   i. $5,216. $1,000 × 5.216 (the factor for ten periods at 14%)
   ii. $1,874. $10,000/5.335 (the factor for eight periods at 10%)
   iii. About five years. $20,000/$5,000 = 4.0, which is the factor for 8% and an unknown number of years. Moving down the 8% column in Table B, we find 3.993, which is the closest factor to 4.0 under 8%.
   iv. About 12%. $10,000/$2,000 = 5.0, which is the factor for eight years and an unknown interest rate. The closest factor in the eight-period row is 4.968, which is the factor for 12%. The true rate is slightly less than 12%.

## ASSIGNMENT MATERIAL

### EXERCISES

**B-1  Computations—present values**  Find the present value of the following sets of payments if the discount rate is as noted for each set.

| Received at End of Year | Set A at 8% | Set B at 10% | Set C at 20% |
|---|---|---|---|
| 1 | | $2,000 | $(3,000) |
| 2 | | 2,000 | 4,000 |
| 3 | | 2,000 | 4,000 |
| 4 | | 2,000 | 4,000 |
| 5 | | 2,000 | 4,000 |
| 8 | $10,000 | | |

**B-2  Missing factors**  Fill in the blanks for each of the following independent investment opportunities.

| Case | Investment Required Now | Periodic Receipt | Number of Years of Receipt | Interest (Discount) Rate |
|------|------|------|------|------|
| A | $16,950 | $3,000 | 10 | ___ |
| B | $16,775 | $___ | 10 | 8% |
| C | $___ | $5,000 | 13 | 18% |
| D | $10,000 | $2,500 | __ | 24% |

**B-3  Computation of bond prices**  You are considering investing in some corporate bonds. Each bond is different, and because the companies are different, you believe you should earn a different rate of interest (effective interest rate) on each investment. The relevant data for each bond are as follows.

| | Bond of Company | | |
|---|---|---|---|
| | A | B | C |
| Face value | $10,000 | $5,000 | $20,000 |
| Nominal (stated) interest rate | 10% | 8% | 6% |
| Years to maturity | 7 | 8 | 7 |
| Interest paid | Annually | Annually | Semiannually |
| Desired interest rate | 12% | 10% | 10% |

**Required**
Compute the price you would pay for each bond.

**B-4  Present values and rates of return**  The following information is available about two investments.

| | A | B |
|---|---|---|
| Required investment now | $10,000 | $20,000 |
| Cash flows, annually for 7 years | $2,500 | $4,700 |

**Required**
1. Compute the approximate IRR for each investment.
2. Compute the present value of each investment if the desired rate of return is 10%.
3. Determine the annual cash flows that would have to be received for each year in the seven-year period to make each investment provide a 16% return.
4. For each investment, determine the number of years that the stated annual cash flows would have to be received to make the investment provide a 20% return.

**B-5  Present values—unusual timing**  Many situations involve cash flows occurring at or near the end of a period. Still others involve flows at or near the beginning of a period. Tables A and B can be used to deal with both types of situations. For each of the following situations, compute the present value of the cash flows described.

(a) A receipt of $5,000 four years from today; the interest rate is 9%.
(b) A receipt of $1,000 per year at the beginning of each of five years beginning today; the interest rate is 8%.
(c) A receipt of $10,000 per year for seven years, the first receipt to arrive exactly six years from today; the interest rate is 12%.

**B-6  Relationships**  Fill in the blanks for each of the following investments.

| Item | Case 1 | 2 | 3 | 4 |
|------|------|------|------|------|
| a. Investment required now | $_____ | $416,250 | $32,280 | $_____ |
| b. Present value at desired rate of return | $_____ | $_____ | $31,080 | $358,000 |
| c. Annual cash receipt | $9,000 | $125,000 | $_____ | $50,000 |
| d. No. of years cash to be received | 16 | 8 | 4 | _____ |
| e. Desired rate of return | 16% | 14% | _____ | 9% |
| f. Rate of return yielded | 20% | _____ | 18% | 14% |

Table A
Present Value of $1

| Number of Periods | Interest Rates | | | | | | | | | | | | |
|---|---|---|---|---|---|---|---|---|---|---|---|---|---|
| | 5% | 6% | 8% | 9% | 10% | 12% | 14% | 16% | 18% | 20% | 22% | 24% | 25% |
| 1 | .952 | .943 | .926 | .917 | .909 | .893 | .877 | .862 | .847 | .833 | .820 | .806 | .800 |
| 2 | .907 | .890 | .857 | .842 | .826 | .797 | .769 | .743 | .718 | .694 | .672 | .650 | .640 |
| 3 | .864 | .840 | .794 | .772 | .751 | .712 | .675 | .641 | .609 | .579 | .551 | .524 | .512 |
| 4 | .823 | .792 | .735 | .708 | .683 | .636 | .592 | .552 | .516 | .482 | .451 | .423 | .410 |
| 5 | .784 | .747 | .681 | .650 | .621 | .567 | .519 | .476 | .437 | .402 | .370 | .341 | .328 |
| 6 | .746 | .705 | .630 | .596 | .564 | .507 | .456 | .410 | .370 | .335 | .303 | .275 | .262 |
| 7 | .711 | .665 | .583 | .547 | .513 | .452 | .400 | .354 | .314 | .279 | .249 | .222 | .210 |
| 8 | .677 | .628 | .541 | .502 | .467 | .404 | .351 | .305 | .266 | .233 | .204 | .179 | .168 |
| 9 | .645 | .592 | .500 | .460 | .424 | .361 | .308 | .263 | .225 | .194 | .167 | .144 | .134 |
| 10 | .614 | .558 | .463 | .422 | .386 | .322 | .270 | .227 | .191 | .162 | .137 | .116 | .107 |
| 11 | .585 | .527 | .429 | .387 | .350 | .287 | .237 | .195 | .162 | .135 | .112 | .094 | .086 |
| 12 | .557 | .497 | .397 | .355 | .319 | .257 | .208 | .168 | .137 | .112 | .092 | .076 | .069 |
| 13 | .530 | .469 | .368 | .326 | .290 | .229 | .183 | .145 | .116 | .093 | .075 | .061 | .055 |
| 14 | .505 | .442 | .340 | .299 | .263 | .205 | .160 | .125 | .099 | .078 | .062 | .049 | .044 |
| 15 | .481 | .417 | .315 | .274 | .239 | .183 | .140 | .108 | .084 | .065 | .051 | .040 | .035 |
| 16 | .458 | .394 | .292 | .251 | .218 | .163 | .123 | .093 | .071 | .054 | .042 | .032 | .028 |
| 20 | .377 | .312 | .215 | .178 | .149 | .104 | .073 | .051 | .037 | .026 | .019 | .014 | .012 |
| 30 | .231 | .174 | .099 | .075 | .057 | .033 | .020 | .012 | .007 | .004 | .003 | .002 | .001 |

Table B
Present Value of $1 Annuity

| Number of Periods | Interest Rates | | | | | | | | | | | | |
|---|---|---|---|---|---|---|---|---|---|---|---|---|---|
| | 5% | 6% | 8% | 9% | 10% | 12% | 14% | 16% | 18% | 20% | 22% | 24% | 25% |
| 1 | .952 | .943 | .926 | .917 | .909 | .893 | .877 | .862 | .847 | .833 | .820 | .806 | .800 |
| 2 | 1.859 | 1.833 | 1.783 | 1.759 | 1.736 | 1.690 | 1.647 | 1.605 | 1.566 | 1.528 | 1.492 | 1.457 | 1.440 |
| 3 | 2.723 | 2.673 | 2.577 | 2.531 | 2.487 | 2.402 | 2.322 | 2.246 | 2.174 | 2.106 | 2.042 | 1.981 | 1.952 |
| 4 | 3.546 | 3.465 | 3.312 | 3.240 | 3.170 | 3.037 | 2.914 | 2.798 | 2.690 | 2.589 | 2.494 | 2.404 | 2.362 |
| 5 | 4.329 | 4.212 | 3.993 | 3.890 | 3.791 | 3.605 | 3.433 | 3.274 | 3.127 | 2.991 | 2.864 | 2.745 | 2.689 |
| 6 | 5.076 | 4.917 | 4.623 | 4.486 | 4.355 | 4.111 | 3.889 | 3.685 | 3.498 | 3.326 | 3.167 | 3.020 | 2.951 |
| 7 | 5.786 | 5.582 | 5.206 | 5.033 | 4.868 | 4.564 | 4.288 | 4.039 | 3.812 | 3.605 | 3.416 | 3.242 | 3.161 |
| 8 | 6.463 | 6.210 | 5.747 | 5.535 | 5.335 | 4.968 | 4.639 | 4.344 | 4.077 | 3.837 | 3.619 | 3.421 | 3.329 |
| 9 | 7.108 | 6.802 | 6.247 | 5.996 | 5.759 | 5.328 | 4.946 | 4.607 | 4.303 | 4.031 | 3.786 | 3.566 | 3.463 |
| 10 | 7.722 | 7.360 | 6.710 | 6.418 | 6.145 | 5.650 | 5.216 | 4.833 | 4.494 | 4.192 | 3.923 | 3.682 | 3.571 |
| 11 | 8.306 | 7.887 | 7.139 | 6.805 | 6.495 | 5.988 | 5.453 | 5.029 | 4.656 | 4.327 | 4.035 | 3.776 | 3.656 |
| 12 | 8.863 | 8.384 | 7.536 | 7.160 | 6.814 | 6.194 | 5.660 | 5.197 | 4.793 | 4.439 | 4.127 | 3.851 | 3.725 |
| 13 | 9.394 | 8.853 | 7.904 | 7.487 | 7.103 | 6.424 | 5.842 | 5.342 | 4.910 | 4.533 | 4.203 | 3.912 | 3.780 |
| 14 | 9.899 | 9.295 | 8.244 | 7.786 | 7.367 | 6.628 | 6.002 | 5.468 | 5.008 | 4.611 | 4.265 | 3.962 | 3.824 |
| 15 | 10.380 | 9.712 | 8.559 | 8.061 | 7.606 | 6.811 | 6.142 | 5.575 | 5.092 | 4.675 | 4.315 | 4.001 | 3.859 |
| 16 | 10.838 | 10.106 | 8.851 | 8.313 | 7.824 | 6.974 | 6.265 | 5.669 | 5.162 | 4.730 | 4.357 | 4.033 | 3.887 |
| 20 | 12.462 | 11.470 | 9.818 | 9.129 | 8.514 | 7.469 | 6.623 | 5.929 | 5.353 | 4.870 | 4.460 | 4.110 | 3.954 |
| 30 | 15.372 | 13.765 | 11.258 | 10.274 | 9.427 | 8.055 | 7.003 | 6.177 | 5.517 | 4.979 | 4.534 | 4.160 | 3.995 |

# COMPANY INDEX

# INDEX

# CHECK FIGURES

2-27    (1b) 833,333, (3) $21.20
2-28    (2) $20
2-29    (2) 45
2-30    (1) a, (2) 2, (3) 77,778
2-31    12,000 April unit sales
2-32    (2) $24,000 increase
2-33    (2) $16
2-34    (2) $39
2-35    (1) $200,000, (2) 56,667
2-36    $38,000 April contribution margin
2-37    (1) $70,000 model 440
2-38    (1) $460, (2) 1,324
2-39    (1) 319,000, (2) 106,333 premium
2-40    $10,250
2-41    (2) $29.60 businesses
2-42    (3a) 48%
2-43    (1) $36,842,105 for normal, (2) $4,500,000 for special
2-44    (2) $36,842,100
2-45    $85,000 total fixed costs
2-46    (1b) 60%
2-47    (2a) 10,800
2-48    $800,000 indifference point
2-49    $1,146,250 income
2-50    (1) 14.9%, (2) $203,000
2-51    (1) $2,755

## Chapter 3

3-7    Variable component = $0.47
3-8    Fixed component = $7,720
3-9    (2) Income = $21,300
3-12   Cost of sales 30% variable
3-13   (1c) $230,000, (2c) $60,000
3-14   (3) $6.77
3-15   (3) $50,000
3-17   (2) 150 sweaters
3-20   (2) $7,622 million
3-21   (3) $5.89
3-22   (3) $93.015
3-23   (6) $400,000, (8) 60,000 units
3-24   Variable rate 5.2%
3-26   Profit, special arrangement at $100 million sales, $4.5 million
3-29   (2) $21
3-30   (1) Lofixed = $200,000
3-33   (2) 16,667
3-34   (2) 11.66%
3-35   (2) $36,000
3-36   (1) Annual income, monthly lease, $78,000
3-37   (2) $280,000
3-38   (2) 80 loaves

## Chapter 4

| | |
|---|---|
| 4-6 | (1) $67,500 to residential |
| 4-7 | Residential shows loss of $6,500 |
| 4-8 | Cost of A3, $280 |
| 4-9 | Cost of A3, $262 |
| 4-10 | (2) $0.45 |
| 4-11 | (2) $21,700 |
| 4-12 | (2) Supermarkets, $336,900 |
| 4-15 | Paper products margin = $290,000 |
| 4-16 | Large customer $624,000 profit |
| 4-17 | Supermarkets profit $86,350 |
| 4-19 | (2) Line B $161,805 |
| 4-20 | (1) Saws $72,000, drill $30,000 |
| 4-21 | Suits margin $15.6 |
| 4-22 | (1) Line C margin $87,660 |
| 4-23 | (2) Domestic margin $220,000 |
| 4-24 | (1) Product 389, cost $55.85 |
| 4-25 | Southern margin $186,400 |
| 4-26 | Hardware margin $707.8 |

## Chapter 5

| | |
|---|---|
| 5-6 | Incremental profit $70,800 |
| 5-7 | Boride $2, Doride -$2 |
| 5-8 | Foride $163,000 |
| 5-9 | (2) $95,000 |
| 5-10 | (2) Walkers at $14,000/month |
| 5-11 | Cost to produce $14 |
| 5-12 | $240,000 gain |
| 5-13 | (2) 11.7% |
| 5-16 | (2) $120 |
| 5-17 | (2) $40,000 |
| 5-18 | (1) Advantage $170 |
| 5-19 | (3) 70,000 units |
| 5-20 | (2) Make 40,000 Zs, 10,000 Qs |
| 5-21 | (2) $80,000 difference |
| 5-22 | (2) $26, $40 |
| 5-23 | (3) Increase $80,000 |
| 5-24 | (3) $14 |
| 5-25 | Difference of $20,340 |
| 5-26 | (2) $445,000 |
| 5-27 | Loss of $46 |
| 5-29 | Public buildings margin $12.8 thousand |
| 5-31 | (1) $67,500 increase |
| 5-32 | (2) 24,474 |
| 5-34 | Advantage $102,000 |
| 5-35 | $8,400 retailers' margin |
| 5-36 | (2) $16.50 |
| 5-37 | $1,257,100 |
| 5-39 | Loss of $20,000 |

5-40    (2) $3,980
5-41    $76,000
5-42    (2) $80,000 increase
5-43    (2) With hardware, $124,000
5-44    (2) $30,000
5-45    (1) 7,000 jars
5-46    (2) Hold two months
5-47    (2) $7.95
5-50    $18,930 difference
5-51    In-house boutique $38,516

**Chapter 6**
6-9     $285,000
6-10    May income $45,000
6-11    March purchases $75,000
6-12    February purchases $72,000
6-13    $64,000
6-14    June profit $7,800
6-15    April purchases $17,400
6-17    Total cost $1,450
6-18    $630
6-19    (2) $29,600
6-20    June $92.5
6-21    Total variance $900
6-22    (3) 14,000 units
6-23    Favorable variance $3,310
6-24    (2) $15,000
6-25    May 40,000
6-26    $1,395,000
6-27    $570,000
6-28    January purchases 110,000
6-29    October purchases 78,500
6-30    $90,600 at 10,000 DLH
6-31    (2) $420, (8) $24,810
6-32    March production 2,300
6-33    Income $26,000
6-34    April production 250
6-35    April sales 4,600, April ending inventory 9,300
6-36    Income $140,800
6-38    (2) March production 22,000
6-40    Operating room revenue $451,200
6-41    Case B $669,000 total cost
6-42    June costs $1,200
6-44    April blank iron purchases $9,000
6-46    (2) 840
6-47    (2) August 21,280
6-48    Total purchases September $20,600

**Chapter 7**
7-8     May $288,000
7-9     June 30 balance $154,000

| 7-10 | April $1,506 |
|---|---|
| 7-11 | February disbursements $69,700 |
| 7-12 | February 28 balance $159,160 |
| 7-13 | February 28 balance $15,200 |
| 7-14 | Total equities $188,000 |
| 7-15 | March 31 balance $14,000 |
| 7-16 | Total equities $400,000 |
| 7-17 | (2) $2,720, (3) $2,054 |
| 7-18 | Total borrowings $1,010 |
| 7-19 | Total equities $2,155 |
| 7-20 | (6) $46,800, (7) $56,200 |
| 7-21 | February disbursements $570,000 |
| 7-22 | March purchases $60,000, March receipts $76,000 |
| 7-23 | (2) $78,000, (4) $3,000, (7) $99,000 |
| 7-24 | October $450 required from work |
| 7-25 | (2) $106 |
| 7-26 | Total assets $185,500 |
| 7-27 | February 28 balance $72,400 |
| 7-28 | March $13,700 available to invest |
| 7-29 | (2) $25.2427 |
| 7-30 | February 28 balance $43,200 |
| 7-31 | August ending balance $87,920 |
| 7-32 | 20X5 gap $159 |
| 7-34 | November 30 cash $55,600 |
| 7-35 | Gap $52,300 |
| 7-36 | Ending February cash $5,000 |
| 7-37 | Ending cash $69,800, total assets $2,855,800 |
| 7-38 | June cash after borrowing $122,496, August balance $123,912 |
| 7-39 | (4) $1,000, (5) $11,250 |
| 7-40 | (4) $1,000, (5) $11,250 |
| 7-41 | June ending balance $63,000 |
| 7-42 | Total assets $1,570 thousand |
| 7-43 | 20X6 gap $11.3 |
| 7-44 | Gap $81,000 |
| 7-45 | Gap $19,145 |
| 7-46 | (4) $36,000, (6) total assets $307,000 |

## Chapter 8

| 8-7 | (2a) $9,500 |
|---|---|
| 8-8 | (1) $2,220 |
| 8-9 | (3) $2,298,755 |
| 8-10 | (3) $4,564 |
| 8-11 | (1) $1,340 |
| 8-12 | (2) about 16% |
| 8-13 | $536,280 |
| 8-14 | (3) 3.0 years |
| 8-15 | (1) -$9,302 |
| 8-16 | B has an NPV of $7,485 |
| 8-17 | NPV $29,736 |
| 8-18 | (b) 4.545 |
| 8-20 | $65,160 |

| 8-21 | (2b) $337,050, (3a) $62,073 |
|---|---|
| 8-22 | Semiautomatic NPV $319,260 |
| 8-23 | (2) $2,656 thousand |
| 8-24 | $1,390,000 |
| 8-25 | -$8,051 |
| 8-26 | (1) PV 10 year $8,603,000 |
| 8-27 | (2) $2,920 |
| 8-28 | (2) 2.797 |
| 8-29 | $2,536.4 |
| 8-30 | 6.22 is the relevant PV factor |
| 8-31 | (2) 3.28 years |
| 8-32 | $266 NPV of buying |
| 8-33 | (1) $976,404 |
| 8-34 | (2) NPV $262,458 |
| 8-35 | $120,825 |
| 8-36 | $1.15 million |
| 8-37 | $3,893,400 |
| 8-38 | (3) Labor intensive process $1,484,080 |
| 8-39 | -$57,338 |
| 8-40 | -$1,584 |
| 8-41 | -$87,320 |
| 8-42 | $8,551,320 |
| 8-43 | (2) $53 |
| 8-44 | (2) $16.1 million |
| 8-45 | NPV accept and expand -$10,742 |
| 8-46 | (1) $1,616,712 |

## Chapter 9

| 9-5 | Project B 1.107 |
|---|---|
| 9-6 | (2) $50,573 |
| 9-7 | (2) NPV $32,366 |
| 9-8 | (2) $125,683 |
| 9-9 | $75,426 |
| 9-10 | -$3,420 |
| 9-11 | $175,440 |
| 9-12 | Semiautomatic 1.228 |
| 9-13 | $21.8 million |
| 9-14 | (2) $43,757 |
| 9-15 | -$11,400 |
| 9-16 | (1) $351,900 for hand-fed machine |
| 9-17 | $1,565,188 for semiautomatic machine |
| 9-18 | (2) $52,946 |
| 9-19 | (2) $54,452, (7) 52,221 units |
| 9-20 | (2b) $110,000, (3f) $90,400 |
| 9-21 | (4) $102,436 |
| 9-22 | $62,474 |
| 9-23 | -$184,952 |
| 9-24 | -$20,644 |
| 9-25 | $343,942 |
| 9-26 | PV of machine A $74,412 |
| 9-27 | -$47,804 |

| | |
|---|---|
| 9-28 | $280.8 thousand |
| 9-29 | Entrol -$1,328,644 |
| 9-30 | (3) $13,691 |
| 9-31 | (2) -$2,016 |
| 9-32 | (2) 31,712 |
| 9-33 | (2) $4.42 |
| 9-34 | (1) $62,850 heart disease |
| 9-35 | (3) 9 years |
| 9-36 | -$437 |
| 9-37 | 207,527 |
| 9-38 | (1) $325,851 |
| 9-39 | PV savings $26,866 |
| 9-40 | (2) $16,250,627 |
| 9-41 | About $1,221 thousand |
| 9-42 | -$128,047 |
| 9-43 | (2) $25,504 favoring dropping the product |
| 9-44 | (1) -$155,160 |
| 9-45 | $268,800 favoring closing |
| 9-46 | $96,080 favors buying |
| 9-47 | $92,779 PV of Rapidgo 350 |
| 9-48 | $515,725 advantage to making |
| 9-50 | $48,185 sell and lease |
| 9-51 | Plan A, NPV $497,400 |

## Chapter 10

| | |
|---|---|
| 10-10 | (1) $240,000 groceries, (2) $172,500 meat |
| 10-11 | $97,850 budget |
| 10-12 | $360,000 HD |
| 10-13 | $417,073 HD |
| 10-17 | $38,000F price variance |
| 10-18 | (1) 12,000, (2) $18.30 |
| 10-19 | (3) $2,000F volume variance |
| 10-20 | $159,500 profit |
| 10-21 | (1) $367,857 trimming, (2) $437,500 trimming, (3) $406,383 trimming |
| 10-22 | $120,000 indoor income |
| 10-26 | (1) $456,000 reimbursement |
| 10-28 | $2,404,400 machining |
| 10-29 | $112,445 controllable costs |
| 10-30 | $212,000U total variance for junior staff |
| 10-31 | $30,800 February income |
| 10-32 | $72,000 contribution margin for saws |
| 10-33 | (2) $160,000 |
| 10-34 | $30,000 profit decrease |
| 10-39 | (1) $285,000 domestic margin, (2) $152,000 product C profit |
| 10-43 | $136 sporting goods margin |
| 10-44 | (2) $3,000 decrease, (4b) $4,500 |
| 10-45 | (2) $208,450 to cleaners |
| 10-47 | $892,000 retailers' income |
| 10-49 | (2) $191 total cost |
| 10-51 | (1) $409,320 for 10% reduction, (2) $957,600 for 5% reduction |

## Chapter 11

11-6    (1) 50,000, (2) 32%
11-7    (1) select B and D
11-8    (1b) $60,000 increase, (2c) $60,000 decrease
11-9    (2) $0.3 million for disinfectants
11-10   (3) games gains $100,000
11-11   (1) laundry 31.5%
11-12   (1) 43,750, (2b) $22.92
11-13   (2) $58.2
11-14   (1) $60 million sales, (2) 21.7%
11-15   Company gains $28,000
11-16   (2) $90,000 drop for Carter, $30,000 increase for Devon
11-17   (1) $23, (3) $32
11-18   (1b) $6 million, (2) 30%
11-19   (A) RI $20, (C) investment $100
11-20   (1d) $500, (3a) $6,000, (5b) $30,000
11-21   (2) $10,000 increase
11-23   (2) 1.6 times, (5) $256,000
11-25   (1) 15% for both, (2a) 0.67
11-26   (2) $5.33, (3) $6
11-27   (2) $60,000
11-28   (1b) $20,000, (2) 85,000, (3b) $11.20
11-32   (2) $1,250
11-33   (1) $1,158.4
11-34   (1) $100,000 reduction
11-35   (2) $8,000 increase
11-36   (1) 21.7% overall ROI
11-38   (1) $150,000 difference to division
11-40   (1) $57,000 increase, (3) $54,000
11-41   (1a) $1,800,000 profit at 4,000,000 cases
11-44   (1) $18,500 income to division
11-46   (1) $88,000 increase to company

## Chapter 12

12-8    MUV $1,200F
12-9    DLEV $500F, VOH budget $400U
12-10   (3) 30,000 units, (6) $675,000 VOH
12-11   MPV $200F, DLEV $560U
12-12   $62,000 paid
12-14   $3,600U spoilage variance, materials
12-16   (2) 0.4453 hours
12-17   7,900 actual hours, (d) 2,000 units
12-18   $22,667F DLEV
12-19   Budget $10,250
12-20   (4) $62,400, (7) $1,600F, (12) $31,300
12-21   VOHEV $1,680U
12-22   Labor efficiency $3,052U
12-23   5.2% reduction
12-24   $1,320F VOHEV
12-25   $25,470U for currently attainable standard
12-26   Total cost, 3rd quarter $1,863

| | |
|---|---|
| 12-27 | $5.16 cost per pound |
| 12-28 | $2,400U efficiency variance for setup-related costs |
| 12-29 | VOHEV $1,600U |
| 12-30 | $194 cost of minor product |
| 12-31 | Indirect labor $538F efficiency variance |
| 12-32 | $7.82 |
| 12-33 | $40,000U DLEV |
| 12-34 | $35,000U |
| 12-36 | $6.4 sales volume variance |
| 12-38 | $4,800U MUV |
| 12-39 | (2) $430,400 |
| 12-40 | $34,000U variances under manager's control |
| 12-41 | $4,300U design change variances |
| 12-42 | $6,020U total variances |
| 12-43 | (3) $4, (4) $38,200, (7) $77,000 |
| 12-44 | (2) profit $346,510 |
| 12-45 | (c) 2,500, (e) $2,250F, (g) $600F |
| 12-46 | $8.838 and $8.343 |
| 12-47 | $376,842 favoring Capital |
| 12-48 | $4.19 |
| 12-49 | (b) $600U, (e) $737U |
| 12-50 | $204,500F sales volume variance, $79,500U MUV |

## Chapter 13

| | |
|---|---|
| 13-7 | (3) JO-8 $250,000 |
| 13-8 | (3) $19,000 underapplied |
| 13-9 | (2) income $70,000 |
| 13-10 | Income $160,000 |
| 13-11 | (1b) $186,000, (4d) 35,000 |
| 13-13 | (2b) $197,000, (4a) $304,000 |
| 13-14 | (4) $396,000 |
| 13-15 | $13,000 underapplied |
| 13-16 | (3) Income $173,500 |
| 13-17 | EI $88,067 |
| 13-18 | Job M-3 cost $146,800 |
| 13-20 | Flake River cost $9,600 |
| 13-21 | (2) $229 overapplied |
| 13-22 | $7,980U volume variance |
| 13-23 | $10,000 underapplied |
| 13-24 | (2) XR-23 cost $152,550 |
| 13-25 | (2) Job 1030 cost $106,800 |
| 13-26 | $259,320 cost of sales |
| 13-27 | (2) $1,092 |
| 13-29 | (2) $1,999,490 |
| 13-30 | $82,810 cost of XY-67 |
| 13-31 | GHK cost $7,380 |
| 13-32 | (3) $609,500 cost of sales, $43,500 EI |
| 13-33 | (2) Profit $18,000 |
| 13-34 | (2) Class III $29.37 |
| 13-35 | Incremental cost $37,500 |
| 13-36 | $9,760 |

13-37    (3) $760,000, (4) $1,000,000
13-38    $1,171.20 price for 5052 Table
13-40    Income $1,250, underapplied overhead $28
13-42    Profit on Randle offer $169,000
13-43    (2) $15,950
13-44    A-16 cost $59,510
13-45    (3) Cost of sales $8,290,000, inventories $838,000
13-46    XT-12 cost $4,620 and $658
13-48    $14,220 and $13,590 bids for job 391
13-49    (2) $39,000
13-50    (2) 3,000, 4,500, and 6,000

## Chapter 14
14-5     (1) Income $70,000
14-6     (2) Income $160,000
14-7     March variable costing income $40,000, April absorption income $20,000
14-8     January incomes $68,000 and $48,000
14-9     Income $2,530,000
14-10    Income $1,630,000
14-11    (2) $60,000F and $180,000U
14-12    (1b) $60,000, (3a) $8
14-13    $80,000 income
14-14    $80,000 and $85,000 incomes
14-15    Incomes are from $30,000 to $30,009
14-16    (1) 20X3 income $100,000
14-17    Profit $115,000
14-18    (1) $5,000 loss, $145,000 profit
14-19    $80,000 loss, $195,000 profit
14-20    $43,000 profit
14-21    35,000 and 16,000
14-22    $1,010,000 and $930,000 incomes
14-23    $770,000 income
14-24    (1b) 70,000, (3d) $105,000
14-25    (1) Profits $29,000, $30,000, and $31,000
14-26    (2) $70,000 income
14-27    (2) $230,000 income
14-28    (3) $2,155,000 income
14-29    Incomes $189,000 and $139,000
14-30    Incomes $305,000 and $280,000
14-31    (d) $12,000F, (g) $3,000U
14-32    $58,400 income
14-33    Income $504.0
14-34    Incomes $484 and $524
14-35    (2a) $900,000, (2d) 10,000
14-36    $71,200 income
14-37    Total assets $1,740,000
14-38    (1) Profit $512,000
14-39    (2) $38.87
14-40    (1) $21.8 March income
14-41    (2) $217,224 income

14-42    $20,000 incremental profit on order
14-43    (3) Income $22,300
14-45    $3,415 and $4,105 total assets
14-46    $85,000 profit
14-47    $154,200 profit
14-48    $684,000 income, $318,400 ending cash, $13,748 total assets
14-49    (2) $4,015,000
14-50    (2) 123,500 units
14-51    $562,500 income
14-52    (2) incomes of -$61,000, -$1,000, $89,000
14-54    Break-even point 1,500,000 units


## Chapter 15
15-3     (3) $5,760, (4) $80,000
15-7     (3) $14,200
15-8     (4) $283,800
15-11    (2) $18,000U, (4) $88,000
15-12    (2) 95,000
15-13    EI $60,600
15-14    EI $61,500
15-15    EI $76,000
15-17    EI $72,000
15-18    (2) $1,620
15-19    (2) $0.22 and $0.67
15-20    (3) $88,600, $883,500
15-21    (1) 2,300
15-22    $28 is best price
15-23    $180,000 income
15-26    Incomes of $2,000, $8,000, and $18,000
15-27    Mixing costs, $0.24 and $0.45
15-28    (2) $51,920
15-29    (1) $360,000 income
15-30    (3) 240,000, (4) $260,000, (7) $9,000U
15-31    (3) 22,000, (4) $72,000
15-32    $4,500 income
15-33    (1) $50,000 income, (3) $40,500 income
15-34    (2) $91,650 income
15-35    (2) $126,980 income
15-36    The order yields $20,000 profit
15-37    Total variances $1,995U
15-38    Incomes $315,112, $302,000, $298,000, $282,000, $292,000
15-39    Incomes $576,888, $588,333, $587,000, $595,000, $588,684
15-40    $244,005 gain on order
15-41    (2) 3,000 units, (5) $9, (7) $18, (10) $10
15-42    (3) $72,788
15-43    $10,000U DLEV
15-44    Incomes $735,000 and $675,000
15-45    $8 unit cost
15-46    (1) 19,000

## Chapter 16

| | |
|---|---|
| 16-6 | (1) 28 minutes |
| 16-7 | (2) 614 hours average time |
| 16-8 | (2) 10,000 A, 4,000 B, 1,500 C |
| 16-9 | $90,000 increased profit |
| 16-11 | (1) $40,960 |
| 16-12 | (2) $72,768 |
| 16-14 | Internal failure: $1,025,000 |
| 16-15 | (1) $207,360 |
| 16-17 | (2) $64,000 |
| 16-18 | Less than 9 days |
| 16-19 | Less than 8 days |
| 16-21 | (3) alpha 50 units, beta 22 units |
| 16-22 | (1) option 2 $1,235 |
| 16-25 | 40 units of X, 70 units of Y |

## Chapter 17

| | |
|---|---|
| 17-6 | $255,000 cash provided by operations |
| 17-7 | $42,000 increase in cash |
| 17-8 | B $992,000, C $870,000 |
| 17-9 | B $798,000 |
| 17-10 | C $2,833,000 |
| 17-13 | Cash provided by operations $331,300 |
| 17-14 | B $72,318 |
| 17-15 | A $819,000 |
| 17-16 | $149,000 cash provided by operations |
| 17-19 | (3) $350,000, (5) $1,240,000 |
| 17-20 | $150,000 cash provided by operations |
| 17-21 | $164,000 increase in cash |
| 17-22 | Profit $45,000 |
| 17-24 | $1,000 increase in cash |
| 17-25 | $288,000 cash provided by operations |
| 17-26 | $581,000 payments for operating expenses |
| 17-27 | $251,500 cash provided by operations |
| 17-28 | $181,000 cash provided by operations |
| 17-29 | $67,000 increase in cash |
| 17-30 | (2) $17,000 increase in cash |
| 17-32 | $10,000 decrease in cash |
| 17-34 | $120 increase in cash |
| 17-35 | $101,000 increase in cash |
| 17-36 | $19.2 decrease in cash |
| 17-37 | $10,000 increase in cash |
| 17-38 | $450 cash provided by operations |

## Chapter 18

| | |
|---|---|
| 18-11 | (1) $500,000, (3a) $300,000, (5) $345,000 |
| 18-12 | (1) 16.0% ROE, (2) $5.25 EPS |
| 18-13 | (1) 9.375% ROA, (2) 15.0% ROE, (3) 10.5% ROE |
| 18-14 | (1) 15%, 21%, 17% ROE |
| 18-15 | (2) 1997 AR turnover: Dell 8.30, Compaq 8.50, Gateway 12.32 |

18-16   (2) $396,000, (3) $1,260,000
18-18   1.8:1 acid-test ratio, 5.6 inventory turnovers, 1.3% dividend yield
18-19   15%, 20%, 12% ROE
18-20   (2) 49, 40 days, (3) 6.7, 7.0 turnovers
18-21   $540 cost of sales, $54 income, $180 receivables
18-23   (1) 1.7:1, 1.1:1 acid-test ratios, 89, 59 days' sales in inventory, (2) 5.9%, 5.5% ROS, 17%, 27.3% ROE, (3) 11, 5.64 times interest earned
18-25   $300,000 net income, $3,000,000 sales, $450,000 inventory, $550,000 long-term debt
18-26   (1) $9.00, $13.00
18-27   (2) $720,000, (3) 11.4%
18-29   $712,000 available to repay loan
18-32   $149 for 20X2 total assets, $177.5 for 20X3
18-33   (2) $744,000, $852,000, (3) 4.55%, 4%